DATE DUE

			PRINTED IN U.S.A.

Literature
Criticism from
1400 to 1800

Guide to Gale Literary Criticism Series

For criticism on	Consult these Gale series
Authors now living or who died after December 31, 1959	*CONTEMPORARY LITERARY CRITICISM (CLC)*
Authors who died between 1900 and 1959	*TWENTIETH-CENTURY LITERARY CRITICISM (TCLC)*
Authors who died between 1800 and 1899	*NINETEENTH-CENTURY LITERATURE CRITICISM (NCLC)*
Authors who died between 1400 and 1799	*LITERATURE CRITICISM FROM 1400 TO 1800 (LC)* *SHAKESPEAREAN CRITICISM (SC)*
Authors who died before 1400	*CLASSICAL AND MEDIEVAL LITERATURE CRITICISM (CMLC)*
Black writers of the past two hundred years	*BLACK LITERATURE CRITICISM (BLC)*
Authors of books for children and young adults	*CHILDREN'S LITERATURE REVIEW (CLR)*
Dramatists	*DRAMA CRITICISM (DC)*
Hispanic writers of the late nineteenth and twentieth centuries	*HISPANIC LITERATURE CRITICISM (HLC)*
Native North American writers and orators of the eighteenth, nineteenth, and twentieth centuries	*NATIVE NORTH AMERICAN LITERATURE (NNAL)*
Poets	*POETRY CRITICISM (PC)*
Short story writers	*SHORT STORY CRITICISM (SSC)*
Major authors from the Renaissance to the present	*WORLD LITERATURE CRITICISM, 1500 TO THE PRESENT (WLC)*

ISSN 0740-2880

Volume 36

Literature Criticism from 1400 to 1800

Critical Discussion of the Works of Fifteenth-, Sixteenth-, Seventeenth-, and Eighteenth-Century Novelists, Poets, Playwrights, Philosophers, and Other Creative Writers

Jelena O. Krstović, Editor

GALE

DETROIT · NEW YORK · TORONTO · LONDON

STAFF

Jelena O. Krstović, *Editor*

Gerald R. Barterian, *Associate Editor*

Aarti Stephens, *Managing Editor*

Susan M. Trosky, *Permissions Manager*
Kimberly F. Smilay, *Permissions Specialist*
Maureen Puhl, *Permissions Associate*
Sarah Chesney, *Permissions Assistant*
Kelly A. Quinn, *Permissions Assistant Co-Op*

Victoria B. Cariappa, *Research Manager*
Laura Bissey, Julia C. Daniel, Tamara Nott, Michele Le Meau, Tracie A. Richardson, Cheryl Warnock, *Research Associates*
Alfred Gardner, *Research Assistant*

Mary Beth Trimper, *Production Director*
Deborah Milliken, *Production Assistant*

Sherrell Hobbs, *Macintosh Artist*
Pamela A. Hayes, *Photography Coordinator*
Randy Bassett, *Image Database Supervisor*
Mikal Ansari, Robert Duncan, *Scanner Operators*

∞™ This book is printed on acid-free paper that meets the minimum requirements of American National Standard for Information Sciences—Permanence Paper for Printed Library Materials, ANSI Z39.48-1984.

Library of Congress Catalog Card Number 94-29718
ISBN 0-7876-1130-1
ISSN 0740-2880
Printed in the United States of America

10 9 8 7 6 5 4 3 2 1

Contents

Preface   vii

Acknowledgments   xi

Preface

*L*iterature Criticism from 1400 to 1800 (LC) presents critical discussion of world authors of the fifteenth through eighteenth centuries. The literature of this period reflects a turbulent time of radical change that saw the rise of modern European drama, the birth of the novel and personal essay forms, the emergence of newspapers and periodicals, and major achievements in poetry and philosophy. Many of these historical forces continue to influence modern art and society. *LC,* therefore, provides valuable insight into the art, life, thought, and cultural transformations that took place during these centuries.

Scope of the Series

LC provides an introduction to the great poets, dramatists, novelists, essayists, and philosophers of the fifteenth through eighteenth centuries, and to the most significant interpretations of these authors' works. Because criticism of this literature spans nearly six hundred years, an overwhelming amount of scholarship confronts the student. *LC* organizes this material into volumes addressing specific historical and cultural topics, for example, "Literature of the Spanish Golden Age," or "Literature and the New World." Every attempt is made to reprint the most noteworthy, relevant, and educationally valuable essays available.

Readers should note that there is a separate Gale reference series devoted exclusively to Shakespearean studies. Although belonging properly to the period covered in *LC,* William Shakespeare has inspired such a tremendous and ever-growing corpus of secondary material that the editors have deemed it best to give his works extensive coverage in a separate series, *Shakespearean Criticism.*

Each author entry in *LC* presents a survey of critical response to a topic or an author's oeuvre. Early criticism is offered to indicate initial responses, later selections document any rise or decline in literary reputations, and retrospective analyses provide students with modern views. The size of each author entry is a relative reflection of the scope of criticism available in English. Every attempt has been made to identify and include the seminal essays on each author's work and to include recent commentary providing modern perspectives.

The need for *LC* among students and teachers of literature and history was suggested by the proven usefulness of Gale's *Contemporary Literary Criticism (CLC), Twentieth-Century Literary Criticism (TCLC),* and *Nineteenth-Century Literature Criticism (NCLC),* which excerpt criticism of works by nineteenth- and twentieth-century authors. There is no duplication of critical material in any of these literary criticism series. Major authors may appear more than once in one or more of the series because of the great quantity of critical material available and because of their relevance to a variety of thematic topics.

Thematic Approach

Beginning with Volume 12, the authors in each volume of *LC* are organized around such themes as specific literary or philosophical movements, writings surrounding important political and historical events, the philosophy and art associated with eras of cultural transformation, and the literature of specific social or ethnic groups. Each volume contains a topic entry providing a historical and literary overview, and several author entries which examine major representatives of the featured period.

Organization of the Book

Each entry consists of the following elements: author or thematic heading, introduction, list of principal works, annotated works of criticism (each preceded by a bibliographical citation), and a bibliography of further reading. Also, most author entries contain author portraits and other illustrations.

- The **Author Heading** consists of the author's name (the most commonly used form), followed by birth and death dates. (If an author wrote consistently under a pseudonym, the pseudonym is used in the author heading, with the real name given in parentheses on the first line of the biographical and critical introduction.) Also located here are any name variations under which an author wrote, including transliterated forms for authors whose native languages use nonroman alphabets. Uncertain birth or death dates are indicated by question marks. Topic entries are preceded by a **Thematic Heading,** which simply states the subject of the entry.

- The **Biographical and Critical Introduction** contains background information that concisely introduces the reader to the author or topic.

- Most *LC* author entries include **Portraits** of the author. Many entries also contain illustrations of materials pertinent to an author's career, including author holographs, title pages, letters, or representations of important people, places, and events in an author's life.

- The **List of Principal Works** is ordered chronologically, by date of first book publication, identifying the genre of each work. In the case of foreign authors whose works have been translated into English, the title and date (if available) of the first English-language edition are given in brackets following the foreign-language listing. Unless otherwise indicated, dramas are dated by first performance, not first publication.

- **Criticism** is arranged chronologically in each author entry to provide a useful perspective on changes in critical evaluation over time. For the purpose of easy identification, the critic's name and the date of first composition or publication of the critical work are given at the beginning of each piece of criticism. Unsigned criticism is preceded by the title of the source in which it appeared. All titles by the author featured in the critical entry are printed in boldface type. Publication information (such as publisher names and book prices) and some parenthetical numerical references (such as footnotes or page and line references to specific editions of works) have been occasionally deleted to provide smoother reading of the text.

- Critical essays are prefaced by **Annotations** as an additional aid to students using *LC*. These explanatory notes provide information such as the importance of a work of criticism, the commentator's individual approach to literary criticism, and a brief summary of the reprinted essay. In some cases, these notes cross-reference the work of critics within the entry who agree or disagree with each other.

- A complete **Bibliographical Citation** of the original essay or book precedes each piece of criticism.

- An annotated bibliography of **Further Reading** appears at the end of each entry and suggests resources for additional study. In some cases, significant essays for which the editors could not obtain reprint rights are included here.

Cumulative Indexes

Each volume of *LC* includes a cumulative **Author Index** listing all the authors that have appeared in the following sources published by Gale: *Contemporary Literary Criticism, Twentieth-Century Literary Criticism, Nineteenth-Century Literature Criticism, Literature Criticism from 1400 to 1800, and Classical and Medieval Literature Criticism,* along with cross-references to the Gale series *Short Story Criticism, Poetry Criticism, Children's Literature Review, Authors in the News, Contemporary Authors, Contemporary Authors Autobiography Series, Contemporary Authors Bibliographical Series, Dictionary of Literary Biography, Concise Dictionary of Literary Biography, Something about the Author, Something about the Author Autobiography Series, and Yesterday's Authors of Books for Children.* Readers will welcome this cumulative author index as a useful tool for locating an author within the various series. The index, which includes authors' birth and death dates, is particularly valuable for those authors who are identified with a certain period but whose death dates cause them to be placed in another, or for those authors whose careers span two periods. For example, F. Scott Fitzgerald is found in *TCLC,* yet a writer often associated with him, Ernest Hemingway, is found in *CLC.*

Beginning with Volume 12, *LC* includes a cumulative **Topic Index** that lists all literary themes and topics treated in *LC, NCLC, TCLC,* and the *CLC* Yearbook. Each volume of *LC* also includes a cumulative **Nationality Index** in which authors' names are arranged alphabetically under their respective nationalities and followed by the numbers of the volumes in which they appear.

Each volume of *LC* also includes a cumulative **Title Index,** an alphabetical listing of all literary works discussed in the series. Each title listing includes the corresponding volume and page numbers where criticism may be located. Foreign-language titles that have been translated followed by the tiles of the translation—for example, *El ingenioso hidalgo Don Quixote de la Mancha (Don Quixote).* Page numbers following these translated titles refer to all pages on which any form of the titles, either foreign-language or translated, appear. Titles of novels, dramas, nonfiction books, and poetry, short story, or essays collections are printed in italics, while individual poems, short stories, and essays are printed in roman type within quotation marks.

A Note to the Reader

When writing papers, students who quote directly from any volume in the Literary Criticism Series may use the following general format to footnote reprinted criticism. The first example pertains to material drawn from periodicals, the second to material reprinted from books.

T. S. Eliot, "John Donne," *The Nation and the Athenaeum,* 33 (9 June 1923), 321-32; excerpted and reprinted in *Literature Criticism from 1400 to 1800,* Vol. 10, ed. James E. Person, Jr. (Detroit: Gale Research, 1989), pp. 28-9.

Clara G. Stillman, *Samuel Butler: A Mid-Victorian Modern* (Viking Press, 1932); excerpted and reprinted in *Twentieth-Century Literary Criticism,* Vol. 33, ed. Paula Kepos (Detroit: Gale

Research, 1989), pp. 43-5.

Suggestions Are Welcome

Since the series began, features have been added to *LC* in response to various suggestions, including a nationality index, a Literary Criticism Series topic index, and thematic organization of entries.

Readers who wish to suggest new features, themes or authors to appear in future volumes, or who have other suggestions or comments are cordially invited to write to the editor (fax: 313 961-6599).

Acknowledgments

The editors wish to thank the copyright holders of the excerpted criticism included in this volume and the permissions managers of many book and magazine publishing companies for assisting us in securing reproduction rights. We are also grateful to the staffs of the Detroit Public Library, the Library of Congress, the University of Detroit Mercy Library, Wayne State University Purdy/Kresge Library Complex, and the University of Michigan Libraries for making their resources available to us. Following is a list of the copyright holders who have granted us permission to reproduce material in this volume of *LC*. Every effort has been made to trace copyright, but if omissions have been made, please let us know.

COPYRIGHTED EXCERPTS IN *LC*, VOLUME 36, WERE REPRODUCED FROM THE FOLLOWING PERIODICALS:

The Historical Journal, v. IX, 1966. Reproduced by permission.—*The Journal of Political Economy*, v. XLVIII, August, 1940. Reproduced by permission The University of Chicago Press.

COPYRIGHTED EXCERPTS IN *LC*, VOLUME 36, WERE REPRODUCED FROM THE FOLLOWING BOOKS:

Babbitt, Irving. From *Democracy and Leadership*. Houghton Mifflin Company, 1924. Copyright 1924 by Irving Babbitt . Renewed 1951 by Esther Babbitt Howe and Edward S. Babbitt. All rights reserved. Reproduced by permission of National Humanities Institute.—Baumgold, Deborah. From "Hobbes's Political Sensibility: The Menace of Political Ambition," in *Thomas Hobbes and Political Theory*. Edited by Mary G. Dietz. University Press of Kansas, 1990. © 1990 by the University Press of Kansas. All rights reserved. Reproduced by permission.—Campbell, R. H., and A. S. Skinner. From *Adam Smith*. St. Martin's Press, 1982. © 1982 R. H. Campbell and A. S. Skinner. All rights reserved. Reproduced by permission.—Campbell, T. D. From *Adam Smith's Science of Morals*. Allen & Unwin, 1971. © George Allen & Unwin Ltd, 1971. Reproduced by permission.—Canavan, Francis. From *Edmund Burke: Prescription and Providence*. Carolina Academic Press, 1987. © 1987 by Francis Canavan. All rights reserved. Reproduced by permission.—Cranston, Maurice. From an introduction to *The Social Contract by Jean-Jacques Rousseau*. Translated by Maurice Cranston. Penguin Books, 1968. Copyright © Maurice Cranston, 1968. Reprinted by permission of the Peters, Fraser & Dunlop Group Ltd.—Cullen, Daniel E. From *Freedom in Rousseau's Political Philosophy*. Northern Illinois University Press, 1993. © 1993 by Northern Illinois University Press. Reproduced with permission of Northern Illinois University Press, DeKalb, IL.—Dewey, John. From "The Motivation of Hobbes's Political Philosophy," in *Thomas Hobbes in His Time*. Ralph Ross, Herbert W. Schneider, Theodore Waldman, eds. University of Minnesota Press, 1974. © copyright 1974 by the University of Minnesota. All rights reserved. Reproduced by permission.—Gauthier, David. From "Hobbes's `Social Contract*'," in *Perspectives on Thomas Hobbes*. Edited by G. A. J. Rogers and Alan Ryan. Oxford at the Clarendon Press, 1988. © David Gauthier 1988. All rights reserved. Reproduced by permission of Oxford University Press.—Greenleaf, W. H. From *Order, Empiricism and Politics: Two Traditions of English Political Thought, 1500-1700*. Oxford University Press, London, 1964. © University of Hull 1964. Reproduced by permission of the University of Hull.—Hollander, Samuel. From *The Economics of Adam Smith*. University of Toronto Press, 1973. © University of Toronto Press 1973. Reproduced by permission of University of Toronto Press Incorporated.—Johnson, David. From *The Rhetoric of "Leviathan": Thomas Hobbes and the Politics of Cultural Transformation*. Princeton University Press, 1986. Copyright © 1986 by Princeton University

PHOTOGRAPHS AND ILLUSTRATIONS APPEARING IN *LC,* VOLUME 36, WERE RECEIVED FROM THE FOLLOWING SOURCES:

Political Theory from the 15th to the 18th Century

INTRODUCTION

Western European political philosophy underwent radical changes in the early modern period, which spanned the late Middle Ages, the Renaissance, and the Enlightenment. In the 400 years from 1400 to 1800, the political notions fundamental to twentieth-century Westerners—individual rights, the nation-state, the social contract—took precedence over the faith in monarchy that had defined the political world of the Middle Ages. Changes in the concepts of political organization reflected and were reflected in changes taking place in many aspects of European life including religion, economics and production, science, and transportation.

The Europe of the late Middle Ages, in 1400, was still largely a continent of powerful monarchies whose peoples believed that the source of political power stemmed from divine right, ordained by God. Many of the nations we recognize today were not yet united, but loosely connected duchies and provinces. The Catholic church ruled Europe virtually unchallenged, shaping political and economic issues with its extensive power. The great age of imperialism was just arising, led into existence by the explorations and conquests made by a powerful Spanish government.

By 1800 a very different world had emerged. Catholicism lost vital battles in France, Germany, the Netherlands, and England, where Protestant sects redefined the individual's relationship to God, sometimes implicitly redefining the nature of hierarchy as well. When English Dissenters challenging the Anglican Church in the seventeenth century executed King Charles I, they irrevocably damaged the belief in divine kingship. The Industrial Revolution and imperialism matched pace with religious upheaval, causing far-reaching shifts in economic and class structure. A merchant and civil class—the bourgeoisie—used its new economic muscle to challenge the traditional social and political dominance of the aristocracy; an embryonic industrial working class, with its all-too-apparent poverty and degradation, led to questions about the appropriateness of subordination and obedience. Medieval notions of hierarchy were further undermined by discoveries by such scientists as Galileo Galilei, Nicolaus Copernicus, and Johannes Kepler, whose ideas changed the worldview from a belief in a universe governed by God's will, to acknowledgment of a mechanical universe.

While different historians emphasize different strands in this dense fabric, each thread contributed in some way to a political world that looked quite novel after four hundred years of change. A revised image of the individual, and of the individual's relationship to power, took its most dramatic form at the end of the eighteenth century, when the American Revolution threw off England's monarchy altogether and when French citizens beheaded their king and created a parliamentary government. Many philosophers sought to explain the breadth and complexity of the forces at work, a few of whom have become representative of modern political philosophy, including Thomas Hobbes, John Locke, Jean-Jacques Rousseau, David Hume, Immanuel Kant, and Edmund Burke. Their works, all hugely influential, struggled with a remarkably consistent set of questions about human society and political power. What is political power?, they ask. What is its source? What is the individual? Is he naturally prone to cooperation and moral behavior or to isolation and violent self-preservation? How did the social contract come into being? What are its parameters?

OVERVIEW

Otto Gierke (essay date 1900)

SOURCE: "The Beginnings of the Modern State," in *Political Theories of the Middle Age*, translated by Frederic William Maitland, 1900. Reprint by Cambridge at the University Press, 1913, pp. 87-100.

[*In the excerpt below, Gierke sketches the transition from the heyday of the Middle Ages to the modern era. Emphasizing concepts rather than individual thinkers, Gierke discusses the emerging sovereignties of the period—that of the state and that of the individual.*]

. . . Everywhere beside the formulation of thoughts that were properly medieval we have detected the genesis of 'antique-modern' ideas, the growth of which coincides with the destruction of the social system of the Middle Age and with the construction of 'nature-rightly' theories of the State. It remains for us to set forth by way of summary this tendency of medieval doctrine to give birth to the modern idea of the State and to transform the previously accepted theory of Communities. We must attend separately to the more important of those points at which this tendency exhib-

1

its itself.

The fundamental fact which chiefly concerns us when we contemplate this process of evolution is that in medieval theory itself we may see a drift which makes for a theoretical concentration of right and power in the highest and widest group on the one hand and the individual man on the other, at the cost of all intermediate groups. The Sovereignty of the State and the Sovereignty of the Individual were steadily on their way towards becoming the two central axioms from which all theories of social structure would proceed, and whose relationship to each other would be the focus of all theoretical controversy. And soon we may see that combination which is characteristic of the 'nature-rightly' doctrines of a later time: namely, a combination of the Absolutism which is due to the renaissance of the antique idea of the State, with the modern Individualism which unfolds itself from out the Christiano-Germanic thought of Liberty.

As regards the question touching the Origin of the State—its origin in time and its origin in law—the Theory of the Social Contract slowly grew. It was generally agreed that in the beginning there was a State of Nature. At that time 'States' were not, and pure Natural Law prevailed, by virtue whereof all persons were free and equal and all goods were in common. Thus it was universally admitted that the Politic or Civil State was the product of acts done at a later time, and the only moot question was whether this was a mere consequence of the Fall of Man, or whether the State would have come into being, though in some freer and purer form, if mankind had increased in numbers while yet they were innocent. By way of investigating the origin of Political Society, men at first contented themselves with a general discussion of the manner in which *dominium* had made its appearance in the world and the legitimacy of its origin; and in their concept of *dominium,* Rulership and Ownership were blent. Then, when the question about Ownership had been severed from that about Rulership, we may see coming to the front always more plainly the supposition of the State's origin in a Contract of Subjection made between People and Ruler. Even the partizans of the Church adopt this opinion when they have surrendered the notion that the State originated in mere wrong. But then arose this further question:— How did it happen that this Community itself, whose Will, expressed in an act of transfer, was the origin of the State, came to be a Single Body competent to perform a legal act and possessing a transferable power over its members? At this point the idea of a Divine Creation of the State began to fail, for however certain men might be that the Will of God was the ultimate cause of Politic Society, still this cause fell back into the position of a *causa remota* working through human agency. As a more proximate cause the 'politic nature' which God has implanted in mankind could be

introduced; and Aristotle might be vouched. We can not say that there were absolutely no representatives of a theory of organic development, which would teach that the State had grown out of that aboriginal Community, the Family, in a purely natural, direct and necessary fashion. Still the weightier opinion was that Nature (like God) had worked only as *causa remota* or *causa impulsiva*: that is, as the source of a need for and of an impulse towards the social life, or, in short, as a more or less compulsory motive for the foundation of the State. More and more decisively was expressed the opinion that the very union of men in a political bond was an act of rational, human Will. Occasionally there may appear the notion that the State was an Institution which was founded, as other human institutions [e.g. monasteries or colleges] were founded, by certain definite Founders, either in peaceful wise or by some act of violence; but, in the main, there was a general inclination towards the hypothesis of some original, creative, act of Will of the whole uniting Community. This joint act was compared to the self-constitution of a corporation. But men did not construct for this purpose any legal concept that was specially adapted to the case. The learning of Corporations developed by the lawyers had no such concept to offer, for they also, despite the distinction between *universitas* and *societas,* [between Corporation and Partnership,] confused the single act whereby a Community unifies itself, with a mere obligatory contract made among individuals, and they regarded the peculiar unity of the Corporation as something that came to it from without by virtue of a concession made by the State. Thus in the end the Medieval Doctrine already brings the hypothetical act of political union under the category of a Contract of Partnership or 'Social' Contract. On the one hand, therefore, proclamation was made of the original Sovereignty of the Individual as the source of all political obligation. In this manner a base was won for the construction of Natural Rights of Man, which, since they were not comprised in the Contract, were unaffected by it and could not be impaired by the State. On the other hand, since the Sovereignty of the State, when once it was erected, rested on the indestructible foundation of a Contract sanctioned by the Law of Nature, conclusions which reached far in the direction of the State's Absolutism could be drawn by those who formulated the terms of the Contract.

If Philosophy was to find the terms of that fictitious Contract which provided a basis of Natural Law for the State and the State's power, it could not but be that the decisive word about this matter would be sought in the purpose which the State and its power are designed to fulfil. If, on the one part, the idea was retained that every individual had a final cause of his own, which was independent of and stood outside and above all political and communal life—and here was a divergence from Classical Antiquity—so, on the other part, the final cause of the State was always being enlarged—and here was a departure from the earlier Middle Age, though at times we may still hear echoes of the old Germanic idea that the State's one function is the maintenance of peace and law. In imitation of classical thought, men defined the State's purpose to be a happy and virtuous life: the realization of the public-weal and civic morality. True, that, according to the prevailing doctrine, the function of the State had a limit, and a necessary complement, in the function of the Church: a function making for a higher aim than that of the State, namely, for inward virtue and supra-mundane bliss. But an always stronger assault was being made upon the Church's monopoly of culture. An independent spiritual and moral mission was claimed for the State, until at length there were some who would ascribe to the State the care for all the interests of the Community, whether those interests were material or whether they were spiritual.

If, however, the contents of the Institutes of Natural Law were to be discovered by a consideration of their final cause, this same final cause would also be the measure of those indestructible rights that pertained to the 'Subjects' of Natural Law. From the final cause of the Individual flow the innate and inalienable rights of liberty, and so from the final cause of the Politic Community flow—and from of old the Church might here serve as a model—the State's innate and inalienable rights of superiority. From the rights thus bestowed Positive Law could take, and to them it could add, nothing. If, as a matter of fact, it contravenes them, it must admit itself over-ruled. The maxim *Salus publica suprema lex* entered on its reign, and a good legal title had been found on which Revolution, whether it came from above or from below, could support itself when it endeavoured to bring the traditional law into conformity with the postulates of the Law of Nature.

In truth Medieval Doctrine prepared the way for the great revolutions in Church and State, and this it did by attributing a real working validity as rules of Natural Law to a system constructed of abstract premisses and planned in accordance with the dictates of expediency. The whole internal structure of the State was subjected ever more and more to criticism proceeding from the Rationalist's stand-point. The value of the structure was tested by reference to its power of accomplishing a purpose and was measured by reference to an ideal and 'nature-rightly' State. The steering of public affairs was likened to the steering of a ship; it is a free activity consciously directed towards the attainment of a goal. Thus there arose the idea of an Art of Government, and people undertook to teach it in detail. There was disputation about the best form of government and the most suitable laws, and out of this grew a demand for such a transformation of Public Law as would bring it into accord with theoretical principles. Through the last centuries of the Middle

Age, alike in Church and Empire, unbroken and always louder, rings the cry for 'Reformation'!

Turning now to the fundamental concepts of Public Law, the resuscitation and further development of the classical idea of Sovereignty will appear to us as the main exploit achieved in this department by the prevalent endeavour to construct constitutions which shall conform to Natural Law. Men found the essence of all political organization in a separation of Rulers and Ruled. Also they took over from the antique world the doctrine of the Forms of Government and of the distinctions that exist between them. And so they came to the opinion that in every State some one visible Ruler, a man or a ruling assembly, is the 'Subject' of a Sovereign Power over the Ruled. And then, when, in contrast to the theory of 'Ruler's Sovereignty,' men developed the theory of a Popular Sovereignty, existing everywhere and always, the partizans of this doctrine did not once more call in question the newly acquired idea of Sovereignty, but transferred it to an Assembly which represents the People. The Medieval notion of Sovereignty, it is true, always differed in principle from that exalted notion which prevailed in after times. For one thing, there was unanimous agreement that the Sovereign Power, though raised above all Positive, is limited by Natural Law. Secondly, it was as unanimously agreed that the idea of the Sovereign by no means excludes an independent legal claim of nonsovereign subjects to participate in the power of the State. On the contrary, advocates of 'Ruler's Sovereignty' expressly maintained a political right of the People, and advocates of the People's Sovereignty expressly maintained a political right of the Ruler, so that even the extremest theories gave to the State somewhat of a 'constitutional' character. Therefore it was thought possible to combine the Sovereignty of the Monarch with what was in principle a Limited Monarchy. Therefore also the idea of a Mixed Constitution could be developed without facing awkward questions. Therefore again the beginnings of a doctrine which teaches the Separation of Powers could be reared on a basis of Popular Sovereignty. And therefore also the Representative System could be theoretically elaborated. None the less, the idea of Sovereignty, when once it had been formulated, irresistibly pressed forwards towards the conclusion that in the last resort some one Ruler or some one Assembly must be the 'Subject' of the Supreme Power, and that in case of conflict the State is incorporate only in this one man or this one Assembly.

The State Power, thus focussed at a single point, made, over all members of the State, ever fresh claims to all such rights of Superiority as were comprised within the idea and measure of the State's final cause and were compatible with those rights of Liberty of which the Individual could not be deprived. And just because the rights of Superiority flowed from the very idea of State Power, that Power, with increasing insistance, claimed to exercise them over all individuals equally and with equal directness and immediacy. If then, on the one hand, the Individual just in so far as he belongs to the Community is fully and wholly absorbed into the State, so, on the other hand, there is a strong tendency to emancipate the Individual from all bonds that are not of the State's making.

There was, moreover, a steady advance of the notion that the State is an exclusive Community. In phrases which tell of the Antique World men spoke of the State simply as 'Human Society.' The State is the all-comprehensive, and therefore the one and only, expression of that common life which stands above the life of the individual.

This thought, it is true, came at once into conflict with the ascription of a higher, or even an equal, right to the Church. And it was only with a great saving-clause for the rights of the Church that the prevalent doctrine of the Middle Age received the antique idea of the State. Still in the fourteenth and fifteenth centuries theory was preparing the way for the subsequent absorption of Church in State. One medieval publicist there was who dared to project a system, logically elaborated even into details, wherein the Church was a State Institution, Church property was State property, spiritual offices were offices of State, the government of the Church was part of the government of the State, and the sovereign Ecclesiastical Community was identical with the Political Assembly of the Citizens. He was Marsilius of Padua. No one followed him the whole way. Howbeit, isolated consequences of the same principle were drawn even in the Middle Age by other opponents of the Hierarchy. Already an unlimited power of suppressing abuses of ecclesiastical office was claimed for the State. Already, with more or less distinctness, Church property was treated as public property and placed, should the *salus publica* require it, at the disposal of the State. Already powers of the State which reach far down even into the internal affairs of the Church were being deduced from the demand that in temporal matters the Church should be subject to the temporal Magistrate. Already the classical sentence which told how the *ius sacrum* was a part of the *ius publicum* was once more beginning to reveal its original meaning.

If, however, we leave out of sight the State's relation to the Church, we see that, when Medieval Doctrine first takes shape, the idea of the State, which had been derived from the Antique World, was enfeebled and well-nigh suffocated by the consequences that were flowing from the medieval idea of the Empire: an idea which itself was being formulated by theory. The thought of a concentration at a single point of the whole life of the Community not only stood in sharp contradiction to actual facts and popular opinions, but also was opposed in theory to what might seem an insur-mountable bulwark, namely to the medieval thought of an harmoniously articulated Universal Community whose structure from top to bottom was of the federalistic kind. Nevertheless that antique concept of the State, when once it had found admission, worked and worked unceasingly and with deadly certainty until it had completely shattered this proud edifice of medieval thought. We may see theory trying to hold fast the mere shadow of this stately idea, even when what should have corresponded to it in the world of fact, the Medieval Empire, had long lain in ruins. And so also we may see in theory the new edifice of the Modern State being roofed and tiled when in the world of fact just the first courses of this new edifice are beginning to arise amidst the ruins of the old.

When Aristotle's *Politics* had begun their new life, the current definition taught that the State is the highest and completest of Communities and a Community that is self-sufficing. It is evident that, so soon as men are taking this definition in earnest, only some one among the various subordinated and superordinated Communities can be regarded as being the State. For a while this logical consequence might be evaded by a grossly illogical device. The . . . *civitas* that the ancients had defined was discovered by medieval Philosophy in a medieval town, and, by virtue of the ideal of the organic structure of the whole Human Race, the community of this . . . *civitas* was subordinated to a *regnum* and to the *imperium*: that is, to higher and wider communities in which it found its completion and its limitations. Thus, no sooner has the medieval thinker given his definition, than he is withdrawing it without the slightest embarrassment: his superlative becomes a comparative, and the absolute attribute becomes relative. Then, on the other hand, the lawyers, with the *Corpus Iuris* before them, explained that the Empire is the one true State; but they defined *civitas* and *populus* and even *regnum* in such a manner that these terms could be applied to provinces and to rural or urban communes; and then, as a matter of fact, they went on applying the concept of 'The State' to communities that were much smaller than the Empire. Still the antique idea, when once it had been grasped, was sure to triumph over this confused thinking. Indeed we may see that the Philosophic Theory of the State often sets to work with the assumption that there cannot be two States one above the other, and that above the State there is no room for a World-State, while below the State there is only room for mere communes. Then in Jurisprudence, from the days of Bartolus onwards, an ever sharper distinction was being drawn between communities which had and those which had not an external *Superior,* and communities of the latter kind were being placed on a level with the *Imperium.* The differences between *civitas, regnum* and *imperium* became mere differences in size instead of being joints in the organic articulation of a single body, and at the same time the concept of the State became the exclusive property of a community which recognizes no external superior (*universitas superiorem non recognoscens*).

Thus already in the Middle Age the idea of the State arrived at theoretical completion, and the attribute of External Sovereignty became the distinguishing mark of the State. The *Imperium Mundi,* which rose above the Sovereign States, had evaporated into an unsubstantial shadow, and at any rate was stripped of the character of a State, even when its bare existence was not denied. For States within the State there was thenceforth no room, and all the smaller groups had to be brought under the rubric 'Communes and Corporations'.

From the concentration of 'State Life' at a single point there by no means follows as logically necessary a similar concentration of all 'Community Life.' The medieval idea of the organic articulation of Mankind might live on, though but in miniature, within each separate State. It might become the idea of the organic articulation of the Nation. And up to a certain degree this actually happened. The Romano-Canonical Theory of Corporations, although it decomposed and radically transmuted the German notion of the autonomous life of communities and fellowships, always insured to the non-sovereign community a certain independent life of its own, a sphere of rights within the domain of Public Law, a sphere that belonged to it merely because it was a community, and lastly, an organic interposition between the Individual and the Community of All. Even among political theorists there were not wanting some who in the last centuries of the Middle Age—centuries brimful of vigorous corporate life—sought to oppose to that centralization which had triumphed in the Church and was threatening the State, a scientific statement of the idea of corporative articulation and a logically deduced justification of the claims that could be made on behalf of the smaller groups as beings with rights of their own and an intrinsic value.

For all this, however, even in the Middle Age the drift of Theory set incessantly towards an exaltation of the Sovereignty of the State which ended in the exclusive representation by the State of all the common interests and common life of the Community. In this direction Philosophy with giant strides was outstripping Jurisprudence.

For those rights of Lordship of Germanic origin which subsisted within the State and beneath the Sovereign's Power, Jurisprudence might long provide a secure place. It had accepted the *ius feudorum,* and was prepared to treat offices as objects of proprietary rights. But Political and Philosophical Theories could find no room whatever in their abstract systems for feudal and patrimonial powers. On the contrary, this was just the point whence spread the thought that all subordinate

public power is a mere delegation of the Sovereign Power. Also this was just the point whence spread a process which transmuted the medieval concept of Office, in such wise that every office appeared merely as a commission to use the Power of the State: to use, that is, in a certain manner, a power which is in substance one and untransferable. When that process is completed, every officer appears as the freely chosen instrument of the Sovereign Will.

A similar attitude was taken by the abstract theories of Politics and Philosophy in relation to those independent Rights of Fellowships which had their source in Germanic Law. For a long time Jurisprudence was prepared to give them a home; but Philosophical Theory looked askance at them. The Doctrine of the State that was reared upon a classical ground-work had nothing to say of groups that mediated between the State and the Individual. This being so, the domain of Natural Law was closed to the Corporation, and its very existence was based upon the ground of a Positive Law which the State had made and might at any time alter. And then as the sphere of the State's Might on the one hand, and the sphere of the Individual's Liberty on the other, became the exclusive and all-sufficing starting-points for a Philosophy of Law, the end was that the Corporation could find a place in Public Law only as a part of the State and a place in Private Law only as an artificial Individual, while all in actual life that might seem to conflict with this doctrine was regarded as the outcome of privileges which the State had bestowed and in the interest of the public might at any time revoke. While the Middle Age endured, it was but rarely that the consequences of these opinions were expressly drawn. Howbeit, Philosophic Doctrine was on the one hand filling itself full of the antique idea of the State, and on the other hand it was saving therefrom and developing the Christiano-Germanic idea of Freedom and depositing this in the theory of Natural Law. And as this work proceeded towards the attainment of ever more distinct results, the keener were the weapons which Medieval Doctrine was forging for that combat which fills the subsequent centuries. A combat it was in which the Sovereign State and the Sovereign Individual contended over the delimitation of the provinces assigned to them by Natural Law, and in the course of that struggle all intermediate groups were first degraded into the position of the more or less arbitrarily fashioned creatures of mere Positive Law, and in the end were obliterated.

Andrew S. Skinner (essay date 1993)

SOURCE: "The Shaping of Political Economy in the Enlightment," in *Adam Smith: International Perspectives,* edited Hiroshi Mizuta and Chuhei Sugiyama, St. Martin's Press, 1993, pp. 113-39.

[The essay that follows, revised for publication from a lecture originally delivered in 1990, looks at political and economic thought together. By considering the works of Smith, Hume, and Steuart, Skinner seeks to determine "the 'shape' which these writers gave to their studies" and ultimately the shape they gave to the course of political thought in general.]

Thirty-five years ago, Alec Macfie addressed the question of the 'Scottish tradition in economic thought'. He sought to isolate a number of characteristic features of the Scottish approach and in so doing drew attention to the sociological, philosophical and historical dimensions which Adam Smith together with his predecessors and successors had brought to the study of economic phenomena. In particular, Professor Macfie gave prominence to a certain penchant for systematic argument, and to an approach which was 'more concerned with giving a broad, well balanced comprehensive picture, seen from different points of view than with logical rigour' (1967, p. 22).

While one might hesitate to describe these approaches to the study of political economy as particularly or even exclusively Scottish, there is no doubt that all are characteristic of the work done by three major figures of the Enlightenment, David Hume, Sir James Steuart and Adam Smith. Adam Smith, the bicentenary of whose death has just passed, proved, in the event, to be the most influential figure: the writer whose choice of 'model' (and there were choices to be made) did most to establish the shape of the early classical system as Alfred Marshall would have known it. Yet there is a sense in which we can claim that all three of the writers named not only shared common intellectual interests, but also produced work of lasting value. It may also be true that we can only attain a true perspective on the measure of Smith's achievement by pausing to review the contributions of his immediate predecessors, both of whom he knew. It is, in any event, certain that we cannot attain an accurate understanding of the tradition which Macfie identified by considering the contribution of Adam Smith in isolation. There is, besides, the intriguing fact that Hume's *Political Discourses* profoundly influenced two writers who were to produce systematic treatises which were quite markedly different in character.

This paper is divided into four main parts. In Part I we consider Hume's contribution. In Parts II and III we examine the different ways in which Steuart and Smith may have reacted to the lead provided by their friend. In Part IV we consider the advantages of the Smithian system and examine the consequences of his dominance as the founder of classical economics, especially as this affected the interpretation of the past. But it is not the intention in this place exhaustively to review the work done by these major figures, and far less to consider in detail their analytical contributions. Rather our concern is with the broad perspectives adopted—the 'shape' which these writers gave to their studies.

I

David Hume's *Discourses* (1752) contain nine essays on economic topics which were conveniently collected and most helpfully introduced by Eugene Rotwein in 1955. The essays cover such subjects as money, the balance of trade, the rate of interest, public finance, taxation and population. The topics were treated as *essays,* a fact which makes it difficult to recover Hume's intention if not his meaning. But as Rotwein has shown, the essays are marked by a unity of purpose and method. They also enable us to identify a number of particular and interdependent themes.

The first theme is broadly methodological and arises from Hume's conviction 'that all the sciences have a relation, greater or less, to human nature, and that however wide any of them may seem to run from it, they still return back by one passage or another' (*EW,* p. xx). The study of human nature was thus to be based upon empirical evidence: as Hume himself made clear, the *Treatise* constituted an attempt to introduce the 'experimental method of reasoning into moral subjects'.

The approach also allowed Hume to state a proposition which was profoundly influential in the eighteenth century, namely that: 'It is universally acknowledged that there is a great uniformity among the actions of men, in all nations and ages, and that human nature remains still the same in its principles and operations.' Among these 'constant principles' Hume was to include a desire for action, for liveliness and, of particular interest to the economist, avarice or the desire for gain; a constant principle of motion which allows the commentator to offer scientific generalizations at least in the sphere of political economy (*Essays,* pp. 12-13).

A second major theme in the *Discourses* relates to Hume's employment of historical materials. From one point of view this perspective is straightforward, in the sense that the study of history is an 'invention' which 'extends our experience to all past ages, and to the most distant nations' (*Essays,* p. 556). But from the point of view of our understanding of economic phenomena, broadly defined, the picture which was to emerge from the 'economic writings' was in fact a complex one.

If Hume did argue that the principles of human nature were constant, he also appreciated that the way in which they found expression would be profoundly affected by the socio-economic environment which may happen to exist, and by habit, customs and manners. While this theme runs throughout the essays, perhaps two examples will suffice for the present purpose.

In the long essay 'Of the Populousness of Ancient Nations', a work which has scarcely received the attention it deserves, Hume addressed a proposition which had been advanced by both Montesquieu and Robert Wallace to the effect that population levels had been higher in ancient as compared to modern times (*EW*, p. 108n.). In deciding in favour of modern society, Hume drew attention to the use of slavery in the classical period as 'in general disadvantageous both to the happiness and populousness of mankind' (*EW*, p. 124), pointing also to the incidence of military conflict and of political instability. But perhaps the most striking aspect of the argument is the attention given to the point that 'Trade, manufactures, industry were no where, in former ages, so flourishing as they are at present in Europe' (*EW*, p. 143). Population is ultimately limited not just by political factors, but also by the food supply, and this in turn by the type of economic organization prevailing.

The same basic theme emerges in the essay 'Of Money' where Hume rejected the conventional wisdom that money can be regarded as wealth (*EW*, pp. 33, 37) and stated the famous relationship between changes in the money supply and the general price level, a relationship which remained substantially unchallenged until the 1920s.

Less familiar is the point that Hume consistently contrasted the situation of a primitive economy with a more sophisticated version. It is, he argued, 'the proportion between the circulating money, and the commodities in the market which determines the prices' (*EW*, p. 42). In the primitive economy, 'we must consider that, in the first and more uncultivated ages of any state, . . . men have little occasion for exchange, at least for money, which, by agreement, is the common measure of exchange' (*EW*, p. 42). But in the state of commerce, in contrast, 'coin enters into many more contracts, and by that means is much more employed' (*EW*, p. 43).

On the other hand, the changed form of economic organization had given a greater scope to individual effort and must therefore massively increase the supply of commodities which are subject to exchange. Hume therefore concluded that although prices in Europe had risen since the discoveries in the West Indies and elsewhere, these prices were in fact much lower than the extent of the increase in the money supply might of itself suggest: 'And no other satisfactory reason can be given, why all prices have not risen to a much more exorbitant height, except that which is derived from a change of customs and manners' (*EW*, p. 44).

The technique which we have just considered is essentially an exercise in comparative statics in the sense that it enables us to contrast and compare the operation of certain economic relationships in different institutional environments. But there was another dimension to Hume's historicism which, if loosely articulated, is none the less more explicitly dynamic in character.

The theme of historical dynamics is addressed primarily in the essays 'Of Commerce' and 'Of Refinement in the Arts', where it is noted that:

> The bulk of every state may be divided into *husbandmen* and *manufacturers*. The former are employed in the culture of the land; the latter work up the materials furnished by the former, into all the commodities which are necessary or ornamental to human life. As soon as men quite the savage state, where they live chiefly by hunting and fishing, they must fall into these two classes though the arts of agriculture employ *at first* the most numerous part of the society.
>
> (*EW*, pp. 5-6)

It was Hume's contention that there had been a gradual progression to a situation where the two main sectors of activity are fully interdependent, supported by merchants: 'one of the most useful races of men, who serve as agents between those parts of the state, that are wholly unacquainted, and ignorant of each other's necessities' (*EW*, p. 52).

The argument is rooted in Hume's deployment of a favourite thesis of the eighteenth century, namely that men have natural wants which gradually extend in a self-sustaining spiral. The tone is best expressed in the essay 'Of Refinement in the Arts' where Hume also contrasts the form of government found in 'rude and unpolished nations' with that likely to be associated with the modern state. In passages which are likely to have caught the attention of both Smith and Steuart, Hume observed that 'where luxury nourished commerce and industry, the peasants, by proper cultivation of the land, become rich and independent; while the tradesmen and merchants acquire a share of property, and draw authority and consideration to that middling rank of men, who are the best and firmest basis of public liberty' (*EW*, pp. 28-9): a development which may be expected further to encourage the rate of economic growth.

The final major theme in Hume's thought relates to the problem of international trade, a theme which, here as elsewhere, unfolds on a number of levels. To begin with Hume drew attention to the general benefits of foreign trade. In the essay 'Of Commerce', for example, he made the point that if 'we consult history, we shall find that in most nations, foreign trade had preceded any refinement in home manufactures, and had given birth to domestic luxury'. In the same context he drew attention to induced changes in taste and to the point that imitation leads domestic manufactures 'to emulate the foreign in their improvements' (*EW*, pp. 13-14, cf. p. 78). Hume continued to note that the encouragement of domestic industry would further enhance the opportunities for trade and economic growth (*EW*, p. 79).

The second aspect of Hume's argument supports his repeated claim for freedom of trade on grounds that are essentially technical. Building upon the analysis in the essay 'Of Money' Hume examined the case of two or more economies *with no unemployed resources* with a view to demonstrating the futility of the mercantile preoccupation with a positive balance of trade. Against this, Hume contended, a net inflow of gold would inevitably raise prices in the domestic economy, while a loss of specie would reduce the general price level elsewhere—thus improving the competitive position in the latter case and reducing it in the former. In the essay 'Of the Balance of Trade' Hume concluded that 'money, in spite of the absurd jealousy of princes and states, has brought itself nearly to a level' (*EW*, p. 66) just as 'all water, wherever it communicates, remains always at a level' (*EW*, p. 63).

The third dimension to Hume's treatment of foreign trade is much more complex. It is based upon the premiss that countries have different characteristics and different rates of growth, thus opening up a different and distinctive policy position as compared to those so far considered. The argument effectively introduced what Hont (1983, Ch. 11) has described as the 'rich country - poor country debate'. Hont has identified no fewer than twelve aspects of the argument (1983, pp. 274-5). But for the present purpose, we may approach the matter in a slightly different way.

While critical of Montesquieu's thesis regarding the role of physical factors, Hume was none the less conscious of the fact that different countries could have different factor endowments, and aware that climate could have some influence upon economic activity (*EW*, p. 17). But there is also a sense in which the rich country-poor country thesis reflects strands of thought which we have already identified in dealing with the comparative static and dynamic branches of Hume's argument.

In this context it is worth recalling that the comparative static technique involves the *comparison of different* economic types, while the dynamic element draws attention to the importance of individual effort and to an accelerating rate of change as institutions and manners themselves change. On the one hand the reader is reminded of the phenomenon of a 'diversity of geniuses, climates and soil' while on the other attention is drawn to the point that the extent to which men apply 'art, care and industry' may vary in one society over time and between different societies at a given point in time. Other factors which will affect the rate of growth

and cause variations in rates of growth in different communities, include the form of government and the degree to which public policies such as trade regulations, taxes and debt are deployed with intelligence.

Hume illustrated this new phase of problem by referring to the issue of regional imbalance (a concern which he shared with Josiah Tucker) citing the case of London and Yorkshire (*EW*, p. 95). The regional dimension is as relevant to the rich country-poor country debate as is the international, although it was upon the latter that Hume chose to place most emphasis.

Hume's treatment of the performance of the modern economy, especially in the context of the essays 'Of Money' and 'Of Interest' implies an increase in productivity which may give the developed economy an advantage in terms of the price of manufactures (cf. *EW*, p. 195). He also recognized that an inflow of gold in the context of a growing economy need not generate adverse price effects (*EW*, pp. 197-8).

But Hume clearly felt that rich countries could lose their competitive edge, in noting that England feels 'some disadvantages in foreign trade by the high price of labour, which is in part the effect of the riches of their artisans, as well as of the plenty of money' (*EW*, pp. 15-16). It was thus recognized that advantages may be eroded, causing the loss in turn of *particular* industries, (*EW*, p. 80), *unless care is taken to preserve them*.

Hume also seems to have felt that the tendency for the prices of labour and provisions to rise over time could lead to a *general* loss of markets and that this could involve a policy of protection to support employment levels, a situation which he contemplated with calm objectivity in noting that 'as foreign trade is not the most material circumstance, it is not to be put in competition with the happiness of so many millions' (*EW*, p. 16).

Hume concluded in the essay 'Of Money' that 'there seems to be a happy concurrence of causes in human affairs, which checks the growth of trade and riches, and hinders them from being confined entirely to one people' (*EW*, p. 34). The point was to be elaborated in correspondence with Lord Kames, and reflects an old preoccupation with the thesis of 'growth and decay' (cf. *EW*, p. 201).

II

Sir James Steuart cited more than fifty authorities in the *Principles* (Skinner, 1966, pp. 739-40) in a list which includes Cantillon, Mirabeau, Montesquieu and Hume. It is not difficult, therefore, to identify Steuart's sources of inspiration in matters of *doctrine*. But it is sometimes forgotten that Steuart faced an acute problem of *organization* in writing the *Principles* (cf. Skinner, 1966, pp. 5-6), a problem which was largely solved by his adoption of the broad methodological perspectives associated with Hume. While Hume was said to have been critical of the 'form and style' of the *Principles,* it is not difficult to understand his pleasure when first he read the work in manuscript form (Skinner, 1966, p. xlv).

Perhaps the use of the historical approach provides the most striking parallel, especially as applied to political subjects where Steuart ascribed to economic development a gradual but fundamental change in the patterns of authority and dependence, deducing that 'modern liberty' had arisen from the 'introduction of industry, and circulation of an adequate equivalent for every service' (Skinner, 1966, p. 209). The change in the balance of power which was the reflection of the same process also led Steuart to the conclusion that 'industry must give wealth and wealth *will* give power' (Skinner, 1966, p. 213). As an earnest of this position Steuart drew attention (in his notes on Hume's *History*) to the reduced position of the Crown at the end of Elizabeth's reign, a revolution which appears 'quite natural when we set before us the causes which occasioned it. Wealth must give power; and industry, in a country of luxury, will throw it into the hands of the commons' (Skinner, 1966, p. 213n).

There is an equally obvious parallel between Steuart and Hume in respect of the treatment of population, where in effect the former sought to extend the analysis of Hume's essay and to place this topic at the centre of his treatment in Book I. In so doing, Steuart stated that the first fundamental principle of population is generation, the next is food (Skinner, 1966, p. 31) from which it followed that where men live by gathering the fruits of the earth (the North American model), population levels must be determined by their extent (pp. 36-7).

Where some effort is applied to the cultivation of the soil (the agrarian stage) Steuart recognized that the output of food, and therefore the level of population, would grow. But here again he drew a distinction between cultivation for subsistence and the application of industry to the soil, as found in the modern situation, where all goods and services command a price and where the potential for economic growth (and therefore population) is enhanced—especially in a situation where the major sectors of activity are fully interdependent (Skinner, 1966, p. 42). It was for these reasons that Steuart was able to side with Hume's judgment against that of Montesquieu and Wallace.

Steuart's account of the stage of commerce also includes a statement which Hume would have instantly recognized when it was noted that:

We find the people distributed into two classes. The first is that of the farmers who produce the subsistence, and who are necessarily employed in this branch of business; the other I shall call the *free hands;* because their occupation being to procure themselves subsistence out of the superfluity of the farmers, and by a labour adapted to the wants of the society, may vary according to these wants and these again according to the spirit of the times.

(Skinner, 1966, p. 43)

The whole process, it was then noted, would be facilitated by the use of money as the means of exchange and further 'by an operation by which the wealth or work, either of individuals or of societies, may, by a set of men called merchants, be exchanged for an equivalent, proper for supplying every want, without interruption to industry, or any check upon consumption' (Skinner, 1966, p. 146).

Hume would have had little difficulty in appreciating these points or the broadly optimistic assessment which Steuart offered with regard to economic growth within this institutional framework. It is readily apparent that Steuart saw no reason to doubt the potential for economic development in the context of the *exchange* economy. Here, and for the first time in an *institutional* sense: 'Wealth becomes *equably distributed;* . . . by *equably distributed* I do not mean, that every individual comes to have an *equal* share, but an equal chance, I may say a certainty, of becoming rich in proportion to his industry' (*Works,* 1805, ii. 156). Steuart also argued that the potential for economic growth was almost without limit or certain boundary in the current 'situation of every country in Europe' (Skinner, 1966, p. 137). An equally dramatic confirmation of the general theme is to be found in the chapter on machines, which he considered to be 'of the greatest utility' in 'augmenting the produce or assisting the labour and ingenuity of man' (p. 125).

Again in the manner of Hume, it was Steuart's contention that the modern economy had encouraged new forms of demand and new incentives to industry. In a passage reminiscent of Smith's *Moral Sentiments* (which he may have read), Steuart drew attention to man's love of ingenuity and to the fact that the satisfaction of one level of perceived wants tends to open up others by virtue of a kind of demonstration effect (Skinner, 1966, p. 157).

The general point at issue is best caught by Steuart's earlier (but recurring) contrast between the feudal and modern systems: 'Men were then forced to labour because they were slaves to others; men are now forced to labour because they are slaves to their own wants' (Skinner, 1966, p. 51). But Steuart was to offer further applications of the thesis in ways which recall Hume's concern with variations in rates of economic performance in different communities.

In the second book Steuart dropped the Humean assumption of the closed economy and proceeded to examine the issue of international trade. Characteristically, he traced the interrelationship between developed and undeveloped nations in terms of the distinction between active and passive trade, which had already been established by Malachy Postlethwayt but in the context of a problem already addressed by Hume.

Steuart was clearly preoccupied with variations caused by 'natural advantages' such as access to materials, transport and the nature of the climate (Skinner, 1966, p. 238), as benefits a close student and admirer of 'the great Montesquieu' (p. 121). To these he added the form of government in arguing that 'trade and industry have been found to flourish best under the republican form, and under those which have come nearest to it' (p. 211). But equally important for Steuart were the spirit of a people and 'the greater degree of force' with which 'a taste for refinement and luxury in the rich, an ambition to become so, and an application to labour and ingenuity in the lower classes of men' manifested themselves in different societies at any one point in time and over time, a thoroughly Humean perspective.

Steuart was acutely conscious of the sheer variety of economic conditions and indeed noted early in the book that:

> If one considers the variety which is found in different countries, in the distribution of property, subordination of classes, genius of people, proceeding from the variety of forms of government, laws, climate, and manners, one may conclude, that the political economy of each must necessarily be different.

(Skinner, 1966, p. 17)

The number of possible 'combinations' opened up by the proposition that growth rates and other characteristics will vary is virtually endless. In recognition of this point Steuart employed three broad classifications, all of which may derive from Mirabeau's *Friend of Man* (1756): the stages of infant, foreign and inland trade. This generalization and clarification of Hume's position reminds us of a further characteristic of Steuart's argument, namely his concern with economic policy.

The duties of the statesman in the economic sphere are clear: having defined the essence of the exchange economy as involving a 'general tacit contract', Steuart went on to note that 'Whenever . . . anyone is found, upon whom nobody depends, and who depends on everyone, as is the case with him who is willing to work for his bread, but who can find no employment, there is a breach of contract and an abuse' (Skinner, 1966, p. 88).

As in the case of Smith, the justification for intervention is market failure, although Steuart's position with respect to the function of the state arises directly from the areas of analysis and policy with which he was primarily concerned.

It is appropriate, first, to recall Steuart's interest in the model of primitive accumulation and in the *emergence* of the exchange economy. Steuart's concern with society in a process of transition is reflected in his attempt to formulate policies designed to deal with the problems generated by *historical* developments, developments which had caused cities to expand, and feudal retainers to be dismissed. It is in this context that the statesman is invited to consider the employment of redundant nobles and of the 'multitudes of poor' together with the all-important issue of the means of communication (such as good roads).

Steuart also suggested that the historical and contemporary record would also provide an invaluable guide to the problems which would confront a statesman who adopted a self-conscious policy of economic *and therefore* of social development. It was Steuart's contention that in many cases the transition from a state of 'trifling industry' and subsistence farming (which could be described as the primitive version of the stage of commerce) could not occur without the interposition of the sovereign (Skinner, 1966, p. 108). Steuart also gave a great deal of attention to policy with respect to international trade, in emphasizing the need for protection in particular cases and freedom of trade in others. The position is conveniently summarized by reference to the 'stages' of trade.

Infant trade, for example, represents an undeveloped economy where the ruling policy must be one of protection (Skinner, 1966, p. 262)—although he also noted that 'the scaffolding must be taken away when the fabric is completed' (*Works,* ii. 235). In the case of *foreign trade,* taken as representing the attainment of a competitive stage, the policies recommended are simply designed to retain the capacity of an economy to compete: here the ruling principles are 'to banish luxury; to encourage frugality; to fix the lowest standard of prices possible; and to watch, with the greatest attention, over the vibrations of the balance between work and demand. While this is preserved, no internal vice can affect the prosperity of it' (Skinner, 1966, p. 263).

Inland trade, on the other hand, represents a situation where a developed nation has lost its competitive edge. Here the basic preoccupation must be the maintenance of the level of employment. Steuart also recognized the importance of the balance of payments in advocating a restrictive monetary policy, and concluded: 'I will not therefore say, that in every case which can be supposed, certain restrictions upon the exportation of bullion or coin are contrary to good policy. This proposition I confine to the flourishing nations of our own time' (Skinner, 1966, p. 581).

Two additional points are worth making before we conclude this sketch. First, we should recall Hume's distinction between the loss of particular markets in international trade and the situation where an *economy* finds itself in an uncompetitive position. Exactly this point was made by Steuart in commenting upon the fact that his 'stages of trade' may apply to economies, or regions, or indeed to particular industries. As he noted:

> We are not to suppose the commerce of any nation confined to any one of the three species. I have considered them separately, according to custom, in order to point out their different principles. It is the business of statesmen to compound them according to circumstances.

> (Skinner, 1966, p. 265)

Second, we should note that Steuart's policy recommendations are always related to *circumstances*. He contended that economic intervention could only be justified in cases of perceived economic necessity. For example, in a passage which applies to nations as well as to sectors or regions within a nation he observed:

> Were industry and frugality found to prevail equally in every part of . . . great political bodies, or were luxury and superfluous consumption everywhere carried to the same height, trade might, without any hurt, be thrown entirely open. It would then cease to be an object of a statesman's care and concern.

> (Skinner, 1966, p. 296)

III

It is now recognized that Smith owed much to Hume (and to Francis Hutcheson) in his approach to ethics, at least in the sense that he developed mechanisms which involved the use of sympathy, reason and imagination in an argument which greatly developed the concept of the spectator. A distinctive feature of the approach is the role ascribed to self-interest, where Smith took the opposite view to Hutcheson in suggesting that a 'regard to our own private happiness and interest . . . appear upon many occasions to be very laudable principles of action' (*TMS*, VIII. ii.3.6).

Smith's analysis placed much emphasis on man's desire for approval, a desire which finds many illustrations in the economic sphere where Smith suggests that the basic drive to better our condition is rooted in the pursuit of status, and further supported by a desire to acquire the imagined conveniences of wealth. These passages in *TMS* reflect the tone of Hume's essay 'Of Refinement in the Arts' regarding the benefits of eco-

nomic growth, and provide a good illustration to Smith's use of the basic thesis of man's insatiable wants. Smith was also at one with Hume in his calm assessment of Bernard Mandeville's provocative argument that private vices were public benefits:

> If the love of magnificence, a taste for the elegant arts and improvements of human life . . . is to be regarded as luxury, sensuality and ostentation, even to those whose situation allows, without any inconvenience, the indulgence of those passions, it is certain that luxury, sensuality and ostentation are public benefits; since without these qualities upon which he thinks it proper to bestow such opprobious names, the arts of refinement could never find encouragement.

> (*TMS*, VII.ii.4.12)

If Smith followed Hume in offering a moral dimension to his system, he agreed with both Hume and Steuart in applying a sociological perspective to his treatment of history, a treatment marked by an interest in the link between economic organization and patterns of authority and dependence. Smith also shared the same interest in the association between economic development and the changing distribution of political power which, in the case of England, had led to the House of Commons assuming a position of dominance, *vis-à-vis* the House of Lords.

But Smith gave the 'history of civil society' a distinct status built in turn upon a distinctive thesis—that of the four stages which he developed in its complete form (Meek, 1976). One example of Smith's historical writing is to be found in the treatment of public jurisprudence in the *Lectures*. A further illustration, possibly of more direct interest to the student of economics, is found in *The Wealth of Nations* (henceforth *WN*), Book III, where Smith set out to trace the rise and fall of the feudal system: a process which culminated in the emergence of the 'present establishments' in Europe.

Following a general description of the feudal state, Smith's account of the process of transition begins with the emergence of the city as a means of establishing a countervailing power *vis-à-vis* the great landed magnates. Smith argues that royal policy had in effect created self-governing institutions with the right to defend themselves, thus establishing an environment within which economic growth was possible (*WN*, III. iii. 12).

In a compact analysis remarkable for its formality, Smith proceeded to argue that economic growth must initially be supported by foreign trade. This would be based at first on the exchange of domestic surpluses in primary products for foreign manufactures. This in turn would be followed, he suggested, by an attempt to introduce manufactures at home based upon foreign materials and, finally, by the gradual refinement of manufactures based upon domestic output (*WN*, III. iii. 20).

It will be noted that the argument gives prominence to a point emphasized by Hume, namely the role of imitation. It is also noteworthy that the whole process depends upon the assumption that trade initially took place between societies at different stages of development, and that the pattern of trade will change as domestic development unfolds in the manner suggested by Steuart in his analysis of what he (unlike Smith) took to be a central problem in international trade.

As is now well known, Smith proceeded to show that the emergence of new forms of activity and of wealth would impinge upon the interests of the great proprietors until a situation was reached where they became 'as insignificant as any substantial burgher or tradesman in a city. A regular government was established in the country as well as in the city, nobody having sufficient power to disturb its operations in the one, any more than in the other' (*WN*, III. iv. 15). Smith thus established a link between commerce and liberty, and in so doing acknowledged a debt to Hume as the 'only writer who, so far as I know, has hitherto taken any notice of it' (*WN*, i. p. 42). In the manner of Steuart and Hume, Smith had established that the modern economy is a two-sector case within which all goods and services command a price, but by a more formal route.

Smith's students would undoubtedly have understood that his treatment of economic questions was to be seen against the background provided by the ethics and by the historical analysis. But when Smith turned to political economy he also made it possible to see this subject as separate and distinct—thus emulating the achievements of Hume and Steuart, while departing from Hutcheson, whose analysis of economic questions is integral with his theory of jurisprudence (cf. Teichgraeber, 1986). But at the same time Smith followed Hutcheson in respect of the *organization* of his argument, featuring as it does a consideration of the division of labour, money, and the analysis of price and allocation (Taylor, 1965, p. 14; Scott, 1900, Ch. 11).

While Smith differs from Hutcheson in respect of trade policy, it is perhaps in this area that he shows some debt to Hume. He cited Hume's authority in connection with the doctrine of the specie-flow (cf. Eagly, 1970), while in addition there is a strong Humean flavour in the claim 'that Britain should by all means be made a free port, that there should be no interruptions of any kind made to foreign trade . . . and that free commerce and liberty of exchange should be allowed

with all nations and for all things' (*LJB,* p. 269).

But at the same time, the lectures were innocent of a clear distinction between factors of productions and categories of return. Absent too was 'the fundamental analysis . . . of saving, investing, capital and money which was to become the central pillar of the classical macro-economics' (Hutchison, 1988, p. 353). These deficiencies may well have been corrected as a result of Smith's contact with the Physiocrats in 1766, and especially by his knowledge of Turgot's *Reflections on the Formation and Distribution of Riches* (cf. Skinner, 1979, Ch. 5).

As far as the purely economic analysis is concerned, the familiar tale need not detain us. It is sufficient to be reminded that in the *Wealth of Nations* the theory of price and allocation was developed in terms of a model which made due allowance for distinct factors of production (land, labour, capital) and for the appropriate forms of return (rent, wages, profit). This point, now so obvious, struck Smith as novel and permitted him to develop an analysis of the allocative mechanism which ran in terms of interrelated adjustments in both factor and commodity markets. The resulting version of general interdependence also allowed Smith to move from the discussion of 'micro' to that of 'macro' economic issues, and to develop a model of the 'circular flow' which relies heavily on the distinction, already established by the Physiocrats, between fixed and circulating capital.

But these terms, which were applied to the activities of individual undertakers, were transformed in their meaning by their application to society at large. Working in terms of period analysis, Smith in effect represented the working of the economic process as a series of activities and transactions which linked the main socio-economic groups (proprietors, capitalists and wage-labour). In Smith's terms, current purchases in effect withdraw consumption and investment goods from the circulating capital of society, goods which were in turn replaced by virtue of productive activity in the same time period.

Looked at from one point of view, the analysis as a whole provides one of the most dramatic examples of the doctrine of 'unintended social outcomes', or the working of the 'invisible hand'. The individual undertaker (entrepreneur), seeking the most efficient allocation of resources, contributes to overall economic efficiency; the merchant's reaction to price signals helps to ensure that the allocation of resources accurately reflects the structure of consumers' preferences; the drive to better our condition contributes to economic growth.

The argument is also buttressed by a series of judgments as to *probable* patterns of behaviour and *actual* trends of events. It was Smith's firm opinion, for example, that in a situation where there was tolerable security, 'The sole use of money is to circulate consumable goods. By means of it, provisions, materials and finished work are bought and sold, and distributed to their proper consumers' (*WN,* II. iii. 23). In the same way he contended that the savings generated during any (annual) period would always be matched by investment (*WN,* II. iii. 18), a key assumption of the classical system which was to follow.

If such a model enabled Smith to isolate the cause of economic growth, with the emphasis now on the supply side, it is also informed throughout by what Hutchison (1988, p. 268) has described as the 'powerfully fascinating idea and assumption of beneficient self-adjustments and self-equilibration'.

Schumpeter may have been correct in his assertion that 'the *Wealth of Nations* does not contain a single analytical idea, principle, or method that was entirely new in 1776' (1954, p. 184). But what is important is the presence of a *system,* the fact that Smith gave political economy a distinctive analytical *shape* which was a dramatic step forward. Looked at from this point of view it is apparent that the concept of the analytical system as a kind of imaginary machine is entirely apt as a description of Smith's contribution and that his particular 'machine' went well beyond those of Hume and Steuart in terms of organization and content.

Smith's contribution made it possible to proceed from one area of analysis to another in a clear and logical order: from the analysis of price to that of distribution, from distribution to the concept of the circular flow and hence to the treatment of dynamics. Moreover, it is apparent that Smith advances through the work by dealing with distinct logical problems in a particular sequence which successfully illustrates the interdependence of economic phenomena.

The quality of *system* was appreciated by some contemporaries, such as Dugald Stewart who noted that 'it may be doubted . . . if there exists any book beyond the circle of the mathematical and physical sciences, which is at once so agreeable in its arrangement to the rules of a sound logic, and so accessible to the examination of ordinary readers' (IV. 2). This is a compliment which Smith would have appreciated, conscious as he was of the 'beauty of a systematical arrangement of different observations connected by a few common principles' (*WN,* V. i. f. 25).

As in the case of Steuart, there is also a policy dimension which reflects the author's areas of interest. But the dimension is now very different and based, in the main, on a series of judgments of an analytical and empirical nature. Smith was concerned essentially to

formulate policies which would *facilitate* the operation of an economy based on exchange. It was of course in this context that he advocated abolition of all impediments to the working of the allocative mechanism and, in the interests of growth, the repeal of regulations in respect of trade.

This feature of Smith's work is also evident in his concern that the state should organize services which would ensure an appropriate and secure *environment,* services such as justice and defence. As is well known, Smith defended the view that the state should encourage public works and institutions designed to facilitate the commerce of society and which were 'of such a nature, that the profit could never repay the expense to any individual or small number of individuals, and which it, therefore, cannot be expected that any individual or small number of individuals should erect or maintain' (*WN,* V. I. c. 1). Education, including military education, was later added to the list.

But there is also another characteristic dimension to the argument which reminds us of the institutional structure which Smith had in mind, his concern that public services be *organized* in such a way as to *induce* efficient delivery (cf. Rosenberg, 1960; Peacock, 1975). It was in this context that Smith argued that public services should, where possible, be paid for by the consumer. He further suggested that public services should be so structured as to respect the point that in every trade and profession 'the exertion of the greater part of those who exercise it, is always in proportion to the necessity they are under of making that exertion' (*WN,* V. i. f. 4).

While the reader interested in this branch of Smith's thought can do no better than to consult Viner (1927), one further point should be noted here on the ground that it reflects Smith's understanding of the nature of the economy with which he had to deal.

Smith was well aware that the modern version of the circular flow depended on paper money and on credit, in effect a system of dual circulation involving a complex of transactions linking producers and merchants, retail dealers and consumers. He was aware that such transactions would involve cash (at the level of the household) and credit (at the level of the firm). It was in this context that he was willing to regulate the small note issue in the interests of a stable banking system and objected to the use of the optional clause (*WN,* II. ii. 94; cf. Checkland, 1975). In the same context, Smith advocated control of the rate of interest, set in such a way as to ensure that 'sober people are universally preferred to prodigals and projectors' (II. iv. 15). The latter proposal was to call down the wrath of Jeremy Bentham (1787), who believed that this particular suggestion was inconsistent with Smith's defence of natural liberty. Apparently Smith remained unconvinced.

IV

This paper has attempted, in general terms, to illustrate the point that Hume, Steuart and Smith all produced works which are important in their own right and which amply illustrate the qualities which Macfie ascribed to the Scottish tradition, especially in the form in which that tradition was established in the Age of Enlightenment.

Hume in particular shows a typical interest in the principles of human nature and thus 'deserves to be remembered . . . for his more fundamental attempts to incorporate economics into a broader science of human experience' (Rotwein, 1955, p. cxi). As we have noted above, the approach is also dominated by Hume's awareness of the variety of human experience over time and by his use of the historical method in dealing with purely economic issues, a point which explains Terence Hutchison's contention that he was 'too deeply committed to historical relativism to accept a single model' (1988, p. 214).

The same feature is to be found in Hume's concern with variations in economic performance, a problem which manifests itself in the *Political Discourses* in the form of an analysis of the rich-country—poor-country relationship. On this view of the economic process, policy prescriptions must always be related to the circumstances prevailing. Hume thus emerges (like Galiani) as a writer who always insisted on the variability of man and the relativity to time and place of all policies; . . . one who was completely free from the paralysing belief, that crept over the intellectual life of Europe, in practical principles that claim universal validity' (Hutchison, 1988, p. 269).

It has also been contended that Sir James Steuart's connection with Hume, and the influence of the latter upon him, have been unduly neglected and further that Steuart may well have organized his *Principles* along the lines suggested by the *Discourses*. There is certainly the same preoccupation with the social and political implications of economic growth, the same emphasis on the role of natural wants, the same style of treatment in the theory of population and when considering the nature of the exchange economy. But Steuart carries the argument further, not just in terms of the analysis of specific problems such as price theory or the theory of money (Vickers, 1960), but also in the sense that he explicitly addressed the issues presented by a socio-economic system in a process of transition. Not for nothing did he make the point that he proposed to follow the historical 'clue' (Skinner, 1966, p. 29) or draw attention to the fact that the process of economic development was causing a wonderful ferment in the remaining fierceness of the feudal constitution. Steuart's is perhaps the only example in the writings of the Scottish Enlightenment of an attempt to address what Perelman (1983) and Kobayashi (1967) have described as the problem of primitive accumulation and as such is deserving of attention.

Steuart went further than Hume in addressing the problems presented by variation in rates of growth both regionally and internationally, an analysis which resulted, as we have seen, in the generalized statement of three 'stages' of trade. As with Hume, the implication is that economic policy must always be related to the circumstances which prevail. To this extent, Steuart would have agreed with Galiani, in his contention that 'policy is a matter of detail. It must always be concerned with particular cases. If it is made universal, it makes for confusion; in particular circumstances, it produces good' (quoted in Hutchison, 1988, p. 270).

In drawing attention to Steuart's lack of confidence in self-regulating mechanisms and to his corresponding fear of unemployment, Hutchison concluded that his stylistic faults were 'brought about by his intellectual virtues, and by his persistent resistance to oversimplification . . . It is easier to write clearly and engagingly when one has a simple system to expound' (1988, p. 350).

When we turn to Smith it is not difficult to find marked parallels with his predecessors in respect of the style of approach. There is clear evidence of similarity in terms of his interest in social psychology and above all in the fact that Smith also addressed the historical dimension in a way which elucidated the processes which had generated the exchange economy and explained changing patterns of dependence and a changing distribution of political power. The analyses and the conclusions are strikingly similar to those offered by Steuart and Hume; especially noteworthy is Smith's (rare) acknowledgment of a debt to the latter in this area of thought.

But there were differences: differences in the degree of formality and of completeness.

Smith also differs from Steuart and Hume in respect of his use of the historical method. In Smith's hands, the history of civil society is essential to our understanding of the exchange economy and of the social and political environment which it may produce. But it is now the *preface* to political economy rather than integral to the treatment. In the event, Smith did not use historical method in dealing with economic questions, a point noted by Rotwein in his discussion of Hume:

> One may say that, despite its pronounced emphasis on economic development, Smith's approach to its more general aspects is less basically genetic or evolutionary than Hume's . . . With regard particularly to his treatment of the theoretical issues of political economy, Smith clearly exhibits the tendency to abstract from the historical influence which was so characteristic of Ricardo and the later

classical economists.

(1955, p. cix; cf; Hutcheison,
1988, pp. 213-14)

Smith also differs from Hume and Steuart in that he did not address the problem of the primitive version of the exchange economy, but rather concentrated on a relatively sophisticated model of a capital-using system. While admitting that rates of growth may vary, both in Book III and in his analysis of the American colonies (cf. Skinner, 1979) this is not a major feature of his treatment of international trade.

Smith had chosen a different path and had given political economy a different shape, a shape which was consistent with analytical completeness and clarity and with a policy prescription which was deceptively simple and attractive. While sharing common interests in the approach to the study of man in society, the contrast with Hume and Steuart in terms of the choice of analytical strategy could hardly be more complete.

It was perhaps for this reason that Smith scarcely acknowledged Hume's work as an economist and chose to ignore entirely Steuart's *Principles*. This was hardly an act of generosity (cf. Raschid, 1982, Skinner, 1988). As Steuart's biographer noted shortly after his death, 'We cannot help lamenting that he should have passed over the *Political Oeconomy* without once bestowing upon it a single mark of public attention' (quoted in Skinner, 1966, p. lii). But the real blow to the reputation of his predecessors came not so much from Smith as from those who were to find *in* Smith the inspiration for a new classical orthodoxy.

The two pillars of Smith's success may be represented as the analytical system and the broad advocacy of free trade. Yet as Teichgraeber has shown, success was not immediate. In a convincing argument, Teichgraeber has indicated that Smith's advocacy of freedom of trade did 'not register any significant victories during his life time' (1987, p. 338), echoing a point already made by Raschid (1982, p. 83). Indeed, Raschid has argued that when success did come, it was largely because Smith's policy prescriptions were peculiarly relevant to British interests (1982, p. 82).
In the same vein, Teichgraeber's research suggests that although there were contemporary admirers (such as Dugald Stewart) there 'is no evidence to show that many people explored his arguments with great care before the first two decades of the nineteenth century' (1987, p. 39). He concluded: 'It would seem that at the time of his death Smith was widely known and admired as the author of the *Wealth of Nations*. Yet it should be noted too that only a handful of his contemporaries had come to see his book as uniquely influential' (1987, p. 363). But if Smith's analytical contribution was understood only by a few at the time of his death, the situation was soon to change. The point is

implied in Hollander's exhaustive work (1973) and further elaborated in O'Brien's excellent account of classical economics (1975). In a later work, O'Brien has noted the *longevity* of Smith's paradigm (1976), a point also made by Boulding (1971) who found in Smith's work the basis of modern economics. It was this perception in the early nineteenth century which did most to consign the work of Smith's predecessors to oblivion, precisely because it led to the belief that the history of the discipline dated from 1776.

Acceptance of the *Wealth of Nations* as shaping the analytical base would also appear to have been accompanied by the acceptance both of Smith's definition of the mercantile system and of his critique of its alleged deficiencies. Even where the flaws of Smith's account have been noted (cf. Pownall, 1776, for an early example) there was acceptance of Smith's point that there was an identifiable system. There was also general acceptance of the basic proposition that: 'no regulation of commerce can increase the quantity of industry in any society beyond what its capital can maintain. It can only divert a part of it into a direction into which it might not otherwise have gone; and it is by no means certain that this artificial direction is likely to be more advantageous to the society than that into which it would have gone of its own accord' (*WN,* IV. ii. 3). Economic historians have long argued that Smith's account of the mercantile system was a straw man, an invention (Coleman, 1969) and little more than free trade propaganda (Heckscher, 1965, ii. 332). A. V. Judges has also argued that, following Smith, the classical economists established a dummy dragon which, 'articulated and endowed with organic functions by its indignant creators, had the fire of life breathed into it by the avenging angels themselves' (1969, p. 36). In the event, acceptance of the view thought to be that of Smith led to a situation where regulation of trade and industry was deplored and, by implication, generally thought to be unenlightened. At best this perception has caused some commentators to view with mild embarrassment the occasional failings of Hutcheison, Hume, and, indeed, Smith himself whose views on the functions of the state are nothing if not complex. At worst, the conventional interpretation generated a situation where Steuart was roundly condemned as a mercantilist (cf. Anderson and Tollison, 1984), thus neatly illustrating Hume's contention that we frequently produce fallacies where a 'collateral effect is taken for a cause' (*EW,* p. 46).

It is a view which made it difficult on occasion for economists to appreciate the perspective of the economic historian which contends that an understanding of the contemporary economic situation may be a better guide to contemporary recommendations than a criticism of policy (Coleman, 1967, p. 15). This is exactly the view which would have been taken by Hume and Steuart.

Other problems followed from the development of a new orthodoxy. As Hutchison has eloquently argued, from an analytical point of view 'the losses and exclusions which ensued after 1776, with the subsequent transformation of the subject and the rise of dominance of the English classical orthodoxy were immense' (1988, p. 370). Among these losses were many of the issues identified by Hume and Steuart. The use of the historical method in addressing theoretical issues was one such loss; another was the concern with unemployment and the model of primitive accumulation, while in addition the classical orthodoxy showed little interest in the problems of differential rates of growth or of underdeveloped economies. If there is a line from Hume to Steuart and from Hume to Smith, the path followed by Steuart was to emerge, for a time at least, as a cul-de-sac to which the analysis of underdeveloped economies was also consigned.

Ironically, the conventional perception of *Smith's* contribution also suffered as a result of the developing orthodoxy, at least in later years. Here attention might be drawn to Smith's concern with *processes* of adjustment rather than with equilibrium *states,* and to his emphasis on uncertainty. It may also be suggested that the rigorous logic of the classical system as developed by Ricardo, unintentionally (for Ricardo expected serious students to read *WN*) helped his successors to lose sight of Smith's broad perspective on the working of the economy. The reference is again to the issue of shape, in this case to Smith's concept of the circular flow with its focus on process analysis, where all magnitudes are dated and set in the context of an environment where all sectors and socio-economic groups are horizontally and vertically integrated.

More serious still was the fact that the classical orthodoxy made it possible to think of economics as quite separate from ethics and history, thus obscuring Smith's true purpose. In referring to these problems Terence Hutchison, in a telling passage, has commented that Adam Smith was unwittingly led by an Invisible Hand to promote an end no part of his intention, that 'of establishing political economy as a separate autonomous discipline' (1988, p. 355). Macfie made a related point when noting that: 'It is a paradox of history that the analytics of Book I, in which Smith took his own line, should have eclipsed the philosophical and historical methods in which he so revelled and which showed his Scots character' (1967, p. 21). While a version of Smith's work vigorously survived, Macfie was suggesting in effect that major aspects of the Scottish tradition did not, at least for a season: i.e. that tradition which Hume, Steuart and Smith had done so much to establish in their different ways.

Yet the elements of the 'tradition' which Macfie identified do not disclose habits of mind which are ex-

clusively Scottish, as he was well aware. They find some expression in the work of the German Historical School, in the contributions of the American institutionalists—and in the work of Englishmen such as Alfred Marshall, whose *Principles* (1890) were celebrated in the last issue of this journal. Marshall's work especially shows how much he was influenced by contemporary work in philosophy, history and biology. The *Principles* in particular exhibits real sensitivity to the complexity of economic phenomena seen in a wider social setting, causing Keynes to describe his work, significantly, as 'a mine rather than a railway', the fruit of 'Marshall's learning and ripe wisdom' (1951, p. 213).

Like Smith, Marshall's concern with realism presented problems for subsequent commentators, leading to Samuelson's claim that the 'ambiguities of Alfred Marshall paralysed the best brains in the Anglo-Saxon branch of our profession for three decades' (1967, p. 109). Hutchison recorded only a matter of fact in pointing out that the work done in the 1920s and 1930s reflected another victory for the mathematical model and the application of 'more rigorous academic standards of logical and terminological tidiness and precision' (1953, p. 315).

As in the case of the immediate post-Smithian period, there were gains in terms of theoretical elegance and precision, but losses to be measured in terms of realism and relevance (Skinner, 1986b). Smith, with his acute understanding of the role of the subjective in science and of the competing claims of the theoretical and the practical, would have been quick to understand such developments. But it may be fitting to leave the last word with a central figure in this story, David Hume, who commented with wry humour:

> Though men are commonly more governed by what they have seen, than by what they foresee, with whatever certainty; yet promises, protestations, fair appearances, with the allurements of present interest, have such powerful influence as few are able to resist. Mankind are, in all ages, caught by the same baits: The same tricks, played over and over again, still trepan them.

> *(EW,* p. 104)

Abbreviations

David Hume's *Writings on Economics,* edited by Eugene Rotwein (1955), are cited as *EW.*

Hume's *Essays Moral Political and Literary,* edited by Eugene Miller (2nd edn, 1987), are cited as *Essays.*

References to Adam Smith conform to the usages of the Glasgow edition. *WN = The Wealth of Nations* with the references given to Book, chapter, section and paragraph. *TMS = The Theory of Moral Sentiments* (1759) with references to Part, chapter, section and paragraph. Stewart = Dugald Stewart's bibliographical memoir and is included in *EPS = Essays on Philosophical Subjects* (1795). In the Glasgow edition, *WN* was edited by R.H. Campbell, A.S. Skinner and W.B. Todd (Oxford, 1976); *TMS* was edited by D.D. Raphael and A.L. Macfie (Oxford, 1976); and *EPS* by D.D. Raphael and A.S. Skinner, acting as general editors to the specialized contributions of J.C. Bryce, I.S. Ross and W.P.D. Wightman (Oxford, 1980).

References

Anderson, G.M. and Tollison, R.D. (1984). 'Sir James Steuart as the apotheosis of mercantilism and his relation to Adam Smith', *Southern Economic Journal,* 51.

Bentham, J. (1787, 1790). *Jeremy Bentham's letters to Adam Smith,* in the *Correspondence of Adam Smith,* eds E.C. Mossner and I.S. Ross. Oxford, 1977.

Boulding, K. (1971). 'After Samuelson, who needs Adam Smith?', *History of Political Economy,* 3. Reprinted in Wood (1983), iii. 247-55.

Checkland, S.G. (1975). 'Adam Smith and the bankers', in *Essays on Adam Smith,* eds A.S. Skinner and T. Wilson. Oxford.

Coleman, D.C. (ed.) (1969). *Revisions in Mercantilism.* London.

Eagly, R. (1970). 'Adam Smith and the specie flow doctrine', *Southern Journal of Political Economy,* 17. Reprinted in Wood (1983), iii. 240-6.

Hecksher, E. (1965). *Mercantilism.* London.

Hollander, S. (1973). *The Economics of Adam Smith.* Toronto.

Hont, I. (1983). 'The rich country-poor country debate in Scottish political economy,' in Hont, I. and Ignatieff, M., *Wealth and Virtue: The Shaping of Political Economy in the Scottish Enlightenment.* Cambridge.

Hutchison, T.W. (1953). *A review of economic doctrines, 1870-1929.* Oxford.

Hutchison, T.W. (1988). *Before Adam Smith: the emergence of political economy, 1662-1776.* Oxford.

Judges, A.V. (1969). 'The idea of a mercantile state', in Coleman (1969), 92-117.

Keynes, J.M. (1951). *Essays in Biography.* London.

Kobayashi, N. (1967). *Sir James Steuart, Adam Smith and Friedrich List.* Tokyo.

Macfie, A.L. (1967). *The Individual in Society.* London.

Meek, R.L. (1976). *Social Science and the Ignoble Savage.* Cambridge.

O'Brien, D.P. (1975). *The Classical Economists.* Oxford.

O'Brien, D.P. (1976). 'The longevity of Adam Smith's vision', *Scottish Journal of Political Economy,* 23. Reprinted in Wood (1983), iii. 377-94.

Peacock, A. (1975). 'The treatment of the principles of public finance in the *Wealth of Nations*', in *Essays on Adam Smith,* eds A.S. Skinner and T. Wilson. Oxford.

Perelman, M. (1983). 'Classical political economy and primitive accumulation', in *History of Political Economy,* 15.

Pownall, T. (1776). *A Letter from Governor Pownall to Adam Smith.* Reprinted in *Correspondence of Adam Smith,* eds I.S. Ross and E.C. Mossner. Oxford, 1977, appendix A.

Raschid, S. (1982). 'Adam Smith's rise to fame: a re-examination', in *The Eighteenth Century, Theory and Interpretation, 23.*

Rosenberg, N. (1960). 'Some institutional aspects of the *Wealth of Nations*', *Journal of Political Economy,* 18. Reprinted in Wood (1983), ii. 105-20.

Rotwein, E. (1955). *David Hume: Economic Writings.* Edinburgh.

Samuelson, P.A. (1967). 'A modern theorist's vindication of Adam Smith', *American Economic Association, Papers and Proceedings,* 67. Reprinted in Wood (1983), iii. 498-509.

Schumpeter, J.A. (1954). *A History of Economic Analysis.* London.

Scott, W.R. (1900). *Francis Hutcheson.* Cambridge.
Skinner, A.S. (1966). *Sir James Steuart; Principles of Political Economy.* Edinburgh and Chicago.

Skinner, A.S. and Wilson, T. (eds) (1975). *Essays on Adam Smith.* Oxford.

Skinner, A.S. (1979). *A System of Social Science: Papers Relating to Adam Smith.* Oxford.

Skinner, A.S. (1986a). 'Adam Smith: then and now', in *Ideas in Economics,* ed. R.D.C. Black. London.

Skinner, A.S. (1986b). 'Edward Chamberlin: the theory of monopolistic competition', *Journal of Economic Studies,* 13.

Skinner, A.S. (1988). 'Sir James Steuart, economic theory and policy', in *Philosophy and Science in the Scottish Enlightenment,* ed. P. Jones. Edinburgh.

Taylor, W.L. (1965). *Francis Hutcheson and David Hume as Precursors of Adam Smith.* Durham, NC.

Teichgraeber, R. (1986). *Free Trade and Moral Philosophy: Re-thinking the Sources of Adam Smith's Wealth of Nations.* Durham, NC.

Teichgraeber, R. (1987). "'Less abused than I had reason to expect': the reception of the *Wealth of Nations* in Britain, 1776-1790", *The Historical Journal,* 30.

Vickers, D. (1960). *Studies in the Theory of Money, 1690-1776.* London.

Vickers, D. (1975). 'Adam Smith and the status of the theory of money', in *Essays on Adam Smith,* eds A.S. Skinner and T. Wilson. Oxford.

Viner, J. (1927). 'Adam Smith and laisser faire', *Journal of Political Economy,* 35. Reprinted in Wood (1983), i. 143-67.

Wood, J.C. (1983). *Adam Smith: Critical Assessments.* London.

Carole Pateman (essay date 1988)

SOURCE: "Contract, the Individual and Slavery," in *The Sexual Contract,* Stanford University Press, 1988, pp. 39-76.

[*A feminist theorist, Pateman challenged the traditional assessment of the social contract with her book* The Sexual Contract. *In the excerpt that follows, she analyzes works of the primary contract theorists—including Locke, Rousseau, and Hobbes—in order to argue that the freedoms and privileges of the social contract did not apply to women.*]

Classic social contract theory and the broader argument that, ideally, all social relations should take a contractual form, derive from a revolutionary claim. The claim is that individuals are naturally free and equal to each other, or that individuals are born free and born equal. That such a notion can seem commonplace rather than revolutionary today is a tribute to the successful manner in which contract theorists have turned a subversive proposition into a defence of civil subjection. Contract theory is not the only example of a theoretical strategy that justifies subjection by presenting it as freedom, but contract theory is remarkable in reaching that conclusion from its particular starting-point. The doctrine of natural individual freedom and equality was revolutionary precisely because it swept away, in one fell swoop, all the grounds through which the subordination of some individuals, groups or categories of people to others had been justified; or, conversely, through which rule by one individual or group over others was justified. Contract theory was the emancipatory doctrine *par excellence,* promising that universal freedom was the principle of the modern era.

The assumption that individuals were born free and equal to each other meant that none of the old arguments for subordination could be accepted. Arguments that rulers and masters exercised their power through God's will had to be rejected; might or force could no longer be translated into political right; appeals to custom and tradition were no longer sufficient; nor were the various arguments from nature, whether they looked to the generative power of a father, or to superior birth, strength, ability or rationality. All these familiar arguments became unacceptable because the doctrine of individual freedom and equality entailed that there was only one justification for subordination. A naturally free and equal individual must, necessarily, *agree* to be ruled by another. The creation of civil mastery and civil subordination must be voluntary; such relationships can be brought into being in one way only, through free agreement. There are a variety of forms of free agreement but, for reasons which I shall explore below, contract has become paradigmatic of voluntary commitment.

When individuals must freely agree or contract to be governed, the corollary is that they may refuse to be bound. Since the seventeenth century, when doctrines of individual freedom and equality and of contract first became the basis for general theories of social life, conservatives of all kinds have feared that this possibility would become reality and that contract theory would therefore become destructive of social order. Children, servants, wives, peasants, workers and subjects and citizens in the state would, it was feared, cease to obey their superiors if the bond between them came to be understood as merely conventional or contractual, and thus open to the whim and caprice of voluntary commitment. Conservatives had both cause to be alarmed and very little cause at all. The cause for alarm was that, in principle, it is hard to see why a free and equal individual should have sufficiently good reason to subordinate herself to another. Moreover, in practice, political movements have arisen over the past three centuries that have attempted to replace institutions structured by subordination with institutions constituted by free relationships. However, the anxiety was misplaced, not only because these political movements have rarely been successful, but because the alarm about contract theory was groundless. Rather than undermining subordination, contract theorists justified modern civil subjection.

The classic social contract theorists assumed that individual attributes and social conditions always made it reasonable for an individual to give an affirmative answer to the fundamental question whether a relationship of subordination should be created through contract. The point of the story of the social contract is that, in the state of nature, freedom is so insecure that it is reasonable for individuals to subordinate themselves to the civil law of the state, or, in Rousseau's version, to be subject to themselves collectively, in a participatory political association. The pictures of the state of nature and the stories of the social contract found in the classic texts vary widely, but despite their differences on many important issues, the classic contract theorists have a crucial feature in common. They all tell patriarchal stories.

Contract doctrine entails that there is only one, conventional, origin of political right, yet, except in Hobbes' theory where both sexes are pictured as naturally free and equal, the contract theorists also insist that men's right over women has a natural basis. Men alone have the attributes of free and equal 'individuals'. Relations of subordination between *men* must, if they are to be legitimate, originate in contract. Women are born into subjection. The classic writers were well aware of the significance of the assumptions of contract doctrine for the relation between the sexes. They could take nothing for granted when the premise of their arguments was potentially so subversive of all authority relations, including conjugal relations. The classic pictures of the state of nature take into account that human beings are sexually differentiated. Even in Hobbes' radically individualist version of the natural condition the sexes are distinguished. In contemporary discussions of the state of nature, however, this feature of human life is usually disregarded. The fact that 'individuals' are all of the same sex is never mentioned; attention is focused instead on different conceptions of the masculine 'individual'.

The naturally free and equal (masculine) individuals who people the pages of the social contract theorists are a disparate collection indeed. They cover the spectrum from Rousseau's social beings to Hobbes' entities reduced to matter in motion, or, more recently, James Buchanan's reduction of individuals to preference and production functions; John Rawls manages to introduce both ends of the spectrum into his version of the contract story. Rousseau criticized his fellow social contract theorists for presenting individuals in the state of nature as lacking all social characteristics, and his criticism has been repeated many times. The attempt to set out the purely natural attributes of individuals is inevitably doomed to fail; all that is left if the attempt is consistent enough is a merely physiological,

biological or reasoning entity, not a human being. In order to make their natural beings recognizable, social contract theorists smuggle social characteristics into the natural condition, or their readers supply what is missing. The form of the state or political association that a theorist wishes to justify also influences the 'natural' characteristics that he gives to individuals; as Rawls stated recently, the aim of arguing from an original position, Rawls' equivalent to the state of nature, 'is to get the desired solution'.[1] What is not often recognized, however, is that the 'desired solution' includes the sexual contract and men's patriarchal right over women.

Despite disagreement over what counts as a 'natural' characteristic, features so designated are held to be common to all human beings. Yet almost all the classic writers held that natural capacities and attributes were sexually differentiated. Contemporary contract theorists implicitly follow their example, but this goes unnoticed because they subsume feminine beings under the apparently universal, sexually neuter category of the 'individual'. In the most recent rewriting of the social contract story sexual relations have dropped from view because sexually differentiated individuals have disappeared. In *A Theory of Justice,* the parties in the original position are purely reasoning entities. Rawls follows Kant on this point, and Kant's view of the original contract differs from that of the other classic contract theorists, although . . . in some other respects his arguments resemble theirs. Kant does not offer a story about the origins of political right or suggest that, even hypothetically, an original agreement was once made. Kant is not dealing in this kind of political fiction. For Kant, the original contract is 'merely an *idea* of reason',[2] an idea necessary for an understanding of actual political institutions. Similarly, Rawls writes in his most recent discussion that his own argument 'tries to draw solely upon basic intuitive ideas that are embedded in the political institutions of a constitutional democratic regime and the public traditions of their interpretation'. As an idea of reason, rather than a political fiction, the original contract helps 'us work out what we now think'.[3] If Rawls is to show how free and equal parties, suitably situated, would agree to principles that are (pretty near to) those implicit in existing institutions, the appropriate idea of reason is required. The problem about political right faced by the classic contract theorists has disappeared. Rawls' task is to find a picture of an original position that will confirm 'our' intuitions about existing institutions, which include patriarchal relations of subordination.

Rawls claims that his parties in their original position are completely ignorant of any 'particular facts' about themselves.[4] The parties are free citizens, and Rawls states that their freedom is a 'moral power to form, to revise, and rationally to pursue a conception of the good', which involves a view of themselves as sources of valid claims and as responsible for their ends. If citizens change their idea of the good, this has no effect on their 'public identity', that is, their juridical standing as civil individuals or citizens. Rawls also states that the original position is a 'device of representation'.[5] But representation is hardly required. As reasoning entities (as Sandel has noticed), the parties are indistinguishable one from another. One party can 'represent' all the rest. In effect, there is only one individual in the original position behind Rawls' 'veil of ignorance'.[6] Rawls can, therefore, state that 'we can view the choice [contract] in the original position from the standpoint of one person selected at random.'[7]

Rawls' parties merely reason and make their choice— or the one party does this as the representative of them all—and so their bodies can be dispensed with. The representative is sexless. The disembodied party who makes the choice cannot know one vital 'particular fact', namely, its sex. Rawls' original position is a logical construction in the most complete sense; it is a realm of pure reason with nothing human in it—except that Rawls, of course, like Kant before him, inevitably introduces real, embodied male and female beings in the course of his argument. Before ignorance of 'particular facts' is postulated, Rawls has already claimed that parties have 'descendants' (for whom they are concerned), and Rawls states that he will generally view the parties as 'heads of families'.[8] He merely takes it for granted that he can, at one and the same time, postulate disembodied parties devoid of all substantive characteristics, and assume that sexual difference exists, sexual intercourse takes place, children are born and families formed. Rawls' participants in the original contract are, simultaneously, mere reasoning entities, and 'heads of families', or men who represent their wives.

Rawls' original position is a logical abstraction of such rigour that nothing happens there. In contrast, the various states of nature pictured by the classic social contract theorists are full of life. They portray the state of nature as a condition that extends over more than one generation. Men and women come together, engage in sexual relations and women give birth. The circumstances under which they do so, whether conjugal relations exist and whether families are formed, depends on the extent to which the state of nature is portrayed as a social condition. I shall begin with Hobbes, the first contractarian, and his picture of the asocial war of all against all. Hobbes stands at one theoretical pole of contract doctrine and his radical individualism exerts a powerful attraction for contemporary contract theorists. However, several of Hobbes' most important arguments had to be rejected before modern patriarchal theory could be constructed.

For Hobbes, all political power was absolute power,

and there was no difference between conquest and contract. Subsequent contract theorists drew a sharp distinction between free agreement and enforced submission and argued that civil political power was limited, constrained by the terms of the original contract, even though the state retained the power of life and death over citizens. Hobbes also saw all contractual relations, including sexual relations, as political, but a fundamental assumption of modern political theory is that sexual relations are not political. Hobbes was too revealing about the civil order to become a founding father of modern patriarchy. As I have already mentioned, Hobbes differs from the other classic contract theorists in his assumption that there is no natural mastery in the state of nature, not even of men over women; natural individual attributes and capacities are distributed irrespective of sex. There is no difference between men and women in their strength or prudence, and all individuals are isolated and mutually wary of each other. It follows that sexual relations can take place only under two circumstances; either a man and woman mutually agree (contract) to have sexual intercourse, or a man, through some stratagem, is able to overpower a woman and take her by force, though she also has the capacity to retaliate and kill him.

Classic patriarchalism rested on the argument that political right originated naturally in fatherhood. Sons were born subject to their fathers, and political right was paternal right. Hobbes insists that all examples of political right are conventional and that, in the state of nature, political right is maternal not paternal. An infant, necessarily, has two parents ('as to the generation, God hath ordained to man a helper'),[9] but both parents cannot have dominion over the child because no one can obey two masters. In the natural condition the mother, not the father, has political right over the child; 'every woman that bears children, becomes both a *mother* and a *lord*.'[10] At birth, the infant is in the mother's power. She makes the decision whether to expose or to nourish the child. If she decides to 'breed him', the condition on which she does so is that, 'being grown to full age he become not her enemy';[11] that is to say, the infant must contract to obey her. The postulated agreement of the infant is one example of Hobbes' identification of enforced submission with voluntary agreement, one example of his assimilation of conquest and consent. Submission to overwhelming power in return for protection, whether the power is that of the conqueror's sword or the mother's power over her newly born infant, is always a valid sign of agreement for Hobbes: 'preservation of life being the end, for which one man becomes subject to another, every man [or infant] is supposed to promise obedience, to him [or her], in whose power it is to save, or destroy him.'[12] The mother's political right over her child thus originates in contract, and gives her the power of an absolute lord or monarch.

The mother's political power follows from the fact that in Hobbes' state of nature 'there are no matrimonial laws.'[13] Marriage does not exist because marriage is a long-term arrangement, and long-term sexual relationships, like other such relationships, are virtually impossible to establish and maintain in Hobbes' natural condition. His individuals are purely self-interested and, therefore, will always break an agreement, or refuse to play their part in a contract, if it appears in their interest to do so. To enter into a contract or to signify agreement to do so is to leave oneself open to betrayal. Hobbes' natural state suffers from an endemic problem of keeping contracts, of 'performing second'. The only contract that can be entered into safely is one in which agreement and performance take place at the same time. No problem arises if there is a simultaneous exchange of property, including property in the person, as in a single act of coitus. If a child is born as a consequence of the act, the birth occurs a long time later, so the child belongs to the mother. A woman can contract away her right over her child to the father, but there is no reason, given women's natural equality with men, why women should always do this, especially since there is no way of establishing paternity with any certainty. In the absence of matrimonial laws, as Hobbes notes, proof of fatherhood rests on the testimony of the mother.

Hobbes' criticism of the natural basis of father-right suggests that there is only one form of political right in the state of nature: mother-right. There can, it seems, be no dominion of one adult over another because individuals of both sexes are strong enough and have wit enough to kill each other. No one has sufficient reason to enter into a contract for protection. But is this so clear? Even if marriage does not exist, are there families in the natural state? Hobbes has been seen, by Hinton for example, as a patriarchalist not an anti-patriarchalist (on the question of paternal right). Hobbes' was 'the strongest patriarchalism because it was based on consent', and he took 'patriarchalism for granted and insert[ed] the act of consent'.[14] Hinton refers to Hobbes' mention of a 'patrimonial kingdom' and to some passages where Hobbes appears to fall back on the traditional patriarchal story of families growing into kingdoms ('cities and kingdoms . . . are but greater families.')[15] The criterion for a 'family-kingdom' is that the family becomes strong enough to protect itself against enemies. Hobbes writes that the family,

> if it grow by multiplication of children, either by generation, or adoption; or of servants, either by generation, conquest, or voluntary submission, to be so great and numerous, as in probability it may protect itself, then is that family called a *patrimonial kingdom,* or monarchy by acquisition, wherein the sovereignty is in one man, as it is in a monarch made by *political institution.* So that whatsoever rights be in the one, the same also be in the other.[16]

Hobbes also writes of 'an *hereditary kingdom*' which differs from a monarchy by institution—that is to say, one established by convention or contract—only in that it is 'acquired by force'.[17]

To see Hobbes as a patriarchalist is to ignore two questions: first, how have fathers gained their power in the state of nature when Hobbes has taken such pains to show that political right is mother-right?; second, why is political right in the family based on force? Certainly, Hobbes is not a patriarchalist in the same sense as Sir Robert Filmer, who claims that paternal right is natural, deriving from procreative capacity or generation, not conquest. Hobbes turns Filmer's social bonds into their opposite: Filmer saw families and kingdoms as homologous and bound together through the natural procreative power of the father; Hobbes saw families and kingdoms as homologous, but as bound together through contract (force). For Hobbes, the powers of a mother in the natural state were of exactly the same kind as those of family heads and sovereigns. Perhaps Hobbes is merely inconsistent when he introduces families into the state of nature. But since he is so ruthlessly consistent in everything else—which is why he is so instructive in a variety of ways about contract theory—this seems an odd lapse. The argument that Hobbes is a patriarchalist rests on the patriarchal view that patriarchy is paternal and familial. If we cease to read Hobbes patriarchally it becomes apparent that his patriarchalism is conjugal not paternal and that there is something very odd about Hobbes' 'family' in the natural condition.

The 'natural' characteristics with which Hobbes endows his individuals mean that long-term relationships are very unlikely in his state of nature. However, Hobbes states in *Leviathan* that in the war of all against all 'there is no man who can hope by his own strength, or wit, to defend himself from destruction, without the help of confederates.'[18] But how can such a protective confederation be formed in the natural condition when there is an acute problem of keeping agreements? The answer is that confederations are formed by conquest, and, once formed, are called 'families'. Hobbes' 'family' is very peculiar and has nothing in common with the families in Filmer's pages, the family as found in the writings of the other classic social contract theorists, or as conventionally understood today. Consider Hobbes' definition of a 'family'. In *Leviathan* he states that a family 'consists of a man and his children; or of a man and his servants; or of a man, and his children, and servants together; wherein the father or master is the sovereign'.[19] In *De Cive* we find, 'a *father* with his *sons* and *servants,* grown into a civil person by virtue of his paternal jurisdiction, is called a *family.*'[20] Only in *Elements of Law* does he write that 'the father or mother of the family is sovereign of the same.'[21] But the sovereign is very unlikely to be the mother, given Hobbes' references to 'man' and 'father' and the necessity of securing patriarchal right in civil society.

If one male individual manages to conquer another in the state of nature the conqueror will have obtained a servant. Hobbes assumes that no one would wilfully give up his life, so, with the conqueror's sword at his breast, the defeated man will make a (valid) contract to obey his victor. Hobbes defines dominion or political right acquired through force as 'the dominion of the master over his servant'.[22] Conqueror and conquered then constitute 'a little body politic, which consisteth of two persons, the one sovereign, which is called the *master,* or lord; the other subject, which is called the *servant*'.[23] Another way of putting the point is that the master and servant are a confederation against the rest, or, according to Hobbes' definition, they are a 'family'. Suppose, however, that a male individual manages to conquer a female individual. To protect her life she will enter into a contract of subjection—and so she, too, becomes the servant of a master, and a 'family' has again been formed, held together by the 'paternal jurisdiction' of the master, which is to say, his sword, now turned into contract. Hobbes' language is misleading here; the jurisdiction of the master is not 'paternal' in the case of either servant. In an earlier discussion, together with Teresa Brennan, of the disappearance of the wife and mother in Hobbes' definition of the family, we rejected the idea that her status was that of a servant.[24] I now think that we were too hasty. If a man is able to defeat a woman in the state of nature and form a little body politic or a 'family', and if that 'family' is able to defend itself and grow, the conquered woman is subsumed under the status of 'servant'. All servants are subject to the political right of the master. The master is then also master of the woman servant's children; he is master of everything that his servant owns. A master's power over all the members of his 'family' is an absolute power.

In the state of nature, free and equal individuals can become subordinates through conquest—which Hobbes calls contract. But in the state of nature there are no 'wives'. Marriage, and thus husbands and wives, appear only in civil society where the civil law includes the law of matrimony. Hobbes assumes that, in civil society, the subjection of women to men is secured through contract; not an enforced 'contract' this time, but a marriage contract. Men have no need forcibly to overpower women when the civil law upholds their patriarchal political right through the marriage contract. Hobbes states that in civil society the husband has dominion 'because for the most part commonwealths have been erected by the fathers, not by the mothers of families'.[25] Or again, 'in all cities, . . . constituted of *fathers,* not *mothers,* governing their families, the domestical command belongs to the man; and such a contract, if it be made according to the civil laws, is called matrimony.'[26]

There are two implicit assumptions at work here. First, that husbands are civil masters because men ('fathers') have made the original social contract that brings civil law into being. The men who make the original pact ensure that patriarchal political right is secured in civil society. Second, there is only one way in which women, who have the same status as free and equal individuals in the state of nature as men, can be excluded from participation in the social contract. And they must be excluded if the contract is to be sealed; rational, free and equal women would not agree to a pact that subordinated women to men in civil society. The assumption must necessarily be made that, by the time the social contract is made, all the women in the natural condition have been conquered by men and are now their subjects (servants). If any men have also been subjected and are in servitude, then they, too, will be excluded from the social contract. Only men who stand to each other as free and equal masters of 'families' will take part.

A story can be constructed that is (almost) consistent with Hobbes' general assumption about individuals, to show why it might come about that men are able to conquer women in the natural condition. In order to combat and turn upside-down the argument that political right followed naturally from the father's generative powers, Hobbes had to argue that mother-right, not paternal right, existed in the natural condition and that mother-right originated in contract. So the story might run that, at first, women are able to ensure that sexual relations are consensual. When a woman becomes a mother and decides to raise her child, her position changes; she is put at a slight disadvantage against men, since now she has her infant to defend too. A man is then able to defeat the woman he had initially to treat with as an equal (so he obtains a 'family'). The problem with the story is that, logically, given Hobbes' assumption that all individuals are completely self-interested, there seems no reason why any woman (or man) would contract to become a lord over an infant. Infants would endanger the person who had right over them by giving openings to their enemies in the war of all against all. Thus, all stories of original social contracts and civil society are nonsense because the individuals in the state of nature would be the last generation. The problem of accounting for the survival of infants is part of a general problem in contractarianism, and I shall return to the wider questions in chapter 6. One might speculate that a thinker of Hobbes' brilliance could have been aware of a difficulty here and was thus prompted to make his remark that, in the state of nature, we should think of individuals as springing up like mushrooms, a comment that Filmer dealt with scornfully and swiftly.

Hobbes is unusual in his openness about the character and scope of political domination or political right in civil society. For Hobbes, the distinction between a civil individual or citizen and an individual in subjection to a master is not that the former is free and the latter bound; 'the subjection of them who institute a commonwealth themselves, is no less absolute, than the subjection of servants.' Rather, the difference is that those who subject themselves to Leviathan (the state) do so because they judge that there is good reason for their action, and so they live in 'a state of better hope' than servants. Their 'hope' arises from the fact that an individual 'coming in freely, calleth himself, though in subjection, a *freeman*', and in civil society free men have 'the honour of equality of favour with other subjects', and 'may expect employments of honour, rather than a servant'.[27] Or, as Hobbes puts the point in another formulation, 'free subjects and sons of a family have above servants in every government and family where servants are; that they may both undergo the more honourable offices of the city or family.'[28] In civil society, Leviathan's sword upholds the civil laws that give individuals protection from forcible subjection, but individuals of their own volition can enter into contracts that constitute 'masters' and 'servants'. Or, more accurately, male individuals can.

In the natural state all women become servants, and all women are excluded from the original pact. That is to say, all women are also excluded from becoming civil individuals. No woman is a free subject. All are 'servants' of a peculiar kind in civil society, namely 'wives'. To be sure, women become wives by entering into a contract, and later I shall explore the puzzle of why beings who lack the status of (civil) individuals who can make contracts nonetheless are required to enter into the marriage contract. The relationship between a husband and wife differs from subjection between men, but it is important to emphasize that Hobbes insists that patriarchal subjection is also an example of *political* right. He stands alone in this. The other classic contract theorists all argue that conjugal right is not, or is not fully, political.

The latter is true even of Pufendorf, who begins, like Hobbes, by including women as 'individuals' in the natural state, but whose consistency soon lapses. Pufendorf argues that although, by nature, 'the male surpasses the female in strength of body and mind',[29] the inequality is not sufficient to give him natural mastery over her. Pufendorf, however, also argues that natural law shows us that marriage is the foundation of social life, and that marriage exists in the state of nature. Women do not have to get married in the natural condition. If a woman wishes merely to have a child and to retain power over it, then she can make a contract with a man 'to give each other the service of their bodies'. If the contract 'has no added convention on continued cohabitation, it will confer no authority of the one over the other, and neither will secure a right over the other'.[30] But marriage, Pufendorf declares, 'square[s] more precisely with the condition of human

nature'.[31] The difference between the sexes is not sufficient to ensure men's natural mastery over women, but it turns out that it is enough to underwrite their conjugal mastery. Pufendorf writes that:

> Whatever right a man has over a woman, inasmuch as she is his equal, will have to be secured by her consent, or by a just war. Yet since it is the most natural thing for marriages to come about through good will, the first method is more suited to the securing of wives, the second to that of handmaids.[32]

The assumption is that a woman *always* agrees to subordinate herself as a wife, because of the man's degree of superior strength, and the fact that the man 'enjoys the superiority of his sex'.[33]

Pufendorf investigates the question whether marriage gives the husband 'sovereignty, or dominion, properly so called'; that is to say, whether he gains a political right. Marriage is like business where, once a business contract is concluded, the will of one party must prevail (although Pufendorf does not mention that there is presumably no fixed rule in business about which of the parties will exercise the right). A husband's power, however, is not that of a political sovereign. His right, like that of the ruling business partner, is limited, and extends only to the marriage itself; 'in matters peculiar to marriage the wife is obligated to adapt herself to the will of her husband, yet it does not at once follow that he necessarily has power over her in other acts as well.' Marriage is what Pufendorf calls 'an unequal league' in which the wife owes the husband obedience and, in return, he protects her.[34] A husband does not require the full sovereign power of life and death over his wife. The husband's right, then, is not properly political. But nor does it arise from nature. Conjugal right originates in 'an intervening pact and voluntary subjection on the part of the wife'.[35] Women's status as 'individuals' is thus immediately undercut in the state of nature. Beings who must always contract to subordinate themselves to others who enjoy a natural superiority cannot stand as free equals, and thus they cannot become civil individuals when the passage is made into civil society.

The matter is more straightforward in the state of nature pictured by Locke. Women are excluded from the status of 'individual' in the natural condition. Locke assumes that marriage and the family exist in the natural state and he also argues that the attributes of individuals are sexually differentiated; only men naturally have the characteristics of free and equal beings. Women are naturally subordinate to men and the order of nature is reflected in the structure of conjugal relations. At first sight, however, Locke can appear to be a true anti-patriarchalist—Hinton claims that he 'countered the patriarchalist case almost too effectively'—and he has even been seen as an embryonic feminist.[36] Locke points out more than once that the Fifth Commandment does not refer only to the father of a family. A mother, too, exercises authority over children; the authority is parental not paternal. More strikingly, Locke suggests that a wife can own property in her own right, and he even introduces the possibility of divorce, of a dissoluble marriage contract. When 'Procreation and Education are secured and Inheritance taken care for', then separation of husband and wife is a possibility; 'there being no necessity in the nature of the thing, nor to the ends of it, that it should always be for Life'. He goes on to say that the liberty that a wife has 'in many cases' to leave her husband illustrates that a husband does not have the power of an absolute monarch.[37]

In civil society, no one enjoys an *absolute* political right, unconstrained by the civil law. The question is not whether a husband is an absolute ruler, but whether he is a ruler at all, and, if he always has a limited (civil) right over his wife, how that comes about. Locke's answer is that conjugal power originates in nature. When arguing with Sir Robert Filmer about Adam and Eve, Locke disagrees about the character of Adam's power over Eve, not that his power exists. The battle is not over the legitimacy of a husband's conjugal right but over what to call it. Locke insists that Adam was not an absolute monarch, so that Eve's subjection was nothing more 'but that Subjection [wives] should ordinarily be in to their Husbands'. We know that wives should be subject, Locke writes, because 'generally the Laws of mankind and customs of Nations have ordered it so; *and there is, I grant, a Foundation in Nature for it.*'[38] The foundation in nature that ensures that the will of the husband and not that of the wife prevails is that the husband is 'the abler and the stronger'.[39] Women, that is to say, are not free and equal 'individuals' but natural subjects. Once a man and a woman become husband and wife and decisions have to be made, the right to decide, or 'the last Determination, i.e., the Rule', has to be placed with one or the other (even though Locke's argument against Filmer and Hobbes is designed to show why the rule of one man is incompatible with 'civil' life). Locke states that 'it naturally falls to the Man's share' to govern over their 'common Interest and Property', although a husband's writ runs no further than that.[40] None of this disturbs Locke's picture of the state of nature as a condition 'wherein all the Power and Jurisdiction is reciprocal, . . . without Subordination or Subjection'. When he states that he will consider 'what State all Men are naturally in', in order to arrive at a proper understanding of the character of (civil) political power, 'men' should be read literally.[41] The natural subjection of women, which entails their exclusion from the category of 'individual', is irrelevant to Locke's investigation. The subjection of women (wives) to men (husbands) is not an example of political domination and subordination. Locke has already made this clear, both in his argument with Filmer over Adam and Eve in the *First Treatise,* and in his opening statement

in chapter I of the *Second Treatise* before he begins his discussion of the state of nature in chapter II. He writes that the power of a father, a master, a lord and a husband are all different from that of a magistrate, who is a properly political ruler with the power of life and death over his subjects. In the *First Treatise,* Locke claims that Eve's subjection

> can be no other Subjection than what every Wife owes her Husband . . . [Adam's] can be only a Conjugal Power, not Political, the Power that every Husband hath to order the things of private Concernment in his Family, as Proprietor of the Goods and Lands there, and to have his Will take place before that of his wife in all things of their common Concernment; but not a Political Power of Life and Death over her, much less over anybody else.[42]

Rousseau, who was critical of so much else in the theories of Hobbes, Pufendorf and Locke, has no difficulty with their arguments about conjugal right. He maintains that civil order depends on the right of husbands over their wives, which, he argues, arises from nature, from the very different natural attributes of the sexes. Rousseau has much more to say than the other classic social contract theorists about what it is in women's natures that entails that they must be excluded from civil life. He elaborates at some length on the reasons why women 'never cease to be subjected either to a man or to the judgements of men', and why a husband must be a 'master for the whole of life' . . . .[43] Several puzzles, anomalies and contradictions, which I shall take up in subsequent chapters, arise from the theoretical manoeuvering of the classic social contract theorists on the question of conjugal right and natural freedom and equality. Perhaps the most obvious puzzle concerns the status of conjugal or sex-right; why, since Hobbes, has it so rarely been seen as an example of political power? In civil society all absolute power is illegitimate (uncivil), so the fact that a husband's right over his wife is not absolute is not sufficient to render his role non-political. On the other hand, a distinguishing feature of civil society is that only the government of the state is held to provide an example of political right. Civil subordination in other 'private' social arenas, whether the economy or the domestic sphere, where subordination is constituted through contract, is declared to be non-political.

There are other difficulties about the origin of conjugal right. The classic contract theorists' arguments about the state of nature contrive to exclude women from participation in the original contract. But what about the marriage contract? If women have been forcibly subjugated by men, or if they naturally lack the capacities of 'individuals', they also lack the standing and capacities necessary to enter into the original contract. Yet the social contract theorists insist that women are capable of entering, indeed, must enter, into one contract, namely the marriage contract. Contract theorists simultaneously deny and presuppose that women can make contracts. Nor does Locke, for example, explain why the marriage contract is necessary when women are declared to be naturally subject to men. There are other ways in which a union between a man and his natural subordinate could be established, but, instead, Locke holds that it is brought into being through contract, which is an agreement between two equals.

Nor do the puzzles end once the marriage contract is concluded. Most of the classic social contract theorists present marriage as a natural relationship that is carried over into civil society. Marriage is not unique in this respect, other contractual relations are held to exist in the natural condition. The curious feature of marriage is that it retains a natural status even in civil society. Once the original contract has been made and civil society has been brought into being, the state of nature is left behind and contract should create civil, not natural, relations. Certainly, the relation between employer and worker is seen as civil, as purely contractual or conventional. But marriage must necessarily differ from other contractual relations because an 'individual' and a natural subordinate enter into the contract, not two 'individuals'. Moreover, when the state of nature is left behind, the meaning of 'civil' society is not independently given, but depends upon the contrast with the 'private' sphere, in which marriage is the central relationship. . . .

Notes

1 J. Rawls, *A Theory of Justice* (Cambridge, MA, Harvard University Press, 1971), p. 141.

2 I. Kant, *Political Writings,* ed. H. Reiss (Cambridge, Cambridge University Press, 1970), p. 79.

3 J. Rawls, 'Justice as Fairness: Political not Metaphysical', *Philosophy and Public Affairs,* 14, 3 (1985), pp. 225, 238.

4 Rawls, *Theory of Justice,* pp. 137-8.
5 Rawls, 'Justice as Fairness', pp. 241, 236.

6 M. Sandel, *Liberalism and the Limits of Justice* (Cambridge, Cambridge University Press, 1982), p. 131.

7 Rawls, *Theory of Justice,* p. 139.

8 Ibid., p. 128.

9 T. Hobbes, *Leviathan,* in *The English Works of Thomas Hobbes of Malmesbury* (hereafter *EW*) (Germany, Scientia Verlag Aalen, 1966), vol. III, ch. XX, p. 186.
10 T. Hobbes, *Philosophical Rudiments Concerning Government and Society* (the English version of *De Cive), EW,* vol. II, ch. IX, p. 116.

11 Ibid., ch. IX, p. 116.

12 Hobbes, *Leviathan,* ch. XX, p. 188.

13 Ibid., p. 187.

14 R. W. K. Hinton, 'Husbands, Fathers and Conquerors', *Political Studies,* XVI, 1 (1968), pp. 62, 57.

15 Hobbes, *Leviathan,* ch. XVII, p. 154.

16 T. Hobbes, *De Corpore Politico, or The Elements of Law, EW,* vol. IV, ch. IV, pp. 158-9.

17 Hobbes, *Philosophical Rudiments,* ch. IX, p. 122.

18 Hobbes, *Leviathan,* ch. XV, p. 133.

19 Ibid., ch. XX, p. 191.

20 Hobbes, *Philosophical Rudiments,* ch. IX, p. 121.

21 Hobbes, *De Corpore Politico,* ch. IV, p. 158.

22 Hobbes, *Leviathan,* ch. XX, p. 189.

23 Hobbes, *De Corpore Politico,* ch. III, pp. 149-50.

24 T. Brennan and C. Pateman, '"Mere Auxiliaries to the Commonwealth": Women and the Origins of Liberalism', *Political Studies* XXVII, 2 (1979), pp. 189-90. I was prompted to look at this again by J. Zvesper, 'Hobbes' Individualistic Analysis of the Family', *Politics* (UK), 5, 2 (1985), pp. 28-33; Zvesper, though, sees Hobbes' 'family' in the state of nature as like a 'family' in civil society, despite the absence of 'matrimonial laws'.

25 Hobbes, *Leviathan,* ch. XV, p. 187.

26 Hobbes, *Philosophical Rudiments,* ch. IX, p. 118.

27 Hobbes, *De Corpore Politico,* ch. IV, pp. 157-58.

28 Hobbes, *Philosophical Rudiments,* ch. IX, p. 121.

29 S. Pufendorf, *On the Law of Nature and Nations,* tr. C. H. and W. A. Oldfather (Oxford, The Clarendon Press, 1934), bk VI, ch. I, § 9, p. 853.

30 Ibid., p. 854.

31 Ibid., § 10, p. 855.

32 Ibid., § 9, p. 853.

[33] Ibid., § 11, p. 860.

[34] Ibid., pp. 859-60.

[35] Ibid., § 12, p. 861.

[36] Hinton, 'Husband, Fathers and Conquerors', p. 66; and M. A. Butler, 'Early Liberal Roots of Feminism: John Locke and the Attack on Patriarchy', *American Political Science Review,* 72, 1 (1978), pp. 135-50.

[37] J. Locke, *Two Treatises of Government,* 2nd edn, ed. P. Laslett (Cambridge, Cambridge University Press, 1967), II, § 183, II, 81-82.

[38] Ibid., I, § 47.

[39] Ibid., II, § 82.

[40] Ibid.

[41] Ibid., § 4.

[42] Ibid., I, § 48.

[43] J-J. Rousseau, *Emile or on Education,* tr. A. Bloom (New York, Basic Books, 1979), pp. 370, 404. In *The Problem of Political Obligation,* I argued that the form of Rousseau's original pact meant that it was not a 'contract'. Rousseau is, however, the leading theorist of the original sexual contract, which certainly is a contract. So, without implying that I have changed my mind about my previous interpretation (which is not the case), I shall refer to Rousseau here as a 'classic contract theorist'.

NATURAL LAW

Irving Babbitt (essay date 1924)

SOURCE: "The Types of Political Thinking," in *Democracy and Leadership*, 1924. Reprint byLiberty Classics, 1979, pp. 49-92.

[*In the following excerpt, Babbitt contends that "naturalism" has defined the rise of modern political philosophy. He studies the leading philosophers of the period, including Machiavelli, Hobbes, Locke, and Montesquieu, in relation to how they understood the function of natural law.*]

. . . The naturalist no longer looks on man as subject to a law of his own distinct from that of the material order—a law, the acceptance of which leads, on the religious level, to the miracles of other-worldliness that one finds in Christians and Buddhists at their best, and the acceptance of which, in this world, leads to the

Wilson Carey McWilliams on political societies:

All political societies are "many," complex unions of individuals and families, skills and interests, so that Aristotle regarded it as a decisive criticism of Plato's *Republic* that it seemed to reduce citizenship to a mere unison rather than a harmony. Yet, just as harmony requires some ordering or ruling principle, every political society is also "one," identifiably different from all others, unique. The unity of a political society is thus tied to its identity, an understanding shared by its members of what collectively they are about, extended over time. It is not visible or material. . . . The members of a public do not necessarily look very much alike, beyond the humanity that unites all peoples, nor are their material interests evidently common. . . . A political society, however, includes complexly related interests that often conflict; in these multinational days, moreover, citizens may very well have some interests that are closer to those of foreigners than to those of their fellows. For both reasons unity can be hard to discern. A political society can be symbolized, but it cannot be seen: It is defined by thought, reflected in speech and especially in law, so that "the one" is ultimately an idea, a quality of spirit that serves as the rule or measure for the quantities that we see in political life.

Wilson Carey McWilliams, in an introduction to "The Constitution of the People": Reflections on Citizens and Civil Society, edited by Robert E. Calvert, University Press of Kansas, 1991.

subduing of the ordinary self and its spontaneous impulses to the law of measure that one finds in Confucianists and Aristotelians. The rise of the individualistic and critical spirit and the resulting break with the medieval and theocratic ideal, from the Renaissance on, might have assumed a religious or humanistic character; it has actually been in the main naturalistic. One important outcome of this naturalistic trend has been the growth of the national spirit. The Protestant religion itself, if one takes a sufficiently long-range view, appears largely as an incident in the rise of nationalism. If one wishes, however, to study, in its purest form, the new nationalistic spirit that was destined finally to destroy the religious unity of medieval Europe, one needs to turn to Machiavelli. He will probably remain the best type in either East or West of the unflinching political naturalist. To understand Machiavelli, one needs to study him in his relation to traditional religion. Christianity, especially in its Pauline and Augustinian forms, has always tended to oppose a stark supernaturalism to a stark naturalism; so that when an austere Christian, such as Pascal, considers man in his fallen estate, man unsupported by divine grace, he quickly arrives at conclusions regarding the secular order and its political problems that are, if possible, more Machiavellian than those of Machiavelli himself.

One seems to have no alternative except to get rid of ethics in getting rid of theology. Moreover, the church, as an actual institution, had such a monopoly of the higher life of man that to seek, like Machiavelli, to give the state a basis independent of the church was to run the risk of giving it a basis independent of morality. Furthermore, Machiavelli was, within certain limits, an extraordinarily shrewd observer. His views reflect the failure of Christianity to control men's actual deeds, either in his own time or in the medieval past with which he was familiar. His intention, as he proclaims it, is "to follow up the real truth of a matter rather than the imagination of it, . . . because how one lives is so far distant from how one ought to live, that he who neglects what is done for what ought to be done sooner effects his ruin than his preservation."[2] The statesman should, therefore, be sternly realistic. As a matter of fact, any one who neglects men's ideals and fine phrases and attends solely to their actual performance is always likely to seem a bit Machiavellian. There is, for example, a strong Machiavellian element in this sense in Thucydides.

The conclusions to which Machiavelli was led by his special type of realism are familiar. The rules of ordinary morality may hold in the relations between man and man, but have only a secondary place in the relations between state and state; what prevails in these latter relations is the law of cunning and the law of force. The ruler who wishes to succeed should, therefore, blend harmoniously in himself the virtues of the lion and the fox.[3] The true essence of any doctrine is revealed finally in the kind of personality in which it becomes incarnate. Machiavelli, as is well known, saw the perfect incarnation of his own conception in Cesare Borgia. He relates, in one place, the detestable treachery by which Borgia trapped and then had strangled several of his political enemies, and then says elsewhere: "When all the actions of the duke are recalled, I do not know how to blame him, but rather it appears to me, as I have said, that I ought to offer him for imitation to all those who, by fortune or the arms of others, are raised to government."[4] One should mark especially the meaning that Machiavelli attaches to the word virtue. He begins an account of the medieval tyrant Castruccio Castricani, in which the main traits that emerge are ruthlessness and cruelty, by praise of his "virtue." The virtue of the Machiavellian political leader plainly has very little in common with humanistic virtue and nothing at all with religious virtue. Christian virtue in particular has its foundation in the law of humility. The man who takes on the yoke of this law enters, at the same time, into a realm of free conscience; he has ceased to be subject to any mundane state and has become a member of a heavenly commonwealth or City of God. This divided allegiance seemed to Machiavelli a source of weakness and effeminacy. Humility should give way to patriotic pride. The ruler above all should have no conscience apart

from the state and its material aggrandizement. Any one who consents to become a passive instrument in the service of any corporation, political, commercial, or religious, to the point of practicing a morality different from that which should rule the individual, is in the Machiavellian tradition. Machiavelli is the ancestor of the German who puts the fatherland "over all," and of his equivalent the one hundred percent American, and in general of those who are so patriotic that they are ready to back their country right or wrong. He embodies, more completely than any one else, what is usually defined as the realistic tradition in European politics. Yet one cannot grant that either Machiavelli or his spiritual descendants, the *Realpolitiker,* are thoroughgoing realists. The Nemesis, or divine judgment, or whatever one may term it, that sooner or later overtakes those who transgress the moral law, is not something that one has to take on authority, either Greek or Hebraic; it is a matter of keen observation. Without asserting that there is no such thing as reason of state and that public and private morality should coincide precisely at all points, nevertheless, one may affirm that it is chimerical to set up a dual code in the Machiavellian sense, to suppose that men can, as a rule, be ruthless in the service of country and at the same time upright as individuals. To be merely a naturalistic realist, to combine, that is, a clear perception of the facts of the material order with spiritual blindness, leads practically to imperialistic dreaming. Machiavelli relates how at the time he was composing *The Prince* he was wont, after a day spent in petty occupations on his small property at San Casciano, to pull off his peasant clothes and don court attire in the evening, and then, retiring into his study, escape from the trivialities of the present to the imperial glories of ancient Rome. This particular land of heart's desire is still that of a certain number of Italians.

Perhaps the most important followers of Machiavelli, in actual practice, have been found among the Germans from Frederick the Great to Bismarck. For the student of political theory, on the other hand, the most significant line of development runs rather through England. Hobbes is possibly even more lacking in ethical perception, even more naturalistic in his conception of human nature, than Machiavelli himself. Strip man of the conventions that have been imposed upon him from without, says Hobbes, and what one discovers as his essence is "a perpetual and restless desire of power after power, that ceaseth only in death."[5] Hobbes reflects, to some extent, in his philosophy the cynicism and disillusion that had been engendered in many by the civil convulsions of seventeenth-century England. If one is to retain a rose-colored view of human nature, it is not well, it should seem, to see it at too close range in periods of great upheaval. La Rochefoucauld, who is also in the Machiavellian tradition by his insistence on the egoistic element even in what appear to be man's fairest virtues, was influenced, we are told, in no small measure by his participation in the Fronde.

Though Hobbes is Machiavellian in his emphasis on the law of cunning and the law of force, he is, unlike Machiavelli, not merely systematic but metaphysical. He seeks to develop the postulates of naturalism into a logical and closed system. The difference between the two men is related to Pascal's distinction between the geometrical spirit and the spirit of finesse. Hobbes's extreme confidence in reasoning of the abstract or geometrical type (*la raison raisonnante*) strikes one as rather un-English, but in other respects he belongs to the great English utilitarian tradition, and points the way to Locke, who is himself, in essential respects, a dogmatic rationalist. For a striking fact about the English utilitarian is that, while professing to appeal from mere theory to experience, he repudiates that whole side of experience that belongs to the realm of the human law. Wishing to be thoroughly positive and critical, he inclines to identify this experience with the traditional forms in which it had become embedded and so to reject it as mere myth and fable; and herein he is at one with the traditionalists themselves who do not admit that the truths of the human law can be disengaged from certain special forms and, like the truths of the natural law, dealt with in a purely critical fashion. As I have tried to show elsewhere, the positivists have failed signally thus far to live up to their own program. Hobbes, for example, opposes to the dogmas and metaphysical assumptions of the traditionalists other assumptions that are almost equally metaphysical. One needs to consider what some of these assumptions are, for, in one shape or other, they have pervaded most political thinking from the time of Hobbes to our own day, even the thinking of those who at first sight seem most opposed to him.

One may take as the first of these metaphysical assumptions the conception of absolute and unlimited sovereignty. When anything absolute is set up, we may know that we are running into metaphysics; for precise observation of life does not give anything absolute. The only thing that approaches the absolute in man is his ignorance, and even that is not quite absolute. Hobbes's assertion of absolute and unlimited sovereignty recalls the medieval notion of sovereignty with a most important difference: it rests upon force and is in this sense imperialistic; it does not, like the sovereignty of the Middle Ages, have a supernatural sanction. For the medieval sovereign, whether pope or emperor, if not responsible to the people, is responsible to God, who is, finally, the only absolute and unlimited ruler. Furthermore, the individual in the state of Hobbes has no refuge from its despotic control in religion, or, what amounts to the same thing, in a domain of conscience set apart from the secular order. Hobbes subordinates the spiritual to the temporal, and, in his dealing with the rival claims of church and state,

is, like Machiavelli, not only unmedieval but un-Christian.

Whence, one may inquire, does the sovereign of Hobbes derive a power so unlimited and irresponsible as to be subversive not only of liberty in the temporal order, but also of the "liberty wherewith Christ hath made us free." The reply is that the sovereign holds his unlimited and irresponsible power, not by the grace of God, but as a result of a contract with the people; and here emerges another metaphysical assumption, that of the social contract, which dominated to an extraordinary degree the political thinking of several generations. This involves, in some form or other, the assumption of a state of nature, in which man is isolated and unsocial, in opposition to a state of society where men escape from their isolation on the basis of a convention or contract. Just as Machiavelli is infinitely below Aristotle in setting up two codes of morality, one for the state and one for the individual, so Hobbes marks a great retrogression from Aristotle in accepting this mythical contrast between man in society and man as he is naturally. According to Aristotle, it is natural for man, being as he is a political animal, to live in society. Hobbes, also, as we have just seen, by running together the things of God and the things of Caesar, compromises the chief advance in political thinking that has been made since Aristotle. As a whole, his work may be described as an attempt to justify metaphysically what would result practically in a violent materialism.

To the social contract, unlimited sovereignty, and the state of nature, we need to add natural rights if we wish to complete the list of abstract and metaphysical conceptions that have dominated so much modern political thinking. The rights that man possesses in the "state of nature" would not seem very valuable, since his life in this state, as conceived by Hobbes, is "solitary, poor, nasty, brutish, and short"; and since, as a result of the dominance of self-love, every one is at war with every one else (*bellum omnium contra omnes*). From the point of view of theory, it is, however, important that man has in the state of nature unlimited liberty, in the sense that he has unlimited sovereignty over his own person, and can, therefore, transfer by the social contract this unlimited sovereignty to the state. Men also tend to be equal in the natural state, since the physically weak may, according to Hobbes, develop a cunning that will in the conflict of egoisms put them more or less on a level with the strong. The state of nature according to Hobbes may, then, be defined as liberty, equality—and war.

Natural rights and the freedom and equality that are supposed to be based upon them become increasingly important with the tendency that appears about the time of Hobbes to interpret more optimistically the state of nature. The origins of this tendency are complex. Perhaps the most important single influence was the revival of Stoical philosophy and the Stoical views regarding *jus naturale* and *jus gentium* that had been incorporated in Roman law. The underlying driving power behind the "return to nature" from the Renaissance down was the rise of the new astronomy and the growing triumphs of physical science. The success of the great revolt on naturalistic lines against the Christian and medieval dualism was due even less perhaps to scientific discovery, and to the type of progress that resulted, than to the positive and critical method by which the progress and the discoveries had been achieved, a method that was in direct conflict with the dogmatic and uncritical affirmations of the traditionalists. In the political theorists of the sixteenth and seventeenth centuries, the naturalistic and Stoical elements are combined in almost every conceivable proportion with elements that derive from the traditional supernaturalism. A mixture of this kind is especially evident in the "De Jure belli et pacis" (1625) of Grotius, the father of international law. The great nationalities, that were arising with the breakdown of medieval theocracy, were plainly in a state of nature as regards one another, so that it was even more important to determine, in the case of the nation than in the case of the individual, whether there can prevail in the state of nature any other law than the law of cunning and the law of force. If one is to refute Machiavelli and Hobbes, one must show that there is some universal principle that tends to unite men even across national frontiers, a principle that continues to act even when their egoistic impulses are no longer controlled by the laws of some particular state supported by its organized force. Whether one starts with a state of nature in which men are conceived as mere isolated units, and then imagines a contract of some kind by which they pass from a state of nature into society, or whether one asserts with Aristotle that man is a political animal, and that it is, therefore, natural for him to live in society, one needs in either case to define with some care the principle of cohesion among men. According to the true Christian, the final counterpoise to egoism, in virtue of which alone men may be drawn to a common center, is submission to the will of God, a submission that is conceived in terms of the inner life. The attempt to find a bond of union among men in a "rule of reason," and the association of this rule of reason with nature, is, strictly speaking, not Christian, but Stoical. It is as natural for a man to serve other men, says Marcus Aurelius in his exposition of Stoical "reason," as it is for the eye to see. This doctrine of service, which the Stoic deems at once rational and natural, does not involve the inner life in the Christian sense. The final appeal is to something outside the individual—namely, to what Cicero, a main source of Stoical influence upon the modern world, calls the "common utility" (*utilitas communis*). The community that one serves may again, according to Cicero, be either one's country or mankind at large (*societas generis humani*). Stoical utili-tarianism is in general highly rationalistic. English utilitarianism, on the other hand (and England is the chief source of utilitarian doctrine in modern times), puts far greater emphasis on the principle of pleasure, and in general on the instinctive side of man, an emphasis that is less Stoical than Epicurean. Cumberland, for example, seeks to refute Hobbes not merely by an appeal to right reason, but by asserting the presence in man of an instinct to promote the common good; thus to serve the community, says Cumberland, combining the new utilitarian conception with the older theology, is to fulfill the will of God.

One finds, however, in writers like Cumberland only the beginnings of the transformation in the very basis of ethics that has taken place in connection with the great movement, partly utilitarian, partly sentimental, that I have defined in its totality as humanitarianism. What is singular about the representatives of this movement is that they wish to live on the naturalistic level, and at the same time to enjoy the benefits that the past had hoped to achieve as a result of some humanistic or religious discipline. They have contradicted religion by asserting in substance that man, in order to rise above his selfish impulses, does not need conversion and the system of supernatural sanctions on which conversion has traditionally rested. They have also sought to refute the egoistic naturalists of the type of Machiavelli and Hobbes, who have maintained that the most fundamental impulse in man is the push for power. The rise of emotional ethics may be studied, especially in the England of the early eighteenth century, in connection with the deistic movement. The trend of deistic moralists like Shaftesbury and Hutcheson is all toward what we should call, nowadays, altruism and social service. With the decline of the doctrine of total depravity, the age of theology is beginning to give way to the age of sociology. The word beneficence gains currency about this time. The sympathetic man, the good-natured man, the man of feeling are emerging and are being held in ever-increasing estimation.

Those who believed in the intrinsic evil of human nature on either theological or naturalistic grounds were still numerous and aggressive. The divergent views concerning the goodness or badness of human nature were combined in almost every conceivable proportion in different individuals. They were so combined in Pope and Voltaire, for example, as to introduce into their writings a central incoherency. A curious attempt to combine the new expansiveness with an attack on the school of Shaftesbury and an affirmation of the egoistic element in man that reminds one of Hobbes and La Rochefoucauld and Machiavelli, is found in Mandeville's *Fable of the Bees*. With the growth of the new philosophy, man was encouraged to indulge more freely his natural desires. At the same time, scientific discovery was making increasingly possible the satisfaction of these desires. It was gradually developing a vast machinery designed to minister to man's material comfort and convenience and destined to culminate in the industrial revolution. Mandeville warned the English, who were entering an era of commercial and imperialistic expansion, that this expansion, with its concomitant growth of luxury, would, so far as the individual is concerned, be an expansion of vice and selfishness. The Stoical notion that mere "reason" can control the selfish passions, he refutes. The assertion of Shaftesbury that there inheres in the natural man a "moral sense" or will to serve, that can prevail over the will to power, or instinct of sovereignty, as he terms it, he dismisses as "romantic and chimerical." He recommends ironically as a remedy a return to the Golden Age and its diet of acorns. The true remedy, he professes to believe, is the most austere Christianity and its renunciation of the lusts of the flesh. The real sting of his argument, however, is in the new turn that he gives to the Machiavellian idea of the double standard. The multiplication of wants, which is bad, considered from the point of view of the individual, may, if properly directed by government, make for the greatness of the state. Private vices are public benefits:

> Thus every part was full of vice.
> Yet the whole mass a paradise.
>   . . . Luxury
> Employ'd a million of the poor,
> And odious pride a million more;
> Envy itself and vanity,
> Were ministers of industry.

Mandeville concludes:

> Fools only strive
> To make a great and honest hive.

In Shaftesbury and Mandeville, we see clearly revealed, for perhaps the first time, the opposition between the romantic idealist and the Machiavellian realist. Much of Shaftesbury's doctrine stands in close relation to that of the ancient Stoics, notably Marcus Aurelius and Epictetus, so that there is truth in Mandeville's accusation that Shaftesbury "endeavored to establish heathen virtue on the ruins of Christianity." Shaftesbury, for example, does not go beyond Stoicism when he hopes, in Mandeville's phrase, to "govern himself by his reason with as much ease and readiness as a good rider manages a well taught horse by the bridle." But Mandeville is not entirely wrong in discovering in Shaftesbury a flattery of human nature beyond what the Stoics or other pagan moralists ever attempted. "He imagines that men without any trouble or violence upon themselves may be naturally virtuous. He seems to expect and require goodness in his species as we do a sweet taste in grapes and China oranges." On the basis of his natural goodness which displays itself in an instinctive affection of man for his own species, Shaftesbury was the first "to maintain virtue without self-

denial." The word sympathy first became current largely as a result of its use by the Greek Stoics, but there is a wide gap between Stoical sympathy and the incipient sentimentalism of a Shaftesbury. So far from encouraging emotional effusion, the Stoic aimed at "apathy," and in his more austere moments would have us serve men, but refrain from pitying them.[6] The moral aestheticism that is beginning to appear in Shaftesbury, though it has no strict parallel in classical antiquity, is Epicurean rather than Stoical. The more advanced type of sentimentalist has, in order to display his "virtue," merely to palpitate deliciously.[7] As a matter of fact, the love or sympathy on which the romantic idealist puts so much emphasis is, as I shall try to show later, a subrational parody of Christian charity.

The moral sense of Shaftesbury and his disciple Hutcheson was developed by Hume and Adam Smith and other exponents of emotional ethics, and is not unrelated to the emphasis that the later utilitarians put on the principle of pleasure. Though Mandeville denied that sympathy of the humanitarian type can prevail over the "instinct of sovereignty," it is well to remember that he was himself an emotional moralist. He even recognizes among man's natural passions a passion of pity that may on occasion be violent. One has only to exalt this passion of pity and, at the same time, to take seriously Mandeville's occasional praises of ignorance and the simple life, to be in sight of the primitivistic solution of the problem of luxury and of civilization itself that Rousseau was to set forth in his two Discourses. Mandeville is on the side of decorum, and yet he admits that decorum is not only "artificial," but is, as Rousseau was to say later, only the "varnish of vice" and the "mask of hypocrisy." He affirms that vice in general is nowhere more predominant than where arts and sciences flourish, and that we shall find innocence and honesty nowhere more widely diffused than among the most illiterate, the "poor silly country people." "Would you banish fraud and luxury? Break down the printing-presses and burn all the books in the Island, except those at the universities where they remain unmolested."

What is being weakened by the realism of Mandeville, as well as by the idealism of Shaftesbury, is the sense of the inner life. And by the inner life, I mean the recognition in some form or other of a force in man that moves in an opposite direction from the outer impressions and expansive desires that together make up his ordinary or temperamental self. The decisive victories of both rationalistic and emotional ethics over the traditional dualism were won in the eighteenth century. At the same time, we must not forget that we have to do with the final stages of a secular process. The political reflex of this process is the passage from a Europe that was unified in theory, and to some extent in practice, by the Roman theocracy to a Europe made up of great territorial nationalities governed in their relations to one another by international law. As conceived by Grotius, international law rests largely upon naturalistic foundations. The publication of his work was followed in a few years by recognition of the new Europe in the Peace of Westphalia (1648). Within the bounds of each separate nationality, the essential aspect of this secular process is the passage from divine right to popular right, from the sovereignty of God to the sovereignty of the people. In the long period of transition, supernaturalist and naturalistic views are blended in almost every possible proportion. For example, Protestants, especially the Calvinists, and Catholics, especially the Jesuits, borrowed naturalistic concepts such as a state of nature, natural rights, and the social compact, but only that they might affirm more effectively the principle of divine sovereignty, with its theocratic implications, in the spiritual order.

Some, to be sure, saw the danger of thus making secular power seem to receive its sanction, not from above, but from below. Thus Filmer says in his *Patriarcha*: "Late writers have taken up too much upon trust from the subtle schoolmen who, to be sure to thrust down the king below the pope, thought it the safest course to advance the people above the king." A doctrine that was opposed to Jesuitical encroachments of this kind, and played an important role in the rise of nationalism, was that of the divine right of kings and of passive obedience. The strict subordination of the spiritual to the temporal power, urged by Erastus, had been encouraged by Luther himself. And Luther's own attitude was related to that of medieval theorists like Occam, who had sought to exalt the emperor and depress the pope. The monarchs, however, to whom the Lutheran inclined to give jurisdiction in matters religious (*cujus regio, ejus religio*), were not like the emperor universal; they ruled by hereditary right over certain limited teritories. The theocratic state of Calvin again is related to the medieval theory that exalted the pope at the expense of the emperor; but here also there is lacking the element of universality. Practically both the Lutheran and the Calvinistic state tend to run together the things of God and the things of Caesar, and to leave the individual without any *civitas dei* in which he may take refuge from the secular power. There is, then, this justification for the opinion of those who look upon Protestantism in all its forms as only an incident in the rise of nationalism.

A defense of divine right that should receive attention as an example, though a very imperfect one, of an important type of political thinking, is the work of Filmer I have just mentioned: *Patriarcha, or the Natural Power of Kings* (1680). The arguments in favor of the patriarchal view of government have indeed never been adequately set forth in the Occident. In spite of all that has been urged by Aristotle and others, we must, if we go by the actual experience of mankind, conclude that the patriarchal conception has enormous

elements of strength. It has been the normal conception of great portions of the human race over long periods of time. Such a study as that of Fustel de Coulanges on the Greek and Roman city-state, and its derivation from the religion of the family, aids us to understand political and social institutions that still survive in countries like China and Japan. Unfortunately, Filmer does not apply an adequate psychological analysis to the patriarchal conception and uncover its deep roots in the actual facts of human nature. He is at once too naturalistic and too theological. By his very subtitle, he proclaims that the patriarchal power is "natural," and, at the same time, he seeks by somewhat grotesque speculations to prove that the actual power of kings is based on their direct descent from Adam.

Filmer seems to have missed the point seriously in seeking to show that the basis of patriarchal and royal power is natural. A more powerful and consistent champion of divine right is Bossuet in his *Politique tirée de l'Ecriture Sainte* (1709). He asserts, indeed, that all laws are founded on the first of all laws, that of nature, conceived as a law of equity and right reason. But in general he opposes to the oncoming naturalistic tide a thoroughgoing supernaturalism. Men are born, not free and equal, but subjects, first of all to their parents. Parental authority itself is the image of that of God, who is the only absolute sovereign. Parental authority serves, in turn, as a model for that of the king. The king's power does not depend upon the consent and acquiescence of his people. It is independent of the pope. But though absolute, it is not arbitrary; for it is controlled from above. Bossuet exalts the monarch in the secular order only to humble him in the sight of God and to lay upon him the weight of an almost intolerable responsibility. "Behold," he says, "an immense people brought together in a single person, behold this sacred, paternal, and absolute power; behold the secret reason which governs all this body of the state. You see the image of God in kings and gain from them the idea of royal majesty. And so, O kings, exercise your power boldly; for it is divine and salutary to mankind; but exercise it with humility. It is laid upon you from without. At bottom it leaves you weak, it leaves you mortal, it leaves you sinful; and burdens you in God's sight with a heavier reckoning." Kings, after all, he goes on to say, are but gods of flesh and blood, of clay and dust. Earthly grandeur may separate men for a moment, but they are all made equal at the end by the common catastrophe of death.

This exercise of the royal office in humble subordination to God was scarcely achieved even by a Saint Louis. As for Louis XIV, one is tempted to say that he took to himself the first part of Bossuet's doctrine (*l'état c'est moi*) and overlooked the humility. Bossuet, in asserting the immediate derivation of the royal power from God, goes back, like other champions of divine right, to the medieval theorists of the empire. But there was only one emperor whose sway was supposed to be universal, whereas there were a number of kings equally absolute in their pretensions, ruling by hereditary right over great territorial nationalities, and clashing, not merely in their secular ambitions, but also, as a result of the Reformation, in their religion. Practically the rulers of these nationalities were in the state of nature with reference to one another, whatever one may conceive the state of nature to be. Bossuet pushed his love of unity to the point of encouraging religious persecution, as manifested, for example, in the Revocation of the Edict of Nantes (1685). Yet his doctrine not only failed to provide an adequate offset to a centrifugal nationalism, it seemed by its insistence on the liberties of the French king and clergy (*les libertés gallicanes*) to make against unity in the church.

In asserting the Gallican liberties, Louis XIV and Bossuet were setting themselves against the main trend of the church since the later Middle Ages. The fourth article of the Declaration of the French clergy, made in 1682 and subscribed by Bossuet, declares that the judgment of the pope is not definitive without the consent of the church. But this type of limited and constitutional Catholicism had been compromised by the breakdown of the conciliar movement. Every significant change from that day to this has been in the direction of greater papal centralization. The theorist of this ultramontane type of Catholicism and the enemy of Bossuet and Louis XIV is Joseph de Maistre. His book on the pope (1819) looks forward to the final triumph of the doctrine of papal infallibility in the Vatican Council (1870). A main element in Christianity from a fairly early period is what one may term Roman imperialistic organization. This element de Maistre develops into a thoroughgoing papal imperialism. The supreme ruler by divine right is the pope. Temporal rulers, so far as they profess to be Catholic, should recognize his hegemony. This conception of rigid outer authority de Maistre proceeds to establish on the ruins of every type of individualism. In contrast to Bossuet, who was in the great central Christian tradition, so much so that one is tempted to call him the last of the fathers of the church, de Maistre, though a man of admirable character, reveals in his writings little sense of the inner life, not much more, it might be maintained, than the rationalists of the eighteenth century whom he was assailing. The subordination of the true Christian is based on humility and charity. The subordination at which de Maistre aims is primarily social. The chief need of society is order, and order, as de Maistre conceives it, must be achieved largely by fear and repression. The ultimate support of the whole social structure, as he tells us in a celebrated chapter, is the executioner. He champions the agencies of the church that are most frankly ultramontane and anti-individualistic—the Index, the Inquisition, and the Jesuits.

Bossuet pushes the doctrine of the divine right of kings about as far as it will go, and no one is ever likely to go beyond de Maistre in asserting the divine right of the pope. The reply to the absolute and unlimited sovereignty, whether of pope or king, based on divine right, was the assertion of the absolute and unlimited sovereignty of the people, based on natural right. The doctrine of popular sovereignty is found even in the Middle Ages, notably in Marsilius of Padua, and at the beginning of the seventeenth century is worked out along rather radical lines by Althusius. Practically, however, the most important precuror of Rousseau in the development of this doctrine is Locke. The first of his two *Treatises of Government* (1690) has lost its interest along with the special form of the doctrine of divine right that he sets out to refute, that of Filmer's *Patriarcha;* the second treatise, however, remains a chief landmark of political thinking. To understand this work in its derivation, one needs to go back to the contrast between nature and convention established by the early Greek thinkers, and to the conception of a law of nature that grew out of this contrast, largely under Stoical influence, and became embodied in Roman law; finally one needs to trace through the centuries the process by which the Roman juristic conception finally became, in writers like Locke, the doctrine of the rights of man. The doctrine of natural rights, as maintained by Locke, looks forward to the American Revolution, and, as modified by Rousseau, to the French Revolution. Locke has to defend natural right not merely against the partisans of royal prerogative, but also against Machiavellian realists like Hobbes. For Hobbes, the state of nature is liberty, equality, and war. He would, therefore, in the interests of peace have the individual enter into a contract by which he renounces once and for all his liberty or unlimited sovereignty over his own person, and enjoy equality under a despot. For Locke, on the other hand, though he has an occasional primitivistic touch, the state of nature is liberty, equality, and reason. It is "a state of peace, good will, mutual assistance, and preservation."[8] In fact the law of nature is identical with the will of God[9] (or, as Pope was to say a little later, "The state of nature was the reign of God"). Locke, indeed, so runs together the spiritual and the temporal order that he speaks of an "appeal to heaven" when he means an appeal to force. He recognizes, however, certain disadvantages in the state of nature, especially in its bearing upon the safety of private property. If property is to be fully secured, men need in addition to the natural law a positive law to be administered by impartial judges who require in turn the force of an organized state to give their decisions due execution. The first aim, therefore, of the contract by which men substitute a settled government for the state of nature, is to secure the common good, which is taken to be identical with the protection of property. The source of property itself, and this is a point of extreme importance to which I shall need to return later, is manual labor. The will of the people, conceived as the will of the majority, is to be supreme. This will, however, is to be expressed not directly but through the legislative, which as the organ of the popular will is to dominate both the executive and the judiciary. Practically, Locke's treatise reflects the upshot of the Revolution of 1688, the transfer, namely, of the final power of the state from the king to Parliament. The legislative is especially vigilant in its control over the executive in all that relates to the common interest, that is, the safety of property. (Taxation without representation is tyranny.)

Even a theorist of divine right like Bossuet admits the danger of an uncontrolled executive. "Let us candidly confess," he says, "that there is no temptation equal to that of power, nor aught more difficult than to refuse yourself anything when men grant you everything, and think only of forestalling or even of stimulating your desires." As for Locke, he does not even deem it worth while to reply to those who maintain that a ruler, though not limited by men, may be limited by his responsibility to what is above him. For him, a king is in a state of nature not only with reference to other kings, but with reference to his own subjects; and being thus unrestrained he is at the same time corrupted with flattery and armed with power. Though Locke is thus on his guard against an uncontrolled royal will, it is hard to see that he has taken any precautions against the opposite danger. However moderately he himself may interpret the sovereignty of the people, it is not easy to discover in his theory anything that will prevent this sovereignty from developing into a new absolutism. The people exercises not only legal control over its legislators, but has the right, if they seem to be acting contrary to the people's interest, to rise up against them in insurrection. In the final analysis, the only check to the evils of an unlimited democracy will be found to be the recognition in some form of the aristocratic principle. Such a recognition is entirely lacking in Locke. The very logic of natural rights runs counter to the idea of deference and subordination, at least on any other basis than that of force. In the state of nature, says Locke, all men are equally kings, and subject to nobody; and this equality does not suffer serious diminution as the result of the social contract. Locke simply dodges the political problem that seems so important to an Aristotle and a Confucius, namely, the problem of leadership. It is characteristic of the English that the radical and egalitarian side of Locke should be slow to develop. The Revolution of 1688, of which he is the theorist, gave the control of government to an oligarchy that owed its power and prestige to the survival of the traditional subordinations. The difficulties of the Whig position, that of carrying on government by an aristocracy that lacks doctrinal justification, became manifest in time. This aristocracy virtually abdicated at the time of the Reform Bill (1832). The full results of the movement that was getting under way in the time of Locke are becoming apparent in our own day. The people, especially the people of the great urban centers, no longer look up with respect to representatives who are themselves so imbued with the utilitarian temper encouraged by Locke that they have perhaps ceased to be worthy of respect. If the aristocratic principle continues to give way to the egalitarian denial of the need of leadership, parliamentary government may ultimately become impossible.

It is Locke's aim to deal with human nature in a more empirical or experimental way than his philosophical predecessors. At the same time he has a strongly rationalistic side that reveals the Cartesian influence. By their assertion of a "reason" in man that can prevail unaided over the imagination and expansive desires, both Locke and Descartes renew the Stoical position. The counterassertion of Pascal that unaided reason cannot win any such easy victory, that on the contrary "imagination rules everything," seems nearer to the observed facts, and, therefore, more truly experimental. According to Locke, imagination becomes embodied in customs and traditions that may from the point of view of reason be dismissed as mere prejudice. By the opposition that he thus establishes between reason and prejudice, Locke becomes, along with Descartes, a main influence on the period of European culture known as the Enlightenment. Although no one perhaps did more for Locke's French and European influence in general than Voltaire, in the field of political theory, on the other hand, this influence is perhaps best studied in Montesquieu.[10] Like Locke, he stands for parliamentary control of the executive, especially in all that relates to taxation and the initiation of money bills. He tends, however, to separate more sharply than Locke the legislative, the judiciary, and the executive, and to make the judiciary and the executive more independent of the legislative, in such wise that the different functions of government may serve as a system of checks and balances upon one another. As is well known, it was this side of Montesquieu that was most influential on early American political theory. At the same time, only an unfriendly critic will see in the framers of the American Constitution pure disciples of Montesquieu. They possessed in a marked degree something that can scarcely be claimed for Montesquieu—practical sagacity. Compared with the political views of a Machiavelli, those of Montesquieu have about them an atmosphere of unreality; so much so that even the angelic Joubert said that one might learn more of the art of government from a page of Machiavelli than from a volume of Montesquieu. Moreover, our own constitutional statesmen did not for the most part share Montesquieu's general philosophy. This philosophy as it appears in *L'Esprit des Lois* (1748) suffers from certain inconsistencies, but on the whole it shows, even when compared with that of Locke, a noteworthy advance in the direction of a pure naturalism. The theological has given way still further to the sociological point of view, so much so that Montesquieu has been regarded by some as the founder of sociology. "He is the least religious spirit that ever was," says Faguet;

and in truth he reveals an almost total lack of sense of the values of the inner life. To be genuinely religious or humanistic, one must assert whether in the form of divine grace or of free moral choice, a power in the heart of the individual that may lift him above physical nature. In the three main forms of government that he recognizes—monarchical, republican, and despotic—Montesquieu gives little weight to any such specifically human factor. Though he does lipservice to Christianity, he leans toward determinism and the empire of physical causes, putting special stress, as is well known, on the relation between climate and national character. His insistence, therefore, that laws must not be regarded as anything absolute, but must coincide in their general spirit with national character, is very different from the Aristotelian emphasis on ethos. For though Aristotle recognizes the influence of climate, he is on the whole less concerned with what nature makes of man than with what man makes of himself. In Montesquieu's view, even religion is largely a matter of climate. Climate determines the parts of the world that are to be Muhammadan or Christian,[11] and within Christianity itself those that are to be Protestant or Catholic.[12] "Good sense" is likewise, it would seem, a matter of climate.[13] This naturalistic relativism implies a revolution in the very basis of ethics. As a matter of fact, Montesquieu has the grace to warn us that he is not using a word like "virtue" in the traditional meaning. "What I call virtue in a republic," he says, "is not a moral or Christian virtue, it is the love of country, that is to say, the love of equality." He develops admirably the thesis that this republican love of equality must not be pushed to a point where it becomes incompatible with the necessary subordinations. The obvious reply of a Bossuet would be that if subordination is to rest on any other principle than force, it must imply the submission of man's ordinary will to some higher will, it must in other words be ultimately rooted in humility. To be sure, Montesquieu seems at times to recognize the relation between republican virtue and religious control. He says in a celebrated sentence: "Rome était un vaisseau tenu par deux ancres dans la tempête—la religion et les moeurs." With the decay of this traditional ethos, luxury increased and liberty declined.[14]

Montesquieu conceives in an external and formalistic fashion the honor that is the informing principle of monarchy. It has little to do with virtue either as he defines it or as it has been traditionally understood. His treatment of this form of the aristocratic principle, however faithfully it may reflect what aristocracy had actually become in the age of Louis XV, can scarcely be said to do justice to the implications of the maxim *noblesse oblige*. In the humanistic poise that the gentleman (*honnête homme*) sought to combine with the cult of honor, he discovers little more than a veneer of politeness that dissimulates the scramble of courtiers for the royal favor.

Since laws and governments, according to Montesquieu, are relative, and relative chiefly to physical causes, one might suppose that not much is to be gained from human interference with the working of these causes. As a matter of fact, there is another side of Montesquieu that suggests that though man cannot modify himself from within along humanistic or religious lines, he may be modified from without not merely by climate but by institutions; and that these institutions may be of a more or less progressive character. He displays, in short, the usual confidence of the man of the Enlightenment in the final triumph of reason over prejudice. His influence can be traced on those persons, especially numerous toward the end of the eighteenth century, who hoped to renovate society by an ingenious manipulation of political machinery, and who had an almost unlimited faith in the efficacy of paper constitutions.

I have just used the word "progressive." As a matter of fact, the idea of progress, which was to give its distinctive note to modern naturalism, was just taking definite shape in the time of Montesquieu. Only the barest beginnings of this idea can be found in the naturalism, whether Stoic or Epicurean, of ancient Greece and Rome. The idea of progress has its ultimate source in the first triumphs of scientific method in the Renaissance. In its early English form, it is associated with the Baconian influence and the founding of the Royal Society (1662), and tends to be practical and empirical. In its early French form, it is associated with the Cartesian influence, and tends to be more abstract and logical. The Baconian and Cartesian currents come together in the eighteenth century, especially in France. The result is an ever-growing confidence in human perfectibility. The Abbé de Saint-Pierre is already a fairly complete specimen of what one may term the professional philanthropist. Diderot and other Encyclopedists set out deliberately to substitute the Baconian kingdom of man for the traditional kingdom of God. At the same time, the new doctrine did not have all that it needed if it was to develop into what has been, for several generations past, the true religion of the Occident—the religion of humanity. The movement thus far had been predominantly rationalistic. Its main achievement had been to develop, largely on Cartesian lines, the idea of universal mechanism, and to oppose nature, conceived as a system of constant and inflexible laws, to the providential interference with natural law that had been asserted, in some form or other, by the older dualists. A Christian supernaturalist like Bossuet was, therefore, justified from his own point of view in putting at the very center of his defense of religion against naturalistic tendency the idea of Providence. The substitution of the idea of law for Providence is not in itself, from the point of view of the strict positivist, a chimerical undertaking.[15] But in that case one would have needed, if the truths of the inner life were to be retained, to assert two laws—a law for man as well as a law for thing. The whole point of the new movement, however, was that it did nothing of the kind. It sought to bring both the natural and the human order under one law, and then, following the lead of Descartes, to reduce this one law to mathematical and mechanical formulae. To be sure, in the deistic movement, an important intermediary stage in the passage from the older dualism to modern monistic conceptions, the idea of Providence is still retained after a fashion. This deistic Providence, however, acts not immediately, as in true Christianity, but mediately through the laws of nature, which Providence was deemed, therefore, to have contrived with a special view to man's benefit. Hence the emphasis that most deists put on the doctrine of final causes, and their consternation at an event like the Lisbon earthquake which scarcely seemed to square with their theory of a Providence that worked for man's good through the natural order.

The deistic movement, and indeed, as I have already said, the whole naturalistic movement from the Renaissance down, had been thus far predominantly rationalistic. Now it has been a constant experience of man in all ages that mere rationalism leaves him unsatisfied. Man craves in some sense or other of the word an enthusiasm that will lift him out of his merely rational self. Even Voltaire, perhaps the outstanding figure of the Enlightenment, declared that illusion is the queen of the human heart. In the field of political thought, the conception of the rights of man remained comparatively inert as long as these rights were derived from a hypothetical state of nature merely by a process of abstract reasoning. "Cold reason," as Rousseau declared, "has never done anything illustrious." Rousseau had many precursors, as appears from what I have already said about the English background, yet it was he who more than any other one person put behind the doctrine of the rights of man the imaginative and emotional driving power it still lacked, and at the same time supplied the missing elements to the religion of humanity. Among those who took up the defense of the traditional order against Rousseau, Burke is easily first, because he too perceived in his own way the truth that cold reason has never done anything illustrious. He saw that the only conservatism that counts is an imaginative conservatism. One may, therefore, without being fanciful, regard the battle that has been in progress in the field of political thought since the end of the eighteenth century as being in its most significant phase a battle between the spirit of Burke and that of Rousseau. And this opposition between Burke and Rousseau will itself be found to turn, in the last analysis, on the opposition between two different types of imagination.

Notes

. . . [2]*The Prince,* chap. 15.

[3]*Ibid.,* chap. 19.

[4]*Ibid.,* chap. 7.

[5]*Leviathan,* pt. 1, chap. 9.

[6] See Seneca, *de Clem.,* II, 4-6.

[7] The following passage from Rousseau (*Emile,* liv. 4) may serve as a sample of the fully developed emotional ethics of which the beginnings are found in Shaftesbury: "Cet enthousiasme de la vertu, quel rapport a-t-il avec notre intérêt privé? . . . Otez de nos coeurs cet amour du beau, vous ôtez tout le charme de la vie. Celui dont les viles passions ont étouffé dans son âme étroite ces sentiments délicieux; celui qui, à force de se concentrer au dedans de lui, vient à bout de n'aimer que lui-même, n'a plus de transports, son coeur glacé ne palpite plus de joie, un doux attendrissement n'humecte jamais ses yeux, il ne jouit plus de rien." This type of "enthusiasm" assumes at times a Platonic coloring, as in *Nouvelle Héloïse,* pt. 2, letter 11. Plato, however, as Gomperz points out (*Griechische Denker,* II, p. 411), "would have utterly despised the sentimentalism of Rousseau."

[8] Bk. 2, chap. 3.

[9] *Ibid.,* chap. 11.

[10] See J. Dedieu: *Montesquieu et la tradition politique anglaise en France.*

[11] *Esprit des Lois,* liv. 24, chap. 26.

[12] *Ibid.,* chap. 5.

[13] *Ibid.,* liv. 14, chap. 3.

[14] Yet in another chapter—and this is a good sample of his inconsistency—he adopts Mandeville's arguments in favor of luxury (*ibid.,* liv. 19, chap. 9).

[15] Buddha, for example, bestowed his final homage not upon Providence in the Christian sense, but upon the Law ("Dhamma"), a law, one scarcely need add, quite distinct from that of physical nature.

Peter J. Stanlis (essay date 1958)

SOURCE: "Natural Law and Revolutionary 'Natural Rights'," in *Edmund Burke and the Natural Law,* The University of Michigan Press, 1958, pp. 14-28.

[*In the excerpt that follows, Stanlis demonstrates the pervasiveness of the notion of Natural Law for all modern political philosophy, from the relatively conservative to the most radical. To explain his thesis, he analyzes the works of Hobbes, Bentham, and Locke.*]

> The bulk of contemporary jurists (particularly those of the positivist school) . . . are really attacking a false idea of natural law, and in exterminating it, exterminate only a man of straw, drawn from the pages of cheap-jack textbooks. . . . The idea of natural law . . . does not go back to the philosophy of the eighteenth century, which more or less deformed it.
>
> Maritain, *The Rights of Man and Natural Law*, p. 59.

In 1789 Jeremy Bentham published his *Introduction to the Principles of Morals and Legislation,* in which he made a famous attack upon the Natural Law: "A great many people are continually talking of the law of nature: and then they go on giving you their sentiments of what is right and what is wrong: and these sentiments, you are to understand, are so many chapters and sections of the law of nature." With so many whimsical and personal projections of moral feelings and aspirations being put forth as the "universal" and "eternal" Natural Law, Bentham concluded, "the expressions *law of nature* and *natural right* are no more than a senseless jargon." Yet four years later, in 1793, Bentham's contempt for Natural Law was wholly contradicted by John Quincy Adams, who in the course of attacking Thomas Paine's *Rights of Man* defended the traditional veneration for Natural Law: "When the glorious Congress of 1774 declared that 'the inhabitants of the English Colonies in North America were entitled to certain rights by the immutable laws of nature' . . . they knew very well what they meant, and were perfectly understood by all mankind."[1] In contrast to Bentham, Adams' assertion is clearly consistent with Aristotle's statement that the Natural Law "does not exist by people's thinking this or that." The differences between Bentham and Adams concerning Natural Law are not so much a matter of belief as of understanding. As a Christian, Adams both understood and believed in the Natural Law, and undoubtedly the utilitarian Bentham would have detested it even if he had understood it. But like secular contemporary sociologists who deny the existence of all moral norms or standards, Bentham could not even distinguish between what Natural Law was in fact, and derivations or violations of Natural Law made in its name. In denying all norms but those of social utility, Bentham was reduced to the absurdity that if men have the power to violate the imperatives of Natural Law, there is no such thing as Natural Law. This common sociological delusion has been well answered by Maritain:

> That every sort of error and deviation is possible in the determination of [Natural Law precepts] merely proves that our sight is weak and that innumerable accidents can corrupt our judgment. Montaigne maliciously remarked that, among certain peoples, incest and thievery were considered virtuous acts. Pascal was scandalized by this. We are scandalized by the fact that cruelty, denunciation of parents, the lie for the service of the party, the murder of old or sick people should be considered virtuous actions by young people educated according to Nazi methods. All this proves nothing against natural law, any more than a mistake in addition proves anything against arithmetic, or the mistakes of certain primitive peoples, for whom the stars were holes in the tent which covered the world, proves anything against astronomy.[2]

Bentham's confusion concerning the Natural Law was not merely intellectual; it was inherent in the historical development of utilitarianism itself. Bentham did not know that his utilitarianism, in its English origins and even in its nature, had much in common with the detested "natural rights" championed by Paine, whose revolutionary "rights" were the antithesis of the traditional Natural Law which Adams had defended.

The same contradictions found in Bentham and Adams exist among modern scholars of the eighteenth century. Henry V. S. Ogden in *The State of Nature and the Decline of Lockian Political Theory in England, 1760-1800* (New York, 1940) contended that in the last four decades of the eighteenth century all appeals to "nature" suffered a sharp decline roughly proportional to the growth of utilitarianism. Yet in 1941 Alfred Cobban said: "Up to the end of the eighteenth century . . . it would have been taken for granted that there is a Natural Law, and that positive law is justified in so far as it derives from the basic principles of Natural Law."[3] Like Bentham and Adams, Ogden and Cobban were each right in a particular way. There were indeed many arbitrary and personal claims made in the name of "nature," and the resulting confusions tended to discredit all appeals to "nature" in favor of Benthamite utilitarianism. Nevertheless, the radical pamphlet literature of England from 1760-1800 reveals that this growth in utilitarianism frequently was combined with appeals to "natural rights." If anything, the emphasis is upon "rights." Priestley's later utilitarianism was built upon a "natural rights" foundation, and Paine's *Rights of Man,* Part I, is purely an argument of abstract "rights," whereas Part II is founded upon social utility. Contradictory or not, there was frequently a parallel development of utilitarianism and of "natural rights." In the next chapter I shall show that the greatest single error of modern scholarship on Burke derives largely from the failure to distinguish between eighteenth-century "natural rights," which was a revolutionary doctrine, and the still vital but submerged and partly deformed traditional conception of Natural Law.

To resolve these confusions it is necessary to return to the revolutionary interpretations of Natural Law propounded by Hobbes and Locke. The key to the problem is provided in two admirable books by Leo Strauss,

The Political Philosophy of Hobbes (1936), and *Natural Right and History* (1953). In the preface to his book on Hobbes, Strauss asks and answers the most crucial question concerning the fate of Natural Law in the last three centuries:

> We must raise the . . . question, whether there is not a difference of principle between the modern and the traditional view of natural law. Such a difference does in fact exist. Traditional natural law is primarily and mainly an objective 'rule and measure,' a binding order prior to, and independent of, the human will, while modern natural law is, or tends to be, primarily and mainly a series of 'rights,' of subjective claims, originating in the human will.[4]

The vital differences between the revolutionary "natural rights" and the traditional Natural Law, Strauss points out, is evident in a comparison of Hobbes's political theory with that of Plato and Aristotle. "Essentially the same result is reached," Strauss adds, "if one compares the doctrines of Locke, Montesquieu, and Rousseau with those of, e.g., Hooker, Suarez, and Grotius."[5] Thus, Hobbes's philosophy is the great dividing line between medieval and modern secular thought; his revolutionary break with the past, his destruction of the primacy of "law" or "reason" in favor of "power" or "will" is the fountainhead of revolutionary social thought.

Historically, the foundations of Hobbes's individual "natural rights" are to be found in nominalism. Hobbes is the seventeenth-century heir of William of Occam, whose denial of universals paved the way for the eventual denial of Natural Law. In his personal development Hobbes first used then abused Aristotle and the Schoolmen; by the time he attacked them in *Leviathan* (1651), his gradual emancipation from their most essential principles was complete. Hobbes's attitude toward tradition in human affairs was as revolutionary as that of Bacon in scientific method. Hobbes's addiction in middle age to Euclid led to his conviction that the methods of physical science, particularly of mathematics, could be applied to social and political thought. Much nonscientific thought was enamored of mathematics during the seventeenth century. Grotius had utilized mathematical method in his presentation of Natural Law;[6] Descartes was a mathematician turned philosopher; Spinoza built on Hobbes in his attempt to bring religion and ethics into harmony with mathematical science. Hobbes, therefore, was but one of many writers who prepared the way for the cult of Newton, whose discoveries were taken by materialists as proof that laws of motion, such as Hobbes had predicated, followed mechanical principles. In presenting his political philosophy in mathematical form, Hobbes contributed greatly to the general confusion in the eighteenth century between ethics and physics, between "nature" as a moral norm and "nature" as an orderly process subject to empirical description.[7] This confusion, together with the passion for abstract mathematical reasoning, characterizes much eighteenth-century radical speculation and obscures the distinction between the classical or Scholastic Natural Law and abstract "natural rights."

Hobbes's part in subverting the traditional understanding of Natural Law is even more clearly evident in his theory of political sovereignty. Ancient and medieval Natural Law thinkers had almost always treated the idea of a "state of nature," a pre-civil state of primitive man, as a hypothetical and ridiculous fiction. Hobbes probably never believed in any historical state of nature,[8] but he posited it as a useful means of illustrating seriously his conception of the social contract as an irrevocable agreement sanctioning the legal sovereignty of established authority. Strauss has noted the important fact that "it is only since Hobbes that the philosophic doctrine of natural law has been essentially a doctrine of the state of nature."[9] Despite Hobbes's personal preference for monarchy, it did not matter in his theory who ruled in his absolute state. As Sabine has said: "Hobbes had been at pains to point out that his views were consistent with any *de facto* government."[10] Hobbes's definition of law in effect denied the existence of Natural Law as understood by his predecessors: "These dictates of Reason [i.e., Natural Law] men use to call by the names of Lawes; but *improperly:* for they are but conclusions, or theorems concerning what conduceth to the conservation and defence of themselves; whereas Law, properly is the word of him, that by right hath command over others."[11] In Hobbes's theory of sovereignty, the absolute will of the sovereign was paramount over right reason and was the only source of law. Clearly, Hobbes's absolutist state left no room for any citizen to appeal to the normative ethical principles of justice which had formerly characterized the Natural Law.

But the greatest blow which Hobbes struck at the classical and Scholastic understanding of Natural Law was in his theory of human nature. Hobbes propounded a mechanistic psychology in which man was conceived as a purely physiological creature whose actions or "motions" were either conditioned responses to sensations, or the spontaneous overflow of infinite and self-generating passions. Hobbes's principles of sensation and of association of ideas anticipated in purer form the better-known empiricism of Locke and later associationalism of Hartley.[12] Hobbes's creature of limitless passions anticipated the Rousseauist man of sensibility. According to Hobbes, man was dominated by the appetites of pride, vanity, and ambition, all of which required "a perpetuall and restlesse desire of power after power, that ceaseth only in death."[13] Such a creature of sensations and passions, without free will or the capability of acting according to "right reason," could not possibly believe in or abide by the traditional Natural Law. Combined with Hobbes's nominalism, state of nature, theory of contract, and conception of sovereignty, this mechanistic view of man made him out to be an asocial individualist whose nature existed prior to the state, and whose membership in society was voluntaristic. Contrary to classical and Scholastic Natural Law teaching, Hobbes's man was not by nature a political animal, born without his consent into an organically developed civil society, and with no civil character apart from his common corporate nature and constitutional inheritance. Although Hobbes stressed the absolute *duty* of each citizen to obey the established power, his theory of sovereignty was totally subordinate as an influence to his theory of human nature, which laid the foundation for modern "natural rights."[14] There had been a traditional "natural rights" doctrine connected with classical and Scholastic Natural Law, but the revolutionary Hobbist theory of "natural rights" was centered in the private will or ego of each individual, and was not limited by the social duties and ethical norms of Natural Law. It remained for Locke and his eighteenth-century disciples to complete the destruction of classical and Scholastic Natural Law by converting it from a bulwark for liberty and justice as an inheritance of constitutional law, to a revolutionary doctrine of liberty and equality as an abstract, inherent, individual "natural right."

Until the extensive work of Strauss, most scholars were so aware that Locke's *Second Treatise* (1690) was meant to refute Hobbes's political theory that they stressed the very obvious party differences between them and ignored or minimized their far more fundamental similarities in principles. Locke's highly favorable reputation as a friend of democracy and Hobbes's defense of absolute monarchy also helped to obscure their great similarities. Indeed, among scholars who make no distinction between the traditional Natural Law and the eighteenth-century development of Hobbes's revolutionary "natural rights," Locke is frequently invoked as an exponent of Natural Law.[15] On the surface there is much to warrant the claim that Locke followed the traditional Natural Law philosophy. He regularly used the vocabulary of Natural Law and natural rights, and all his life he believed ardently and sincerely in some apparently normative "nature." Locke's indebtedness to Hooker and through him to St. Thomas Aquinas and ultimately to Aristotle is a commonplace of scholarship on Locke. Yet it is precisely this commonplace that Strauss has doubted, and his answer to the question whether Locke meant the same thing as his predecessors when he appealed to "nature" is crucial to every scholar who would understand the fate of Natural Law in the eighteenth century:

> Hooker's conception of natural right is the Thomistic conception, and the Thomistic conception, in its turn, goes back to the Church Fathers, who, in their turn, were pupils of the Stoics, of the pupils of pupils of Socrates. We are then apparently confronted with an unbroken tradition of perfect respectability that stretches from Socrates to Locke. But the moment we take the trouble to confront Locke's teaching as a whole with Hooker's teaching as a whole, we become aware that, in spite of a certain agreement between Locke and Hooker, Locke's conception of natural right is fundamentally different from Hooker's. The notion of natural right had undergone a fundamental change between Hooker and Locke. . . . The period between Hooker and Locke had witnessed the emergence of modern natural science . . . and therewith the destruction of the basis of traditional natural right. The man who was the first to draw the consequences for natural right from this momentous change was Thomas Hobbes. . . . At first glance Locke seems to reject altogether Hobbes' notion of natural law and to follow the traditional teaching. . . . [But] his teaching seems to endanger the very notion of a law of nature . . . Locke cannot have recognized any law of nature in the proper sense of the term. This conclusion stands in shocking contrast to what is generally thought to be his doctrine, and especially the doctrine of the second *Treatise.* . . . However much Locke may have followed tradition in the *Treatise* . . . a comparison of its teaching with the teachings of Hooker and of Hobbes would show that Locke deviated considerably from the traditional natural law teaching and followed the lead given by Hobbes.[16]

Hobbes's nominalism, his posit of the state of nature and theory of contract, his conception of sovereignty and mechanistic view of human nature, were assumed independently or adopted from Hobbes by Locke, who modified and greatly softened the most pessimistic and cynical elements in Hobbes's philosophy, and popularized throughout the eighteenth century the modern secular theory of "natural rights."

It is ironical that Hobbes, the conscious enemy of traditional Natural Law, provoked by his militant rashness a host of defenders of the Natural Law,[17] so that by his radical opposition he kept vital the philosophy he wished to destroy. Locke, the presumed friend of Natural Law, by his superior "common sense" prudence, his rational simplicity, and moderation, softened and made palatable the basic "natural rights" principles of his professed enemy Hobbes, and popularized them throughout Europe. Whether Locke arrived at his principles independently or in conscious imitation of Hobbes is not relevant here. As Plamenatz has said: "We need not wonder . . . if we find in the political writings of Locke most of the ideas of Hobbes, except those explicitly rejected by the younger philosopher."[18] Both thinkers were nominalists and both felt compelled to seek for universal ethical certainty in the current methods of mathematical science.[19] The result in both philosophers was that love of rational simplicity in all things, that passion for (abstract logical speculation) so characteristic of eighteenth-century radical thought. But the fundamental similarity between Locke and Hobbes is their common empirical theory of knowledge and mechanistic conception of human nature. Locke's empiricism and denial of innate ideas is indistinguishable from Hobbes's basic principle that all knowledge is derived from sensations of external objects.[20] In this, Locke contradicts both his professed faith in Christian revelation and his declared belief in the innate rights to "life, liberty and estate" of traditional Natural Law. This contradiction between Locke's theory of knowledge and his social thought makes his whole political philosophy endlessly equivocal.

But it is in his mechanistic conception of human nature, with its implicit "greatest happiness" principle, that the utilitarian strain in Locke's thought joins hands with Hobbes's Epicurean ethics. Where Hobbes had made "fear of death" man's dominant passion, the far more optimistic Locke posited the correlative principle of the "pursuit of pleasure." As Strauss has shown, the desire for power is the common denominator of their common hedonism.[21] The similarities in their egocentric conception of man, and of Locke's popularization of their hedonism, are well summarized by Sabine:

> The psychology which in the eighteenth century grew out of Locke's theory of mind was fundamentally egoistic in its explanation of human behavior. It ran in terms of pleasure and pain, and not like Hobbes's in terms of self-preservation—a doubtful improvement—but the calculation of pleasure was exactly as self-centered as the calculation of security. Hobbes's better logic had its way in spite of Locke's better feeling.[22]

In man's desire for self-preservation, Hobbes had practically identified self-interest and the Natural Law; Locke did the same concerning his "greatest happiness" principle. The necessary means of self-preservation and of the pursuit of happiness is the possession of power; as these are identified with "natural rights," the revolutionary "natural rights" are nothing more than a disguised principle of power. In the traditional sense, the "natural rights" of Hobbes and Locke are not rights at all. Hobbes and Locke merely call powers "rights," and then treat them as if they were what Cicero or Hooker would have called rights. Although few writers used the terms "law of nature" and "natural rights" more frequently than Hobbes and Locke, it is clear that their egocentric conception of human nature left no place for the Natural Law of classical and Scholastic tradition.

Compared with these common philosophical principles, the differences between Hobbes and Locke in political theory are superficial and extraneous. Locke's optimistic interpretation of the "state of nature," his greater willingness to treat it as an actual historical phenomenon, is no less destructive to traditional Natural Law than Hobbes's darker and more hypothetical "state of nature." If anything, Locke is more revolutionary than Hobbes; he minimizes civic duties further by making the social contract revocable at will. Also, from the viewpoint of constitutional political sovereignty based upon Natural Law Hobbes and Locke are alike revolutionists. Both exalted private will above normative law: Hobbes upheld the absolute and arbitrary will of the monarch, based upon hereditary or acquired right, and Locke championed the equally absolute and arbitrary will of parliament, based upon popular support.[23] Under Natural Law the "divine right of freeholders" is no more valid than the "divine right of kings." Until the time of Hobbes, the tradition of Natural Law had been essentially theistic. The natural rights introduced by Hobbes and popularized by Locke exalted man's private reason and will above any eternal and unchangeable divine law. Under the added impact of natural science and deistic speculation, as the eighteenth century unfolded the classical and Scholastic Natural Law was ripped completely loose from its divine origin, so that from a law fitted to the spiritual nature of man, as a being of supernatural destiny, it became merely a fancied description of the physical order of nature, or a hedonistic and utilitarian precept for the survival of man as a biological creature in the jungle of nature. Nothing was so instrumental in bringing about this vital change as the development of physical science.

There is a direct connection between the abandonment of the theistic conception of Natural Law and the supremacy of mathematical logic and self-sufficiency of private reason in natural rights. Every philosopher from Aristotle to Hooker had posited as the basis of his faith in Natural Law a belief in God's being and beneficence. Grotius was the first modern to say, for illustrative purposes, that Natural Law would be valid even if God did not exist. A. P. D'Entreves has summarized the historical development of this hypothesis:

> Grotius . . . proved that it was possible to build up a theory of laws independent of theological presuppositions. His successors completed the task. The natural law which they elaborated was entirely 'secular.' They sharply divided what the Schoolmen had taken great pains to reconcile. The doctrine of natural law which is set forth in the great treatises of the seventeenth and eighteenth centuries—from Pufendorf's *De Jure naturae et gentium* (1672) to Burlamaqui's *Principes du droit naturel* (1747), and Vattel's *Droit des gens ou principes de la loi naturelle* (1758)—has nothing to do with theology. It is a purely rational construction. . . . God is increasingly withdrawn from immediate contact with men. . . . What Grotius had set forth as a hypothesis has become a thesis. The self-evidence of natural law has made the existence of God perfectly superfluous.[24]

The revolutionary belief that Natural Law was a product of private reason opened the way for arbitrary claims to be made in its name. This belief caused men to regard Natural Law not as a practical but as a purely speculative science, like mathematics. As practical affairs involved a great variety of circumstances, the traditional method of judging men's actions by the Natural Law involved moral prudence rather than mathematical logic. St. Thomas Aquinas had said on this vital point: "Laws are laid down for human acts dealing with singular and contingent matters which have infinite variations. To make a rule fit every case is impossible."[25] Traditional Natural Law left much room for infinite variations of circumstances and was therefore capable of absorbing the constantly changing conditions of civil society. John Wu, an eminent twentieth-century representative of traditional Natural Law, has summarized how "the speculative and rationalistic philosophers of the eighteenth century . . . treated the natural law as if it were geometry":

> The modern speculative, rationalistic philosophies of Natural Law are aberrations from the highroad of the scholastic tradition. . . . It is most regrettable that practically all of the seventeenth, eighteenth and nineteenth century philosophers of Natural Law departed from this great tradition. They proceeded *more geometrico;* they wove whole systems of so-called Natural Law just as a spider would weave a net out of its own belly. To mention a few, Hobbes, Spinoza, Locke, Pufendorf, Christian Wolff, Thomasius, Burlamaqui, Kant, Hegel, and even Bentham with his felicific calculus, all belong to the speculative group. Many of the nineteenth century judges in America abused the name of Natural Law by identifying it with their individualistic bias.[26]

Hobbes and Locke were among the earliest and most important "speculative" and "rationalistic" theorists to believe that an ideal system of laws, based upon uniformity in reason and mathematical method, could be established for all men everywhere. Strauss has shown that as a result of this notion, "modern political philosophy in contrast to classical political philosophy . . . claimed unconditional applicability (applicability under any circumstances) for its theories."[27] Ironically, this secular parody of Natural Law, this divergence by Hobbes, Locke, and others from the norms of Natural Law prudence, was taken by later positivist critics as the norm, and whereas Hobbes rejected traditional Natural Law because it was not based upon infallible mathematics, later critics rejected the supposed traditional natural law of Hobbes because it did claim mathematical certainty.

An equivalent fate overtook the traditional Natural Law in France during the eighteenth century.[28] In England, following the lead of Hobbes and Locke, Hume and the utilitarians completed the philosophical revolution begun by the physical sciences and augmented by the mathematical method of Hobbes and Locke's empiricism. The full significance of

Hobbes's revolutionary method and "natural rights" was greatly obscured by his use of the traditional vocabulary of Natural Law.[29] For reasons of habit and prudence, and because Natural Law enjoyed such great prestige, Hobbes could not abandon the language of Natural Law, even though he emptied it of all its traditional moral content. Locke and his eighteenth-century disciples also retained the vocabulary, and even the ethical overtones, of traditional Natural Law, though it would have been far better if they had devised a terminology more suitable to their hedonist psychology.[30]

I have noted the profound difference in content between traditional Natural Law and the revolutionary "natural rights." Despite the appeal to "nature" common to the "natural rights" of both Hobbes and Locke,[31] there was in each man a deep strain of utilitarian thought. The later supposed antithesis between "natural rights" and utilitarianism is merely a verbal illusion. Bentham was undoubtedly right to condemn traditional Natural Law as "nonsense on stilts," but in his failure to perceive his own kinship with the radical "natural rights" theory he revealed great ignorance of his philosophical ancestors. As Plamenatz observed, it would "have been as easy to prove that the spiritual ancestor of Bentham was Locke rather than Hobbes." Sir Frederick Pollock was one of the few later critics of utilitarianism to perceive that although Bentham was the first utilitarian to consciously break with the vocabulary of "nature" and of "rights," his principles added up to a pure "natural rights" philosophy.[32] Halévy, perhaps the most eminent scholar to deal with eighteenth-century philosophical radicalism, took Bentham at his own word; he saw that claims of private "natural rights" and social utility were often incompatible, and therefore concluded that their basic principles were historically antithetical. It is no paradox, however, that as the heir of Hobbes and Locke, Bentham was the great enemy of classical and Scholastic Natural Law precisely because he accepted their revolutionary "natural rights." Bentham merely converted Hobbes's and Locke's hedonistic philosophy into the language of social utility. By developing Hutcheson's principle of "the greatest good of the greatest number," Bentham socialized the individual "natural rights" of his predecessors, recast their hedonistic premises into language more suitable to their principles and more acceptable to the taste of the nineteenth century.

. . . In retrospect and summary there emerge certain basic facts concerning the fate of the Natural Law in eighteenth-century England. The fundamental change in the meaning of appeals to "nature" is most evident in the revolutionary character of the new doctrine of "natural rights." Under the influence of physical science, the conscious attacks of Hobbes and the inept compromises of Locke, traditional Natural Law as a system of normative ethics centered in God's being and man's "right reason" was replaced by or confounded with a purely materialist view of the universe and a hedonistic conception of individual "natural rights." The external attacks of Hobbes were probably less disastrous to traditional Natural Law than the apparent allegiance of Locke, who hastened its dissolution from within. By employing the traditional language of "nature" in popularizing Hobbes's egocentric philosophy, Locke left standing the shell of traditional Natural Law principles, with their religious imperatives and idealistic connotations, but he unwittingly destroyed the meaning which Natural Law had carried for almost twenty centuries. But the moral norms and imperatives of traditional Natural Law did not perish. The final effect of Hobbes's and Locke's philosophies was not to destroy the Natural Law, but to involve it in hopeless confusion with alien principles and arbitrary claims made in its name. In the last half of the eighteenth century, when various political movements of reform and revolution were justified by frequent appeals to Lockian doctrines of "natural rights," utilitarians such as Bentham, Godwin, and Mill, who often sympathized with radical movements, treated with contempt all appeals to "nature" and individual "rights." . . .

Notes

1. John Quincy Adams, *An Answer to Paine's Rights of Man* (London, 1793), p. 17. This work has been attributed frequently to his father, John Adams.

2. Jacques Maritain, *The Rights of Man and Natural Law*, tr. Doris C. Anson (New York: Charles Scribner's Sons, 1943), p. 36.

3. Alfred Cobban, *The Crisis of Civilization* (London: J. Cape, 1941), p. 85.

4. The revolutionary implications of this point were drawn by Leo Strauss: "During the modern period natural law became much more of a revolutionary force than it had been in the past. This fact is a direct consequence of the fundamental change in the character of the natural law doctrine itself" (*Natural Right and History* [Chicago: University of Chicago Press, 1953], p. 183).

5. Leo Strauss, *The Political Philosophy of Hobbes* (Chicago: University of Chicago Press, 1952), p. xii.

6. See A. P. D'Entreves, *Natural Law* (London: Hutchinson's University Library, 1951), pp. 51-53 and 58-59. "The tendency to regard natural law in moral and legal science as analogous to axioms in geometry was well settled in seventeenth-century thought after Grotius" (George Sabine, *A History of Political Theory*

[New York: Henry Holt, 1937], p. 530).

7. For an example of the common failure among scholars to cut through the eighteenth-century confusions regarding "nature," see Carl Becker, *The Heavenly City of the Eighteenth-Century Philosophers* (New Haven: Yale University Press, 1932), pp. 54-63.

8. See Strauss, *The Political Philosophy of Hobbes,* p. 104.

9. Strauss, *Natural Right and History,* p. 184. See also p. 185.

10. Sabine, *A History of Political Theory,* p. 456. Hobbes's absolute sovereignty would sanction a popular or democratic despotism quite as much as a monarchical or oligarchical despotism. See Strauss, *Natural Right and History,* pp. 192-193.

11. Thomas Hobbes, *Leviathan,* ch. 15.

12. See William Hazlitt, *The Complete Works of William Hazlitt,* ed. P. P. Howe (London, 1930), II, 123-191; XVI, 123; and XX, 69-83.

13. Hobbes, *Leviathan,* ch. 2.

14. For Hobbes's secular "natural rights" in his social thought see Strauss, *Natural Right and History,* pp. 120-164. Strauss is not sufficiently aware that Hobbes's theory of human nature is paramount in his "natural rights" philosophy.

15. For example, Ernest Barker asserts that Locke is "the exponent of the sovereignty of Natural Law." Yet the ambiguities in Locke's political philosophy compel Barker to admit that "Locke has no clear view of the nature or residence of sovereignty" (*Essays on Government* [London: Oxford University Press, 1951], pp. 94 and 102-103).

16. Strauss, *Natural Right and History,* pp. 165-166, 202-203, and 220-221. See also pp. 207, 222-226. To a certain extent Strauss was anticipated by Sabine, who noted that "Locke had to adopt into his social philosophy a large part of Hobbes's premises." Sabine also pointed out "the inherent contrariety of what he took from Hooker and what he took from Hobbes" (*A History of Political Theory,* pp. 525 and 531; see also pp. 533 and 535).

17. In Britain outstanding refutations of Hobbes were written by Whichcote, Culverwell, Henry More, John Smith, Ralph Cudworth, Shaftesbury, Clarke, and Cumberland. In France François d'Aube, Montesquieu, and the Abbé Claude-Marie Guyon, among others, defended the traditional conception of Natural Law.

[18]. John Plamenatz, *The English Utilitarians* (Oxford: Blackwell, 1949), p. 20.

[19]. Hobbes's attempt to place ethics on a foundation of geometry was first noted in 1686 by Leclerc in the *Bibliothèque universelle et historique.*

[20]. See William Hazlitt, *The Complete Works of William Hazlitt,* II, 123-191; XX, 69-83.

[21]. Strauss, *Natural Right and History,* pp. 249-251.

[22]. Sabine, *A History of Political Theory,* p. 529. Willmoore Kendall also noted that Locke's disagreement with Hobbes and other ethical hedonists was largely verbal, because "the law of nature is . . . a law which commands its subjects to look well to their own interests" (*John Locke and the Doctrine of Majority-Rule* [Urbana, Ill.: University of Illinois Press, 1941], p. 77).

[23]. See Kendall, *op. cit.,* pp. 66-67, 106, and 112.

[24]. A. P. D'Entreves, *Natural Law,* pp. 52-53. Ernest Barker stated that in Gierke's great study of the modern natural law "the Natural Law which is in question is a secular Natural Law." It is noteworthy that as the eighteenth century unfolded, the term "natural law" was replaced by "natural rights" in many treatises on jurisprudence.

[25]. Thomas Gilby, *St. Thomas Aquinas* (New York: Oxford University Press, 1951), p. 364.

[26]. John C. H. Wu, "Natural Law and Our Common Law," *Fordham Law Review,* XXIII (March, 1954), 21-22.

[27]. Strauss, *The Political Philosophy of Hobbes,* p. 164.

[28]. In France, reinforced by Cartesian scientific philosophy, the deism of Voltaire and Diderot was extended into atheistic materialism by such *philosophes* as Holbach, Helvetius, La Mettrie, and Meslier. These *enragé* admirers of Locke, together with the separate influences of Spinoza and Rousseau, completed the circle back to Hobbes, whose influence upon French thought in the eighteenth century was perhaps second only to that of Locke. The *philosophes* did not merely believe in materialism; they openly and defiantly professed their atheism. In their writings the term "Natural Law" was generally replaced by "law of nature" or "natural rights." Like Hobbes and Locke they appealed to "nature," but their universal moral law was assimilated into or annihilated by the "law of nature" pervading the Newtonian universe of the deists or the Spinozist universe of the pantheists.

[29]. "Hobbes used a traditional vocabulary unsuited to his political theory, and it was precisely this vocabulary that the utilitarians abandoned. That is why the difference between them appears so much greater than it is" (Plamenatz, *The English Utilitarians,* p. 16).

[30]. "Since the nineteenth century, readers of Locke have found it hard to understand why . . . he stated his doctrines in terms of natural law" (Strauss, *Natural Rights and History,* p. 246).

[31]. For Hobbes on natural right, see Strauss, *Natural Right and History,* pp. 166-202; for Locke on natural right, see pp. 202-251.

[32]. Sir Frederick Pollock, *History of the Science of Politics* (New York: J. Fitzgerald, 1883), pp. 111-112.

EMPIRICISM

W. H. Greenleaf (essay date 1964)

SOURCE: W. H. Greenleaf, "Empiricism and Politics," in *Order, Empiricism and Politics: Two Traditions of English Political Thought, 1500-1700,* Oxford University Press, London, 1964, pp. 157-205.
[*In the excerpt below, Greenleaf looks at changes in political philosophy within the context of changes in philosophy in general—particularly the theories of observation and knowledge described by empiricism. Greenleaf concludes that empiricism cultivated the advocation of "mixed government" among most modern philosophers.*]

Doubt about the transcendental order led, as I have explained, to the distinction between the spheres of God and nature. Man as a political animal belonged to the latter realm, a view reinforced perhaps by the traditional procedure of comparing the body politic to various aspects of the macrocosm. It was consequently implied that the study of man and society could be carried on by the same empirical method that was being used so successfully to investigate the processes of the material world. The facts of man's nature and his history, as these were influenced by the physical environment in which he lived, could, it was thought, be analysed to reveal the permanently operating factors of political and social life. Indeed, the great progress achieved by natural science helped to stimulate the anticipation that a genuine, empirically based political science was possible. A good example of this optimistic expectation was provided by Bishop Sprat, who declared that although nature alone was first to be considered by the empirical method (because this was the easiest and least contentious field of investigation), in the end all other areas of enquiry would be studied as well and reduced to order in the same way.[28] Such a science of politics, when it was developed, would not necessarily reach the same conclusions as traditional moral and political theory. These were based on theology which, in terms of the fideistic distinction, had nothing to say about the sphere of second causes. The laws of the human world could not be determined in advance of the investigation which was supposed to elicit them. And the analysis of experience would not be undertaken merely to show how traditional tenets might be more effectively applied, how men might be directed into the paths of orthodox conduct. It would, in the end, be a basis for independent generalization, and would produce its own ideas about the best form of government, moral criteria and so forth.

The cluster of ideas produced I call the political theory of empiricism, for there was a certain degree of uniformity of conclusion among those who claimed to be building something new on the basis of inductively considered experience. Not a complete community of views, naturally, but a sufficient measure of agreement to be distinctive. Of course, what was done was not wholly new at all; and despite all protestations of scientific objectivity to the contrary, the conclusions reached were no doubt both influenced by traditional norms and premeditated independently of the evidence—as what political theories are not? But this experience-based prudence provided the foundation of the moderate, fairly conservative, trimmer-type political attitude of many seventeenth-century Englishmen. It was concerned to free society from the more undesirable claims of absolute monarchy and to show how a stable and prosperous political system could be established; just as Baconian empiricism had as its scientific objective the freeing of man's mind from the cramping effects of established intellectual authority and the foundation of sound, useful and progressive learning. It was not really radical and made no appeal to natural rights, conscience and such-like 'non-scientific' conceptions. And so, like the scientific methodology on which it was based, its politics was rather out of touch with the future. Which is why it is important to examine it carefully.

What, then, were the tenets of the political theory of empiricism? It meant basically, as I have said, the collection of appropriate facts as a basis for inductive generalization. I shall first review the types of experience on which the political empiricist drew in support of his conclusions, and then go on to indicate what these conclusions were in the field of morals and politics. Then, as I did with the political theory of order, I shall illustrate the doctrine in more detail by looking at some of the exponents of the creed.

Empirical data were the basis of the inductive analysis and there were two main kinds of human experience used for the purpose of political and ethical generali-

zation: personal experience, and vicarious experience. 'Experience is either personal knowledge gained by our own action, or the knowledge acquired by what we have seen, read, heard of, in others.'[29] To this there had to be added the study of those natural factors which influenced human affairs.

Personal experience consists of what may be called 'autobiography' and 'introspection', that is to say, experience of various kinds, both external and psychological, which is acquired during the course of an individual's life. The wider a man's external experience, the better he is able to assess the conduct of others and to form accurate generalizations about politics. For this reason, the literature of the time continually urged a broadening of contacts and suggested that as much as possible should be seen of all sorts and conditions of men in different lands. In consequence, travel was considered an essential part of the training of men whose duty it was to be concerned with public affairs. As Robert Molesworth put it, '*Travel* seems as necessary to one who desires to be useful to his Country, as practising upon other Men's Distempers is to make an able Physician. . . . ' Hence the growing fashion for the grand tour as an essential part of the education of young men of quality. The authority of Aristotle's *Rhetoric* was invoked, in which it was stated that a sound political education depended on the understanding of different systems of government.[30] This could be obtained by travelling in foreign countries and making careful political observations. In this spirit, too, books were written to guide and instruct the intending traveller about what he should look for and try to learn during his journey so as to maximize its value. For example in 1598 Philip Jones published his *Certain briefe, and speciall Instructions,* the object of which was to train observers to note and analyse during their voyages abroad a long list of topics covering every feature which could contribute to their knowledge: they should look especially at a country's geography, 'navigation', agriculture, politics, religion, learning and so on. Among the many other works of the same kind two typical and popular examples were Robert Johnson's translation of Botero's *The Travellers Breuiat* (1601) and Sir Robert Dallington's *A Method for Travell* (1605?).

'Introspection' or personal psychological experience was, of course, a particular aspect of 'autobiography'. By examining his own feelings, motives and thought-processes a man could, it was thought, acquire valuable insight into human nature generally. For men (at least those with a common culture and environment) were not so different that their psychological attributes were not basically the same. 'The history of one mind is the history of many.' Hence the importance attributed to the dictum 'know thyself'; self-knowledge could provide valuable data for political and ethical generalization.[31]

But, of course, personal experience was bound to be limited. It was especially immediate in its impact and the impressions it made were likely to be deep and long-lasting, but in the nature of things it could not be as wide as was desirable, especially when measured against the vast range of possible experience. Time, energy and money were too little. So while valuable, personal experience was too narrow a basis for really adequate or safe generalization, and it was necessary to draw on the bank and capital of vicarious experience of all kinds. There were two major sources of such information provided by the literature of history and of travel.

The belief in the didactic value of history was important here. This has already been described,[32] and it need only be added that the same developments were taking place in historiography as in many branches of natural science. The legendary and miraculous elements were being critically examined, attention was being concentrated on detailed studies of specific problems rather than on the production of universal conspectuses, auxiliary aids were being developed, and direct inspection of original material was becoming more common. The result was a more extensive and reliable mass of historical data as an empirical basis for discussion and as a source of authoritative examples and precedents.

The literature of travel also provided an important source of vicarious experience and was, in addition, vital to the understanding of the effects on man and society of 'nature' or 'climate'. A man could not travel in time, so he made up the deficiency by reading history. If he could not travel abroad and go to see for himself the customs, manners and methods of other countries, he read accounts of journeys which had been made by other men. These geographical handbooks often embodied historical accounts of the countries concerned, for in Bodinian fashion the geopolitical link between history and geography was recognized to be very close. To this mixed genre belongs the type of book represented by the travelogue-histories of Richard Hakluyt, Samuel Purchas, Thomas Coryate, Fynes Morison, Peter Mundy and so on. A good representative example from the pen of Botero was commended to the English reader in terms which showed what was expected from such accounts:

> Our Author deserves rather to bee numbred among the Polititians, than amongst the Historians or *Geographers*. Tis to his purpose sometimes to deliver you the situation of the Country he discourses upon; so to shew you, first the Greatnesse of each kingdome. Secondly, how formidable or helpefulle each Prince is likely to prove to his next neighbour; out of which two considerations, arise most of these leagues, Alliances, and those other Tyes of State, betwixt Kingdome and Kingdome. Thirdly, wee hence learne, how suddenly either Forces or Merchandizes may bee transported from one Nation

to another. And all these help him [i.e. the author] to relate of the Greatnesse and Riches of each Kingdome; which to doe, bee two of his maine purposes. The *Historie* that hee makes use of is to shew you the valours of people, the power of taking opportunities, the advantages of the use of severall weapons, &c. and that is also to his purpose. Both *Geographie* and *History* together (which bee the two favourite studies of the times) doe serve finally for the delight of the *Reader;* and doe altogether make up our Author into a complete and fine companion for Gentlemen, for Souldiers, for Schollers, and for all men to passe the time withall. . . . [33]

Like the histories of the time, the travel books were intended, therefore, to serve a didactic purpose, and many of them were politically oriented in this way. Dallington's books on France and Tuscany were like this; so were the Elzevir and other similar series of travel books, and to mention but one specific example of the same period, Giles Fletcher's *Of the Russe Commonwealth* (1589) was a complete account of Russian geography, laws, religion, military system, politics and society generally, intended to instruct the reader who was unable to visit Russia himself.

The result of all this was that by the middle of the seventeenth century it was possible to buy a reasonably good account of nearly every important European country and of many outside Europe.[34] Particularly numerous were the descriptions of states like Venice and the United Provinces, which were supposed to be models of stable government in a free society. One most remarkable feature was the 'sinomania' to which travellers' and missionaries' accounts gave rise. As a result of their descriptions Chinese civilization acquired a great reputation, and its culture, institutions and ideas were much in vogue as examples to be imitated.[35]

This considerable body of literature, the production of which was deliberately stimulated by the Royal Society after the Restoration, had a number of important effects on the discussion of political ideas. For one thing, it provided a great deal of detailed information about man in the state of nature. Many of the notions about pre-social man, like those of Hobbes and Locke, were conditioned by the state of contemporary anthropological knowledge. Similarly, conceptions of the noble savage were formed, at least in part, under the influence of accounts of explorers.[36] And while many monarchists found evidence to support their particular political views, arbitrary kingship was not the system of government which travellers most often noted among primitive men, at least during the latter part of the early modern period.[37] One early-eighteenth-century traveller, Cadwallader Colden, held that the Indian nations of North America, which showed exactly the most ancient and original condition of every society, demonstrated the errors of the patriarchal theory of government.[38] A book called *Civil Polity,* which was published anonymously in 1703, specifically defended the Lockeian notions of government on the basis of information provided by 'the Records that are left us by the Ancients; and by the Voyages, Travels, Discoveries, and Observations of the Moderns.'[39] Then, this travel literature stimulated the comparative method of studying man and society in all their variations, in the way that, at a much earlier time, Alexander's collections moved Aristotle and others to classify and systematize them in an attempt to discover general principles. Of course, this approach was not confined to the political sphere. Lord Herbert of Cherbury, for instance, was one of those who searched the religions of the world for the essential truths of 'rational religion' common to all of them. But in the study of politics, the essence of this attitude was reflected by Sir William Temple who, in his famous essay *Of Heroic Virtue* (1690), had written of the invaluable things to be learned from such wide-ranging study.[40] His own writings about law and government were good illustrations of the empirical approach, especially as he helped to extend its scope and to break new ground by widening the basis of analysis beyond the framework of conventional scholarship, which tended to concentrate on the European scene. Although Temple thought that Europe, and especially its classical period, was important, it also seemed too narrow a basis for political and moral generalization. He therefore suggested the systematic consideration as well, of the experience of other parts of the world. He said he was inclined to believe that some out-lying countries, which were unknown to the ancients and often overlooked by modern scholars, could provide 'as much matter of action and speculation, as the other scene so much celebrated in story.' He went on to explain that he meant this not only in respect of their size and geographical diversity, but also in connexion with their political arrangements.[41] Temple himself studied with great care a wide variety of contemporary travel literature in order to gain knowledge of the political and legal systems and the moral ideas of different and distant lands. He paid particular attention to Arabia, China, Scythia and Peru, not simply because these were the areas oversea about which he had most information, but rather because they were representative of the four corners of the world and so, he thought, a most adequate basis for inductive generalization.

Not that Temple neglected the lessons that could be learned from a comparative study of the major European powers of the day. Because of his diplomatic training and experience, he was especially suited for the kind of analysis involved and attempted an outline in his *A Survey of the Constitutions,* probably written in 1671. Any government, he said, ought to know about and reflect upon 'the constitutions, forces, and conjunctures' of neighbouring states, so that it was aware of the interests and power of the various countries which might affect its own policy and position.[42] It is almost certain that he wrote and published his *Memoirs* (1691) with the same sort of purpose in mind. This is also true of his *Observations upon the United Provinces* (1672), one of his longest works and one in which the empirical style of analysis is particularly evident. In the resolutive fashion its method consisted in studying Dutch history to see in 'the glasse of time and experience' the 'natural springs' of the country's rise and decline.[43] The tone of the discussion may be indicated by quoting the outline of the heads of analysis with which Temple ended his preface:

> . . . whereas the greatness of their strength and revenues grew out of the vastness of their trade, into which their religion, their manners and dispositions, their situation and the form of their government, were the chief ingredients; . . . it will be necessary, for the survey of this great frame, to give some account of the rise and progress of their State . . . ; to discover the nature and constitutions of their government in its several parts, and the motions of it, from the first and smallest wheels; to observe what is peculiar to them in their situations or dispositions, and what in their religion; to take a survey of their trade, and the causes of it; of the forces and revenues which composed their greatness, and the circumstances and conjunctures which conspired to their fall.[44]

Of course, Temple's efforts in this comparative field were not unique. Many similar collations had appeared earlier in the century, for instance, Pierre d'Avity's *The Estates, Empires, and Principalities of the World,* published in translation in 1615, and Peter Heylin's *Cosmographie,* which appeared in 1652. There were many others. Indeed the production of such surveys of the resources, defences, trade and of the geographical and other features of foreign countries, must always have been part of the work of civil servants and statesmen. In this sense the idea of a comparative study of politics may be seen simply as an extension of normal diplomatic and administrative practice.[45] It is no surprise, therefore, to find the idea exemplified in the writings of such men of affairs as Machiavelli, Bacon, Halifax, Temple, Petty, and later of Bolingbroke. Often the general effect of reading about such diversity of manners and institutions was to lead men to question the validity of those of their own country. If other political systems than absolute monarchy and if other religions than Anglicanism, or even than Christianity, seemed to provide the necessary conditions of civil order and prosperity, then why should existing institutions of Church and state be regarded as the one and only norm?

Underlying these implications was frequently a type of historical and natural determinism or, better, conditioning: the belief that the form taken by laws and institutions was moulded by circumstances. This was a doctrine of relativity. Political systems could vary according to the history, situation, habits and needs of the people concerned; and the actions of men were likewise no longer seen as being formed directly under the uniform order of God's design, but as a function of a number of empirical variables. Thus the single and simple picture of a world of unity and order was split up and diversified. If, beneath all this variation, there was any uniformity at all, it could only be perceived by a careful and extensive collection of all the factual data with a view to their comparison and conflation. If, for instance, the picture of an ideal system of laws and government was sought, then, in the words of Bodin's *Methodus,* there was only one way to proceed: to 'bring together and compare the legal framework of all states, or of the more famous states, and from them to compile the best kind.'[46]

When the empiricist carried out such a comparative or historical analysis of diverse systems of law and government, he invariably concluded that amid all the differences which he observed, the best, because most stable, form of constitution was one in which there was a mixture of monarchy, aristocracy and democracy. The connexion between his style of thinking and a belief in mixed government was often remarked at the time. Hobbes and Filmer were particularly scathing about the seditious effect of reading books of classical history and policy where, as we shall see, the claims of mixed government were often strongly advanced.[47] Similarly, royalists were by no means unaware that the study of England's past could prove fertile ground for the culture of hostility to the throne: such research did not necessarily lay stress on the importance of obedience to the ruler, as was the case with the Tudor histories discussed in an earlier chapter. This was why in 1604 the government dissolved the Society of Antiquaries, and why in 1629 its agents searched Sir Robert Cotton's library of manuscripts for seditious material and then sequestered the collection and restricted access to it. For this library and the work it made possible was a potent political weapon, being a major source of the precedents on which the parliamentarians rested so much of their case against the Crown. The same sort of reason led to the suppression of Selden's *History of Tythes.*[48]

This idea of mixed government could, as Bodin showed, hide certain ambiguities. Indeed, the precise system of institutions which the term was intended to describe could vary considerably. For one thing, advocacy of this system was compatible with republicanism, insofar as the monarchical function did not have to be carried out by an hereditary or even an elected king. It could be performed by a Protector, Doge, Chancellor, Consul or some similar nominated or elected first minister, or even by a committee or council. Then, in

its simplest form, mixed government meant a fusion of the main features of the three elements without intending their equal participation in control of affairs. The germ of such an arrangement may be seen in the Aristotelian 'polity' where one group played a dominant part (though there was, it is true, a blend only of the rule of the few and of the many). Taking up this idea, some later writers often suggested that one of the three parts should be preponderant. Machiavelli, for instance, seems to have believed that in a republic founded for expansion, this major component should usually be the popular one.[49] But in a perhaps more sophisticated version, the intention was that the three elements should balance one another. Polybius was probably the first to express this idea fully. Having said 'it is evident that we must regard as the best constitution a combination of all . . . three varieties' of government, he urged that the Spartan precedent should be followed. There, the force of each component was 'neutralized by that of the others', so that none could 'prevail and outbalance another'. The object of this device was that the constitution should remain for as long as possible in a state of equilibrium 'like a well-trimmed boat, kingship being guarded from arrogance by the fear of the commons, . . . and the commons on the other hand not venturing to treat the kings with contempt from fear of the elders. . . . ' The outcome was that by drawing up his constitution in this way, Lycurgus 'preserved liberty at Sparta for a longer period than is recorded elsewhere.'[50] From this and other classical sources like Cicero, Dionysius of Halicarnassus, Plutarch and Livy, the various notions about mixed government passed to Aquinas, Machiavelli, Soderini, Paruta and other moderns.[51]

In England during the sixteenth and seventeenth centuries, the term mixed government was very often, probably usually, equated with a limited or constitutional monarchy. In this system the royal power was restricted by the authority of Parliament which, as it consisted of both Lords and Commons, represented the aristocratic and popular elements. There was also, however, an important trend of republican thought which asserted the virtues of the non-monarchical form and was represented by men like Harrington, Sidney, Russell and Milton.

I shall now go on to indicate the factors which contributed to the development and prevalence of the idea of mixed government in this country during the early modern period. This analysis will show in more detail the characteristic connexion of the idea with the empirical style of thinking, and will also lead in particular to a review of the special pattern of English history which supporters of this kind of constitution formulated for themselves.

As the preceding paragraphs will have indicated, many of the arguments used were a legacy of the classical revival, ancient authority contributing both a philosophical justification of the mixed system and some of the most influential illustrations of its virtues. The theoretical assertion, such as it was, was that no 'pure' or 'simple' form of being could remain long undecayed and that stability and longevity were the characteristics only of 'mixed' or 'composite' bodies which contained elements of more than one simple form. So far as political organization was concerned, the logical implication of this view was that no simple type of government could exist for any length of time. It was thought possible, indeed, to observe a continual process of decline and renewal. Once again, the clearest and most influential statement of the theme by a classical writer was probably that of Polybius, who wrote in *The Histories* that 'Monarchy first changes into its vicious allied form, tyranny; and next, the abolishment of both gives birth to aristocracy. Aristocracy by its very nature degenerates into oligarchy; and when the commons inflamed by anger take vengeance on this government for its unjust rule, democracy comes into being; and in due course the licence and lawlessness of this form of government produces mob-rule to complete the series.'[52] Finally, of course, the confusion or anarchy thus created needed the firm rule of one man to restore peace and order; monarchy reappeared; and so, apparently, *ad infinitum.* Yet there was, perhaps, a way in which this seemingly unending constitutional cycle might be interrupted and a degree of relatively long-lasting stability obtained. This was to combine features of each pure form of government to make a mixed, and therefore more stable, body. For example, Sidney wrote that 'History and daily Experience' showed all governments to be subject to corruption and decay 'but with this difference, that Absolute Monarchy is by principle led unto, or rooted in it; whereas mix'd or popular Governments are only in a possibility of falling into it'.[53]

It was not, however, in any metaphysical terms that the claims of the composite political body were most widely argued. The main appeal, as Sidney's reference shows, was to the lessons of experience; and the history in particular of the ancient world (through the key examples of Sparta and republican Rome) was taken to show indubitably the superior virtues of the mixed system. Harrington reflected a common theme when he contrasted '*ancient Prudence,*' which he linked with these virtues, and '*modern Prudence,*' with which he associated a belief in absolute monarchy or aristocracy.[54]

But modern as well as classical experience was nonetheless prayed in support of mixed government. Indeed, the lessons of contemporary experience were in many respects crucial, the political system of Venice being singled out as a key example of a mixed polity which, because of its adherence to this system, had endured for a very long time and enjoyed peace and prosperity on a grand scale. Harrington's friend, Marvell, hailed its wisdom:

> To the serene Venetian state I'll go,
> From her sage mouth famed principles to
> know.

This 'Venetian myth', as Professor Fink has called it,[55] was spread by popular native writers like Paruta and Contarini, and it was firmly established in England by the end of the sixteenth century. The reasons for its popularity are fairly obvious. Venice was admired not merely for what was taken to be the harmony and stability of its political life, but also in a number of other ways, ranging from praise for the beauty of its location and its buildings to appreciation of its role in guarding Europe against the Turk. Similarly, the dependence of Venice's prosperity on trade and sea-power produced obvious parallels with this country, as did its conflicts with papal authority. Certainly, reference to Venetian institutions and practices was much in vogue among Parliament-men in their quarrels with the king, and, during the Commonwealth when constitution-making was a popular pastime, the 'most serene republic' was much invoked as an example to be followed. The myth only began to lose its hold after the Restoration, though it was still strikingly employed by Whigs like Henry Nevile during the Exclusion crisis and was indeed still used in the mid-eighteenth century. In addition to the Venetian case, it is probable that the ideas about the ancient French constitution, limited monarchy and mixed government which were produced in France during the religious troubles, had some effect on the propagation of these notions in England, for example through the influence of Hotman's *Franco-Gallia,* the *Vindiciae Contra Tyrannos* and similar works produced by both the Huguenots and Ligeurs.

Further, the experience of England itself was by no means ignored in putting the case against absolute monarchy. During the early modern period there was, as we have already seen, much discussion of this country's historical tradition and from various points of view. Innumerable references were made to the ancient constitution (which was a mixed constitution) and to the fundamental law which were thought by many scholars and lawyers to be embodied in that tradition. From these categories opponents of royalism derived both a constitutional doctrine and a particular version of English history.

The constitutional theory had two aspects, being linked with medieval notions of political pluralism and also with the idea of the king's two bodies which similarly flourished in England during the later Middle Ages. Traditionally, private persons and institutions had been recognized to have established rights in their 'property'. These privileges were protected by the fundamental law (as embodied, for instance, in Magna Carta), by parliamentary control of taxation, and by the diffusion of political and social authority. Such authority was regarded as not belonging to the king alone but to the nation, and as being distributed among a number of related but separate, almost independent, institutions representative of different interests. Thus there were the coexistent authorities of king, council, Parliament, Church, courts, chartered boroughs, universities, inns of court, and so forth. Under the ancient constitution of the realm each of these bodies had its proper place and its own distinct function and power and was not supposed to encroach on any other. This view was used by those who opposed Stuart attempts to strengthen the royal position, for instance during the controversies over ecclesiastical courts and royal proclamations. The common lawyers led by Coke often based their case against the king on such traditional usages and distinctions. In terms of the key political problem, that is the problem of the relations between king and Parliament, the solution sought by opponents of absolute monarchy was, in large part, the maintenance of this conventional balance of authority. Here there is an obvious link with the other factor, the medieval doctrine of the king's two bodies. This was a sort of political nestorianism which distinguished between the king's natural person and will on the one hand, and his being the representative of the immortal body politic, of the *dignitas* of the impersonal Crown, on the other. The 'king' was not the same as the 'King'. Hobbes disdainfully called this notion 'an university quibble', but it was nevertheless quite common. Since the beginning of the fifteenth century at least and following the lead given by this idea, many commentators had taken to defining the body politic in terms not of the king or head alone, but of the king combined with his council and Parliament, which together constituted a mixed or composite body. In 1559 John Aylmer reflected this view when he wrote, in *An Harborowe for Faithful and True Subjects,* that the 'regiment of England' was not 'a mere monarchy' nor was it 'a mere oligarchy, nor democracy, but a rule mixed of all these'.[56] The specifically dualist theory was naturally used as a counter to claims made on behalf of the king. In 1610, during the debate on impositions when the king's right to levy duty without parliamentary consent was challenged, the House of Commons was told that

> The soveraigne power is agreed to be in the king: but in the king is a two-fold power; the one in parliament, as he is assisted with the consent of the whole state; the other out of parliament, as he is sole, and singular, guided merely by his own will. And if of these two powers in the king, one is greater than the other, and can direct and controule the other; that is *suprema potestas,* the soveraigne power, and the other is *subordinata.* It will then be easily proved that the power of the king in parliament is greater than his power out of parliament; and doth rule and controule it. . . . [57]

At this particular stage of the constitutional controversy, during the early-seventeenth century, what the parliamentary forces demanded was their traditional share of the supreme power. But as the quarrel intensified, the more extreme Puritans and lawyers increasingly whittled down the sphere in which they were prepared to acknowledge that the king's will could rule by itself. Parliament began to entrench on prerogative matters, to tender advice on religious, economic and even foreign policy and, up to a point, James I and Charles I were forced to give way. On the eve of the Civil War and in the face of growing parliamentary claims, Charles was even driven to concede that the constitution was one involving a balance of three co-ordinate powers. This was a considerable modification of the arguments deployed by his father and the less moderate of his own supporters. But it was also a case which had the advantage of being, perhaps, legally and traditionally more correct. It also had the virtue of confining the Commons to a more narrow competence than that which they were coming to assert.[58] When in the end hostilities began, the anti-royalist forces thereby clearly indicated that they were not prepared to leave to God or to chance the responsibility for restraining the king within traditional bounds. They assumed the divine prerogative themselves, saying that they were defending the 'King' against the 'king'. For the king as a person had tried to usurp for himself what only rightfully belonged to the Crown represented by the king in Parliament. To say the monarch was under the fundamental law was not enough. The law had to be interpreted and protected, and Parliament (or the People) was to do this. Under the pressures of war, it was but a short step openly to claim the supreme power for Parliament itself without the king, or even for the Commons alone. This was an absolutism as untraditional as that pursued by the Stuarts. And it was the hallowed, conventional balance or mixture of governmental authorities that, to a large degree, the Restoration was intended to achieve. Though the manner in which Locke argued the case was rather different, when he wrote the *Second Treatise* he restated the essence of the traditional position including the two-fold aspect of the single executive.[59] And it was, at least in part, by reference to numerous precedents drawn from English and other constitutional history that, at the time of the Exclusion crisis, the Whig pamphleteers supported the case for keeping the Duke of York off the throne.[60] The same is true of the way in which, in the late-seventeenth and early-eighteenth centuries, the common-wealthmen like Attwood and Somers urged that the powers of the monarchy should be limited.

In such a fashion as this, then, the opponents of royalism looked to the lessons of the past, to the wisdom of the ancient constitution which the course of English history showed to be a balance of the rights and duties of all concerned. Consequently, to the supporters of the traditional system of limited monarchy, English history was a major source of argument and evidence and, like their constitutional adversaries, they contrived a characteristic version of its development.

One interpretation was that sustained by Coke and many of the other common lawyers, who found evidence in the British history itself of the native and immemorial custom embodied in the common law of the land. The books and treatises of the common laws of the ancient Britons had all been lost, 'an inestimable loss' Coke called it. But this unhappy privation was not allowed to inhibit reference to these old precedents. They were often assumed to establish the antiquity and independent authority of Parliament, by demonstrating that it had existed time out of mind and that it could not, therefore, have originated in any specific act of the royal will. Considerable restrictions on the king's power could thus be suggested to have the blessing of very ancient practice indeed. At the same time Parliament was not left in possession of an unfettered authority either, for it too was subject to the fundamental law. The courts would always interpret statutes in accordance with the accepted principles of reason and justice which that ancient law embodied and in this sense control legislation.[61]

Similar to this attitude but distinct in important ways, was the so-called Gothic view of English history, the most important of the non-royalist variations. It was being expounded by parliamentarians at least as early as the middle of the sixteenth century, and subsequently became widespread. The term Gothic (and the various synonyms somewhat loosely used in its place, such as Saxon, Jutish, Germanic and so on) referred to an ancient culture said to have developed outside the classic, Roman stream. Tacitus, who had been almost unknown in the Middle Ages, was growing in popularity and served to stimulate and represent this trend. Bodin and others like Richard Verstegan had elaborated the theory that, because of 'climatic' influences, the northerners or Goths were naturally disposed to be hardy, vigorous and liberty-loving. And antiquarian research was used to substantiate the story that the forbears of this island's inhabitants were Goths or Saxons who, when they invaded Britain, brought with them their traditional racial characteristics and free institutions. The scholarship involved was sometimes loose in the extreme. In many cases, often where it suited the polemical purpose in mind, the Goths were confused with the Britons they supplanted; and indeed the term Gothic came often to be associated with any non-Roman or non-Latin people and influence. But on the whole the specific political point was not blurred. It was that the old Gothic constitution was a system of mixed government and that Parliament had descended from the tribal assemblies or folk-moots of the Saxons. Moreover, the Saxon kings were not hereditary rulers but elected leaders chosen originally for the purpose of

commanding in a war, and thus limited by the temporary and conditional nature of their authority. They were, therefore, by no means absolute and their power derived from the people over whom they ruled and by whom they might be removed. Despite the Danish and Norman invasions and the attempts of various kings to destroy popular assemblies and rights, these had a continuous and unbroken history; Parliament could be traced back directly to the Witenagemot. There are many examples of these themes, which became more common as the seventeenth century wore on.[62] Here two illustrations must suffice to show the use made of these Gothic ideas by anti-royalists: Algernon Sidney's championing of the theory in his *Discourses concerning Government* and Philip Hunton's *A Treatise of Monarchy*.

Like Locke, Sidney set out to destroy Filmer's theory which had become the official defence of the royalist case during the Exclusion crisis. But unlike Locke, Sidney did not produce a document the essence of which was rationalistic. His book was much more in the normal empirical style, depending for its arguments on the evidence of experience and of history, ancient and modern, sacred and profane. It was a mass of detailed references to the Bible, books of travel and the story of other countries. Sidney explained his preferences in respect of systems of government in many passages, of which the following may be taken as typical:

> If it be true, which perhaps may be doubted, that there have bin in the world simple Monarchys, Aristocracys or Democracys legally establish'd, 'tis certain that the most part of the Governments of the world (and I think all that are or have bin good) were mix'd. Part of the Power has bin confer'd upon the King, or the Magistrate that represented him, and part upon the Senat and People, as has bin prov'd in relation to the Governments of the *Hebrews, Spartans, Romans, Venetians, Germans,* and all those who live under that which is usually call'd the Gothic Polity.[63]

This polity he took to be traditionally established in England, whose liberties he traced as far back as the times of ancient Britain. But more emphasis was given to the heritage of the Saxons 'from whom we chiefly derive our Original and Manners'. Sidney took from Tacitus the view that the Germans 'liv'd free under such Magistrats as they chose, regulated by such Laws as they made, and retain'd the principal powers of the Government in their general or particular Councils. Their Kings and Princes had no other power than what was confer'd upon them by these Assemblys, who having all in themselves could receive nothing from them who had nothing to give.'[64] And he thought that if the Saxons were free in their own country 'they must have bin so when they came hither.' Our 'later Historys show, that as soon as the *Saxons* came into this Country, they had their . . . general Assemblys of the Noble and Free men, who had in themselves the Power of the Nation'. These assemblies 'were evidently the same in power with our Parliaments'.[65] Sidney did not bother to examine the question whether the Commons had always been part of these ancient assemblies, contenting himself with the remark that as supreme power belonged to these bodies they could have included the popular element whenever they wished. In fact, he inclined to think that the Commons had always had a part in the government. He was sure, however, that the balance should properly lie with the aristocratic element: 'in all the legal Kingdoms of the North, the strength of the Government has always been plac'd in the Nobility'. This was not the peerage of his day, but a real nobility of 'strength and vertue', rather like Harrington's aristocracy of authority.[66]

The other example is Hunton's *A Treatise of Monarchy,* first published in 1643 and reissued in later years including 1689. It was concerned to reject the royalist case, and to do this discussed the various types of kingship. 'Simple' forms of government were when the supreme power rested in the hands of either one person, the nobility or the community. The writer then went on to argue thus:

> Now experience teaching people, that several inconveniencies are in each of these, which is avoided by the other: as aptness to tyranny in simple monarchy, aptness to destructive factions in an aristocracy, and aptness to confusion and tumult in a democracy. As on the contrary, each of them hath some good which the others want, *viz.* unity and strength in a monarchy; counsel and wisdom in an aristocracy; liberty and respect of common good in a democracy. Hence the wisdom of men deeply seen in state matters guided them to frame a mixture of all three, uniting them into one form; that so the good of all might be enjoyed, and the evil of them avoided. And this mixture is either equal, when the highest command in a state, by the first constitution of it, is equally seated in all three; and then . . . it can be called . . . but by the general style of a 'mixed state': or if there be priority of order in one of the three . . . it may take the name of that which hath the precedency.

The author thought that stability could only emerge from the latter, as in a so-called 'mixed monarchy', where, though all three powers shared in government and none could become exorbitant, the king was predominant.[67] Then, discussing the nature of the particular monarchy of England, it was stated that, 'as our histories record', the Saxons,

> coming into the kingdom, drove out the Britons, and by degrees planted themselves under their commanders, and no doubt continued the freedom they had in Germany; unless we should think, that by conquering they lost their own liberties to the

kings, for whom they conquered, and expelled the Britons into Wales. Rather I conceive, the original of the subject's liberty was by those our fore-fathers brought out of Germany: where, (as Tacitus reports,) . . . 'their kings had no absolute, but limited power'; and all weighty matters were dispatched by general meetings of all the estates. Who sets not here the antiquity of our liberties, and frame of government? So they were governed in Germany, and so here, to this day; for, by transplanting themselves, they changed their soil, not their manners and government.[68]

Although, as I have said, Saxon was often confused with Briton, both as enemies of Rome, this Gothic interpretation was usually made to contrast with the royalist, order-dominated view of history. This had made much of the Britons and had seen the Saxons as barbarians overwhelming the Britain of Arthur. The Gothicist, on the other hand, was inclined to regard the old British history as so much legend and saw the invaders as the founders of the country's liberties, simple democrats overthrowing the sinful and autocratic Britons. 'God . . . abated the nobility of the Britons, who had recourse to force rather than to law [and] delivered the kingdom to the humblest and simplest of all the neighbouring nations: to wit, the Saxons, who came to conquer it from the parts of Almaine . . . And they . . . chose from among themselves a king to reign over them . . . to maintain and defend their persons and goods by the rule of right.' [69] This rejection of direct descent from the aboriginal Britons may well have been associated, at least in part, with growing knowledge of primitive peoples. It seems quite likely, for instance, that the discovery of the Red Indians of North America helped to persuade many people that the ancient Britons must have been just as primitive and savage. [70] In any event, to champion the Saxon heritage obviously implied criticism of the stories which had grown up around the figure of Arthur, whose place as the paragon of all the virtues was taken by Alfred. The rejection of this pseudo-history of the Britons could be conveniently and easily associated with attacks on the Tudor despotism with which the Arthurian legend was linked, and so with anti-royalist sentiment in general. It was thus no accidental association of ideas which led Milton, when considering the composition of an historical epic, to switch his interest from Arthur to Alfred, a change paralleled by his realization that he had parliamentary sympathies. The controversy between these contrasting views was amusingly parodied by the author of the mid-seventeenth-century comedy *Hey for Honesty,* in which one character claimed 'my lice are of the noble breed, Sprung from the Danes, Saxons, and Normans' blood', while another improved on this boast by evoking a parasitic ancestry 'ap Brutus, ap Sylvus, ap Aeneas' which fought in the wars of Troy. [71] The Gothic view also differed from the Cokean in that while it accepted the free constitution as being of venerable and pre-Conquest origin, it did not regard it as being so ancient as Coke had suggested. It was of more definite and recent foundation (in fact in the traditional invasion year of A.D. 449), though still owing nothing to royal initiative and power. An additional contrast was that the Gothicist sought the mixed system's origin in a foreign and not a native source.

A major difficulty, which had to be faced by both Cokean and Gothic schools of thought, was presented by the Norman Conquest, for it was necessary to explain how this shattering event had not prevented the continuance of the immemorial—or Gothic—constitution and its laws. One explanation provided involved, in effect, a denial that there had been any real conquest or basic change at all. It was suggested that William had agreed to accept the laws of St Edward the Confessor and that his successors had from time to time confirmed their continuance. [72] A variation of this theory played up particularly the 'Men of Kent' who, because the Jutes had originally landed in that county, were supposed to be especially liberty-loving. They were never conquered by the Normans and only yielded themselves on the condition 'that they might retaine their ancient customes unviolated'. [73] Magna Carta (taken, in fact, as many of the royalist historians like Brady saw, quite anachronistically out of its feudal context) played an important role in the supposed continuation of ancient liberties. Until 1688 the coronation oath contained a promise to obey the ancient law of St Edward— 'that noble Transcript of the Original Contract' as Attwood called it—and the assumption by the king of this obligation had the same effect as the original imposition of Magna Carta. John Pym provided one of the most well-known expressions of 'the myth of the confirmations' in the debate on the case of Manwaring in 1628:

> . . . there are plain footsteps of those Laws in the Government of the *Saxons,* they were of that vigor and force as to overlive the Conquest, nay to give bounds and limits to the Conqueror . . . the assurance and possession of the Crown he obtained by composition, in which he bound himself to observe these and the other antient Laws and Liberties of the Kingdom, which afterwards he likewise confirmed by oath at his Coronation: from him the said Obligation descended to his Successors. It is true, they have been often broken, [yet] they have been often confirmed by Charters of Kings, by Acts of Parliaments; but the Petitions of the Subjects, upon which those Charters and Acts were founded, were ever Petitions of Right, demanding their antient and due Liberties, not suing for any new. [74]

In consequence, remote precedents were continually invoked in the political controversies which led up to the civil wars, and indeed in the interminable antiquarian exegesis which accompanied the constitutional crises of the later part of the century.

The Gothic belief in the golden age of Anglo-Saxondom had other than constitutional implications. It had cultural and artistic aspects and was also associated with the defence of Protestantism. It was not simply that it was very closely related to the idea that German purity led to the triumph of Luther over the decadence of the Roman Church or that this was the repetition, which had been prophesied, of the ancient Gothic victory, the establishment of the fifth, everlasting monarchy foretold in the Book of Daniel. There was also a specific English version, albeit somewhat confused with the stories about the early church of the Britons. The Society of Antiquaries, or rather the group founded in 1572 by Archbishop Parker to which the origins of the Society may perhaps be traced, was established specifically to extend research into Anglo-Saxon Church charters and to try to maintain the historicity and rights of the native Church against that dominated from Rome. The 'English Scholars' similarly believed that an indigenous form of Christianity had flourished before the arrival of Augustine, after which this pure and uncorrupt form of worship and ecclesiastical polity was overwhelmed and fell under foreign, Romish domination not to be finally freed until the Reformation. [75]

In fine, then, it may be suggested that the exponents of mixed government or limited monarchy frequently argued their case by calling to their aid appropriate classical authority, the experience of states both old and new, and the lessons of history. And, in general, it may be seen how the political ideas associated with this empiricism stood in contrast to the political theory of order and its own special style of argument. Monarchy was regarded not as the best and most natural form of government, for it was unstable and likely to degenerate into tyranny and disorder. Here, of course, there was a certain superficial similarity with the order theory, but the remedies prescribed for this instability differed markedly. The royalist urged the re-establishment on a firmer basis of authority of the pure form of absolute monarchy; the empiricist held that the monarchical element in the constitution should be merged as one component merely of a system of shared sovereignty. The exponents of mixed government were prepared to concede that one of the three elements might be predominant, but it was frequently the aristocratic or popular element of which they spoke in this connexion and not the monarchical. Moreover, the mixed theory made it quite easy to argue that if the king claimed too much power he was upsetting the traditional balance and so might legitimately be resisted by the other groups. Further the theory could be and was used in an even more extreme fashion as an argument for republicanism. Finally, the idea that a system of government could be instituted, by a legislator for example, implied that political organization was not natural or God-given but artificial, in the sense that it was made by man in the form he considered appropriate. . . .

Notes

[28] T. Sprat, *History of the Royal Society,* ed. Cope and Jones (London, 1959), p. 17; cf. Sprat's own statement of the method, ibid., p. 31.

[29] Vives, op. cit., p. 228. The division was an empirical commonplace and was expressed, e.g., in very similar terms over a century and a half later in R. Molesworth, *An Account of Denmark* (London, 1694), sig. a[I] verso.

[30] Aristotle, *Rhetoric,* 1360[a] 30; the preceding quotation is from Molesworth, op. cit., sig. a2 verso.

[31] e.g. Montaigne, op. cit., iii.331, Hobbes, op. cit., p. 6; cf. Hobbes's *The English Works,* ed. Molesworth (London, 1839-45), i.73-75, a passage which also describes the 'analytical' and 'synthetical' (i.e. the resolutive-compositive) method. On the general importance of 'intense introspection' cf. W. Haller, *The Rise of Puritanism* (New York, 1947), pp. 90-100.

[32] See above pp. 95-106.

[33] G. Botero, *The Travellers Breuiat* (London, 1601), sigs. A2 verso-A3 verso.

[34] G. N. Clark, *Science and Social Welfare in the Age of Newton* (2nd ed., Oxford, 1949), p. 129.

[35] See A. O. Lovejoy, *Essays in the History of Ideas* (Baltimore, 1948), ch. vii, and W. W. Appleton, *A Cycle of Cathay: the Chinese Vogue in England in the Seventeenth and Eighteenth Centuries* (New York, 1951), where references will be found. A characteristic opinion was Temple's high praise of Confucian philosophy and the Chinese system of government in his essay 'Of Heroic Virtue' in *Works,* ed. cit., iii.325-45.

[36] J. L. Myres, 'The Influence of Anthropology on the Course of Political Science', *University of California Publications in History,* iv (1916), pp. 22-33.

[37] R. W. Frantz, *The English Traveller and the Movement of Ideas 1660-1732* (Lincoln, Nebraska, 1934), p. 130.

[38] Frantz, op. cit., p. 126, where passages are cited from Colden's *The History of the Five Indian Nations* (New York, 1727).

[39] [Peter Paxton] *Civil Polity. A Treatise Concerning the Nature of Government. Wherein the Reasons of that Great Diversity to be observed in the Customs, Manners, and Usages of Nations, are Historically Explained* (London, 1703), p. 193.

[40] Temple, op. cit., iii.321-2; cf. Molesworth, op. cit., sigs. [a5] recto-verso.

[41] Temple, op. cit., iii.322-4.

[42] Ibid., ii.209.

[43] Ibid., i.41-42, 82.

[44] Temple, op. cit., i.38-39.

[45] See, e.g., 'Mr. Faunt's Discourse touching the office of Principal Secretary of Estate, etc.' (1592) in J. R. Tanner (ed.), *Constitutional Documents of the Reign of James I A.D. 1603-1625* (Cambridge, 1960), pp. 120-3.

[46] Bodin, *Method for the Easy Comprehension of History,* tr. Reynolds (New York, 1945), p. 2. This was the object outlined also in Bodin's *Juris Universi Distributio* (1580).

[47] Hobbes, *Leviathan,* ed. cit., pp. 140-1, 214; cf. *The English Works,* ed. cit., vi. 168, 192-3, 233, 362; Filmer, *Patriarcha and other Political Works,* ed. Laslett (Oxford, 1949), pp. 277-8, cf. p. 188.

[48] On this general question see, e.g., Fussner, op. cit., ch. 5; H. Butterfield, *The Englishman and his History* (Cambridge, 1945), pp. 37-38, 63; R. F. Brinkley, *Arthurian Legend in the Seventeenth Century* (Baltimore, 1932), pp. 31-33. Cf. the comment about Selden's *History* in T. Randolph, *Poetical and Dramatic Works,* ed. Hazlitt (London, 1875), ii.485.

[49] *The Discourses of Niccolo Machiavelli,* ed. Walker (London, 1950), i.220, 226-7; though he also thought that in a state which did not wish to expand, the aristocracy might with advantage play the major role, ibid., i.220-2.

[50] Polybius, *The Histories* (Loeb ed., London, 1922ff.), VI.iii.7-9, x.7-11. The idea of a Lycurgean 'Legislator' here expressed is found frequently in the writings of supporters of mixed government, such as Machiavelli, Harrington, Milton, Temple and Nevile.

[51] The general theme and the transmission of ideas involved is admirably described by Z. S. Fink, *The Classical Republicans* (2nd ed., [Evanston], 1962), pp.

2-10.

[52] Polybius, op. cit., VI.iv.8-11; cf. the more detailed account at VI.v-ix.

[53] Sidney, *Discourses concerning Government* (2nd ed., London, 1705), pp. 131-2; cf. p. 96 and also Machiavelli's *Discourses,* ed. cit., i.211-16, 459-60.

[54] *James Harrington's Oceana,* ed. Liljegren (Heidelberg, 1924), pp. 12-13. Sir Leslie Stephen noticed the association between support of mixed government and the appeal to experience and history, see *History of English Thought in the Eighteenth Century* (3rd ed., New York, 1949), ii.134.

[55] On the importance of the Venetian example, see Fink, op. cit., esp. chs. ii, v and vii, on which I have drawn for most of this paragraph.

[56] Quoted in G. R. Elton (ed.), *The Tudor Constitution: Documents and Commentary* (Cambridge, 1960), p. 16; cf. Sir Thomas Smith, *De Republica Anglorum,* ed. Alston (Cambridge, 1906), pp. 46-47, 48.

[57] *A Complete Collection of State-Trials* (4th ed., London, 1776-81), xi.53. It has recently been suggested that this mixed-state theory, so common under the Tudors, was 'to a significant degree in abeyance' from roughly the accession of James I until 1642. See R. W. K. Hinton, 'The Decline of Parliamentary Government under Elizabeth I and the Early Stuarts', *The Cambridge Historical Journal,* xiii (1957), pp. 121-2, 130, and also his 'English Constitutional Theories from Sir John Fortescue to Sir John Eliot', *The English Historical Review,* lxxv (1960), esp. pp. 423-4. Yet the idea of the fundamental law, which Mr Hinton suggests tended at the time in question to eclipse the theory of mixed government as a means of limiting royal power, surely embodied the notion of the balanced, mixed constitution: it was argued that the king was breaking the fundamental law because he was trying to do out of Parliament what could properly only be done in and with Parliament.

[58] See Charles's 'Answer to the Nineteen Propositions' in J. Rushworth, *Historical Collections* (London, 1659-1701), Part III vol. i, pp. 725-35, esp. p. 731; also the discussions by C. C. Weston, 'The Theory of Mixed Monarchy under Charles I and After', *The English Historical Review,* lxxv (1960), pp. 427-30, 436-7, and by H. Hulme, 'Charles I and the Constitution' in W. A. Aiken and B. D. Henning (eds.), *Conflict in Stuart England* (London, 1960), pp. 120-3.

[59] See, e.g., Locke's *Two Treatises of Government,* ed. Laslett (Cambridge, 1960), p. 386 (§151).

[60] O. W. Furley, 'The Whig Exclusionists: Pamphlet Literature in the Exclusion Campaign, 1679-81', *The Cambridge Historical Journal,* xiii (1957), pp. 25-27. On the importance of the idea of mixed monarchy at the same time see B. Behrens, 'The Whig Theory of the Constitution in the Reign of Charles II', ibid., vii (1941-3), pp. 50-55.

[61] See, e.g., *The Reports of Sir Edward Coke, Knt.* (ed. Thomas and Fraser, London, 1826), The Third Part (vol. ii), 'To The Reader', pp. xiv-xxiii, and the prefaces to the Sixth, Eighth and Ninth Parts, *passim.*

[62] See S. Kliger, *The Goths in England* (Cambridge, Mass., 1952), chs. i, ii.

[63] Sidney, op. cit., p. 321.

[64] Ibid., p. 347.

[65] Ibid., p. 348, cf. pp. 211, 270. Nor did the Conquest interrupt the Saxon tradition, ibid., pp. 271, 298-9.

[66] Ibid., pp. 349-54.

[67] Hunton, *A Treatise of Monarchy,* quoted from the anonymous reprint of 1689 in *The Harleian Miscellany* (London, 1808-13), vi.335-6.

[68] Hunton, op. cit., *The Harleian Miscellany* (London, 1808-13), vi.340.

[69] Horn's *The Mirror of Justices,* ed. Whittaker (Selden Society, London, 1895), vol. vii, p. 6. Originally written in the thirteenth century, this book was translated only in 1646 but had always been used by parliamentarian and non-royalist lawyers.

[70] T. D. Kendrick, *British Antiquity* (London, 1950), pp. 120-5.

[71] T. Randolph, op. cit., ii.431, 432. And see the general discussion of the Trojan-Saxon controversy in R. F. Brinkley, *Arthurian Legend in the Seventeenth Century* (Baltimore, 1932), chs. ii and iii, a pioneer study.

[72] See, e.g., Sidney, op. cit., pp. 298-9, 349, 371; and Hunton, op. cit., vi.341.

[73] William Camden, *Britannia,* tr. Holland (London, 1637), p. 325; and see Kliger, op. cit., pp. 21-25.

[74] Rushworth, op. cit., Part I, p. 596. Attwood's phrase is from *The Fundamental Constitution of the English Government* (London, 1690), p. iv. Other assertions of the myth can be seen in e.g. one of Ireton's contributions to the Putney Debates in 1647 in A. S. P. Woodhouse (ed.), *Puritanism and Liberty* (London, 1951), p. 52 (2nd pagination); Sir Matthew Hale, *Reflections on Mr Hobbes His Dialogue of the Lawe* (c. 1670-5?) reprinted in W. S. Holdsworth, *A History of English Law* (London, 1903ff.), v.507, 511; W. Petyt, *The Antient Right of the Commons of England Asserted* (London, 1680), pp. 71-72; H. Nevile, *Plato Redivivus* (London, 1681), pp. 106-7; *The Character of a Popish Successor* (1681) in *State-Tracts* (London, 1692-3), Part I, p. 163; and Lord Somers, *The Judgment of Whole Kingdoms and Nations* (London, 1713), pp. 6, 18, 22.

[75] D. C. Douglas, *English Scholars 1660-1730* (2nd ed., London, 1951), pp. 19-20, 52-53, 197ff.; Kliger, op. cit., pp. 79-91, 119.

FURTHER READING

Anthologies

Barker, Ernest, ed. *Social Contract: Essays by Locke, Hume, and Rousseau.* London, Oxford, and New York: Oxford University Press, 1960, 307 p.

> Reprint of Locke's *An Essay Concerning the True Original, Extent and End of Civil Government,* Hume's *Of the Original Contract,* and Rousseau's *The Social Contract.* Barker's introduction provides a detailed overview and historical context.

Sigmund, Paul E., ed. *Natural Law in Political Thought.* Cambridge, Mass.: Winthrop Publishers, 1971, 214 p.

> Excerpts many of the primary statements concerning natural law, including selections from Locke, Rousseau, Bentham, and Kant. Each section begins with introductory essays.

Criticism

Abbo, John A. *Political Thought: Men and Ideas.* Westminster, Md.: The Newman Press, 1960, 452 p.

> Surveys the history of political philosophy from ancient Greece to the twentieth century, with several sections devoted to the primary figures of the early modern period.

Boucher, David, and Paul Kelly. *The Social Contract from Hobbes to Rawls.* London and New York: Routledge, 1994, 276 p.

> Presents academic essays by scholars writing from positions ranging from Marxist to feminist and new historicist. Many treat the dominant figures of modern political philosophy, including Hobbes, Locke, Hume, and Rousseau.

Dunn, John. *The History of Political Theory and Other essays.* Cambridge: Cambridge University Press, 1996, 235 p.

> Tells the history of political philosophy while engaging with many of its key theoretical aspects, including a chapter on "Contractualism."

Gough, J. W. *The Social Contract: A Critical Study of Its Development.* Oxford: Oxford at the Clarendon Press, 1957, 259 p.

> An authoritative history of the social contract by a prominent scholar. Central chapters treat the period from the late Middle Ages to the eighteenth century.

Laslett, Peter, ed. *Philosophy, Politics and Society.* New York: Macmillan, 1956, 184 p.

> Presents ten largely theoretical essays on different aspects of political philosophy, including Margaret Macdonald on "Natural Rights."

Lessnoff, Michael. *Social Contract.* London: Macmillan, 1986, 178 p.

> Provides a detailed history of the social contract, as well as an assessment of how recent critiques have understood that history and revived the idea of the contract.

Macpherson, C. B. *The Political Theory of Possessive Individualism: Hobbes to Locke.* Oxford: Oxford at the Clarendon Press, 1962, 310 p.

> Looks at the history of political philosophy via the concept of possessive individualism, which Macpherson contends to be fundamental to even the most diverse thinkers of modern history.

Medina, Vicente. *Social Contract Theories: Political Obligation or Anarchy?* Savage, MD: Rowman & Littlefield Publishers, 1990, 179 p.

> Takes each of the major figures—from Hobbes through Rawls—in turn before the author addresses the primary theoretical issues surrounding the idea of the social contract.

Skinner, Quentin. *The Foundations of Modern Political Thought.* : Volume One: *The Renaissance.* Cambridge, London, New York: Cambridge University Press, 1978, 405 p.

> Combines a history of early modern political philosophy with an attempt to "indicate something of the process by which the modern concept of the State came to be formed."

Wolin, Sheldon S. *Politics and Vision: Continuity and*

Innovation in Western Political Thought. Boston and Toronto: Little, Brown and Company, 1960, 529 p.

An extensive, in-depth discussion of the history of political philosophy, the last half of which treats the modern era. Wolin investigates politics in relation to other significant fields, including religion, imperialism, economics, and "the social."

Edmund Burke

1729-1797

British political philosopher and statesman.

The following entry provides critical discussion of Burke's writing on political theory. For additional information on Burke's life and works, see *Literature Criticism from 1400 to 1800*, Volume 7.

INTRODUCTION

A philosopher and statesman, Burke ranks as a preeminent figure in western political thought. Long regarded as the father of modern conservatism, his career as a polemicist and politician spanned years of significant political turmoil in England and the West. Writing and speaking passionately about actual and potential excesses of state authority, Burke espoused the desirability of limited, divided government. He feared the threat to liberty posed by concentrations of governmental power whether wielded autocratically by the Crown or collectively by radical reformers in democratic assemblies. Burke conceived of the state as a divinely-ordered hierarchy where an elite of property owners sitting in Parliament, mindful of tradition and owing allegiance to the past, would collectively posses the forbearance to govern wisely. While affirming the need for constitutional government to adjust to new circumstances, Burke believed that reform should be prudent, practical, and specific—not predicated on abstract theories of natural rights. Writing in the Age of Enlightenment, Burke parted rank from such philosophers as John Locke, who championed a faith in the perfectibility of humankind and effectively erased the idea of original sin. Rejecting revolutionary change predicated on a facile faith in individual will, Burke held a particular disdain for Jean Jacques Rousseau, who argued that all rights and liberties were inherent in individuals in a pre-social state, and that political allegiance was a voluntary exercise that could be revoked if the state no longer served the general will of the people. Although his age was one of increasing secularization and faith in individual volition, Burke's political philosophy had deep religious underpinnings as he believed that the original covenant between God and man both prefigured and predestined the nature of all social contracts. Thus, government had a positive duty to provide a moral framework for the cultivation of a virtuous society. Burke's spirited and thoughtful defense of faith, order, and historical continuity distinguish his contribution to political thought, while his eloquence and cogency continue to engage new readers in each generation.Biographical InformationBurke was born in

Dublin in 1729 to Richard Burke, a prominent attorney and a Protestant, and to Mary Nagle Burke, a staunch Roman Catholic. His Irish heritage and the influence of his mother's Catholicism played an important role in defining his political attitudes and shaping his moral sensibilities. He attended a Quaker school in Dublin before graduating from Trinity College with a degree in Classics. At his father's urging, Burke went to London in 1750 to study law, but soon became captivated by literary and philosophical pursuits. Much to his father's disappointment, Burke never joined the bar. Soon married and a father himself, Burke was unable to support his family solely by writing and editing, even though his literary talents were championed by such writers as Samuel Johnson. To increase his financial security, Burke first turned to politics in 1761, when he enlisted in the service of the Earl of Halifax. But his political future was decisively cast when he became the private Secretary to the Marquis of Rockingham, Charles Watson Wentworth. A prominent Whig, Lord Rockingham led the conservative opposition party most favored by the Crown. Burke's alliance with the influential leader led to his securing a seat in Parliament in 1765, where he soon established a reputation as a gifted orator and thoughtful statesman. While Burke focused much of his energy on domestic politics, he was frequently preoccupied with events outside of Britain. He was especially sympathetic to the complaints of the American colonists in their grievances over the Crown's taxation policies, insisting that much of the colonists's discontent stemmed from their perception that, as the descendants of Englishmen, their rights and liberties were being infringed. Burke also took up the cause of Indian subjects under British rule. In his speeches he continually railed against Parliament for its failure to provide proper oversight to the Indian population. For seven years Burke played a major and often controversial role in the long impeachment trial of Governour Warren Hastings for alleged abuses and neglect of the basic needs of the Indian subjects under his charge. Burke insisted that governments had positive obligations to colonized people, whether that meant building roads, schools, or hospitals. Burke's attitudes were shaped in part by his status as an outsider, for his Irish ancestry had precluded full acceptance into British society. Having a lifelong interest in the plight of the Irish, Burke especially criticized the Crown's penal laws, which were harshly punitive to Catholics in limiting their ability to amass wealth. As a statesman, he believed in voting in the interest of the entire realm, and refused to be influenced by the narrow interests of any one borough; as a result, he often grew unpopular with local constituencies whose concerns were naturally parochial. Thus he was unable to permanently hold onto any single seat in Parliament, and never achieved much personal political power. Yet Burke's writings and speeches were widely read throughout the West during much of his lifetime, and, despite never achieving high office, he enjoyed widespread acknowledgment of his work, and publicly debated through pamphlets with such men as Thomas Paine. After Hastings was acquitted in his impeachment trial in 1794, Burke resigned from Parliament and retired to his rural estate in Beaconsfield, Buckinghamshire, where he kept up correspondence and writing before succumbing to stomach cancer within three years.

Major Works

Burke's allegiance to the Whigs meant that he was politically allied with the minority party through almost all his tenure in Parliament. *Thoughts on the Cause of the Present Discontents* (1770), Burke's first major political essay, was largely a defense of the necessity of political parties to channel oppositional thought, check the power and prerogatives of the Crown, and secure balanced legislation. In his *Speech on American Taxation* (1774) Burke eloquently urged his peers to reconsider retaliatory measures aimed at the colonists for their militant opposition to the Crown's tax poli-

cies. He believed the colonists had just cause in resisting a government too willing to over-reach and meddle. While he did not support the idea of colonial independence, he warned his colleagues that oppressive Parliamentary measures might result in revolution. In his *Speech on Moving His Resolutions for Conciliation with the Colonies* (1775) Burke appealed to reason and circumstance by using historical data to shore up his arguments for the benefits of British-colonial trade. While defending the Crown's right to tax the colonists, Burke urged the repeal of repressive measures that would only further exacerbate strained relations. Burke's most famous essay, *Reflections on the Revolution in France and on the Proceedings in Certain Societies in London Relative to That Event* (1790) was a passionate diatribe denouncing the radical ends of French revolutionaries. Burke cautioned against radical change and held up the British constitution as a model which provided for responsible government reform. His polemic prompted Thomas Paine to reply with his *Rights of Man* (1791) pamphlet. In *An Appeal from the New, to the Old Whigs* (1791) Burke (writing anonymously) addressed critics of his anti-revolutionary tracts by reiterating his contention that all members of civil society live with an incumbent duty to constitutional fidelity, and that other moral obligations are not a matter of choice in an divinely ordered world.

Critical Reception

Burke was generally well-received and respected by peers in Parliament who admired his eloquence and cogency even though they frequently voted against him. But when policy debates turned to Anglo-Irish affairs, Burke's ancestry led to charges that his perceptions were unbalanced, biased and shaped by emotion. His laborious persistence in the impeachment pursuit of Hastings contributed to the perception that he often became zealously single-minded. Perhaps the most painful political breach for Burke occurred when he parted ways with many of his former Whig colleagues over the French Revolution. These quarrels spilled over into ongoing discussions of English politics, exacerbating competing interpretations of the Glorious Revolution and its consequences for British constitutionalism. Placing a much heavier emphasis on tradition and historical continuity, Burke defended long-standing institutions such as the aristocracy, the Church, and the state, but these only put him at odds with the revolutionary spirit of his times. He further asserted that the sovereignty of the Crown had not been diminished with the ascension of Parliament, but only its powers circumscribed. Other Whigs held that Revolution was necessary to assert the supremacy of the people. Thus, at the end of his life, he was philosophically more aligned with the modern-day Tories. Neglected for the most part during the nineteenth-century, Burke is enjoying a significant revival in the latter half of the twentieth century, especially by neo-conservative critics. The emergence of dictatorships following political revolutions in the modern era has, according to these critics, vindicated Burke's mistrust of radical reform predicated on rational faith and utopian promises. A current theme in Burkean scholarship is the extent to which he was a disciple of Adam Smith, and the degree to which he believed government should intervene in the economy. It is a testament to the depth and breadth of Burke's political legacy that his writings remain a rich source for scholarship and that they continue to engender vigorous debate.

PRINCIPAL WORKS

A Free Briton's Advice to the Free Citizens of Dublin (essay) 1748

A Vindication of Natural Society; or, A View of the Miseries and Evils Arising to Mankind from Every Species of Artificial Society (essay) 1756

A Philosophical Enquiry into the Origin of Our Ideas of the Sublime and Beautiful (essay) 1757

The Annual Register (journal) 1759-65

An Essay towards an Abridgement of the English History (unfinished history) 1760

Thoughts on the Cause of the Present Discontents (essay) 1770

Speech on American Taxation, April 19, 1774 (essay) 1775

Speech on Moving His Resolutions for Conciliation with the Colonies (essay) 1775

A Letter from Edmund Burke, Esq., One of the Representatives in Parliament for the City of Bristol,

to John Farr and John Harris, Esqrs., Sheriffs of That City, on the Affairs of America (essay) 1777

Speech...on Presenting, on the 11ᵗʰ of February 1780— a Plan for the Better Security of the Independence of Parliament and the Economical Reformation of the Civil and Other Establishments (essay) 1780

Mr. Burke's Speech, on the 1ˢᵗ December 1783, upon the Question for the Speaker's Leaving the Chair, in Order for the House to Resolve Itself into a Committee on Mr. Fox's East Indian Bill (essay) 1784

Articles Exhibited by the Knights, Citizens, and Burgesses in Parliament Assembled, in the Name of Themselves, and of All the Commons of Great Britain, against Warren Hastings...In Maintenance of Their Impeachment against Him for High Crimes and Misdemeanors [with others] (essays) 1787

Reflections on the Revolution in France and on the Proceedings in Certain Societies in London Relative to That Event (essay) 1790

An Appeal from the New, to the Old Whigs, in Consequence of Some Late Discussions in Parliament, Relative to the Reflections on the French Revolution (essay) 1791

A Letter from the Right Honourable Edmund Burke to

a Noble Lord, on the Attacks Made Upon Him and His Pension, in the House of Lords, by the Duke of Bedford and the Earl of Lauderdale, Early in the Present Sessions of Parliament (essay) 1796

Two Letters...on the Proposals for Peace, with the Regicide Directory of France (essays) 1796

**Thoughts and Details on Scarcity Originally Presented to the Right Hon. William Pitt in the Month of November, 1795* (essay) 1800

Works of the Right Honourable Edmund Burke. 16 vols. (essays and letters) 1803-27

The Correspondence of Edmund Burke. 10 vols. (letters) 1958-78

***The Writings and Speeches of Edmund Burke* (essays and letters) 1981-

Selected Letters of Edmund Burke (letters) 1984

---

*This journal was edited by Burke through 1789, and may have been written entirely by him through 1765.

**This work was written in 1795.

***This is an ongoing, multi-volume series published by the Oxford University Press.

CRITICISM

John MacCunn (essay date 1913)

SOURCE: John MacCunn, "Religion and Politics," in *The Political Philosophy of Burke*, Edward Arnold, 1913, pp. 122-43.

[*In the essay below, MacCunn outlines Burke's belief in a divinely-ordered society and the inseparability of church and state.*]

Burke's political religion has its roots deep in three convictions. The first is that civil society rests on spiritual foundations, being indeed nothing less than a product of Divine will; the second, that this is a fact of significance so profound that the recognition of it is of vital moment, both for the corporate life of the State and for the lives of each and all of its members; and the third, that whilst all forms of religion within the nation may play their part in bearing witness to religion, this is peculiarly the function of an Established Church, in which the 'consecration of the State' finds its appropriate symbol, expression, and support.

On the first of these convictions it would be needless to enlarge. Enough to reinforce what has been already said by a single sentence which contains the sum of the whole matter: 'They'—he is speaking of both reflecting and unreflective men—'conceive that He who gave our nature to be perfected by our virtue, willed also the necessary means of its perfection. He willed therefore the State. He willed its connection with the source and original archetype of all perfection.'[1] It follows that the problem how to unite the secular and the sacred in the life of the State, much as it may perplex many minds, is not one that, in its general aspect at any rate, troubles Burke. As the product of Divine will and of the 'stupendous wisdom' that operates throughout the ages, the State is in itself inherently and inalienably sacred. It is not an institution, secular in its nature and then made sacred by an 'alliance' with a Church. This is the very fallacy he rejects when touching incidentally on the large and thorny topic of Church and State: 'An alliance between Church and State in a Christian commonwealth is, in my opinion, an idle and a fanciful speculation. An alliance is between two things that are in their nature distinct and independent, such as between two sovereign States. But in a Christian commonwealth, the Church and the State are one and the same thing, being different integral parts of the same whole.'[2] And this 'whole,' this State in the larger and more comprehensive sense of the word, is always, in its entire constitution, and not merely in its ecclesiastical institutions, however important and august, the result of that 'Divine tactic' which presides over the evolution of a nation. It is needless, however, to labour this point further. For if civil society does not rest on theistic and (we may add) on Christian foundations, if it be not vitalised through and through by the spirit of God, it must be evident by this time that Burke's political teaching is false precisely where he most passionately believed it to be true.

But if this be fact; if God, Providence, stupendous wisdom, Divine tactic, be of a verity thus operative in the growth and gradual organisation of civil society, it is not a matter to which the citizens of any State can afford to shut their eyes. On the contrary, its recognition by every citizen, small or great, is fraught with results of momentous significance. So, at least, Burke will have it. And if we grant his premises, his inference is unimpeachable. It is not credible that the citizens of any commonwealth can see the will of God in the history of their country, in the institutions under which they live, in the civic functions they discharge, in the ends to which they give their lives, without their attitude being influenced thereby. With the belief that 'God willed the State,' if it be indeed a real, and not a merely notional belief, there inevitably comes a reverent and dutiful, and even at times a quietistic spirit, such as can hardly be expected where the social system is regarded as begotten, sustained, and sanctioned by merely secular forces and a merely secular utility. For however true it may be—and happily there is no need to deny it—that even the most secularly minded of citizens may love his country, respect its laws, and if need be lay down his life for it, there must always be a difference in political motive between him and his genuinely religious-minded neighbour. For, of course, political motive, like all motive, reflects the nature of

the object that evokes it; and, so long as this is so, it is idle to suppose that the citizen who accepts his station and its duties as prescribed by the supreme object of human worship will not be profoundly influenced thereby. As man and as citizen, he will most certainly be different; and there are no differences between man and man that go deeper than differences in constitution of motive.

But Burke goes much further than this. Not only did he believe that religion makes a difference; he was convinced that it makes a better citizen. And the peculiar interest of his writings here lies, not in mere eloquent generalities, but in his specification of the quite definite ways in which the vitality of the religious spirit must influence the citizen's outlook on the world of politics.

The difficulty of doing full justice to him here is that the glowing sentences of his rhetoric lose so much by translation into the cold and cut-and-dried statements of abbreviated exposition. But, *per contra,* it is just because critics are apt to think eloquence is not argument, that it is important to note how definite and how forcible are the reasons which here, as in so many of Burke's pages, underlie the rhetoric. First and central is the bold assertion that it is only a religious consciousness that can appreciate in its true significance the persistence and continuity of national life. This sounds audacious. But on no point is Burke more insistent. In one passage we have the affirmation that, were the religious consciousness destroyed, 'no one generation could link with another,' and 'men become little better than the flies of a summer';[3] and in another the sweeping prediction that 'the commonwealth itself would, in a few generations, crumble away, be disconnected into the dust and powder of individuality, and at length dispersed to all the winds of heaven.'[4] Words can no further go. If these be true, the conscious dependence of the human on the Divine, and the continuity of a nation's life stand and fall together.

Not that Burke was unaware that there are other resources by which generation may be made to link with generation. 'Prescriptive constitution,' 'entailed inheritance,' 'bank and capital of the ages,' 'experience of the species,' and other phrases of like import, are all of them conceptions suggestive of ways in which political continuity may be sustained and fostered. The point is that Burke, though himself the prolific author of such phrases, is convinced that more is needed. They may suggest that the national life is a legacy: they do not, or at any rate not sufficiently, suggest that it is a supreme trust. They bear witness to the fact that a nation has a history: they do not enough convey the still more strengthening reminder that it has an assured leading and destiny, in the light of which its traditions and achievement gain an enhanced significance. For it is never enough for Burke that social organisms should be thrust forwards to an astonishing pitch of development by the mere *vis a tergo* of natural evolutionary forces, which, so far as evolutionists can tell, may quite possibly be fortuitous and aimless. He craves for more. To illuminate the struggles of the past, to dignify and intensify the responsibilities of the present, and to guarantee the future against the decadence and defeat with which, in a world of turbulent human wills, it is constantly menaced, it seemed to him the sheet anchor of a true political faith that the whole great drama of national life should be reverently recognised as ordered by a Power to which past, present, and future are organically knit stages in one Divine plan. 'There is an order that keeps things fast in their place; it is made to us, and we are made to it,'[5] so runs his creed.

Results follow. For a belief such as this transfigures at a stroke the idea of the service of the State; and it does this, he tells us, especially in the case of 'persons of exalted station.' There is a paradox in Plato which declares that it is in vain to expect any man to be a great statesman unless he cares for something greater than politics. And though it may seem foolhardy to apply it to Burke, to whom politics were as the breath of his nostrils, it is none the less applicable. For both thinkers see the pitfalls that all too obviously lie in wait for the mere secular politician—the absorption in affairs, the greed for power, the sinister promptings of self-interest, the spirit of faction. And both would look for remedy in the same direction—in that purification of motive that springs from the elevation of the vocation of the statesman into nothing less than a ministry of the unseen. 'All persons possessing any portion of power,' so run the words, 'ought to be strongly and awfully impressed with an idea that they act in trust; and that they are to account for their conduct in that trust to the one great Master, Author, and Founder of society.'[6] The words are in the very spirit of Plato, if we do but translate the language of a theistic faith into the reasoned terminology of Platonic metaphysics.

But it is not to 'persons of exalted station' alone that this line of thought applies. In truth, it never applies with so much force and urgency as in democracies, where political power has been cut up into minute fragments and portioned out in wide franchises. For it is just the wide distribution of political power that may disastrously impair the sense of individual responsibility. Burke has some weighty sentences here. The people, he points out, are, to a far less extent than are princes and other persons of exalted station, 'under responsibility to one of the greatest controlling powers on earth, the sense of fame and estimation. The share of infamy that is likely to fall to the lot of each individual in public acts is small indeed; the operation of opinion being in the inverse ratio to the number of those who abuse power. Their own approbation of their own acts has to them the appearance of a public judgment in their favour. A perfect democracy is therefore

the most shameless thing in the world. As it is the most shameless, it is also the most fearless. No man apprehends in his person he can be made subject to punishment. Certainly the people at large never ought: for as all punishments are for example towards the conservation of the people at large, the people at large can never become the subject of punishment by any human hand.'[7]

Few will deny that in this passage Burke touches with a sure hand one of the dangers of democracy. It is so much easier for human nature to be eager to share power than to take its share of responsibility in using it. Nor would it be difficult to point the moral by reference to the capriciousness, or the levity, or the indifference that is too often found in the democratic electorates which have come into being since Burke's day. The question with many is to find the remedy. And the remedy to which Burke would have us turn is characteristic. The only adequate safeguard against these dangers of popular power is to be found in the vitality of the religious spirit in the class or classes whose will is law. For that, and that alone, can bring the citizen to realise that, in the giving of vote or the duties of office, he is fulfilling what Burke does not hesitate to call a 'holy function.' The words, no doubt, must sound extravagant to secular minds, to whom politics altogether is nothing more than a matter of most mundane business, and very far indeed from being 'holy.' But they are not the less on that account significant of the civic importance of religion as understood by one of the greatest of all its exponents. Reverently religious in his own life, convinced by his diagnosis of human nature that man is 'a religious animal,' and insistent always that religious institutions are an organic element in the body-politic, it was inevitable that Burke should recoil from a merely secular citizenship as unequal to the demands and burdens which the State imposes on its members. Secular minds may reject his teaching. To them it can only seem a devout imagination. But they can be in no doubt, if they have read his pages, that to leave this aspect out would make his political message a wholly different, and, in his eyes, an impoverished thing.

Nor, perhaps, is it rash to assume that the vast majority of the religious world would be in substantial sympathy with Burke's insistence on the political value of religion, so far at any rate as we have considered it. Presumably all religious organisations, including such as are frankly, and even bitterly, hostile to established Churches, unite in the aspiration that the religious spirit may permeate life, of which political life is not the least part, from end to end. Even those who protest that politics ought to be kept separate from religion, and religion from politics, must be aware, no matter how sharply they distinguish secular and religious organisations and their work, that they carry their religion with them in the constitution of their motives, as these operate in the performance of all important work done by them for the world. That any citizen should be religious, and that he should *not* be influenced thereby in motive, even in the most secular of transactions, can only mean that in certain departments of life he is not religious. Fullness of life, and of strife, may have made the Churches many, yet one must do them the justice of supposing that they all alike desire to leaven the entire social system with Christian conscience and Christian charity. And if this be so, they can hardly fail to sympathise with the spirit of Burke's teaching as a plea for the alliance of citizenship and religion.

Burke, however, as is well known, would have his readers go a step further. Neither the sanctuaries of the heart nor the sanctuaries of voluntary Churches are enough for him. For, as he found the Church of England in possession of its prescriptive inheritance, material and spiritual, he insists, with all the argument and eloquence in his resourceful treasury, that it ought to stand as a recognition of religion by the nation in its corporate capacity. Convinced, as we have seen, that civil society as an organic whole is a sacred institution, he pled for a national and visible recognition of that fact. The 'corporate fealty and homage' of the State to religion was to him simply the public acknowledgment that 'God willed the State.' And this general principle was backed by arguments as definite as they are forcible.

One is the claim, which controversy has made familiar, that religion—and not least because of the intimacy of its connection with education—is too momentous a national interest to be left to what he calls 'the unsteady and precarious contribution of individuals.'

Another is the plea that the clergy of an established Church occupy a position which effectively strengthens their hands as upholders of morality and moral valuations. Not only can they bring the consolations of religion to the hapless and heavily burdened poor; not only can they minister, no less, to 'the distresses of the miserable great'; they can also, from a position of independence, such as he thinks is not enjoyed by a clergy directly dependent on popular support, instruct 'presumptuous ignorance' and rebuke 'insolent vice,' whether in high estate or low. 'The people of England,' he declares, 'will not suffer the insolence of wealth and titles, or any other species of proud pretension, to look down with scorn upon what they look up to with reverence; nor presume to trample on that acquired personal nobility which they intend always to be, and which often is, the fruit, not the reward (for what can be the reward?) of learning, piety, and virtue.'[8] And it is but an extension of this democratic demand for an independent aristocracy of the spirit that leads him on to welcome the 'modest splendour and unassuming state, the mild majesty and sober pomp' of religious ceremonial, and to justify an ecclesiastical hierarchy

such as may (to quote a phrase that has become familiar) 'exalt its mitred front in courts and parliaments.'

A third point is that it is when a clergy enjoys the recognised position, and the financial independence which the establishment of religion gives, that they are best placed to resist all temptations to yield to tyrannical pressure either from above or from below, and, by consequence, peculiarly well fitted to stand for a genuine political liberty. 'The English,' he says, 'tremble for their liberty from the influence of a clergy dependent on the Crown; they tremble for the public tranquillity from the disorders of a factious clergy, if it were made to depend upon any other than the Crown. They therefore made their Church, like their king and their nobility, independent.'[9]

Nor, finally, could he regard it as other than a good application of public money, and not least in the interests of the poorer classes, that it should be devoted to religious purposes. He puts the point with unqualified directness: 'For those purposes they (*i.e.* those who believe that God willed the State) think some part of the wealth of the country is as usefully employed as it can be in fomenting the luxury of individuals. It is the public ornament. It is the public consolation. It nourishes the public hope. The poorest man finds his own importance and dignity in it, whilst the wealth and pride of individuals at every moment makes the man of humble rank and fortune sensible of his inferiority, and degrades and vilifies his condition. It is for the man in humble life, and to raise his nature, and to put him in mind of a state in which the privileges of opulence will cease, when he will be equal by nature, and may be more than equal by virtue, that this portion of the general wealth of his country is employed and sanctified.'[10]

Nor does it in the least shake him in this that the Church, thus supported by the general wealth, should have its own tenets and tests, and that these should exclude the conscientious nonconformist. Invoking the Lockian principle, which no one is likely to dispute, that a voluntary society can exclude any member she thinks fit on such conditions as she thinks proper, he transfers the principle, with a surprising indifference to the significance of the transition, to the Church that claims to be national.[11] It is precisely on this ground, indeed, that he argues, in 1772, against the petition, in which not only certain of the clergy of the Church, but doctors and lawyers, claimed to be relieved from subscription to the Articles. And the line he took here is all the more remarkable, because he was far from thinking that the Church was perfect. Both Articles and Liturgy, he frankly admits, are 'not without the marks and characters of human frailty.'[12] This was, of course, to be lamented; but it was not enough to precipitate a change. Against a change he urges that there is no real grievance—none for the petitioning clergy, who may easily find pulpits and congregations to suit their views in one or other of the many Churches that are tolerated; and none for the taxpayer, who, if he be one of a minority who dissent from the creed of the Church, is not to be supposed to subscribe to the creed because he consents to pay his tax. Nor has he much difficulty in showing that, in suggesting subscription to Scripture as substitute, the petitioners were opening up as many difficulties as those they wished to escape. *Some* test of membership, he insists, every Church must impose; men must not expect to be paid by taxation 'for teaching, as Divine truths, their own particular fancies.' And this being so, he would rather have subscription to the Articles, with all their imperfections, than anything that can be put in their place.

There is much in this that will no doubt invite criticism in days when both Church establishment and Creed subscription are more burning questions than they were then. But it is not necessary to embark here on either of these highly controversial topics. Enough if what has been said makes it clear how far Burke carried his repugnance to anything that savoured of the secularisation of the State.

For it is not Burke's defence of Church establishment that is the central interest in his apologia for religion in politics; it is rather the grounds on which this rests—grounds which will appeal to many besides those who stand for established religions. Is it true that the belief that God has willed the State is fraught for citizens with these momentous issues which Burke ascribes to it? Is it a fact that the State is a sacred thing? Is it incontrovertible that the trite distinction between secular and sacred is a pernicious and false dualism? Is it the case that religion is the basis of civil society? These are questions that go deeper far than the vexed controversy about Church establishments. For it is not the adherents of established Churches alone, it is the whole religious world that finds itself nowadays in the presence of critics and assailants more numerous, more formidable, more scientific than the atheists and infidels of Burke's abhorrence and denunciation. For the nineteenth century has seen the advent, not to say—for not a few would say it—the triumph, of naturalism. And in political theory naturalism, of course, means not only that the social organism, like other organisms, comes to its maturity through the action of biological laws, but that the prolonged process of struggle and survival through which it emerges, finds all the explanation available in the operation of quite secular conditions and causes, possibly in the last resort mechanical, but at any rate such as leave no room for the agency of any final cause or providential agency whatsoever. Nor is it doubtful that any such notion as that the course of history and the evolution of nations are 'the known march of the providence of God,' would receive but a chilling welcome at the hands of naturalism. If so, the practical inference is obvious. Ill would

it become the statesman to cherish one thought, or utter one word, about a 'Divine tactic,' 'a stupendous wisdom,' a 'Divine Disposer,' or what not. Let the will of evolution be done! Enough for him to be content, as the naturalistic thinkers are content, to learn from experience what the facts and forces are that are thrusting on his country he knows not whither. Enough for him to shape these facts and control these forces in the interests of the public good, or whatever other end he can find, and sufficiently believe in, to vitalise the civic will to strenuous service. Nor presumably would either theoretical or practical naturalism resent the imputation that it leads to a thoroughgoing secularisation of the State.

Nor can it be denied that it would be in vain to seek for a refutation of naturalism in the pages of Burke. He does not prove, he never dreams of proving that man is a religious animal, or that the object of religious faith is real. His religion is a faith, not a philosophy; and those who wish to find these fundamentals of the faith made good by proof, must go, not to Burke but to the theologians, or to the idealistic philosophers who are not afraid to give the world a philosophy of religion. And yet Burke's teaching has its claims upon the thinker. It suggests a problem which is theoretically, as well as practically, of the first rank. For, by the passionate conviction and definiteness of statement wherewith he specifies the ways in which the vitality of the religious consciousness influences the attitude of the citizen of all ranks and grades towards his station and its duties—a matter on which he could speak with the voice of experience—he prompts the question as to what is likely to happen should religious belief suffer eclipse. Will that consciousness of imperious political obligation, which so often has had its root in theism, survive? Will the faith that men and nations have a destiny no less assured and divinely guided than their past history, still play its part in fostering that belief in ideals in which lies the nerve of political struggle? Will an unselfish devotion to the public good still persist? Hardly can it be denied that hitherto the resolute and dutiful civic spirit has thriven, not only in illustrious instances, but amongst masses of the people, in close alliance with religion. To quicken and sustain it, more has seemingly been needed than the consciousness of ties to home, to comrades, to neighbourhood, to nation, to humanity. The appeal to altar has been as potent as to hearth. 'It is in the form of imagination,' says a writer on political obligation, who never ventured on a statement till he felt that his foot was planted on experience,[13] 'the imagination of a supreme, invisible, but all-seeing ruler that, in the case at least of all ordinary good people, the idea of an absolute duty is so brought to bear upon the soul as to yield an awe superior to any personal inclination.' If this be true, how is the gap to be filled should this article of practical faith become in the eyes of 'all ordinary good people,' as doubtless it already is to naturalistic scrutiny, no better than an imaginative figment best relegated to the scrap-heap of past, or passing, phases of metaphysical illusion? For the strength and vitality of motives depends ultimately upon the objects to which they attach themselves, and by which they are fed and fostered. And so long as this is so, it would seem something of a venture to remove a God, a 'Divine Disposer,' a 'Providence,' a 'Divine tactic,' from the human horizon without finding some substitute.

This, indeed, seems to be well recognised, for naturalistic minds do not revolt against political theism without putting something in the place of the deity deposed and the 'Divine tactic' superseded. Sometimes it is the Nation which, following a French lead, they set on the secular altar of civic devotion.[14] And sometimes, and not by any means only amongst avowed positivists, it is Humanity. Nor is it to be doubted that both are great and enduring objects to which the minds and hearts of men will never look in vain for incentive and support.

This, however, is not a statement that Burke of all men would have been likely to challenge. There is abundant room in his scheme of life, as we have already seen,[15] both for the nation and humanity. No writer in our language, or in any language, is less open to the charge of underestimating the strength of the patriotic motive. To this we need not return. But then it has to be remembered that it was not the nation as a merely secular institution that aroused this passion of patriotism, but the nation consecrated in his imagination as product and instrument of the Divine will. It is not worth asking whether his patriotism would have survived the destruction of his theism, because in his mind the two things are one and indivisible.

Similarly with the larger, though far less closely knit, object, humanity. Burke was not blind to it. Despite his denunciations of French fraternity, he never failed, as we have seen,[16] to recognise that his own country, and all countries, were parts of a larger whole. But this larger whole was not the humanity of positivism or naturalism; it was 'the great mysterious incorporation of the human race'; and the mystery that encompassed it was not the mystery that, to the agnostic, shuts out the faith that the fortunes of the race are shaped and controlled by spiritual forces, but the mystery which, however dark and inscrutable (the words are his own), is still compatible with the belief that the course of civilisation is 'the known march of the ordinary providence of God.' Certainly for the mind of Burke there could be no ultimate rest in the idea of humanity. How could there be, when it was to him of the essence of humanity, by the perennial vitality of the religious consciousness, to bear its witness to the dependence of the human on the Divine? It needs no words to prove that if man be 'a religious animal,' if atheism be against both human instincts and human reason, as Burke

declared it was, 'humanity' was ill fitted to be offered to the world as a *substitute* for God. For, though it may need few words to prove that, if humanity be severed by the sword of science from divinity, and God left out as but an ancient idol, the apotheosis of humanity is the deposition of divinity; it is not less obvious that the idea of a humanity, in every individual soul of which the belief in God is eternal and ineradicable, is the strongest of all securities against the secularisation of human life. Yet nothing less than this was the creed of Burke, to whose profoundly religious spirit the attempted secularisation of history and politics was nothing less than a conspiracy to denationalise the nation and to dehumanise the race.

Notes

[1] *Reflections.*

[2] Speech, May 11, 1792.

[3] *Reflections.*

[4] *Ibid.*

[5] Speech, May 7, 1782.

[6] *Reflections.*

[7] *Reflections.*

[8] *Reflections.*

[9] *Reflections.*

[10] *Reflections.*

[11] Speech on the Acts of Uniformity.

[12] *Ibid.*

[13] Professor T. H. Green.

[14] *E.g.* Pearson in *National Life and Character.*

[15] P. 23 *et seq.*

[16] P. 27.

Charles Parkin (essay date 1956)

SOURCE:Charles Parkin, "The Natural Relation of Society and Government," in *The Moral Basis of Burke's Political Thought: An Essay*, 1956. Reprint by Russell & Russell, 1968, pp. 30-53.

[*Below, Parkin explains why Burke believed in the*

natural suitability of a Parliament composed of members of the aristocracy, and discusses Burke's ideas about the principles by which they should govern.]

The lower and higher natures in man are held in unity by the 'great primeval contract of eternal society'. For the individual, therefore, apprehension of the moral order comes to him through his instinctive nature.

> Dark and inscrutable are the ways by which we come into the world. The instincts which give rise to this mysterious process of nature are not of our making. But out of physical causes, unknown to us, perhaps unknowable, arise moral duties, which, as we are able perfectly to comprehend, we are bound indispensably to perform.[1]

This order is the source of all moral relations; as the law of human nature, it is not created by, or subject to, human will. 'We have obligations to mankind at large, which are not in consequence of any special voluntary pact. They arise from the relation of man to man, and the relation of man to God, which relations are not matters of choice.'[2] The concrete sphere of the moral life and activity of the individual is given to him by the human position into which he is born; it is created by the 'mysterious process of nature'. His place in the order of human lives is in no sense arbitrary or accidental, it is a purposeful dispensation of the supreme ruler who sustains the created order.

> I may assume, that the awful Author of our being is the Author of our place in the order of existence; and that having disposed and marshalled us by a divine tactic, not according to our will, but according to his, he has, in and by that disposition, virtually subjected us to act the part which belongs to the place assigned us.[3]

The primary sphere of moral relations within the great contract is the small society through which the individual comes into the order of lives—the family. This is the first natural community. 'Men come in that manner into a community with the social state of their parents, endowed with all the benefits, loaded with all the duties of their situation.'[4] Beyond this, a wider unity of rights and duties, is civil society.

> If the social ties and ligaments, spun out of those physical relations which are the elements of the commonwealth, in most cases begin, and always continue, independently of our will, so, without any stipulation on our own part, are we bound by that relation called our country, which comprehends (as it has been well said) 'all the charities of all'. Nor are we left without powerful instincts to make this duty as dear and grateful to us, as it is awful and coercive.[5]

The commonwealth, as a moral essence, is not a mere geographical entity or a fortuitous assemblage of unrelated units; it is a network of moral relations, a stable and traditional social unity of ordered superiority and subordination and diversity. 'Our country is not a thing of mere physical locality. It consists, in a great measure, in the ancient order into which we are born . . . The place that determines our duty to our country is a social, civil relation.'[6] The situation of the individual in this natural order is the preceptor of his duty,[7] because it is the means of his fullest participation in the moral law. 'If you ask, *quem te Deus esse jussit?* you will be answered when you resolve this other question, *humana qua parte locatus es in re?'*[8] The relations of the individual to the family and to the traditional community are on the same footing of moral obligation; a man contracts as much into the latter by being born into it as he does into the former.[9] Equally the two societies afford to him the possibility of instinctive self-expression. The feelings by which he is attached to the small and the large society are therefore directly and intimately linked and interdependent. Love of the whole, the large society, is built on the private and local affections, and grows out of them.

> To be attached to the subdivision, to love the little platoon we belong to in society, is the first principle (the germ as it were) of public affections. It is the first link in the series by which we proceed towards a love to our country, and to mankind.[10]

The superior and subordinate ties do not flourish at one another's expense, they subsist together in a pro portioned whole, so that the charities of the state and the hearth are combined and mutually reflected.[11]

> We begin our public affections in our families. No cold relation is a zealous citizen. We pass on to our neighbourhoods, and our habitual provincial connections . . . The love to the whole is not extinguished by this subordinate partiality. Perhaps it is a sort of elemental training to those higher and more large regards.[12]

The type of civil society within which the individual finds his sphere of natural morality is a stable traditional community, a unified hierarchy of ranks, which is erected and sustained by durable instincts and prejudices. In his place, he can exert his moral self and achieve his true natural rights of family life and possession of property. Such a society is a variegated unity of superior and subordinate ranks, in which individuals find their strength in their diversity of conditions. But if this natural harmony between individual and community is damaged, both suffer; it was therefore the great care of the ancient legislators to respect the diversity of ranks and conditions in which they found men.[13]

The unity of direction of society, to be in accordance with the moral order, must arise out of the natural structure of society, and seek to maintain it. That is, it must be based on the natural union of rights and duties embodied in the society of status. The leading role in the direction of society will fall on the superior ranks of the hierarchy, the group in the community which Burke calls a 'natural aristocracy'. The natural aristocracy are 'the wiser, the more expert, and the more opulent' of society,[14] and they must be qualified in character to conduct, enlighten, and protect the subordinate orders. In presenting this conception, Burke is advocating the predominance of those in whom the primary ties of self-interest and duty are traditionally and closely identified with the good of society as a whole—that is, the long-standing propertied aristocratic families. It is a necessary feature of this 'dominion of natural interests' that it should include a hierarchy of property: the greater accumulations of property form the natural defence for the less:

> The characteristic essence of property, formed out of the combined principles of its acquisition and conservation, is to be *unequal*. The great masses therefore which excite envy, and tempt rapacity, must be put out of the possibility of danger. Then they form a natural rampart about the lesser properties in all their gradations.[15]

Burke believes that this is a natural ordering of society, and not a dangerous one, because the natural forms of self-interest, which are natural precisely because they contain or imply acceptance of obligations, are limited and satisfiable, and do not develop into that appetite for domination which springs from illegitimate desire and mere wilful self-interest. The predominance of a natural aristocracy is therefore at the opposite pole from any type of tyrannous authority. In his conception of the natural authority of an aristocracy of virtue, intelligence, and wealth, Burke is once again affirming a union and harmony of legitimate individual self-interest and the general good: he presupposes a very intimate relation of private and public interests.

The idea of a natural aristocracy is to be sharply distinguished from the conception of a rule of the privileged or of the rich, or any type of oligarchic ascendancy. Burke often makes it clear that his advocacy of the value of an aristocracy is purely for its place in the unity of a moral society, not for its own sake. As a system of government, aristocracy is an 'austere and insolent domination',[16] and Burke insists that he is no friend to aristocracy in that sense. The aristocratic order, meaning the peers, is an absolute necessity in the constitution, but only good when kept within its proper bounds; but if aristocracy is to be defined as merely the self-interested rule of the rich and powerful, Burke proclaims himself its enemy.[17] On occasion, as in the **Speech on Economical Reform,** he is scathing in his contempt for those among the nobility who are 'as perfectly willing to act the part of flatterers, tale-bearers, parasites, pimps, and buffoons, as any of the lowest and vilest of mankind can possibly be'; or, as in the **Letter to a Noble Lord,** for the obtuseness which blinds some aristocrats to their own real interests.

As opposed to all forms of aristocratic self-interested domination, a natural aristocracy exists in the interests of the rest of society, not against them:

> this nobility in fact does not exist in wrong of other orders of the state, but by them, and for them.[18] A true natural aristocracy is not a separate interest in the state, or separable from it. It is an essential integrant part of any large body rightly constituted.[19]

Such an ascendancy is not a form of benevolent aristocratic despotism or paternal rule, or indeed a rule of any sort. It is a type of leadership, in which the interests of leaders and led are the same, that is, the maintenance of the harmony which is to be found by each individual in the acceptance of the duties and rights of his station. Burke therefore deprecates attempts to oppose the aristocratic interest to that of the people, to inflame the poor against their 'guardians, patrons, and protectors',[20] or to make separate parties of the higher and lower orders.[21] He claims that the success of the historical struggles for liberty in England has been due to the traditional leadership provided by a natural aristocracy:

> that while the landed interest, instead of forming a separate body, as in other countries, has, at all times, been in close connection and union with the other great interests of the country, it has been spontaneously allowed to lead, and direct, and moderate, all the rest.[22]

The value of such a natural aristocracy is to provide a discipline in society, the steadiness which can only come from a traditional position and the sense of social continuity which that gives. Expressing his beliefs through the mouth of Keppel, Burke says:

> he felt, that no great commonwealth could by any possibility long subsist, without a body of some kind or other of nobility, decorated with honour, and fortified by privilege. This nobility forms the chain that connects the ages of a nation, which otherwise (with Mr Paine) would soon be taught that no one generation can bind another. He felt that no political fabric could be well made without some such order of things as might, through a series of time, afford a rational hope of securing unity, coherence, consistency, and stability to the state.[23]

This social union in which a natural aristocracy exists and fulfils its proper role is Burke's conception of a 'people': 'when great multitudes act together, under that discipline of nature, I recognise the PEOPLE', and he calls it 'this harmony . . . this beautiful order, this array of truth and nature, as well as of habit and prejudice'.[24] It is the moral harmony of status expressed in terms of the unity of direction in society.

> To enable men to act with the weight and character of a people, and to answer the ends for which they are incorporated into that capacity, we must suppose them (by means immediate or consequential) to be in that state of habitual social discipline in which the wiser, the more expert, and the more opulent conduct, and by conducting enlighten and protect, the weaker, the less knowing, and the less provided with the goods of fortune.[25]

Such a society does not embody economic or political equality, and Burke rejects any suggestion that the leadership of society can be dissociated from economic or social weight, still more the legitimacy of an assault on property by the poor, such as is taking place in France. The natural society of ranks provides the only true equality, which is moral equality, 'the happiness that is to be found by virtue in all conditions'.[26] Happiness is to be sought in the natural sphere of rights and duties offered to the individual, not in envy or contempt of the position of others. There is a more genuine equality between the ranks of the natural hierarchy than can be created by any artificial equalisation of the conditions of material life or of political power.

The system of government which is erected on this natural form of community will be a government of reason; it will spring from the moral harmony embodied in the natural 'people', and maintain it. 'The foundation of government . . . is laid in a provision for our wants, and in a conformity to our duties; it is to purvey for the one: it is to enforce the other.'[27] It is to refine the general good out of the multiplicity of primary, local and partial feelings and interests. These are all minor goods, and the necessary elements out of which the good of the whole is to be elicited. It follows from the assumption of a harmony between the true self-interest of the individual and the general good that acceptance of the variety and complexity of individual forms of expression and endeavour is a necessary means to arrival at a final harmony. There cannot be any suggestion of an ultimate collision between the expression of the natural capacities of the individual and the demands of the general interest. 'Expedience is that which is good for the community, and good for every individual in it.'[28]

There is therefore a necessarily intimate relation of the people to government. Government originates from the people and rests on their consent. It has no other end than their happiness and only they can be the judges of its success by their own feelings. 'The object of the state is (as far as may be) the happiness of the whole . . . The happiness or misery of mankind . . . is, and ought to be, the standard for the conduct of legislators towards the people.'[29] Negatively at least, their feelings are true and accurate: they are the judges of oppression:

> What I have always thought of the matter is this— that the most poor, illiterate, and uninformed creatures upon earth are judges of a *practical* oppression. It is a matter of feeling; and as such persons generally have felt most of it, and are not of an over-lively sensibility, they are the best judges of it.[30]

Burke goes so far as to maintain that the only test of a free government is, practically speaking, what the people think is so,[31] though his meaning seems to be the same, that the people can judge by their feelings of the weight of government, not that they are, positively, to formulate a concept of freedom out of their feelings. Elsewhere he affirms that it is rare for men to be wrong in their feelings concerning public misconduct, though he adds immediately that they are equally rarely right in their speculations upon the cause of it.[32] The reason for this basic accuracy of feeling of the governed is that the natural feelings are in accord with the general good of society and with the government which maintains it; 'the people have no interest in disorder'.[33] Their feelings do therefore embody a type of reason.

Nor is it only that the feelings of the people are in an ultimate sense the test of the wisdom of government. Government ought further to realise their desires, so far as they are legitimate. 'To govern according to the sense and agreeably to the interests of the people is a great and glorious object of government.'[34] In all the forms of government the people is the true legislator, in the sense that the remote and efficient cause of law is their actual or implied consent.[35] But their feelings and opinions in fact exercise a much closer and more powerful influence on the formal legislative body of the community, since they determine the effective scope and limits of legislative rights: 'no . . . part of legislative rights can be exercised, without regard to the general opinion of those who are to be governed. That general opinion is the vehicle, and organ of legislative omnipotence.'[36] Government as law-maker is thus finally dependent on the organised and clarified feelings of the community: 'In effect, to follow, not to force, the public inclination; to give a direction, a form, a technical dress, and a specific sanction, to the general sense of the community, is the true end of legislature.'[37]

Nevertheless, the feelings of the people, however violent or general, are only legitimate and binding upon government so far as they are within the bounds of the moral law. Burke unites the subordination of the legislative power to the general feeling of the community, and the subordination of that feeling to the moral law, in the strongest terms in a single sentence: he speaks of 'the demands of the people, whose desires, when they do not militate with the stable and eternal rules of justice and reason, (rules which are above us and above them), ought to be as a law to a house of commons.'[38] This bound is set, in Burke's mind, by a religious sense of an ultimate objective moral standard. If the people are not to be suffered to imagine that their will is the standard of right and wrong,[39] if the opinions of even the greatest multitudes are not the standard of rectitude, it is because 'it may be doubted whether Omnipotence itself is competent to alter the essential constitution of right and wrong'.[40] So far as the desires of the people threaten to overstep this boundary, it is the duty of government to oppose them. It ought to be responsive to the popular wish and even the popular humour, but not at the expense of justice.

> No man carries further than I do the policy of making government pleasing to the people. But the widest range of this politic complaisance is confined within the limits of justice. I would not only consult the interest of the people, but I would cheerfully gratify their humours . . . But I never will act the tyrant for their amusement.[41]

Within this fundamental bound, there is a difficult and subtle, yet all-important, distinction to be drawn between the real and the apparent desires of the people, between the capricious tides of feeling against which government is to stand firm and that general sense of the community to which it is to be responsive. It is the function of government to safeguard the interest of the people, but 'the will of the many and their interest, must very often differ'.[42] Popular desire can seldom express itself in spontaneous and natural form; it will be evoked, stimulated and distorted by many factors, including the deliberate fomenting of passions by agitators; thus the desires of the people may be, as Burke claims they were in the Economical Reform movement of 1780, 'partly natural and partly infused into them by art'.[43] The chief test of the genuine sense of the community must be its steadiness as compared with transient fluctuations of feeling. The constitutional organisation of the state should be designed to separate the one from the other. Of a proposal for constitutional reform, Burke says, 'I most heartily wish, that the deliberate sense of the kingdom on this great subject should be known. When it is known, it *must* be prevalent.' But that general wish must be sought with deliberation and without haste. 'Sure I am, that no precipitate resolution on a great change in the fundamental constitution of any country can ever be called the real sense of the people.'[44]

Both needs, the expression of popular feeling, and the separation of purely transient and local prejudice from genuine and general sense, must be provided for by the representation of the people in government. The structure of representation in the natural society and government is erected on the local communities, the minor and primary natural associations. The Member of Parliament is the channel through which the people's wishes and complaints are to reach government. It is the prerogative of the people that they should have personal choice of him, because judgment of persons is within their competence; they must be represented by someone whom they know and trust.[45] The House of Commons cannot think or act as a self-originated magistracy, independent of the opinions and feelings of the people.[46] It is not merely that it receives its power from the people; that is true of government as a whole. It is that its essence consists in its being the 'express image of the feelings of the nation', or bearing at least 'some stamp of the actual disposition of the people at large'.[47]

On the other hand, the Member of Parliament is not a mere delegate, transmitting the will of the people to government as commands. Instruction to representatives is a doctrine unfounded in reason, destructive of the constitution.[48] Such a procedure would not arrive at a good of the whole in which genuine and natural expressions of self-interest found reconciliation, but in a collision and struggle of unresolved wills. The representative owes a deference and alertness to the opinions of those he represents, but his responsibility is for their interest. This is something both more permanent and more objective than transient humours, which are not only inconstant but are less accurate perceptions of true self-interest. Burke expresses the paradoxical nature of the representative's task in his defence of his own conduct in that capacity.

> I did not obey your instructions: No. I conformed to the instructions of truth and nature, and maintained your interest against your opinions, with a constancy that became me. A representative worthy of you ought to be a person of stability. I am to look, indeed, to your opinions; but to such opinions as you and I *must* have five years hence. I was not to look to the flash of the day.[49]

This is to say that the representative is not the servant of the people to the extent that he ought to sacrifice his judgment to theirs. He cannot fulfil his function of contributing to the discovery of the rational good if he submits himself to the will of those for whom he speaks.

> It is his duty to sacrifice his repose, his pleasures, his satisfactions, to theirs; and above all, ever, and in all cases, to prefer their interest to his own. But, his unbiased opinion, his mature judgment, his enlightened conscience, he ought not to sacrifice to you . . . Your representative owes you, not his industry only, but his judgment; and he betrays, instead of serving you, if he sacrifices it to your

opinion . . . Government and legislation are matters of reason and judgment, and not of inclination; and what sort of reason is that, in which the determination precedes the discussion?[50]

The people's legitimate role is limited to the choice of those who are to defend their diverse interests and to reconcile them into a whole; they are well capable of that choice, and it is imperative that they should have it, but they cannot themselves perceive the common good. They are within their rights in expressing their local and personal interests and demands; but they must surrender the task of harmonising will and reason in the community to others.

The relation of the Member of Parliament to the elector is of the same nature as that of the electors to the unenfranchised. Both M.P. and elector are 'virtual representatives' for the unenfranchised, in the sense in which Burke defines the idea.

> Virtual representation is that in which there is a communion of interests, and a sympathy in feelings and desires between those who act in the name of any description of people, and the people in whose name they act, though the trustees are not actually chosen by them.[51]

There is communion of interests and feelings in the basic sense that representative, elector, and unenfranchised all share the natural wish for maintenance of the moral harmony of society; and this communion ensures that the former will not oppose his own interest to that of those for whom he speaks, but will perceive the two to be on the same ground. This common sentiment will enable the legitimate interests of the unenfranchised to be provided for without the dangers involved in a constitutional expression of their transient humours and excited passions. The most poor, illiterate, uninformed members of the community are judges of oppression, but they cannot grasp its real cause or appropriate remedy, and they ought therefore to be shut out of council:

> because their reason is weak; because, when once roused, their passions are ungoverned; because they want information; because the smallness of the property, which individually they possess, renders them less attentive to the consequence of the measures they adopt in affairs of moment.[52]

The uniform principle that the discovery of the general good lies through the expression of steady rational self-interest, and its separation from all forms of transient feeling and appetite, provides the justification for the foundation of political representation on property, and especially on landed property. This, the traditional base of the English constitution, is in Burke's eyes the secret of its stability and efficacy. Landed property is 'in its nature the firm base of every stable government'.[53] This is because the acquisition and possession of property constitutes a proof of a natural and steady self-interest and a guarantee against the untrammelled operation of irrational or changeable feeling. The desire of acquisition is, as Burke says, 'a passion of long views',[54] and it sustains in the property-owner a calm, steady perception of his own interest and of the limits set to it by the rights of others and of the community. The Whig party, being connected with the solid, permanent, long-possessed property of the country, 'by a temper derived from that species of property' is attached to the ancient tried usages of the kingdom.[55] The argument for the connection of political power with property is more than just a claim for the ascendancy of *the propertied,* those with the largest stake in the country. They are an important, but still a partial, interest. It is a belief that property in all its gradations represents the stable rational self-interest from which the good of the whole community is to be elicited. The importance of 'settled permanent substance'[56] does not therefore exclude the principle of numbers, because the legitimate needs of the poorest in the community are a factor in the general good.

> The numbers ought never to be neglected; because (besides what is due to them as men) collectively, though not individually, they have great property: they ought to have therefore protection: they ought to have security: they ought to have even consideration: but they ought not to predominate.[57]

The supreme arbiter in the task of discovering the general good is Parliament. It is for the legislature to reconcile the feelings of the people with the rational permanent good of the community; or rather to detect in the confused voice of the people that steady utterance which is their own awareness of their best good, 'to separate the feelings of the people from their judgment, to consider their interest with their real intentions'.[58] It is therefore necessary that while popular complaint should receive anxious attention from Parliament, the people must be submissive to the legislature as to a superior wisdom.

> Faithful watchmen we ought to be over the rights and privileges of the people. But our duty, if we are qualified for it as we ought, is to give them information, and not to receive it from them; we are not to go to school to them to learn the principles of law and government.[59]

Though they are in an ultimate sense the legislative power,

> the people, indeed, are presumed to consent to whatever the legislature ordains for their benefit; and they are to acquiesce in it, though they do not

clearly see into the propriety of the means, by which they are conducted to that desirable end. This they owe as an act of homage and just deference to a reason, which the necessity of government has made superior to their own.[60]

Nor can they rationally judge of policy. The situation in France, where the gallery and the mob domineer over the National Assembly, is an inversion of true order:[61] the people are not

> under a false show of liberty, but, in truth, to exercise an unnatural, inverted domination, tyrannically to exact, from those who officiate in the state, not an entire devotion to their interest, which is their right, but an abject submission to their occasional will.[62]

Crude popular desire cannot be regarded as binding on Parliament; it will always be necessary to seek for a real cause of complaint which may be concealed or disguised in the flux and tumult of inflamed feelings. To pursue popular desire in a spirit of literal obedience may even militate with the very principle of that desire.[63] The people are the sufferers, Burke says, they tell the symptoms, the Members of Parliament can alone diagnose the illness and prescribe the remedy; or, changing the metaphor, 'the people are the masters. They have only to express their wants at large and in gross. We are the expert artists; we are the skilful workmen, to shape their desires into perfect form.'[64] That will include distinguishing their real feelings from 'the bad use which artful men may make of an irritation of the popular mind.'[65] Hence Burke's defence of his own policy in the Economical Reform agitation is that 'It was my aim to give to the people the substance of what I knew they desired, and what I thought was right, whether they desired it or not, before it had been modified for them into senseless petitions.'[66] If the confusion of popular feeling is extreme, it is indeed superficial to wish to please everybody. 'In such a discordancy of sentiments, it is better to look to the nature of things than to the humours of men.'[67] Parliament cannot allow itself to be drawn hither and thither by every distortion and distraction of popular feeling.

> I reverentially look up to the opinion of the people, and with an awe that is almost superstitious. I should be ashamed to show my face before them, if I changed my ground, as they cried up or cried down men, or things, or opinions; if I wavered and shifted about with every change, and joined in it, or opposed, as best answered any low interest or passion; if I held them up hopes, which I knew I never intended, or promised what I well knew I could not perform.[68]

It must not even seem to follow too obviously a popular inclination; Burke is careful to say that 'I cannot indeed take upon me to say I have the honour *to follow* the sense of the people. The truth is, *I met it on the way,* while I was pursuing their interest according to my own ideas.'[69] The better-informed must sometimes resist the sense of the people when they appear to be misled;[70] the American war, for example, was originally a war of the people, and was put a stop to, not by them, but by the virtue of the House of Commons, who took upon themselves to end it.[71] When, as in the Gordon Riots, mere mob pressure is brought to bear on Parliament to reverse its deliberate resolutions, the exhortation to attend to popular prejudice and opinion is wholly inapplicable.[72] In particular, as the deliberative assembly for the whole nation, the House of Commons must not allow its unity and integrity to be destroyed by an excessive emphasis on the local interests which constitute its units. They have their place and must receive due attention, but they are subordinate to the general good which is to be constructed out of them. Constituents must allow their representatives to act on enlarged views, not confine them to a strict adherence to these local interests for which they speak, or else the House of Commons will be degraded into a 'confused and scuffling bustle of local agency'.[73] Too exclusive an attention to local interest will conceal that single general good within which lesser goods have their place and on which they depend. It will prevent that refinement of reason out of the multiplicity of expressions of feeling without which government cannot be conformable to the natural order.

> Parliament is not a *congress* of ambassadors from different and hostile interests . . . but parliament is a *deliberative* assembly of *one* nation, with *one* interest, that of the whole; where, not local purposes, not local prejudices ought to guide, but the general good, resulting from the general reason of the whole.[74]

Holding this belief in the pre-eminence and unique function of Parliament, Burke, while welcoming lesser associations within the community, is suspicious of political unions which seem to challenge the supremacy of Parliament as the sole repository of national wisdom, virtue, and wealth.[75]

The principle on which the direction of society is to rest is that the structure of government should grow out of the natural order of society itself. The community is a unity with a single rational good, and the feelings and desires of each individual are a necessary contribution to the discovery of the good; but men are to participate in the search for it according to the degree that their self-interest is expressed in stable rational form and purged of transient passion or whim. Besides the foundation of representation on property, the frequency of elections is designed to allow the voters the opportunity to pass judgment on those who defend their interests, while protecting the popular

House from every flux of emotion outside. Parliament, by the union of permanence and change in its personnel, imitates in the sphere of government the natural character of society as a whole.

> Nothing is more beautiful in the theory of parliaments, than that principle of renovation, and union of permanence and change, that are happily mixed in their constitution: That in all our changes we are never either wholly old or wholly new: That there are enough of the old to preserve unbroken the traditionary chain of the maxims and policy of our ancestors, and the law and custom of parliament; and enough of the new to invigorate us and bring us to our true character, by being taken fresh from the mass of the people.[76]

Reform of the structure of government will be necessary from time to time in the course of social change, but it must respect the natural order of society, in order to preserve the unity of feeling and obligation. While giving expression to new forms of natural interest it will exclude transient and irrational impulse. Popular control of Parliament is, in the abstract, a good; but so far as frequent elections involve the danger of greater corruptibility in both representative and elector, and hence the subversion of natural feeling, they will hinder rather than assist the discovery of the rational good.[77] For the same reason an increase in the franchise is not to be favoured, if this is merely to enlarge the scope of corruption; on the contrary it might be more in the spirit of the constitution to increase the weight and independence of voters by lessening their numbers.[78]

Nor is the natural feeling of the community necessarily conformable to any abstract type of organisation. Criticism of inequality of representation as between places betrays an excessive preoccupation with the secondary question of arithmetical equality and symmetry. What matters is not the formal, but the moral and efficient aspect of institutions.[79] If there is a moral and political equality, this is all that is required; and such an equality exists as long as the representatives are all equally interested in the prosperity of the whole, all involved in the general interest and the general sympathy.[80] If indeed the natural feeling and rational self-interest from which the general good is elicited should be corrupted, it cannot be supplied by a greater formal balance or symmetry of organisation. The machine will work if the materials are sound, but no virtue can ensue from 'the arrangement of *rottenness*'.[81]

The extreme danger to the natural society of ranks and orders in which the individual realises his true moral self within his status, is presented by those schemes for reform of representation based on the argument of abstract natural right. This claim, 'founded on the right of self-government in each individual'[82] destroys the natural structure of government, because it implies some system of representation of persons, not of property. This is to subvert the ancient and wise tradition of the British constitution, which regards rather property than persons in provincial elections;[83] it undermines the authority of the House of Commons, which is not, and never has been, representative of the people as a collection of individuals.[84] It represents 'the great danger of our time, that of setting up number against property'.[85] The claim of abstract natural right is an attempt to found government not on stable individual self-interest which can recognise its limited place within the general good, but on changeable and irrational caprice and wilfulness. Neither steady government nor stable social order can rest on such a basis.

Notes

[1] VI, 206

[2] VI, 206

[3] VI, 205-6

[4] VI, 207

[5] VI, 207

[6] VI, 207

[7] II, 9; cf. IV, 44

[8] VI, 208; cf. *Corr.* II, 276

[9] VI, 208

[10] V, 100

[11] V, 80

[12] V, 352

[13] V, 330-1

[14] VI, 216

[15] V, 107-8

[16] II, 246

[17] X, 138-9

[18] VIII, 68

[19] VI, 217

[20] VII, 415

[21] VII, 265

[22] VIII, 400

[23] VIII, 67; cf. *Corr.* I, 381.

[24] VI, 219

[25] VI, 216

[26] V, 84-5

[27] VI, 257-8

[28] X, 100

[29] X, 46

[30] VI, 346

[31] III, 183

[32] II, 226; cf. III, 294

[33] II, 224

[34] X, 73

[35] IX, 350

[36] III, 179

[37] III, 180

[38] III, 236

[39] V, 179

[40] III, 422

[41] III, 422-3

[42] V, 109

[43] VIII, 18

[44] IX, 321-2

[45] II, 304-5

[46] X, 64

[47] II, 287-8

[48] *Cavendish,* I, 287-8

[49] III, 374

[50] III, 18-19

[51] VI, 360

[52] VI, 346-7

[53] VIII, 400

[54] IX, 389

[55] *Corr.* III, 388

[56] VI, 371

[57] VI, 371

[58] *Cavendish,* I, 308

[59] X, 76

[60] IX, 350-1

[61] V, 137

[62] V, 179

[63] III, 249

[64] III, 344

[65] VI, 347

[66] VIII, 19

[67] III, 357

[68] X, 76

[69] III, 249

[70] *P.H.* XXIV, 944

[71] *P.H.* XXVIII, 477

[72] III, 420-3

[73] III, 360

[74] III, 20

[75] VIII, 14

[76] *Corr.* IV, 465

[77] X, 82-3, 88-9

[78] II, 135-6

[79] IX, 65

[80] X, 101-3

[81] *Corr.* II, 383-4

[82] X, 95

[83] VI, 370

[84] X, 95

[85] VI, 371

Works Cited

Works, Rivington edition, 16 vols., 1826-27.

Correspondence, edited by Fitzwilliam and Bourke, 4 vols., 1844.

Sir Henry Cavendish's Debates of the House of Commons, ed. by J. Wright, 2 vols., 1841-43.

Alfred Cobban characterizes Burke as an enigmatic political thinker:

Burke has held rather a dubious position in the history of political thought. A political philosopher who is also a practical politician is apt to be regarded as somewhat of an anomaly and to be treated accordingly by other politicians during his life and by philosophers after his death. Of Burke we may say that had he been less of a theorist he would have met with higher rewards in his Parliamentary career, while had he been a less violent partisan his political ideas might have been granted a juster appreciation by those who studied them in the subsequent century. So intermingled with advocacy of party policy is his exposition of political principles, that those who set out to treat him as a theorist in the light of pure reason have generally ended by applauding or denouncing him as a politician in the light of latter-day politics. Mostly it has been applause, but of rather a self-regarding nature. In a political way of speaking, all things to all men, to Liberals such as Morley, Burke has seemed a Gladstonian who went wrong towards the end of his days; while to Conservatives like Lord Hugh Cecil the vision has been revealed of the great Whig as spiritually one with Disraeli and Young England.

Alfred Cobban, in his Edmund Burke and the Revolt against the Eighteenth Century: A Study of the Political and Social Thinking of Burke, Wordsworth, Coleridge and Southey, *The Macmillan Company, 1929.*

Francis Canavan (essay date 1987)

SOURCE: Francis Canavan, "Prescription and Government," in *Edmund Burke: Prescription and Providence,* Carolina Academic Press, 1987, pp. 113-35.

[In the following essay, Canavan explains how Burke's theory of prescription led to his belief that preexisting moral obligations in a divinely-willed state both supersede and underpin the rights and liberties of individuals secured through social contracts.]

In relating the political order of civil society to the created order of the world, Burke's theory of prescription of government plays an important role. He says explicitly that "the doctrine of prescription . . . is a part of the law of nature."[1] But as the variety of scholarly interpretations of his doctrine of prescription testifies, what he meant by it and in what sense it is part of the law of nature, is by no means clear, certainly not to all who read Burke.

Paul Lucas has described Burke's theory of prescription as his "idea about the way in which an adverse possession of property and authority may be legitimated by virtue of use and enjoyment during a long passage of time."[2] The description is accurate so far as it goes. Burke certainly held that if one had held uncontested possession as the owner of a piece of property for a sufficiently long period of time, no earlier title to the property, however valid, could be revived and made to prevail against the occupant's title. Through the passage of time the occupant had acquired a title by prescription, and this in Burke's eyes was "the soundest, the most general, and the most recognized title . . . a title, which . . . is rooted in its principle, in the law of nature itself."[3] He applied the same principle, by analogy, to the possession of political authority.

Lucas goes on to say that Burke "revolutionized the meaning of prescription"[4] and that "it was through his conception of prescription that Burke attacked the natural and common laws."[5] This writer disagrees with Lucas's propositions that Burke attacked the natural law, that he "believed that prescription possessed an immanent justification,"[6] and that in his mind "time alone became the material and efficient cause of prescription."[7] This chapter, however, is not a rebuttal of Lucas's contention that Burke's "key and characteristic doctrine of prescription is not to be found in the old writings on the natural law," or in the Roman civil law, the Roman Catholic canon law, the English common law, or the many expositions of the various French "civil" or feudal laws.[8] All that is intended here is to set forth Burke's doctrine and his reasons for it, whether it is to be found in previous writings or not.

Burke's doctrine of prescription of government, as Fennessy remarks, "is by no means an anti-rational defence of existing institutions, based on feelings of reverence for antiquity. It is a theoretical answer to a problem of political theory."[9] Burke was not speculating in a vacuum when he spoke of a prescription of government; he was arguing against what he regarded as a false and dangerous theory of the origin and nature of political authority. Burke's defense of authority as prescriptive, therefore, must be understood in the light of the theory to which it was a reply. To try to understand the Burkean doctrine of prescription in itself, without reference to the opposing doctrine, is to run the risk of missing its point.

For the present purpose, what is important is not so much what Burke's opponents really meant as what he thought they meant. There is, in fact, no reason to believe that he seriously misunderstood them, even though for polemic reasons he did reduce their arguments to their simplest and most radical form. It would be hard to oversimplify Thomas Paine's thesis in *The Rights of Man,* but it was doubtless unfair of Burke to take Paine as the exponent of the view of all the English sympathizers with the French Revolution. Nonetheless, to understand what Burke meant by prescription, we must first understand the position against which he directed the doctrine of prescription, and we must understand it as he did.

He had summarized that position several years before the French Revolution in his **Speech on the Reform of the Representation of the Commons in Parliament**. Since that speech will be the subject of the following chapter, we may leave full discussion of it until then, and not only that Burke said in it that most of those seeking reform claimed the right to vote for members of Parliament as one of "the supposed rights of man as man."[10] Such an argument, as Burke pointed out, led logically not only to reform of the representation in one house of Parliament, but to popular sovereignty clear across the constitutional board. By the time Burke came to write his **Reflections on the Revolution in France** in 1790, the argument, as he understood it, had in fact taken that form. "They have 'the rights of men,'" he said, and continued:

> Against these there can be no prescription; against these no argument is binding: these admit no temperament, and no compromise: any thing withheld from their full demand is so much of fraud and injustice. Against these their rights of men let no government look for security in the length of its continuance, or in the justice and lenity of its administration. The objections of these speculatists, if its forms do not quadrate with their theories, are as valid against such an old and beneficent government as against the most violent tyranny, or the greenest usurpation. They are always at issue with governments, not on a question of abuse, but a question of competency, and a question of title.[11]

The point at issue between Burke, on the one hand, and the revolutionists and the whole "natural rights" school of political thought, on the other, was not a question of what made a constitution good or when authority was abused. It was "a question of title." They held that there was one and only one legitimate title to political authority: "the rights of men." Burke's counterargument was that "*prescription* . . . gives right and title."[12] In the passage in which he used that phrase, he was speaking of the title to real estate, but he explained in another place: "Prescription is the most solid of all titles, not only to property, but, which is to secure that property, to Government."[13] Prescription, according to Burke, gave "right and title" not only to real property but to inherited liberties, religion, and political authority. We therefore do not understand the dispute between Burke and his "rights of men" opponents unless we see that the point at issue was precisely one of the *title* to political authority.

In the context of this dispute, the "rights of men" were reducible to one: the sovereign right of every individual in the state of nature to govern himself. From this natural right of the individual it followed that society, or at least *civil* society endowed with the authority to govern, was formed and legitimately could only be formed by a voluntary compact among individuals. The compact brought into being a sovereign people which, being composed of originally sovereign and politically equal individuals, was of necessity governed by majority rule. The people, acting by majority, were the authors and always remained the masters of the society's constitution and government.

Burke explained this doctrine of his opponents in the following terms in the sequel to the **Reflections,** which he published in 1791 under the title **An Appeal From the New to the Old Whigs:**

> These new whigs hold, that the sovereignty, whether exercised by one or many, did not only originate *from* the people (a position not denied, nor worth denying or assenting to) but that, in the people the same sovereignty constantly and unalienably resides; that the people may lawfully depose kings, not only for misconduct, but without any misconduct at all; that they may set up any new fashion of government for themselves, or continue without any government at their pleasure; that the people are essentially their own rule, and their will the measure of their conduct; that the tenure of magistracy is not a proper subject of contract; because magistrates have duties, but no rights; and that if a contract *de facto* is made with them in one age, allowing that it binds at all, it only binds those who are immediately concerned in it, but does not pass to posterity.[14]

This theory, according to Burke, rested on two false principles which he restated later in the same work. The first was "that the *people,* in forming their commonwealth, have by no means parted with their power over it."[15] The other was the "principle of the right to change a fixed and tolerable constitution of things at pleasure."[16] The words to be underscored in this phrase are, once again, *at pleasure.* The object of Burke's attack was the idea that the will of a majority of the people, told by the head, was its own supreme rule.

Against this notion Burke expounded a theory of political authority derived from an Aristotelian theory of the state set in the framework of the Christian doctrine of creation. "His conception of 'nature' and the 'natural' is in its essence Greek to the core," says John MacCunn. "It is the Aristotelian conception of the organized 'natural' municipal State read into the life of the modern nation."[17] Between the Greek *polis* and the eighteenth-century national state there is, as the French say, a certain distance, and Burke did not take over Aristotle's *Politics* in its entirety. Yet he did base his notion of the state on a teleological conception of nature, as the following passage with its Aristotelian echoes reveals:

> The state of civil society . . . is a state of nature; and much more truly so than a savage and incoherent mode of life. For man is by nature reasonable; and he is never perfectly in his natural state, but when he is placed where reason may be best cultivated, and most predominates. Art is man's nature. We are as much, at least, in a state of nature in formed manhood, as in immature and helpless infancy.[18]

Hence, while society is indeed a contract, as Burke said in the *Reflections,* it is no ordinary contract. It is "a partnership in every virtue, and in all perfection."[19] Society has a natural end or purpose, from which its fundamental law is derived, and that end is the full intellectual and moral development of human nature.

Aristotle has said as much. But Burke also saw man as a creature of God "who gave us our nature, and in giving impressed an invariable Law upon it."[20] God, as the Creator of human nature, is also the ultimate author of the state. Even though the state might be founded by a voluntary compact among men—"which in many cases it undoubtedly was," Burke was willing to admit[21]—the binding force of the compact nevertheless came from God because "if no supreme ruler exists, wise to form, and potent to enforce, the moral law, there is no sanction to any contract, virtual or even actual, against the will of prevalent power."[22]

Therefore, as Fennessy has put it, "the natural foundation of society is, for Burke, the given moral relation between men, imposed and sanctioned by the act of creation."[23] Burke's ideological opponents also acknowledged Nature and Nature's God. "Both he and they," in MacCunn's words, "believe that, behind the struggles and the flux of politics, there is an objective order which (to revert once more to Burke's words) holds all things fast in their place, and that to this objective order men and nations are bound to adapt themselves."[24] But for Burke's opponents the objective moral order was the foundation of the natural and imprescriptible rights of men and therefore of the untrammeled sovereignty of the people. Burke's task was to show that, on the contrary, the moral order was the source of political obligations that bound even the people.

To this task he addressed himself with his most closely reasoned argument in *An Appeal From the New to the Old Whigs*. The objective, divinely-founded moral order, he there argues, is the source of duties as well as of rights, and duties are not subject to the will of those who are bound by them. Some duties are assumed voluntarily, but the most basic ones are not; and even voluntarily assumed duties do not for that reason fail to be obligations.[25]

"We have obligations to mankind at large," says Burke, "which are not in consequence of any special voluntary pact. They arise from the relation of man to man, and the relation of man to God, which relations are not matters of choice."[26] They are consequences of God having created men as human beings whose very nature entails morally binding relationships. Why is a man bound to act morally in his relationships with other men? Because, Burke argues, he is a man—a free, rational, and social being—and his nature as a man obliges him to act according to the relationships inherent in that nature. But why must he respect what is inherent in his nature? Because his nature is created by God who has written His will into it as its constitutive law.

The most basic moral obligations thus rest upon the metaphysics of a created universe and are the source of all subsequent and subordinate obligations: "the force of all the pacts which we enter into with any particular person or number of persons amongst mankind, depends upon those prior obligations." The pacts to which Burke refers are relations among persons established by consent. But other derived and subordinate relations are involuntary, yet nonetheless give rise to "compulsive" duties:

> When we marry, the choice is voluntary, but the duties are not matter of choice. They are dictated by the nature of the situation. . . . Parents may not be consenting to their moral relation [to their children]; but consenting or not, they are bound to a long train of burthensome duties towards those with whom they have never made a convention of any sort. Children are not consenting to their relation [to their parents], but their relation, without their actual consent, binds them to its duties; or rather it implies their consent, because the presumed consent of every rational creature is in unison with the predisposed order of things.[27]

Two fundamental principles are laid down in this passage. First, that a relationship may be established by consent, as marriage is, yet once established it creates obligations that are independent of and superior to consent. Second, that a relationship established without consent, like that of a child (who did not ask to be conceived) toward his parents, nevertheless creates obligations. What is more, the obligations not only bind the child without his prior consent, they command his consent because "the presumed consent of every rational creature is in unison with the predisposed order of things." The child is obliged by his nature as a rational creature to consent to his obligations to his parents and to other duties that flow from this initial obligation. The consent, of course, cannot become actual until he reaches the age of reason, but in the meantime it is legitimately presumed because it is obligatory and cannot morally be refused.

In Burke's moral universe, therefore, obligation is antecedent to consent and compels consent. We *must* consent, rationally and freely, to the morally obligatory relationships that are knit into "the predisposed order of things." This order of things is, in its most fundamental meaning, the frame of the world, and, specifically, of the human world as created by God. Derivatively, it is the contingent part of that human world into which a man is born.

To illustrate this last point, one may remark that there is nothing in the nature of man as man that requires that a particular family should exist at a given time and place and in a given social situation. The particular family, therefore, is a contingent reality. Nonetheless, children are born, not to man as man, but to some particular parents who, normally at least, are the founders of a particular family. It is through them that their children get their place in society, with its duties as well as its rights. "Men come . . . into a community with the social state of their parents, endowed with all the benefits, loaded with all the duties of their situation."[28] This situation is, to be sure, contingent inasmuch as it need not have existed. But it does exist, and by existing, it creates obligations for its participants, to which their consent is mandatory.

The root of the obligations is "that the awful author of our being is the author of our place in the order of existence; and that having disposed and marshalled us by a divine tactick, not according to our will, but according to his, he has, in and by that disposition, virtually subjected us to act the part which belongs to the place assigned us."[29] The divine act of creation extends itself in history through the providence by which God governs the world and establishes particular as well as universal obligations.

If, in this manner, we are "loaded with all the duties" of our family's situation, "so without any stipulation on our own part, are we bound by that relation called our country." For "our country is not a thing of mere physical locality. It consists, in a great measure, in the antient order into which we are born." An order is a relation or, more accurately, a network of relations and, like other human relations, it creates obligations.

"The place that determines our duty to our country is a social, civil relation."[30]

It is immaterial, therefore, that "civil society might be at first a voluntary act." Even if it was, what counts is that "its continuance is under a permanent standing covenant, co-existing with the society; and it attaches upon every individual of that society, without any formal act of his own."[31] The generation that voluntarily founded a civil society are bound by that to which they consented, as are partners in marriage. Later generations are born into the society, not only physically, but morally: they are born to the covenant or constitution and its legal political obligations. As Fennessy says, for Burke "it was not consent that made the social bond, but a created social bond that demanded the consent of free and rational creatures."[32]

These obligations may be conceived, as the men of the eighteenth century commonly did conceive them, as contractual in nature. Even so, Burke argued, a social contract is a moral engagement and does not leave certain members of the society free to change the contract merely because they are the majority:

> Neither the few nor the many have a right to act merely by their will, in any matter connected with duty, trust, engagement, or obligation. The constitution of a country being once settled upon some compact, tacit or expressed, there is no power existing of force to alter it, without the breach of the covenant, or the consent of all the parties. Such is the nature of a contract. And the votes of a majority of the people, whatever their infamous flatterers may teach in order to corrupt their minds, cannot alter the moral any more than they can alter the physical essence of things.[33]

This was a rather narrowly legalistic argument, however, and leaves the impression that the people are obliged to maintain the social contract merely because contracts are morally binding. Burke's argument rested, however, on the wider and deeper premise that man is by nature rational and, because rational, social. In saying that the Creator willed the state as the necessary means to human nature's full development and perfection, Burke meant that God willed the historically-evolved social order.

The particular form that the state took depended on "the circumstances and habits of every country."[34] But once the state, with its particular and historically conditioned form, had come into existence, its constitution became a contingent part of the moral order and was endowed with the binding force of the universal, divinely-willed moral law.

One may feel here that Burke is engaging in intellectual sleight of hand. What justifies this slide from the universal moral order, in all its majesty and perfection, to the constitution of a particular state, with its all too human imperfections, as if they were morally both of one piece? The answer, in Burke's view, is that they are of one piece.

Universal moral imperatives are, as such, abstractions and become actual only in the concrete and particular. As was said above, children are born, not to man as man, but to particular parents in a particular family. They have natural obligations, not, however, to parenthood or to parents in general, but to *their* parents. So, too, while marriage is a natural relationship and carries with it natural obligations, marriage as such exists nowhere. In the real world, Man does not marry Woman. All that happens or can happen is that John marries Mary. They thereby contract marital obligations that are rooted in the complementary natures of the two sexes. But the obligations are not to the opposite sex as such, but to each other as individual persons.

Similarly, while it is meaningful to say that God wills the state because man's rational nature requires civil society, civil society cannot exist in the abstract and simply as such. If civil society implies moral obligations, those obligations can take concrete form and become actually binding only in a particular state under a particular constitution. "Constitutions," as Burke once put it, "furnish the civil means of getting at the natural."[35] Or, as he said in praise of the British constitution, "The foundation of government is there laid, not in imaginary rights of men, . . . but in political convenience, and in human nature; either as that nature is universal, or as it is modified by local habits and social aptitudes."[36] In the created universe, the necessary is realized in the contingent, the universal in the particular, the natural in the conventional. The distinctions among these are valid, but in actual existence they are all of one piece. The universal moral order is the order of a real, historically-existing world.

Burke thus speaks the language of the social contract theory, but with a difference. He begins his most oft-quoted passage on the roots of political obligation with the words, "Society is indeed a contract."[37] Yet, as C. E. Vaughan points out, with some exaggeration, in Burke's hands the implications of the contract undergo a profound change:

> The mere act of consent, which to Locke was all in all, has ceased to be of any importance. It has, in fact, come to stand for something very different; an obligation which is binding upon all men, whether they choose to recognise it or no. It is no longer the consent itself, but the thing to which consent has been given—no longer the contract, but the particular obligation contracted—that counts. Under these circumstances, the consent, the contract, is manifestly no true consent, no contract at all. The consent, so far from being actually given, is tacitly assumed. The contract, so far from being matter of

choice, is imposed by the necessities of man's nature.[38]

The derivation of the bond of civil society from the necessities of man's nature shifts the emphasis, not only from consent to obligation, but also from rights to purposes. With Burke, the inquiry into the source of political obligation no longer begins with men's pre-political rights in a state of nature, but with the purposes of civil society. The "*real* rights of men," says Burke, are not the abstract original rights of men, but the benefits that civil society can and should confer on them. They are the goals or purposes of civil society, rooted ultimately in the nature of man and in the creative act of God. These goals are not only men's rights but, as Burke explained in *An Appeal,* are also the source of their obligations in civil society:

> Men without their choice derive benefits from that association; without their choice they are subjected to duties in consequence of these benefits; and without their choice they enter into a virtual obligation as binding as any that is actual. Look through the whole of life and the whole system of duties. Much the strongest moral obligations are such as were never the results of our option.[39]

To say this is not to deny that men have rights, nor even that these rights are in a valid sense natural. But it is to deny that the authority of civil society derives from the consent of men who were by nature independent of any civil bond and who therefore retain the natural right to make and unmake the civil bond at pleasure. The structure of authority and the form of government are framed, not in the light of the original independence and equality of men in the state of nature, but with a view to the benefits which civil society exists to confer upon them. "Government is not made in virtue of natural rights, which may and do exist in total independence of it. . . . Government is a contrivance of human wisdom to provide for human *wants.* Men have a right that these wants should be provided for by this wisdom."[40]

The constitution of civil society is determined by human needs, not by original rights. Consequently, "the whole organization of government becomes a consideration of convenience,"[41] i.e., of aptitude for satisfying those needs, and "the true statesman . . . thinks of the place in which political power is to be lodged, with no other attention, than as it may render the more or the less practicable, its salutary restraint, and its prudent direction."[42] A properly made constitution is one that places power in the hands of those who have the requisite wisdom and virtue to direct society in such a way as to provide for men's genuine needs.

But the needs which civil society exists to satisfy are many and varied, and so its constitution cannot be framed for any single or narrow purpose. "The nature of man is intricate; the objects of society are of the greatest possible complexity; and therefore no simple disposition or direction of power can be suitable either to man's nature, or to the quality of his affairs."[43] It is the ends of civil society, not its origins, that shape its constitution, but those ends are complex and so, too, should the constitution be.

But, however complex the ends of civil society, they may be subsumed under one general goal: the good of the people. This goal is the only one that government may legitimately intend: "all political power which is set over men, . . . being wholly artificial, and for so much a derogation from the natural equality of mankind at large, ought to be some way or other exercised ultimately for their benefit."[44] End or purpose, however, is a coin the obverse side of which is result or effect. Political power is not justified by the ends it merely intends, but by those it actually achieves. The good of its members is the purpose of civil society but the purpose is morally inadequate unless it becomes an accomplished result.

"The practical consequences of any political tenet go a great way in deciding upon its value," Burke said. ". . . What in the result is likely to produce evil, is politically false: that which is productive of good, politically true."[45] It was on this basis that he passed judgment on the French Revolution. "I cannot think that what is done in France is beneficial to the human race," he said. But, he admitted, "if it were, the English constitution ought no more to stand against it than the antient constitution of the kingdom in which the new system prevails."[46] He used the same criterion for old institutions, but all the more easily because their results were already visible. "Old establishments are tried by their effects. If the people are happy, united, wealthy, and powerful, we presume the rest. We conclude that to be good from whence good is derived."[47]

To summarize, in his critique of the natural rights-social contract theory Burke shifted the basis of political authority from original rights, individual consent, and the sovereignty of the popular majority to the purposes and achieved results of civil society. Civil society, though in itself an artificial and conventional human construct, has a natural claim on men's obedience because it has a natural and God-given purpose: to serve the needs of human nature. Political obligation is therefore in principle antecedent to political consent. Since, however, civil society as such is an abstraction and has real existence only in concrete and historically-conditioned forms, men are obliged to accept and respect the particular constitution to which they are born. But the obligation, in the concrete, is not absolute and unqualified. That constitution has a claim on men's obedience which in fact has served them well or at least, in the exceptional case of a jus-

tified revolution, gives solid promise of doing so.

It is in this intellectual framework, which Burke went to great pains to establish, that we must set his thesis that prescription is a title to political authority. There have been those who found the framework, like the doctrine of prescription itself, mystifying. For example, G. P. Gooch says that "despite his passionate denunciation of metaphysical politics, Burke's own philosophy is suffused with mysticism. His profoundly religious temper led him to regard the moral relations and duties of man and the order of society as of divine institution."[48] Such language can be used, however, only by those who cannot tell the difference between metaphysics and mysticism. There is nothing particularly mystical about Burke's metaphysics. As Russell Kirk says, his "view of the cosmos may be true, or it may be delusory; but it is not obscure, let alone incomprehensible."[49] But without it, his doctrine of prescription is indeed incomprehensible.

Burke did not mean by prescription of government—despite what he seemed to say—that government gained authority merely by lasting a long time or that men's rights and obligations in civil society were independent of natural law. He did not mean this even in his *Speech on the Reform of the Representation of the Commons in Parliament,* where he said that the sole authority of the British constitution was that it had existed time out of mind.[50]

What he was getting at may be gleaned from a speech he wrote for delivery in the Commons in 1792:

> The foundations, on which obedience to government is founded, are not to be constantly discussed. That we are here, supposes the discussion already made and the dispute settled. We must assume the rights of what represents the Publick to control the individual, to make his will and his acts to submit to their will, until some intolerable grievance shall make us know that it does not answer its end, and will submit neither to reformation nor restraint.[51]

The centuries-old existence of the British constitution was sufficient proof that the nation had already decided where political authority was to be lodged. That decision was not to be reopened with every new generation, but must be taken as right and binding until some intolerable and irremediable grievance showed that government was not answering its end and was refusing to achieve the purpose for which it was instituted.

But the established constitution, however long it has endured, cannot be its own self-sufficient norm of goodness. Burke's position on this point is indicated by his answer to Warren Hastings during the latter's impeachment as the East India Company's Governor-

General in India. Hastings had argued that when the Company acquired sovereignty over Indian states, it had accepted despotic and arbitrary power which he, Hastings, exercised in its name. For such was the traditional constitution of Asia and such, given the conditions of Asiatic society, was the only way in which Asiatics could be ruled.

If a prescriptive constitution were established by mere passage of time, Hasting's argument would be conclusive, at least for Burke. But Burke replied that neither the Company nor the British government could have acquired or given arbitrary power, "because arbitrary power is a thing, which neither any man can hold nor any man can give." All power is from God and

> is bound by the eternal laws of Him, that gave it, with which no human authority can dispense; . . . The title of conquest makes no difference at all. No conquest can give such a right; for conquest, that is force, cannot convert its own injustice into a just title, by which it may rule others at its pleasure.[52]

We notice once again that the unforgivable sin is to claim the right to rule at pleasure. It matters not whether the government be constitutionally democratic or despotic:

> Despotism if it means any thing, that is at all defensible, means a mode of government, bound by no written rules, and coerced by no controlling magistracies, or well settled orders in the state. But if it has no written law, it neither does, nor can, cancel the primeval, indefesible, unalterable law of nature, and of nations; and if no magistracies control its exertions, those exertions must derive their limitation and direction either from the equity and moderation of the ruler, or from downright revolt on the part of the subject by rebellion, divested of all its criminal qualities.[53]

"There is a sacred veil to be drawn over the beginnings of all governments," according to Burke, and he was willing to contend that "prudence and discretion make it necessary to throw something of the same drapery over more recent foundations" such as British rule in India.[54] Nonetheless, in accepting governmental powers from the Mogul Empire, the East India Company accepted the responsibility "to observe the laws, rights, usages, and customs of the natives; and to pursue their benefit in all things. For this duty was inherent in the nature, institution, and purpose of the office which they received."[55]

The authority of government thus turns out once more to depend on its fulfillment of its natural purposes, and no prescription derived from mere duration will suffice to justify a government that frustrates these purposes. The prescriptive constitution is the constitution that has proved itself not only by long but by good performance, and the good performance is more decisive than the long. As Gerald W. Chapman says, prescription "makes the point that in all the depth of existence, past and present, there is no ground and sanction for any constitution or state except as by a prescriptive use it is found to be good."[56]

The same point is made by Burke's assertion that prescription can be anticipated. Speaking of the French Revolution, he said:

> If they had set up this new experimental government, as a necessary substitute for an expelled tyranny, mankind would anticipate the time of prescription, which, through long usage, mellows into legality governments that were violent in their commencement. All those who have affections which lead them to the conservation of civil order would recognise, even in its cradle, the child as legitimate, which has been produced from those principles of cogent expediency to which all just governments owe their birth, and on which they justify their continuance.[57]

Burke, of course, did not admit that the traditional French monarchy was a tyranny or that the revolutionary substitute for it was necessary. On the contrary, he said of the Revolution, "It is a recent wrong, and can plead no prescription."[58] But he did say that a revolution could be justified by "those principles of cogent expediency to which all just governments owe their birth, and on which they justify their continuance." "Then what is the standard of expedience?" he asked in another context. "Expedience is that, which is good for the community, and good for every individual in it."[59]

Now, if all just governments are founded on cogent expediency, among them must be even those governments that were violent and unjust in their commencement, but which prescription, through long usage, has mellowed into legality. Unjust in their beginnings, they have become just and have acquired a prescriptive title by their service to the people whom they govern. This is why prescription can be anticipated: the principles of cogent expediency may be operative from the beginning in a violent but necessary change of government.

Prescription of government, therefore, does not depend upon the possession of authority in good faith from the beginning. It does not answer the question whether the predecessors of those who now hold authority acquired it rightfully or whether the existing constitution was originally conceived in justice. Prescription rules out these questions as irrelevant to the only point that is now at issue: is the existing constitution legitimate and does government established under it have the right to rule? The doctrine of prescription answers that question with a qualified affirmative: yes, if it governs for the welfare of the community.

Prescription does not mean that old institutions must be preserved merely because they are old, as if, in Lucas's words, "time alone became the material and efficient cause of prescription." Burleigh Wilkins has pointed out that "Burke's opposition to slavery and the slave trade . . . shows that the historicity of an institution or a practice is not always in his opinion a fact of moral significance in favour of the institution or practice in question let alone a sufficient condition of its moral worth."[60]

Burke himself explicitly says: "'Monopoly' is contrary to 'Natural Right.' . . . No monopoly can, therefore, be prescribed in; because contrary to common right." He allows that the state "may grant a monopoly" because, "representing all its individuals," it "may contract for them." But nothing follows from this except that persons may by their own consent or that of their agents surrender the exercise of at least some of their natural rights. Burke adds that the state "ought not to grant this monopoly on arbitrary principles, but for the good of the whole."[61] The basic principle remains that prescription cannot maintain a monopoly contrary to the claims of natural or common right.

Nor is age alone a sufficient reason for preserving institutions of government, as Burke explained in his *Speech on Economical Reform* in 1780. When the reason for having them is gone, he said, "it is absurd to preserve nothing but the burthen of them."[62] It is not only absurd, but dangerous, for "there is a time, when men will not suffer bad things because their ancestors have suffered worse. There is a time, when the hoary head of inveterate abuse will neither draw reverence, nor obtain protection."[63]

On the other hand, age counts for a great deal in judging the value of institutions, and it is therefore wise to recognize it. As Burke said in the same speech, "People will bear an old establishment when its excess is corrected, who will revolt at a new one."[64] There is a still deeper reason for respecting and conserving what is old. All government, Burke was convinced, "stands upon opinion,"[65] because "the only firm seat of all authority is in the minds, affections, and interests of the people."[66] But, "if we must resort to prepossessions for the ground of opinion, it is in the nature of man rather to defer to the wisdom of times passed, whose weakness is not before his eyes, than to the present, of whose imbecility he has daily experience. Veneration of antiquity is congenial to the human mind."[67]

It is to be noticed in this and the numerous other passages where Burke praises veneration of antiquity, that he presents it, not as being in itself the prescriptive title to authority, but as an explanation of why people are willing to accept authority. The statesman, there-fore, is not obliged to preserve what is old merely because it is old. But it is wisdom on his part to recognize the advantage offered him by what is old, to preserve it insofar as he can, and to modify it when he must rather than abolish it. Reform, per se, is preferable to revolution.

Prescription, then, is no bar to reform. During the crisis between Great Britain and her American colonies, Burke never questioned Britain's prescriptive right to legislate for the Americans, though he urged great moderation in its use. In 1777, for example, he wrote to the Sheriffs of Bristol, whose representative in Parliament he then was:

> When I first came into a publick trust, I found your parliament in possession of an unlimited legislative power over the colonies. I could not open the statute book without seeing the actual exercise of it, more or less, in all cases whatsoever. This possession passed with me for a title. It does so in all human affairs. No man examines into the defects of his title to his paternal estate, or to his established government.[68]

But Burke could contemplate a change in the prescriptive constitution, as is shown by the following passage from an *Address to the British Colonists in North America,* which he drafted as a last-minute attempt at reconciliation, probably in 1777:

> This Constitution has . . . admitted innumerable improvements, either for the correction of the original scheme, or for removing corruptions, or for bringing its principles better to suit those changes, which have successively happened in the circumstances of the nation, or in the manners of the people.

> We feel that the growth of the Colonies is such a change of circumstances; and that our present dispute is an exigency as pressing as any, which ever demanded a revision of our Government. Publick troubles have often called upon this Country to look into its Constitution. It has ever been bettered by such a revision. If our happy and luxuriant increase of dominion, and our diffused population, have outgrown the limits of a Constitution made for a contracted object, we ought to bless God, who has furnished us with this noble occasion for displaying our skill and beneficence in enlarging the scale of rational happiness, and of making the politick generosity of this Kingdom as extensive as its fortune.[69]

Even the French Revolution, while it certainly strengthened Burke's devotion to the traditional order of things, did not lead him to make any fundamental change in the above conception of the constitution. The British constitution, he said in *An Appeal,* "is the result of the thoughts of many minds, in many ages."[70] Let us, then, he urged,

> follow our ancestors, men not without a rational, though without an exclusive confidence in themselves; who, by respecting the reason of others, who, by looking backward as well as forward, by the modesty as well as by the energy of their minds, went on, insensibly drawing this constitution nearer and nearer to its perfection by never departing from its fundamental principles, nor introducing any amendment which had not a subsisting root in the laws, constitution, and usages of the kingdom.[71]

The prescriptive constitution does not rule out change; indeed, its development and even its survival depend on change. But it does rule out radical change, the kind of change that either is or pretends to be a clean break with the past. For it is continuity with the past that makes the constitution a predisposed order of things to which men are born and which has an antecedent claim on their obedience and consent. There is no predictable limit to the changes that a prescriptive constitution may undergo, provided that the direction of change continues to be set by the controlling end, the good of the people. But the changes must be gradual and evolutionary, "insensibly drawing [the] constitution nearer and nearer to its perfection by never departing from its fundamental principles."

Finally, prescription does not mean that authority cannot be lost by abuse. Burke urged taking political power in India away from the East India Company on a general principle that would apply against any government, however ancient, that had become inimical to the purposes of all just governments:

> that this body, being totally perverted from the purposes of its institution, is utterly incorrigible; and because they are incorrigible, both in conduct and constitution, power ought to be taken out of their hands; just on the same principles on which have been made all the just changes and revolutions of government that have taken place since the beginning of the world.[72]

What the doctrine of prescription really means, therefore, is that the abuse of political authority is the only moral ground on which it can be lost. Power is rightly taken from a government which has become "totally perverted from the purposes of its institution." But that the constitution of a state originated in wrong, or that it contains no mechanism for registering the formal consent of a majority of the present generation, is irrelevant. These are "speculative," not "real" grievances in Burke's eyes, and they do not suffice to justify the refusal of political obedience.

Yet to assert that prescriptive authority can be lost only by abuse is not to deny that all just governments depend on the consent of the governed. Burke, at any rate, thought that the two propositions were reconcilable. In his early treatise, *A Tract relative to the Laws against Popery in Ireland,* he expounded a thesis which is consistent with and throws light upon his later political theory in this respect.

Having described how the penal laws against Catholics, who were the bulk of the Irish population, deprived them of their elementary human rights, Burke remarked: "A Law against the majority of the people is in substance a Law against the people itself: its extent determines its invalidity."[73] In other words, "a Law directed against the mass of the Nation" simply lacks the authority of the law. The reason that Burke gives for this principle is significant:

> In all forms of Government the people is the true Legislator; and whether the immediate and instrumental cause of the Law be a single person, or many, the remote and efficient cause is the consent of the people, either actual or implied; and such consent is absolutely essential to its validity.[74]

This conception of the people as the ultimate authors of all law is as compatible with monarchy or aristocracy as with democracy. Burke's point here is that, under any form of government, the people, whose actual or implied consent is necessary, cannot be understood to consent to a law that excludes them "not from favours, privileges and trusts, but from the common advantages of society."[75] When the people subject themselves to government, "it is their judgment they give up, not their right."

It is their judgment they give up. . . . Burke explains:

> The people, indeed, are presumed to consent to whatever the Legislature ordains for their benefit; and they are to acquiesce in it, though they do not clearly see into the propriety of the means, by which they are conducted to that desirable end. This they owe as an act of homage and just deference to a reason, which the necessity of Government has made superiour to their own.[76]

The necessity of government (founded in the nature of man and the will of God) requires the people to submit their judgment to the superior reason of those who govern. The consent of the governed is a rational consent, not an arbitrary one which the people may give or withhold at pleasure. Yet neither the government nor the people themselves have a "right to make a Law prejudicial to the whole community . . . because it would be made against the principle of a superiour Law, which it is not in the power of any community, or of the whole race of man, to alter—I mean the will of Him, who gave us our nature, and in giving impressed an invariable Law upon it."[77]

The consent of the people, in short, is given by implication, and is therefore legitimately presumed, to whatever is done for their benefit. But what is clearly not done for their benefit cannot have their consent, and so is invalid. This theory of the relationship between political obligation and consent harmonizes with Burke's later statements and is not an early position that he later abandoned.

It is consistent with his later contention that the fact that "a nation has long existed and flourished under" a "settled scheme of government . . . is a better presumption even of the *choice* of a nation, far better than any sudden and temporary arrangement by actual election."[78] It is consistent with his statement in the **Reflections:** "There is no qualification for government but virtue and wisdom, actual or presumptive."[79] And it leads into his argument, in *An Appeal,* that the upper classes enjoy a legitimate presumption in favor of their wisdom and virtue. He there maintains that the state of civil society, which is man's truly natural state, necessarily generates a class structure which in turn generally produces a natural aristocracy of the wise and good. The members of this aristocracy "form in nature, as she operates in the common modification of society, the leading, guiding, and governing part." To deprive them of authority, in the name of the political equality of all citizens, is "a horrible usurpation."[80]

All government, for Burke, is a trust to be exercised for the benefit of the people by those who are qualified for the task by wisdom and virtue. That a nation has long existed and flourished under a constitution is an indication that the trust has been and is being fulfilled. It is also an indication that the people consent to the trustees and their government. But if, for the moment, a majority of them do not consent, it is no matter. Their consent is legitimately presumed because the natural law requires their consent to a good government. Prescription of government is a part of the law of nature.

Burke's conception of the natural aristocracy is obviously anti-democratic and has been criticized, reasonably enough, on the ground that it too facilely identifies the wise and the good with the well-born and the well-to-do. His defense of the unreformed representative system in Great Britain is simply out of date today. So, too, is his interpretation of the British constitution as a contract to which King, Lords, and Commons are parties. But his doctrine of prescription, though used to justify those governmental arrangements, has a significance that transcends them and is still relevant to political theory.

It is a continuing theoretical problem why men should be morally obliged to obey other men in civil society.

The myth of the state of nature and the social contract has almost wholly disappeared from formal political thought by now. Yet the assumptions of liberal individualism which that myth embodied remain as the premises of much of contemporary political discourse, as Alexander Bickel pointed out. To those who find individualism an inadequate basis for explaining either the facts or the obligations of political life, Burke's doctrine of prescription offers an alternative that could be developed in a contemporary political theory. Without attempting such a development here, one may suggest that its central theme would be the priority of purpose to consent as the source of political obligation.

Notes

[1] *Works,* 5: 276.

[2] "On Edmund Burke's Doctrine of Prescription," *Historical Journal,* 11 (1968): 36.

[3] *Works,* 9: 449.

[4] "On Burke's Doctrine of Prescription," p. 36.

[5] Ibid., p. 35.

[6] Ibid., p. 40-41.

[7] Ibid., p. 62.

[8] Ibid., p. 36. Burke is in flat disagreement with Warburton, who holds that "the Law of Prescription directly contradicts the Law of Nature and Nations." *Alliance of Church and State,* p. 127.

[9] *Burke, Paine, and Rights of Man,* p. 131-132.

[10] *Works,* 10: 93.

[11] Ibid., 5: 119-120.

[12] *Correspondence,* 6: 95.

[13] *Works,* 10: 96.

[14] Ibid., 6: 147. Cf. ibid., 7: 18. In this chapter, subsequent references to *An Appeal from the New to the Old Whigs* will be by short title and page number in *Works,* vol. 6.

[15] Ibid., p. 200.

[16] Ibid., p. 230.

[17] *Political Philosophy of Burke,* p. 54.

[18] *Appeal,* p. 218.

[19] *Works,* 5: 184.

[20] Ibid., 9: 349-350.

[21] *Appeal,* p. 205.

[22] Ibid.

[23] *Burke, Paine,* p. 110.

[24] *Political Philosophy of Burke,* p. 144.

[25] *Appeal,* pp. 204-207.

[26] Ibid., p. 206.

[27] Ibid., pp. 206-207.

[28] Ibid., p. 207.

[29] Ibid., p. 206.

[30] Ibid., p. 207.

[31] Ibid., p. 205.

[32] *Burke, Paine,* p. 114.

[33] *Appeal,* p. 201-202. Cf. *Works,* 5:57-58.

[34] *Appeal,* p. 133.

[35] *Works,* 9: 112.

[36] *Appeal,* p. 257.

[37] *Works,* 5: 183.

[38] *Studies in the History of Political Philosophy before and after Rousseau,* ed. A. G. Little, 2 vols. (Manchester: University of Manchester Press, 1925), 2: 53.

[39] P. 205.

[40] *Works,* 5: 122-123.

[41] Ibid., 5: 123.

[42] *Appeal,* p. 203.

[43] *Works,* 5: 125.

[44] Ibid., 4: 11.

[45] *Appeal,* p. 210.

[46] *Works,* 7: 114-115.

[47] Ibid., 5: 310.

[48] "Europe and the French Revolution," *Cambridge Modern History,* 13 vols. (New York: Macmillan, 1907-1911), 8: 757.

[49] "Burke and the Philosophy of Prescription," *Journal of the History of Ideas,* 14 (1953): 368.

[50] *Works,* 10: 96.

[51] Ibid., 10: 51.

[52] Ibid., 13: 166-167.

[53] Ibid., 13: 169-170.

[54] Ibid., 13: 95-96.

[55] Ibid., 13: 24.

[56] *Edmund Burke: the Practical Imagination* (Cambridge, Mass.: Harvard University Press, 1967), p. 166.

[57] *Works,* 5: 298.

[58] Ibid., 8: 189-191.

[59] Ibid., 10: 100.

[60] *The Problem of Burke's Political Philosophy* (Oxford: Clarendon Press, 1967), p. 237. Cf. *Works,* 9: 276-315.

[61] "Notes on Copy-Right Bill and Monopolies Generally," *Correspondence of the Right Honourable Edmund Burke,* ed. Charles William, Earl Fitzwilliam, and Sir Richard Bourke, 4 vols. (London: Francis and John Rivington, 1844), 4: 459-460.

[62] *Works,* 3: 278.

[63] Ibid., 3: 246-247.

[64] Ibid., 3: 313.

[65] Ibid., 10: 93.

[66] Ibid., 9: 178.

[67] Ibid., 9: 370.

[68] Ibid., 3: 177.

[69] Ibid., 9: 212.

[70] P. 261.

[71] Ibid., p. 265-266.

[72] *Works,* 4: 111.

[73] Ibid., 9: 347-348.

[74] Ibid., 9: 348.

[75] Ibid., 9: 349.

[76] Ibid., 9: 348-349.

[77] Ibid., 9: 349-350.

[78] Ibid., 10: 96.

[79] Ibid., 5: 106.

[80] *Appeal*, pp. 217-19.

Works Cited

Works. The Works of the Right Honourable Edmund Burke. 16 vols. London: F. C. and J. Rivington, 1803-1827. (A new and definitive edition, *The Writings and Speeches of Edmund Burke*, under the general editorship of Paul Langford, began publication by the Clarendon Press at Oxford in 1981 but, since at the time of this writing it was still incomplete, I have used the Rivington edition for the sake of uniformity of reference.)

Correspondence. The Correspondence of Edmund Burke. Edited by Thomas W. Copeland. 10 vols. Cambridge: At the University Press; Chicago: University of Chicago Press, 1958-1970.

Samuels, *Early Life*. Samuels, Arthur P. I., *The Early Life, Correspondence, and Writings of the Rt. Hon. Edmund Burke*. Cambridge: At the University Press, 1923.

Parliamentary History. The Parliamentary History of England, from the Earliest Period to the year 1803. 36 vols. London: T. C. Hansard, 1806-1820.

Peter J. Stanlis (essay date 1991)

SOURCE:Peter J. Stanlis, "Burke and the Moral Natural Law," in *Edmund Burke: The Enlightment and Revolution*, Transaction Publishers, 1991, pp. 3-61.

[*In the following excerpt, Stanlis examines how Burke's concept of a moral natural law guided both his domestic political policies and his view of Parliament's affairs with the American colonies, Ireland, India, and France.*]

. . . Since "very early youth," Burke confessed in 1780 to a gentleman interested in reforming parliament, he had "been conversant in reading and thinking upon the subject of our laws and constitution, as well as upon those of other times, and other countries," and a decade before his death he stated in parliament that "he had in the course of his life looked frequently into law books on different subjects." Burke's interest in the law began at least as early as 1747, when his father entered his name at the Middle Temple. Early in 1750 Burke went to London to study law, and although he soon abandoned his studies to take up first literature and then an active life in politics, his speeches reveal that he had acquired a profound knowledge and enduring respect for the law. "No man here," he said in 1770, "has a greater veneration than I have for the doctors of the law," and four years later, in his speech on American taxation, he voiced his greatest tribute to the law: "The law . . . is, in my opinion, one of the first and noblest of human sciences; a science which does more to quicken and invigorate the understanding than all other kinds of learning put together; but it is not apt, except in persons very happily born, to open and to liberate the mind exactly in the same proportion." Burke always believed that nothing sharpened the mind like the study of the law; he therefore cautioned his colleagues in March 1775 not to underestimate the resources of the American colonists, who had bought as many copies of Blackstone's *Commentaries* as the British: "This study [law] renders men acute, inquisitive, dexterous, prompt in attack, ready in defence, full of resources." . . .

Burke's knowledge of the law is most clearly revealed in his innumerable quotations and references to the ancient records, charters, legal treatises, statutes, procedures, and decisions that comprised the common law of England. His understanding of English common law is pertinent in determining his conception of the Natural Law merely as an abstract code of ethics perceived directly by the naked reason. To Burke the spirit of the Natural Law was embodied in the rules of equity that governed English common law, and was transmitted through legal precedents and prescription, particularly through the Constitution. Although Burke by no means identified English common law and the Natural Law, he used his knowledge of both to illuminate their close reciprocal relationship. It is important to know, therefore, how well Burke knew the common law. In 1773 he candidly admitted in parliament: "I have studied, . . . God knows: hard have I studied, even to the making dog-ears of almost every statute book in the kingdom . . . the letter as well as the spirit of the laws, the liberties, and the constitution of this country."[27] . . .

Burke's legal erudition was so well known and respected among his colleagues in the House of Commons, his mastery of English common law was so complete, that he was the fittest man among them to handle the enormous legal problems entailed in the impeachment of Warren Hastings. Nothing but a profound ignorance of Burke's thought and career could have induced Sabine to write that "he was unaware of the relation of his own ideas, or of the system of natural law that he opposed, to the whole intellectual history of modern Europe." Indeed, as an examination of Burke's appeals to the Natural Law will reveal, no British statesman of his time was more aware than he of the relationship between his intellectual inheritance and the Natural Law.

To appreciate fully Burke's appeals to the moral Natural Law in Irish, American, domestic, and Indian affairs, it is necessary to understand the historical conditions and immediate circumstances that called forth his pleas, and to examine the manner in which Burke sought to establish the principles of Natural Law through practical political action. It is generally conceded by historians of all schools of thought that during most of the eighteenth century Ireland was to England as an abject slave to a proud master. Morley has clearly summarized the essential nature of the problem Ireland faced:

> After the suppression of the great rebellion of Tyrconnel by William of Orange, nearly the whole of the land was confiscated, the peasants were made beggars and outlaws, the Penal Laws against the Catholics were enacted and enforced, and the grand reign of Protestant Ascendancy began in all its vileness and completeness. The Protestants and landlords were supreme; the peasants and the Catholics were prostrate in despair. The Revolution brought about in Ireland just the reverse of what it effected in England. Here it delivered the body of the nation from the attempted supremacy of a small sect. There it made a small sect supreme over the body of the nation.[33]

Even in the last decade of the century, after a series of mild reforms, Burke could lament that sectarian differences kept the people of Ireland as much apart as if they were not only separate nations, but separate species. To complicate and intensify the differences in religion and the tyranny of the penal laws, Ireland, like the American colonies at a later date, was subjected to a commercial policy by which England severely restricted her industry and fettered her economic productivity to enrich Bristol and Manchester merchants. The greater part of the people of Ireland lived out their lives in extreme poverty, often without even the elemental necessities of life.

Since Ireland was much weaker than America and closer to England, the abstract "right" of the king and parliament to rule there by arbitrary will was far more successful and tyrannical, and was intensified by differences in religion. Burke observed that in his coronation oath "the king swears he will maintain . . . 'the laws of God.' I suppose it means the natural moral laws." Burke complained, nevertheless, that under

English kings Ireland had suffered "penalties, incapacities, and proscriptions from generation to generation," and was "under a deprivation of all the rights of human nature."[34] Burke summarized the "vicious perfection" of the system by which England deprived her Irish subjects of their natural rights:

> It was a complete system, full of coherence and consistency; well digested and well composed in all its parts. It was a machine of wise and elaborate contrivance; and as well fitted for the oppression, impoverishment, and degradation of a people, and the debasement in them of human nature itself, as ever proceeded from the perverted ingenuity of man.[35]

Those in Britain who wished to rule by arbitrary will found that the best means of depriving the Irish of the rights of nature was to exclude them from the protective benefits of the constitution. Burke objected strongly to this policy:

> Our constitution is not made for great, general, and proscriptive exclusions; sooner or later it will destroy them, or they will destroy the constitution. . . . This way of proscribing men by whole nations as it were, from all the benefits of the constitution to which they were born, I never can believe to be politic or expedient, much less necessary for the existence of any state or church in the world.[36]

The long-standing great political pretexts for exercising arbitrary power were that the Irish people were by nature turbulent, and that the authority of the English state had to be maintained. Burke denied the first charge, and said of the second: "The coercive authority of the state is limited to what is necessary for its existence."[37] This did not include the statutes of persecution against Irish liberty, property, trade, and manufactures, nor the suppression of their education, professions, and religion. "Nothing can be more absurd and dangerous," wrote Burke, "than to tamper with the natural foundations of society in hopes of keeping it up by certain contrivances," and he appealed to Britain to "restore nature to its just rights and policy to its proper order."[38] He agreed with Dr. Johnson in hating England's stern debilitating policy against Ireland, and would have preferred to see the authority of the English government perish rather than be maintained by such iniquity.

Burke knew that the ultimate grounds for persecuting Ireland were religious, and in appealing to the moral Natural Law against the arbitrary will of rulers he defended the religious rights of Ireland's Catholics on the same grounds that he defended the Protestant Dissenters' claims of conscience in the Relief Bill of 1773. At that time Burke invoked "an author who is more spoken of than read, I mean Aristotle," and he applied the Greek philosopher's distinction between power and moral right: "Yes . . . you have the power; but you have not the right" because "this bill is contrary to the eternal laws of right and wrong—laws that ought to bind all men, and above all men legislative assemblies."[39] Burke's attack on the English government's failure in Irish affairs to distinguish between its power and moral rights, implies his belief in the moral Natural Law. Except in Indian affairs, Burke's belief in the Natural Law is perhaps nowhere more explicit than in the **"Tract on the Popery Laws,"** which resulted from his two winters in Dublin, 1761 to 1762 and 1763 to 1764. The time is important, because it shows that the fundamental principles of Burke's political philosophy were fixed in his mind even before he entered British public life. In the **"Tract on the Popery Laws"** the distinction between political power and moral right, between Hobbes's theory of arbitrary will and Cicero's right reason, underscores Burke's strong appeals to the Natural Law:

> It would be hard to point out any error more truly subversive of all the order and beauty, of all the peace and happiness, of human society than the position that any body of men have a right to make what laws they please; or that laws can derive any authority from their institution merely and independent of the quality of the subject-matter. No arguments of policy, reason of state, or preservation of the constitution, can be pleaded in favour of such a practice. They may, indeed, impeach the frame of that constitution; but can never touch this immovable principle. This seems to be, indeed, the principle which Hobbes broached in the last century, and which was then so frequently and so ably refuted. Cicero exclaims with the utmost indignation and contempt against such a notion; he considers it not only as unworthy of a philosopher, but of an illiterate peasant; that of all things this was the most truly absurd, to fancy that the rule of justice was to be taken from the constitutions of commonwealths, or that laws derived their authority from the statutes of the people, the edicts of princes, or the decrees of judges. . . . Everybody is satisfied that a conservation and secure enjoyment of our natural rights is the great and ultimate purpose of civil society; and that therefore all forms whatsoever of government are only good as they are subservient to that purpose to which they are entirely subordinate. Now, to aim at the establishment of any form of government by sacrificing what is the substance of it; to take away, or at least to suspend, the rights of nature . . . is preposterous in argument . . . and cruel in its effect.[40]

The Hobbist theory of sovereignty, that the will of the state is the ultimate measurement of law, is nowhere more false, according to Burke, than in religion:

> Religion, to have any force on men's understandings, indeed to exist at all, must be supposed paramount to laws, and independent for its substance upon any

human institution. Else it would be the absurdest thing in the world; an acknowledged cheat. Religion, therefore, is not believed because the laws have established it; but it is established because the leading part of the community have previously believed it to be true.[41]

In Ireland more than four-fifths of the people adhered to their inherited Catholicism: "This religion, which is so persecuted in its members, is the old religion of the country, and the once established religion of the state." Compared with a claim based on such historical prescription, wrote Burke, "An opinion at once new and persecuting is a monster." The whole of Burke's objection to such religious persecution, based on the theory that arbitrary legislative will, rather than moral Natural Law, is the foundation of social justice, is summarized in one sentence in his **"Tract on the Popery Laws":** "They have no right to make a law prejudicial to the whole community . . . because it would be made against the principle of a superior law, which it is not in the power of any community, or of the whole race of man, to alter.—I mean the will of Him who gave us our nature, and in giving impressed an invariable law upon it."[42] Nothing is more plain than that Burke's defense of religious conscience and freedom in Ireland rests on the moral Natural Law.

Burke applied the same Natural Law principles in attacking the economic restrictions and civil disabilities imposed upon Ireland. For him, the right of holding private property in Ireland, no less than that of following religious conscience, depended not upon the will of any legislators, but was secured "on the solid rock of prescription, the soundest, the most general, and the most recognized title between man and man . . . a title in which not arbitrary institutions, but the eternal order of things gives judgment; a title which is not the creature, but the master, of positive law; a title which . . . is rooted in its principle in the law of nature itself, and is, indeed, the original ground of all known property; for all property in soil will always be traced to that source, and will rest there."[43] The Irish penal laws, which "disabled three-fourths of the inhabitants from acquiring any estate of inheritance for life"; which excluded Catholics from military service, the legal profession, and all public office; which prohibited any private or public education and proscribed the clergy; were a total "depravation of society," and Burke's arguments for their repeal are based throughout on the eternal law of reason and general justice, the moral Natural Law.

Had Burke's utilitarian critics read his **"Tract on the Popery Laws"** with greater care, they would have found that in this early work he expressly rejected the principle that utility is the sole source, test, and ultimate foundation of thought. Although Burke had a principle of utility, he was no utilitarian. He generally gave prior consideration to equity in law, because the necessary legal means of achieving any social end had to be grounded in the moral law before Burke would consider the social consequences. The following passage proves that for him both equity and utility were derived from "the substance of original justice," the moral Natural Law:

> In reality there are two, and only two, foundations of law; and they are both of them conditions without which nothing can give it any force; I mean equity and utility. With respect to the former, it grows out of the great rule of equality, which is grounded upon our common nature, and which Philo, with propriety and beauty, calls the mother of justice. All human laws are, properly speaking, only declaratory; they may alter the mode and application, but have no power over the substance of original justice. The other foundation of law, which is utility, must be understood, not of partial or limited, but of general and public utility, connected in the same manner with, and derived directly from, our rational nature; for any other utility may be the utility of a robber.[44]

To reinforce his assertion that "law is a mode of human action respecting society and must be governed by the same rules of equity which govern every private action," Burke quoted supporting passages from Cicero, Paulus, and Suarez. Throughout his argument the primacy of equity to utility, and the subordination of both to Natural Law, is clearly evident.

Burke confessed that among the first thoughts that crossed his mind on being elected to parliament in 1765 was the hope that he might achieve some measure of justice for his native land. His political career bears out his hope. The affairs of Ireland called forth Burke's powers as a practical statesman on several important occasions, and vitally influenced his own career. Throughout his life Burke maintained a correspondence with Irishmen such as Dr. Leland and Lord Kenmare, whose major interest was religious emancipation, and he wrote private and public letters to Edmund Pery, Thomas Burgh, William Smith, and Sir Hercules Langrishe, all members of the Irish parliament. Burke and Lord Nugent obtained some small commercial favors for Ireland in 1778, and further concessions were made in 1779. Burke was instrumental in drawing up the Savile Act of 1778, which eased restrictions on Catholics in England and became the model for similar legislation in Ireland. In the Parliamentary session of 1779-80, the grievous restrictions on the Irish export trade were repealed, and in 1782 additional economic and religious disabilities were slightly lifted, and greater legislative independence was achieved by the Irish parliament. Burke's part in these reforms was auxiliary to the crisis brought on by the American war, which compelled the English government to conciliate Ireland.

His active attempt to "fix the principles of free trade in all the parts of these islands, as founded in justice, and beneficial to the whole," cost him his Bristol constituency in 1780, but he saw his principle fulfilled in 1785 in Pitt's famous Irish propositions, based on Adam Smith's theory of free trade. The French Revolution provoked yet another crisis in Irish affairs. To the last month of his life Burke labored to prevent Ireland from resorting to Jacobin principles of revolution. His lifelong struggle to extend the benefits of equal citizenship to Ireland under the British constitution is an important practical manifestation of his belief that Natural Law supplied the ethical norms of every just society.

In practically every discussion of Burke's part in American colonial affairs, it has been the universal opinion of positivist scholars that against George III's claim of an abstract right to tax the colonies, Burke took his stand almost completely on the principle of utilitarian expediency, and that therefore he rejected all belief in "natural rights" based on moral Natural Law.[45] Burke certainly did attack the metaphysical abstract "right" of taxation assumed by Townshend, Grenville, and Lord North, and his own words reveal precisely how far "expediency" applied in his attack:

> I shall not now enquire into the right of Great Britain to tax her colonies; all that is lawful is not expedient, and I believe the inexpediency of taxing our colonies, even supposing it to be lawful, is now evident to every man.[46]

> I am resolved this day to have nothing at all to do with the question of the right of taxation. . . . I put it totally out of the question. . . . I do not examine, whether the giving away a man's money be a power excepted and reserved out of the general trust of government; and how far all mankind, in all forms of polity, are entitled to an exercise of that right by the charter of nature. Or whether, on the contrary, a right of taxation is necessarily involved in the general principle of legislation, and inseparable from the ordinary supreme power. These are deep questions, where great names militate against each other; where reason is perplexed; and an appeal to authorities only thickens the confusion. For high and reverend authorities lift up their heads on both sides; and there is no sure footing in the middle. This point is the "great Serbonian bog, betwixt Damiata and Mount Casius old, where armies whole have sunk." I do not intend to be overwhelmed in that bog, though in such respectable company.[47]

The first passage reveals that expediency was an important practical element in Burke's attack, while the second shows that Burke believed in the existence of rights under "the charter of nature," but that out of fear of a useless quarrel in metaphysics, he did not wish to discuss the American problem in terms of abstract rights. Nothing could be more false than the conclusion of Morley and the "respectable company" of critics who have followed him that these passages prove Burke made expediency the complete antithesis of natural rights, that he rested his case on expediency and therefore denied all belief in Natural Law. Later we shall see that Burke's "expediency" is not the expediency of the utilitarian calculator, but a manifestation of practical moral prudence, which is not contrary to the Natural Law, but an essential part of its practical fulfillment.

Certainly the American colonies never considered it merely inexpedient to be taxed without their legislative consent. To them, as to Burke, the abstract "right" of taxation without representation was positively unjust. It was a constant threat to or actual violation of their property rights, and the attempt to enforce unjust taxation resulted in threats to their lives and liberty under the British constitution which they, like Burke, believed was founded on Natural Law:

> It is the glory of the British Prince and the happiness of all his subjects that their constitution hath its foundation in the immutable laws of nature; and as the supreme legislature, as well as the supreme executive, derives its authority from that constitution, it should seem that no laws can be made or executed which are repugnant to any essential law of nature.[48]

This memorable appeal to Natural Law was spoken by James Otis in 1768. Whereas the colonists, in their petitions of grievances, came more and more to appeal directly to the Natural Law, Burke's appeals were almost always indirect, through the British constitution, which was for him merely the practical and specific means of guaranteeing the rights of moral Natural Law throughout the empire. "Our constitution," Burke said in parliament, "was a provident system, formed of several bodies, for securing the rights, the liberties, the persons and the properties of the people."[49] In both domestic and American affairs Burke felt that George III and his ministers, in trying to make the power of the crown supreme, had placed their arbitrary will above the constitution and therefore had violated the sovereignty of Natural Law. "The same baneful influence," said Burke in 1770, "under which this country is governed, is extended to our fellow sufferers in America; the constitutional rights of Englishmen are invaded" and the "unalienable rights of their constituents" are defeated by "ministerial requisitions that are altogether arbitrary and unjust."[50] In February 1772, Burke said in parliament: "When tyranny is extreme, and abuses of government intolerable, men resort to the rights of nature to shake it off."[51] Burke regretted and opposed the arbitrary principles and policies of parliament, and favored the American cause not because the colonists had an abstract right to rebel against British rule, as

Tom Paine and Dr. Price had argued, but because the British parliament had imprudently invoked its sovereign power as an abstract right to tax and rule the colonists by arbitrary decrees, and above all, because the king and parliament were themselves in rebellion against rules of prudence in the Natural Law by their denial of the colonists' civil rights under the constitution.

Burke believed that constitutional liberty in England would stand or fall upon the outcome of the struggle with America; that if the British government succeeded in destroying liberty abroad, English citizens would soon have none at home. In March 1775, he said: "In order to prove that the Americans have no right to their liberties, we are every day endeavouring to subvert the maxims which preserve the whole spirit of our own."[52] Before seeing how the king's "oppressive stretches of power" in America were paralleled in Britain, it will be useful to summarize Burke's reactions to the arbitrary decrees passed against the colonies. In March 1774, the Boston Port Bill was passed, taking away the city's trade and in effect revoking its charter. Burke promptly attacked it: "I call this bill unjust, for is it not fundamentally unjust to prevent the parties who have offended from being heard in their own defence? Justice . . . is not to be measured by geographical lines nor distances." Such an act, he added in private, is "the doctrine of devils"; it is "contrary to the nature of man and the nature of things." "Franchises," he continued, "are for the preservation of men's liberties, properties, and lives. . . . It is bad to take away a charter; it is worse to take away a city." Such a "proscription of whole cities and provinces is to take away from them benefits of nature, . . . deprive them of their civil privilege, and . . . strip them of their judicial rights."

When the bill was extended to all New England, Burke again objected: "You sentence . . . to famine at least 300,000 people in two provinces, at the mere arbitrary will and pleasure of two men." In short, these acts of parliament toward America "take away the rights of men" and prove that when power becomes arbitrary, when legislative authority is placed above constitutional and Natural law, "a man may be regulated out of his liberty, his property and his life."[53] As with British rule in Ireland, Burke charged that in her American policy Britain was "endeavouring to invert the order of nature," and that her claimed "right" to rule the colonies by arbitrary decrees was totally opposed to the British constitution and Natural Law.

Burke's practical endeavors to restrict the arbitrary powers of the king and to preserve civil liberty in America are among the best-known episodes of his political career. Almost from the moment he entered parliament in 1765 he was absorbed in American affairs, and as the intellectual guide and manager of the

Rockingham Whigs he did more than any other man to make his colleagues and the British public aware of the fatal course they were following. The one measure of tax relief enjoyed by America in the decade before the Revolution was passed by the short-lived Rockingham administration of 1766, which repealed Grenville's odious Stamp Act. It was on this occasion that Burke, in his first appearance in the House of Commons, revealed his political greatness. On 9 March 1766, Dr. Johnson wrote of Burke's initial speech: "He has gained more reputation than perhaps any man at his first appearance ever gained before. He made two speeches in the House for repealing the Stamp Act, which were publicly commended by Mr. Pitt, and have filled the town with wonder. Mr. Burke is a great man by nature, and is expected soon to attain civil greatness."[54]

From 1766 until the conclusion of hostilities with America Burke continued to fill the political world with wonder. In pamphlets such as his early masterpiece *Thoughts on the Cause of the Present Discontents* (1770), in parliamentary speeches such as his *Speech on Conciliation* (1775), and in public essays such as his *Letter to the Sheriffs of Bristol* (1777), he struggled to maintain the natural rights of Americans under English constitutional law. In 1771 Burke became the agent in parliament for the colony of New York. Through this post he acquired a complete mastery of details and knowledge of the civil temper of the colonists, which he utilized throughout his exposition of constitutional and Natural Law principles. Burke's writings on American affairs received Morley's unqualified admiration: "It is no exaggeration to say that they compose the most perfect manual in our literature, or any literature, for one who approaches the study of public affairs, whether for knowledge or for practice."[55] Despite the eloquence and wisdom of Burke's efforts on America's behalf, he did not succeed in convincing the British public that great empires can best endure when grounded upon the solid foundation of constitutional and Natural Law. The principles Burke taught were learned from the bitter lessons of history; afterwards, his words remained as a constant reminder and depository of political wisdom for those who were to rule the British Empire in the nineteenth century.

In the spring of 1768 began the first great domestic constitutional issue to arise after Burke entered parliament—the Wilkes affair. In 1764 John Wilkes had been convicted of publishing an inflammatory pamphlet, the famous *North Briton,* number forty-five, but he had fled to France to escape sentence. Wilkes returned to England in 1768 and was elected to the House of Commons for Middlesex, but before he took his seat the court sent him to prison on his old conviction. In November 1768, Wilkes appeared before the House to plead his innocence and to be admitted as a member, but the House voted 219 to 136 to expel him. Wilkes was elected twice more for Middlesex and each time

was immediately voted out of the House. When he was elected for the fourth time, the House of Commons, over the opposition of the Middlesex freeholders' petition, ordered that Wilkes's defeated opponent, Colonel Luttrell, be declared elected and seated. In "the rights of election invaded in Middlesex," and in the king's refusal to grant redress to the freeholders' petition, Burke saw a deep threat to free elections under the constitution:

> I stand up to . . . bear my testimony to its injustice, as well as to its inexpediency; to support the unquestionable birthright of the British subject, and to defend the sanctity of our laws. . . . They [the London freeholders] could neither prostitute their parts nor their principles to the arbitrary fiat of an all-directing favourite. . . . Till the sacred right of election, wrested from their hands, filled the freeholders of Great Britain with universal apprehension for their liberties, they never disturbed the royal repose with their complaints. . . . By what rule, then, does the majority of this House square its conduct, when it acts in direct opposition to the majority of the people? . . . That the people should not choose their own representatives, is a saying that shakes the constitution. . . . The question amounts to this, whether you mean to be a legal tribunal, or an arbitrary and despotic assembly. . . . The substance of the question is, to put bounds to your own power by the rules and principles of law.[56]

Burke knew that given good reason the House had the right to expel a member, but it had no constitutional authority to alter the election results, nor to seat the defeated candidate. For the Commons to declare any elected member unworthy at its arbitrary discretion "is to corrupt judicature into legislature." Burke drew out the logical implication in the Commons' claim: "Whatever it decides is de jure law." He then concluded; "Nobody will, I hope, assert this, because the direct consequence would be the entire extinction of the difference between true and false judgments. For if the judgment makes the law, and not the law directs the judgment, it is impossible there should be such a thing as an illegal judgment given."[57] The main thesis of a theory of sovereignty based on will rather than on law is that a de facto judgment is de jure law, and Burke's opposition to the king and Commons in the Wilkes affair proves that he did not believe a law was good because government willed it, but that government was morally obliged to will only that which was good. The ethical code of the Natural Law and the legal traditions of the English constitution provided Burke with the normative standards of what government should or should not will.

The most important domestic constitutional issue during the last three decades of the eighteenth century was the growing popular agitation for a shorter duration of parliaments and a greater extension of the franchise. Nothing so illustrates Burke's veneration of the British constitution as a prescriptive instrument perfectly suited to fulfill the functions of just government as his refusal to set aside experience in favor of radical innovation. "The great object of most of these reformers," Burke declared on 7 May 1782, "is to prepare the destruction of the constitution, by disgracing and discrediting the House of Commons." He noted that by far the largest segment of these reformers made their plea "in the nature of a claim of right, on the supposed rights of man as man." In a highly significant passage, Burke analyzed the claim that personal representation in government is a natural right:

> They who plead an absolute right cannot be satisfied with anything short of personal representation, because all *natural* rights must be the rights of individuals, as by *nature* there is no such thing as politic or corporate personality; all these ideas are mere fictions of law, they are creatures of voluntary institution; men as men are individuals, and nothing else. They, therefore, who reject the principle of natural and personal representation are essentially and eternally at variance with those who claim it. As to the first sort of reformers, it is ridiculous to talk to them of the British constitution upon any or upon all of its bases; for they lay it down that every man ought to govern himself, and that, where he cannot go, himself, he must send his representative; that all other government is usurpation, and in so far from having a claim to our obedience, it is not only our right, but our duty, to resist it. Nine tenths of the reformers argue thus—that is, on the natural right.[58]

In attacking the reformers' claim that personal representation is a natural right, Burke was not rejecting the natural rights of the classical and Scholastic moral Natural Law, as so many scholars have supposed; he was merely denying one of the many false and arbitrary claims put forth during the eighteenth century in the name of natural right. Burke also was distinguishing between *civil* and *natural* rights, not in order to reject natural rights, as MacCunn supposed, but to show that the franchise belongs to the civil order. The franchise was a derivative right, not of man as man, but of man as citizen. The conditions under which it was exercised were determined by the constitution and the civil conventions of any given society. Therefore, the reformers' claim of an abstract right of representation, paramount to the constitution itself, was a revolutionary innovation. As the English constitution was itself based upon traditional Natural Law, Burke's attack on the false claims of revolutionary natural rights was a direct defense of the prescriptive English constitution and an indirect defense of the traditional Natural Law.

Burke's most cherished belief concerning the British constitution was that it was the largest national legal frame of reference for judging Englishmen's political behavior, and that it was derived from and in harmony with the moral Natural Law. In his criticism of Pitt's Regency Bill (1790), he asserted that in the hierarchy of moral and legal values, the constitution stood just below the Natural Law: "The framers of it [Pitt's bill] first proceeded to a violation of precedents, next to a violation of law, then to a violation of the constitution, and now they had arrived at a climax of violence; a violation of the law of nature." The greatest single right of nature that the constitution sought to protect was that of life: "As self-preservation in the individuals is the first law of nature, the same will prevail in societies." And again: "Defence is the natural right of man,—nay, the first of all his rights, and which comprehends them all."[59] From the absolute natural right to life Burke derived those civil rights that were necessary and convenient to men's social existence, particularly liberty and property, and these in turn were the basis of other lesser civil rights, such as protection from libel: "Undoubtedly the good name of every man ought to be under the protection of the law, as well as his life, and liberty and property." The highly whimsical English laws on libel, Burke thought, should be made to reflect more closely the spirit of the moral Natural Law: "It is high time to fix the law in such manner as to resemble, as it ought, the great Author of all law, in whom there is no variableness nor shadow of turning."[60] The British constitution established the basic rights of nature, and all derived civil rights, by protecting all people equally from the encroachments of arbitrary power. As Burke said, it set limits to power by saying to rulers and ruled alike, "Thus far shalt thou go, and no farther."

Burke's eulogy of the British constitution reveals it as the great bulwark guarding the traditional moral and legal rights of individuals against arbitrary power:

> The constitution . . . says to an encroaching prerogative, your sceptre has its length, you cannot add an hair to your head, or a gem to your crown, but what an eternal law has given to it. Here it says to an overweening peerage,—your pride finds banks that it cannot overflow: here to a tumultuous and giddy people,—there is a bound to the raging sea. Our constitution is like our island, which uses and restrains its subject sea; in vain the waves roar. In that constitution I know, and exultingly I feel, both that I am free, and that I am not free dangerously to myself or to others. I know that no power on earth, acting as I ought to do, can touch my life, my liberty, or my property.[61]

Therefore, the constitution was necessarily opposed to *all* claims to absolute or arbitrary power, whether that of the king against the colonies, the lords against the people, the Commons against Wilkes, or such advocates of popular power as Tom Paine, Dr. Price, and Dr. Priestley against constituted limited monarchy. Nor did it make any difference to Burke that any of these persons or groups claimed such power by an appeal to abstract rights, as did both George III and Paine. "Strict right," said Burke, "must necessarily be arbitrary, and could admit of no modification." As in Irish and American affairs, Burke sought to limit arbitrary power in England's domestic and constitutional conflicts, so that the basic natural rights to life, liberty, and property under the moral Natural Law would be maintained. The whole issue in Burke's objective is contained in one sentence: "Arbitrary power . . . is a subversion of natural justice, a violation of the inherent rights of mankind."[62]

No connection has ever been noted between Burke's views on economics and his belief in the Natural Law. In his **Letter to a Noble Lord** Burke confessed that he had studied "political economy" from early youth to the end of his service in parliament, but as economics was a new subject he never acquired a fully developed theory of it. Most scholars, following a strong hint from Adam Smith, have claimed that Burke simply believed in the laissez faire principles of Smith's *Wealth of Nations* (1776),[63] while Halévy and Laski thought they found utilitarianism at the heart of Burke's economic principles.[64] Burke certainly adhered to three vital and closely related principles in Smith's theory—free trade, the "natural identity of interests," and the passive or negative function of the state in individual economic relationships—but it is nonsense to claim from this that Burke was a Benthamite in economics. Bentham was indeed the logical heir of Smith's theory, but Burke's understanding of these three principles, centered in the Natural Law, was vitally different from that of Bentham and even to some extent from Smith himself.

In Burke's thought, free trade was not based upon utility but on justice. "But that to which I attached myself the most particularly," Burke declared, "was to fix *the principle* of a free trade in all the ports of these islands, as founded in justice, and beneficial to the whole." To Burke justice was the foundation and social utility was the consequence of free trade, a position the reverse of Bentham's utilitarianism. Burke attacked the "zealots of the sect of regulation" not on utilitarian grounds, or because he believed in the natural goodness of man in economic affairs, but because natural justice took precedence in economic liberty over any restraints or controls imposed by the state. Burke favored a large measure of personal liberty in economics, a full use of the natural faculties that God has given to all people. In Indian affairs he came to see the need of state intervention because personal liberty had been converted by the East India Company agents into a limitless avarice. But there was a clear distinction between necessary legal regulation and arbitrary suppression of trade. The East India Company confounded being morally controlled with being legally suppressed, and criticized Burke as an enemy of free trade;

Burke's Bristol constituents defended the suppression of Irish trade as necessary control, and rejected Burke's argument for free trade.

To appreciate Burke's position toward India and Ireland, and to see how his economic principles were consistently centered in moral Natural Law, it is necessary to understand his conception of wealth. He rejected totally the Rousseauist theory, shared by Bentham and some of his Bristol constituents, that wealth was limited in quantity, that the enrichment of one person or nation necessarily impoverished others:

> I know that it is but too natural for us to see our own *certain* ruin in the *possible* prosperity of other people. It is hard to persuade us that everything which is *got* by another is not *taken* from ourselves. But it is fit that we should get the better of these suggestions, which come from what is not the best and soundest part of our nature, and that we should form to ourselves a way of thinking more rational, more just, and more religious. Trade is not a limited thing; as if the objects of our mutual demand and consumption could not stretch beyond the bounds of our jealousies. God has given the earth to the children of men, and He has undoubtedly, in giving it to them, given them what is abundantly sufficient for all their exigencies; not a scanty, but a most liberal, provision for them all. The Author of our nature has written it strongly in that nature, and has promulgated the same law in His written word, that man shall eat his bread by his labor; and I am persuaded that no man, and no combination of men, for their own ideas of their particular profit, can, without great impiety, undertake to say that he shall not do so—that they have no sort of right either to prevent the labor or to withhold the bread.[65]

In economic affairs Burke posited a faith in God's providential nature toward man; the ultimate foundation of Burke's economic theory rests not in any human contrivances but in the moral Natural Law.

There is no doubt that Burke believed in a divinely directed "natural" identity of self-interests and social benevolence in economic affairs: "The benign and wise Disposer of all things . . . obliges men, whether they will or not, in pursuing their own selfish interests, to connect the general good with their own individual success."[66] Yet he was not an optimistic economic determinist; he was simply more convinced than most that in economic affairs the power of human reason and will is strongly circumscribed by both physical and moral Natural Laws. Because God has established "the nature of things with which we shall in vain contend," in economic self-fulfillment human institutions play a role secondary to nature:

> To provide for us in our necessities is not in the power of government. It would be vain presumption in statesmen to think they can do it. The people

maintain them, and not they the people. It is in the power of government to prevent much evil; it can do very little positive good in this, or perhaps in anything else.[67]

Burke certainly knew that political power is very important in regulating human affairs, that it is the final court of practical appeal in disputes, but he also understood that "the nature of things is a sturdy adversary," that fixed created conditions of environment and resources had far more to do with determining economic happiness or misery than any human contrivances. As he said in the **Reflections,** "I do not like to compliment the contrivances of men with what is due in a great degree to the bounty of Providence." This distinction, habitually ignored by rationalists, was obscured in the economic crisis that struck Britain in 1794 and 1795, and which called forth various "projects" to manipulate the economy. To combat these schemes Burke wrote **"Thoughts and Details on Scarcity"** (1795), in which he explicitly stated his belief that economics rests upon Natural Law:

> We, the people, ought to be made sensible, that it is not in breaking the laws of commerce, which are the laws of nature, and consequently the laws of God, that we are to place our hope of softening the Divine displeasure to remove any calamity under which we suffer.[68]

God's reason and will, which Burke called "the law of laws and the sovereign of sovereigns," applies in economics as in everything, and Burke believed that man's part in fulfilling a sound economy was clearly subordinated to the moral Natural Law.

Burke's speeches in Indian affairs reveal his legal erudition at its best and also provide the clearest expression of the Natural Law in his political philosophy. Burke was actively concerned in the affairs of India from at least 21 March 1780, when he spoke on the renewal of the East India Company's charter, until 23 April 1795, when Hastings was acquitted. His first important appeal to the Natural Law occurred on 1 December 1783, in his speech supporting Fox's East India bill. "This bill," Burke said, was "intended to form the Magna Charta of Hindostan," yet he noted that those who opposed it did so on the grounds "that the bill is an attack on the chartered rights of men."[69] Here, for the first of several times in Indian affairs, he made a vital distinction between what he considered the true natural rights derived from the classical and Scholastic Natural Law, and false or arbitrary claims to abstract rights. Because the word "rights" was an abstraction, and subject to various interpretations, Burke approached his problem semantically. "The phrase of 'the chartered rights of men,'" he noted, "is very unusual in the discussion of privileges conferred by charters of the present description." All previous charters, he continued, such as those of King John and Henry III, "may, without any deceitful ambiguity, be very fitly called *the chartered rights of men*," because they are merely written documents expressly recognizing the sanctity of the Natural Law, to which all public measures should conform:

> The rights of men, that is to say, the natural rights of mankind, are, indeed, sacred things; and if any public measure is proved mischievously to affect them, the objection ought to be fatal to that measure, even if no charter at all could be set up against it. If these natural rights are further affirmed and declared by express covenants, if they are clearly defined and secured against chicane, against power and authority, by written instruments and positive engagements, they are in a still better condition: They partake not only of the sanctity of the object so secured, but of that solemn public faith itself, which secures an object of such importance. Indeed, this formal recognition, by the sovereign power, of an original right in the subject, can never be subverted, but by rooting up the holding radical principles of government, and even of society itself.[70]

But, Burke remarked, "the charter of the East India Company" is "formed on principles the *very reverse* of those of the great charter." He elaborates this crucial point:

> Magna Charta is a charter to restrain power, and to destroy monopoly. The East India charter is a charter to establish monopoly, and to create power. Political power and commercial monopoly are *not* the rights of men; and the rights of them derived from charter, it is fallacious and sophistical to call "the chartered rights of men." These chartered rights . . . do at least suspend the natural rights of mankind at large; and in their very frame and constitution, are liable to fall into a direct violation of them.[71]

If the East India Company had governed in India "under the control of the sovereign imperial discretion, and with the due observance of the natural and local law," Burke would have opposed revoking its charter. But the company refused to recognize the Natural Law and the local laws of India, which guaranteed the natives' rights; it insisted that the charter granted by parliament left its officials free to govern India as they saw fit. The company, Burke concluded, had violated its "subordinate derivative trust," had "notoriously, grossly abused" its power; parliament could not stand by in total indifference to the moral law, nor make a sale of its duties, but should adopt Fox's bill and "provide a real chartered security for the *rights of men* cruelly violated under that charter."[72] For Burke the issue was of conflicting claims to sovereignty, and his choice is clear: "If I kept faith . . . with the Company," he said, "I must break the faith, the covenant, the solemn, original, indispensable oath, in which I am bound, by the eternal frame and constitution of things, to the whole human race." Burke's eloquent appeal to the natural rights of traditional Natural Law enabled him, in his first great attack on abuses in India, to transcend the commercial and national powers that sacrificed men's rights to a narrow self-interest.

In February 1785, two years after Fox's bill had been rejected in the House of Lords, Burke made his famous speech exposing the hoax of the Nabob of Arcot's debts.[73] There is only one appeal to nature in this long speech, but it is an explicit defense of the enduring character of moral Natural Law:

> The benefits of heaven to any community ought never to be connected with political arrangements, or made to depend on the personal conduct of princes. . . . The means of subsistence of mankind should be as immutable as the laws of nature, let power and dominion take what course they may.[74]

In a short speech in March 1787 Burke made a general protest against those in parliament who wished to obstruct Hastings's impeachment: "I rise in support of the eternal principles of truth and justice, and those who cannot or dare not support them are endeavouring to cough them down." Hastings had a small group of powerful friends, most of whom were skilled lawyers, and they succeeded in throwing up an endless series of legal impediments to keep the impeachment from coming to an issue. "The greatest obstruction of all," Burke lamented, "proceeded from the body of the law. There was no body of men for whom he entertained a greater respect. . . . For the profession itself he felt a degree of veneration, approaching almost to idolatry." However, when the lawyers among the opposition tried to invalidate the impeachment by dissolving parliament, Burke protested: "These gentlemen of the law, driving us from law to law, would, in the end, leave us no law at all." As Burke wrote to Dundas in December 1787, these obstructions were further complicated because "all the local knowledge of India is in the hands of the person prosecuted by the House of Commons," and Hastings had suppressed or destroyed the main sources of information. Burke secured a large body of detailed evidence on India from Philip Francis, Hastings's mortal enemy and prejudiced accuser, and also from the records of the India House. But as manager of the impeachment Burke took his stand against Hastings mainly on the Natural Law, and Hastings himself supplied him with material for his most severe indictments.

Burke made it clear that Hastings's defense ultimately rested on the argument that he had the right to rule India through arbitrary power. Hastings claimed this right on two accounts; first, because parliament, through the East India Company, had granted him unlimited power to rule in India, and second, as Burke summarized him, because "the whole history of Asia is nothing more than precedents to prove the invariable exercise of arbitrary power."[75] Throughout his impeachment speeches Burke frequently reminded his hearers of Hastings's claim:

> Mr. Hastings comes before you. . . . He says, "I had arbitrary power to exercise, and I exercised it. Slaves I found the people, slaves they are; they are so by their constitution; I did not make it for them; I was unfortunately bound to exercise it, and I did exercise it. . . ." In India, to use the words of Mr. Hastings, the power of the sovereign was everything, the rights of the people nothing. . . . The prisoner . . . assumes to exercise a power which extended to the property, liberty, and life of the subject. . . . He makes the corrupt practices of mankind the principles of his government; he collects together the vicious examples of all the robbers and plunderers of Asia, forms the mass of their abuses into a code, and calls it the duty of a British governor.[76]

As manager for the prosecution, Burke saw that he was obliged to destroy Hastings's assumption that sovereignty rested solely in a governor's arbitrary will, a principle that totally contradicted the ethical norms of Natural Law.

Burke's most extended and eloquent attack on Hastings's claim of arbitrary power, made on 16 February 1788, derives wholly from his ardent faith in Natural Law:

> Will you ever hear the rights of mankind made subservient to the practice of government? It will be your lordships' duty and joy—it will be your pride and triumph, to teach men, that they are to conform their practice to principles, and not to derive their principles from the wicked, corrupt, and abominable practices of any man whatever. Where is the man that ever before dared to mention the practice of all the villains, of all the notorious depredators, as his justification? To gather up, and put it all into one code, and call it the duty of a British governor? I believe so audacious a thing was never before attempted by man. "He had arbitrary power!" My lords, no man can govern himself by his own will; much less can he be governed by the will of others. We are all born—high as well as low—governors as well as governed—in subjection to one great, immutable, pre-existing law, a law prior to all our devices and all our conspiracies, paramount to our feelings, by which we are connected in the eternal frame of the universe, and out of which we cannot stir. This great law does not arise from our combinations and compacts; on the contrary, it gives to them all the sanction they can have. Every good and perfect gift is of God: all power is of God; and He who has given the power, and from whom alone it originates, will never suffer it to be corrupted. Therefore, my lords, if this be true—if this great gift of government be the greatest and best that was ever given by God to mankind, will he suffer it to be the plaything of man, who would place his own feeble

and ridiculous will on the throne of divine justice? It is not to be overturned by conquest; for by conquest, which is the more immediate designation of the hand of God, the conqueror succeeds to that alone which belonged to the sovereign before him. He cannot have absolute power by succession; he cannot have it by compact; for the people cannot covenant themselves out of their duty to their rights. . . .[77]

The whole of Burke's argument against Hastings's theory of sovereignty is contained in a few aphorisms infused with the Natural Law: "Law and arbitrary power are at eternal hostility. . . . We should be brought back to our original situation; we should be made to know ourselves as men born under law. He that would substitute will in the place of law is a public enemy to the world. . . . Against law, no power can be set up." "There never was a man who thought he had no law but his own will, who did not also find that he had no ends but his own profit."[78] To Burke, who maintained that since the introduction of the Roman law into Britain "the law of nature and nations (always a part of the law of England) came to be cultivated," nothing could be more destructive of the ethical norms necessary for a just society than Hastings's theory of sovereignty based upon arbitrary will.

Hastings's claim that arbitrary power was the normal mode of rule in Asia implied that there was no universal law of just conduct on essential principles, as taught by the moral Natural Law. Burke emphatically rejected such a contention:

> This gentleman has formed a geographical morality, by which the duties of men in public and private stations are not to be governed by their relation to the great Governor of the universe, and by their relation to one another, but by climates. After you have crossed the equinoxal line, all the virtues die. . . . Against this geographical morality I do protest, and declare therefore, that Mr. Hastings shall not screen himself under it, because . . . the laws of morality are the same everywhere; and actions that are stamped with the character of peculation, extortion, oppression, and barbarity in England, are so in Asia, and the world over.[79]

Burke's great sympathy for the people of India was only exceeded by his fear that Hastings's friends, in defending him, would introduce his "Eastern" principles into England: "The doctrine that in the East there are no laws, no rights, no liberties, is a doctrine which has not only been stated by the prisoner at the bar, but has been disseminated with a wicked activity throughout this country." Burke valued his public services in Indian affairs above anything else in his political career, because in addition to his primary aim of bringing Hastings to justice and reclaiming national honor, he wished to destroy the corrupting influence against the constitution that the English nabobs had come to

exercise in parliament. Although Hastings was acquitted and later came to be held in high honor, Burke purified parliament of Hastings's Eastern morality and raised the moral level of British colonial policy abroad. These larger derivative consequences of Hastings's trial were enormously important in preserving Britain's constitutional liberty and colonial supremacy.

To disprove Hastings's contention that basic morality varied in time and place, Burke read widely in Oriental jurisprudence. He read the Koran, the Shasta, and the Heyada; he quoted Tamerlane's *Institutes,* recently translated by Major Davy, Hastings's former secretary; he used Joseph White's translations of the *Institutes of Timour* (Oxford, 1783), and Jean Baptiste Tavernier's *Travels into Persia and the East Indies* (1677). Burke placed the results of his reading before the House of Lords: "The morality of the East, my lords, as far as respects governors, is as pure as our own. . . . Mr. Hastings finds no authority for his practice, either in the Koran or in the Gentoo law. . . . The same laws, the same sacredness of principle, however they may be disobeyed, both in Europe and in Asia, are held and strictly maintained." Burke finally concluded:

> Mr. Hastings has no refuge—let him run from law to law; let him fly from common law, and the sacred institutions of the country in which he was born; let him fly from acts of parliament; . . . still the Mohammedan law condemns him. . . . Let him fly where he will—from law to law—law, thank God, meets him everywhere—arbitrary power cannot secure him against law; and I would as soon have him tried on the Koran, or any other eastern code of laws, as on the common law of this kingdom.[80]

Against Hastings's theory of geographical morality and arbitrary power, Burke set the traditional conception of moral Natural Law, and like all of his predecessors back to Aristotle he insisted that its imperative ethical norms are universally valid.

Since Hastings's acts were, in Burke's words, "crimes . . . against those eternal laws of justice which you [the judges] are assembled here to assert," it was necessary for his prosecutors to follow "rules drawn from the fountain of justice," and to condemn him in terms of the eternal Natural Law. "I impeach him," said Burke, "in the name and by the virtue of those eternal laws of justice, which ought equally to pervade every age, condition, rank, and situation in the world." Burke believed that the function of courts of law was to reflect through human institutions the spirit of the divine Natural Law: "Courts of justice were links of that great chain of which the first and great link was Divine Justice." Despite the fact that many parts of Burke's speeches were reported in the third person, and give only an approximate idea of his principles and argument, nothing is clearer than that the appeal to Natural Law is at the heart of his impeachment of Hastings:

> Mr. Burke next entered into a disquisition upon the nature of government, of which we lament our inability to give an adequate idea; but we will endeavour . . . to give the general scope of his reasoning. He first laid it down as a general principle, that all law and all sovereignty were derived from Heaven; for if the laws of every nation, from the most simple and social of the most barbarous people, up to the wisest and most salutary laws of the most refined and enlightened societies, from the Divine laws handed down to us in Holy Writ, down to the meanest forms of earthly institution, were attentively examined, they would be found to breathe but one spirit, one principle, equal distributive justice between man and man, and the protection of one individual from the encroachments of the rest. The universality of this principle proved its origin. Out of this principle laws arose, for the execution of which sovereignty was established; and all, viz. that principle, those laws, and that sovereignty, were thus evidently derived from God. . . . If, then, laws and sovereignty were sacred, as being the gift of God for the benefit of the people; and if the laws and sovereignty of India were, as he contended them to be, founded upon the same principle of universal justice, then Mr. Hastings, as a British governor, sent, not to conquer or extirpate, but to preserve and cherish, was bound to protect the people of that country in the use of those laws, and shield that sovereignty from encroachment or usurpation.[81]

Since the East India Company was a state in the disguise of a merchant, Burke's strictures on Hastings's violations of Natural Law principles and sovereignty were doubly significant, because he believed that above all other men legislators stood in the place of God and were accountable to him in the practical uses of political power, and were therefore most bound by the moral dictates of the Natural Law. To understand the deepest implications to Burke's political philosophy in his life-long devotion to the Natural Law, one must examine his reaction to the French Revolution.

In 1769, exactly two decades before the French Revolution, Burke had predicted in his *Observations on "The Present State of the Nation"* that the chronically desperate financial condition of France would culminate in "some extraordinary convulsion" that would shake the whole system of government and would have a tremendous effect on all Europe. In 1789 Burke was the first public man in Britain to realize that the revolution was far more than an alteration in the government of France. He wrote to his son in November 1792 that the revolution was "an event which has nothing to match it, or in the least to resemble it, in history." He felt that the revolution violated "the whole system of policy on which the general state of Europe has hitherto stood," that the revolutionists tried to make

themselves "paramount to every known principle of public law in Europe," and that they sought to establish "principles subversive of the whole political, civil, and religious system of Europe." In 1796 Burke summarized his impressions of the strange and powerful effect the revolution had produced on men's imaginations; he found it "a vast, tremendous, unformed spectre" that "subdued the fortitude of man," and went "straight forward to its end, unappaled by peril, unchecked by remorse, despising all common maxims and all common means." For Burke 1789 was "a revolution in dogma"; it was "a total departure . . . from every one of the ideas and usages, religious, legal, moral, or social, of this civilized world."[82] So catastrophic was the French Revolution that it compelled him, against his will and temperament, to become a political theorist in defense of the traditional principles of civilized society, among which the Natural Law held a preeminent position.

Throughout Burke's writings on French revolutionary affairs, more often than not his belief in the Natural Law was implicitly assumed, and supplied the spirit that permeates all of his references to God and discussions of religion, society, church, and state, the nature of the social contract, political sovereignty, and the security of private and corporate liberty and property. It is too frequently forgotten that Burke's initial response to the French Revolution," revealed in October 1789 in his "Letter to M. Depont on the French Revolution," was warm-hearted, cautious, and friendly.[83] In this letter Burke expressed his unwillingness to form a positive opinion upon matters with which he was imperfectly acquainted. He agreed with his young friend's hope that the French deserved liberty, and stated that if, under the new order of things, law is made paramount to will, if prescriptive rights to life, liberty, and property are maintained, if civil liberty is regarded as a human birthright rather than the reward of merit or industry, as something inherent in man rather than a favor granted from the state, or a subject for endless metaphysical speculations about political power and social systems, he would look with favor upon the revolution.[84]

True liberty, Burke cautioned, is "not solitary, unconnected, individual, selfish liberty, as if every man was to regulate the whole of his conduct by his own will." Such "liberty" was but another name for arbitrary power, such as George III and the British parliament had claimed over the colonies, or Hastings over India, and Burke knew it could not be reconciled to civil liberty under Natural Law. Like Aristotle, Burke believed man was by nature a social and political animal, so that true liberty must be "social freedom," a condition that required restriction on raw will and prevented anyone from exercising arbitrary power. Such liberty, said Burke to his young friend, was but another name for justice, and was consonant with the supremacy of

Natural Law, of right reason over the "dangerous dominion of will." If in France he found that "the citizen . . . is in a perfect state of legal security with regard to his life, to his property, to the uncontrolled disposal of his person," he would share the general joy in such a reformation.

Burke's hope for France lasted less than four months. Before the beginning of 1790 Jacobin doctrinaire radicalism had begun its attacks on religion, private property, and traditional political and legal institutions. Events across the channel gradually convinced Burke that the revolutionists had no respect for the classical and Scholastic tradition of Natural Law, which was the whole foundation of civil society in all Europe. In place of Natural Law legal principles, such as that prescription formed the best claim to property, the revolutionists invoked egalitarian speculations centered in the abstract "rights of man" to sanction the arbitrary seizure of corporate and private property. When Englishmen professed to admire these French methods of reform, Burke assumed the offensive against the revolution. An occasion presented itself on 9 February 1790 during the debates on estimates for the army, for Burke to attack the violations of property in France:

> They . . . laid the ax to the root of all property, and consequently of all national prosperity, by the principles they established, and the example they set. . . . They made and recorded a sort of *institute* and *digest* of anarchy, called the rights of man, in such a pedantic abuse of elementary principles as would have disgraced boys at school.[85]

As Burke's great object was to warn his compatriots against the principles and example of the French, his speech on the army estimates revealed in miniature the essential argument he was to follow in his struggle to maintain the principles of traditional Natural Law against the revolutionary "natural rights" of France. Although many scholars have failed to grasp this fundamental distinction between traditional Natural Law and revolutionary natural rights, Burke understood the distinction perfectly and left no doubt that the basis of his attacks on the revolutionists was that they violated the Natural Law: "They are naturally pointed out, not by their having rebelled against the state, as a state, but by their having rebelled against the law of nature, and outraged man as man."[86] Burke wrote this sentence in October 1793, and it may be taken as the touchstone in all that he wrote of French affairs, from February 1790 through his posthumous *Fourth Letter on a Regicide Peace* (1797).

Although the Natural Law is most explicitly stated in Burke's writings on Irish and Indian affairs, its tacit assumption and intense moral spirit is clearly evident throughout his most famous work, the *Reflections on the Revolution in France,* which appeared in November 1790. Before considering Burke's subtle appeals to the Natural Law in the *Reflections,* the historical importance of this great work should be understood. Alfred Cobban did not exaggerate in calling the *Reflections* "the greatest and most influential political pamphlet ever written." If we consider only Burke's immediate practical intention, to warn against French revolutionary principles and to exalt a Christian and Natural Law conception of civil society, the *Reflections* was the most successful book of the eighteenth-century Enlightenment, and it was almost totally opposed to the prevailing spirit of the age.

So clearly and eloquently did Burke analyze the basic issues and social theories raised by the revolution, that the people of Britain were almost immediately divided into two distinct groups for or against it.[87] The first British edition sold 12,000 copies in the first month; in less than a year there were eleven editions, and by 1796 over 30,000 official copies had been sold. For that era, when a book was circulated among many readers and was frequently read to large public groups, this was a phenomenal achievement. So remarkable was the immediate effect of the *Reflections* that it became the focal point for all private and public discussions of the revolution. Wilberforce, the ardent advocate of emancipation for slaves, praised Burke as the man who "had stood between the living and the dead until the plague was stayed."[88] Reynolds and Gibbon greatly admired the *Reflections,* the latter writing of it: "Burke's book is an admirable medicine against the French disease. I admire his eloquence; I approve his politics; I adore his chivalry; and I can almost forgive his reverence for church establishments."[89] Of course the king said in public that it was "a very good book" that "every gentleman ought to read." In November 1796, Earl Fitzwilliam wrote to Burke and estimated the practical effect his *Reflections* and other writings on French affairs had produced in Britain: "You, my dear Burke, by the exertion of your great powers, have carried three-fourths of the public. . . . Your labours . . . have produced an effect in the country beyond expectation."[90] The French translation, reputed to have been done in part by the imprisoned Louis XVI, enjoyed an even greater contemporary triumph throughout Europe.[91] Letters of congratulations were sent to Burke by Catherine the Great of Russia and King Stanislas of Poland. For over a century and a half the *Reflections* has been used extensively in dealing with the French Revolution, and it remains as great a source of political wisdom as when it first appeared.

Among the revolutionists in France, Burke was of course strongly denounced. Mirabeau, who had visited Burke at Beaconsfield, spoke warmly against the *Reflections* in the National Assembly, and Jean Baptiste Cloots, the eccentric Prussian Jacobin, sent Burke an ironic invitation to France: "Quittez votre île, mon cher

Burke; venez en France, si vous voulez jouir du plus magnifique spectacle dont l'entendement du philosophe puisse être frappé."[92] As Morley noted, when the fourteenth edition of the *Reflections* appeared, Romilly "wondered whether Burke was not rather ashamed of his success." In Britain the immediate political consequence of Burke's book was a sharp split in the Whig party. Burke assumed the unofficial leadership of the anti-revolutionary Whig minority, while Fox and Sheridan, his lifelong political friends, headed the Whig majority. Their differences were hotly debated through many issues on the floor of parliament, and came to a climax on 21 April 1791, when Burke solemnly renounced Fox's friendship.

Within three years Burke's eloquence and the dire events in France that he had predicted with such amazing accuracy had drawn most of the nation and Fox's supporters to Burke's side. But as Edmond Malone noted in May 1794, personal animosities continued unabated: "We are now so distracted by party there [at the Literary Club], in consequence of Burke and Windham, and I might add the whole nation, being on one side, and Fox and his little phalanx on the other, that we in general keep as clear of politics as we can."[93] If such friction existed among Burke's friends, one may well understand the intense revulsion provoked by the *Reflections* among English radical admirers of the revolution. Such well-known reforming zealots as Dr. Price, Dr. Priestley, the Godwins, Mrs. Catherine Macaulay Graham, and Thomas Paine—as well as the more moderate Mackintosh, George Rous, and Earl Stanhope—savagely attacked his work. In addition there were "replies" from many obscure pamphleteers, such as Joel Barlow, William Belsham, Sir Brooke Boothby, Benjamin Bousfield, Thomas Broome, Thomas Cooper, Norman MacLeod, Charles Pigott, Major John Scott, the political agent of Hastings, Thomas Spence, Francis Stone, Joseph Towers, Mark Wilks, David Williams, and Christopher Wyvill. Exclusive of the many anonymous tracts published by the various radical clubs, there were at least four hundred "replies" and several defenses of the *Reflections*.[94] Burke's book was the center of perhaps the greatest debate ever carried on in English over first principles in politics, and a careful reading of the *Reflections* will reveal that he took his stand on the ground of Aristotle, Cicero, St. Thomas Aquinas, and the traditional conception of the Natural Law.

Burke's appeals to the Natural Law in Indian affairs demonstrated his belief that all persons are born "in subjection to one great, immutable, pre-existing law, a law . . . paramount to our feelings, by which we are connected in the eternal frame of the universe. . . ." The rest of this passage revealed that implicit in man's connection with this immutable law is a conception of divine contract. "This great law does not arise from our combinations and compacts," Burke wrote, but "on the contrary, it gives to them all the sanction they can have." In effect he said that God contracted with himself never to be unjust to man. Thus, the Natural Law was the moral standard in all human contracts. This conception of a divine contract and of the ethical norm of Natural Law underscored Burke's statement in Indian affairs that the greatest and best gift of God to man was government, for the state was the necessary means by which people could live according to the Natural Law. In Burke's *Reflections* all of these ideas are to be found more fully developed in his conception of the social contract.

To Burke, man's relationship to civil society is a moral necessity; it cannot be voluntaristic, for that would exalt will above right reason; nothing could be more false and wicked than the Lockian theory of a voluntary and revocable social contract based upon a hypothetical state of nature. The moral primacy and binding necessity of the Natural Law, as the true basis of the social contract, has never been more eloquently expressed, even by Cicero, than in the *Reflections*:

> Society is indeed a contract. Subordinate contracts for objects of mere occasional interest may be dissolved at pleasure but the state ought not to be considered as nothing better than a partnership agreement in a trade of pepper and coffee, calico or tobacco . . . to be taken up for a little temporary interest, and to be dissolved by the fancy of the parties. It is to be looked on with other reverence; because it is not a partnership in things subservient only to the gross animal existence of a temporary and perishable nature. It is a partnership in all science; a partnership in all art; a partnership in every virtue, and in all perfection. As the ends of such a partnership cannot be obtained in many generations, it becomes a partnership not only between those who are living, but between those who are living, those who are dead, and those who are to be born. Each contract of each particular state is but a clause in the great primaeval contract of eternal society, linking the lower with the higher natures, connecting the visible and invisible world, according to a fixed compact sanctioned by the inviolable oath which holds all physical and all moral natures, each in their appointed place. This law is not subject to the will of those who by an obligation above them, and infinitely superior, are bound to submit their will to that law. The municipal corporations of that universal kingdom are not morally at liberty at their pleasure, and on their speculation of a contingent improvement, wholly to separate and tear asunder the bands of their subordinate community, and to dissolve it into an unsocial, uncivil, unconnected chaos of elementary principles. It is the first and supreme necessity only, a necessity that is not chosen, but chooses, a necessity paramount to deliberation, that admits no discussion, and demands no evidence, which alone can justify a resort to anarchy. This necessity is no exception to the rule; because this necessity itself is

a part of that moral and physical disposition of things, to which man must be obedient by consent or force: but if that which is only submission to necessity should be made the object of choice, the law is broken, nature is disobeyed, and the rebellious are outlawed, cast forth, and exiled, from this world of reason, and order, and peace, and virtue, and fruitful penitence, into the antagonist world of madness, discord, vice, confusion, and unavailing sorrow.[95]

This vital passage contains in essence all that Burke said about the social contract throughout many parts of his **Reflections**. It reveals his belief in a transcendent moral duty beyond all will or power, a duty imposed by the "primaeval contract" of God's "inviolable oath," binding man through the Natural Law to his civil obligations. "The great ruling principle of the moral and natural world," said Burke, is not "a mere invention to keep the vulgar in obedience." He clearly agreed with Pufendorf's principle that "by the observance of *Natural Law,* it must be supposed that God laid an obligation on man to obey this *law,* as a *means* not arising from Human invention or changeable at Human pleasure."[96] Burke regarded the Natural Law as a divinely ordained imperative ethical norm that, without consulting man, fixed forever his moral duties in civil society.

Throughout the **Reflections** the spirit of the Natural Law and Burke's conception of the divine contract that binds all men appears in various forms—in his discussions of the English constitution, in his principle of political sovereignty, in his idea that civil liberty is an inheritance and private property is secured by prescription, and above all, in his conception of the divine and social functions of church and state. He states that Britain's "constitutional policy" works "after the pattern of nature" and that her "political system is placed in a just correspondence and symmetry with the order of the world" and is held together "by the disposition of a stupendous wisdom, moulding together the great mysterious incorporation of the human race. . . ." By "preserving the method of nature in the conduct of the state," deliberation is made "a matter not of choice, but of necessity," and political justice is thus secured.[97]

Even more explicitly than in Indian affairs Burke insists in the **Reflections** on the divine origin of the state: "He who gave our nature to be perfected by our virtue, willed also the necessary means of its perfection.—He willed therefore the state.—He willed its connection with the source and original archetype of all perfection."[98] Indeed, church and state are for Burke but two aspects of the same thing—God-given instruments to bring people to their highest spiritual and social perfection, through which they become united to the Godhead: "Every sort of moral, every sort of civil, every sort of politic institution, aiding the rational and

natural ties that connect the human understanding and affections to the divine, are not more than necessary, in order to build up that wonderful structure, Man." Through the church, Burke continues, the state is consecrated, "that all who administer in the government of men, in which they stand in the person of God himself, should have high and worthy notions of their function and destination." Clearly, his conception of the divine contract in human affairs implies that all power is a divine trust: "All persons possessing any portion of power ought to be strongly and awfully impressed with an idea that they act in trust; and that they are to account for their conduct in that trust to the one great Master, Author, and Founder of society. . . . Power . . . to be legitimate must be according to that eternal, immutable law, in which will and reason are the same."[99] The belief that power is a divine trust is evident in Burke's conception of the function of church and state; it reappears throughout his extensive discussions of political sovereignty.

In Burke's discussions of Irish affairs, he regarded prescription in property rights as one of the great derived principles of Natural Law. In 1772 he had said in parliament: "If the principle of prescription be not a constitution of positive law, but a principle of natural equity, then to hold it out against any man is not doing him injustice."[100] In the **Reflections** he repeated this principle: "By the laws of nature, the occupant and subduer of the soil is the true proprietor; there is no prescription against nature."[101] But the revolutionists in the National Assembly, through their false conception of natural rights, declared that all property was usurped that was not held on terms consistent with man's "original" nature. Their contention overturned legal prescription as the basis of ownership:

> With the National Assembly of France, possession is nothing, law and usage are nothing. I see the National Assembly openly reprobate the doctrine of prescription, which one of the greatest of their own lawyers [Domat] tells us, with great truth, is a part of the law of nature. He tells us, that the positive ascertainment of its limits, and its security from invasion, were among the causes for which civil society itself has been instituted. If prescription be once shaken, no species of property is secure, when it once becomes an object large enough to tempt the cupidity of indigent power. I see a practice perfectly correspondent to their contempt of this great fundamental part of natural law.[102]

The National Assembly, said Burke, left nothing but their own arbitrary pleasure to determine what property was to be protected and what subverted. He admitted that he saw no reason why landed estates could not be held otherwise than by inheritance. In opposing the wholesale confiscations of church lands in France, Burke warned his countrymen against the example established by the National Assembly in its violation of the Natural Law:

> I hope we shall never be so totally lost to all sense of the duties imposed upon us by the law of social union, as, upon any pretext of public service, to confiscate the goods of a single unoffending citizen. Who but a tyrant . . . could think of seizing on the property of men, unaccused, unheard, untried, by whole descriptions, by hundreds and thousands together?[103]

To Burke one of the great means of fulfilling the Natural Law was through prescription, which maintained the law of social union by protecting the private property of men and institutions.

It is not necessary here to go into the negative side of Burke's appeals to the Natural Law, centered in his attacks on the revolutionary "rights of man." It is sufficient to note than in the *Reflections* he explicitly distinguished between the false, revolutionary, abstract rights of man and the specific valid natural rights of traditional Natural Law: "Far am I from denying in theory, full as far is my heart from withholding in practice (if I were of power to give or to withhold,) the *real* rights of men. In denying their false claims of right, I do not mean to injure those which are real, and are such as their pretended rights would totally destroy."[104]

What are the *real* natural rights of man? Burke agreed with his predecessors in the classical and Scholastic Natural Law tradition that the protection of life, liberty, and property constituted the most fundamental human rights. But more than perhaps any other Natural Law thinker, Burke insisted upon the concrete realization of man's natural rights in civil society, through the incorporation of basic moral principles in constitutional law. He therefore rejected totally, even for illustrative purposes, the Hobbist and Lockian hypothesis of a pre-civil "state of nature," maintaining that a veil was thrown over the origins of civil society and that "men cannot enjoy the rights of an uncivil and of a civil state together." He was profoundly skeptical of all logical arguments based upon abstract mathematical reasoning, maintaining that "in politics the most fallacious of all things was geometrical demonstration."[105] Since "government is not made in virtue of natural rights, which may and do exist in total independence of it," Burke believed there was no use of discussing a man's abstract right to food or medicine. The abstract perfection and clarity that could be established through mathematical reasoning concerning such a "right" was its practical defect in civil society, where the farmer and the physician, not the professor of metaphysics, would determine the means of procuring food and administering medicine.

Burke always refused to treat moral and political questions of rights as materials for a speculative and theo-retical science:

> These metaphysical rights entering into common life, like rays of light which pierce into a dense medium, are, *by the laws of nature,* refracted from their straight line. Indeed, in the gross and complicated mass of human passions and concerns, the primitive rights of men undergo such a variety of refractions and reflections, that it becomes absurd to talk of them as if they continued in the simplicity of their original direction.[106]

To Burke the fulfillment of natural rights is determined by political prudence, as set by the limits of man's fallible nature and the variety of circumstances found in every civil society. The Natural Law itself decrees that people recognize the variety of conditions under which life exists. Since man in every state is by nature a political animal, the real human natural rights are a matter of practical political prudence, and are to be found only within the objectives and conventions of civil society.

In the *Reflections,* among people's natural and derivative civil rights in civil society, Burke included all the advantages that accrue by virtue of civil society being established. Specifically, he noted the right to justice under law, and the rights of all to the fruits of their industry and to the means of making their industry fruitful. All people were entitled by right "to the acquisitions of their parents; to the nourishment and improvement of their offspring; to instruction in life, and to consolation in death. Whatever each man can separately do, without trespassing upon others, he has a right to do for himself; and he has a right to a fair portion of all which society, with all its combinations of skill and force, can do in his favor."[107] Burke distinguished between equity as the basis of common rights within a range of social conditions, and that fictitious "equality" that would reduce all people to the same status. He refused to separate considerations of rights from social circumstances, or to define real rights in any abstract terms: "The rights of men are in a sort of *middle,* incapable of definition, but not impossible to be discerned. The rights of men in governments are their advantages; and these are often in balances between differences of good; in compromises sometimes between good and evil, and sometimes between evil and evil."[108] Moral prudence was the principle by which Burke believed the true natural rights of people in civil society could best be realized.

Practically everything that Burke wrote in the *Reflections* about the divine contract, Natural Law, and natural rights, about prescription, civil liberty, political sovereignty, and church and state; is either assumed or restated with variations throughout his other writings on French affairs. His famous attack on Rousseau's sensibility in *A Letter to a Member of the National*

Assembly (January 1791) was prefigured in the *Reflections,* and embodies Burke's conviction that unrestrained emotion implies an intuitive and voluntaristic conception of moral duty contrary to the "right reason" of Natural Law. His sequel to the *Reflections, An Appeal from the New to the Old Whigs* (July 1791), contains an exposition of his faith in a divine contract, and of the moral duties it imposes upon man, second in importance only to his declaration in the *Reflections:*

> I allow, that if no supreme ruler exists, wise to form, and potent to enforce, the moral law, there is no sanction to any contract, virtual or even actual, against the will of prevalent power. On that hypothesis, let any set of men be strong enough to set their duties at defiance, and they cease to be duties any longer. . . . The awful Author of our being is the Author of our place in the order of existence; and . . . having disposed and marshalled us by a divine tactic, not according to our will, but according to his, he has, in and by that disposition, virtually subjected us to act the part which belongs to the place assigned us. We have obligations to mankind at large, which are not in consequence of any special voluntary pact. They arise from the relation of man to man, and the relation of man to God, which relations are not matters of choice. On the contrary, the force of all the pacts which we enter into with any particular person or number of persons amongst mankind, depends upon these prior obligations. In some cases the subordinate relations are voluntary, in others they are necessary—but the duties are all compulsive. . . . Dark and inscrutable are the ways by which we come into the world. The instincts which give rise to this mysterious process of nature are not of our making. But out of physical causes, unknown to us, perhaps unknowable, arise moral duties, which, as we are able perfectly to comprehend, we are bound indispensably to perform.[109]

This important passage reaffirms and extends Burke's belief in the Natural Law principle that God is the ultimate source of all law and duty, and that the validity of every human contract depends upon the divinely established moral law that all people are obliged to obey.

Beginning with his *Thoughts on French Affairs* (December 1791), Burke became more and more concerned with the international relations between revolutionary France and her neighbors, and with the problem of maintaining a balance of power in Europe. His appeals to the law of nations are a vital part of his belief in the Natural Law. But his primary concern continued to be England, and all that he wrote in the last five years of his life reflected his fear that French revolutionary principles would be accepted by the English. When the enormously wealthy Duke of Bedford declared his approval of the French Revolution, with its confisca-

tions of inherited landed estates, Burke immediately perceived the irony and in *A Letter to a Noble Lord* (1796) invoked prescription to save the duke from his own folly:

> The Duke of Bedford will stand as long as prescriptive law endures: as long as the great stable laws of property, common to us with all civilized nations, are kept in their integrity. . . . The whole revolutionary system, institutes, digest, code, novels, text, gloss, comment, are not only not the same, but they are the very reverse . . . fundamentally, of all the laws on which civil life has hitherto been upheld in all the governments of the world. The learned professors of the rights of man regard prescription, not as a title to bar all claim, set up against all possession—but they look on prescription as itself a bar against the possessor and proprietor. They hold an immemorial possession to be no more than a long-continued, and therefore an aggravated injustice.[110]

In his *Letters on a Regicide Peace* (1796-1797), the whole revolutionary legal system of the French Jacobins was attacked as a violation of prescription, of the established sovereignty of independent nations, and even of the Natural Law itself:

> They made, not law, not conventions, not late possession, but physical nature, and political convenience, the sole foundation of their claims. . . . With them it is not for the states of Europe to judge of their title: the very reverse. In their eye the title of every other power depends wholly on their pleasure. . . . It is a declaration not made in consequence of any prescription on her side, not on any cession or dereliction . . . of other powers. . . . In other words, their will is the law, not only at home, but as to the concerns of every nation. . . . Without the least ceremony or compliment, they have sent out of the world whole sets of laws and lawgivers. They have swept away the very constitutions under which the legislators acted, and the laws were made. Even the fundamental sacred rights of man they have not scrupled to profane. They have set this holy code at nought with ignomiony and scorn. Thus they treat all their domestic laws and constitutions, and even what they had considered as a law of nature; but whatever they have put their seal on for the purpose of their ambition, and the ruin of their neighbours, this alone is unvulnerable, impassible, immortal.[111]

Burke's attack on arbitrary power or will as an alternative to the Natural Law forms the dominant theme of his *Letters on a Regicide Peace:* "It appears as if the contract that renovates the world was under no law at all." "As to the right of men to act anywhere according to their pleasure, without any moral tie, no such right exists." "The law of this their empire is anything rather than the public law of Europe." "This strong hand is the law, and the sole law, in their state."[112]

When the revolutionists, under the slogan "the rights of man," seized Savoy, Burke remarked ironically in parliament: "This gentle people, in adding the country of their neighbors to their own dominions, only follow the mild laws of nature.[113] In contrast to the new order in France, wrote Burke, the institutions of the Holy Roman Empire had long taught "the great, the rich, and the powerful . . . to submit their necks to the imperial laws, and to those of nature and of nations."[114] The Jacobins exalted arbitrary will above the ethical norms of Natural Law because they would "not acknowledge the existence of God as a moral governor of the world."[115] This is what is behind Burke's extensive and violent attacks on the *philosophes* and the Jacobins' "atheism by establishment." To Burke the moral Natural Law was so basic to the ancient inherited social order of Europe that its subversion was enough proof that the revolution was the most extensive project ever launched against all religion, law, property, and real civil order and liberty.

Before drawing any conclusion concerning Burke's appeals to the Natural Law, it is worth noting a significant development that occurred in his relationship with James Mackintosh. Among the many "replies" that the *Reflections* provoked was Mackintosh's *Vindiciae Gallicae,* which appeared in April 1791. Between the time of his reply and Burke's death in 1797, Mackintosh experienced a slow, reluctant, painful disillusionment in the French Revolution, similar to that which overtook Wordsworth, Coleridge, Southey, and many other ardent youths. Mackintosh's disillusionment was intensified by the partisan triumph he had enjoyed over Burke with his *Vindiciae Gallicae.* William Hazlitt testified in *The Spirit of the Age* to the popularity and esteem with which Mackintosh's book was received: "It was cried up by the partisans of the new school, as a work superior in the charms of composition to this undoubted rival: in acuteness, depth, and soundness of reasoning, of course there was supposed to be no comparison." Soon after its publication Burke wrote to his friend Dr. Laurence: "I have not read, or even seen Mackintosh;—but Richard tells me that it is Paine at bottom; and that indeed all the writers against me are, either Paines, with some difference in the way of stating, or even myself."[116] Richard Burke's report to his father was not strictly accurate. Mackintosh's work was really a mixture of Paine's natural rights theory and the current utilitarianism; it was an intelligent and liberal "new" Whig expression of the glowing optimism and widespread hope that the revolution had inspired up to April 1791. Burke must have read Mackintosh some time afterwards, because in December 1792 he complained in the House of Commons that Sheridan, like "Mr. Mackintosh and other writers of less eminence" garbled him by "taking a detached passage without explaining it by what followed or went before it." Orally and in print, Burke and Mackintosh continued their war of words during the three or four years following the French Revolution.

Even more than Burke's writings, events across the channel caused Mackintosh gradually to modify his original enthusiasm for the Revolution. When the first three of Burke's *Letters on a Regicide Peace* appeared late in 1796, Burke was pleasantly suprised to note the grave decorum, candor, and moderation with which the Scotsman criticized his work in letters to the *Monthly Review* for November and December 1796. Mackintosh met Dr. Laurence in London and they discussed a possible meeting between Burke and his young critic. From Beaconsfield Burke wrote to Dr. Laurence early in December and expressed some ambivalent feelings about the apparent change in Mackintosh's political views:

> I forgot to speak to you about Mackintosh's supposed conversion. I suspect by his letter, that it does not extend beyond the interior politics of this island, but that, with regard to France and many other countries, he remains as frank a Jacobin as ever. This conversion is none at all; but we must nurse up these nothings, and think these negatives advantages as we can have them. Such as he is, I shall not be displeased if you bring him down.[117]

Burke arranged through Dr. Laurence to have Mackintosh visit him during Christmas 1796. According to Hazlitt, who had a strong animus against Burke's interpretation of the French Revolution, the Scotsman was drawn wholly into Burke's political orbit and became an obsequious satellite: "He sent an invitation to the writer to see him; and in the course of three days' animated discussion of such subjects, Mr. Mackintosh became a convert not merely to the graces and gravity of Mr. Burke's style, but to the liberality of his views, and the solidity of his opinions.—The Lincoln's Inn Lectures were the fruit of this interview."[118] Hazlitt attributed the "sudden and violent change in Sir James' views and opinions" to his "personal interview" with Burke. Before their meeting Burke's doubts concerning Mackintosh's recantation were centered in the Scotsman's view of international relations. It is therefore significant that the first series of Mackintosh's thirty-nine "Lincoln's Inn Lectures," which resulted from his discussions with Burke, were called *A Discourse on the Law of Nature and Nations* (London, 1799). In this work Mackintosh's original utilitarianism was wholly abated, and he attacked as "fanciful chimeras" the utopian aspirations of the revolutionary doctrines of equality, based upon the rights of man. At the same time he appealed frequently to Burke and to such ancient proponents of the classical natural Law as Aristotle and Cicero. In contrast to his *Vindiciae Gallicae,* in which he had praised Hobbes for introducing the method of mathematics in political reasoning, Mackintosh made much of moral prudence in his second book and revealed great skepticism toward abstract speculations. Undoubtedly Burke was not the sole cause of all these important changes in Mackintosh's political principles. But there is incontrovertible evidence that Mackintosh's lectures owed much to Burke; through his *A Discourse on the Law of Nature and Nations,* Burke's mighty spirit, like Caesar at Philippi, still walked abroad in triumph after death.

The most serious error in the interpretation of Burke's political philosophy and practical career in parliament has been the general failure to perceive his full and lifelong acceptance of the classical and Scholastic conception of the moral Natural Law. Utilitarian and positivist critics, who made no distinction between the ethical norms of traditional Natural Law and the revolutionary eighteenth century "rights of man" doctrines derived from a supposed state of nature, accepted Burke's attacks on abstract rights as a rejection of the Natural Law, and claimed him as a conservative utilitarian. Yet Burke had an encyclopedic knowledge of the tradition of Natural Law in Western thought, and of the common law in England, which is saturated with the spirit of Natural Law. What is more, by Natural Law he always meant essentially the same thing, and he applied it as the ultimate test of justice and liberty in all human affairs. As a practical statesman he feared abstractions and was reluctant to take his mind from concrete political problems. But to Burke no *moral* problem was ever an *abstract* question; therefore, he conceived of statecraft as the practical application in concrete human affairs of primary moral principles, clearly evident to man's right reason. It is in this vital sense that the Natural Law is implicitly affirmed in all of Burke's great parliamentary concerns.

Generally, Burke was content to fulfill the Natural Law indirectly, through the concrete constitutional, legal, and political instruments of the state. But when the state itself was corrupted from its true function, and became the instrument of arbitrary tyranny and injustice, as in the penal code against Ireland, the rule of Hastings in India, and of the revolutionists in France, Burke's appeals to the Natural Law became explicit. In its relative simplicity as a code of ethical principles, and in its enormous complexity in practical application, the Natural Law absorbed Burke's whole intellectual and emotional nature. It was so deeply rooted in him, so refined through his sensitive temperament, that even when it was not explicitly mentioned it appeared as his basic instinct and conviction. The Natural Law was his moral anchor, securing him to the most vital and enduring religious and political traditions of Europe from ancient times to his own era.

Burke's faith in the Natural Law supplied the religious spirit that infuses his entire political philosophy. He was the foremost modern Christian humanist in politics because he saw the world and the nature of man through the revelations of Christianity and the right reason of Natural Law. His world of right reason and nature was the Stoical world of Aristotle and Cicero and the Christian world of St. Thomas Aquinas and Hooker, and not the Cartesian rationalistic world of eighteenth-century nature, based upon mathematical science and Locke's empirical-rational philosophy, and systematized into an optimistic deism or pantheism. Burke's vision of reality was not centered in natural science, in the cosmos, or in the visible world of physical things, but in the divinely created and humanly developed world of people, the transfigured and complex world of civil institutions, with its laws and customs, its art and corporate wisdom, its invisible tissue of loyalties and prejudices, all of which gave cohesion and concreteness to the divine contract, which connected man in the eternal frame of the universe. Man was essentially a religious and political being, born in subjection to one great, immutable, preexistent law; his primary duty as citizen and statesman was to determine, obey, and promote in civil society the divine law ordained by God for his spiritual and temporal benefit. Only by accepting the supernatural or natural laws of God, and the divinely given instruments of civil society, could men and women flourish and bring themselves to that degree of perfection that gave them an exalted yet subordinate place in the creation.

Notes

[27] Burke, *Speeches,* vol. 1, p. 172. . . .

[33] Morley, *Burke,* pp. 22-23. See also pp. 24-27.

[34] See Burke, "A Letter to Sir Hercules Langrishe," pp. 311, 315. Hereinafter this will be cited as "Letter to Langrishe." See also Burke, "On the Penal Laws Against Irish Catholics," p. 289. Hereinafter this will be cited as "Laws Against Irish Catholics."

[35] Burke, "Letter to Langrishe," p. 343. For a detailed account of this English system of persecution, see Morley, *Edmund Burke: A Historical Study,* pp. 180-86, 191-93.

[36] Burke, "Letter to Langrishe," pp. 305, 317. See also pp. 303-307, 319, 331-38. See also Burke, "Tract on the Popery Laws," p. 24. Hereinafter this will be cited as "Popery Laws."

[37] Burke, "Popery Laws," p. 34.

[38] Ibid., pp. 48, 45.

[39] Burke, *Speeches,* vol. 1, p. 151. See also p. 328. Yet as in American affairs, Burke rested the practical side of his case for Ireland on moral prudence rather than on abstract right: "I do not put the thing on a question of right" ("Letter to Langrishe," p. 334).

[40] Burke, "Popery Laws," pp. 21-22, 29-30. To enforce this appeal to Natural Law Burke quoted Cicero's *De legibus.*

[41] Burke, "Popery Laws," pp. 32-33.

[42] Ibid., p. 21.

[43] Burke, *A Letter to Richard Burke,* p. 80. See also "Letter to Langrishe," p. 324.

[44] Burke, "Popery Laws," p. 22.

[45] For example, see Morley, *Edmund Burke: A Historical Study,* pp. 135-52.

[46] Burke, *Speeches,* vol. 1, p. 20. This idea recurs frequently in Burke's speeches on American affairs.

[47] Ibid., pp. 303-304.

[48] House of Representatives of Massachusetts to Conway, Feb. 13, 1768, in Almon, *Prior Documents,* pp. 181-82.

[49] Burke, *Speeches,* vol. 4, p. 136. See also vol. 1, pp. 214, 237, 257.

[50] Ibid., vol. 1, pp. 16-17. See also p. 327. The king had so corrupted the House of Commons, Burke lamented, that "the ground and pillar of freedom is . . . held up only by the treacherous underpinning and clumsy buttresses of arbitrary power" (p. 195).

[51] Ibid., p. 110. See also p. 111.

[52] Ibid., p. 295. See also pp. 20, 298.

[53] For these passages see respectively Burke, *Speeches,* vol. 1, pp. 176, 233; *Correspondence,* vol. 4, Appendix, pp. 493, 474, 476-77, 488-89, 490-93; *Speeches,* vol. 1, p. 270; and *Correspondence,* vol. 4, Appendix, p. 495.

[54] Boswell, *Life of Samuel Johnson* (New York: Dutton, 1949), vol. 1, p. 320.

[55] Morley, *Burke,* p. 81.

[56] Burke, *Speeches,* vol. 1, pp. 35-37, 70-74. See also pp. 75-76, 79.

[57] Ibid., p. 78.

[58] Burke, *Speech on the Reform of Representation in the House of Commons,* p. 145.

[59] Burke, *Speeches,* vol. 3, p. 414; vol. 4, pp. 57, 66.

[60] Ibid., vol. 1, pp. 84, 88.

[61] Ibid., vol. 3, p. 360. See also p. 51.

[62] Burke, *Correspondence,* vol. 4, p. 463.

[63] See Dixon Wecter, "Adam Smith and Burke," *Notes and Queries,* 174 (30 April 1938): 310-11; Alfred Cobban, *Edmund Burke and the Revolt Against the Eighteenth Century* (London, 1929), pp. 189-97; William C. Dunn, "Adam Smith and Edmund Burke; Complementary Contemporaries," *The Southern Economic Journal,* 7 (January 1941), pp. 330-46.

[64] Halévy, *The Growth of Philosophic Radicalism,* pp. 230-31 and *passim;* Harold Laski, *Political Thought in England from Locke to Bentham* (New York: Henry Holt, 1920), p. 236.

[65] Burke, *Two Letters to Gentlemen in Bristol,* pp. 51-52.

[66] Burke, "Thoughts and Details on Scarcity," p. 89. Hereinafter this will be cited as "Thoughts on Scarcity." See also pp. 92, 107-108. See also *Letters on a Regicide Peace,* pp. 315-16. Hereinafter this work will be cited as *Regicide Peace.* See also "A Second Letter to Sir Hercules Langrishe," p. 58.

[67] Ibid., p. 83.

[68] Ibid., p. 100.

[69] Burke, *Speeches,* vol. 2, pp. 409; 413.

[70] Ibid., p. 410.

[71] Ibid. A fragment on monopoly found among Burke's papers is worth noting here: "'Monopoly' is contrary to 'Natural Right.' Monopoly is the power . . . of exclusive dealing in a commodity . . . which others might supply if not prevented by that power. No monopoly can, therefore, be prescribed in; because contrary to common right. . . . The State, representing all its individuals, may contract for them; and therefore may grant a monopoly" (*Correspondence,* vol. 4, Appendix, p. 459; see also pp. 460-62; *Speeches,* vol. 4, p. 310).

[72] Ibid., pp. 412-13. See also pp. 428, 476, 478, 486-87, 490.

[73] For a good account of this fraud, see Morley, *Edmund Burke: A Historical Study,* pp. 205-207.

[74] Burke, *Speeches,* vol. 3, p. 162. See also p. 163. This passage may be interpreted as a reference to *physical* rather than *moral* laws of nature, in which case

the reference is merely an analogy.

[75] Ibid., vol. 4, p. 356. See also p. 357; *Speeches,* vol. 2, pp. 446-47; vol. 3, p. 66.

[76] Ibid., pp. 354, 472, 479, 367. In securing absolute rule, Burke noted that Hastings acted on a principle of sovereignty centered in power alone: "He declares that in a division between him and the Nabob 'the strongest must decide.'" (*Speeches,* vol. 2, p. 434). The same applied in divisions with England: "Here Mr. Burke read from parts of the defence of Mr. Hastings, passages, stating, that whenever he thought the laws of England militated against the interests of the Company, he was at liberty to violate them" (*Speeches,* vol. 4, pp. 476-77).

[77] Ibid., pp. 357-58.

[78] Ibid., pp. 374-75. For other examples in Indian affairs of Burke's attack on the theory of sovereignty based upon arbitrary power, see *Speeches,* vol. 2, pp. 429, 431-32, 434, 446-47, 460, 473, 475-76; vol. 3, pp. 57, 68, 74, 86, 99, 175-76, 223-25, 266, 280; and vol. 4, pp. 307, 313, 328, 354-63, 368, 374-75, 475-76, 478-79, 489-91, 499.

[79] Ibid., vol. 4, p. 354.

[80] Ibid., pp. 366-67. See also p. 481.

[81] Ibid., p. 477.

[82] See Burke, *Correspondence,* vol. 4, p. 24, Appendix, pp. 519, 544, 547. See also *Regicide Peace,* pp. 155, 215.

[83] For the various theories concerning M. Depont's identity, see Thomas Copeland, *Our Eminent Friend Edmund Burke* (New Haven: Yale University Press, 1949), pp. 190-245. Professor Copeland subsequently retracted his theory.

[84] See Burke, *Correspondence,* vol. 3, pp. 102-121, especially pp. 107-17.

[85] Burke, *Speech on the Army Estimates,* p. 275. See also pp. 276-78. Burke's italics.

[86] Burke, *The Policy of the Allies,* p. 453.

[87] For the division of public opinion between Burke and his opponents, see Samuel Bernstein, "English Reactions to the French Revolution," *Science and Society,* 9, no. 2 (1945), pp. 147-71.

[88] William Wilberforce, *Diary* (London, 1897), vol. 1, p. 284.

[89] Quoted by James Prior, *Life of the Rt. Hon. Edmund Burke,* 5th ed. (London: Henry G. Bohn, 1854), p. 315.

[90] Burke, *Correspondence,* vol. 4, pp. 356, 359.

[91] "Le succès de cette publication avait été immense; trente mille exemplaires s'étaient vendues dans une seule année, et tous les peuples de l'Europe avaient pu lire cette oeuvre remarquable, traduite dans toutes les langues des son apparition. . . . La première traduction française, faite d'après la 3e édition anglaise, parut à Paris en 1790. Le manuscrit fut distribué, par parties, à trois imprimeries et imprimé en huit jours. On fit cinq éditions de cette traduction de 1790 à la fin de 1791" (René Bazin, "Edmund Burke et la révolution," *Revue de l'Anjou* [nouvelle série], 4 [January 1882]: 33).

[92] Jean Baptiste Cloots, *Addresse d'un Prussien à un Anglais* (Paris, 1790), p. 12. See also p. 49.

[93] Quoted by Donald C. Bryant, *Edmund Burke and His Literary Friends* (St. Louis: Washington University, 1939), p. 42.

[94] Carl B. Cone in "Pamphlet Replies to Burke's *Reflections,*" *Social Science Quarterly,* 26 (June 1945), pp. 22-34, made use of twenty-one replies. Ernest Barker noted "some forty answers to the *Reflections.*" In the course of my studies on Burke I have discovered and read forty-eight replies to the *Reflections* and Burke's other writings on French affairs, out of about 400.

[95] Burke, *Reflections on the Revolution in France,* pp. 368-69. Hereinafter this work will be cited as *Reflections.* See also p. 370. Charles E. Vaughan dismissed this passage as "a mere metaphor," and F. J. C. Hearnshaw condemned it as "resounding nonsense." H. V. S. Ogden stated that "Burke was imbued with the importance of the differences between peoples, and for him the contract is an *ex post facto* abstraction of particular validity, not an initiating act of universal application." Ogden concluded by agreeing with Vaughan: "A contract between the dead, the living and the unborn is only a contract by metaphor." John A. Lester called this passage "the work of Burke's moral idealism," a criticism too abstract to be meaningful. He too failed to mention the Natural Law. It is ironical that the positivist Morley, who also never mentioned the Natural Law in Burke, recognized in a general way, and apart from any consideration of contract, that the ultimate basis of Burke's politics lay in a "mysticism" that transcended a naturalistic explanation of life: "at the bottom of all his thoughts about communities and governments there lay a certain mysticism. It was no irony, no literary trope, when he talked of our having taught the American husbandman 'piously to believe in the mysterious virtue of wax and parchment.' He

was using no idle epithet, when he described the disposition of a stupendous wisdom, 'moulding together the great mysterious incorporation of the human race.' To him there actually was an element of mystery in the cohesion of men in societies, in political obedience, in the sanctity of contract; in all that fabric of law and charter and obligation, whether written or unwritten, which is the sheltering bulwark between civilization and barbarism. When reason and history had contributed all that they could to the explanation, it seemed to him as if the vital force, the secret of organization, the binding framework, must still come from the impenetrable regions beyond reasoning and beyond history" (*Burke,* p. 165). This was the closest Morley ever came to recognizing the sovereignty of Natural Law in Burke's political philosophy.

[96] Pufendorf, *Of the Law of Nature and Nations* (Oxford, 1703), p. 117. Pufendorf's italics.

[97] Burke, *Reflections,* pp. 307-309.

[98] Ibid., p. 370.

[99] Ibid., pp. 364-66.

[100] Burke, *Speeches,* vol. 1, p. 114. See also *Annual Register* (1767), pp. 290, 293-94.

[101] Burke, *Reflections,* p. 493. See also p. 492; *Letter to Richard Burke,* p. 80.

[102] Ibid., p. 422. See also p. 423.

[103] Ibid., p. 377. See also pp. 378-79.

[104] Ibid., p. 331. Burke again distinguished between "the pretended rights of man" and "the rights of the people" in his *An Appeal from the New to the Old Whigs,* p. 95. Hereinafter this work will be cited as *New to the Old Whigs.* Burke's distinction recurs in *The Policy of the Allies,* p. 417; *Letter to a Noble Lord* (hereinafter cited as *Noble Lord*), p. 150; *Regicide Peace,* p. 305.

[105] Ibid., p. 444. See also pp. 452, 454, 467.

[106] Ibid., p. 334. My italics.

[107] Ibid., p. 332.

[108] Ibid., p. 335.

[109] Burke, *New to the Old Whigs,* p. 79. See also pp. 80-81.

[110] Burke, *Noble Lord,* p. 137. See also pp. 138-39.
[111] Burke, *Regicide Peace,* pp. 168, 172, 176-77. See also pp. 178, 185-86, 206-7, 406, 414-15; *Preface to M. Brissot's Address,* pp. 524-26. Burke denied that

prescription applied to recent conquests: "A recent wrong . . . can plead no prescription. It violates the rights upon which not only the community of France, but those on which all communities are founded, . . . principles which are as true in England as in any other country" (*Regicide Peace,* p. 219).

[112] Ibid., pp. 211, 216, 304, 400.

[113] Burke, *Speeches,* vol. 4, p. 73.

[114] Burke, *Letter to William Elliot,* p. 75.

[115] Burke, *Regicide Peace,* p. 207. Burke's basic conviction that "God is the all-wise but mysterious Governor of the world" is a recurring theme in this work. See pp. 236, 277, 322, 326, 353.

[116] Burke, *The Epistolary Correspondence of Edmund Burke,* ed. Dr. French Laurence (London, 1827), p. 241. Hereinafter this work will be cited as *Laurence Correspondence.*

[117] Ibid., pp. 106-107.

[118] William Hazlitt, *The Spirit of the Age, in The Complete Works of William Hazlitt,* ed. P. P. Howe (London, 1930), vol. 2, p. 100. For Burke's letter to Mackintosh see Robert M. Mackintosh, *Memoirs of the Life of Sir James Mackintosh* (Boston: Little Brown, 1853), vol. 1, pp. 88-90. Hazlitt's account agrees with that of Lois Whitney, *Primitivism and the Idea of Progress,* pp. 224-26. For a different account of the origin of Mackintosh's lectures, see B. Sprague Allen, "Minor Disciples of Radicalism in the Revolutionary Era," *Modern Philology,* 30 (1923-1924), p. 294.

FURTHER READING

Bibliography

Gandy, Clara I. And Stanlis, Peter J. *Edmund Burke: A Bibliography of Secondary Studies to 1982.* New York and London: Garland Publishing, 1983, 357 p.
  An exhaustive catalog of secondary material, including theses and dissertations, published prior to 1982.

Biography

Copeland, Thomas W. *Our Eminent Friend: Edmund Burke.* New Haven: Yale University Press, 1949, 251p.
  Focuses on Burke's character.

Criticism

Barrington, Donald Patrick Michael. "Edmund Burke as

an Economist," *Economica*, New Series, 21(1954):252-58.
Discussses Burke as a *laissez-faire* economist.

Bickel, Alexander. "Constitutional Government and Revolution," in *Edmund Burke: Appraisals and Applications*, edited by Daniel E. Ritchie, pp. 131-45. New Brunswick, N.J.: Transaction Publishers, 1990.
Describes Burke's criteria for effective and legitimate constitutional government.

Cameron, David R. *The Social Thought of Rousseau and Burke: a Comparative Study*. Toronto: University of Toronto Press, 1973. 242 p.
Discusses the philosophers' competing views of human nature and social organization.

Cone, Carl B. "Pamphlet Replies to Burke's *Reflections*," *Social Science Quarterly*, XXXVI(June, 1945):22-34.
Examines published responses to Burke's anti-revolutionary politics.

Conniff, James. "Burke on the Nature and Extent of State Authority." In *The Useful Cobbler: Edmund Burke and the Politics of Progress*. Albany: State University of New York, 1990, pp. 113-36.
Descusses Burke's belief in reform initiatives being grounded to concrete, practical ends rather than theories of abstract rights.

Kirk, Russell. "Reforming Party and Government," in

Edmund Burke: A Genius Reconsidered, Arlington House, 1967, pp. 75-103.
Important essay in which Kirk discusses Burke's belief in the role of oppositional parties to act as a check against improvident legislation.

Lucas, Paul. "On Edmund Burke's Doctrine of Prescription," *Historical Journal* 11(1968): 35-36.
Challenges interpretations of Burke that suggest he drew sharp distinctions between the "natural law" and "natural rights" traditions.

Reid, Christopher. "The Politics of Taste." In *Edmund Burke: Appraisals and Applications*, edited by Daniel E. Ritchie, pp. 57-72. New Brunswick, N.J.: Transaction Publishers, 1990.
Discusses how Burke's aesthetics informed and shaped his politics.

Robinson, Nicholas K. *Edmund Burke: A Life in Caricature*. New Haven: Yale University Press, 1997, 214 p.
An art book that contains numerous caricatures of Burke and his ideas gleaned from contemporary periodicals.

Weston, John C. "Edmund Burke's View of History," *Review of Politics* 23(1961):203-29.
Explains the roles of divine providence, free will, and constitutional government in Burke's philosophy.

Additional coverage of Burke's life and career is contained in the following sources published by Gale research: *Literature Criticism from 1400 to 1800*, Vol. 7, *Discovering Authors, Discovering Authors: British, Discovering Authors:Canadian*, and *World Literature Criticism*.

Thomas Hobbes

1588-1679

English philosopher, political theorist, essayist, critic, scientist, and autobiographer.

INTRODUCTION

Considered one of England's most important philosophers, Hobbes was the author of *Leviathan, Or The Matter, Forme, & Power of a Common-Wealth Ecclesiasticall and Civill* (1651), a work Michael Oakeshott calls "the greatest, perhaps the sole, masterpiece of political philosophy written in the English languange." Although Hobbes wrote many of his works in Latin, the language of choice for such intellectual matters in his time, it was his decision to write *Leviathan* in English that deemed the language suitable for any area of inquiry. It was in *Leviathan* that Hobbes wrote the famous description of man's life in nature as "solitary, poor, nasty, brutish, and short." To free themselves from this natural state of warfare, men join in a compact with one another, make a social contract, and set up a sovereign. The sovereign, called the Leviathan by Hobbes, exercises absolute power over his subjects and maintains the peace. Succinct and contentious, Hobbes enraged many readers with such statements as "The universe is corporeal; all that is real is material, and what is not material is not real." Hobbes also asserted that the Church must be subject to the State. Such ideas, expressed so confidently and in an uncommonly accessible style, created an instant uproar, especially in ecclesiastical circles. Contemptuously dismissing Aristotle and his followers, Hobbes declared himself the creator of civil philosophy, what would today be called political science. Heavily influenced by his friend Galileo Galilei, Hobbes was a mechanist who viewed the world as matter in motion and man as movement of limbs. His Machiavellian insistence on looking at things as they are, not as they should be, his contention that expediency rather than morality motivated political obedience, and his unshakable secularism fueled countless attacks by his critics. As contradictory as they were original, Hobbes's ideas are debated to this day.

Biographical Information

Hobbes was born April 5, 1588, in Malmesbury, England. He claimed that his mother gave birth to him upon hearing the rumor that the Spanish Armada was set to destroy the nation. She gave birth to twins, Hobbes wrote,—himself and fear. His father, also named Thomas, was an uneducated clergyman prone

to quarrel. Biographers have posited that both timidity and argumentativeness were notable traits of Hobbes throughout his lifetime. After Hobbes's father abandoned his parish and family, young Thomas and his brother and sister were raised by their uncle Francis Hobbes, who was successful enough to see that Thomas received a fine education. At the age of six, Hobbes was learning Greek and Latin. At fourteen he translated Euripides's *Medea* and was sent to Oxford. Although an adequate student, Hobbes disliked the university, rejected much of what he read there, and went on to criticize universities in much of his later writing. According to his first biographer, John Aubrey, Hobbes took delight in saying that if he had read as much as other men, he would know as little as other men. Upon receiving a degree in 1608, Hobbes became tutor to William Cavendish, the son of the first Earl of Devonshire. Through this association Hobbes made his first trip to the continent and became inspired to study the classics. He was employed as Roger Bacon's secretary in 1623-24. In 1628 Hobbes published his translation of Thucydides's history of the Peloponnesian

War, an important improvement to what had previously circulated, and intended by Hobbes to serve as a warning to the English of the dangers inherent in Democracy. Hobbes worked for and tutored many men, including three Cavendishes, until 1640. During his teaching career he enjoyed much leisure time and three three-year stays on the continent. It was there that he met and became friends with Galileo. He met other great minds as well, including Ben Jonson, Abbe Mersenne, and Pierre Gassendi, and became fascinated with the study of motion. Profoundly stirred by his chance discovery of Euclid, Hobbes considered applying the science of geometry to politics. He wrote a treatise in 1640 on citizenship and absolutism, *The Elements of Law Natural and Politique,* which circulated widely in manuscript form. Fearing for his safety at the hands of Parliament, Hobbes fled to Paris, where he promptly composed numerous objections to René Descartes's *Meditations,* which he saw before publication. He began work on a proposed trilogy on the body, the man, and the citizen. After the publication of *Leviathan* in 1651, Hobbes returned to England, notorious but respected at the same time, and carried on years of controversies, notably with Bishop John Bramhall on free will and on mathematics with John Wallis, the inventor of algebra. Hobbes, considered an atheist by many in Parliament, was saved from a charge of Christian heresy by the intercession of the King, who ordered Hobbes to refrain from further publishing any inflammatory works. In 1672 Hobbes wrote a brief, compelling autobiography and in 1675, at age 86, translated the *Iliad* and the *Odyssey.* Hobbes died December 4, 1679.

Major Works

Critics have always characterized Hobbes as a mature writer, with his first original book, *Elementorum Philosophiae Sectio Tertia De Cive* (1642), being published when he was fifty-four. The case has recently been made that three of the *Discourses* are the product of a young Hobbes, the work originally having been included in an anonymous volume of 1620, *Horae Subsecivae.* These discourses demonstrate the strong influence of Bacon and Nicollò Machiavelli. The execution of the King in 1649 spurred Hobbes's desire to provide guidance for his country, and he published *Human Nature* and *De Corpore Politico* (1650), which included much of *The Elements of Law,* a work that would not be published in its entirety until 1889. England, Hobbes felt, had gone wrong, and war had been the result. *Leviathan,* the strongest and boldest statement of his political thought, was offered to show that there was an alternative. According to Hobbes, people are more or less equals in strength and intelligence. Mankind are driven by the desire to fulfill their wants and needs. In satisfying themselves, however, they will inevitably encroach on others attempting to fulfill their own wants and needs. Therefore, people will constant-

ly be at odds, and the essentially matched strengths of the opponents will ensure a constant state of warfare, which to Hobbes included the tendency to war and the lack of assurance to the contrary. Hobbes proposed that there is an even more powerful drive, the fear of death, and that to assuage this fear, people join in a compact with one another, make a social contract, and set up a sovereign. The sovereign will have absolute power; virtually all say is surrendered by the citizens. This sovereign, called the Leviathan by Hobbes, will keep his subjects in check and protect them from their enemies. Where once good and bad were relative values decided by individuals, there would now be a common rule since all were under the sovereign and his total control, which would allow no review. In *De Corpore* (1655, *The Body*) Hobbes turned to the philosophy of motion and to the idea that life as well as thought were merely motion. His utterly mechanistic view of life in these works was the source of great contention. In 1668 Hobbes finished a history of the Long Parliament and submitted it to the King, who denied it publication because of Hobbes's dangerous political suggestions; *Behemoth, the History of the Causes of the Civil Wars of England, from 1640. to 1660.* did not reach the public until 1682, buried in a composite edition of his treatises.

Critical Reception

Hobbes's influence on Western political thought was profound. His successors could and did disagree with him, but they could not escape being compared to and measured against him. In his writing, Hobbes was not timid: many readers were provoked to opposition upon first exposure. Hobbes met the criticism either directly, responding vigorously, as he did to John Bramhall's *Catching of Leviathan,* or indirectly, with disdainful, silent superiority. Hobbes's emphasis on the secular over the theological was particularly infuriating to his detractors. Any relation to God, even if by way of an intermediary, as in the Catholic Church, was denied. He wrote, "If a man consider the original of the great ecclesiastical dominion, he will easily perceive that the Papacy is no other than the ghost of the deceased Roman Empire sitting crowned upon the grave thereof." The title of one response exemplifies some of the reaction to Hobbes: "The Brief View of the Dangerous and Pernicious Errors to Church and State in Mr. Hobbes's book." Hobbes was called an atheist, and for years "Hobbism" was the term applied when attempting to denigrate any example of scepticism or free thought. In 1683 *De Cive* and *Leviathan* were condemned as heretical books and burned at Oxford; Hobbes's enemies also prevented him from becoming a fellow of the Royal Society. Despite his tempestuous life, Hobbes's works were respected and admired by many of his contemporaries. However, his ideas were still considered radical for half a century after his death, and it was not until the mid-eighteenth century that Hobbes's works could be written about dispassionately. Since then, he has held his place among the most important political philosophers of the western tradition, and his works continue to spark interest and debate.

PRINCIPAL WORKS

Discourses [In *Horae Subsecivae;* published anonymously] (philosophy) 1620

Eight Books of the Peloponnesian Warre Written by Thvcidides the sonne of Olorvs. Interpreted with Faith and Diligence Immediately out of the Greeke [translator] (history) 1629

The Elements of Law Natural and Politique (treatise) 1640

"Objectiones tertiæ" ["Objections Made against the Foregoing Meditations"] in René Descartes, *Meditationes de Prima Philosophia, in qva Dei Existentia, & animæ immortalitas demonstratur* (criticism) 1641

Elementorum Philosophiae Sectio Tertia De Cive [*Philosophicall Rudiments Concerning Government and Society. Or, A Dissertation Concerning Man in his severall habitudes and respects, as the Member of a Society, first Secular, and then Sacred*] (philosophy) 1642

De Corpore Politico. Or the Elements of Law, Moral & Politick, with Discourses upon several Heads (philosophy) 1650

Human Nature: Or, The fundamental Elements of Policie (philosophy) 1650

Leviathan, Or The Matter, Forme, & Power of a Common-Wealth Ecclesiasticall and Civill (philosophy) 1651

Of Libertie and Necessitie: A Treatise, wherein all Controversie concerning Predestination, Election, Freewill, Grace, Merits, Reprobation, &c. is fully decided and cleared, in answer to a Treatise written by the Bishop of London-derry, on the same subject (philosophy) 1654

Elementorum Philosophiae Sectio Prima De Corpore [*Elements of Philosophy, the First Section, Concerning Body*] (philosophy) 1655

The Questions Concerning Liberty, Necessity, and Chance. Clearly Stated and Debated Between Dr. Bramhall Bishop of Derry, and Thomas Hobbes of Malmesbury (philosophy) 1656

Elementorum Philosophiae Sectio Secunda De Homine (philosophy) 1658

Examinatio & Emendatio Mathematica Hodiernæ. Qualis explicatur in libris Johannis Wallisii Geometriæ Professoris Saviliani in Academia Oxoniensi. Distributa in sex Dialogos. (essay) 1660

Homer's Odysses [translator] (poem) 1675

Homer's Iliads in English [translator] (poem) 1676

Thomæ Hobbessii Malmesburiensis Vita. Authore Seipso ["The Life of Thomas Hobbes of Malmesbury"] (autobiography) 1679

Behemoth, the History of the Causes of the Civil Wars of England, from 1640. to 1660. [In *Tracts of Mr. Thomas Hobbs of Malmsbury* (philosophy) 1682

English Works of Thomas Hobbes. 11 vols. (treatises, essays, philosophy, poetry) 1839-45

Opera Philosophica. 5 vols. (philosophy) 1961

The Correspondence of Thomas Hobbes (correspondence) 1994

CRITICISM

Sir Leslie Stephen (essay date 1904)

SOURCE: "The State," in *Hobbes,* 1904. Reprint by The University of Michigan Press, 1961, pp. 173-236.

[*In the following excerpt, Stephen examines Hobbes's conception of both the law of nature and the social contract.*]

THE STATE [1]

1. Contemporary Controversies

We come now to the third part of Hobbes's philosophy. He is to base a science of politics upon the doctrines already expounded. We become aware that there is a certain breach of continuity. To understand his line of thought, it is necessary to take note both of the problems in which he was specially interested, and the form into which the arguments had been moulded by previous thinkers. He applies to the questions of the day certain conceptions already current in political theory, though he uses them in such a way as materially to alter their significance.

Hobbes's theory in the first place involves the acceptance of a so-called "Law of Nature." "Nature," as we know, is a word contrived in order to introduce as many equivocations as possible into all the theories, political, legal, artistic, or literary, into which it enters. The "Law of Nature," as writers upon jurisprudence tell us, was invented by Roman lawyers with the help of Stoic philosophers. The lawyers, having to deal with the legal systems of the numerous races which came into contact with Rome, were led to recognise a certain body of laws common to all. Such law came to be considered as laid down by Nature. It was a product of the human nature common to Greeks and Romans, and not affected by the special modifications by which Romans are distinguished from Greeks. It belonged to the genus man, not to the species nation. The philosopher, meanwhile, took the Law of Nature to be law imposed by the divine author of nature, discoverable by right reason, and therefore common to all reasoning beings. The law in either case is "natural" because universally valid. But this may cover two diverging conceptions. To the man of science "nature" means everything actually existing. One quality cannot be more "natural" than another, though it may be more widely diffused. A scientific investigator of jurisprudence would inquire what systems of law prevail in different countries, and would seek to discover the causes of uniformity or difference. The inquirer is so far simply concerned with the question of fact, and to him the exceptional is just as much a natural product as the normal legislation. The scientific point of view is that from which one might expect Hobbes to treat the question. He accepts, however, the Law of Nature in another sense. It meant an ideal, not an actual law, and tells us what ought to be, not what is. There may of course be a presumption that a law (if there is such law) which is universally accepted is also dictated by reason; or a state may be so happily constituted that the perception that a law is reasonable may involve its acceptance in the actual system. But in any case the Law of Nature is supposed to be the type to which the actual law should be made to conform, and therefore implies a contrast and occasional conflict between the two systems.

Hobbes's view implies another distinction. Every one admits that laws may rightly vary according to circumstances within certain limits. There are laws, we may say, which it is right to obey because they are the law, and others which are the law because it is right to obey them. In England the law of the road tells carriages to keep to the left, and in France to keep to the right. We clearly ought to obey each rule in its own country. But there are other cases. In some countries the law permits or enforces rules of marriage which in other countries are held to be immoral and revolting. Is it true in this case also that each law is right in its own country, or is one set of laws to be condemned as contrary to the Law of Nature? Given the Law of Nature, that is, how are we to decide what sphere of discretion is to be left to the legislator? Can he deal with the most vital as well as the most trivial relations, or how is his proper sphere of authority to be defined? Where does "positive" law begin and natural law end? This involves the problem, how far does the power of the legislature extend, or what is the relation between the sovereign and the subject. That was a problem which had not been discussed in the classical philosophy. Man as a "political animal" was so identified with the State that citizenship was an essential part of him. Different forms of government might be compared, but the individual could not be conceived as existing independently of the State. To Hobbes the State had become an "artificial" construction, and therefore its relation to the units of which it was constructed had to be settled and was vitally important.

The theory of sovereignty had become interesting when there were rival claimants to sovereignty. The Christian Church, beginning as a voluntary association outside the State, and appealing to men in their individual capacity, had become a gigantic organisation with an elaborate constitution and legal system. It had come into collision, alliance, and rivalry with the empire. According to the accepted theory, both powers had legitimate claims to allegiance. Pope and emperor were compared to the sun and moon, though it might be disputed which was the sun and which was the moon, or whether they were not rather two independent luminaries. In the great controversies which arose, the Church had an obvious advantage. It derived its authority from direct revelation. It represented on earth the supreme Being, and was entrusted by him with power to enforce the moral laws which coincide with the Law of Nature. As the empire could claim no special revelation, the advocates of its claims had to find some independent support for them in the Law of Nature. To the question, then, whence is derived the obligation to obey the State, or rather the ruler, there was but one obvious answer. "All obligation," says Hobbes, "derives from contract." It is part of the Law of Nature that man should observe compacts. If therefore the relation between sovereign and subject depends upon a compact, there is a sufficient obligation to obedience though the ruler has not a special commission from God. It could not, it is true, be proved that such a compact had ever been made, nor that, if made in one generation, it would be binding on the next, nor was it possible to say what were the exact terms of the supposed compact. But such cavils were trifles. They could be met by saying that there was an "implicit" contract, and that it, no doubt, prescribed reasonable terms. This theory was gradually developed in the middle ages, and when Hobbes was a young man it had acquired especial currency from the great book in which Grotius had adopted it, when applying the Law of Nature to regulate the ethics of peace and war.[2]

This set of conceptions gives Hobbes's starting-point, though in his hands the Law of Nature and the social compact received a peculiar development, or, indeed, seemed to be turned inside out. He applied them to the great controversies in which he and his contemporaries were specially interested. The complicated struggles of the Reformation period had raised issues which were still undecided. Church and State, whatever the theory of their relations, were so closely connected as to form parts of one organism, and a separation of them, such as is contemplated by modern speculation, was unthinkable. If the two bodies had conflicting claims, they were also reciprocally necessary. Their systems of legislation were not independent, but interpenetrating. Each implied the other, and the State was bound to suppress heresy, as the Church to condemn rebellion. The disruption of the old system implied both civil and foreign war. The lines of cleavage ran through both Church and State, and in each fragment the ecclesiastical and secular system had to readjust their relations. When in England Henry VIII. renounced the authority of the pope, he had to become a bit of a pope himself. In Scotland the Church, though it might suppose that it had returned to primitive purity, could not be expected for that reason to relinquish its claims to authority over the laity. In the famous "Monarchomachist" controversy, Jesuits agreed with Scottish Protestants and French Huguenots in defending tyrannicide. They had a common interest in limiting the claims of the secular power. Jacques Clement and Ravaillac gave a pointed application in France to the Jesuit doctrine; and the Scots had to make a case against Queen Mary. Meanwhile the claims of the Catholic Church were the cause or the pretext of the warfare which culminated in the Spanish Armada. The patriotic Englishman regarded the pope as the instigator or accomplice of the assailants of our national independence. Persecution of priests seemed to be necessary, even if cruel, when priests were agents of the power which supported hostile fleets and inspired murderous conspiracies. Throughout the seventeenth century the protestant Englishman suffered from "papacy" on the brain, and his fear flashed into panic for the last time when Hobbes was dying. During his youth the keenest controversy had been raging over the claims of the papacy. James I. himself and his most learned divines, such as Andrewes and Donne, were arguing against the great Catholic divines, Suárez and Bellarmine. The controversy turned especially upon the imposition of the oath renouncing the doctrine of the right of the pope to depose kings. To that right was opposed the "divine right of kings": thereby being meant, not that kings had a "right divine to govern wrong," but that the king's right was as directly derived from Heaven as the rights of the Church.

Hobbes, as we shall see, was deeply impressed by these problems. The power of the Catholic Church to enforce its old claims was rapidly disappearing; but men are often most interested in discussing the means of escaping the dangers of the day before yesterday. While Hobbes was elaborating his system, great political issues seemed to turn upon the relation between the spiritual and secular authority. Meanwhile the purely political were inextricably mixed up with ecclesiastical questions. James's formula, "no bishop, no king," expressed the fact. The Church of England was in the closest alliance with the royal authority; "passive obedience" to the king became almost an essential doctrine, even with liberal Anglican divines; and the rebellion was the outcome of the discontent in both spheres. In England the claim of parliament to a share of power came first, but the power was to be applied on behalf of religious Puritanism. In Scotland the Church question was most prominent; but the Church, in the rule of which, as James complained, Tom, Dick, and Harry had claimed to have a voice, also represent-

ed the aspirations of the nation. The political problem was equally important, whatever might be the motives for demanding political power. The question in England was whether the ancient parliamentary institutions were to be preserved and developed, or to be allowed to fall into decay as in other European countries where the State was being organised on different lines. In later days, writers, who held the British Constitution to be an embodiment of perfect wisdom, naturally venerated the Hampdens and Eliots as representatives of the ultimately victorious, and therefore rightful cause.

As Hobbes altogether condemned their principles, we must remind ourselves how things appeared at the time. To men who desired a vigorous national government—which is surely a very reasonable desire—the claims of the parliamentary party appeared to be a hopeless obstacle. All men admitted that the king was to have the fullest authority over the national policy; he might make war or peace without consulting anybody; and if he could make it at his own expense, parliament had no ground for interference. The only thing which it could do was to refuse money if he wanted it for a policy which it disliked. It was as if the crew of a ship of war gave the command unreservedly to the captain, but, if they disliked the direction in which he was steering, showed disapproval by turning off the steam. That obviously would be a clumsy method. Parliament did not superintend or give general directions, but could throw the whole system out of gear when it pleased. We know, of course, how the struggle resulted in the supremacy of parliament, and of that party organisation which enabled it to act as a unit, and to regulate the whole national policy with a certain continuity of purpose. In Hobbes's time not only could such a system, as historians agree, occur to no one, but if it had occurred it would have been impracticable. To be efficient it required, not merely an exposition of principles, but the development of a mutual understanding between the different classes, which was not less essential because not expressed in any legal document. The art of parliamentary government has to be learnt by practice.

Another remark is now pretty obvious. The British people managed to work out a system which had, as we all believe, very great advantages and may justify some of the old panegyrics. Men could speak more freely—if not always more wisely—in England than elsewhere, and individual energy developed with many most admirable, if with some not quite admirable consequences. But the success was won at a cost. The central authority of the State was paralysed; and many observers may admit that in securing liberty at the price of general clumsiness and inefficiency of all the central administrative functions, the cost has been considerable. It is desirable to remember this point when we come to Hobbes's special theories. To him the demands of the parliamentary party appeared to imply a hopeless disorganization of the political machinery. His political writings, though professing to be a piece of abstract logic, are also essentially aimed at answering these questions. The vital problem involved was, as he thought, what is sovereignty and who should be sovereign? The State, on one side, was struggling with the Church—whether the Church of Rome or the Church of Scotland,—and, on the other hand, the supreme power was claimed for king alone, for parliament alone, and for some combination of the two. What will a scientific analysis enable us to say as to the general nature of the supreme power and as to the best constitution of a body politic. The country, as he says, for some years before the civil war, "was boiling over with questions concerning the rights of dominion and the obedience due from subjects": a state of things which "ripened and plucked" from him the third part of his philosophy before the other parts were ready.

2. *The Social Contract*

Hobbes's political theories are expounded in the *De Corpore Politico* (the little treatise of 1640), the *De Cive,* and the *Leviathan*. The title of the last of these works is suggested by certain words in the Book of Job: *"Non est potestas super terram quæ comparetur ei."* They are printed at the head of the quaint allegorical title-page, where a composite giant, his body made of human beings, holds the sword in one and a crosier in the other hand, while beneath him is a wide country with a town, a fort, and a church in the foreground, and below it are various symbols of temporal and spiritual power. The great Leviathan, he tells us, is that mortal god to which we owe, under the immortal God, our peace and defence. But he is also a machine. We are to take him to pieces in imagination, as we actually take to pieces a watch to understand its construction. We have already seen the statement of Hobbes's method. It is impossible to deduce the properties of this complex mechanism by the synthetical method; but by analysing the observed "motions of the mind" we can discover its essential principles. Justice, he says, means giving to each man his own. How does a man come to have an "own"? Because community of goods breeds contention, while reason prescribes peace. From the regulation of the "concupiscible" nature by the "rational" arises the system of moral and civil laws embodied in the great Leviathan. We have to examine this process in detail. Men have, as we have seen, "a perpetual and restless desire of power after power." In the next place, men are naturally equal. The weakest in body, at any rate, may kill the strongest, and there is a still greater equality in mind. This doctrine of natural equality he tries to establish by rather quaint arguments. "Every man," he says, "thinks himself as wise, though not as witty or learned as his neighbours. What better proof can there be of equality of distribution than that every man is contented with his share?" That

is hardly convincing; but what Hobbes means to say is that no man has such a superiority over his fellows as would make him secure in the chaotic struggle of "the state of nature." When two men want the same thing, therefore, each will have a chance. Competition, diffidence (a distrust of each other), and glory (the desire, we may say, for prestige) are the three principal causes of quarrel. "The first maketh men invade for gain; the second for safety; the third for reputation." When there is no common power to overawe, there will be a "war of every man against every man." War, he explains, is not confined to actual fighting, but exists where there is a "known disposition thereto" and "no assurance to the contrary." So long as this state continues, "there is no place for industry, because the fruit thereof is uncertain," and (besides many other wants) "no arts, no letters, no society, and which is worst of all, continual fear and danger of violent death; and the life of man solitary, poor, nasty, brutish, and short." Do you object to this account of man? Look at experience. Does not a man arm himself when he is going a journey? Does he not lock the chests in his own house, although he knows that there are public officers to protect them? What opinion does that imply of his fellow subjects or of his servants? "Does he not as much accuse mankind by his actions, as I do by my words?"

But was there ever such a "state of nature"? Not perhaps over the whole world, though in America many savages live in this nasty and brutish fashion. If, however, that were not so with particular men, "yet in all times kings and persons of sovereign authority, because of their independency, are in continual jealousies, and in the state and posture of gladiators; having their weapons pointing and their eyes fixed on one another—that is their forts, garrisons, and guns upon the frontiers of their kingdoms—and continual spies upon their neighbours." The argument is certainly not obsolete, nor the remark which follows. "Because they uphold thereby the industry of their subjects, there does not follow from it that misery which accompanies the liberty of particular men." Now where every man is at war with every man, "the notions of right and wrong, justice and injustice, have no place. Where there is no common power there is no law; where no law, no injustice. Force and fraud are in war the two cardinal virtues." Justice and injustice "relate to men in society, not in solitude." In such a state of things, there can be "no *mine* and *thine* distinct, but only that to be every man's that he can get and for so long as he can keep it."

> " . . . the good old rule
> Sufficeth them, the simple plan,
> That they should take who have the power,
> And they should keep who can,"

as Wordsworth puts it. This is the "ill condition" in which man is placed "by mere nature." There is a possibility of his getting out of it, partly because some passions, fear of death, desire of comfort, and hope of securing it induce men to peace, and partly because "reason suggesteth convenient articles of peace."

This is Hobbes's famous theory that the "state of nature" is a state of war. It does not imply, he says, that men are "evil by nature." The desires are not themselves wicked, though at times they may cause wicked actions. "Children grow peevish and do hurt if you do not give them all they ask for; but they do not become wicked till, being capable of reason, they continue to do hurt." A wicked man is a child grown strong and sturdy; and malice is a defect of reason at the age when reasonable conduct is to be expected. Nature provides the faculties but not the education. The doctrine should be tested by its truth, not by its pleasantness. Hobbes accepts in part the method of Machiavelli, who clearly announced that he was concerned with what actually happened, not with what ought to happen. To adopt that plan is to undertake to tell unpleasant truths, and to tell unpleasant truths is, according to most readers, to be "cynical." Hobbes incurred the blame; but, at least, he was so far pursuing the truly scientific method. Up to this point, indeed, he was taking the line which would be followed by a modern inquirer into the history of institutions. Warfare is part of the struggle for existence out of which grow states and the whole organisation of civilised societies. A modern would maintain, like Hobbes, that in admitting the part played by selfish force in the development of society, he does not assert the wickedness of human nature. He only asserts that the good impulses cannot acquire the desirable supremacy until a peaceful order has been established by the complex struggles and alliances of human beings, swayed by all their passions and ambitions. But here we come upon an element in Hobbes's theory of which I have already spoken, namely, the Law of Nature. The "laws of human nature," in the scientific sense, expressing the way in which human beings actually behave, are identified with the Law of Nature as an ideal or divine law, which declares how men ought to behave. Hobbes professes to show that the sovereign has certain "rights" as well as certain powers; and, moreover, that those rights are far from being recognised in many countries and especially in England. He is not simply pointing out how it came to pass that Charles I. and his parliament had got into conflict, and thence inferring the best mode of settling the disputed points; but he desires to show that the "Law of Nature" decides the question of their conflicting rights. The "Nature" which prescribes the right cannot be identical with the "Nature" which gives the power and determines the facts.

Hobbes's next point, therefore, is to show what are the "Laws of Nature." Every man has a right, he says, to use his own power for his own preservation. A "Law of Nature" is a precept found out by reason, forbidding

him to do the contrary: that is, to destroy himself or his means of self-preservation. Now, in the "state of nature" just described, every man has a right to everything—even to another man's body. He has a "right," that is, because nature makes self-preservation the sole aim of each man, even when it implies the destruction of others. But it is plain that, while this is the case, no man's life or happiness is secure. "Nature," therefore, orders men to get out of the "state of nature" as soon as they can. Hence we have the twofold principle. It is the "fundamental *law* of nature" that every man should "seek peace and follow it"; and the fundamental "*right* of nature" is that a man should defend himself by every means he can. Peace makes self-defence easy. It follows that a man should "lay down his right to all things" if other men will lay down theirs. This is identified by Hobbes with the "law of the Gospel": *"Whatsoever you require that others should do to you, that do ye to them"* or (which he takes to be equivalent), *"Quod tibi fieri non vis alteri ne feceris."* A man may simply renounce or he may transfer a right. In either case, he is said to be "obliged" not to interfere with the exercise of a right by those to whom he has abandoned or granted it. It is his "duty" not to make his grant void by hindering men from using the right; and such hindrance is called "injustice." We thus have Hobbes's definitions of Obligation, Duty, and Justice. Injustice, he observes, is like an absurdity in logic. It is a contradiction of what you had voluntarily asserted that you would do.

From these definitions, Hobbes proceeds to deduce other "Laws of Nature," and finds no less than nineteen. The third law (after those prescribing peace and self-defence) is that men should keep their "covenants." He afterwards deduces the duties of gratitude, sociability, admission of equality—the breach of which is pride—equity, and so forth. If, he says, the "deduction" seems "too subtile," they may all be regarded as corollaries from the "golden rule." That rule, however, is itself deducible from the rule of "self-preservation." We do good to others in order that they may do good to us. "No man giveth," as he says, by way of proving that gratitude is a virtue, "but with intention of good to himself." . . . "Of all voluntary acts, the object is to every man his own good." That, one would rather have supposed, is a reason for not being "grateful" to anybody. We must interpret "gratitude" in the prospective sense—with an eye to the favours to come. It is prudent to pay your debts in order to keep up your credit. In one case he seems to deviate a little from his egoism. Justice means keeping covenants—obedience, that is, to his "third law." A man who does a just action from fear, as he remarks, is not therefore a just man; his "will is not framed by the justice, but by the apparent benefit of what he is to do. That which gives to human actions the relish of justice is a certain nobleness or gallantness of courage, rarely found, by which a man scorns to be beholden for the contentment of his life to fraud or breach of promise." He should have held, it would seem, that the will is always framed by the "apparent benefit." The inconsistency (if there be one, for even this appears to be a case of "glory") is explicable. Hobbes has to deduce all the "Laws of Nature" from the law of self-preservation. That, no doubt, may show the expediency of making a "covenant" with your neighbours, and even the expediency of generally keeping it. But it must also be granted that there are occasions in which expediency is in favour of breaking covenants. The just man, the ordinary moralist would say, is a man who keeps his word even to his own disadvantage. That, on the strictest interpretation of Hobbes, is impossible. Nobody can do it. Justice, however, in the sense of "covenant-keeping," is so essential a part of his system, that he makes an implicit concession to a loftier tone of morality, and admits that a man may love justice for its own sake. This, however, seems to be an oversight. Hobbes is content to take for granted that each man will profit by that which is favourable to all, or that the desire for self-preservation will always make for the preservation of society. The Law of Nature, we see, is simply an application of the purely egoistic law of self-preservation. It represents the actual forces which (in Hobbes's view) mould and regulate all human institutions. But in sanctioning so respectable a virtue as "justice," it takes a certain moral colouring, and may stand for the ideal Law of Nature or Reason to which the actual order ought to conform.

There is another reserve to be made: the laws of nature are not properly laws. They are only "theorems concerning what conduceth" to self-preservation. They become laws proper when they are "delivered in the Word of God"; and he proceeds in the *De Cive* to prove them by a number of texts, and comes to the edifying conclusion that the "Law of Nature" is the Law of Christ. It is a theorem, for example, that to keep your word tends to self-preservation. But law means the command of a rightful superior; and until such a command has been given, it is not properly a "Law of Nature" that you should keep your word. The laws are always binding *in foro interno:* you are always bound to desire that they should come into operation; but they are not always binding *in foro externo;* that is, you are not always bound to "put them in act." Self-preservation is the fundamental law. But till other people keep the laws, obedience to them does not tend to self-preservation. If you are peaceful and truthful when other men are not, you will "procure your own certain ruin, contrary to all the Laws of Nature." That obviously will be the case in the "state of nature" where fraud and force are the cardinal virtues. There is, no doubt, a truth in this contention. The moral law, to become operative in fact, requires a certain amount of reciprocity. Actual morality clearly depends upon the stage of social evolution. In a primitive society, where men have to defend themselves by the strong hand, we

can hardly condemn the man who accepts the standard methods. Achilles would be a brutal ruffian to-day; but when Troy was besieged, he was a hero deserving admiration. He was perhaps in the true line of development. The chief of a savage tribe is, on the whole, preparing the way for a peaceful order. Even in the present day a philanthropist living in one of the regions where the first-comer is ready to shoot him at sight, might think it right to carry a revolver in his pocket, and, if necessary, to anticipate the shooting. Moral rules become useful in proportion as society perceives their value, and is more or less inclined to adopt them in practice. Otherwise, the man whose morality was of a higher type would be thrown away or summarily stamped out. Ought a man to be several generations in advance of his time? That is a pretty problem which I do not undertake to solve. In any case, Hobbes had a real and important meaning. He saw, that is, that the development of morality implies the growth of a certain understanding between the individuals composing the society, and that until this has been reached ideal morality proper to a higher plane of thought is impracticable if not undesirable. This leads to the theory of the social contract—the mutual agreement by which the great Leviathan is constructed.

The Law of Nature prescribes peace as a condition of security. But the law is "contrary to our natural passions," and "covenants without the sword are but words and of no strength to secure a man at all." It is therefore essential to create a common power to keep men in awe. Such creatures as bees and ants do, indeed, live at peace with each other and are therefore called by Aristotle "political creatures." Why cannot men do so? Because men compete and have private aims different from the common good. Men too can talk and therefore reason; they are "most troublesome when most at ease," because they then love to show their wisdom and control their rulers. The great difference, however, is that their agreement is "by covenant, which is artificial," whereas bees agree by "nature." By "artificial" we must here understand what is made by reason. Since men can live, for they do sometimes live in a "state of nature," a political society is not essential to man as man. It is a product of his voluntary action, and therefore implies a conscious deliberation. The only way, then, in which the common power can be erected and security established, is that men should "confer all their power and strength upon one man or one assembly of men." Then wills will be "reduced into one will, and every man acknowledge himself to be the author of whatsoever is done by the ruler so constituted." "This is more than consent or concord; it is a real unity of them all in one and the same person, made by covenant of every man with every man; in such manner as if every man should say to every man: *'I authorise and give up my right of governing myself to this man, or this assembly of men, on this condition that thou give up thy right to him, and authorise all his actions in like manner.'"* The Leviathan, or mortal god, is instituted by this covenant. He is the vital principle of political association, and from it Hobbes will proceed to deduce the whole of his doctrine.

Before considering its terms, one remark may be made. It is sometimes asked whether the expounders of the "social contract" in various forms meant to be understood historically. Did they mean to assert that at some remote period a number of men had held a convention, like the American States, and signed articles of association, to bind themselves and their posterity? Occasionally they seem to be driven to accept that position. Hobbes, however, can hardly have entertained such a belief. He is as ready as anybody to give an historical account of the origin of actual constitutions. In his *Dialogue upon the Common Law,* for example, he, like Montesquieu, traces the origin of the British Constitution to the forests of Germany, and the system once prevalent among the "savage and heathen" Saxons. He recognises in the *Leviathan* that governments may arise from conquest or the development of the family as well as by "institution," and endeavours to show that the nature of sovereignty will be the same in whatever way it may have originated. A contract, it always has to be admitted, may be "implicit" (that is, may really be no contract at all), and there can be no doubt that, in point of fact, the social contract, if it exists, must at the present day be of that kind. Nobody is ever asked whether he will or will not agree to it. Men, as members of a political society, accept a certain relation to the sovereign, and unless they did so the society would be dissolved. That such an understanding exists, and is a condition of the existence of the State, would be enough for Hobbes, whatever the origin of the understanding. As we shall presently see, he would be more consistent, if not more edifying, if he threw the contract overboard altogether.

We must look more closely at the terms of the hypothetical contract. The first point is that Hobbes's version differs from the earlier forms in this, that it is not a contract between the subject and the sovereign, but between the subjects themselves. The sovereign is created by it, but is not a party to it. This is Hobbes's special and most significant contribution to the theory. His reason is plain. Men, in a state of nature, that is, not acknowledging any commòn authority, cannot make a contract collectively. They are, in that case, simply a "multitude." His own theory, he says in a note to the *De Cive,* depends upon clearly understanding the different senses in which this word may be used. A multitude means first a multitude of men. Each has his own will and can make compacts with his neighbours. There may be as many compacts as there are men, or pairs of men, but there is then no such thing as a common will or a contract of the multitude considered as a unit. This first becomes possible when they have each agreed that the will of some one man or of a majority shall be taken for the will of all. Then the multitude becomes a "person," and is generally called a "people." One man is a "natural person," and their common representative is an "artificial person," or, as he puts it, "bears the person of the people." It is, therefore, impossible to take the social contract as made between the sovereign and the subjects. Till they have become an "artificial person" they cannot make a contract as a whole. This social contract is presupposed in all other contracts. It must be at the foundation of all corporate action, and a compact between the sovereign and the subjects would suppose the previous existence of a unity which is only created by the contract itself. In the "state of nature" men can promise but cannot make a binding contract. A contract means an exchange of promises, and in a "state of nature" neither party can depend upon the other keeping his word. Obligation follows security. It seems rather difficult, perhaps, to see how you can ever get out of the state of nature, or why the agreement of each man to take the sovereign will for his own, is more likely to be observed than any other agreement. Hobbes, however, assumes that this is possible; and when the Leviathan has once been constructed, it embodies the common will. The multitude becomes a person, and law, natural and civil, becomes binding.

3. *The Leviathan*

We have thus got our sovereign. His will is the will of all. He is under no obligation to his subjects, but is the source of all obligation. The ultimate justification of his existence, however, is still the desire for self-preservation, and for peace as an essential condition. Hence, indeed, arise the only limitations to the power of the sovereign which Hobbes admits. Since I aim at my own security, I cannot lay down the right of resisting men who would kill me, or even men "who would inflict wounds or imprisonment." I may indeed agree that you shall kill me, but I cannot agree that I will not resist you. A criminal may be properly put to death, for he has agreed to the law; but he must be guarded on his way to execution, for he has not bargained not to run away. He adds another quaint exception. A man may refuse to serve as a soldier, at least if he can offer a substitute. "And," he adds, "there is allowance to be made for natural timorousness, not only to women, of whom no such dangerous duty is expected, but also to men of feminine courage." (They may have been born in 1588.) In such cases, it seems, disobedience does not "frustrate the end for which sovereignty was ordained." The principle applies to the case of *de facto* government—when the sovereign cannot defend me I need not obey him.

With these exceptions, the power of the sovereign is unlimited. The "mortal god" is omnipotent. The covenant once made is indefeasible. The parties to it cannot make a new covenant inconsistent with it. They cannot transfer their allegiance without the consent of the sovereign. Since there is no power of revising the covenant, it cannot be broken without injustice. Hobbes, we see, speaks of the sovereign as "representing" the subjects. But he does not "represent" them as a member of parliament represents his constituents, or as a delegate bound to carry out their wishes. He "represents" them in the sense that whatever he does is taken to be done by them. They are as responsible for all his actions as though he was their volition incorporated. It follows that his power can never be forfeited. The subjects have done whatever he has done, and in resisting him would be calling themselves to account. The social contract, considered as a covenant with the ruler, was alleged as a justification of rebellion. Hobbes inverts the argument. It can never be right to allege a "covenant" with the ruler because that would justify rebellion. Since there is no common judge in such a case, this would mean an appeal to the power of the sword, and the power of the sword is what you have abandoned in covenanting. No individual again can dissent. If he does, he "may justly be destroyed" by the rest. If he consented to covenant, he implicitly consented to the covenant actually made. But, if not, he is left in the state of nature and may, therefore, "without injustice be destroyed by any man whatsoever."

The Leviathan, thus constituted, has therefore an indefeasible title and is irresponsible. He is the ultimate authority from whom all rights are derived. The end of his institution is peace. A right to the end implies a right to the means. The sovereign may do whatever promotes peace. Since men's actions proceed from their opinions, he may suppress the publication of opinions tending in his opinion to disturb the peace. Since contention arises from the clashing of rights, he must determine men's rights; or, in other words, must be the supreme legislator. The law means the command of the sovereign, and whatever he commands is therefore law. He must, again, have the "right of judicature"; the right to hear and decide all controversies arising out of the law. The sword of justice belongs to him, and "the sword of justice must go with the sword of war." The sovereign has to protect the people against foreign enemies as well as to protect each man against his neighbour. He must decide upon war and peace; and when war is necessary must decide what forces are necessary; and, further, must decide how much money is required to pay for them. "The command of the militia" (the military forces in general), "without other institution, maketh him that hath it sovereign; and, therefore, whosoever is made general of an army, he that hath the sovereign power is always generalissimo." Other powers, such as the appointment of ministers, the distribution of honours, and the infliction of punishments, obviously follow.

The Leviathan, thus invested with fullest power of legislature, judicature, and military command, with authority over opinion, and right to levy taxes, appeared to Hobbes's contemporaries to be a terrible portent. Charles I., trying to dispense with parliaments, Cromwell ruling by armed force, Louis XIV. declaring himself to be the State, might be taken as avatars of the monster. Lovers of liberty of thought or action were shocked by a doctrine fit only for the graceless and abject courtiers of the Restoration. The doctrine, however, must be considered on more general grounds. Hobbes, in the first place, is not here arguing for one form of government more than for another. He prefers monarchy; but his special point is that in every form, monarchic, aristocratic, or democratic, there must be a "sovereign"—an ultimate, supreme, and single authority. Men, he says, admit the claim of a popular State to "absolute dominion," but object to the claim of a king, though he has the same power and is not more likely, for reasons given, to abuse it. The doctrine which he really opposes is that of a "mixed government." As "some doctors" hold that there are three souls in one man, others hold that there can be more souls than one in a commonwealth. That is virtually implied when they say that "the power of levying money, which is the nutritive faculty," depends on a "general assembly"; the "power of conduct and command, which is the motive faculty, on one man; and the power of making laws, which is the rational faculty, on the accidental consent, not only of those two last, but of a third": this is called "mixed monarchy." "In truth it is not one independent commonwealth, but three independent factions; nor one representative person but three. In the Kingdom of God there may be three persons independent without breach of unity in God that reigneth; but where men reign that be subject to diversity of opinions, it cannot be so. And therefore if the king bear the person of the people, the general assembly bear the person of the people, and another assembly bear the person of a part of the people, they are not one person, nor one sovereign, but three persons and three sovereigns." That is to say, the political, like the animal organism, is essentially a unit. So far as there is not somewhere a supreme authority, there is anarchy or a possibility of anarchy. The application to Hobbes's own times is obvious. The king, for example, has a right to raise ship-money in case of necessity. But who has a right to decide the question of necessity? If the king, he could raise taxes at pleasure. If the parliament, the king becomes only their pensioner. At the bottom it was a question of sovereignty, and Hobbes, holding the king to be sovereign, holds that Hampden showed "an ignorant impatience of taxation." "Mark the oppression! A parliament man of £500 a year, land-taxed 20s." Hampden was refusing to contribute to his own defence. "All men are by nature provided of notable multiplying glasses, through which every little payment appeareth a great grievance." Parliament remonstrated against arbitrary imprisonment, the Star Chamber, and so forth; but it was their own fault that the king had so to act. Their refusal to give money "put him (the king) upon those extraordinary ways, which they call illegal, of raising money at home." The experience of the Civil War, he says in the *Leviathan,* has so plainly shown the mischief of dividing the rights of the sovereign that few men in England fail to see that they should be inseparable and should be so acknowledged "at the next return of peace."

Men did in fact come to acknowledge it though not for some generations, and then by virtually transferring sovereignty from the king to the parliament. A confused state of mind in the interval was implied in the doctrine which long prevailed, of the importance of a division between the legislative, executive, and judicial powers, and in the doctrine that the British Constitution represented a judicious mixture of the three elements, aristocracy, monarchy, and democracy, whose conflicts were regulated by an admirable system of checks and balances. Whatever truth may have been expressed in such theories, they were erroneous so far as inconsistent with Hobbes's doctrine. A division of the governmental functions is of course necessary, and different classes should be allowed to exercise an influence upon the State. But the division of functions must be consistent with the recognition of a single authority which can regulate and correlate their powers; and a contest between classes, which do not in some way recognise a sovereign arbitrator, leads to civil war or revolution. Who is the sovereign, for example, was the essential question which in the revolt of the American colonies, and in the secession of the Southern States, had to be answered by bullets. So long as that question is open, there is a condition of unstable equilibrium or latent anarchy. The State, as Hobbes puts it, should have only one soul, or as we may say, the political organism should have the unity corresponding to a vital principle.

The unity of the Leviathan seemed to imply arbitrary power. Since the king had the power of the sword, said Hobbes, he must also have the power of the purse. The logic might be good, but might be applied the other way. The true Englishman was determined not to pay the money till he knew how it was to be spent; and complained of a loss of liberty if it was taken by force. Hobbes's reply to this is very forcible and clears his position. He agreed with Johnson that the cry for liberty was cant. What, he asks, in his *De Cive,* is meant by liberty? If an exemption from the laws, it can exist in no government whatever. If it consist in having few laws, and only those such as are necessary to peace, there is no more liberty in a democracy than in a monarchy. What men really demand is not liberty but "dominion." People are deceived because in a democracy they have a greater share in public offices or in choosing the officers. It does not follow that they have more liberty in the sense of less law. Hobbes was putting his finger upon an ambiguity which has contin-

ued to flourish. Liberty may either mean that a man is not bound by law or that he is only bound by laws which he has made (or shared in making) himself. We are quite aware at the present day that a democracy may use the liberty, which in one sense it possesses, by making laws which are inconsistent with liberty in the other sense.

The problem, so much discussed in our times, as to the proper limits of government interference had not then excited attention. Hobbes seems to incline towards non-interference. Subjects grow rich, he says, by "the fruits of the earth and water, labour and thrift" (land, labour, and capital), and the laws should encourage industry and forbid extravagance. The "impotent" should be supported and the able-bodied set to work; taxes should be equal, and laid upon consumption, which (as he thinks) will encourage saving, and extravagance should be punished. So far his principles are those which his contemporaries fully accepted. But he adds emphatically that the laws should not go too far. "As water enclosed on all hands with banks, stands still and corrupts, so subjects, if they might do nothing without the command of the law, would grow dull and unwieldy." They must not, however, be left too much to themselves. "Both extremes are faulty, for laws were not invented to take away but to direct men's actions, even as nature ordained the banks not to stay, but to guide the course of the stream; it is therefore against sound policy that there should be more laws than necessarily serve for the good of the magistrate and his subjects." Laws, moreover, should be clear, simple, and directed not to revenge, but to correction. "Leaders of a commotion should be punished; not the poor seduced people. To be severe to the people, is to punish that ignorance which may in great part be imputed to the sovereign, whose fault it was that they were no better instructed." This is, perhaps, the only remark of Hobbes which would be endorsed by Tolstoi. Hobbes was in favour of a despotic rule; but he was anxious that it should be thoroughly humane, and was fully sensible that the English laws were in great need of reform.

Such questions, however, were then in the background. The real issue with his contemporaries was different. Although his theory of sovereignty is avowedly independent of the particular form of government, he has a leaning to monarchy. He confesses that he has not proved this advantage demonstratively: "the one thing in the whole book," he adds, in regard to which he will make that modest admission. His grounds are mainly that a king has a direct interest in promoting the welfare of his subjects, while popular leaders are prompted by vain glory and jealousy of each other, and popular assemblies are swayed by orators, for whom he always expresses contempt. "A democracy is no more than an aristocracy of orators, interrupted sometimes with the temporary monarchy of one orator": a Pym or a Gladstone. Hobbes's dislike to popular rule may be due in part to a certain intellectual difficulty. A sovereign must needs be a unit. But Hobbes is not comfortable with abstractions, or with so vague a body as the sovereign in a complex political system. He likes to have a king—a concrete, tangible individual in whom his principles may be incarnated. This prevents him from recognising one development of his theory which none the less was implied from the first. He perceives with perfect clearness and asserts in the most vigorous way that the division of sovereignty was the real weakness of the English system. His prejudices lead him to throw the whole blame upon the popular leaders. But a man of science should see that it is little to the purpose to blame individuals. Their discontent is a fact: a philosophical reformer should aim not at denouncing the symptoms, but at removing the causes of discord. It was clearly hopeless to persuade either side that it was in the wrong; but he might have tried to give an impartial diagnosis of the disease. He might then have admitted that the true solution might be, not to give the power of the purse to the king, but to give the power of the sword to the parliament. If he had contemplated that proposition, he might have foreseen (I do not mean that any human being could wholly have foreseen) that his theory would apply to a radically changed order.

In fact, Hobbes's *Leviathan* represents what is called "the modern State." Supremacy of the law, absolute authority of the governing power, and unity of the administrative system may be most fully realised when the "sovereign" is not an individual but an organic body. Government represents or "bears the person of the people," not in Hobbes's sense, that whatsoever the sovereign wills becomes their will, but in the inverse sense, that whatever they will becomes his will. Similar consequences follow in either version. Hobbes, for example, believes in the equality of man. It is one of his laws of nature that "every man acknowledge another for his equal by nature." Even if men were not equal, they would only make the compact on conditions of equality. Inequality of subjects, he says elsewhere, is made by the sovereign; and therefore all must be equal before the sovereign, as kings and subjects are equal before the King of Kings. Crimes of great men are "not extenuated but aggravated by the greatness of their persons." If they are favoured, "impunity maketh insolence; insolence hatred; and hatred an endeavour to pull down all oppressing and contumelious greatness, though with the ruin of the commonwealth." No subject can acquire any rights which will impede the full exercise of the sovereign power. The property of subjects in lands, for example, "consisteth in right to exclude all other subjects from the use of them, and not to exclude their sovereign, be it an assembly or a monarch." If land is not to be nationalised, the landowner's right is never absolute. So in all "systems subject—that is, in all associations of any kind—no power can be enjoyed except what the sovereign chooses to allow." They must be thoroughly subordinate to

his will, though in practice they have an awkward tendency to independence. Among the diseases of a commonwealth, Hobbes reckons great towns able to furnish an army (London, of course, is in his mind) "as well as the great number of corporations which are, as it were, many lesser commonwealths in the bowels of the greater, like worms in the entrails of a natural man." The principle is evidently fatal to privileged estates or corporations. The king or sovereign may call in councillors; but they must remain councillors only. That, for example, is the case with the House of Commons. But the House of Lords has no better claim. "Good counsel comes not by inheritance." The claim of certain persons to have a place in the highest council by inheritance is derived "from the conquests of the ancient Germans." Their chiefs were able to extract privileges for their posterity. Such privileges, however, are inconsistent with sovereign power, and if men contend for them as a right, they "must needs by degrees let them go," and be content with the honour due to their natural abilities.

This consequence of the supremacy of the sovereign illustrates one curious contrast between Hobbes and his opponents. The parliamentary party had to defend privilege against prerogative; and privilege has to be defended by precedent. The party, therefore, which would in modern phrase claim to be the "party of progress," justified itself by appealing to antiquity. When, indeed, you cut off a king's head you have to appeal to general principles. Constitutional precedents are not available. Milton had to claim indefeasible rights for the people, and men like honest John Lilburne used language which anticipated Paine's *Rights of Man*. But in the earlier stages of the quarrel, Coke's gigantic knowledge of old records, and superstitious reverence for the common law, that is, for tradition and custom, was a stronghold of the party. Hobbes rejects the whole doctrine. An absolute political theory could not fit into the constitutional tradition or justify the heterogeneous products of historical accidents. His treatise on the common law expresses his aversion to Coke. He had already quoted him in the *Leviathan* to show how men's judgments were "perverted by trusting to precedent." "If the man who first judged, judged unjustly, no injustice can be a pattern of justice to succeeding judges." No custom, again, can justify itself. If "use obtaineth the authority of a law, it is not the length of time that maketh the authority, but the will of the sovereign signified by his silence." The tacit consent of a ruler may make a custom law. But "many unjust actions and unjust sentences go uncontrolled for a longer time than any man can remember." Only "reasonable" customs should be law, and evil customs should be abolished. The sovereign must decide what is reasonable and what should be abolished.

According to Hobbes, then, all political machinery is absolutely subordinate to the sovereign. His power is the sole working force, and every resisting element must be ejected or brought under control. The law is the expression of his will, and though he may enforce rules which have grown up independently, they can only exist on sufferance or by his tacit consent. In that respect Hobbes was at one with the most thorough-going revolutionists who ever proposed to rearrange the political order upon an ideal plan, and to abolish all traditional law which is not in conformity with the dictates of reason. As a matter of fact, Hobbes's legal doctrine came to life again in the hands of Bentham and his follower, Austin, the legal lights of the "philosophical radicals." Maine observes that they had scarcely anything to add to Hobbes's analysis of the meaning of law. Hobbes puts his theory with all possible clearness in the *De Cive* and the *Leviathan*. "A law is a command of that person, whose precept contains in it the reason of obedience." The "civil law" is the command of the sovereign. We are bound to obey it, because it is his command, as soon as we know it to be his. It must therefore be promulgated in order that we may know it, and have a "penalty annexed to it" in order that we may obey it; for "vain is that law which may be broken without punishment." When we are solemnly informed that a law is a command of the sovereign, enforced by a "sanction," the impulse of the unregenerate mind is to reply, "that is what I always supposed." Parliament and the policeman are phenomena too obvious to be overlooked; the great manufactory which is always turning out laws, and the rod which will smite us if we do not obey are always with us. What else should a law be than a rule made by one and enforced by the other? We are told in reply that great confusion has arisen by confounding such laws with "Laws of Nature," laws which are supposed to exist in some transcendental world, and yet to supply the necessary basis for the laws of actual life, and which have to be applied to life by the help of such shifty and ambiguous hypotheses as the social contract. I do not doubt that that is true, but it suggests one question. Austin and his disciples were always exposing the absurdity of the Law of Nature and the social contract, and yet their own doctrine coincides with that of Hobbes, who professes to make these theories an integral part of his system.

The explanation is simple, and gives the essence of Hobbes. According to Hobbes, in fact, the Law of Nature has a singularly limited sphere of action. It only exists, one may say, in order to repeal itself. Before the social contract, he says, every man has a right to everything, which is practically equivalent to nobody having a right to anything; for if the same thing belongs to two men, neither has a right against the other. But the contract is itself made by every man resigning all his rights to the sovereign. When he has thus made them over, he can no longer make any claims under the Law of Nature. The sovereign may command him to do anything (except, indeed, to help to hang him-

self) and he is bound to obey. The Law of Nature orders him to obey the positive law, and does nothing else. This comes, however, of being thoroughly logical, after making one initial error. The Law of Nature is simply the law of self-preservation, and whatever necessarily follows from it. But in what sense of "law" can we call self-preservation a law? In one sense it is what Hobbes calls a "theorem," not a law. It is (assuming its truth) a statement of fact. All men do aim at self-preservation. That is their one actual and, indeed, their one possible principle. If so, it cannot be a "law" at all in the ethical or strictly legal sense. It expresses an essential condition of man's nature, and not a law imposed upon him from without. Men act for their own preservation as stones fall by gravitation. It is a way they have, and they cannot have any other. Taking for granted the truth of the "theorem," it will enable us to show how political institutions and "civil laws" have come into existence, but it does not show that they are right or wrong. It is as irrelevant to introduce that confusion as it would be to say that the angles of a triangle ought to be equal to two right angles. Hobbes's real theory comes out when we drop the imaginary contract altogether. We assume "self-preservation" as the universal instinct and, moreover, we must provisionally accept Hobbes's thoroughgoing egoism. Then so long as there is no common superior, the instinct produces competition and war, and implies the nasty, brutish "state of nature." How do men get out of it? Historically, he replies, governments may be made by conquest or developed out of the family, "which is a little monarchy." In both cases sovereignty is acquired by "force" and the subjects submit from fear. Governments, also, are made by "institution," that is, by the social contract; and in this case the motive is still fear, but fear of one another. Admitting, then, that even as an historical fact, sovereignty has been made by "institution" or contract, the essential motive is still the same. Each man sees that he will be better off, or preserve his life and means of living better if he and his will obey a sovereign than if they remain masterless. The hypothesis that States were deliberately contrived and made by a bargain between the separate atoms is, of course, absurd historically, but is also irrelevant to Hobbes. The essential point is simply that settled order is so much more favourable to self-preservation than anarchy that every one has a sufficient interest in maintaining it. Peace, as he tells us, means all the arts and sciences that distinguish Europeans from Choctaws. The original contractors can scarcely be supposed to have foreseen that. But at least it gives a very good reason for obedience.

This comes out curiously in Hobbes's "exceptions" to the obligation of the contract. Men are not bound to kill themselves because the tacit "consideration" for accepting the contract was the preservation of life and the means of life. He was logically bound to go further. If upon that ground they may repudiate the contract, they may break it whenever the end is frustrated, that is, whenever by keeping it they will be in a worse position. Moreover, since nobody ever acts, except for his own good, they certainly will break it whether it is binding or not. In other words, the supposed contract is merely another version of the first principle of egoism: a man will always do what seems to be for his own interest. By calling it a contract he gets the appearance of extending the obligation to a wider sphere—to cases, that is, in which a man's interest is opposed to his contract. But it is only an appearance. It is indeed true that when a sovereign has once been set up, fraud and force cease to pay, as a general rule, and honesty becomes the best policy. But that is more simply expressed without reference to a contract. It merely means that the most selfish of mankind finds that it is worth while to have a policeman round the corner. Indeed the more selfish he is the greater may be the convenience. By abandoning my supposed right to all things, I get an effectual right to most things; and that may be called a bargain, but it is a bargain which I shall only keep, and indeed can only keep, according to Hobbes, so long as the balance of profit is on my side. That is, it is not a bargain at all.

The facts, however, remain, and Hobbes manages to state a clear and coherent scheme. His position may be compared to that of the old economists. They used to maintain that in taking for granted the selfishness of mankind they were making a legitimate abstraction. Men, it is true, are not simply selfish, they have other motives than a love of money; but the love of money is so prominent an instinct in economic masses that we may consider it as the sole force at work, and so we may get a theory which will be approximately true, though requiring correction when applied to concrete cases. Hobbes virtually considers the political system in so far as it is based upon selfish motives and is worked by individual interests. No doubt such motives are tolerably prevalent. The obvious and most assignable motive for obeying the law is fear of the hangman; and all manner of selfish interests are furthered by maintaining a settled system of government. He thus obtains a clear conception of one important aspect of the political order. It means organised force. The State is held together by armies which protect us from invasion, and by the administrative system which preserves order at home. These are undeniable facts which it is as well to recognise clearly, and which are most vigorously set forth in Hobbes's *Leviathan*.

Certain limits to the value of his theory are equally plain. In the *Leviathan* Hobbes says that the "public ministers" are parts organical of the commonwealth, and compares the judges to the "organs of voice," the executive to the hands, ambassadors to eyes, and so forth. The analogy between the political and the individual organism is implied in the whole theory. But the Leviathan is an "artificial" body, and "artificial" means mechanical construction. The individual is the ultimate unit, and though he resigns his rights to the sovereign, it is always for his own personal advantage. The comparison to a body suggests the modern phrase "the social organism," but the "artificial" indicates that Hobbes does not really interpret the Leviathan as an organism. It is a big machine or set of atoms held together by external bonds. Hobbes's egoism forces him to the doctrine that the particles gravitate together simply from fear—fear of the magistrate or fear of your neighbour. Sympathy is ignored, and such sentiments as patriotism or public spirit or philanthropy are superficial modifications of selfishness, implying a readiness to adopt certain precautions for securing our own lives and properties. This involves a one-sided view of the conditions of social and political welfare. It may be fully admitted that organised force is essential to a civilised society, that it cannot exist or develop without its military and judicial bodies, its soldiers and its judges, its hangmen, gaolers, and policemen, its whole protective apparatus. An animal cannot live without its teeth and claws. What is overlooked is the truth that other parts of the system are equally essential, and that there is a reciprocal dependence indicated by the word "organic." Society is held together not simply by the legal sanctions, but by all the countless instincts and sympathies which bind men together, and by the spontaneous associations which have their sources outside of the political order. It may be granted to Hobbes that peace is an essential condition of progress, and that the sovereign must be created to keep the peace. It is equally true that the sovereign derives his power from other sources than mutual "fear" or dread of the "legal sanctions." Society could not get on without the policeman; but the policeman could not keep order by the simple force of his truncheon. Force must be "organised," but it cannot be organised out of simple egoism and fear. So when Hobbes defines law as the command of the sovereign, he is stating what in a fully developed State is an undeniable fact. The law is the system of rules promulgated and enforced by the sovereign power in spite of any conflicting customs. Historically speaking, laws are not the less the product of customs which have grown up spontaneously; they are the causes, not the effects of the sovereign's authority; and in the last resort the sovereign power must still rest upon custom; that is, upon all the complex motives from which arises loyalty to the State, and upon which its vitality depends.

Hobbes's position was indeed inevitable. The conception of sociology as a science, in which the political order is regarded as only part of the whole social system, had not yet arisen. That could not happen until historical methods of inquiry had begun to show their power, and the necessity of treating political questions in connection with the intellectual or the industrial evolution began to be perceived. The "social contract" theory helped Hobbes to pass over in summary fashion the great historical problems as to the way in which the State has actually been developed; and therefore the State itself could be regarded as held together by the purely political and legal forces. When he had deduced the sovereign power from the principle of self-preservation, he seemed to himself to have explained everything. He had got to the one force which held the units together, as gravitation holds together the solar system. The relation between subject and sovereign is the one bond from which all others may be deduced. The thoroughgoing acceptance of this assumption leads to some of the singular results by which he startled his contemporaries, though he announces them with superlative calmness as demonstrated truths.

There are, as he has to admit, two sets of laws which may occasionally conflict with the laws of the State. In the first place, there is the moral law. Hobbes was perfectly well aware that a king might be a fool or a brute. It seemed to follow that laws might be contrary to the dictates of morality. His opponents could point out to him that some of the Roman emperors had been far from model characters. Besides their other weaknesses, they had occasionally thought it right to give Christians to lions. Again, the Christian Church claimed obedience, and Hobbes was an orthodox Christian. What is the subject to do if his sovereign orders him to break the moral law or to deny the truth of religion?

4. *The Moral Law*

Hobbes does not shrink from the logical result of his principles. The moral law, he holds, is the Law of Nature. The Law of Nature, as we have seen, means essentially the law of self-preservation, and from that is deduced the "virtue" of justice, from which all other laws of nature are corollaries. Justice means keeping covenants, which becomes operative when a "coercive power" is constituted; that is, at the institution of the social contract. This contract therefore is at the base of all moral as well as of all political relations. It is presupposed in all particular contracts. Justice, the cardinal or rather the sole virtue, means keeping covenants, but also keeping the primitive contract to which all others owe their binding force. It implies, therefore, unconditional obedience to the sovereign who is the social contract incarnate. The sovereign cannot be unjust to a subject; for every subject is himself author of all that the sovereign does. Laws are the "rules of just and unjust; nothing being reputed unjust that is not contrary to some law." "The Law of Nature and the civil law contain each other and are of equal extent." "Justice, gratitude, and other moral virtues" are merely "qualities that dispose men to peace and obedience" until the commonwealth is instituted. Then they become laws, "for it is the sovereign power that obliges men to obey them." Thus the Law of Nature is part of the civil law, and "reciprocally the civil law is part of the dictates of nature."

Nobody, I believe, ever followed Hobbes in this audacious identification of law and morality. I must try to make some apology for a most estimable old gentleman misled by an excessive passion for logic. In the first place, it may be held that, whatever be the ultimate meaning of morality, the actual morality of a race is evolved in constant correlation with its social organisation. Hobbes, who substituted the social contract for this process, and regarded sovereignty as the sole bond of union, could only approximate to this doctrine by making moral obligations a product of the sovereign will. It would be outrageous, no doubt, to suppose that a sovereign could make the moral law at his pleasure, so that lying might become a virtue or gratitude a vice if the lawgiver chose to alter the law. That is not Hobbes's meaning. Honesty, gratitude, and the like are, we see, useful qualities and parts of the Law of Nature as tending to self-preservation. The sovereign of course cannot alter that fact. What he can do is to make them obligatory by establishing the state of security which makes their exercise possible or prudent for the individual. In the "state of nature" the conduct would be self-destructive which, when the commonwealth is formed, becomes self-preservative. But, we may ask, will the power thus constituted aim at the end for which it was instituted? May not the sovereign do wrong? May he not be a brutal tyrant, or lay down laws which are immoral, because inconsistent with the welfare of the people? Is it in that case our duty to obey them? Must we submit to oppression or enslave our neighbours because the sovereign, whether king or parliament, commands it? Hobbes admits the possibility. "They that have the sovereign power may commit iniquity, but not injustice or injury in the proper signification." That is, the sovereign's immorality gives no right to the subject to disobey or even to protest. The reason is that the only alternative is anarchy. Bad laws are better than no laws. "Good," as we have seen, means what a man desires and evil what he eschews. "One counts that good which another counts evil; and the same man what now he esteemed for good, he immediately after looks on as evil; and the same thing which he calls good in himself he terms evil in another." There is no such thing as absolute good. Hence it is impossible to make a common rule from the tastes of "particular" men. We have to consider what is reasonable; but "there are no other reasons in being but those of particular men and that of the city; it follows that the city is to determine what with reason is culpable." We are bound to obey the laws before we know what the laws are; for the State must precede the law. Therefore "no civil law whatever can be against the Law of Nature." The Law of Nature may forbid theft and adultery; but till we have civil laws we do not know what theft and adultery are. When the Spartans permitted their youth to take other men's goods, the taking was not theft. In other words, all law becomes positive law, for the Law of Nature only orders us to obey the law of the sovereign. It has been said that "whatsoever a man does against his conscience is sin." That is true in the "state of nature," where a man has no rule but his own reason. "It is not so with him that lives in a commonwealth, because the law is the public conscience by which he hath already undertaken to be guided." Otherwise nobody would obey further than it seemed good in his own eyes.

The subject, then, hands over the whole responsibility to the sovereign. Then "it is in the laws of a commonwealth as it is in the laws of gaming; whatsoever the gamesters all agree on is injustice to none of them." Are then the laws as arbitrary as the laws of a game? To that Hobbes has his answer: "The safety of the people is the supreme law." The sovereign is "obliged by the Law of Nature" to procure this end, "and to render an account thereof to God and to none but Him." Remembering the peculiarity of Hobbes's theology, it may seem that this responsibility is perhaps illusory. It is more to his purpose that, as he puts it, "the good of the sovereign and people cannot be separated." "It is a weak sovereign that has weak subjects, and a weak people whose sovereign wanteth power to rule them at his will." It is clearly to the interest of the sovereign, as it is also his duty, to maintain order. But to maintain order is, according to Hobbes, to enforce morality. The sovereign has to instruct his people in the "fundamental rights" of his office. To do so is "not only his duty, but his benefit also, and security against the danger that may arise to himself in his natural person from rebellion." He proceeds in his quaint fashion to point out that this duty of instructing the people is the duty of impressing upon them the Ten Commandments. Since kings are mortal gods, the commandments of the first table are applicable to them as well as to the Supreme Being. Clearly a man who proves that kings not only should but naturally will adopt the Ten Commandments is preaching a sound morality.

It is necessary, however, to remember Hobbes's general ethical conception. Every man acts simply for his own good. Every man, again, interprets "good" as that which pleases him. Order can only be established when every man sees that he will get more good for himself by submitting to a common authority. When that is securely established, the individual will be repaid for sacrificing that right to everything which he could not enforce. But when that is done, the moral law is made supreme. For morality, according to Hobbes, is summed up in justice; that is, in observing the general contract according to which the distribution of good things is regulated and men are obliged to keep their particular contracts. Equality before the law and equality of taxation are also implied, for inequality leads to discontent. But in other respects every man may, and of course will be guided by his own conceptions of "good." As I have said before, Hobbes is not in favour of extending the sphere of legislation. Laws are "like hedges," set "not to stop travellers but to keep them in their

way. And therefore a law which is not needful, having not the true end of law, is not good." "Unnecessary laws are not good laws, but traps for money; which, where the right of sovereign power is acknowledged, are superfluous; and where it is not acknowledged, insufficient to defend the people."

This, it seems, is the essential meaning of Hobbes's identification of law and morality. They are, according to him, different aspects of the virtue which he calls justice. That means that a man acts morally so far as he pursues his own ends without harming his neighbour; and legally, so far as he obeys the sovereign who enforces the security without which it is not a man's interest to act morally. No doubt this is a totally inadequate view of morality. It is the legal or purely external conception which supposes that the moral, like the positive law, is satisfied by obeying certain "sanctions" which make bad conduct unprofitable. But it does not imply that the moral law is "arbitrary" or made at will by the sovereign. It is the law of "self-preservation" regarded from a purely egoistic point of view. . . .

Notes

[1] Hobbes's political theory is given in three books: the *De Corpore Politico,* which was the second part of his first treatise, and is reprinted in the fourth volume of the English works; the *De Cive,* which is in the Latin works, vol. iii., and an English translation of which, by Hobbes himself, forms the second volume of the English works; and the *Leviathan,* which forms the third volume of the English works.

[2] A very remarkable book, the *Politics of Johannes Althusius* (1557-1636), that appeared in 1603, anticipated much that Hobbes afterwards said, and played a considerable part in the evolution of the theory of "Naturrecht." Professor Gierke's most learned and interesting book upon Althusius gives a full account of his doctrine and of his relation to Hobbes among many others.

A. E. Taylor (essay date 1908)

SOURCE: "Empirical Psychology—The Nature of Man," in *Thomas Hobbes,* Archibald Constable & Co Ltd, 1908, pp. 76-101.

[*In the following excerpt, Taylor explores Hobbes's views regarding humankind's transition from a "state of anarchy into a state of settled order."*]

We have seen, in the last chapter, what is Hobbes's conception of the 'state of nature,' the condition in which man found himself at the dawn of civilisation, and into which he tends to degenerate when the bonds of political allegiance are gravely relaxed. It is a condition in which the machinery provided by government for the restraint of men's fundamentally anti-social impulses is entirely absent, and in which there is nothing to take its place. How, then, could any number of men ever pass out of this state of anarchy into a state of settled order? Hobbes replies that there is a possibility to escape from the state of nature into one of civil society which is founded partly on men's passions, partly on men's reason. Partly on their passions, since among these there are several which make for peace and orderly existence, such as 'fear of death, desire of such things as are necessary to commodious living, and a hope by their industry to obtain them.' (*Leviathan,* c. xiii.) Partly on reason, since it is reason which suggests to mankind the proper means of securing gratification for these unbellicose passions, or as Hobbes puts it, 'suggesteth convenient articles of peace upon which men may be drawn to agreement' (*Ib.*). We might, perhaps, ask how men living by the unregulated promptings of egoistic appetite ever come to listen to these 'suggestions' of reason, but here, too, Hobbes is ready with an answer. We, all of us, he says, have our calmer moments when rational reflection is undisturbed by passion, and it is then that the voice which suggests 'articles of peace' makes itself heard.

Like the great majority of the political theorists from Hooker in the sixteenth century to Rousseau in the eighteenth, Hobbes thus assumes that the transition from savagery to civil society must have began with an express agreement or contract, the so-called 'social compact.' Hence with him, as with the others, it becomes the first object of political theory to discover the terms of this original contract—the 'articles of peace' already mentioned—since it is by these terms that we have to ascertain the limits of the rightful authority of political rulers. The ruler is legitimately entitled to just so much authority over his subjects, and no more, as can be logically deduced from the examination of the terms of the contract by which civil subjection was first instituted. Whatever in the practice of actual rulers is not covered by these terms is usurpation. This method of deducing the rights of a government over its subjects from a supposed original contract, which had, in point of fact, come down to the thinkers of the sixteenth century from the mediæval legists and schoolmen, who were seeking a rational basis for their various theories of the division of power between the Pope and the secular authorities, or between the Pope and the general councils, received its deathblow towards the end of the eighteenth century from Bentham and Burke, both of whom insist, in different ways, that the rights of governments must be based on the actual needs of society, and not on any theory of the primitive rights of man. Bentham's arguments, which will be found in his *Fragment on Government,* are mainly directed against Blackstone's attempt to determine the rights of the British Crown by deductions from the compact between king and people supposed to be made in the coronation oath, Burke's, against the onslaught of the French Revolution, acting in the name of the 'rights of man' upon the vested interests, which he chooses to regard as established 'rights,' of the nobility and clergy. In the nineteenth century, the growth of historical research into social origins made the conception of government as having arisen at a definite time by means of a definite voluntary compact even more unreal, by revealing the enormous extent to which definite political institutions have arisen out of an earlier stage of 'customary' law. Indeed, when we look the matter squarely in the face, it becomes evident that free association by voluntary agreement belongs to the culmination rather than to the beginnings of civilisation, and that the recognition of the binding force of such agreements presupposes the existence of a highly organised public opinion against their violation, so that contract depends upon society more than society upon contract. It is therefore quite impossible for us to take Hobbes's account of the compact by which savagery is ended and civilised life begun as serious historical fact. Yet it is possible to suspect that the reaction against theories of the origin of government in contract may perhaps have been carried too far even on the historical side. History itself, at least, gives us reason to believe that many a famous community has sprung from combinations of 'broken men,' relics, in a period of general disintegration, from many distinct ruined tribes or cities, who have somehow been thrown together and entered into a new alliance among themselves, and in such cases the new community must clearly have rested upon the voluntary agreement to unite in mutual support. But, in any case, the substance of Hobbes's reasoned plea for absolutism is quite independent of the largely mythical form in which it is clothed by the author. However governments originate, it is at least true that their permanency depends upon the recognition by governors and governed alike of certain general principles defining the functions of the governor and the obligations of the governed, and such recognition may not unsuitably be represented to the imagination as an implicit bargain. These principles Hobbes and the seventeenth century publicists in general call by a name borrowed from the Roman lawyers, who in their turn had borrowed it from the Stoic philosophers, the 'laws of nature,' the curious result of this appeal to the terminology of the Roman jurists being that, in effect, the theorists of the 'social contract' contrive to apply to political institutions of a very un-Roman character the doctrines of the Roman law of corporations. There is, of course, no inconsistency between the phrase 'laws of nature' and Hobbes's doctrine that a law, in the sense of a command by a superior, is impossible until the creation of a public authority to give the command, since Hobbes is careful to explain that 'laws of nature' are not commands, but 'rules of reason,' true universal propositions as to the conditions upon which settled wellbeing is obtainable. They are laws in the sense in which we apply the name to the principle of Excluded Middle or to that of the syllogism, not in the sense in which it is given to the Statute of Mortmain or the British North America Act: 'A law of nature (*lex naturalis*), is a precept, or general rule found out by reason, by which a man is forbidden to do that which is destructive of his life, or taketh away the means of preserving the same, and to omit that by which he thinketh it may best be preserved' (*Leviathan,* c. xiv.). Hobbes's employment of the word 'forbidden' in this sentence is, of course, metaphorical. His meaning is simply that since every man desires to live, reflection shows us that it would be irrational to endanger our lives or to fail to protect them. It is in this, and not in any mere idealistic sense, that we have to understand the declaration, in the first chapter of the *De Corpore Politico,* that the law of nature is identical with reason. It is not that reason is thought of as supplying us with ends of action: the ends of action are already given by the fundamental brute passions and appetites. What reason does is to indicate general rules as to the means by which such foregone ends may be most certainly obtained.

Of such 'general rules found out by reason,' there are, according to Hobbes, a considerable number, but all are deducible from a single supreme rule, 'that every man ought to endeavour peace as far as he has hope of obtaining it, and where he cannot obtain it, that he may seek and use all helps and advantages of war. The first branch of which rule containeth the first and fundamental *law* of nature, which is *to seek peace, and follow it*; the second the sum of the *right* of nature, which is, *by all means we can to defend ourselves'* (*Leviathan,* c. xiv.). (Of course, by saying that we 'ought' to seek peace, Hobbes means no more than that, in virtue of the hazards and dangers of the 'war of all against all,' it is manifestly to our advantage to do so where we can.) An immediate corollary, which figures as the second law of nature, is that each of us should be willing, when the rest are equally willing, to abandon the general claim to act exactly as he thinks fit, so far as the renunciation is necessary for peace; 'that a man be willing, when others are so too, as far forth as for peace and defence of himself he shall think it necessary, to lay down this right to all things, and be contented with so much liberty against other men as he would allow other men against himself' (*Ib.*) Briefly, then, the second law is 'do not to others what you are not prepared to allow them to do to you', a precept which Hobbes, characteristically enough, confuses with the 'golden rule' of the Gospel. It is upon this rule that the whole possibility of contract, and, consequently, according to Hobbes, of political society, depends. For what the rule provides for is the laying aside by each member of a body of men of some part of his original right, as described in the first of Hobbes's 'rules of

reason,' to act exactly as he thinks fit. Now rights laid aside are either merely renounced, or, when they are resigned for the benefit of an expressly designated person or persons, *transferred* to that person or persons. Such transference, being a voluntary act, is necessarily interested, since the object of every voluntary act is some good to myself. The contracting parties, then, in every case, act each with a view to his own ultimate advantage. Also, since there are certain things for the surrender of which no man can receive an equivalent, there are things which cannot be made the subjects of contract, rights which cannot be transferred. A man cannot *e.g.* divest himself of the right to resist an assault upon his life, or an attempt to wound or imprison him. More generally, since the whole object of a transference of rights is to obtain an increased security of life and the means of enjoying life, no act or word of mine can reasonably be interpreted as showing an intention of divesting myself of the means of self-preservation. These considerations will meet us again as furnishing some limits even to the power of the sovereign.

Hobbes now proceeds to deduce from this second law a third, which is the immediate foundation of the rest of his social theory. When two parties make a bargain for their mutual advantage, it frequently happens that one of them is called upon to perform his part of the contract first and to trust the other to discharge his part at some future time. In this case the contract is called, from the point of view of the second party, a *covenant.* From the second law of nature we can then deduce a third, which Hobbes treats as the foundation of all moral obligation, 'that men perform their covenants made' (*Leviathan,* c. xv.). This follows, because if I break my agreement with you, then, since your object in the original agreement was to secure some good to yourself, and my failure to perform what I undertook has frustrated that object, you have no longer any inducement to fulfil your part of the bargain. Thus the whole purpose of making covenants has been defeated; 'covenants are in vain, and but empty words, and, the right of all men to all things remaining, we are still in the condition of war' (*Ib.*). On this law of the sacredness of a covenant depends the distinction of justice from injustice, and, indirectly, the whole of social morality, since 'the definition of injustice is no other than the not performance of covenant. And whatsoever is not unjust is just.' (*Ib.* Note, incidentally, that Hobbes thus, like Schopenhauer, treats wrongdoing as a concept logically prior to right-doing.) This definition explains what Hobbes had meant by saying that in 'a state of nature' there can be no injustice. Injustice is breach of covenant, but the mutual trust upon which the making of covenants depends, is only possible when there is a coercive power which can affect breaches of covenant with penalties severe enough to make it to my interest to abstain from them, *i.e.* under a civil government. For the same reason it is only under civil government that there can be property. It is a natural question why, if the motive for loyalty to my agreements is always some prospect of advantage to myself, I should be morally bound to keep them in cases where treachery promises to be still more advantageous. The fact of the obligation Hobbes does not dispute; he even maintains expressly that a promise to a brigand to pay a certain sum on condition of being released is binding unless declared invalid by a properly constituted court of law; but he is not altogether successful in the reasoning by which he supports his view. Partly he replies that a promise-breaker is *not* likely to gain in the long-run, since no one will trust him after his detection; partly he obscurely hints that there may be a final judgment of God to be reckoned with. Apparently this suggestion is not merely made for the benefit of the orthodox reader but represents a laudable inconsistency in the author's own views, a belief that honesty is not merely the best policy, but has a higher sanctity of its own which Hobbes's analysis of morality fails to account for. Perhaps he was more deeply influenced than he knew by the traditional English hatred of a lie, as something inherently base.

Hobbes now enumerates no less than sixteen subsidiary 'laws of nature,' that is, conditions without which peaceable common existence would be impossible. The general character of these 'laws' is negative; they are prohibitions of various forms of behaviour which may be expected to lead to a breach of the peace, and the deduction, in each case, takes the form of an appeal to self-interest. *E.g.* if I show myself revengeful, or arrogant, or unwilling to refer a dispute between myself and my neighbour to a disinterested and impartial arbitrator, I am doing what lies in me to prolong the 'state of war,' and am thus losing the increased security of life and enjoyment of its good things which peace would have given me. The whole body of the nineteen 'laws,' Hobbes says, may be summed up in the simple formula which had already been given as an equivalent for the second 'law': 'To leave all men unexcusable, they have been contracted into one easy sum, intelligible even to the meanest capacity, and that is, *Do not that to another which thou wouldest not have done to thyself;* which sheweth him that he has no more to do in learning the laws of nature, but when, weighing the actions of other men with his own, they seem too heavy, to put them into the other part of the balance and his own into their place, that his own passions and self-love may add nothing to the weight; and then there is none of these laws of nature that will not appear unto him very reasonable' (*Leviathan,* c. xv.).

We see, then, that Hobbes's 'laws of nature,' looked at as a whole, afford a fair formulation of the fundamental negative condition upon which the maintenance of social order depends; no man is to expect more from his neighbours than he is willing that they should ex-

pect from him, and no man is to interfere with the doings of his neighbours in any way in which they may not equally interfere with his. The competitors in the great struggle of life are to start fair, and to 'play the game.' What we should seek in vain in any of Hobbes's expositions of his social doctrine is the great Hellenic conception of the state or community as having a further positive function, a duty to ennoble the lives of its members, so that each of them may, if he will, climb to spiritual heights which he could not have sealed alone. Hobbes can hardly be said to have any real belief in social institutions as the instruments and bearers of progressive civilisation, he treats them as merely so much machinery for the preservation of a *status quo*. He has mastered only the first half of Aristotle's famous dictum that 'the city comes into being that men may live, but continues to be that they may live well.'

We may now pass at once to a demonstration of the necessity of the organised state and its machinery. The 'laws of nature' are, indeed, in themselves a sufficient code of conduct, and if they were always observed, peaceful social existence would be guaranteed with all its accompanying benefits. But in the 'state of nature' we can have no security that they will be obeyed. They 'oblige in *foro interno;* that is to say, they bind to a desire they should take place; but in *foro externo,* that is, to the putting them in act, not always,' since a man who persisted in keeping them while all his neighbours broke them, would infallibly lose by his conduct, and it is impossible, on Hobbes's theory of human nature, that a man should persist in doing what he knows to be contrary to his private interest. Thus they are, rightly speaking, not as yet *laws,* so long as men remain in a 'state of nature.' For a law means a command given and enforceable by a definite person. 'These dictates of reason men use to call by the name of laws, but improperly; for they are but conclusions or theorems concerning what conduceth to the conservation and defence of themselves, whereas law properly is the word of him that by right hath command over others' (*Leviathan,* c. xv.). What is needed, then, to secure actual obedience to them is that they should be converted into commands issued by an authority which has rightful claims to obedience, and has also sufficient force at its disposal to secure obedience by the infliction of such penalties for disobedience as may make it always to a man's own advantage to obey. What is needed is, in fact, the institution of a ruler, or sovereign, and with the creation of the ruler we have passed at once into a state of civil society, or political subjection. This is why, with Hobbes, the creation of a ruler or chief magistrate is identical with the creation of society itself, and rebellion against the ruler equivalent to the dissolution of the social bond itself.

Before we go on to examine the way in which the ruler is created, there are two points to which it is essential to call attention if Hobbes is not to be greatly misjudged. In spite of his insistence upon the view that the 'dictates of reason' do not become actual commands until there is some one to enforce them, Hobbes is not justly chargeable with the identification of the moral law with the caprices of an autocrat. The validity of the moral law, though not its character as '*law*,' is with him anterior to the establishment of the ruler, and depends upon what he takes to be the demonstrable coincidence of morality with the general interest. What the ruler is needed for is to provide the individual with a standing adequate *incentive* to behave morally, and Hobbes is at great pains to urge that his favourite constitution, an absolute monarchy, is precisely the form of society in which the ruler is least likely to have any personal interest independent of the well-being of the community, and may therefore be most safely trusted to see that his 'laws' embody nothing but the conditions necessary for peace and security.

And again, though Hobbes's argument amounts to a defence of absolutism, the defence is throughout based on rationalistic and, consequently, democratic grounds. He is entirely free both from the superstition of a 'divine hereditary right' inherent in monarchs, such as the Stuarts laid claim to, and from the doctrine that mere force itself constitutes right. His object is to show that the absolute authority of the sovereign has a foundation in right by tracing it back to its supposed origin in a voluntary 'transference of right' on the part of the subject, a transference made in the interests of the subject himself, and so to legitimate absolutism by giving it a utilitarian basis. The *jure divino* royalists were thus completely justified in their instinctive distrust of Hobbes. When once it is granted that absolute sovereignty is only defensible *if* it can be shown to be for the general interest, the door is opened for further inquiry whether absolutism really *is* for the general interest or not, and, if it can be shown that it is not, for the rejection of absolutism itself. Thus Hobbes's theories really contain the germs of the constitutionalism which he combated. To declare that absolutism requires an utilitarian justification is to be already half-way on the road to revolution; there is much more community of spirit between Hobbes and Locke or Sidney, or even Rousseau, than between Hobbes and Filmer.

The immediate object of Hobbes's deduction of the rights of the sovereign is closely connected with the political controversies of his own time. He is anxious to disprove the claims made by Parliament against the British Crown to be, in a special sense, the *representative* of the people and of popular rights. He therefore sets himself to argue that, in every society, the supreme executive authority is already itself the true representative of the whole community; the community, consequently, cannot be again 'represented' by any other institution, and all claims made by such institutions to authority co-ordinate with, or superior to, that

of the executive, on the plea of their 'representative' character, must be nugatory. To effect this proof, he has recourse to the technical terms of the Roman law of corporations and their legal representation. He starts with the legal definition of a *person*. A person means any being whose words and acts are considered in law as issuing either from himself or from any other man or thing to whom they are attributed. In the latter case, where the words and acts of such a person are legally regarded as belonging to some other being or beings, whom he *represents,* the representer is an *artificial* person (*e.g.* an advocate, speaking from his brief, is an artificial person, who represents his client; what he says is taken in law as if it were uttered by, and committed, not the advocate himself, but his client). When the being thus represented by another owns the words and acts of his representative, he is said to authorise them, and the representative speaks and acts with *authority,* so that an act done by authority always means an act 'done by commission or license from him whose right it is.' This at once leads to the conclusion that, by the 'law of nature,' any being who has 'authorised' another to represent him is bound by all engagements entered into by his representative on his behalf, so far as they come within the scope of the authorisation, exactly as if they were his own words or acts. To repudiate them is to be guilty of a breach of the law that covenants when made are to be kept.

This point being granted, it only remains to establish the proposition that all governments must be regarded as originating in a commission bestowed by a whole community upon the government to 'represent' it, and the logical defence of absolutism is complete. Accordingly Hobbes now proceeds to reason as follows. An aggregate of individual men can only become a true *society* in so far as it exhibits a unity of will and purpose. It is this unity of will which constitutes the multitude into a community. But there is, properly speaking, no such thing as a 'general' will, or will of society at large, which is not that of individuals. Only by a legal fiction can we speak of anything but individual beings as endowed with will. Consequently, the unity of society is only possible by means of representation. The 'will' of the society becomes a real thing when the original aggregate agree to appoint a determinate man, or body of men, their representative, *i.e.* to take the volitions of that man, or that body of men, as 'authorised' by every individual composing the aggregate.

In this way, and only in this way, an aggregate may, by legal fiction, become one *person, i.e.* a collective subject of legal rights and duties. 'A multitude of men are made *one* person when they are by one man, or by one person, represented so that it be done with the consent of every one of that multitude in particular. For it is the unity of the *Representer,* not the unity of the *Represented,* that maketh the person one. And it is the Representer that beareth the person, and but one person; and unity cannot otherwise be understood in multitude. And because the multitude naturally is not one but many, they cannot be understood for one, but many, authors of everything their representative saith or doth in their name, every man giving their common representer authority from himself in particular, and owning all the actions the representer doth' (*Leviathan,* c. xvi.). The only way, then, in which an aggregate of men can form themselves into a society for mutual defence against outsiders, and against one another's anti-social tendencies, is by unanimous agreement to appoint some definite man, or number of men, to act as their representative, whose commands each of the aggregate is henceforth to regard as issuing from himself, and by whose actions each henceforth is to regard himself as bound, exactly as though they had been performed by himself. In this way, the 'laws of nature,' the conditions of peace and security, become actually operative, since by making such an agreement, the represented implicitly authorise their representer to employ their united physical force, as though it were his own, in restraint of all disobedience to his commands, and thus create a coercive power adequate enough to give every individual personal motives to obey.

'The only way to erect such a common power . . . is to confer all their power and strength upon one man, or upon one assembly of men, that may reduce all their wills, by plurality of voices, unto one will; which is as much as to say, to appoint one man, or assembly of men, to bear their person; and every one to own and acknowledge himself to be the author of whatsoever he that so beareth their person shall act or cause to be acted in those things which concern the common peace and safety, and therein to submit their wills to his will and their judgments to his judgment. This is more than consent or concord; it is a real unity of them all in one and the same person, made by covenant of every man with every man. . . . This done, the multitude, so united in one person, is called a *Commonwealth.* . . . This is the generation of that great *Leviathan,* or rather, to speak more reverently, of that mortal God, to which we owe, under the immortal God, our peace and defence. For by this authority, given him by every particular man in the Commonwealth, he hath the use of so much power and strength conferred on him, that by terror thereof he is enabled to form the wills of them all to peace at home and mutual aid against their enemies abroad. And in him consisteth the essence of the Commonwealth, which, to define it, is one person, of whose acts a great multitude, by mutual covenants one with another, have made themselves every one the author, to the end that he may use the strength and means of them all as he shall think expedient for their peace and common defence. And he that carrieth this person is called *Sovereign* and said to have sovereign power, and every one besides, his *subject*' (*Leviathan,*

c. xvii.).

One or two points in this deduction call, perhaps, for special remark. (1) It should be clear that, in spite of his absolutist leanings, what Hobbes is trying to express by the aid of his legal fictions is the great democratic idea of self-government. The coercive powers of the ruler are only legitimated in his eyes by the thought that they give effect to what is at heart the will of the whole people over whom he rules; the sovereign is, in effect, the incarnation of the national will. But as his philosophy will not allow him to admit the reality of any purpose which is not that of a definite man, he has to conceive of this national spirit and purpose as having no actual existence until it is embodied in a representative of flesh and blood. The nation is one man, with a will and purpose of its own, but it is one only by the legal fiction which treats the acts of an agent or representative *as if* they were those of that which he represents. To borrow an analogy from the case of the individual, the soul of the great artificial 'body politic' is not diffused over the whole organism, 'all in every part,' but definitely located in a central organ, or brain. This is why Hobbes is so careful to insist that legitimate sovereignty must be based on an express or tacit consent of every member of the subject body, and also why he is afterwards at great pains to argue that his favourite form of government, the absolute sovereignty of a single man, is just the one in which, from the nature of the case, the ruler is least likely to have any private interests of his own distinct from those of the community, and, in fact, is most nearly a mere mouthpiece of the national will.

(2) With Hobbes, as we see, the creation of a commonwealth, and the creation of a central coercive or executive power, form one and the same act. It is by the constitution of an executive that the 'laws of nature,' which bid men to seek peace and ensue it, cease to be amiable but impracticable ideals and become operative realities. He is thus the author of the doctrine, revived in the nineteenth century by Austin and his disciples, that sovereign power is in its nature one and indivisible, and that there can be no real distinction between the different functions of government, so that the making of laws may belong to one set of persons, the enforcing them by penalties to a second, and the interpretation of them in particular cases to a third. It is on this point that Hobbes's political theory is most strikingly at variance with those of his best-known successors. When Locke formulated the philosophy of the Revolution Whigs in his treatises on *Civil Government,* he was inevitably led, in the attempt to justify resistance to a chief magistrate who violates his trust, to make a distinction which is opposed to the central thought of Hobbes. With Locke the fundamental and original 'social compact' consists simply in the determination of a number of men to live in future under a known and common law of action instead of being

guided by the uncertain and fluctuating dictates of individual judgment, *i.e.* in the will to establish a common *legislature*. The appointment of a definite set of persons armed with power to put the decisions of this legislature into act—the creation of executive officials—is a later proceeding, and the chief magistrate thus becomes a mere delegate of the legislature, a trustee, who may lawfully be removed whenever he transgresses the limits of the powers delegated to him. Locke is thus the author of the famous doctrine of the 'division of powers' between distinct 'branches' of government,' and of the theory of the importance of 'constitutional checks,' by which one 'branch' may be hindered from usurping the functions of the others.

(3) We might perhaps add that in virtue of his definition of the ends of government as exhausted by the preservation of 'peace and common defence,' Hobbes may be regarded as a forerunner of the negative *laisser aller* doctrine of the functions of the state. The sovereign is there, in fact, to remove certain standing obstacles to the secure prosecution by his subjects of their individual aims, to keep society from relapsing into primitive anarchy. With his defective theory of volition, Hobbes can naturally find no place for any conception of the state as an organisation for the positive promotion among its members of the 'good life' or 'civilisation' or 'progress,' or whatever else we may please to call that ideal of life, by which the rationally free man is distinguished from the barbarian. The very existence of moral and social progress is, in fact, just the one striking feature of historical civilisation which his account of human nature, to be consistent with itself, is bound to ignore.

G. P. Gooch (essay date 1914-15)

SOURCE: "Hobbes," in *Political Though in England: From Bacon to Halifax*, Thorton Butterworth Limited, 1914, pp. 35-57.

[In the following excerpt, Gooch offers an overview of Hobbes's political philosophy and suggests that he was instrumental in the "atmospheric change which substituted the secular for the theological standpoint."]

While James proclaimed the divinity of lawful kings and Bacon preached the ideals of the Tudor monarchy, Hobbes, the author of the first comprehensive political system produced in England, derived his theory of the State neither from theology nor from tradition, but from the study of human nature. The most interesting as well as the most explosive English thinker in the seventeenth century stood aloof from the contending factions. No man of his time occupied such a lonely position in the world of thought, and it was only in the nineteenth century that his importance was fully grasped and the startling modernity of his cardinal principles

was realised. While the divine right of kings perished with the theological age which gave it birth, the sovereignty of the State exhibits every characteristic of robust and undiminished vitality.

Born in the year of the Armada, Hobbes learned as little at Oxford as most of his contemporaries. Becoming tutor to the son of the first Earl of Devonshire, with whom he visited France and Italy, he established the happy relations with the Cavendish family which only terminated seventy years later with his death. He enjoyed ample leisure, and roamed at will over the wide expanses of philosophy and classical literature. It was in these years that he made the acquaintance of Bacon, who, as Aubrey records, used to walk up and down the gardens of Gorhambury in contemplation. When an idea entered his mind he would at once communicate it to one of his attendants; and he used to say that Hobbes was quicker than any one in seizing his meaning and conveying it to paper in an intelligible form. The chief product of his early studies was a translation of Thucydides, whose pregnant analysis of the problems of government commanded his admiration, and whose vivid pictures of political confusion confirmed his conviction of the necessity of a strong ruler. A second and third journey abroad enabled him to study the France of Richelieu at close quarters. In Italy he made the acquaintance of Galileo, and in Paris formed an enduring friendship with Mersenne, the henchman of Descartes, Gassendi and other French scholars. Returning to England in 1638 he associated with the famous group of lawyers, poets and divines who gathered round Falkland at Great Tew and freely discussed problems of government and religion. He watched the gathering storm, and in 1640 felt impelled to sketch out a political theory differing widely from that held either by King or Parliament.

The little work entitled **The Elements of Law Natural and Politic,** though not written for publication, circulated freely in manuscript copies; and the author later declared that if the Short Parliament had not been dissolved, his life would have been in danger. The Opposition had more serious work on hand than to rend an unknown philosopher; but the timid thinker fled in panic to France, where he remained till Charles had lost his head. The book, which consists of two parts, the first entitled **Human Nature,** the second **De Corpore Politico,** is distinguished by the clearness and pregnant brevity which he never lost. Though it was directly prompted by the controversies of the day, there is no reference to current events and no trace of polemical purpose. The first part describes the different elements in human nature, and urges the necessity for men to find security against each other. "The cause which moveth a man to become subject to another is the fear of not otherwise preserving himself." At this point the second part begins. The state of nature, which is a state of war, passes into political society when it is agreed that a majority, or a few or one, shall represent the will of all, either for a limited time or for ever. The Government, whatever its nature, must have the power of coercion; "for the wills of most men are governed by fear." In every State there is an absolute and indivisible sovereignty, which can neither be punished nor resisted. Obedience to the sovereign is terminable only by exile or conquest; for "every man may lawfully defend himself that hath no other defence." Though monarchy is not the only possible form of government, it is the least subject to passion or to dissolution by civil war. To avoid uncertainty in the succession the sovereign may name his successor. He must also decide controversies in religion, controlling not, indeed, the consciences of men, but their words and actions; for he is the immediate ruler of the Church under Christ, and all other authorities are subordinate to him. In a chapter on the Causes of Rebellion he rebukes the contention that in certain cases the sovereign may be resisted. If exceptions are made to the plain rule of obedience, the door is opened to confusion and peril. In words which recall the "True Law of Free Monarchies," he declares that the ruler is required by God to rule well and wisely under pain of eternal death, and that his punishment is the affair of God, not of man. But while James claimed impunity for lawful rulers alone, Hobbes claims it for all alike. The distinction of *de jure* and *de facto* is brushed aside. The duty of the sovereign is to keep men from cutting each others' throats; and that duty can be discharged as efficiently by a usurper as by the anointed descendant of a hundred kings.

It is not surprising that the little treatise impressed its readers; for its doctrines came as a sharp challenge to the parties that were girding themselves for battle in the spring of 1640. The doctrine of indivisible sovereignty and of law as the command of the sovereign had been proclaimed by Bodin during the wars of religion in France; but the idea was still unfamiliar in England. From the votaries of divine right he was separated by his purely secular view of the origin of kingship, and by his refusal to concern himself with the legal title of the sovereign. From the Parliamentary leaders he was still more deeply sundered by his contempt for fundamental laws and by his uncompromising repudiation of limited monarchy. Though both King and Parliament saw some of their cherished convictions assailed, the latter was the more deeply outraged. The message of the book was that the King had the right to do whatsoever he pleased. From the safe anchorage of Paris he followed the crisis with anxious interest, and occupied himself with the composition of the *De Cive,* which appeared in Latin in 1642.

Though the dedication to his patron, the Earl of Devonshire, announces that he is careful not to meddle with the laws of any special nation, the Preface makes it clear that the book was written throughout with English politics in the author's mind. He speaks of the "errors" that a tyrant may be killed, a prince deposed, a king's commands discussed by private citizens before they obey, and of the fearful mischief they bring in their train. In classical times the supreme power was reverenced and obeyed. "They little used, as in our days, to join themselves with ambitions and hellish spirits to the utter ruin of the State. They could not entertain so strange a fancy as not to desire the preservation of that by which they were preserved." The state of nature being a mere war of all against all, instinct compels the desire to escape from "this misery." Though monarchy is the most convenient government, the beginning of wisdom is to recognise that in every State there must be a supreme power to which obedience is due in all things, as well spiritual as temporal.

When the *De Cive* was launched Hobbes began a third and still more detailed exposition of his political philosophy. While engaged on the *Leviathan* he was appointed mathematical tutor to the Prince of Wales, and laid the foundation of an acquaintance which was to be of no small value in later years. The execution of the King in 1649 stirred him to offer guidance to his afflicted country. In 1650 he at last allowed the *Elements of Law* to be printed, and in 1651 he published an English translation of the *De Cive*. Later in the same year the *Leviathan* appeared in London. He no longer hid his counsels in Latin, but appealed directly to his fellow-countrymen. Shortly after its appearance Charles II reached Paris a hunted fugitive, and was presented by the author with a manuscript copy. Though the gay young King shirked the massive treatise, certain members of the royal circle were more curious and raised such a hue and cry that Hobbes fled from Paris.

In his attack on the *Leviathan,* written many years after in his final exile, Clarendon declared that he had conversed with Hobbes on the eve of the appearance of the book, and asked him how he could publish such doctrines. The philosopher replied, half in jest, half in earnest, "The truth is I have a mind to go home." Even if the conversation is correctly reported it can only have been a joke; for the principles of the *Leviathan* are those of the little treatise of 1640, and Hobbes was the last man wilfully to risk offending the King. In like manner the charge brought against him after the Restoration that the book was "writ in defence of Oliver's title" is refuted by dates. While he was putting the finishing touches to the treatise in 1650, England was governed by the Rump. The real cause of his expulsion was not his politics but his theology and his contemptuous treatment of ecclesiastical pretensions. "All honest men here," wrote the King's Secretary, Sir Edward Nicholas, "are very glad that the King hath at length banished from his court that father of atheists Mr. Hobbes." The philosopher made his submission to the Council of State, and spent the remainder of his long life in England.

The Leviathan or the Matter, Form and Power of a Commonwealth Ecclesiastical and Civil, is not only the fullest presentation of Hobbes's theory of the State, but one of the great books of the world. Its originality and power, its clarity of thought and pregnancy of phrase secure it a place among the classics of political philosophy beside "The Prince," the "Essays on Civil Government" and the "Contrat Social." The frontispiece strikes the keynote of the book. A gigantic crowned figure, with a sword in the right hand and a crozier in the left, rises behind a hill at the bottom of which lies a stately city. Above the head of the sovereign are the resounding words, *Non est potestas super terram quæ comparetur ei.* The great Leviathan, declares the Introduction, is the State, "which is but an artificial man, though of greater stature and strength than the natural, for whose protection and defence it was intended."

The first of the four books deals with Man, and passes in review his faculties and capacities, his virtues and defects. He pronounces men to be by nature so nearly equal in the faculties of mind and body that, while they all long for power, none can claim any benefit to which another may not pretend. From equality proceeds rivalry, and from rivalry proceeds war—not war in the organised sense, but a perpetual struggle of all against all. The desires and passions from which this anarchy arises are in themselves no sin, nor are the actions that result from them a crime till they are forbidden by law. But no laws can be made till men agree who shall make them. The state of primitive society or the state of nature was intolerable—"no industry, no arts, no letters, no society, and continual fear and danger of violent death." The life of man was "solitary, poor, nasty, brutish, short." Notions of right and wrong, justice and injustice, had no place. "Where there is no common power there is no law; where no law, no injustice." As the state of nature proved to no one's interest—for the weakest is strong enough to kill the strongest—it was natural that a way of escape should be sought. This could only be attained by every individual surrendering his right to do what he liked to a single man or body of men. Thus the war of all against all was exchanged for political society. The community became a state, the control of which was vested in the sovereign, the Leviathan or mortal God. The contracting parties are not the community and the sovereign, but subject and subject. The sovereign is the result of the pact, not a party to it. Hobbes defends this curious departure from the common theory on the ground that men in a state of nature, acknowledging no common authority, cannot make a contract collectively. The multitude is not a unit, and no "people" exists till a government has been formed.

The sovereign is chosen and endowed with power in the expectation that he will introduce peace and security; but though his authority is derived exclusively from those over whom he rules, he is bound by no obligations to them. The anti-social instincts of mankind are too insistent to be checked except by absolute authority; and any attack on that authority would involve an instant relapse into the barbarism which was deliberately abandoned. His will is law, and his subjects have only a right to do what he does not forbid. There is no limit to his power, though Hobbes allows an individual to resist an attempt to kill, wound or imprison him. The covenant once made cannot be terminated or revised. As he embodies the will of all, his actions are virtually their actions. A limited monarchy is a contradiction in terms. His task is to protect his subjects against foreign enemies and internal commotions, to decide on war and peace, and to levy the necessary taxation. The law embodies his command, and he must decide on its interpretation. He must suppress the publication of opinions which he deems dangerous to social peace. As he was instituted to defend the people against themselves, he must perform his task in his own way and without let or hindrance.

In the *Leviathan,* as in its predecessors, Hobbes takes infinite pains to establish that the sovereign is supreme, not less in spiritual than in temporal affairs. He will suffer no rival near the throne. Such subordination was of course implicit in his theory of the original contract; but his conviction of its necessity was emphasised by the claims of his Catholic and Puritan contemporaries. His gospel was the indivisibility of sovereignty, and sacerdotal pretensions to a co-ordinate or even subordinate authority were sternly repudiated. He trains his heaviest artillery against the claims of the Roman Church, because he realises the strength of its insidious appeal. The spiritual authority finds its opportunity in the weakness of the average man, with whom "the fear of darkness and ghosts is greater than other fears," and whose nerves are agitated by the threat of everlasting damnation. Against such a danger the sovereign must defend himself and his subjects, lest there be a struggle in every man's breast between the Christian and the subject. Naked Erastianism forms a vital part of the system; but Hobbes goes further than his argument actually requires. He endeavours to show that there never was a divinely instituted spiritual authority independent of the State, and that even among the Jews the secular sovereign was supreme. The Christian Church only obtained legal status by the gift of the Emperor, and its claim to supernatural authority is therefore baseless. Priests increased their power by encouraging the tendency to superstition latent in every man. He adds the celebrated sentence that has been quoted by a hundred Protestant historians: "If a man consider the original of this great ecclesiastical dominion, he will easily perceive that the Papacy is no other than the ghost of the deceased Roman Empire sitting crowned upon the grave thereof." Behind the elaborate parade of scriptural texts it is easy to detect not only an indignant repudiation of ecclesiastical pretensions, but something like contempt for the dogmas of the Churches. He would have welcomed Gibbon's historic sneer that all religions were to the believer equally true, to the philosopher equally false, to the magistrate equally useful. Religion was of value when it was employed not to challenge the decisions of the State but to teach men to live in peace.

If the rule of *Leviathan* should seem as intolerable as the anarchy from which it offered an escape, the reply was that the Government would interfere but little in the routine of daily life. While possessing the right and power to determine every detail, it would in practice permit whatever did not tend to disturb the peace. The laws should be few and simple. "As nature ordained the banks not to stay but to guide the course of a stream, so it is against sound policy that there should be more laws than necessarily serve for the good of the magistrate and his subjects." In like manner while the expression of opinion was subject to the will of the sovereign, thought itself remained free. There must be outward conformity to the worship ordained by law; but a man might believe as much or as little as he liked. For instance, he might reject "those acts that have been given out for miracles." There was, in fact, no need to molest a conforming sceptic like the philosopher of Malmesbury.

The *Leviathan* provoked an outburst of indignation in royalist and ecclesiastical circles, and hard words were used of its audacious author. They detested his anti-clericalism, his secularism, his contempt for the Universities. They were incensed by his doctrine that theology was a branch of politics, not politics of theology. For many years every sort of scepticism or free-thought was denounced as Hobbism. Evelyn records that the gentle physicist, Robert Boyle, entertained feelings of antipathy for but one person in the world, and that was Hobbes. Bentley was later to ascribe the decay of morality to Hobbes, and Dr. Sacheverell to class him with Spinoza as an atheistical monster. Hobbes's dislike of the clergy was only equalled by their detestation of him. The most substantial and authoritative reply came from the greatest of royalists. The "Brief View of the Dangerous and Pernicious Errors to Church and State in Mr. Hobbes's book," written by Clarendon in exile in 1670, was dedicated to Charles II. "I could not think of anything of more importance to Your Majesty's service than to confute Hobbes." To his personal worth he offers a warm testimonial. "A man of excellent parts, of great wit, of some reading and somewhat more thinking, Hobbes is one of the most ancient acquaintances I have in the world, and of whom I have always had a great esteem as one who, besides his eminent parts of learning and knowledge, hath been

always looked upon as a man of probity and a life free from scandal." To his teaching, however, he shows no mercy. Liberty, religion and justice were only empty words. Moreover, his theory of the contract did not even close the door to rebellion. If there was a revolt the ruler could not complain, for his subjects thereby broke no promise made to him. The old exile naturally repudiates the doctrine that a usurper once possessed of the sceptre should be implicitly obeyed. If a subject might and must submit to his new master as soon as the old one was unable to protect him, loyalty was torn up by its roots. The contemptuous treatment of religion provokes scarcely less indignation. He concludes with a wish that it should be burnt. "I never read any book which contained so much sedition, treason and impiety."

Passing from contemporary controversialists, a modern critic would begin by challenging the foundation on which the system rests. The necessity for absolute government is stated over and over again to lie in human nature itself as revealed in primitive society. But neither Hobbes nor his contemporaries knew anything of the actual life of primitive communities. His terrifying picture of a war of all against all corresponds to no reality. No community lives or could live in the state which he describes. For Hobbes there is no middle term between anarchy and absolutism. He was not aware that custom preceded law, and that the sanction of the one is as potent as of the other. He rightly rejected sentimental rhapsodies on the noble savage and the golden age of innocence and virtue; but he was unaware that the elements of social life are never absent among human beings, and that savages possess a rudimentary morality without any political organisation. The unit of primitive society was not, as he imagined, the individual, but the family or some other group, and the life of primitive man was far more fettered by tradition and rule than that of England under the Stuart kings. Progress towards a more complex organisation occurred not because the conditions were unbearable but owing to the emergence of new needs and aptitudes, often stimulated by peaceful or hostile intercourse with other communities. Hobbes expressly declares that in drawing a darkly shadowed picture of early society he is bringing no indictment against human nature; but in focussing attention on self-preservation he completely overlooks the complementary instinct of mutual aid. For him man is neither a moral nor a political animal. Behind every theory of absolute government lurks a disparaging view of mankind, and Hobbes is no exception to the rule.

With the destruction of his vision of primitive society the case for the iron yoke of a Leviathan falls to the ground. But even assuming the necessity of escaping from an unbearable situation, Hobbes fails to convince his readers that the only course was the unconditional surrender of "natural" rights. In his famous treatise

"De Rege," the Spanish Jesuit Mariana, who anticipated Hobbes in his description of the state of nature and traced civil society to the failings of mankind, declared that the community reserved more power than it surrendered. Hooker, again, who had shared the view that the compact was between the members of the group, not between ruler and subject, had declined to draw the inference that they had beggared themselves. His argument that no collective action was possible is controverted by his own version of events. The determination to escape from the state of nature was a collective volition, and the transference of rights to a sovereign was a collective action. His contention that men parted with their natural rights without the smallest security for the future is an affront to common sense. If men were capable of contracting out of their rights towards one another, they were equally capable of giving general directions to the ruler of their choice. The doctrine of the original contract in its usual form, though a pure fiction, found favour for many centuries precisely because it satisfied the sense of equity. It proclaimed the gospel of government by consent. As subjects owed a reasonable obedience to the ruler, so the ruler owed good government to his subjects. No unconditional and irrecoverable surrender of natural rights could take place. Some were surrendered in order to guarantee the rest. No generation could bind its successors for ever. The same demand for a better life which led to the selection of a ruler carried with it the right to test his actions by the measure in which they secured that object. In Hobbes's scheme, on the other hand, neither subject nor sovereign undertakes any obligations to the other.

The theory of an absolute sovereign, as has been pointed out, was almost equally unacceptable to the contending factions into which England was divided while Hobbes was writing his treatises. Clarendon speaks bitterly of his "notorious ignorance in the law and constitution of England"; and indeed the spirit is rather that of a continental than a British publicist. He was wrong in his contention that there is and always must be a sovereign in every State. There was no sovereignty in his sense in the Middle Ages, when power was divided between Church and State, between the King and his feudatories. His conviction that mixed government involves anarchy has been disproved by experience. Yet his doctrine, which seemed so extravagant in the seventeenth century, was capable of adaptation to the circumstances of a widely different age. Though he repeatedly spoke of monarchy as the "most commodious" form of government, he declares that the sovereign might be a king or an assembly. His mission was to attack the division of power. With whom that power rested was of minor importance. Thus a doctrine which sounded almost monstrous when predicated of a single man would wear a very different aspect when applied to a representative assembly; and the fame of Hobbes, after a long period of obscuration, was revived by the Philosophic Radicals of the early nineteenth century. The division of power between king and Parliament was, as he maintained, a source of danger; and the only means of terminating it was to settle which should be supreme. The events of 1688 having finally decided against the King, Parliament gradually came to occupy the position of undisputed sovereign. The conditions of Hobbes are fulfilled not less by a democratic Parliament in a country which possesses no written constitution than by the monarchy of Louis XIV. This capacity for adaptation to totally different circumstances distinguishes his position from that of his royalist contemporaries.

A further aspect of his teaching is also strangely modern. Hobbes recognised no law but the will of the actual sovereign. "Laws of nature" were simply "rules of reason," generalisations from experience, principles discovered to be essential to life and prosperity, but possessing in themselves no power of securing recognition. While paying lip-service to the authority of scripture, he reserved to the sovereign the monopoly of its interpretation. He rejects, moreover, the appeal both to fundamental laws of a peculiarly sacred character, such as Magna Charta, and to precedent. Like Halifax, Burke and Bentham, he teaches that the powers of government must be based on the needs of society, not on any theory of primitive rights. In the *Dialogue of the Common Laws,* written in old age, he remarks concisely that it is not wisdom but authority that makes a law. Laws made in past times have no validity without the approval and support of the reigning sovereign. Of the Law of Nature, on which thinkers of many schools erected their structure and by which they tested existing conditions, Hobbes will hear nothing; for, assuming it to exist, it could be interpreted by every man in his own way, and a conflict would at once arise between natural and positive law. The doctrine that law is the command of a superior, and that no law can be recognised which is not enforceable by punishment, was taken over bodily by Austin and forms the kernel of his teaching.

The worst part of Hobbes's system is that it allows the State no positive function. Its sole duty is the maintenance of order. Leviathan is the policeman, not the instructor. He has no vision of the Greek ideal of a State as a work of art, or of Burke's splendid conception of an association in all science, in all art, in all perfection. He accepts the Aristotelian maxim that the State comes into being that man may live, but ignores the equally vital truth that it continues in order that he may live well. His State is a necessary evil, an instrument to defend men against their savage instincts, not to achieve a free and progressive civilisation. His ideal was the rigid absolutism of the Bourbons, not freedom slowly broadening down from precedent to precedent.

When Hobbes returned to England in 1651 and made

his peace with the Commonwealth, he was acting in strict consistency with his teaching. Directly a sovereign ceased to be able to protect his subjects, his claim to their allegiance was at an end. Though the *Leviathan* was not written in the interest of the Commonwealth, its counsels of submission to a *de facto* government were highly opportune. In 1656 the philosopher claimed credit for "turning the minds of a thousand gentlemen to a conscientious obedience to the present government, which otherwise would have wavered." Though he detested the confusion which followed the Protector's death, the approach of the Restoration aroused lively apprehensions for his safety. But though he had many enemies at Court he possessed a steady friend in Charles II, who recognised his old tutor in the streets on his arrival in London and raised his hat in kindly greeting. Loving the society of wits, he ordered that the veteran thinker should be admitted whenever he appeared at Court, and used to greet him with the words, "Here comes the bear to be baited." "After the King's return," records Clarendon, "he came frequently to the Court, where he had too many disciples, and he once visited me." Though the omnipotent minister hated both his absolutism and his scepticism, men of less austerity delighted in the company of one who, in the words of his devoted friend Aubrey, was "marvellous happy and ready in his replies." With the rising tide of reaction, however, his position became increasingly insecure; and when the Plague and the Great Fire upset the nerves of the public, a bill was introduced to suppress atheism and profaneness, and a committee was chosen to examine the *Leviathan*. Though the bill, which passed the Commons, was dropped, Hobbes, always timid and now an old man of seventy-eight, was thoroughly scared. He burned some of his papers, wrote an essay to prove that he could not be lawfully executed for heresy, and ostentatiously attended the private chapel of the Earl of Devonshire. The King prevented his enemies proceeding to extremities, but forbade him to publish any more controversial books.

Hobbes's last important work, *Behemoth, or a Dialogue on the Civil Wars,* written in 1668, was printed without his knowledge a few months before his death in 1679, from an imperfect copy of his manuscript. The work is extraordinarily fresh and vigorous for a man of eighty, and it is of considerable interest for his judgment of the earth-shaking events of the middle decades of the century. While naturally attributing the main responsibility for the catastrophe to the champions of Parliament, he sharply castigates the royalists who thought the government of England was not an absolute but a mixed monarchy and attempted to impose limitations on the prerogative. The attack on the constitutional lawyers was repeated in the *Dialogue of the Common Laws,* written about the same time. Once again he states that the King is the supreme judge and the sole legislator, and that he cannot be controlled by his subjects. Yet it was by a sound instinct that the champions of authority looked askance at the prophet of absolutism; for Hobbes was above all a rationalist, and rationalism is the mortal foe of the mysticism on which the bolder claims of kings and Churches ultimately rest. To a far greater degree than Bacon he was the author of the atmospheric change which substituted the secular for the theological standpoint throughout the boundless realms of thought and speculation.

Works Cited

Leslie Stephen, *Hobbes*; Croom Robertson, *Hobbes*; A. E. Taylor, *Hobbes*; Tönnies, *Hobbes* (ed. of 1912); Aubrey's *Lives,* Vol. I.

Bertrand Russell (essay date 1945)

SOURCE: "Hobbes's *Leviathan*," in *A History Western Philosophy, and Its Connection with Political and Social Circumstances from the Earliest Times to the Present Day*, Simon & Schuster, 1945, pp. 546-57.

[*In the following essay, Russell examines the doctrines of* Leviathan, *noting that Hobbes's main limitations are his fear of anarchy, overemphasis on the national interest, and misunderstanding of relations between states.*]

Hobbes (1588-1679) is a philosopher whom it is difficult to classify. He was an empiricist, like Locke, Berkeley, and Hume, but unlike them, he was an admirer of mathematical method, not only in pure mathematics, but in its applications. His general outlook was inspired by Galileo rather than Bacon. From Descartes to Kant, Continental philosophy derived much of its conception of the nature of human knowledge from mathematics, but it regarded mathematics as known independently of experience. It was thus led, like Platonism, to minimize the part played by perception, and over-emphasize the part played by pure thought. English empiricism, on the other hand, was little influenced by mathematics, and tended to have a wrong conception of scientific method. Hobbes had neither of these defects. It is not until our own day that we find any other philosophers who were empiricists and yet laid due stress on mathematics. In this respect, Hobbes's merit is great. He has, however, grave defects, which make it impossible to place him quite in the first rank. He is impatient of subtleties, and too much inclined to cut the Gordian knot. His solutions of problems are logical, but are attained by omitting awkward facts. He is vigorous, but crude; he wields the battle-axe better than the rapier. Nevertheless, his theory of the State deserves to be carefully considered, the more so as it is more modern than any previous theory, even that of Machiavelli.

Hobbes's father was a vicar, who was ill-tempered and uneducated; he lost his job by quarrelling with a neighbouring vicar at the church door. After this, Hobbes was brought up by an uncle. He acquired a good knowledge of the classics, and translated The *Medea* of Euripides into Latin iambics at the age of fourteen. (In later life, he boasted, justifiably, that though he abstained from quoting classical poets and orators, this was not from lack of familiarity with their works.) At fifteen, he went to Oxford, where they taught him scholastic logic and the philosophy of Aristotle. These were his bugbears in later life, and he maintained that he had profited little by his years at the university; indeed universities in general are constantly criticized in his writings. In the year 1610, when he was twenty-two years old, he became tutor to Lord Hardwick (afterwards second Earl of Devonshire), with whom he made the grand tour. It was at this time that he began to know the work of Galileo and Kepler, which profoundly influenced him. His pupil became his patron, and remained so until he died in 1628. Through him, Hobbes met Ben Jonson and Bacon and Lord Herbert of Cherbury, and many other important men. After the death of the Earl of Devonshire, who left a young son, Hobbes lived for a time in Paris, where he began the study of Euclid; then he became tutor to his former pupil's son. With him he travelled to Italy, where he visited Galileo in 1636. In 1637 he came back to England.

The political opinions expressed in the *Leviathan,* which were Royalist in the extreme, had been held by Hobbes for a long time. When the Parliament of 1628 drew up the Petition of Right, he published a translation of Thucydides, with the expressed intention of showing the evils of democracy. When the Long Parliament met in 1640, and Laud and Strafford were sent to the Tower, Hobbes was terrified and fled to France. His book *De Cive,* written in 1641, though not published till 1647, sets forth essentially the same theory as that of the *Leviathan*. It was not the actual occurrence of the Civil War that caused his opinions, but the prospect of it; naturally, however, his convictions were strengthened when his fears were realized.

In Paris he was welcomed by many of the leading mathematicians and men of science. He was one of those who saw Descartes' *Meditations* before they were published, and wrote objections to them, which were printed by Descartes with his replies. He also soon had a large company of English Royalist refugees with whom to associate. For a time, from 1646 to 1648, he taught mathematics to the future Charles II. When, however, in 1651, he published the *Leviathan,* it pleased no one. Its rationalism offended most of the refugees, and its bitter attacks on the Catholic Church offended the French government. Hobbes therefore fled secretly to London, where he made submission to Cromwell, and abstained from all political activity.

He was not idle, however, either at this time or at any other during his long life. He had a controversy with Bishop Bramhall on free will; he was himself a rigid determinist. Over-estimating his own capacities as a geometer, he imagined that he had discovered how to square the circle; on this subject he very foolishly embarked on a controversy with Wallis, the professor of geometry at Oxford. Naturally the professor succeeded in making him look silly.

At the Restoration, Hobbes was taken up by the less earnest of the king's friends, and by the king himself, who not only had Hobbes's portrait on his walls, but awarded him a pension of £100 a year—which, however, His Majesty forgot to pay. The Lord Chancellor Clarendon was shocked by the favour shown to a man suspected of atheism, and so was Parliament. After the Plague and the Great Fire, when people's superstitious fears were aroused, the House of Commons appointed a committee to inquire into atheistical writings, specially mentioning those of Hobbes. From this time onwards, he could not obtain leave in England to print anything on controversial subjects. Even his history of the Long Parliament, which he called **Behemoth,** though it set forth the most orthodox doctrine, had to be printed abroad (1668). The collected edition of his works in 1688 appeared in Amsterdam. In his old age, his reputation abroad was much greater than in England. To occupy his leisure, he wrote, at eighty-four, an autobiography in Latin verse, and published, at eighty-seven, a translation of Homer. I cannot discover that he wrote any large books after the age of eighty-seven.

We will now consider the doctrines of the *Leviathan,* upon which the fame of Hobbes mainly rests.

He proclaims, at the very beginning of the book, his thorough-going materialism. Life, he says, is nothing but a motion of the limbs, and therefore automata have an artificial life. The commonwealth, which he calls Leviathan, is a creation of art, and is in fact an artificial man. This is intended as more than an analogy, and is worked out in some detail. The sovereignty is an artificial soul. The pacts and covenants by which "Leviathan" is first created take the place of God's fiat when He said "Let Us make man."

The first part deals with man as an individual, and with such general philosophy as Hobbes deems necessary. Sensations are caused by the pressure of objects; colours, sounds, etc. are not in the objects. The qualities in objects that correspond to our sensations are motions. The first law of motion is stated, and is immediately applied to psychology: imagination is a decaying sense, both being motions. Imagination when asleep is dreaming; the religions of the gentiles came of not distinguishing dreams from waking life. (The rash reader may apply the same argument to the Christian religion, but Hobbes is much too cautious to do so himself. [Elsewhere he says that the heathen gods were created by human fear, but that our God is the First Mover.]) Belief that dreams are prophetic is a delusion; so is the belief in witchcraft and in ghosts.

The succession of our thoughts is not arbitrary, but governed by laws—sometimes those of association, sometimes those depending upon a purpose in our thinking. (This is important as an application of determinism to psychology.)

Hobbes, as might be expected, is an out-and-out nominalist. There is, he says, nothing universal but names, and without words we could not conceive any general ideas. Without language, there would be no truth or falsehood, for "true" and "false" are attributes of speech.

He considers geometry the one genuine science so far created. Reasoning is of the nature of reckoning, and should start from definitions. But it is necessary to avoid self-contradictory notions in definitions, which is not usually done in philosophy. "Incorporeal substance," for instance, is nonsense. When it is objected that God is an incorporeal substance, Hobbes has two answers: first, that God is not an object of philosophy; second, that many philosophers have thought God corporeal. All error in *general* propositions, he says, comes from absurdity (i.e., self-contradiction); he gives as examples of absurdity the idea of free will, and of cheese having the accidents of bread. (We know that, according to the Catholic faith, the accidents of bread *can* inhere in a substance that is not bread.)

In this passage Hobbes shows an old-fashioned rationalism. Kepler had arrived at a general proposition: "Planets go round the sun in ellipses"; but other views, such as those of Ptolemy, are not logically absurd. Hobbes has not appreciated the use of induction for arriving at general laws, in spite of his admiration for Kepler and Galileo.

As against Plato, Hobbes holds that reason is not innate, but is developed by industry.

He comes next to a consideration of the passions. "Endeavour" may be defined as a small beginning of motion; if towards something, it is *desire,* and if away from something it is *aversion.* Love is the same as desire, and hate is the same as aversion. We call a thing "good" when it is an object of desire, and "bad" when it is an object of aversion. (It will be observed that these definitions give no objectivity to "good" and "bad"; if men differ in their desires, there is no theoretical method of adjusting their differences.) There are definitions of various passions, mostly based on a competitive view of life; for instance, laughter is sudden glory. Fear of invisible power, if publicly allowed, is religion; if not allowed, superstition. Thus the decision as to what is religion and what superstition rests with the legislator. Felicity involves continual progress; it consists in prospering, not in having prospered; there is no such thing as a static happiness—excepting, of course, the joys of heaven, which surpass our comprehension.

Will is nothing but the last appetite or aversion remaining in deliberation. That is to say, will is not something different from desire and aversion, but merely the strongest in a case of conflict. This is connected, obviously, with Hobbes's denial of free will.

Unlike most defenders of despotic government, Hobbes holds that all men are naturally equal. In a state of nature, before there is any government, every man desires to preserve his own liberty, but to acquire dominion over others; both these desires are dictated by the impulse to self-preservation. From their conflict arises a war of all against all, which makes life "nasty, brutish, and short." In a state of nature, there is no property, no justice or injustice; there is only war, and "force and fraud are, in war, the two cardinal virtues."

The second part tells how men escape from these evils by combining into communities each subject to a central authority. This is represented as happening by means of a social contract. It is supposed that a number of people come together and agree to choose a sovereign, or a sovereign body, which shall exercise authority over them and put an end to the universal war. I do not think this "covenant" (as Hobbes usually calls it) is thought of as a definite historical event; it is certainly irrelevant to the argument to think of it as such. It is an explanatory myth, used to explain why men submit, and should submit, to the limitations on personal freedom entailed in submission to authority. The purpose of the restraint men put upon themselves, says Hobbes, is self-preservation from the universal war resulting from our love of liberty for ourselves and of dominion over others.

Hobbes considers the question why men cannot cooperate like ants and bees. Bees in the same hive, he says, do not compete; they have no desire for honour; and they do not use reason to criticize the government. Their government is natural, but that of men can only be artificial, by covenant. The covenant must confer power on one man or one assembly, since otherwise it cannot be enforced. "Covenants, without the sword, are but words." (President Wilson unfortunately forgot this.) The covenant is not, as afterwards in Locke and Rousseau, between the citizens and the ruling power; it is a convenant made by the citizens with each other to obey such ruling power as the majority shall choose. When they have chosen, their political power is at an end. The minority is as much bound as the majority, since the covenant was to obey the government chosen by the majority. When the government has been chosen, the citizens lose all rights except such as the government may find it expedient to grant. There is no right of rebellion, because the ruler is not bound by any contract, whereas the subjects are.

A multitude so united is called a commonwealth. This "Leviathan" is a mortal God.

Hobbes prefers monarchy, but all his abstract arguments are equally applicable to all forms of government in which there is one supreme authority not limited by the legal rights of other bodies. He could tolerate Parliament alone, but not a system in which governmental power is shared between king and Parliament. This is the exact antithesis to the views of Locke and Montesquieu. The English Civil War occurred, says Hobbes, because power was divided between King, Lords, and Commons.

The supreme power, whether a man or an assembly, is called the Sovereign. The powers of the sovereign, in Hobbes's system, are unlimited. He has the right of censorship over all expression of opinion. It is assumed that his main interest is the preservation of internal peace, and that therefore he will not use the power of censorship to suppress truth, for a doctrine repugnant to peace cannot be true. (A singularly pragmatist view!) The laws of property are to be entirely subject to the sovereign; for in a state of nature there is no property, and therefore property is created by government, which may control its creation as it pleases.

It is admitted that the sovereign may be despotic, but even the worst despotism is better than anarchy. Moreover, in many points the interests of the sovereign are identical with those of his subjects. He is richer if they are richer, safer if they are law-abiding, and so on. Rebellion is wrong, both because it usually fails, and because, if it succeeds, it sets a bad example, and teaches others to rebel. The Aristotelian distinction between tyranny and monarchy is rejected; a "tyranny," according to Hobbes, is merely a monarchy that the speaker happens to dislike.

Various reasons are given for preferring government by a monarch to government by an assembly. It is admitted that the monarch will usually follow his private interest when it conflicts with that of the public, but so will an assembly. A monarch may have favourites, but so may every member of an assembly; therefore the total number of favourites is likely to be fewer under a monarchy. A monarch can hear advice from anybody secretly; an assembly can only hear advice from its own members, and that publicly. In an assem-

bly, the chance absence of some may cause a different party to obtain the majority, and thus produce a change of policy. Moreover, if the assembly is divided against itself, the result may be civil war. For all these reasons, Hobbes concludes, a monarchy is best.

Throughout the *Leviathan,* Hobbes never considers the possible effect of periodical elections in curbing the tendency of assemblies to sacrifice the public interest to the private interest of their members. He seems, in fact, to be thinking, not of democratically elected Parliaments, but of bodies like the Grand Council in Venice or the House of Lords in England. He conceives democracy, in the manner of antiquity, as involving the direct participation of every citizen in legislation and administration; at least, this seems to be his view.

The part of the people, in Hobbes's system, ends completely with the first choice of a sovereign. The succession is to be determined by the sovereign, as was the practice in the Roman Empire when mutinies did not interfere. It is admitted that the sovereign will usually choose one of his own children, or a near relative if he has no children, but it is held that no law ought to prevent him from choosing otherwise.

There is a chapter on the liberty of subjects, which begins with an admirably precise definition: Liberty is the absence of external impediments to motion. In this sense, liberty is consistent with necessity; for instance, water *necessarily* flows down hill when there are no impediments to its motion, and when, therefore, according to the definition, it is free. A man is free to do what he wills, but necessitated to do what God wills. All our volitions have causes, and are in this sense necessary. As for the liberty of subjects, they are free where the laws do not interfere; this is no limitation of sovereignty, since the laws could interfere if the sovereign so decided. Subjects have no right as against the sovereign, except what the sovereign voluntarily concedes. When David caused Uriah to be killed, he did no injury to Uriah, because Uriah was his subject; but he did an injury to God, because he was God's subject and was disobeying God's law.

The ancient authors, with their praises of liberty, have led men, according to Hobbes, to favour tumults and seditions. He maintains that, when they are rightly interpreted, the liberty they praised was that of sovereigns, i.e., liberty from foreign domination. Internal resistance to sovereigns he condemns even when it might seem most justified. For example, he holds that Saint Ambrose had no right to excommunicate the Emperor Theodosius after the massacre of Thessalonica. And he vehemently censures Pope Zachary for having helped to depose the last of the Merovingians in favour of Pepin.

He admits, however, one limitation on the duty of submission to sovereigns. The right of self-preservation he regards as absolute, and subjects have the right of self-defence, even against monarchs. This is logical, since he has made self-preservation the motive for instituting government. On this ground he holds (though with limitations) that a man has a right to refuse to fight when called upon by the government to do so. This is a right which no modern government concedes. A curious result of his egoistic ethic is that resistance to the sovereign is only justified in *self*-defence; resistance in defence of another is always culpable.

There is one other quite logical exception: a man has no duty to a sovereign who has not the power to protect him. This justified Hobbes's submission to Cromwell while Charles II was in exile.

There must of course be no such bodies as political parties or what we should now call trade unions. All teachers are to be ministers of the sovereign, and are to teach only what the sovereign thinks useful. The rights of property are only valid as against other subjects, not as against the sovereign. The sovereign has the right to regulate foreign trade. He is not subject to the civil law. His right to punish comes to him, not from any concept of justice, but because he retains the liberty that all men had in the state of nature, when no man could be blamed for inflicting injury on another.

There is an interesting list of the reasons (other than foreign conquest) for the dissolution of commonwealths. These are: giving too little power to the sovereign; allowing private judgement in subjects; the theory that everything that is against conscience is sin; the belief in inspiration; the doctrine that the sovereign is subject to civil laws; the recognition of absolute private property; division of the sovereign power; imitation of the Greeks and Romans; separation of temporal and spiritual powers; refusing the power of taxation to the sovereign; the popularity of potent subjects; and the liberty of disputing with the sovereign. Of all these, there were abundant instances in the then recent history of England and France.

There should not, Hobbes thinks, be much difficulty in teaching people to believe in the rights of the sovereign, for have they not been taught to believe in Christianity, and even in transubstantiation, which is contrary to reason? There should be days set apart for learning the duty of submission. The instruction of the people depends upon right teaching in the universities, which must therefore be carefully supervised. There must be uniformity of worship, the religion being that ordained by the sovereign.

Part II ends with the hope that some sovereign will read the book and make himself absolute—a less chimerical hope than Plato's, that some king would turn

philosopher. Monarchs are assured that the book is easy reading and quite interesting.

Part III, "Of a Christian Common-wealth," explains that there is no universal Church, because the Church must depend upon the civil government. In each country, the king must be head of the Church; the Pope's overlordship and infallibility cannot be admitted. It argues, as might be expected, that a Christian who is a subject of a non-Christian sovereign should yield outwardly, for was not Naaman suffered to bow himself in the house of Rimmon?

Part IV, "Of the Kingdom of Darkness," is mainly concerned with criticism of the Church of Rome, which Hobbes hates because it puts the spiritual power above the temporal. The rest of this part is an attack on "vain philosophy," by which Aristotle is usually meant.

Let us now try to decide what we are to think of the *Leviathan*. The question is not easy, because the good and the bad in it are so closely intermingled.

In politics, there are two different questions, one as to the best form of the State, the other as to its powers. The best *form* of State, according to Hobbes, is monarchy, but this is not the important part of his doctrine. The important part is his contention that the *powers* of the State should be absolute. This doctrine, or something like it, had grown up in Western Europe during the Renaissance and the Reformation. First, the feudal nobility were cowed by Louis XI, Edward IV, Ferdinand and Isabella, and their successors. Then the Reformation, in Protestant countries, enabled the lay government to get the better of the Church. Henry VIII wielded a power such as no earlier English king had enjoyed. But in France the Reformation, at first, had an opposite effect; between the Guises and the Huguenots, the kings were nearly powerless. Henry IV and Richelieu, not long before Hobbes wrote, had laid the foundations of the absolute monarchy which lasted in France till the Revolution. In Spain, Charles V had got the better of the Cortes, and Philip II was absolute except in relation to the Church. In England, however, the Puritans had undone the work of Henry VIII; their work suggested to Hobbes that anarchy must result from resistance to the sovereign.

Every community is faced with two dangers, anarchy and despotism. The Puritans, especially the Independents, were most impressed by the danger of despotism. Hobbes, on the contrary, was obsessed by the fear of anarchy. The liberal philosophers who arose after the Restoration, and acquired control after 1688, realized both dangers; they disliked both Strafford and the Anabaptists. This led Locke to the doctrine of division of powers, and of checks and balances. In England there was a real division of powers so long as the king had influence; then Parliament became supreme, and ultimately the Cabinet. In America, there are still checks and balances in so far as Congress and the Supreme Court can resist the Administration; but the tendency is towards a constant increase in the powers of the Administration. In Germany, Italy, Russia, and Japan, the government has even more power than Hobbes thought desirable. On the whole, therefore, as regards the powers of the State, the world has gone as Hobbes wished, after a long liberal period during which, at least apparently, it was moving in the opposite direction. Whatever may be the outcome of the present war, it seems evident that the functions of the State must continue to increase, and that resistance to it must grow more and more difficult.

The reason that Hobbes gives for supporting the State, namely that it is the only alternative to anarchy, is in the main a valid one. A State may, however, be so bad that temporary anarchy seems preferable to its continuance, as in France in 1789 and in Russia in 1917. Moreover the tendency of every government towards tyranny cannot be kept in check unless governments have some fear of rebellion. Governments would be worse than they are if Hobbes's submissive attitude were universally adopted by subjects. This is true in the political sphere, where governments will try, if they can, to make themselves personally irremovable; it is true in the economic sphere, where they will try to enrich themselves and their friends at the public expense; it is true in the intellectual sphere, where they will suppress every new discovery or doctrine that seems to menace their power. These are reasons for not thinking only of the risk of anarchy, but also of the danger of injustice and ossification that is bound up with omnipotence in government.

The merits of Hobbes appear most clearly when he is contrasted with earlier political theorists. He is completely free from superstition; he does not argue from what happened to Adam and Eve at the time of the Fall. He is clear and logical; his ethics, right or wrong, is completely intelligible, and does not involve the use of any dubious concepts. Apart from Machiavelli, who is much more limited, he is the first really modern writer on political theory. Where he is wrong, he is wrong from over-simplification, not because the basis of his thought is unreal and fantastic. For this reason, he is still worth refuting.

Without criticizing Hobbes's metaphysics or ethics, there are two points to make against him. The first is that he always considers the national interest as a whole, and assumes, tacitly, that the major interests of all citizens are the same. He does not realize the importance of the clash between different classes, which Marx makes the chief cause of social change. This is connected with the assumption that the interests of a monarch are roughly identical with those of

his subjects. In time of war there is a unification of interests, especially if the war is fierce; but in time of peace the clash may be very great between the interests of one class and those of another. It is not by any means always true that, in such a situation, the best way to avert anarchy is to preach the absolute power of the sovereign. Some concession in the way of sharing power may be the only way to prevent civil war. This should have been obvious to Hobbes from the recent history of England.

Another point in which Hobbes's doctrine is unduly limited is in regard to the relations between different States. There is not a word in *Leviathan* to suggest any relation between them except war and conquest, with occasional interludes. This follows, on his principles, from the absence of an international government, for the relations of States are still in a state of nature, which is that of a war of all against all. So long as there is international anarchy, it is by no means clear that increase of efficiency in the separate States is in the interest of mankind, since it increases the ferocity and destructiveness of war. Every argument that he adduces in favour of government, in so far as it is valid at all, is valid in favour of international government. So long as national States exist and fight each other, only inefficiency can preserve the human race. To improve the fighting quality of separate States without having any means of preventing war is the road to universal destruction.

John Dewey (essay date 1954?)

SOURCE: "The Motivation of Hobbes's Political Philosophy," in *Thomas Hobbes in His Time,* Ralph Ross, Herbert W. Schneider, Theodore Waldman, eds., University of Minnesota Press, 1974, pp. 8-30.

[*In the following excerpt, Dewey examines Hobbes's political philosophy in historical context. Because the editors were unable to determine the exact date of this essay, Dewey's death date has been used.*]

It is the object of this essay to place the political philosophy of Hobbes in its own historic context. The history of thought is peculiarly exposed to an illusion of perspective. Earlier doctrines are always getting shoved, as it were, nearer our own day. We are familiar with the intellectual struggles of our own time and are interested in them. It is accordingly natural to envisage earlier thought as part of the same movement or as its forerunner. We then forget that that earlier period had its own specific problems, and we proceed to assimilate its discussions to our present interest. Hobbes has been especially subject to this temporal displacement. For over a century the chief question in social philosophy has centered about the conflict between individual freedom and public and institutional control. The central position of the theory of sovereignty in Hobbes's thought has made it easy to translate his political philosophy into terms of this debate; the issue which was really acute in his day—the conflict of church and state—now lacks actuality for English and American writers at least.

I

To prove this statement as to the central issue of Hobbes's day would require more than the space allotted to this paper. In general, I can only refer to the voluminous political discussions of the seventeenth century and to the overt history of England during the time of the civil wars. Specifically, let me note the admirable studies of Mr. Figgis.[1] They are enough to relieve my statement from any charge of exaggeration. Some quotations from Mr. Figgis will, then, be used to introduce the discussion. He points out that the controversy regarding the divine right of kings belongs to a day when politics, by common consent, was a branch of theology, and goes on to say, "All men demanded some form of divine authority for any theory of government . . . Until the close of the seventeenth century, the atmosphere of the supporters of popular rights is as theological as that of the upholders of the Divine Right of Kings."[2] And again, "There is no more universal characteristic of the political thought of the seventeenth century than the notion of non-resistance to authority. 'To bring the people to obedience' is the object of writers of all schools. When resistance is preached, it is resistance to some authority regarded as subordinate. Nor is the resistance permitted at the pleasure or judgment of private individuals. It is allowed only as a form of obedience, as executing the commands of some superior and ultimate authority, God, or the Pope, and the Law."[3]

In other words, everybody worked upon an assumption of a supreme authority, of law as command by this authority, and duty as ultimately obedience. Not these conceptions, but rather the special content given them, mark off Hobbes. There was, of course, a party which opposed such centralization as Hobbes argued for, but the opposition was not in the name of the individual, but of something very different, the people.

So far as I can discover, the term *people* still had its meaning fixed by the traditional significance of *Populus*—a meaning very different from that of *plebs* or the French *peuple*. This notion, as defined, say, by Cicero, was a commonplace among the "civilians" and those trained in scholastic philosophy. In Cicero's words, the people is "not every gathering of men, assembled in any way whatsoever, but is the multitude associated by a common sense of justice and by a common interest." It is a *universitas,* not a *societas,* much less a mere aggregate of individuals. And the appeal of the upholders of popular against royal government was to the *authority* of this organized body, of which the Commons was frequently (but not always) taken to be the representative. The following words from Lawson, taken from *An Examination of the Political Part of Mr. Hobbes, His Leviathan* (1657) are worth quoting: "The liberty which the English have challenged and obtained with so much expense of blood is . . . that which is due unto us by the constitution of the State, Magna Charta, the Laws, and the Petition of Right. It is but the liberty of subjects, not sovereigns; when he hath said all he can, we are not willing to be slaves or subject ourselves to

Kings as Absolute Lords. . . . By liberty Aristotle meant such a privilege as every subject might have in a free state . . . where it is to be noted that one and the same person who is a subject, and at the best but a Magistrate, hath a share in the sovereign power. Yet this he hath not as a single person, but as one person jointly with the whole body or major part at least of the people" (pp. 67-68). This correlativity of three things: the people, a society organized through laws and especially through the fundamental law, or constitution, and liberty is in marked opposition to Locke's conceptions of a natural right or authority found in the individual himself. It is not, I think, paradoxical to say that Locke derived this conception of a natural right belonging to the individual as such from Hobbes rather than from Hobbes's popular opponents.

It is noteworthy that Cumberland, the chief systematic opponent of Hobbes on rationalistic grounds, objects to the latter's political philosophy because "Hobbes's principles overthrow the Foundations of all Government"; they would not suffer any man to enter into civil society; they excite subjects to rebellion. In short, it is Hobbes's psychological and moral individualism rather than his theory of sovereignty to which objection is taken. The same is true of a much less effective writer, Tenison, in his *Creed of Mr. Hobbes Examined* (1670). He says that since Hobbes identifies the law of nature with the counsels of self-interest "the Fundamentals of your Policy are hay and stubble, and apter to set all things into blaze than to support government" (p. 156); and again, "Woe to all the Princes on earth, if this doctrine be true and becometh popular; if the multitude believe this, the Prince . . . can never be safe from the spears and barbed irons which their ambition and presumed interest will provide." Hobbes's principles, in their appeal to self-interest, are but "seeds of sedition" (pp. 170-171). That Hobbes himself was aware that, as matter of fact, a government is not likely to retain enough strength to secure obedience unless it has regard to the commonweal, will appear in the sequel—though naturally he never made this moral explicit.

Let us hear from Mr. Figgis again. "It is true that with the possible exception of Hobbes, all the political theorists up to the end of the seventeenth century either have religion as the basis of their system, or regard the defense or supremacy of some form of faith as their main object."[4] Now Hobbes is precisely the exception which proves the rule. He is theological in motive and context in the sense that he is deliberately anti-theological. Along with his exclusive self-interest doctrine, it was his theory of a secular basis for sovereignty, not the doctrine of a supreme authority, which brought him into disrepute.[5] His familiar title was atheist, so that even the royalists who might be supposed, on purely political grounds to welcome his support, found it necessary to disclaim him. Compare the following from a contemporary letter: "All honest men who are lovers of monarchy, are very glad that the King hath at last banisht his court that father of atheists Mr. Hobbes, who it is said hath rendered all the queen's court, and very many of the Duke of York's family, atheists."[6] In the apologetic dedication of his *Seven Philosophical Problems* to the king after the Restoration in 1662, Hobbes in defending himself against this charge says of his *Leviathan,* "There is nothing in it against episcopacy. I can not therefore imagine what reason any episcopal man can have to speak of me, as I hear some of them do, as of an atheist or man of no religion, *unless it be for making the authority of the church depend wholly upon the regal power.*" In the words which I have italicized Hobbes flaunts his ground of offense.

II

Postponing, for the moment, the important point in Hobbes, his attempt to secularize morals and politics, I take up his own sayings regarding the immediate occasion of his political writings. Croom Robertson and Tönnies have made it clear that the first of his writings[7] dates from 1640 and is substantially what we have in his *Human Nature* and *De Corpore Politico.* In his *Considerations upon the Reputation of T. Hobbes* (1662) Hobbes says this little treatise "did set forth and demonstrate that the said power and rights were inseparably annexed to the sovereignty," and that the treatise was so much talked of, although it was not printed, that if the king had not dissolved Parliament, it would have brought him into danger of his life.[8] There is here, indeed, no reference to just what the points were in the quarrel about the regal power, but his *Behemoth; or the Long Parliament* leaves no doubt. There he says that the Parliament of 1640 "desired the whole and absolute sovereignty. . . . For this was the design of the Presbyterian ministers, who taking themselves to be, by divine right, the only lawful governors of the Church, endeavored to bring the same form of government into the civil state. And as the spiritual laws were to be made by their synods, so the civil laws should be made by the House of Commons."[9] And at the beginning of this work, in stating the causes of the corruption of the people which made the civil wars possible, he puts first the Presbyterians, second the Papists, and third the Independents.[10]

In the *Considerations* already referred to he says he "wrote and published his book *De Cive,* to the end that all nations which should hear what you and your Con-Coventanters were doing in England, might detest you." Not less significant is his letter, from Paris, in 1641 to the Earl of Devonshire. He says, "I am of the opinion that ministers ought to minister rather than govern; at least, that all Church government depends on the state, and authority of the kingdom, without which there can be no unity in the church. Your lordship may think this but a Fancy of Philosophy, but I am sure that Experience teacheth thus much, that the dispute for (the word is variously read preference and precedence) between the spiritual and civil power, has of late more than any other thing in the world been the cause of civil war."[11] Of the **Leviathan,** he says: "The cause of my writing that book was the consideration of what the ministers before, and in the beginning of the civil war, by their preaching and writing did contribute thereunto" (VII, 35). And it may be worth noting that considerably over one-half of the **Leviathan** is explicitly devoted to the bearing of religious and scriptural matters upon politics as they touch upon the relation of church and the civil power.

In his controversy with "the egregious professors of the mathematics in the University of Oxford" he remarks of the **De Cive:** "You know that the doctrine therein taught is generally received by all but the clergy, who think their interest concerned in being made subordinate to the civil power" (VII, 333). Again he expresses his surprise that some even of the episcopal clergy have attacked him, and thinks it can be explained only as a "relic still remaining of popish ambition, lurking in that seditious division and distinction between the power spiritual and civil" (IV, 429). Most significant of all, perhaps, are his remarks in the preface of the **Philosophical Rudiments,** where after saying that he does not "dispute the position of divines, except in those points which strip subjects of their obedience, and shake the foundations of civil government," he goes on to say, "These things I found most bitterly excepted against: That I made the civil powers too large, but this by ecclesiastical persons. That I had utterly taken away liberty of conscience, but this by sectaries. That I had set the princes above the laws, but this by lawyers" (II, xxii-xxiii). In no enumeration of the criticisms brought against his teachings does he mention the principle of absolute sovereignty, nor does he set his doctrine of sovereignty in antithesis to any doctrine except that of divided sovereignty—divided, that is, between the spiritual and temporal power. Locke's doctrine of a sovereignty limited by prior natural rights of those who were its subjects had neither provocation nor justification till after the revolution of 1688 called for some theoretical explanation.

One can hardly, of course, accept Hobbes as an unbiased witness to the way in which his doctrine was received. But Eachard's *Mr. Hobbes's State of Nature Considered* (1696) (a genuinely witty work) gives corroborative evidence that it was not the doctrine of sovereignty which aroused dissent, for he repeatedly states that that was old matter dressed in new form. "Your book called Dominion chiefly consists of such things as have been said these thousands of years." And again, "it might easily be shown how all the rest (so much as is true) is the very same with the old plain

Dunstable stuff which commonly occurs in those who treated of Policy and Morality." Aside from the aspersion on human nature contained in Hobbes's doctrine of self-interest, what Eachard objects to is Hobbes's "affected garbs of speech, starched mathematical method, counterfeit appearances of novelty and singularity."[12] How habitually the ideas of the evils of divided sovereignty were in Hobbes's mind appears from a note in the **Rudiments.** "There are certain doctrines wherewith subjects being tainted, they verily believe that obedience may be refused to the city, and that by right they may, nay, ought, to oppose and fight against chief princes and dignitaries. Such are those which, whether directly and openly, or more obscurely and by consequence, require obedience to be given to others besides them to whom the supreme authority is committed. I deny not that, but this reflects on that power which many, living under other government, ascribe to the chief head of the Church of Rome, and also on that which elsewhere, out of that Church, bishops require in theirs to be given to them; and last of all, on that liberty which the lower sort of citizens, under pretence of religion, do challenge to themselves. For what civil war was there ever in the Christian world, which did not either grow from, or was nourished by this root?" (II, 79n)

As an *argumentum ad hominem* in his own time, it is impossible to overestimate the force of his argument. All Protestants united in declaiming against the claim of the Roman Church to interfere in matters temporal. Yet some of the episcopalian bishops declared that in matters of religious actions, such as rites, appointments, preferments, the church represented God, not man, and had a superior right to obedience. The Presbyterians in general were committed to a dual theory of authority and obedience. Yet all of these ecclesiastical institutions united in reprimanding the fifth monarchy men, Anabaptists, Levellers, etc., who claimed that their personal conscience as enlightened by the indwelling presence of the Holy Spirit was the ultimate source of knowledge of divine law, and hence the rule for obedience. Luther, Calvin, English bishop, and Scotch presbyter alike attacked this doctrine as anarchic and immoral. Hobbes, in effect, points out that all churches are in the same anarchic class, for they all appeal to something other than publicly instituted and proclaimed law.

In connection with the sectaries, it is interesting to note that they expressly cried out for "natural rights derived from Adam and right reason." According to this view, "all men are by nature the sons of Adam, and from him have derived a natural propriety (property), right, and freedom. . . . By natural birth all men are equally free and alike born to like propriety, liberty, and freedom; and as we are delivered of God by the hand of nature into this world, every one with a natural innate freedom and propriety, even so we are to live, every one equally and alike, to enjoy his birth-right and privilege."[13] That this anarchic doctrine of the Levellers was wrought by Locke into a stable foundation for a reasonably conservative Whig doctrine, testifies to his altered background and outlook. There is no evidence that Hobbes was influenced by the doctrine, but it is more than a coincidence that he makes a precisely similar notion of natural rights the origin of the war of all upon all, and the basis of demand for absolute sovereignty. If he had this notion in mind in his picture of the state of nature, it adds a piquant irony to his sketch, as well as to his repeated assertions that there was no difference of principle between the sectaries' appeal to the court of private judgment and the doctrines of Papist, Presbyterian, and of such Episcopalians as did not recognize that the authority of the Established Church was by grace of the political sovereign and not by divine right.

Lawson was one of the better tempered and more moderate opponents of royal sovereignty, an episcopalian rector with obvious sympathies with Cromwell. He admits as a "certain truth" that sovereignty is above all civil law, but asserts the supreme legislator "is subject to the superior will of God"—which, of course, was Hobbes's own doctrine. "All the sovereignty's power of making laws, judgments, *etc.*, are from God. . . . Men may give their consent that such a man or such a company of men shall reign, but the power is from God, not them." From this doctrine, it is not a long step to his statement that the true believer in God "may, must within himself, even of laws, so far as they are a rule, and bind him, enquire, examine, and determine whether they are good or evil. Otherwise, he can perform only a blind obedience even to the best; and if he conform unto the unjust, he in obeying man disobeys God, which no good man will do. Romans, xii, 14-15." Subsequently he adds, "Nor does this doctrine anyways prejudice the civil power, nor encourage any man to disobedience and violation of the civil laws, if they be just and good as they ought to be; and the subject hath not only liberty, but a command to examine the laws of his sovereign, and judge within himself and for himself, whether they be not contrary to the laws of God."[14] Yet Lawson joins in the common animadversions upon the leveling sectaries. Moreover, Lawson deplores the disorder and divisions of the time. "Our form of government is confounded by the different opinions of common lawyers, civilians, and divines who agree neither with one another, nor amongst themselves." Nor can the history of England be appealed to as an umpire—as many were doing, for as Lawson, clearer-headed than most, perceived, it shows "only as matter of fact how sometimes the King, Counties, and Barons, sometimes the Commons were predominant and ascendant." And he concludes, "Yet for all this, a free parliament of just, wise, and good men might rectify all this, and *unite the supreme power so miserably divided to the hazard of the state.*"[15] In a situation

where a writer sees that the great need is for a unified authority or sovereignty, and yet argues in support of that very principle of private judging of laws which had been a large factor in bringing about the situation he deplores, Hobbes's case almost states itself.

III

A few words are now to be said about another motif in Hobbes's ardent assertion of a unified sovereignty. The part of his doctrine which was not directed against the claim of the churches to obedience was aimed at the claim of the authority of Law set up by the lawyers. To go fully into this matter would require a summary of certain phases of parliamentary history in England, beginning in the time of Elizabeth and becoming highly acute in the reign of James. On the one side were the lawyers and judges, and on the other were the claims of the legislature representing statute law, and of the chancellor representing equity. The king then largely dominated Parliament, and this made the party of the judges against Parliament essentially the popular party of later controversy. In the earlier words of Aristotle, and the later words of the Constitution of Massachusetts, they proclaimed a government "which was a government of laws, not of men."[16]

Consider, for example, such a statement as this of John Milton, arguing against Salmasius: "Power was therefore given to a king by the people, that he might see by the authority committed to him that nothing be done against law, and that he keep our laws and not impose upon us his own. Therefore, there is no regal power but in the courts of the kingdom and by them." And Harrington's constant contention is that only a commonwealth is a government of laws, since law must proceed from will, and will be moved by interest; and only in a commonwealth is the whole will and the whole interest expressed. In a monarchy or oligarchy, the laws are made in the interest of a few, so that what exists is a government of men. Harrington, however, is an innovator in connecting law with legislation rather than with the courts. "Your lawyers, advising you to fit your governments to their laws, are no more to be regarded than your tailor if he should desire you to fit your body to his doublet"—another point of sympathy between him and Hobbes.

It was lawyer's law then which was usually meant—the law of courts, not of legislation. As Figgis says, speaking of the reliance of the popular party upon government by law, "Nor is it of statute law that men are thinking; but of the common law . . . which possesses that mysterious sanctity of prescription which no legislator can bestow. The common law is pictured invested with a halo of dignity, peculiar to the embodiment of deepest principles and to the highest expression of human reason and of the law of nature implanted by God in the heart of man. As yet men are not clear that an Act of Parliament can do more than declare the common law."[17] It is with this doctrine in mind that Hobbes is so insistent that the sovereign is absolved from all law save the moral law—which, as we shall see later, is for him the law of an enlightened hedonism. But Hobbes is not just begging the question. Bacon before him had pointed out many of the defects of common law and the need of codification and systematized revision. The demand for legislative activity was constantly increasing; the Long Parliament in effect restated the common law. Courts of equity had been obliged to assume an extensive activity, and it is not unimportant that the chancellor's court was essentially a royal court and followed the law "of reason," the law "of nature," the law of conscience and of God. Hobbes's essential rationalism was shocked at calling anything law which expressed, as did the common law, merely custom and precedent (III, 91).

Hobbes does away at one sweep with any alleged distinction between written and unwritten law. All law is written, for written *means* published. And as published, it proceeds only from him (or them) who has authority—power to require obedience. And that, of course, is the sovereign. "Custom of itself maketh no laws. Nevertheless, when a sentence has once been given, by them that judge by their natural reason, . . . it may attain to the vigor of a law . . . because the sovereign power is supposed tacitly to have approved such sentence for right. . . . In like manner those laws that go under the title of *responsa prudentum,* the opinions of lawyers, are not, therefore, laws because *responsa prudentum,* but because they are admitted by the sovereign" (IV, 227).[18]

But Hobbes is most explicit in a work, too infrequently made use of by historians of philosophy, entitled *A Dialogue between a Philosopher and a Student of the Common Law of England* (VI). This dialogue opens with an attempt to prove that it is the king's reason which is the soul even of the common law. He quotes Coke's saying (and it is to be recalled that Coke had been on the lawyers' side against King James) that law is reason, although an artificial reason, got by long study and observation; such a perfection of reason, however, that "if all the reason that is dispersed into so many several heads were united into one, yet could he not make such a law as the law of England is, because by many successions of ages it hath been fined and refined by an infinite number of grave and learned men." As against this view, Hobbes inserts his usual caveat; it was not the succession of lawyers or judges that made the law, but the succession of kings who created the judges and who enforced the decisions. "The king's reason, when it is publicly upon advice and deliberation declared, is that *anima legis,* and that *summa ratio,* and that equity . . . which is all that is the law of England." And even more emphatically: "There is not amongst men a universal reason agreed upon in any nation, besides the reason of him that hath the sovereign power. Yet though his reason be but the reason of one man, yet it is set up to supply the place of that universal reason which is expounded to us by our Saviour in the Gospel; and consequently our King is to us the legislator both of statute law and of common law" (VI, 14 and 22).[19] Later he suggests that common law and its lawyers are the chief source of excessive litigation "on account of the variety and repugnancy of judgments of common law," and because "lawyers seek not for their judgments in their own breasts, but in the precedents of former judgments," and also in the liberty they have to scan verbal technicalities (VI, 45). Still later his aversion to reference to mere custom and precedent becomes more marked, and he even goes so far as to say that all courts are courts of equity in principle if not in name (VI, 63)—than which it would be hard to find a doctrine more obnoxious to lawyers—all of which throws light upon the opening sentence of his book, that the study of law is less rational than the study of mathematics, and possibly suggests a slight irony in his reference to the reason of kings as the source of the supreme rationality of common law claimed for it by such a writer as Coke.

IV

When I first became aware of these specific empirical sources for Hobbes's political philosophy, I was inclined to suppose that he had made the latter a necessary part of a deductive system from that inordinate love of formal system to which philosophers are given. And the closing words of the *Leviathan* seem to bear out the impression, when, as if in a relieved tone, he says that having brought to an end his discourse on Civil and Ecclesiastical Government "occasioned by the disorders of the present time," he is now free to "return to my interrupted speculation of bodies natural." Croom Robertson, no mean judge where Hobbes is in question, says "the whole of his political doctrine . . . has little appearance of having been thought out from the fundamental principles of his philosophy. Though connected with an express doctrine of human nature, it doubtless had its main lines fixed when he was still an observer of men and nature, and not yet a mechanical philosopher. In other words, his political theory is explicable mainly from his personal disposition, timorous and worldly, out of sympathy with all the aspirations of his time."[20]

Further study led me, however, to a different position, to the position that Hobbes was satisfied that (even if his ideas had arisen in his own experience) he had given them a strict scientific or rational form. And while this point is of no great importance as merely an item in Hobbes's biography, it is, I think, of fundamental importance in the theme that Hobbes's great work was in freeing, once for all, morals and politics from subservience to divinity and making them a branch of natural science. So I offer no apology for setting forth the evidence that Hobbes himself believed in the scientific status of his politics.

As a point of departure, take the following passage from the preface to his **Rudiments** (the original **De Cive**). "I was studying philosophy for my mind's sake and I had gathered together its first elements in all kinds, and having digested them into three sections by degrees, I had thought to have written them, so as in the first I would have treated of body . . . ; in the second of man . . . ; in the third of civil government and the duties of subjects. . . . It so happened in the interim, that my country, some few years before the civil war did rage, was boiling hot with questions regarding the rights of dominion and the obedience due from subjects; and was the cause which, all those other matters deferred, ripened and plucked from me this third part" (II, xix-xx).[21] And in a letter written in 1646 to Mersenne, speaking of his delay in completing his first part, namely, that on Body, he says that laziness is in part the cause, but chiefly because he has not yet been able to satisfy himself in the parts relating to the senses, and adds, "for that which I hope I have done in moral doctrine, that I am anxious to do in First Philosophy and in Physics."[22]

More specifically we have the claims he puts forth for his **De Cive** (claims which he continued to put forth even after he was aware that they exposed him to the accusation of actuation by egregious vanity) that it was the first treatise to put morals and politics on a scientific basis. Molesworth quotes from an unpublished manuscript on *Optics* the following concluding paragraph. "If it be found to be true doctrine, I shall deserve the reputation of having been the first to lay the grounds of two sciences: this of *Optiques,* the most curious, and the other of natural justice, which I have done in my books **De Cive,** the most profitable of all other." In the epistle dedicatory to his **Elements of Philosophy,** in which he executed his plan to give a systematic treatment of his entire philosophy, he says that geometrical science dates from antiquity; natural philosophy from Galileo, while "civil philosophy is much younger, being no older (I say it provoked, and that my detractors may know how little they have wrought upon me) than my own book **De Cive**" (I, ix).

The matter becomes one of more than biographical importance when we recall Hobbes's conception of science or demonstrative knowledge and the importance attached by him to science. Science is reasoning from cause to effect, and hence universal and certain, while empirical knowledge, or prudence, reasons from effect to cause, and is but probable and hypothetical. The end or object of science is power, control, for if we know the generation or cause of things, we have it in our power to determine them. The question of the

scientific character of morals and politics is, then, a question of the possibility of enduring social security and safety—"peace." Unless men attained to first principles from which any one could proceed, as by mathematical reasoning, to determinate conclusions, politics would remain still a matter of opinion, uncertainty, controversy, in short, of war. It is in this light that we have to understand his assertion that geometry, physics, and morals form one science, as the "British, the Atlantic, and the Indian seas . . . do altogether make up the ocean" (II, iv). Strictly speaking, moreover, *natural* philosophy cannot be a science, for in it we must, perforce, reason from effects to causes, and thus arrive only at what "may be." "The science of every subject is derived from a precognition of the causes, generation, and construction of the same; and consequently where the causes are known, there is place for demonstration. . . . Geometry, therefore, is demonstrable, for the lines and figures from which we reason are drawn and described by ourselves; and civil philosophy is demonstrable, because we make the commonwealth ourselves" (VII, 184).[23]

Moreover, the situation of the times made Hobbes's belief, whether it were rightly grounded or not, of more than academic import. We have already seen the extent to which private and variable opinion was to him the source of the ills from which the state suffered. Scientific demonstration is the sole alternative to the continuation of the troubled regime of opinion. Hobbes is in the somewhat paradoxical opinion of holding that while all order proceeds from the unquestioned authority of the sovereign, the permanent and settled institution of sovereignty itself depends upon a recognition of the scientific truths of morals and politics as set forth by him. While his controversies with Wallis and Ward doubtless gave asperity to his attacks on the universities, there is no questioning the fact that they were sincerely actuated by the belief that the doctrines of morals and politics therein taught were largely responsible for the evils of the time. They are to England as the Wooden Horse to Troy; the core of rebellions; the source of opinions contrary to the peace of mankind; the shops and operatories of the clergy; the fountains of civil and moral doctrine.[24] Hobbes was equally sincere in believing that the new science of morals and politics ought to be taught in the universities, and that such inculcation was a precondition of lasting social security.[25] If this nation was "very lately an anarchy and a dissolute multitude of men, doing every one what his own reason or imprinted light suggested" (IV, 287), a considerable part of the remedy is to be found in the control, in the future, of instruction by the civil authority. "Because opinions, which are gotten by education and in length of time are made habitual, can not be taken away by force and upon the sudden; they must, therefore, be taken away also by time and education." And then he goes on, as usual, to charge the universities with having been the corrupters of opinion, and to add that if the true doctrine of a body politic and of law were taught to young men "whose minds are as white paper," they would teach it to the people even more sedulously than false doctrine is now taught (IV, 219). It is in this context, then, that we have to take Hobbes's famous contention that the practical utility of moral science is to be found more in what men have suffered from its absence than in what they have gained by its presence, and his contention that he is the first in morals to "reduce the doctrine to the rules and infallibility of reason."[26]

V

Such are some of the grounds for thinking that the final importance of Hobbes's political philosophy is found in its attempt to make the subject secular and scientific. Not merely in external matters was he motivated by the conflict of civil and ecclesiastic power, but even more in intellectual aim and method. We fail to get the full force of Hobbes's conception of sovereignty until we see that to Hobbes the logical alternative is setting up the private opinions of individuals and groups of individuals as the rule of public acts—a method whose logical inconsistency has division and war for its practical counterpart.

There exists, indeed, a paradox in Hobbes. On one hand, we have the doctrine of the sovereign's arbitrary institution of duties, and rights and wrong. On the other, we have his doctrine of the strictly scientific character of morals and politics. In view of the seeming contradiction it is little wonder that his opponents—notably Cudworth and his school—passed over the latter strain and assumed that the whole content of Hobbes consisted in an assertion of the purely arbitrary character of all moral distinctions. Nevertheless Cudworth's view is thoroughly one-sided. Cumberland, not Cudworth, was Hobbes's most intelligent opponent, and in his *De Legibus Naturae* we find an attempt to meet Hobbes on his own ground in a way which reveals the positive influence of Hobbes's conception of morals as a branch of natural science. In speaking of the natural light and innate ideas of the Platonizers, he remarks scornfully, "I have not been so happy as to learn the laws of nature in so short a way." He argues for an order of logical precedence in moral laws from the analogy of the laws of motion in natural science. He expressly points out that other writers, in reasoning from approved sentiments and the common consent of mankind (e.g., Grotius and his followers), had reasoned from effects to causes only, and in his search for laws of nature commits himself to the essentially Hobbesian conception that they are "the foundations of all moral and civil knowledge" in such a way as to compel the use of a deductive method. He differs radically as to substance of the fundamental axioms, but agrees as to the form of

morals as a science. He "abstains" from theological matters, because he will prove the laws of nature only from reason and experience. He believes that "the foundations of piety and moral philosophy are not shaken, but strengthened by Mathematics and the Natural Philosophy" that depends thereon. In making benevolence, or regard for the happiness of all, his fundamental principle, instead of egoistic regard for private happiness, the influence of Hobbes may be seen in the fact that he, too, starts from Power, but argues that the effective power of man in willing his own happiness is limited to willing it *along with* the happiness of others. And since Hobbes had held that the desire for purely personal good contradicts itself when acted upon, the transformation upon the basis of Power of Hobbes's axiom of self-love into one of benevolence was not difficult.

VI

I do not mean, however, that Hobbes is free from the paradox mentioned. On the contrary, his position is precisely the paradox of attempting to derive by mathematical reasoning the authority of the sovereign to settle arbitrarily all matters of right and wrong, justice and injury, from rational, universal axioms regarding the nature of good and evil. His method of dealing with the paradox takes us to the meaning given by him to natural law, and to his conception of the aim and purpose, or "offices" of sovereignty. Both sides of the matter are worth attention because they reveal a thoroughgoing utilitarianism.

The mistake of so many of Hobbes's critics in thinking that he identified morals with the commands of the sovereign because he identified justice and injustice, right and wrong, with the latter, arises from overlooking the fundamental distinctions which Hobbes draws between *good* and *right,* and between intention and act—or *forum internum* and *forum externum.* Good is simply, to Hobbes, that which pleaseth a man; that which is agreeable to him—which, in turn, means "whatsoever is the object of any man's appetite or desire." It follows, of course, that since men differ in constitution and circumstance from one another, conflict or the state of war ensues; from difference of constitution, because what one man calls good another man finds evil; from circumstance, because when two men find the same object good it ofttimes cannot be shared or mutually possessed. But besides the good of passion or desire of appetite, which is immediately determined by the momentary desire, whatever that may be, there is the good of reason, or rational good. To Hobbes, of course, the rational good does not differ from the sensible good in kind or quality; it is as much the pleasing as is the good of appetite. But it differs in being the object of a survey which includes *time,* instead of being a momentary estimate. For since finding good in present appetite brings a man into conflict with others, it puts his life and possessions in jeopardy; in seeking present pleasure he exposes himself to future evils "which by strict consequence do adhere to the present good," or even to destruction of life. Hence, when a man is in a "quiet mind" he sees the good of present passion to be evil, and is capable of perceiving that his true good lies in a condition of concord or agreement with others—in peace which preserves his body and institutes secure property. "They, therefore, who could not agree concerning a present, do agree concerning a future good; which indeed is a work of reason; for things present are obvious to the sense, things to come to our reason only" (II, 44, 47-48).[27]

Moral laws,[28] laws of nature, are then equivalent to the counsels or precepts of prudence, that is to say, of judgment as to the proper means for attaining the end of a future enduring happiness. The rules of good and evil are the procedures which any man, not perturbed by immediate passion, would perceive to be conducive to his future happiness. Let it be remembered that according to Hobbes all reason (in matters natural as well as moral) is simply a sequence of thoughts directed toward an end which regulates the sequence. Hobbes, then, really believes in laws (or at least counsels) of morality which in their origin are wholly independent of the commands of the sovereign. He ascribes to these all the eulogistic predicates which were scholastically current regarding the laws of nature: they are eternal, immutable, divine, etc. Right reason is the "act of reasoning, that is, the true and peculiar ratiocination of every man concerning those actions of his which may redound to the damage or benefit of his neighbors. . . . I call it true, that is, concluding from true principles rightly framed, because that the whole breach of the laws of nature consists in the false reasoning, or rather folly of those men who see not those duties they are necessarily to perform towards others in order to their own conservation" (II, 16n).[29]

It is not easy to estimate just how sincerely meant were all of Hobbes's professions of piety. I think it may safely be assumed, however, that whether or no he believed in a theological God, he did believe that reasoning was divine, and that there is a sincere piety toward reason in his regarding rational precepts as divine; and that accordingly he believed in some genuine sense that God was reason. There is something besides accommodation in the following language: "Finally, there is no law of natural reason that can be against the law divine: for God Almighty hath given reason to man to be a light unto him. And I hope it is no impiety to think that God Almighty will require a strict account thereof at the day of judgment, as of the instructions which we were to follow in our peregrinations here, notwithstanding the opposition and affronts of supernaturalists nowadays to rational and moral conversation" (IV, 116).

One of the necessary conclusions of such ratiocination on future well-being and conservation is the conclusion that it is not safe for any individual to *act* upon the moral law—which in effect is not to do anything to another which one would not have him do unto us—until he has some guarantee that others will do likewise. A person so acting renders himself exposed to evil from others. Hence suspicion and mistrust, even on the part of one disposed to regard the happiness of others, are inevitable where there is no power or authority which can threaten the evilly minded with such future pains as to give assurance as to their conduct. Hence, it is one of the laws of sound reasoning to enter into a civil state, or to institute a sovereign authority with power to threaten evil doers with evils in return, to such extent as to influence their conduct.[30]

Hence it follows in Hobbes, quite as much as with any of the upholders of the popular theory, that the end or purpose of the state is the "common good." He but insists upon the correlativity of this good with implicit obedience to the commands of a protecting power. To set up any private judgment about the *acts* by which the common good is to be attained is to weaken the protective power, and thereby to introduce insecurity, mutual fear, and discord—all negations to the attaining of that happiness for whose sake the state was instituted. No matter how arbitrary the sovereign's acts, the state is at least better than the anarchy where private judgments as to good (that is to say, immediate appetite and passion) reign.

But there are other checks. The sovereign is himself under the law of nature: that is to say, he is subject to the "sanctions" of utility. As a reasoning creature, he will perceive that his interests as sovereign coincide with the prosperity of the subjects. "The profit of the sovereign and the subject goeth always together" (IV, 164). Hobbes uniformly lays down certain precepts which bind the sovereign's conscience. In his **Leviathan** he develops at length the "Offices of the sovereign." They include equality of taxes, public charity, prevention of idleness, sumptuary laws, equality of justice to all, and the care of instruction. In his earliest writing he mentions all these, and also lays emphasis upon the duty of the civil authority to foster husbandry, fishing, navigation, and the mechanical arts.[31] In his discussion of the need that the state take charge of education, he clearly recognizes the limitations placed upon power to control action through positive commands appealing to fear. *Allegiance to the state is not a matter of positive command, but of moral obligation.* "A civil law that shall forbid rebellion (and such is all resistance to the essential rights of the sovereignty) is not, as a civil law, any obligation but by virtue only of the law of nature that forbiddeth the violation of faith." Hence, its ground has to be diligently and truly taught; it cannot "be maintained by any civil law, or terror of legal punishment" (III, 323-324).[32]

Moreover, there are natural, or utilitarian, checks to the exercise of the power of sovereignty. In the first place, it cannot affect, and (except through education) is not intended to affect inner inclinations or desires, but only acts—which are external. There is always a distinction between the just *man* and a just *act;* the former is one who means to obey the law or to act justly to others, even if by infirmity of power or by reason of circumstance he fail to do so. Even more significant is the check upon despotic action on the part of sovereignty in the mere fact that all acts *cannot* be commanded. "It is necessary that there be infinite cases which are neither commanded nor prohibited, but every man may either do or not do them as he lists himself. . . . As water, inclosed on all hands with banks, stands still and corrupts; having no bounds it spreads too largely, and the more passages it finds the more freely it takes its current; so subjects, if they might do nothing without the commands of the law, would grow dull and unwieldy; if all, they would be dispersed; and the more that is left undetermined by the laws, the more liberty they enjoy. Both extremes are faulty; for laws were not invented to take away, but to direct men's actions; even as nature ordained the banks not to stay, but to guide the course of the stream" (II, 178). [33] The sovereign who attempts too much dictation will provoke rebellion.

This summary account should make it clear that Hobbes deduces the need, the purpose, and the limits of sovereign power from his rationalistic, or utilitarian, premises. Undoubtedly a certain arbitrariness of action on the part of the sovereign is made possible. It is part of the price paid, the cost assumed, in behalf of an infinitely greater return of good. Right and wrong are nothing but what the sovereign commands, but these commands are the means indispensable to procuring good, and hence have a moral or rational sanction and object. To use Hobbes's own words: "In sum all actions and habits are to be esteemed good or evil by their causes and usefulness in reference to the commonwealth" (VI, 220). No franker or more thoroughgoing social utilitarianism could be found.

When we seek for Hobbes's natural historical associates, we should turn not to the upholders of political absolutism for its own sake, but to Jeremy Bentham. They are one in opposition to private opinion, intuition, and *ipse dixitism* as sources of the rules of moral action; they are one in desire to place morals and politics upon a scientific basis; they are one in emphasis upon control of present and private good by reference to future and general good, good being understood by both as pleasure. Their unlikenesses flow from the divergent historic settings in which their ideas were generated. To Hobbes the foe was ecclesiastic interests, the source of divided allegiance and of the assumption of a right of private judgment over against a public law of right and wrong. His remedy was a cen-

tralized administrative state. Bentham found the foe in vested economic interests which set private or class happiness above the general good, and which manipulated the machinery of the state in behalf of private advantage. His remedy was a democratizing of government to be obtained by a mass participation in it of individuals, accompanied by a widening of personal initiative in the choice and pursuit of happiness to the maximum possible limit. To both, however, moral science was one with political science, and was not a theoretical luxury, but a social necessity. It was the common fate of both to suffer from a false psychology, from an inadequate conception of human nature. But both are protagonists of a science of a human nature operating through an art of social control in behalf of a common good. Progress beyond them comes not from a hostile attitude to these conceptions, but from an improved knowledge of human nature.

Notes

[1] *The Divine Right of Kings* and *From Gerson to Grotius.*

[2] *Divine Right of Kings*, p. 11.

[3] *Ibid.,* p. 221. Technically, discussions centered on the nature of *Jus.* The ambiguity of Jus, meaning both command and law on one side, and right, on the other side, has been frequently noted. At this time, it was not so much ambiguity which existed as two sides of one notion. Jus is primarily *authority,* and secondarily *authorization,* depending, of course, upon authority.

[4] *Ibid.,* p. 219.

[5] See, for example, the quotations from royalist writers, Falkner and Filmer, in *ibid.,* pp. 388-389.

[6] Quoted by Tönnies in *Archiv für Geschichte der Philosophie* (1890), p. 223.

[7] Now published (from manuscript) by Tönnies under the title of *The Elements of Law Natural and Politic* (London, 1889).

[8] William Molesworth, ed., *The English Works of Thomas Hobbes* IV (London, 1839; first, published, 1655), 414. References to the *Works* will hereafter be cited in the text by volume and page numbers.

[9] Tönnies's edition, p. 75. See also pp. 63, 57, 49, 95, 172, etc.

[10] *Ibid.,* pp. 2-3.

[11] Quoted by Tönnies in *Archiv,* XVII, 302. See also *Works,* IV, 407.

[12] Harrington, on the contrary, who was a genuinely democratic writer with an interest which was modern, economic, and secular, in differing radically from Hobbes as to respective merits of royal and popular government, says, "In most other things I believe Mr. Hobbes is, and in future ages will be, accounted the best writer in this day in the world."

[13] Quoted from Ritchie, *Natural Rights,* p. 9. He quotes from the preface of Firth to the *Clarke Papers.*

[14] Lawson, *An Examination of the Political Part of Mr. Hobbes, His Leviathan,* pp. 96, 123, 127. When one considers the prevalence of this idea of the duty of private judgment, one is almost inclined to align Hobbes's criticism of it with that passed by Auguste Comte upon Protestantism.

[15] *Ibid.,* pp. 133-134. Italics mine.

[16] As Hobbes saw, this doctrine is either a negation of sovereignty or works out practically (as it has done so largely in this country) in placing the judges in the seat of sovereignty—a "government of lawyers, not of men," to paraphrase the old saying. Locke comes close to this legal position, and historically is half way between Hobbes's location of sovereignty and Rousseau's ascription of sovereignty to the legislative body alone.

[17] Figgis, *Divine Right of Kings,* p. 229. See his note for references in support of the text.

[18] See also *Works,* VI, 194-195.

[19] In the *Leviathan (Works,* III, 256), he criticizes this definition of Coke's on the ground that long study only increases error unless the foundations are true and agreed upon.

[20] *Hobbes* (London, 1886), p. 57.

[21] See also *Works,* II, xxii, in which he says that there is only one point not *demonstrated* in the whole book—namely, the superior commodiousness of monarchy; for, as we must remember, Hobbes always means mathematical method by demonstration.

[22] Tönnies, *Archiv,* p. 69.

[23] I think that there is more than a shadowy reminiscence of Hobbes in Locke's contention that morals and mathematics are the two demonstrative subjects. What we "make ourselves" and general notions which, being the "workmanship of the understanding," are their own archetypes, are not, after all, far apart.

[24] *Works,* VI, 213, 236; III, 330; VII, 345; III, 713. See also IV, 204.

[25] *Works,* III, 713, for his suggestion to Cromwell to have his doctrines taught in the universities; see *ibid.,* VII, 343-352, for a defense of the proposal.

[26] In his dedication to the Earl of Newcastle, dated in 1640, where men's agreement in mathematics, due to dependence on reason, is contrasted with their controversies and contradictions in policy and justice, due to their following passion.

[27] Compare with this the following from the *Leviathan*: "For all men are by nature provided with notable multiplying glasses, that is, their passions and self-love, through which, every little payment appeareth a great grievance; but are destitute of those prospective glasses, namely, moral and civil science, to see afar off the miseries that hang over them, and can not without such payments be avoided" (III, 170).

[28] They are called laws only metaphorically, since only a command is a law. But in the sense in which the faculty of reason is a gift of God, and God may be said to command us to act rationally, they are true laws or commands.

[29] In his own day, Hobbes had logically the benefit of the fact that "self-preservation" was laid down by practically all writers as the first article of the law of nature. Moral laws are "eternal" to Hobbes in exactly the same way as are geometrical propositions. They flow from original definitions whose subjects include their predicates in such a way that the latter cannot be denied without falling, at some point, into formal self-contradiction. The absolute "obligation" which the subject is under not to withdraw from the compact by which he entered the State is the obligation not to contradict his own premises.

[30] Hobbes never attributes physical omnipotence to the sovereign, but only a power to threaten and to enforce threats which arouses enough fear to influence men's outer conduct. His whole position very closely resembles that of Kant regarding the relation of the moral and the legal, much as the two differ in their conception of the moral.

[31] *Leviathan,* pt. II, chap. XXX. Vol. III, chap. XIII, "Concerning the Duties of Them That Rule." See also vol. IV, *De Corpore Politico,* chap. IX, which sets out from the proposition, "This is the general law for sovereigns, that they procure, to the uttermost of their endeavour, the good of the people."

[32] It is in the same vein when Hobbes says that rebellion is not an offense against the civil law, but against the moral or natural law, for they violate the obligation to obedience which is before all civil law—since the institution of civil law depends upon it (*Works,* II, 200).

[33] Compare the *Leviathan,* III, 335.

Quentin Skinner (essay date 1966)

SOURCE: "The Ideological Context of Hobbes's Political Thought," in *The Historical Journal,* Vol. IX, No. 3, 1966, pp. 286-317.

[In the following excerpt, Skinner explores Hobbes's contemporary reputation and rejects the claim that he was isolated ideologically.]

The modern reputation of Hobbes's *Leviathan* as a work 'incredibly overtopping all its successors in political theory'[1] has concentrated so much attention on Hobbes's own text that it has tended at the same time to divert attention away from any attempt to study the relations between his thought and its age, or to trace his affinities with the other political writers of his time. It has by now become an axiom of the historiography[2] that Hobbes's 'extraordinary boldness'[3] set him completely 'outside the main stream of English political thought' in his time.[4] The theme of the one study devoted to the reception of Hobbes's political doctrines has been that Hobbes stood out alone 'against all the powerful and still developing constitutionalist tradition',[5] but that the tradition ('fortunately')[6] proved too strong for him. Hobbes was 'the first to attack its fundamental assumptions',[7] but no one followed his lead. Although he 'tried to sweep away the whole structure of traditional sanctions',[8] he succeeded only in provoking 'the widespread re-assertion of accepted principles',[9] a re-assertion, in fact, of 'the main English political tradition'.[10] And the more *Leviathan* has become accepted as 'the greatest, perhaps the sole masterpiece'[11] of English political theory, the less has Hobbes seemed to bear any meaningful relation to the ephemeral political quarrels of his contemporaries. The doctrine of *Leviathan* has come to be regarded as 'an isolated phenomenon in English thought, without ancestry or posterity'.[12] Hobbes's system, it is assumed, was related to its age only by the 'intense opposition' which its 'boldness and originality' were to provoke.[13]

The view, however, that Hobbes 'impressed English thought almost entirely by rousing opposition',[14] and that consequently 'no man of his time occupied such a lonely position in the world of thought'[15] seems to be much in need of re-examination. For it can be shown that complex and ambiguous relationships between Hobbes and the other political writers of his age have in this way become misleadingly oversimplified. It has not been recognized that to set against the hostility of his numerous critics there was also a popular following for Hobbes's doctrines, particularly on the continent. It has not been realized that Hobbes's theory of obligation was also critically studied at the same time, and treated as authoritative, by a whole group of *de facto* theorists in the English Revolution. The fact that these aspects of Hobbes's contemporary reputation have been overlooked, moreover, can be shown to have given rise to a misleading view about the intentions even of his critics.

These affinities between Hobbes's doctrine and its intellectual milieu have never been investigated.[16] The attempt to see Hobbes against this ideological background, however, will not only produce an historically more complete picture. It can also be shown to be relevant in itself to questions about the nature of Hobbes's own contribution to political theory. For Hobbes's views have tended to get evaluated in a misleadingly unhistorical way. He has been treated as a figure in complete isolation, the inventor of 'an entirely new type of political doctrine'.[17] He has thus come to seem an inevitable influence, a necessary point of departure, for other political writers of the time, including Harrington and even Locke.[18] All such judgements, however, become arbitrary or unhistorical when it is shown that Hobbes was in fact drawing on and contributing to existing traditions in political ideology, as well as helping to refine and modify them. The prevailing view, moreover, about the meaning of Hobbes's own political doctrine depends in effect on discounting all such evidence about his contemporary intellectual relations. It can be shown, similarly, that this in itself must reduce considerably the plausibility of such interpretations. It is the aim, in short, of the following study to show from an investigation of Hobbes's contemporary reputation that it is not possible to disconnect questions about the proper interpretation of Hobbes's views from questions about the ideological context in which they were developed.

The accepted view of Hobbes as a complete outcast from the intellectual society of his time, 'the bête noire of his age,'[19] has arisen at least in part from a misleading restriction of the investigation. Although there have been valuable studies of the numerous attacks made on Hobbes by his clerical enemies in England, there has never been any study[20] of Hobbes's reception in his own time on the continent. It has in general been assumed that Hobbes's views 'proved equally noxious and combustible'[21] abroad, and that he 'received the same hard usage' as in England.[22] It is clear, however, that there is in fact an important distinction to be drawn between the many critics whom Hobbes provoked at home and the many admirers he was to gain on the continent, especially in France.

Hobbes himself remarked with some bitterness in his later years on the contrast between his reputation abroad, which 'fades not yet',[23] and the opposition he continued to arouse in the English universities and in the Royal Society. The Royal Society always contrived to ignore him. But the foreign *savants* were to show no such hostility. When Pierre Bayle came to summarize so much of their achievement at the end of the century, in his Dictionary, he was to single Hobbes out as 'one of the greatest minds of the seventeenth century'.[24] And perhaps the greatest of the foreign *savants,* Leibniz himself, cited 'the famous Hobbes' with his 'extreme subtlety' on many points.[25] Leibniz completely disagreed with Hobbes's ethical and political theory, 'which, if we were to adopt it, would bring nothing but anarchy'.[26] Yet he still placed Hobbes among the highest, for (as he remarked in one of the *Meditations*) 'what could be more acute than Descartes in physics, or Hobbes in ethics?'[27]

Hobbes had first gained this high reputation among the continental *savants* a generation earlier, during his eleven years' exile from the civil wars in England. He was then a frequent visitor at Mersenne's cell, which served during the 1640s as perhaps the most important *salon* for the learned. Many of the scientists and philosophers Hobbes is known to have met there were to become avowed followers and popularizers of his political theories. Several of them corresponded with Hobbes and even visited him after his return to England in 1651.[28] Hobbes met there the physician Sorbière, who was to publish the first French translation of Hobbes's *De Cive,* as well as a translation of *De Corpore Politico,* both with fulsome prefaces in praise of Hobbes's political system.[29] He also met the mathematician Du Verdus, who was later to produce a further translation of *De Cive,* with a preface recommending it to Louis XIV as suitable for use in all French schools.[30] He met Gassendi, whose remarks about the freedom and clarity of Hobbes's political thought were to be inserted in the second edition of *De Cive*.[31] Mersenne himself wrote similarly of 'the incomparable Hobbes', whose *De Cive* had shown that politics could be made a study as scientific as geometry.[32] A large number of letters sent to Hobbes at this time by other French admirers reveal the extent of his popularity and ideological relevance in France, as well as the efforts which these disciples made to ensure that the works of 'this great politician' became widely known.[33]

This continental acceptance of the relevance of Hobbes's doctrine was to be reflected in the political propaganda of the De Witt party in Holland[34] as well as among the apologists for absolutism in France. In Holland Velthuysen welcomed the publication of *De Cive* with a dissertation in the form of a letter to its 'most celebrated' author, pointing out 'how much you will see my own views bear the closest affinity to the views of the great Hobbes'.[35] 'The famous Hobbes' is cited throughout this *Dissertatio* as the authority on the nature of man, on the relations between natural and human laws, and on the power of the civil magistrate.[36] In France Merlat similarly used the viewpoint of 'that famous Englishman, Hobbes' as a basis for the argument of his *Traité du Pouvoir Absolu*.[37] Although he claimed to disagree strongly with Hobbes on the question of man's natural unsociability, his own view of

the origins and the necessary form of political society both cited and closely followed Hobbes's characteristic account. Hobbes was 'undoubtedly correct' to see that 'the malice of most men would ruin a Society', and so was correct to deduce not only that this 'established in general the need for political power', but also that it required that such power should be absolute. And for further elucidation Merlat simply referred 'the curious' to Hobbes's own works.[38]

Hobbes's political theory was to be critically studied as well as merely popularized among his contemporaries on the continent. His sympathetic readers, moreover, included some of the greatest names. It is a commonplace that Spinoza's *Tractatus Politicus* shows the effects of 'a critical reflection on Hobbes's theory' in 'its content and terminology as well as its method'.[39] The affinity was recognized at the time, particularly by critics, who often bracketed Spinoza together with Hobbes in a general denunciation.[40] It is known from his correspondence that Spinoza himself recognized his affinities with Hobbes.[41] It is known from Aubrey's biography that Hobbes himself (anticipating much modern commentary)[42] recognized in Spinoza's political theory an equally pessimistic but even more rigorous development of his own assumptions.[43] It was among the continental jurists, however, that Hobbes's political doctrines were to set off the strongest echoes. Even the hostile traditionalists were to acknowledge his immediate impact. Samuel Rachel, professor of Law at Holstein in the 1660s, remarked—very instructively—on the dangerous fact that while 'many learned and good men in England have been roused' against 'this novel philosophy of Hobbes', yet it 'has been greedily swallowed by some in France and the Netherlands, and even in Germany'.[44] The jurists were sometimes hostile to Hobbes's views, but in their works he none the less joins the ranks of the great—a name to cite with the Ancients, and to stand with Grotius and Pufendorf among modern authorities. Gundling was to use Hobbes as a source throughout his works, and in his *De Jure Oppignorati Territorii* cited Hobbes as his authority both in discussing the problems of establishing political society and on the need for a monopoly of power within it.[45] Textor in his *Synopsis Juris Gentium* gave Hobbes, along with Pufendorf, as the authority to be cited in discussing both the distinction between 'the Natural Law of Man and of States' and 'the origins of Kingdoms and the ways in which they are acquired under the Law of Nations'.[46] Beckman in his *Meditationes Politicae* gave a list of authorities on political theory in which he singled out, as 'the two incomparable men to be consulted in these matters', Hugo Grotius and Thomas Hobbes.[47] Grotius was conventionally the greatest name to cite in discussions about *ius gentium,* but Beckman was later to decide that it was Hobbes's name which 'deserved to be praised before all others'.[48]

The most careful student of Hobbes among the seventeenth-century jurists was to be Pufendorf himself, in his effort to construct a systematic jurisprudence out of a 'reconciliation between the principles of Grotius and Hobbes'.[49] His great treatise of 1672, *De Jure Naturae et Gentium,* treated Hobbes throughout as an authority on many of the points at which (in Pufendorf's favourite phrase) 'scholars are not yet agreed',[50] as well as providing perhaps the most intelligent analysis by a contemporary of Hobbes's political theory. Pufendorf was frequently critical of Hobbes, whose basic political axiom, he felt, was 'unworthy of human nature'.[51] He was prepared, nevertheless, to defend even this part of Hobbes's system, since he felt (as did Leibniz)[52] that Hobbes had been unfortunate in being 'interpreted with very great rigour, and with very little reason, by some learned men'.[53] Pufendorf remained close and sympathetic to Hobbes's views, moreover, at two important points, corresponding to Book II of his Treatise, on man and society, and Book VII, on the establishment of States. In Book II, although Pufendorf remained sceptical about 'that War of all men against all which Hobbes would introduce', he conceded that Hobbes 'has been lucky enough in painting the insecurities of such a state', and concluded that if the theory is treated 'only by way of hypothesis' it may well have a distinct relevance and cautionary value.[54] In Book VII Pufendorf is even closer to Hobbes—closer, perhaps, even than his acknowledgments suggest. He begins by agreeing that 'what Mr Hobbes observes concerning the genius of Mankind is not impertinent to our present argument: that all have a restless desire after power'. And, though he remained hostile to the theory of obligation which Hobbes deduced, he concluded (with extensive quotation from *Leviathan*) that 'Mr Hobbes hath given us a very ingenious draft of a civil State, conceived as an artificial man'.[55]

It becomes clear that the immediate reception of Hobbes's political theory on the continent was much less hostile than in England. There was a clearer sense of the relevance as well as the importance of his doctrine. The distinction has been largely ignored in modern commentary. It was recognized at the time, however, not only by Hobbes himself, but by the first of his biographers, his friend John Aubrey. When Aubrey came to draw up his list of Hobbes's 'learned familiar friends' for his biography, he treated it as a sad but undoubted fact that 'as a prophet is not esteemed in his own country, so he was more esteemed by foreigners than by his countrymen'.[56]

The relations of Hobbes's political thought to the ideologies of the English Revolution have been obscured as well as illuminated by the tendency of scholars to concentrate exclusively on the fulminations of Hobbes's numerous clerical opponents. It is true, of course, that among his contemporaries Hobbes was particularly marked out for his originality, particularly denounced

for his heterodoxy. It is evident, none the less, that his impact has been viewed in a misleading perspective. It can be shown (quite apart from the central issue of Hobbes's following) that the treatment of Hobbes's critics as 'representative' of political theory at the time has been misleading in two important respects. It is a view based, in the first place, on a misleading oversimplification of the nuances and complexities of different political ideologies of the time. For despite the many attacks Hobbes also gained a serious reputation as an authority on political matters among many of the learned—even among the learned orthodox who remained uncommitted to any of his views. The accepted view of Hobbes's reputation has been based, in the second place, on a mistaken impression of the assumptions, and even the intentions, of Hobbes's critics. It has not been recognized how much they feared not merely Hobbes's dangerous doctrines, but their serious ideological purchase, not to mention their popular following.

The serious reputation of Hobbes among 'the solemn, the judicious' was conceded at the time even by his enemies.[57] By the end of the century Hobbes had come to be accepted as an authority even among philosophers of avowedly opposed temperament. 'Tom Hobbes', as Shaftesbury was to admit, 'I must confess a genius, and even an original among these latter leaders in philosophy.'[58] By this time Hobbes had attained the recognition he had always hoped for, in having his works placed (though amidst much controversy) in the libraries of his own university.[59] Within his own lifetime he was not without a similar recognition. Selden and Osborne, who both revealed in their writings a markedly 'Hobbesian' strain, were also (according to Aubrey) amongst the earliest serious students of Hobbes's political works. Osborne wrote of Hobbes as one of the men who had 'embellished the age',[60] while Selden is known to have sought Hobbes's acquaintance on the strength of reading *Leviathan*.[61] In a similar spirit Hobbes's friend Abraham Cowley 'bestowed on him an immortal Pindaric Ode',[62] the fulsome sentiments of which were to be echoed by Blount's remarks on Hobbes as 'the great instructor of the most sensible part of Mankind'.[63]

Although such tributes to Hobbes mainly came from his less conventional friends, his recognition was not confined to them. Hobbes had a number of clerical admirers,[64] among whom must be counted that very type of a Restoration bishop, Seth Ward. Ward was suspicious of *Leviathan,* disliking its attack on the universities. Yet he acknowledged 'a very great respect and a very high esteem' for its author,[65] and possibly wrote the Epistle prefacing *De Corpore Politico,* in which Hobbes's 'excellent notions' on 'the grounds and principles of Policy' are 'commended as the best that ever were writ'.[66] James Harrington wrote of Hobbes in a very similar way. Although suspicious and critical of *Leviathan* he nevertheless agreed 'that Mr Hobbes is and will in future ages be accounted the best writer at this day in the world'. [67] And, while Harrington looked to future ages, a reference by Webster to Hobbes and the Ancients completes the eulogy. There was no need, Webster claimed, to revere too much the views of the Ancients on statecraft. Although they had produced works 'of singular use and commodity', yet 'even our own countryman Master Hobbes hath pieces of more exquisiteness and profundity in that subject than ever the Grecian wit was able to reach unto'. [68]

These anticipations of Hobbes's modern reputation were echoed at the time even among his critics. These acknowledgments of Hobbes's stature have been suppressed in modern commentary. Even the critics agreed, however, in seeing Hobbes not only as 'a man of excellent parts', [69] a man 'singularly deserving in moral and socratical philosophy', [70] but even as a writer 'of as eminent learning and parts as any this last age hath produced'. [71] *Leviathan,* as even its bitterest critics allowed, was the work of 'a universal scholar'. [72] The recognition of its author's 'mighty *acumen ingenii*', [73] moreover, caused the critics to move with some circumspection in their attacks. Hobbes was 'a man with so great a name for learning', as one critic admitted, that the best he could hope to do was to 'fling my stone at this giant, and I hope hit him'. [74] Clarendon, too, prefaced his statesmanlike attack by conceding how difficult it was to contest the 'great credit and authority' which *Leviathan* had gained 'from the known name of the author, a man of excellent parts'. As much as any follower, he joined the other critics in acknowledging *Leviathan*—with whatever alarm—to be a work 'which contains in it good learning of all kinds, politely extracted, and very wittily and cunningly digested, in a very commendable method, and in a vigorous and pleasant style'. [75]

It is clear, moreover, that what disturbed the critics was not merely the serious reputation or even the alarming content of Hobbes's doctrines, but their ideological purchase, and their even more alarming popularity. This point has been submerged under the weight given to the contemporary attacks on Hobbes—though the number of attacks might in itself be thought to offer some paradoxical guide to Hobbes's continuing popularity. The popular acceptance of Hobbes's views, however, was a point which weighed with his critics from the start. As early as 1657 Lawson was to note how much *Leviathan* was 'judged to be a rational piece' both by 'many gentlemen' and by 'young students in the Universities'. [76] Within two years of its publication Rosse had expected to be attacked himself for denouncing so fashionable a work. [77] By 1670 Tenison felt obliged to admit that 'there is certainly no man who hath any share of the curiosity

of this present age' who could still remain 'unacquainted with his name and doctrine'. [78] Clarendon noted at the same time how much Hobbes's popularity continued to weather every attack, how much his works 'continue still to be esteemed as well abroad as at home'. [79] By the time of his death Hobbes had grown 'so great in reputation', as Whitehall angrily remarked, that even apparently 'wise and prudent' men had come to accept his political views, which 'are daily undertaken to be defended'.[80]

Hobbes's enemies doubtless wished to emphasize the menace, but there is independent evidence about the extent of Hobbes's contemporary popularity. A catalogue of 'the most vendible books in England' which happens to survive for the year 1658 included all of Hobbes's works on political theory, and showed him one of the most popular of all the writers listed under 'humane learning', surpassed in the number of his entries only by Bacon and Raleigh. [81] Twenty years later Eachard was to make the figure of Hobbes in his *Dialogue* reply to his detractors by pointing out that despite their strictures on his works they 'have sold very well, and have been generally read and admired'. [82] The printing history for all of Hobbes's political works certainly bears this out. [83] *De Corpore Politico,* originally published in 1650, reached a third edition by 1652, was immediately translated, and in its French version went through two further editions within the year. *De Cive* was first published in a very small edition in 1642, but on being re-issued five years later it went through three editions in one year. It was published again in 1657, again in 1669, as well as appearing in the two-volume collection of Hobbes's *Opera Philosophica* which went through two editions in 1668. Translated into French in 1649, it had attained a third edition by 1651 and a new translation by 1660. *Leviathan* went through three editions in its first year of publication, and by 1668 the book (as Pepys noted) was so 'mightily called for' that he had to pay three times the original price to get a copy, [84] even though there had in fact been two further editions of the work in the same year. It is a record of publication not even rivalled by Locke (to take the most famous case from the next generation), within whose lifetime the *Two Treatises* reached only three English and two French editions.[85]

The failure to acknowledge this element of popularity has tended to give a misleading impression of the intentions of Hobbes's contemporary critics. They have been treated as attacking a single source of heterodox opinion. It can be shown, however, that they concentrated on Hobbes not because he was seen as the 'singlehanded' opponent of tradition, but rather because he was seen to give the ablest and most influential presentation to a point of view which was itself gaining increasingly in fashionable acceptance and in ideological importance. To the more hysterical critics it even seemed possible to believe that 'most of the bad principles of this Age are of no earlier a date than one very ill Book, are indeed but the spawn of the *Leviathan*'. [86] By the time of the 1688 Revolution, when the question of allegiance to *de facto* power was again (as when *Leviathan* was first published) the central issue of political debate, it seemed to the last exponents of passive obedience that the 'authority and the reasons' of Hobbes's political theory 'are of a sudden so generally received, as if the doctrine were Apostolical'. [87] By this time (according to Anthony à Wood, Hobbes's old Oxford enemy) *Leviathan* had already 'corrupted half the gentry of the Nation'. [88] The suspicion of Hobbes's leading contribution to 'the debauching of this generation' [89] was the moving spirit even with some of Hobbes's most statesmanlike critics. Richard Cumberland excused his long philosophical attack on Hobbes with the hope that he might limit the increasing acceptance of Hobbes's political views. [90] Even Clarendon, from the bitterness of his second exile, claimed to trace 'many odious opinions' back to *Leviathan,* 'the seed whereof was first sowed in that book'. [91]

A more realistic—and more revealing—assumption was that the reason for Hobbes's doctrines being so 'greedily sought and cried up' [92] was rather 'the prevalence of a scoffing humour' in 'this unhappy time'. [93] When Francis Atterbury came to reflect a generation later on the ease with which the 'false and foolish opinions' of that age had 'gotten footing and thriven', he had no doubt that there had been 'something in them which flattered either our vanity our lust or our pride, and fell in with a daring inclination'. And he particularly mentioned Hobbes as a man who had 'owed all his reputation and his followers' to this 'skill he had in fitting his principles to men's constitutions and tempers'. [94] Earlier critics had nearly all made the same point. According to Lucy the popularity of *Leviathan* merely indicated 'the genius that governs this age, in which all learning, with religion, hath suffered a change, and men are apt to entertain new opinions in any science, although for the worse, of which sort are Mr Hobbes his writings'. [95] And according to Eachard—Hobbes's rudest, shrewdest critic—the age itself had thrown up so many 'who were sturdy, resolved practicants in Hobbianism' that they 'would most certainly have been so, had there never been any such man as Mr Hobbes in the world'. [96]

To some Hobbes was the leading symptom, to others the sole cause, of the increasingly rationalist temper of political debate. But the point on which all critics agreed was that Hobbes's popularity reflected a more widespread endorsement of his outlook. It was not Hobbes himself whom they were even mainly concerned to denounce, but rather Hobbes as the best example of the alarming and increasing phenomenon of 'Hobbism'. Within Hobbes's own lifetime the word 'Hobbism' was already in popular currency to denote 'a wild, atheistically disposed' attitude to the powers that be, [97] while the 'Hobbists' were recognized as wanting to 'subvert our laws and liberties and set up arbitrary power'. [98] The 'Hobbist' villain became a familiar parody on the Restoration stage: in Farquhar's *Constant Couple* he reads what appears to be *The Practice of Piety,* but is in fact *Leviathan* under plain cover. [99] The 'Hobbist' was also recognized, more seriously, as the political rationalist who assumed that God had left it 'arbitrary to men (as the Hobbeans vainly fancy)' [100] to establish their own political societies 'according to the principles of equality and self-preservation agreed to by the Hobbists'. [101] Locke in his *Essay* contrasted the 'Hobbist' with the Christian, as a man who would justify his keeping of 'compacts' not by saying 'because God, who has the power of eternal life and death, requires it of us', but 'because the public requires it, and the Leviathan will punish you if you do not'. [102] Bramhall similarly addressed his *Catching of Leviathan* not merely to Hobbes, but to the man 'who is thoroughly an Hobbist', with the aim of showing him that 'the Hobbian principles do destroy all relations between man and man, and the whole frame of the Commonwealth'. [103]

The 'Hobbists' and the followers of Hobbes, so alarming to contemporaries, have been almost totally discounted by modern commentators. The positive ideological affinities between the political views of Hobbes and his contemporaries have in consequence received no attention. The one analysis of the relations between 'Hobbes and Hobbism' has claimed, in fact, that in Hobbes's own time there was to be only one 'favourable' as against fifty-one 'hostile' published reactions to Hobbes's political views. [104] It is evident, however, that a great deal of information has been missed here. It has not always been recognized, in the first place, that most of Hobbes's critics (apart from the mathematicians) were concerned not so much with his political doctrines as with the allegedly atheistic implications of his determinism. [105] Only half of the twelve tracts entirely aimed at Hobbes during his own lifetime were even mainly concerned with his political thought. [106] This did not mean that Hobbes's specifically political doctrines were to receive less notice in his own time. It can be shown that Hobbes had important affinities and connexions with other strands of contemporary political debate, and that these were both recognized and sympathetically discussed. It can also be shown that Hobbes came to be cited and accepted within his own lifetime—independently of any close critical study—simply as an authority on matters of political theory, even among writers who might never have read his works, or had read only to confute them.

It was his famous attempt to explain political association in terms of man's need to mediate his nasty and brutish nature which was to give Hobbes his immediate place in the accepted canon of writers on political theory. He became labelled as the writer who had thought of deducing the necessary form of the state from the imagined chaos of a 'state of Nature'. Just as Aristotle retained a reputation in the seventeenth century—even among his fashionable denigrators—as the first writer who had emphasized man's natural sociability, so Hobbes gained a reputation as the first writer to reverse this traditional emphasis. The point was often made even by writers who wished to repudiate it, or who wished to leave it an open question (as one writer put it) whether 'as it was said of old' man was 'naturally sociable', or whether 'as a learned modern has said' he is 'compelled into Society merely for the advantages and necessities of life'....[107]

Notes

[1] R. G. Collingwood, *The New Leviathan* (Oxford, 1942), p. iv.

[2] For studies of Hobbes's reception, see J. Laird, *Hobbes* (London, 1934), part III, pp. 243-317, esp. 247-57; H. R. Trevor-Roper, 'Thomas Hobbes' and 'The Anti-Hobbists', in *Historical Essays* (London, 1957), pp. 233-8, 239-43; J. Bowle, *Hobbes and his Critics* (London, 1951); S. I. Mintz, *The Hunting of Leviathan* (Cambridge, 1962), and incidental discussions in other works cited below.

[3] Trevor-Roper, 'Thomas Hobbes', p. 233.

[4] Bowle, op. cit. p. 13.

[5] Ibid. p. 42.

[6] Ibid. p. 47.

[7] Ibid. p. 42.

[8] Ibid. p. 43.

[9] Ibid. p. 13.

[10] Ibid. p. 14.

[11] Thomas Hobbes, *Leviathan,* ed. M. Oakeshott (Oxford, 1946), Introduction, p. x.

[12] Trevor-Roper, 'Thomas Hobbes', p. 233.

[13] Mintz, op. cit. p. 155.

[14] Leslie Stephen, *Hobbes* (London, 1904), p. 67.

[15] G. P. Gooch, *Political Thought in England: Bacon to Halifax* (London, 1915), p. 23.

[16] Bowle's book simply treats Hobbes's critics as 'representative' of a political tradition which Hobbes is alleged 'singlehandedly' to have challenged. For a brilliant discussion, however, of the relations between Hobbes's intellectual *assumptions* and their appropriate *social* context, see Keith Thomas, 'The Social Origins of Hobbes's Political Thought', in *Hobbes Studies,* ed. K. C. Brown (Cambridge, Mass., 1965), pp. 185-236.

[17] Leo Strauss, *Natural Right and History* (Chicago, 1953), p. 182.

[18] For this assumption, see esp. ibid. pp. 202-51; C. B. Macpherson, *The Political Theory of Possessive Individualism* (Oxford, 1962), pp. 265-70; R. H. Cox, *Locke on War and Peace* (Oxford, 1960), esp. pp. 136-47 on the relations between Commonwealths, where it is claimed that Locke's doctrine 'tacitly follows Hobbes', p. 146.

[19] Mintz, op. cit. p. vii.

[20] Except for the brief, though valuable, remarks in Laird, op. cit. part III.

[21] Mintz, op. cit. p. 62.

[22] Ibid. p. 57.

[23] Thomas Hobbes, 'Considerations', *The English Works,* ed. Sir W. Molesworth (London, II vols., 1839-45), IV, 435.

[24] Pierre Bayle, *Dictionnaire Historique et Critique* (Rotterdam, 4 vols., 1697), III, 99-103. Note: in this and all following quotations from seventeenth-century sources all translations are mine, all spelling and punctuation are modernized.

[25] G. W. Leibniz, *Opera Omnia* (Geneva, 6 vols., 1768), I, 5, 256.

[26] Ibid. IV, 360.

[27] Ibid. VI, 303.

[28] On visits, see Thomas Birch, *The History of the Royal Society* (London, 4 vols., 1756), I, 26-7; S. Sorbière, *A Voyage to England* (London, trans. 1709), pp. 26-7.

[29] See, in *Elements Philosophiques du Citoyen* (Amsterdam, 1649), Sorbière's translation of *De Cive; Le Corps Politique ou les Elements de la Loi Morale et Civile* (Amsterdam, 1652), his translation of *De Corpore Politico.*

[30] See, in *Les Elements de la Politique de Monsieur*

Hobbes (Paris, 1660), Du Verdus's translation of *De Cive*.

[31] Gassendi to Sorbière: printed in Thomas Hobbes, *Elementa Philosophica De Cive* (Amsterdam, 1647), sig., 10a-b.

[32] Mersenne to Sorbière; printed in ibid. sig., IIa-b.

[33] For a special study of this group and its correspondence with Hobbes, see my article, 'Thomas Hobbes and his Disciples in France and England', *Comparative Studies in Society and History,* VIII (1966), 153-67.

[34] See Johan de la Court, *Consideratien van Staat* (n.p., 1661); A. Wolf, 'Annotations', *Correspondence of Spinoza* (London, 1928), p. 446.

[35] Lambertino Velthuysen, *Epistolica Dissertatio* (Amsterdam, 1651), p. 2.

[36] Ibid. pp. 35 ff., 136 ff., 175 ff.

[37] E. Merlat, *Traité du Pouvoir Absolu des Souverains* (Cologne, 1685).

[38] Ibid. pp. 219-22.

[39] Benedict de Spinoza, *The Political Works,* trans. and ed. A. G. Wernham (Oxford, 1958), Introduction, pp. 1, 12.

[40] E.g. Richard Baxter in *The Second Part of the Non-Conformists Plea for Peace* (London, 1680); William Falkner in *Christian Loyalty* (London, 1679); and Regnus à Mansvelt, as cited in the Introduction to *The Moral and Political Works of Thomas Hobbes* (London, 1750), p. xxvi n.

[41] See Wolf, op. cit. Letter 50, p. 269.

[42] E.g. S. Hampshire, *Spinoza* (London, 1951), pp. 133-6.

[43] See John Aubrey, *Brief Lives,* ed. A. Clark (Oxford, 2 vols., 1898), I, 357.

[44] Samuel Rachel, *Dissertation on the Law of Nature and of Nations* (1676), trans. in J. B. Scott (ed.), *The Classics of International Law* (Washington, 2 vols., 1916), II, 75.

[45] N. H. Gundling, *De Jure Oppignorati Territorii* (Magdeburg, 1706), p. 16. Also mentioned Hobbes in *De Praerogativa* (n.d.) and in *Dissertatio de Statu Naturali* (1709).

[46] J. W. Textor, *Synopsis of the Law of Nations* (1680), trans. in L. von Bar (ed.), *The Classics of International Law* (Washington, 2 vols., 1916), II, 9 and 82.

[47] J. C. Beckman, *Meditationes Politicae* (Frankfort, 1679), p. 7.

[48] J. C. Beckman, *Politica Parallela* (Frankfort, 1679), p. 417.

[49] Laird, *Hobbes,* p. 276.

[50] Samuel Pufendorf, *Of the Law of Nature and Nations* (London, trans. 1710). Cited Hobbes as authority on Law of Nature (in Book II, ch. IV, and in VIII, I); on consensus (II, III); on contracts (V, II); on sovereignty (VII, VII).

[51] Ibid. p. 87.

[52] Leibniz, op. cit. V, 468.

[53] Pufendorf, op. cit. p. 112.

[54] Ibid. Book II, pp. 84-8.

[55] Ibid. Book VII, pp. 518-26.

[56] Aubrey, op. cit. I, 373.

[57] J. Eachard, *Some Opinions of Mr Hobbes Considered.* Introduction distinguished Hobbes's serious and popular following, anatomizing 'Hobbists' into pit, gallery and box 'friends'. See sig. A, 4a-b.

[58] A. A. Cooper, 3rd earl of Shaftesbury, *The Life, Unpublished Letters and Philosophical Regimen,* ed. B. Rand (London, 1900), Letter to Stanhope, p. 414.

[59] See Thomas Hearne, *Remarks and Collections* (Oxford, 11 vols., 1885-1921), X, 75 and 322.

[60] Francis Osborne, *A Miscellany* (London, 1659), sig. A.

[61] Aubrey, op. cit. I, 369.

[62] Ibid. p. 368.

[63] Charles Blount, *The Oracles of Reason* (London, 1693), p. 104.
[64] Aubrey's list of Hobbes's closest friends included four clergymen (see Aubrey, op. cit. I, 370).

[65] Seth Ward, *A Philosophical Essay* (Oxford, 1652), sig. A, 3a.

[66] Thomas Hobbes, 'To the Reader', *De Corpore Politico* (London, 1650). Cf. Thomas Hobbes, *The Ele-*

ments of Law, ed. F. Tönnies (London, 1889), Introduction, p. vii.

[67] J. Harrington, 'The Prerogative of Popular Government', *Works* (London, 1771), p. 241.

[68] J. Webster, *Academiarum Examen* (London, 1654), p. 88.

[69] Alexander Rosse, *Leviathan Drawn out with an Hook* (London, 1653), sig. A, 12a.

[70] Philip Scot, *A Treatise of the Schism of England* (London, 1650), p. 223.

[71] Roger Coke, *A Survey of the Politics* (London, 1662), sig. A, 4a.

[72] John Dowel, *The Leviathan Heretical* (Oxford, 1683), sig. A, 2a.

[73] William Lucy, *Observations, Censures and Confutations of Notorious Errors in Mr Hobbes his Leviathan* (London, 1663), p. 117.

[74] William Lucy, *Examinations, Censures and Confutations of Divers Errors in the Two First Chapters of Mr Hobbes his Leviathan* (London, 1656), sig. A, 5a.

[75] Edward Hyde, earl of Clarendon, *A Brief View and Survey of . . . Leviathan* (Oxford, 1676), sig. A, 1b.

[76] George Lawson, *An Examination of the Political Part of Mr Hobbes his Leviathan* (London, 1657), sig. A, 2b.

[77] Rosse, op. cit. sig. A, 4b.

[78] Thomas Tenison, *The Creed of Mr Hobbes Examined* (London, 1670), p. 2.

[79] Clarendon, op. cit. sig. A, 3a.

[80] John Whitehall, *The Leviathan Found Out* (London, 1679), p. 3.

[81] W. London, *A Catalogue of the Most Vendible Books in England* (London, 1658), sig. T, 3a, to sig. Z, 1b.

[82] John Eachard, *Mr Hobbes's State of Nature Considered,* ed. P. Ure (Liverpool, 1958), p. 14.

[83] For following details, cf. H. Macdonald and M. Hargreaves, *Thomas Hobbes: a Bibliography* (London, 1952), pp. 10-14, 16-22, 30-6, 76-7.

[84] Samuel Pepys, *The Diary,* ed. H. B. Wheatley (London, 8 vols., 1904-5), VIII, 91. The 'three editions' of *Leviathan* in 1651 may of course be slightly misleading, as the second two are evidently false imprints—contemporary, but precise dates unknown.

[85] See John Locke, *Two Treatises of Government,* ed. P. Laslett (Cambridge, 1960), Introduction, appendix A, pp. 121-9.

[86] Charles Wolseley, *The Reasonableness of Scripture-Belief* (London, 1672), sig. A, 4a.

[87] Abednego Seller, *The History of Passive Obedience since the Reformation* (Amsterdam, 1689), sig. A, 4a.

[88] Anthony à Wood, 'Thomas Hobbes', *Athenae Oxoniensis* (London, 2 vols., 1691-2), II, 278-483.

[89] J. Lymeric, life of Bramhall in *Works of . . . John Bramhall* (Dublin, 1676), sig. N, 1b.

[90] Richard Cumberland, *A Treatise of the Laws of Nature* (1672) (trans. London, 1727), Introduction, sect. xxx.

[91] Clarendon, op. cit. sig., 3a.

[92] Baxter, op. cit. p. 8.

[93] Anonymous, *Inquiry,* cited from Mintz, op. cit. p. 136.

[94] Francis Atterbury, *Maxims, Reflections and Observations* (London, 1723), p. 66.

[95] Lucy, *Examinations,* sig. A, 3b.

[96] Eachard, *Some Opinions,* sig. A, 3b.

[97] R.F., *A Sober Enquiry* (London, 1673), p. 51.

[98] John Crowne, *City Politics* (London, 1683), p. 50.

[99] T. Farquhar, *The Constant Couple* (London, 1700), p. 2: Vizard, 'This Hobbes is an excellent fellow'. On this point generally, see L. Teeter, 'The Dramatic Use of Hobbes's Political Ideas', *E.L.H.* III (1936), 140-69.

[100] Anonymous, *A Letter to a Friend* (London, 1679), p. 6.

[101] Anonymous, *The Great Law of Nature or Self-Preservation Examined* (n.p., n.d.) (B.M. Catalogue gives 1673), p. 6.

[102] John Locke, *An Essay Concerning Human Understanding* (London, 1690), Book I, ch. 3, para. 6.

[103] John Bramhall, *The Catching of Leviathan* (London, 1658), heading to ch. II, p. 503.

[104] S. P. Lamprecht, 'Hobbes and Hobbism', *American Political Science Review,* XXXIV (1940), 31-53, esp. p. 32.

[105] A point excellently made in Mintz, op. cit. p. vii, but also *passim.*

[106] See checklist in ibid. pp. 157-60.

[107] Anonymous, *Confusion Confounded* (London, 1654), p. 9.

Michael Oakeshott (essay date 1975)

SOURCE: An introduction to *Hobbes on Civil Association*, Basil Blackwell, 1975, pp. 1-74.

[*In the following excerpt from his introduction to* Leviathan, *Oakeshott discusses what philosophy meant to Hobbes, and how to approach reading him.*]

THE CONTEXT OF *LEVIATHAN*

Leviathan is the greatest, perhaps the sole, masterpiece of political philosophy written in the English language. And the history of our civilization can provide only a few works of similar scope and achievement to set beside it. Consequently, it must be judged by none but the highest standards and must be considered only in the widest context. The masterpiece supplies a standard and a context for the second-rate, which indeed is but a gloss; but the context of the masterpiece itself, the setting in which its meaning is revealed, can in the nature of things be nothing narrower than the history of political philosophy.

Reflection about political life may take place at a variety of levels. It may remain on the level of the determination of means, or it may strike out for the consideration of ends. Its inspiration may be directly practical, the modification of the arrangements of a political order in accordance with the perception of an immediate benefit; or it may be practical, but less directly so, guided by general ideas. Or again, springing from an experience of political life, it may seek a generalization of that experience in a doctrine. And reflection is apt to flow from one level to another in an unbroken movement, following the mood of the thinker. Political philosophy may be understood to be what occurs when this movement of reflection takes a certain direction and achieves a certain level, its characteristic being the relation of political life, and the values and purpos-es pertaining to it, to the entire conception of the world that belongs to a civilization. That is to say, at all other levels of reflection on political life we have before us the single world of political activity, and what we are interested in is the internal coherence of that world; but in political philosophy we have in our minds that world and another world, and our endeavour is to explore the coherence of the two worlds together. The reflective intelligence is apt to find itself at this level without the consciousness of any great conversion and without any sense of entering upon a new project, but merely by submitting itself to the impetus of reflection, by spreading its sails to the argument. For, any man who holds in his mind the conceptions of the natural world, of God, of human activity and human destiny which belong to his civilization, will scarcely be able to prevent an endeavour to assimilate these to the ideas that distinguish the political order in which he lives, and failing to do so he will become a philosopher (of a simple sort) unawares.

But, though we may stumble over the frontier of philosophy unwittingly and by doing nothing more demonstrative than refusing to draw rein, to achieve significant reflection, of course, requires more than inadvertence and more than the mere acceptance of the two worlds of ideas. The whole impetus of the enterprise is the perception that what really exists is a single world of ideas, which comes to us divided by the abstracting force of circumstances; is the perception that our political ideas and what may be called the rest of our ideas are not in fact two independent worlds, and that though they may come to us as separate text and context, the *meaning* lies, as it always must lie, in a unity in which the separate existence of text and context is resolved. We may begin, probably we must begin, with an independent valuation of the text and the context; but the impetus of reflection is not spent until we have restored in detail the unity of which we had a prevision. And, so far, philosophical reflection about politics will be nothing other than the intellectual restoration of a unity damaged and impaired by the normal negligence of human partiality. But to have gone so far is already to have raised questions the answers to which are not to be found in any fresh study of what is behind us. Even if we accept the standards and valuations of our civilization, it will be only by putting an arbitrary closure on reflection that we can prevent the consideration of the meaning of the general terms in which those standards are expressed; good and evil, right and wrong, justice and injustice. And, turning, we shall catch sight of all that we have learned reflected in the *speculum universitatis.*

Now, whether or not this can be defended as a hypothetical conception of the nature of political philosophy, it certainly describes a form of reflection about politics that has a continuous history in our civilization. To establish the connections, in principle and in detail, directly or mediately, between politics and eternity is a project that has never been without its followers. Indeed, the pursuit of this project is only a special arrangement of the whole intellectual life of our civilization; it is the whole intellectual history organized and exhibited from a particular angle of vision. Probably there has been no theory of the nature of the world, of the activity of man, of the destiny of mankind, no theology or cosmology, perhaps even no metaphysics, that has not sought a reflection of itself in the mirror of political philosophy; certainly there has been no fully considered politics that has not looked for its reflection in eternity. This history of political philosophy is, then, the context of the masterpiece. And to interpret it in the context of this history secures it against the deadening requirement of conformity to a merely abstract idea of political philosophy.

This kind of reflection about politics is not, then, to be denied a place in our intellectual history. And it is characteristic of political philosophers that they take a sombre view of the human situation: they deal in darkness. Human life in their writings appears, generally, not as a feast or even as a journey, but as a predicament; and the link between politics and eternity is the contribution the political order is conceived as making to the deliverance of mankind. Even those whose thought is most remote from violent contrasts of dark and light (Aristotle, for example) do not altogether avoid this disposition of mind. And some political philosophers may even be suspected of spreading darkness in order to make their light more acceptable. Man, so the varied formula runs, is the dupe of error, the slave of sin, of passion, of fear, of care, the enemy of himself or of others or of both—

> *O miseras hominum mentes, O pectora*
> *caeca*

—and the civil order appears as the whole or a part of the scheme of his salvation. The precise manner in which the predicament is conceived, the qualities of mind and imagination and the kinds of activity man can bring to the achievement of his own salvation, the exact nature and power of civil arrangements and institutions, the urgency, the method and the comprehensiveness of the deliverance—these are the singularities of each political philosophy. In them are reflected the intellectual achievements of the epoch or society, and the great and slowly mediated changes in intellectual habit and horizon that have overtaken our civilization. Every masterpiece of political philosophy springs from a new vision of the predicament; each is the glimpse of a deliverance or the suggestion of a remedy.

It will not, then, surprise us to find an apparently contingent element in the ground and inspiration of a political philosophy, a feeling for the exigencies, the cares, the passions of a particular time, a sensitiveness to the dominant folly of an epoch: for the human predicament is a universal appearing everywhere as a particular. Plato's thought is animated by the errors of Athenian democracy, Augustine's by the sack of Rome, and what stirs the mind of Hobbes is 'grief for the present calamities of my country', a country torn between those who claimed too much for Liberty and those who claimed too much for Authority, a country given over into the hands of ambitious men who enlisted the envy and resentment of a 'giddy people' for the advancement of their ambitions.[1,2] And not being surprised at this element of particularity, we shall not allow it to mislead us into supposing that nothing more is required to make a political philosopher than an impressionable political consciousness; for the masterpiece, at least, is always the revelation of the universal predicament in the local and transitory mischief.[3]

If the unity of the history of political philosophy lies in a pervading sense of human life as a predicament and in the continuous reflection of the changing climate of the European intellectual scene, its significant variety will be found in three great traditions of thought. The singularities of political philosophies (like most singularities) are not unique, but follow one of three main patterns which philosophical reflection about politics has impressed upon the intellectual history of Europe. These I call traditions because it belongs to the nature of a tradition to tolerate and unite an internal variety, not insisting upon conformity to a single character, and because, further, it has the ability to change without losing its identity. The first of these traditions is distinguished by the master-conceptions of Reason and Nature. It is coeval with our civilization; it has an unbroken history into the modern world; and it has survived by a matchless power of adaptability all the changes of the European consciousness. The master-conceptions of the second are Will and Artifice. It too springs from the soil of Greece, and has drawn inspiration from many sources, not least from Israel and Islam. The third tradition is of later birth, not appearing until the eighteenth century. The cosmology it reflects in its still unsettled surface is the world seen on the analogy of human history. Its master-conception is the Rational Will, and its followers may be excused the belief that in it the truths of the first two traditions are fulfilled and their errors find a happy release. The masterpiece of political philosophy has for its context, not only the history of political philosophy as the elucidation of the predicament and deliverance of mankind, but also, normally, a particular tradition in that history; generally speaking it is the supreme expression of its own tradition. And, as Plato's *Republic* might be chosen as the representative of the first tradition, and Hegel's *Philosophie des Rechts* of the third, so *Leviathan* is the head and crown of the second.

Leviathan is a masterpiece, and we must understand it

according to our means. If our poverty is great, but not ruinous, we may read it not looking beyond its two covers, but intent to draw from it nothing that is not there. This will be a notable achievement, if somewhat narrow. The reward will be the appreciation of a dialetical triumph with all the internal movement and liveliness of such a triumph. But *Leviathan* is more than a *tour de force*. And something of its larger character will be perceived if we read it with the other works of Hobbes open beside it. Or again, at greater expense of learning, we may consider it in its tradition, and doing so will find fresh meaning in the world of ideas it opens to us. But finally, we may discover in it the true character of a masterpiece—the still centre of a whirlpool of ideas which has drawn into itself numberless currents of thought, contemporary and historic, and by its centripetal force has shaped and compressed them into a momentary significance before they are flung off again into the future.

THE MIND AND MANNER

In the mind of a man, the [*súnolon*] of form and content alone is actual; style and matter, method and doctrine, are inseparable. And when the mind is that of a philosopher, it is a sound rule to come to consider the technical expression of this unity only after it has been observed in the less formal version of it that appears in temperament, cast of mind and style of writing. Circumstantial evidence of this sort can, of course, contribute nothing relevant to the substantiation of the technical distinctions of a philosophy; but often it has something to contribute to the understanding of them. At least, I think this is so with Hobbes.

Philosophy springs from a certain bent of mind which, though different in character, is as much a natural gift as an aptitude for mathematics or a genius for music. Philosophical speculation requires so little in the way of a knowledge of the world and is, in comparison with some other intellectual pursuits, so independent of book-learning, that the gift is apt to manifest itself early in life. And often a philosopher will be found to have made his significant contribution at an age when others are still preparing themselves to speak or to act. Hobbes had a full share of the *anima naturaliter philosophica,* yet it is remarkable that the beginning of his philosophical writing cannot be dated before his forty-second year and that his masterpiece was written when he was past sixty. Certainly there is nothing precocious in his genius; but are we to suppose that the love of reasoning, the passion for dialectic, which belong to the gift for philosophy, were absent from his character in youth? Writers on Hobbes have been apt to take a short way with this suggestion of a riddle. The life of Hobbes has been divided into neat periods, and his appearance as a philosopher in middle life has been applauded rather than explained. Brilliant at school, idle at the university, unambitious in early life, later

touched by a feeling for scholarship and finally taking the path of philosophy when, at the age of forty, the power of geometric proof was revealed to him in the pages of *Euclid*: such is the life attributed to him. It leaves something to be desired. And evidence has been collected which goes to show that philosophy and geometry were not coeval in Hobbes's mind, evidence that the speculative gift was not unexercised in his earlier years.[4] Yet it remains true that when he appears as a philosophical writer, he is already adult, mature in mind; the period of eager search of tentative exploration, goes unreflected in his pages.

The power and confidence of Hobbes's mind as he comes before us in his writings cannot escape observation. He is arrogant (but it is not the arrogance of youth), dogmatic, and when he speaks it is in a tone of confident finality: he knows everything except how his doctrines will be received. There is nothing half-formed or undeveloped in him, nothing in progress; there is no promise, only fulfilment. There is self-confidence, also, a Montaigne-like self-confidence; he has accepted himself and he expects others to accept him on the same terms. And all this is understandable when we appreciate that Hobbes is not one of those philosophers who allow us to see the workings of their minds, and that he published nothing until he was fifty-four years old. There are other, more technical, reasons for his confidence. His conception of philosophy as the establishment by reasoning of hypothetical causes saved him from the necessity of observing the caution appropriate to those who deal with facts and events.[5] But, at bottom, it springs from his maturity, the knowledge that before he spoke he was a match for anyone who had the temerity to answer back. It belonged to Hobbes's temperament and his art, not less than to his circumstances, to hold his fire. His long life after middle age gave him the room for change and development that others find in earlier years; but he did not greatly avail himself of it. He was often wrong, especially in his lighthearted excursions into mathematics, and he often changed his views, but he rarely retracted an opinion. His confidence never deserted him.

But if the first impression of Hobbes's philosophical writing is one of maturity and deliberateness, the second is an impression of remarkable energy. It is as if all the lost youth of Hobbes's mind had been recovered and perpetuated in this pre-eminently youthful quality. One of the more revealing observations of Aubrey about him is that 'he was never idle; his thoughts were always working.' And from this energy flow the other striking characteristics of his mind and manner—his scepticism, his addiction to system and his passion for controversy.

An impulse for philosophy may originate in faith (as with Erigena), or in curiosity (as with Locke), but with Hobbes the prime mover was doubt. Scepticism was, of course, in the air he breathed; but in an age of sceptics he was the most radical of them all. His was not the elegiac scepticism of Montaigne, nor the brittle net in which Pascal struggled, nor was it the methodological doubt of Descartes; for him it was both a method and a conclusion, purging and creative. It is not the technicalities of his scepticism (which we must consider later) that are so remarkable, but its ferocity. A medieval passion overcomes him as he sweeps aside into a common abyss of absurdity both the believer in eternal truth and the industrious seeker after truths; both faith and science. Indeed, so extravagant, so heedless of consequences, is his scepticism, that the reader is inclined to exclaim, what Hobbes himself is said to have exclaimed on seeing the proof of the forty-seventh theorem in *Euclid,* 'By God, this is impossible.' And what alone makes his scepticism plausible is the intrepidity of Hobbes himself; he has the nerve to accept his conclusions and the confidence to build on them. Both the energy to destroy and the energy to construct are powerful in Hobbes.

A man, it is generally agreed, may make himself ridiculous as easily by a philosophical system as by any other means. And yet, the impulse to think systematically is, at bottom, nothing more than the conscientious pursuit of what is for every philosopher the end to be achieved. The passion for clearness and simplicity, the determination not to be satisfied with anything inconsequent, the refusal to relieve one element of experience at the cost of another, are the motives of all philosophical thinking; and they conduce to system. 'The desire of wisdom leadeth to a kingdom.' And the pursuit of system is a call, not only upon fine intelligence and imagination, but also, and perhaps pre-eminently, upon energy of mind. For the principle in system is not the simple exclusion of all that does not fit, but the perpetual re-establishment of coherence. Hobbes stands out, not only among his contemporaries, but also in the history of English philosophy, as the creator of a system. And he conceived this system with such imaginative power that, in spite of its relatively simple character, it bears comparison with even the grand and subtle creation of Hegel. But if it requires great energy of mind to create a system, it requires even greater not to become the slave of the creation. To become the slave of a system in life is not to know when to 'hang up philosophy', not to recognize the final triumph of inconsequence; in philosophy, it is not to know when the claims of comprehension outweigh those of coherence. And here also the energy of Hobbes's mind did not desert him. When we come to consider the technicalities of his philosophy we shall observe a moderation that, for example, allowed him to escape an atomic philosophy, and an absence of rigidity that allowed him to modify his philosophical method when dealing with politics; here, when we are considering informally the quality of his mind, this ability appears as resilience, the energy to

be perpetually freeing himself from the formalism of his system.

Thinking, for Hobbes, was not only conceived as movement, it was felt as movement. Mind is something agile, thoughts are darting, and the language of passion is appropriate to describe their workings. And the energy of his nature made it impossible for him not to take pleasure in controversy. The blood of contention ran in his veins. He acquired the lucid genius of a great expositor of ideas; but by disposition he was a fighter, and he knew no tactics save attack. He was a brilliant controversialist, deft, pertinacious and imaginative, and he disposed of the errors of scholastics, Puritans and Papists with a subtle mixture of argument and ridicule. But he made the mistake of supposing that this style was universally effective, in mathematics no less than in politics. For brilliance in controversy is a corrupting accomplishment. Always to play to win is to take one's standards from one's opponent, and local victory comes to displace every other consideration. Most readers will find Hobbes's disputatiousness excessive; but it is the defect of an exceptionally active mind. And it never quite destroyed in him the distinction between beating an opponent and establishing a proposition, and never quite silenced the conversation with himself which is the heart of philosophical thinking. But, like many controversialists, he hated error more than he loved truth, and came to depend overmuch on the stimulus of opposition. There is sagacity in Hobbes, and often a profound deliberateness; but there is no repose.

We have found Hobbes to possess remarkable confidence and energy of mind; we must consider now whether his mind was also original. Like Epicurus, he had an affectation for originality. He rarely mentions a writer to acknowledge a debt, and often seems oversensitive about his independence of the past in philosophy. Aristotle's philosophy is 'vain', and scholasticism is no more than a 'collection of absurdities'. But, though he had certainly read more than he sometimes cared to admit—it was a favourite saying of his that if he had read as much as other men he should have known no more than other men—he seems to have been content with the reading that happened to come his way, and complained rather of the inconvenience of a want of conversation at some periods in his life than of a lack of books. He was conscious of being a self-taught philosopher, an amateur, without the training of a Descartes or the background of a Spinoza. And this feeling was perhaps strengthened by the absence of an academic environment. One age of academic philosophy had gone, the next was yet to come. The seventeenth century was the age of the independent scholar, and Hobbes was one of these, taking his own way and making his own contacts with the learned world. And his profound suspicion of anything like authority in philosophy reinforced his circumstantial independence. The guidance he wanted he got from his touch with his contemporaries, particularly in Paris; his inspiration was a native sensitiveness to the direction required of philosophy if it were to provide an answer to the questions suggested by contemporary science. In conception and design, his philosophy is his own. And when he claimed that civil philosophy was 'no older than my own book *De Cive'*, [6] he was expressing at once the personal achievement of having gone afresh to the facts of human consciousness for his interpretation of the meaning of civil association, and also that universal sense of newness with which his age appreciated its own intellectual accomplishments. But, for all that, his philosophy belongs to a tradition. Perhaps the truth is that Hobbes was as original as he thought he was, and to acknowledge his real indebtedness he would have required to see (what he could not be expected to see) the link between scholasticism and modern philosophy which is only now becoming clear to us. His philosophy is in the nature of a palimpsest. For its author what was important was what he wrote, and it is only to be expected that he should be indifferent to what is already there; but for us both sets of writing are significant.

Finally, Hobbes is a *writer,* a self-conscious stylist and the master of an individual style that expresses his whole personality; for there is no hiatus between his personality and his philosophy. His manner of writing is not, of course, foreign to his age; it belongs to him neither to write with the informality that is the achievement of Locke, nor with the simplicity that makes Hume's style a model not to be rejected by the philosophical writer of today. Hobbes is elaborate in an age that delighted in elaboration. But, within the range of his opportunities, he found a way of writing that exactly reflected his temperament. His controversial purpose is large on every page; he wrote to convince and to refute. And that in itself is a discipline. He has eloquence, the charm of wit, the decisiveness of confidence and the sententiousness of a mind made up: he is capable of urbanity and of savage irony. But the most significant qualities of his style are its didactic and its imaginative character. Philosophy in general knows two styles, the contemplative and the didactic, although there are many writers to whom neither belongs to the complete exclusion of the other. Those who practice the first let us into the secret workings of their minds and are less careful to send us away with a precisely formulated doctrine. Philosophy for them is a conversation, and, whether or not they write it as a dialogue, their style reflects their conception. Hobbes's way of writing is an example of the second style. What he says is already entirely freed from the doubts and hesitancies of the process of thought. It is only a residue, a distillate that is offered to the reader. The defect of such a style is that the reader must either accept or reject; if it inspires to fresh thought, it does so only by opposition. And Hobbes's style is imaginative, not merely on account of the subtle imagery that fills his pages, nor only because it requires imagination to make a system. His imagination appears also as the power to create a myth. *Leviathan* is a myth, the transposition of an abstract argument into the world of the imagination. In it we are made aware at a glance of the fixed and simple centre of a universe of complex and changing relationships. The argument may not be the better for this transposition, and what it gains in vividness it may pay for in illusion. But it is an accomplishment of art that Hobbes, in the history of political philosophy, shares only with Plato.

THE SYSTEM

In Hobbes's mind, his 'civil philosophy' belonged to a system of philosophy. Consequently, an enquiry into the character of this system is not to be avoided by the interpreter of his politics. For, if the details of the civil theory may not improperly be considered as elements in a coherence of their own, the significance of the theory as a whole must depend upon the system to which it belongs, and upon the place it occupies in the system.

Two views, it appears, between them hold the field at the present time. The first is the view that the foundation of Hobbes's philosophy is a doctrine of materialism, that the intention of his system was the progressive revelation of this doctrine in nature, in man and in society, and that this revelation was achieved in his three most important philosophical works, *De Corpore, De Homine* and *De Cive*. These works, it is suggested, constitute a continuous argument, part of which is reproduced in *Leviathan;* and the novel project of the 'civil philosophy' was the exposition of a politics based upon a 'natural philosophy', the assimilation of politics to a materialistic doctrine of the world, or (it is even suggested) to the view of the world as it appeared in the conclusions of the physical sciences. A mechanistic-materialist politics is made to spring from a mechanistic-materialist universe. And, not improperly, it is argued that the significance of what appears at the end is determined at least in part by what was proved or assumed at the beginning. The second view is that this, no doubt, was the intention of Hobbes, but that 'the attempt and not the deed confounds him'. The joints of the system are ill-matched, and what should have been a continuous argument, based upon a philosophy of materialism, collapses under its own weight.

Both these views are, I think, misconceived. But they are the product not merely of inattention to the words of Hobbes; it is to be feared that they derive also from a graver fault of interpretation, a false expectation with regard to the nature of a philosophical system. For what is expected here is that a philosophical system should conform to an architectural analogue, and consequently what is sought in Hobbes's system is a foundation and a superstructure planned as a single whole, with civil philosophy as the top storey. Now, it may be doubted whether any philosophical system can properly be represented in the terms of architecture, but what is certain is that the analogy does violence to the system of Hobbes. The coherence of his philosophy, the system of it, lies not in an architectonic structure, but in a single 'passionate thought' that pervades its parts. [7] The system is not the plan or key of the labyrinth of the philosophy; it is, rather, a guiding clue, like the thread of Ariadne. [8] It is like the music that gives meaning to the movement of dancers, or the law of evidence that gives coherence to the practice of a court. And the thread, the hidden thought, is the continuous application of a doctrine about the nature of philosophy. Hobbes's philosophy is the world reflected in the mirror of the philosophic eye, each image the representation of a fresh object, but each determined by the character of the mirror itself. In short, the civil philosophy belongs to a philosophical system, not because it is materialistic but because it is philosophical; and an enquiry into the character of the system and the place of politics in it resolves itself into an enquiry into what Hobbes considered to be the nature of philosophy.

For Hobbes, to think philosophically is to reason; philosophy is reasoning. To this all else is subordinate; from this all else derives. It is the character of reasoning that determines the range and the limits of philosophical enquiry; it is this character that gives coherence, system, to Hobbes's philosophy. Philosophy, for him, is the world as it appears in the mirror of reason; civil philosophy is the image of the civil order reflected in that mirror. In general, the world seen in this mirror is a world of causes and effects: cause and effect are its categories. And for Hobbes reason has two alternative ends: to determine the conditional causes of given effects, or to determine the conditional effects of given causes. [9] But to understand more exactly what he means by this identification of philosophy with reasoning, we must consider three contrasts that run through all his writing: the contrast between philosophy and theology (reason and faith), between philosophy and 'science' (reason and empiricism) and between philosophy and experience (reason and sense).

Reasoning is concerned solely with causes and effects. It follows, therefore, that its activity must lie within a world composed of things that are causes or the effects of causes. If there is another way of conceiving this world, it is not within the power of reasoning to follow it; if there are things by definition causeless or ingenerable, they belong to a world other than that of philosophy. This at once, for Hobbes, excludes from philosophy the consideration of the universe as a whole, things infinite, things eternal, final causes and things known only by divine grace or revelation: it excludes what Hobbes comprehensively calls theology and faith. He denies, not the existence of these things, but their

rationality.[10] This method of circumscribing the concerns of philosophy is not, of course, original in Hobbes. It has roots that go back to Augustine, if not further, and it was inherited by the seventeenth century (where one side of it was distinguished as the heresy of Fideism: both Montaigne and Pascal were Fideists) directly from its formulation in the Averroism of Scotus and Occam. Indeed, this doctrine is one of the seeds in scholasticism from which modern philosophy sprang. Philosophical explanation, then, is concerned with things caused. A world of such things is, necessarily, a world from which teleology is excluded; its internal movement comprises the impact of its parts upon one another, of attraction and repulsion, not of growth or development. It is a world conceived on the analogy of a machine, where to explain an effect we go to its immediate cause, and to seek the result of a cause we go only to its immediate effect. [11] In other words, the mechanistic element in Hobbes's philosophy is derived from his rationalism; its source and authority lie, not in observation, but in reasoning. He does not say that the natural world is a machine; he says only that the rational world is analogous to a machine. He is a scholastic, not a 'scientific' mechanist. This does not mean that the mechanistic element is unimportant in Hobbes; it means only that it is derivative. It is, indeed, of the greatest importance, for Hobbes's philosophy is, in all its parts, pre-eminently a philosophy of *power* precisely because philosophy is reasoning, reasoning the elucidation of mechanism and mechanism essentially the combination, transfer and resolution of forces. The end of philosophy itself is power—*scientia propter potentiam*. [12] Man is a complex of powers; desire is the desire for power, pride is illusion about power, honour opinion about power, life the unremitting exercise of power and death the absolute loss of power. And the civil order is conceived as a coherence of powers, not because politics is vulgarly observed to be a competition of powers, or because civil philosophy must take its conceptions from natural philosophy, but because to subject the civil order to rational enquiry unavoidably turns it into a mechanism.

In the writings of Hobbes, philosophy and science are not contrasted *eo nomine*. Such a contrast would have been impossible in the seventeenth century, with its absence of differentiation between the sciences and its still unshaken hold on the conception of the unity of human knowledge. Indeed, Hobbes normally uses the word science as a synonym for philosophy; rational knowledge is scientific knowledge. Nevertheless, Hobbes is near the beginning of a new view of the structure and parts of knowledge, a change of view which became clearer in the generation of Locke and was completed by Kant. Like Bacon and others before him, Hobbes has his own classification of the *genres* of knowledge, [13] and that it is a classification which involves a distinction between philosophy and what we have come to call 'science' is suggested by his ambiguous attitude to the work of contemporary scientists. He wrote with an unusually generous enthusiasm of the great advances made by Kepler, Galileo and Harvey; 'the beginning of astronomy', he says, 'is not to be derived from farther time than from Copernicus'; [14] but he had neither sympathy nor even patience for the 'new or experimental philosophy', and he did not conceal his contempt for the work of the Royal Society, founded in his lifetime. But this ambiguity ceases to be paradoxical when we see what Hobbes was about, when we understand that one of the few internal tensions of his thought arose from an attempted but imperfectly achieved distinction between science and philosophy. The distinction, well known to us now, is that between knowledge of things as they appear and enquiry into the fact of their appearing, between a knowledge (with all the necessary assumptions) of the phenomenal world and a theory of knowledge itself. Hobbes appreciated this distinction, and his appreciation of it allies him with Locke and with Kant and separates him from Bacon and even Descartes. He perceived that his concern as a philosopher was with the second and not the first of these enquiries; yet the distinction remained imperfectly defined in his mind. But that philosophy meant for Hobbes something different from the enquiries of natural science is at once apparent when we consider the starting-place of his thought and the character of the questions he thinks it necessary to ask. He begins with sensation; and he begins there, not because there is no deceit or crookedness in the utterances of the senses, but because the fact of our having sensations seems to him the only thing of which we can be indubitably certain. [15] And the question he asks himself is, what *must* the world be like for us to have the sensations we undoubtedly experience? His enquiry is into the cause of sensation, an enquiry to be conducted, not by means of observation, but by means of reasoning. And if the answer he proposes owes something to the inspiration of the scientists, that does nothing to modify the distinction between science and philosophy inherent in the question itself. For the scientist of his day the world of nature was almost a machine, Kepler had proposed the substitution of the world *vis* for the word *anima* in physics; and Hobbes, whose concern was with the rational world (by definition also conceived as the analogy of a machine), discovered that some of the general ideas of the scientists could be turned to his own purposes. But these pardonable appropriations do nothing to approximate his enquiry to that of Galileo or Newton. Philosophy is reasoning, this time contrasted, not with theology, but with what we have come to know as natural science. And the question, What, in an age of science, is the task of philosophy? which was to concern the nineteenth century so deeply, was already familiar to Hobbes. And it is a false reading of his intention and his achievement which finds in his civil philosophy the beginning of sociology or a science of politics, the beginning of that movement of thought

that came to regard 'the methods of physical science as the proper models for political'. [16]

But the contrast that finally distinguishes philosophy and reveals its full character is that between philosophy and what Hobbes calls experience. For in elucidating this distinction Hobbes shows us philosophy coming into being, shows it as a thing generated and relates it to its cause thereby establishing it as itself a proper subject of rational consideration. The mental history of a man begins with sensation, 'for there is no conception in a man's mind, which hath not at first, totally, or by parts, been begotten upon the organs of sense'. [17] Some sensations, perhaps, occupying but an instant, involve no reference to others and no sense of time. But commonly, sensations, requiring a minimum time of more than a single instant, and reaching a mind already stored with the relics of previous sensations, are impossible without that which gives a sense of time—memory. [18] Sensation involves recollection, and a man's experience is nothing but the recollected afterimages of sensations. But from his power to remember man derives another power, imagination, which is the ability to recall and turn over in the mind the decayed relics of past sensation, the ability to experience even when the senses themselves have ceased to speak. Moreover imagination, though it depends on past sensations, is not an entirely servile faculty; it is capable of compounding together relics of sensations felt at different times. Indeed, in imagination we may have in our minds images not only of what we have never actually seen (as when we imagine a golden mountain though we have seen only gold and a mountain), but even of what we could never see, such as a chimera. But imagination remains servile in that 'we have no transition from one imagination to another whereof we never had the like before in our senses'. [19] Two things more belong to experience; the fruits of experience. The first is History, which is the ordered register of past experiences. The second is prudence, which is the power to anticipate experience by means of the recollection of what has gone before. 'Of our conceptions of the past, we make a future.' [20] A full, well-recollected experience gives the 'foresight' and 'wisdom' that belong to the prudent man, a wisdom that springs from the appreciation of those causes and effects that time and not reason teaches us. This is the end and crown of experience. In the mind of the prudent or sagacious man, experience appears as a kind of knowledge. Governed by sense, it is necessarily individual, a particular knowledge of particulars. But, within its limits, it is 'absolute knowledge'; [21] there is no ground upon which it can be doubted, and the categories of truth and falsehood do not apply to it. It is mere, uncritical 'knowledge of fact': 'experience concludeth nothing universal'. [22] And in all its characteristics it is distinguished from philosophical knowledge, which (because it is reasoned) is general and not particular, a knowledge of consequences and not of facts, and conditional and not absolute.

Our task now is to follow Hobbes in his account of the generation of rational knowledge from experience. In principle, experience (except perhaps when it issues in history) is something man shares with animals and has only in a greater degree: memory and imagination are the unsought mechanical products of sensation, like the movements that continue on the surface of water after what disturbed it has sunk to rest. In order to surmount the limits of this sense-experience and achieve reasoned knowledge of our sensations, we require not only to have sensations, but to be conscious of having them; we require the power of introspection. But the cause of this power must lie in sense itself, if the power is to avoid the imputation of being an easy *deus ex machina*. Language satisfies both these conditions: it makes introspection possible, and springs from a power we share with animals, the physical power of making sounds. For, though language 'when disposed of in speech and pronounced to others' [23] is the means whereby men declare their thoughts to one another, it is primarily the only means by which a man may communicate his own thoughts to himself, may become conscious of the contents of his mind. The beginning of language is giving names to after-images of sensations and thereby becoming conscious of them; the act of naming the image is the act of becoming conscious of it. For, 'a name is a word taken at pleasure to serve as a mark that may raise in our minds a thought like some thought we had before'. [24]

Language, the giving of names to images, is not itself reasonable, it is the arbitrary precondition of all reasoning: [25] the generation of rational knowledge is by words out of experience. The achievement of language is to 'register our thoughts', to fix what is essentially fleeting. And from this achievement follows the possibility of definition, the conjunction of general names, proposition and rational argument, all of which consist in the 'proper use of names in language'. But, though reasoning brings with it knowledge of the general and the possibility of truth and its opposite, absurdity, [26] it can never pass beyond the world of names. Reasoning is nothing else but the addition and subtraction of names, and 'gives us conclusions, not about the nature of things, but about the names of things. That is to say, by means of reason we discover only whether the connections we have established between names are in accordance with the arbitrary convention we have established concerning their meanings.' [27] This is at once a nominalist and a profoundly sceptical doctrine. Truth is of universals, but they are names, the names of images left over from sensations; and a true proposition is not an assertion about the real world. We can, then, surmount the limits of sense-experience and achieve rational knowledge; and it is this knowledge, with its own severe limitations, that is the concern of philosophy.

But philosophy is not only knowledge of the universal, it is a knowledge of causes. Informally, Hobbes describes it as 'the natural reason of man flying up and down among the creatures, and bringing back a true report of their order, causes and effects.' [28] We have seen already how, by limiting philosophy to a knowledge of things caused (because reasoning itself must observe this limit) he separates it from theology. We have now to consider why he believed that the essential work of reasoning (and therefore of philosophy) was the demonstration of the cause of things caused. Cause for Hobbes is the means by which anything comes into being. Unlike any of the Aristotelian causes, it is essentially that which, previous in time, brings about the effect. A knowledge of cause is, then, a knowledge of how a thing is generated. [29] But why must philosophy be a knowledge of this sort? Hobbes's answer would appear to be, first, that this sort of knowledge can spring from reasoning while it is impossible to mere experience, and, secondly, that since, *ex hypothesi*, the data of philosophy are effects, the only possible enlargement of our knowledge of them must consist in a knowledge of their causes. If we add to the experience of an effect a knowledge of its generation, a knowledge of its 'constitutive cause', [30] we know everything that may be known. In short, a knowledge of causes is the pursuit in philosophy because philosophy is reasoning. [31]

The third characteristic of philosophical knowledge, as distinguished from experience, is that it is conditional, not absolute. Hobbes's doctrine is that when, in reasoning, we conclude that the cause of something is such and such, we can mean no more than that such and such is a possible efficient cause, and not that it is the actual cause. There are three criteria by which a suggested cause may be judged, and proof that the cause actually operated is not among them. For reasoning, a cause must be 'imaginable', the necessity of the effect must be shown to follow from the cause, and it must be shown that nothing false (that is, not present in the effect) can be derived. [32] And what satisfies these conditions may be described as an hypothetical efficient cause. That philosophy is limited to the demonstration of such causes is stated by Hobbes on many occasions; it applies not only to the detail of his philosophy, but also to the most general of all causes, to body and motion. For example, when he says that the cause or generation of a circle is 'the circumduction of a body whereof one end remains unmoved', he adds that this gives 'some generation [of the figure], though perhaps not that by which it was made, yet that by which it might have been made'. [33] And when he considers the general problem of the cause of sensations, he concludes, not with the categorical statement that body and motion are the only causal existents, but that body (that is, that which is independent of thought and which fills a portion of space) and motion are the hypothetical efficient causes of our having sensations.

If there were no body there could be no motion, and if there were no motion of bodies there could be no sensation; *sentire semper idem et non sentire ad idem recidunt.* [34] From beginning to end there is no suggestion in Hobbes that philosophy is anything other than conditional knowledge, knowledge of hypothetical generations and conclusions about the names of things, not about the nature of things. [35] With these philosophy must be satisfied, though they are but fictions. Indeed, philosophy may be defined as the establishment by reasoning of true fictions. And the ground of this limitation is, that the world being what it is, reasoning can go no further. 'There is no effect which the power of God cannot produce in many several ways,' [35] verification *ad oculos* is impossible because these causes are rational not perceptible, and consequently the farthest reach of reason is the demonstration of causes which satisfy the three rational criteria.

My contention is, then, that the system of Hobbes's philosophy lies in his conception of the nature of philosophical knowledge, and not in any doctrine about the world. And the inspiration of his philosophy is the intention to be guided by reason and to reject all other guides: this is the thread, the hidden thought, that gives it coherence, distinguishing it from Faith, 'Science' and Experience. It remains to guard against a possible error. The lineage of Hobbes's rationalism lies, not (like that of Spinoza or even Descartes) in the great Platonic-Christian tradition, but in the sceptical, late scholastic tradition. He does not normally speak of Reason, the divine illumination of the mind that unites man with God; he speaks of reasoning. And he is not less persuaded of its fallibility and limitations than Montaigne himself. [37] By means of reasoning we certainly pass beyond mere sense-experience, but when imagination and prudence have generated rational knowledge, they do not, like drones, perish; they continue to perform in human life functions that reasoning itself cannot discharge. Nor, indeed, is man, in Hobbes's view, primarily a reasoning creature. This capacity for general hypothetical reasoning distinguishes him from the animal, but he remains fundamentally a creature of passion, and it is by passion not less than by reasoning that he achieves his salvation. [38]

We have considered Hobbes's view of philosophy because civil philosophy, whatever else it is, is philosophy. Civil philosophy, the subject of **Leviathan,** is precisely the application of this conception of philosophy to civil association. It is not the last chapter in a philosophy of materialism, but the reflection of civil association in the mirror of a rationalistic philosophy. But if the *genus* of civil philosophy is its character as philosophy, its *differentia* is derived from the matter to be considered. Civil philosophy is settling the generation or constitutive cause of civil association. And the kind of hypothetical efficient cause that civil philosophy may be expected to demonstrate is determined by the fact that civil association is an artifact: it is artificial, not natural. Now, to assert that civil association is an artifact is already to have settled the question of its generation, and Hobbes himself does not begin with any such assertion. His method is to establish the artificial character of civil association by considering its generation. But in order to avoid false expectations it will be wise for us to anticipate the argument and consider what he means by this distinction between art and nature.

Hobbes has given us no collected account of his philosophy of artifice; it is to be gathered only from scattered observations. But when these are put together, they compose a coherent view. A work of art is the product or effect of mental activity. But this in itself does not distinguish it securely from nature, because the universe itself must be regarded as the product of God's mental activity, and what we call 'nature' is to God an artifact; [39] and there are products of human mental activity which, having established themselves, become for the observer part of his natural world. More firmly defined, then, a work of art is the product of mental activity considered from the point of view of its cause. And, since what we have to consider are works of human art, our enquiry must be into the kind of natural human mental activity that may result in a work of art; for the cause of a work of art must lie in nature; that is, in experience. It would appear that the activities involved are willing and reasoning. But reasoning itself is artificial, not natural; it is an 'acquired' not a 'native' mental activity, [40] and therefore cannot be considered as part of the generation of a work of art. [41] We are left, then, with willing, which, belonging to experience and not reasoning, is undoubtedly a natural mental activity. The cause (hypothetical and efficient, of course) of a human work of art is the will of a man. And willing is 'the last desire in deliberating', deliberating being mental discourse in which the subject is desires and aversions. [42] It is a creative activity (not merely imitative), in the same way as imagination, working on sensations, creates a new world of hitherto separated parts. Both will and imagination are servile only in that their products must be like nature in respect of being mechanisms; that is, complexes of cause and effect. [43] Moreover, will creates not only when it is single and alone, but also in concert with other wills. The product of an agreement between wills is no less a work of art than the product of one will. And the peculiarity of civil association, as a work of art, is its generation from a number of wills. The word 'civil', in Hobbes, means artifice springing from more than one will. Civil history (as distinguished from natural history) is the register of events that have sprung from the voluntary actions of man in commonwealths. [44] Civil authority is authority arising out of an agreement of wills, while natural authority (that of the father in the family) has no such generation and is consequently of a different character. [45] And civil association is itself contrasted on this account with the appearance of it in mere natural gregariousness. [46]

Now, with this understanding of the meaning of both 'civil' and 'philosophical', we may determine what is to be expected for a civil philosophy. Two things may be expected from it. First, it will exhibit the internal mechanism of civil association as a system of cause and effect and settle the generation of the parts of civil association. And secondly, we may expect it to settle the generation, in terms of an hypothetical efficient cause, of the artifact as a whole; that is, to show this work of art springing from the specific nature of man. But it may be observed that two courses lie open to anyone, holding the views of Hobbes, who undertakes this project. Philosophy, we have seen, may argue from a given effect to its hypothetical efficient cause, or from a given cause to its possible effect. Often the second form of argument is excluded; this is so with sensations, when the given is an effect and the cause is to seek. But in civil philosophy, and in all reasoning concerned with artifacta, both courses are open; for the cause and the effect (human nature and civil association) are both given, and the task of philosophy is to unite the details of each to each in terms of cause and effect. Hobbes tells us [47] that his early thinking on the subject took the form of an argument from effect (civil association) to cause (human nature), from art to nature; but it is to be remarked that, not only in **Leviathan,** but also in all other accounts he gives of his civil philosophy, the form of the argument is from cause to effect, from nature to art. But, since the generation is rational and not physical, the direction from which it is considered is clearly a matter of indifference. . . .

Notes

1 *E.W.,* II, i-xxiv.

2 *L.,* pp. 3, 274, 549. Hobbes had also in mind the situation in late sixteenth-century France.

3 *L.,* p. 271.

4 L. Strauss, *The Political Philosophy of Hobbes.*

5 *L.,* p. 554.

6 *E.W.,* I, ix.

7 Confucius said, 'T'zu, you probably think that I have learned many things and hold them in my mind.' 'Yes,' he replied, 'is that not true?' 'No,' said Confucius; 'I have one thing that permeates everything.'—Confucius, *Analects,* XV, 2. *L.,* p. 19.

8 *E.W.,* II, vi.

9 *E.W.,* I, 65-6, 387.

10 *L.,* p. 80; *E.W.,* I, 10, 410.

11 *E.W.,* II, xiv.

12 *E.W.,* I, xiv; *O.L.,* I, 6.

13 *L.,* p. 64.

14 *E.W.,* I, viii.

15 It will be remembered that the brilliant and informal genius of Montaigne had perceived that our most certain knowledge is what we know about ourselves, and had made of this a philosophy of introspection.

16 J. S. Mill, *Autobiography,* p. 165.

17 *L.,* p. 11.

18 *E.W.,* I, 393.

19 *L.,* p. 18.

20 *E.W.,* IV, 16.

21 *L.,* p. 64.

22 *E.W.,* IV, 18.

23 *E.W.,* I, 16.

24 *E.W.,* I, 16.

25 This is why introspection that falls short of reasoning is possible. *E.W.,* I, 73.

26 Since truth is of propositions, its opposite is a statement that is absurd or nonsensical. Error belongs to the world of experience and is a failure in foresight. *L.,* p. 34.

27 *O.L.,* V, 257.

28 *E.W.,* I, xiii.

29 *E.W.,* VII, 78.

30 *E.W.,* II, xiv.

31 Hobbes gives the additional reason that a knowledge of causes is useful to mankind. *E.W.,* I, 7-10.

32 *Elements of Law,* Appendix II, §1, 168.

33 *E.W.,* I, 6, 386-7.

34 *O.L.,* I, 321.

[35] *L.,* pp. 49-50.

[36] *E.W.,* VII, 3. It may be observed that what is recognized here is the normally unstated presupposition of all seventeenth-century science: the Scotist belief that the natural world is the creation *ex nihilo* of an omnipotent God, and that therefore categorical knowledge of its detail is not deducible but (if it exists) must be the product of observation. Characteristically adhering to the tradition, Hobbes says that the only thing we can know of God is his omnipotence.

[37] *L.,* p. 34.

[38] *L.,* p. 98.

[39] *L.,* p. 5.

[40] *L.,* p. 29.

[41] The expression 'natural reason' is not absent from Hobbes's writings, but it means the reasoning of individual men contrasted with the doubly artificial reasoning of the artificial man, the Leviathan. e.g. *L.,* pp. 5, 42, 233, 242; *E.W.,* I, xiii.

[42] *L.,* p. 38.

[43] *L.,* p. 8.

[44] *L.,* p. 64.

[45] *L.,* p. 153.

[46] *L.,* p. 130.

[47] *E.W.,* II, vi, xiv.

The texts of Hobbes's works referred to are, with the exceptions of *Leviathan* and the *Elements of Law,* those published in the *English Works of Thomas Hobbes,* edited by Molesworth, 11 volumes, 1839 (referred to as *E.W.*), and in the *Opera Latina,* edited by Molesworth, 5 volumes, 1845 (referred to as *O.L.*). References to *Leviathan* (*L.*) are to the pages of the Clarendon Press reprint (1909) of the edition of 1651. References to the *Elements of Law* are to the edition by Tönnies, Cambridge, 1928.

David Johnston (essay date 1986)

SOURCE: "Theory and Transformation: The Politics of Enlightment," in *The Rhetoric of "Leviathan": Thomas Hobbes and the Politics of Cultural Transformation,* Princeton University Press,1986, pp. 114-33.

[*In the following excerpt, Johnston considers Hobbes's*

purpose in presenting the theological arguments in the second half of Leviathan.]

Apart from the vigor and vividness of its language, the feature of *Leviathan* that distinguishes it most clearly from Hobbes's earlier political works is the great extent and detail of the attention it devotes to Scriptural exegesis and theological argumentation. In *The Elements of Law,* a work of twenty-nine chapters, Hobbes had devoted two chapters to a discussion of potential conflicts between religious and political authority. In *De Cive* he expanded this discussion considerably, creating a new division of four chapters on religious subjects, which he placed at the end of his book. Even with this expansion of their role, however, Scriptural and religious questions remained a distinctly subordinate subject in Hobbes's work. Their status in *Leviathan* is very different from that which they had held in these earlier compositions. *Leviathan* includes a new chapter on religion in general, placed in a pivotal position at the end of Hobbes's account of human nature and immediately before the portrait of the state of nature with which his theory of the generation of a commonwealth begins. Of four parts into which he now divided his treatise, the third and longest is devoted almost entirely to Scriptural interpretation, while the fourth is concerned mainly with the diagnosis of spiritual errors. In short, Scriptural and religious questions occupy more space in *Leviathan* than any other topic discussed in the work, including Hobbes's theory of the commonwealth itself.

What is the significance of Hobbes's introduction of these new arguments into the body of his work? What bearing do they have upon the political argument detailed in parts I and II of his book? Until very recently these questions received scant attention in the critical literature. The traditional interpretation has been that the theological views developed in parts III and IV of *Leviathan,* however interesting they may be in themselves, are of no real significance for his political philosophy. The foundation of that philosophy, according to this interpretation, is entirely naturalistic. Hobbes develops his political argument out of an analysis of human nature, especially the passions, and its consequences for social interaction. He does not derive it from a set of theological presuppositions, as political philosophers had customarily done since early medieval times. From this viewpoint, then, the theological arguments adumbrated in *Leviathan* appear to be mere appendages to the true work. They are addressed to concerns that are local and transitory, by contrast with the more enduring concerns of Hobbes's political philosophy in the proper sense. [1] While many adherents to this interpretation regard these theological arguments as mere trappings, designed to make Hobbes's doctrines palatable to a nation of Christian believers, it has also been maintained by critics who have taken them to be an elaboration of his sincere religious beliefs. [2] Raymond Polin has expressed the essence of this interpretation clearly and forcefully by arguing that Hobbes's theology is "superimposed" upon his political philosophy, and should in no sense be regarded as an integral part of that philosophy. [3]

This interpretation was strongly challenged some years ago, mainly as a result of Howard Warrender's thorough and carefully argued study of Hobbes's theory of obligation. Warrender argued that the pivotal concept in Hobbes's theory of obligation was that of natural law. The laws of nature are the basis upon which men acquire all their obligations, including those toward their civil sovereign. In this sense they provide the foundation for all commonwealths and all civil laws. But these laws of nature, he suggested, are intelligible only as expressions of divine will. Furthermore, the obligation to obey them, which must exist prior to and independently of all acquired obligations, cannot be understood without reference to divine sanctions. No obligation can be operative or valid unless those obliged by it have a sufficient motive to obey. The only motive sufficient to validate men's obligation to obey the laws of nature is provided by the divine sanction of salvation. Hence the theological concepts of divine will and divine sanctions are basic to Hobbes's entire political philosophy, the foundations of which are in this sense essentially theological rather than naturalistic.[4]

Warrender and others who have advocated this revisionist interpretation have provided many new insights into the structure of Hobbes's political argument, and some of these have proven themselves to be valuable correctives to the traditional view of Hobbes. But their thesis that the foundation of that argument is religious or theological rather than naturalistic is unconvincing. The general source of the confusion is not difficult to identify. Advocates of this revisionist interpretation have focused their attention sharply upon the juridical concepts and language of Hobbes's political philosophy. By so doing they have forced defenders of the traditional, naturalistic view to take this language much more seriously than they have sometimes done in the past. At the same time, however, the revisionists have tended to neglect the behavioral and causal language that is also an integral component of Hobbes's political argument, and have thus underestimated the importance of this entire dimension of his political philosophy, which is encapsulated, among many other places, in his characterization of the laws of nature as "dictates of Reason, . . . or Theoremes *concerning what conduceth to the conservation and defence of themselves.*" [5]

The most curious thing about this revisionist interpretation, however, is that its advocates have made almost no effort to draw upon the voluminous evidence of Hobbes's own theological argumentation in parts III and IV of **Leviathan**. In spite of their claims about the importance of Hobbes's theological concepts or religious beliefs to his political philosophy, these revisionists seem to have accepted, either tacitly or expressly, the traditional view that those portions of **Leviathan** are of no very great or enduring interest. [6] While postulating that his theological views are integral to, or indeed the very foundation of, his political philosophy as a whole, these revisionist critics have actually had little more to say about Hobbes's own theological argumentation than their traditionalist adversaries.

Only very recently has a new cohort of scholars, more interested in and sensitive to the historical context and concreteness of Hobbes's political philosophy than earlier generations of critics, begun to rectify this omission. The seminal work on this point was an essay on Hobbes's religious and historical views by J.G.A. Pocock. Analyzing Hobbes's argument in the latter half of **Leviathan** more closely than any previous critic in recent times, Pocock was led to conclude that this second half of the work is neither strictly subordinate to the political argument of its first half, as most defenders of the traditional interpretation have asserted, nor an elaboration of views that form the theoretical foundation of that political argument, as advocates of the revisionist view have claimed. Instead, he argues, Hobbes simply "embarks on a new course" at the midpoint of **Leviathan**. The first half of that work deals with the domain of nature and reason, while its second half deals with the historical domain of prophecy and faith; and this latter domain is not, in spite of the usual opinion to the contrary, "reabsorbed" into the former. For Pocock, then, **Leviathan** is in effect two separate works, composed in two distinct languages, which stand side by side, neither being subordinate to the other.[7]

Perhaps the greatest virtue of Pocock's work is that it demonstrates emphatically the importance of taking Hobbes's words in the latter half of **Leviathan** seriously. But taking his words seriously is not the same thing as taking him at his word, as Pocock also tends to do. Thus, for example, he argues that Hobbes would never have written "chapter after chapter of exegesis with the proclaimed intention of arriving at the truth about it" had he not believed that the Christian Scriptures constitute the true prophetic word of God. [8] This argument from bulk is unconvincing, if only because it underestimates Hobbes's capacity for political wile. Pocock is absolutely right to chastise most previous scholars for ignoring what Hobbes actually wrote about the Scriptures and sacred history, [9] but his own methodological dictum that critics should concern themselves less with Hobbes's sincerity of conviction than with the effects his words seem designed to produce does not lead to the conclusions he reaches in his essay.

From a strictly logical point of view, the traditional interpretation, according to which parts III and IV of *Leviathan* are a mere appendage to the "real" political argument of that work, is substantially correct. The theological argumentation of Hobbes's work is neither the foundation nor in any other sense an integral part of his political philosophy, if we understand that philosophy to be an abstract, timeless scheme for the organization of political society. That scheme is constructed by interweaving a set of observations about human behavior and interaction, formulated as theoretical propositions, with a set of legalistic or juridical propositions about the grounds, origins, and distribution of rights and obligations. In no essential way does it involve or rest upon theological concepts or religious beliefs. From this point of view, then, the second half of the book is indeed a superimposition, which can be explained only by going outside the bounds of its central argument.

But this conclusion flows from the adoption of assumptions about the nature of Hobbes's work that are different from those held by Hobbes himself. For him, as I have sought to suggest, *Leviathan* was not simply and exclusively a work of "science" or abstract speculation about the causes and organization of political society. It was above all else a work of political persuasion and engagement, which sought to shape popular opinion in ways designed to benefit the cause of peace.

Considered as a political act, the metaphysical, theological, and historical argumentation of parts III and IV of *Leviathan* are integral to the design of Hobbes's book as a whole. Indeed, from this practical point of view it can be argued that they constitute the core of, and lay the foundation for, his project in *Leviathan*. If, in other words, we focus upon the effects Hobbes's words seem designed to produce, we find that (Pocock's investigations notwithstanding) there is a close, even intimate, relationship between the argumentation of the second half of the book and that of its first half. The second half of *Leviathan* is designed to shape the thoughts and opinions of its readers in ways that will make the argumentation of the first half persuasive and compelling. In this sense, parts III and IV lay the groundwork upon which the practical effects envisaged in parts I and II of the work are to arise. [10] The balance of this chapter will sketch the reasoning behind my interpretation, while the chapters that follow will attempt to demonstrate its validity by examining the content and implications of Hobbes's metaphysical, theological, and historical argumentation.

THE STRUGGLE FOR ENLIGHTENMENT

The discrepancy between the theoretical model of man upon which Hobbes had drawn to build the initial version of his political theory and the descriptive portrait of man developed in *Leviathan* opened up a problem of fundamental importance for Hobbes's political philosophy. If men are ignorant, superstitious, and irrational, none of the basic mechanisms upon which his political argument relies will be likely to work. Men who do not fear death, or at least do not allow their fear of death to override all conflicting passions, cannot be relied upon to live together in peace under the authority of an acknowledged sovereign. Fear of death is the ultimate basis of sovereign power and the ultimate inducement for men to remain at peace with one another. If men allow their imaginations to subordinate their fear of death to any other passion or end, the whole basis of sovereign power and civil peace is destroyed.

One possible response to this discrepancy would have been for Hobbes to throw out the theoretical model of man that had underpinned his initial political philosophy. If man had shown himself to be a different creature from the one depicted in his model, Hobbes might have reacted by scrapping that model and making a new beginning. Yet he did not. Instead, as we have seen, he formulated a portrait of man characterized by a systematic opposition between two models. One of these was the model of man as an egoistic, rational being that had underlain his political philosophy from the beginning. The other was a descriptive model of man as an ignorant, superstitious, irrational being. The first model had been an integral component of Hobbes's political philosophy from the outset. The second, descriptive model was subversive of that philosophy in the sense that it depicted man as a creature who could not be tamed by the arguments, threats, and punishments Hobbes had originally envisaged. Perhaps as a consequence of the years of civil war and violent sectarianism, Hobbes was more acutely conscious than he had initially been of how far from his original model of man human behavior could stray. Yet he continued to cling to his initial model of man as an egoistic, rational actor. Why, in the face of all the evidence that had accumulated against it, did he do so? Why, in other words, did he think that the basis of his political philosophy could be saved?

The answer is that Hobbes believed actual human behavior might, in time, come to resemble the pattern described by his model. In the present, men were ignorant, superstitious, and irrational. Their behavior was poles apart from the pattern described by his model and required by his political theory. But Hobbes did not think that men were essentially and permanently irrational beings. They remained for him potentially rational actors of the kind described by his model of human nature. The discrepancy between that model and Hobbes's description of actual men as irrational beings might have led him to abandon both the model and the theory of political society that rested upon it. In fact his reaction was the reverse. Instead of treating observed reality as a given datum and adjusting his political theory accordingly, Hobbes held fast to his theory of human nature and politics. The inconsistency between that theory and observed behavior called for a change in the behavior, not an alteration of the theory. If actual men were ignorant and irrational, they remained rational beings in potential. The validity of Hobbes's theory rested upon the assumption that the irrationality which seemed to characterize human behavior in the present was neither an essential nor a permanent feature of human nature.

This response was, of course, entirely consistent with Hobbes's idea of science. Like that of a geometrical theorem, the truth of a scientific proposition about human nature was not dependent, for him, upon its accuracy as a representation of empirical reality. As long as there was a chance that reality could be reshaped in accordance with the dictates of theory, there was reason for Hobbes to hope that his science of politics could prove its validity through practical use.

Hobbes had strong reasons for supposing that such a chance existed. He believed himself to be living in the opening stages of a new age of discovery and science. He was extremely conscious of the impact that the discoveries and inventions of modern times had left upon the practical arts and the societies that supported them. Already in his manuscript of 1640 he had cited the achievements of these practical arts as the features that distinguish a civilized society from a savage one:

> For from the studies of these men hath proceeded, whatsoever cometh to us for ornament by navigation; and whatsoever we have beneficial to human society by the division, distinction, and portraying of the face of the earth; whatsoever also we have by the account of times, and foresight of the course of heaven; whatsoever by measuring distances, planes, and solids of all sorts; and whatsoever either elegant or defensible in building: all which supposed away, what do we differ from the wildest of the Indians?[11]

The shape of a society, for Hobbes, was dependent upon the state of its practical arts; and the achievements of these arts flowed from advances in learning. In the recent experience of European society these advances had been dramatic. The techniques of navigation that had led to the great voyages of discovery would not have been possible without a relatively modern European invention, the compass. Mapmaking had advanced in great strides during the age, and even during Hobbes's own lifetime, aided both by the discoveries of navigators and by the invention of new mathematical techniques for portraying the earth's geography on a flat surface.[12] The new, Gregorian calendar began to come into general use during the first half of the seventeenth century, and the science of astronomy was revolutionized by acceptance of the Copernican view of the universe during the same period.[13] Hobbes's life was a time of discovery and rare excitement, and no one was more affected by the spirit of intellectual ferment than he.

This spirit is captured by the letter of dedication Hobbes affixed to *De Corpore,* the lengthy study of natural philosophy he began working on in the late 1630's or early 1640's and completed four years after finishing *Leviathan*. Geometry, logic, and astronomy, he argues, had all been developed to very advanced stages of learning by scientists in ancient times. Later on, however, many of these ancient achievements had been "strangled with the snares of words" by ignorant, meddling scholastic philosophers. The chain of learning they had broken had begun to mend only in recent times. Copernicus, Galileo, and William Harvey were the great heroes of its revival; indeed, Harvey was the only one of these who, "conquering envy, hath established a new doctrine in his life-time." Before these men, Hobbes argues, there was "nothing certain" in natural philosophy; but since their time "astronomy and natural philosophy in general have, for so little time, been extraordinarily advanced by Joannes Keplerus, Petrus Gassendus, and Marinus Mersennus," all of whom were contemporaries of Hobbes. "Natural philosophy is therefore but young; but Civil Philosophy yet much younger, as being no older . . . than my own book *De Cive*."[14]

Hobbes had some reason, then, to imagine that great things might flow from the recent revival of learning. That revival was new and fresh; who could say what achievements it might produce? Already it had led to numerous improvements in many specific practical arts. To have an impact upon the prospects of his political philosophy, however, the new wave of learning would have to achieve an even broader effect: the forging of a new and more rational cast of mind, not only within scientific and intellectual circles, but among ordinary people as well.

Formidable obstacles to the achievement of such a vast effect existed, as Hobbes very plainly understood. For in the first place, the seeds of superstition and irrationality, he suggests in *Leviathan,* lie deeply imbedded in human nature. Reason, after all, is an acquired skill, not a natural gift. It is far easier to remain ignorant than to become informed and enlightened. Superstitions arise naturally, without any conscious effort on the part of those who hold them. The imagination is naturally lively and uncontrolled. Magical pseudo-explanations appeal to it, since their falsity cannot be revealed without deliberate and careful scrutiny. The human mind is ripe ground for the "Weeds, and common Plants of Errour and Conjecture."[15] It is not enough merely to implant the seed of reason into the minds of men and expect it to flourish without further cultivation. The weeds of error will crowd and eventually extinguish the life of that seed unless they are forcibly uprooted and destroyed.

Yet, in the second place, there are many men who inadvertently propagate these weeds, and some who deliberately cultivate them. The minds of ordinary people are like clean paper, but only if they have not been "tainted with dependance on the Potent, or scribbled over with the opinions of their Doctors."[16] In practice few people enjoy the clarity of thought and openness of mind needed to make them receptive to the rational teachings of science. Most have been subjected to delusive, confusing doctrines propagated by people who have an interest in maintaining the ignorance of others. "The Enemy has been here in the Night of our naturall Ignorance," sowing and cultivating the weeds of superstition and darkness.[17] That darkness cannot be dispelled unless its authors can be identified and routed.[18]

The magnitude of these obstacles to reason and enlightenment, and the strength with which he emphasizes them, have contributed to the view that in *Leviathan,* at least, Hobbes must have regarded supernatural beliefs—understood either in a Machiavellian way as myths and illusions or in a pious manner as truths of Christian faith—as an appropriate source for the ideological foundations that must underpin any political society.[19] But this conclusion is neither stated by Hobbes himself nor implied necessarily by what he does say. Those seeds of superstition which cannot be "abolished out of humane nature" are only, when reduced to their most primitive core, "an opinion of a Deity, and Powers invisible."[20] The shape these opinions assume when they have matured into a fully grown plant is very much dependent upon the precise way in which they have been cultivated. Belief in God, in itself, is in no way inimical to science or truth, since reason, too, leads us to the conclusion that a deity must exist.[21] And with sufficient cultivation and care even a belief in invisible powers could probably be refined into a form entirely consistent with the truths of science. After all, Hobbes himself habitually attempted to explain physical phenomena by invoking the idea that space is filled with an enormous number of tiny, invisible particles.[22] Properly cultivated, even the seeds of superstition can be transformed into ideas consistent with reason and science.

The real obstacle to any such transformation lay in the entrenched positions of those who opposed it. Yet there was some reason for hope here, too. The forces of darkness had not always held such a tight stranglehold over the minds of ordinary people, and there were grounds for believing that their grip was beginning to loosen. Throughout *Leviathan* there are signs that Hobbes believed he was living in a time of virtually unprecedented ferment and cultural transition—a view that is hardly surprising, given the extraordinarily millenarian atmosphere that had enveloped the English imagination by the time of his writing. [23] Philosophy and the sciences had begun to break loose of their theological shackles, as the achievements of Copernicus, Galileo, Harvey, and others showed. Their revival was still a fragile one, as Hobbes suggests in the opening paragraph of *De Corpore:*

> Philosophy seems to me to be amongst men now, in the same manner as corn and wine are said to have been in the world in ancient time. For from the beginning there were vines and ears of corn growing here and there in the fields; but no care was taken for the planting and sowing of them.

Yet a foothold had been gained, and it opened up a greater opportunity both for the advancement of scientific learning—or, as Francis Bacon had called it, the true "natural magic" [24]—and for the broader enlightenment of ordinary people than any that had occurred for centuries.

The benefits of such a general enlightenment, if it could be achieved, would be very great. By drawing men away from the superstitious habits of thinking to which they had long been accustomed, a movement toward enlightenment would be helping to lay the foundations for a new kind of common-wealth, stronger and more lasting than any that had ever existed before. Instead of resorting to myths and fables, as the founders of past commonwealths had done, the architects of a modern state could rest it upon the firmer, more permanent basis of enlightened, rational self-interest.

Hobbes did not imagine, therefore, that he would have to fall back upon myth to provide the ideological underpinnings of the commonwealth he envisaged. He was acutely aware of the power of myth, but he also believed that rational self-interest, once established as the principal motive of an enlightened people, would prove itself a more enduring foundation for political society than any fable or superstitious fabrication could ever be. He emphasized the magnitude of the obstacles to enlightenment because, unlike Bacon, he was convinced that it would never be achieved without an immense and bitter struggle. A victory would clear the way for philosophy and enlightenment to flourish together, and for commonwealths to be laid upon new, more rational foundations; a defeat would strangle these achievements before they had had a chance to establish strong roots. The struggle for enlightenment, Hobbes believed, was coming to a head in his own lifetime. Its outcome would be of historic importance; but at mid-century, when he was completing *Leviathan,* that outcome was not secure.

THE POLITICS OF CULTURAL TRANSFORMATION

By becoming linked with the historic struggle for "enlightenment," as he conceived it—a struggle he might easily have traced back to Erasmus and other representatives of earlier Renaissance humanism—Hobbes's political philosophy acquired a temporal dimension that had not been present in its initial formulation. In *The Elements of Law,* he had analyzed the commonwealth and the distribution of rights and obligations within it in essentially ahistorical and abstract terms. He had based a timeless theory of government and politics upon an equally timeless model of human nature. In *Leviathan* he clung to all the essential features of that theory. But the discrepancy between that model of human nature and his portrait of man as an irrational being gives *Leviathan* an historical dimension that had been lacking from Hobbes's earlier works. His theory of the commonwealth still had an abstract, timeless quality about it, but the model of man upon which it rested was now linked to a specific historical moment. Hobbes's theory would not achieve practical realization until men became the rational actors they had always had the potential to be. This would not occur until knowledge had triumphed over ignorance, reason had driven out superstition, and enlightenment had vanquished the forces of darkness. The practical realization of Hobbes's political philosophy had become linked to a possible event in future time: the transformation of human beings into the relatively enlightened, rational creatures that had always been the inhabitants of his vision of political society.

This possible future transformation of man became, for Hobbes, the crucial event in human history. The prospects for a commonwealth as he envisaged it were vitally dependent upon the outcome of the struggle between superstition and enlightenment. His theory of the state could not fully be put into practice before the movement toward enlightenment had triumphed. Yet there was no certainty that this triumph would take place. Hence Hobbes was led by what seemed to be inexorable necessity to a basic reformulation of the design of his political theory. His original aim had been to demonstrate the proper distribution of rights and obligations in a commonwealth. This demonstration, he hoped, would help convince men of the need for absolute sovereignty. Now, however, Hobbes saw that he would have to take on aims much broader than these original ones. To promote enlightenment itself, an entire outlook and approach to life, became an integral part of Hobbes's political purpose. His original theory was now encapsulated within a project of even grander design. The cultivation of rational modes of thought and action was an essential step toward the realization of his political aims. It became an aim in itself, distinct from, but inseparably wedded to, the original purposes of Hobbes's political theory.

This new aim generated a stratum of argument that was new in *Leviathan*. Hobbes had touched upon certain religious themes and used Scriptural arguments in both of the earlier versions of his political theory. But in each of these previous works the religious and Scriptural argumentation had been strictly subordinated to his central political aims. Its purpose had been to show that there could be little or no conflict between a man's duties to God and his obligations to his earthly sovereign, and thereby to remove one important potential obstacle to civil obedience. Though Hobbes reproduces many of the arguments of these earlier works in *Leviathan,* the theological argumentation in that work as a whole has a very different character from that which it had before. The doctrines of Christianity, as he portrays them, have been infiltrated over the centuries by many superstitious and magical traditions. As taught by some of the established churches, Christianity has become a carrier of superstition and spiritual darkness. The struggle for enlightenment is, in very large measure, a struggle against these tendencies within established Christian doctrine. The theological argumentation of *Leviathan* is essentially different from that of Hobbes's earlier works because the central aim of that argumentation is new. That new aim was to expose the superstitious and magical elements in Christianity so that these could be expelled from Christian doctrine. Ultimately, it was to lay the groundwork for a fundamental change in the habits of thought and action that had prevailed throughout most of the Christian era—amounting almost to a transformation of the human psyche that would prepare men and women to be assembled, for the first time in history, into a truly lasting political society.

The formulation of this new aim was the pivotal event in the development of Hobbes's political philosophy. It stands behind all the alterations that distinguish *Leviathan* from his earlier works. The new ambition to appeal to a large, public audience and thus shape popular opinion directly; the vividness of language, designed to leave a deep and lasting impression upon his readers; the new stratum of theological argumentation, so vastly more developed than it had been in his previous works—all these changes were linked to this one great shift in Hobbes's aims. The philosophical treatise that was designed to show the need for absolute sovereignty by means of logical demonstration, and that had constituted the main content of *The Elements of Law,* is contained in *Leviathan* as well. But in *Leviathan* that treatise is merely one part of a work of much larger extent and scope. The opposition between reason and rhetoric had been Hobbes's basic theme in *The Elements of Law*. In *Leviathan,* it was replaced by a new theme, that of the struggle between enlightenment and superstition, between the forces of light and the forces of darkness. And the form in which he presents this theme is less that of a philosophical argument in the ordinary sense than that of an epic, with all the grandeur of conception that term implies.[25]

The fact that Hobbes presents this theme in a new

form is intimately related to the reorientation of his aims. "The Sciences," he points out, "are small Power. . . . For Science is of that nature, as none can understand it to be, but such as in a good measure have attayned it." [26] This observation is especially applicable when the aim is not so much to demonstrate the truth of a scientific conclusion from principles that are already accepted as to establish the validity of those principles themselves. For the principles of science, as Hobbes often remarks, cannot be demonstrated by scientific methods. They are self-evident truths, and must simply be presented to the reader in the hope that he or she will recognize them as such: "For this kind of Doctrine, admitteth no other Demonstration." [27] Science cannot prove that the principles upon which it rests are true. But this limitation inherent in the nature of science need not prevent its advocates from using other means to persuade their readers to accept those principles as truths. The vigor and vividness of Hobbes's language in *Leviathan,* as well as the extremely polemical cast of his theological argumentation, are designed to accomplish just this aim. The language of *Leviathan* was necessarily rhetorical, in a deeper sense than the language of his earlier works of political philosophy had been, because the aim of that work was not merely to demonstrate the truth of Hobbes's political argument. That aim, rather, was to establish the authority of science, and through it to promote rational modes of thought and action, with a superstitious people. The form in which Hobbes presents his argument was a consequence of his adoption of this new and extra-scientific aim. In this sense *Leviathan* is at least as much a polemic *for* science and enlightenment as it is an instance of scientific or philosophical argument.

By recasting his argument into this new form, Hobbes effected a synthesis between some of the possibilities inherent in his own idea of science, on the one hand, and the rhetorical lessons he had imbibed during the years before he had conceived that idea, on the other. From the beginning, his idea of science had left open the question of what was to be done to reconcile discrepancies between scientific theory and empirical reality. In fact, the geometrical archetype implied that such discrepancies should be interpreted as signs of the imperfection of reality, not evidence of defective theory. The analogy with geometry did not immunize the theorems of science from empirical criticism entirely, of course, since for Hobbes any science should be capable of proving its mettle through its usefulness in changing and controlling reality. Until an opportunity to apply its theorems had been seized, however, empirical criticism of science would remain meaningless. Recasting the argument of *Leviathan* was a way of helping to create such an opportunity for his political theory. By drawing upon the lessons of the rhetorical tradition, which emphasized the power of the vi-

sual image or "speaking picture" in contrast to the weakness of merely conceptual discourse for creating mental impressions, Hobbes was attempting to create conditions under which the validity of his own theory of government and politics could be confirmed through its practical realization.

Hence the change in form and methods that distinguishes the argumentation of *Leviathan* from that of his earlier works of political philosophy represents neither an abandonment nor in any essential sense a modification of his original purposes. The truth is that this change is a sign and consequence of Hobbes's increased determination to achieve those purposes. The final aim—to bring into being a commonwealth based upon firmer, more rational foundations than any that had ever existed before—remained unchanged. But attainment of this aim now seemed to be contingent upon a prior cultural transformation. The polemical defense of science and enlightenment against magic and superstition was designed to help bring about this transformation, to implant those (in Hobbes's view, rational) habits of thought and action which were required if his scheme for the organization of political society was to work. This defense led Hobbes to offer interpretations of the metaphysical, prophetic, and historical dimensions of human existence as well as the assessment of man's political situation already expressed in earlier versions of his political philosophy. The next three chapters will explore these interpretations and their implications for his political philosophy.

Notes

[1] Polin, *Politique et Philosophie chez Hobbes;* Strauss, *Political Philosophy of Hobbes;* Oakeshott, *Hobbes on Civil Association,* p. 48. Strauss adopts a somewhat different view in his later essay, "On the Basis of Hobbes's Political Philosophy," in *What Is Political Philosophy?* (Glencoe, Ill.: The Free Press, 1959), pp. 170-196.

[2] Paul J. Johnson, "Hobbes's Anglican Doctrine of Salvation," in Ralph Ross, Herbert W. Schneider, and Theodore Waldman, eds., *Thomas Hobbes in His Time* (Minneapolis: University of Minnesota Press, 1974), pp. 102-125.

[3] *Hobbes, Dieu, et les hommes* (Paris: Presses Universitaires de France, 1981), p. 61.

[4] *The Political Philosophy of Hobbes: His Theory of Obligation* (Oxford: Clarendon Press, 1957), esp. pp. 99-100, 272-277.

[5] *Leviathan,* ch. 15, pp. 216-217 [80], emphasis added.

[6] In addition to Warrender, cf. on this point F. C. Hood,

The Divine Politics of Thomas Hobbes (Oxford: Clarendon Press, 1964), esp. p. 252.

[7] "Time, History, and Eschatology in the Thought of Thomas Hobbes," in J.G.A. Pocock, *Politics, Language, and Time* (New York: Atheneum, 1973), pp. 148-201, esp. pp. 159, 167, 191.

[8] "Time, History, and Eschatology," pp. 167-168.

[9] "Time, History, and Eschatology," pp. 160-162.

[10] The nearest approach to this interpretation in the existing literature is that offered by Eisenach in *Two Worlds of Liberalism*. Like Pocock, however, Eisenach greatly exaggerates the disjunction between the two halves of *Leviathan,* going so far as to argue that the work "contains two separate languages, logics, psychologies, and politics" (p. 70). This claim arises out of his acceptance of Pocock's assumption that faith and prophecy constitute a form and realm of knowledge for Hobbes, whereas in fact Hobbes treats faith as a form of mere opinion, not as knowledge, and seeks to undermine the entire concept of prophecy, as the argument of Chapters 6 and 7, below, attempts to show. For another attempt to revise Pocock's interpretation in a similar direction, see Patricia Springborg, "*Leviathan* and the Problem of Ecclesiastical Authority," *Political Theory* 3 (1975), pp. 289-303.

[11] *Elements* I.13.3.

[12] In his autobiography Hobbes reports that as a young student in Oxford he took great interest in maps and the voyages of discovery. See J. E. Parsons, Jr. and Whitney Blair, trans., "The Life of Thomas Hobbes of Malmesbury," *Interpretation* 10 (1982), pp. 1-7. Hobbes also drew up a map of his own to accompany his translation of Thucydides, and makes a special point of its accuracy and reliability in *Thucydides,* p. x.

[13] For general account of many of these discoveries, see Marie Boas, *The Scientific Renaissance, 1450-1630* (New York: Harper and Row, 1962).

[14] *De Corpore,* Epistle Dedicatory, pp. viii-ix. Hobbes cites *De Cive* rather than *The Elements of Law* presumably because the former work was published in 1642, eight years before the latter, even though *The Elements of Law* was written first.

[15] *Leviathan,* ch. 46, p. 683 [368].

[16] *Leviathan,* ch. 30, p. 379 [176].

[17] *Leviathan,* ch. 44, p. 628 [334].

[18] *Leviathan,* ch. 47, esp. pp. 704-706 [381-382].

[19] Tarlton, "The Creation and Maintenance of Government"; Eisenach, *Two Worlds of Liberalism* and "Hobbes on Church, State, and Religion."

[20] *Leviathan,* ch. 12, p. 179 [58].

[21] *Leviathan,* ch. 11, p. 167 [51].

[22] Brandt, *Thomas Hobbes' Mechanical Conception, passim.*

[23] This view is elaborated in Chapter 8, below.

[24] *Advancement of Learning,* p. 97.

[25] Cf. Sheldon Wolin, *Hobbes and the Epic Tradition of Political Theory* (Los Angeles: Clark Memorial Library, 1970), which argues a thesis similar to that of this and the following paragraph.

[26] *Leviathan,* ch. 10, p. 151 [42].

[27] *Leviathan,* Introduction, p. 83 [2]; cf. *De Corpore* I.6.5, 13, 15.

Arlene W. Saxonhouse (essay date 1995)

SOURCE: Arlene W. Saxonhouse, "Hobbes and the Beginnings of Modern Political Thought," in *Thomas Hobbes, Three Discourses: A Critical Modern Edition of Newly Identified Work of the Young Hobbes,* edited by Noel B. Reynolds and Arlene W. Saxonhouse, The University of Chicago Press, 1995, pp. 123-54.

[*In the following excerpt, Saxonhouse discusses three newly-attributed, pre-scientific writings of the young Hobbes.*]

INTRODUCTION

There are many ways to read the three ***Discourses:*** for what they tell us about the social and religious life of the English aristocrat in the early decades of the seventeenth century, for what they tell us about where people traveled comfortably (and not so comfortably), for an understanding of the development of the literary genres of the essay and the discourse. Our purpose here, though, is briefly to explore the political ideas of the author whose later writings are masterpieces of political theory and whose work gave rise, in part, to the principles underlying modern liberalism. The ***Discourses,*** by offering us Hobbes's early reflections on the political questions that will engage him for the rest of his life, help us understand the challenges that confronted those moving from a medieval, religiously focused worldview to modern, secular models built on an infinite universe that is at the foundation of liberal political thought. [1]

The *Discourses*—admittedly immature when compared to Hobbes's mature writings and certainly inconsistent at times—point to the central concern of modern thought: how to identify the secular sources of a political power that might provide for security and stability in a world of constant flux. The **"Discourse upon the Beginning of Tacitus"** faces this challenge directly while the **"Discourse of Laws"** explores how to integrate a legal system based on human rather than divine reason into a political system founded on human choice and will. As such, these *Discourses* not only offer insights into the intellectual development of Thomas Hobbes; they also enlighten us about the beginning of liberalism itself and the contradictions that this new political outlook must address.

One of the most salient features of the *Discourses* is the affinity they reveal between Hobbes and Niccolò Machiavelli. [2] Leo Strauss is not the only theorist to suggest that the modern political perspective emerged in Machiavelli's work a century before Hobbes wrote the *Discourses*. As he states in his introduction to the second American edition of his book on Hobbes: "Hobbes appeared to me [at the time of the first edition] as the originator of modern political philosophy. This was an error: not Hobbes, but Machiavelli, deserves this honor" (1952, xv). This self-correction, though, provides us with a key to understand the novelty of Hobbes's human-centered world where political order is imposed against, rather than in conformity with, nature. These modest writings allow us now to see Hobbes standing at the watershed of modern political thought well before he brought methods of geometry or physics to his analysis of political events. [3] The *Discourses,* by allowing us to read the "pre-scientific" Hobbes, enable us to speculate briefly on the impact that the scientific turn had on Hobbes's political thought. The interest that he develops later in the scientific method and the study of bodies in motion is an accretion to his motivating interest in things political displayed in the *Discourses*. It is, without doubt, an accretion that allows him to formulate in novel and important ways his mature ideas concerning political life, but it does not significantly alter the primary concerns and orientations that he developed as a young man.

The *Discourses* should not be read simply as the immature expression of ideas later presented more fully by Hobbes, for they reveal how the ideas themselves were generated. At the birth of modern political thought is Hobbes's insight that political order can emerge as the result of human rather than divine efforts. In the *Discourses* he analyzes the efforts of the prince—the one skilled in policy—and of the lawmakers to bring about order. Instead of accepting the traditional view and assuming an inherent natural order that needs to be discovered and implemented through the laws and the institutions of the political community, Hobbes reinterprets the past and introduces new theories about the present by pointing to political orders dependent on human will. Here, in his writings at the beginning of the seventeenth century, Hobbes describes how the prince—the new prince—makes certain critical choices and thereby replaces chaos with order.

The *Discourses* suggest a serious Hobbes who is struggling with some of the same questions that will engage him when he writes *Leviathan* some thirty years later. We see him in the *Discourses* working to free himself from the conventional thought of the time, not always successfully or consistently. But the incompatibility of the old worldview and the demands of a political world without foundations in religion or precedent pose for him challenges that he acknowledges here and that his later work will attempt to resolve.

A DISCOURSE UPON THE BEGINNING OF TACITUS

The political concern for defining and determining the origins of political communities and authority within them drives the *Discourses* and especially the discourse devoted to the first four paragraphs of Tacitus' *Annales*. The study of human history looks to origins rather than to ends, to causes rather than to conclusions, to examples rather than to precepts (Strauss 1952, chap. 6). Science, as the study of causes or origins, later helps clarify for Hobbes how to analyze political questions, but the young Hobbes turned originally to history to explore the causes of political order and disorder in pre-Christian Rome.

In some ways Tacitus can be described as the Roman Thucydides, and Hobbes's translation of Thucydides published some ten years later continues his interest in historical writing from the ancient world. [4] But Thucydides provides Hobbes with quite a different window on political life. Thucydides' recounting of the Peloponnesian War and the transformation of the Athenian polity during that war gives insight into the causes of war, its execution, and its consequences. But apart from its introductory chapters, or so-called "archaeology," on which Hobbes does not comment directly in his own introductory remarks, Thucydides' history does not address the issue of foundations. The beginning of the *Annales* poses just that question and enables Hobbes to question the causes of order before he turns to Thucydides to study the causes of disorder. Hobbes is clearly already asking these questions about causes, well before he adopts the more systematic models concerning causes in the natural world that arise from his interactions with the emerging scientific communities of the seventeenth century. [5]

According to the standard biographies and his own accounts written late in life, [6] Hobbes spent the early decades of the seventeenth century in pleasurable trav-el and light pursuits, not in serious philosophical study (LW: I.xii-xiv; I.lxxxviii). Hobbes reports that after coming back from his first trip abroad, [7] he turned to the historians and the poets, with the frequent use of grammatical commentaries, in order to be able to com-pose moderately good Latin. Aubrey supports Hob-bes's presentation of himself when he comments: "Be-fore Thucydides, he spent two years reading romances and playes, which he haz often repented and said that these two years were lost of him—perhaps he was mistaken. For it might furnish him with copie of words" (1898: 351). [8]

Hobbes's sentence-by-sentence commentary on Taci-tus' *Annales* follows a tradition that was established in the sixteenth century and continued well into the sev-enteenth century. Hobbes's decision to comment only on the first four paragraphs of the *Annales* makes his analysis of Tacitus' history unique; it indicates the questions that engage him and displays his early ef-forts at providing answers to those questions. Through his analysis of Tacitus, Hobbes offers a series of Machiavellian maxims as guides for the founders of political orders. In doing so, he also demonstrates his commitment to discovering the sources of political order.

Tacitus, the Roman historian who detailed in clipped Latin prose the iniquities of the Roman emperors of the first century A. D., became especially popular in the sixteenth century. His *Annales* and *Histories* were published, translated, commented upon, and the com-mentaries were translated and commnted upon in turn. The first English translation of Tacitus appeared in 1591 and within the next forty-nine years this transla-tion went through five more editions (Womersley 1991, 313). As one scholar notes, between 1580 and 1700 more than 150 authors wrote commentaries on Tacitus, with most of those coming in the first half of the sev-enteenth century (Burke 1969, 150). Tacitus' popular-ity rested in part on a reading of his works as tirades against the corruption of monarchical power and thus as a call for the republican form of government that had been lost when Augustus established the Princi-pate. For many of these commentators, Tacitus served as the basis for their antityrannical tracts that explored justifications for rebellion against evil kings, a theme that the Protestant Reformation had brought to the forefront of political thinking.

In addition, Tacitus emerged as a cover for Machiavel-lian themes. While Machiavelli wrote his commentary on the beginning of Livy's history (or the first ten books of it), he also uses Tacitean aphorisms at critical points. [9] To cite Machiavelli directly—the incarnation of evil from whom, according to the stage productions of the time, the devil learned his tricks (Raab 1964)—in the sixteenth or even seventeenth century was dan-

gerous, though a few like Bacon showed no hesitation or worry about incurring the unfavorable notice such attention to and respect for the Florentine might entail (Orsini 1936). To cite Tacitus, however, entailed no such danger. Justus Lipsius, the Dutch author who edited the authoritative edition of Tacitus in the six-teenth century, wrote his *Politicorum, sive, Civilis doctrinae libris sex* relying heavily on Tacitus. Indeed, the work is almost an unending and uninterrupted string of Tacitean aphorisms. As Lipsius' English translator noted in 1594: "Gentle reader, if thou please, thou mayest with one view, behold those authors, from whom this discourse is gathered. Amongst the which Cornelius Tacitus has the preeminence, being recited extraordinarily" (Lipsius 1594 [spelling modernized]). [10] Authors such as Giuseppe Toffanin ([1921] 1972) have argued that there were two separate strands of Tacitism; Toffanin called them the black and the red. The former entailed drawing republican lessons from Tacitean aphorisms, the latter Machiavellian ones from many of the same aphorisms. Though Toffanin's claims are now seen as exaggerated (Burke, 1969), a pattern does exist in the sixteenth century of aligning Tacitus with Machiavelli as well as with antityrannical authors. In one version, Tacitus is the exponent of Machiavel-lian themes of "reason of state" and offers a catalogue of the crimes necessary to preserve whatever regime is in power. In the other version, Tacitus points to the dangers of tyranny, and his stories of the violence and immorality of the Roman princes seem to justify rebel-lions against tyrants. [11] So popular was Tacitus in England and on the Continent that a whole school of anti-Tacitus literature appeared as well. [12].

While others found in Tacitus a way to express their views on the political events of the day, Hobbes's Tacitus is primarily a resource for explaining political foundations. Hobbes says little about "reasons of state," less about the dangers of tyranny, and nothing about justifications for rebellion; rather, he examines the account of Augustus' ascension to and assertion of political power to illuminate the origins of states and the challenge of political foundations. The section on which Hobbes comments is the very brief introduction to the *Annales* in which Tacitus quickly describes the transition from the Republic to the Principate under Augustus. Most of the lengthy *Annales* and what con-cerned most of the others who used Tacitus as a store-house of aphorisms relates the actions of the series of princes who followed Augusts—Tiberius, Claudius, Nero, and on down the line of abhorrent rulers. Hob-bes's focus is directly on the institutional origins of the Principate rather than its sordid development in the reigns of subsequent rulers.

Hobbes's fascination with Augusts as he appears in the brief introductory remarks by Tacitus focuses on Augustus' role as a new prince in a new state (255, 257)[13] who is confronted by the difficulties of asserting authority and winning the support of his subjects. A new prince in a state that was once free faces the challenges engendered by making enemies of those who were once eager for change and must now settle for what is. To quote Machiavelli: "But the difficulties reside in the new principality. . . . Its instability arises in the first place from a natural difficulty that exists in all new principalities. This is that men willingly change their masters in the belief that they will fare better: this belief makes them take up arms against him, in which they are deceived because they see later by experience that they have done worse." [14] It is precisely this challenge that confronts Augustus. He is not able to turn, as a king of the seventeenth century could, to foundations in divine right.

James I, writing about the time the *Discourses* were composed, expresses at least the official theory of the source of political authority. In a passage addressed to his son, he admonishes him: "Learn to know and love God, to whom ye have a double obligation; first for that he made you a man; next, for that he made a little God to sit on His Throne, and rule over other men" (McIlwain 1918, 12; spelling and punctuation modernized). In the verse introduction to *Basilikon Doron*, James portrays again the divine source of political power: "God gives not kings the style of gods in vain, / For on his throne his scepter do they sway; / And as their subjects ought them to obey, / So kings should fear and serve their God again" (McIlwain 1918, 3).

Augusts cannot rely on such divine support in his assertion of political power over the Roman state, but neither is he restrained by any such limits as James articulates for his son. Instead, neither supported nor restrained by a divine order, Augustus uses his own skills—or in the loaded term of the time, "policy" (Raab 1965, 78)—to transform the chaotic liberty of the Republic to the ordered model of the Principate. Thus we learn of, and are urged to admire, Augustus' efforts to root out the "stout patriots" who, unapt to bend to the needs of a new regime governed by a new prince, wanted to defend liberty. In good Machiavellian fashion Hobbes asserts that even if they had been allies and members of Augustus' own faction, they could not "be left alive" (264). Such "stubborn companions," had they not been gotten "rid of" (265), would have demanded participation in the new authority and thus they would have divided sovereignty. The rest will "accept the present with security, rather than strive for the old, with danger" (267). Augustus knew he had to "extinguish" the fiercer men and allure the gentler sort.

The Hobbesian message here—whether we see it as building on Machiavellian beneficent violence or as foreshadowing *Leviathan*—is that before the construction of the state neither vice nor virtue exist. The language of *Leviathan* 13 is foreshadowed in these sections of the *Discourses:* "Where there is no common power, there is no law: where no law, no injustice. . . . Justice and injustice are none of the faculties neither of body nor mind." And as Hobbes points out in discussing the regicides who killed the last Roman king as the prelude to the founding of the Republic: "But I shall never think otherwise of it than thus; *Prosperum et felix scelus virtus vocatur*" (228).

Likewise, in language that again recalls Machiavelli, Hobbes notes that traditional virtues are vices and vices are virtues. Liberality costs a country liberty (258) and as a variety of stories from Rome illustrate, generosity leads to absolute sovereignty (259-60).[15] The standards for virtues and vices as traditionally understood do not limit the founding of states, because there are no such standards before such foundings. For the modern authors like Hobbes and Machiavelli the central human task of political founding precedes the moral order. The latter comes only as the result of a political foundation, not as the prior limit on its construction. The security that a James I might have felt with the backing of divine authority for his own ascension to political power and his position as king entailed as well the moral limits on his actions that such a backing required. The open world that Machiavelli envisioned and that Hobbes recalls in his praises for Augustus allows for a freedom of political action denied to those whose security comes from the nature of God and not from their own efforts. Hobbes emphasizes in this discourse the openness at the moment of founding; Tacitus' *Annales* chronicles how subsequent rulers failed to use this openness effectively, earning moral condemnation from their contemporaries and later writers and being unable to provide the political stability Augustus achieved at the start of the Principate.

Hobbes, in his reflections on the fall of the kings which led to the establishment of the Roman Republic, finds fault not with the form of monarchical government that was overthrown in the name of liberty, but with the private excesses of the king's son, excesses which offended and threatened otherwise obedient subjects. The limits on the monarch suggested here do not come from natural law or divine restraints but from what we find later in chapter 30 of *Leviathan* and can call "monarchical prudence." As Hobbes argues in his early discourse: "It is not the [form of] government [in this case, monarchy] but the abuse that makes the alteration be termed Liberty" (229). Monarchy is approved insofar as it retains the support of the king's subjects, not insofar as it follows any moral principles of political authority. It can retain the allegiance of its subjects, however, only insofar as the regime respects their private interests. When the king's son rapes the wife of one of the leading subjects, such an action may well bring about revolution. The issue is not the right or wrong of the action in an absolute sense; the issue thus framed is the degree to which the ruler's acts support or hinder the security of the political authority, be it aristocratic, republican, or monarchical.[16]

As this discourse makes clear, the instability of regimes dominates Hobbes's thought long before England is racked by civil war. The challenge he sees for political leaders is how to ensure a stability that does not reside in the natural order of things by founding a regime in which the people "apply themselves wholly to the Arts of service, whereof obsequiousness is the chief" (307). The Roman Republic, with its exaltation of liberty, offers a model of the instability that emerges from equality, where men "study no more the Art of commanding which had been heretofore necessary for any Roman Gentleman, when the rule of the whole might come to all of them in their turns" (307). Hobbes drawing on Tacitus' two brief phrases describing the beginning of the Republic ("Liberty and the Consulship Lucius Brutus brought in" and "The Decemviri passed not two years" [227, 231]) points out that the people, freed from the rule of kings, "grew perplexed at every inconvenience, and shifted from one form of government to another." They are like a sick man with a fever who, he says, often tosses "to and fro in his bed" (231). It was a regime that loved change and a variety of government (234). Such tossing and such shifting bring on civil war, what Hobbes, long before he himself has experienced it, calls "the worst thing that can happen to a State" (239). It is the liberty of the Republic that allows for the chaos, and only after "the Commonwealth relinquished her liberty, and confessed herself subdued" (250) does the order of the state emerge.

Augustus did not make the same mistakes the founders of the Republic made. Once he established himself in a position of power, through policy, through purgings, through the manipulation of opinions and desires, indeed through violence as well, only then could the populace of Rome enjoy the "sweetness of ease" and only then could they welcome the "vacancy of War" (260). Augustus, not temporary leaders like Cinna or Sulla, knew how to use violence to transform the chaos of the Republic and civil war to a regime that lasted more than a year or two. He transformed a people once accustomed to equality to a people who now realize that "striving for equality, is not the best of their game, but obedience, and waiting on the command of him that had power to raise, or keep them low at his pleasure" (306), and a people as well who recognize that in the "subject of a Monarch, obedience is the greatest virtue" (307). Cinna and Sulla, the usurpers of political power in the early years of the first century while Rome was still a republic, failed "to have mollified or extinguished the fiercer, allured the gentler sort." Thus, they could not assure "to themselves by politic provisions" what "they had obtained by arms" (235).

In contrast, the story of Augustus' founding becomes in Hobbes's hands a "mirror of princes" as he identifies in Machiavellian fashion the necessary first principles of a stable political regime. What might in the traditional discourse be considered personal virtues are less relevant than knowledge concerning the crafts or arts of politics. And Hobbes makes clear that virtue is no assurance of a good ruler: "though he might prove no ill man, he might be nevertheless an ill governor" (297). In particular, we might note Hobbes's extended gloss on the Tacitean phrase "with the title of Prince" which in Hobbes's hands turns into a discourse on the priority of what appears to be over what is, on the prince's need to control minds and wills as "the noblest and surest command of all other" (254). As he notes: "Most men receive as great content from Title, as substance" (240), and "in a multitude, seeming things, rather than substantial, make impression" (241). Augustus, Hobbes explains, knew that the aggrandizement of personal power does not stir men to sedition as "insolent titles" do, and thus he chose a title that would not remind them of their kings. "To give them then content in words, which cost him neither money, nor labor, he thought no dear bargain" (241). Later in the story, Hobbes comments on Augusts' willingness to shed the title "triumvir" since the title itself would evoke recollections of the civil wars, "and a new Prince ought to avoid those names of authority, that rub upon the Subjects' wounds, and bring hatred, and envy" (255).

Hobbes's assertion that a founder must rely on appearances for the security of his position is a euphemism for a ruler's need to deceive. For writers of this time, chapter 18 of *The Prince* captured the heart of Machiavelli's teaching. "In What Mode Faith Should be Kept by Princes" Machiavelli asked, and in answer he makes clear that faith need not be kept; rather, the prince must remember that "men are so simple and so obedient that he who deceives will always find someone who will let himself be deceived" and that "Men in general judge more by their eyes than by their hands. . . . Everyone sees how you appear, few touch what you are."[17]

Sixteenth- and seventeenth-century Europe believed that Machiavelli's approbation of deceit captured the central message of his teaching (Raab 1965), and Hobbes, in this most Machiavellian of discourses, does not hesitate to recommend deceit when it is necessary for political foundings. Augustus "turns to dissimulation, which was in those times held an inseparable accident of a politic Prince" (285). The wise prince does not take away "all the show of their liberty at one blow." Rather, he gradually eases his subjects into accepting their servitude (261). No apologies are offered—just admiration for Augustus' success at political founding. Evaluating the qualities of Agrippa—the prince who would not become emperor because of his untimely death—Hobbes notes Agrippa's lack of just those skills that he finds in Augustus: "the Art of conforming to times, and places, and persons . . . to contain and dissemble his passions, and purposes; and this was then thought the chief Art of government" (297). It is almost as if he were quoting from the twenty-fifth chapter of *The Prince* when he taxes Agrippa for lacking these qualities. In contrast to Agrippa, Tiberius (who does succeed Augustus) knows "best of all men how to dissemble his vices" (317).

In Hobbes's later writings, he will not urge on his rulers the personal exercise of deception; it will not be necessary. With the exercise of complete authority and with an epistemology that questions the existence of any truth outside deductions from first principles, dissimulation will have no meaning and cannot be central to the ensuring of political power. Control of public opinion, however, is crucial. The sovereign who neglects to define words for his subjects will find himself displaced by those who claim to have definitions for such terms as "justice" and "liberty" that are superior to or more attractive than those of the sovereign. "The common people's mind, unless they be tainted with dependence on the potent, or scribbled over with the opinions of their doctors, are like clean paper, fit to receive whatsoever by public authority shall be imprinted in them" (Hobbes [1651] 1968, chap. 30, 221). It is the new sovereign who must tell the people what they are to think, but since there is no longer any truth apart from the ruler's speech, this speech can no longer take on the personal and moral tones of the word "dissimulation." The sovereign of *Leviathan* is protected from any moral evaluation. In the *Discourses* Hobbes, in a sense, is more daring; here the moral language is not excluded but faced head-on, and Hobbes is willing to assert the unfashionable claim that the new prince must dissimulate in order to acquire power and, more important, secure it over time.

In a passage that well captures Hobbes's movement towards a world devoid of the traditional moral limits on political rule, he comments on Augustus' execution of war, beginning with claims concerning the just war, namely, that wars are just only if they are undertaken in defense of our lives, right, or honor; and he mocks those who set the "Law of State before the Law of God" (301-2). But in looking at the particular war against the Germans, an aggressive war with no injury to justify retribution, Hobbes concludes: "For oftentimes Kingdoms are better strengthened and defended by military reputation, than they are by the power of their Armies" (302). Despite the pieties noted a few lines above, the real issue is the preservation of the empire, not justice. And, just to be sure we recognize that, Hobbes adds almost as an afterthought: "And besides this, Augustus might find commodity in this war, by employing therein the great and active spirits, which else might have made themselves work at home, to the prejudice of his authority" (303). In a similar vein, towards the end of the discourse he recognizes

how men "commonly measure their own virtues, rather by the acceptance that their persons find in the world, than by the judgment which their own conscience makes of them" (318-19). What establishes a reputation is "as often vicious as virtuous. For there is almost no civil action, but may proceed as well from evil as from good" (319).

Much of the first book of Tacitus' *Annales* addresses the problem of succession. Augustus, having established himself as the prince of the new regime, must identify the person who is to follow him in control of the state. The story Tacitus tells is of a founding prince who identifies a series of successors only to lose each one to an untimely death (287-95). Finally, Augustus is left with his less than pleasing stepson Tiberius. The problem of princely succession confronts Hobbes here. He has identified the principles of political foundings and pointed to the skills of one prince as the source of that founding against a disordered natural world. But individual skills alone are unable to sustain a regime beyond the time of the prince's death—or even the anticipation of death, for "when he dies, they are of necessity to begin again, and lay their foundation anew in the next" (310). The key development in Hobbes's political thought will be the generalization to a multitude of actors of the principles that he articulates here with reference to an individual. For Machiavelli this multitude becomes the basis for his republican theories as they appear in his own *Discourses,* a republic that he saw thriving on the conflict and disorder that inhered in regimes that prized their liberty. For Hobbes, the multitude did not lead to a theory of republicanism but to the search for a surer support for political order where one does not need to depend on the skills of one man to exercise *virtù;* where, in the language of the Dedicatory Epistle to *Leviathan,* all that was necessary was that the sovereign be there, like the geese on the Capitol who saved the Romans "not because they were they, but there."

The study of Augustus, the founder of the Principate, as sketched by Tacitus, shows how political foundings may come from the exercise of skills outside the traditional standards of moral behavior, but the history that follows and that Hobbes ignores in these early reflections identifies the problems of permanence for a regime so founded. Hobbes must progress beyond the model of the new prince embodied by Augustus to a regime founded on the basic power of all to recognize the need for order and to exercise the crafts or employ the intellectual efforts necessary to establish that order on their own.

The history that Tacitus records shows the wisdom of Augustus' efforts to identify a successor to prevent civil discord and to kill "the seeds of ambitious and traitorous hopes in those that think of alteration" (274). But identifying a successor cannot replace the security ensured by the establishment of principles or rules of authority that transcend the individual. The degeneration of the Roman Principate described in such vivid detail in Tacitus' writings demonstrates that the regime founded by the most politic of princes cannot last. As it turned out, that regime depended on the skill of one man; Hobbes's later writings acknowledge that the challenge of political order must go beyond the efforts of the one man skilled in the political crafts to include all members of the community, or as he puts it in *Leviathan,* men as the makers as well as the matter of the commonwealth.

After Hobbes wrote this discourse, he continued to use history as the basis for his political speculations and political exhortations at least through his decision to publish the translation of Thucydides in 1627, finally contenting himself that it would be of interest to the "few and better sort of readers" (Hobbes 1975, 9). In his autobiography he writes that he was an enthusiastic reader of ancient and modern history during the period when he composed the *Discourses* (*LW* 2:lxxxviii). As Machiavelli recognized, though, the study of the polities of the ancient world gives us insights into human behavior before the religious and moral impact of Christianity transformed the expectations of political leaders and rulers; it offers insights into foundings and institutions where issues of Christian doctrine can be set aside. But already Hobbes recognizes the limits that must attend the study of history itself as a guide to political understanding and action. It is limited, in particular, by the interests of the historian. Though Tacitus, in the famous phrase, claims to write his history *sine ira, sine studio* (without spleen, without partiality), most historians do not present the whole story or provide accurate lessons from which one can learn, but offer partial accounts driven by flattery or slander. Given men's passions, histories may obscure rather than illuminate the real causes of events. The sciences to which Hobbes later attaches himself escape the private passions of any particular story or storyteller. Histories ultimately turn out to be unreliable since "most men measuring others by themselves, are apt to think that all men will not only in this, but in all their actions more respect what conduces to the advancing of their own ends, than of truth, and the good of others" (249). The sciences appear to escape this problem; and as Hobbes comes to perceive it, the vanities of authors are not caught up in the stories that scientists tell. Discovering the sciences of geometry and physics, Hobbes finds a world where writers appear to work *sine ira, sine studio.* He thus discovers a new source in his search for historical maxims that will lead to order and protection from "the worst evil that can befall a State" (239).

History, so dependent on the personal passions of the storyteller, is likewise limited by its focus on the particular, the particular prince, the particular regime. Geometry as the deductive science which Hobbes dis-

covered by chance on a trip to Europe in the early 1630s,[18] provides Hobbes with an escape from the particularity of history and suggests a way to generalize and equalize. In so doing, however, geometry and the other sciences to which Hobbes turns do not change the questions that he asks and the critical assumptions that lie at the core of those questions. Geometry allows for a universalized response to the problem of political foundings by generalizing to all the qualities attributed to the single founder. As the principles of political foundation are generalized, it will be the efforts of all, through authorization, that accomplish the transformation from chaos to order. It will not be the one leader who manipulates but all those who have learned from Hobbes the true, original source of political order. Nevertheless, the science of geometry does not change the problem that Hobbes (and Machiavelli) had put at the center of the study of modern politics: how order emerges from chaos or how regimes can be instituted on the ashes of political conflict. **"A Discourse upon the Beginning of Tacitus"** shows us what his original questions and assumptions were—and why he saw the answers as insufficiently grounded.

A DISCOURSE OF ROME

Significantly, Hobbes studies political foundations in the first discourse through a careful sentence-by-sentence commentary on a historical text from pagan antiquity. In the second of the discourses published in the volume of the *Horae Subsecivae* Hobbes takes us to Rome. He had visited the Continent as tutor to William Cavendish, a trip that apparently included numerous nations and cities, but we have only his reflections on Rome, a city which as he phrases it had survived "a diversity of governments" (325).

Though much of the discourse purports to be about Roman sites, the introductory remarks make clear that once again it is political foundations that intrigue Hobbes, while the title reminds us of another discourse of Rome, that by Machiavelli on the founding of Rome as reported in the first ten books of Livy. An audience for secular travel literature in English appears to have developed in the first decades of the seventeenth century. In part, this literature on Italy and Europe in general may have been a response to the desire for descriptions of the voyages of discovery (Haynes 1986, 27). A number of weighty volumes were published about the time that Hobbes would have been writing this discourse on Rome (Coryat 1611, Sandys 1615, and Moryson 1617).[19] Most of these works contained long descriptions of journeys, inns and food, of customs and folktales, of ruins and castles—or as one author says about Coryat, "half travel-diary, half guidebook" (Sells 1964). The publisher's note to Coryat's 1611 edition of his work comments: "On his return he proposed to publish his book of travels, but finding it difficult to induce any bookseller to undertake its publication, he applied to many eminent men to write 'panegyricke verses upon the Authour and his booke'" (1611, ix). The "panegyrickes" fill a fair number of pages and ensured publication of this particular travel book.[20]

Hobbes's discourse describing Rome is one of the earliest pieces reporting on an Englishman's travel to Rome.[21] His fascination with Rome comes, he claims, in part from the "divine power" (325) it had in antiquity, when Rome became "so great an empire" and its subsequent transformation through the Donation of Constantine into an empire of the popes. In that donation, Hobbes finds the "true Original" (327) of the dominion of the popes, a greatness claiming "supremacy in all causes, through all Kingdoms in the world" that has "more risen by encroachment than right" (328-29). In the previous discourse Hobbes had reflected on and learned from the establishment of political power by a political prince. In this discourse, he eschews speculation on the source of political power except to suggest that perhaps it was the "fate of this place, that has ever been, or aimed to be the Mistress of the world" (329). What begins as a travelogue and continues in that fashion, nevertheless keeps reverting to issues of political power and its foundations. The study of the religious center of the Catholic world continues the study of political foundings, albeit of a very different sort.

Thus, a brief note on the harshness of the land turns into a disquisition on the effects of such a terrain on the morals and character of a people. More particularly, though, Hobbes reflects on how the ease and comfort afforded by pleasant surroundings lead to a stagnancy of effort on behalf of one's country and a lethargy that precipitates the loss of autonomy. By nature, he tells us, men are "prone to an active life"; it is "custom" that brings on the lethargy and the effeminacy that make men subjects where they ought to rule (333). The language again recalls that of Machiavelli, who, at the beginning of his own discourses, reflects on the impact of Rome's topography on the moral qualities of the early Romans. The observation that the luxury of a fertile land leads to servile populations is not unusual, but Hobbes's emphasis is not on morality or the lack of it, but on action as natural and inaction as unnatural; he is concerned with the life of public energy rather than with private affairs.

This section of the discourse shows that Hobbes still accepts the traditional models which extolled the worth of public service and the honors that accrue to the one who serves his state. The aristocratic pursuit of honor and glory tugs hard at his understanding here, as when he criticizes the "easeful life" which will dull the mind and lead a man to "grow retired, applying himself to his own contents" (335-36). For such men, "memory dies with them." And then Hobbes adds language that

will startle any reader who interprets *Leviathan* as a primer of egoism: "for no man is born only for himself" (336). Hobbes here contrasts public service for the public good, which brings honor, with what will later be called the bourgeois value of private ends, which brings comforts to the individual without special regard for or impact on the public welfare. The hard life produces the former, the energy to act on behalf of the welfare of the whole; the "easeful" life brings the latter, the focus on the self which brings no honor.

The contrast as Hobbes presents it, though, has its own complexities, especially if we refer back to the beginning of Machiavelli's own *Discourses* and if we look forward to Hobbes's later writings. In Hobbes's **"Discourse of Rome,"** he notes that ease and comfort have reduced men to a complacency that makes them subject to the encroachments of others; harshness would encourage an energy for public service. According to Machiavelli, the fertility of the land and the serenity of the climate can reduce a people to complacency and consequently subjection. But more significantly, Christianity, not the topography and the climate, offered the Italians peace in the future and a comfort that did not depend on the world at hand, leading them to ignore the oppression and enslavement that they were suffering. Machiavelli reminds the Italians that they have lost their freedom, that their complacency has made them slaves. The comfortable topography of their lives coming from Christian doctrine has withered the energy they need to save themselves. Machiavelli's self-imposed task is to make the Italians uncomfortable. Similarly in Hobbes's later writings the state of nature is designed to point readers to the discomforts which religion may hide, to the conditions from which they must protect themselves through the creation of civil society. He is in effect admonishing the English that, though they may live in the comfort of a stable government, they must remember the suffering, the harshness that lurks behind that comfort lest they allow themselves to be reduced to the brutishness of the natural condition of mankind or to the turmoil of civil war, the worst evil a state can experience.

One way to read Hobbes's mature political theory is to think of it as encouraging all to engage in an intellectual exercise that reminds us of what we have too casually forgotten: the nasty and brutish natural condition of mankind is like the harsh topography around Rome, an incentive to action, an incentive to the ambition to ameliorate the discomfort through political foundings. Ease may lead us to forget the necessity for political authority just as those whose wealth and luxury appear to come to them by nature, without effort, become enervated and unable to defend their possessions. The former will soon lose the ease and find themselves back in the natural condition; the latter will soon find their luxuries stolen by those with the energy to acquire. In the **"Discourse of Rome"** we see an early indication of the thought experiment Hobbes will later urge on his readers.

In these early writings, the honor attendant on public service still underlies Hobbes's vision of one's proper relationship to the political realm. In his later writings the individual concern with honor and glory is identified as destructive of political order rather than a prod to beneficial actions. Again, perhaps, we can see the equalizing effects of a science which he discovers more than a decade later and which led him to abandon distinctions between degrees of birth. All—not just those nobly motivated—must experience the ambition that leads them to transform the harsh into the pleasant, the state of nature into civil society. In his early writings Hobbes can still extol the notion of honorable public service that brings "memory" or glory to an individual; later that honor inheres not in the actions of any individual, but is ascribed to individuals by the sovereign. On the other hand, the glory of creation belongs to all who in their equal assertion against a harsh nature become the creators of the leviathan; the task belongs not just to those nobly inspired by the hope of eternal fame.

Following a catalogue of the numerous statues and monuments he observed throughout Rome, Hobbes reflects again on glory and reputation, revealing his early belief that noble action derives from promises of renown. He marvels that the statues show a people more enthralled with virtue than with greatness and concludes that the expectation of continued fame among men "produced better effects of virtue and valor, than Religion, and all other respects do in our days" (356). The concern with reputation appears here a potent incentive to noble action. But it is an incentive which will be rejected by the later Hobbes, who will find in such a concern the denial of the equality that must lie at the heart of the founding of the state. That a desire to be first and foremost, whether in reputation or in anything else, is destructive of the state must be pointed out to Hobbes's later readers. Here, still under the spell of aristocratic notions of public service and Machiavellian visions of glory, Hobbes extols what he later condemns. [22]

Yet, the feisty, contrary Hobbes emerges in this essay as well—the Hobbes who mocks common, self-satisfied opinions and prejudices. He derides those who ridicule these monuments built in recognition of noble deeds. They scorn the ancients who, lacking any higher notion of eternal life, depend on such monuments for their immortality. Hobbes defends the ancients, who "had some sense of the immortality of the soul" (361), though they were "only learned in natural sciences, and had no inspiration from above" (361-62); in turn, he scorns those of his contemporaries who in their "strange blindness . . . have such a mist before their

eyes . . . that they will still turn the image of the incorruptible God, into the likeness of a corruptible man, which in any natural understanding, seems foolish" (363).

In the middle of the discourse, Hobbes's catalogue of sites again turns to broad reflections, this time on human credulity. While we should expect anti-popish pronouncements from an Englishman of Hobbes's religious upbringing, the peculiar focus of these pronouncements should intrigue us, as they are directed specifically to epistemological questions. He expresses alarm at the ease with which men are controlled by "shadows to conclude truth" (375) and how easily men are blinded by form and deceived into believing impossibilities as they give credence to miracles. These reflections come from Hobbes's observations upon religious antiquities and the relics in Rome, but also from "the gloriousness of their Altars, infinite numbers of images, priestly ornaments, and the divers actions they use in that service; besides the most excellent and exquisite Music of the world, that surprises our ears" (389-90). The Church having access to such wondrous displays is able "to catch men's affections, and to ravish their understanding" (389) and by repeating tales of miracles—even those which are proved false—churchmen "delude the people" (391). At one point Hobbes suggests, "A man might spin out a long discourse of such a subject" (377-78). Indeed, he later does so when he begins ***Leviathan*** with "concerning the thoughts of men," and when he concludes that lengthy book with a detailed section on the Kingdom of Darkness. In this discourse the "miracle of the two chains" (373-74) leads to his awe at human credulity. It is just this credulity that leads to the instability of polities; it is this credulity that must be replaced with the firm epistemological foundations of Hobbes's empiricism.

Hobbes's tone when describing the Roman's belief in miraculous causes and the attribution of such miracles to some saint or another is scornful, but even when mocking men's credulity Hobbes never loses sight of his search for causes. He sees the Romans, attempting to understand their world and the proximate causes for the events in it, accepting the Church's explanation of saints and direct divine intervention into their daily activities. Such credulity precludes efforts at true understanding and remains unsatisfactory, worthy of ridicule. The search for causes, though, so unsatisfactorily practiced in the Rome of the popes, does dominate Hobbes's thought as he later turns to science for causes independent of any divine intervention.

While Hobbes's travelogue illustrates the epistemological turn to his intellect, and while his observations illuminate the religious role of Rome as devoted to the salvation of the human soul, he also analyses the city of Rome as a purely political institution. He asks of the city political questions: can it protect itself from invasion, what sort of "government" does it have, how wealthy is it? (395-96). The answers to these questions in turn lead to reflections on how similar the Church is in its actions to the temporal princes. With its ambassadors and its goings and comings, with its outward aspects of honor, it is "behind none" of the "greatest Princes" of the world (398). The temporal ambitions and pride of the popes and of the cardinals bring Hobbes to a critique of Rome on political grounds. The pope and his cardinals are proud and ambitious, like the ambitious man writ large, the one Hobbes warned us about in the **"Discourse upon the Beginning of Tacitus"** who is a danger to any honest man that stands behind him or before him, destroying the former out of fear, the latter out of hope (300). Such men become the teachers, by example, of what they oppose by precept, educating their followers to "ambitious thoughts, and unsatisfied desires after the wealth and glory of this world" (404). The ambitions of the Church become more than a simple political hazard in the relations between nations. By its own example the Church educates people in just those vices that are destructive of civil order, just those qualities of character against which the Hobbesian laws of nature advise (*Leviathan,* chap. 15). The attack on the Roman Church goes well beyond doctrine; indeed, apart from the discussion of miracles, little is included in this discourse about doctrine. It is rather the politics of Rome that intrigues Hobbes and gives this discourse its place in his early political thought.

A DISCOURSE OF LAWS

In his **"Discourse upon the Beginning of Tacitus,"** Hobbes searches for the sources of political order in the personal actions of a new prince in a new state. He points to the policy of a prince who can "extinguish" his former allies and can lure his subjects to obedience with the "vacancy of war" and with grain for their tables. In the midst of the discussion of the harsh and sometimes duplicitous measures that Augustus took in order to assure order in the newly founded state, Hobbes refers to the laws in effect at the time of the Roman Republic. They are like "Spiders' webs, only to hold the smaller Flies" (272) and cannot function to restrain the strong or to ensure the stability that a new prince can provide. When Augustus took power he had to put his "authority" behind the preexisting laws so that they would no longer be so easily disregarded. Laws in the discourse on Tacitus, then, appear as part of the tool kit of the new prince. In his **"Discourse of Laws,"** Hobbes appears to be considerably more sanguine about the potential that laws may have to structure society and protect a political order in which men live peaceful and secure lives. In a sense, the laws here replace the prince from the discourse on Tacitus. [23] They are the "Princes we ought to serve, the Captains we are to follow" (506).

Despite its optimistic view of what laws can accomplish, the discourse on laws makes evident what life without laws would be like and so demonstrates why we need political authority and political restraints, why "by the fear, and terror of them, men's audacities might be repressed" (507). Hobbes offers us an early adumbration of what he will later call the natural condition of mankind. In the discourse on Tacitus we have allusions to civil wars that plagued the Romans under the Republic. In the discourse on laws we find a more general statement of that condition. Hobbes uses words like "confusion" (507, 514), "convulsion," and "dissolution" (516), and phrases such as "an overthrow to conversation, and commerce amongst men" and "all right would be perverted by power, and all honesty swayed by greatness" (507) to describe a world in which men are not restrained by the rule of law. Laws protect us from "all such violent and unlawful courses, as otherwise liberty would insinuate" (508). At one point he claims, "For where Laws be wanting, there neither Religion, nor Life, nor society can be maintained" (517), strongly suggesting religion's dependence on laws. But it is his warning that "a man had better choose to live where no thing than where all things be lawful" (516) that captures what will characterize his later presentation of the state of nature and our need to escape it.

Where all things are lawful, there men enjoy the rights to all things and there confusion and convulsion follow. There we can rightly ask: "who is it that can say, 'This is my House, or my Land, or my money, or my goods'?" (519). There men will measure their actions not "by the rule of *Aequum* and *Iustum,* but by the square of their own benefit, and affections" (508). Hobbes here performs the mental exercise that he urges us to do in his later political works when he asks us to imagine the state of nature—we are to imagine places where the laws do not restrain. To imagine such a place is to recognize that property does not exist by nature, that it depends on the voice of the lawmaker(s). To imagine such a place is to recognize that justice is not self-enforcing; self-interest is. Men not restrained by power act as "their own wills, and inclination would give them leave to effect" (508), to the detriment of a life of security, not to mention prosperity.

To claim, as Hobbes does frequently throughout this discourse, that without laws human society dissolves is hardly a novel argument. For support Hobbes can return to such classical authorities as Plato and Heraclitus; he can cite readily the relevant passages from their works (and he does, 509-10). But while the language that Hobbes uses to emphasize the chaos resulting from the absence of justice and secure property foreshadows the language we find later in his treatment of political society, the more significant aspect of these sections of the discourse is the suggestion that law acts in opposition to nature. [24] For Plato and Heraclitus, and for medieval natural-law theory as well, law is reason and reason derives from nature. There is no opposition between that which is natural and that which the laws command. For Hobbes there is—and there is not. In other words, the **"Discourse of Laws"** suggests that Hobbes has not yet resolved the relationship among law and reason and nature as he will in his later writings. The resolution that he offers later with his presentation of the various laws of nature is among the most radical of his redefinitions of traditional language, but here in his early work we see him still struggling with an opposition between a nature that provides no natural grounds for property or justice and a nature that gives us the reason to discover laws.

On the one hand, Hobbes argues that "we receive much more benefit from Laws in this kind [those that bridle the claims of others], than from Nature" (520). On the other hand, he accepts the language of traditional natural-law theory whereby our laws derive from our reason which derives from nature. Hobbes tells us in this discourse that by nature men are affected "with a violent heat of desires, and passions and fancies"; by "natural inclination" men are prone to "all manner of hazards and ill" (520). These are the natural inclinations and passions that the laws created or "invented" (522) by men and applied by human officers must restrain. The opposition is between nature and human art. Order is not inherent in the natural world; it is imposed by human effort and human reason. In the discourse describing the rise of Augustus it was the individual policy of the prince that could impose order on the disorder left by the conflicts of civil war; in this discourse, a quieter and tamer work, Hobbes focuses on laws as the mechanism for human restraint; laws once created and written by humans can outlast their authors but still impose an order that is contrary to nature. To capture the thrust of these early writings, we must attend to the way in which he establishes the imposition of order on a disordered universe as the central human challenge. Augustus illustrates one way; laws as human exercises in control over "confusion" and "convulsion" illustrate another.

The complexity emerges, however, when Hobbes draws into his discourse on laws the language of natural-law theory that unites law with nature in a way that contradicts his earlier portrait of a naturally disordered world. In a section that could almost come from St. Thomas Aquinas, Hobbes discusses the law of nature which is "common to every living creature, and not only incident to Men: as for example, the commixture of several sexes . . ." (518). He discusses the "fountains of natural Justice" from which the infinite variety of laws derive (524-25) and describes the unity of law and reason (531). [25] Whereas elsewhere he will combine law and reason, in this discourse he, on occasion, unites law and nature.

While this embrace of natural law may be disconcerting for those eager to find in these discourses the Hobbes known as the critic of defenders of common law such as Coke and the precursor of positive-law theory, we do, nevertheless, find in the elaboration of this point the direction in which Hobbes will move. After his assertion of natural law along scholastic lines, Hobbes quickly turns to civil and municipal law. These are the laws over which his attention lingers as he speaks of the origins of Roman law (i.e., pre-Christian law); he reiterates that it is law—now municipal law—that defines property, the mine and thine of civil society. The ties of generation, for instance, are inadequate to ensure the passing of wealth from parent to child. "Whatsoever is left unto us by Testament of another, it is impossible we should ever keep it as our own, if Law restrained not others' claims, and confirmed them not unto us" (519-20). Nature by itself accounts for nothing; the natural desire to leave what is ours to our descendants is not self-enforcing. Only the laws which depend on the "dispensers and interpreters" (521) for their existence and enforcement can ensure the satisfaction of our natural desires.

A section of the discourse that analyzes the spur to making laws—be it fear or reason—is followed by a section that describes the infinite variety of laws that derive from the fountains of natural justice (524-25). Here the civil law attached to the particularities of place and time comes not from the authority of the prince, the speech of Augustus, for example, but from those fountains of natural justice. Differences in laws in different states arise not because of the authority of different speakers but because the landscape through which the waters from the fountain of natural justice run will differ from place to place, giving a different taste to the laws of each state. The metaphor is purple and forced, and the consistency of argument so characteristic of the later Hobbes is missing.

Before Hobbes can reach the classic Hobbesian understanding of natural law and of the place of law within the political community, he will need to shed a natural-law theory that posits a natural and perceptible justice from which civil laws derive. The tension in the **"Discourse of Laws"** partly arises from a mind still accepting a natural-law theory as articulated in the medieval period but recognizing that law is constructed by humans to restrain nature in order to build an unnatural order. There is no evidence here of the magical transformation Hobbes will later perform when he unites law and nature to describe the exercise of human reason discovering the principles of self-preservation. Here he still writes about the fountains of natural justice and, for the moment, with quotes from Cicero, defines law as reason applied to the particularities of the situation (531).

The common source of law in reason does confront

Hobbes with the difficulty of explaining the varieties of laws. This is easy whether he uses the fountain and stream image noted above or when he makes reference to different intentions of the "first Planters" (533) of polities. But this challenge does lead Hobbes to address the precise origins of these diverse laws, and he proposes to use ancient Rome as an example, offering a typology of the variety of sources for that state's laws, from those ordained by the power of the Senate (the *senatus consultum*) to those given as "commandments of the General in the Field" (536-38). The typology of Roman law makes explicit the origin of law in speech. In this discussion he has left behind the question of the specific law's relation to the fountain of natural justice and its dependence on the local landscape. That which pleases the prince, *principium placita,* goes along with laws propounded by the people as a *plebiscitum.*

As if to confound us, however, Hobbes turns this discussion of Roman law to a consideration of the unwritten laws or customs which arise over time and which have no "known Author" (541). [26] To these he grants the same power and authority as those laws which come from the official actions of the political units. The discourse ends, then, with a discomforting equation of common law based on custom with law that is based on civil statutes. Hobbes's embrace of both forms of law, giving each full authority and legitimacy, will slacken as his thought matures. He will recognize the threat to political obedience and political obligation that emerges from allowing the validity of common law (Herzog 1989, 137). Indeed, custom and common law will disappear from his model, and statutes whose "author" is "known" will be the only way to ensure that the "confusions" and "convulsions" that laws prevent do not destroy the security and prosperity that men seek. The contradictions that Hobbes poses in this discourse will be resolved as he clarifies his own analyses of political origins and institutions. But these contradictions show what challenges must be met in the movement from the medieval worldview to the deeply rationalistic foundations of Hobbes's later political thought, as well as of liberal thought in general.

These early writings by Hobbes leave us with the question of how his ideas developed as the result of his subsequent encounters with other intellectual traditions, in particular the scientific concerns of his contemporaries in England and on the Continent. The *Discourses* help us to structure that question. What we have here is Hobbes's thought unaffected by scientific models; it thus puts us in a position to evaluate how the scientific method altered (or did not alter) the issues Hobbes raised and the answers he provided. The answer to this question should lead us to a deeper understanding of the basis of modern political thought. I would suggest that the questions at the core of his

thought are vividly present in these prescientific writings; Hobbes's later search was primarily for a method appropriate to address these issues. In science he found the abstraction from and the absence of *ira* and *studium* that created difficulties with historical sources of knowledge. But this new epistemological base does not mean the abandonment of the puzzle he defines early in his writings—the puzzle of the sources of political order. What he gains is new insight into how the modern world might address this puzzle; what he began with was a recognition of the challenges the modern world faced.

Notes

[1] Koyré (1959:vi) perhaps most elegantly describes this transformation in the pattern of thought that reached its apex in the seventeenth century: "[T]he destruction of the cosmos and the geometrization of space, that is the substitution for the conception of the world as a finite and well-ordered whole, in which the spatial structure embodied a hierarchy of perfection and value, that of an indefinite or even infinite universe no longer united by the identity of its elements and basic components." See also Greenleaf (1964).

[2] That Hobbes uses the discourse form and title for his reflections is itself interesting; the discourse had not yet become a popular literary genre in English literature by the time Hobbes was writing. In contrast, the essay, the form which comprises the first half of the *Horae Subsecivae,* had quickly taken hold in England in the late sixteenth and early seventeenth centuries, most prominently in Bacon's writing. Among a variety of other definitions, the *OED* describes the discourse as "a dissertation, treatise, sermon, homily, or the like" and refers to a 1581 text. The use of discourse in the actual title of a work occurs in 1575: "A brief Discourse off the Troubles . . . abowte the Booke off Common Prayer and Ceremonies," and, of course, it appears in the discourse found not to be by Hobbes that appears in the *Horae Subsecivae,* the "Discourse against Flatterie," which was published separately and anonymously in 1611 (Pollard 1946, no. 6906), but the form was not nearly as familiar as the essay at this time. By the end of the century the discourse is a common form, especially for theological treatises. The most familiar work written in the discourse form at the time that Hobbes was writing his own discourses would have been the *Discorsi* of Machiavelli.

[3] The *Discourses* also show Hobbes interested in these questions of order well before the crises of the English civil war made even more vivid the need to identify the new sources of political authority.

[4] It is unclear when Hobbes decided to publish his translation of Thucydides. In his verse autobiography

he says of his readings of the classical authors, poets, historians, playwrights, both Greek and Roman, that Thucydides pleased him the most. (L W 1: lxxxviii.) This was during the time that he enjoyed the friendship and leisure entailed in acting as the tutor of the William Cavendish who was to be the second earl of Devonshire. In the Preface to the Reader introducing his translation, Hobbes remarks about it: "After I had finished it, it lay long by me; and other reasons taking place, my desire to communicate it ceased" (Hobbes 1975, 8-9).

[5] Numerous scholars have focused on one influence or another as the basis for Hobbes's full philosophical and political system. Whether it be the "resolutive-deductive" system of Watkins (1965), or the geometric method of Goldsmith (1966), or the aristocratic sensibilities noted by Strauss ([1936] 1952) and Thomas (1965), or the impact of reading Descartes (Tuck 1988), any such assessments of the influences on Hobbes's thought will need to return to these early *Discourses* and address the defining influences that may surface from a careful reading of these writings.

[6] Aubrey (1898, 395) affirms that the prose autobiography is by Hobbes, noting in his introduction: "This was the draught that Mr. Hobbes did leave in my hands, which he sent for about two years before he died, and wrote that which is printed by Dr. Richard Blackburn."

[7] Noel Malcolm (1984) provides new evidence that this trip to the Continent took place from the autumn of 1614 to the spring of 1615, rather than in 1610 as had originally been conjectured by most scholars.

[8] We do know that Hobbes's modest description of his intellectual concerns prior to the publication of the Thucydides translation is not quite accurate, since during that time he was translating letters written in Italian by Fra Fulgenzio Micanzio, a Venetian, who had begun a lengthy correspondence with the second earl of Devonshire. The letters, dating from 1615 to 1628, contain detailed discussions of the political conditions in Venice, as well as extensive commentaries on the works of Bacon. Two manuscripts of these letters are known to us, one in the library at Chatsworth, the other in the British Museum (add. MS 11,309). Neither of these is written in Hobbes's hand, but the manuscript at Chatsworth has on the flyleaf, in Hobbes's writing: "Translated out of the original Italian Letters by Th: Hobbes Secretary to ye Lord Cavendish." Malcolm (1984) and Sommerville (1992, 76-78) discuss these letters at some length.

[9] Though Machiavelli seldom cites Tacitus directly, there are some key passages from Tacitus in Machiavelli's texts, e.g., compare Chapter 13 of *The Prince* and Tacitus' *Annales* 13.19; see also Machiavelli's *Discourses* 1.10 where Machiavelli lifts a paragraph

directly from the introduction to Tacitus' *Histories;* compare *Discourses* 1.29 and *Histories* 4.3, and see especially *Discourses* 3.19 where Tacitus is cited as the author who feels that severity is more important for a ruler than gentleness. Mansfield (1979, 373-86) comments extensively on this passage, as does Strauss (1958, 160-65). Womersley (1991, 316) goes so far as to argue that "a powerful knowledge of Machiavelli's *The Prince*" enabled a sixteenth-century translator of Tacitus to fill "up the blanks and spaces left by his source."

[10] According to Hamilton (1978, 450) this book was in the Hardwick Library where Hobbes would have had frequent access to it as a member of the Cavendish household.

[11] Womersley (1991, 326-27) cites an edition of the Huguenot *Vindiciae Contra Tyrannos* published in Basel that appeared bound with a Latin translation of *The Prince,* with the explanation that Machiavelli is the counsellor of the "true prince" and not of tyrants. As such, Machiavelli can help identify the false princes who must be overthrown. In general, Womersley clearly explains the relation between Machiavelli and Tacitus and the use of these authors to justify rebellion.

[12] Bywaters and Zwicker (1989) follow the pro- and anti-Tacitean movements in England in particular.

[13] The page numbers refer to the original pagination of the 1620 edition of the *Horae Subsecivae* and are included in Hobbes's text printed above.

[14] Machiavelli (1985), *The Prince,* Chapter 3 (Mansfield translation, 7-8). On the availability of Machiavelli's writings, see Praz ([1928] 1973) and Raab (1964, chap. 2).

[15] See *The Prince,* Chapter 16 in particular, and Orwin (1978).

[16] This section of the *Discourses* where Hobbes praises monarchical rule suggests difficulties with certain of Strauss's conclusions concerning Hobbes's early thought ([1936] 1952). In particular, Strauss argues that Hobbes at first emphasized an "affinity between monarchy and paternal authority" (62) and that it was only his increased interest in representation that led to a change of view from monarchy as the best natural state to the best artificial state. While references to the patrimonial justifications for monarchy do appear in Hobbes's *Elements of Law* (*EW* II. v. 3) and *De Cive* (II. x. 3), Strauss's claim that "Hobbes came only gradually to cast them aside and . . . at first he considered [patrimonial] monarchy to be the only natural form of authority" (60) does not find support in the *Discourses*. Similarly, Strauss argues that Hobbes only gradu-

ally moved to a "wholehearted rejection of the idea of a mixed constitution. His original opinion will have been that the absolute monarch is by no means obliged, but would do well, to set up an aristocratic or democratic council, and thus unite the advantages of monarchy with those of aristocracy or democracy" (68). Such a claim finds no support in this discourse, although Hobbes would have had ample opportunity to praise a mixed regime such as that found in the Roman Republic, the primary model for the mixed form. Instead, from his earliest writings, Hobbes is firm in his presentation of the advantages of monarchical rule—but not monarchical rule based on the analogy with divine rule over the universe or paternal rule in the family.

[17] Mansfield translation, pp. 70-71.

[18] If we are to believe Aubrey (1898 1:332).

[19] Moryson refers in his introduction to his "Discourses of severall commonwealths," but none of the authors of this travel literature uses the term "discourse" in the title of his book.

[20] See Parr (1992) for a full discussion of Coryat and the emergence of the travelogue/guidebook in English literature.

[21] As Hobbes suggests in his discourse (408-17), travel to Rome was seen as not without its dangers for a Protestant Englishman. Others traveling in Italy at this time describe attempts to disguise themselves so as not to be thought infidels. See especially Stoye (1952, 110-12, 119-22).

[22] This discourse especially offers support for Strauss's (1936) central thesis concerning the aristocratic origins of Hobbes's moral theory and gives weight to Thomas's (1965) effective garnering of passages from Hobbes's texts that clearly demonstrate his ties and debts to the intellectual life and social mores of the aristocrats among whom he lived.

[23] The word "replace" may suggest a chronological order to the essays. We cannot make such a claim and cannot know in which order the discourses published in this volume were composed. It may be that the discourse on Tacitus is a later work and as such moves directly into the theoretical principles at the basis of Hobbes's thought, and that the "Discourse of Laws" shows Hobbes's early explorations where laws still seem more than "spiders' webs" and have the potential to bring order to disorder.

[24] Bobbio (1993, 36) writing about Hobbes's later thought phrases it this way: "Artifice no longer imitates nature, but is equal to it. This change is a sign that things made by human beings, and human industry in general, are now seen in a new light and valued more highly." This insight is appropriate to the *Discourses* as well.

[25] The laws of nature that will figure in Hobbes's later works on politics are likewise related to reason, as deductions of reason (e.g., *Leviathan,* esp. chaps. 14 and 15), but the definition of reason has changed radically from that used for natural-law theory of the medieval period. It is in Hobbes's appropriation of the terms "reason" and "law of nature" that we might identify his inversion of traditional thought rather than his continuation of it. See Bobbio (1993, 118); but also Fuller (1990), who suggests affinities between St. Thomas Aquinas and Hobbes in terms of their understandings of the relation of law to reason.

[26] As Cropsey (1971, 11) notes, Hobbes does not become involved in a controversy with Coke over the position of common law during Coke's tenure as chief justice. The explicit rejection of Coke's views comes in *Leviathan* and in *A Dialogue between a Philosopher and a Student of the Common Laws of England,* probably written well after the completion of *Leviathan* (Cropsey 1971, 3).

FURTHER READING

Bibliography

Hinnant, Charles H. *Thomas Hobbes: A Reference Guide.* Boston: G. K. Hall & Co., 1980, 275 p.

  Lists editions of Hobbes's writings and annotates works about Hobbes published in English, Latin, French, and German between 1679 and 1976.

Biography

Hobbes, Thomas. "The Life of Thomas Hobbes of Malmesbury." Translation of "Thomæ Hobbessii Malmesburiensis Vita. Authore Seipso" (1679) by J. E. Parsons, Jr., and Whitney Blair. *Interpretation* 10, No. 1 (January 1982): 1-7.

  Account of Hobbes's life, originally written and published in Latin verse when he was eighty-four.

Criticism

Baumgold, Deborah. "Hobbes's Political Sensibility: The Menace of Political Ambition." In *Thomas Hobbes and Political Theory,* edited by Mary G. Dietz, pp. 74-90. Lawrence: University of Kansas Press, 1990.

  Identifies the elite's desire for power as central to Hobbes's political theories, and discusses Hobbes's views on the causes of civil war.

Brown, K. C., ed. *Hobbes Studies*. Oxford: Basil Blackwell, 1965, 300 p.
  Wide-ranging collection of post-World War II essays.

Dietz, Mary G., ed. *Thomas Hobbes and Political Theory*. Lawrence: University Press of Kansas, 1990, 211 p.
  Collection of essays that focuse on Hobbes's political ideas.

Gauthier, David P. *The Logic of Leviathan: The Moral and Political Theory of Thomas Hobbes*. Oxford: Clarendon Press, 1969, 217 p.
  Incorporates "games theory" and the "Prisoners' Dilemma" in analysis of Hobbes's state of nature and natural law.

—. "Hobbes's Social Contract." In *Perspectives on Thomas Hobbes*, edited by G. A. J. Rogers and Alan Ryan, pp. 125-52. Oxford: Clarendon Press, 1988.
  Analyzes problematic aspects of Hobbes's social contract argument.

Hampton, Jean. *Hobbes and the Social Contract Tradition*. Cambridge: Cambridge University Press, 1986, 299 p.
  Attempts to rethink and restate Hobbes's political argument in order to understand its failings.

Hinnant, Charles H. "Leviathan." In his *Thomas Hobbes*, pp. 96-131. Boston: G. K. Hall & Co., 1977.
  Compares and contrasts *Leviathan* with Hobbes's earlier work, particularly *The Elements of Law*.

Kavka, Gregory S. *Hobbesian Moral and Political Theory*. Princeton, N. J.: Princeton University Press, 1986, 460 p.
  With *Leviathan* as its source, examines morality in its relationship to self-interest, emphasizing that Hobbes writes of a limited morality of minimal standards of conduct.

Kraus, Jody S. *The Limits of Hobbesian Contractarianism*. Cambridge: Cambridge University Press, 1993, 334 p.
  Critiques the views of Hobbes's contract expounded by Jean Hampton, Gregory Kavka, and David Gauthier.

Laird, John. *Hobbes*. 1934. Reprint. New York: Russell & Russell, 1968, 324 p.
  Discusses Hobbes's life, philosophy, and influence.

Macpherson, C. B. *The Political Theory of Possessive Individualism: Hobbes to Locke*. Oxford: Clarendon Press, 1962, 310 p.
  Study of the theory of political obligation.

Mintz, Samuel I. *The Hunting of Leviathan: Seventeenth-Century Reactions to the Materialism and Moral Philosophy of Thomas Hobbes*. Cambridge: Cambridge University Press, 1962, 189 p.
  Examines contemporary English criticism of the "Monster of Malmesbury."

Oakeshott, Michael. "The Moral Life in the Writings of Thomas Hobbes." In his *Rationalism in Politics,* pp. 248-300. London: Methuen & Co Ltd, 1962.
  Examines assorted interpretations of Hobbes and the contradictions that result.

Peters, Richard. *Hobbes*. 1956. Reprint. Westport, Conn.: Greenwood Press, 1979, 271 p.
  Critically acclaimed, comprehensive study by an important Hobbes scholar.

Pocock, J. G. A. "Time, History and Eschatology in the Thought of Thomas Hobbes." In his *Politics, Language and Time: Essays on Political Thought and History,* pp. 148-201. New York: Atheneum, 1973.
  Analyzes the apocalyptic in Hobbes's theology.

Robertson, George Croom. "The 'System' and 'Anti-Hobbes'." In *Hobbes*, pp. 75-159, 207-22. William Blackwood and Sons, 1886.
  Discusses Hobbes's notions of state and of the social contract, and offers an overview of the arguments of Hobbes's opponents.

Ross, Ralph, Herbert W. Schneider, and Theodore Waldman, eds. *Thomas Hobbes in His Time*. Minneapolis: University of Minnesota Press, 1974, 150 p.
  Collection of essays that includes a chronology and a bibliography of recent criticism.

Sommerville, Johann P. *Thomas Hobbes: Political Ideas in Historical Context*. New York: St. Martin's Press, 1992, 234 p.
  Examination of Hobbes's political views; includes chronology and an extensive bibliography.

Sorell, Tom. *Hobbes*. London: Routledge & Kegan Paul, 1986, 163 p.

  Emphasizes Hobbes's philosophy of science.

Spragens, Thomas A., Jr. *The Politics of Motion: The World of Thomas Hobbes*. Lexington: The University Press of Kentucky, 1973, 224 p.
  Considers what Hobbes borrowed from Aristotle, what he altered, and what he rejected.

Springborg, Patricia. "Hobbes, Heresy, and the *Historia Ecclesiastica*." *Journal of the History of Ideas* 55, No. 4 (October 1994): 553-71.
  Focuses on Hobbes's religious doctrines and his *Ecclesiastical History*.

Strauss, Leo. *The Political Philosophy of Hobbes: Its Basis and Its Genesis*. Translated by Elsa M. Sinclair. Oxford: Clarendon Press, 1936, 172 p.
  Seminal work in Hobbes studies. Strauss contends

that the basis for Hobbes's philosophy was not modern science.

Tuck, Richard. *Hobbes*. Oxford: Oxford University Press, 1989, 127 p.

Overview that also contains a survey of Hobbes's important critics.

Warrender, Howard. *The Political Philosophy of Hobbes: His Theory of Obligation*. Oxford: Clarendon Press, 1957, 346 p.

Controversial work that rejects the linking of Hobbes's philosophy with his political theories.

Watkins, J. W. N. *Hobbes's System of Ideas: A Study in the Political Significance of Philosophical Theories*. London: Hutchinson, 1973, 140 p.

Traces Hobbes's political theory to his philosophical ideas.

Nicollò Machiavelli

1469-1527

(Full name Niccolò di Bernardo Machiavelli.) Italian essayist, dramatist, historian, biographer, novella writer, and poet.

The following entry provides critical discussion of Machiavelli's writings on political theory. For additional information on Machiavelli's life and works, see *Literature Criticism from 1400 to 1800*, Volume 8.

INTRODUCTION

A Florentine statesman and political theorist, Machiavelli remains one of the most controversial figures of political history. Although his writings address a wide range of political and historical topics, he has come to be identified almost exclusively with his highly controversial manual of state *Il principe* (1532; *The Prince*). This straightforward, pragmatic treatise on political conduct and the application of power has, over the centuries, been variously hailed, denounced, and distorted to such an extent that Machiavelli's name has become synonymous with ruthless and unscrupulous political tactics. Seldom has a single work generated such divergent and fierce commentary from such a wide assortment of writers. Commenting on Machiavelli's colorful critical heritage, T. S. Eliot has remarked that "no great man has been so completely misunderstood."

Biographical Information

Machiavelli was born in Florence, in what is present-day Italy, to an established, though not particularly affluent, middle-class family whose members had traditionally filled responsible positions in local government. While little of the author's early life has been documented, it is known that as a boy he learned Latin and that he quickly became an assiduous reader of the classics. Among these, he highly prized his copy of Livy's history of the Roman Republic. Machiavelli's first recorded involvement in the volatile Florentine political scene occurred in 1498, when he joined the political faction that deposed Girolamo Savonarola, then the dominant religious and political figure in Florence. Machiavelli was subsequently appointed to the second chancery of the republic. As chancellor and secretary to the Ten of Liberty and Peace, a sensitive government agency dealing chiefly with warfare and foreign affairs, Machiavelli participated both in domestic politics and in diplomatic missions to foreign governments. These posts afforded him innumerable opportunities over the next fourteen years to closely examine the inner

workings of government and to meet prominent individuals, among them Cesare Borgia, who furnished the young diplomat with the major profile in leadership for *The Prince*. Machiavelli's political stature and influence increased quickly and by 1502 he was a well-respected assistant to the republican *gonfalonier,* or head of state, Piero Soderini. In 1512, however, the Florentine political climate changed abruptly when Spanish forces invaded Italy. The Medici—for centuries the rulers of Florence, but exiled since 1494—seized the opportunity to depose Soderini and replace the republican government with their own autocratic regime. Machiavelli was jailed and tortured for his well-known republican sentiments, and finally banished to his country residence in Percussina, where he spent his enforced retirement writing the small body of political writings that insured his literary immortality. Completed between 1513 and 1519, *Discorsi . . . sopra la prima deca di Tito Livio* (1531; *Discourses on Livy*) and *The Prince* were not published until after Machiavelli's death, though both works circulated in manuscript. Around 1518 he turned from discursive prose to drama. Like the author's other writings, *Comedia di Callimaco: E di Lucretia* (1518; *The Mandrake Root*) is firmly predicated on an astute, unsentimental awareness of human nature as flawed and given to self-centeredness. The play was popular with audiences throughout much of Italy for several years. His next effort, a military treatise entitled *Libro della arte della guerra* (1521; *The Art of War*), was the only historical or political work published during Machiavelli's lifetime. After several attempts to gain favor with the Medici (including dedicating *The Prince* to Lorenzo), Machiavelli was appointed official historian of Florence in 1520 and subsequently entrusted with minor governmental duties. His prodigious *Historie di Nicolo Machiavegli* (1532; *The History of Florence*) carefully dilutes his republican platform with the Medicean bias expected of him. In 1525 Pope Clement VII recognized his achievement with a monetary stipend. Two years later, the Medici were again ousted, and Machiavelli's hopes for advancement under the revived republic were frustrated, for the new government was suspicious of his ties to the Medici. Disheartened by his country's internal strife, Machiavelli fell gravely ill and died, his dream of an operational republic still unrealized.

Major Works

Commentators have found it ironic that the fiercely republican Machiavelli should have written a handbook advising an autocratic leader how best to acquire and maintain power and security. Machiavelli was acutely aware of foreign threats to Italian autonomy and thus deemed it necessary for a strong prince to thwart French and Spanish hegemony. Hence *The Prince,* addressed to the ruling Medici. Machiavelli believed that a shrewd head of state, exemplified by Borgia, was essential to sublimating self-interest to common welfare. Since handbooks of conduct meeting monarchal needs had become immensely popular by the 1400s, the external form of *The Prince* was neither startling nor particularly remarkable to Machiavelli's contemporaries. Yet, from its initial appearance, *The Prince* proved no mere manual of protocol nor, for that matter, of even conventional strategy. In its chapters, Machiavelli delineated a typology of sovereignties and the deployment of available forces—military, political, or psychological—necessary to acquire and retain them. Many of the ideas contained in *The Prince* were and continue to be quite shocking. For example, Machiavelli suggested that a prince should not categorically omit murder as an option if it serves his purposes; that a prince only needed to *appear* virtuous; and that a leader need only keep promises and alliances as long as these served the interests of the state. *The Prince* is the first political treatise to divorce statecraft from ethics. As Machiavelli wrote: "How one lives is so far removed from how one ought

to live that he who abandons what one does for what one ought to do, learns rather his own ruin than his preservation." Adding to his unflinching realism the common Renaissance belief in humanity's capacity for determining its own destiny, Machiavelli posited two fundamentals necessary for effective political leadership: *virtu* and *fortuna. Virtu* refers to the prince's own abilities (ideally a combination of force and cunning), and *fortuna* to the unpredictable influence of fortune, or luck. In a significant departure from previous political thought, the designs of God play no part in Machiavelli's scheme. On issues of leadership hitherto masked by other political theorists in vague diplomatic terms, Machiavelli presented his theses in a direct, candid, and often passionate manner, employing easily grasped metaphors and structuring the whole in an aphoristic that which lends it a compelling authority. For sheer volume and intensity, studies of *The Prince* have far exceeded those directed at Machiavelli's *Discourses,* though the latter work has been acknowledged an essential companion piece to the former. All of the author's subsequent studies treating history, political science, and military theory stem from this voluminous dissertation containing the most original thought of Machiavelli. Less flamboyant than *The Prince* and narrower in its margin for interpretation, the *Discourses* contains Machiavelli's undisguised admiration for ancient governmental forms, and his most eloquent, thoroughly explicated defense of freedom and republicanism, sentiments which would not have been popular among the many monarchical, absolutist rulers of the Renaissance period. Commentators have noted the presence of a gravity and skillful rhetoric that at times punctuate *The Prince* but are in full evidence only in that work's final chapter, constituting a memorable exhortation to the Medicis to resist foreign tyranny. The *Discourses* also presents that methodical extrapolation of political theory from historical documentation which is only intermittent in *The Prince.* Max Lerner has observed that, "if *The Prince* is great because it gives us the grammar of power for a government, *The Discourses* are great because they give us the philosophy of organic unity not in a government but in a state, and the conditions under which alone a culture can survive."

Critical Reception

Reaction to *The Prince* was initially—but only briefly—favorable; Catherine de Medici is said to have enthusiastically included it among other of Machiavelli's writings in the educational curriculum of her children. But within a short time the book fell into widespread disfavor, becoming viewed as a handbook for atheistic tyranny. *The Prince,* and Machiavelli's other writings as well, were placed in the Papal Index of Prohibited Books in 1559. Further denigrated toward the close of the sixteenth century in *Discours sur les moyens de bien gouverner et maintenir en paix un royause, ou autre principaute. Contre Nicolas Machiavel, florentin*, by Innocenzo Gentillet in France, *The Prince* was held responsible for French political corruption and for widespread contribution to any number of political and moral vices. Gentillet's interpretation of *The Prince* as advocating statecraft by ruthlessness and amoral duplicity was disseminated throughout Britain through the works of such popular, highly influential dramatists as William Shakespeare and Christopher Marlowe. In the Prologue to Marlowe's *The Jew of Malta* (1589?), "Machevil" addresses the audience at length, at one point encapsulating the Elizabethan perception of Machiavelli by saying, "I count religion but a childish toy, / And hold there is no sin but ignorance." Here and in the works of Marlowe's contemporaries, Machiavelli was depicted as an agent of all that Protestant England despised in Catholic, High-Renaissance Italy. Hostile English interpreters so effectively typified Machiavelli as an amalgam of various evils, which they described with the still-used term "Machiavellian," that fact and fabrication still mingle today. Rarely, until the nineteenth century, did mention of *The Prince* elicit anyting other than unfounded and largely unexamined repugnance, much less encourage objective scrutiny of its actual issues. As Fredi Chiappelli has aptly summarized: "Centuries had to elapse before the distinction between moral moment and political moment, between technical approach and moralistic generalities, and even between the subject matter of the book and the author's person were finally achieved." Modern critics, noting these crucial distinctions, have engaged in a prolonged and animated discussion concerning Machiavelli's intent in *The Prince*. A seventeenth-century commentator, philosopher Pierre Bayle, found it "strange" that "there are so many people, who believe, that Machiavel teaches princes dangerous politics; for on the contrary princes have taught Machiavel what he has written." Since Bayle's time, further analysis has prompted prolonged and animated discussion relating to Machiavelli's purpose in writing the work. Was the treatise, as Bayle suggested, a faithful representation of princely conduct which might justifiably incriminate its subjects but not its chronicler? Or had Machiavelli, in his manner of presentation, devised the volume as a vehicle for his own commentary? A single conclusion concerning the author's motive has not been drawn, though patterns of conjecture have certainly appeared within Machiavelli's critical heritage. Lord Macaulay, in emphasizing the writer's republican zeal and those privations he suffered in its behalf, has contended that it is "inconceivable that the martyr of freedom should have designedly acted as the apostle of tyranny," and that "the peculiar immorality which has rendered *The Prince* unpopular . . . belonged rather to the age than to the man." Others have echoed this suggestion, examining the work in its historical context. Many have urged that Machiavelli intended the treatise as a veiled satiric

attack on the methods of Italian tyranny or, by abstruse methods, its converse—a paean to patriotism and sensible government, grounded in a clear-sighted knowledge of the corrupt human condition. While ultimately unable to agree on the underlying purpose of *The Prince*, nearly all critics have nonetheless been persuaded of its masterful composition, even when unwilling to endorse its precepts. Macaulay has affirmed that the "judicious and candid mind of Machiavelli shows itself in his luminous, manly, and polished language." And Francesco De Sanctis has determined that "where he was quite unconscious of form, he was a master of form. Without looking for Italian prose he found it." A decided influence on the philosophies of Thomas Hobbes and Sir Francis Bacon and on the thought of such modern political theorists as Vilfredo Pareto, Gaetano Mosca, Georges Sorel, and Robert Michels, Machiavelli has been called the founder of empirical political science, primarily on the strength of the *Discourses* and *The Prince*. Taken in historical perspective, it is understandable that *The Prince* should have dwarfed Machiavelli's other works. For with this slim treatise the author confronted the ramifications of power when its procurement and exercise were notably peremptory—not only in his own country but throughout Europe as well. Commentators have come to weigh the integrity of Machiavelli's controversial thought against the pressing political conditions which formed it. Some, like Roberto Ridolfi, have endeavored through their studies to dislodge the long-standing perception of Machiavelli as a ruthless character: "In judging Machiavelli one must . . . take account of his anguished despair of virtue and his tragic sense of evil. . . . [On] the basis of sentences taken out of context and of outward appearances he was judged a cold and cynical man, a sneerer at religion and virtue; but in fact there is hardly a page of his writing and certainly no action of life that does not show him to be passionate, generous, ardent and basically religious."

PRINCIPAL WORKS

Comedia di Callimaco: E di Lucretia [*The Mandrake Root*] (drama) c. 1518

Libro della arte della guerra [*The Art of War*] (essay) 1521

La clizia [*Clizia*] (drama) 1525

*Discorsi di Nicolo Machiavelli ... sopra la prima deca di Tito Livio, a Zanobi Buondelmonte, et a Cosimo Rucellai [*Discourses on Livy*] (essay) 1531

†*Historie di Nicolo Machiavegli* [*The History of Florence*] (history) 1532

‡*Il principe di Niccholo Machivello* [*The Prince*] (essay) 1532

§*La vita di Castruccio Castracani da Lucca ... Il modo che tenne il Duca Valentino per ammazar Vitellozo, Oliverotto da Fermo il S. Paolo et il Duca di Gravi-*

ni Orsini in Senigaglia [*The Life of Castruccio Castracani of Lucca* and *The Meanes Duke Valentine Us'd to Put to Death Vitellozzo Vitelli, Oliverotto of Fermo, Paul, and the Duke of Gravina*] (biography and essay) 1532

Favola: Belfagor arcidiavolo che prese moglie [*A Fable: Belfagor, the Devil Who Took a Wife*] (novella) 1559

The Literary Works of Machiavelli (drama, poetry, and novella) 1961

Machiavelli: The Chief Works and Others. 3 vols. (essays, history, dramas, biography, and prose) 1965

---

*This work was written between 1513 and 1519.

†This work is also known as *Istorie Fiorentine.*

‡This work was written in 1513 and circulated in manuscript before being published.

§*La vita di Castruccio Castracani . . .* and *Il modo che tenne il Duca Valentino . . .* were appended to and originally appeared in print with the first edition of *The Prince.*

CRITICISM

M. D. Petre (essay date 1917)

SOURCE: "Machiavelli and Modern Statecraft," in *The Edinburgh Review*, Vol. 226, No. 461, July, 1917, pp. 93-112.

[*Below, Petre presents an overview of the main characteristics of Machiavelli's thoughts on dipolmacy and government as exhibited in* The Prince.]

The work by which Nicholas Machiavelli is best known is *Il Principe*: a treatise popularly regarded as the standard manual of unscrupulous diplomacy. The word Machiavellism, like its counterpart Jesuitism, is a current term with a definite meaning: the former may be employed by an admirer of Machiavelli, as the latter by a lover of the Jesuits. It signifies a philosophy of pure expediency; the subordination of every moral and human consideration to the political needs of the hour.

The Prince is a work as characteristic of its author as any of the others; though we may add that it will be best understood by those to whom it is not the only one with which they are acquainted. Some students of Machiavelli have, indeed, tried to place this book in a special category: they have regarded it as ironical; or as a description of the vices of princely rulers cast into the illusory form of a treatise for their guidance; or even as just a time-serving effort to enter into grace with the Medicis, when thus alone its author could hope to obtain public employment.

This last motive may, indeed, have had something to do

with the actual form of the work; but as for the other interpretations they are surely uncalled for. If ever a writer was clear and consistent and characteristic throughout his works, it is Machiavelli; we may not always like his meaning, but we can never mistake it. Some of the most unscrupulous passages from *The Prince* could be set beside others from the *Discourses on Livy* though the first is on tyrannical and the second on popular government. Thus in chap. xviii. of *The Prince* having given reasons why a prince cannot always keep his word, Machiavelli concludes that a prudent ruler 'neither can nor ought to keep faith when to do so would be to his disadvantage, and when the motives for which he made his promise are no longer existent.'

But in the *Discourses on Livy* Machiavelli applies the same principle of expediency to the conduct of the loyal citizen:

'No sensible person will reproach anyone for however extraordinary an action that is directed to the well-ordering of a kingdom or the founding of a republic.'

And in another place: 'When the salvation of our country is at stake all questions of justice and injustice, of mercy and cruelty, of honour and dishonour must be set aside; every other consideration must be subordinated to the one aim of saving her life and preserving her honour.'

We need not multiply examples. The consensus of opinion is that, whatever else he also was, Nicholas Machiavelli was Machiavellian: as Machiavellian as Bismarck; as Machiavellian as the German General Staff; as Machiavellian as the rest of us, and the best of us, in the realm of diplomacy, unconsciously or protestingly, are to some extent bound to be.

Machiavelli was a diplomat: a statesman in so far as his position permitted of it; and, in all his strivings, a state-builder. He was in love with ancient Rome, with all her works, and all her pomps; with her wisdom and her perfidy; her magnanimity and her ruthlessness. He studied, with passion and admiration, the story of her political evolution; of the emergence of a self-governing people from the warfare of conflicting sects. He held that men changed but little in the course of history, and that what had been done could be done again. He dreamed of a modern Florence fashioned according to the lessons of Livy: a free, strong, democratic and austere republic. But with Latin sincerity he set forth his doctrine of ways and means, and in that doctrine is the philosophy of Machiavellism, though, as we shall see, there is also something besides.

But once again, just because he was a thorough Latin, his subject interested him for its own sake, apart from its practical bearings. Thus in dealing with the question of tyrannical government, even had there been no living tyrants with whom he had to reckon, the subject would have interested him for its own sake, and he would have set forth the rules that should guide the conduct of a prince, who aimed at despotic power for purely selfish ends, just as calmly and fully as though he were advocating tyranny as his own ideal.

To the ordinary English mind this moral detachment is perplexing and misleading, like much else in the Latin temperament. The Englishman is more truthful than the Latin, but he is not so great a lover of truth. The Latin thinks it and speaks it as his intellect moves him to do, the Englishman speaks it because he holds that he ought to do so; his moral life is more vigorous, his intellectual life is not so keen. Hence the quiet indifference with which a Latin will declare certain actions—to have been admirably fitted to the attainment of their own end, without uttering or implying further comment: the manner, for instance, in which Machiavelli describes the clever trapping and murdering of his enemies, Vitellozzo Vitelli and three others, by the Duke of Valentinois, will confuse the Anglo-Saxon, but not the Latin, to whom it is the fact, and not its moral bearings, that presents the main intellectual interest.

But even with this proviso Machiavellism remains a distinct code of action, of ethical as well as intellectual import: a statement of politics and diplomacy not originated by its namesake, but by him put into work and system. Therefore, the first thing we want to understand in Machiavelli is his Machiavellism, and its relation to modern statecraft; only then can we see whether, and how far, Machiavelli is greater than Machiavellism, just as we can also, by a frank estimate of our own Machiavellism, best appreciate how far our own policy is set towards higher ends.

One of the first and most fundamental characteristics of Machiavellism is its estimate of human nature. The majority of men are mean, cowardly, and self-interested; this is the primary fact with which the statesman has to deal. He may start with another view if he likes, but he does it at his own risk and that of his country.

> It may be said of men in general [he writes in **The Prince**] that they are ungrateful, plausible, deceitful, cowardly, and avaricious; so long as you benefit them they are yours—they offer you their blood, their possessions, their life, their children, while danger is distant; but when it comes too near, they turn. And then the Prince, who has made no other provision than his trust in them, is ruined.' (Ch. xvii.)

There are two ways of dealing with men, he tells us in the next chapter: by law and by force. Law is properly for men, and force for beasts; but since human beings are in part beasts, the prince must be fox and lion as well as man. It is a fine thing to keep faith, but only

with those who are correspondingly loyal. Mutual distrust is a primary principle of sound diplomacy.

The next guiding principle of Machiavellism is the avoidance of half measures. 'He who would be a tyrant, but slays not Brutus, and he who would free his country, but slays not the sons of Brutus, is doomed to failure.' (Discorsi, Bk. III. ch. iii.)

Nor is it enough to kill some of the children of Brutus and leave others; all must go. Machiavelli often refers to the downfall of his friend Piero Soderini, one time Gonfaloniere of Florence, as the consequence of an admixture of human with political motives; while the Duke of Valentinois (Cesare Borgia) was, even from the humanitarian standpoint, more successful, in virtue of his swift and ruthless action.

Krieg ist Krieg; for Machiavellism there is no other conception of war. For war is, indeed, the supreme occasion in which it is man as beast, and not man as man, with whom we are dealing. Law, as Machiavelli has already stated, is for man; force is for the brute. If, between ruler and people, occasions arise on which the bestial and not the human element is to be taken into count, how much more is this the case when it is with avowed enemies that we have to deal. We have yet to see if, in the philosophy of Machiavelli, there be any hint of pacifist tendencies; but in war itself he allows no place for half-measures. For him peace was peace, and war was war:

'You cannot call it peace,' he says, 'when States are continually falling on one another with armies; nor can you call it war when men are not killed, cities are not ravaged, governments are not destroyed.' And he adds regretfully that war at one time became so decadent, 'that it was undertaken without fear, waged without danger, and concluded without loss.' (Istorie Florentine, Bk. V.)

To be thorough, and also to be fearless and to be swift: this is Machiavellian wisdom. The *Pecca fortiter* of Luther, which has been so wholeheartedly adopted as a German motto, is in perfect consonance with this principle of moral fearlessness. Machiavelli relates, with pity and contempt, how Giovampagolo Baglioni, having the opportunity of murdering Pope Julius II. and a number of his cardinals through the rashness of the former, failed to take advantage of it. Machiavelli would not have blamed him had he been a good man, deterred from the crime by conscientious motives. But, as he explains:

> It was not his goodness nor his conscience that restrained him; there was no room for considerations

of duty in the breast of a wicked man who lived with his own sister, and had murdered his cousins and nephews in order to reign; but the fact is that few men are capable of being honestly bad or perfectly good, and, when a bad deed demands a certain measure of greatness and generosity, they are incapable of it (Discorsi, Bk. I. ch. xxvii.).

Machiavelli implies, in this chapter, that Julius II. proved himself in every sense the greater, and the stronger, and even the better man, by daring his lesser adversary to commit a crime whose greatness appalled him, though its actual wickedness would have counted but little. Baglioni desired the end, but he shrank from the means; and no greater sin can be committed against the principles of Machiavellism.

Yet this same doctrine of the means to the end as consistently reprobates useless daring as it commends that which can be successful. No vain sacrifices, in the name of courage and honour, can find place in Machiavellian policy. To die for your country—yes, a hundred times if need be—but only provided your death truly saves her. A military expedition, however desperate and daring, when necessity demands it, and when there is some hope of success; but no sheer waste for however honourable a cause. The good of the country is the supreme end; 'whether by glory or by humiliation she is to be served and saved.' (Discorsi, Bk. III. ch. xii.)

It is in this chapter that he refers to the advice given by Lentulus to the Roman Army trapped within the Caudine Forks; surrender might be ignoble, and those who advocated it might be accused later on of regard for their own skins, but in this way alone could Rome be saved. A good end, according to Machiavellism, may justify questionable means; but the best of ends cannot justify hopeless and inadequate measures.

Machiavellism manifests that kind of respect for religion which we have seen advocated in recent years by a modern French school. 'Princes and republics that would preserve their State from corruption must, above all things, maintain the ceremonies of religion incorrupt, and treat them with veneration; for there is no more emphatic sign of the ruin of a province than the contempt of divine worship.' (Discorsi, Bk. I. ch. xii.)

And the next chapter is entitled: 'How the Romans made use of religion for the good order of the city, for the success of their enterprises and the suppression of tumults.'

But, at the same time, the character of the Christian religion may prove dangerous to the State, for whereas in Pagan religions the brute element of man had its share, in the Christian religion the human and the divine elements are supreme:

They [i.e. ancient religions] lacked neither pomp nor magnificence of ritual, but to these was added the practice of bloody and ferocious sacrifices, in which multitudes of animals destroyed one another; which awful sight inspired similar sentiments in the beholders. Also ancient religions only beatified men full of worldly glory—such as military captains and political leaders. Our religion has glorified the humble and contemplative rather than the energetic. It has placed the highest good in humility, abjection, and the contempt of human things; while pagan religion aimed at greatness of soul, strength of body, and everything that contributed to velour. And though our religion would have us strong, yet it asks of us rather to suffer than to act as though we were strong. This manner of life appears therefore to have weakened the world and left it the prey of wicked men, who can easily control their fellow beings, seeing that the majority of the latter, for the sake of Paradise, are more ready to support illtreatment than to revenge themselves. (Discorsi, Bk. II. ch. ii.).

SS. Francis and Dominic, who, in the view of Machiavelli, saved Christianity from utter extinction, by reanimating its early fervour, also, incidentally, encouraged the vices of prelates; for they taught the people 'that it is evil to speak evil of the bad, and that it is better to live in obedience, and 'leave the punishment of wicked superiors to God; as a result of which doctrine these latter have done the worst they could, since they had no dread of a punishment they neither saw nor believed in.' It may be remarked, in passing, that the contemporary Pope and prelates, who allowed the writer of this passage to go by unchastised, must, in spite of the vices of their day, have exercised a tolerance of which our own age does not always show examples.

Yet Machiavelli will not allow that this is the last word in the matter. He was a cynical Churchman, but a believing Christian; and he goes on to say, after the former of these two passages:

Though it would therefore appear as though the world were effeminate and heaven disarmed, this result arises, in reality, from the meanness of men, who have been influenced by sloth, and not by virtue, in their interpretation of religious teaching. For if they remembered how our religion permits us to glorify and defend our country they would see that she expects us to love and honour it, and make ourselves such that we are able to defend it.' (Discorsi, Bk. II. ch. ii.).

As Machiavellism distrusts men in general, so also it contains special warnings against the danger to the State of over-powerful individuals. On this point Machiavelli treats princes and republics to the same advice: not because he esteems them equally, but because their case and its dangers are the same. Men are out for their own ends, and the individual is out for individual ends:

this is the teaching of Machiavellism, then as now. Hence king and republic must jealously watch their own best servants, and must put an end to them, whatever their claims to gratitude, if they are taking advantage of their credit for the satisfaction of their private ambition.

There is, in one case he introduces, a curious similarity to one of recent occurrence in our own country. The Florentines had made the mistake of sending two envoys to treat with France of the restitution of Pisa. Giovambattista Ridulfi was the better known man, and consequently the chief; Antonio degli Albizi was the more really capable. But this second, seeing that the other overshadowed him, took refuge in silence, and did nothing for the good of the mission. As Machiavelli remarks, he gratified his vanity and ambition not by opposition, but by silence and disdain; and only exerted his superior powers when the other man was withdrawn.

Machiavelli, as was natural in those days of mercenary armies, was particularly alive to the danger accruing to a ruler from a successful general. It is painful to kill the man who has led his armies to victory; it is happier for him if the same should die in a natural manner; but, on the whole, there is but one way of avoiding the dilemma, and that is for the prince to lead his expeditions himself. We shall see, later on, in what way a republic was to avoid the same danger.

We are reminded once more of things that have taken place in a neighbouring country when Machiavelli warns statesmen of the need of suspecting even pious and charitable works, which may contribute to the excessive power of those who direct them.

Last among the main principles of Machiavellism which we will select for its better definition, may be placed its deep sense and acknowledgment of Fate; of the restriction of human power by the great *Hinterland* of uncontrollable forces and circumstances. Fate, or Fortune, as Machiavelli calls it, limits the attainable and narrows the domain of conscience and ethics. In by no means the best of worlds neither can a man always do his best. The *ought* and the *must* are to be measured by the *can*. Men may 'follow fortune, but not oppose her; they can weave her webs, but not break them.' It is the fool, and not the wise man, who, ignoring 'the just bounds of hope, and looking not to what can be done, but to what he would wish to do, is brought to ruin.'

Machiavelli's description of the ever recurring round of good and evil in human life almost suggests the 'Ewige Wiederkehr' of Nietzsche.

> Nature [he says] allows not of rest. So soon as earthly things have attained perfection they begin to sink, because they can rise no further; and when, through disorder, they have fallen as low as they can, not

being able to descend further, they begin again to rise and thus they swing perpetually from good to bad and from bad to good. For virtue begets tranquillity, tranquillity sloth, sloth disorder, and disorder ruin; and similarly, from ruin springs order, from order virtue. and from virtue happiness and glory. (Istorie Fiorentine, Bk. V.)

So much for some of the main principles of Machiavellism. It is hard to resist the temptation of giving much fuller quotations from the mass of shrewd wisdom, truly Italian wisdom, which the works contain. In the more intellectual days of English life, when the young man with pretensions to a good education made his tour of Europe, the works of French and Italian wisdom were more familiar to our country than they now are. The keen Latin intellect had its share in moulding the richer Anglo-Saxon mind and clarifying its power of utterance. We are more left to our own intellectual resources in these days, though we are now looking forward to better times, of fuller intellectual community.

And now we have to see whether Machiavelli can teach us anything besides Machiavellism. That he systematised the policy that bears his name is undoubted; but that his philosophy also contains principles that morally and spiritually transcend it, will be, I think, to any careful student of his works, equally positive. And for those who believe that nearly all statecraft yet contains its admixture of Machiavellism, this will be a question of high interest; for what we shall want to know is whether an unavoidable blend of Machiavellism precludes, in any State philosophy, the hope of eventual development into a more human system from which such elements may be finally eliminated.

'In what,' asks Cosimo Rucellai of Fabrizio Colonna, 'would you have us copy the ancients?'

Fabrizio replies that he would have the modern State 'honour and reward virtue; not despise poverty; respect the methods and laws of military discipline; compel citizens to love one another, to avoid factions, and to set the public above the private good.'

The speaker goes on to maintain that such ideals are not mere dreams, but have only to be rightly set forth in order to be accepted. 'Their truth,' he says, 'is so evident that the most ordinary intelligence can perceive it. And to labour for such an end is to plant trees under which mankind could rest with greater peace and joy than the present state of things can afford.' (Arte della Guerra, Bk. I.)

In the same work, speaking of that very Cosimo, Machiavelli says of him, as the highest praise he could bestow: 'I know not what thing that belonged to him, not even excepting his own soul, he would have refused to his friends; I know not what enterprise would have daunted him if he had seen in it some good to be achieved for his country.'

The statesman that planned for his city such an ideal of well-being, and planned it even while composing a treatise on war, aimed at something more than mere Machiavellian prosperity. This man, diving amidst that turmoil to which one of the fairest and most intellectual lands of Europe had been reduced by the quarrels of her neighbours, and the rival ambitions of Pope and Emperor, kings and small princes, cast a yearning glance back through history to the days of Roman greatness and liberty. Not even an American president, in these democratic days, can be more convinced that the greatest menace to 'peace and freedom lies in the existence of autocratic governments, backed by organised force which is 'controlled wholly by their will and not by the will of the people,' than Machiavelli, who believed that in freedom alone could political salvation be found. A republic was, for him, the highest form of government; but his was too unprejudiced a mind not to see that liberty has been consistent also with the well-constituted government of a monarch. And this was to him a truth of considerable moment; for his aim was practical and immediate, not abstract and remote: he wanted the good of his own beloved Florence; and if he could not have it, in the best way, by means of a republic, he would have it in the second best way, by forming good rulers. He distinctly sets forth in one place (Discorsi, Bk. I. ch. ix.) his belief that, for certain crises of growth or transformation, the' government of one man is best; though for the continuance of the State the republican form is alone satisfactory.

In one of his most eloquent passages he invites reigning princes to look back on the days of Nerva and Marcus Aurelius, to compare them with those that went before and those that came after, and to ask themselves in which time they would have chosen to live and reign. In those days of good rulers you may see

> a prince secure amidst a secure people, a world filled with justice and peace. You will behold the Senate established in authority and magistrates in honour. The rich there enjoy their own riches; virtue and nobility are exalted; peace and goodness prevail; rancour, licence, corruption and ambition are extinguished. Those were the golden times in which each one could hold and defend his own opinion. Then did the world triumph, for the prince was full of reverence and glory, the people of love and confidence. Glance, then, at the state of things under the other emperors, and you shall see terrible wars, discords and seditions; cruelty in peace and in war; princes slain by the sword, civil dissensions, foreign wars; a sorrowful Italy torn by misfortune, with her cities ravaged and ruined. You shall see Rome burnt, the Capitol destroyed by the citizens, the ancient temples desolate, their ceremonies neglected, the town filled with adulterers, the sea covered with exiles, her rocks stained with blood. . . . You shall

> see informers rewarded, slaves seduced against their masters, servants against their patron while those who have no enemies are persecuted by their friends. Then you will know what Rome, Italy, and the world owed to Caesar. . . . Indeed, if a prince seek worldly glory he should desire to rule a corrupt city: not to spoil it like Caesar, but to re-order it like Romulus.
> (*Discorsi*, Bk. I. ch. x.)

And later on: 'The true salvation of a republic or a kingdom is not to have a prince who rules it wisely in his lifetime, but one who orders it in such manner that it goes on well after his death.'

But such princes are rare, and, in the opinion of Machiavelli, the hereditary principle is fatal to the chances of finding them. 'That the sins of the people are caused by their princes,' is the title of one chapter of the *Discorsi*, in which he goes on to warn princes that they have no right to complain of the faults of their people, which arise from their own negligence or from similar faults in themselves. In another chapter he tells us that the people are wiser and more constant than princes; in the following one that republics keep faith better than kings.

Thus Machiavelli would have endorsed a recent utterance, according to which 'a steadfast concert for peace can never be maintained except by the partnership of democratic nations. No autocratic government could be trusted to keep faith within it or observe its covenants.'

In chapter xviii. of *The Prince* his very counsels lightly cloak his intimate conviction that the government of one man is too unavoidably selfish to be really clean and honourable. That it is praiseworthy in a prince to keep faith and practice honesty rather than fraud is obvious. Nevertheless, we see by the experience of our own day that those princes have done best who made light of their promises.'

Elsewhere he describes the misery that a prince is forced to inflict upon the State over which he would tyrannise. He must change everything, upset all peace and happiness; behave not only as an enemy of Christ but as the foe of mankind. 'It were surely better,' he adds, 'to live as a private citizen, than to rule at the cost of so much human misery;' but there is no middle course. The despot must renounce his ambition or take the necessary means to its fulfillment. Machiavelli hated tyrants; but he more than hated—he despised—the man who tried to satisfy his conscience as well as his greed: an attempt that ended in greater misery to others as well as personal failure. Rather would he follow such a man as the Duke of Valentinois than a pious tyrant. Knowing too well the selfishness of man to suggest to the Medicis, at a certain crisis in Florentine affairs, that they should actually free the city, he submitted to Leo X. a scheme that would, he hoped, satisfy both objects.

They were to prepare the State, during their lifetime, for the exercise of republican freedom, into which it was to enter at their death. But the scheme was, of course, too noble for their moral reach.

As to the individual citizen, he would, in the ideal State, enjoy freedom and happiness, but it would be at the price of loyal and devoted citizenship.

Machiavelli speaks little of the rights and much of the duties of citizens in a free State: their glory is in the service they can render and not in the power they can exercise. It was not of his age to lay stress on the claims of the individual: it is not, perhaps, of any age with strong idealistic tendencies. Freedom for him was of a corporate and not a private character; and the main privilege of free citizenship was co-operation to the good of the State. He lauds the great Roman dictator generals, who faced danger in the moment of national emergency, and, after their hour of glory, returned to their little farms. 'Restored to private life, they became frugal, humble, careful administrators of their modest possessions, obedient to the magistrates, reverent to their betters; it was indeed a marvel to see one man capable of sustaining two such different lives.'

A story is told of General Joffre that is not unworthy of this passage. When after the battle of the Marne, some one said to him 'General, you have gained a great victory!' his reply was 'I hope that I have gained the right to return to my country farm.'

To maintain this character of true citizenship Machiavelli regarded poverty as essential. The austere ideal of Roman republicanism was ever before him. And as the true citizen was to serve, but not for reward, so he was 'to forget private injuries for the love of his country.'

In Machiavelli's days the notion of a 'concert of peace' would have been an anachronism. Furthermore, in the actual waging of war Machiavelli is thoroughly Machiavellian. For him, indeed, war was war, and he would not have attached much importance to the greater or less ferocity with which it was carried on. Yet he was, even in those savage days, no militarist; and if he could not advocate universal peace yet he dealt a solid blow at the idea of war for war's sake by his endeavour to substitute a national for a foreign and mercenary army. This was a really remarkable effort at that time. Europe was ploughed up by a professional and mercenary soldiery, as deadly, in the end, to those who employed them as to those against whom they were led. Owing to the hopelessness of his circumstances Machiavelli's attempt was unsuccessful, but it was a noble failure.

Not only did he aim at the formation of a national army, but he would have had it constituted on territorial lines: the soldiers were to be well acquainted with one another and with their leaders; for only amongst those who have been born and have lived in the same place does there exist that confidence which makes for success.

Though he wrote a treatise on *The Art of War* yet he opens it with a protest against regarding war as an art; for it is by so doing that war becomes prized for its own sake, and creates the demand for a professional soldiery. Professional soldiers, he says, 'are scandalous, idle, undisciplined, irreligious, fugitives from paternal rule, blasphemers, gamblers, badly educated, . . . which characteristics are the very opposite of what is needed for a strong and efficient army.' And to those who feared an armed people his advice was to govern them well, and then there would be nothing to apprehend.

Though war admits of fraud, yet such fraud must only be practiced 'against those who do not trust you '; to break faith with those who believe in you may indeed be profitable, but it is inglorious.

Also there is such a thing as magnanimity in victory. Like the old Roman leader, the general must be too proud to take advantage when the enemy is at his feet. He cites from Livy the words put in the mouth of Scipio, who granted to Antiochus, after a further defeat, the very terms he had previously refused; for 'Romani, si vincuntur, non minuuntur animis, nec si vincunt insolescere solent.'

In religion he was cynical, as those must have been who saw their country ruined by the ambition of the Church. And yet the sum of his charge, in one remarkable chapter, is not that the Church has directly ruined the State, but that her ambition has ruined religion, and thereby, indirectly, weakened and corrupted the State.

He speaks first of the piety and reverence of ancient Rome; of the strictness with which she upheld all religious laws and ceremonies. Had the Christian Church protected religious observance in the same way—

> Christian republics would be happier and more united than they are. Nor can we better gauge the decline of religion than by seeing how those countries that are nearest to the Roman Church, the head of our religion, are the least religious. . . .
>
> And whereas some maintain that the good of Italy depends on the Roman Church, I will refute this view by the arguments that occur to me.
>
> The first is that, through the evil example of that Court, this country has lost all her piety and religion, which is the cause of immense inconveniences and disorders. . . . So that the first obligation we Italians owe the Church and her priests is to have become through them irreligious and bad; but there is yet another and a greater one, the true cause of our ruin—that is, that the Church has kept, and still keeps, our country in a state of division. . . . Not

being powerful enough to hold Italy herself, nor allowing any other power to hold her, the country has not been able to come under one rule. . . .

This is what we Italians owe to the Church, and to no one else. And if any would prove the matter, and were strong enough to send the Roman Court to dwell in Switzerland, with the same power that it possesses in Italy, they would soon see how in that land, where at present the people live, both in religious and military matters, most like the ancients, there would result greater disorders from the evil customs of that Court than could arise from any other cause. (Discorsi Bk. I. ch. xii.)

In sum, the ideal State of Machiavelli was one in which the people should be self-governing, but should sacrifice private aims to the welfare of their country; one in which property should be protected, but in which the citizens should be poor and austere. The highest privilege of their freedom would be the right to serve their country while co-operating in her government. They should be fully equipped for her defence, but should defend her themselves at the cost of their own peace and comfort, with no mercenary army to suggest war for its own sake or for purely ambitious ends. Yet in his Machiavellism its author faces the un-ideal state of things that actually existed: he takes count of the selfishness of mankind; and gives precepts as to how, given the psychological and physiological facts of human nature, the bark of the State is to be steered with safety and success.

Thus do we find in Machiavelli, first of all Machiavellism in the most cold-blooded and inhuman sense of the word; but afterwards the germ and promise of a state-craft inspired by more human and spiritual ideals. To Machiavelli the former was a necessary constituent of the latter, and in his highest flights of idealism he would not have denied those maxims of selfish, worldly wisdom, simply because to have done so would have been, for him, not to deny an immoral principle, but to deny a non-moral fact.

Actually, is not all state-craft even yet in the same predicament? Can statesmen, of whatever country, safely and patriotically act on the assumption that men in general are good and unselfish and disinterested? Can a diplomatist successfully eschew all vulpine wisdom? Can a general restrain, in himself or his soldiers, all that savours of the ferocity of the lion? Can war be waged without fraud and violence or without the sacrifice of the innocent and helpless? Must a government put blind trust in even the best of its own citizens? Must not the most gentlemanly of our politicians sacrifice, at times, their own high code to the exigencies of diplomacy? Do not half-measures prove as fatal now as they did in the days of Machiavelli? Is not a disregard for unpleasant and immoral facts as disastrous as ever in its

results? Is not ruthlessness, now as then, sometimes more merciful in its results than a half-hearted severity? To sum up these questions in one, Can or does any State, even in our more civilised days, behave in its corporate capacity as a man of perfectly noble character can behave in his individual capacity? Can it exercise meekness, altruism, brotherly love in its dealings with neighbouring States, or even with its own citizens? Can a State behave like a perfect Christian or even like a perfect gentleman?

We know quite well what is the only truthful answer to such a question, but what we are persistently unwilling to admit is that, in so far as state-craft precludes the acceptance of an unreservedly human and a wholly Christian[1] ideal, so far also does it necessitate an admixture of Machiavellian principles and practice.

That another political attitude is possible and imperative is the claim of Christian idealists, first among whom may be named Tolstoi, who has followers, nowadays, amongst the genuine conscientious objectors.[2] To this school the human ideal so entirely transcends all claims of mere patriotism that they would ask of their country, as they would ask of an individual, the sacrifice of life for so noble a cause. The early Christians were, in the opinion of Roman politicians, a danger to the State from their contempt of the State religion. Therefore the State endeavoured to exterminate them, as it would now exterminate those who prize their own moral judgments above their duties of citizenship. The early Christians proved that men could be good citizens, and even good soldiers, without belief in the Pagan religion of the State; but the misgivings of their rulers were justifiable, for indeed Rome, without her religion, was bound to become, at last, another Rome. Christianity was an enemy to the Pagan State.

So, too, is the full spirit of Christianity hostile to the modern State, and the Tolstoyan, or genuine conscientious objector, is a proof of the fact. The State cannot do with him, for the State is not wholly Christian; it has as much right to persecute him as he has a right to maintain his own principles at the cost of his life as a citizen.

Yet the conscientious objector, or the unqualified pacifist, is probably not the one who does best for the promotion of his own ideals. Good is not worked in isolation, and there are truer forms of humanism, humbler forms of Christianity, more hopeful forms of pacifism, which do not wholly deny the fact and the duties of citizenship; which accept the moral resulting obligations of having drawn life and education and nurture from a certain country; and which therefore admit of the corresponding necessity to share the moral inadequacies, even the sins of that country.
'Justum est bellum quibus necessarium, et pie arma

quibus nisi in armis nulla spes est.' Such pacifism will not allow of abstention in the hour of our country's need; though it will unrestingly endeavour to transform the politics of the world in accordance with its ideal.

But, on the other hand, I would urge that pacifists, whether of the former or of the latter category, are consistent: just as those who admit that the prevailing state-craft inevitably contains certain non-Christian and non-human elements are consistent. But those, on the contrary, who would maintain that state-craft can admit of diplomacy, in the classical sense, without any admixture of Machiavellism, or of warfare that can be termed Christian, are not consistent nor sincere; and they justify the position of the unqualified pacifist, as those do not who confess that the best of us are yet far from the attainment of a purely human and Christian ideal in politics. To deny Machiavellism is to deny facts.

But as in the philosophy of Machiavelli, so in modern statecraft, the question is not, does it actually and always set forth a wide and human and disinterested policy? but does it admit of it? The philosophy of Machiavelli did—the philosophy of his Machiavellian disciple Bismarck did not; for the former aimed at the formation of a free, self-contained State, with an army for defensive purposes, and citizens whose pride it would be to govern and to serve; while the latter set himself to constitute a powerful autocratic government, strong for purposes of world-dominion.

Even the Mid-Europe policy, as set forth by Friedrich Naumann, which is not indeed wholly and heartlessly Machiavellian, is yet exclusive of any widely human policy. Not a great wall, but a great ditch, is to include the German State of the future, and all its dependent States, and to exclude the rest of the world from a share in German wealth and power.

The ideal citizen of Naumann is, indeed, to live for the State, but not as the austere and disinterested citizen of Machiavelli, who has his ever active share in the shaping of her destiny. For Naumann's citizen it is a question of commercial success: 'For the sake of personal interest he becomes a member of an impersonal institution and works for it as for himself. . . . Individualism is fully developed, but it is then carried up into the next higher form of economic co-operative existence.'

The State, on the other hand, uses individuals for her purpose, as those same individuals seek their purpose in her. 'For it is only by means of healthier, better educated, and better nourished masses that the military, financial, and civilised Mid-Europe of which we dream can come into existence.'

Mr. Bertrand Russell, in 'Principles of Social Reconstruction,' has divided the impulses of political life into two groups: 'the possessive and the creative, according as they aim at acquiring or retaining something that cannot be shared, or at bringing into the world some valuable thing—such as knowledge, or art, or goodwill—in which there is no private property.'

'Ecco chi crescera i nostri amori,' said Machiavelli's great countryman, in describing that love which knows not envy nor rivalry. To act as though such love could be the law of political life, before its sun has risen above our horizon, is the dangerous mistake of the idealist without a sense of facts. But this same idealist would be less excusable if our State philosophers had the candour to confess the Machiavellism they cannot avoid. Then would they be justified in demanding of the citizen that he should not be too good for the country to which he owes the protection of his life and his interests; that he should work along with her, but not apart from her, in the pursuit of a greater international ideal.

That ideal has at last found expression in the mouth of a statesman who has not disregarded facts, on the lips of a pacifist who has accepted the necessity of war:

> We are glad [said President Wilson] now that we see facts with no veil of false presence about them, to fight thus for the ultimate peace of the world. . . . The world must be safe for democracy. . . . We desire no conquests and no dominion. We seek no indemnities for ourselves, and no material compensation for sacrifices we shall freely make. . . . Right is more precious than peace, and we shall fight for the things we have always carried nearest our hearts—for democracy, for the right of those who submit to authority to have a voice in their own government, for the rights and liberties of small nations, for the universal dominion of right by such a concert of free peoples as will bring peace and safety to all nations and make the world itself at last free.

It would be rash to take these words as the absolute due of our own cause, just and righteous as that cause may be. It is through a higher fatality than our own statesmanship that we are now fighting alongside of an emancipated Russia, and not a Czar. We are yet in a state of confusion in regard to national and international ideals which is significant of effort rather than attainment. In all our talk of a new Europe there has been, as yet, but little preoccupation with the ideal of a new Africa, with a new standard for the treatment of native races. Until Russia found her soul there was yet the danger that her alliance might be rewarded regardless of the true interests of some of the lesser nations.

These words of the American President are rather the noble expression of a deep and universal human aspiration than of the actual policy of any one of us, and we should be nearer the attainment of that higher policy if we believed it. As George Tyrrell writes in his 'Essays on Faith and Immortality':

> 'This is the meaning of Christ Crucified—man agonising for goodness and truth even unto death, and thereby fulfilling the universal law of God in Nature and in himself. . . . Hence, instead of hell-fire, I should preach the hollowness of the self-life in and out, up and down, till men loathed it and cried *"Quis me liberabit?"'*

Such cannot yet be the spirit of diplomacy; but for those who believe in the union of nations, and in a world-wide policy inspired by human love, it is on these lines that their ideal is to be sought.

It is a frightening thought that a few men will, by and by, sit round a table to settle the welfare of the world. It would be a still more alarming thought if we believed that they really would settle it, and that the visible actors on the world's stage were as potent as they appear to be. Yet their opportunity is a great one, and could we hope that fifty percent of the future Peace Conference would be inspired by the temper of President Wilson's speech; that disinterestedness, altruism, humanity, and a pride magnanimous but not boastful, would be their character-istics; then, indeed, their efforts, seconded by a greater fate and by the pressure of those nobler aspirations that are stirring in the heart of the world, might bring good from the most awful happenings that our lives have known.

One quality we would wish them for the performance of their weighty task, and that is unflinching moral courage: a courage that will not shrink from the ac-knowledgment of unpleasant facts; that will not en-deavour to clothe the acts of self-interest, unavoid-able as they may be, in the garment of human love; a courage that will give them the strength to ac-knowledge wherein each country yet seeks her own, even at the expense of her friends. But their courage must go farther still, and, just as it shrines not from admitting what we are, so must it also boldly state what we would be; having acknowledged the un-pleasant truths of worldly prudence it must go on to enunciate fearlessly the nobler truths of human wis-dom and love.

Notes

[1] I use here the word Christian in a moral sense, as denoting a principle of unselfish love and devotion.

[2] I believe that such exist, though not all who refuse military service on those grounds deserve the name.

Leo Strauss (essay date 1958)

SOURCE: "Machiavelli's Intention: *The Prince*," in *Thoughts on Machiavelli*, 1958. Reprint by The Uni-versity of Chicago Press, 1978, pp. 54-84.

[*In the following excerpt, Strauss carefully analyzes* The Prince'*s structure and themes, discussing how the work relates to Machiavelli's other works, particularly* Discourses upon the First Decade of T. Livius.]

Many writers have attempted to describe the intention of the *Prince* by using the term "scientific." This de-scription is defensible and even helpful provided it is properly meant. Let us return once more to the begin-ning. In the Epistle Dedicatory Machiavelli gives three indications of the subject-matter of the book: he has incorporated in it his knowledge of the actions of great men both modern and ancient; he dares to discuss princely government and to give rules for it; he pos-sesses knowledge of the nature of princes. As appears from the Epistle Dedicatory, from the book itself, and from what the author says elsewhere,[1] knowledge of the actions of great men, i.e., historical knowledge, supplies only materials for knowledge of what princely government is, of the characteristics of the various kinds of principalities, of the rules with which one must comply in order to acquire and preserve princely pow-er, and of the nature of princes. It is only knowledge of the latter kind that the *Prince* is meant to convey. That kind of knowledge, knowledge of the universal or general as distinguished from the individual, is called philosophic or scientific. The *Prince* is a scientific book because it conveys a general teaching that is based on reasoning from experience and that sets forth that rea-soning. That teaching is partly theoretical (knowledge of the nature of princes) and partly practical (knowl-edge of the rules with which the prince must comply). In accordance with the fact that the *Prince* is a scien-tific, and not an historical book, only three of twenty-six chapter headings contain proper names.[2] When referring to the *Prince* in the *Discourses,* Machiavelli calls it a "treatise."[3] For the time being we shall de-scribe the *Prince* as a treatise, meaning by "treatise" a book that sets forth a general teaching of the character indicated. To the extent that the *Prince* is a treatise, it has a lucid plan and its argument proceeds in a straight line without either ascending or descending. It consists at first sight of two parts. The first part sets forth the science or the art of princely government while the second takes up the time honored question of the lim-its of art or prudence, or the question of the relation of art or prudence and chance. More particularly, the *Prince* consists of four parts: 1) the various kinds of principalities (chs. 1-11), 2) the prince and his enemies (chs. 12-14), 3) the prince and his subjects or friends (chs. 15-23),[4] 4) prudence and chance (chs. 24-26). We may go a step further and say that the *Prince* appears, at the outset, not only as a treatise but even as a scho-lastic treatise.[5]

At the same time, however, the book is the opposite of

a scientific or detached work. While beginning with the words "All states, all dominions which have had and have sway over men," it ends with the words "the ancient valor in Italian hearts is not yet dead." It culminates in a passionate call to action—in a call, addressed to a contemporary Italian prince, to perform the most glorious deed possible and necessary then and there. It ends like a tract for the times. For the last part deals not merely with the general question concerning the relation of prudence and chance, but it is concerned with the accidental also in another sense of the term. The chapters surrounding the explicit discussion of the relation between prudence and chance (ch. 25) are the only ones whose headings indicate that they deal with the contemporary Italian situation. The *Prince* is not the only classic of political philosophy which is both a treatise and a tract for the times. It suffices to refer to Hobbes' *Leviathan* and Locke's *Civil Government*. But the case of the *Prince* is not typical: there is a striking contrast between the dry, not to say scholastic, beginning and the highly rhetorical last chapter which ends in a quotation from a patriotic poem in Italian. Could Machiavelli have had the ambition of combining the virtues of scholasticism with those of patriotic poetry? Is such a combination required for the understanding of political things? However this may be, the contrast between the beginning of the *Prince,* or even its first twenty-five chapters, and its end forces us to modify our remark that the argument of the book proceeds in a straight line without ascending or descending. By directly contrasting the beginning and the end, we become aware of an ascent. To the extent to which the *Prince* is a treatise, Machiavelli is an investigator or a teacher; to the extent to which it is a tract for the times, he assumes the role of an adviser, if not of a preacher. He was anxious to become the adviser of the addressee of the *Prince* and thus to rise from his low, and even abject condition.[6] The movement of the *Prince* is an ascent in more than one sense. And besides, it is not simply an ascent.

In contradistinction to the *Discourses,* the *Prince* comes first to sight as a traditional or conventional treatise. But this first appearance is deliberately deceptive. The antitraditional character of the *Prince* becomes explicit shortly beyond the middle of the book, and after remaining explicit for some time, it recedes again. Hence the movement of the *Prince* may be described as an ascent followed by a descent. Roughly speaking, the peak is in the center. This course is prefigured in the first part of the book (chs. 1-11): the highest theme of this part (new principalities acquired by one's own arms and virtue) and the grandest examples (Moses, Theseus, Romulus, Cyrus) are discussed in chapter 6, which is literally the central chapter of the first part.

But let us follow this movement somewhat more closely. At first sight, the *Prince* belongs to the traditional genre of mirrors of princes which are primarily addressed to legitimate princes, and the most familiar case of the legitimate prince is the undisputed heir. Machiavelli almost opens the *Prince* by following custom in calling the hereditary prince the "natural prince." He suggests that the natural is identical with the established or customary, the ordinary and the reasonable; or that it is the opposite of the violent. In the first two chapters he uses only contemporary or almost contemporary Italian examples: we do not leave the dimension of the familiar. We cannot help noting that in the *Discourses,* which open with his declaration that he will communicate therein new modes and orders, the first two chapters are devoted to the remote beginnings of cities and states: we immediately transcend the dimension of the familiar. In the third chapter of the *Prince,* he continues to speak of "the natural and ordinary" and "the ordinary and reasonable" but he now makes it clear that nature favors the established no more than the disestablishment of the established or, more generally stated, that the natural and ordinary stands in a certain tension to the customary: since the desire for acquisition is "natural and ordinary," the destruction of "natural" princes, "the extinction of ancient blood," by an extraordinary conqueror is perhaps more natural than the peaceful and smooth transition from one ordinary heir to another.[7] In accordance with this step forward, foreign and ancient examples come to the fore: the Turks and above all the Romans appear to be superior to the Italians and even to the French. Provoked by the remark of a French Cardinal that the Italians know nothing of war, and thus justified, Machiavelli replied, as he reports here, that the French know nothing of politics: the Romans, whose modes of action are discussed in the center of the chapter, understood both war and politics. Furthermore, he transcends the Here and Now also by referring to a doctrine of the physicians, for medicine is an achievement of the ancients,[8] and by opposing the wise practice of the Romans to "what is everyday in the mouth of the sages of our times." But he is not yet prepared to take issue with the opinion held by more than one contemporary according to which faith must be kept. In chapters 4-6, ancient examples preponderate for the first time. Chapter 6 is devoted to the most glorious type of wholly new princes in wholly new states, i.e., to what is least ordinary and most ancient. The heroic founders discussed therein acquired their positions by virtue, and not by chance, and their greatness revealed itself by their success in introducing wholly new modes and orders which differed profoundly from the established, familiar, and ancient. They stand at the opposite pole from the customary and old established, for two opposite reasons: they were ancient innovators, ancient enemies of the ancient. Chapter 6 is the only chapter of the *Prince* in which Machiavelli speaks of prophets, i.e., of men to whom God speaks. In the same chapter there occurs the first Latin quotation. Compared with that chapter, the rest of the first part marks a descent. The hero of chapter 7 is Cesare Borgia, who acquired his principality by means of chance. He is presented at the outset as simply a model for new princes. But, to say nothing of the fact that he failed because of a grave mistake of his, he was not a wholly new prince in a wholly new state: he is a model for such new princes as try to make changes in ancient orders by means of new modes rather than for such new princes, like the heroes of chapter 6, as try to introduce wholly new modes and orders. Accordingly, the emphasis shifts to modern examples from this point on.[9] As for chapters 8-11, it suffices to note that even their chapter headings no longer contain references to new princes; the princes discussed therein were at most new princes in old states. The last two chapters of the first part contain, as did the first two chapters, only modern examples, although the last two chapters contain also examples other than Italian.

The second part (chs. 12-14) marks an ascent from the end of the first part. The first part had ended with a discussion of ecclesiastical principalities, which as such are unarmed. We learn now that good arms are the necessary and sufficient condition for good laws.[10] As Machiavelli indicates through the headings of chapters 12-13, he ascends in these chapters from the worst kind of arms to the best. We note in this part an almost continuous ascent from modern examples to ancient ones. This ascent is accompanied by three references to the question as to whether modern or ancient examples should be chosen; in the central reference it is suggested that it would be more natural to prefer ancient examples.[11] Machiavelli now takes issue not only with specific political or military errors committed by "the sages of our times" but (although without mentioning his name) with his contemporary Savonarola's fundamental error: Savonarola erroneously believed that the ruin of Italy was caused by religious sins, and not by military sins. In this fairly short part (about 10 pages) Machiavelli refers six times to ancient literature while he had referred to it in the considerably more extensive first part (about 37 pages) only twice. Only in the second part does he come close to referring deferentially to the highest authorities of political or moral thought. He refers, not indeed to the New Testament, but to the Old, and not indeed to what the Old Testament says about Moses but to what it says about David, and not to what it says about David literally but to what it says about David, or in connection with David, figuratively. And he refers, not indeed to Aristotle, or to Plato, but to Xenophon whom he regarded however as the author of the classic mirror of princes. Besides, the Old Testament citation in chapter 13 merely supplies at most an additional example of the correct choice of arms; Xenophon's *Education of Cyrus,* mentioned at the end of chapter 14, however, is the only authority he refers to as setting forth a complete moral code for a prince. To say the least, the height reached at the end of the second part recalls the height reached in the center of the first part: the second part ends and culminates in a praise of Cyrus—one of the four "grandest examples" spoken of in chapter 6. In the first part, Machiavelli leisurely ascends to the greatest doers and then leisurely descends again; in the second part he ascends quickly to the origins of the traditional understanding of the greatest doers.

Right at the beginning of the third part (chs. 15-23) Machiavelli begins to uproot the Great Tradition. The emphasis is on a change in the general teaching: the first chapter of the third part is the only chapter of the *Prince* which does not contain any historical examples. Machiavelli now takes issue explicitly and coherently with the traditional and customary view according to which the prince ought to live virtuously and ought to rule virtuously. From this we begin to understand why he refrained in the second part from referring to the highest authorities: the missing peak above the Old Testament and Xenophon is not the New Testament and Plato or Aristotle but Machiavelli's own thought: all ancient or traditional teachings are to be superseded by a shockingly new teaching. But he is careful not to shock anyone unduly. While the claim to radical innovation is suggested, it is made in a subdued manner: he suggests that he is merely stating in his own name and openly a teaching which some ancient writers had set forth covertly or by using their characters as their mouthpieces.[12] Yet this strengthens Machiavelli's claim in truth as much as it weakens it in appearance: one cannot radically change the mode of a teaching without radically changing its substance. The argument ascends from chapter 15 up to chapters 19 or 20 and then descends again. In chapter 17 Machiavelli begins to speak again of "new princes," after a pause of 10 chapters, and he continues to do so in the three subsequent chapters; at the beginning of chapter 21 he still refers to "a quasi-new prince," but in the rest of the third part this high theme disappears completely: Machiavelli descends again to ordinary or second rate princes.[13] This movement is paralleled by a change regarding modern or ancient examples. Up through chapter 19, there is, generally speaking, an increase in emphasis on the ancient; thereafter modern examples preponderate obviously.[14] The last two-thirds of chapter 19, which deal with the Roman emperors, may be said to mark the peak of the third part. The passage is introduced as a rejoinder to what "many" might object against Machiavelli's own opinion. Chapter 19 is literally the center of the third part, just as the peak of the first part was literally its center (ch. 6). This is no accident. Chapter 19 completes the explicit discussion of the founder while chapter 6 had begun it. Hence we may justly describe chapter 19 as the peak of the *Prince* as a whole, and the third part as its most important part.[15] Chapter 19 reveals the truth about the founders, or the greatest doers almost fully.[16] The full revelation requires the universalization of the lesson derived from the study of the Roman emperors, and this universalization is presented in the first section of chapter 20. Immediately thereafter the descent begins. Machiavelli refers there to a saying of "our ancients," i.e., of the reputedly wise men of old Florence, and rejects it in an unusually cautious manner:[17] after having broken with the most exalted teaching of the venerable Great Tradition, he humbly returns to a show of reverence for a fairly recent and purely local tradition. Shortly afterwards he expresses his agreement with "the judgment of many," and immediately before questioning the wisdom of building fortresses and before showing that the practice of building fortresses had wisely been abandoned by a considerable number of Italian contemporaries, he says that he praises the building of fortresses "because it has been used from ancient times."[18] He shows every sign of wishing to pretend that he believes in the truth of the equation of the good with the ancient and the customary. Acting in the same spirit he expresses there a belief in human gratitude, respect for justice, and honesty[19] which is quite at variance with everything that went before, and especially with what he said in the third part.

Just as the movement of the argument in the third part resembles that in the first part, the movement of the argument in the fourth part (chs. 24-26) resembles that in the second part. In contrast to the last chapters of the third part, the fourth part is marked by the following characteristics: Machiavelli speaks again of the "new prince," and even "the new prince in a new principality" and he again emphasizes ancient models. Philip of Macedon, "not the father of Alexander, but the one who was defeated by Titus Quintus," i.e., an ancient prince who did not belong to the highest class of princes, is presented as vastly superior to the contemporary Italian princes who also were defeated. While the central chapter of the fourth part contains only modern examples, it compensates for this, as it were, by being devoted to an attack on a contemporary Italian belief, or rather on a belief which is more commonly held in contemporary Italy than it was in the past. In the last chapter, Moses, Cyrus, and Theseus, three of the four heroic founders praised in chapter 6, are mentioned again; Moses and Theseus had not been mentioned since. In that chapter Machiavelli speaks in the most unrestrained terms of what he hopes for from a contemporary Italian prince or from the latter's family. But he does not leave the slightest doubt that what he hopes for from a contemporary new prince in a new state is not more than at best a perfect imitation of the ancient founders, an imitation made possible by the survival of the Italians' ancient valor: he does not expect a glorious deed of an entirely new kind, or a new creation. While the last chapter of the *Prince* is thus a call to a most glorious imitation of the peaks of antiquity within contemporary Italy, the general teaching of the *Prince,* and especially of its third part, i.e., Machiavelli's understanding of the ancient founders and of the foundation of society in general, is the opposite of an imitation, however perfect: while the greatest deed possible in contemporary Italy is an imitation of the greatest deeds of antiquity, the greatest theoretical achievement possible in contemporary Italy is "wholly new,"[20] We conclude, therefore, that the movement of the *Prince* as a whole is an ascent followed by a descent.

It is characteristic of the *Prince* to partake of two pairs of opposites: it is both a treatise and a tract for the times, and it has both a traditional exterior and a revolutionary interior. There is a connection between these two pairs of opposites. As a treatise, the book sets forth a timeless teaching, i.e., a teaching which is meant to be true for all times; as a tract for the times, it sets forth what ought to be done at a particular time. But the timelessly true teaching is related to time because it is new at the particular time at which it is set forth, and its being new, or not coeval with man, is not accidental. A new teaching concerning the foundations of society being, as such, unacceptable or exposed to enmity, the movement from the accepted or old teaching to the new must be made carefully, or the revolutionary interior must be carefully protected by a traditional exterior. The twofold relation of the book to the particular time at which it was composed or for which it was composed explains why the preponderance of modern examples has a twofold meaning: modern examples are more immediately relevant for action in contemporary Italy than ancient examples, and a discussion of modern examples is less "presumptuous"[21] or offensive than is a discussion of the most exalted ancient examples or of the origins of the established order which are neither present nor near. This must be borne in mind if one wants to understand what Machiavelli means by calling the *Prince* a "treatise."[22] As matters stand, it is necessary to add the remark that, in describing the *Prince* as the work of a revolutionary, we have used that term in the precise sense: a revolutionary is a man who breaks the law, the law as a whole, in order to replace it by a new law which he believes to be better than the old law.

The *Prince* is obviously a combination of a treatise and a tract for the times. But the manner in which that combination is achieved is not obvious: the last chapter does come as a surprise. We believe that this difficulty can be resolved if one does not forget that the *Prince* also combines a traditional surface with a revolutionary center. As a treatise, the *Prince* conveys a general teaching; as a tract for the times, it conveys a particular counsel. The general teaching cannot be identical, but it must at least be compatible, with the particular counsel. There may even be a connection between the general and the particular which is closer than mere compatibility: the general teaching may necessitate the particular counsel, given the particular circumstances in which the immediate addressee of the *Prince* finds himself, and the particular counsel may required the general teaching of the *Prince* and be incompatible with any other general teaching. At any rate, in studying the general teaching of the *Prince* we must never lose sight of the particular situation in which Lorenzo finds himself. We must understand the general in the light of the particular. We must translate every general rule which is addressed generally to princes, or a kind of prince, into a particular counsel addressed to Lorenzo. And conversely, we must work our way upward from the particular counsel which is given in the last chapter to its general premises. Perhaps the complete general premises differ from the general premises as explicitly stated, and the complete particular counsel differs from the particular counsel as explicitly stated. Perhaps the unstated implications, general or particular, provide the link between the general teaching as explicitly stated and the particular counsel as explicitly stated.

What precisely is the difficulty created by the counsel given in the last chapter of the *Prince*? As for the mere fact that that chapter comes as a surprise of some kind, one might rightly say that in the *Prince* no surprise ought to be surprising. In the light of the indications given in the first chapter, chapters 8-11 come as a surprise, to say nothing of other surprises. Besides, one merely has to read the *Prince* with ordinary care, in order to see that the call to liberate Italy with which the book ends is the natural conclusion of the book. For instance, in chapter 12 Machiavelli says that the outcome of the Italian military system has been that "Italy has been overrun by Charles, plundered by Louis, violated by Ferdinand, and insulted by the Swiss," or that Italy has become "enslaved and insulted."[23] What other conclusion can be drawn from this state of things than that one must bend every effort to liberate Italy after having effected a complete reform of her military system, i.e., that one ought to do what the last chapter says Lorenzo ought to do? The last chapter presents a problem not because it is a call to liberate Italy but because it is silent as to the difficulties obstructing the liberation of Italy. In that chapter it is said more than once that the action recommended to Lorenzo, or urged upon him, will not be "very difficult": almost everything has been done by God; only the rest remains to be done by the human liberator. The chapter creates the impression that the only things required for the liberation of Italy are the Italians strong loathing of foreign domination, and their ancient valor; the liberator of Italy can expect spontaneous cooperation from all his compatriots and he can expect that they will all fly to arms against the foreigners once he "takes the banner." It is true that Machiavelli stresses even here the need for a radical reform of the Italian military system. In fact, he devotes the whole center of the chapter, i.e., almost half of the chapter, to the military conditions for the liberation of Italy. But all the more striking is his complete silence as to its political conditions. What would be gained by all Italians becoming the best soldiers in the world if they were to turn their skill and prowess against one another or, in other words, if there were not first established a strict unity of command, to say nothing of unity of training? It is absurd to say that Machiavelli's patriotic fervor temporarily blinds him to the hard practical problems: his patriotic fervor does not prevent him from speaking in the last

chapter very prosaically and even technically about the military preparation. The liberator of Italy is described as a new prince, for the liberation of Italy presupposes the introduction of new laws and new orders: he must do for Italy what Moses did for the people of Israel. But, as Machiavelli had been at pains to point out in the earlier chapters of the book, the new prince necessarily offends many of his fellow countrymen, especially those who benefit from the customary order of things, and his adherents are necessarily unreliable. In the last chapter he is silent on the subject of the inevitable offensiveness of the liberator's actions, as well as concerning the powerful resistances which he must expect. The liberator of Italy is urged there to furnish himself with his own troops who will be all the better if they see themselves commanded by their own prince: will the Venetian or the Milanese troops regard the Florentine Lorenzo as their own prince? Machiavelli does not say a word about the difficulties which might be created for the liberator by the various Italian republics and princes. He merely alludes to those difficulties by raising the rhetorical question, "what envy will oppose itself to him?" and by speaking once of "the weakness of the chiefs" in Italy. Does he mean to say that the patriotic fervor of the Italian people will suffice for sweeping aside those weak chiefs, however envious they might be? He certainly implies that before the liberator can liberate Italy, he would have to take not merely a banner, as is said in the text of the chapter, but Italy herself, as is said in the heading. It is a rare if not unique case in Machiavelli's books that the heading of a chapter should be more informative than its body.

Apart from chapters 26 and 24, the headings of which refer us to contemporary Italy, only one chapter heading in the *Prince* contains proper names and thus draws our attention to the particular. Chapter 4 is entitled: "Why the Kingdom of Darius which Alexander had seized did not rebel against Alexander's successors after his death."[24] As a consequence, the place of the chapter within the plan of the general teaching as indicated in chapter 1, is not immediately clear. Chapter 4 is the central one of three chapters which deal with "mixed principalities," i.e., with the acquistion of new territory by princes or republics, or, in other words, with conquest. The primary example in chapter 3 is the policy of conquest practiced by King Louis XII of France; but the country in which he tried to acquire new territory was Italy. In chapter 3, Machiavelli discusses the difficulties obstructing foreign conquests in Italy, a subject most important to the liberator of Italy. By discussing the mistakes which the French king committed in attempting to make lasting conquests in Italy, Machiavelli undoubtedly gives advice to foreigners contemplating conquest in his own fatherland.[25] This might seem to cast a reflection on his patriotism. But one might justly say that such advice is only the reverse side, if the odious side, of advice as to how to defend Italy against foreign domination, or how to liberate Italy. It appears from Machiavelli's discussion that but for certain grave mistakes committed by the French king, he could easily have kept his Italian conquests. The French king committed the grave mistakes of permitting the minor Italian powers to be destroyed and of strengthening a major Italian power, instead of protecting the minor Italian powers and humiliating that major power. We are forced to wonder what conclusion the liberator of Italy would have to draw from these observations. Should he destroy the minor Italian powers and strengthen the major Italian powers? The destruction of the minor powers which Machiavelli has in mind was effected by Cesare Borgia whose actions he holds up as models for Lorenzo. But would not the strengthening of the other major Italian powers perpetuate, and even increase, the difficulties of keeping the foreigner out of Italy? It is this question which is taken up in an oblique way in chapter 4. Machiavelli there distinguishes two kinds of principality: one like the Persia conquered by Alexander the Great, in which one man is prince and all others are slaves, and another kind, like France, which is ruled by a king and barons, i.e., in which powers exist that are not simply dependent on the prince but rule in their own right. He makes this distinction more general by comparing the French monarchy to Greece prior to the Roman conquest. What he is concerned with is then the difference between countries ruled by a single government from which all political authority within the country is simply derived, and countries in which there exists a number of regional or local powers, each ruling in its own right. Seen in the light of this distinction, Italy belongs to the same kind of country as France. In discussing Alexander's conquest of Persia, Machiavelli is compelled to discuss the conquest of a country of the opposite kind, i.e., the conquest of France. This, however, means that he is enabled to continue surreptitiously the discussion, begun in the preceding chapter, of the conquest of Italy.[26] Chapter 4 supplies this lesson: while it is difficult to conquer Persia, it is easy to keep her; conversely, while it is easy to conquer France, it is difficult to keep her. France (for which we may substitute in this context Italy) is easy to conquer because there will always be a discontented baron (state) that will be anxious to receive foreign help against the king (against other states within the country). She is difficult to keep because the old local or regional loyalties will always reassert themselves against the new prince. Secure possession of the country is impossible as long as the ancient blood of the local or regional lords or dukes or princes has not been extinguished. One might think for a moment that what is good for the foreign conqueror of a country of the kind under discussion is not necessarily good for the native liberator of such a country. But, as Machiavelli indicates in chapter 3, the superiority of France to Italy in strength and unity is due to the extirpation of the princely lines of Burgundy, Brittany, Gascony and Normandy. Given the urgency arising from foreign domination of Italy, the liberator cannot afford to wait until the other princely families

have become extinct in the course of centuries. He will have to do on the largest scale what Cesare Borgia had done on a small scale:[27] in order to uproot the power of the old local and regional loyalties which are a major source of Italian weakness, one must extinguish the families of the obnoxious Italian princes. Cesare Borgia performs a crucial function in the *Prince* for the additional reason that he is the link between the foreign conqueror of Italy and her native, patriotic liberator: since he was not simply an Italian, he could not well be regarded as a potential liberator of his fatherland.[28] As for the Italian republics, we learn from chapter 5, the last chapter devoted to the subject of conquest, that the only way in which a prince, or a republic, can be sure of the loyalty of a conquered republican city with an old tradition of autonomy is to ruin it, and to disperse its inhabitants, and that this holds true regardless of whether the conqueror and the conquered are sons of the same country or not.[29]

The information regarding the political prerequisites of the liberation of Italy is withheld in the chapter which is explicitly devoted to the liberation of Italy because Machiavelli desired to keep the noble and shining end untarnished by the base and dark means that are indispensable for its achievement. He desired this because the teaching that "the end justifies the means" is repulsive, and he wanted the *Prince* to end even more attractively than it began. The information withheld in the last chapter is supplied in the section on conquest. To that section above all others we must turn if we desire to know what kinds of resistance on the part of his countrymen the liberator of Italy will have to overcome, and what kinds of offense against his fellow countrymen he will have to commit. To liberate Italy from the barbarians means to unify Italy, and to unify Italy means to conquer Italy. It means to do in Italy something much more difficult than what Ferdinand of Aragon had done in Spain, but in certain respects comparable to it.[30] The liberator of Italy cannot depend on the spontaneous following of all inhabitants of Italy. He must pursue a policy of iron and poison, of murder and treachery. He must not shrink from the extermination of Italian princely families and the destruction of Italian republican cities whenever actions of this kind are conducive to his end. The liberation of Italy means a complete revolution. It requires first and above everything else a revolution in thinking about right and wrong. Italians have to learn that the patriotic end hallows every means however much condemned by the most exalted traditions both philosophic and religious. The twenty-sixth chapter of the *Discourses,* which has already supplied us with more than one key to the *Prince,* confirms our present conclusion. Its heading says: "A new prince, in a city or country taken by him must make everything new." From its text we learn that just as Cesare Borgia did not become master of the Romagna except by "cruelty well used," Philip of Macedon did not become within a short time "prince of Greece" except by the use of means which were inimical not only to every humane manner of life but to every Christian manner of life as well.[31]

The major Italian power which the would-be foreign conqueror, Louis XII, mistakenly strengthened instead of humiliating, was the Church. The native liberator of Italy on the other hand, is advised to use his family connection with the then Pope Leo X in order to receive support for his patriotic enterprise from the already greatly strengthened Church. He is advised, in other words, to use the Church ruled by Leo X as Cesare Borgia, the model, had used the Church ruled by Alexander VI. But this counsel can be of only a provisional character. To see this, one has to consider Machiavelli's reflections on Cesare's successes and failures. Cesare's succusses ultimately benefited only the Church, and thus increased the obstacles to the conquest or liberation of Italy. Cesare was a mere tool of Alexander VI and hence, whatever Alexander's wishes may have been, a mere tool of the papacy. Ultimately, Alexander rather than Cesare represents the contemporary Italian model of a new prince. For Cesare's power was based on the power of the papacy. That power failed him when Alexander died. Cesare's failure was not accidental, considering that the average length of a Pope's reign is ten years, that the influence of any Italian prince on the election of a new Pope is not likely to be greater than that of the great foreign powers and, above all, considering that the Church has a purpose or interest of its own which casts discredit on and thus endangers the use of the power of the Church for purposes other than strengthening the Church.[32] The liberation of Italy which requires the unification of Italy eventually requires therefore the secularization of the Papal states. It requires even more. According to Machiavelli, the Church is not only through its temporal power the chief obstacle to the unity of Italy; the Church is also responsible for the religious and moral corruption of Italy and for the ensuing loss of political virtue. In addition, Machiavelli was very much in fear of the Swiss, whose military excellence he traced partly to their sturdy piety. He draws the conclusion that if the Papal Court were removed to Switzerland, one would soon observe the deterioration of Swiss piety and morals and hence of Swiss power.[33] He seemed to have played with the thought that the liberator of Italy would have to go beyond secularizing the Papal states; he might have to remove the Papal Court to Switzerland and thus kill two birds with one stone. The liberator of Italy must certainly have the courage to do what Giovampagolo Baglioni was too vile to do, namely, "to show the prelates how little one ought to respect people who live and rule as they do and thus to perform an action whose greatness obliterates every infamy and every danger that might arise from it." He must make Italy as united as she was "in the time of the Romans."[34] The addressee of the *Prince* is advised to imitate Romulus among

others. To imitate Romulus means to found Rome again. But Rome exists. Or could the imitation of Romulus mean to found again a pagan Rome, a Rome destined to become again the most glorious republic and the seminary and the heart of the most glorious empire? Machiavelli does not answer this question in so many words. When he mentions for the second time, in the last chapter of the *Prince,* the venerable models whom the addressee of the *Prince* should imitate, he is silent about Romulus.[35] The question which he forces us to raise, he answers by silence. In this connection we may note that, whereas in the *Discourses* "We" sometimes means "We Christians," "We" never has this meaning in the *Prince*. At any rate, both the explicit general teaching and the explicit particular counsel conveyed by the *Prince* are more traditional or less revolutionary than both the complete general teaching and the complete particular counsel. The two pairs of opposites which are characteristic of the *Prince,* namely, its being both a treatise and a tract for the times and its having both a traditional exterior and a revolutionary center, are nicely interwoven. The *Prince* is altogether, as Machiavelli indicates at the beginning of the second chapter, a fine web. The subtlety of the web contrasts with the shocking frankness of speech which he sometimes employs or affects. It would be better to say that the subtle web is subtly interwoven with the shocking frankness of speech which he chooses to employ at the proper time and in the proper place.

So much for the present regarding the character of the *Prince*. The subject of the book is the prince but especially the new prince. In the Epistle Dedicatory, Machiavelli indicates that his teaching is based upon his knowledge of the actions of great men; but the greatest examples of great men are new princes like Moses, Cyrus, Romulus and Theseus, men "who have acquired or founded kingdoms." In the first chapter, he divides principalities into classes with a view to the differences of materials and modes of acquisition rather than to differences of structure and purpose. He thus indicates from the outset that he is chiefly concerned with men who desire to acquire principalities (either mixed or wholly new), i.e., with new princes. There is a twofold reason for this emphasis. The obvious reason is the fact that the immediate addressee of the book is a new prince, and one who is, moreover, advised to become prince of Italy and thus to become a new prince in a more exalted sense. But what at first glance seems to be dictated merely by Machiavelli's consideration for the needs and prospects of his immediate addressee proves, on reflection, to be necessary for purely theoretical reasons as well. All principalities, even if they are now elective or hereditary, were originally new principalities. Even all republics, at least the greatest republics, were founded by outstanding men wielding extraordinary power, i.e., by new princes. To discuss new princes means then to discuss the origins or foundations of all states or of all social orders, and therewith the nature of society. The fact that the addressee of the *Prince* is an actual or potential new prince somewhat conceals the eminent theoretical significance of the theme "the new prince."

The ambiguity due to the fact that the *Prince* sometimes deals with princes in general and sometimes with new princes in particular is increased by the ambiguity of the term "new prince." The term may designate the founder of a dynasty in a state already established, i.e., a new prince in an old state, or a man who "seizes" a state, like Sforza in Milan or Agathocles in Syracuse or Liverotto in Fermo. But it may also designate a new prince in a new state or "a wholly new prince in a wholly new state," i.e., a man who has not merely acquired a state already in existence but has founded a state. The new prince in a new state in his turn may be an imitator, i.e., adopt modes and orders invented by another new prince, or in other ways follow the beaten track. But he may also be the originator of new modes and orders, or a radical innovator, the founder of a new type of society, possibly the founder of a new religion—in brief, a man like Moses, Cyrus, Theseus, or Romulus. Machiavelli applies to men of the highest order the term "prophets."[36] That term would seem to fit Moses rather than the three others. Moses is indeed the most important founder: Christianity rests on a foundation laid by Moses.

At the beginning of the chapter which is devoted to the grandest examples, Machiavelli makes unambiguously clear the fact that he does not expect the addressee of the *Prince* to be or to become an originator: he advises his reader to become an imitator or to follow the beaten track or to be a man of second rate virtue. This is not surprising: an originator would not need Machiavelli's instruction. As he states in the Epistle Dedicatory, he wishes that Lorenzo would "understand" what he himself "had come to know and had come to understand": he does not expect him to have come to know the most important things by himself. Lorenzo may have an "excellent" brain; he is not expected to have a "most excellent" brain.[37] However this may be, being "a prudent man," he is exhorted to "follow the track beaten by great men and to imitate those who have been most excellent," i.e., men like Romulus and Moses. On the other hand, the precepts which Machiavelli gives to Lorenzo are abstracted from the actions, not of Romulus or Moses, but of Cesare Borgia.[38] For, to say nothing of other considerations, Lorenzo's hoped-for rise depends upon his family connection with the present head of the Church and therewith on chance, just as Cesare's actual rise depended on his family connection with a former head of the Church, whereas Romulus and Moses rose to power through virtue as distinguished from chance. In imitating Cesare Borgia, Lorenzo would admit his inferiority to Cesare: Machiavelli's book would be somewhat out of place if meant for a man of Cesare's stature and lack of scruples. Still, Lorenzo is advised to imitate men of the stature of Romulus and of Moses. As appears from the last chapter, however, that imitation is expected less of Lorenzo by himself than of the illustrious house to which he belongs.

In the last chapter the emphasis is altogether on Moses. Machiavelli says there that God was a friend of Moses, Cyrus and Theseus. The description is applied to Moses with greater propriety than to Cyrus and to Theseus. Lorenzo is then exhorted to imitate Moses. The notion of imitating the prophets of old was familiar to Machiavelli's contemporaries: Savonarola appeared as a new Amos or as a new Moses, i.e., as a man who did the same things which the Biblical prophets had done, in new circumstances. This is not to say that there is no difference between the imitation of Moses as Savonarola meant it and the imitation of Moses as Machiavelli understood it. In order to encourage Lorenzo to liberate Italy, Machiavelli reminds him of the miracles which God had performed before their eyes: "The sea has been divided. A cloud has guided you on your way. The rock has given forth water. Manna has rained." The miracles of Lorenzo's time which indeed are attested to by Machiavelli alone, imitate the miracles of Moses' time. More precisely, they imitate the miracles which were performed, not in Egypt, the house of bondage, but on the way from Egypt to the promised land—to a land to be conquered. Differing from Savonarola, Machiavelli does not predict that Florence, or her ruler, will become the ruler of Italy,[39] for the success of the venture now depends alone on the exercise of human virtue which, because of man's free-will, cannot be foreseen. What may be imminent, Machiavelli suggests, is the conquest of another promised land, the land which Machiavelli has half-promised to Lorenzo. But alas, the imitation of Moses is bad for Lorenzo; for Moses did not conquer the promised land: he died at its borders. In this dark way, Machiavelli, the new sibyl, prophesies that Lorenzo will not conquer and liberate Italy.[40] He did not regard the practical proposal with which he concluded the *Prince* as practicable. He had measured the forces of contemporary Italy too well to have any delusions. As he states in the two Prefaces of the companion book, which in this respect takes up the thread where the *Prince* drops it, "of that ancient virtue [which is political] no trace has been left" in Italy. Not the short range project suggested at the end of the *Prince,* but rather the long range project indicated throughout the *Discourses* offers hope for success. Many writers have dismissed the last chapter of the *Prince* as a piece of mere rhetoric. This assertion—if it were followed up by an intelligent account of the enigmatic conclusion of the *Prince*—could be accepted as a crude expression of the fact that that chapter must not be taken literally or too seriously.

Machiavelli is not content with indicating his opinion by leading us to think of the inauspicious character of the imitation of Moses in respect of the conquest of a promised land. While stressing the imitative character of the work to which he exhorts Lorenzo, he stresses the fact that the liberator of Italy must be an originator, an inventor of new modes and orders, hence not an imitator. He himself hints at some far-reaching tactical innovations. But it is clear that the innovator or the inventor in these matters would be Machiavelli, not Lorenzo. The cryptic prediction of Lorenzo's failure, if he were to attempt to liberate Italy, can therefore be restated as follows: only a man of genius, of supreme virtue, could possibly succeed in liberating Italy; but Lorenzo lacks the highest form of virtue. This being the case, he is compelled to rely too much on chance. Machiavelli indicates and conceals how much Lorenzo would have to rely on chance by the religious language which he employs in the last chapter. He mentions God as often there as in all other chapters of the *Prince* taken together. He refers to the liberator of Italy as an Italian "spirit"; he describes the liberation of Italy as a divine redemption and he suggests its resemblance to the resurrection of the dead as depicted by Ezekiel; he alludes to the miracles wrought by God in Italy. However much we might wish to be moved by these expressions of religious sentiment, we fail in our effort. Machiavelli's certainty of divine intervention reminds us of his expectation of a spontaneous all-Italian rising against the hated foreigners. Just as that expectation is at variance with what earlier chapters had indicated as to the certainty of powerful Italian resistance to the liberator and unifier of Italy, so the expression of religious sentiment is at variance with earlier explicit remarks. According to those remarks, fear of God is desirable or indispensable in soldiers and perhaps in subjects in general, while the prince need merely appear religious, and he can easily create that appearance considering the crudity of the large majority of men. In the last chapter itself, Machiavelli calls the God-wrought contemporary events which resemble certain Biblical miracles not "miracles" but "extraordinary" events "without example"[41]: he thus denies the reality of those Biblical miracles and therewith, for an obvious reason, the reality of all Biblical miracles. Without such a denial, his own free invention of the contemporary "extraordinary" events would not have been possible: those invented miracles have the same status as the Biblical miracles. According to the *Prince,* miracles are happenings which are neither common nor reasonable. They are happenings that cannot be traced to secondary causes but only to God directly. Near the beginning of chapter 25 Machiavelli suggests that what is generally meant by God is in truth nothing but chance. Hence the suggestion made in chapter 26, that a number of miracles had happened in contemporary Italy is the figurative equivalent of the assertion, made explicitly in chapter 25, that chance is particularly powerful in contemporary Italy. More specifically, many "miraculous losses" have been sustained in contemporary Italy.[42] In the last chapter Machiavelli enumerates seven astonishing defeats suffered in the immediate past by Italian troops.[43] Since there is no defeat without a vic-

tor, one may speak with equal right of "miraculous losses and miraculous acquisitions" being the necessary consequence of the preponderance of Fortuna's power in contemporary Italy.[44] This means that, given the poverty of the Italian military system and the ensuing preponderance of chance, a well advised and industrious prince might have astounding temporary successes against other Italian princes, just as Pope Julius II had such successes against his cowardly enemies. In particular, Lorenzo might succeed in building up a strong power in Tuscany. But the thought of defeating the powerful military monarchies which dominate parts of Italy remains for the time being a dream.[45]

One cannot understand the meaning of the last chapter, and therewith of the *Prince* as a whole, without taking into consideration the position, the character and the aspirations of the other partner in the relationship, not to say in the dialogue, which is constitutive of the book. In proportion as the status of Lorenzo is lessened, the stature of Machiavelli grows. At the beginning, in the Epistle Dedicatory, Lorenzo appears as dwelling on the wholesome heights of majesty whereas Machiavelli must inhale the dust at his feet: the favorite of Fortuna is contrasted with her enemy. Machiavelli presents himself as a man who possesses information which princes necessarily lack and yet need. He describes that information in a way which is surprising not only to those who are forced by disposition or training to think of statistical data. He claims to possess knowledge of the nature of princes: just as one sees mountains best from a valley and valleys best from a mountain, so one must be a prince in order to know well the nature of peoples, and one must be a man of the people in order to know well the nature of princes. In other words, while Lorenzo and Machiavelli are at opposite ends of the scale of Fortuna, they are equal in wisdom: each possesses one half of the whole of political wisdom; they are born to supplement each other. Machiavelli does not say that they should pool their resources in order to liberate Italy. Nor does he wish to hand over his share of political wisdom to Lorenzo as a pure gift. He desires to receive something in return. He desires to better his fortune. Looking forward to the end of the book, we may say that he desires to better his fortune by showing Lorenzo how to better his fortune through becoming prince of Italy. For, as he says already in the Epistle Dedicatory, chance and Lorenzo's other qualities promise him a greatness which even surpasses his present greatness. He dedicates the *Prince* to Lorenzo because he seeks honorable employment. He desires to become the servant of Lorenzo. Perhaps he desires to become an occasional or temporary adviser to Lorenzo. Perhaps he is even thinking of the position of a permanent adviser. But the absolute limit of his ambition would be to become the minister of Lorenzo, to be to Lorenzo what Antonio da Venafro had been to Pandolfo Petrucci, prince of Siena. His desire would be wholly unreasonable if he did not see his way toward convincing his master of his competence. The proof of his competence is the *Prince*. But competence is not enough. Lorenzo must also be assured of Machiavelli's loyalty or at least reliability. Machiavelli cannot refer, not even in the Epistle Dedicatory, to the fact that he had once had honorable employment in which he served loyally. For he was a loyal servant of the republican regime in Florence, and this by itself might compromise him in the eyes of his prince. He faces this difficulty for the first time in the chapter on civil principalities, i.e., on the kind of principality of which Lorenzo's rule is an example. He discusses there the question of how the prince ought to treat the notables among his subjects. He distinguishes three kinds of notables, the central one consisting of men who do not commit themselves entirely to the cause of the prince because they are pusillanimous and have a natural defect of courage. Machiavelli advises the prince to employ men of this kind provided they are men of good counsel, "for in prosperity you are honored on account of this and in adversity you have nothing to fear from them." Men of good counsel will have the required pusillanimity if the power of the prince has strong popular support: the few who can see with their own eyes "do not dare to oppose themselves to the opinion of the many who have the majesty of the state on their side." Since Machiavelli was suspected of having participated in a conspiracy against the Medici, it was particularly necessary for him to show through the *Prince* that men of his kind would never have the temerity to engage in such dangerous undertakings for they would think only of the probable outcome of the deed and not of its possible intrinsic nobility. He almost presents the spectacle of a conversation between himself and a potential conspirator against the prince in which he tries to convince the conspirator of the folly of his imaginings—a spectacle the very suggestion of which must have edified and reassured Lorenzo should he have read the *Prince*. Eventually, Machiavelli does not refrain from speaking explicitly about how a new prince should treat men who in the beginning of his reign had been suspect because of their loyalty to the preceding regime. He urges the prince to employ men of this kind. "Pandolfo Petrucci, prince of Siena, ruled his state more with those who were suspected by him than with others." The mere fact that such men are compelled to live down a past makes them willing to be reliable servants of the prince. But by proving so completely his reliability in addition to his competence, Machiavelli might seem to have overshot the mark. His potential employer might well wonder whether a man of Machiavelli's cleverness, if employed as an adviser or minister, would not receive all credit for wise actions of the government and thus by contrast render the less wise prince rather contemptible. Machiavelli reassures him, as well as he can, by setting up the infallible general rule that a prince who is not himself wise cannot be well advised.[46] Considering the great hazards to which Machiavelli exposes himself by trying to enter the service of a new prince, one may wonder whether according to his principles he ought not to have preferred poverty and obscurity. He answers this question in the *Discourses* since it cannot be answered with propriety in the *Prince*. Men in his position, he indicates, live in continuous danger if they do not seek employment with the prince; in trying to give advice to the prince, they must indeed "take things moderately," i.e., they must avoid standing forth as the chief or sole promoters of a bold scheme. Only if the bold scheme is backed by a strong party can some risks be safely taken.[47] The particular counsel which Machiavelli gives to Lorenzo explicitly, i.e., the counsel which he gives in the last chapter of the *Prince,* is moderate both because it is silent concerning the extreme measures required for the liberation of Italy and because it cannot but be very popular with very many Italians.

We have not yet considered Machiavelli's strange suggestion that he possesses one half of political wisdom, namely, knowledge of the nature of princes, whereas Lorenzo may possess the other half, namely, knowledge of the nature of peoples. He makes this suggestion in the same context in which he declares his intention of giving rules for princely government. But to give rules to princes as to how they ought to rule, means to teach them how they ought to rule their peoples. Machiavelli cannot then teach princes without possessing good knowledge of the nature of peoples as well. In fact, he gives much evidence of his possessing such knowledge inasmuch as he transmits it in the *Prince* to his princely pupil. He knows then everything of relevance that the prince knows, and in addition he knows much that is relevant of which the prince is ignorant. He is not merely a potential adviser of a prince but a teacher of princes as such. In fact, since more than one of his precepts is not required for princes at all, because princes would know such things without his instruction, he also, through the *Prince,* teaches subjects what they should expect from their prince, or the truth about the nature of princes.[48] As an adviser of a prince, he addresses an individual; as a teacher of political wisdom, he addresses an indefinite multitude. He indicates his dual capacity and the corresponding duality of his addressees by his use of the second person of the personal pronoun: he uses "Thou" when addressing the prince, and even the man who conspires against the prince, i.e., when addressing men of action, while he uses "You" when addressing those whose interest is primarily theoretical, either simply or for the time being. The latter kind of addressees of the *Prince* are identical with the addressees of the *Discourses,* "the young."[49]

Machiavelli mentions only one teacher of princes, namely, Chiron the centaur who brought up Achilles and many other ancient princes. Machiavelli's own model is a mythical figure: he returns to the beginnings not only by making the heroic founders his most exalted theme and the foundation of society his most fundamental theme, but likewise in understanding his own doing. His model is half beast, half man. He urges princes, and especially new princes, first to make use of both natures, the nature of the beast and the nature of man; and in the repetition, simply to imitate the beast, i.e., to use the person of the fox and the lion, or to imitate those two natures.[50] The imitation of the beast takes the place of the imitation of God. We may note here that Machiavelli is our most important witness to the truth that humanism is not enough. Since man must understand himself in the light of the whole or of the origin of the whole which is not human, or since man is the being that must try to transcend humanity, he must transcend humanity in the direction of the subhuman if he does not transcend it in the direction of the superhuman. *Tertium*, i.e., humanism, *non datur*. We may look forward from Machiavelli to Swift whose greatest work culminates in the recommendation that men should imitate the horses,[51] to Rousseau who demanded the return to the state of nature, a sub-human state, and to Nietzsche who suggested that Truth is not God but a Woman. As for Machiavelli, one may say with at least equal right that he replaces the imitation of the God-Man Christ by the imitation of the Beast-Man Chiron. That Beast-Man is, as Machiavelli indicates, a creation of the writers of antiquity, a creature of the imagination. Just as Scipio, in imitating Cyrus, in fact imitated a creation of Xenophon,[52] so the princes in imitating Chiron, will in fact imitate, not Chiron, but the ancient writers, if the carrying out of a teaching can justly be called an imitation of that teaching. But whatever may be true of princes or other actors, certainly Machiavelli, by teaching princes what Chiron was said to have taught, imitates Chiron or follows the creators of Chiron. Yet, as we have noted before, merely by teaching openly and in his own name what certain ancient writers had taught covertly and by using their characters as their mouthpieces, Machiavelli sets forth an entirely new teaching. He is a Chiron of an entirely new kind.

As a teacher of princes or of new princes in general, Machiavelli is not especially concerned with the particular problems facing contemporary Italian princes. Those particular problems would be of interest to him only as illustrations of typical problems. The primary purpose of the *Prince* then is not to give particular counsel to a contemporary Italian prince, but to set forth a wholly new teaching regarding wholly new princes in wholly new states, or a shocking teaching about the most shocking phenomena. From that fact we understand the meaning of the last chapter. The particular counsel there given serves the purpose of justifying the novel general teaching before the tribunal of accepted opinion: a general teaching, however novel and repulsive, might seem to be redeemed if it leads up to a particular counsel as respectable, honorable and praiseworthy as that of liberating Italy. But how is this transformation achieved? Machiavelli does not merely suppress mention of the unholy means which are required for the achievement of the sacred end. He surreptitiously introduces a new end, an end not warranted by the argument of the first twenty-five chapters. He urges Lorenzo to liberate Italy on patriotic grounds or, to use a term to which he alludes near the beginning of chapter 26, on grounds of the common good. He thus creates the impression that all the terrible rules and counsels given throughout the work were given exclusively for the sake of the common good. The last chapter suggests then a tolerable interpretation of the shocking teaching of the bulk of the work. But the first twenty-five chapters had observed complete silence regarding the common good. The allusion to the common good near the beginning of chapter 26 has the same status as the other surprising features of that chapter: the expectation of a spontaneous all-Italian rising against the foreigners and the expression of religious sentiment. It is only when one subjects the particular counsel given in the last chapter to political analysis along the lines demanded by the earlier chapters that one realizes that one must have broken completely with traditional morality and traditional beliefs in order even to consider that counsel. But the judicious reader cannot be satisfied with raising the question of how that particular counsel could be put into practice and thereafter whether it can be put into practice under the given circumstances. He must raise this further and more incisive question: would Machiavelli condemn the immoral policies recommended in the bulk of the book if they did not serve a patriotic purpose? Or are those immoral policies barely compatible with a patriotic use? Is it not possible to understand the patriotic conclusion of the *Prince* as a respectable coloring of the designs of a self-seeking Italian prince? There can be no doubt regarding the answer; the immoral policies recommended throughout the *Prince* are not justified on grounds of the common good, but exclusively on grounds of the self-interest of the prince, of his selfish concern with his own well-being, security and glory.[53] The final appeal to patriotism supplies Machiavelli with an excuse for having recommended immoral courses of action. In the light of this fact, his character may very well appear to be even blacker than even his worst enemies have thought. At the same time however, we are not forced to leave the matter with the remark that the last chapter of the *Prince* is a piece of mere rhetoric, i.e., that he was not capable of thinking clearly and writing with consummate skill.

These observations are not to deny that Machiavelli was an Italian patriot. He would not have been human if he had not loathed the barbarians who were devastating and degrading his fair country. We merely deny that his love for his fatherland, or his fatherland itself, was his most precious possession. The core of his being was his thought about man, about the condition of man and about human affairs. By raising the fundamental questions he of necessity transcended the limitations and the limits of Italy, and he thus was enabled to use the patriotic sentiments of his readers, as well as his own, for a higher purpose, for an ulterior purpose. One must also consider an ambiguity characteristic of Machiavelli's patriotism. In the *Prince* there are eight references to "the fatherland." In one case Italy is described as a fatherland. In six cases the fatherlands mentioned are, not countries, but cities. In one case, four fatherlands are mentioned; two are cities (Rome and Athens) and two are countries; one of the countries is Persia; as regards the other country, the fatherland nobilitated by Moses, it is unclear whether it is Egypt or Canaan, the land of his birth or the land of his aspiration.[54] When we apply this observation to Machiavelli, we become aware of a tension between his Italian patriotism and his Florentine patriotism. Or should one not rather speak of a tension between his Roman patriotism and his Tuscan patriotism? There exists a close connection between the transpatriotic core of his thought and his love for Italy. Italy is the soil out of which sprang the glory that was ancient Rome. Machiavelli believed that the men who are born in a country preserve through all ages more or less the same nature. If the greatest political achievement which the world has ever known was a fruit of the Italian soil there is ground for hope that the political rejuvenation of the world will make its first appearance in Italy: the sons of Italy are the most gifted individuals; all modern writers referred to in either the *Prince* or the *Discourses* are Italians. Since that political rejuvenation is bound up with a radical change in thought, the hope from Italy and for Italy is not primarily political in the narrow sense. The liberation of Italy which Machiavelli has primarily in mind is not the political liberation of Italy from the barbarians but the intellectual liberation of an Italian elite from a bad tradition. But precisely because he believed that the men who are born in a country preserve through all ages more or less the same nature, and as the nature of the Romans was different from that of the Tuscans, his hope was also grounded on his recollection of Tuscan glory:[55] the old Etrurians had made a decisive contribution to the religion of the Romans. He seems to have regarded himself as a restorer of Tuscan glory because he too contributed toward supplying Rome with a new religion or with a new outlook on religion. Or perhaps he thought of Tarquinius Priscus who, coming from Etruria, strengthened the democratic element of the Roman polity.

Furthermore, once one grasps the intransigent character of Machiavelli's theoretical concern, one is no longer compelled to burden him with the full responsibility for that practical recklessness which he frequently recommends. The ruthless counsels given throughout the *Prince* are addressed less to princes, who would hardly need them, than to "the young" who are concerned with understanding the nature of society. Those true addressees of the *Prince* have been brought up in teachings which, in the light of Machiavelli's wholly new teaching, reveal themselves to be much too confident of human goodness, if not of the goodness of creation, and hence too gentle or effeminate. Just as a man who is

timorous by training or nature cannot acquire courage, which is the mean between cowardice and foolhardiness, unless he drags himself in the direction of foolhardiness, so Machiavelli's pupils must go through a process of brutalization in order to be freed from effeminacy. Or just as one learns bayoneting by using weapons which are much heavier than those used in actual combat,[56] one learns statecraft by seriously playing with extreme courses of action which are rarely, if ever, appropriate in actual politics. Not only some of the most comforting, but precisely some of the most outrageous statements of the *Prince* are not meant seriously but serve a merely pedagogic function: as soon as one understands them, one sees that they are amusing and meant to amuse. Machiavelli tries to divert the adherence of the young from the old to the new teaching by appealing to the taste of the young which is not the best taste or, for that matter, to the taste of the common people:[57] he displays a bias in favor of the impetuous, the quick, the partisan, the spectacular, and the bloody over and against the deliberate, the slow, the neutral, the silent, and the gentle. In the *Prince* he says that a prince who has conquered a city which was wont to live free must destroy that city if he cannot make it his residence. In the *Discourses* he says that precisely a prince (if he is not a barbarian) as distinguished from a republic would spare and protect conquered cities and would leave their autonomy intact, as much as possible.[58] Another resolute course of action recommended in the *Prince* is to avoid neutrality when two powerful neighbors come to blows: to take sides is always better than to remain neutral. Machiavelli gradually discloses the limitations of this advice. He admits first that neutrality is not always fatal. He then states that because of the power of justice, to take sides is safer than to remain neutral. Thereafter he makes clear that under certain conditions it is most unwise to abandon neutrality in case of conflict between two powerful neighbors. Finally he admits that no course of action is perfectly safe or, in other words, that the power of justice is not as great as he previously indicated.[59] He suggests very strongly in the *Prince* that the one thing needful is good arms; he speaks less loudly of the need for prudence.[60]

We must return once more to Machiavelli's suggestion that he possesses adequate knowledge of the nature of princes, whereas Lorenzo may possess adequate knowledge of the nature of peoples. As we have said, this suggestion is absurd: since to be a prince means to rule the people, it is impossible to know princes well without knowing peoples well; to say nothing of the facts that Machiavelli displays knowledge of the nature of peoples throughout the *Prince* and, as he says explicitly in the *Discourses,* there is no difference of nature between princes and peoples.[61] Since he knows well the nature of peoples, he intimates by his strange suggestion that he is a prince. This intimation will appear strange only to those who lack familiarity with Xenophon or Plato: he who knows the art of ruling is more truly a ruler than men who rule merely by virtue of inheritance or force or fraud or election by people who know nothing of the art of ruling.[62] But if Machiavelli is a prince, he is a new prince and not one who imitates the modes and orders found by others, but rather an originator, a true founder, a discoverer of new modes and orders, a man of supreme virtue. In fact, if it is proper to call prophet the founder of a new social order which is all-comprehensive and not merely political or military, then Machiavelli is a prophet. Not Lorenzo, but Machiavelli is the new Romulus-Numa or the new Moses, i.e., a man who does not merely repeat in new circumstances what Romulus-Numa or Moses had done in the olden times, but who is as original as they were. In the last chapter of the *Prince,* he attests to certain miracles which had happened somewhere in contemporary Italy—miracles which resemble those of the time of Moses. The ancient miracles happened on the way from the house of bondage to the promised land: they happened immediately before the revelation on Mount Sinai. What is imminent, Machiavelli suggests then, is not the conquest of a new promised land, but a new revelation, the revelation of a new code, of a new decalogue. The man who will bring the new code, cannot be Lorenzo or any other prince in the vulgar sense. The bringer of the new code is none other than Machiavelli himself: he brings the true code, the code which is in accordance with the truth, with the nature of things. Compared with this achievement, the conquest of the promised land, the liberation of Italy, is a *cura posterior*: it can wait, it must wait until the new code has regenerated the Italians. The new Moses will not be sad if he dies at the borders of the land which he had promised, and if he will see it only from afar. For while it is fatal for a would-be conqueror not to conquer while he is alive, the discoverer of the all-important truth can conquer posthumously.[63]

Concerning prophets in general, Machiavelli remarks that all armed prophets have conquered and the unarmed prophets have failed. The greatest armed prophet is Moses. The only unarmed prophet mentioned is Savonarola. But as is shown by the expression "all armed prophets . . . and the unarmed ones," he thinks not only of Savonarola. Just as he, who admired so greatly the contemporary Muslim conquerors, could not help thinking of Muhammad when speaking of armed prophets, so he must have thought of Jesus when speaking of unarmed prophets. This is perhaps the greatest difficulty which we encounter when we try to enter into the thought of the *Prince:* how can Machiavelli, on the basis of his principles, account for the victory of Christianity? Certain of his successors attempted explicitly to explain the victory of Christianity in purely political terms. To quote from a present-day historian: "In the most starkly Erastian utterance of the [seventeenth] century, [Henry] Parker all but maintained that it was Constantine, and not the preaching or the miracles of the early Church, that won Europe to the Chris-

tian fold."[64] But we cannot bring ourselves to believe that a man of Machiavelli's intelligence would have been satisfied with an answer of this kind, which merely leads to this further question: what motivated Constantine's action? must Christianity not already have been a power in order to become an attraction or a tool for a politician? To see how Machiavelli could have accounted for the victory of Christianity, we have to consider a further difficulty which is no less obvious. All unarmed prophets, he says, have failed. But what is he himself if not an unarmed prophet? How can he reasonably hope for the success of his enormous venture—enormous in itself and productive of infinite enormities—if unarmed prophets necessarily fail? This is the only fundamental question which the *Prince* raises in the reader's mind without giving him even a suspicion of Machiavelli's answer. It reminds one of the question, likewise left unanswered in the *Prince,* as to how new modes and orders can be maintained throughout the ages.[65] For the answer to it, we must turn to the *Discourses*.

Notes

[1] Letter to Vettori, December 10, 1513.

[2] Of the 142 chapter headings of the *Discourses,* 39 contain proper names.

[3] *Discourses* II 1 (234), III 19 and 42; cf. II 20 beginning.

[4] Cf. *Prince,* ch. 15 beginning.

[5] See page 23 above.

[6] Cf. the Epistle Dedicatory of the *Prince.*

[7] We are thus not unprepared to find that the most extraordinary conqueror, Alexander (the Great), is mentioned twice in the heading of the following chapter.

[8] *Discourses,* I pr.

[9] The tacit emphasis on ancient examples in ch. 9 has a special reason. It draws our attention to the impropriety of discussing in the *Prince* the most important modern example of civil principalities i.e., the rule of the Medici. Machiavelli leaves it at discussing the ancient counterpart: Nabis of Sparta. Cf. ch. 21 (73).

[10] Compare also the chief example of ch. 10 (the German cities which are free to the highest degree) with the remark about the Swiss in ch. 12 (the Swiss are armed to the highest degree and free to the highest). This distinction is developed somewhat more fully in *Discourses* II 19 (286-287).

[11] Chs. 12 (41) and 13 (43, 44). Cf. the letter to Piero Soderini of January 1512.

[12] Chs. 17 (52) and 18 (55). In the only intervening reference to literature—ch. 17 (54)—Machiavelli attacks "the writers" and no longer merely as he did at the beginning of ch. 15, "many" writers. Incidentally, "many writers" are attacked in the *Discourses* as early as the tenth chapter; the break with the tradition becomes explicit in the *Discourses* proportionately much earlier than in the *Prince*.

[13] Cf. the relation of princes and ministers as it appears in ch. 22 with the relation of Cesare Borgia and his minister as presented in ch. 7 (24).

[14] Chs. 20, 22 and 23 contain only modern examples. The explicit emphasis on modern examples in ch. 18 (How princes should keep faith) has a special reason just as had the tacit emphasis on ancient examples in ch. 9: Machiavelli draws our attention to the modern form of faithlessness or hypocrisy which strikingly differs from the Roman form (cf. *Discourses* II 13 end). There is a connection between this thought and the reference to "pious cruelty" in ch. 21. Machiavelli indicates that the argument of ch. 18 requires a special act of daring (56).

[15] Ch. 19 is the center not only of the third part but of the whole section of the *Prince* which follows the discussion of the various kinds of principality, i.e., of that whole section which in the light of the beginning of the *Prince* comes as a surprise (cf. ch. 1 where the theme "the various kinds of principality" is announced with the beginnings of chs. 12, 15 and 24). Whereas the first, second, and fourth parts of the *Prince* each contain one Latin quotation, the third part contains two of them.—Compare the beginning of ch. 6 with the beginnings of chs. 21-23 in the light of the observation made in the text.

[16] Cf. pages 46-47 above.

[17] Ch. 20 (67-68). The opinion described there as held by "our ancients" is described in *Discourses* III 27 (403) as a modern opinion held by "the sages of our city sometime ago."

[18] Shortly before, Machiavelli mentions "natural affection" for a prince. He had not used that expression since early in ch. 4. But there he had spoken of the natural affection of the subjects for the French barons, their lords from time immemorial; now he speaks of natural affection for a new prince. The transition is partly effected by what he says in ch. 19 (60) about the hatred, founded in fear, of the French people against the French magnates.

[19] Ch. 21 (72). Cf. ch. 3 end.

[20] The most unqualified attack in the *Prince* on ancient writers in general ("the writers")—ch. 17 (54)—occurs within the context of a praise of ancient statesmen or captains.—The fourth part of the *Prince* contains one Latin quotation and the only Italian quotation occurring in the book.

[21] *Prince* chs. 6 (18) and 11 (36).

[22] To "treat" something means to "reason" about it (*Prince*, ch. 2 beginning and ch. 8 beginning). Machiavelli calls his discourse on the Decemvirate, which includes an extensive summary of Livy's account of the Decemvirate and therefore in particular of the actions of the would-be tyrant Appius Claudius, the "above written treatise" (*Discourses* I 43), whereas he calls his discourse on the liberality of the senate "the above written discourse" (*Discourses* I 52 beginning). In *Discourses* II 32 (323) *trattato* means "conspiracy." He calls Xenophon's *Hiero* a "treatise" on tyranny (II 2) while he calls Dante's *Monarchia* a "discourse" (I 53). In *Florentine Histories* II 2, he calls the First Book of that work *nostro trattato universale*.

[23] Compare also the end of ch. 13 with ch. 25.—In the first chapter Machiavelli indicates 13 subjects whose treatment might seem to require 13 chapters, and he indicates in the fifteenth chapter 11 subjects whose treatment might seem to require 11 chapters.

[24] Chs. 26 and 4 of the *Prince* begin with practically the same word.

[25] Cf. *Discourses* I 23 (153).

[26] Only at the end of ch. 4 does Machiavelli allude to Italy by mentioning the failure of Pyrrhus, i.e., his failure to keep his conquests in Italy.

[27] *Prince* ch. 7 (23-25); cf. *Opere* I 637. Consider Machiavelli's statement on the pernicious character of the feudal nobility in *Discourses* I 55.

[28] The term "fatherland" which occurs in chs. 6, 8 and 9 is avoided in ch. 7, the chapter devoted to Cesare Borgia.

[29] The subject-matter of ch. 5 is slightly concealed (see the unobtrusive transition from states in general to cities i.e., republics, near the beginning: *volerli . . . ruinarle*). It almost goes without saying that almost all examples in this chapter are ancient. All the more striking is Machiavelli's silence about the Roman mode of ruling republican cities by making them allies; see *Discourses* II 24 (303) and 19 (285); he tacitly rejects this mode in the *Prince* because it is impracticable for a prince who is to become prince of a united Italy.—When discussing the badness of mercenary armies, Machiavelli uses almost exclusively examples which

show that mercenary armies have ruined or endangered republics. He thus shows in effect that mercenaries can be eminently good for a leader of mercenary armies, like Sforza who by being armed became a new prince; compare ch. 12 with chs. 7 (21) and 14 (36). As we learn from Livy (XXXVII 27.15), Nabis of Sparta whom Machiavelli praises, placed the greatest confidence in his mercenary troops. (This report of Livy precedes almost immediately his account of Philopoemen which Machiavelli uses in *Prince* ch. 14). These remarks taken together with those about the soldiers of the Roman emperors in ch. 19 and about the impossibility of arming all able-bodied Italian subjects in ch. 20 (67) reveal a possibility which deserves attention. In this connection one should also consider what Machiavelli says toward the end of the ninth chapter, immediately after having praised (the tyrant) Nabis of Sparta, about the superiority of absolute principalities, i.e., about the kind of principality which was traditionally called tyranny (*Discourses* I 25 end), and compare it with the confrontation of the Turkish and the French monarchies in *Prince* ch. 4 (14).

[30] Compare ch. 25 (79) with chs. 18 end and 21 beginning, as well as *Discourses* I 12 (130).

[31] Compare *Discourses* I 26 with *Prince* chs. 7 (24), 8 (30), 13 end, 17 and 21 beginning. Just as Philip became "from a little king, prince of Greece" by the use of the most cruel means, Ferdinand of Aragon became "from a weak king, the first king of the Christians" by the use of "pious cruelty."

[32] *Prince* chs. 3 (11-13), 7 (23,26), II (37-38); cf. *Discourses* III 29. We note in passing that in the *Prince* ch. 16 (50-51) Machiavelli holds up "the present king of France," "the present king of Spain," and Pope Julius II but not the present Pope, Leo X, who possesses "goodness and infinite other virtues," (ch. 11 end) as models of prudent stinginess which is the indispensable condition for "doing great things." Cf. Ranke, *Die Roemischen Paepste,* ed. by F. Baethgen, I, 273 on Leo X's extravagance.—In the *Prince* Machiavelli tells two stories about private conversations which he had had (chs. 3 and 7). According to the first story Machiavelli once told a French cardinal that the French know nothing of politics, for otherwise they would not have permitted the Church to become so great (through the exploits of Cesare Borgia). The second story deals with what Cesare told Machiavelli on the day on which Pope Julius II was elected, i.e., on which Cesare's hopes were dashed through his insufficient control of the Church: Cesare had in fact committed the same mistake as the French, but he had the excuse that he had no choice. In *Florentine Histories* I 23, Machiavelli alludes to the possibility that the papacy might become hereditary. Could he have played with the thought that a new Cesare Borgia might redeem Italy after having himself become Pope and the founder of a papal dynas-

ty?

[33] *Discourses* I 12. Cf. the letter to Vettori of April 26, 1513.

[34] *Discourses* I 27; *Opere* I 683.

[35] Machiavelli prepares for the silence about Romulus in ch. 26 in the following manner: in ch. 6 he enumerates the four heroic founders three times and in the final enumeration he relegates Romulus to the end. Cf. *Florentine Histories* VI 29.

[36] *Prince* chs. 1, 6 (17-19), 8 (29-30), 14 (48), 19 (66), 20 (67) and 24 (77); cf. *Art of War* VII (616-617).

[37] Cf. *Prince* ch. 22.

[38] Ch. 7 (21-22). Cf. pages 22-23 above.

[39] Letter to [Ricciardo Bechi], March 8, 1497.

[40] The shift in *Prince* ch. 26 from Lorenzo to his family can be understood to some extent from the point of view indicated in the text. As for the unreliability of promises stemming from passion, cf. *Discourses* II 31; as for the popularity of grand hopes and valiant promises, cf. *Discourses* I 53.

[41] This is not to deny the fact that the miracles attested to by Machiavelli are without example insofar as their sequence differs from the sequence of the Mosaic miracles.

[42] *Prince* chs. 3 (13), 12 (39,41), 18 (56-57) and 25 (80-81); cf. *Discourses* I 27. One can express the progress of the argument in the last part of the *Prince* as follows: 1) everything depends on virtue (ch. 24); 2) very much depends on chance but chance can be kept down by the right kind of man (ch. 25); 3) chance has done the most difficult part of the work required for liberating Italy, only the rest needs to be done by means of virtue (ch. 26).

[43] The 7 real defeats must be taken together with the 4 invented miracles if one wants to grasp Machiavelli's intimation.

[44] *Discourses* II 30 end.

[45] In the "highest" part of the *Prince* Machiavelli speaks of "us Florentines," (chs. 15 and 20) while in the other parts of the book he speaks of "us Italians" (chs. 2, 12, 13 and 24).—The tyrant Nabis had destroyed the freedom of many Greek cities (Justinus XXXI, 1); by his assassination that freedom was restored. Cf. note 9 above.

[46] *Prince* chs. 9 (32), 18 (57), 19 (58-59), 20 (68-

69) and 23 (76-77). In each of the two chapters, 20 and 21, Machiavelli gives five rules to princes; the fourth rule in ch. 20 concerns the employment of men who were suspect at the beginning of the reign of a new prince; in the fourth rule given in ch. 21 the prince is urged to honor those who are excellent in any art.

[47] *Discourses* III 2 end and 35 (422-423).

[48] Compare *Discourses* I 30 (163) with 29 (160-161).

[49] Apart from the Epistle Dedicatory and ch. 26 where Machiavelli, speaking of Lorenzo to Lorenzo uses the plural of reverence, he uses the second person plural only in connection with verbs like "seeing," "finding," "considering," and "understanding." There are, I believe, 11 cases of the latter kind in the *Prince* while in the *Discourses,* if I remember well, there are only 2 (I 58 [221] and II 30 [317]): in the *Discourses* which are addressed to potential princes, the need to distinguish between doers and thinkers does not arise to the same extent as it does in the *Prince.* Consider *Discourses* II pr. (230). In the chapter of the *Prince* on flatterers—ch. 23 (75)—Machiavelli uses Thou when speaking of the prince to the prince, while he uses the third person when speaking of the prudent prince: he is not a flatterer. Ch. 3 (10-11) beautifully illustrates how Machiavelli the teacher works together with his readers in examining certain things as well as how his contribution differs from that of his readers.

[50] *Prince* chs. 18 (55) and 19 (62).

[51] Swift's Houyhnhnms, being reasonable horses, are centaurs if a centaur is a being which combines the perfection of a horse with the perfection of man. In order to understand what the recommendation to imitate these beast-men means in *Gulliver's Travels,* one would have to start from the facts that the relation between Lilliput and Brobdingnag imitates the relation between the moderns and the ancients, and that the same relation is imitated again on a different plane in the last two parts of the work.

[52] Compare *Prince* ch. 14 end with *Discourses* II 13.

[53] Machiavelli does not even suggest that Cesare Borgia, the model, was animated by patriotism or concerned with the common good. It is true that he contrasts Cesare with the criminal Agathocles by not calling Cesare a criminal. But if one looks at the actions of the two men, the contrast vanishes: in describing Agathocles as a criminal, he provi-

sionally adopts the traditional judgment on that man, whereas there does not yet exist a traditional judgment on Cesare. The traditional condemnation of Agathocles was partly based on the fact that he had risen to princely power from "a base and abject condition." Machiavelli refers to a similar consideration when explaining the failure of Maximinus—*Prince* ch. 19 (64-65)—but it is irrelevant for his own judgment as can be seen from *Discourses* II 13, to say nothing of the Epistle Dedicatory to the *Prince* where he describes himself as "a man of low and base state." The main reason why Machiavelli had to speak of a criminal ruler was that he was compelled to indicate that he was questioning the traditional distinction between the criminal and the non-criminal as far as founders are concerned. He thus presents Agathocles as the classical example of the criminal ruler, as a breaker of all divine and human laws, a murderer and a traitor, a man without faith, mercy and religion; Agathocles possessed indeed greatness of mind; although a most excellent captain, he cannot be counted among the most excellent men; his actions could acquire for him empire but not glory; he benefited indeed his subjects, or rather the common people, but he did this of course entirely for selfish reasons. In the sequel Machiavelli retracts everything he had said in connection with Agathocles about the difference between an able criminal ruler and an able non-criminal ruler. The first step is the praise of Nabis whom he calls a prince in the *Prince* while he calls him in the *Discourses* a tyrant: Nabis' policy was fundamentally the same as that of Agathocles (compare *Prince* chs. 9 [33] and 19 [58] with *Discourses* I 10 [122] and ch. 40 [187]). The second step is the questioning of the difference between "most excellent captain" and "most excellent man": good arms are the necessary and sufficient condition of good laws, and Agathocles had good arms; Cyrus, the excellent man most emphatically praised, is not said to have possessed faith, mercy and religion, but he is distinguished by greatness of mind, i.e., by a quality which Agathocles also possessed. One reason why Agathocles cannot be counted among the most excellent men is his savage cruelty and inhumanity; but Hannibal who is likewise characterized by inhuman cruelty is a most excellent man. (Compare *Prince* chs. 12 [38-39], 14 [47-48], 17 [54], 26 [81] with *Discourses* II 18 [280] and III 21 end). The last step is to show that glory can be acquired by crime or in spite of crime. This is shown most clearly by the case of Severus (see pages 46-47 above), but hardly less clearly by *Prince* ch. 18 toward the end, to say nothing of Machiavelli's observations regarding Giovampagolo Baglioni in *Discourses* I 27.

[54] *Prince* chs. 6 (18), 8 (27,29,30), 9 (31,33), 26 (84).

[55] *Prince* ch. 26 (83); *Discourses* II 4 toward the end and III 43; *Art of War,* at the end; compare *Discourses* I 1 end with Livy I 34. 12-35. 12, also Livy V 15.

Cf. note 45 above.

[56] Cf. *Art of War* II (489).

[57] Cf. *Discourses* I 53.

[58] *Prince* ch. 5; *Discourses* II 2 (239-240). In the preceding chapter of the *Discourses* (234) there occurs one of the few references to the *Prince*; the reference is to the third chapter i.e., to the section which deals with conquest.

[59] *Prince* ch. 21 (71-73).

[60] *Prince* chs. 12 (38-39) and 19 (58); *Discourses* I 4 (103); *Opere* II 473.

[61] *Prince* chs. 3 (6), 6 (19), 9 (31,32), 10 (35-36), 17 (53), 18 (57), 23 (75), 24 (78); *Discourses* I 57 and 58 (217-219). In the *Prince* chs. 7 (22) and 8 (28) he applies expressions to Cesare Borgia and to Agathocles which he had applied to himself in the Epistle Dedicatory.

[62] Cf. *Discourses* Epistle Dedicatory and the letter to Vettori of December 10, 1513.

[63] The 11 pairs of moral qualities mentioned in ch. 15 and the 11 rules of conduct discussed in chs. 20-21 prove on examination to be 10.—Compare Hobbes' re-writing of the decalogue in *Leviathan,* ch. 30.

[64] W. K. Jordan, *Men of Substance* (Chicago: The University of Chicago Press, 1942). p. 82.

[65] Compare *Discourses* III 35 beginning with *Prince* ch. 6 (19).

Benito Mussolini describes Machiavelli's pessimistic view of human nature:

Men . . . are evil, more attached to material possessions than to their own kin, ever ready to change their sentiments and their convictions.

Turning now to human selfishness, I find the following statement in his miscellaneous papers: 'Men complain more of losing a fortune than of losing a brother or a father, for we forget our grief over a death but never over a loss of property. The reason is obvious. Everyone knows that if there is a change of government it will not restore his brother to life, but it may restore a lost estate.' And in the third chapter of his *Discourses*: 'As all those who have written of political affairs have pointed out, and as all history shows by numerous examples, a man who founds a republic and drafts the laws that govern it must assume that all men are evil and prone to indulge their evil impulses whenever they are free to do so. Men never guide their conduct by ideal motives, but by necessity. But wherever liberty abounds and license is possible, a country is at once filled with confusion and disorder.'

I might multiply similar quotations, but it is not necessary. The citations I have made are sufficient to prove that Machiavelli's low opinion of men is not accidental and occasional, but fundamental in his philosophy of life. It recurs in all his works; it represents the fixed conviction of an experienced and disillusioned mind. We must keep in view this initial and essential fact if we are to follow intelligently the successive development of Machiavelli's thought.

Benito Mussolini, in "Prelude to Machiavelli,"
in The Living Age, Vol. CCCXXIII, No. 4194,
November 22, 1924.

John Plamenatz (essay date 1972)

SOURCE: "In Search of Machiavellian 'Virtu'," in *The Political Calculus: Essays on Machiavelli's Philosophy*, edited by Anthony Parel, University of Toronto Press, 1972, pp. 157-78.

[*In the essay below, Plamenatz examines Machiavelli's concept of virtue, put forth in* The Prince *and* Discourses upon the First Decade of T. Livius. *The critic argues that Machiavelli approaches a philosophical understanding of humankind, but he exalts heroic qualities at the expense of important human traits.*]

The most vilified of political thinkers is also the one of whom it has been said that he 'concentrated all his real and supreme values in what he called *virtù*.'[1] There is nothing here to be surprised at; for those who have been shocked by Machiavelli have been so, not only by his seeming to justify murder, cruelty, and treachery, but by

his way of speaking about virtue.

Machiavelli is no longer shocking, and it is widely agreed that those who were shocked by him in the past misunderstood him. But he is still a subject of controversy. In particular, there are differences of opinion about what he called *virtù*. These differences are, I think, less about what is to be understood by the term, what qualities it refers to, than about the place of *virtù* in Machiavelli's political thought generally and his conception of man. Some ninety years ago Villari said that Machiavelli 'always used the word *virtue* in the sense of courage and energy both for good and evil. To Christian virtue in its more general meaning, he rather applied the term *goodness,* and felt much less admiration for it than for the pagan virtue that was always fruitful of glory.'[2] Later scholars, though they have qualified this verdict, have not disagreed with it substantially—though they have sometimes believed that they were doing so. It is not true that Machiavelli always used the word *virtù* in this general sense, or in narrower senses that fall within its scope. He sometimes used it in quite other senses. It has been questioned whether he admired *virtù* more than he did goodness, and it is doubtful whether what he understood by goodness (*bontà*) has much that is peculiarly Christian about it. Still, though writers since Villari's time have gone further than he did in distinguishing the various senses that Machiavelli gave to *virtù*, they have not seriously challenged his account of it. They have tried rather to improve on it.

No one has gone further than Meinecke in treating the idea of *virtù* as the key to understanding Machiavelli's conceptions of man and of the state. Meinecke distinguishes two important senses in which Machiavelli uses the term. Sometimes he has in mind what is nowadays called *civic virtue,* and sometimes something altogether more rare and excellent—a virtue peculiar to rulers and leaders of men, and especially to founders of states and religions. This second virtue, to distinguish it from the first, we might call *heroic*—though Meinecke does not give it that name. Heroic and civic virtue are not mutually exclusive; indeed, they are closely related in the sense that each sustains the other or gives scope to it, but they are different.

If, among Machiavelli's twentieth-century interpreters, Meinecke makes the most of *virtù,* Professor Whitfield seems to make the least. 'There is,' he says, 'no doctrine of *virtù* in Machiavelli. If there were it would be easy to discover in his works, but Machiavelli was not given to such theorizing, and he himself would be the first to be surprised at the stir the word has caused.'[3] Whitfield, in his English way, felt perhaps a certain impatience with other scholars 'theorizing' about a writer who, in his eyes, has the merit of not being 'given to theorizing.'

Professor Whitfield is right; there is no doctrine of *virtù* in Machiavelli. Machiavelli does not define the word, even in the most general way, let alone distinguish different senses in which he uses it. Nor is it part of a systematic theory about man and the state, for Machiavelli has no such theory. There is no more a doctrine of *virtù* in Machiavelli than there is a doctrine of *vertu* in the plays of Corneille. Still, what each expresses by the word is worth, and has received, close scrutiny; for this scrutiny is one way, and a good way, of getting at how they think and feel about man.

Neither Meinecke, who says that Machiavelli 'concentrates his real and supreme values in *virtù,*' nor Whitfield, who denies that he has a doctrine of it, disagrees with Villari that part of what Machiavelli understands by *virtù* is energy or strength of will. No moderately attentive reader of **The Prince** and the **Discourses** can help but notice that Machiavelli finds *virtù* both in the Roman citizen devoted to the republic and in such men as Romulus, Lycurgus, Moses, and Numa Pompilius,

the 'founders' of states or religions. Though Machiavelli does not define either the virtue of the citizen or that of the maker or restorer of a state or religion, though he does not point to the differences between them, there can really be no doubting that he does not attribute the same range of qualities to the citizen and to the heroic creator or preserver of what brings order to men.

Thus, though there is no doctrine of *virtù* in Machiavelli, there is no denying that he uses the word in related and yet different senses, and that the attempt to explain how they differ and how they are connected with his other ideas about man, the human condition and the state, is an attempt to interpret what can properly be called a philosophy. Because a writer produces no systematic theory, it does not follow that he has nothing that deserves to be called philosophy—for his ideas may be coherent and may have implicit in them a comprehensive attitude or way of looking at the human condition, either at all times and everywhere or within broad limits of time and territory. Of course, there are inconsistencies and obscurities in Machiavelli; but then there are also in the much more systematic Hobbes, who loved to define and to distinguish. And it may be that Machiavelli was not the less consistent and lucid of the two.

Though Machiavelli did not 'theorize' about *virtù,* Whitfield does so for some thirteen pages and to good purpose. Machiavelli, he says, sometimes contrasts *virtù* with *viltà,* and at least once with *ozio,* but more often with *fortuna.*[4] Now, *viltà* is cowardice, or faint-heartedness, and sometimes baseness or meanness, and *ozio* is idleness. So that Whitfield agrees with Villari that *virtù* is, first and foremost, courage and energy; for courage is the opposite of cowardice, and energy of idleness. And though courage and energy are not properly the *opposites* of fortune, they can be *opposed* to it. Machiavelli speaks of fortune, sometimes, as if it were a person, as if it had purposes of its own, benevolent or malevolent, and at other times as if it were opportunity that a man may take or not take; and he speaks of it also as whatever in human affairs is unforeseen and must be faced when it comes. He speaks of it as sailors, in the old sailing days, spoke of the sea, as if it were both friend and enemy, propitious and threatening, itself unconquerable but the occasion of human defeats and victories. Fortune is what man is 'up against'; and *virtù* is opposed to it in the sense that it makes the best of it, either by taking advantage of what it brings or by bearing up under it. Here again *virtù* is courage and energy, and something more besides; it is fortitude, or courage in adversity, and also intelligence and resourcefulness, the ability to recognize how you are placed and to act in time and effectively. There is nothing that Whitfield says or implies about *virtù* to which either Villari or Meinecke need disagree.

This is not to suggest that he only repeats what they,

who wrote before he did, said. For example, he shows how close Machiavelli stands to other writers, earlier or later, who never, as he did, shocked posterity. He quotes from Cicero's *De Officiis* (II, X, 320): 'For they [men] do not despise everyone of whom they think ill. They think ill of those who are wicked, slanderous, fraudulent, ready to commit injustices, without indeed despising them. Wherefore, as I said, those are despised who, as the saying goes, are of no use either to themselves or others, in whom there is no exertion, no care for anything.'[5] This is good, and to the point. At least since Villari's time, Machiavelli's 'pagan' idea of *virtù* has been contrasted with the 'Christian' idea of *bontà*. Yet even the best of Christians does not despise all that he blames; he does not despise, any more than Machiavelli did, courage and energy, fortitude and resourcefulness—even in the wicked, even when he blames what they could not have done had they not had these qualities. Actions that require *virtù*, though sometimes evil, are never despicable. Cicero said it, or rather implied it, long before Machiavelli did.

Excellent, too, and to the point, are Whitfield's quotations from La Rochefoucauld: 'Weakness is more opposed to virtue than is vice,' or 'No one deserves the name of good unless he has strength and boldness enough to be wicked—all other goodness is most often a form of idleness or of impotence of the will,' or 'There are evil heroes as well as good ones.'[6] The virtue that La Rochefoucauld speaks of is not Machiavelli's *virtù*, but the two ideas have a good deal in common. Where there is virtue, for La Rochefoucauld as for Machiavelli, there is strength of will. But Professor Whitfield goes too far when he suggests that what passes uncondemned in Cicero and La Rochefoucauld (and in others) is found shocking in Machiavelli. The Frenchman never said, and Whitfield does not show that the Roman did either, that actions ordinarily held to be wicked are justified when they are committed for the founding or preserving of the state. This doctrine—whatever is to be said for or against it—is not to be found in La Rochefoucauld and is not implied by the passage that Whitfield quotes from Cicero. But it is to be found in Machiavelli or at least it has seemed so to those who have accused him of condoning wickedness. To quote from some of the great 'moralists' to make clearer what Machiavelli meant by *virtù* is an excellent idea but to use the quotations to suggest that he is no more open than they are to the accusation that he justifies immorality is to misuse them.

I have touched briefly on the views of three writers, Villari, Meinecke, and Whitfield, who have all in their different ways thrown light upon what Machiavelli meant by *virtù*. They do not all three say the same things. Neither Villari nor Whitfield distinguishes, as Meinecke does, *civic* from what might (for want of a better word) be called *heroic* virtue. Indeed, Meinecke himself does not go far in making this distinction; he rather suggests

that it ought to be made than puts himself to the trouble of making it, for he does not explain in detail how the two sorts of virtue differ. He goes no further in this direction than to say: 'it [*virtù*] therefore embraced the civic virtues and those of the ruling class; it embraced a readiness to devote oneself to the common good, as well as the wisdom, energy and ambition of the great founders and rulers of states.'[7] But 'common good' is a vague term, and the founder and the ruler may be as ready as the ordinary citizen to promote it. Civic virtue is perhaps better described as a readiness to perform the duties of one's office or role in the state than as devotion to a common good. The citizen, and not only the ruler, needs 'energy' if he is to be a good citizen, and even some measure of wisdom. As for ambition, I doubt, for reasons that I shall give later, whether it is to be included in Machiavellian *virtù*.

We may regret that Meinecke did not explain more adequately and fully the difference between these two kinds of 'virtue,' but we cannot deny that they differ considerably and are closely related, and that both are important in the thought of Machiavelli. Nor can we go far in disagreeing with Meinecke's account of what they consist in, for he says too little about them to allow us to do that. He neither repeats what Villari said nor contradicts him, and is not contradicted by Whitfield. Where he goes wrong—so at least it seems to me—is not so much in his meagre account of what Machiavelli meant by *virtù*; it is rather in some of the conclusions he draws from it. The distinction he makes between *civic* and what I have called *heroic* virtue is one that needs to be made, though it ought to be made more clearly than he makes it. But to say, as he does, that 'the ethical sphere of his (Machiavelli's) *virtù* lay in juxtaposition to the usual moral sphere like a kind of world on its own'[8] which was, for Machiavelli, a 'higher world' is to misinterpret Machiavelli, attributing to him beliefs and attitudes which there is no good reason to believe were his. And it is just as misleading to say that 'the development and creation of *virtù* was for Machiavelli the ideal, and completely self-evident, purpose of the state.'[9] There are no better scholars in the world than the Germans. Yet the weight of German scholarship sometimes lies heavy on what it studies, pushing it out of shape. How it does so in this case I shall try to show later. But first let us look at some examples of how Machiavelli speaks of *virtù* in the two most often read of his books, **The Prince** and the **Discourses**.

If we read only English translations of Machiavelli, we are hard put to it to discover what he meant by *virtù*. For his translators, more often than not, do not render *virtù* by 'virtue.' They have an excellent excuse for not doing so; for *virtù*, as Machiavelli uses it, often does not mean what 'virtue' means in the English of our day. So they render *virtù* by some other word, such as valour, ability, merit, courage, or genius, or by some combination of words. Take for example the nineteenth chapter of the first book of the *Discourses,* which in most editions, both Italian and English, is from two to three pages long. In it Machiavelli speaks of *virtù* ten times; Detmold, in one of the most widely used of English translations, renders *virtù* by 'virtue' only twice, and on both occasions adds the word 'valour,' presumably in the hope of coming closer to the original; while Allan Gilbert, the most recent and perhaps the most accurate of Machiavelli's translators into English, abstains altogether from the word 'virtue' in his version of this chapter.[10] On all ten occasions he renders *virtù* by ability, leaving it to the reader to judge from the context what kind of ability is in question. Detmold renders *virtù* by 'character,' 'virtue and valour,' 'vigour and ability,' 'genius and courage,' 'good qualities and courage,' 'great abilities and courage,' 'military ability,' 'merits.' If we take only this chapter, Gilbert is the more prudent translator of the two, and also the more faithful to the original. Yet *virtù,* as Machiavelli uses the word, has not quite the same meaning, or range of meanings, as the broader and more colourless English word 'ability.' Which is not to suggest that Gilbert was wrong to prefer it to the more varied expressions to which Detmold resorted.

In the third chapter of *The Prince,* Machiavelli praises the Romans for their foresight. He says of them that 'seeing their troubles far ahead, [they] always provided against them, and never let them continue in order to avoid war, because they knew that such a war is not averted but is deferred to the other's advantage . . . Nor did they approve what all day is in the mouths of the wise men of our age: to profit from the help of time; but they did profit from that of their own vigor [*virtù*] and prudence.'[11] Here *virtù* is associated with prudence. The Romans looked far ahead, taking resolute and timely action. What, according to Machiavelli, do the wise—the falsely-wise—mean by 'the help of time'? They mean that we can see only a little way ahead, and that therefore difficult decisions are best left untaken. This is the excuse of the pusillanimous. True, we cannot be sure of the future, but we must look ahead as far as we can, seeing what is to be done for the best, and doing it in good time. With the old Romans, at least in the eyes of Machiavelli, foresight, energy, and courage went naturally together.

In the sixth chapter of *The Prince,* speaking of men who have become rulers, Machiavelli says: 'they had from Fortune nothing more than opportunity, which gave them matter into which they could introduce whatever form they chose; and without opportunity, their strength of will [*la virtù dello animo loro*] would have been wasted, and without such strength, the opportunity would have been useless';[12] and then, a little further on, he continues: 'Their opportunities then made these men prosper, since their surpassing abilities [*la eccelenza virtù loro*] enabled them to recognize their opportuni-

ties. As a result, their countries were exalted and became very prosperous.'[13] Here *virtù* consists, in the first place, of strength of will or mind, and in the second, of insight. The possessor of *virtù* sees his chance to mould something to his own design, not some inert or physical thing, but something human, some community or some aspect of communal life; he has imagination and intelligence enough to see what can be done, to see what is invisible to others, and strength of purpose enough to do it. He is strong, bold, and of good judgment, to his own great advantage and to the advantage of his people or community.

This is not to say that, in the opinion of Machiavelli, these qualities fail to qualify as *virtù* unless their possessor actually gets what he wants for himself or his people. Courage, energy, and intelligence do not cease to be what they are when they fail of their purpose. Small men have small purposes and are often successful, but their success is no evidence of *virtù* in them, and great men—who are great because their courage, energy, and intelligence are out of the ordinary—sometimes fail. One of the meanings that Machiavelli gives to *virtù* is the capacity to form large and difficult purposes, and to act resourcefully and resolutely in pursuit of them. *Virtù,* in this (the heroic) sense, is imagination and resilience as well as courage and intelligence. There is no scope for it except where there are difficulties, where there are risks to be taken; and where risks are taken, there is a chance of failure. Machiavelli's feelings towards the most notorious, and (in some eyes) the most oddly chosen, of his heroes varied considerably. There was a time when he came close to despising Cesare Borgia—not because Borgia failed of his purpose but because he lost his nerve and his dignity when things went against him.

Villari is right when he says that Machiavellian *virtù* is 'fruitful of glory.' The actions it inspires are of the kind that bring fame or reputation: fame where *virtù* is heroic and reputation where it is civic. But it is a mistake to include, as Meinecke does, ambition among the qualities that make up *virtù.* I have found no example of Machiavelli using the word in such a way as to suggest that ambition is itself a part of *virtù.* True, he thought well of ambition, and was himself ambitious. The desire for glory promotes *virtù*; it is the strongest of the forces that move men to display it, especially the heroic kind. And even the citizen who displays only civic *virtù* is concerned for his good name; and this concern, though it is not what is ordinarily called ambition, is akin to it. But to hold that ambition is a prime mover of *virtù* is still not to treat ambition as a part of *virtù.*

In some of the most discussed pages he wrote, in the eighth chapter of *The Prince.* Machiavelli denies that a really wicked man who achieves a great ambition can be said to be virtuous, even though he displays great strength of mind and courage. This denial has been called half-hearted, and is certainly ambiguous. Speaking of Agathocles, a potter's son who by ruthless means became tyrant of Syracuse, Machiavelli says: 'It cannot, however, be called virtue [*virtù*] to kill one's fellow-citizens, to betray friends, to be without fidelity, without mercy, without religion; such proceedings enable one to gain sovereignty but not fame. If we consider Agathocles' ability [*se si considerassi la virtù di Agatocle*] in entering into and getting out of dangers, and his greatness of mind in enduring and overcoming adversities, we cannot see why he should be judged inferior to any of the most excellent generals [*a qualunque eccelentissimo capitano*]. Nevertheless, his outrageous cruelty and inhumanity . . . do not permit him to be honoured among the noblest men [*che sia infra li eccelentissimi uomini celebrato*].'[14] The translator, in a footnote to the passage I have quoted, suggests that the first *virtù* means moral excellence, and the second, the kind attributed to Agathocles, courage and prudence. This, no doubt, is why he renders only the first as 'virtue.'

Now, the other great 'captains'—for example, Romulus or Cesare Borgia—to whom Machiavelli attributes *virtù* were not morally excellent. Or at least, he was not pointing to their moral excellence when he spoke of their *virtù*. He was pointing to much the same qualities in them as he found in Agathocles—to their courage, energy, fortitude, and ability to see and to seize opportunities. These qualities are, of course, compatible with moral excellence just as they are with cruelty, murder, and perfidy. They are qualities that men, wherever they recognize them for what they are, are disposed to admire. It is not peculiar to Machiavelli that he admired them. They are also, so Machiavelli tells us (and surely he is right?), qualities that men are the readier to recognize and to admire, the better they like, or the more they come to accept, their effects. That is why the crimes of the man of heroic *virtù* are so often excused when his achievement is recognized, and why he is admired in spite of them. He is not admired for being murderous, perfidious, and cruel. For the cowardly, the irresolute, and the stupid, and those who lose their heads in the face of danger or unexpected difficulties, may also kill, betray, and be cruel. He is admired for the largeness and boldness of his purpose, for his resolution, courage, and skill in carrying it out, for daring to do what has to be done to achieve it. Yet there are limits to this admiration; it is sometimes given grudgingly or even withheld from someone of whom it cannot be denied that he possesses these rare qualities. Not because he lacks moral excellence; for the others, the honoured, the *celebrati,* may do so too. Borgia, as Machiavelli describes him, is not less selfish than Agathocles. But because his purpose, when achieved—no matter what his motives in pursuing it—is not accepted by others, is not found good by them or does not attract their sympathy, or else because, in pursuing it, he commits unnecessary crimes. If he is wantonly cruel or treacherous, or if his purpose or achievement is unintelligible to others or awakens no response in them, then his qualities are not admired or perhaps even recognized, or are so grudgingly, even though they are of a kind ordinarily much admired. *Virtù*, wherever it is recognized, is apt to be admired because it consists of qualities that most men understand and wish they had. Why then was it not admired in Agathocles? Why the reluctance to admit that he had it? Was it because he lacked moral excellence? Or because he was entirely selfish? I doubt whether Machiavelli had such reasons as these in mind when he wrote the eighth chapter of *The Prince*. Not that he cared nothing for moral excellence or unselfishness. But these things, I suggest, seemed irrelevant to him when he was asking how it came about that Agathocles was less admired than other men of no greater strength of purpose, resourcefulness and courage than himself.

The *virtù* that Machiavelli speaks of in *The Prince* is for the most part not civic but heroic. In the *Discourses* he has more to say about the *virtù* of the citizen, and what he says there allows us to draw some conclusions about how the two kinds of *virtù* are connected. In the eleventh chapter of book I he says: 'Kingdoms depending on the vigor [*virtù*] of one man alone are not very lasting because that vigor departs with the life of that man . . . It is not, then, the salvation of a republic or kingdom to have a prince who will rule prudently while he lives but to have one who will so organize it that even after he dies it can be maintained.'[15] And in the first chapter of the same book he says: 'Those who read in what way the city of Rome began, and by what lawgivers and how she was organized, will not marvel that so much vigor was kept up in that city for so many centuries [*che tanta virtù si sia per più secoli mantenuta in quella città*] and that finally it made possible the dominant position to which that republic rose.'[16]

The *virtù* 'of one man alone' is the *virtù* of the ruler or of the founder of a state or religion, whereas the *virtù* that survived in Rome for centuries was widespread among the citizens. Clearly, there are here two kinds of *virtù* in question; they may have something in common but they also differ. If a state is to be well organized or reformed, it must have a founder or restorer who has the first and rarer kind of *virtù*. But, unless it is well organized or reformed, its citizens are unlikely for long to have much of the second kind, the kind that many can share. So much is, I think, clearly implied by Machiavelli in these and other chapters of the *Discourses,* even though he never distinguishes between two kinds of *virtù*.

Speaking in the *Discourses* (book I, chapter 4) of the dissensions between patricians and plebeians in the Roman republic, he says that a republic cannot 'in any way be called unregulated [*inordinata*] where there are so many instances of honorable conduct [*dove sieno tanti esempli di virtù*]; for these good instances have their origin in good education; good education in good laws; good laws in those dissensions that many thoughtlessly condemn. For anyone who will properly examine their outcome will not find that they produce any exile or violence damaging to the common good, but laws and institutions conducive to public liberty.'[17] The examples of *virtù* are examples of devotion to the republic and respect for her laws, of civic virtue, and we are told that they abounded in Rome, not only in spite of dissensions, but indeed—though indirectly, no doubt—because of them. Dissension sometimes enhances respect for law, and therefore civic virtue, since this respect is part of that virtue; and sometimes has the opposite effect. In the *History of Florence* (book III, chapter 1), Machiavelli enquires why discord between the nobles and the people strengthened the republic in ancient Rome and weakened it in Florence. It was, he thinks, because the Roman people, unlike the Florentines, were moderate and content to share power with the nobles. Thus 'through the people's victories the city of Rome became more excellent [*virtuosa*] . . . and . . . as she increased in excellence [*virtù*], increased in power.' Whereas in Florence, the nobles, deprived of office by the people, when they tried to regain it 'were forced in their conduct, their spirit, and their way of living not merely to be like the men of the people [*popolani*] but to seem so . . . [so much so that] the ability in arms [*virtù dell'armi*] and the boldness of spirit [*generosità di animo*] possessed by the nobility were destroyed, and these qualities could not be rekindled in the people, where they did not exist, so that Florence grew always weaker and more despicable.'[18]

It would seem, then, that even civic virtue is, or may be, aristocratic in origin, and later acquired by the people from the nobles, provided that the people are moderate. The *virtù* of the citizen is more than just respect for the laws and institutions, and more than courage and devotion to the community; it is also a kind of wisdom or self-restraint which it would be misleading to call *prudence,* as that word is now used in English.

The *virtù* of the citizen does not consist of all the qualities in him that help to make the state strong; it consists only of qualities that he exhibits when he acts as a citizen. The Romans, at least in the days of the republic, were (so thought Machiavelli) a religious people, and Rome was the stronger for their being so. Yet being religious is no part of *virtù*, as Machiavelli conceives of it. For religion sustains both goodness (*bontà*), or what might be called private morals, and civic virtue. We are told in the ***Discourses*** (I, 55) that: "Where this goodness [*bontà*] does not exist, nothing good can be expected, as nothing good can be expected in regions that in our time are evidently corrupt, as is Italy above all, though in such corruption France and Spain have their share. If in those countries fewer dis-

orders appear than we see daily in Italy, the cause is not so much the goodness of the people—which for the most part no longer exists—as that they have a king who keeps them united, not merely through his ability [*virtù*] but also through the still unruined organization of these kingdoms. In Germany this goodness and this religion are still important among the people. These qualities enable many republics to exist there in freedom and to observe their laws so well that nobody outside or inside the cities dares to try to master them.'[19] It is the *virtù* of its citizens that makes a state formidable, and this *virtù* is sustained by religion and good morals. It is sustained also by good laws and institutions, for if a state were not well organized (*ordinata*) *virtù* could not survive for long inside it. Thus good laws and civic virtue support one another, and both are supported by religion and morals.

The well-ordered state is not—so Machiavelli implies—the slow work of time, the undesigned effect of human endeavour that men learn to value as they come to appreciate its benefits. It is the achievement of one, or of at most a few, clear-sighted and bold men who see further and dare more than other men do. These men, the founders and restorers of states and religion, possess a *virtù* far rarer than that of the ordinary citizen, even at his Roman best. They have greater foresight and insight, more firmness of purpose, more ruthlessness (*ferocia*), and a courage that most men—even the brave—lack. They can set aside scruples to achieve some large aim. They may not be good men, but it is good that there should be such men; for if there were not, there would exist no well-ordered states, and therefore little scope for either the more ordinary virtue of the citizen or for the goodness that Machiavelli always praises except when it endangers the state. This goodness, which he attributes to the old Roman and to the German of his own day, is not quite goodness as the Christian understands it, or as many who are not Christians have understood it, whether in our times or in others. He says so little about it that we cannot be sure quite what it consists of. He says much less about it than about *virtù*—which does not in the least mean that he holds it of little account. On the contrary; for he tells us that no community can do without it—can for long have either internal security or be formidable to other communities. All this he tells us, though he also tells us that sometimes it takes a man willing to set this goodness aside to establish or to save a community.

If we do Machiavelli the simple justice of attributing to him only opinions that he expressed or clearly implied, we must not even say that he valued goodness, as distinct from *virtù*, merely for its political effects. We must say only that he had more to say about its political effects than about its nature—which is perhaps not surprising in a historian and a writer on politics.

It is a pity that Meinecke should say that, for Machiavelli, the 'ethical sphere of *virtù* is 'higher' than the 'usual moral sphere' because it is 'the vital source of the state,' or that 'the development and creation of *virtù* is for him the 'self-evident purpose of the state.'[20] In spite of this and other attempts to make a German philosopher of him, Machiavelli remains obstinately an Italian of the Renaissance.

Certainly, he tells us that it takes a man of rare *virtù* to found, preserve, or restore a state, and that such a man, to achieve his purpose, may have to do what is ordinarily condemned as an atrocious crime. But to say this is not to imply that there is an 'ethical sphere' higher than ordinary morality. Nothing that Machiavelli says about *virtù,* so far as I can see, justifies Meinecke's attributing this belief to him. No doubt, Machiavelli does imply that there is a sphere of action in which ordinary moral rules do not always apply. He implies also that, unless the men who act in this sphere disregard these rules when they have to, the other sphere, in which the rules do always apply, cannot be established or preserved. That, more or less, is his position as it is usually, and no doubt correctly, interpreted.[21] There are two spheres, and they are, as Meinecke says, 'juxtaposed'—for neither can exist without the other. In a world without scope for heroic virtue, there would be no scope for civic virtue either. Though Machiavelli does not say this in so many words, it is a fair inference from what he does say, especially in the *Discourses*. But it is not a fair inference that he considered one of these spheres 'higher' than the other.

Indeed, we might well ask, higher in what sense? For Meinecke does not tell us. He points to nothing in Machiavelli's argument that could justify our concluding that, in his eyes, one sphere—the one that allows of 'necessary crimes'—is higher (or for that matter lower) than the other. The belief imputed to him by Meinecke follows from nothing he said. Among the many respectable defenders of Machiavelli quoted by Lord Acton in his introduction to Burd's edition of *The Prince* is Fichte, the champion of another kind of virtue. 'Questions of political power are never,' says Fichte, 'least of all among a corrupt people, to be solved by moral means, so that it is stupid [*unverständig*] to cry down *The Prince*. Machiavelli had a ruler to describe and not a monk.'[22] Must we say, then, that Fichte also believed in a 'politico-ethical' sphere *higher* than the sphere of ordinary morality? Or if we refuse to say so, must we then conclude that he wrote these sentences in a moment of aberration?

There is no warrant, either, for saying that, for Machiavelli, 'the development and creation of *virtù*' is 'the self-evident purpose of the state.' Nowere does he speak of any such purpose. There is to be found in his writings no conception of a good or a best life for man, and therefore no attempt to justify the state on the ground that it makes possible that kind of life. What is the *virtù*

that Meinecke has in mind when he attributes this belief to Machiavelli? Is it what he calls civic virtue? Or is it the *virtù* that he says is of a higher order, the kind that I have called heroic? On the face of it, it would seem to make better sense to treat civic virtue, rather than the other, as the purpose of the state; for it is the virtue that flourishes in the state. It can exist only in a political community; and so we can speak of it without absurdity as an end to which the political community, the state, is a means. We need not speak of it in this way, not even if, following Aristotle, we speak of the state as a means to 'the good life'; for our conception of that life may include much more than civic virtue. Still, we can so speak of it. But how does the state stand to the *virtù* which is—as Meinecke interprets Machiavelli—of a higher order? This is the *virtù* that establishes or restores the state, and so the state is its product. How then can this *virtù* be the purpose or end of the state? Does the worth of the state consist above all in the fact that the making and preserving of it are occasions for certain kinds of excellence? Is the state to be valued wholly—or at least primarily—as a work of art? Or rather (which is not quite the same thing) as an effect of *virtù;* of rare courage, strength of mind, insight and foresight?

There is no shred of evidence that Machiavelli thought of *virtù,* whether civic or heroic or both together, as the end of the state. On the contrary, there is evidence in plenty that he valued the *virtù* of the ruler or leader largely because it establishes or preserves the state. Only the creation or preservation of the state excuses actions that would otherwise be inexcusable. In the *Discourses* (I, 10) he says: 'those men are infamous and detestable who have been destroyers of religions, squanderers of kingdoms and republics, enemies of virtue [*delle virtù*],[23] of letters, and of every art that brings gain and honor to the human race . . . And no one will ever be so foolish or so wise, so bad or so good, that . . . he will not praise what is to be praised and blame what is to be blamed.'[24] If the 'purpose' of the state were only to give occasion for displays of *virtù,* this purpose might sometimes be achieved in destroying it and not in establishing or restoring it; for the business of destruction can require as much *virtù,* especially of the heroic kind that Meinecke says is the higher in the Machiavellian scale, as the business of construction: as much and as rare courage, tenacity of purpose, foresight and skill. It all depends on what is being destroyed or created. Though it takes a Titian to paint a picture by Titian but not to destroy one, it may take a Caesar to destroy a Roman republic.

Though Machiavelli never enquires what is the purpose of the state, he does in the *Discourses* (I, 3) say that the lawgiver must assume that all men are evil. He then quotes the saying 'that hunger and poverty make men industrious, and the laws make them good.'[25] But in the next sentence he qualifies what he has said by suggesting that where there is a good custom, there is no need of law. In the idiom of a later age, we can attribute to him the belief that good laws and good customs make men good—that is to say, disposed so to behave that they do not harm but benefit others and themselves. If he had been asked what the state should do for men, he would probably have answered that it should give them security, and perhaps have added that it should dispose them to goodness. It is much more likely, I suggest, that he would have given this answer to a question he never put to himself than the answer that Meinecke attributes to him.

It is also misleading to say, as Villari does, that Machiavelli 'like the ancients . . . sacrifices the individual to the state, but in his opinion the state is indifferent to every activity save the political and the military, and is solely engaged in guarding the security of its own existence and increasing its own strength.'[26] For this, too, is to assume that Machiavelli raised questions he did not raise, and gave or implied certain answers to them. No doubt, he admired the Romans for their willingness to make great sacrifices for the republic. But he never enquired what the citizens should be willing to do for the political community he belongs to. He made no attempt, as later writers were to do, to define the limits of the duty of the individual to the state, or to argue that there are no limits. If we take the political writers most concerned for the individual, his rights and aspirations—such liberals as Constant, Humboldt, and the younger Mill—we do not find them denying that the citizen ought to be called upon to risk his life for the state, or to make other great sacrifices for it. They do, of course, define the obligations of the state to its citizens, and they argue or imply that citizens have a moral right, under certain circumstances, to disobey or resist their rulers. That is why we call them liberals. They do what Machiavelli never attempted. But that does not give us the right to conclude that Machiavelli, who addressed his mind to quite other problems, took up a position opposed to theirs. If to sacrifice the individual to the state is to approve his risking his life in defence of it, them most liberals sacrifice him; and if it is to deny that he ever has the right to resist his rulers, then Machiavelli does not sacrifice him. To say that he does or does not is equally misleading: for it is to suggest that he answers a question that he never even puts to himself.

The writers who speak of him in this way are perhaps moved to do so by what he says about *virtù*. Since the questions of deepest concern to him in both *The Prince* and the *Discourses* relate to the state and its establishment and preservation, it is only to be expected that he should attend particularly to the qualities which he believes men must possess if the state is to be well-ordered and strong. These are the qualities that make up what he calls *virtù*. He admires them, or some of them, very much, even when they are manifest in what he thinks are necessary 'crimes.' He expresses much louder admiration for these qualities than he does for goodness as distinct from *virtù*. But then they are more directly relevant to the questions he puts and tries to answer. There is no warrant for saying that he looks upon *virtù* as higher than goodness, or thinks of it as the purpose of the state, or that he sacrifices the individual to the state—whatever that may mean.

Chabod says that Machiavelli's absorbing passion is for politics, and that he takes little interest in anything else. This is substantially true; for Machiavelli, though he speaks of other things, especially in his plays and letters, speaks of them much as he does of politics. As, for example, when he speaks of love—or, rather, of the pursuit of women. Here too there is something definite to be attained, and the pursuer must be resourceful, skilful, and bold if he is to attain it. Love, as Machiavelli speaks of it, is an activity less absorbing, less admirable, less fruitful of glory, than government and war, but in several respects it is similar. It is a game, perhaps, a distraction, and yet is not unlike the serious business from which it distracts. I speak, of course, not of any theory about love to be found in Machiavelli's writings, nor of his treatment of women, but only of an attitude to love revealed in his two plays and some of his letters.

'The truth,' says Chabod, 'is that Machiavelli leaves the moral ideal intact and he does so because it does not concern him.'[27] Perhaps it would be better to say that it does not concern him directly; for, as we have seen, he holds that a community cannot be well ordered for long, nor formidable to others, unless its members are honest and good—unless, like the old Romans and the Germans of his day, they have *bontà* and not merely *virtù*. And *bontà* has more of morality about it than has *virtù*. But Machiavelli has little to say about it, and has nowhere a word of sympathy for the troubled conscience. As Chabod puts it, 'he is ignorant, not only of the eternal and the transcendent, but also of the moral doubt and the tormenting anxiety that beset a conscience turned in upon itself.'[28]

Ridolfi expresses a different opinion, and speaks of 'the intimate religious foundation of his conscience which breathes from all his works.'[29] It seems to have breathed for few besides Ridolfi. By all means, let us take care how we speak of Machiavelli. Let us not say that he was without religion or that he was untroubled by conscience, or—as some have said—that his **Exhortation to Penitence** was not a moment of piety in his life but a 'frivolous joke.' Chabod, taken literally may well be wrong; Machiavelli was perhaps not 'ignorant of the eternal and transcendent' and was almost certainly (being intelligent, sensitive, and self-critical) often a prey to moral doubt and anxiety. No man reveals all that is in him in the writings he leaves behind him. But the fact remains that Machiavelli has much to say about *virtù* and little about moral goodness, and that *virtù,* as he speaks of it, has nothing to do with conscience. Machiavelli was not entirely a political animal; no man ever is. Yet the spirit that 'breathes from all his works' is political.

Notes

[1] F. Meinecke, *Machiavellism: The Doctrine of Raison d'Etat and Its Place in Modern History,* tr. Douglas Scott (London & New Haven 1957), 31

[2] P. Villari, *Life and Times of Machiavelli,* tr. Linda Villari, 4 vols (London, n.d.), II, 92

[3] J.H. Whitfield, *Machiavelli* (Blackwell 1947), 95

[4] Ibid., 97

[5] Ibid., 100

[6] Ibid., 100-1. Whitfield quotes from La Rochefoucauld in French, but I give these quotations, as all others in this article, in English.

[7] Meinecke, *Machiavellism,* 32

[8] Ibid., 33

[9] Ibid., 34

[10] For Detmold's rendering see his translation of the *Discourses* in the Modern Library College edition of *The Prince* and the *Discourses,* 172-4; for Gilbert's see *Machiavelli: The Chief Works and Others,* tr. Allan H. Gilbert, I, 244-5.

[11] Gilbert, *Chief Works,* I, 17. I shall quote only from Allan Gilbert's translation of Machiavelli, putting the word *virtù* or other Italian words or phrases in brackets next to Gilbert's renderings of them.

[12] Ibid., 25

[13] Ibid., 26

[14] Ibid., 36

[15] Ibid., 226

[16] Ibid., 192

[17] Ibid., 203—I do not know why Gibert has translated *esempli* by *instances* rather than *examples,* for Machiavelli is speaking here of conduct which he thinks is exemplary.

[18] Ibid., III, 1141

[19] Ibid., I, 307

[20] Meinecke, *Machiavellism,* 33-4

[21] The sociologist might argue that, even in the case of the most ordinary of mortals, life consists of several interdependent spheres, and that rules that apply to one sphere often do not apply to another.

[22] *Il Principe,* ed. L. Arthur Burd (Oxford 1891), xxxvii. Surely, Fichte ought not to have said that such questions are *never* solved by moral means. Machiavelli did not say it. How these German philosophers, even the best of them, exaggerate!

[23] As Professor Whitfield points out, Machiavelli seldom uses *virtù* in the plural; when he does so, he has in mind, not the *virtù* discussed in this article, but good or evil qualities more generally. See Whitfield, *Machiavelli,* 98.

[24] Gilbert, *Chief Works,* I, 220

[25] Ibid., 201

[26] Villari, *Life and Times of Machiavelli* bk.II, ch.2, 95

[27] Federico Chabod, *Machiavelli and the Renaissance,* tr. D. Moore (London 1958), 142

[28] Ibid., 93

[29] Roberto Ridolfi, *The Life of Niccolò Machiavelli,* tr. Cecil Grayson (London 1963), 253

Harvey C. Mansfield, Jr. (essay date 1985)

SOURCE: An introduction to *The Prince,* by Niccolo Machiavelli, translated by Harvey C. Mansfield, Jr., The University of Chicago Press, 1985, pp. vii-xxiv.

[*In the following essay, Mansfield provides an overview of* The Prince, *describing the work as "the most famous book on politics when politics is thought to be carried on for its own sake, unlimited by anything above it."*]

Anyone who picks up Machiavelli's **The Prince** holds in his hands the most famous book on politics ever written. Its closest rival might be Plato's *Republic,* but that book discusses politics in the context of things above politics, and politics turns out to have a limited and subordinate place. In **The Prince** Machiavelli also discusses politics in relation to things outside politics, as we shall see, but his conclusion is very different. Politics according to him is not limited by things above it, and things normally taken to be outside politics—the "givens" in any political situation—turn out to be much more under the control of politics than politicians, peoples, and philosophers have hitherto assumed. Machiavelli's *The Prince,* then, is the most famous book on politics when politics is thought to be carried on for its own sake, unlimited by anything above it. The renown of *The Prince* is precisely to have been the first and the best book to argue that politics has and should have its own rules and should not accept rules of any kind or from any source where the object is not to win or prevail over others. *The Prince* is briefer and pithier than Machiavelli's other major work, *Discourses on Livy,* for *The Prince* is addressed to Lorenzo de' Medici, a prince like the busy executive of our day who has little time for reading. So *The Prince* with its political advice to an active politician that politics should not be limited by anything not political, is by far more famous than the *Discourses on Livy*.

We cannot, however, agree that *The Prince* is the most famous book on politics without immediately correcting this to say that it is the most infamous. It is famous for its infamy, for recommending the kind of politics that ever since has been called Machiavellian. The essence of this politics is that "you can get away with murder": that no divine sanction, or degradation of soul, or twinge of conscience will come to punish you. If you succeed, you will not even have to face the infamy of murder, because when "men acquire who can acquire, they will be praised or not blamed" (Chapter 3). Those criminals who are infamous have merely been on the losing side. Machiavelli and Machiavellian politics are famous or infamous for their willingness to brave infamy.

Yet it must be reported that the prevailing view among scholars of Machiavelli is that he was not an evil man who taught evil doctrines, and that he does not deserve his infamy. With a view to his preference for republics over principalities (more evident in the *Discourses on Livy* than in *The Prince,* but not absent in the latter), they cannot believe he was an apologist for tyranny; or, impressed by the sudden burst of Italian patriotism in the last chapter of *The Prince,* they forgive him for the sardonic observations which are not fully consistent with this generous feeling but are thought to give it a certain piquancy (this is the opinion of an earlier generation of scholars); or, on the basis of Machiavelli's saying in Chapter 15 that we should take our bearings from "what is done" rather than from "what should be done," they conclude that he was a forerunner of modern political science, which is not an evil thing because it merely tells us what happens without passing judgment. In sum, the prevailing view of the scholars offers excuses for Machiavelli: he was a republican, a patriot, or a scientist, and therefore, in explicit contradiction to the reaction of most people to Machiavelli as soon as they hear of his doctrines, Machiavelli was not "Machiavellian."

The reader can form his own judgment of these excuses for Machiavelli. I do not recommend them, chiefly because they make Machiavelli less interesting. They transform him into a herald of the future who had the luck to sound the tunes we hear so often today—democracy, nationalism or self-determination, and science. Instead of challenging our favorite beliefs and forcing us to think, Machiavelli is enlisted into a chorus of self-congratulation. There is, of course, evidence for the excuses supplied on behalf of Machiavelli, and that evidence consists of the excuses offered by Machiavelli himself. If someone were to accuse him of being an apologist for tyranny, he can indeed point to a passage in the *Discourses on Livy* (II 2) where he says (rather carefully) that the common good is not observed unless in republics; but if someone else were to accuse him of supporting republicanism, he could point to the same chapter, where he says that the hardest slavery of all is to be conquered by a republic. And, while he shows his Italian patriotism in Chapter 26 of *The Prince* by exhorting someone to seize Italy in order to free it from the barbarians, he also shows his fairmindedness by advising a French king in Chapter 3 how he might better invade Italy the next time. Lastly, it is true that he sometimes merely reports the evil that he sees, while (unnecessarily) deploring it; but at other times he urges us to share in that evil and he virtuously condemns halfhearted immoralists. Although he was an exceedingly bold writer who seems to have deliberately courted an evil reputation, he was nonetheless not so bold as to fail to provide excuses, or prudent reservations, for his boldest statements. Since I have spoken at length on this point in another place, and will not hesitate to mention the work of Leo Strauss, it is not necessary to explain it further here.

What is at issue in the question of whether Machiavelli was "Machiavellian"? To see that a matter of the highest importance is involved we must not rest satisfied with either scholarly excuses or moral frowns. For the matter at issue is the character of the rules by which we reward human beings with fame or condemn them with infamy, the very status of morality. Machiavelli does not make it clear at first that this grave question is his subject. In the Dedicatory Letter he approaches Lorenzo de' Medici with hat in one hand and *The Prince* in the other. Since, he says, one must be a prince to know the nature of peoples and a man of the people to know the nature of princes, he seems to offer Lorenzo the knowledge of princes he does not have but needs. In accordance with this half-serious promise, Machiavelli speaks about the kinds of principalities in the first part of *The Prince* (Chapters 1-2) and, as we learn of the necessity of conquest, about the kinds of armies in the second part (Chapters 12-14). But at the same time (to make a long story short), we learn that the prince must or may lay his foundations on the people (Chapter 9) and that while his only object should be the art of war, he must in time of peace pay attention to moral qualities in such manner as to be able to use them in time of war (Chapter 14, end).

Thus are we prepared for Machiavelli's clarion call in Chapter 15, where he proclaims that he "departs from the orders of others" and says why. For moral qualities are qualities "held good" by the people; so, if the prince must conquer, and wants, like the Medici, to lay his foundation on the people, who are the keepers of morality, then a new morality consistent with the necessity of conquest must be found, and the prince has to be taught anew about the nature of peoples by Machiavelli. In departing from the orders of others, it appears more fitting to Machiavelli "to go directly to the effectual truth of the thing than to the imagination of it." Many have imagined republics and principalities, but one cannot "let go of what is done for what should be done," because a man who "makes a profession of good in all regards" comes to ruin among so many who are not good. The prince must learn to be able not to be good, and use this ability or not according to necessity.

This concise statement is most efficacious. It contains a fundamental assault on all morality and political science, both Christian and classical, as understood in Machiavelli's time. Morality had meant not only doing the right action, but also doing it for the right reason or for the love of God. Thus, to be good was thought to require "a profession of good" in which the motive for doing good was explained; otherwise, morality would go no deeper than outward conformity to law, or even to superior force, and could not be distinguished from it. But professions of good could not accompany moral actions in isolation from each other; they would have to be elaborated so that moral actions would be consistent with each other and the life of a moral person would form a whole. Such elaboration requires an effort of imagination, since the consistency we see tells us only of the presence of outward conformity, and the elaboration extends over a society, because it is difficult to live a moral life by oneself; hence morality requires the construction of an imagined republic or principality, such as Plato's *Republic* or St. Augustine's *City of God*.

When Machiavelli denies that imagined republics and principalities "exist in truth," and declares that the truth in these or all matters is the effectual truth, he says that no moral rules exist, not made by men, which men must abide by. The rules or laws that exist are those made by governments or other powers acting under necessity, and they must be obeyed out of the same necessity. Whatever is necessary may be called just and reasonable, but justice is no more reasonable than what a person's prudence tells him he must acquire for himself, or must submit to, because men cannot afford justice in any sense that transcends their own preservation. Machiavelli did not attempt (as did Hobbes) to formulate a new definition of justice based on self-preservation. Instead, he showed what he meant by not including justice among the eleven pairs of moral qualities that he lists in Chap-

ter 15. He does mention justice in Chapter 21 as a calculation of what a weaker party might expect from a prince whom it has supported in war, but even this little is contradicted by what Machiavelli says about keeping faith in Chapter 18 and about betraying one's old supporters in Chapter 20. He also brings up justice as something identical with necessity in Chapter 26. But, what is most striking, he never mentions—not in *The Prince,* or in any of his works—natural justice or natural law, the two conceptions of justice in the classical and medieval tradition that had been handed down to his time and that could be found in the writings on this subject of all his contemporaries. The grave issue raised by the dispute whether Machiavelli was truly "Machiavellian" is this: does justice exist by nature or by God, or is it the convenience of the prince (government)? "So let a prince win and maintain a state: the means will always be judged honorable, and will be praised by everyone" (Chapter 18). Reputation, then, is outward conformity to successful human force and has no reference to moral rules that the government might find inconvenient.

If there is no natural justice, perhaps Machiavelli can teach the prince how to rule in its absence—but with a view to the fact that men "profess" it. It does not follow of necessity that because no natural justice exists, princes can rule successfully without it. Governments might be as unsuccessful in making and keeping conquests as in living up to natural justice; indeed, the traditional proponents of natural justice, when less confident of their own cause, had pointed to the uncertainty of gain, to the happy inconstancy of fortune, as an argument against determined wickedness. But Machiavelli thinks it possible to "learn" to be able not to be good. For each of the difficulties of gaining and keeping, even and especially for the fickleness of fortune, he has a "remedy," to use his frequent expression. Since nature or God does not support human justice, men are in need of a remedy; and the remedy is the prince, especially the new prince. Why must the new prince be preferred?

In the heading to the first chapter of *The Prince* we see that the kinds of principalities are to be discussed together with the ways in which they are acquired, and then in the chapter itself we find more than this, that principalities are classified into kinds by the ways in which they are acquired. "Acquisition," an economic term, is Machiavelli's word for "conquest"; and acquisition determines the classifications of governments, not their ends or structures, as Plato and Aristotle had thought. How is acquisition related to the problem of justice?

Justice requires a modest complement of external goods, the equipment of virtue in Aristotle's phrase, to keep the wolf from the door and to provide for moral persons a certain decent distance from necessities in the face of which morality might falter or even fail. For how can one distribute justly without something to distribute? But, then, where is one to get this modest complement? The easy way is by inheritance. In Chapter 2, Machiavelli considers hereditary principalities, in which a person falls heir to everything he needs, especially the political power to protect what he has. The hereditary prince, the man who has everything, is called the "natural prince," as if to suggest that our grandest and most comprehensive inheritance is what we get from nature. But when the hereditary prince looks upon his inheritance—and when we, generalizing from his case, add up everything we inherit—is it adequate?

The difficulty with hereditary principalities is indicated at the end of Chapter 2, where Machiavelli admits that hereditary princes will have to change but claims that change will not be disruptive because it can be gradual and continuous. He compares each prince's own construction to building a house that is added on to a row of houses: you may not inherit all you need, but you inherit a firm support and an easy start in what you must acquire. But clearly a row of houses so built over generations presupposes that the first house was built without existing support and without an easy start. Inheritance presupposes an original acquisition made without a previous inheritance. And in the original acquisition, full attention to the niceties of justice may unfortunately not be possible. One may congratulate an American citizen for all the advantages to which he is born; but what of the nasty necessities that prepared this inheritance—the British expelled, Indians defrauded, blacks enslaved?

Machiavelli informs us in the third chapter, accordingly, that "truly it is a very natural and ordinary thing to desire to acquire." In the space of a few pages, "natural" has shifted in meaning from hereditary to acquisitive. Or can we be consoled by reference to Machiavelli's republicanism, not so prominent in *The Prince,* with the thought that acquisitiveness may be natural to princes but is not natural to republics? But in Chapter 3 Machiavelli praises the successful acquisitiveness of the "Romans," that is, the Roman republic, by comparison to the imprudence of the king of France. At the time Machiavelli is referring to, the Romans were not weak and vulnerable as they were at their inception; they had grown powerful and were still expanding. Even when they had enough empire to provide an inheritance for their citizens, they went on acquiring. Was this reasonable? It was, because the haves of this world cannot quietly inherit what is coming to them; lest they be treated now as they once treated others, they must keep an eye on the have-nots. To keep a step ahead of the have-nots the haves must think and behave like have-nots. They certainly cannot afford justice to the have-nots, nor can they waste time or money on sympathy.

In the Dedicatory Letter Machiavelli presents himself to Lorenzo as a have-not, "from a low and mean state"; and one thing he lacks besides honorable employment, we learn, is a unified fatherland. Italy is weak and divided. Then should we say that acquisitiveness is justified for Italians of Machiavelli's time, including him? As we have noted, Machiavelli does not seem to accept this justification because, still in Chapter 3, he advises a French king how to correct the errors he had made in his invasion of Italy. Besides, was Machiavelli's fatherland Italy or was it Florence? In Chapter 15 he refers to "our language," meaning Tuscan, and in Chapter 20 to "our ancients," meaning Florentines. But does it matter whether Machiavelli was essentially an Italian or a Florentine patriot? Anyone's fatherland is defined by an original acquisition, a conquest, and hence is always subject to redefinition of the same kind. To be devoted to one's native country at the expense of foreigners is no more justified than to be devoted to one's city at the expense of fellow countrymen, or to one's family at the expense of fellow city-dwellers, or, to adapt a Machiavellian remark in Chapter 17, to one's patrimony at the expense of one's father. So to "unify" one's fatherland means to treat it as a conquered territory—conquered by a king or republic from within; and Machiavelli's advice to the French king on how to hold his conquests in Italy was also advice to Lorenzo on how to unify Italy. It appears that, in acquiring, the new prince acquires for himself.

What are the qualities of the new prince? What must he do? First, as we have seen, he should rise from private or unprivileged status; he should not have an inheritance, or if he has, he should not rely on it. He should owe nothing to anyone or anything, for having debts of gratitude would make him dependent on others, in the widest sense dependent on fortune. It might seem that the new prince depends at least on the character of the country he conquers, and Machiavelli says at the end of Chapter 4 that Alexander had no trouble in holding Asia because it had been accustomed to the government of one lord. But then in Chapter 5 he shows how this limitation can be overcome. A prince who conquers a city used to living in freedom need not respect its inherited liberties; he can and should destroy such cities or else rule them personally. Fortune supplies the prince with nothing more than opportunity, as when Moses found the people of Israel enslaved by the Egyptians, Romulus found himself exposed at birth, Cyrus found the Persians discontented with the empire of the Medes, and Theseus found the Athenians dispersed (Chapter 6). These famous founders had the virtue to recognize the opportunity that fortune offered to them—opportunity for them, harsh necessity to their peoples. Instead of dispersing the inhabitants of a free city (Chapter 5), the prince is lucky enough to find them dispersed (Chapter 6). This suggests that the prince could go so far as to make his own opportunity by creating a situation of necessity in which no one's inherited goods remain to him and everything is owed to you, the new prince. When a new prince comes to power, should he be grateful to those who helped him get power and rely on them? Indeed not. A new prince has "lukewarm defenders" in his friends and allies, because they expect benefits from him; as we have seen, it is much better to conciliate his former enemies who feared losing everything (compare Chapters 6 and 20).

Thus, the new prince has virtue that enables him to overcome his dependence on inheritance in the widest sense, including custom, nature, and fortune, and that shows him how to arrange it that others depend on him and his virtue (Chapters 9, 24). But if virtue is to do all this, it must have a new meaning. Instead of cooperating with nature or God, as in the various classical and Christian conceptions, virtue must be taught to be acquisitive on its own. Machiavelli teaches the new meaning of virtue by showing us both the new and the old meanings. In a famous passage on the successful criminal Agathocles in Chapter 8, he says "one cannot call it virtue to kill one's fellow citizens, betray one's friends, to be without faith, without mercy, without religion." Yet in the very next sentence Machiavelli proceeds to speak of "the virtue of Agathocles."

The prince, we have seen in Chapter 15, must "learn to be able not to be good, and to use this and not use it according to necessity." Machiavelli supplies this knowledge in Chapters 16 to 18. First, with superb calm, he delivers home-truths concerning the moral virtue of liberality. It is no use being liberal (or generous) unless it is noticed, so that you are "held liberal" or get a name for liberality. But a prince cannot be held liberal by being liberal, because he would have to be liberal to a few by burdening the many with taxes; the many would be offended, the prince would have to retrench, and he would soon get a name for stinginess. The right way to get a reputation for liberality is to begin by not caring about having a reputation for stinginess. When the people see that the prince gets the job done without burdening them, they will in time consider him liberal to them and stingy only to the few to whom he gives nothing. In the event, "liberality" comes to mean taking little rather than giving much.

As regards cruelty and mercy, in Chapter 8 Machiavelli made a distinction between cruelties well used and badly used; well-used cruelties are done once, for self-defense, and not continued but turned to the benefit of one's subjects, and badly used ones continue and increase. In Chapter 17, however, he does not mention this distinction but rather speaks only of using mercy badly. Mercy is badly used when, like the Florentine people in a certain instance, one seeks to avoid a reputation for cruelty and thus allows disorders to continue which might be stopped with a very few examples of cruelty. Disorders harm everybody; executions harm only the few or the one who is executed. As the prince may gain a name for liberality by taking little, so he may be held merciful by

not being cruel too often.

Machiavelli's new prince arranges the obligation of his subjects to himself in a manner rather like that of the Christian God, in the eye of whom all are guilty by original sin; hence God's mercy appears less as the granting of benefits than as the remission of punishment. With this thought in mind, the reader will not be surprised that Machiavelli goes on to discuss whether it is better for the prince to be loved or feared. It would be best to be both loved and feared, but, when necessity forces a choice, it is better to be feared, because men love at their convenience but they fear at the convenience of the prince. Friends may fail you, but the dread of punishment will never forsake you. If the prince avoids making himself hated, which he can do by abstaining from the property of others, "because men forget the death of a father more quickly than the loss of a patrimony," he will again have subjects obligated to him for what he does not do to them rather than for benefits he provides.

It is laudable for a prince to keep faith, Machiavelli says in Chapter 18, but princes who have done great things have done them by deceit and betrayal. The prince must learn how to use the beast in man, or rather the beasts: for man is an animal who can be many animals, and he must know how to be a fox as well as a lion. Men will not keep faith with you; how can you keep it with them? Politics, Machiavelli seems to say, as much as consists in breaking promises, for circumstances change and new necessities arise that make it impossible to hold to one's word. The only question is, can one get away with breaking one's promises? Machiavelli's answer is a confident yes. He broadens the discussion, speaking of five moral qualities, especially religion; he says that men judge by appearances and that when one judges by appearances, "one looks to the end." The end is the outcome or the effect, and if a prince wins and maintains a state, the means will always be judged honorable. Since Machiavelli has just emphasized the prince's need to appear religious, we may compare the people's attitude toward a successful prince with their belief in divine providence. As people assume that the outcome of events in the world is determined by God's providence, so they conclude that the means chosen by God cannot have been unworthy. Machiavelli's thought here is both a subtle attack on the notion of divine providence and a subtle appreciation of it, insofar as the prince can appropriate it to his own use.

It is not easy to state exactly what virtue is, according to Machiavelli. Clearly he does not leave virtue as it was in the classical or Christian tradition, nor does he imitate any other writer of his time. Virtue in his new meaning seems to be a prudent or well-taught combination of vice and virtue in the old meaning. Virtue for him is not a mean between two extremes of vice, as is moral virtue for Aristotle. As we have seen, in Chapter 15 eleven virtues (the same number as Aristotle's, though not all of them the same virtues) are paired with eleven vices. From this we might conclude that virtue does not shine of itself, as when it is done for its own sake. Rather, virtue is as it takes effect, its truth is its effectual truth; and it is effectual only when it is seen in contrast to its opposite. Liberality, mercy, and love are impressive only when one expects stinginess (or rapacity), cruelty, and fear. This contrast makes virtue apparent and enables the prince to gain a reputation for virtue. If this is so, then the new meaning Machiavelli gives to virtue, a meaning which makes use of vice, must not entirely replace but somehow continue to coexist with the old meaning, according to which virtue is shocked by vice.

A third quality of the new prince is that he must make his own foundations. Although to be acquisitive means to be acquisitive for oneself, the prince cannot do everything with his own hands: he needs help from others. But in seeking help he must take account of the "two diverse humors" to be found in every city—the people, who desire not to be commanded or oppressed by the great, and the great, who desire to command and oppress the people (Chapter 9). Of these two humors, the prince should choose the people. The people are easier to satisfy, too inert to move against him, and too numerous to kill, whereas the great regard themselves as his equals, are ready and able to conspire against him, and are replaceable.

The prince, then, should ally with the people against the aristocracy; but how should he get their support? Machiavelli gives an example in the conduct of Cesare Borgia, whom he praises for the foundations he laid (Chapter 7). When Cesare had conquered the province of Romagna, he installed "Remirro de Orco" (actually a Spaniard, Don Remiro de Lorqua) to carry out a purge of the unruly lords there. Then, because Cesare thought Remirro's authority might be excessive, and his exercise of it might become hateful—in short, because Remirro had served his purpose—he purged the purger and one day had Remirro displayed in the piazza at Cesena in two pieces. This spectacle left the people "at the same time satisfied and stupefied"; and Cesare set up a more constitutional government in Romagna. The lesson: constitutional government is possible but only after an unconstitutional beginning.

In Chapter 9 Machiavelli discusses the "civil principality," which is gained through the favor of the people, and gives as example Nabis, "prince" of the Spartans, whom he calls a tyrant in the *Discourses on Livy* because of the crimes Nabis committed against his rivals. In Chapter 8 Machiavelli considers the principality that is attained through crimes, and cites Agathocles and Oliverotto, both of whom were very popular despite their crimes. As one ponders these two chapters, it becomes more and more difficult to find a difference

between gaining a principality through crimes and through the favor of the people. Surely Cesare Borgia, Agathocles, and Nabis seemed to have followed the same policy of pleasing the people by cutting up the great. Finally, in Chapter 19, Machiavelli reveals that the prince need not have the support of the people after all. Even if he is hated by the people (since in fact he cannot fail to be hated by someone), he can, like the Roman emperor Severus, make his foundation with his soldiers (see also Chapter 20). Severus had such virtue, Machiavelli says, with an unobstrusive comparison to Cesare Borgia in Chapter 7, that he "stupefied" the people and "satisfied" the soldiers.

Fourth, the new prince has his own arms, and does not rely on mercenary or auxiliary armies. Machiavelli omits a discussion of the laws a prince should establish, in contrast to the tradition of political science, because, he says, "there cannot be good laws where there are not good arms, and where there are good arms there must be good laws" (Chapter 12). He speaks of the prince's arms in Chapters 12 to 14, and in Chapter 14 he proclaims that the prince should have no other object or thought but the art of war. He must be armed, since it is quite unreasonable for one who is armed to obey one who is disarmed. With this short remark Machiavelli seems to dismiss the fundamental principle of classical political science, the rule of the wise, not to mention the Christian promise that the meek shall inherit the earth.

Machiavelli does not mean that those with the most bodily force always win, for he broadens the art of war to include the acquisition as well as the use of arms. A prince who has no army but has the art of war will prevail over one with an army but without the art. Thus, to be armed means to know the art of war, to exercise it in time of peace, and to have read histories about great captains of the past. In this regard Machiavelli mentions Xenophon's "Life of Cyrus," as he calls it (actually "The Education of Cyrus"), the first and best work in the literature of "mirrors of princes" to which *The Prince* belongs. But he calls it a history, not a mirror of princes, and says that it inspired the Roman general Scipio, whom he criticizes in Chapter 17 for excessive mercy. Not books of imaginary republics and principalities, or treatises on law, but histories of war, are recommended reading for the prince.

Last, the new prince with his own arms is his own master. The deeper meaning of Machiavelli's slogan, "one's own arms," is religious, or rather, antireligious. If man is obligated to God as his creature, then man's own necessities are subordinate or even irrelevant to his most pressing duties. It would not matter if he could not afford justice: God commands it! Thus Machiavelli must look at the new prince who is also a prophet, above all at Moses. Moses was a "mere executor of things that had been ordered by God" (Chapter 6); hence he should be admired for the grace that made him worthy of speaking with God. Or should it be said, as Machiavelli says in Chapter 26, that Moses had "virtue," the virtue that makes a prince dependent on no one but himself? In Chapter 13 Machiavelli retells the biblical story of David and Goliath to illustrate the necessity of one's own arms. When Saul offered his arms to David, David refused them, saying, according to Machiavelli, that with them he could not give a good account of himself, and according to the Bible, that the Lord "will deliver me out of the hand of this Philistine." Machiavelli also gives David a knife to go with his sling, the knife which according to the Bible he took from the fallen Goliath and used to cut off his head.

Must the new prince—the truly new prince—then be his own prophet and make a new religion so as to be his own master? The great power of religion can be seen in what Moses and David founded, and in what Savonarola nearly accomplished in Machiavelli's own time and city. The unarmed prince whom he disparages in Chapter 6 actually disposes of formidable weapons necessary to the art of war. The unarmed prophet becomes armed if he uses religion for his own purposes rather than God's; and because the prince cannot acquire glory for himself without bringing order to his principality, using religion for himself is using it to answer human necessities generally.

The last three chapters of *The Prince* take up the question of how far man can make his own world. What are the limits set on Machiavelli's political science (or the "art of war") by fortune? At the end of Chapter 24 he blames "these princes of ours" who accuse fortune for their troubles and not their own indolence. In quiet times they do not take account of the storm to come. but they should—they can. They believe that the people will be disgusted by the arrogance of the foreign conquerors and will call them back. But "one should never fall in the belief you can find someone to pick you up." Whether successful or not, such a defense is base, because it does not depend on you and your virtue.

With this high promise of human capability, Machiavelli introduces his famous Chapter 25 on fortune. He begins it by asking how much of the world is governed by fortune and God, and how much by man. He then supposes that half is governed by fortune (forgetting God) and half by man, and he compares fortune to a violent river that can be contained with dikes and dams. Turning to particular men, he shows that the difficulty in containing fortunes lies in the inability of one who is impetuous to succeed in quiet times or of one who is cautious to succeed in stormy times. Men, with their fixed natures and habits, do not vary as the times vary, and so they fall under the control of the times, of fortune. Men's fixed natures are the special problem, Machiavelli indicates; so the problem of overcoming

the influence of fortune reduces to the problem of overcoming the fixity of different human natures. Having a fixed nature is what makes one liable to changes of fortune. Pope Julius II succeeded because the times were in accord with his impetuous nature; if he had lived longer, he would have come to grief. Machiavelli blames him for his inflexibility, and so implies that neither he nor the rest of us need respect the natures or natural inclinations we have been given.

What is the new meaning of virtue that Machiavelli has developed but flexibility according to the times or situation? Yet, though one should learn to be both impetuous and cautious (these stand for all the other contrary qualities), on the whole one should be impetuous. Fortune is a woman who "lets herself be won more by the impetuous than by those who proceed coldly"; hence she is a friend of the young. He makes the politics of the new prince appear in the image of rape; impetuous himself, Machiavelli forces us to see the question he has raised about the status of morality. Whether he says what he appears to say about the status of women may be doubted, however. The young men who master Lady Fortune come with audacity and leave exhausted, but she remains ageless, waiting for the next ones. One might go so far as to wonder who is raping whom, cautiously as it were, and whether Machiavelli, who has personified fortune, can impersonate her in the world of modern politics he attempted to create.

A. J. Parel (essay date 1991)

SOURCE: "The Question of Machiavelli's Modernity," in *The Review of Politics*, Vol. 53, No. 2, Spring, 1991, pp. 320-39.

[*In the essay below, Parel contends that the arguments which support Machiavelli's "new" ideas, are "based on premodern cosmology and anthropology."*]

That Machiavelli is an innovator of political philosophy is universally acknowledged. The program of innovation is outlined in *The Prince,* chapter 15: he wants to depart from the orders of his predecessors. The goal of the new philosophy is "effectual truth," and not the imagination of it. Actual states, not "imagined republics and kingdoms" are its real concerns. The distinction between how one lives and how one ought to live is still made, but only in order to point out that what is done should never be abandoned for what should be done. Preservation of the state has emerged as the new *summum bonum,* in the interest of which everything becomes permitted. The distinction between virtue and vice is no longer important; and the new type of ruler, if he is good, must learn how to be not good. The Preface to *Discourses* I also proposes a similar program: he is determined "to enter a path not yet trodden by anyone" and to introduce "new modes and orders."[1]

The question is whether being an innovator necessarily makes Machiavelli a modern? Is being new the same as being modern? Most critics who speak of him as an innovator do not address this specific question. He is not one of the ancients, they agree, but they are not clear whether he is one of the moderns. The critic who has persistently argued that his newness constitutes his modernity, however, is Leo Strauss.[2] He is followed on this point by Harvey C. Mansfield, Jr., Allan Bloom, and others. Modern political philosophy, Strauss claims, arose out of the war against the classics and Christianity, against Athens and Jerusalem, and the person who first declared this war was Machiavelli. Out of this war emerged a new mode of thought, philosophic in character, but no longer Greek. "It is in trying to understand modern philosophy that we come across Machiavelli."[3] Machiavelli, not Hobbes, is the founder of modern political philosophy,[4] and "all specifically modern political science rests on the foundations laid by Machiavelli."[5] According to Strauss, his modernity consists, first, in his attack on the classical political philosophy of Plato and Aristotle, and in his antitheological passion against Christianity; secondly, in lowering the standards of politics from what ought to be to what is; thirdly, in his plan to conquer fortune or chance; and finally, in his wanting "to make probable, if not certain, the actualization of the right or desirable social order."[6] In support of his claims, he asserts that there is "a hidden kinship between Machiavelli's political science and the new natural science."[7]

The validity of Strauss's claim, however, can be ascertained only after we have examined Machiavelli's view of nature and human nature, that is, his cosmology and his anthropology.

Machiavelli's Cosmology

A number of premodern cosmological assumptions underlie Machiavelli's political theory. The first and most important of these is the assumed distinction between heaven and earth, between the heavenly bodies and the sublunar world. The two are related causally, as superior to subordinate. All motions in the sublunar world, both natural and human, are thought to depend on the motions emanating from heaven, the planets and the stars. This is the key assumption underlying his historiography. History in part is a function of the natural motions of celestial bodies, and in part the product of human causation. This is stated in the carefully drafted Preface to *Discourses* I, the only portion of the work we have in Machiavelli's autograph. The movement of history is not the outcome of fully autonomous human

motion; history is dependent on "heaven, the planets and the elements" for its "motion, order and power." This dependency on cosmic motion accounts for not only the regularity and the predictability but also the pattern of the rise and fall of civilizations, states, and religions. The validity of the Machiavellian theory of "imitation" of virtue also depends on this alleged fact. The "error" of his contemporaries was that they did not accept this view of history. This lack of acceptance, according to him, was due to Christianity which taught a linear view of history. And one of the grand strategies of his innovation is to reinstate the older, premodern theory of history, such that imitation of *virtù* becomes morally possible. The remedy to modern corruption is the practice of antique *virtù*. Forgetting this "truth" about history and politics, his "corrupt" Christian contemporaries read history for amusement, not moral instruction. "From this it comes that great numbers who read take pleasure in hearing of various events they (histories) contain, without thinking at all of imitating them, judging that imitation is not merely difficult but impossible, as if the heaven, the sun, the elements, men, were changed in motion, order and power from what they were in antiquity."[8] It is to get humans out of this error that he has decided to write on Livy's *History,* according to his "knowledge of ancient and modern things" (*secondo le cognizione delle antique e moderne cose).*[9]

Everything that happens in history, then, happens according to the laws of cosmic motion. Strictly speaking history is a conjoint product of cosmic and human motions, in which the one plays the superior, and the other, the subordinate role. Insofar as this is Machiavelli's position, the phenomenon of cycle of political regimes, described in *Discourses* I. 2, should also be seen as occurring according to the general laws governing history.

Applying the theory of cosmic motion to politics, Machiavelli points out how the imitation of virtue can be successful only if it takes place at a time when the country in question is in the right period of its history. For countries follow the pattern of rise and fall, virtue and corruption; they have their upward and their downward phases. Imitation, to be efficacious, should occur when the country in its upward phase.

> Since human affairs (*le cose umane*) are always in motion, either they rise or they fall. So a city or province can be organized for well planned government by some excellent man, and for a time, through that organizer's *virtù*, it can keep on always growing better. He who is then born in such a state and praises ancient times more than modern ones deceive himself. . . . But they who are born later in that city or province, when the time has come for it to descend towards a worse condition, do not then deceive themselves.[10]

The theory is stated comprehensively in the *History of Florence:*

> In their normal changes, countries generally go from order to disorder and then from disorder move back to order, because, since nature does not allow things of the world (*mondane cose*) to remain fixed, when they come to their utmost perfection and have no further possibility of rising, they must go down. Likewise, when they have gone down and through their defects have reached the lowest depths, they necessarily rise, since they cannot go lower. So always from good they go down to bad, and from bad rise up to good. Because *virtù* brings forth quiet; quiet, leisure; leisure, disorder; disorder, ruin; and likewise from ruin comes order; from order, *virtù*; from the last, glory and good fortune.[11]

The questions of war and peace also come within the purview of cosmic motion. That is to say, according to Machiavelli, war and peace have more than just human causes: the dispositions of heaven also have something to do with them. States have a natural tendency to be expansionist which varies with the "influence" of heaven over them. Given this, the more rational policy would be to prepare for expansion than for staying stationary. "But since all human things (*tutte le cose umane*) are in motion and cannot remain fixed, they must needs rise up or sink down; to many thing to which reason does not bring you, you are brought by necessity."[12] Even "if heaven is so kind to a state that it does not have to make war," the effect might be that leisure (*ozio*) would make it "effeminate or disunited." In either case, danger to the country is very real. Accordingly, it is not possible to balance international affairs and to keep exactly to a middle way. The most honorable way is to be powerful and expansionist so that "if necessity causes states to grow, they can keep what they have conquered."[13] The point not to be missed is that even Machiavelli's analysis of war, peace and foreign policy presupposes the operation of natural "necessity" (stemming from cosmic causes) operating in human affairs.

Machiavelli also adheres to a premodern concept of heaven's naturalistic "providence" over human affairs including the fortunes of religions or "sects." This is stated in general terms in *Discourses* II. 5. Natural calamities such as floods, famine and pestilence are seen as caused by heaven in order to keep the human species relatively healthy. The pressure of population increases on land, "so that men cannot live where they are and cannot go elsewhere, since all places are settled and filled full, and when human craft and malice have gone as far as they can go, of necessity the world is purged." And this is brought about by the causality exercised by heaven: "As to the causes that come from heaven, they are those that wipe out the race of men and bring down to a few the inhabitants of part of the world, either through plagues or through famine or through a flood."[14]

These demographic purgations are part of the "natural" process at work under the superintendence of heaven. The outcome is that "by becoming few and humble, men can live more commodiously and grow better." In other words, heaven sees to it that the material conditions of existence are favorable to the human species, and periodic destruction of a "part of the world" through natural calamities is one way of achieving that end.

Heaven's naturalistic "providence" extends not only to humankind in general, but also to particular states. In *Discourses* II. 29, he analyzes the fortunes of the early Roman republic in terms of naturalistic "providence." And the example of Rome, Machiavelli makes clear, simply illustrates a general rule. In the Gallic war of 390 B. C., heaven is pictured as "testing" the virtue of the Roman republic. "If we observe carefully how human affairs (*le cose umane*) go on, many times we see that things come up and events take place against which the heavens do not wish any provisions to be made." And if this happened to Rome, he notes, "it is not strange" that such things happen more often in cities or countries which are inferior to Rome. He takes the Gallic war for detailed analysis, because it is "very noteworthy for showing heaven's power over human things." Heaven for some reason wished the Romans to know its power; and it was because of the astral causes, he asserts, that Rome made so many diplomatic and military blunders, all carefully catalogued in the chapter in question. Presumably, with heaven's favor, the Romans passed the "test" and the tide turned into Rome's favor, and she survived.

The Gallic War of 390 B. C. is not the only example of heaven's "providence" that Machiavelli provides. The French invasion of Italy of 1494 and the political disasters that struck Italy subsequently are also presented in terms of fate and astral displeasure. This is made clear in the *First Decennale,* especially in its Dedicatory Letter and the opening lines. In the Dedicatory Letter, addressed to Alamanno Salviati, Machiavelli states that Italy's political tribulations were unavoidable because they were due to "necessity of fate" (*necessità del fato*). In the Latin version of this letter the point is made even more sharply. Italy's tribulations were due to the "necessity of fate, whose power could not be restrained" ("necessitudine fati, cujus vis refringi non potest").[15] And the opening lines of the poem make it clear that fate here means the "will" of the stars: "I shall sing Italian hardships for those two lustres now just over, under stars hostile to her good."[16]

There are two other examples of heaven's "providence" over Italian politics that Machiavelli mentions. Of these the first refers to the rise to prominence of the Colonna and the Orisini families. This example is very striking because of its bearings on the papacy. The implication is that even the fortunes of the papacy were subject to naturalistic "providence."

> The heavens (knowing a time would have to come when the French and the Germans would abandon Italy and that land would remain entirely in the hands of the Italians) in order that the Pope, when he lacked opposition from beyond the Alps, might not make his power solid or enjoy it, raised up in Rome two very powerful families, the Colonna and the Orisini; with their power and their proximity these two were to keep the papacy weak.[17]

The second example concerns the rise of the notorious factionalism of Florentine politics. This was due, he avers, to Florence's "fated families." But having fated families is not something peculiar to Florence: every republic, says Machiavelli, has its "fated families," only Florence had more than its share of them. "It is given from on high (*i.e.,* heaven), in order that in human things there may be nothing either lasting or at rest, that in all republics there are fated families (*famiglie fatali*), born for their ruin. Our republic, more than any other, has abounded in these."[18] Thus the struggles between the Buondelmonti and the Uberti, the Donati and the Cerchi, the Ricci and the Albizzi, not to mention the Medici and the Albizzi, are also seen from the point of view of cosmic laws operating in Florentine politics.

When we shift our attention from politics to religion, here too we see Machiavelli invoking the causality exercised by heaven. Thus the origin of the religion of the Romans is attributed to the "judgment" of the heavens: "the heavens judged (*giudicando i cieli*) that the laws of Romulus would not be sufficient for so great an empire."[19] They, therefore, inspired the senate to appoint Numa Pompilius as Romulus's successor and as the founder of the institutions of Roman religion. The instrumental character of religion, as one may infer from this passage, has its foundation in Machiavelli's cosmology. It is the heavens that judged that religion was necessary to supplement politics. Apparently, according to this pattern of thought, religion has no other end. Understood in this way, those in charge of religion, whether they be the senate or the consuls or the augurs, may legitimately exploit it for political ends. In particular they may exploit, without scruple, both the human fear of the unknown and the credulity of humankind. The Romans did exactly this. The institutions of the Roman religion—oracles, omens, behavior of sacred "chickens"—left a lot to the interpretation of those who had knowledge of "natural things" (*cose naturali*). The implication is that the effects of natural phenomena sometimes appeared as signs sent by heaven. The soothsayers and the augurs often "spoke so as to please the powerful."[20] All this was proper and legitimate in Machiavelli's eyes, basically because religion was intended by heaven to be at the service of the state. Though the state may exploit religion for its own ends, it does not mean that religion itself is a human invention. In its origin or "inspiration" it is transmundane; but in its use, it is entirely civil and mundane.

This brings us to Machiavelli's famous attack on Christianity.[21] No doubt, the attack is based in part on the political role which the Italian church had played in Italy, and in part on the moral lapses of the Italian Christian elite, especially the clergy. But these are objections directed at practices, corrigible by reform. The question is whether the roots of his criticism originate in his cosmology. His fundamental attack is directed not at the practices but at the theory of Christianity, namely that it is a supernatural religion, not dependent on the judgment of heaven. And because it does not originate in the judgment of heaven, it could not properly be turned into an instrument of politics. Its origin is in the Uncreated Logos, superior to the planets and the heavens. It is this fact which renders invalid any treatment of Christianity as a cosmic, natural religion. Christianity is not compatible with Machiavellian politics, because it does not originate in the "judgment" of heaven. That is why it could legitimately maintain the superiority of contemplation over political action; introduce the notion of another *patria,* superior to the temporal one; propose another *summum bonum* in addition to the *summum bonum* of politics; oppose *mondana gloria* to spiritual glory; and value the good of the soul more than that of the body.

There is a suggestion in ***Discourses*** II. 2 that Machiavelli saw Christianity not as a supernatural religion but as a cosmic, natural religion. For he hints that Christianity's appearance coincided with "the world becoming effeminate and the heaven becoming disarmed." This is the closest that he comes to suggesting that Christianity had its origin in the judgment of the heavens, that it appeared at a time when heaven and earth were in a specific astrological condition. In contemporary astrological thought Christianity was thought to have been the outcome of the conjunction of Jupiter and Mercury. And Mercury was held to be the planet favoring thought and contemplation. The "weakness" which Machiavelli says Christianity has allegedly introduced into the world and its contemplative bent, then, have their natural basis in cosmological causes.

The astrological pattern of thought, as it applies to religion, reappears in ***Discourses*** II. 5: all religions, he states, "change two or three times in five or six thousand years." The practice of calculating and predicting the duration of religions was a favorite past time of astrological natural philosophy. Savonarola, for example, in his *Treatise on Astrology,* ridiculed these calculations: Abu'Mashar, according to Savonarola, had calculated 1460 years to be the lifespan of Christianity, while Habraz had put it at 1444.[22] While in ***Discourses*** II. 5, Machiavelli does not subscribe to a particular date for Christianity's demise, he seemed to imply that Christianity has a limit to its duration. In the meantime, however, what Christians had to do was to interpret Christianity according to *virtù,* that is, as a natural religion, something which Christians had failed to do. If it could be interpreted politically rather than theologically, it could, for the remainder of its duration, become a politically aggressive religion. Christian rulers would then be able to manipulate Christianity the way the Roman senate had manipulated paganism. But he was afraid that Christian theology stood in the way of this ever happening. For Christianity countered the cosmological notion of the heaven (*il cielo*) with the theological notion of paradise (*paradiso*): "This (the Christian) way of living, then, has made the world weak and turned it over as prey to the wicked men, who can in security control it, since the generality of men (*l'universalità degli uomini*), in order to go to paradise, think more about enduring their injuries than about avenging them."[23] The contra-position of *il cielo* and *paradiso* highlights the contrast between Machiavelli's political cosmology and Christian theology.

A cosmological argument also lies at the basis of Machiavelli's celebrated theory of renewal, of "returning to the beginning."[24] Although "all the things of the world" (*tutte le cose del mondo*) have a limit (*il termine*) to their life, some of them can prolong it, if they can periodically renew themselves by going back to their beginning. The things that can prolong their lives in this way are, of course, "the mixed bodies"—republics, monarchies, and religions. The crucial point to be noted here is that these bodies, no less than natural bodies, are subject to the laws "ordained for them by heaven." These too are subject "to the process of time," and time, as Machiavelli is never tired of saying, does injure or disorder all human collectivities, whether religious or secular.[25] However, human causation can work within the limit imposed by the motions of heaven, and if it does, it will result in the temporary renewal of the entity in question. The point that ought not to be overlooked here is that Machiavelli ties his very theory of renewal, to the premodern notion of going back to the origin of the entity that is to be renewed. In other words, Machiavellian renewal is not something that looks forward but rather it is something that looks backward. Even though in *Discourses* I. 39, he clearly indicates that such renewal can bring forward new remedies, such notions of newness have still to be interpreted in the light of the fundamental notion, expressed in *Discourses* II (Preface). It is that "the world has always gone on in the same way and that there has been as much good as bad, but that this bad and this good have varied from land to land."[26] The sum of good and bad remains constant, the only difference is that the good or *virtù* migrates from country to country—in Machiavelli's list, from Assyria, to Media, to Persia, to ancient Italy, to Turkey, France and parts of Germany and Switzerland.

The examples of renewal cited in *Discourses* III. 1, are those of the early Roman republic, the Franciscan and the Dominican movements within the Catholic church, and contemporary French monarchy. Certainly, in each case, specific human agencies were at work. Thus in the case of Rome there were such external accidents as the Gallic War of 390 B. C., as well as the internal renewal brought about by the Roman *ordini,* harshly executed. In the case of the Franciscan and the Dominican movements, there were, of course, the examples set by St Francis, St Dominic and their followers. The striking point about Machiavelli's interpretation of this instance of Christian renewal is that it too, by implication, was subject to the course ordained for them by heaven. In other words, Machiavelli prefers to see Christian renewal not in theological, but in cosmological terms. Here it may be useful to remember that according to contemporary astrological natural philosophy, the Franciscan and the Dominican reforms were thought to have begun with the planetary conjunction of 1226. No less an orthodox figure than Cardinal Pierre D'Ailly (c. 1350-c. 1420), chancellor of the University of Paris, believed this on the basis of astrological calculations.[27] The cosmological context of Machiavelli's notion of renewal makes it doubtful whether he thought of these renewals as fully autonomous human activities. Yet there are those who think that Machiavelli's notion of renewal is to be understood in terms of the search for human autonomy.[28] Harvey C. Mansfield, Jr., sees in Machiavelli's idea of renewal, and the related notion of the perpetual republic, the basis for interpreting Machiavelli as the initiator of the modern notion of progress and progressivism (contra John Pocock and Quentin Skinner). "States will rise and fall," he writes, "but the whole will remain strong and mankind will progress in a condition Machiavelli calls 'the perpetual republic.'"[29] Given Machiavelli's cosmology, and his rejection of the linear theory of history, it is difficult to see how the idea of modern progress can be read into Machiavelli. As we have already noted, his notion of renewal looks more to the beginning than to the future. The Machiavellian notion of the perpetual republic, it seems, should be interpreted both in the context of Machiavelli's cosmological principle, and in the specific context of *Discourses* III. 1, which, as the title indicates, is speaking only of prolonging the life (*viva lungamente*) rather than of perpetuating it. It is true that Machiavelli does say that if certain conditions can be met, a republic could carry on without corruption, and be perpetual. Two conditions are mentioned. The first, mentioned in *Discourses* I. 2, is that a republic be not conquered and absorbed by another. But we know, from *Discourses* I. 6, that this condition cannot be met, since nothing in human affairs can be perpetual, and since all states are subject to the cycle of growth, decline and fall. Decline of power tempts the stronger states to conquests. And the stronger states themselves will eventually succumb to the disintegrating, natural, process of time. The second condition to be met, mentioned in *Discourses* I. 20, *Discourses* III. 1, and *Discourses* III. 22, is the availability of good laws and good rulers. But such a condition can be met only if the republic itself is virtuous. Thus in *Discourses* I. 20, the argument is that if an infinite number of virtuous rulers can follow one another such a virtuous succession (*virtuosa successione*) could make a republic perpetual. That is to say, in order to have a virtuous perpetual republic, there should be an infinite number of virtuous rulers, which condition can be met only if the republic is perpetually virtuous. The argument involves circularity and, therefore, cannot be taken seriously. The same defect characterizes the other two cases. However, *Discourses* III. 17 denies the possibility of a perpetual republic: "And because no certain remedy can be given for such troubles that rise in republics, it follows that a perpetual republic cannot be established; in a thousand unexpected ways her ruin is caused." Briefly, Machiavelli's cosmology is not hospitable to the modern notion of progress; and the renewal he speaks of is not the outcome of sole human activity, but the outcome of conjoint activity of human and celestial causes.

One of the arguments in favor of Machiavelli's modernity, as noted already, is based on the claim that he paves the way for the conquest or, at least the control, of fortune, understood as chance. His famous metaphor of fortune as woman, who should be beaten into submission, is often cited as proof. As Strauss puts it, "Fortuna can be vanquished by the right kind of man."[30] But the claim regarding chance warrants a close scrutiny of Machiavelli's treatment of fortune. The first thing to notice is his pattern of treating fortune throughout his works. We find him speaking of the fortune of individuals and the fortune of countries. The best example of this is chapter 25 of *The Prince*. In the first part of this chapter the fortune of countries—Germany, France, Spain, and Italy—is discussed. This is followed, in the second part, by a discussion of the fortune of individuals, in this case that of Julius II. Of the two metaphors used in this chapter, the first, that of the river in spate, refers to the fortune of countries, and the second, that of woman, refers to the fortune of individuals. The remedy against fortune varies depending on which fortune is being discussed. In the case of the fortune of countries, *ordinata virtù*—military power and preventive measures and preparations symbolized by dams, dikes and canals—can deal with chance events that occur to them. This was shown in a positive way by the example of Spain, Germany and France, and in a negative way, by that of Italy. The Roman republic also, as shown in *Discourses* II. 1, owed its greatness, more to its *ordinata virtù* than to fortune. But in the final analysis, countries, however powerful, are subject to the laws of the cycle of rise and fall. There is no question, then, of vanquishing the fortune of countries.

As regards the fortune of individuals, altogether different considerations are given. Military power and preparations can hardly help an individual stricken by the blows of misfortune. What is needed instead is the right quality of time, and the right temperament or humor, and their harmonization. In other words, Machiavelli's explanation relies on the astrologically laden concepts of quality of time and humors. Julius II succeeded in all that he did because his time and his temperament (which was choleric) always harmonized. And he would have failed, Machiavelli warns us, if he had to face a time which required a different type of temperament. The point of the warning is that one cannot go against one's temperament, that is, one is obliged to work within one's given temperament. And, of course, it is one's fortune, not free will or choice, that sees to it that one's time and one's temperament harmonize. That is to say, as far as the fortune of individuals is concerned, the chances of mastering fortune depends on fortune itself. The metaphor of the woman, if studied closely, says as much. Even though the youth is asked to beat the woman into submission, it is premised on the prior notion that fortune likes that this be so. Or, as Machiavelli states, "one sees that she lets herself be won more by the impetuous than by those who proceed coldly."[31] The point is that humans, not having control over the quality of their times, nor over the humor with which they are born, are dependent on fortune, who (or which) controls both the times and temperament. This is the pessimistic conclusion that Machiavelli reaches, not only in *The Prince* 25, but also elsewhere, for example, in his analysis of Cesare Borgia, Piero Soderini, Castruccio Castracani, Fabius Maximus, and others.[32]

We have already referred to the astrological language of Machiavelli's analysis of fortune. But there is more to his use of such language. For where else but in Ptolemy's *Tetrabiblos* do we find the original source of treating fortune in the twofold manner? It is in this master work of classical astrology, widely read in Florence for centuries (Salutati and Savonarola, for instance used to refer to Ptolemy as "the prince of astrologers"), that we find the scope of astrology being divided into "universal" or catholic and particular or genethliacal.[33] The first concerns the fortunes of countries, cities and nations, and the second, those of individuals. Now it is remarkable that *The Prince,* chapter 25, in passing from the first part of the chapter to the second, uses the Ptolemaic terminology of the universal and the particular.[34] Whether Machiavelli actually read Ptolemy or not, is not the question; the question is whether in his treatment of the subject, he appears to follow the mode of dividing astrology into the general and the particular. And the answer seems to be in the affirmative. And if this is true, it follows that his treatment of fortune is based on a premodern cosmology.

There is another aspect of Machiavelli's treatment of

fortune which also casts doubts on the claim that he conquers fortune. It is that he uses fortune in at least two distinct senses. The first refers to fortune as a superhuman power, and the second, as the fortuitous. Fortune in the superhuman sense is the personified and deified goddess *Fortuna,* symbolizing the power of the heavenly bodies. Machiavelli sometimes used fortune in this sense: for example in *Discourses* II. 29, where fortune and heaven are identified. And in *The Prince* 25 where it is claimed that fortune is the arbiter of half of our actions, and that she leaves the other half, or almost that, for us to govern. Fortune in the second sense is used more frequently by him, as in *The Prince,* chapters 1 and 7, *Discourses* II. 30 and *Discourses* III. 31, where it is opposed to *virtù. Virtù* can and should do everything possible within its sphere of effectiveness. One should not resign oneself to chance events that might occur in one's life, but should do everything that one can. But there is a limit to what one can do, and that limit is set by one's temperament and one's time. Thus to the question, Does Machiavelli overcome chance?, the answer needs to be based on a fundamental distinction between these two senses of fortune. Machiavelli wants humans to be activists, not fatalists. But the activism in question, as we shall see presently discussing his anthropology, is predicated on a premodern concept of human nature. It is, therefore, difficult to agree with Allan Bloom and others like him, who assert that there is an ideological continuity between Machiavelli, Bacon, Descartes, Danton, and the modern-day ideologue of scientism. Danton's *de l'audace, encore de l'audance, toujours de l'audace,* Bloom writes, "is but a pale, merely political duplicate of Machiavelli's original call to battle. Bacon's assertion that the goal of science is to 'ease man's estate,' Descartes' assertion that science will make man 'master and possessor of nature,' and the commonplace that science is the conquest of nature are offsprings of Machiavelli's revolution and constitute the political face adopted by modern philosophy." [35]

MACHIAVELLI'S ANTHROPOLOGY

There is no formal analysis of human nature in Machiavelli. But there is, no doubt, a coherent view of human nature underlying his political philosophy. Considered negatively, he does not conceive of humans as animals naturally destined for virtuous life to be lived in political society. As is evident from *Discourses* I. 2, humans come to recognize justice, goodness, and virtue, only after the "state" has been established on the basis of the need for security and power. In other words, his conception of human nature is neither Platonic nor Aristotelian nor Christian. But does this mean that it is modern?

Where he makes positive statements on human nature, we notice that the language used is often borrowed from premodern natural philosophy. Perhaps the most famous

of these statements is found in *Discourses* I. 3: founders of republics should presuppose that "all men are evil (*rei*) and that they are always going to act according to the malignity of their spirit (*animo*) whenever they have free scope; and when any malignity remains occult for a time (*occulta un tempo*), the reason is some occult cause (*occulta cagione*) which, in the lack of any experience of the contrary, is not recognized, but then its discovery is brought out by time (*il tempo*), which they say, is the father of every truth."[36] The key concepts contained in this remarkable statement—the absence of any predisposition toward the good, the predisposition, on the other hand, of the *animo* to act according to the malignity of time, the operations of an occult cause in nature and the human world—are all derived from contemporary astrological natural philosophy. The occult cause in question is the nonphysical, but supposedly real "influence" that heaven, the stars and the planets are alleged to exercise on human behavior. As the quality of their "influence" varies with their positions, the human propensity to evil also varies. It remains occult for a time, that is, it remains manifest only when the planetary conditions are correct. There is no mention here of the soul (*anima*); instead, the spirit (*animo*) is mentioned. Spirit in astrological natural philosophy was a psychic capacity capable of forming intentions, but not capable of surviving the dissolution of the body. The implication is that humans are not only subject to the occult influences but also that there is no truly immaterial power in their constitution, such as the power of the soul, a power that can resist the "influences" of heaven. It goes without saying that this is neither the classical nor the Christian view of human nature; but neither is it the modern view, insofar as the latter does not recognize the operations of any occult cause in nature.[37]

The second set of significant statements on human nature are found in the *Ghiribizzi* and in *The Prince*. In the *Ghiribizzi,* written in September 1506 to his friend Giovan Baptista Soderini,[38] the enquiry centers on the question of fortune: and its bearings on our successes and failures. How is it that moral virtues do not have anything to do with the successes or failures of politics?

> We have seen and see every day that kingdoms and sovereignties are gained or lost according to fortuitous accidents. . . . A man who was praised while he was successful is reviled when he fails, and frequently after long prosperity a man who finally fails does not in any way blame himself but accuses heaven and the disposition of fate. But the reason why different ways of acting are sometimes equally effective and equally damaging I do not know, but I should much like to know. So in order to get your opinion I shall be so presumptuous as to give mine.[39]

This is the context of Machiavelli's enquiry in the

Ghiribizzi. And Machiavelli's answer is the following:

> I believe that as nature has given each man an individual face, so she has given him an individual "mind" (*diverso ingegno*)[40] and individual imagination (*diversa fantasia*). From this it results that each man governs himself according to his *ingegno* and *fantasia.* On the other hand, because times vary and affairs are of varied type, one man's desires come out as he had prayed they would; he is fortunate who harmonizes his behavior with his time, but on the contrary, he is not fortunate who in his behavior is out of harmony with his time and the type of its affairs. Hence it can well happen that two men working differently come to the same end, because each of them adapts himself to what he encounters, for affairs are of as many types as there are provinces and states. Thus, because times and affairs change universally and individually (*universalmente et particularmente,* shades of Ptolemy here?) and men do not change their fantasies and their behavior, it happens that a man at one time has good fortune and at another time bad.[41]

The astrological context of this analysis becomes evident thanks to the reference to the famous astrological dictum of the Middle Ages and the Renaissance: "the wise man shall overcome the stars" (*vir sapiens dominabitur astris*). Astrological natural philosophy believed that this formula would solve the problem of astral determinism and free will. The wise man was the astrologer, that is, the scientist who knew the positions of the stars, and who, on the basis of such knowledge could anticipate the evil "influences" of the stars and could take preventive measures against them. In this sense he was thought to be able to "overcome" the stars. But both in the *Ghiribizzi* and in *The Prince,* Machiavelli rejects this classical astrological solution: "because there never as such wise men, since men in the first place are shortsighted and in the second place cannot command their nature, it follows that fortune varies and commands men and holds them under her yoke."[42] These ideas, first developed in the *Ghiribizzi,* are refined and restated in *The Prince,* chapter 25; as well.[43] But the rejection of the astrological formula does not mean that he rejected the astrological mode of analysis in terms of times and temperament.

What is striking in this mode of analysis is the shift that Machiavelli introduces in the theory of human action. The classical and scholastic theory of practical reason, *phronesis,* and *recta ratio* is abandoned in favor of *ingegno* and *fantasia.* However, action springing from these new foundations is subject to two new limitations. The first arises from the humor or temperament of each person, and the second, from the "quality" of the times under which each person operates. Both these limitations have their origin in astrological anthropology. Any one familiar with Durer's "Melancholia" knows how deeply the ideas of humors and temperament had

influenced the Renaissance conception of personality. Melancholy was the humor which was under the influence of Saturn; but Jupiter could neutralize its malignant "influence." Whether the melancholic person produced works of genius or not depended on the "influences" of the planets in question. All such theory was the common patrimony of the Renaissance, and one should not be surprised if one sees reflections of it in the *Ghiribizzi, The Prince,* and the *Discourses.* Julius II succeeded in all that he did, Machiavelli argues, because his temperament and his times harmonized.[44] This was also true of the successes of Fabius Maximus, Hannibal and Scipio. "Men in their conduct, and so much more in their great actions, ought to think of the times and adapt themselves to them. Those who because of a bad choice or natural inclination are out of harmony with the times, generally live in misfortune and their actions have a bad outcome; it is the opposite with those who are in harmony with the times."[45]

The consequence this theory of action has for free will (*libero arbitrio*) is considerable. Free will in the scholastic sense was rational desire, enjoying the freedom of indifference. Such a notion of freedom is not to be found in Machiavelli. For the Machiavellian personality is incapable of going against its natural inclination set by its humor and temperament. "You always act as nature forces you."[46] Fabius Maximus Cunctator conducted himself the way he did in the Punic Wars, "through nature and not through choice."[47] Julius II acted according to his choleric temperament: "and because the times fitted him well, his enterprises succeed—all of them. But if times requiring a different plan had come, of necessity he would have fallen, because he would not have changed for two reasons: one, that we cannot counteract that to which nature inclines us; the other, that when with one way of doing a man has prospered greatly, he cannot be persuaded that he can profit by doing otherwise."[48] Manlius Torquatus "was forced to proceed so severely by those extraordinary commands to which nature inclined him . . . being impelled first by his nature, then by his desire that what his natural inclination had made him arrange should be carried out."[49] The only change that Machiavelli recognizes as possible for humans are those which are caused by humor and temperament: "men are bored in good times and complain of bad ones."[50] We cannot hold to the middle way, "because our nature does not allow it."[51]

No doubt Machiavelli has lowered the standards of conduct: he has brought them down from *recta ratio* and *phronesis* to imagination and *ingegno,* temperament and times. But Strauss's argument is that this lowering has made the actualization of human desires more probable, even certain. But is this so? When we look closely at Machiavelli's account of the successes and failures of Julius II, Soderini, Castruccio Castracani, Cesare Borgia, Fabius Maximus, Scipio, Han-

nibal, Marius, Sulla, Manlius Torquatus, and Manlius Capitolinus—individuals whose actions he has
examined more or less closely—we see that successes and failures were the outcome of coincidence of
temperament and times rather than that of will and
autonomy. Their successes had nothing to do with the
lowering of standards. Moreover, Machiavelli accounts for them with the aid of an outmoded anthropology, the anthropology of astrological natural philosophy, and not with the aid of a modern type of
anthropology.

CONCLUSION

We now return to the question raised at the beginning
of this paper: Does the newness of Machiavelli imply
or require modernity? No doubt, Machiavelli's political theory introduces many new things. It rejects,
for example, the teachings springing from Plato, Aristotle and the Scholastics. It has changed the meaning of virtue in general and of *phronesis* in particular. But the arguments by means of which this is
accomplished are based on premodern cosmology and
anthropology; they are not based on arguments derived from modern science. If modernity requires
the acceptance of a post-seventeenth-century concept of physical nature and human nature, then
Machiavelli cannot be considered a modern. Only
with the new concept of physical nature and human
nature does modernity constitute itself. Insofar as
this is true, Machiavelli's newness does not amount
to modernity. Consequently, Strauss was correct
when he wrote that Hobbes was the founder of
modern political philosophy, and mistaken when he
later revised this position and declared that the hon-
or should go to Machiavelli.

There is still another point which Strauss raises and
which needs to be addressed. It is his claim that there
is a hidden kinship between Machiavelli's political
science and the new natural science of the seventeenth century. But can even a hidden kinship exist
between Machiavelli and the moderns when the open
differences between them are so fundamental? Can
two parties disagree on the nature of reality itself and
still maintain any significant agreement between them,
hidden or otherwise? To have a significant agreement
there must be, for a minimum, a prior agreement on
the nature of reality. Between Machiavelli and the
moderns, however, no such agreement seems possible. Insofar as this is the case, one does not see how
any significant hidden kinship can exist between the
two.

Notes

The Editors thank Oxford University Press for permission to publish this article which is to appear in
Tom Sorell's *Early Modern Philosophy* (forthcom-
ing).

[1] All references to Machiavelli's writings are to Niccolò Machiavelli, *Tutte le opere,* ed. Mario Martelli
(Florence, 1971); hereafter Martelli. I have given my
own translation of Machiavelli's texts, but in doing
so, I have consulted Allan Gilbert's translation of
Machiavelli: The Chief Works and Others, 3 vols.
(Durham, NC: Duke University Press, 1965). *Discourses on the First Decade of Titus Livius,* hereafter *Discourses.*

[2] Strauss, Leo, *The Political Philosophy of Hobbes*
(Chicago: University of Chicago Press, 1952), p. xix;
Natural Right and History (Chicago: University of
Chicago Press, 1953), pp. 178-79; *What Is Political
Philosophy? And Other Studies* (Glencoe, IL: Free
Press, 1959), pp. 41-47; *Thoughts on Machiavelli* (Se-
attle, 1969), passim; *On Tyranny* (Ithaca: Cornell, 1963),
PP. 24, 110-11, 196-97, 205; *History of Political Phi-
losophy* (Chicago: University of Chicago Press, 1987),
pp. 296-318.

[3] Strauss, *History of Political Philosophy,* p. 297.

[4] Strauss, *Political Philosophy of Hobbes,* p. xix; *What
Is Political Philosophy,* p. 40.

[5] Strauss, *On Tyranny,* p. 24.

[6] Strauss, *What Is Political Philosophy,* pp. 46-47.

[7] *Ibid.,* p. 47.

[8] ". . . come se il cielo, il sole, li elementi, li uomini,
fussino variati di moto, di ordine e di potenza, da quello
che gli erono antiquamente" (*Discourses,* I. Preface,
Martelli, p. 76).

[9] Note Machiavelli's use of the notion of ancients and
moderns here. "Modern things" (*moderne cose*) are
recent or contemporary events that are understood and
explained according to the principles of Christian culture, whereas "ancient things" are things that are understood and explained according to the principles of
classical or pre-Christian culture. Christianity for Machiavelli is part of modernity. The contrast between
ancients and moderns occurs very frequently in his
writings.

[10] *Discourses,* II. Preface, Martelli, p. 145.

[11] Martelli, p. 738; for the parallel passage see *The
Golden Ass,* chap. 5, Martelli, p. 967.

[12] *Discourses,* I. 6, Martelli, p. 86.

[13] *Ibid.*

[14] Martelli, pp. 154-55.

[15] For both the Italian and the Latin versions of this letter, dated 8 November 1504, see Martelli, p. 939.

[16] "Io canterò l'italiche fatiche, / segùite già ne' duo passati lustri / sotto le stelle al suo bene inimiche" (*Ibid.*, p. 940).

[17] *History of Florence,* I. 25, Martelli, pp. 649-50.

[18] *Ibid.,* III. 5, Martelli, p. 694.

[19] *Discourses,* I. 11, Martelli, p. 93.

[20] *Discourses,* I. 12, Martelli, p. 95.

[21] *Discourses,* I. 12, *Discourses,* II, 2; *The Prince,* chap. 12, *History of Florence,* I. 9.

[22] Girolomo Savonarola, *Contra Astrologiam Divinatricem,* Tract III, chap. 4. I have used the 1497 edition of this work, preserved at the Houghton Library of Harvard University.

[23] *Discourses,* II. 2, Martelli, pp. 149-50.

[24] *Discourses,* III. 1, Martelli, p. 195.

[25] *Discourses,* III. 9, Martelli, p. 212.

[26] *Discourses,* II. Preface, Martelli, p. 145.

[27] See Lynn Thorndike, *History of Magic and Experimental Science* (New York: Macmillan, 1934), 4: 107.

[28] A case for full autonomy is made by Hanna Pitkin in her *Fortune Is a Woman: Gender and Politics in the Thought of Niccolò Machiavelli* (Berkeley: University of California Press, 1984), p. 7, passim.

[29] See Harvey C. Mansfield, Jr., "Machiavelli's Political Science," *American Political Science Review* 75 (1981): 294 n. 3 and 305 n. 55.

[30] Strauss, *Thoughts on Machiavelli,* p. 216.

[31] *The Prince,* chap. 25, Martelli, p. 296.

[32] See *The Prince,* chap. 7; *Discourses,* III. 9; and *The Life of Castruccio Castracani of Lucca.*

[33] See Ptolemy, *Tetrabiblos,* ed. and trans. F. E. Robins, (London: The Loeb Classical Library, 1980), II. 1.

[34] "E questo voglio basti avere detto quanto allo opporsi alla fortuna, *in universali.* Ma restringendomi più a' *particulari,* dico come si vede oggi questo principe felicitare, e domani ruinare, sanza averli veduto mutare natura o qualità alcuna" (Martelli, p. 295. Emphasis added).

[35] Allan Bloom, *The Closing of the American Mind* (New York: Simon and Schuster, 1987), p. 286.

[36] Martelli, p. 81.

[37] In the poem *On Fortune,* Machiavelli points out the connection of"*occulta virtù*" by which we are "governed" by heaven: see Martelli, p. 978.

[38] For the text see Martelli, pp. 1082-83.

[39] *Ibid.*

[40] *Ingegno* here is the Italian of the Latin *ingenium.* Note Descartes's use of this word in *Regulae ad directionem ingenii.* The difficulty in translating this word into English may also be noted: G. R. T. Ross translates it as both "intelligence" and "mind." See *Descartes: The Philosophical Works,* trans. Elizabeth S. Haldane and G. R. T. Ross (Cambridge: Cambridge University Press, 1968), 1: x and 1. Machiavelli uses the word *ingegno* here to refer to the cognitive power of human beings. But given his astrological natural philosophy, it should be understood that this power is not a power of the soul but of the body, and that it works in tandem with imagination.

[41] Martelli, p. 1083.

[42] *Ibid.*

[43] See Martelli, p. 296.

[44] *The Prince,* 25, Martelli, p. 296.

[45] *Discourses,* III. 6, Martelli, p. 212.

[46] *Discourses,* III. 9, Martelli, p. 213.

[47] *Ibid.*

[48] *Ibid.*

[49] *Discourses,* III. 22, Martelli, p. 228.

[50] *Discourses,* III. 21, Martelli, p. 227; *Ghiribizzi,* 1083.

[51] Martelli, p. 227.

FURTHER READING

Biography

Hale, J. R. *Machiavelli and Renaissance Italy.* New York: Collier Books, 1960, 220 p.

 Biographical and critical study of Machiavelli's life and works.

Criticism

Berlin, Isaiah. "The Originality of Machiavelli," in *Studies on Machiavelli,* edited by Myron P. Gilmore, pp.149-206. G. C. Sansoni Editore, 1972.

 Important essay that provides a comprehensive overview of Machiavelli's thought.

Burnham, James. "Machiavelli: The Science of Power," in *The Machiavellians,* pp. 29-80. New York: The John Day Co., 1943.

 Discusses Machiavelli's goals, methods, conception of history, and reputation. Burnham argues that Machiavelli's principal aim was the unification of Italy and that he divorced politics from transcendental ethics in order to locate both politics and ethics in the "real world of space and time and history."

Cochrane, Eric W. "Machiavelli: 1940-1960," *The Journal of Modern History* XXXIII, No. 2 (June 1961): 113-36.

 Surveys trends in scholarly writing on Machiavelli, noting interest in such topics as the relationship between politics and Christian morality, method, language, and the connections between Machiavelli's ideas and life experiences.

Colish, Marcia L. "The Idea of Liberty in Machiavelli," *Journal of the History of Ideas* XXXII, No. 3 (July-September 1971): 323-50.

 Analyzes Machiavelli's use of the word *libertà* in an effort to understand what he meant by that term and its relation to his other political ideas.

Grazia, Sebastian de. *Machiavelli in Hell.* Princeton, N. J.: Princeton University Press, 1989, 497 p.

 Extensive survey and analysis of Machiavelli's political thought.

Hariman, Robert. "Composing Modernity in Machiavelli's *Prince.*" *Journal of the History of Ideas* 50, No. 1 (January-March 1989): 3-29.

 Argues that Machiavelli was the key figure in the transition to modern political thinking because he "invented the peculiar assumption informing modern political consciousness that power is an autonomous, material force."

Hulliung, Mark. *Citizen Machiavelli.* Princeton, N. J.: Princeton Unviersity Press, 1983, 299 p.

 Discusses Machiavelli's thoughts on republicanism

and argues that if popular culture is mistaken about what Machiavelli promoted in his writings, scholars efforts to redeem him have been even more misleading.

Mansfield, Harvey C., Jr. "Machiavelli's Political Science." *The American Political Science Review* 75, No. 2 (June 1981): 293-305.

 Discusses Machiavelli's role in the formation of modern political science. In his analysis, Mansfield focuses on *The Prince* and the *Discourses.*

——. "Machiavelli and the Modern Executive." In *Taming the Prince: The Ambivalence of Modern Executive Power,* pp. 121-49. New York: Free Press, 1989.

 Analyzes Machiavelli's understanding of nature, his attack on the Christian religion, and his concept of the executive. Mansfield argues that Machiavelli "was the first writer on politics to use the word 'execute' frequently and thematically in its modern sense."

Parel, A. J. "Machiavelli's Notions of Justice: Text and Analysis." *Political Theory* 18, No. 4 (November 1990): 528-44.

 Analyzes Machiavelli's "Allocution Made to a Magistrate." Parel argues that "Allocution" demonstrates Machiavelli's thorough knowledge of Christian and classical justice and contends that "two different conceptions of justice coexist in his writings."

——. *The Machiavellian Cosmos.* New Haven: Yale University Press, 1992, 203 p.

 Explores the themes of heaven—in the Renaissance sense of physics and cosmology—and humours—in the pre-modern sense of the medical study of human nature. Parel contends that the study of these themes informs Machiavelli's political thought as a whole.

Strauss, Leo. "Niccolo Machiavelli." In *History of Political Philosophy,* edited by Leo Strauss and Joseph Cropsey, pp. 271-92. Chicago: University of Chicago Press, 1973.

 Examines Machiavelli's political thought in the context of prior and subsequent political thinkers.

Villari, Pasquale. "Chapter II: The *Prince* and the *Discourses.*" In *The Life and Times of Noccolo Machiavelli,* translated by Linda Villari, pp. 94-132. 1892. Reprint. New York: Greenwood Publishers, 1968.

 Discusses Machiavelli's ideas regarding politics and the state in the two works, and relates them to the overall context of renaissance notions of political science.

Whitfield, J. H. *Machiavelli.* Oxford: Basil Blackwell, 1947, 167 p.

 Critical overview of Machiavelli's life and works,

focusing on *The Prince, The Discourses on Livy,* and the context in which he wrote.

————. "The Politics of Machiavelli." In *Discourses on Machiavelli,* pp. 163-79. Cambridge, England: W. Heffer & Sons, 1969.

Examines the history of and meaning attached to the word "politics," arguing that its connotations have changed considerably since Machiavelli's time.

Additional coverage of Machiavelli's life and career is contained in the following sources published by Gale Research: *Literature Criticism from 1400 to 1800,* Vol. 8; *Discovering Authors*; *Discovering Authors:British*; *Discovering Authors:Canadian.*

Jean-Jacques Rousseau

1712-1778

Swiss-born French essayist, autobiographer, novelist, dramatist, and poet.

The following entry provides critical discussion of Rousseau's writing on political theory. For additional information on Rousseau's life and works, see *Literature Criticism from 1400 to 1800,* Volume 14.

INTRODUCTION

Rousseau was a French philosopher and political theorist who is recognized as one of the greatest thinkers of the French Enlightenment. A prolific writer on many subjects, he has been variously cited as the intellectual father of the French Revolution, founder of the Romantic movement in literature, and engenderer of many modern pedagogical movements. The broad influence of his thought originates not only from his best-known political and philosophical treatises—*Du contrat social; ou principes du droit politique* (*The Social Contract*; 1762), *Discours sur les sciences et les arts* (*Discourse on the Sciences and the Arts*; 1750), and *Discours sur l'origine et les fondaments de l'inégalité parmi les hommes* (*Discourse upon the Origin and Foundation of the Inequality among Mankind*; 1755)— but also from his eloquent novels and autobiographical writings—*La Nouvelle Héloïse* (1761), *Émile, ou de l'éducation* (*Émile*; 1762), and *Les Confessions de J. J. Rousseau* (*The Confessions of J. J. Rousseau*; 1782-89). Rousseau's attempts to reconcile individual freedom with political unity gives his political writings an enigmatic quality that often leaves his readers questioning the degree of coherence between his ideas. Despite this, however, Rousseau's political writings have made a tremendous impact on Western thought.

Biographical Information

Rousseau was born in 1712 to Isaac Rousseau, a Genevese watchmaker, and Suzanne Bernard, the daughter of an upper-middle-class Genevese family. Rousseau's mother died a few days after his birth, and until age ten he lived with his father, who educated him by reading Calvinist sermons and seventeenth-century romance novels aloud to him. Rousseau's father subsequently abandoned him to the tutelage of an uncle, who apprenticed him at age thirteen to an abusive engraver. Having endured three miserable years of apprenticeship, Rousseau fled Geneva in 1728, and advised by a Roman Catholic Priest, went to the town of

Annecy. There, Rousseau met 29-year old Mme. de Warens, who supported herself by taking in and encouraging Catholic converts. Under her protection, Rousseau was sent to a hospice in Turin, where he converted to Catholicism, and thereby forfeitted his Genevese citizenship. Rousseau returned to Annecy the following spring intending to enter the priesthood, but instead he taught music to girls from the wealthiest families in the neighborhood. In 1731, after an unsuccessful search for employment in Paris, he once again returned to Mme. de Warens, who now lived near Chambéry, where Rousseau claimed he passed the happiest years of his life. He became her lover and stayed with her until 1740. During that time he studied music, read philosophy, science, and literature, and began to compose and write. Rousseau returned once more to Paris in late 1742, when he presented (without success) a new system of musical notation to the Académie des Sciences. In 1743, with the publication of his *Dissertation de la musique moderne*, together with the compositions of an opera and a comedy, Rousseau was appointed private secretary to the French ambassador in Venice; he lost the position the following year.

In 1745, he met Thérèse Levasseur, a chambermaid who became his lifelong companion, and with whom he reputedly had five children. In Paris, Rousseau came to know prominent Encyclopedists and philosophers, including Voltaire and Denis Diderot. Rousseau's career as an essayist began in 1749 when, on the way to visit Diderot in prison, he saw an announcement for an essay contest sponsored by the Dijon Academy. In his winning essay, the *Discourse upon the Sciences and the Arts,* Rousseau argued that culture had ruined morality. The essay brought him immediate fame and provoked a number of literary disputes. During the following decade, Rousseau wrote most of his other important works, including the *Discourse on the Origin and Foundation of the Inequality among Mankind, La Nouvelle Héloïse,* the *Lettre à d'Alembert sur les spectacles* (*Letter to d'Alembert on the Theater*; 1758), *Émile,* and *The Social Contract.* In 1756 he briefly returned to Geneva to re-embrace Calvinism and recover his citizenship. He then returned to France and settled at the "Hermitage," a house at Montmorency, offered to him by Mme. d'Épinay, a friend of the Encyclopedists. He was forced to flee France in 1762, when the Parliament of Paris condemned both *Émile* and *The Social Contract.* He went back to Geneva, only to find that there, too, his works were banned and he was banished. He defended his writings in the *Lettre à Christophe de Beaumont* (1763), which attacked the archbishop of Paris who had condemned *Émile,* and *Lettres écrites de la montagne* (1764), which responded to the Council of Geneva's decree that *Émile* and *The Social Contract* be burned. In 1766, and under considerable mental distress, Rousseau fled to England and was offered refuge by David Hume. Rousseau soon grew paranoid and suspected Hume of collusion with his perceived enemies. Paranoid and panicked, Rousseau returned to France in 1767 under an assumed name: Renou. He wandered about France, never remaining anywhere for long, married Thérèse, and wrote his *Confessions.* In 1770 he returned to Paris and resumed hisreal identity unmolested. Determined to defend himself against the "conspirators," Rousseau publicly read excerpts from his *Confessions.* He was forced to stop the readings when Mme. d'Épinay requested police intervention. Rousseau's madness lessened during the last two years of his life, and he lived in seclusion with Thérèse. He wrote *Les Rêveries du promeneur solitaire* (*The Reveries of a Solitary Walker*). Rousseau continued to write until his death on July 2, 1778.

Major Works

From 1751 to 1759 Rousseau worked on a large project that was to be called *Institutions politiques.* Though he never finished the project as such, several essays within the *Institutions* were among his most famous. The first of these was his follow-up to the *First Discourse,* the *Discourse on the Origins of Inequality.* This *Second Discourse,* a second essay for the Dijon Academy, was essentially a diatribe against despotism and private property. He sought to expose and denounce artificially instituted social inequality by describing a hypothetical state of natural man. He believed that human beings are essentially good and potentially perfect. Human faults arise from the corrupting influences of conventional society—inequality, despotism, and privately-owned property—which, he claimed, progressively restrict freedom and lessen moral virtue. In order to restore humanity to its natural goodness, Rousseau called for a return to nature so far as is possible, but he also stressed that individual freedom can be reconciled with political unity. Rousseau's novels also expressed and elaborated on his ideas about the state of nature. *La Nouvelle Héloïse* demonstrated the triumph of a primitive family unit over the corruption of modern society, while *Émile* explicated his scheme for "natural" education in which man would preserve his fundamentally good instincts. Much of his subsequent political writing, notably *The Social Contract,* was an attempt to resolve the problem of freedom by reconciling the ideal freedom in the state of nature with the freedom possible in a civil society. Beginning with the famous phrase, "Man is born free and everywhere in chains," *The Social Contract* outlined the social order that would enable human beings to be natural and free—acknowledging no other bondage save that of natural necessity. While much of his writing was abstract and theoretical, Rousseau was keenly aware of current political events, especially in his native Geneva. Despite his twenty-year loss of citizenship and persecution by the Genevan authorities, Rousseau always considered himself a Genevan. The dedication of the *Second Discourse* was addressed to his fellow Genevans, and his *Discours sur l'oeconomie politique* (*Discourse on Political Economy*; 1758), written for the *Encyclopédie,* explicitly took the Genevan Republic as an example. Other concrete political treatises were the *Projet de constitution pour la Corse* (*Project for a Constitution for Corsica*; 1765) and *Considérations sur le gouvernement de Pologne et sur sa réformation projetté* (*Considerations on the Government of Poland*; 1782), which was requested by the Polish Confederation of the Bar, a group of noble Polish nationalists.

Critical Reception

Critics have long considered much of Rousseau's work extremely controversial, if not decidedly revolutionary. Moreover, Rousseau's works have been subject to various and contradictory interpretations. Rousseau himself maintained in his *Confessions,* however, that his *oeuvre* was consistent and coherent, and that any apparent inconsistencies were superficial. In the years after Rousseau's death, he was seen as a champion of individualism by both counter-revolutionaries and radicals. Conversely, Hippolyte Taine wrote in his

Ancien Régime that Rousseau's collectivism led inevitably to tyranny and despotism. In general, Rousseau's writings were widely read and critically acclaimed throughout Europe well into the nineteenth century, after which point interest waned until the early twentieth century. As the bicentenary of Rousseau's birth approached, English commentators began to reassess the import of the writer's life and ideology and critics focused on the contradictory nature of much of his thought. There have been periodic attempts, such as Ernst Cassirer's 1932 essay The Problem of Rousseau, to extract from the variety of his writings the fundamental unity of thought that Rousseau himself claimed existed. Rousseau continued (and continues) to be read as providing a foundation for a range of political ideologies, including modern democracy, socialist collectivism, totalitarianism, and individualist anarchy. In recent years, critical attention has shifted from a "paternity" approach—study of Rousseau's "formative influence" on modern society as the father of certain ideas, movements, and events—to attempts at lucid interpretation of the actual meaning of his thought, but he remains a complex or contradictory figure whose ideas and eloquence continue to resonate powerfully with those reading him from the economic and social vantage point of the late twentieth century.

PRINCIPAL WORKS

Dissertation sur la musique moderne (essay) 1743

Discours qui a remporté le prix à l'Académie de Dijon. En l'année 1750. Sur cette Question proposée par la même Académie: Si le rétablissment des Sciences et des Arts a contribué à épurer les moeurs [Discourse on the Sciences and the Arts; also called First Discourse] (essay) 1750

Le Devin du village [The Cunning Man] (operetta) 1752

Lettre sur la musique français (criticism) 1753

Discours sur l'origine et les fondements de l'inégalité parmi les hommes [A Discourse upon the Origin and Foundation of the Inequality among Mankind; also called Second Discourse] (essay) 1755

Oeuvres diverses de M.J.J. Rousseau de Genève.2 vols. [The Miscellaneous Works of Mr. J.J. Rousseau, 5 vols.] (essays and letters) 1756

*A M. D'Alembert de l'Académie Françoise de l'Académie Royale des Sciences de Paris, de celle de Prusse, de la Société Royale de Londres, de l'Académie Royale des Belles-Lettres de Suéde & de l'Institut de Bologne. Sur son Article Genève dans le VIIᵉᵐᵉ Volume de l'Encyclopédie, et particulièrement, sur le projet d'établir un Théatre de Comédie en cette ville [A Letter from M. Rousseau to M. D'Alembert concerning the effects of theatrical entertainments on the manners of mankind] (essay) 1758

Discours sue l'oeconomie politique [Discourse on Political Economy] 1758

Lettre de J.J. Rousseau à Monsieur de Voltaire (letter) 1759

†Lettres de deux amans, habitans d'une petite ville au pied des Alpes. 6 vols.; also published as La Nouvelle Héloïse (novel) 1761

Du contrat social: ou principes du droit politique [The Social Contract] (essay) 1762

Émile, ou l'éducation. 4 vols. [Émile] (novel) 1762

Manuscrit de Genève [Geneva Manuscript] (essay) 1762

Jean Jacques Rousseau, citoyen de Genève, à Christophe de Beaumont, Archevegue de Paris [An Explanatory Letter from J. J. Rousseau to C. de Beaumont, Archbishop of Paris] (letter) 1763

Lettres écrites de la montagne (essays) 1764

Projet de constitution pour la Corse [Project for a Constitution for Corsica] (essay) 1765

Dictionnaire de musique [Dictionary of Music] (dictionary) 1768

Lettres Nouvelles de J.J. Rousseau, sur le motif de sa retraite la campagne, addressées à M. de Malesherbes, et qui paroissent pour la première fois: suivies d'une relation des derniers momens de ce grand Homme (letters) 1780

Rousseau juge de Jean Jacques: Dialogues (autobiography) 1780

Considérations sur le gouvernement de Pologne et sur sa réformation projettée [Considerations on the Government of Poland] (essay) 1782

‡Les Rêveries du promeneur solitaire [The Reveries of a Solitary Walker] (essays) 1782

Les Confessions de J.J. Rousseau [The Confessions of J.J. Rousseau] (autobiography) 1782-89

Ouevres complètes de J.J. Rousseau, classées par ordre de matières, avec des notes. 38 vols. (essays, poems, novels, and autobiographies) 1788-93

Nouvelles lettres de J.J. Rousseau [Original Letters of J.J. Rousseau] (letters) 1789

Ouevres complètes. 4 vols. (essays, novels, poems, and autobiographies) 1959-64

Correspondance complète. 45 vols. (letters) 1965-86

*This work is commonly referred to in French as Lettre à d'Alembert sur la spectacles and in English as Letter to d'Alembert on the Theater.

†This work is sometimes referred to as Julie: ou la Nouvelle Héloïse.

‡This work first appeared with the publication of Les Confessions in 1782.

CRITICISM

Maurice Cranston (essay date 1968)

SOURCE: An introduction to The Social Contract, by Jean Jacques Rousseau, translated by Maurice Cranston, Penguin Books, 1968, pp. 9-43.

[*In the following excerpt, Cranston discusses Rousseau's* Social Contract *in the context of Rousseau's other works and in the works of his contemporaries.*]

The political views of the *philosophes* were as distasteful to Rousseau as were most of their opinions. Like their master, Francis Bacon, they believed in strong government; the doctrine of planning called for a ruler with enough power to put plans into effect; and just as Bacon himself once dreamed of converting James I to his way of thinking and then using magnified royal prerogative to enact his proposals, so the *philosophes* of the eighteenth century based their hopes for success on influencing powerful monarchs to do what they suggested. The current name for this was *le despotisme éclairé;* to Rousseau, the champion of freedom, any kind of despotism was anathema, and the so-called enlightened sort seemed rather worse than others.

In 1755 Rousseau addressed a letter to a pastor in Geneva who had conceived the idea of launching a literary periodical: 'Believe me, Sir, this is not the sort of work for you,' he wrote. 'Serious and profound writings may do us credit, but the glitter of that trivial philosophy which is fashionable today is wholly unbecoming to us. Great themes such as virtue and liberty enlarge and fortify the mind; little things, like poetry and the fine arts, give it more delicacy than subtlety.'[1]

The great themes of liberty and virtue were the themes of the *Social Contract*. This is why Rousseau attached so much importance to the book; and also, perhaps, why it got him into trouble. It might seem to the reader that Rousseau started to write the *Social Contract* as a book about liberty and ended up with a book about virtue; in truth it is the argument of the whole book that once men have entered into society, freedom comes to be inseparable from virtue.

Some time between the writing of the *Discours sur l'inégalité* and the writing of the *Social Contract,* Rousseau read the works of Thomas Hobbes. His only reference in the *Social Contract* to Hobbes are fleeting and hostile ones, but Professor Robert Derathé[2] has shown that Rousseau was not in the habit of acknowledging his intellectual debts, and that his debts were particularly great both to the legal theorists, or jurisconsults, of earlier generations, to Grotius,[3] Pufendorf,[4] Barbeyrac,[5] and Burlamaqui,[6] and also to the political philosophers, especially Hobbes and Locke. The second title of Rousseau's *Social Contract* is the same as the main title of one of Burlamaqui's books: *Principes du droit politique.* This *droit politique,* which I have been obliged for lack of a better alternative (there is no English equivalent of *le droit*) to translate as 'political right', Burlamaqui employed as a semi-technical expression to designate the general abstract study of law

and government, and Rousseau uses the word in the same sense.

The main title of Rousseau's *Social Contract* refers to a concept which all these jurisconsults and political philosophers invoked. They all believed that the state was the outcome of a covenant or agreement among men. The purpose of the state was the protection of those people to which it owed its being, and the same theorists also agreed that the sovereign must have enough power to provide such protection. Most of the theorists sought at the same time to limit this power of sovereigns under one principle or another, and even to divide sovereignty between several elements. Hobbes stood apart from the others in insisting that sovereignty must be unified and absolute. Hobbes said that men must choose: either they were ruled or they were free; they could not be both; liberty went with anarchy and security with civil obedience.

Rousseau accepted Hobbes's argument on one point; he agreed that sovereignty must be absolute or nothing, but he could not bring himself to accept Hobbes's notion that men must choose between being governed and being free. Rousseau, who loved liberty so much, believed he could show that it was possible for men to be at once free and members of a political society. Indeed the *Social Contract* may be read as an answer to Hobbes by an author whose mind was stimulated by the brilliance of Hobbes's reasoning, but who could not stomach Hobbes's conclusion.

It is important to note what Rousseau is doing in the *Social Contract*. He explains it clearly at the beginning: 'My purpose is to consider *if,* in political society, there can be any legitimate and sure principle of government, taking men as they are, and laws as they might be.' The *if* is crucial. Rousseau is not offering a plan for reform,[7] nor is he writing the kind of history and sociology he provides in his *Discours sur l'inégalité*. He is dealing with *right* rather than with *fact,* though fact comes into it, because he undertakes to deal with men 'as they are'. In the *Social Contract* Rousseau is dealing, in the hypothetical mood, with abstract problems which seem to him to emerge from philosophical reflection on the actual nature of man and the possible order of laws and government. The social contract discussed in the *Social Contract* is not the actual historical contract described in the *Discours sur l'inégalité,* that *imposture*[8] made to consolidate the advantages of the rich. It is a genuine and legitimate contract, which is to the benefit of everyone, since it unites liberty with law and utility with right.

Now Rousseau not only rejects Hobbes's claim that men must choose between being free and being ruled, he positively asserts that it is only through living in civil society that men can experience their fullest freedom. This is the connexion between freedom and virtue. Here we may detect a modification of the argument of the *Discours sur l'inégalité*. In the earlier work Rousseau stresses both the freedom and the innocence of man in the state of nature. In the *Social Contract* he still says that men have freedom in the state of nature, but he treats it as freedom of a crude and lesser kind. Such freedom is no more than independence. And while he does not accept Hobbes's picture of man in the state of nature as an aggressive and rapacious being, Rousseau (having read Hobbes) speaks less of the innocence and more of the brutishness of man in a state of nature. Man in the state of nature, as he is depicted in the *Social Contract,* is a 'stupid and unimaginative animal'; it is only by coming into a political society that he becomes 'an intelligent being and a man'. Assuredly, as a result of the growth of passions and sophistry which society breeds, men have generally grown worse with the passage of time; but that is because society, instead of improving men, has corrupted them. Society is bound to change men, and if it does not do what it is meant to do, and improve them, it will worsen them. Nevertheless, according to Rousseau, it is only by leaving the state of nature and becoming a social being in the fullest sense, that is to say, in becoming a citizen, that man can realize his own nature as man.

Rousseau never abandons the belief, put forward in his *Discours sur l'inégalité,* that men are happy in the state of nature. He continues to think it possible for them to be good. Men cannot, however, be virtuous in the state of nature, virtue being a characteristic of men who are conscious of morality. Unlike Hobbes, Rousseau does not suggest that it is fear which drives men to quit the state of nature; but he does say that it is man's weakness which makes him social.[9] Rousseau also suggests both that Providence has to intervene by creating natural disasters and shortages to force men to cooperate and also that there is a certain natural pressure within men to actualize those social and moral qualities which are mere potentialities in a state of nature.

Here one might suspect a certain equivocation in Rousseau's use of the word 'nature'. But what he is saying is that the state of nature is man's *original* state, not his natural state; for man can only realize his full nature as a man by making the social compact and living under law. Rousseau's ambiguity reflects a common ambiguity in the word 'nature', which is sometimes used to refer to what is, and sometimes to refer to what should be. Rousseau uses the word 'nature' at different times in either of these two senses.

In a way, Rousseau's solution to the problem posed by Hobbes is wonderfully simple. Men can be both ruled and free if they rule themselves. For what is a free man but a man who rules himself? A people can be free if it retains sovereignty over itself, if it enacts the rules or laws which it is obliged to obey. Obligation in such circumstances is wholly distinct from bondage; it is a moral duty which draws its compulsion from the moral will within each man. In this argument, we can detect a striking departure from the 'social contract' theorists who preceded Rousseau. The jurisconsults and Hobbes and Locke all rejected the well-established theories that sovereignty was based on nature or on divine right, and they all argued in one way or another, that sovereignty derived its authority from the assent of the people. But these earlier theorists also held that sovereignty was transferred from the people to the ruler as a result of the social contract. Rousseau is original in holding that no such transfer of sovereignty need or should take place: sovereignty not only originates in the people; it ought to stay there.[10]

Rousseau's solution to the problem of how to be at the same time ruled and free might plausibly be expressed as democracy. I have already spoken of the importance to him of what is commonly named 'democracy' in Switzerland. But Rousseau himself used the word 'democracy' in a rather distinctive fashion,[11] because of the emphasis he puts on the difference between the two departments, as he sees them, of government. Ruling, in the strict sense of making rules or laws, is the function which he says that the people must retain; for thus, and only thus, does sovereignty express itself. Every act of the sovereign is a law, and anything which is not a law is not an act of sovereignty. From this function of law-making, Rousseau distinguishes the administration, or executive management, of government. And he does *not* demand, as a prerequisite of liberty and legitimacy, that this administration shall be conducted by the whole body of citizens. On the contrary, he thinks it might be best done by a limited number. The conduct of administration by the whole body of the citizens he seems to consider too utopian an arrangement. And this is the arrangement which in the *Social Contract* he calls 'democracy', and of which he is thinking when he says that democracy is for gods, not men.[12]

Rousseau is undoubtedly a democrat in the sense that 'democracy' means legislative rule by the whole body of the citizens; but as he himself used the word in another sense, it might be less confusing to speak of him as a 'republican' or champion of 'popular sovereignty'. One of the reasons why he distinguishes so carefully between the legislative sovereign body and the executive or administrative body is his consciousness of the abiding danger to the legislative which the administrative body constitutes. For while it is convenient that the business of government should be entrusted to a council of magistrates or commissioners, those magistrates will naturally tend, with the passage of time, to encroach on the sacred territory of legislation, and thus to invade the sovereignty and destroy the republican nature of the state. As a matter of empirical fact, Rousseau even suggests that this is bound to happen.[13]

Nowhere in the *Social Contract* does Rousseau offer any short definition of liberty, although there are several often-quoted epigrams about it. In his *Lettres écrites de la montagne* (published two years after the *Social Contract*) he provides the most succinct account of what he means by this key word:

> Liberty consists less in doing one's own will than in not being subject to that of another; it consists further in not subjecting the will of others to our own. . . . In the common liberty no one has a right to do what the liberty of any other forbids him to do; and true liberty is never destructive of itself. Thus liberty without justice is a veritable contradiction. . . . There is no liberty, then, without laws, or where any man is above the laws. . . . A free people obeys, but it does not serve; it has magistrates, but not masters; it obeys nothing but the laws, and thanks to the force of the laws, it does not obey men.[14]

It is partly because of this intimate connexion between liberty and law that the freedom of man in a state of nature is so inferior. The freedom of the savage is no more than independence; although Rousseau speaks of the savage being subject to natural law, he also suggests that the savage has no consciousness of natural law; thus Rousseau can speak of a man being 'transformed', as a result of his entry into civil society, from a brutish into a human, moral being. A moral being is, or can be, free in another sense than the political; if, instead of being a slave of his passions, he lives according to conscience, lives according to rules he imposes on himself, then he has a liberty which only a moral being can enjoy. The savage has no sense of this; for one thing, the passions only begin to develop with society, which explains why society can mark the beginning of a change for the worse as well as the beginning of a change for the better. One of the new passions which emerges with society is pride or *amour-propre*, which Rousseau sees as an evil mutation of the perfectly innocent sentiment of self-love or *amour-de-soi*. It is a characteristic of modern sophisticated culture to be dominated by pride. The emphasis on 'going back to nature' in Rousseau's treatise on education, *Émile,* is the result of his belief that cultural environment, not natural inclination, breeds such harmful passions. Here we may notice a contrast between Rousseau's views and Hobbes's. Whereas Hobbes holds that pride is natural to man, Rousseau holds that it is artificial; whereas Hobbes says that war prevails among men in the state of nature because of men's pride, Rousseau says that war is a product of conflicts about property, and therefore cannot exist in the state of nature, where there is no property.

On the other hand, Rousseau seems to be entirely at one with Hobbes when he says that under the pact by which men enter into civil society everyone makes a total alienation of all his rights. However, it must be remembered that Rousseau regarded this alienation as a form of exchange, and an advantageous one; men give up their natural rights in exchange for civil rights; the total alienation is followed by a total restitution; and the bargain is a good one because what men surrender are rights of dubious value, unlimited by anything but an individual's own powers, rights which are precarious and without a moral basis; in return men acquire rights that are limited but legitimate and invincible. The rights they alienate are rights based on might; the rights they acquire are rights based on law.

It might be supposed that Rousseau is contradicting Locke when he says that men alienate all their rights when they make the social contract, Locke having said that men make the social contract only to preserve their rights. But Rousseau is really thinking in different terms from Locke. Rousseau does not think that men have in the state of nature the kind of natural rights which Locke supposes—the right, for example, to property. For Rousseau there is only *possession* in the state of nature; property (by definition, rightful possession) comes into being only when law comes into being. Nor does Rousseau think, like Locke, of liberty as one of men's rights. Indeed he says, quite as emphatically as Locke, that men *cannot* alienate their liberty. If Locke and Rousseau were thinking in the same terms, it would be a contradiction for Rousseau to say, as he does, that the social contract entails the total alienation of rights, and that men cannot alienate their liberty. In truth, what Rousseau is saying is that instead of surrendering their liberty by the social contract, they *convert* their liberty from independence into political and moral freedom, and this is part of their transformation from creatures living brutishly according to impulse into men living humanly according to reason and conscience.

There is no more haunting paragraph in the whole of the *Social Contract* than that in which Rousseau speaks of forcing a man to be free.[15] But it would be wrong to put too much weight on these words, in the manner of those who consider Rousseau, whether early-fascist or early-communist, at all events a totalitarian.[16] Rousseau is nothing so simple. He is authoritarian, but the authority he favours is explicitly distinguished from mere power; it is based on conscious and vocal assent, and is offered as something wholly consistent with liberty. There is no necessary antithesis, as some writers assume, between liberty and authority as such; for authority is a form of potency which rests on the credence and acceptance of those who respect it, and Rousseau insists that if authority is to be legitimate the credence and acceptance must be both universal and unconstrained. There is no resemblance between Rousseau's republic and the actual systems of twentieth-century totalitarian states, where the various devices of party rule, government by edict, brain-washing and secret police are manifestations of what Rousseau regarded as despotism and vigorously condemned. Indeed for those who seek the theoretical ancestry of present-day totalitarian ideology, the optimistic *despotisme éclairé* of the *philosophes* may well be worth as much attention as the pessimistic republicanism of Rousseau.

Rousseau does not say that *men* can be forced to be free in the sense that a whole community may be forced to be free; he says that *a* man may be forced to be free, and he is thinking here of the occasional individual who, as a result of being enslaved by his passions, disobeys the voice of the law, or of the general will, within him. The general will is something inside each man as well as in society as a whole, so that the man who is coerced by the community for a breach of the law, is, in Rousseau's view of things, being brought back to an awareness of his own true will. Thus in penalizing a law-breaker, society is literally correcting him, 'teaching him a lesson' for which, when he comes to his senses, the offender should be grateful. Legal penalties are a device for helping the individual in his own struggle against his own passions, as well as a device for protecting society against the anti-social depredations of law-breakers. This explains the footnote to Chapter 2 of Book IV of the **Social Contract,** where Rousseau writes: 'In Genoa the word *Libertas* may be seen on the doors of all the prisons and on the fetters of the galleys. This use of the motto is excellent and just.'

In arguing thus, Rousseau may be seen as adopting and elaborating an argument used by Locke against Hobbes. Hobbes in his plain, robust way, says that to be free is to be unopposed and unconstrained in doing what one wants to do; the law is a form of constraint, so that the less the law forbids, the more free a man is: 'The liberty of the subject is the silence of the laws.' Locke rejects this; he holds that the law does not diminish men's freedom, but effectively enlarges it, both by protecting a man from anarchic invasions of his liberty and by preventing collisions between one man's use of his liberty and another's. Locke even accepts the notion, though he never uses the words, of forcing a man to be free, because he mentions the case of a man who is prevented by *force majeure* from crossing a bridge which is dangerous and which he does not know to be dangerous; as soon as the man learns the true situation, he is grateful to those who have taken hold of him, and no longer feels that his freedom has been invaded. This is the kind of situation that Rousseau has in mind—albeit on a much larger scale—when he speaks of forcing a man to be free. The recalcitrant, to Rousseau, is someone who is out of joint with himself and with society, and thus to use physical restraint on him is not to harm, or injure, him, but, on the contrary, to help or heal, to recover him for reason, and therefore, at the same time, for freedom. It is difficult, assuredly, to reconcile this way of thinking with Rousseau's partiality for the death penalty.

In the discussion of liberty, Rousseau's whole emphasis is different from Locke's. Locke is not worried, as Rousseau is, by corruption; and he does not hanker after virtue. Locke thinks that a system of positive law set up by a constitutional state can enlarge men's liberty, but he also thinks that many systems of positive law do diminish men's liberty. For Locke there are good laws and bad laws. Good laws are the ones that recognize and defend men's natural rights, bad laws are the ones that neglect or abuse those rights. And therefore for Locke the problem is to have positive laws that secure men's rights and avoid laws that imperil men's liberty. But Rousseau has a different approach, or rather he has two distinctive approaches to law. When he is speaking of law as right, a law, for him, is by definition just; and even when he characterizes a law as an expression of the general will, it is still by definition just because the general will is by definition righteous. But, secondly, when Rousseau is thinking about the kinds of law he sees in the real world, when he is thinking, so to speak, as an empirical social scientist, he notes that all actual systems of law can be seen to be unjust. In a footnote to Book IV of *Émile* he writes: 'The universal spirit of laws in all countries is to favour the stronger against the weaker, and those who have against those who have nothing: this disadvantage is inevitable and without exception.'[17]

There is thus for Rousseau a radical dichotomy between true law and actual law, between law as it should be and law as it is seen in the existing world. And it should not be forgotten that the law he is writing about in the **Social Contract** is law in the true sense. Thus laws, as he explains them in these pages, are rules made by a people in its capacity of sovereign and obeyed by the same people in its capacity as subject. Rousseau thinks it axiomatic that such rules will never be oppressive for the simple reason that a people, being at the same time sovereign and subject, would never forge fetters for itself. The only thing he fears is that the people, being ignorant, might forge fetters unwittingly: hence the need for the lawgiver.

The distinction between true law and actual law corresponds to the distinction Rousseau draws between the general will and the will of all. The general will is a normative concept, its connexion with right is a matter of definition. The will of all is an empirical concept; the only test of the will of all is what, in fact, all will. Having been so severe on Grotius for failing to distinguish between fact and right, Rousseau is careful not to make the same mistake himself.

Why should I abide by the decision of the majority?

Because by the deed of the social contract itself, to which *everyone* subscribes and pledges (there is no question of a majority here; you either subscribe or you are not in civil society at all), everyone agrees to accept the decision of the majority in the formulation of the law. But it is also understood that the members of the majority whose decision is accepted do not ask themselves what do *I,* as an individual, demand, but what does the general will demand; thus it is the majority *interpretation* of the general will which is binding and not the majority will. This is how it can be morally obligatory for the minority to accept.

Rousseau borrows from Hobbes the argument that sovereignty is an absolute power; it cannot be divided and remain sovereign; and it cannot be subject to 'fundamental laws' and remain sovereign. At the same time Rousseau takes from Locke and the jurisconsults the notion that sovereignty is limited. Sovereignty is absolute, but not unlimited. The limits are those imposed by natural law and by the considerations of public good. 'Sovereignty does not pass the bounds of public advantage.' As an example of what Rousseau means by a natural law limitation, we may note his argument in the *Social Contract* that no agreement to enter into slavery could be a valid one because any agreement which is wholly to the advantage of one party and wholly to the disadvantage of the other is void in natural law.

Several commentators, including C. E. Vaughan,[18] say that Rousseau eliminates natural law, but Professor Derathé has drawn attention to certain passages from Rousseau's writings which illustrate the importance he attaches to natural law. Derathé quotes Rousseau's claim, in the course of his controversy with D'Alembert, that he recognizes three authorities higher than the sovereign authority of the state: 'that of God, that of the natural law which derives from the constitution of man, and that of honour'.[19] Again, in the *Lettres écrites de la montagne* Rousseau writes: 'It is no more permissible to violate natural law by the social contract than it is permissible to violate positive law by private contracts.'[20] Thirdly, in his *Considérations sur le gouvernement de Pologne* (written in 1771), Rousseau speaks of '. . . Natural law, that holy imprescriptable law which speaks to the heart and reason of man . . .'[21]

Against all this, it must be noticed that Rousseau in the *Social Contract* offers no possibility of an appeal to natural law. It is all very well to say, as he does, that the sovereign must not violate natural law, but this raises the question of who is to be judge of any such violation. In several of his writings, Rousseau emphasizes the supremacy of the individual conscience; he even goes so far as to speak of conscience as infallible. 'Conscience never deceives us.'[22] This might lead one to expect that he would agree with those theorists who hold that the individual conscience must ultimate-

ly decide where to draw the line between justice and injustice. In fact, in the *Social Contract* Rousseau takes up the position of Hobbes, namely, that the citizen can have no other guide but the civil law and the public conscience. The general will is itself the arbiter of just and unjust. Here there seems to be a contradiction between the argument of the *Social Contract* and that of the *Profession de foi* and other writings. In the *Social Contract* the general will is the moral authority; elsewhere individual conscience is represented as the innate principle of justice.

This points to another and even more striking contradiction between what Rousseau says in the *Social Contract* and what he says elsewhere. Rousseau as he appears in the *Profession de foi* and indeed in most of his writings, published and unpublished, is clearly a Unitarian or Socinian, like Locke or Malebranche, regarding the minimal creed as a genuine, if not the only genuine, form of Christianity. Rousseau plainly detested the atheism of Diderot and the *philosophes*; his belief in the love of God and the life to come was profoundly important to him. He often said that he could not live without such religious faith. He also believed, much as Locke did, that such Christianity is reasonable.

In the *Social Contract,* however, his attitude is very much closer to that of Machiavelli than it is to that of Locke. What the state needs, Rousseau says in his chapter on the civil religion, is a religion subordinate to the state and designed to teach patriotic, civic and martial virtues. And Christianity, he says, quite as boldly as Machiavelli, is no good for this purpose; it teaches men to love the kingdom of heaven instead of their own republic on earth, and it teaches them to suffer but not to fight. It teaches the wrong virtues. Assuredly, Rousseau makes clear that he is talking here about civil religion, not private religion, and he admits that 'the religion of the Gospel' is the word of God for the private person. But the state religion is the more important, and the state religion must be supreme; Rousseau even goes so far as to propose a death penalty for those whose conduct is at variance with the religious principles they proclaim.

Up to a point Rousseau's argument is perfectly logical; he thinks that men will not become virtuous without the aid of religious institutions—a cult, a church— and since Christianity does not teach the civic virtue that is needed for the kind of republic he favours—a state on the model of Sparta or Rome—Rousseau is perfectly consistent in proposing, with Machiavelli, some kind of neo-pagan cult to match the needs of such a state. But how can he reconcile this with his professed faith in Christianity? Conceivably he is saying only that neo-paganism is useful and Gospel Christianity is true, and that the two belong to different logical categories, to be judged by different standards, the one by the standard of social utility and the other by that of truth; but if this is so, Rousseau is putting the useful above the true, and what then becomes of his criticism of his atheistic contemporaries, that they put utility in the place of morality?

An even more serious criticism of Rousseau can, I think, be levelled against his whole theory of liberty. On the one hand, he belongs to a certain tradition of moral philosophers who argue that to be free is not to be left to do what you want to do but to be enabled to do what you ought to do. Everything that Rousseau says about freedom being inseparable from justice, and about the necessary connexion between liberty and virtue, puts him in this school of morality. This theory of freedom, which has its origins in religious thought, claims to offer a superior, higher, more true and exalted analysis of what freedom is. Rousseau stands squarely in this tradition when he speaks of the higher, and more specifically moral freedom that men attain when they quit the state of nature and enter civil society.

But at the same time, Rousseau reveals an attachment to a less exalted idea of what freedom is. This is when he says that freedom is not being subject to any other *man*. Here one may suspect that Rousseau retained from the experiences of his life the simple notion—which might well be the occupational notion of domestic servants—that being dependent on another man is slavery and that freedom is simply having no master. To be dependent on things or institutions is quite different, and wholly unobjectionable. Throughout the *Social Contract* it is clear that Rousseau never sees institutions as a threat to freedom. The image of a King or Prince in Rousseau's eyes is the image of a master, and he sees such monarchs as enemies of liberty. But the image of the state touches him quite differently. There is a sentence in Book II (Chapter 12) of the *Social Contract* which illustrates this forcefully: this is where he says that things should be so arranged that every citizen is perfectly independent from all his fellow citizens and excessively dependent on the republic'. The word 'excessive' is significant. And why does Rousseau use it? Because he thinks such dependence can never be too great; because dependence on the state guarantees men against all dependence on men, against '*toute dépendance personnelle*'.

Is this a philosopher's concept of freedom? Perhaps; but is it not also like that of a footman? The dream of liberty in the servants' hall is the dream of the elimination of the master; translated into political terms, this becomes the republican fantasy that freedom lies in the elimination of the King. Of course Rousseau says a great deal more than this about freedom. He says that to be free means to live under a law of one's own enactment. But one does not have to progress very far through the pages of the *Social Contract* to see how modest this role of enactment is allowed to

become. Men, he insists, are ignorant. The general will is morally sound, it is always rightful, but it is unenlightened. Men cannot be trusted to frame or devise their own laws. They need a Law-giver to make laws for them. Their part in the enactment of laws is limited to *assent* to those laws. Thus freedom for Rousseau consists of putting oneself willingly under rules devised by someone else.

The measure of confidence that Rousseau has in his fellow men is made clear in *Émile*. At the very end of that long book, when the hero is grown up, and his exemplary education has produced its paragon, the young man, who is married and about to have a child, begs his tutor to stay with him: 'Advise and control us,' he implores the tutor, ' . . . as long as I live I shall need you. I need you more than ever now that I am taking on the duties of manhood.'[23]

And just as the Tutor is the dominant figure of *Émile* so does the Lawgiver become the dominant figure of the *Social Contract*. Indeed the Lawgiver repeats in the state the role that the Tutor performs for the individual.[24] He is needed for the same reason; men left alone will be led by their own passions and folly into disaster; they need someone to save them from themselves.

It is a bad thing to have a master; for that is the reverse of freedom. But it is a good thing to have a tutor, so long as we follow him willingly and gladly. For Rousseau the way to liberty is the path of voluntary submission. 'The King is dead; long live the Lawgiver!' Is this, in the end, the battle cry of the republic? Does Rousseau wish us to say: 'Advise and control us, O *Législateur*. As long as we live we shall need you. We need you more than ever now that we are taking on the duties of self-government.'?

Many readers may find the *Social Contract* a frustrating book. What is offered with one hand is taken away with the other. It is theoretically possible for a political system to be so devised that men become more free by entering into it. This is to 'take laws as they might be'. On the other hand, it is hard, indeed impossible, to see how such a system could avoid being spoiled. This is to 'take men as they are'. Rousseau enlarges our vision and perhaps also our insight; at the same time he diminishes our expectations.

Notes

[1] Rousseau to Jacob Vernes, 2 April 1755. Quoted in Georges May, *Rousseau par lui-même,* Paris, 1963, p.26.

[2] *Jean-Jacques Rousseau et la science politique de son temps,* Paris, 1950.

[3] Hugo Grotius (1583-1645), Dutch jurist; author of *De jure belli et pacis* (1625).

[4] Samuel Pufendorf (1632-94), German jurist; author of *Elementa jurisprudentiae universalis* (1660), *De jure naturae et gentium* (1672), *De officio hominis et civis* (1673).

[5] Jean Barbeyrac (1674-1744), French jurist, translator and commentator on the works of Grotius and Pufendorf.

[6] Jean-Jacques Burlamaqui (1694-1748), Genevan jurist; author of *Principes du droit naturel* (1747), *Principes du droit politique* (1754).

[7] Rousseau deals with practical politics in his *Projet de Constitution pour la Corse* (written 1764-5) and his *Considérations sur le gouvernement de Pologne* (written June 1771).

[8] For a discussion of this see J. Starobinski, 'Du Discours de l'inégalité au Contrat social' in *Journées d'Étude sur le Contrat Social*, Paris, 1964.

[9] 'It is the weakness of man which renders him social: it is our common miseries which carry our hearts towards humanity.' *Émile*, Book IV, p. 249 Paris, 1524.

[10] See Derathé, op. cit., p. 47.

[11] In a letter to Madame d'Épinay, dated March 1756, Rousseau wrote: 'Learn my dictionary, my good friend, if you want to have us understand each other. Believe me, my terms rarely have the ordinary sense.' Quoted in C. W. Hendel, *Citizen of Geneva: Selected Letters of Jean-Jacques Rousseau*, New York, 1937, p. 140.

[12] See Book III, Chapter 4.

[13] Bertrand de Jouvenel has drawn attention to a contradiction here between Rousseau as a philosopher and Rousseau as a political scientist. Rousseau the political philosopher argues that legitimate government is possible only if sovereignty remains in the hands of the citizens. Rousseau the political scientist puts forward as an empirical law of development that the executive or administrative body must in the long run invade the legislative body and capture the sovereignty. Jouvenel cites a passage from Rousseau's *Lettres écrites de la montagne* (Part 1, Letter 6): '. . . since sovereignty tends always to slacken, the government tends always to increase its power. Thus the executive body must always in the long run prevail over the legislative body; and when the law is finally subordinate to men, there remains nothing but slaves and masters, and the republic is destroyed.' Jouvenel stresses that the 'must' in this paragraph is a scientific must; so that Rousseau the political scientist is denying the possibility of the

continued existence in the real world of the one form of political association which unites liberty with government. See B. de Jouvenel on 'Rousseau' in *Western Political Philosophers,* ed. M. Cranston, London, 1964, and Jouvenel's introduction to his edition of *Du Contrat social,* Geneva, 1947.

[14] *Lettres écrites de la montagne,* Letter 8, Pléiade, vol. 3, pp. 841-2.

[15] Book I, Chapter 7.

[16] See, for example, J. L. Talmon, *The Origins of Totalitarian Democracy,* London, 1952. For a rejoinder to Talmon see R. A. Leigh, 'Liberté et autorité dans le Contrat social' in *Jean-Jacques Rousseau et son œuvre,* Paris, 1963.

[17] *Émile,* Classiques Garnier, Paris, 1924, p. 270.

[18] C. E. Vaughan, *The Political Writings of Jean-Jacques Rousseau,* Cambridge University Press, 2 volumes, 1915.

[19] Derathé, op. cit., p. 157.

[20] *Lettres écrites de la montagne,* Letter 6, Pléiade, vol. 3, p. 807.

[21] *Political Writings,* ed. C. E. Vaughan, vol. 2, p. 445.

[22] *Profession de foi du vicaire savoyard,* ed. Beauvalon, Paris, 1937, pp. 134-5

[23] *Émile,* ed. cit., p. 596.

[24] See Judith N. Shklar, 'Rousseau's Images of Authority', *American Political Science Review,* December 1964, p. 919, and Pierre Burgelin, 'Le Social et Le Politique chez Rousseau' in *Journées d'Étude,* ed. cit., p. 173.

Judith N. Shklar (essay date 1969)

SOURCE: "'One Nation, Indivisible . . .'," in *Men and Citizens: A Study of Rousseau's Social Theory,* Cambridge at the University Press, 1969, pp. 165-214.

[*In the following excerpt, Shklar discusses Rousseau's idea of the body politic, one of his political personifications.*]

THE POLITICS OF PREVENTION

The Great Legislator practices preventive politics in much the same way as the tutor gives Emile a negative education. Both create an external environment that

---

Rousseau comments on social order in *On the Social Contract, or Principles of Political Right*:

Man is born free, and everywhere he is in chains. He who believes himself the master of others does not escape being more of a slave than they. How did this change take place? I have no idea. What can render it legitimate? I believe I can answer this question.

Were I to consider only force and the effect that flows from it, I would say that so long as a people is constrained to obey and does obey, it does well. As soon as it can shake off the yoke and does shake it off, it does even better. For by recovering its liberty by means of the same right that stole it, either the populace is justified in getting it back or else those who took it away were not justified in their actions. But the social order is a sacred right which serves as a foundation for all other rights. Nevertheless, this right does not come from nature. It is therefore founded upon convention.

Jean Jacques Rousseau, in The Basic Political Writings, *translated and edited by Donald A. Cress, Hackett Publishing Company, 1987.*

---

will forestall the moral deformation that has been the lot of 'man in general'. Both also manage to create a deep attachment to themselves in their respective charges. Their influence is thus as profound as it is apparently effortless. There is, however, a rather obvious difference. The tutor is raising one child, while the Legislator is dealing with 'a people', that is, with a considerable number of adults. The startling fact is that Rousseau spoke of 'the people' as if it were Emile. That, indeed, was only one of his personifications. The sovereign, the public happiness (*'le bonheur publique'*), the general will and the body politic are all personifying metaphors, and very conventional ones at that. Together they form the main subject of Rousseau's political thought. That in itself is not particularly odd. All political thought is a matter of metaphors. The complexity of an endless series of relations between people could not be imagined, could not even be felt, without such organizing images.

The mere fact that Rousseau concentrated consistently on a few political personifications is not, in itself, notable. It is what he did with them that is entirely peculiar to him. The personifications allowed him to bring his moral and social psychology to bear on the great question of politics: can civil society be justified? And his quite deliberate use of traditional metaphors permitted him to show just how damaging and erroneous all prevalent answers were. In giving these well-worn commonplaces new meanings he carried his psychology into a political context, and also exposed the falseness of the conventions that these metaphors had embodied. It was a marvellous exercise in rhetor-

ical economy, but it did not succeed perfectly. For, as Rousseau realized with some bitterness, few readers were able to understand the *Social Contract*. Its elusiveness has become notorious.

There is nothing neutral about Rousseau's personifications. They are neither ornaments, nor descriptions. On the contrary, they are part of that 'moral truth' that reveals how people feel in specific situations, and in that exposure there is a judgment. What matters is the moral impact of situations on those who must live within them. Rousseau's moral psychology always involved consumers and creators of social environments. That was unalterable. Society always makes people. The question is not whether society should or should not mould its members. The real issue is how to imagine an environment that benefits those who must bear its pressures. How is one to envisage a social cure for the diseases of association? How might the rift between inclination and duty within each person be healed? The biography of Everyman was a 'genealogy of vice'. Under what conditions might Everyman be restored to a condition free of his traditional miseries? That is the subject of political psychology. It also makes Rousseau's use of personifications far less bizarre than it might seem. They are collective patients.

Rousseau's view of 'the people' is that of an outside observer. The Legislator considers only the physical and social conditions that must be created for it. The reactions of the people, of Everyman, are only what one would expect of most persons in these situations. The interplay between situation and individual is known in its main movements, even if the 'individual' is a composite 'man in general'. He is not any special person, in his entirety, but only the bearer of a number of responses common to all men in society. The sovereign also is treated in terms of the conditions which permit, or rather fail to permit, the exercise of the people's civic rights and duties. The happiness of the people is again not a personal feeling peculiar to any person, but the sum of circumstances which allow simple people to feel secure and contented. The general will, like any will, is that faculty, possessed by all men, that defends them against destructive impulses and influences. It is general because each citizen can guard himself and his fellow citizens against the dangers of *amour-propre,* the empire of opinion and institutionalized inequality. Everyman's overriding self-interest is to prevent inequality and his will is pitted against all those forces within and outside himself that promote it. The body politic, lastly, only shows the conditions under which governments aid or destroy the people. The first function of all these personifications is to illustrate how man might respond to a civil order and to show what a legitimate society would be like. For that Rousseau had to consider only the conditions which were likely to stimulate the least painful responses to the inevitable inconveniences of civil life.

Although there is nothing anthropomorphic in Rousseau's metaphors they have their disadvantages. Even though it is clear that he had no notion of a group mind or of any social purposes apart from those of the individual citizens, his personifications do create an impression of excessive civic uniformity. Rousseau, of course, did think that, in spite of men's natural differences, they were in many aspects quite alike. This was true especially of the vast majority of people who possessed no exceptional talents. It is for them that civic society exists. Their similarity is most notable in their reactions to the process of association. That is what gives Everyman's agonized passage into civilization and Emile's education their plausibility. Rousseau may very possibly have overestimated the pain caused by inner and social conflict. He believed that nothing was more terrible than the tension between nature and society, and that social iniquity was mainly responsible for that suffering. Given these assumptions, he can hardly be accused of ignoring individual needs in favour of public ends dissociated from feelings. 'Everything that destroys social unity is worthless; all institutions that put a man in contradiction with himself are worthless.'[1] This harsh sentence against Christianity could just as readily be applied to civilization as a whole. It expressed completely what Rousseau meant to prevent in his vision of a just civil order. It is not social cohesion as an end in itself. The end is the unity within each man. Social peace is merely the reflection of that inner harmony which had marked natural men in contrast to the civilized. Because this need was a general one, it could be described in a composite figure of a man, or of 'the people', without unduly distorting the experience of actual men.

The great convenience of Rousseau's personifications for joining his moral psychology and his vision of justice does not exhaust their uses. Because they were all rich in conventional associations, Rousseau could, by redefining them, express, in a word, the full extent of his radicalism, and his utter contempt for prevailing political opinion. Who were 'the people' in common usage? They were everybody who was nobody, the vulgar multitude, the 'feet' of the body politic. That was not Rousseau's meaning. 'The people is mankind; those who do not belong to the people are so few in number that they are not worth counting. Man is the same in every station of life; if that be so, those ranks to which most men belong deserve most honor.' The European peasants, not their masters, are to be the object of all consideration and their welfare the sole end of politics. No one else matters at all. 'If all the kings and all the philosophers were removed they would scarcely be missed and things would go on none the worse.'[2] When Rousseau spoke of the people the word was not just meant to cover, without discrimination, all those who might be living in a given place at a given time. It meant those who are now the poor, and quite specifically, *not* the rich in talent or goods.

The 'sovereignty of the people' is also a metaphor containing a negation. The word sovereignty has scarcely any meaning at all apart from absolute monarchy. It is the chief attribute of the man who can say *tel est mon plaisir*, and make it stick. That he should be able to do this was no less the will of God than it was necessary for social order; such was the meaning of sovereignty in the old régime. By taking this fear- and awe-inspiring power, so wholly associated with monarchical government, and attributing it to the people Rousseau was able to tell simple men in a phrase how immense he thought their rightful claims were. The sovereign people implies the destruction of sovereignty as a relation between rulers and ruled. It is the anti-monarchy, and not a new sovereignty in any intelligible sense.

The general will was certainly Rousseau's most original contribution to the language of politics. The phrase has remained his own and rightly so. However, both Montesquieu and Diderot had used it before him.[3] Montesquieu used it vaguely to signify public opinion. That was Rousseau's meaning as well, though by no means a casual one. The initial purpose of his notion of the general will was to reject Diderot's idea. For Diderot the general will expressed a vague benevolence felt quite naturally by men for mankind in general. For Rousseau the general will pursued nothing but hard personal interest, even if it was an interest that citizens shared. Nor was its content vague; 'it always tended to equality'. Far from concerning itself with all mankind, it owed its inspiration to xenophobia. It can come to men only when they acquire that *moi commun* which arises out of close and exclusive association with their fellow-citizens.[4] It is general because the prevention of inequality is the greatest single interest that men in society share, whatever other ends they might have. Nothing could be more remote from the cosmopolitan and aristocratic values of Voltaire and the Parisian intellectuals. As d'Alembert had noted, it was a 'ridiculous heresy' to say that the *philosophes* believed in general equality.[5] It was not a mistake Rousseau was likely to make about them. He knew perfectly well that they spoke for the interests of exceptional men, and that his alone was the 'voice of the people'.[6] That also was why his definition of the 'public happiness' began with a rejection of conquest and commerce as fit objects of policy. These serve only the interests of the great and proud. What peasants want is to live in security and abundance. That is the public happiness, derived from life in a civic order, and expressed in a quiet satisfaction with things as they are.[7]

The body-politic was the oldest and the most tradition-ridden of all Rousseau's metaphors. Partly he meant to show, as that personification had always done, that governmental authority could be justified. He did that by taking the magistrates out of the head or soul, and reducing them to mere organs of the body, with no will of their own. That was enough to undo the traditional view of monarchical authority.[8] For *Leviathan* more was needed. To dispose of Hobbes' 'atrocious despotism', government had to be pictured, less as a member of the body politic, than as the principal cause of its diseases and ultimate death. As the body dies, so does the artificial man, the state, and it is government that inevitably brings about the destruction, unless it is checked with improbable zeal by 'the people' as a whole.[9]

Negative in this as in everything, Rousseau's metaphors are the vehicles that took human needs into battle against the forces of inequality. Even when Rousseau wrote about a policy or an institution that he recommended, it was always a matter of attacking the existing system. Not equality, but the destruction of inequality matters, all the more so since the psychological predisposition to inequality is a manifest part of the experience of association. That is why the Legislator must instruct a people before it is even capable of knowing what citizenship means. When one remembers who 'the people' are, the necessity for a Legislator becomes all the more evident.

The people, as Rousseau never forgot, are not very intelligent. It may know its own interests, but it needs help if it is to defend them effectively.[10] Without a Legislator to guide men, they will never acquire a character or become aware of themselves as a people, who 'collectively' are citizens subject only to laws they have made for themselves.[11] Like Emile at adolescence the people needs instruction and examples. Interest brings men together, but to become all that they might be as a people requires more. To be ready for its Lycurgus the people must not yet have rooted prejudices, must be 'pliable', isolated from foreigners and, in sum, have the 'simplicity of nature joined to the needs of society'.[12] Only such a people can be saved for liberty and from the master's yoke. To avoid that is indeed its main aim.[13] To that end it needs civic pride, while Emile needs Stoic self-control. Both, however, know how to find their fulfillment in isolation.

The best way to avoid both war and inner confusion is simply to keep the people apart from all others. Philosophers, to be sure, pretend to love Tartars and other distant nations, but that is only to save themselves the trouble of having to love their fellow-citizens. For ordinary people it is more important to avoid foreigners, indeed to dislike them. To prevent that dreadful 'mixed-state', half social and half natural, the people needs a 'smaller social group, firmly united in itself and dwelling apart from others, [that] tends to withdraw itself from the larger society. Every patriot hates foreigners; they are only men, and nothing to him.' It is not a perfect situation, but it does avoid the perpetual war and despotism of monarchies and the cold indifference of philosophers.[14] These are the conditions the Legislator must, at all costs, prevent from arising.

Commerce and conquest, the policies of monarchical states, are far from the people's interest. The Legislator induces the people to be neither so rich as to tempt other nations, nor so poor as to be itself tempted to engage in these forms of international relations. A modest self-sufficiency is the first condition to be met.[15] There are also powerful psychological reasons for isolation. Emulation is always bound to lead to trouble. Nations only copy each other's vices.[16] Had not the French corrupted the Swiss?[17] Emile might be allowed to travel: he is not a citizen, but even he must be warned against the dangers of foreign influence to his inner integrity.[18] Self-possession, like civic loyalty, is frail. Lord Eduard is pleased that the English are nothing but Englishmen, since they have no need to be men. An Englishman's prejudices spring from pride, not from *amour-propre* as do those of Frenchmen.[19] This idea came to Rousseau from Montesquieu, who in one of his panegyrics on England, had noted that 'free nations are haughty, others may properly be called vain'.[20]

Like many of his contemporaries Rousseau enjoyed comparing the 'character' of various peoples. He very much regretted the uniformity to which life in the capitals of Europe had reduced their inhabitants. Only isolated peoples can retain ways that are integrally their own and express their particular experiences.[21] The masked people of capitals are not just faceless; they are without character or self-esteem. The Legislator must see to it that the people acquires a character suited to it and capable of withstanding foreign influences which simply disintegrate that independence that comes from having a clearly felt sense of self-hood.[22] In prehistoric times, for which Rousseau had a real understanding, the bare needs for subsistence and all that bears upon it, climate and soil, mould men entirely. That is, however, not men's condition now.[23] For Rousseau climate was not, as it was for Montesquieu, a perpetual influence upon men's lives. Once they emerge from animality, moral forces dominate their lives and characters. The history of the Jews had taught Rousseau that.[24] In history, it is psychological, not physical resources that cause a people to survive or to perish.

The people's character, for Rousseau, was in no way separable, either as an end of policy, or as a subject of study, from the ways of its individual members. To show how shared conditions affect the behavior and opinions of individual persons was all he had to show. That is why he talked not of Spartan maternal behavior, but of just one truly awful Spartan mother. That, also, is one of Lord Eduard's roles in the *Nouvelle Héloise*. Rousseau did more than just put Montesquieu's phrases about England into his mouth. He made Lord Eduard a perfect embodiment of those traits that Montesquieu believed the English owed to their liberty.

Without illusions about himself or his country, Eduard is wealthy, but never acquisitive. As Montesquieu had noted, opulence and personal merit are all that matter in England. Lord Eduard is as generous as he is rich, takes no pride in his ancestors, serves the laws rather than the king, loathes the court and is totally indifferent to public opinion. He immediately recognizes Saint-Preux's worth and the two become the closest of friends. To be sure, he is no Wolmar, far from it. He has violent passions, and his deep Stoicism cannot save him from them. His manners are direct and the same toward all. No false politeness and no delicacy for him. He is not at all stupid, but completely unintellectual. Because he is proud, and not arrogant, he has none of the class prejudice that dominates Julie's father. And it is he who denounces the latter mercilessly for having sold his military services to the king of France and for adhering to tyrannical notions. No one buys Lord Eduard—nor does he buy others. He himself is a model of personal independence because the people still count for something in England; even the simple sailors whom Saint-Preux meets have a feeling for real merit and a sturdy character. Freedom creates character, even in modern England.

Nevertheless, it is Lord Eduard, quite in keeping with Montesquieu's own pessimism, who notes that the laws do not rule in England; it is merely the last country in which they still exist.[25] Above all, it is he who in dissuading Saint-Preux from suicide, brings out with great force how enormous a distance separates modern man from the heroes of antiquity.[26] The republic and its virtue are so remote from modern man that its heroes cannot be copied. Self-control and a melancholy awareness of present ills are all that the ancients can now teach us. It is the English hero who must recognize this most perfectly, because he was the only conceivable rival to the moral supremacy of ancient virtue. Montesquieu had wavered. Rousseau was certain: Rome was incomparably greater than England.

The historical reasons for the character of the English or any other people were beyond Rousseau's range of thought. It was not his ambition to be an inferior Montesquieu. Psychology was what he understood and it enabled him to create a living character who also personified English freedom. Lord Eduard, quite apart from his intrinsic interest as one of the best drawn figures in the **Nouvelle Héloise,** is important for an understanding of Rousseau's notion of a people's character. In spite of the enormous differences in their style of thought, Rousseau's debt to Montesquieu was enormous. It was Montesquieu who had shown that a people's character is not the cause of its collective conduct, but part of a social whole which it reflects and sustains. It is both an expression of a people's physical and political experience, and also its chief source of

strength in maintaining those institutions which best suit it. It is that active force that must inform the law if it is to be appropriate to the physical and moral needs of the people. It is, moreover, a sensitive disposition, which like the personality of a human being can be crushed, as despotism can crush people who once were free. In that complex of related and mutually dependent actions and responses that are summed up in the word 'society', the character of a people plays the most vital part in maintaining the integrity of the whole. That is why Rousseau felt so strongly, knowing the true lesson of Montesquieu, that a people must be given a character by the Legislator. It must be moulded for strength and survival. *Secretly,* therefore, when he seems to concern himself with regulations, that master psychologist stimulates the mores and opinions of the people which alone can give it an enduring character and institutions capable of enduring.[27]

Character is pride and the structuring of the people's opinions has no more important end than to replace *amour-propre* with self-esteem.[28] That is a sense of inner self-appreciation that makes people indifferent to the opinions of outsiders, as it guards individuals against that servile and self-destructive Parisian concern for 'what is done'. To feel secure men must have a sense of the importance of their own part in the social whole. How else can pride be extended to public objects? Only in a small society is that ever possible. People cannot even have an awareness of society as a single whole unless they know each other.[29] In large states, where people are strangers to each other, public sentiment just evaporates.[30] To be sure, citizens should not be crowded together as they are in Paris and other large cities, 'where man's breath is fatal to man'.[31] They should meet regularly, but live apart. The agrarian republic is perfect for that. Men do not live in cities there; they only meet to conduct public affairs in them. Then they return to their own land, which their simple minds identify directly with the fatherland. That is why patriots grow in the soil.[32]

Size is not only important in creating attachments to the land and fellow-citizens. It makes the assertion of rights and the identification of interests much less difficult. Interest is what brings men into society and keeps them there.[33] The consciousness of common interests is citizenship. Justice itself is not divorced from *amour-propre*. It is, like pride, only well-understood, expanded and properly directed self-interest.[34] In a small state this is not difficult because the identity of interests is genuine and evident.[35] Given very meagre intellectual capacities of the people, the scope of society should not exceed their faculties.[36] If they cannot understand what is going on people will dissociate themselves from their fellows. Moreover, a man's vote does not matter much to him, or to anyone else, if it is only one among many.[37] He then feels powerless and loses interest in the state. Size and complexity thus always work against the interests of the people and in favour of those who have special abilities and wealth.[38] Rousseau had learned that in Paris. That, indeed, is why the cohesive community is very much the anti-capital. Its virtues arise mainly from the absence of those conditions which created Paris and its counterparts all over Europe.[39]

In the absence of social bonds, moreover, the *esprit d'état* of the magistrates will assert itself and they will become overbearing with no active public to restrain them and no patriotism to shame them.[40] In addition to that, the difficulties of governing a large territory and a huge population cannot but increase the need for concentrated governmental power. The inevitable result, as Montesquieu had shown, was that large states are ruled by monarchs who presently become despots.[41] In short, everything that has gone into the making of the old régime was to be avoided. The small, isolated city, the peasant republic, its opinions and mores carefully instilled by a Legislator and maintained by patriotic feeling, is the sole defense against civilized tyranny.

The conditions that impinge so deeply upon the people's feelings and ways are part of a psychological strategy. These defenses against inner and outer threats are, however, useless unless those interests which lead men to join in a social contract continue to be served. That is why the Polish project is such a superficial fantasy; as Rousseau well knew.[42] Polish patriotism does not support the military policies of the ancients and it does nothing for the vast majority of the people, who are excluded from its political life. Without sovereignty, in fact, the people has exactly nothing. The Legislator's art is described in loving detail in the Polish project, but it says nothing about the real ends of republicanism. For that one must read the ***Economie Politique,*** the true Spartan utopia. It has its Legislator, but it also has a general will and a *vox populi, vox dei,* which alone make it possible for the people to achieve its permanent interests. Without freedom and justice no republic can be said to exist. And without equality there is no liberty.[43] All the hypnotic powers of the Legislator were in vain if inequality, the root of all vice, was not checked. Rousseau never doubted the truth of Montesquieu's remark that 'a free nation may have a deliverer: a nation enslaved can only have another oppressor'.[44] No single savior can replace the conditions necessary for freedom.

To illuminate the conditions required for justice, Rousseau turned from the Legislator and the character of the people to another personification, the sovereign. Rousseau admitted explicitly that for him the words 'the sovereign' was a personification. It was his name for 'the will of all [which] is the order, the supreme rule' in society.[45] The writers of the monarchical tradition, and above all Hobbes, had certainly paid their respects to that will as it was expressed in the social

contract which establishes civil societies. Rousseau entirely agreed with that, but for purposes of his own. What he wanted to show was that these contracts, so long misinterpreted by absolutist theory, were invalid because they were never enforced and could not be enforced unless the people was sovereign. That is why, in spite of the title of his most celebrated book, the social contract itself plays an insignificant part in his political thought. It is the ordinary people, 'the all' whose will rules, that matters most. Their sovereignty is meant to express their supremacy within civil society, a supremacy which it is always in their interest to retain and which must always be protected against usurpation. Sovereignty thus personifies the most important interest of all. And it is never anything apart from the interests of the men who come together to live in society, and who recognize the rules under which their interests are to be secured.[46] The justifiable civil society is one in which the people's interests, and none other, determine the rules: not kings and not representative parliaments, but the people are sovereign. That is the chief value of the personification. It brings home, as no other word could, whom the people, the nobodies, are to replace. The great question of politics is how to protect the people against its own incompetence, and against fraud and usurpation.

All societies are based on some agreement, some commonly accepted conventions. That is merely a definition of society. Moreover, men generally come together for the same sorts of reasons: to ensure their preservation and to supply their needs.[47] The contract, the decision to create a civil society, expresses nothing else. It does not come from any new moral awareness or civic sense. It creates these eventually, and the differences between societies depend on that development. The terms of the contract are, in fact, exactly the same for every civil society, whatever its moral and political quality may be.[48] In every case it is an agreement that replaces possession with property.[49] Instead of having to defend his person and his things as best he can, each man now agrees to respect the possessions of every other man and to join with everyone in protecting these. From now on his safety and his goods are his, not because he has the strength to ward off attacks upon them, but because his potential aggressors have agreed that they are his to have and hold in undisturbed peace. He, in turn, not only recognizes their right to this, but all join together in order to protect each one whenever the need for it arises. *If* this arrangement really comes to mean in actuality what it says, it is a very advantageous exchange in which all gain.[50] 'All' means, of course, those who are not exceptionally strong and shrewd: the people. For them only, after all, is it true that 'no one' loses anything to any other person, since all give up identical powers and all gain an identical security.[51] They, indeed, give up only a precarious hold on their safety in return for collectively assured protection. The easy possibility of aggression was of no use to them, in any case. To be sure, if a man now fails to abide by his agreement he may be punished. That is implicit in the accepted obligation to protect each person through collective action against any aggressor.[52]

This is the origin of every civil society. It is also the birth of law and justice. Without property, without mutuality of rights and duties, there can be no sense of justice. Any individual will, like little Emile, feel a sense of injustice when someone simply deprives him of the work of his own hands. Justice, as a general social feeling, as the sense of what is due to others, no less than to oneself, can arise only out of rules that establish property, that define 'mine' and 'thine' and the rights and duties implicit in those words. However, unless we also learn to care for our brothers as we do for ourselves it is ineffective.[53] The emergence of a sense of justice is transforming for those who enter civil society, *any* civil society. It is not, however, a feeling that can prosper under all circumstances.

It is only when men *really* recognize and accept mutual obligations, and when the rules *really* apply to everyone of them in exactly the same way, that justice can be said to be more than a frustrated hope.[54] If the strong continue to dominate the weak, and the rules do not replace, but only legalize the power of masters, then nothing at all has been gained by anyone but the rich. A man obeys himself only if he follows a rule that he knows to be necessary and advantageous. If he follows rules that limit him, but impose no restraints on other men, then the rules are not in his interest and he cannot be presumed to have agreed to them simply because he is silent. Consent may not be the most uncomplicated word in the political vocabulary, but it does not mean slavish endurance of domination. To have said so was the atrocious error of that 'untruthful child', Grotius.[55]

Not the mere existence of a social contract, but mutuality of obligations under rules that are impersonal demands, and not the wishes of any one person, makes justice. That is also what is meant by replacing the inequality of physical powers by civil equality.[56] It is not mere consent that imposes obligation. Only an agreement that binds all equally, and therefore excludes the possibility of personal domination, is obliging.[57] Only this condition makes the social contract a plausible justification for the 'chains' of civil society.

The real problem of justifying civil society is, then, to find ways of making the social contract effective. As usual, Rousseau's mind took a negative turn. What he really wanted to make clear, after all, was how unjust all actual societies were. He therefore concentrated on the conditions that reduce the contract to futility at best, and to an instrument of enslavement at worst. Without the work of the Legislator no contract can ever come to much. The people cannot be expected to

have the wits needed to protect its newly awakened sense of justice against its own *amour-propre* or against the wiles of the conspiratorial few.[58] In fact, most social contracts are fraudulent, mere deceptions, as Rousseau showed in the ***Discourse on Inequality***. All societies at present live under rules designed by the rich in order to oppress the poor.[59] The poor were lured into submitting to a contract by the rich. The pretense of the contract to bind all equally deceives them. In fact when there are rich and poor the effect of the contract is to prevent the poor from attacking the rich without inhibiting the powers of the rich in any way whatever. When there are rich and poor there are always two kinds of rule, the legal one set by the contract, and the real one exercised by the rich who dominate everyone and everything without restraint.[60] Such a contract merely accelerates the abuses of inequality, of which despotism is the ultimate one.[61]

Fraud is not the only means of rendering the contract ineffective. Since it is not a simple agreement, but the creation of a new civic consciousness, it is imperative that the sense of justice should be sustained and continually asserted. The people cannot develop an artificial social conscience, which is justice, spontaneously. Mere natural compassion is not enough now. Justice is an attitude that has to be nurtured. It is a question of the psychological growth of 'the sovereign'. Civic obligations must not just be accepted once and for all, but must be explicitly and regularly reassessed and reaffirmed. Not only must every citizen participate in the original contract, but he must at any time be free to reconsider his allegiance. If he rejects it, he should be free to reconsider his allegiance and should be free to leave the polity, without hindrance, difficulty or fear for himself or his family. Without that, tacit consent is a fraud, not merely a silence. For consent to be explicit, genuine and personal, the possibility of opting out must exist. Once a man has accepted the contract he obviously cannot leave to escape from his duties, whether they be personal debts or military service in time of war.[62] That would be a private act of war against the polity, not a free act of dissociation. With that in mind, however, no one is bound by the contract who has not agreed to it.[63] All contracts say that. Few mean it.

The contract also lapses if the people cannot assemble at stated times to consider the rules that bind all of them, and to reaffirm their intention to abide by them. There is no other way in which the sense of justice can be kept alive. It is also the only way of keeping governments within their legitimate bounds. That, indeed, is the main political function of these assemblies.[64] The purpose of the assemblies of the people has nothing to do with modern notions of legislation. They are not called to make or remake laws, but to reassert the people's willingness to abide by the contract and to live in justice. That is why the fewness and antiquity of laws is the very best proof of their validity and worth.[65] There is nothing wrong with tacit consent so long as the opportunity to make it vocal is always present.[66] The open and frequent affirmation of faith in the rules is an expression of the sense of justice that the rules have kindled and a means to their preservation. The sovereign *does* very little. Sovereignty is the people's determination to live without masters and under rules accepted by it, even if fashioned for it by the Legislator. This is what separates an 'association' from a mere 'aggregation'.[67] The acts of periodic recollection are not a blind adherence to tradition as such; on the contrary, by returning to its foundations the people reinvigorates a present and immediate commitment to justice, to a single virtue.

Justice is also not a matter of self-government in any very extensive sense. It does not imply any sort of action or adaptation to change. It is, rather, an effort to prevent all change. The sovereign people abides by an ethos that has been created for it by the Legislator. It is he who is the sole 'architect' of the edifice that the people maintains.[68] That is why Rousseau quoted Montesquieu with such approval: 'At the birth of societies the chiefs of the republics make institutions, and later the institutions make the chiefs.'[69] The psychology of justice demands participation in public acts of civic loyalty and defense against usurpation. It does not call upon the people, for all its sovereignty, to make new laws or to exercise governmental functions. It does mean that the *moi commun* is sustained, that each citizen, even the least important, is treated with the consideration due a 'sovereign', and that the citizens, because they are equal and just, care for each other.[70] These dispositions are found only among the people, not among privilege-seeking groups. That is why the people is fit for sovereignty, and why the great in their cruelty and the intellectuals in their indifference are not.[71] Justice is, in short, a state of mind created by civic experience. Its ultimate victory comes when the little *moi humain* is totally absorbed by love of the public good. This is what sovereignty does for the people.

If Rousseau had been able to abandon the traditional vocabulary of politics occasionally, he might have saved his readers at least one confusion. Because the term sovereign has as its corollary the term subject, Rousseau thought it necessary to put it to at least some use. The just society is evidently a society without subjection. Rousseau wanted to say just that. The citizen is the very antithesis of the usual subject. What he did say was that the people consists of citizens who are the sovereign, and of subjects who submit to the law of the state.[72] This disastrous explication seems almost to make the people as neurotic as the Vicar at his self-divided worst. In fact, exactly the very opposite is implied. Not two selves, but an undivided self is the mark of the citizen, who, being tormented by neither *amour-propre* nor oppression, finds that his duty is also his inclination. He is internally whole because he lives in a social environment in which his interests are perfectly served, and subject and sovereign are 'identical correlations united in the term, citizen'.[73]

If he expressed himself awkwardly, Rousseau, however, did not misrepresent a very essential aspect of his view of citizenship by speaking of sovereign subjects. It brings out perfectly the extent to which the people is a beneficiary of justice in society, rather than its creator. In the perfect Spartan republic the people is taught to understand and even to love its laws by carefully constructed preambles.[74] That is how men absorb the meaning of their laws, as Plato had so well explained.[75] Such an education is nothing if not wise in a patriotic republic, as the Legislator well knows. It also says something about the people's sovereignty. It is a condition free from personal oppression, but it is not self-determination in a politically active sense.

The people is, quite in keeping with Rousseau's psychology, reactive and passive in its moral life. Its activity, important though it be, is at most defensive. It must assert itself constantly, but only to prevent usurpation. It does little else. Personification has, thus, the effect of seeing the people as subjects of a social situation that has been created for them. To be sure, they experience it as beneficiaries, not as victims. The individualizing tendencies of Rousseau's psychology are also evident here. Each citizen is like every other in being just. Justice is, however, described as an external condition and as an inner state of mind. At no time is there a sense of relations *between* people. The 'others' are the situation for the individual citizen, and he remains an isolated entity who reacts to them. Their justice creates that absence of oppression which is the essential feature of a legitimate society. For the individual it is a framework, not a set of relationships. He helps to maintain the structure, but he does so primarily by keeping his own inner civic self intact. The only visible actors in society are the Legislator and the enemies of the people who compete for its opinions. Social change after the initial institution of a people is always a decline, therefore. That is inherent in Rousseau's utopia.

The conspiratorial few are not the only agents of degeneration. Gradually, as the memory of the Legislator fades so do the character and opinions that he gave the people. He is, after all, only a brief interruption in the normal course of history which is a tale of otherwise unmitigated popular self-destruction. Indeed, neither he nor his utopia have any purpose other than to illuminate what might be, in a glaring contrast to what is, was and will be. The picture of a legitimate civil society is that of laws as they might be, men being what they are. It is the interplay between these two, between the unrealized possibility and history, that makes the personification of politics into a dramatic morality play.

Of all Rousseau's celebrated 'bipolarities' none is more dramatic than the confrontation of the possible with the probable.[76] Just because fate is character, a failure of the human will, it is insurmountable, as any doom must be. The dramatic intensity of Rousseau's style of thought is not in its admitting alternative and incompatible moralities. It is not the either/or of Sparta or the Golden Age, but *either* one of these, when it is pitted against men's actual moral poverty, that illuminates, without solving, the deepest and most universal tensions. The juxtaposition of what is and what might be is not a call for action, but a revelation, a psychological event, not an historical one. The sinister accidents that drive men out of the Golden Age and out of Sparta are all of their own making. That is their most significant aspect, because it ensures their recurrence. To understand and to condemn are the only fit responses to this spectacle and Rousseau knew no others. He was not interested in showing how men gradually mould each other. That is the subject of historical narrative. The drama of irresoluble confrontations alone could express warnings, imprecations and denunciations, and, above all, Rousseau's infinite revulsion.

THE WILL AGAINST INEQUALITY

Since the people does not do very much with its sovereignty, why does it need a will? Could Rousseau not have saved his readers from confusion by replacing the term, general will, with the more simple word, consent? He could not, because the latter does not in the least express his meaning. The general will is Rousseau's most successful metaphor. It conveys everything he most wanted to say. It ties his moral psychology and political theory together as no other words could. And the unity of morality and politics was a matter of no small importance to Rousseau.[77] The general will is a transposition of the most essential individual moral faculty to the realm of public experience. Like the personal will it is not directed at the external world or even immediately toward manifest action. It is a regulative power, the defensive force that protects the self against the empire of opinion that threatens it from within and without. On the level of public life that means that the republican people is on its guard against all other states, and that its will protects it against them.[78] It is, as a will, the very antithesis of Diderot's general will, which encompassed the rights of all mankind. It is also an internal faculty, because it defends the people against those disruptive groups that yearn for inequality. As such there is nothing mysterious about the general will. It is the will against inequality. That is also why it is general. It pursues the interests of man in general against those 'particular' wills which lead men to seek privileges, especially by forming groups that aim at inequality. The general will

is, thus, a specific form of the human faculty of willing, and one that each citizen ought to possess.

The nature and functions of the will as a psychological power, rather than its 'generality', really explain why Rousseau had to attribute a will to the people in its position of sovereignty. The people, the nobodies of this world, is *'par état'* in favor of justice and equality. It knows perfectly well that if exceptions to the rules are made it is not in its favor or to its advantage.[79] That realization is not too difficult, even for men of the most limited intelligence. One does not have to be particularly shrewd to feel cheated and to wish to avoid it. There is nothing complicated about peace, unity and equality. Anyone can appreciate them.[80] Only the *arcana imperii* require subtle minds. The real interests of the people are more easily grasped. There is no great need to alter men's opinions on this score. Let each man have his own opinion and 'what is most pleasing in itself will always secure most votes'.[81] And equality is certainly what is most pleasing to the people, since that is its main interest. There is nothing excessively confident in this. The problem is not that the people does not see its interests, but that it is no match for those who want to deceive and mislead it.[82] That is why the force of circumstances, the external pressures upon the people, always tends toward inequality.[83] That is why the people needs a Legislator so desperately to enlighten it. What happens without him is only too well known.

There is, moreover, a psychological dynamism at work, even in the best of republics, that disorients every citizen. *Amour-propre* arises out of association as such. It is stimulated in the just no less than in the unjust society. Only the family does not arouse it. The people, each individual citizen, that is, cannot be protected against the emergence of competitive feelings. In the ***Social Contract,*** Rousseau conceded that a self-oriented, advantage- and privilege-seeking particular will remains alive within each citizen. As long as this tendency is not allowed to play any significant part in civic life, it is not a serious obstacle to the prevalence of the spirit of justice, but it must be limited and diverted.[84] To keep particular wills in check within the citizens is the greatest achievement of the Legislator's educative art. That is why he also is said to submit to the general will.[85] The strengthening of opinions that prevent institutionalized inequality is, indeed, his main task.

The fostering of an unwavering will is by no means easy, for nothing was clearer to Rousseau than the feebleness of this faculty. The timid instinct of conscience and the artificially created sense of justice are alike in their weakness. Both emerge best when the individual withdraws into himself for quiet introspection. If conscience is to be awakened, the pains of remorse must be recalled. If justice is to move a citizen, he must remember the dangers of inequality. To achieve these recollections men must withdraw from their fellows and return to themselves. That is why the citizen before voting should consult with no one, but only bethink himself.[86] In both cases the individual, whether he be a man or a citizen, pursues only a strategy of self-fulfillment. It is, however, only if his duty and his personal inclinations are really at one that men can feel both free and virtuous.[87] If the citizen is to prefer the general to the particular will, he must really see that his own interest is served by such a choice. That requires two inseparable conditions: that he live in a society where there are no rich and poor and that he be educated to see his enduring interest in preventing inequality. In an unequal society to be just is far from one's real interest. That is why the mixed state is so painful. Justice is known but not practicable. The just Emile feels a duty toward his native land, unjust though it be, because the very fact that he *does* live in *a* society has given him a sense of obligation and justice. *Any* society, after all, arouses the capacity for justice, even those that deny it. Where justice does not prevail, however, the just man feels his duty as something he owes to himself, to his own self-respect, to his idea of what a man should be. It is evidently no part of his non-existent civic life. That is why a just man must suffer, for his sense of justice is perpetually insulted and outraged. He wisely withdraws to the Golden Age.[88] Only in a republic is it in the social, as well as emotional interest, of the citizen to be just and civic-minded.

The mores engraved upon the hearts of the citizens, the opinions instilled in them by the Legislator, fortify them against *amour-propre* and against the empire of opinion. Without that the social contract is meaningless. Without the new rules that instill new opinions men will have no common feeling for justice and no means of 'forgetting their primitive conditions.' The pull of nature will overwhelm that of duty, which, within society, can lead only to competition and institutionalized inequality.[89] However, the will to maintain the republic can become a lively personal motive in a properly educated people, for it is not difficult to share the ends of those whom we like. The youth's education in perfect equality, the elimination of the family and the selfish partiality it creates, the incessant games and assemblies, the military exercises and constant stimulation of a common pride in a shared past, all have as their end the redirection of *amour-propre* toward civic self-esteem, and the replacing of opinions that tend to inequality with those that prevent it.[90] The tendency of men's spontaneous reaction to society is toward personal preference; education must counteract it. For their enduring interest is to maintain equality, without which liberty is meaningless.[91] Once there are rich and poor, all is lost.[92] As long as a man feels part of the sovereign, as long as he is actively engaged in some sort of public activity with his fellow citizens, he

is likely to remember his and their common interest in defending the republic against the forces of inequality.[93] When he leaves the rites and assemblies, however, he will again think of himself as a particular person, not as a citizen, and his mind will turn to personal advantages, rather than to civic interest.[94] The whole policy of patriotism is to make these moments of civic dissociation rare, and to prevent their becoming accepted modes of conduct.[95]

The instilling of proper mores and opinions would be an impossibility, if they did not correspond to the genuine social interests of men. The present 'mixed condition' is morally tormenting because our duty never corresponds to our interests. Men cannot be moved by anything but their interests; their self-preserving instincts and their will cannot respond to anything that ignores and defies these.[96] The general will must, therefore, express the fundamental common interests that all men can accept as both their advantage and duty: the prevention of inequality. The general will is a 'tendency to equality'.[97] Personal non-civic interests survive, but as long as they are not organized into privilege seeking groups, they cancel each other out.[98] The general will, in any case, is not determined by the number of voices that can, at any moment, be heard, but by the one interest that unites the citizens—which may momentarily be forgotten.[99] What that interest is, however, is very well known. It is the replacement of the inequalities of nature by civil equality.[100]

Social disunity is therefore a sign that some members are not as aware of the necessity for justice as they ought to be. That also is why unanimity is a sign of civic vigor in the people. If all agree to a rule it can only mean that all are served by it. Competition divides, shared interests unite. That is evident enough. Unanimity is a sign of concord—except in monarchies where it is a sign of despotism. Absence of conflict is all the more a proof of civic well-being since the general will is not directed at political action which may involve prudential calculations. It is not concerned with government and policy. The general will is, like the personal will, a state of mind, not a specific motive for action. The will creates, sets and strengthens character and standards of conduct. Specific courses of action are left to the determination of magistrates, even when peace and war are at stake.[101]

The difference between moral purpose and government is particularly clear in the military aspects of civil life. Rousseau was more than enamored of the military spirit. 'Every citizen must be a soldier as a duty and none may be so by profession.'[102] It is a sign of young peoples that they have a militia, not a professional army, which is typical of despotic regimes.[103] At one time Geneva had its citizen army; now the magistrates repress it, as inequality has come to destroy the city.[104] Equality and the armed citizenry were as inseparable as were inequality and professional armies. Had not, as Lord Eduard notes, Saint-Preux's father fought for his country, while Julie's had sold his services to the king of France? Who stood, then, for real valor?[105] The social contract of the far from cosmopolitan people, therefore, makes it a right and duty of each citizen to defend the polity against aggression.

Since there can be no law between polities, but only among individuals within a polity, justice has nothing to say about war and peace. The relations between states are not subject to law and justice. There are neither just nor unjust wars. War is a matter of preservation or destruction.[106] In a just society it is never anything but defensive, since conquests are a danger to the people. However, the duty to fight for one's polity is, under a social contract, always absolute. For wars may be a political mistake, but they are never lawful or unlawful. Citizens must fight for their country just as much as they must pay debts and protect each other's lives and goods. In addition, patriotism is a military virtue, and the Legislator who wants the contract to flourish can base it on no firmer ground than the spirit of martial valor. Military service is therefore a part of civic education and a fundamental duty and right. War and peace, however, are merely questions of prudence and may, therefore, be left to the magistrates. It need hardly be added that military obligation, like any other, is real only within a society that is ruled by a living social contract. In fraudulent civil orders there are no civic obligations or rights, only prudential calculations among which fear plays the most significant part.

Acts of sovereignty are declarations of principle. They sustain the spirit of the laws upon which civic society rests. The sovereign people assembled has only one function, 'to maintain the social pact' in its military and proprietal aspects. In considering government the sovereign has to answer only two questions, whether the form of government is acceptable, and whether the men who conduct its affairs are faithful to the social contract binding all citizens.[107] Moral self-defense, not action, is the concern of the general will. That is why agreement among the citizens is so valuable. It proves that they are not competing for private gains, but are really concentrating on common interests. However, unanimity is required only for the original contract.[108] The principle of majority rule may be accepted for all future decisions.[109] Majorities may, to be sure, be diverted from the pursuit of equality. They may be overcome especially by organized privilege-oriented particular wills.[110] When that becomes the habitual state of affairs the republic is dead, because evidently the citizens no longer care for justice.[111] The social bond is then broken and no real grounds for obligation are left, only considerations of prudence and fear.[112] These, to be sure, must determine the moral strategies that each person pursues. They do not liberate men from

the instinct of conscience, but that is not the voice of public obligation.

When an individual citizen or even several of them find themselves at odds with the majority, no one need feel aggrieved, nor is the republic in danger. They have accepted majority rule and if their notions are at odds with the general will they have erred, which is only human. To be in a minority does not deliver these men into political servitude, it only forces them to accept, as they knew they would have to, the will of the majority.[113] In a free society, if there is no war and they have no debts, they can always leave if they wish. In such a society the problem of minority rights is not a real one. The supreme interest of the people and the whole aim of the general will is to prevent inequality, and that demands a single state of mind. To reject that spirit is to reject civil society. One may do that perfectly freely, but one may not conduct war against the people by forming privilege-oriented groups which usurp its sovereignty.[114]

In a society that accepts inequality as desirable or inevitable the enforcement of minority rights is indeed the essence of liberty. That was, however, not Rousseau's idea of a just society. The individual is protected in his rights, but the pursuit of inequality is not among these. The people is sovereign only as long as it can and does prevent institutionalized inequality. To that end the majority of the citizens must share a common will. The protection of groups that are opposed to civil equality, its most fundamental interest, can hardly be one of the sovereign's aims. The general will is, in its tendency to equality, opposed to the particular will which strives for inequality. The general will maintains the spirit of the republic, its opinions and mores. The particular wills in the polity oppose them. The former stands for inner unity, the latter for public disintegration. Where only a minority cares for the republic and has a will against inequality its rule is not conceivable. A reign of virtue cannot be imposed. Either the sovereign people protects its interests or it fails to do so, in which case all legitimacy lapses. A lawbreaking individual can be coerced to abide by the conditions of freedom, but not a majority of citizens, since freedom is defined as its will to be free.

It is clear why the people has to have a will. What makes that will general? Partly it is general because it is the will of 'man in general' and not of exceptional men. Mostly, however, generality is a set of limitations upon the scope of the will. It is not any will, but a will to impersonality and to fairness toward all. Sovereignty being a condition, rather than a way of exercising power, is not only inactive, it is also limited by its purposes. The general will can only express itself in rules which apply to every member of civil society, and in an identical manner.[115] For all its sacred inviolability the sovereign may not burden one subject more than another, nor deprive anyone of any liberties and goods except those freely ceded to the civil order in the social contract. No person and no group may be singled out for special burdens or privileges.[116] That not only prevents the emergence of 'estates'. It also precludes arbitrariness. General rules even in unjust societies and even when they aim at socially harmful ends have at least one virtue: they treat those who are affected 'without preferences', without whims. That is why Rousseau thought that even the worst law was better than the best master.[117] In that he may well have been mistaken, but it certainly illustrates how profoundly he distrusted personal subservience of any sort. Clearly he felt that all personal acts of domination were humiliating in a way that even general oppression was not. Rousseau, to be sure, spoke for the people and for himself as an apprentice and footman. Certainly he knew what he was talking about when he spoke about masters. The Legislator is unique just because he inspires laws, as his very name implies.

The absence of preferences and the impersonality of general rules are not the only limitation on a will that is to be general. It cannot, by definition, impose duties that are not genuinely useful to the citizens.[118] Rousseau admitted somewhat ruefully that the decision about what was in fact useful was ultimately up to the sovereign. Who, after all, could decide what the people needed, except the people itself? Is utility not also a convention and an opinion? Rousseau was troubled by this because he was so deeply aware of the people's stupidity. He comforted himself with the thought that if the people were ever to suffer from its own errors, it would hasten to correct them.[119] That is a mechanical evasion, since no one knew better than Rousseau that moral self-injury cannot simply be undone. Moral and social errors are irreversible. The sovereign people need only follow its own interests to live in justice, but there is no guarantee that it will do so. The best hope is to save it from the wiles of its seducers by providing it with good opinions at the time of its civil formation. Without the Legislator the will cannot be sustained or attain generality, which demands more intelligence than the people can command. To know what is really useful is beyond the wits of the people. That is why the rich can dupe it so easily into accepting a false contract. That is also why it needs the Legislator so desperately.

The generality of the sovereign's will is its impersonality, its expression in the form of rules which apply to all. That is what its justice and civic equality mean. The great lesson Montesquieu had taught Rousseau was that justice without law is unimaginable. It was Montesquieu who had insisted that it was 'only by the protection of the laws that the equality of nature can be recovered in society'.[120] That was also why Spartan society was no extension of the family. The virtue of republicans owes nothing to the natural partiality of parents. Citizens are bound by impersonal bonds of mutual obligation, and if they learn to love each other it is because they have no other erotic ties. The 'sublime virtue' of republican magistrates arises on the annihilation of parental affection.[121] To think that a republic can be built on the model of the family can have only one result: a society ruled by a prince in whom the love of domination takes the place of an affection he certainly does not feel for his subject-children.[122] Civil society thrives on the redirection of erotic energy, not on its spontaneous movement. Nothing in Rousseau's vision of Spartan community life suggests the extended family group. There is nothing cozy about Rome or Sparta. For those who long for the warmth of family life a retreat to the Golden Age offers the only hope—and an unattainable one. Who, however, is happy in a place such as Sparta? Are Caius and Lucius in their inner integrity as citizens no longer men at all? Do they not yearn for some sort of felicity?

Since happiness is the sole object of men's striving, the legitimate society, like any other human enterprise must be judged in terms of its ability to satisfy the most universal aspiration. Rousseau did not forget it. The sovereign people must feel a 'public happiness'. Like the general will it is a metaphor of personification. For happiness is the most individual and personal of feelings, as Rousseau realized very well.[123] This evidently made it difficult to speak of it as something 'public', and after worrying the notion of *'le bonheur publique'* in several fragments, he used it rather sparingly in his finished political writings. His difficulties with the notion are, however, very interesting, because they reveal how and why he used his metaphors as he did. It also shows how aware he was of the complexities that his subtle moral psychology created for political judgments.

The first and the greatest obstacle to a notion of the public happiness was that Rousseau did not believe that happiness was ever attainable. It is not for men. At best a man's happiness is 'a negative state, measured by the fewness of his ills'.[124] 'Man is born to suffer, that is what it means to be a man.'[125] The closest Rousseau could come to recalling a moment of joy was the memory of watching some peasants celebrating a holiday.[126] Certainly happiness could not be taught. Emile's tutor does not attempt anything of the sort. Emile learns how to cope with adversity and to evade misery. His emotional equilibrium is due to a balance between his needs and his powers. He does not yearn for anything outside his reach. 'Then alone a man is not unhappy.'[127] Even natural man is a stranger to happiness. Absence of pain, health and freedom are all he enjoys.[128] At least he, unlike social man, does not busily create his own misery. The best strategy is to follow him in that, and to avoid the worst form of misery, that for which we are alone to blame.[129] Our happiness consists in self-content which depends on our ability to avoid abusing our powers.

What can the public order contribute to such an inward state? Does the happiness of each person not depend on his particular 'powers', his personality? Rousseau admitted that readily. Happiness is like religious belief in that it depends entirely on those aspects of a man's character and disposition which are uniquely his and which differ greatly from man to man. Governments cannot force men to be happy.[130] Public control is, in the complete absence of identity of feeling and need among individuals, an intolerable imposition. Certainly there is no abstract or collective notion of happiness that could be dissociated from the feelings of the individuals who compose the public. What they all want in common is 'peace and abundance' which are conditions necessary for happiness.[131] However, that is not happiness itself, private or public.

As with all his personifications, the 'public happiness' was thus a situation created for people in which they might achieve something they desired. In this case it was reduction of misery, a relief from the tensions created within men between nature and society, inclination and duty, interest and virtue.[132] The public happiness then would be much like that absence of pain in which man lives in nature. However, Rousseau did not choose to leave it at that. He also wanted to show that there must be some sort of peculiarly 'public' state of felicity, which was different from private joy, at least in its source, just as the general will differs from the personal will. As one might expect, he began his investigation of that possibility on a negative note. What are the false notions of public happiness now being pursued? Some states, monarchies for example, have no interest at all in the felicity of the people.[133] Others claimed that wealth or conquest contributed to the public happiness. Wealth is a relative notion whose meaning depends on the existence of poverty. The state that seeks wealth through commerce must not only impoverish other states, but also comes to depend on them. Commerce, moreover, makes the use of money necessary, which allows for accumulation of wealth among individual citizens. Domestic inequality is thus the inevitable result of trade between nations. As such it is scarcely a contribution to public happiness.[134] As for conquest, it creates misery among conquerors and conquered alike. Excessive power inevitably accrues in the hands of military and civil officials who plan and carry out conquests. If they are not despots when they begin, they will certainly be that before long. Nothing compares to the misery of conquering peoples, ruined by mercenary soldiers and enslaved by ambitious proconsuls.[135] These are the abuses of civil power that pretend to promote the public happiness. So much for *raison d'état*.

To avoid these now prevalent paths to assured misery was a contribution in itself to the public happiness.

The public happiness, like all Rousseau's metaphors, carried a criticism within it. The whole idea of commercial wealth and territorial expansion so avidly promoted by 'benevolent' despots and their publicists had to be exposed. Voltaire might admire Catherine the Great and Frederick of Prussia, but not Rousseau. He could see perfectly that the happiness of the people was not even part of what they promoted. What was the alternative? Clearly Rousseau did need one if he was to appropriate the phrase so glibly misused by 'enlightened' despots for their own ends. A people finds its happiness in perfect obscurity and in independence from all other states. It avoids war and commerce.[136] To that extent the public happiness is the mere avoidance of present policy. Autonomy for the people is what it is for Emile, the proper use of one's powers and the limitation of one's needs.

However, the truly Spartan order must offer more than that. It must have a public happiness that is more than the sum of personal felicities. That would merely be an aggregation of feeling, not a union. The happiness of citizens must emerge from their new relations to each other and the civil law engraved in their heart. It is a pool, as it were, from which each draws his happiness rather than creating his own as best he can.[137] People find their fulfillment in public, not private places. Rousseau did not develop this notion. He abandoned it, in fact. To be sure, public activity is a source of pleasure to citizens, as justice is the necessary condition for well-being. The public assembly was not, however, where he finally looked for signs of happiness. To find out if people are happy one ought not to listen to what they say in any case. People complain when they are free, not when they are miserable.[138] To know whether they are really well off one must look somewhere else. The only one objective proof of good government, the only true sign that a people feels at ease, is a general willingness to have a lot of children.[139] When people feel as well off as is humanly possible, they procreate, willingly and frequently.

In the end then, happiness, even if it is stimulated by a favorable civil situation, expresses itself in the most personal way. Happiness remains individual. In the just society the sort of happiness that man as man, and not as a particular person with particular sensibilities, can feel in response to his social environment, is a form of security. And men express that feeling in a simple and direct way. Everyone does the same thing in the absence of socially created anxieties; they multiply— whether for their own or the republic's sake is not clear. In any case, there is one common way of showing happiness, rather than perhaps consciously feeling it. In this way one can tell when the harmony of man within nature has really been recreated for the citizen within the republic.

It is clear that the achievements of the civil state, for

all the virtue and justice that it engenders, are not really so much greater than that of the Age of Gold. If public virtue is justified by so modest a form of felicity, then denaturation hardly seems worth the trouble. And indeed, it is only thinkable as an alternative to our present miseries. It is, moreover, no more enduring than the Age of Gold. The polity is a body because it also dies. It can function well only as long as the will against inequality is strong enough within each citizen to quell *amour-propre* and to protect him against the empire of opinion. When the will built up within each citizen by the Legislator slackens, when mores weaken and particular wills assert themselves against equality, the republic is dead. The citizens live as persons, the people remains, but its sovereignty, its laws and its inner unity are gone. The sense of justice survives. Its reign is over.

TWO BODIES POLITIC

The body politic was of all metaphors of personification the one Rousseau used most frequently. Sometimes he mentioned it quite casually simply to refer to civil society. Occasionally, however, he went into full anatomical detail and then he had very specific purposes in mind. Moreover, he gave the metaphor much thought, and at least in one fragment, subjected it to a devastating critical analysis. That did not prevent him from doing with it what he had done with other traditional metaphors. He turned it upside down.

Rousseau used the body politic, as it had been so often used before, to demonstrate the necessity of government in a healthy society. However, when he drew his body he assigned to government a bodily function infinitely less important than the head or soul that had so often stood for monarchs, whether absolute or not. That, however, was not Rousseau's only contribution to political physiology. He also provided a second picture of the body politic, one in decay. Far from enjoying *Leviathan's* 'artificial eternity' which only unruly subjects and conquest could end, Rousseau's second body politic was born to die.[140] It dies not because the people disappears, but because the general will is subverted by the magistrates, and justice and equality are destroyed. This body politic was made to convey Rousseau's most radical thoughts. All the earlier bodies politic had defended rulers; his alone attacked all governments. If one of his bodies politic tried to overcome the conflict between authority and equality, the second exposed it. In this there is no real conflict. Rousseau knew that government was necessary, no less than he understood that rulers were the enemies of the people.

In the history of political theory the body politic had enjoyed an immense popularity. Writers as different as John of Salisbury, Thomas Aquinas and Thomas Hobbes all adopted it. In medieval thought the body politic was the social microcosm, which, as such, shared the essential traits of all God's creations. It was a model of hierarchical harmony, created out of human diversity by a beneficent authority, which assigned a proper place to each person and group so that all could perform their functions in maintaining the whole. Everyone has his preordained place in an organism which reflects the divine order.[141] It is a creation, but in no sense is it a forced union. For it corresponds to a common need and end. 'There can be no faithful or firm cohesion', wrote John of Salisbury, 'where there is not an enduring union of wills and, as it were, a cementing together of souls.'[142] The head, however, wears a crown and the soul a mitre in a body of which the peasants are merely the feet.[143] The king has, moreover, responsibilities that no one can share. It is he who has 'the function and duty to bring different acts into harmony by allotting them to different individuals to whom they are appropriate'.[144] Authority from above is what keeps this body together. Such also was Thomas Aquinas' body politic. The efficiency of a monarchical soul was clear to him, both within an established social body, and when a new polity is to be created, as Romulus had once created Rome.[145]

Above all there was *Leviathan* so boldly engraved and described on the opening pages of the book that Rousseau carried like a cross on his back. That artificial monster in the picture has a body made up of men, but the head is not composed thus. It is just a head and it wears a crown. The sovereign, not visible, is said to be the soul. In the full anatomical account the head is not mentioned at all, but it is implicit throughout, that monarchy fits *Leviathan* as no other cranium could. The body politic made monarchical government appear an integral necessity, even if not at all a logical one, when one considers that it was by 'pacts and covenants' that this body was 'first made, set together and united'. It allowed Hobbes from the first to pretend that monarch and sovereign were indistinguishable.[146]

On one occasion Rousseau used the old metaphor in a medieval way, but not to justify political authority. Marriage was, in his view, necessarily a union between unequal partners. The authority of husband over wife was perhaps no more natural than marriage itself, but it was necessary for their harmony. The husband is thus the head while the wife is the eyes of this social body.[147] Rousseau resorted readily to the traditional form of the metaphor when he wanted to express an old-fashioned prejudice. In his political writings he found no occasion to do so.

The fullest account of the body politic, in minute anatomical detail, occurs in the *Economie Politique,* Rousseau's most complete and perfect Spartan utopia.[148] It is also a violent attack upon the intellectual establishment and, indeed, a continuation of the *First Discourse*. The patriot is pitted against the unfeeling, cosmopolitan philosopher, and Cato is again raised above Socrates.[149] The perfect unity of this Spartan polity is due, in no small degree, to the identity of interests between the people and its 'chiefs'.[150] Rousseau liked to speak of rulers whom he admired as 'chiefs'. That seemed to take the sting out of political authority. Clearly neither the functional hierarchy of the medieval monarchy, nor the absolutism of Hobbes could have much application to a society composed of citizens who have no interest other than equality and liberty. There might be no feasible solution to the problem of government under law. The rule of law might be as difficult to devise as the squaring of the circle.[151] The most perfect personal rule might be the only tolerable alternative to 'austere democracy' as Rousseau admitted in a despairing letter.[152] But Sparta was neither. It might be unrealizable, but it was *the* only satisfactory polity that could be imagined at all. *Leviathan* might appeal to all the intellectual valets of the 'enlightened' despots, but he was not Rousseau's idol. Sparta was his answer to those who chose to flatter Frederick and Catherine the Great.

His own body politic was a distorting mirror of all its predecessors, but most especially of *Leviathan*. Rousseau's body had no soul. That locus of the Catholic Church in John of Salisbury's body is simply eliminated. The sovereign is in the head. It does not, like *Leviathan's* sovereign, take the place of the Church in the soul. There is also no place left, the head being already occupied by the sovereign people, for a monarch. The rest of the body politic is not unlike *Leviathan*. The magistrates are the mere organs of the faculties which are lodged in the head and so cannot move unless the sovereign wills it. However, they are only joints in *Leviathan* also. To be sure, in Rousseau's body they are even less than that. Only the citizens make the body move and work. The main physical difference between Rousseau's *Leviathan* and Hobbes' is that there is no place for a crown on the former. The head contains all those powers of feeling and understanding which react to bodily and sensory stimulation and it is, therefore, not only the seat of life itself, it is sovereign because the people, the total body, affects it constantly. Clearly democracy was the only form of government for such a body politic. And, indeed, Rousseau readily recognized that democracy was the form of political organization that best corresponded to the will of his robot. The example of Athens' turbulence did not discourage him. Athens was no democracy, but an aristocratic tyranny governed by intellectuals and orators.[153] Only in democracy, after all, does the sovereign feel pain when any member of the polity is hurt, as does the head of this body politic.
There was, however, more than a subtle caricature of *Leviathan* here. Rousseau was also covering a difficulty with a metaphor. The subordinate physical position of the magistrates only illustrates that they cannot move

without the will of the people. It says nothing of their activities. And those are extremely extensive in a Spartan order. The chiefs are to make the people happy by a wise political economy, a term that covers all the relations of government to persons and things.[154] Commerce, industry and agriculture are the mouth and stomach of the body politic and public finance is the blood which a wise economy, performing the functions of the heart, pumps throughout the body politic. The later part of the ***Economie Politique*** is devoted to this economy, which it emerges, is conducted by the magistrates. Clearly the magistracy is an organ, but, though this is not made at all clear by the metaphor itself, that organ is the heart of the body politic.

Government enforces the law against any deviant member, and it is responsible for every aspect of public policy.[155] It is government that instils patriotism. Old magistrates and soldiers educate the young. Government protects the poor against the rich, and prevents the excessive accumulation of riches. It protects the safety and prosperity of the citizens, and it administers a system of taxation, agrarian laws and public finances in general.[156] In fact, once the Legislator has done his work, it does everything. The chiefs are said to be well-intentioned, to be sure.[157] Everything, in fact, depends on that. This miracle is the result of law, the bond that keeps the body united.[158] That, however, only describes a republic: a people united by mores and moved by a will that prevents inequality and assures an identity of interests. It does not explain it. And indeed in that respect the picture of Rousseau's *Leviathan* is not so unlike Hobbes'; both are attempts to evade conclusions implicit in their respective social contracts.

Sparta and Rome were hardly ungoverned republics; both were aristocracies. Rousseau accepted that as their essential character and as a necessary part of their social triumph: the transformation of men into citizens. The body politic metaphor allowed Rousseau to strengthen the impression that the republic thus artificially recreated the state of nature. The body politic, like healthy man in nature, does not neglect its self-preservation. An integrated whole, it does no injury to itself, but on the contrary avoids any source of pain.[159] When the health of this body is gone, then its instincts, the people's self-love, no longer operates effectively. That is why despotism is not a body politic at all. It is only a master and slaves united neither by law nor love. It is a mere aggregation of people, not a people and its chiefs. It is that combination alone which may properly be called a body politic.[160]

What of equality, however, in this body? Is it not, after all, just like all those medieval bodies politic, a justification of governmental authority, even if not of monarchy? In fact, it is just that. The chiefs may have no interests apart from the general will, but there is a vast difference between those who rule and those who are ruled. The body politic merely seems to show that government is necessary for republican survival. Identity of interests, benevolence and unity, however, are not equality, natural or social.

In his most violent attack on the intellectuals Rousseau had claimed that the well-governed society was so free from *amour-propre* that the conditions of natural equality were totally restored. Not even moral differences are given public recognition; just as in nature psychological inequalities find no occasion to flourish. 'In a well constituted state', he wrote, 'men are so busy that they have no time for speculation. They are so equal that no one can be preferred as the more learned or shrewd. At most he is the best, and even that is often dangerous, because it makes cheats and hypocrites.' No desire for distinction is, therefore, lighted in the hearts of the citizens at all.[161] Now *that* really *is* equality.

To deny the public relevance of moral inequality, to refuse any public recognition to the difference between good and bad is indeed the ultimate step in egalitarianism. In a mood of furious anger and self-deception Rousseau was driven to accept anarchy. That was not his normal attitude. However, the notion that equality meant identity was not merely a passing thought. It was something he had often said and always believed. The state of nature was not one of mutuality, but of isolated men identical because subject to a situation that rendered them uniformly alike. Underdeveloped man has no talents; that is why there is no inequality. The great differences in men's abilities remain dormant. They are alike in their utter dullness. In a society in which the general will is dominant that identity is partially recreated by making men equal, and so, alike in their rights or duties. If that means that not even moral powers are allowed to differentiate men in their public life, then one really has a staggering degree of equality. In such a society election to office must be by lot and government a 'true democracy'. Rousseau recognized that clearly. He also knew that no such polity could exist.[162] He might have added that the Spartan body politic does not even try to be egalitarian in that sense.

The patriotic, the virtue-creating state that reconciles men to society, makes equality impossible. The heroic republic with its Brutus and Cato does not disregard moral differences. It is in fact an extremely competitive society that uses rewards to stimulate moral athleticism among its citizens.[163] Moreover, Sparta is a single-value society. Virtue, whether it be an end in itself, or the means toward ending men's inner conflicts, allows for only one standard of judgment. Patriotic devotion, essentially martial in character, is the only attribute which has any worth. Additional values might, of course, destroy the inner harmony of the

citizens. However, by demanding that all citizens strive to achieve one character and to acquire one sort of excellence only, inequality is made inevitable. For certainly all men had never been, nor did Rousseau pretend that they could have been, equal in their capacity for patriotic devotion, military heroism and statesmanship or even in physical agility and toughness, which were so important to the Spartan model citizen. Governments, moreover, not only administer the system of rewards that encourages competition in virtue, its offices are rewards for virtue. Cato is the perfect magistrate, after all, not an ordinary citizen. Was not Brutus a 'chief'? The pursuit of virtue integrates citizens, prevents the rise of destructive opinion and mores, and it restrains rulers. It does not, and was not expected to, create equality.

All this was perfectly clear to Rousseau. Equality of political rights and duties was all that distributive justice demanded in the public sphere. That meant no exceptions to the rules, no special privileges. The inequality to be fought, moreover, was not inequality of authority, but of wealth. Not distinctions as such, but distinctions based on wealth were obnoxious. The government pictured in the *Economie Politique* is legitimate, and expressive of the general will, because all its public policies have one end: the elimination of the power of the rich. As long as the rich cannot buy the poor and the laws are not mere instruments for promoting the interests of the wealthy, the will against inequality is in effect.[164] Only power based on wealth, not power based on authority, is illegitimate. Only wealth reduces the contract to a fraud.[165] The will against inequality is a will against wealth and privilege, not against political rulership.

Governments may prevent economic inequalities that are sufficiently great to make the poor the bought servants of the rich. However, equality does not characterize governments. And as Rousseau knew only too well, the psychology of *ésprit de corps* is always a danger to the people in general. It is not money that corrupts individual magistrates. Each one of them may be a man of the utmost integrity. Collectively, however, they have a will of their own, an interest particular to themselves. In defense of that there is no injustice they will not commit. In the *Economie Politique* Rousseau chose to forget it, to pretend that, as long as no pecuniary ambition existed, the magistrates shared and promoted the interests of the people.[166] In short, they are 'chiefs', not masters. Why, however, should they be satisfied with that? They do not love their subjects as fathers love their children; they need a sterner virtue.[167] Why should they submit to it, and to laws that only inhibit their interests? Rousseau did feel compelled to offer an argument here. They are likely to obey the law, since it is by law that they hold authority.[168] It is not a good answer. If they have the enormous powers that the law gives them, they are perfectly free to use it as they please, to protect or to destroy the law and the people whom it serves. He knew that and admitted, even as he contemplated Spartan perfection, that personal interest is always contrary to duty and that lesser associations find their interests served by defying the popular will.[169]

The unity of will that binds a people and its chiefs is based on the strength of virtue, mores and the *moi commun* which all citizens must possess. However, since the interests of governments are not those of the people, magistrates soon cease to be 'chiefs'. The picture of the body politic, which makes magistrates passive organs of the will, gives them an apparent insignificance, and justifies their existence by their lack of independence and power. It is not a true picture of Sparta with its ephors and kings or of Rome with its consuls and tribunes. That hardly mattered to Rousseau. Was Cato not a greater man than Socrates? Was not the great censor incomparably superior to the opinion-makers of modern Europe? Does Rome not show what manner of men the 'chiefs' were able to create? Were they not in every way better and happier than the enervated and enslaved Parisian poor? That was enough. The Spartans and Romans had not been perfect. They were men. That is precisely why they shame modern civilization so, and that was all they were meant to do.

The full body politic that justifies political 'chiefs' was not the only one for which Rousseau had some use. His rhetorical ingenuity went well beyond that. Eventually he invented a body politic that showed government to be the seat, not of public life, but of death. He developed this new metaphor rather gradually. It was at first forced upon him by those critics of the *Discourse on Inequality,* who insisted that man was a political animal. To this Rousseau replied that civil society had come late in the history of mankind and that this was not a natural development comparable to the aging of a man. Our relatively recent history is not a necessary bodily growth, but the consequence of external circumstances, many of which even depend on the will of men. He did not, however, as one might have expected, abandon the body politic metaphor entirely at this point. Instead he replaced the old organic body with his own artificial one. Government is what a crutch is to an old man. If mankind is senile then it needs an artificial limb. In short, mankind can be said to be in decay, but it is an artificially induced state and one that depends on man-made devices. That has its advantages. What men have done cannot be undone, but they can at least be warned against continuing on their disastrous course. They can also avail themselves of artificial devices for survival, such as civil society.[170]

Another common appearance of the natural body politic was in conventional law of nations thinking. Rousseau was torn by conflicting urges in this case. On one hand he detested the cosmopolitanism of the intellectuals and admired the martial spirit of Sparta; on the other he hated war and conquest which were, as he knew well, the instruments of despotism. The isolated polity, economically and militarily self-reliant, bound by no ties to any other state was the only answer to these various demands. It provided martial virtue without war and bloodshed. War itself was only the manifestation of incomplete socialization. It was not natural. Men in nature do not fight, they are too aloof from each other. This alert autarchy is what the artificial body politic must imitate. Where law is impossible, the situation of nature, which is *not* a state of war, but one of isolation, is the only safe alternative. The body politic should artificially model itself upon the natural condition of man.

This 'natural' policy among peoples is not open to any states except just republics. To think that the actual states of Europe could be anything but at war was pure folly. Nothing could exceed the stupidity of the Abbé de Saint Pierre's notion of a law binding sovereign states, and absolute monarchies at that. The deceptions invented by Grotius were worse. His laws of war and rights of conquest were lies that enslaved. Invented to flatter kings and fleece the people, this law of nations was neither law nor did it bind states. Rousseau disliked Grotius particularly because the real social basis of law, the social contract between free persons, could never be understood unless conventional jurisprudence was shown up for what it was; a fantasy at best, a crude deception at worst.[171]

The law of nations which purports to rule the conduct of states in peace and war is, first of all, no law at all. Sovereign states have never been known to live in anything but a state of war. Peace occurs only when the stronger state can see some advantage in not attacking the weaker.[172] In this, however, they do not behave as individuals who have a fight. War is a social phenomenon in which men, organized and policed, are forced to fight men who are in the same condition as their own. The state, whether in active or dormant war is, thus, in no sense like a natural body. It is subject to none of the limitations, physical or psychological, that restrain individuals, even highly aggressive ones. The horror of our present 'mixed condition' arises out of this situation. As individuals men are forced to live under laws. As subjects of lawless absolute monarchs they are forced by these very laws, which correspond to none of their needs, to fight and kill men with whom they have absolutely no quarrel whatever. The conflicts are between the ambitions of only a very few men, the absolute sovereigns of Europe. However, as sovereigns they control 'artificial' bodies politic with which they can engage in military enterprises which are completely unlike private violence. It is again precisely because the body politic is artificial, and not organic, that it is not subject to law. Instead, its members are exposed to force and to the despotism that comes with war. Governments in their relations to each other and to the citizens, in short, are always potential sources of death to the body politic. For despotism, conquest and revolution kill bodies politic, even artificial ones. The people continues to survive, but not the polity.[173]

The artificiality of the body politic explains why in the present 'mixed', semi-social condition, government is a perpetual threat to the survival of the people. Indeed royal government had ruined men so utterly that no monarchy could be reformed.[174] The artificial character of republican bodies politic, however, had its advantages. Their decline could be slowed by cautious citizens in a way that natural death could not be.[175] That was why Rousseau felt it was worth warning the Genevan people against its magistrates. The *Social Contract,* Rousseau explained in the *Confessions,* had two ends in mind.[176] It was to show how government under law might be achieved, and how necessary this was, since men are whatever governments make them. This is what the first part does. It shows, 'laws as they might be'. Standards are set according to which civil society could be justified, 'men being what they are'.[177] The second purpose of the book was to warn Geneva against the dangers of government unchecked by law. In fact, Rousseau managed to denounce *all* governments in warning the Genevans against theirs.[178]

The *Social Contract* is not a Spartan utopia like the *Economie Politique*. It is the continuation of the *Discourse on Inequality,* as the former completed the *Discourse on the Arts and Sciences*. As such it is not directed at the intellectual servants of despotism; it attacks the masters directly. It deals not with the corruption spread by art and science, but with the burdens of injustice and oppression borne by the people. It does not, therefore, offer a picture of republican perfection, though the standards of political judgment presented in it are drawn from the Spartan model. The *Social Contract* is, especially in its many chapters on government, an account of how republics degenerate and die. It is the political part of the 'genealogy of vice'. That is why Rome is here not described as the perfect city of the *Economie Politique,* but as a polity tense with conflict. All its virtue rests in the assemblies of the rural people. The city is full of rabble. The patricians hate the people. Though the rich are fined for ostentation, there are both rich and poor people in Rome. Eventually the tribunes betray the people and the people begins to sell its votes. That was the predictable end. Nevertheless, with all its faults Rome was completely inimitable in the modern age. The Genevans were not to imagine that the Romans were models for them. They could not even hope to be Athenians.[179] If Rome fell, what hope was there for republics so infinitely less virtuous? The political fatalism is profound. For while he attacked governments as deadly, Rousseau continued to insist that they were necessary. With

this the body politic returns to the stage.

The 'body politic' of the *Social Contract* bears no resemblance to *Leviathan* at all. It is not presented in all its parts. The body politic has to be integrated and it needs a 'force' in order to move and act. That force is government.[180] The second characteristic of the body politic is its inevitable end. 'The body politic like that of man begins to decay at birth.'[181] For all his skill in destroying the persuasiveness of the 'natural' body politic of his opponents, Rousseau did not want to discard the organic associations of the metaphor entirely. Its death was not more natural than its life, but life and death are natural experiences. They are also the most dramatic. And Rousseau wanted to bring that to bear upon the spectacle of justice created and destroyed.

The active agent of destruction is government. When it has finally succeeded in overstepping its legally assigned powers, the body politic is paralyzed, but it is not dead. Only when a society has completely dissolved does that occur. Anarchy is not the usual condition of the people, however. Paralysis is more common.[182] It is, in fact, the condition of all unjust, that is all actual, states. The sense of justice is alive in the people, but its will cannot be asserted. The people is powerless and it cannot make the body politic move because the government is completely indifferent to the general will. The mind and soul of a paralyzed person are active. He has a will, but it is of no practical use to him, because he cannot move his limbs. He is impotent, as is the people in an unjust polity. The general will must unite government and people as the soul and body must be one in a living body.[183] When that link breaks, the man may live, but not well.

When Rousseau introduced government into the true civil society he was explicit about its character. It was to be aristocratic, a body with a real life with a *moi particulier* apart from that of the people and a sensibility, a force and a will common only to its members, and designed to preserve it and to keep its members united. Government means assemblies, councils, rights, titles and exclusive privileges, and no turbulent interference from the people.[184] No wonder that governmental usurpation is the vice that inevitably 'from the birth of the body politic tends relentlessly to destroy it'. It is the one form of organized particular will that is unavoidable, but which, like all such wills, incessantly assaults the general will.[185] Government was, however, necessary, not because it was legitimate, but because 'austere democracy' was not possible and, perhaps, not even desirable, for 'men as they are'. Nevertheless, for all its inevitability, government could not be justified positively. All the arguments that Rousseau raised against those representative bodies which, like Parliament, had feudal roots were perfectly applicable to any form of government. It is not the dangerous notion of shared sovereignty, nor the false belief that people are bound by a fundamental contract to their rulers that made Parliament so dangerous to law and justice. It was, rather, that like any association set apart from the people as a whole, its members possessed interests contrary to the general will. Even as mere agents of the sovereign, magistrates have a particular self and will.[186] The reason why Rousseau came to assert that there is no best government, that everything depends on time and place, seems to have been grounded in the belief that all were bad, if not always equally so.[187] When he was really interested only in standards of justice, he said nothing about government at all.[188]

Because the *Social Contract* was less a utopia than a book of warnings, Rousseau took great care to admit all the germs of future destruction to this body politic. There is, at the beginning, legitimacy based on equality which alone can create liberty. However, it is at once made clear that this equality has its limits. No inequalities, apart from those recognized by law or held in virtue of rank, are to mark the distribution of power. No inequalities of wealth that permit the rich to buy the poor and force the poor to sell themselves are to exist. That does not, however, exclude governmental powers at all and it is not inconsistent with those conflicts between rich and poor that led to the decline and fall of the Roman Republic. Such degrees of inequality *can*, unlike those of contemporary society, be regulated and controlled to slow down the steady march to destruction.[189] It justified Rousseau's enterprise. There was room for anger and denunciation, but not for hope or action. 'Austere democracy' might alone be justifiable, but it had to be dismissed so that the body politic might live and die.

It was, however, by no means easy for Rousseau to shake himself free from his rustic dreams. He had made it far too clear that the bonds that tie citizens to each other and to their polity depend on equality and mutuality and not on governmental power.[190] All the virtue, mores and opinions of republican men are ephemeral without these. A people remains a people, with or without its chiefs.[191] And only in a democracy does the execution of laws follow immediately upon the expression of the public will.[192] In short, here alone is there no particular will to misguide, or disrupt the general will or to keep it from its ends. There is no gap between the interests of the people and the conduct of the body politic. No one is imposing anything upon anyone. This is the 'government without government', fit only for angels. Men good enough to govern themselves would need no government. That is only another way of saying that democratic government and gerontocracy, which is another form of election by lot, are not possible for 'men as they are'.[193] That may well mean that no civil order can ever be legitimate, if all need governments. For the rustic simpletons, who 'live

without masters, indeed almost without laws', are those heads of large families, those happy men of the Golden Age, the peasants of Neufchatel, 'perhaps unique on earth'.[194] If only democracy can be legitimate then civil society is not justifiable, because it depends on rulers. Rustic bliss, however, has nothing to say to socialized men. Pre-social life was moral because it was psychologically satisfying, but men in their stupidity abandoned that condition. Now they need medicine. And civil society is only the cure for social disease. It also is no permanent abode for men.

Of Emile it is said, when he reached adolescence, that he was 'now in the world of morals, the door to vice is open'.[195] It is so with mankind as a whole. Once they come together morality is before men and so is evil, and neither can be wholly evaded. Before joining civil society men might have been 'good and just without knowing what goodness and virtue are'.[196] In this, the true rustic democracy, there is an equality that is more than a struggle against inequality. It is also a world in which men live without ever feeling anything, without really being men at all, in fact. In it 'we would have died without having lived; all our happiness would have consisted in not knowing our misery; there would have been no goodness in our hearts, nor morality in our actions and we would never have tasted the most delicious sentiment of the soul which is the love of virtue'.[197] Rustic man is evidently a 'stupid and limited' creature and not a man or a citizen.[198] We are in this respect worse off than he was, however. For we will not 'become men until we are citizens'.[199] We are like rustic man in being less than human, and worse in every other respect. For having destroyed our capacity for unconscious goodness, we have not created the conditions for conscious virtue.

All of Rousseau's radicalism and all his resentment are in that phrase: 'we will not become men until we are citizens'. That is the voice of the watchmaker's son. The Spartan model was a marvellous blunt instrument to hurl against the powerful, the rich, and especially at their polished literary footmen. All of them professed to admire antiquity, but, with the sole exception of Montesquieu, they had chosen to forget the social conditions of republican virtue. To admire Cato meant to love the republic, to despise the intellectuals and to hate Paris. The voice of Cato did not go unheard, however. It found a ready response among those whose interests he was supposed to defend. If Catonism has often been the ideology of a declining gentry, it has also had a genuine appeal for the peasantry.[200] Rousseau certainly had them in mind. He was not in the least interested in protecting Baron d'Etange. The peasants had to be rescued from civilization. Wolmar tries to do that, but he is not merely a model landlord, he is God, and even he fails, because he cannot defend his family against the consequences of their world. Sparta fails and the Golden Age is frail, neither can be restored and both illuminate the situation of men who are torn helplessly between nature and society. The intimate society, the wholly un-Spartan friendship group that Rousseau longed for, and that every man really needs, is a mere day-dream. There could be no society 'according to my heart' or indeed to any heart.[201] Self-knowledge had taught Rousseau that Clarens, or some version of the Golden Age, was the most fundamental human need. Public understanding and hatred of oppression moved him to remind men of Sparta. Neither one is actually attainable. History is the story of mankind's inability to achieve either peace or justice.

Rousseau knew that a revolution was on its way, but it promised nothing. He did not need to speak of popular corruption; the stupidity of the people suffices to condemn it to servitude once rustic simplicity has been lost. The freedom for which the intellectual classes hoped was not in its interest. Rousseau was no defender of intolerance or intellectual repression, but the interests of the intellectuals are not those of the people. The people has an interest in maintaining an order in which there are no intellectuals at all, in which there are, in fact, Catos to see that none appear. Once the learned classes exist, the conditions for popular felicity are already gone. The interests of the clever and talented support civilization. The people have every reason to prefer rural simplicity. Rousseau was far from being deaf to art and learning; he just did not choose to pretend that these embellishments contributed to the moral well-being of mankind. In a corrupt world they are necessary, but there is nothing to be said in favor of that world as a whole. The world as it is demands resignation and prudence, and a careful attention to a conscience that keeps us from causing harm to those around us. It offers no occasion for happiness or civic virtue. Nevertheless, Rousseau did feel bound to do more: to speak the truth, both about 'the history of the human heart' and the world men had made. When he called upon his readers to choose between man and the citizen he was forcing them to face the moral realities of social life. They were asked, in fact, not to choose, but to recognize that the choice was impossible, and that they were not and would never become either men or citizens.

Notes

1 Vaughan, II, 128-9 *(Contrat Social)*.

2 *Emile*, 186-7.

3 Montesquieu, *The Spirit of the Laws*, I, XI, 153; Diderot, *Droit Naturel*, in Vaughan, I, 429-33.

4 Vaughan, I, 460 *(Première Version)*; Vaughan, II, 33-5 *(Contrat Social)*. For more detailed accounts of Rousseau's response to Diderot see René Hubert, *Rousseau et l'Encyclopédie* (Paris, 1928), 31-49, and Jacques

Proust, *Diderot et l'Encyclopédie*, 359-99.

5 Grimsley, *Jean d'Alembert*, 183.

6 Vaughan, I, 243 *(Economie Politique)*.

7 *Ibid.* 325-9 *(Fragment)*.

8 *Ibid.* 241 *(Economie Politique)*.

9 Vaughan, II, 91 *(Contrat Social)*.

10 *Ibid.* 50-1 *(Contrat Social)*.

11 *Ibid.* 34 *(Contrat Social)*.

12 *Ibid.* 60 *(Contrat Social)*.

13 *Ibid.* 40 *(Contrat Social)*.

14 *Emile*, 7; Vaughan, I, 251 *(Economie Politique)*; 326 *(Fragment)*.

15 Vaughan, II, 58-9 *(Contrat Social)*.

16 *'Préface' à Narcisse*, 964.

17 Vaughan, II, 323 *(Corsica)*.

18 *Emile*, 418.

19 *N.H.*, Part II, Letter IX; *Emile*, 416. Rousseau was evidently familiar with much of the 'national character' literature of his time. Lord Eduard was, however, a specifically political figure and Montesquieu alone had concentrated wholly on that aspect of the English scene. To miss that is to miss both what Lord Eduard is meant to convey and the immense influence of Montesquieu upon Rousseau. That is why the purely literary approach in general does such scant justice to the *Nouvelle Héloise*, e.g. George R. Havens, 'Sources of Rousseau's Eduard Bomston', *Modern Philology*, XVII, 1919, 125-39; see also Albert Schinz, *La Pensée de Jean-Jacques Rousseau*, 339-41.

20 *Spirit of the Laws*, I, XIX, 315.

21 *Emile*, 415-18.

22 Vaughan, II, 428-30, 432 *(Poland)*.

23 E.g. *Essai sur l'Origine des Langues*, 383-95.

24 Vaughan, I, 351-7 *(Fragment)*.

25 *N.H.*, Part I, Letters XLV, LX, LXII; Part II, Letter II; Part III, Letters XXII, XXIII; Part V, Letter I; Appendice I, 'Les Amours de Milord Eduard Bomston.' *Spirit of the Laws*, I, XI, 156-7. Thus Montes-

quieu did not choose to 'examine whether the English actually enjoy this liberty or not . . . it is established by their laws; and I inquire no further'. I, XI, 162; XIX, 307-15.

26 *N.H.,* Part II, Letters XXII, XXIII; *Lettres Ecrites de la Montague,* IX, 255.

27 Vaughan, I, 322 *(Fragment);* II, 64 *(Contrat Social).* (My italics.)

28 *Ibid.* II, 344-5 *(Corsica).*

29 *Ibid.* I, 251-2 *(Economie Politique)*

30 *Ibid.* 294 *(L'état de guerre).*

31 *Emile,* 26.

32 Vaughan, II, 110-13 *(Contrat Social);* 347, 351 *(Corsica); Emile,* 326.

33 Vaughan, I, 455, 470, 493-4 *(Première Version);* II, 32 *(Contrat Social).*

34 *Emile,* 215.

35 Vaughan, I, 484-5 *(Première Version);* II, 56-8 *(Contrat Social).*

36 *Ibid.* I, 126 *(Inégalité);* II, 57 *(Contrat Social).*

37 *Ibid.* II, 66 *(Contrat Social); Emile,* 427-8.

38 Vaughan, II, 66-8 *(Contrat Social).*

39 *Emile,* 286-7, 418.

40 Vaughan, II, 431-8, 472 *(Poland).*

41 *Spirit of the Laws,* I, VIII, 120; Vaughan, II, 77-81 *(Contrat Social).*

42 Vaughan, II, 443 *(Poland).*

43 *Ibid.* 61 *(Contrat Social).*

44 *Spirit of the Laws,* II, VIII, 309.

45 *Letters Ecrites de la Montagne,* VI, 203.

46 Vaughan, I, 457 *(Première Version);* II, 35 *(Contrat Social).*

47 *Ibid.* I, 455 *(Première Version);* II, 32 *(Contrat Social).*

48 *Ibid.* I, 181 *(Inégalité);* II, 31-2 *(Contrat Social); Emile,* 424; *Lettres Ecrites de la Montagne,* VI, 205.

49 Vaughan, I, 245 *(Economie Politique);* II, 37-9 *(Contrat Social).*

50 Vaughan, I, 456-7 *(Première Version).*

51 *Ibid.* II, 32-3 *(Contrat Social).*

52 *Ibid.* I, 457 *(Première Version);* II, 36, 46-8, 63 *(Contrat Social).*

53 *Ibid.* I, 259 *(Economie Politique);* 494-5 *(Première Version);* II, 48-9 *(Contrat Social).*

54 *Ibid.* I, 471-4 *(Première Version);* 44-6 *(Contrat Social).*

55 *Emile,* 421-2; Vaughan I, 130 *(Fragment);* II, 25-31, 41-2 *(Contrat Social).*

56 Vaughan, I, 459-60 *(Première Version);* II, 39 *(Contrat Social).*

57 *Ibid.* I, 274 *(Economie Politique);* 467, 475 *(Première Version);* II, 45 *(Contrat Social).*

58 *Ibid.* I, 183-9 *(Inégalité).*

59 *Ibid.* 190 *(Inégalité);* Vaughan II, 39 *(Contrat Social).*

60 Vaughan, I, 181-3 *(Inégalité);* 268 *(Economie Politique);* II, 346 *(Corsica).*

61 *Ibid.* I, 190-1 *(Inégalité).*

62 *Ibid.* II, 102, 105, 44-6 *(Contrat Social).*

63 *Emile,* 424.

64 *Lettres Ecrites de la Montagne,* VII, 230.

65 *Confessions,* IX, 404-5; Vaughan, II, 91-3 *(Contrat Social); Lettres Ecrites de la Montagne,* VII, 231.

66 Vaughan, II, 40, 91 *(Contrat Social).*

67 *Ibid.* 31 *(Contrat Social).*

68 *Ibid.* 54 *(Contrat Social).*

69 *Ibid.* 51 *(Contrat Social).*

70 *Ibid.* I, 126 *(Inégalité);* 241, 250-1, 253-4, 256 *(Economie Politique).*

71 Vaughan, I, 242-3 *(Economie Politique).*

72 *Ibid.* II, 34 *(Contrat Social).*

73 *Ibid.* 93-4 *(Contrat Social);* I, 493 *(Première Ver-*

sion).

[74] *Ibid.* I, 246 (*Economie Politique*); II, 453, 459 (*Poland*).

[75] *The Laws,* 723.

[76] Jean Wahl, 'La Bipolarité de Rousseau', *Annales Jean-Jacques Rousseau,* XXXIII, 1953-5, 49, 55. I completely disagree with this effort to impose Hegel on Rousseau, and I have only borrowed the excellent term, bipolarity, from it.

[77] *Emile,* 197-8, 422.

[78] Vaughan, I, 243 (*Economie Politique*).

[79] *Lettres Ecrites de la Montagne,* IX, 263.

[80] Vaughan, II, 102 (*Contrat Social*).

[81] *Emile,* 306.

[82] *Ibid.* 239, 243, 248; Vaughan, II, 50-1 (*Contrat Social*).

[83] Vaughan, II, 61 (*Contrat Social*).

[84] Vaughan, II, 103-4 (*Contrat Social*); I, 278 (*Economie Politique*).

[85] *Ibid.* I, 247 (*Economie Politique*); 481 (*Première Version*).

[86] *Ibid.* II, 42 (*Contrat Social*). See *supra,* Ch. 2.

[87] *Ibid.* I, 248-9, 278 (*Economie Politique*).

[88] *Emile,* 436-8.

[89] Vaughan, I, 474, 476-7 (*Première Version*); II, 50-1, (*Contrat Social*).

[90] *Ibid.* 248, 250, 255-7, 275 (*Economie Politique*); II, I22 (*Contrat Social*); 344-6 (*Corsica*).

[91] *Ibid.* I, 460 (*Première Version*); 61 (*Contrat Social*).

[92] *Ibid.* II, 330 (*Corsica*).

[93] *Ibid.* I, 457 (*Première Version*).

[94] *Ibid.* 460 (*Première Version*); II, 40 (*Contrat Social*); *Emile,* 426.

[95] Vaughan, II, 95-6 (*Contrat Social*).

[96] *Ibid.* 456, 477 (*Poland*).

[97] *Ibid.* 39-40 (*Contrat Social*).

[98] *Ibid.* 42 (*Contrat Social*).

[99] *Ibid.* 45 (*Contrat Social*).

[100] *Ibid.* 39 (*Contrat Social*).

[101] *Ibid.* 40-1, 76-7 (*Contrat Social*).

[102] Vaughan, II, 486-7 (*Poland*).

[103] *Ibid.* I, 308-9 (*Fragment*).

[104] *Ibid.* II, 488-9 (*Poland*).

[105] *N.H.,* Part I, Letter LXII.

[106] Vaughan, I, 294-305 (*L'état de guerre*); 448-54 (*Première Version*); II, 37-9, 46 (*Contrat Social*).

[107] Vaughan, II, 102 (*Contrat Social*).

[108] *Ibid.* 105 (*Contrat Social*).

[109] *Ibid.* 32 (*Contrat Social*).

[110] *Ibid.* 42-3 (*Contrat Social*).

[111] *Ibid.* 105-6 (*Contrat Social*).

[112] *Ibid.* 26-7 (*Contrat Social*).

[113] *Ibid.* 105-6 (*Contrat Social*).

[114] Vaughan, II, 42-3 (*Contrat Social*).

[115] *Ibid.* 46 (*Contrat Social*).

[116] *Ibid.* 44-6, 49, 98-9 (*Contrat Social*); *Emile,* 425-6.

[117] *Lettres Ecrites de la Montagne,* VIII, 228.

[118] Vaughan, II, 44, 131 (*Contrat Social*); *Lettres Ecrites de la Montagne,* VI, 202-3.

[119] *Lettres Ecrites de la Montagne,* IX, 263.

[120] *The Spirit of the Laws,* I, VIII, III.

[121] Vaughan, I, 240 (*Economie Politique*).

[122] *Ibid.* II, 24 (*Contrat Social*).

[123] *Ibid.* I, 326 (*Fragment*).

[124] *Emile,* 44.

[125] *Ibid.* 183.

[126] *Rêveries*, IX, 1085; *Letter to d'Alembert*, 126.

[127] *Emile*, 44-5.

[128] *Ibid.* 140.

[129] *Ibid.* 362.

[130] Vaughan, I, 328-9 *(Fragment)*; *Lettres Ecrites de la Montagne*, III, 146; Vaughan, II, 133 *(Contrat Social)*.

[131] *Ibid.* I, 348-9 *(Fragment)*.

[132] Vaughan, I, 326 *(Fragment)*.

[133] *Ibid.* II, 77 *(Contrat Social)*.

[134] *Ibid.* I, 329, 344-9 *(Fragment)*.

[135] *Ibid.* 263-5 *(Economie Politique)*; II, 485-92 *(Poland)*.

[136] Vaughan, I, 328-9, 348-9 *(Fragment)*; II, 308-9 *(Corsica)*.

[137] *Ibid.* I, 450 *(Première Version)*; 326-7 *(Fragment)*.

[138] *Ibid.* 327-8 *(Fragment)*.

[139] *Ibid.* II, 87 *(Contrat Social)*.

[140] *Leviathan*, ed. by Michael Oakeshott (Oxford, 1947), 127, 209-18.

[141] Anton-Hermann Chroust, 'The Corporate Idea and the Body Politic in the Middle Ages', *The Review of Politics*, 1947, IX, 423-52.

[142] John of Salisbury, *The Statesman's Book*, ed. and trans. by John Dickinson (New York, 1963), 71.

[143] *Ibid.* 64-5.

[144] *Ibid.* 73-5.

[145] Saint Thomas Aquinas, *On the Governance of Rulers*, trans. by Gerald B. Phelan (London and New York, 1938), 36, 40-2, 91-4.

[146] *Leviathan*, 5, 112, 113-20, 121-9.

[147] *Emile*, 340.

[148] Vaughan, I, 241 *(Economie Politique)*.

[149] *Ibid.* 250-1 *(Economie Politique)*, *Discours sur les Science et les Arts*, 8.

[150] Vaughan, I, 244 *(Economie Politique)*.

[151] *Ibid.* II, 427 *(Poland)*.

[152] 'Lettre à M. le Marquis de Mirabeau', 26 juillet 1767, *C.G.*, XVII, 155-9.

[153] Vaughan, I, 243 *(Economie Politique)*.

[154] *Ibid.* 240, 258 *(Economie Politique)*.

[155] *Ibid.* 244 *(Economie Politique)*.

[156] *Ibid.* 246, 248, 250, 254-5, 257, 259-60, 265, 272-3 *(Economie Politique)*.

[157] *Ibid.* 247, 258 *(Economie Politique)*.

[158] *Ibid.* 239, 240, 242-3 *(Economie Politique)*.

[159] *Lettres Ecrites de la Montagne*, VI, 202.

[160] Vaughan, II, 31 *(Contrat Social)*.

[161] 'Preface' à Narcisse, 965.

[162] Vaughan, II, 107-8 *(Contrat Social)*.

[163] *Ibid.* I, 246, 248-50 *(Economie Politique)*; 334 *(Fragment)*; II, 345-6 *(Corsica)*; 433-41, 477-80 *(Poland)*.

[164] Vaughan, I, 267-8 *(Economie Politique)*; II, 436, 438-9, 474 *(Poland)*.

[165] *Ibid.* II, 346 *(Corsica)*.

[166] See *supra*, Ch. III; Vaughan I, 247, 261-3 *(Economie Politique)*.

[167] Vaughan, I, 239 *(Economie Politique)*.

[168] *Ibid.* 244-5 *(Economie Politique)*.

[169] *Ibid.* 242-3 *(Economie Politique)*.

[170] Vaughan, I, 223-4 *(Lettre à M. Philopolis)*.

[171] Vaughan, I, 447-54 *(Première Version)*; II, 37, 41-2 *(Contrat Social)*.

[172] 'Lettre à M. de Malesherbes', 3 novembre 1760, *C.G.*, 247-8.

[173] Vaughan, I, 293-305 *(L'état de guerre)*; I, 389-91 *(Jugement sur la Paix Perpétuelle)* II, 29-31 *(Contrat Social)*.

[174] *Ibid.* 416-17 *(Jugement sur la Polysynodie)*.

[175] *Ibid.* II, 91 *(Contrat Social).*

[176] *Confessions,* IX, 404-5.

[177] Vaughan, II, 23 *(Contrat Social).*

[178] *Lettres Ecrites de la Montagne,* VI, 203-5; VII, 208-9.

[179] Vaughan, II, 104, 113-15, 117-19 *(Contrat Social); Lettres Ecrites de la Montagne,* IX, 254-5.

[180] Vaughan, II, 64 *(Contrat Social); Lettres Ecrites de la Montagne,* VI, 202.

[181] Vaughan, II, 91 *(Contrat Social).*

[182] *Ibid.* I, 301 *(L'état de guerre);* 318 *(Fragment);* II, 91, 29-30 *(Contrat Social).*

[183] Vaughan, II, 65 *(Contrat Social).*

[184] *Ibid.* 68 *(Contrat Social); Letters Ecrites de la Montagne,* VIII, 224; 'Lettre à M. Marcet de Mézieres', 24 juillet, 1762, *C.G.,* VIII, 35-8.

[185] Vaughan, II, 88 *(Contrat Social); Lettres Ecrites de la Montagne,* VI, 204-5.

[186] Vaughan, II, 68, 95-7, 99 *(Contrat Social).*

[187] *Ibid.* 82-7 *(Contrat Social); Lettres Ecrites de la Montagne,* VI, 205-6; *Emile,* 422.

[188] The *Première Version* breaks off just at the point where 'public force' enters. This was to begin the discussion of government in the final version of the *Contrat Social.* In *Corsica* only a vague reference to 'guardians of the law' disturbs the rustic peace. Vaughan, I, 461-2 *(Première Version);* II, 64 *(Contrat Social);* 351 *(Corsica).*

[189] Vaughan, II, 61 *(Contrat Social).*

[190] E.g. Vaughan, II, 317, 321-2 *(Corsica).*

[191] Vaughan, I, 468 *(Première Version).*

[192] *Ibid.* II, 75, 100 *(Contrat Social).*

[193] Vaughan, II, 72-4, 108 *(Contrat Social).*

[194] *Ibid.* 320-1 *(Corsica); Letter to d'Alembert,* 60.

[195] *Emile,* 65.

[196] Vaughan, II, 321 *(Corsica).*

[197] *Ibid.* I, 449 *(Première Version).*

[198] *Ibid.* II, 36 *(Contrat Social).*

[199] *Ibid.* I, 453 *(Première Version).*

[200] Barrington Moore, Jr., *The Social Origins of Dictatorship and Democracy* (Boston, 1966), 491-505.

[201] *N.H.,* Part IV, Letter X; *Confessions,* IX, 414; *Rousseau Juge de Jean-Jacques,* II, 827; *Lettres à Malesherbes,* I, 1132.

> **Rousseau discusses the signs of a good government in *On the Social Contract, or Principles of Political Right:***
>
> When the question arises which one is absolutely the best government, an insoluble question is being raised because it is indeterminate. Or, if you wish, it has as many good answers as there are possible combinations in the absolute and relative positions of peoples.
>
> But if it is asked by what sign it is possible to know that a given people is well or poorly governed, this is another matter, and the question of fact could be resolved. . . .
>
> What is the goal of the political association? It is the preservation and prosperity of its members. And what is the surest sign that they are preserved and prospering? It is their number and their population. Therefore do not go looking elsewhere for this much disputed sign. All other things being equal, the government under which . . . the citizens become populous and multiply the most, is infallibly the best government. That government under which a populace diminishes and dies out is the worst. . . .
>
> *Jean Jacques Rousseau, in* The Basic Political Writings, *translated and edited by Donald A. Cress, Hackett Publishing Company, 1987.*

Vincente Medina (essay date 1990)

SOURCE: "Rousseau," in *Social Contract Theories: Political Obligation or Anarchy?*, Rowman & Littlefield Publishers, Inc., 1990, pp. 43-61.

[*In the following excerpt, Medina discusses Rousseau as an advocate of contractarianism.*]

Rousseau's views are open to several different interpretations. Four of these may be referred to as the Hobbesian, the Lockean, the Kantian, and the Marxist interpretation. Each stresses one or two aspects of his thought. For example, the Hobbesian interpretation emphasizes the concept of absolute sovereignty. The Lockean interpretation emphasizes the idea of popular sovereignty: that the will of the sovereign is concretely determined by the will of the majority. The Kantian interpretation emphasizes the concept of freedom as respect for moral law. The Marxist interpretation emphasizes Rousseau's political egalitarianism and his criticism of excessive private property and inequality in general. Which of these four interpretations is correct? The answer is paradoxical—all and none. All are correct insofar as each stresses some essential aspect(s) of Rousseau's political philosophy. But none is correct insofar as each attempts, but does not succeed, in presenting a comprehensive view of it.

Rousseau is an innovator in political philosophy. His political philosophy constitutes a bridge from the Natural Law tradition to the Idealist School. He is an original thinker, and if we try to encapsulate his political ideas within the parameters of any particular tradition, they lose much of their flavor and originality. Although Rousseau is an indisputable representative of the social contract tradition, he is not a representative of the "liberal individualist tradition" or what C. B. Macpherson refers to as "possessive individualism." To be an individual is to be a proprietor, an owner of oneself and one's capacities without any debts to society.[1] Liberal individualists define liberty in terms of negative freedom—freedom from subjection to the wills of others. The individual is considered a self-made and self-contained atomic unit with rights and duties independent of society. These are, I believe, essential characteristics of liberal individualism or libertarianism. If so, I maintain that Rousseau is not a liberal individualist in this sense. If he is not a liberal individualist, what is he?

Stephen Ellenburg, in his book, *Rousseau's Political Philosophy,* offers a good characterization of Rousseau's position as nonindividualist and egalitarian.[2] Ellenburg argues that Rousseau is neither a traditional liberal individualist nor a collectivist. For Rousseau the individual and society are necessarily interdependent: one cannot exist apart from the other. Rousseau's individual realizes his nature in and through society. Moreover, Rousseau is, as Ellenburg indicates, a *radical political egalitarian* because he defends the principle of *absolute self-government.* For Rousseau, individuals are free only if they can govern themselves. Therefore, according to Rousseau, any form of representative government would be considered a form of political subservience.

Rousseau presents the essence of his political philosophy in three works: ***Discourse on the Origin and Foundation of Inequality Among Men (Second Dis-***

course), 1754; ***Discourse on Political Economy,*** 1758; and ***The Social Contract,*** 1762. All of his other works are related to his political theory, but these three are sufficient to understand it.

I shall concentrate first on Rousseau's concept of the state of nature. He, like Hobbes and Locke, uses this expression for at least three different purposes: (1) to refer to prepolitical society, where there is no commonly recognized political power or authority; (2) to assist in the development of his concept of human nature; (3) to assist in his explication of the origin of civil society. He also uses this concept in a fourth way: to explicate the origin of political inequalities and private property.

In *Second Discourse,* Rousseau discusses human nature in its original "primitive state" or "pure state of nature," as contrasted with human nature in civil society. To carry out this mental experiment, he strips the individual of all traits acquired only in society. What remains is, according to Rousseau, natural or primitive people—people in their original condition. Nonetheless, he recognizes that separating that which is artificial from that which is natural in people is extraordinarily difficult.[3] He proceeds to present his account of how civilization imprinted its rubric on natural individuals, and how they in consequence have been transformed from a state of innocence to a corrupted state of sin.

I agree with Ramon Lemos when he claims that Rousseau's discussion of the state of nature is more extended than, and its purpose different from, that of Hobbes or Locke.[4] Rousseau is more radical in his analysis of the state of nature than either Hobbes or Locke, since he wants to understand human nature in its original primitive condition, as contrasted with human nature in civil society. Thus Rousseau argues that most philosophers have not gone far enough in their analysis of the state of nature and accuses them of transferring to men in "the state of nature the ideas they acquired in society. They spoke about savage man, and it was civil man they depicted." He goes on to say that "it did not even occur to most of our philosophers to doubt that the state of nature had existed."[5] This unfair accusation is understandable because Rousseau uses the term "the state of nature" in a sense different from Locke's. He uses it to indicate the absence of all forms of social relations, whereas Locke uses it to indicate only the absence of political society.

For Rousseau the concept of the state of nature is hypothetical:

> the investigations that may be undertaken concerning this subject should not be taken for historical truths, but only for hypothetical and conditional reasonings, better suited to shedding light on the nature of things

than on pointing out their true origin, like those our physicists make everyday with regards to the formation of the world.[6]

Rousseau's hypothesis of the state of nature is also an attempt to present a theory of human civilization from its genesis to its actual state of corruption. People, according to him, have evolved from a pure state of nature to a highly complex and corrupt state of society. Human goodness has been corrupted by society. If, however, people are naturally good and society is made up of people, then it seems paradoxical to argue, as Rousseau does, that even though people are naturally good they can corrupt themselves. John Plamenatz recognizes this problem when he writes:

> Men are first brought together by the need to satisfy their natural wants, and this coming together starts a train of events which, through no fault of their own and no calamity, both develops and corrupts their faculties. Society, at least, is not naturally good even if man is so.[7]

Rousseau tries to explain this paradox by arguing that inequality is the main, although not the only, source of corruption in society. Natural individuals differ in their physical abilities and mental capacities (*natural inequalities*). Thus when they start a process of social interaction their natural inequalities necessarily lead them to the development of social and economic differences (*artificial inequalities*). These artificial inequalities, together with the development of metallurgy and agriculture and the emergence of private property with its division of labor, bring about the corruption of people in society.

In *Second Discourse,* Rousseau presents a detailed exposition of how the transformation from the state of nature to a state of social corruption came about. For this purpose he divides the state of nature into several stages. The first stage is the presocial, primitive, or pure state of nature where there are absolutely no forms of social intercourse. The second is a quasi-social state; this state, however, can be divided into different stages, where different forms of social relations gradually evolve from the simplest form of social intercourse, such as family relations, to a more complex form, such as tribal relations. The third is a more highly developed social state, in which there is a division of labor and in which significant inequalities exist. In this stage private property is instituted and class antagonism emerges as a serious threat to social harmony.

Natural, primitive, or original individuals in the presocial state of nature are not, according to Rousseau, acquisitive, fearful, violent and egoistic, as Hobbes depicted them. On the contrary, for Rousseau a natural individual is solitary, peaceful, healthy, happy, good, and free. People in this presocial state do not rec-

ognize any rules or laws; they do not even recognize other fellow humans because they do not need them for the fulfillment of their basic needs. These needs are few and simple. Natural individuals are similar to animals with one essential difference: their freedom. Rousseau puts it succinctly when he says:

> Therefore it is not so much understanding which causes the specific distinction of man from all other animals as it is his being a free agent. Nature commands every animal, and beasts obey. Man feels the same impetus, but he knows he is free to go along or to resist. . . .[8]

This ability to choose is what makes a person a perfectible being and a potential moral agent. Both freedom and perfectibility are what distinguish human beings from other animals. Yet the more important of the two is freedom, since it is a necessary condition for actualizing the capacity for self-perfection.

It is important to note the way in which Rousseau uses the concept of freedom in *Second Discourse*. Maurice Cranston, in his book *Jean-Jacques,*[9] presents a good tripartite distinction of this concept. Natural individuals are free, according to Cranston's interpretation, in three different senses: (1) metaphysical, (2) anarchical, and (3) personal. Metaphysical freedom is possessed by all people at any stage of the state of nature, prepolitical society or political society. This freedom amounts to the ability to choose. Anarchical freedom is possessed only by those living in the state of nature; this amounts to the absence of moral, legal, or governmental rules. Personal freedom is the absence of dependence on others and can be exercised only in the pure state of nature where each individual lives a solitary and self-sufficient life.

These three kinds of freedom are species of natural freedom. I call them natural because, with the exception of metaphysical freedom, which can be exercised in either the state of nature or political society, the other two can be exercised only in the state of nature. Furthermore, personal freedom can be exercised only in the pure state of nature.

Metaphysical freedom, however, is a special case of natural freedom because it is natural in two different senses: (1) it can be exercised in the state of nature, and (2) it is an essential aspect of human nature regardless of one's station in the state of nature or in society. This kind of freedom is, I believe, the ground for the natural right to liberty in Rousseau's political philosophy. If so, this freedom is of paramount importance, since liberty, according to Rousseau, is a fundamental value that one ought not to give up because, in doing so, one is giving up one's moral agency. Rousseau argues that since natural individuals are only potentially rational, one cannot, properly speaking, ascribe rights and duties to them in their original presocial state. In this state the concepts of right and wrong, justice and injustice do not apply. In this respect Rousseau's ideas coincide with those of Hobbes, although for different reasons. Hobbes argues that in the state of nature, "The notions of Right and Wrong, Justice and Injustice have there no place." He goes on, "Justice, and Injustice are none of the Faculties neither of the Body, nor Mind. If they were, they might be in a man that were alone in the world, as well as his Senses, and Passions." He stresses that justice and injustice "are Qualities, that relate to men in Society, not in Solitude."[10]

Rousseau, for his part, maintains that natural individuals in the original or primitive state of nature are characterized by two fundamental qualities: self-love (*amour de soi*) and commiseration. The first "makes us ardently interested in our own well-being and our self-preservation," whereas the latter "inspires in us a natural repugnance to seeing any sentient being, especially our fellowman, perish or suffer."[11] From these two qualities it follows, according to him, that the traditional golden rule, "*Do unto others as you would have them do unto you,*" should be replaced by a maxim of natural goodness, "*Do what is good for you with as little harm as possible to others.*"[12] The quality of natural pity or commiseration makes natural individuals essentially good.

If natural individuals are essentially good, and if the original state of nature was such a peaceful state, why did people depart from their original state? There are two basic answers. (1) Human beings in general possess the faculty of perfectibility or self-perfection. This makes any future development of a person's potentialities possible, including the development of rational self-love. (2) Natural events such as earthquakes, floods, and population growth compelled primitive individuals to enter into some rudimentary forms of social intercourse in order to survive. This marked the end of the presocial state of nature and the beginning of the quasi-social state of nature. From then on, an irreversible process of social interdependence developed, and in the process natural individuals lost their personal freedom or freedom from dependence on others. Natural individuals, according to Rousseau, embarked on a process of slow but progressive social bondage.

It was only at the quasi-social stage that the institution of the family emerged. At this same stage people started to live and work together. Rousseau calls this stage "emerging or nascent" society. During this stage tribal relations develop towards more complex forms of social relations. But there is yet only a mild dependence on others, since people still have a sense of self-sufficiency. According to Rousseau, this is the "*golden age*" of humanity. It is a middle position between "the in-

dolence of our primitive state and the petulant activity of our egocentrism."[13]

Even though this middle position would have been the best state for people to remain in, they unfortunately began to cultivate the land and, as a result, brought about the development of both metallurgy and agriculture. With the latter, a fatal division of labor between metal workers on the one hand and farmers on the other became a reality. This in turn created an upsurge of social interdependence among metal workers and farmers. Concurrently, private property was instituted and, as a result, civil society emerged. According to Rousseau:

> This first person who, having enclosed a plot of land, took it into his head to say *this is mine* and found people simple enough to believe him, was the true founder of civil society.[14]

After the foundation of civil society, Rousseau argued, the *natural inequalities* among people, such as differences of age, health and talent, necessarily led to a highly disproportionate level of *artificial inequalities*: differences in power, prestige, and privileges.[15] The natural inequalities among people together with their desire for recognition in society brought about an increase in artificial inequalities and hence a radical change in human nature. From peaceful and benevolent beings natural individuals were transformed into ambitious and contentious beings. The defining characteristics of natural individuals, self-love and natural pity, were transformed into *amour propre* and selfishness. The latter stems from the development of human rationality and the increase of social interdependence.

Thus, entering civil society, individuals lose their last vestiges of personal freedom and natural independence. They become, Rousseau argues, not only the slaves of new artificial needs but of other people as well. Social individuals are now faced with an inescapable dilemma: On the one hand, if they are rich, they need the service of the poor; on the other hand, if they are poor, they need the help of the rich.[16] Social individuals are inescapably condemned to depend on others. Consequently, people in entering civil society exchange personal freedom for social bondage.

According to Rousseau, social individuals are essentially unhappy and alienated. At least four reasons can be adduced for this: (1) they are alienated from their original nature—from peaceful and benevolent beings, they have been transformed into selfish and belligerent individuals; (2) they are alienated from their natural freedom or independence—no longer able to act as they please, they are now bound by the norms and rules of society; (3) they are alienated from economic and spiritual self-sufficiency—they now depend on the recognition and labor of others for subsistence in society; and (4) their natural inequalities are transformed into greater artificial inequalities in civil society.

Significantly, however, Rousseau does not condemn *inequality* in general; he simply condemns those artificial inequalities, such as the excessive economic ones, that bring about political inequalities. For political equality, he argues, two basic conditions must be fulfilled: (1) the ascription of equal rights and duties to all citizens before the law, and (2) an equal opportunity for all citizens to change or modify the laws under which they live regardless of their differences in power, property, or prestige. Moreover, he condemns any kind of artificial inequality which might lead to forms of political inequality. This is why Rousseau advocates a simple way of life rather than the great accumulation of wealth.

> What is most necessary and perhaps the most difficult in the government is rigorous integrity in dispensing justice to all and especially in protecting the poor against the tyranny of the rich. The greatest evil is already done when there are poor people to defend and rich men to keep in check. It is only at intermediate levels of wealth that the full force of the law is exerted.

> It is one of the most important items of business for the government to prevent extreme inequality of fortunes, not by appropriating treasures from their owners, but by denying everyone the means of acquiring them, and not by building hospitals for the poor but by protecting citizens from becoming poor.[17]

Rousseau opposes great accumulations of wealth because it brings about political inequalities. Those with greater wealth also have greater access to political power and, therefore, they have greater freedom. They have the freedom to influence and perhaps even oppress those who have less political power. This is unjust, Rousseau contends. Justice is only possible when people enjoy political equality and have an equal opportunity to enact or change the laws.

Rousseau is not, however, against all kinds of inequalities; he defends the view that inequalities of rank and prestige are just if they are proportional to natural inequalities. In this sense, he is not a radical egalitarian. But he is a radical egalitarian in the political sense, because he believes that all citizens ought to have the same rights and duties before the law and an equal opportunity to participate in enacting or changing it. In short, he is a radical political egalitarian but not a radical economic egalitarian.

For Rousseau, natural as well as artificial inequalities are inevitable in civil society because people, once united in civil society, "are forced to make compari-

sons among themselves" and to take account of their differences in "wealth, rank, power and personal merit." Of these differences, wealth is the most important because it can buy rank and power in society.[18]

Although Rousseau is against amassing great wealth, he is not against private property *per se*. In fact he considers the right to private property "the most sacred of all the citizens' rights."[19] Nor does he advocate that all citizens have the same degree of wealth. On the contrary, he writes:

> With regard to equality, we must not understand by this word that the degrees of power and wealth should be absolutely the same; but that, as to power, it should fall short of all violence, and never be exercised except by virtue of station and of the laws; while, as to wealth, no citizen should be rich enough to be able to buy another, and none poor enough to be forced to sell himself.[20]

Rousseau is searching for the middle ground or the golden mean between the very rich and the very poor. Thus, in order to establish a state of social equilibrium in civil society, he favors a moderate middle class.

> If, then, you wish to give stability to the state, bring the two extremes as near together as possible; tolerate neither rich people nor beggars. These two conditions, naturally inseparable, are equally fatal to the general welfare; from the one class spring tyrants, from the other, the supporters of tyranny.[21]

It follows from these considerations that a necessary condition for creating a just political order is bridging the gap between the rich and the poor. In a society where there is a great difference between the "haves" and the "have-nots" political equality is simply an illusion. He argues:

> Under bad governments this equality is only apparent and illusory; it serves only to keep the poor in their misery and the rich in their usurpations. In fact, laws are always useful to those who possess and injurious to those who have nothing; whence it follows that the social state is advantageous to men only so far as they all have something, and none of them have too much.[22]

For Rousseau private property must serve a social function. It is permissible only if and so long as it promotes the well-being of the community. Political justice is possible, according to him, only if economic justice is also possible, and vice versa; one cannot exist without the other. Although we can conceive of political justice in abstraction, apart from and independent of economic justice, and vice versa, in reality both forms of justice are intertwined. They are in fact directly proportional to one another. Accordingly, Rousseau argues that "the social state is advantageous to men only when all have something and none have too much." Justice in general is possible only in a classless society.

The concept of the social contract is essential to Rousseau's political philosophy. He uses this concept in two different ways: (1) to explain the nature of legitimate political authority, and (2) to explain the genesis of the state, or how political society emerged from prepolitical society to protect and legalize the possessions of the rich. The poor agree to the institution of political society without realizing that they are instituting a positive legal system which sanctions the wealth of the rich and perpetuates their own misery. Arguing against this "*evil contract,*" Rousseau writes:

> the origin of society and laws, which gave new fetters to the weak and new forces to the rich, irretrievably destroyed natural liberty, established forever the law of property and of inequality, changed adroit usurpation into an irrevocable right, and for the profit of a few ambitious men henceforth subjected the entire human race to labor, servitude and misery.[23]

I agree with Iring Fetscher's interpretation of Rousseau on this point.[24] He contends that, according to Rousseau, a necessary condition for the fulfillment of a "good" social contract is a degree of social and political equality among the citizens. Without this, the contract and hence the institution of political society would be unjust, for when there is conflict as a result of great socio-economic and political inequalities, a social contract is used simply as a subterfuge to end the conflict and perpetuate the *status quo.*

On the other hand, in **The Social Contract,** Rousseau uses the concept of a contract as a political and moral device to transform the unjust *status quo* of actual political life into a just political order. His main purpose in this book is to reconcile the claims of freedom with the claims of justice, the claims of right with the claims of self-interest, "so that justice and utility may not be severed." In order to do this, he proposes to take "men as they are and laws as they can be made."[25] That is to say, he wants, while recognizing the power of self-interest, to form a political association in which laws enacted by all of its members will protect the interest of each without transgressing the interests of others. These laws will also protect and promote the freedom of all. He proposes the following enigmatic formula:

> To find a form of association which may defend and protect with the whole force of the community the person and property of every associate, and by means of which each, coalescing with all, may nevertheless obey only himself, and remain as free as before.[26]

The problem with this formula is to explain how one can enter an association which imposes obligations on its members and, at the same time, obey only one's self. Clearly, at some point there is going to be some conflict between what a person wants to do or refrains from doing and what the association requires or forbids be done.

Rousseau believes that this is not necessarily the case because, given the plasticity of human nature, it is possible through education and legal constraint to encourage the members of the association to will or desire only that which is compatible with the *general will* of the association. So that if someone refuses to abide by the general will, "he shall be forced to be free."[27] This is precisely the point—how can we be free, and obey only ourselves, when we are being coerced to act against our will?

The answer to this paradox is to be found in Rousseau's concept of liberty. He distinguishes among three kinds of liberty: *natural, civil,* and *moral.* I have already discussed natural liberty and its three different species: *metaphysical, anarchical,* and *personal.* Civil liberty, as contrasted with natural liberty, exists only where there are rules and norms to be respected. It involves acting according to the rules, norms, and social customs of a particular civil society. Moral liberty, on the other hand, consists, according to Rousseau, in "obedience to a self-prescribed law."[28] Moral liberty differs from civil liberty in that the latter establishes a relation between the individual and the rules or norms prescribed by the community, whereas moral liberty is primarily a relation between person and conscience.

Apparently, the kind of liberty Rousseau has in mind when he uses the expressions "obeying only oneself" and "being forced to be free," is moral as well as civil. However, moral liberty is the highest kind of liberty, since it "renders man truly master of himself." Rousseau maintains that a person "ought to bless . . . the happy moment that released him from it [the state of nature] forever, and transformed him from a stupid and ignorant animal into an intelligent being and a man."[29]

Rousseau's distinction between liberty and independence is important. He indicates this in his **Letters from the Mountain** when he writes:

> When everyone does what he pleases, he often does what displeases others; and that is not called a condition of freedom. Liberty consists less in doing what we want than in not being subjected to another's will; it also consists in not subjecting another's will to our own.[30]

For Rousseau independence, unlike liberty, consists in acting as one pleases without respect for others, whereas liberty is the ability to act according to self-prescribed rules that respect the rights of others. That being the case, the self-prescribed rules of an individual in a society must not conflict with the self-prescribed rules of others in this society. Otherwise liberty and independence would be synonymous. Freedom as independence is basically egoistic. This kind of freedom creates conflicts among individuals. For example, one is free in this sense only when one is able to satisfy wants and desires without any regard for other people's wants or desires. On the other hand, one is morally free only when one's self-prescribed rules are compatible with those of others.

What can guarantee that one's self-prescribed rules are not in conflict with the self-prescribed rules of the other members of society? At this point the idea of a collective self and the concept of *the general will* become crucial to an understanding of Rousseau's ideas. When he refers to the notion of moral freedom as involving self-prescribed moral rules, the term *"self"* is ambiguous, for it refers to the self of each particular member of the body politic and also to the self as a *"moral or collective self."* This collective self emerges as a product of the social pact when "Each of us puts in common his person and his whole power under the supreme direction of the general will; and in return we receive every member as an indivisible part of the whole."[31] The collective self emerges when associates give themselves and all of their rights to the community in order to preserve and promote the common good or general welfare. The means by which this collective self preserves and promotes the common good are through exercising the general will. This will, like that of each individual, aims at self-preservation.

The moral or collective self prescribes laws to the citizens. However, since this moral self is a product of the unity of the citizens' wills as each aspires to the common good, it follows that the moral self is simply an extension of the wills of particular selves as they aspire to generality. Moreover, the particularity or generality of a will depends on its object. If its object is the common good, it is general. If it is some private interest, it is particular.

We obey ourselves only when we act according to the preservation and promotion of the general will, since this will is simply an extension of individual wills as they aspire to generality or the common good. Whenever the citizens act contrary to the general will, they are acting for the sake of their egoistic wants and desires. In this sense, according to Rousseau, they are not morally free. They are slaves of their passions and appetites. They are morally free only when they act according to self-prescribed laws, that is to say, when they act according to the general will. Hence, Rousseau argues, whenever the citizens' actions are incompatible with the general will they must be *forced to be free,* which is to say that they must be constrained by

the law to act according to the general will. But since the citizens consent to abide by the general will when they become participants in the social contract, and since this contract guarantees that all have a free and equal voice in the making of the law, it follows that they are not in fact constrained. Where there is consent there cannot be coercion, since a necessary condition of coercion is the absence of consent. This is true if one assumes, as Rousseau seems to do, that once one consents to a particular state of affairs one is bound by it to eternity. This, however, is too strong an assumption, since it undermines one's moral autonomy by disregarding future moral considerations that might outweigh the moral importance of one's initial act of consent. Consent, like promise, is an open-ended concept, and thus it cannot have absolute moral weight.

Iring Fetscher, in the spirit of Robert Derathé, argues that Rousseau is operating with a dual concept of reason.

> Reason has a dual and sometimes even contradictory aspect, according to whether it is exercised in the service of the passions of *amour propre* or, "when the passions are silent," is considered with the perception of "order."[32]

Fetscher recognizes that the concept of reason which serves the passions is similar to the Humean concept of reason. He sees it as passive reason. However, reason as a perception of order is not passive but active. This is practical reason.

The above distinction corresponds to Rousseau's distinction between a will that is particular and a will that is general. When we are motivated by our selfish interests, our wills are particular. As a result we are unfree, according to Rousseau, because we are the slaves of our passions. On the other hand, when we are motivated by a will that is general, we are concerned with the common good or general welfare. At this level, active or practical rationality is operating. We are operating with a concept of a moral order. Therefore, it is at this level that we are morally free. This anticipates Kant's notions of freedom as respect for the moral law and practical rationality. According to both Rousseau and Kant, we are morally free insofar as we perform our duties for duty's sake and we are rational to the extent that we are moral.

Rousseau is rejecting the notion of freedom as the maximization of our selfish wants and desires—the result of egoism or *amour propre.* On the contrary, his concept of freedom as respect for the moral law is radically different from this egoistic concept of freedom. Since this law is discovered and instituted by the general will, it follows that we are free, in Rousseau's sense, only if and so long as we act according to the general will. The freedom of the citizen consists, as

Fetscher argues, "in his not being dependent on any single man and his whim, but dependent solely upon the law,"[33] which is a law that each citizen helps to establish. Furthermore, virtue consists, according to Rousseau, in acting in accordance with the moral law and hence also with the general will. I am a virtuous citizen provided that I am morally free, and vice versa. Thus Rousseau claims that if we want the general will to be accomplished, we must

> make all private wills be in conformity with it. And since virtue is merely this conformity of the private to the general will, in a word make virtue reign.[34]

Later he says,

> A country cannot subsist without liberty, nor can liberty without virtue, nor can virtue without citizens. You will have everything if you train citizens; without this you will merely have wicked slaves.[35]

The body politic must therefore educate its citizens to be virtuous—to be morally free.

The function of the law, in Rousseau's ideal Republic, is to protect and promote the common good rather than some private or class interest. Therefore, if the law in fact promotes or protects any private or class interest at the expense of the common good, it will lose its legitimacy and the social contract will be broken. This is why Lucio Colletti argues that Rousseau's social pact is different from the liberal natural law tradition:

> while to Locke and Kant and the whole liberal-natural-law tradition in general, the contract "is not an innovation in the natural-legal order but tends to consolidate it . . . ," to Rousseau, on the other hand, "the contract means the renunciation of the state and freedom of nature and the creation of a new moral and social order."[36]

If Rousseau's ideal Republic is to be realized, the terms of the social contract must be unconditionally observed. Rousseau argues for this when he asserts, "The clauses of this contract are so determined by the nature of the act that the slightest modification would render them vain and ineffectual." Moreover, if this pact is violated, "each man regains his original rights and recovers his natural liberty, while losing the conventional liberty for which he renounced it."[37] By the terms "original rights" and "natural liberty," Rousseau refers to rights and liberties people enjoyed before entering political society. He does not, however, refer to a person's natural rights to life and liberty, since such a person is the bearer of these rights in virtue of his or her nature and, as such, they are inalienable. Only those social or conventional rights possessed in civil society are alienable. He defends the natural rights to life and liberty,

although, unlike Locke, he considers the right to property to be a conventional rather than a natural right.[38] Moreover, in *The Social Contract* he argues against the institution of slavery and defends the natural right to liberty on these grounds:

> To renounce one's liberty is to renounce one's quality as a man, the rights and also the duties of humanity. . . . Such a renunciation is incompatible with man's nature, for to take away all freedom from his will is to take away all morality from his action.[39]

Rousseau's contract is intended to guarantee both the enjoyment of civil and political freedom and the right to private property. It guarantees, among other things, the right to have an equal voice in the making of laws and hence the right to vote. Moreover, the right to political freedom derives from the natural right to liberty.

In *The Social Contract* Rousseau presents a dual account of freedom. Freedom has both a *positive* and a *negative* aspect. The latter consists in being independent of the will of others, the former in acting according to self-prescribed rules. These two aspects of freedom are necessary but not sufficient to exercise one's right to political liberty within the body politic. Two further conditions must be met if a citizen is to be politically free: (1) each citizen must be equally treated before the law, and (2) each must have an equal voice in the making of the laws. It follows that Rousseau favors literal self-government. People are politically free only if they can govern themselves. In this sense, Rousseau is a radical political egalitarian, since he advocates literal self-government or direct democracy. For Rousseau sovereignty is *inalienable;* it remains forever with the people.

Rousseau, like Hobbes, rejects the dichotomy between the *social contract* and the *contract of government.* Both postulate a single contract: a contract of society. This idea of a single contract constitutes, as Colletti contends, a revolutionary approach in political theory: "it implies that the government no longer appears as the 'receptacle' of a sovereignty transferred to it by the people . . . , but as a mere executive organ, or precisely a 'commission.'"[40]

The government, Rousseau argues, has "nothing but a commission," and its task is to respond to the needs and interests of the sovereign, which is the collectivity of citizens. Sovereignty remains always with the people. It is inalienable, indivisible, and incapable of representation. The supreme power of the state remains always in the hands of the sovereign, i.e., in the hands of the people. The sovereign can always, through its general will as expressed through the law, modify, limit, or even dismiss the government whenever it chooses.

The sovereign is therefore above the law.

> it is contrary to the nature of the body politic for
> the sovereign to impose on itself a law which it
> cannot transgress . . . whence we see that there is
> not, nor can there be any kind of fundamental law
> binding upon the body of the people, not even the
> social contract.[41]

Later Rousseau argues this point more explicitly when
he writes:

> there is in the State no fundamental law which
> cannot be revoked, not even the social compact; for
> if all citizens assembled in order to break this
> compact by a solemn agreement, no one can doubt
> that it would be quite legitimately broken.[42]

Otto Gierke argues that Rousseau's concept of popular
sovereignty amounts to "the declaration of a permanent right of revolution, and a complete annihilation of
the idea of the constitutional State."[43] However, by the
phrase "permanent revolution" Gierke does not mean a
violent transformation of the body politic, but the al-
ways-present possibility of its legal restructuring. The
sovereign can even, for example, choose to revoke the
contract. But this can be accomplished only if there is
a unanimous agreement to invalidate it. Thus Rousseau, unlike Locke, does not postulate a right to revolution against tyranny. He does not need this right
because sovereignty remains always with the people.
In Rousseau's Republic, tyranny or any sort of gross
injustice on the part of the sovereign would be impossible. The general will of the people can never be unjust,
"since no one is unjust to himself."[44] The sovereign
therefore is always what "it ought to be."[45]

Rousseau believes he has found the formula to reorga-
nize the body politic in such a way that it will necessarily be a just society. For this society the general
welfare will be above private interests. Moreover, formal or ideal justice will also coincide with distributive
or material justice. Therefore, ideal and material justice will become functions of the law as it is expressed
by the acts of the general will. For Rousseau, what the
general will determines is what it *ought to be*.

To have moral weight, the law must be just. Otherwise
the citizens are not obliged to obey it. The general
will, however, is always right. Therefore, for Rousseau, unlike Locke, the citizens do not need to appeal
to "heaven" for justice. They appeal instead to the
general will which is determined by the will of the
majority.[46] The problem with Rousseau's principle of
majority rule, however, is that neither he nor anybody
else can guarantee that the majority will always be
right nor that it will not impose its own will on the
minority. That is to say, Rousseau's political theory
does not provide any safeguards to avoid the tyranny

of the majority. Locke provides at least for the right to
revolution. He does so by maintaining that the citizens
can delegate their sovereignty to a legislative body
provided that this body does not violate their natural
rights. Rousseau, as we have seen, cannot provide for
this right because his ideal Republic is necessarily just,
and therefore sovereignty is essentially inalienable.

This last claim is doubtful. For, as stated above, if the
general will is concretely determined by the will of the
majority, there is always a danger that the will of the
majority, and thus the general will, will not be just,
and that the majority will eventually tyrannize the
minority. Rousseau might counter by claiming that if
the will of the majority is not just, then it is not the
general will, since this is always necessarily just. Yet
if the only empirical test we have to determine the
content of the general will is the will of the majority,
then what will prevent this will from being recognized
as having the moral and legal imperativeness of the
general will? I do not think Rousseau presents a satisfactory answer to this question.

Colletti is partially right, I believe, when he argues
that Rousseau's political theory leads to "the abolition
or withering away of the State."[47] There are two other
possibilities. Rousseau's political theory might also lead
to the tyranny of the majority over the minority, and to
legal anarchism.

The withering away of the state is possible because,
according to Rousseau, even though there is a distinction between the citizens and their government, the
citizens have an inalienable right to enact the laws by
which they will be ruled. Hence, they also have the
right to appoint or dismiss their government. Nonetheless, he recognizes the need of government as an executive agency to administer the laws enacted by the
sovereign. For Rousseau legislation is a function of
sovereignty rather than government, which has only
executive and judicial functions.

The tyranny of the majority is possible because if the
general will is concretely determined by the will of the
majority, as Rousseau argues, there is always the possibility that the majority might end up imposing its
views on the minority. But no matter what the majority
decides, it can never rightly suppress the rights of the
minority to express its views and to vote. If the majority tries to do so, the social contract is violated and the
minority ceases to be obliged by it.

Legal anarchism is the least probable of the three, but
there is always the remote possibility that it might occur:
since the citizens have the right to enact laws, they
may start enacting and abolishing too many of them
too often thus creating a feeling of insecurity and frustration among themselves. If this were to happen, it
would bring about, as Otto Gierke indicates, "a com-

plete annihilation of the idea of the constitutional state."

Rousseau's notion of the social contract is extremely important for his political philosophy for, like Locke, he grounds political obligation on the principle of consent. Thus, for Rousseau, the citizens are politically obliged to obey the law so long as the terms of the contract are observed: (1) the citizens are equally allowed to express their views publicly, and (2) they are equally allowed to vote in order to determine the content of the *general will.* It is clear in Rousseau's political philosophy that the citizens have an inalienable right to decide whom they are going to obey and the rules they are going to follow. If a citizen or a group of citizens violates this right by attempting to impose his views on the rest of society without their prior consent, the social pact is broken and the people are no longer obliged to abide by it. Whether the notion of the *social contract* can in fact justify *political obligation* remains to be seen.

At least three immediate objections can be raised against Rousseau's notion of *consent,* and since the *social contract* depends upon the latter notion, these objections will apply to it as well. First, Rousseau's notion of consent is hypothetical, and hypothetical consent is not actual consent and thus no consent at all. Second, even assuming citizens at some point in time consent to abide by the *general will,* it does not follow that, under different conditions, they will continue to consent to abide by it. Third, to claim that when citizens refuse to abide by the *general will* society, by punishing them, is *"forcing them to be free"* is simply to leave the door open for justifying coercion disguised as freedom. Punishment always constitutes an infringement of freedom, and since, regardless of what Rousseau says, the general will is always concretely determined by the will of the majority, nothing and nobody can prevent the majority from imposing its views on others by appealing to the idea of a so-called higher freedom.

Notes

[1] C. B. Macpherson, *The Political Theory of Possessive Individualism,* 8th ed. (1962; rpt., Oxford: Oxford Univ. Press, 1979), p. 3.

[2] See Stephen Ellenburg, *Rousseau's Political Philosophy* (Ithaca: Cornell Univ. Press, 1976).

[3] Jean-Jacques Rousseau, *Discourse on the Origin of Inequality (Second Discourse),* in *On the Social Contract,* trans. Donald A. Cress (Indianapolls: Hackett, 1983), p. 113.

[4] Ramon M. Lemos, *Rousseau's Political Philosophy* (Athens: University of Georgia Press, 1977), p. 6.

[5] *Second Discourse,* p. 118.

[6] Ibid., pp. 118-19.

[7] John Plamenatz, *Man and Society,* I (New York: McGraw Hill, 1963), pp. 374-75.

[8] *Second Discourse,* p. 125.

[9] Maurice Cranston, *Jean-Jacques* (New York: W. W. Norton, 1983), p. 295.

[10] Thomas Hobbes, *Leviathan* (New York: E. P. Dutton, 1950), p. 105.

[11] *Second Discourse,* p. 115.

[12] Ibid., p. 135.

[13] Ibid., p. 145.

[14] Ibid., p. 140.

[15] Ibid., p. 138.

[16] Ibid., p. 147.

[17] Jean-Jacques Rousseau, *Discourse on Political Economy,* in *On the Social Contract,* p. 176.

[18] *Second Discourse,* p. 157-58.

[19] *Political Economy,* p. 179.

[20] Jean-Jacques Rousseau, *The Social Contract,* ed. Lester G. Crocker (New York: Washington Square Press, 1967), p. 55.

[21] Ibid.

[22] Ibid., p. 26.

[23] *Second Discourse,* p. 150.

[24] Iring Fetscher, "Rousseau's Concept of Freedom in the Light of his Philosophy of History," in *Nomos IV: Liberty,* ed. Carl J. Friedrich (New York: Atherton Press, 1962), p. 37.

[25] *The Social Contract,* p. 5.

[26] Ibid., pp. 17-18.

[27] Ibid., p. 22.

[28] Ibid., p. 23.

[29] Ibid., pp. 22-23.

[30] Jean-Jacques Rousseau, "Letters from the Mountain," in *Man and Society* by John Plamenatz, vol. 1 (New York: McGraw-Hill, 1963), p. 402.

[31] *The Social Contract,* pp. 18-19.

[32] "Rousseau's Concept of Freedom in the Light of his Philosophy of History," p. 42.

[33] Ibid., p. 51.

[34] "Political Economy," p. 171.

[35] Ibid., p. 176.

[36] Lucio Colletti, *From Rousseau to Lenin,* trans. John Merrington and Judith White (New York: Monthly Review Press, 1974), p. 152.

[37] *The Social Contract*, p. 18.

[38] *Second Discourse*, p. 154.

[39] *The Social Contract*, pp. 12-13.

[40] *From Rousseau to Lenin*, p. 183.

[41] *The Social Contract*, p. 20.

[42] Ibid., p. 106.

[43] Otto Gierke, *Natural Law and the Theory of Society*, I, trans. Ernest Barker (London: Cambridge Univ. Press, 1934), p. 150.

[44] *The Social Contract*, p. 40.

[45] Ibid., p. 21.

[46] Ibid., pp. 112-13.

[47] *From Rousseau to Lenin*, p. 184.

Daniel E. Cullen (essay date 1993)

SOURCE: "The Achievement of Democratic Freedom," in *Freedom in Rousseau's Political Philosophy,* Northern Illinois University Press, 1993, pp. 70-116.

[*In the following excerpt, Cullen analyzes Rousseau's concept of "negative" (in the state of Nature) liberty and its relationship to democracy.*]

Are free relations possible? Can the avoidance of personal dependence characteristic of solitude somehow be imported into community? Rousseau's political thought is devoted to finding a form of association that avoids the inherent tendency of social relations toward domination and submission; its project is negative in that political relations are regarded as defensive relations designed to protect citizens from mutual domination.

Rousseau indicates that freedom might be susceptible to a political form, that there are circumstances in which freedom, nature, citizenship, and virtue might be compatible.

> There are two sorts of dependence: dependence on things, which is from nature; dependence on men, which is from society. Dependence on things, since it has no morality, is in no way detrimental to freedom and engenders no vices. Dependence on men, since it is without order, engenders all the vices, and by it, master and slave are mutually corrupted. If there is any means of remedying this ill in society, it is to substitute law for man and to arm the general wills with a real strength superior to the action of every particular will. If the laws of nations could, like those of nature, have an inflexibility that no human force could ever conquer, dependence on men would then become dependence on things again; in the republic all of the advantages of the natural state would be united with those of the civil state, and freedom which keeps man exempt from vices would be joined to morality which raises him to virtue.[1]

Democratic freedom will involve putting the laws above men, a problem that Rousseau likens to squaring the circle.[2] While a free society can be based only on the will of its members, the latter must will what is right if the conditions of freedom are to be maintained. The people must freely will the kind of yoke that alone may guarantee them against dependence on men. But the achievement of the condition of freedom will be the work of wisdom rather than of will. Rousseau describes putting the laws above men as a suprahuman task, by definition beyond the capacity of a self-governing people.

THE LAST STAGE OF THE STATE OF NATURE

From the origin of man and natural freedom, we turn to the origin of political society and civil freedom. Rousseau describes how men have become what they are before turning to the legitimate principles of right. Understanding that process discloses the obstacles to the establishment of a community of right by revealing what the people must be in order to live according to its principles.

The rupture of the natural condition is coeval with the disequilibrium of power and need that renders the individual dependent on others. Rousseau assumes human development to have reached a point where self-preservation compels men to unite; but in becoming dependent, they remain selfish and uncooperative. In a chapter of the **Geneva Manuscript** that was omitted from the **Social Contract,** Rousseau depicts the unsociability of men as radically as possible, thereby underlining what it means to "take men as they are" as the elements of a new association: "Our needs bring us together in proportion as our passions divide us, and the more we become enemies of our fellow men, the less we can do without them. Such are the first bonds of general society."[3] This fortuitous combination of "Hobbesian" individuals, generated by mutual need rather than by right, is wholly disordered.

> This new order of things gives rise to a multitude of relationships lacking order, regulation and stability, which men alter and change continually— a hundred working to destroy them for one working to establish them. And since the relative existence of man in the state of nature in this later stage is dependent on a thousand continually changing relationships, he can never be sure of being the same for two moments in his life.[4]

From an individual who is entirely for himself, who acts on fixed and invariable principles, man becomes a relative and inconstant being, dependent and miserable. The kind of society that mutual need engenders aggravates this condition, and man "finally perishes as a victim of the deceptive union from which he expected happiness."[5]

In Rousseau's analysis of the last stage of the state of nature, a new dimension of natural freedom comes to light. By the "natural order of things" Rousseau now means a condition that is social (dependent) but pre-civil. In one sense, freedom has simply been lost and men are entangled in the relations of domination occasioned by *amour-propre*. But since the mutual subjection of slaves and masters is devoid of legitimacy, men retain natural freedom in the sense that they have not given up their power and discretion to provide for their needs.[6] Still, natural freedom has ceased to mean independence based on isolation. Men retain their diverse quotients of power, but the latter is no longer in harmony with needs. Consequently, they find themselves in a vicious dilemma. Need exceeds individual power, compelling the assistance of others; but the latter corrupts and degrades by generating relations of "masters and slaves."[7] The final stage of the state of nature resembles the Hobbesian war of all against all.[8]

In the **Social Contract,** Rousseau initially confines the "inconvenience" of the state of nature to the proliferation of obstacles to self-preservation and the inadequacy of individual power to surmount them. The problem is couched in terms of social physics:

> I assume that men have reached the point where obstacles to their self-preservation in the state of nature prevail by their resistance over the forces each individual can use to maintain himself in that state. Then that primitive state can no longer subsist and the human race would perish if it did not change its way of life.

> Now since men cannot engender new forces, but merely unite and direct existing ones, they have no other means of self-preservation except to form, by aggregation, a sum of forces that can prevail over the resistance; set them to work by a single motivation; and make them act in concert.[9]

Now one might imagine a solution to the problem of preservation that did not require the union of forces to have a *single* motivation. That was the very point of Adam Smith's famous dictum that the butcher and baker work to someone else's advantage while being wholly uninterested in his well-being. But while Rousseau appreciates the ingenuity of asocial sociability, he condemns it for cementing a system of dependence that is spiritually debilitating. His exposition of the social contract is unique in its concern to exclude personal dependence in the new, civil mode of being.[10]

THE TUG-OF-WAR BETWEEN NATURE AND RIGHT

In a situation where each individual sees his maximum advantage in others' adhering to the law while he remains free of obligation, there appears to be no hope that the common good might prevail against particular interest.[11] Contradicting the dominant thought of his time, Rousseau suggests that interest is a principle of separation rather than of union.[12] Their disorderly evolution away from the pure state of nature leaves men competing in a zero-sum game. "The reason of each individual dictates to him maxims directly contrary to those that public reason preaches to the body of society, and . . . each man finds his profit in the misfortune of others."[13]

Outside the pure natural condition, the "state of things" or the "new order of things" puts men at cross-purposes.[14] No collection of such beings can be a community, and no mere sum of their interests can constitute a common good. "There are a thousand ways to bring men together; there is only one way to unite them."[15] An aggregation is not a viable political form, because the interest of each remains separate. "It has neither public good nor body politic."[16] Establishing civil association would appear to be an insoluble problem.[17] The qualities of men as they are in the final stage of the state of nature seem inimical to a common good. Rousseau keeps those dangerous propensities before our eyes:

> Indeed, each individual can, as a man, have a private

will contrary to or differing from the general will he has as a citizen. His private interest can speak to him quite differently from the common interest. His absolute and naturally independent existence can bring him to view what he owes the common cause as a free contribution, the loss of which will harm others less than its payment burdens him. And considering the moral person of the State as an imaginary being because it is not a man, he might wish to enjoy the rights of the citizen without fulfilling the duties of a subject, an injustice whose spread would cause the ruin of the body politic.[18]

In his critique of Diderot's understanding of natural right, Rousseau offers a stark portrayal of the problem of social cooperation. Diderot had argued that the existence of natural right was evident to any reflective person, although its precise determination might be elusive. Because the "general will" was "a pure act of understanding which reasons in the silence of the passions," the rules of natural right were accessible to any rational being. One who "refused to reason" would be guilty of "renouncing his human status" and would have to be regarded as a "denatured being."[19]

Rousseau replied that man's moral disposition is not, as Diderot supposed, a concomitant of his humanity. The consequence of man's natural asociality is that morality has no ground outside of society. Futhermore, while morality indeed implies that man consults his reason before heeding his inclinations, reason only directs him to seek his own good. Rousseau accepts Diderot's "violent reasoner" as the representative rational individual, and concludes that deliberation among such merely mirrors a recalcitrant egoism. Precisely so long as they listen only to their reason, men will fail to progress beyond considerations of private interest, to a common good.

> Even if the general will is determined by a pure act of the understanding which reasons in the silence of the passions about what man can demand of his kind . . . where is the man who can thus separate himself from himself? And if the concern for his own preservation is the first precept of nature, how can he be forced to look at the species in general, to impose on himself some duties whose connection with his own constitution he does not see in the least?[20]

Whereas Diderot spoke of natural right as the expression of a "general will" or, more precisely, a universal understanding that signified the needs and goods of all men everywhere, Rousseau spoke of "political right," which could only be the expression of the will of a particular political community.[21] Diderot believed that the general will could be discovered in the laws of "all nations." Rousseau insisted that a general will could only be attributed to this or that nation, for it is a will that one has in common with one's fellow *citizens* rather

than one's fellow men.[22] Morality is a political construct.

The way out of the final stage of the state of nature thus required a "new association" that would express the general will of a particular people, respect the *qualité d'homme* (defined as freedom rather than reason), and "denature" man into a citizen. Rousseau opposed Diderot's cosmopolitanism not out of a truculent misanthropy but on the basis of a superior political sense. The principles of political right must be rooted in a particular political context if they are to avoid the defect of natural law that is, in the final analysis, promulgated to no one: "It is only from the social order established among us that we derive ideas about the one we imagine. We conceive of the general society on the basis of our particular societies; the establishment of small republics makes us think about the large one, and we do not really begin to become men until after we have been citizens."[23] Rousseau anticipates Edmund Burke, who declared, in a celebrated phrase, that our first attachment is to "our little platoon."[24]

The *Social Contract* conceives a rapprochement between individual and general interest.

> The engagements that bind us to the social body are obligatory only because they are mutual, and their nature is such that in fulfilling them one cannot work for someone else without also working for oneself. Why is the general will always right and why do all constantly want the happiness of each, if not because there is no one who does not apply this word each to himself, and does not think of himself as he votes for all? Which proves that the equality of right, and the concept of justice it produces, are derived from each man's preference for himself and consequently from the nature of man.[25]

The play on the words "each" and "all" indicates that the social contract "cancels yet preserves" *amour de soi* in effecting the transition from individualism to social unity. But there is an important difference between the coincidence of individual and general interest and an identification of the two. At the beginning of the *Social Contract,* Rousseau insists that duty and interest not be divided. Since the great maxim of morality is "to avoid situations which put our duties in opposition to our interests," the terms of the contract must be acceptable to "men as they are," men with no prior disposition to duty.[26] The free will of precivil man is the exclusive source of right and the sole ground of civic obligation.[27] Each will consent to bind himself to authority only if it is manifestly in his interest, that is, if it conduces to his self-preservation and freedom.

Now "the total alienation of each associate, with all his rights, to the whole community" is not initially associated with an act of morality or virtue. As Rousseau first describes it, adherence to the contract appears to require nothing more of anyone than that he prefer himself.[28] On the basis of Rousseau's preliminary account, solidarity with the *moi commun* rests upon the coincidence rather than the identification of public and private interests. However, as long as the citizen secretly regards his own good, while ostensibly considering the good of the whole, he has not adopted a "civic disposition" and not achieved a general will. The fact that the political good is contingent upon a civic orientation is a grave defect that repeats the very flaw Rousseau criticized in the "bourgeois" social contracts, which left men with one foot in and one foot out of civil association.[29]

Rousseau initially suggests that the social contract has the internal resources to withstand a secret appeal to each individual's calculation: "It is so false that the social contract involves any true renunciation on the part of private individuals that their situation, by the effect of this contract, is actually preferable to what it was beforehand."[30] Each contractor (who has not surrendered his independent reason) will presumably recognize that the social pact is an advantageous bargain. This scenario is subsequently revealed to be facile.

To accomplish its purpose, the social contract must "lift" its adherents to a new plane that transcends the calculation of interest. It aims to integrate the individual into a community, to change the perspective of "each" to that of "us." Rousseau hints at the magnitude of this change in describing the social order in terms of "sacred right," but, as we shall see, its full significance emerges only gradually and in response to an inherent dilemma of the social contract.[31]

The political community is a new order of right in which individuals no longer relate to each other qua individuals. Each part must "act for an end that is general and relative to the whole."[32] As Rousseau puts it: "Instantly, in place of the private person of each contracting party, this act of association produces a moral and collective body, composed of as many members as there are voices in the assembly, which receives from this same act its unity, its common *self*, its life and its will."[33]

The social contract gives birth to a "moral being," with qualities separate and distinct from the natural beings who constitute it.[34] As the operative principles of the *moi commun* are elaborated, it becomes clear that a new *identity* is in the making: "The general will, to be truly such, should be general in its object as well as in its essence; . . . it should come from all and apply to all; and . . . it loses its natural rectitude when it is directed toward any individual, determinate object. Because then, judging by what is foreign to us, we have no true principle of equity to guide us."[35] Citizens are now so far removed from their antecedent individ-

ualism that partiality toward individual interests is deemed alien to their (collective) judgment: it has become "foreign to us."[36] Such is the goal of the juridical community that would repair the defects in the natural order of things.

THE LOGIC OF CIVIL ASSOCIATION

Since they are compelled to establish a common power over themselves, and since there exists no natural basis for authority, nor even any predisposition toward social life, men will consent only to a form of association that leaves each as free as he was before. However, the pact of association involves the total alienation of each associate (with all his rights and powers) to the whole community. In what sense could this leave the individual free?

The peculiarity of Rousseau's contractual formula stems from the requirement that it reconcile individual and common good while avoiding *personal relations:*

> This formula shows that the act of association includes a reciprocal engagement between the public and private individuals, and that each individual, contracting with himself so to speak, finds that he is doubly engaged, namely toward private individuals as a member of the sovereign and toward the sovereign as a member of the State.[37]

The contract is not an ensemble of mutual obligations one with another, but a form of contract with oneself. When "each unites with all," mutual relations are superseded by an exclusive relation of each part to the whole.[38] Political relations are such that "each" encounters "all," but never "another," and so the individual preserves his independence in the very act of association.[39] Each contractor considers himself in the relation of sovereign to individuals, or as subject to sovereign, but never as one individual toward another. For his own emphatic reason, Rousseau insists on the liberal-democratic principle of a government of laws and not of men. The fundamental purpose of civil association is to escape the evil of personal dependence, to restore the condition of natural freedom.

We may now appreciate the sense in which the social contract might fulfill the mandate to reconcile what right permits with what interest prescribes.[40] On the level of *right* (as opposed to "the natural order of things"), the gulf between private and general interest can be bridged: "The Sovereign, formed solely by the private individuals composing it, does not and cannot have any interest contrary to theirs."[41] The tie that binds individual and public is so tight that the citizen may regard the *moi commun* as his own self writ large. Since sovereignty is deemed to be fully compatible with the concern for self-preservation, and since it guarantees freedom from individual rulers, it can be said to restore the principal features of the natural condition.

But whereas the precivil mode of being was individualized, civil life must be socialized so that the common force has a single source and a single end. Only in this way can each individual, though uniting with all, obey only himself and remain as free as he was before.[42] As Rousseau put it in the *Second Discourse,* "It is the fundamental maxim of all political right, that peoples have given themselves chiefs to defend their freedom and not to enslave themselves."[43] If the purpose of civil association were merely utilitarian, the union of individual powers would not need to be absolute. One might, for instance, acquire in ad hoc fashion whatever assistance one needed under some market arrangement.[44] However, in Rousseau's scheme, civil man must ascend to the plane of right if the tendency of *amour-propre* toward competition and domination (in a struggle for personal recognition) is to be forestalled. Existence on this level requires that a new disposition arise, one capable of adding force to "public reason." *Amour-propre* itself will have to be modified so that it attaches rather than detaches "men as they are."[45]

THE GENERAL WILL

The logic of Rousseau's demand for the total alienation of the individual to the *entire* community emerges once the general will is understood to fulfill the structural requirements of natural freedom in a new form. Rousseau describes the general will sometimes as a will to generalize on the part of the individual who, as a natural being, may have a particular or private will, and sometimes as the predicate of a collectivity with a "moral personality."[46] The general will is presented as both the subject and the object of political activity. In the first instance, the general will is an attribute of the individual as a newly constituted moral subject.[47] In the second instance, the general will is the outcome of a process of voting subject to certain strictures.[48]

Rousseau portrays the social problem arising out of the destruction or corruption of the natural. The *Second Discourse* employs the myth of the statue of Glaucus to suggest that the original human soul has been so altered by society's effects ("a thousand continually renewed causes") that man no longer acts by "fixed and invariable principles."[49] But in submitting to "the supreme direction of the general will," men may once again act according to a fixed and invariable principle, and recapture their original "constancy" as *citizens*. As Rousseau explains, the general will is "toujours droite"; if one follows it, rather than the variable principle of particular interest, one will always act rightly.[50] When all submit to the direction of the general will, society will be governed exclusively on the basis of the common good.[51]

Rousseau juxtaposes the particular and general wills, emphasizing the latter's superior constancy: "The order of human things is subject to so many revolutions, and ways of thinking as well as ways of being changed so easily, that it would be foolhardy to affirm that one particular will, will want tomorrow what one wants today; and if the general will is less subject to this inconstancy, nothing can protect the private will from it."[52] Because the citizen's good is bound up with the good of the *moi commun,* the general will becomes his pole star. It is "always right and always tends toward the public utility," which is to say, "the most general will is always the most just."[53] The general will may be regarded as a collectivized form of *amour de soi.*[54] Like the latter, the general will is "always constant, unalterable, and pure."[55]

Through the social contract, the citizen exchanges one "fixed and invariable principle" for another.[56] Thus "the remarkable change" produced by the transition from the final stage of the state of nature to the civil state nevertheless preserves an important feature of the *original* natural condition.[57] Before the contract, the individual is exclusively self-regarding and merely follows his desires; after the contract, he is "forced to act upon other principles and to consult his reason before heeding his inclinations."[58]

The reference to force must be put in context. Rousseau means that the individual qua contractor chooses to submit to a new necessity, to act according to a new principle. Whereas natural man was immediately dependent on nature (and thereby independent of men), civil man must bring his immediate desires into agreement with the artificial necessity of laws to regain that independence. Since his particular interests and desires have unnaturally proliferated, and now subject him to the will of others, only adherence to law enables him to avoid such private constraints. As we have seen, in Rousseau's mind necessity is not inimical to human freedom so long as it excludes all traces of personal oppression. Accordingly, Rousseau envisions an equal subordination, on the plane of right, to the general will that restores individuals to the same footing they enjoyed in the natural condition. In the words of Eric Weil, "The general will is, in this sense, nature recovered, the human cosmos in whose bosom the individual is free."[59]

The order of right reflects the natural condition of freedom and equality. Each individual wills that order in willing the general, in submerging his particular interests and desires, in acting as "an indivisible part of the whole."[60] The general will is "toujours droite" because it is the expression of a community that exists *by right.* It can be declared only by citizens who regard themselves as members of a collective body, never by individuals who define their good "idiosyncratically." According to the logic of principles of right, the sovereign "by the sole fact of being, is always what it ought to be."[61]

Patrick Riley has argued that a general will is a philosophical and psychological contradiction in terms: "Will is a conception understandable, if at all, only in terms of individual actions."[62] Rousseau does suggest that will can be predicated of collective entities: the general will is "the will of the people as a body."[63] At the same time, the general will can be expressed only if "each citizen gives only his own opinion."[64] Rousseau himself certainly did not perceive a contradiction in the simultaneous attribution of the general will to the individual and to the collective, for he regarded it as a positive virtue: "Why is the general will always right and why do all constantly want the happiness of each, if not because there is not one who does not apply this word *each* to himself, and does not think of himself as he votes for all?"[65]

One purpose of the social contract is to blur the distinction between individual and collective altogether.[66] Hence, when Rousseau states that the general will must be general in its essence or source, he plays on the latter's ambiguity: "It should come from all to apply to all."[67] He might as well have said, "It should come from each and apply to all." If we resort to the "expansiveness" of moral freedom at this juncture, we can, I think, account for the ambiguities surrounding the "authorization" of the general will.

Riley's chief objection to Rousseau's formulation is that it requires the object of the will to be general ("will must take the form of general laws"), whereas "will tends to the particular."[68] However, Rousseau does not say that will *simpliciter* tends toward the particular but, rather, that "The particular will tends by its nature to preferences, and the general will tends by its nature to equality."[69] Or again, "Indeed each individual can, as a man, have a private will contrary to or differing from the general will he has as a citizen."[70] The former will emanates from the individual's "absolute and naturally independent existence"; but the transformation that civil man undergoes invests him with a "moral existence," and the latter is the source of his general will, manifested in his capacity for moral freedom.[71] Rousseau later distinguishes no fewer than three "essentially different" wills in the person of the magistrate.

> First the individual's own will, which tends only toward his private advantage. Second, the common will of the magistrates, which relates uniquely to the advantage of the prince; which may be called the corporate will, and is general in relation to the government and private in relation to the State, of which the government is a part. The will of the people or the sovereign will, which is general both in relation to the State considered as the whole and in relation to the government considered as part of the whole.

> In perfect legislation, the private or individual will should be null; the corporate will of the government very subordinate; and consequently the general or sovereign will always dominant and the unique rule of all the others.[72]

As Rousseau observed in the *Political Economy,* all private individuals who constitute the political association may also be members of other, partial associations: "A given man can be a pious priest, or a brave soldier, or a zealous lawyer, and a bad citizen."[73] Conversely, the good citizen suppresses his possible particular wills when they might conflict with his general will. He cleaves to the civic identity, which is impersonal and general: "Several men together . . . [must] consider themselves to be a single body, so that they have only a single will, which relates to their common preservation and the general welfare."[74]

On the whole, the *Social Contract* is indeed more concerned with the object of the general will than with its source, because Rousseau is after a defense mechanism rather than a positive mode of "agency." In the apt formulation of Judith Shklar, Rousseau conceives "a politics of prevention." The object of the will must be general—the general will must never apply to individuals—to accomplish the condition of negative freedom.[75] To summarize: Each individual, by generalizing his will, prescribes the law to himself and obeys only himself in an act of moral freedom. As a citizen and member of the sovereign, he is free in adhering to the general will because the latter can be said to be his own. His individual will qua citizen blends into the single will of the whole.

SOVEREIGNTY OF THE PEOPLE

The *Social Contract* bears the subtitle *Principles of Political Right*. The goal is a community of right, rather than an association that is permanently challenged by the assertion of prepolitical rights. Herein lies the important difference between the Rousseauian and Hobbesian contracts. From Rousseau's perspective, Hobbesian civil society accomplishes nothing. It is both informed and limited by the right of the individual to self-preservation; but that right has no place inside the state so long as the sovereign maintains internal peace. In Hobbes's scheme, the people alienate their sovereignty for the sake of peace and prosperity; but the political consequence is merely the "neutralization of the war of all against all" rather than the institution of right.[76] Right is only residual, an ultimate limit to a public order resting on force; there is no *relation of right* between the people and the sovereign.

Rousseau reconceives the form and purpose of sovereignty by attributing it to the people themselves and by barring its transfer to an agent. Hobbes acknowledged that the union of the people's wills was the legitimate basis of the civil order, but he thought that it could be "sure" only if the united popular will was alienated to a monarch. For Rousseau, sovereignty cannot be alienated from a collective to an individual, because while the former is only a moral being, the latter must remain a natural being. Sovereignty "consists in the general will, and the will cannot be represented."[77] The significance of Rousseau's refusal to countenance such a transfer is that sovereignty no longer authorizes the domination of a monarch, but serves instead as the foundation of popular freedom. The revised purpose of sovereignty is to call into being a new (social) existence *in right* by confining human relations to relations *of right*. With Rousseau, the function of sovereignty shifts from being the principle of differentiation within the body politic to the principle that defends against differentiation: "The sovereign knows only the nation as a body and makes no distinctions between any of those who compose it. What really is an act of sovereignty then? It is not a convention between a superior and an inferior, but a convention between the whole body and each of its members."[78] The political condition of freedom joins the force of sovereignty to the freedom of the people, so that "they obey and no one commands, that they serve and have no master, and are all the freer, in fact, because under what appears as subjugation, no one loses any of his freedom except what would harm the freedom of another."[79] In relations of right, equality guarantees that sovereignty remains a principle of freedom rather than domination; political freedom will be egalitarian or democratic.

Rousseau's turn to *popular* sovereignty also underscores his abiding concern for negative freedom, for the avoidance of subjection to alien rule. In attributing sovereignty to the people collectively, Rousseau revises the traditional conception of sovereignty as a relation of ruler and ruled; as a consequence, he rigorously distinguishes sovereignty and government.[80] The sovereign must never govern, because government involves administration or the cognizance of particulars, with the attendant threat of personal domination. To the criticism that the individual is powerless before an absolute sovereign, Rousseau replies that the one thing sovereign authority cannot do is oppress individuals: "The general will . . . changes its nature when it has a particular object; and as a general will, it cannot pass judgement on either a man or a fact."[81] Indeed, the sovereign may not even punish one who has broken the social treaty.[82] The absolute authority of the sovereign is designed as a guarantee against dependence on others. In Rousseau's view, it is individual authority or "private government" that truly menaces individuals, whereas the force of the state preserves the freedom of its members.[83] Relations of right must be "enforced" because they establish only an artificial order that remains vulnerable to violation.

The absolutism of Rousseauian sovereignty is a corollary to the absolutizing of convention, which removes men from the last stage of the state of nature into new relations of right. No individual can be secure from the depredations of private power so long as some men remain in the state of nature while others are subject to the civil condition, or so long as all are only partly "civilized." It is the general and complete immersion in the civil order that prevents men from becoming wolves to one another.[84] Identification with the sovereign authority, and adherence to its legitimate commands, is the only way for men who have become social and desire to avoid mutual oppression to recoup their independence. The sovereign people create the law that obliges them, and they are related to one another only through that medium. Law is the regulative principle of human relations on the plane of right.[85]

The purpose of Rousseau's democratic constitution is to avoid oppression, but for that reason it cannot dispense with force. The social contract would be an ineffectual guarantee against *private* oppression (the ruthless politics of difference) if it did not include sanctions. Citizens are admonished only to keep their word, to abide by the terms of their own contract. That is the straightforward reasoning behind the notorious injunction that whoever refuses to obey the general will must be forced to be free. Rousseau means that such a person would be "compelled" to obey *his* will, qua citizen. Since it is his will, the recalcitrant individual continues to obey only himself; but he now regards himself *as citizen* and no longer as private man in his relations with others. These are, again, right or moral relations. By Rousseau's lights, the force-freedom paradox arises only because the civil condition may need to be reattuned to the original condition of independent relations; public force aims only to defend everyone against the failure of anyone to be moral, and so merely elaborates what membership in the community of right entails. [86] To force someone to be free is to pitchfork him into the condition of freedom on the civil plane. Rousseau believes that because this manifestly serves the individual's good, it is therefore not against his will. Let us turn next to the precise relation of morality and freedom in the context of defensive politics.

THE POLITICAL SIGNIFICANCE OF MORAL FREEDOM

If both natural and civil freedom appear to be negative, one might still expect moral freedom to involve a positive project, and to point to a mode of being that transcends the desire for independence. Yet moral freedom is auxiliary to civil freedom; it, too, serves the goal of independence. Moral freedom is defined as obedience to self-prescribed law.[87] The latter can refer only to general laws, which is to say, to expressions of a general will. In Rousseau's conception, a moral will is a general will, in contra-distinction to the particular will of a "natural" and independent being. When he remarks early in the **Social Contract** that "to take away man's freedom of will is to take away all morality from his actions," Rousseau does not mean that anything a man might freely will must be considered moral.[88] His point is negative and fundamentally political: there can be nothing legitimate about an act that represents a concession to sheer force, and no one can alienate his freedom to a master.

According to Rousseau, the height of immorality is to subject oneself to another. Only free conventions have moral weight.[89] When Rousseau finally considers how one's actions do acquire moral status, he reveals that morality is indeed conferred by the operation of will, but it is a will aimed exclusively at general objects. The "moralization" of man signifies his admission into a community of right that entails adherence to the general will on the part of each individual.[90]

Moral freedom does emphasize one aspect of the general will: its source, as opposed to its object. Moral freedom involves the stance of the individual toward his particular civil obligation. Here the question for the citizen is not so much, How can acts of the sovereign collective be confined to general rather than particular objects? but, rather, Will *I* prefer the general will I have as a citizen and moral being to the particular will I continue to have as a "natural person"? Moral freedom involves "mastery of self" in the sense of preferring the *moi commun* to the *moi particulier;* the moral conquest is the victory of one's *moi commun* in achieving the vantage point from which one can then prefer the general to the personal. It is an elaboration of Rousseau's understanding of political existence on the plane of right.

Seen in this light, moral freedom is a precondition of civil freedom. The latter requires that the individual choose to regard himself as part of the whole, or regard himself under a new aspect. Through the practice of moral freedom, the citizen reaffirms his original integration in the civil unity. Rousseau analyzes this dimension of contractual obligation in the following passage from **Political Economy:**

> If . . . men are trained early enough never to consider their persons except as related to the body of the State, and not to perceive their existence, so to speak, except as part of the State's, they will eventually come to identify themselves with this larger whole; to feel themselves to be members of the homeland; to love it with that delicate sentiment that any isolated man feels only for himself.[91]

Moral freedom aims at the achievement of an inner disposition modeled on that of *l'homme isolé,* who was independent outside the state. But the citizen can establish his independence only *within* the state on the basis of a polemical confrontation with his own *volonté particulier. L'homme isolé,* innocent and pure without effort because he lacks the corruption of social life, is the model for the citizen who must struggle to purge himself of the corruption that natural existence (in the last stage of the state of nature) threatens to import into civil existence. The "dualism" that menaced original man or *l'homme isolé* was that he would fall into social existence and become other-regarding; the dualism that menaces the citizen is that he will fall out of civic existence into a corrupt form of self-regardingness.

Civil freedom rests on the unique relation of the individual to the whole community and the consent of each to the supreme direction of the general will; but that relation, and that consent, assume a prior transformation in the relation of the individual to himself. If we unfold the concept of the general will, we discover that each individual must first prescribe it to himself. The general will emerges out of opposition to one's private and particular will.

Because the citizen never really sheds his natural and independent existence, and because "the private will tends by its nature toward preferences," moral freedom is a permanent political requirement. Preferences must be routinely examined and brought into conformity with equality, which is to say, the particular will must be generalized.[92] Rousseau indicates that this cannot be accomplished once and for all.[93] It is to the habit of self-scrutiny that Rousseau refers when he states that civil man is forced "to consult his reason before heeding his inclinations."[94]

Given Rousseau's fundamental assumptions about the goodness of the natural inclinations, as a stance toward oneself, the disciplinary act of moral freedom makes sense only as a means toward civil unity and civil freedom. The latter make possible the escape from the last stage of the state of nature, in which natural inclinations have become corrupt and disordered. Man must become "master of himself" because the victory against his particularity is a prolegomenon to rightful relations with others. The only moral will that concerns Rousseau is a general will; morality is inherently political. It provides no detachable ethics of individual conduct.[95]

I argued earlier that the Kantian perspective errs in construing the new imperative of moral freedom as a "higher will" that is somehow beyond the individual's good, or even at odds with his happiness. The "moralization" that the citizen undergoes, and that requires the suppression of particularity in his will, is understood by Rousseau to be in his interest as a member of a new association. To correctly appreciate the significance of Rousseauian moral freedom, instead of imagining a "higher self," we should picture a "larger self," the self "in association": a *moi commun.*

It is because Rousseau regards freedom in terms of a condition to be achieved that he subsumes moral freedom under political considerations. But then those very considerations come to overwhelm the activity of moral freedom itself. Because it is "a permanent political requirement," Rousseau seeks to *guarantee* the outcome of moral freedom, to do away with its contingency. As we shall see, this move becomes the recurrent tendency in Rousseau's political thinking.

"In order for the general will to be well expressed, it is . . . important that there be no partial society in the State, and that each citizen give only his own opinion."[96] As an instance of self-legislation, moral freedom required that law conform to a person's will or, more precisely, that each freely prefer the general to an exclusive preference of his own. Moral freedom appeared as a "moment" of political freedom in which the individual gives the law to himself "before" expressing it as part of the sovereign. Political freedom per se requires that the law express the will of everyone who belongs to the community. In expounding on that criterion, Rousseau introduces a new attribute of the good citizen: the "constant will."

Rousseau explicitly denies that the "natural individual" has a constant preference for the general will over his particular will. "Though it is not impossible for a private will to agree with the general will on a given point, it is impossible, at least, for this agreement to be lasting and unchanging"; hence the need for recurrent exhibitions of moral freedom.[97] Anticipating that at least some members of the community may find themselves at odds with the authoritative expression of the general will, Rousseau suggests that they remain free even while being forced to obey laws to which they have not consented. We are told that such members really have consented through their "constant will": "The citizen consents to all the laws, even to those passed against his will, and even to those that punish him when he dares to violate one of them. The constant will of all the members of the State is the general will, which makes them citizens and free."[98] This thought echoes the suggestion that an individual might be "forced to be free." On what grounds can Rousseau adduce a constant will to conform to the general will when he had denied such constancy in particular individuals?

Rousseau defends his conclusion by introducing a distinction between choice and discovery.

> When a law is proposed in the assembly of the people, what they are being asked is not precisely whether they approve or reject the proposal, but whether it does or does not conform to the general will which is their own. Each one expresses his opinion on this by voting, and the declaration of the general will is drawn from the counting of the votes. Therefore when the opinion contrary to mine prevails, that proves nothing except that I was mistaken, and what I thought to be the general will was not. If my private will had prevailed, I would have done something other than what I wanted. It is then that I would not have been free.[99]

The implict reasoning is that in the circumstances in which my particular will prevails, *I will not be in a condition of freedom* because I will have left the plane of right for the plane of "natural existence." In other words, the activity of moral freedom, which was to keep the individual from "relapsing" into the wrong existence, is now assumed. My mistaken choice is not a *moral* failure but merely an error that can be overlooked because my good has been accomplished by the majority decision. Once again the substitution of what is good for a person for what that person wills, signifies that Rousseau's goal is the reestablishment of a condition; the *agency* that brings it about becomes a subordinate matter.

The notion of a constant will derives from the distinction between a private will and a general will. As a member of the sovereign body, the citizen is asked only to express a general will. In the terms of our earlier account, the citizen is presumed to have made the moral determination to choose the general over the particular (one might say that he has made a "general determination"). The argument also trades on another previous point: "The general will alone can guide the forces of the State according to the end for which it was instituted, which is the common good."[100] Qua citizen, no individual wants his private will to dominate, because his interest is freedom, which can be secured only if the general will prevails exclusively.

> What really is an act of sovereignty then? It is not a convention between a superior and an inferior, but a convention between the body and each of its members. A convention is legitimate because it has the social contract as a basis; equitable, because it is common to all; useful, because it can have no other object than the general good; and solid, because it has the public force behind it. As long as subjects are subordinated only to such conventions, they do not obey anyone, but solely their own will.[101]

The latter phrase refers to the people's own general will. Such a will is constant in that, qua citizen, no one can want anything other than the general good, for that is his insurance against harm.[102] Rousseau can therefore maintain that "What generalizes the will is not so much the number of votes as the common interest that unites them."[103]

The common interest of each citizen is to avoid oppression, so there is really no objective disproportion between the individual good and the common good. Rousseau reasons from the perspective of the democratic citizen rather than of the free rider who seeks an advantage in every relation. The former's desire not to be oppressed gives him an interest in justice. The people desire only to be left alone.[104] Rousseau suggests that democratic man seeks equality because it guarantees freedom, whereas the powerful and the rich want exemptions from general rules because, for them, the pleasure of domination exceeds the desire for freedom.

But what of the occasion when some individuals mistake what the common interest requires? Rousseau anticipated that eventuality in the following passage from the **Geneva Manuscript**:

> But even if the bond of which I speak were as well established as possible, all the difficulties would not disappear. The works of men—always less perfect than those of nature—never go so directly toward their end. In politics as in mechanics one cannot avoid acting more weakly or more slowly, and losing force over time. The general will is rarely the will of all, and the public force is always less than the sum of the private forces, so that in the mechanism of the State there is an equivalent of friction in machines.[105]

The general will is not always the will of all because "the people's deliberations" are sometimes flawed.[106] Rousseau explains that while one always wants one's good, one does not always see it. The people's good is nonoppression, and the general will always serves it. But since the people are made of flesh and blood, they are prone to substitute their private wills for the general will, or to fail to properly generalize their private wills. Even if the latter converge, the "will of all" remains the mere sum of private wills and forfeits its "rightfulness."

Rousseau suggests that to desire to follow one's private will in the civil order is to forsake one's own interest and, so to speak, to confuse one mode of being with another. He repeatedly reminds us that the state is only a "moral being," and that its members remain private persons, "whose life and freedom are naturally independent of it."[107] But citizens must act *as if* they were "moral beings" with a general rather than a private will. The latter must now be viewed as a counterfeit relic of "natural independence," which has become "uncertain" and "precarious." Rousseau emphasizes the advantage in substituting the new "manner of existence" for the old by characterizing it as the exchange of independence for freedom. By the time civil relations have become necessary, man's "natural independence" no longer means his literal isolation, but merely his personal "right" and capacity to fend off others. That kind of independence no longer guarantees nonoppression, and thus no longer serves the individual's

good.[108]

The great danger now is that relations of right will be ruptured by men who want to do as they please on the civil plane. It seems to be Rousseau's thought that it is not enough to punish violations, to force recalcitrants to be moral. It is necessary that no real violations be found, that political recalcitrance and the moral failure it reflects be explained away as *errors*.

What can account for this strange insistence? A possible explanation emerges when we recall that all "works of men" (as opposed to the works of nature) are peculiarly vulnerable. Because they are merely conventions, the relations of right are fragile. Presumably, repeated ruptures by some will eventually erode the hard-won disposition of others to live justly. The civil condition would be shattered, and individuals would revert to the old form of relations, dominating where they can, submitting where they must. Apart from reasoning such as this, it is difficult to account for Rousseau's desire for unity (for an implicit unanimity) rather than a norm of generality that would punish or correct violations. The appeal to a "constant will" seems designed to preserve the fiction that there are no authentic violations, that all citizens have "good will" or pure intentions, even when they fail to choose the general. Rousseau appears to transmute the *actual* expression of a free will into the *assumption* of a constant will because the latter guarantees a condition of independence, whereas the former necessarily leaves it contingent.

In a passage from **Letters Written from the Mountain,** Rousseau sharply distinguished "independence" from "freedom," asserting that "these things are so different as to be mutually exclusive." This statement seems to undermine the thesis that Rousseau's "ideal" is the condition of independence. However, seen in the context of the transition from the *last* stage of the state of nature to the civil condition, the difficulty is resolved. For it is only when mankind has progressed to the point where civil association becomes necessary that freedom and independence (understood as following one's private will) are at odds. Rousseau elaborates as follows:

> When each person does as he pleases, he often does what displeases others, and that cannot be called a free condition. Freedom consists less in doing one's will than in not being subjected to the will of another; it consists further in not subjecting the will of another to our own. Whoever is a master cannot be free, and to rule is to obey. Your magistrates know that better than anyone, they who, like Otho, omit nothing servile in order to command. I would only regard as truly free a will which no one had the right to resist; in the common freedom no one has the right to do what the freedom of another forbids. Thus freedom without justice is a veritable contradiction; because however one looks at it,

everything prevents the execution of a disordered will.

> Therefore, there is no freedom without Laws, nor where anyone is above the Laws: even in the state of nature, man is free only because of the natural Law which commands everyone. A free people obeys, but it does not serve; it has leaders, but not masters; it obeys Laws, but it obeys only Laws and *it is by the force of Laws that it does not obey men* . . . In a word, freedom is always tied to the fate of Laws, it reigns or it perishes with them; I know of nothing more certain.[109]

These remarks show that political freedom does not represent an entirely new value for Rousseau. It is not really distinguishable from independence, so long as one bears in mind the latter's fundamental meaning of insulation from the will of others. In the context of legitimate civil society, it is accurate to say that freedom from oppression is made more secure, because formerly it had been a mere fact of existence, which became nullified in the last stage of the state of nature. Through the social contract, that fact is converted into a right that cannot be canceled under any circumstances.

The essential identity of independence and freedom is clearly indicated in the following passage from Book 2 of the **Social Contract**: "Each citizen is in a position of perfect independence from all the others and of excessive dependence upon the City. This is always achieved by the same means, because only the force of the State creates the freedom of its members."[110]

Civil freedom is a new *form* of independence. It consists not in the power to do what one pleases but in the condition of independence from the particular wills of others. As we saw above, this is how the democratic citizen defines his good. And it is in this light that Rousseau concludes that "The constant will of all the members of the State is the general will, which makes them citizens and free."[111]

THE SUPERIOR INDIVIDUAL

If the general will is a constant will, could it not be declared by an individual of superior constancy? Would not the declaration of the most virtuous citizen be the greatest safeguard of the integrity of the general will? Since there will always be friction in the political machine, since some citizens will inevitably either lose sight of their constant will or fail in their constancy, why rely on voting to discover the general will in each legislative situation? Granted that the general will alone should guide the forces of the state according to the ends of preservation and mutual independence, is it not a separate question as to who should declare it?[112]

Rousseau defends the inalienability of sovereignty by claiming that while a private will may sometimes agree with the general will, it is impossible for that agreement to be lasting.[113] The reason is that the two are different sorts of will which pertain to different "modes of being": the former to a "natural and independent existence," the latter to a civil and communal existence. In the very place where Rousseau concedes a crucial role in the polity for "superior intelligence," he explains why such a person is disqualified from ruling. The Legislator's task is to convert man's natural and independent existence into a moral existence.[114] But this artificer of the moral personality remains outside the moral horizon he creates; that is, *he* remains a natural, albeit superior, being. Rousseau understands sovereignty to be an attribute of moral beings exclusively, and he denies that moral personality can be predicated of an individual: "It is apparent . . . that the sovereign is by its nature only a moral person, that it has only an *abstract and collective* existence, and that the idea attributed to this word cannot be likened to that of a simple individual."[115]

Even assuming that the Legislator is the equivalent of Plato's philosopher-king, he cannot have any role *within* the polity. Rousseau insists that one who has authority over men should not have authority over laws; and, conversely, one who has authority over laws should not have authority over men. "Otherwise his laws, ministers of his passions, would often only perpetuate his injustices, and he could never avoid having private views alter the sanctity of his work."[116] Since he stands apart from the collective moral personality, even the superior individual remains someone whose good is not united with that of others. Although Rousseau imagined a "superior intelligence, who saw all of men's passions yet experienced none of them," he recognized that such a being's happiness was independent of the people's.[117] Such godlike indifference could never be a regular part of the polity; greatness of soul is incompatible with democratic equality.[118]

The people must have leaders who will, inevitably, exhibit the passions of men. The best of such leaders will be tied to the people by affection; but they should all be subordinate to the laws as well. Rousseau makes this point in distinguishing natural or paternal authority from magistracy:

> Although the functions of the father of a family and of the prince should be directed toward the same goal, the paths they take are so different, their duties and rights are so dissimilar, that one cannot confuse them without forming the most erroneous ideas about the principles of a society, and without making mistakes that are fatal to the human race. Indeed, while heeding nature's voice is the best advice a father can heed to fulfill his duties, for the magistrate it is a false guide, working continuously to separate him from his people. . . . To do what is right, the

former need only consult his heart; the latter becomes a traitor the moment he heeds his. Even his own reason should be suspect to him and he should follow only the public reason, which is the law.[119]

A correct understanding of the "principles of a society" excludes any authoritative individual expression of "the public reason" or, more precisely, the public will.[120] When it comes to securing the people against oppression, there is greater safety in numbers than in the virtuous self-restraint of a few. Hence Rousseau's skepticism about the superior man: "Even if one were to suppose that this man had existed and worn a crown, does reason allow the rule for governments to be established on a marvel?"[121]

Considerations of prudence aside, as a matter of right, Rousseau flatly denies that sovereignty is transferable: "The people itself cannot, even if it wanted to, divest itself of this incommunicable right, because according to the fundamental compact, only the general will obligates private individuals, and one can never be assured that a private will is in conformity with the general will until it has been submitted to a free vote of the people."[122]

If the ascription of sovereignty to an individual, even a superior one, is illegitimate, how can Rousseau defend the undeniable dependence of the sovereign people on the activity of the Legislator?[123] How can authority and will be reconciled? Rousseau's answer involves distinguishing dependence on the Legislator's wisdom from dependence on his will. While the latter would be destructive of democratic freedom, the former is not incompatible with it. The role of wisdom is to re-create the order within which freedom will be maintained. All of Rousseau's superior "artificers" (the Legislator, the tutor, Wolmar) are "ordinateurs."[124] The wisdom of the latter consists in knowing how to remain faithful to the standard of nature, even in unnatural circumstances; they strive to make their artificial constructions perfect after the model of nature.[125] Although the Legislator "denatures" citizens to fit them for "moral relations," he can be said to "renature" the civic milieu by restoring the order conducive to freedom.

THE PROBLEM OF SOCIAL UNITY

Rousseau's concern with wisdom or a superior intelligence reflects the conclusion he reached in his argument with Diderot about the essential incapacity of the individual to adopt a common or general perspective. That deficiency, we recall, was rooted in the relative power of reason and feeling. In another passage from the first version of the *Social Contract*, Rousseau elaborated on it:

Since the social union has a determinate object, its

fulfillment must be sought as soon as the union is formed. In order for each person to want to do what he ought to do according to the engagement of the social contract, each must know what it is that he ought to want. What he ought to want is the common good; what he ought to avoid is the public ill. But since the state has only an ideal and conventional existence, its members have no natural, common sensitivity by means of which they are promptly alerted to receive a pleasant impression from what is useful to it and a painful impression as soon as it is harmed.[126]

Citizenship has a foundation in reason by virtue of the legitimate principles of political right; but the reason of "men as they are" only reinforces the feeling of particularity. This problem left the social contract subject to contingency, which in turn led to Rousseau's elaboration of a new form of (civil) existence that might escape it. Relations of right are a solution for men as they are, but they must undergo a "remarkable change" in order to make the transition from a disordered social existence (in the last stage of the state of nature) to the new order of right.

The political condition to be achieved is clear: "As long as several men together consider themselves to be a single body, they have only a single will, which relates to their common preservation and the general welfare."[127] However, this corporate sensibility is a prodigious requirement that turns out to involve the "denaturation" of man by means of "public education." In the words of *Émile,* "Good social institutions are those that best know how to denature man, to take his absolute existence from him in order to give him a relative one and transport the 'I' into the common unity, with the result that each individual believes himself no longer one but a part of the unity and no longer feels except within the whole."[128]

The deep antagonism between the individual and society is the starting point of Rousseau's philosophy. As we have seen, he condemns not merely the injustice of this or that historical society but the social situation itself.[129] Nevertheless, for human beings in their present predicament, "everything is radically connected to politics."[130] It is because men's circumstances now require the perfection of the political order that Rousseau declares, "Everything that destroys social unity is worthless. All the institutions which put man in contradiction with himself are worthless."[131]

The latter point suggests that in the present condition, social unity and individual unity are linked. If Rousseau's principal concern is individual integrity, the latter now requires a seamless "integration" of the individual into the social whole.[132] Social unity must be perfected so that the individual experiences others only as part of the undifferentiated whole to which he also belongs. As in the state of nature, where the individual's life is consumed in the activity of *amour de soi,* there is no

"I-thou" relation in the perfected social state. The ego is fully integrated into a "moi commun," so that the "moi" imperceptibly becomes "nous." In a *perfect* metamorphosis, the utter self-regardingness of *amour de soi* would be collectivized without any rupture in the individual's consciousness of unity and independence. Civil man could avoid contradiction with himself so long as his ego was represented to him exclusively as a *moi commun*. The oblivion of otherness, which was characteristic of the natural order, is the extraordinary goal of Rousseau's political order. But the other to be avoided now includes a dimension of the self; in the civil condition, one's own particularity represents a threat no less than the particular wills of others. In Rousseau's considered judgment, the function of moral freedom is taken up by civic education, and the Legislator becomes the true artificer of the moral personality.[133]

While principles of right dictate that social contract be the indispensable foundation of political existence, contract does not by itself achieve the *perfection* of political order. We have seen that Rousseau's plan appears to hold out for nothing less. In conformity with the principles of political right, the perfection of generality must be *willed*, but Rousseau indicates that citizens will not freely choose the political remedy they desperately need. Notice that Rousseau does not say that "So long as men continue to submerge their particular wills and will only the general, they will have but a single will." That would imply that their community is, in the words of Renan, "a plebiscite every day," or that the community is indeed the ongoing project of a common will. Rousseau holds the opposite: men must regard themselves as a unified body *if* they are to have that will. The coming into being of community is not the effect of the unified will but its precondition. This fact is explicitly granted in the *Social Contract:*

> For a nascent people to feel [*sentir*] the great maxims of justice and the fundamental rules of statecraft, the effect would have to become the cause, the social spirit which must be the product of the founding would have to preside over the founding itself, and men would have to be prior to the laws that which they ought to become by means of them.[134]

It might be suggested that the foregoing dilemma is confined to the problem of a nascent people, that is, to the circumstances of founding alone. It might then follow that after certain minimum conditions were established, the people would develop the capacity to legislate the common good on the basis of their own deliberations. But for Rousseau, the problem of founding reflects the essential problem of politics as such. For justice and interest to be reconciled, the diversity or plurality of men (in which none sees beyond self-interest) must give way to a unity that apprehends a common good. But *individuals* reject the common good

even while seeing it, because understanding fails to move the will. The perfect political order can be conceived in theory, but its actualization depends on the denaturing art of the Legislator because man's "natural constitution" resists the disengagement of the self from its own particularity.

To be both legitimate and reliable, democracy must rest on contract and community. Rousseau's plan synthesizes a politics of obligation and a politics of solidarity, and strives to satisfy their respective imperatives. The requirement of solidarity arises from the inability of the rational will to lead each individual to choose on the basis of right (to will the general rather than particular interest), even though such a choice is both just and advantageous. On the level of right, the sovereign is always what it ought to be and the general will is always right; but men as they are must first ascend to that level. Rousseau is forced to confront the psychological obstacles to the community of right, and to consider how men as they are might be made to identify with the *moi commun*. In response to this problem he elaborates the politics of virtue.

THE POLITICS OF VIRTUE

As to the relation of virtue and civic education, the first thing to be said is that, for Rousseau, the polity does not exist for the promotion of virtue; rather, virtue exists for the sake of the polity. Virtue consists in putting the good of the whole before one's particular good; it aims at the same goal as the generalizing of one's will. Virtue involves a suppression of one's natural existence in favor of a different identity.[135] Rousseau took over from Montesquieu an understanding of civic virtue as a passion for self-renunciation.[136]

We recall that, initially, the social contract was to avoid any real renunciation.[137] To participate in the general will, the citizen was only to consult his reason.[138] But as the *Social Contract* unfolds, we learn that citizenship must have a foundation in the passions, and that the formation of citizens is a task not for principles of right but for political art. The intervention of the Legislator is required to denature men, to transform them from individuals who prefer themselves into members of a body who cannot conceive of themselves apart from it, to create "a larger whole from which [the] individual receives, in a sense, his life and his being."[139] This requirement is "concealed" in the original statement of the terms of the contract; it comes to light if we unfold the notion of "moral freedom," which Rousseau does not choose to do in the *Social Contract*. One reason for that hesitation may be that civic virtue is overtly problematical in a way that moral freedom was not. Virtue cannot be accounted for by the principles of political right, because citizens do not make themselves virtuous through an exercise of choice. Civic virtue is the work of the Legislator, and thus cannot be grounded in the civil constitution.[140] The denaturing of men into citizens who choose the common good involves educating or "conditioning" the will rather than expressing it. This requirement indicates the gulf between the legitimate and the reliable constitution of the state. To use more familiar language, the constitutional framework must be supported by a "political culture."[141]

Rousseau conceives civic education as a process that takes over the function and purpose of moral freedom in the operations of "political economy." "If it is good to know how to use men as they are, it is better still to make them what one needs them to be. The most absolute authority is that which penetrates to the inner man and is exerted no less on his will than on his actions. It is certain that people are in the long run what the government makes them."[142] The function of government extends beyond the execution of the sovereign will to encompass the formation of citizens inclined to will the common good. As we shall see, the activity of the Legislator is merely the first instance of a continuing "governmental" function devoted to strengthening the social tie.

Civic education is a disciplinary management of the passions, but one that emphatically does not involve the subordination of the passions to reason. The passions themselves are to be manipulated or redirected, by reconstituting their objects. As Émile's tutor declares: "One has a hold on the passions only by means of the passions. It is by their empire that their tyranny must be combatted; and it is always from nature itself that the proper instruments to regulate nature must be drawn."[143] Passion can be made to counteract passion. "Love of country can be more ardent than love of a mistress."[144] Once modified, *amour-propre* can become the foundation of civic virtue; its force can be harnessed for the common good.[145] A skillful manipulation of this passion can inspire enthusiasm for the laws.[146]

Rousseau was not the first to contemplate the management of the passions; Descartes had already indicated the path toward transforming virtue into a science of the passions.[147] But Rousseau advocates the kind of *dirigisme* that Michel Foucault would later associate with the "disciplinary society." Rousseau's regime resembles a *dirigiste* or plebiscitary democracy, with the twist that the citizen submits willingly, indeed *lovingly,* to discipline. The themes of **Poland, The First Discourse,** and Rousseau's meditations on civic virtue in general point to the disciplinary society as the sine qua non of democratic freedom:[148]

> Do you want the general will to be fulfilled? Make sure that all private wills are related to it; and since virtue is only this conformity of the private will to the general, to say the same thing briefly, make

virtue reign.

> If political theorists were less blinded by their ambition, they would see how impossible it is for any establishment whatever to function in the spirit of its institution if it is not directed in accordance with the law of duty.[149]

Civic virtue is not part of the legitimate constitution, but it is nevertheless in tune with its spirit. Without virtue, citizens will fail to regard themselves as a single body, and they will consequently lose the freedom guaranteed by the sovereignty of the general will.

The operation of civic education and the rule of virtue make what ought to be the *effect* of civil life become its *cause.* But must not free men be their own cause? This is the question mark left after moral freedom is absorbed by civic education. If the "moralization" of men is the effect of political economy or "governance" rather than of their own reason, does not civic virtue eclipse the freedom of the citizen altogether by superseding the function of the will?[150]

Rousseau's answer appears to be that civic education serves the free regime by protecting the sovereign will from the danger of its own contingency. In one sense the very purpose of civic education is to overcome the obstacle that sovereignty presents to the perfection of the disciplinary regime or, more generally, to reconcile will and order. Sovereignty by its nature inescapably weakens the force of the law. The yoke of the laws is a fiction, since the sovereign citizenry remains paramount to all laws, including the social contract; will is inherently threatening to order, and a disorderly or particular willfulness permanently threatens to rupture the relations of right that guarantee freedom. It is because Rousseau understands freedom as a condition of order rather than an agency that wills (always contingently) order into being that he emphasizes the stability of sovereignty over its activity. Rousseau's political economy imagines how to perfect *the illusion* of being bound by law, and finds the answer in attaching citizens to their country by their passions.[151] The goal is to bind the heart of the citizen with its own enthusiasm for the law, to exploit the spontaneity of the affections by directing *them* toward what ought to be the object of the will: the maintenance of civil order; the effect (allegiance) becomes the cause.

This conception is clearly at odds with the model of a citizenship understood as the exercise of rational will.[152] "Political economy" and "political right" constitute separate spheres. The latter concerns the legitimate foundations of political institutions, while the former concerns their artful design and operation. The tension between freedom and authority inheres in this distinction. The principles of political right make freedom the cause and the effect of political obligation. The contract is "the most voluntary act in the world," and leaves each contractor "as free as he was before." The ineluctable meaning of sovereignty is that men remain above the law. However, when Rousseau reflects on the requirements of political *order,* he finds that the best social order puts the law above men.[153] Civic virtue aims to resolve this dilemma by changing the perspective of men such that when they look up, they see the law they must obey as an inflexible necessity. Although his sovereignty is incontrovertible, the virtuous citizen regards the law as his master.

For Rousseau, obedience to law *enables* freedom: "the force of the State creates the freedom of its members." It is only the sovereignty of the general will that guarantees the citizen against all personal dependence. By causing the citizen to generalize his will, "by giving each citizen to the *patrie,*" civic virtue becomes the fence to freedom.[154]

Whereas rational or deliberative citizenship is legitimate, passionate citizenship is "sure." Without denying that citizens, by right, are masters of their laws, Rousseau argues that the practice of citizenship must nonetheless involve a passionate affirmation of the laws that seems incompatible with genuine choice. At stake, then, in this scheme is the conception of citizenship as a rational choice versus the product of spontaneous identification. Rousseau's hesitation about the capacity of reason to produce the remarkable change in man, his conviction about the primacy of the sentiments, his equivocation about the rank order of laws and *moeurs* as the regulative principles of civil relations—all these ambivalences can be traced to the difficulty of reconciling legitimacy and reliability, of perfecting political order. Genuine choice calls for the exercise of deliberation, but Rousseau regards the latter more as an opportunity to *undo* the general will than to express it.

Rousseau's perfected constitution thus entails a community of right and a parallel "community of the heart" which promotes political freedom by ensuring that the general will is not menaced by eruptions of partiality. In the democratic regime, strict fidelity to constitutional forms is one barrier to the "unforming" of the general will; but that formalism must be supplemented by a disposition of communal sentiment which transcends respect for formal procedures. The planes of right and fact must be joined in such a way that men as they are act *as if* they considered justice alone.

Rousseau elaborates on this requirement in his discussion of the Legislator and the character of the people. The relative existence of the citizen in the community of right, which is a relation only to a whole, is reiterated for the patriotic citizen through membership in a community of the heart. Political freedom is refracted in these two theoretically distinct but experientially united communities. Each fulfills a requirement of freedom (will and order), but on separate planes. This dualism accounts for the complexity of Rousseau's political formulas.[155]

THE TWO POLES OF DEMOCRATIC FREEDOM

In light of the dual imperatives informing the design of the free regime, two separate questions arise: What would the terms of a free association be? And what kind of government would be required to make men respect those conditions? We have seen how Rousseau struggles to conceive a reestablishment of freedom in a political condition, and we have tried to unravel his logic in articulating the operative assumptions of the sovereignty of the general will. The *Social Contract* strains even more, however, when it addresses the second question, for it concerns the issue of political economy or governance, which cannot be approached with the same directness and confidence as matters of political right.[156] One might say that the complete argument of the *Social Contract* evinces both a liberal concern for protecting individuals from oppression (albeit predicated on Rousseau's redefinition of the threat) and a conservative regard for the character of the people, but not out of an ambivalence concerning the relative merits of individualism and collectivism. Both concerns arise out of the present crisis of human affairs; their divergence bespeaks the underlying dilemma of human relations as such: men are not naturally suited for social relations.

Rousseau first grapples with the problem by casting the question of social relations in the precise terms of contract: What sort of contract will be legitimate and reliable from the standpoint of free men? This orientation signals what James Miller has called an "epochal transvaluation" of democracy. As Miller describes it, that transvaluation is rooted in a conviction that "all human beings possess, in their own free will, the capacity and the desire for goodness essential to govern themselves."[157] But Rousseau also problematizes that very assumption. Although the autonomy and integrity of the principles of political right (to say nothing of human beings themselves) would seem to be fatally compromised if their actualization required something beyond consent, Rousseau is persuaded of that requirement. He reveals that the social contract faces a communitarian imperative, which it cannot fulfill through the agency of contract alone. Legitimate principles of political right depend on a practice of virtue, which itself is without legitimate foundation.[158] Men require a certain education, a discipline of their opinions, passions, and interests, in order to be capable of respecting their contractual obligations. This requirement that the free regime be "governable" is not concealed in the *Social Contract,* but its full significance emerges belatedly. In the *Political Economy,* Rousseau acknowledged the need forthrightly:

The homeland cannot subsist without freedom, nor

freedom without virtue, nor virtue without citizens. You will have all these if you train citizens; without doing so, you will only have wicked slaves, beginning with the leaders of the State. Now training citizens is not accomplished in a day, and to have them as men they must be taught as children. Someone may tell me that anyone who has to govern men should not seek, outside of their nature, a perfection of which they are not capable; that he should not want to destroy their passions; and that the execution of such a project would not be any more desirable than it is possible. I will agree the more strongly with all this because a man who had no passions would certainly be a very bad citizen. But it must also be agreed that although men cannot be taught to love nothing, it is not impossible to teach them to love one thing rather than another, and what is truly beautiful rather than what is deformed. If, for example, they are trained early enough never to consider their persons except as related to the body of the State, and not to perceive their own existence, so to speak, except as part of the State's, they will eventually come to identify themselves in some way with this larger whole.[159]

In this seminal passage, Rousseau describes a synergy among political stability, freedom, and virtue. Citizenship is the key to freedom and stability of right. Recognition of the true principles of political right requires that political life be constituted on a foundation of reason and law rather than of force and violence, and the *Social Contract* offers a juridical doctrine which accomplishes precisely that. At the same time, reason and law must be supplemented by a force in the soul for which the principles of right do not account.

Citizens must be virtuous enough to prefer the common good to their particular good. In Rousseau's terminology, the virtuous citizen will be a good subject.[160] The suppression of private interest manifests itself in obedience to law, which becomes the emblem of the citizen's identification with the *moi commun*. Rousseau maintains that the citizen is simultaneously sovereign and subject.[161] But since sovereignty consists in the maintenance of the general will, dutiful obedience becomes the "effectual truth" of citizenship. The task of the citizen is not to participate in the steering of the general will from issue to issue but to identify with it. For this reason, the relation between the collective citizenry qua sovereign and the same collective qua subject is, in Starobinski's words, "almost narcissistic."[162]

Contract and community involve two separate and contradictory operations. Citizens must be denatured to accept the dictates of *droit politique,* and "renatured" to become members of a *patrie.* Although an austere stance toward oneself is required for the moral choice of the general against the particular, Rousseau's patriot will also be a citizen by inclination and passionate choice. Democratic freedom thus oscillates between the logics of legitimacy and reliability, vibrat-

ing here with forms of a legitimate constitution and there with the spontaneity of a community of feeling.[163] This variation might be unobjectionable were spontaneous feeling only a reinforcement of legitimate democratic procedures; but the former threatens to supplant the latter altogether by supplying the consensual unity that democratic procedures aim at but cannot guarantee.

The argument of the *Social Contract* consequently shifts from juridical to "sociological" considerations.[164] Whereas contract and community are initially portrayed as coeval, their simultaneity is later acknowledged to be fictitious. On the juridical level, members unite in an association of free and equal partners. But that association, to be a true community, must be rooted in a unity of feeling. The sovereignty of the general will is the first principle of political right, but the latter abstracts from what the people must be in order to express a unified will. Only contract can confer sovereignty, because civil association must be voluntary; however, only the Legislator's art can give rise to solidarity, without which sovereignty is unreliable.[165] Contract itself does not give rise to community.

THE PROMISE OF POLITICAL ART

Already in his early writings, Rousseau had indicated the usefulness of "political and moral researches." "The mind revolts," he wrote in the preface to the *Discourse on Inequality,* at "the violence and oppression of society."[166] Yet there was evidence that "All these vices belong not so much to man as to man badly governed."[167] "It is certain that peoples are in the long run what the Government makes them be." Indeed, Rousseau's plan for a comprehensive political teaching began from this conviction:

> I came to see that everything was connected radically to politics, and that however one took it, any people would only be what the nature of its government would make of it, thus this great question of the best possible government seemed to me to reduce itself to this. What is the nature of Government capable of forming a People, the most virtuous, the most enlightened, the wisest, and ultimately, the best, taking this word in its widest sense.[168]

These considerations suggested to Rousseau that men might be bound together in an association without succumbing to domination and servility. The *Social Contract* is an exploration of that possibility. It inquires whether men as they are can be united and subjected to authority, and yet remain free. But how is submission to authority compatible with freedom? Rousseau asked and answered this question in the first version of the *Social Contract:* "By what inconceivable art could the means have been found to subjugate men in order to make them free; . . . to bind their will by their own consent? . . . How can it be that all obey while none commands, that they serve and have no master? . . . These marvels are the work of the laws."[169]

Rousseau's proposed reconciliation of freedom and authority was already implied in his famous statement of the fundamental political problem: "Each one, uniting with all, nevertheless obeys only himself and remains as free as before."[170]

The act of identification with the whole is the means of reconciling the requirements of authority and freedom.[171] While Rousseau maintains the distinction between "participants" in authority and "subjects" of authority, he means to erase the distinction between one or some privileged members of the political association and others; the sovereign is no longer understood as someone apart from the people, and obedience no longer appears as submission to an alien will.[172] But this abolition of the traditional sovereign-subject separation is predicated on the unification of "each" to "all," which is fraught with difficulties.

The idiom of governability pervades Rousseau's discussion of what the people must be in order to bear the civil constitution of freedom. He refers to "subjection to laws," "discipline," "molding," overcoming the "centrifugal force" of each people, "the true yoke of the laws."[173] The physical nature of the task is exemplified in a military analogy: "For the time when the State is organized, like that when a battalion is formed, is the instant when the body is least capable of resisting and easiest to destroy."[174] The genesis of democracy is the creation of an identity, which may entail the destruction of the old. But, his forthright avowal of force notwithstanding, Rousseau's exemplary founding advances against minimal resistance. The people will be docile, passive, and accepting.[175] The force of the Legislator must be sufficient to create a new identity, but not so great as to break the free spirit of the people. Presumably, if the latter experience their subjection to law as a *painful* yoke, they may become either rebellious or slavish as a consequence. Rousseau suggests that the discipline of law is eased by the preexisting habits of communal identity, although this chronology would seem to lie outside real political time.[176] Together, law and communal character make a people free and governable.

GOVERNMENT

The foregoing considerations amply testify to Rousseau's clear-eyed appraisal of the political problem. A social contract is necessary to restore human beings to a condition of freedom, but men as they are, are disinclined to take contract seriously. Government, in the most comprehensive sense, is devoted to instilling that disposition. Is the cause of freedom betrayed by an overriding concern for the governability of democracy, for the inculcation of conservative habits? Rousseau challenges the dichotomy by conceiving (and implicitly justifying) civic virtue as the fence to freedom. The government or management of the people is dedicated to preserving a civic identity that is indispensable to the general will (that is its sole rationale); and it is only the mutual subordination to the supreme direction of the general will that guarantees each individual against all personal dependence.

However, this apology for authority does not yet render it safe. Beyond the founding activity of the Legislator, the need for ordinary government imports a dangerous inequality into real political time. While acknowledging its exigency, Rousseau wants to limit the inequality of the government and the governed, and, to some extent, disguise it. He is adamant that the institution of government in no way implies a pact of submission.[177] Government necessarily entails inequality, and Rousseau maintains that it can be legitimated only by consent. Government is only a device that the sovereign requires as a mediator of its relations with subjects, who are the same individuals considered under a different aspect.[178] Rousseau's model aims to avoid the subordination to government that characterized previous sovereign-subject relations. The evils of traditional politics stemmed from the confusion of government and sovereignty, a false connection that Rousseau severs. As a consequence, government fulfills a single function, regardless of its form.

On the basis of Rousseau's reinterpretation, the form of government is no longer a regime question, and governmental power is somewhat disguised by the impersonality of the rule of law. No one emphasized more than Rousseau the distinction between a government of laws and a government of men. The law embodies no other will than our own, and it guarantees us against personal dependence. But there remains the necessity for particular applications of general rules, which entail the exercise of power by a separate and distinct political body. Although the *Social Contract* evinces a superficial hostility to government, Rousseau does not flinch at what the governability of democracy may require. If things can be so arranged that *tout va tout seul* (everything goes of itself), if the people govern themselves through *moeurs* and right opinion, the weight of the laws will be light and the need for government diminished. On the other hand, Rousseau acknowledges that circumstances might require a period of dictatorship to repair the essential defects of a government of laws.[179]

The question of government is a matter of "social physics," and Rousseau precisely calculates the appropriate quotient of "strength" required for good government. Some readers may see in this exercise only an arcane enthusiasm for mathematics; but Rousseau's recondite discussion points up a fundamental issue.[180] The state is artificial, and consequently permanent vigilance must be exercised over the forces acting upon this "moral body." It turns out that numerous departures from direct democracy are required to preserve the free regime: the Legislator, fundamental law, formalism, tribunes, elective aristocratic government, a redesigned Roman Senate, censorship, civil religion— all of these devices (or their equivalents) may be necessary to the stability of democracy.

Rousseau's republicanism thus has a pronounced *conservative* strain. His vaunted radicalism stems from an insistence on legitimacy; however, his practical political proposals are crafted in response to the defect of political legitimacy. Consequently, Rousseau's model of popular participation is very much an exercise in "legitimation," in both its positive and pejorative senses. When it comes to the civil order, Rousseau is no anarchist, despite his essential objection to relations of rule. On the civil plane he condemns not government simply, but arbitrary and illegitimate government. His aim in books III-IV of the **Social Contract** is to show how institutional hierarchies can serve freedom rather than destroy it.

The complexity and ambivalence of Rousseau's thoughts on government derive from the vexatious problem that political inequality poses for legitimacy. His tendency is to portray inequalities as *hierarchies,* not to exacerbate their power but to mitigate it. Rousseau intuited that the sacred character of authority masks its occasional illegitimacy and softens its effect.[181] Masks are necessary insofar as the political problem is to get a free people "to obey with freedom and bear with docility the yoke of public felicity."[182] The basic dilemma is evident in the notion of "legitimate chains." Rousseau declares early in the **Social Contract** that "the social order is a sacred right," and later notes that founders are moved to attribute their wisdom to communication with the divine. In the **Poland,** Rousseau identifies Numa, who created Rome's religion, as Rome's true founder.[183] Although the fundamental legislative task is accomplished at the beginning, it must be continuously shored up: "A thousand situations for which the legislator has made no provision can arise."[184] Civil religion routinizes the activity of the Legislator, as does, to a lesser extent, the function of the Tribunate.[185] Democracy's need for civil religion is one of the most controversial aspects of Rousseau's political theory; but its rationale can be traced to the essential reliance of the free regime on authority. Rousseau proposes civil religion out of a sense that the power of the sacred could provide the "legitimate and surest way" to preserve the condition of democratic freedom.[186]

CONCLUSION

In Rousseau's account of civil association, the analytical task of elucidating the terms of the social contract gives way eventually to the managerial task of forming citizens who will take their contract seriously by submitting themselves to the supreme direction of the general will. The principles of political right themselves require a movement away from active or autonomous citizenship. Certainly Rousseau invests the democratic citizen with an unprecedented dignity; but at the same time, his role is carefully circumscribed and managed by a tutelary power.

I have suggested that Rousseauian freedom is ill understood as the activity of moral autonomy or self-realization, in the sense made popular by Kant. Rousseauian citizenship is similarly distorted when regarded as the *fons et origo* of participatory democracy. Rousseau's unique moral and political perspective is nicely captured in the following fragment from the **Project on the Corsican Constitution:** "I will not preach morality to them because sermons do not make one act. I will not order them to have the virtues, but I will *put them in such a position* that they will have the virtues without knowing the word; and they will be good and just without having to know what justice and goodness are."[187] Citizens will be good without knowing it, virtuous without virtue. In Rousseau's theory, virtue first appears as a way to achieve the condition of freedom at the cost of a devaluation of genuine willing, or freedom as agency. In the final reckoning, civic virtue itself depreciates.

As Rousseau thinks through the difficulties of a legitimate and reliable democratic freedom, his conception of citizenship declines from the activity of rational deliberation, to virtuous dedication to the common good, to patriotic enthusiasm for one's own. A comprehensive political art guarantees the result that citizens will the common good. And although this scheme to "determine" the will threatens to undermine its integrity, Rousseau seems convinced of its necessity. "It is not enough to say to citizens, be good. They must be taught to be so. . . . Patriotism is the most effective means. . . . for every man is virtuous when his private will conforms on all matters with the general will, and we willingly want what is wanted by the people we love."[188]

Rousseau may have regarded this formula as an adequate resolution of the aforementioned difficulty. Both virtue and freedom are served by the conformity of the private will to the general will, which is nevertheless achieved by passion. Since men can be taught to love one thing rather than another, they can be made to love their country. And because we freely will what is willed by the people we love, patriotism does not appear to offend against the legitimate principles of political obligation. This reasoning reassigns to love the legitimate capacities of will. In this model, passion is central and love of country bridges the gulf between the (internal) consent of the individual and the common good, which is external to the individual and is embodied in the *patrie*. Rousseau hopes through civic education, "[c]itizens will learn . . . to love one another as brothers, never to want anything other than what society wants."[189]

> In this way, an attentive and well-intentioned government, ceaselessly careful to maintain or revive patriotism among the people, prevents from afar the evils that sooner or later result from the indifference of citizens concerning the fate of the republic, and confines within narrow limits that personal interest which so isolates private individuals that the state is weakened by their power and cannot hope to gain anything from their good will.[190]

Just as Émile's tutor "prepares from afar the reign of freedom," government guarantees that citizens will will what they ought to will.

Rousseau was fully aware of the obvious objection. "Whatever sophisms may be used to disguise all this, it is certain that if someone can constrain my will I am no longer free."[191] He distinguishes constraining the will from binding the will with its own consent. On the other hand, Rousseau forthrightly acknowledges that government involves a tutelage of the will. The true statesman extends his *respectable* dominion over wills even more than actions, and

> If he could create a situation in which everyone did what was right, he himself would have nothing further to do, and the masterpiece of his works would be to remain idle. It is certain, at least, that the greatest talent of leaders is to disguise their power to make it less odious, and to manage the State so peacefully that it seems to have no need for managers.[192]

Disguised power is a continuing theme in Rousseau's writings, and many critics have duly condemned it as the seed of totalitarianism. Yet Rousseau had his reasons: it is precisely the regime of democratic freedom in which power requires the mantle of respectability. Although freedom and authority are not antithetical, for Rousseau, authority must be made respectable *in the eyes of citizens,* that is, in the greatest possible accord with legitimacy. The principles of political right exclude disguised power from the sphere of legitimacy. The defect of legitimacy occasions Rousseau's search for an "authoritarianism" that does not constrain the will. The search for a political path to freedom led Rousseau occasionally to cross (if not forget) the boundary between freedom and authority: "The most absolute authority is that which penetrates to the inner man and is exerted no less on his will than on his actions."[193]

"By what inconceivable art could the means be found to subjugate men in order to make them free?" Rousseau's political theory is an attempt to think the unthinkable, which explains its paradoxical character. The elaboration of democratic freedom begins with the kind of contract to which individuals will consent autonomously, and then shifts to the kind of community that will respect such a contract. Antinomies are generated at each stage of the argument: precivil man lacks the identification with the whole that would dispose him to generalize his will; the patriotic citizen identifies so much with the whole that his will appears to be coopted.

While Rousseau's cosmopolitan contemporaries undoubtedly regarded his rehabilitation of patriotism as an irony, or perhaps a rustic eccentricity, it was in fact both a serious and an ingenious attempt to cope with a dilemma of the human condition as Rousseau understood it. His model of citizenship is Janus-faced because it confronts the dichotomous requirements of contract and community, freedom and governability. The pervasive tension in Rousseau's political theory arises out of his effort to attune the political to the natural condition. The philosophic center of his political theory is the revaluation of the natural condition in protest against the conclusions of previous political thought. In the theories of Hobbes and Locke in particular, it is the *deficiencies* of the natural condition that inform the construction of the civil state; the state of nature becomes the *negative* standard for civil society. But on the basis of his revaluation of the state of nature, Rousseau makes the natural condition positively normative—as a condition of freedom. The complexity and perplexity of his thought stem from the effort to *perfect* that condition on the civil plane.

Abbreviations

CGP *Considérations sur le gouvernement de Pologne*

CS *Du contrat social*

DI *Discours sur l'inégalité*

DSA *Discours sur les sciences et les arts*

E *Émile*

EOL *Essai sur l'origine des langages*

EP *Discours sur l'économie politique*
MG *Manuscrit de genéve*

R *Les rêveries du promêneur solitaire*

O.C. Jean-Jacques Rousseau, *Oeuvres complètes,* Bernard Gagnebin and Marcel Raymond, eds., 4 vols. (Paris: Pléiade, 1964-). Roman numeral after abbreviation indicates volume number. The works listed above, with the exception of EOL, are found in this edition.

Citations are normally first to the Pléiade edition of the *Complete Works,* followed by page reference to an English translation, if available. For example, EP 242/ 210 refers first to the Pléiade text and then to the corresponding page in the Roger Masters translation of *Political Economy.* Quotations in the text are from available translations in the editions cited below. I have occasionally modified them for greater literalism. Other translations are my own. I have used the following translations of Rousseau's works:

Émile or On Education, Allan Bloom, ed. (New York: Basic Books, 1979).

The First and Second Discourses, Roger Masters, ed. (New York: St. Martin's Press, 1964).

The First and Second Discourses and the Essay on the Origin of Languages, Victor Gourevitch, ed. (New York: Harper & Row, 1986), for EOL and preface to *Narcissus.*

On the Social Contract, with Geneva Manuscript and Political Economy, Roger Masters, ed. (New York: St. Martin's Press, 1978).

Politics and the Arts: Letter to D'Alembert on the Theatre, Allan Bloom, ed. (Ithaca, N.Y.: Cornell University Press, 1960).

The Reveries of the Solitary Walker, Charles Butterworth, ed. (New York: Harper & Row, 1979).

Notes

[1] E 311/85; cf. 362-63/119-20, "There is no subjection so perfect as that which keeps the appearance of freedom," and CS II.7.10, ". . . so that the peoples, subjected to the laws of the state as they are subjected to those of nature, and recognizing the same power in the formation of man and in that of the city, obey freely and wear docilely the yoke of public happiness."

[2] CGP 955.

[3] MG 1.2.2. The most accessible meaning of the term "men as they are" appears in the second chapter of the first version of the *Social Contract,* "On the General Society of the Human Race." Intended as a reply to Diderot's article "Natural Right" in the *Encyclopedia,* Rousseau rejects Diderot's version of the "general will of the human race" and clarifies his own. He here unites the topics of laws as they can be and men as they are. In the final text, Rousseau does not attend to this question until the second book, where he devotes chapters to the Legislator and the people. The Legis-

lator's activity is the bridge between men as they are and laws as they can be. In the *Social Contract* Rousseau takes up the latter issue first, outlining the community of right before asking, "What people then is suited for legislation?" CS II.8.5.

[4] MG I.2.3.

[5] MG I.2.4.

[6] CS I.4.1: "No man has natural authority over his fellow man." See also Rousseau's statement that civil men lose their natural freedom, which was limited only by their power. CS I.8.2.

[7] Cf. CS I.1.1. Rousseau routinely uses these loaded terms to emphasize the calamity of social dependence.

[8] Note that Rousseau denied that this antagonism existed in the pristine natural condition. See DI 193/180: ". . . this is not the original condition of man . . . it is the spirit of society alone."

[9] CS I.6.1-2.

[10] CS I.6.3-8. These six paragraphs were added in the final version of the *Social Contract.*

[11] It is false that in the state of independence, reason leads us to cooperate for the common good out of a perception of our own interest. Far from there being an alliance between private interest and the general good, they are mutually exclusive in the natural order of things, and social laws are a yoke that each wants to impose on the other without having to bear himself." MG I.2.10.

[12] Preface to *Narcissus,* pp. 104-05.

[13] DI note I, 202/194.

[14] MG I.2.3.

[15] MG I.5.1.

[16] CS I.5.1. Rousseau employs the organic metaphor "body politic" only to emphasize the distinction between an aggregation and an association. He knows very well that it is imprecise. Indeed, a true association is best described as an artificial being rather than an organism, for its foundation cannot be simply natural.

> If the general society did exist somewhere other than in the systems of philosophers, it would be . . . a moral being with qualities separate and distinct from those of the particular beings constituting it, somewhat like chemical compounds which have properties that do not belong

to any of the elements composing them. . . . The public good or ill would not merely be the sum of private goods and ills as in a simple aggregation, but would lie in the liaison uniting them. It would be greater than this sum, and public felicity, far from being based on the happiness of private individuals, would itself be the source of this happiness. MG I.2.9.

Michel Launay has noted that Rousseau uses three metaphors for political association in the *Social Contract:* the first is organic, the second mechanical (political machine), the third architectural (political edifice). "L'Art de l'écrivain dans le *Contrat social,*" in *Études sur le contrat social* (Paris: Société Belles Lettres, 1964).

[17] Cf. David Braybrooke, "The Insoluble Problem of the Social Contract," which adopts a "rational choice" perspective and outlines in a sophisticated manner the dilemma on which Rousseau meditated in the *Geneva Manuscript. Dialogue* 15 (March 1976).

[18] CS I.7.7.

[19] "Renonçant à la qualité d'homme, doit être traité comme un être dénaturé." Denis Diderot, "Droit naturel," in *Political Writings of Rousseau,* C. E. Vaughan, ed. (New York: John Wiley and Sons, 1962 rpt.; 1915) vol. 1, pp. 430-31. Rousseau would later invest Diderot's categories—general will, *qualité d'homme, être dénaturé*—with his own meanings. See Edna Kryger, *La notion de la liberté chez Rousseau* (Paris: Librairie A. G. Nizet, 1978), p. 173.

[20] MG I.2.14. See Terence Marshall, "Rousseau and Enlightenment," *Political Theory* 6 (November 1978), 429-30.

[21] See Patrick Riley, *The General Will before Rousseau,* (Princeton: Princeton University Press, 1986), pp. 202-11, and Roger Masters, *The Political Philosophy of Rousseau,* (Princeton: Princeton University Press, 1986), pp. 257-76.

[22] Hence Rousseau's rejection of natural law in favor of the particularity of the conventions of this or that community. See DI, preface, for his critique of natural law. Rousseau could not subscribe to Diderot's universalism for two related reasons. Will had to be distinguished from reason or understanding. Will can be predicated only of a "moral being," and Diderot's alleged "general society of the human race" does not qualify, since universal humanity remains an abstraction rather than a covenanted body. Second, a "law of reason" is an incoherent concept since the development of reason is preceded by the emergence of passions that neutralize it. "Concepts of the natural law, which should rather be called the law of reason, begin

to develop only when the prior development of the passions renders all its precepts impotent." MG I.2.8.

[23] MG I.2.15.

[24] Thomas H. D. Mahoney, ed. Quoted in Charles Murray, *In Pursuit of Happiness and Good Government* (New York: Simon and Schuster, 1988), p. 260. Murray avers that

> Strongly bound communities, fulfilling complex public functions, are not creations of the state. They form because they must. Human beings have needs as individuals (never mind the "moral sense" or lack of it) that cannot be met except by cooperation with other human beings. To this degree, the oft-lamented conflict between "individualism" and "community" is misleading. The pursuit of individual happiness cannot be an atomistic process; it will naturally and always occur in the context of communities. The state's role in enabling the pursuit of happiness depends ultimately on nurturing *not* individuals, but the associations they form. (italics in the original)

From a Rousseauian perspective, Murray's political conclusion is generally correct, but his crucial assumption is wrong. One ought indeed to forgo appeals to the moral sense and concentrate on the pull of mutual needs in conceiving civil association; and, second, that association must be "nurtured." But according to Rousseau, *strongly* bound communities *are* political constructs precisely because "the pursuit of individual happiness" is no longer natural and does not naturally point to community. Furthermore, it is the very unnaturalness of human needs that will require "strong community," not in order to satisfy those needs so much as to keep them in check. Cf. Michael Ignatieff, *The Needs of Strangers* (Hammondsworth, U.K.: Penguin Books, 1984), pp. 110, 114: "For Rousseau, the spiral of needs is a tragedy of alienation. . . . For what Rousseau saw so clearly was that the very processes which freed men from their enslavement to natural scarcity in turn enslaved them to social scarcity."

[25] CS II.4.5.

[26] OC I, 56.

[27] One meaning of the phrase "man is born free" is that man acknowledges no duty from a source outside himself.

[28] In the first version of the passage quoted above, Rousseau explained that the general will is always right, and all constantly want the happiness of each because "there is no one who does not *secretly* apply this word 'each' to himself." MG I.6.6; my emphasis.

[29] Cf. OC III, 510; E 249/40.

[30] CS II.4.10.

[31] CS I.1.2. I.7.3. refers to the "sanctity of the contract," and IV.8 describes the "sacred dogmas" of civil association. Cf. DI 186/170: "Human governments" need "a base more solid than reason alone." "Divine will" must "give sovereign authority a sacred and inviolable character." It is the need for an *inviolable* commitment from a free will that generates a political conundrum.

[32] MG I.2.8.

[33] CS I.6.10.

[34] See Derathé's useful discussion of the concept of "des êtres moraux" in his *Jean-Jacques Rousseau et la science politique de son temps* (Paris: Presses Universitaires de France, 1950), appendix.

[35] CS II.4.5.

[36] In the first version Rousseau wrote, "judging what is not us," thereby emphasizing even more the idea of a new "personality." What is individual is no longer part of the collective identity. MG I.6.6.

[37] CS I.7.1.

[38] CS I.6.4.

[39] In Rousseauian democracy, the "encounter with difference" is the one thing to be avoided. Cf. Sheldon Wolin, *The Presence of the Past* (Baltimore: Johns Hopkins University Press, 1989), p. 191.

[40] CS I. pref. 1.

[41] CS I.7.5.

[42] CS I.6.4.

[43] DI 181/164.

[44] On the Smithian vision of achieving independence *through* market transactions, see Ignatieff, *The Needs of Strangers,* p. 121.

[45] Rousseau explained, in his more practical works, how *amour-propre* might be redirected away from discrete individuals toward the civic whole, so that the "fureur de se distinguer" (the furious desire to distinguish oneself) would play itself out in heroic service to the polity. This patriotic strategy is developed very clearly in both *Corsica* and *Poland;* the theoretical foundation for the rechanneling of *amour-propre* is expressed in *Émile* IV: "Let us extend *amour-propre* toward others, we will transform it into a virtue." E 547/252.

[46] Compare CS I.7.7 with I.6.10.

[47] CS I.8.1. One might say that with the passage of the individual into the *moi commun,* Rousseau's primary focus shifts accordingly from the psychology of the individual contractor to "the people," although his attention does oscillate back and forth between them.

[48] See chapter 4 below.

[49] DI 122/91. Rousseau identified those principles as *amour de soi* and pity, both of which are anterior to reason; however, pity turns out to be only a variation of *amour de soi,* an application of it, so to speak. Pity involves the identification of *oneself* with the suffering of another being. DI 126/95, 155-56/131-32.

[50] CS II.3.1.

[51] CS II.1.1.

[52] MG I.4.4.

[53] CS II.3.1; EP 246/213.

[54] Bertrand de Jouvenel, "Essai sur la politique de Rousseau," in *Du Contrat social* (Genève: Éditions Cheval-Ailé, 1947), p. 98.

[55] CS IV.1.6.

[56] DI 122/91. Apropos the general will, Rousseau states flatly: "Either the will is general or it is not." CS II.2.1.

[57] Turning to the metamorphosis associated with citizenship, Rousseau writes: "This passage from the state of nature to the civil state produces a remarkable change in man, by substituting justice for instinct in his behavior and giving his actions the morality they previously lacked. Only then, when the voice of duty replaces physical impulse and right replaces appetite, does man, who until that time only considered himself, find himself forced to act upon other principles and to consult his reason before heeding his inclinations." CS I.8.1.

By "civil state" Rousseau means the community of right established by the social contract rather than the general condition wrought by mankind's historical evolution. A sense of justice must forestall any citizen's attempt to use the laws to private advantage. Similarly, being "forced to act upon other principles" is but an elaboration of the meaning of being forced to be free; "right" and "duty" are characteristic of man's new juridical personality. Whereas in the natural order of things men experienced "a multitude of relationships lacking order, regulation and stability," their passage into the community of right endows them with moral relationships that they did not have before.

[58] CS I.8.1.

[59] Eric Weil, "Rousseau et sa politique," in *Pensée de Rousseau,* Gerard Genette and Tzvetan Todorov, eds. (Paris: Éditions du Seuil, 1984), p. 16.

[60] CS I.6.9.

[61] CS I.7.5.

[62] Patrick Riley, "A Possible Explanation of Rousseau's General Will," *American Political Science Review* 64 (March 1970), 86.

[63] CS II.2.1; cf. I.6.10.

[64] CS II.3.4.

[65] CS II.4.5.

[66] See CS I.6.9.

[67] CS II.4.5.

[68] Riley, "A Possible Explanation," p. 95.

[69] CS II.1.3: "car la volonté particulière tend par sa nature aux préférences, et la volonté générale à l'égalité."

[70] CS I.7.7.

[71] CS II.7.3.

[72] CS III.2.5-6.

[73] EP 246/212.

[74] CS IV.1.1.

[75] CS II.4.5; II.6.6. Judith Shklar, *Men and Citizens,* 2nd ed. (Cambridge: Cambridge University Press, 1985), pp. 165-84. In his critique of populist or "Rousseauist" democracy, William H. Riker fails to notice that the general will is intended to express a negative freedom, the value promoted by contemporary "libertarians." *Liberalism against Populism: A Confrontation Between the Theory of Democracy and the Theory of Social Choice* (San Francisco: W. H. Freeman, 1982). For Riker, "The theory of social choice is a theory about the way the tastes, preferences, or values of individual persons are amalgamated and summarized in the choice of a collective group or society." Ibid., p. 1. But the issue between "Rousseauist democracy" and the "liberal" (Madisonian) system advocated by Riker is precisely the assumption that preferences be understood as given, that is, as intractable to political leadership and considerations of justice or "right." Rousseau's goal is to reconcile what right permits with what

interest prescribes (CS, preface), which foreshadows his argument that while particular wills must be acknowledged, they are not to be regarded as sacrosanct. Rousseau's teaching is that on the latter premise, freedom cannot be established at all. I am indebted to William T. Bluhm for this point. See his "Liberalism and the Aggregation of Individual Preferences: Problems of Coherence and Rationality in Social Choice," in *The Crisis of Liberal Democracy,* Kenneth Deutsch and Walter Soffer, eds. (Albany: State University of New York Press, 1987), pp. 280-90.

[76] Weil, "Rousseau et sa politique," p. 29.

[77] CS III.15.5; cf. II.1.

[78] CS II.4.8.

[79] EP 248/214.

[80] Shklar, *Men and Citizens,* p. 168.

[81] CS II.4.6.

[82] CS II.5.5.

[83] CS II.12.3.

[84] To prevent men from harming one another, each must live as a "moral person" rather than as a "man." CS II.5.4.

[85] CS II.12.1.

[86] CS I.7.8. For twentieth-century thematic discussions of membership, see Joseph Tussman, *Obligation and the Body Politic* (New York: Oxford University Press, 1960), pp. 23-57; and Michael Walzer, *Spheres of Justice* (New York: Basic Books, 1983), pp. 31-63.

[87] CS I.8.3.

[88] CS I.4.6.

[89] CS I.4.1. The original version of this discussion should be consulted. MG I.5.10.

[90] CS I.8.1.

[91] EP 259/222. Rousseau's conception would seem to differ from "the self-forgetting of the modern idealist," whose cause, according to Harvey C. Mansfield, Jr., is "not the public good but always someone else's good." "Thomas Jefferson," in *American Political Thought: The Philosophic Dimension of American Statemanship,* Morton J. Frisch and Richard G. Stevens, eds. (Dubuque, Iowa: Kendall/Hunt, 1971), p. 50. The citizen's cause is the public good, but for reasons linked to his own good. The general will remains in service to the

individual's own good by guaranteeing him against personal dependence. Once again, the fact that Rousseau maintains a connection between happiness and independence would seem to mark a decisive break between his project and that of Kant and post-Kantian idealism.

[92] See Hilail Gildin, *Rousseau's Social Contract* (Chicago and London: University of Chicago Press, 1983), pp. 53-57.

[93] CS II.1.3.

[94] CS I.8.1.

[95] On Rousseau's view of ethics as a branch of politics, see Kryger, *La Notion de la liberté,* pp. 162-63.

[96] CS II.3.4.

[97] CS II.1.3.

[98] CS IV.2.8.

[99] Ibid.

[100] CS II.1.1. Rousseau expressed his point more clearly in the first draft, when he added, "Now since the will always tends toward the good of the being who wills, since the private will always has as its object private interest and the general will common interest, it follows that this last alone is or ought to be the true motivation of the social body." MG I.4.2.

[101] CS II.4.8.

[102] "A general will cannot pass judgement on a man or a fact." CS II.4.6.

[103] CS II.4.7.

[104] Cf. Aristotle, *Politics,* bk. VI, and Niccolo Machiavelli, *Discourses on Livy,* bk. I, ch. 5.

[105] MG I.4.6.

[106] CS II.3.1.

[107] CS II.4.2. In the first draft, Rousseau said, less confusingly, "life and existence." MG I.6.3.

[108] CS II.4.10.

[109] O.C. III, 841-42; my emphasis.

[110] CS II.12.3.

[111] CS IV.2.8. Once again, the Rousseauian case against

Rikerian social choice theory would emphasize the folly of granting an unlimited domain to preference. For if we understand freedom (as libertarianism seems to) as an infinitely variable preference, we can never establish it in a political regime. The latter requires that freedom or independence be construed as a constant preference to which variable preferences must accede.

[112] CS II.1.1. Pousseau concedes that sometimes the general will need not be positively expressed by the people themselves: "This is not to say that the commands of leaders cannot pass for expressions of the general will, as long as the sovereign, being free to oppose them, does not do so. In such a case one ought to presume the consent of the people from universal silence." CS II.1.4. This concession opens the door to the possibility that the people might legitimately be confined to a passive, or at least reactive, legislative role.

[113] CS II.1.3.

[114] CS II.7.3.

[115] MG I.4.1; my emphasis. See also *Letters écrites de la montagne,* O.C. III, 807. I have profited from Robert Derathé's illuminating "La Notion de personnalité morale et la théorie des êtres moraux," which traces Rousseau's formulations to Samuel Pufendorf and the early modern school of natural right. *Jean-Jacques Rousseau et la science politique de son temps,* pp. 397-413.

[116] CS II.7.4.

[117] CS II.7.1.

[118] Cf. E 546-48/252-53, where the same theme is introduced from a different perspective.

[119] MG I.5.7.

[120] Rousseau occasionally equates these terms. Cf. MG I.2.14.

[121] MG I.5.7.

[122] CS II.7.7. Eventually, the "free vote of the people" will (as we saw above) be interpreted in such a way as to reflect a constant preference for the general on the part of all, thereby calling into question Rousseau's commitment to freedom qua agency. In the passage under consideration, Rousseau cleaves to the requirements of legitimacy and resists the conclusion that sovereignty be in any way represented. As we shall see, the tension between what is legitimate and what will make the good reliable will become irrepressible in Rousseau's theory.

[123] While he admits that "a people is always the master

to change its laws—even the best laws," Rousseau concedes that the best laws will be the gift of the Legislator. CS II.12.2; II.7.1.

[124] Cf. Shklar, *Men and Citizens,* ch. 4.

[125] Order, in Rousseau's mind, is associated with an "artful" fidelity to the natural. In its perfect expression such an order confounds the distinction between nature and artifice. As Julie teaches Saint-Preux, who is awed by her garden: "Nature has done everything, but under my direction, and there is nothing there that I have not ordered." *La Nouvelle Héloise,* O.C. II, 472.

[126] MG I.7.2.

[127] CS IV.1.1.

[128] E 249/40.

[129] Biographers and psychologists have little difficulty presenting evidence that Rousseau himself experienced the evils he condemns, but one cannot conclude that he merely rationalized his personal resentment in his social criticism. Rousseau's historical and autobiographical portraits are indeed evidentiary. They point, however, to what Baczko has called "general anthropological questions: the relation of man to nature and his own history; human freedom and man's alienation from his products and activities." Bronislaw Baczko, *Solitude et communauté* (Paris: Mouton, 1974), p. 290.

[130] *Confessions* IX, O.C. 1, 404.

[131] CS IV.8.17.

[132] As Derathé observes in his annotation of this passage, Rousseau develops the theme of avoiding contradiction with oneself at length in *Émile.* O.C. III, 1503. Arthur Melzer has made the theme of unity of soul the centerpiece of his interpretation of Rousseau's thought and the key to his explanation of the natural goodness of man. See "Rousseau and the Problem of Bourgeois Society," *American Political Science Review* 74, no. 4 (December 1980); and *The Natural Goodness of Man,* (Chicago: University of Chicago Press, 1990), pp. 20-23.

[133] CS II.7.3.

[134] MG II.2.13.

[135] EP 259-60/222-23, 314, 381; E 248-49/39-40 (but cf. 600-01/290-91).

[136] Montesquieu's paradigmatic community of virtue was the ascetic monastery. "Why do monks love their order so much? It is precisely due to what makes it unbearable for them. Their rule deprives them of all the things the ordinary passions press after: there remains therefore this passion for the very rule which afflicts them. The more austere it is, that is to say, the more it cuts off their inclinations, the more force it gives to the only one left to them." *Spirit of the Laws* IV.12. Cf. Thomas Pangle, *Montesquieu's Philosophy of Liberalism* (Chicago and London: University of Chicago Press, 1973), pp. 81-83.

[137] CS II.4.10.

[138] CS I.8.1,I.8.3,

[139] CS II.7.3.

[140] CS II.7.4.

[141] CS II.12.5.

[142] EP 251/216.

[143] E 654/327.

[144] EP 255/219.

[145] As an artificial passion, *amour-propre* is malleable; it can express itself as civic pride as well as vanity. O.C. III, 937-38.

[146] EP 251-52/16-17.

[147] See Richard Kennington, "René Descartes," in *History of Political Philosophy,* Leo Strauss and Joseph Cropsey, eds., 2nd ed. (Chicago: Rand McNally, 1972).

[148] Leo Strauss described this aspect of Rousseau's vision as the "totalitarianism of a free society." *What Is Political Philosophy? and Other Essays* (Glencoe, Ill.: The Free Press, 1953), p. 51.

[149] EP 252/217.

[150] Michel Foucault coined the term "governmentality" to characterize Rousseau's political economy. See his essay by that title in *Ideology and Consciousness* 6 (1979). Cf. James Miller, *Rousseau: Dreamer of Democracy* (New Haven: Yale University Press, 1984), pp. 196-98.

[151] Cf. Reinhart Kosselleck, *Critique and Crisis: Enlightenment and the Pathogenesis of Modern Society* (Cambridge, Mass.: MIT Press, 1988), p. 164: "The citizen gains his freedom only when he participates in the general will, but as an individual this same citizen cannot know when and how his inner self is absorbed by the general will. Individuals might err, but the *volonté générale* never does."

[152] Cf. F. M. Barnard and Jene Porter, "Will and Polit-

ical Rationality in Rousseau," paper presented at the 1983 annual meeting of the Canadian Political Science Association, Vancouver, Canada.

[153] Letter to Mirabeau, 26 July 1767, in *Political Writings,* Vaughan, ed. vol. 2, pp. 159-62.

[154] CS I.7.8.

[155] Cf. Riley, *The General Will Before Rousseau,* pp. 182, 205, 208-10, 245, 247.

[156] Roger Masters has stressed Rousseau's distinction between "maxims of politics" and "rules of right." *The Political Philosophy of Rousseau,* pp. 291-93, 369-409.

[157] Miller, *Rousseau: Dreamer of Democracy,* p. 203; Riley, *The General Will Before Rousseau,* p. 245: "Do Rousseau's notions of education—private and civic—leave will as the autonomous producer of moral effects that he originally defines it as?"

[158] On the relation of educative authority to will, see Riley, *The General Will Before Rousseau,* pp. 245-48; cf. Miller, *Rousseau: Dreamer of Democracy,* pp. 196-98.

[159] EP 259/222.

[160] CS I.6.10.

[161] Ibid.

[162] Samuel Baud-Bovy, ed., *Jean-Jacques Rousseau* (Neuchâtel: Éditions de la Baconnière, 1962), p. 96.

[163] The latter topic is treated in detail in chapter 4.

[164] See Bernard Groethuysen, *Jean-Jacques Rousseau* (Paris: Gallimard, 1949), p. 109.

[165] Sovereignty is created out of the wills of dissociated, precivil men; its being derives solely from contract. CS I.7.3.

[166] DI 127/97.

[167] Preface to *Narcissus,* p. 106.

[168] *Confessions,* O.C. I, 404-05.

[169] MG I.7.3.

[170] CS I.6.4.

[171] Cf. Richard Flathman, *The Practice of Political Authority* (Chicago and London: University of Chicago Press, 1980), pp. 197-201.

[172] CS I.6.10.

[173] CS II.8.

[174] CS II.10.3.

[175] CS II.10.5.

[176] Since "civilization" must await the preparation of a common identity, only in rare circumstances will a people be ripe for subjection to laws. Rousseau points out the mistake by Peter the Great, who attempted to civilize his people prematurely. "He wanted first to make Germans and Englishmen, whereas it was necessary to begin by making Russians." CS II.8.5.

[177] CS III.16.4.

[178] CS I.7.1.

[179] CS IV.6.6.

[180] For a careful treatment of Rousseau's political geometry, see Masters, *The Political Philosophy of Rousseau,* pp. 340-48; and Richard Carter, "Rousseau's Newtonian Body Politic," *Philosophy and Social Criticism,* 7 (1980), 143-67.

[181] Notice that the Legislator must pretend to intercede with the divine to effectively communicate with the people. CS II.7.10.

[182] Ibid.

[183] CGP, ch. 2. Cf. Machiavelli, who was prepared to disguise inequality by manipulating titles while preserving actual power. *Discourses on Livy* I.2.

[184] CS IV.6.1.

[185] The Tribunate resembles the Legislator himself. It is not a constituent part of the city, and it has no portion of the legislative or executive power. Yet in its role as defender of the laws it is, according to Rousseau's description, more sacred and revered than either the sovereign or the prince. CS IV.5.3.

[186] Cf. CS IV.6.10 on Cicero's "error."

[187] O.C. III, 948; my emphasis.

[188] EP 254/218.

[189] EP 261/223.

[190] EP 262/224.

[191] EP 248/214.

[192] EP 250/215.

[193] EP 251/216.

FURTHER READING

Biography

Starobinski, Jean. *Jean-Jacques Rousseau: Transparency and Obstruction*. Translated by Arthur Goldhammer. Chicago: University of Chicago Press, 1988, 464 p.

A psychological and philosophical study of Rousseau's life and works.

Criticism

Bloom, Allan. "Jean Jacques Rousseau: 1712-1778." In *History of Political Philosophy*, edited by Leo Strauss and Joseph Cropsey, second edition, pp. 532-53. The University of Chicago Press, 1973.

Discusses Rousseau's political and social theory, focusing on the tension between the individual within a civil society and society as a whole.

Cassirer, Ernst. *The Question of Jean-Jacques Rousseau*. Translated by Peter Gay. Bloomington: Indiana University Press, 1954, 129 p.

This noted essay attempts to make sense of contradictory interpretations of Rousseau's writings by making an objective analysis of his work as a whole.

Cranston, Maurice, and Richard S. Peters. *Hobbes and Rousseau: A Collection of Critical Essays*. New York: Doubleday and Co., 1972, 505 p.

A collection of essays on Rousseau by several critical noted scholars.

Crocker, Lester G. An introduction to *The Social Contract and Discourse on the Origin of Inequality*. New York: Simon and Schuster, 1967, 258 p.

An overview of two of Rousseau's major works, that examines the relationship of his ideas to totalitarian thinking.

Della Volpe, Galvano. *Rousseau and Marx*. Translated by John Frasser. New Jersey: Humanities Press, 1979, 206 p.

Compares problems associated with Rousseau's idea of individual merit and social rewards with Marxist ideas.

Ellenburg, Stephen. *Rousseau's Political Philosophy: An Interpretation from Within*. Ithaca: Cornell University Press, 1976, 335 p.

Argues for the coherence of Rousseau's political philosophy, explores its core framework of non-individualism, and contrasts it to traditional liberalism.

Ellis, Madeline B. *Rousseau's Socratic Aemilian Myths*. Columbus: Ohio State University Press, 1977, 433 p.

Analyzes the relationship between *The Social Contract* and *Émile*.

Fetscher, Irving. "Rousseau's Concept of Freedom in the Light of His Philosophy of History." In *Nomos IV: Liberty*. Edited by Carl J. Friedrich, pp. 29-56. New York: Atherton Press, 1962.

Analyses the relationship between social equality and the effectiveness of the social contract.

Ferrara, Alessandro. *Modernity and Authenticity: A Study in the Social and Ethical Thought of Jean-Jacques Rousseau*. Albany: State University of New York Press, 188 p.

Study of Rousseau's thought that both elucidates "the interpretive frame of reference used for reconstructing the unity of Rousseau's *oeuvre*" and investigates certain tendencies of today's culture "through *Denkfiguren* typical of Rousseauean social theory."

Green, F. C. *Jean-Jacques Rousseau: A Critical Study of his Life and Writings*. Cambridge: Cambridge University Press, 1955, 376 p.

Offers a useful examination of the personal and political contexts for the development of Rousseau's ideas and works.

Jones, W. T. "Rousseau's General Will and the Problem of Consent." *Journal of the History of Philosophy* 25 (January 1987): 105-30.

Discusses the problem of individual liberty with respect to Rousseau's concept of the general will.

Lemos, Ramon M. *Rousseau's Political Philosophy: An Exposition and Interpretation*. Athens: University of Georgia Press, 1977, 262 p.

A comprehensive analysis of the philosophical ideas in the *Discourses* and *The Social Contract*.

Melzer, Arthur. "Rousseau and the Problem of Bourgeois Society." *American Political Science Review* 74, vol. 4 (December 1980): 1018-33.

Compares Rousseau's ideas of the unity of the soul with those on the natural goodness of man.

Masters, Roger D. "The Structure of Rousseau's Political Thought." In *Hobbes and Rousseau: A Collection of Critical Essays*. Edited by Maurice Cranston and Richard S. Peters, pp. 401-36. Garden City, New York: Anchor Books, 1972.

Analyzes *The Social Contract* in order to gauge the structure and development of Rousseau's political thought.

Miller, James. *Rousseau: Dreamer of Democracy*. New

Haven: Yale University Press, 1984, 272 p.
Compares Rousseau's thought with concepts of modern democracy.

Mitchell, Joshua. "Rousseau: The History of Diremption and the Politics of Errancy." In *Not By Reason Alone: Religion, History, and Identity in Early Modern Political Thought*, pp. 98-124. Chicago: University of Chicago Press, 1993.
Examines Rousseau's secular conception of atonement.

Noone, John B., Jr. *Rousseau's "Social Contract": A Conceptual Analysis*. Athens: University of Georgia Press, 1980, 222 p.
This study aims to clarify contradictory interpretations of *The Social Contract* by "extract[ing] a [logical] system of ideas from what too often seem to be random, casual and even purposeless particulars."

Riley, Patrick. *Will and Political Legitimacy: A Critical Exposition of Social Contract Theory in Hobbes, Locke, Rousseau, Kant, and Hegel*. Cambridge: Harvard University Press, 1982, 294 p.
Examines Rousseau's social contract theory in the context of modern political thought.

———. *The General Will Before Rousseau: The Transformation of the Divine into the Civic*. Princeton: Princeton University Press, 1986, 272 p.
Important study of the transformation of the idea of "the general will of God to save all men into a political [idea], the general will of the citizen to place the common good of the city above his particular will as a private self, and thereby to 'save' the polity."

Russell, Bertrand. "Rousseau." In *A History of Western Philosophy*, pp. 684-701. New York: Simon and Schuester, 1945.
An overview and analysis of Rousseau's major political and theological ideas, and description of his place in the Western philosophical tradition.

Wolker, Robert. "Rousseau's Two Concepts of Liberty." In *Lives, Liberties, and the Public Good: New Essays in Political Theory for Maurice Cranston*. Edited by George Feaver and Frederick Rosen, pp. 61-100. London: The Macmillan Press, 1987.
Closely examines Rousseau's concepts of "positive" and "negative" liberty.

Additional coverage of Rousseau's life and career is contained in the folowing sources published by Gale Research: *Literature Criticism from 1400 to 1800*, **Vol. 14;** *Discovering Authors*; *Discovering Authors: British*; *Discovering Authors: Canadian*; **and** *World Literature Criticism.*

Adam Smith

1723-1790

Scottish economist, philosopher, nonfiction writer, and essayist.

INTRODUCTION

Often referred to as the founder of the science of political economy, Smith is best known as the author of *An Inquiry into the Nature and Causes of the Wealth of Nations* (1776), which is generally recognized as the first comprehensive and systematic examination of the economic forces in Europe that gave birth to capitalism in the eighteenth century. Combining theoretical analysis with policy recommendations, *The Wealth of Nations* is partly a history of European economics and partly a description of the state of manufacture and trade in Smith's day. Explaining in detail the reasons for the breakdown of feudal Europe and the growth of the newly emerging world of industry, Smith offered suggestions for achieving rapid economic development in contemporary circumstances. His advocacy of freedom from government restriction of the economic process — what has since become known as the laissez-faire doctrine — appealed to the individualistic consciousness of Europe's rising capitalist class, and their enthusiasm for Smith's policy proposals in *The Wealth of Nations* greatly contributed to the book's enormous impact on Western economic thought and institutions. Smith was also known among his contemporaries as a prominent moral philosopher. His study of ethics, particularly as revealed in *The Theory of Moral Sentiments* (1759), helped to define the meaning and attributes of moral behavior in an age when traditional religious teachings were being replaced by secular values. Like *The Wealth of Nations*, *The Theory of Moral Sentiments* has been widely praised for its insight into the psychology of human behavior and its expression of leading intellectual currents of Smith's day.

Biographical Information

Smith was born in the seaport town of Kirkcaldy, Scotland. His father, a customs official, died shortly before his birth, and he was raised by his mother, with whom he enjoyed a close relationship until her death in 1784 at the age of ninety. When he was fourteen, Smith entered the University of Glasgow, where he became a favorite pupil of Francis Hutcheson, whose teaching of moral philosophy greatly influenced Smith's thought throughout his career. In his lectures on moral philosophy, Hutcheson emphasized themes that later

became prominent in Smith's writing: the notion that moral and aesthetic judgments are based on feelings, not reason; faith in the fundamental value and divine origin of an ethical law of nature; and the recognition of benevolence and justice as important human virtues. Smith left the University of Glasgow in 1740 and enrolled at Oxford, where he remained for seven years, pursuing a course of study that was largely self-directed. He moved to Edinburgh in 1748 at the suggestion of Lord Henry Home of Kames, who had invited him to deliver a series of public lectures there on rhetoric and belles lettres. It is believed that Smith repeated or revised many of these lectures, which encompass aesthetic subjects as well as history, jurisprudence, government, and science, during his subsequent teaching career at the University of Glasgow, first as a professor of logic in 1751 and later as a professor of moral philosophy from 1752 to 1764. Since Smith ordered his literary executors to burn his manuscripts, only a portion of these lectures are extant; some are printed in *Essays on Philosophical Subjects* (1795), and others, dating from 1762-63, appear in *Lectures on Justice,*

Police, Revenue and Arms (1896; also referred to as *Lectures on Jurisprudence*) and *Lectures on Rhetoric and Belles Lettres* (1963). As Chair of Moral Philosophy at the University of Glasgow, Smith not only taught ethics, but also carefully considered the social aspects of the subjects of government and law. His study of jurisprudence led him to conclude that economic liberty was a fundamental human right, a theme he was to expand upon in *The Wealth of Nations*. Smith's first book, *The Theory of Moral Sentiments*, was drawn from his lectures at the University of Glasgow dealing properly with ethics. A critical and popular success that also elicited the admiration of Smith's peers, among them the philosophers David Hume and Edmund Burke, the work so impressed the politician Charles Townsend that he offered Smith the position of tutor to his stepson, Henry Scott, the Duke of Buccleuch. Smith accepted the assignment, resigning from his professorship in 1764, and accompanied the Duke on a two-year visit to France and Switzerland. Upon his return to Scotland, Smith settled in Kirkcaldy, where he spent the next ten years working on *The Wealth of Nations*. The immediate success of this book derived in large part from the popularity of its policy recommendations, which favored the rising capitalist class in Europe, and a variety of governments sought Smith's economic advice. During the remaining years of his life, Smith enjoyed recognition as a prominent economist and man of letters. He hosted regular Sunday dinners attended by important writers and other distinguished guests and devoted careful attention to his duties as commissioner of customs for Scotland, an appointment he received in 1778. He died in 1790, three years after his election to the office of Rector of Glasgow University.

Major Works

Smith's reputation as a writer rests on his success in formulating systems in the realm of the social sciences to explain human behavior. In *The Theory of Moral Sentiments*, Smith examined the nature and origin of ethical judgments, and in his masterpiece, *The Wealth of Nations*, he explored the motivations of economic actors operating in a free market. Smith's system of moral philosophy, as outlined the *The Theory of Moral Sentiments*, is founded on the sentiment of sympathy, which, Smith maintained, forms the basis for humankind's judgments about both the propriety and merit of people's actions and feelings. According

to Smith, it is sympathy, in the sense of imagining oneself in another person's situation, that shapes our judgments about whether another person's actions and feelings are right or wrong, deserving of praise or blame. As Smith points out, in order to form sound judgments about the conduct of others, individuals must be able to make judgments about their own behavior

that are free of self-interest. In what is considered the most original aspect of Smith's ethical theory, he argued that the only way to avoid self-deception in our assessments of ourselves is to view our own actions through the eyes of an "ideal impartial spectator," a person possessed of perfect virtue who knows all the relevant facts but is not personally involved and who adheres to a set of general rules about what is considered socially appropiate behavior. In Smith's system, these general rules derive from accepted social virtues, such as benevolence and justice; sympathy, a natural human phenomenon, is the ultimate source of virtuous sentiments. While *The Theory of Moral Sentiments* deals with humankind's struggle to achieve happiness on a moral level, *The Wealth of Nations* concerns humankind's material welfare. Smith's primary objective in *The Wealth of Nations* was to define the ways and means of producing national wealth and to outline the conditions for rapid economic development in terms of national income. He rejected the mercantilist theory that money, in the form of gold and silver, is wealth, maintaining instead that wealth is measured in terms of consumer goods. Smith emphasized that the greatest amount of trade will take place among countries that possess surplus stocks of consumer goods, or the raw materials necessary to produce them, and he argued that the best way to maximize a country's capital accumulation is to increase productivity through a division of labor whereby individual workers are assigned specialized functions in the manufacture of a particular product. It follows from Smith's analysis that producers, in an effort to ensure that all of their material wants will be supplied, will concentrate on the manufacture of goods for which there is the greatest demand. Thus, Smith views self-interest as the primary motivation of economic agents in a capitalist society. He writes, "It is not from the benevolence of the butcher, the brewer, or the baker, that we expect our dinner, but from their regard to their own self-interest." Smith adds, however, that economic actors, through no design of their own, actually help to promote the general welfare by producing and selling the goods that satisfy the greatest needs of the people: the capitalist "intends only his own gain" but is "led by an invisible hand to promote an end which was no part of his intention." In Smith's view, then, there exits a natural order in the universe whereby individual selfishness adds up to the maximum social good. He therefore concluded that government attempts to disrupt this natural order in the form of restrictions on free trade should be abolished. One of the major themes of *The Wealth of Nations*—and the one that most appealed to the capitalist class that was coming to power in Europe at the time of the book's publication—is economic liberalism and the need to remove the government controls on individual economic agents that had survived from feudal and mercantilist times.

Critical Reception

Smith is widely viewed as the philosopher of the capitalist revolution for his achievement in *The Wealth of Nations*. Scholars generally agree that Smith's genius lie in his ability to bring together into a coherent whole a vast range of topics that had been treated in the economic literature of his day and to fashion a system that explained the forces that were then at work forging a new economic order in Europe. Among Smith's contemporary audience, *The Wealth of Nations* was more applauded for its practical recommendations than for its analytic aspects. The acceptance of Smith's policy proposals by Europe's rising capitalist class helped to put in place economic practices and institutions that still survive and that continue to be associated with Smith's name. From a modern standpoint, however, Smith's lasting legacy is his economic analysis, which has been the subject of a vast amount of literature written by both professional and academic economists all over the world. In addition to discussing specific aspects of Smith's theory, most notably his ideas concerning the division of labor and the proper role of government in a free market economy, scholars have studied the philosophical foundations of his thought. Another prominent topic in the literature on Smith is the relationship between *The Wealth of Nations* and *The Theory of Moral Sentiments*. While it is almost unanimously agreed that both works attest to Smith's keen understanding of human psychology, critics have debated whether Smith's moral outlook has any bearing on his economic analysis. While some critics have argued that the concept of sympathy in *The Theory of Moral Sentiments* is in direct conflict with the idea of self-interest in *The Wealth of Nations*, others have found that Smith's notions of justice and benevolence as formulated in the earlier work are the key to an understanding of Smith's economic analysis. The ongoing controversy over whether Smith's moral and economic systems can be reconciled has not detracted from the critical stature of either *The Wealth of Nations* or *The Theory of Moral Sentiments*. *The Theory of Moral Sentiments*, like *The Wealth of Nations*, continues to be analyzed by critics on its own merits, for its theory and methodology as well as for the light it sheds on the Scottish philosophical tradition. Smith's fame, however, rests almost entirely on *The Wealth of Nations*. The economic system Smith developed in this work became the model for capitalist societies all over the globe, and today Smith is ranked with Thomas Robert Malthus, David Ricardo, John Stuart Mill, and Karl Marx among the world's greatest classical economists.

PRINCIPAL WORKS

The Theory of Moral Sentiments (philosophy) 1759; revised editions, 1761, 1767, 1774, 1781, 1790

An Inquiry into the Nature and Causes of the Wealth of Nations (nonfiction) 1776; revised editions, 1778, 1784, 1786, 1789

Essays on Philosophical Subjects (essays and lectures) 1795

The Works of Adam Smith. 5 vols. (nonfiction, philosophy, essays, and lectures) 1811-12

Lectures on Justice, Police, Revenue and Arms, Delivered in the University of Glasgow by Adam Smith, Reported by a Student in 1763 (lectures) 1896

Lectures on Rhetoric and Belles Lettres Delivered in the University of Glasgow by Adam Smith, Reported by a Student in 1762-63 (lectures) 1963

The Glasgow Edition of the Works and Correspondence of Adam Smith. 6 vols. (nonfiction, philosophy, essays, lectures, and correspondence) 1982-87

CRITICISM

Francis W. Hirst (essay date 1904)

SOURCE: "The Theory of Moral Sentiments," in *Adam Smith*, Macmillan & Co., Limited, 1904, pp. 46-67.

[*In the following excerpt from a chapter on* The Theory of Moral Sentiments *in Hirst's full-length study of Smith's career, Hirst focuses on Smith's notion of virtue, discussing the primary components of his system of ethics, sympathy, and the conscience.*]

. . . With all its faults, the *Theory of Moral Sentiments* is still one of the most instructive and entertaining of all our English treatises on ethics. There is plenty of warmth and colour. The argument is never bare; you follow its thread through a wondrous maze, till your perplexities are solved, and you finally congratulate yourself as well as the author on having rejected all the errors and collected all the wisdom of the ages. When the main theme threatens to be tedious he entertains you with an imaginary portrait, or digresses into some subsidiary discussion upon fortune, or fashion, or some other of the currents that turn men from their purpose. It has been observed that the strongest antagonists of Smith's central doctrine are enthusiastic in praising his skill in the analysis of human nature. The truth is, that the most absent-minded was also the most observant of men. He seems to have watched the actions and passions of his acquaintances with extraordinary precision. Motives interested him at least as much as conduct; he rather blames philosophers for having of late years given too much attention to the tendency of affections, and too little to the relationship in which they stand to their causes.

His immediate predecessors and contemporaries in the field of ethics were principally concerned with the origin and authority of right and wrong. Why does mankind generally agree as to what is right and what is wrong; whence are the notions of "ought" and "ought not" derived if not from the church or the Bible? At the time Smith wrote, English moralists were divided upon this point into two main schools. Of the first, who derived all moral rules from self-interest, Hobbes, Mandeville, and Hume were the principal exponents. The second school sought for a less variable standard, and have been called Intuitionalists, because they believed either with Clarke and Price that moral truths are perceived like axioms of Euclid, by the intellect, or with Shaftesbury and Hutcheson, that there is innate in us a moral sense or taste (developed by Bishop Butler into conscience) which prompts us to do right and tells us the difference between good and evil.

Moralists were equally divided upon the question, "In what does virtue consist?" His old teacher Hutcheson had answered that it consisted in benevolence; others thought that prudence was the true mark of the good man. In Adam Smith's view, prudence and benevolence are equally essential ingredients in the constitution of a perfectly virtuous character. With virtue he associates happiness, and his individual view of both is based partly upon the Greek philosophy of an independent leisure, partly upon the Christian conception of doing good to others; and we feel that he does not always succeed in reconciling the new ideal with the old. "Happiness," he says, "consists in tranquillity and enjoyment. Without tranquillity there can be no enjoyment." Tranquillity, he thinks, is "the natural and usual state of a man's mind." But the tranquillity to be desired was as far removed from indolence or apathy as from avarice or ambition. It was the active tranquillity of a well furnished mind and a benevolent heart.

Peace of mind, family peace, a country free from civil, religious, and foreign strife,—these he thought in their order the things most momentous to happiness. Yet he would not allow the leisurely philosopher to bask in the selfish sunshine of tranquillity. "The most sublime contemplation of the philosopher will scarce compensate the neglect of the smallest act of virtue." The study of politics tends to promote public spirit, and political disquisitions are therefore the most useful of all speculations. The trade of the vulgar politician was often ignoble and deceitful; but the best happiness attended the patriotism and public spirit of those who sought to improve government and extend trade. The leader of a successful party may do far more for his country than the greatest general. He may re-establish and reform its constitution, and from the doubtful and ambiguous character of a party leader he may assume "the greatest and noblest of all characters, that of the reformer and legislator of a great state," who by the wisdom of his institutions secures the international tranquillity and happiness of his fellow-citizens for many succeeding generations.

For the man of system in politics Smith has no liking. Wise in his own conceit, such a man "seems to imagine that he can arrange the different members of a great society with as much ease as the hand arranges the different pieces upon a chessboard." He forgets that "in the great chessboard of human society every single piece has a principle of motion of its own, altogether different from that which the legislature might choose to impress upon it."

A true son of Oxford in his admiration for Aristotle, he was fond, as we have seen, of appealing to common life and popular opinion. But another of Aristotle's methods, that of the eclectic who arrives at the truth by choosing out and combining what is good in other philosophers, may almost be said to be the foundation of *The Moral Sentiments*. When, after explaining his system, he comes in his last (seventh) part to describe and criticise his predecessors, it is apparent that he considers his own theory to be an assemblage or reconciliation in one harmonious whole of all the happiest efforts of ethical speculation:—

> If we examine the most celebrated and remarkable of the different theories which have been given concerning the nature and origin of our moral sentiments, we shall find that almost all of them coincide with some part or other of that which I have been endeavouring to give an account of; and that if everything which has already been said be fully considered, we shall be at no loss to explain what was the view or aspect of nature which led each particular author to form his particular system. From some one or other of those principles which I have been endeavouring to unfold, every system of morality that ever had any reputation in the world has, perhaps, ultimately been derived.

A good example of this eclecticism is his treatment of Mandeville, an author from whom Smith no less than Rousseau derived many fruitful ideas. In the first edition of *The Moral Sentiments* he writes:—

> There are, however, some other systems which seem to take away altogether the distinction between vice and virtue, and of which the tendency is upon that account wholly pernicious: I mean the systems of the Duke of Rochefoucauld and Dr. Mandeville. Though the notions of both these authors are in almost every respect erroneous, there are, however, some appearances in human nature which, when viewed in a certain manner, seem at first sight to favour them. These, first slightly sketched out with the elegance and delicate precision of the Duke of Rochefoucauld, and afterwards more fully represented with the lively and humorous, though

coarse and rustic, eloquence of Dr. Mandeville, have thrown upon their doctrine an air of truth and probability which is very apt to impose upon the unskilful.

Bishop Butler, more justly, classed Rochefoucauld with Hobbes. But in Smith's sixth edition (1790) the name of Rochefoucauld was omitted, at the instance of the Duke's grandson, who pointed out that the author of the Maxims is not really in the same category with Mandeville. Coarse and licentious, but entertaining and ingenious, the author of the *Fable of the Bees* hit human nature hard. He traced virtuous actions to vanity, and whittled away the distinction between vice and virtue, until he reached the paradox that private vices are public benefits. But this profligate system could never have caused so much stir and alarm in the world "had it not in some respects bordered upon the truth." We are very easily imposed upon by the most absurd travellers' tales about distant countries. But falsehoods about the parish we live in must, if they are to deceive us, bear some resemblance to the truth, nay, "must even have a considerable mixture of truth in them." A natural philosopher has an analogous advantage over the speculator in ethics. The vortices of Descartes passed for nearly a century as a most satisfactory account of the revolutions of heavenly bodies, though they neither existed nor could possibly exist, and though if they did exist they could not produce such effects as were ascribed to them. But the moral philosopher is no better off than the parish liar. He is giving an account of things that are constantly before us, around us, and within us. "Though here, too, like indolent masters who put their trust in a steward that deceives them, we are very liable to be imposed upon, yet we are incapable of passing any account which does not preserve some little regard to the truth."

In describing those systems which make virtue consist in propriety, Smith displays a profound knowledge of Plato, Aristotle, and the later schools of Greek philosophy. His admiration of Zeno and Epictetus is almost unbounded, especially when he contemplates their confident opinion that a man should always be able to support worldly misfortunes. "They endeavour to point out the comforts which a man might still enjoy when reduced to poverty, when driven into banishment, when exposed to the injustice of popular clamour, when labouring under blindness, deafness, in the extremity of old age, upon the approach of death." He holds that the few fragments which have been preserved of this philosophy are among the most instructive remains of antiquity. "The spirit and manhood of their doctrines make a wonderful contrast with the desponding, plaintive, and whining tone of some modern systems." Chrysippus, on the other hand, did but

reduce stoicism into a scholastic or technical system of artificial definitions, divisions, and subdivisions, "one of the most effectual expedients, perhaps, for extinguishing whatever degree of good sense there may be in any moral or metaphysical system."

Admirable as were the best stoics and epicureans and those Roman writers who, like Cicero and Seneca, direct us to the imperfect but attainable virtues, they quite misunderstood nature. "By nature, the events which immediately affect that little department in which we ourselves have some little management and direction, which immediately affect ourselves, our friends, our country, are the events which interest us the most and which chiefly excite our desires and aversions, our hopes and fears, our joys and sorrows." Here and in similar passages he follows his favourite, Pope:—

> God loves from whole to parts; but human soul
> Must rise from individual to the whole.
> Self-love but serves the virtuous mind to wake,
> As the small pebble stirs the peaceful lake;
> The centre mov'd, a circle straight succeeds,
> Another still, and still another spreads;
> Friend, parent, neighbour, first it will embrace;
> His country next; and next all human race.

Every moralists's, even Epictetus's, description of virtue is just as far as it goes. But Smith claims to have been the first to give any precise or distinct measure by which the fitness or propriety of affection can be ascertained and judged. Such a measure he finds in the sympathetic feelings of the impartial and well-informed spectator. Here, then, we have the central and peculiar doctrine that stamps with originality Adam Smith's *Theory of Moral Sentiments*.[1]

That sympathy or fellow-feeling is a primary instinct of man appears from the commonest incidents of life. Do we not shrink when a blow is aimed at another, do not the spectators wriggle as they follow a rope-dancer's contortions, are we not moved by tears, is not laughter infectious? Sympathy is agreeable. We like to give it, and we long for it. It is too instinctive to be explained (though some would do so) by a refinement of self-love. Yet it is not a mere reflection or shadow. Generally speaking, we only sympathise when our sentiments and feelings correspond with those of another. Sympathy means approval. To give it is to praise, to withhold it to blame. How, then, does Adam Smith account for the growth of moral sentiments in the man, and for the progress of morality in mankind? He holds that what we call conscience, or the sense of duty, arises from a certain reflex action of sympathy. We apply to ourselves the moral judgements we have learned to pass on others. We imagine what they will say and think about our own thoughts and words and actions. We try to look at ourselves with the impartial eyes of other people, and seek to anticipate that judgment which they are likely to pass upon us. This is the first stage. But men have very different degrees of morality and wisdom. One man's praise or blame carries infinitely more weight than another's. Thus what is called conscience, that is our idea of the impartial spectator, insensibly develops. The impartial spectator becomes more and more our ideal man, and we come to pay more homage to his still small voice than to the judgment of the world. The pangs of conscience are far more terrible than the condemnation of the market-place. Praiseworthiness comes to be better than praise; blameworthiness comes to be worse than blame. The true hell is the hell within the breast; the worst tortures are those that follow the sentence of the impartial spectator. One feature in the phenomena of sympathy, which Smith points out, perhaps constitutes a weak point in his theory. The spectator's emotions are apt to fall short of the sufferer's. Compassion is never exactly the same as original sorrow.

Smith, like Kant, has his own way, and a curious one it is, of putting the rule of Christ. "As to love our neighbour as we love ourselves is the great law of Christianity, so it is the great precept of nature to love ourselves only as we love our neighbour, or what comes to the same thing, as our neighbour is capable of loving us." Our philosopher readily admits that there are passions, like love, which, "though almost unavoidable in some part of life," are not at first sight very agreeable to his theory. He says we cannot enter into the eagerness of a lover's emotions. They are always "in some measure ridiculous." "The passion appears to everybody but the man who feels it entirely disproportioned to the value of the object." Ovid's gaiety and Horace's gallantry are pleasant enough, but you grow weary of the "grave, pedantic, and long-sentenced love of Cowley and Petrarca."

Resentment provides him with a better illustration. The counterpart of gratitude, it is a very difficult passion to realise in a proper degree. "How many things," he exclaims, "are requisite to render the gratification of resentment completely agreeable and to make the spectator thoroughly sympathise with our revenge?" First, the provocation must be such that if unresented we should become contemptible and be exposed to perpetual insults. Second, smaller offences had better be neglected. Third, we should resent from a sense of propriety and of what is expected of us. Above all, we should diligently consider what would be the sentiments of the cool and impartial spectator.

Though the love of the lover has to be belittled for the purpose of this theory, friendship and all the social and benevolent affections are dear to sympathy and "please the indifferent spectator upon almost every occasion." True friendship is one of the virtues which prove the limitations of the utilitarian theory: "There is a satisfaction in the consciousness of being beloved which to a person of delicacy and sensibility is of more importance to happiness than all the advantage which he can expect to derive from it."

As Smith goes through the list of virtues and vices his "Impartial Spectator" constantly reminds us of Aristotle's theory that every virtue is a mean between two extremes. The impartial spectator dislikes excess. The rise of the upstart, for example, is too sudden an extreme, nor does his behaviour often conciliate our affections:—

> If the chief part of human happiness arises from the consciousness of being beloved, as I believe it does, those sudden changes of fortune seldom contribute much to happiness. He is happiest who advances more gradually to greatness, whom the public destines to every step of his preferment long before he arrives at it, in whom, upon that account, when it comes, it can excite no extravagant joy, and with regard to whom it cannot reasonably create either any jealousy in those he overtakes or any envy in those he leaves behind.

The Impartial Spectator is rather a fickle and illogical person; he does not like unexampled prosperity, but he is always ready to sympathise with trivial joys. "It is quite otherwise with grief. Small vexations excite no sympathy, but deep affliction calls forth the greatest." It takes a great grief to enlist our sympathy, for "it is painful to go along with grief, and we always enter it with reluctance." So when we hear a tragedy we struggle against sympathetic sorrow as long as we can, and when we finally give way, carefully conceal our tears! In a letter of July the 28th, 1759, from which we have already quoted, Hume made some objections to this part of Smith's theory:—

> I am told that you are preparing a new edition, and propose to make some additions and alterations in order to obviate objections. I shall use the freedom to propose one; which, if it appears to be of any weight, you may have in your eye. I wish you had more particularly and fully proved that all kinds of sympathy are agreeable. This is the hinge of your system, and yet you only mention the matter cursorily on p. 20. Now it would appear that there is a disagreeable sympathy as well as an agreeable. And, indeed, as the sympathetic passion is a reflex image of the principal, it must partake of its qualities, and be painful when that is so. . . .

> It is always thought a difficult problem to account for the pleasure from the tears and grief and sympathy of tragedy, which would not be the case

if all sympathy was agreeable. An hospital would be a more entertaining place than a ball. I am afraid that on p. 99 and 111 this proposition has escaped you, or rather is interwoven with your reasoning. In that place you say expressly, "It is painful to go along with grief, and we always enter into it with reluctance." It will probably be requisite for you to modify or explain this sentiment, and reconcile it to your system.

In the following spring (April 4th) Smith wrote from Glasgow to Strahan, Millar's [Andrew Millar, the publisher of *The Theory of Moral Sentiments*] young and very able partner, about the second edition, for which he had sent "a good many corrections and improvements." He asks Strahan to take care that the book is printed "pretty exactly according to the copy I delivered to you." Strahan, it seems, had offered his services as a critic, and Smith was a little afraid that he might find unauthorised alterations in the text. He will be much obliged to his publisher for suggestions, but cannot consent to surrender "the precious right of private judgment, for the sake of which your forefathers kicked out the Pope and the Pretender. I believe you to be much more infallible than the Pope, but as I am a Protestant, my conscience makes me scruple to submit to any unscriptural authority."

The second edition was issued soon afterwards. It has been erroneously described as a reprint of the first.[2] As a matter of fact, the corrections and alterations made in it were very numerous and it was set up in much smaller type, so that the 551 pages of the first edition are compressed, in spite of some enlargements of the text, into 436 pages. What is particularly noteworthy is that the author, without altering any of the passages criticised by Hume, does make what we conceive to be a perfectly satisfactory answer in an important footnote on page 76 of the second edition after the sentence, "It is painful to go along with grief, and we always enter into it with reluctance." We give the note in full in order that the reader may judge for himself:—

It has been objected to me that as I found the sentiment of approbation, which is always agreeable, upon sympathy, it is inconsistent with my system to admit any disagreeable sympathy. I answer, that in the sentiment of approbation there are two things to be taken notice of: first, the sympathetic passion of the spectator; and secondly, the emotion which arises from his observing the perfect coincidence between this sympathetic passion in himself, and the original passion in the person principally concerned. This last emotion, in which the sentiment of approbation properly consists, is always agreeable and delightful. The other may either be agreeable or disagreeable, according to the nature of the original passion, whose features it must always, in some measure, retain. Two sounds, I suppose, may each of them,

taken singly, be austere, and yet, if they are perfect concords, the perception of their harmony and coincidence may be agreeable.

Of modern philosophers, those to whom Smith is most indebted are certainly Mandeville, his old master Hutcheson, and his friend Hume, "an ingenious and agreeable philosopher who joins the greatest depth of thought to the greatest elegance of expression, and possesses the singular and happy talent of treating the abstrusest subjects not only with the most perfect perspicuity, but with the most lively eloquence." (Was it the religious prejudice against Hume that left his name unmentioned in the *Theory*?) All four were in a greater or less degree utilitarians. But Smith denies that the perception of a distinction between virtue and vice originates in the utility of the one and the disadvantageousness of the other. Hume would explain all virtues by their usefulness to oneself or society. But Smith only regards utility as a powerful additional reason for approving virtue and virtuous actions. It influences our ideas of virtue, as custom and fashion influence our ideas of beauty. Usefulness is seldom the first ground of approval, and "it seems impossible that we should have no other reason for praising a man than that for which we commend a chest of drawers." Even our approval of public spirit arises at first rather from a feeling of its magnificence and splendour than of its utility to the nation, though a sense of utility greatly strengthens our approval. Adam Smith notes, by the way, what Hume had not observed, that the fitness of a thing to produce its end is often more admired than the end itself. Most people prefer order and tidiness to the utility which they are intended to promote.

Buckle has remarked on a contrast between Smith's theory of morals and his theory of economics. In the first, sympathy is the premise, and he works out the principle of sympathy to its logical conclusions. In the *Wealth of Nations,* on the contrary, the word sympathy scarcely occurs. He assumes self-interest as the sole motive of the economic man, and works out all the consequences without troubling about that other-regarding principle which is the foundation and measure of morality, though he shows, it is true, that the motive of self-interest, if sufficiently enlightened, will result in the general good. Without denying that Buckle's contention is suggestive, we may observe that Smith distinctly refuses to confine virtue to benevolence, and parts company on this very point from "the amiable system" of Hutcheson. "Regard to our own private happiness, and interest too, appear," says he, "upon many occasions very laudable principles of action. The habits of economy, industry, discretion, attention, and application of thought are generally supposed to be cultivated from self-interested motives, and at the same time are apprehended to be very praiseworthy qualities, which deserve the esteem and approbation of everybody."[3] Benevolence may perhaps be the sole principle of action in the Deity, but an imperfect creature like man must and ought often to act from other motives.

To the third edition of the **Moral Sentiments** (1767) was appended an essay on the formation of Languages and the different genius of original and compounded languages. It is the fruit of his philological studies, and contains no doubt the substance of lectures that he had read in Edinburgh and Glasgow. He starts with the proposition that names of objects, that is to say, nouns substantive, must have been the first steps toward the making of a language. Two savages who had never been taught to speak would naturally begin to make their mutual wants intelligible by uttering certain sounds, as cave, tree, fountain, whenever they wanted to denote particular objects. What was at first a proper name would thus be extended to similar objects, by the same law which leads us to call a great philosopher a Newton. Similarly, "a child that is just learning to speak calls every person who comes into the house its papa or its mamma." Smith could call to mind a clown "who did not know the proper name of the river which ran by his own door." It was "*the* river." This process of generalisation explains the formation of those classes and assortments called genera and species in the schools, "of which the ingenious and eloquent M. Rousseau of Geneva finds himself so much at a loss to account for the origin."[4] In his account of the dual number, which he finds in all primitive and uncompounded languages, he says that in the rude beginnings of society, *one, two,* and *more,* might possibly be all the numerical distinctions which mankind would have any occasion to take notice of. But these words, though custom has rendered them familiar to us, "express perhaps the most subtle and refined abstractions which the mind of man is capable of forming." His purpose through all this ingenious train of reasoning was to suggest a new mode of approaching a subject which, in itself so fascinating, had been reduced to a dull routine. He is very severe on the Minerva of Sanctius and on some other grammarians who, neglecting the progress of nature, had expended all their industry in drawing up a number of artificial rules so as to exclude exceptions. He sees that languages are the products not of art but of nature or circumstance. He explains how the modern dialects of Europe arose from conquest, migration, and mixture—through Lombards trying to speak Latin, or Normans trying to speak Saxon. In this way the older tongues were decomposed and simplified in their rudiments while they grew more complex in composition. The processes of linguistic development provoke a comparison of philology with mechanics:—

All machines are generally, when first invented, extremely complex in their principles, and there is often a particular principle of motion for every particular movement which, it is intended, they should perform. Succeeding improvers observe, that one principle may be so applied as to produce several of those movements, and thus the machine becomes gradually more and more simple, and produces its effects with fewer wheels, and fewer principles of motion. In Language, in the same manner, every case of every noun, and every tense of every verb, was originally expressed by a particular distinct word, which served for this purpose and for no other. But succeeding observation discovered that one set of words was capable of supplying the place of all that infinite number, and that four or five prepositions, and half a dozen auxiliary verbs, were capable of answering the end of all the declensions, and of all the conjugations in the antient Languages.

The comparison, however, suggests a contrast. The simplification of machines renders them more perfect, but the simplification of languages renders them more and more imperfect, and less proper (in his opinion) for many of the purposes of expression. Thus in a decomposed and simple language, he observes, we are often restrained from disposing words and sounds in the most agreeable order. When Virgil writes

Tityre tu patulae recubans sub tegmine fagi,

we can easily see that *tu* refers to *recubans,* and *patulae* to *fagi,* though the related words are separated from one another by the intervention of several others. But if we translate the line literally into English, *Tityrus, thou of spreading reclining under the shade beech,* Œdipus himself could not make sense of it, because there is no difference in termination to assist us in tracking out the meaning. In the same way Milton's exquisite translation of Horace, "Who now enjoys thee, credulous all gold," etc., can only be interpreted by aid of the original. We may dissent when he goes on to denounce "the prolixness, constraint, and monotony of modern languages." Yet it would be as unfair to estimate the scientific value of these speculations by the accumulated achievements of modern philologists, as to sneer at his essay on the **"Imitative Arts"** or at Burke's treatise on the *Sublime and Beautiful,* because Lessing has helped inferior men to see so much further.

Notes

[1] The crude theory that sympathy is the foundation of altruism was noticed by Hutcheson. In his *System of Moral Philosophy* (B. I. ch. iii.) he writes: "Others say that we regard the good of others, or of societies . . . as the means of some subtiler pleasures of our own by sympathy with others in their happiness." But this sympathy, he adds, "can never account for all kind affections, tho' it is no doubt a natural principle and a beautiful part of our constitution."

[2] Mr. Rae's *Life of Adam Smith,* pp. 148-9. Mr. Rae also says that it contained none of the alterations or additions that Hume expected, and expresses surprise that the additions, etc., which had been placed in the printer's hands in 1760 were not incorporated in the text until the publication of the sixth edition thirty years afterwards. On the other hand, he says that the "Dissertation on the Origin of Languages" was added. But the "Dissertation" was first appended in the third edition (1767).

[3] See *Moral Sentiments,* 1st edition, p. 464.

[4] *Origine de l'inégalité. Partie première,* pp. 376, 377. *Édition d'Amsterdam des œuvres diverses de J. J. Rousseau.* The reference is from *Moral Sentiments,* 3rd ed. p. 440.

Albion W. Small (essay date 1907)

SOURCE: "The Economics and Sociology of Labor," in *Adam Smith and Modern Sociology: A Study in the Methodology of the Social Sciences,* The University of Chicago Press, 1907, pp. 79-154.

[*In the following excerpt, Small comments on the extent to which extra-economic factors such as sociology and psychology enter into Smith's analysis in* The Wealth of Nations, *and also compares Smith's economic theories with those of Karl Marx.*]

. . . [*The Wealth of Nations*] was primarily a technological inquiry, with the ways and means of producing national wealth as its objective; it assumed that this interest had a value of its own; at the same time it assumed that this interest in production is tributary to the interest in consumption; it assumes, further, that the wealth interest in general is but a single factor in the total scheme of human and divine purposes, and that, whatever the technique of satisfying the wealth interest may prove to be, the place of that interest in the whole harmony of human relations has to be established by a calculus in whose equations the formulas of economic technique are merely subordinate terms.

All of this was understood by Smith's friend Dugald Stewart, and it was uttered by him with sufficient clearness more than a century ago. It may assist our own insight to recall some of his words:[1]

> The foregoing very imperfect hints appear to me to form not only a proper, but in some measure a necessary introduction to the few remarks I have to offer on Mr. Smith's *Inquiry;* as they tend to illustrate a connection between his system of commercial politics [*sic*], and those speculations of his earlier years in which he aimed more professedly at the advancement of human improvement and happiness. It is this view of political economy that

can alone render it interesting to the moralist, and can dignify calculations of profit and loss in the eye of the philosopher. Mr. Smith has alluded to it in various passages of his work, but he has nowhere explained himself fully on the subject; and the great stress he has laid on the division of labour in increasing its productive powers, seems at first sight, to point to a different and very melancholy conclusion:—that the same causes which promote the progress of the arts, tend to degrade the mind of the artist; and, of consequence, that the growth of national wealth implies a sacrifice of the character of the people.

> The fundamental doctrines of Mr. Smith's system are now so generally known, that it would be tedious to offer any recapitulation of them in this place, even if I could hope to do justice to the subject, within the limits which I have prescribed to myself. I shall content myself, therefore, with remarking, in general terms, that the great and leading object of his speculations is, to illustrate the provisions made by nature on the principles of the human mind, and in the circumstances of man's external situation, for a gradual and progressive augmentation in the means of national wealth; and to demonstrate that the most effectual plan for advancing a people to greatness, is to maintain that order of things which nature has pointed out, by allowing every man, as long as he observes the rules of justice, to pursue his own interest in his own way, and to bring both his industry and his capital into the freest competition with those of his fellow citizens. Every system of policy which endeavours either by extraordinary encouragements to draw toward a particular species of industry a greater share of the capital of the society than what would naturally go to it, or, by extraordinary restraint, to force from a particular species of industry some share of the capital which would otherwise be employed in it, is, in reality, subversive of the great purpose which it means to promote.

In other words, what we know of Adam Smith's whole scheme of thinking justifies the interpretation that, as it presented itself to his mind, what we now formulate as the general sociological problem might be explained as follows:

The destiny of mankind is to work out a certain moral achievement. The great intellectual task is to understand the conditions and implications of that destiny. There are certain grand divisions of that task. Not touching upon those which belong within the scope of so-called natural or physical science, the first division of the intellectual problem of discovering the conditions and implications of human destiny—that is, the terms in accordance with which mankind must learn how to achieve well-being, or happiness, or progress, or whatever term we may prefer to use as the algebraic x to denote the content of that undetermined resultant of human endeavor toward which we look when we employ the concept destiny—the first division of the problem of human life in the large, is religious. Human life is conditioned by its relations to a divine order and purpose. That divine purpose must be investigated, and so far as possible understood, in order to get the bearings of human life. Then, without attempting to put into Smith's theory details about which we cannot get information, we have evidence enough to show that, whether as a subordinate section of religious relations, or as a division of relations somehow parallel with the religious relations, there was an *ethical* division of life. If we were to judge merely from the essay on the moral sentiments, we should be left to the impression that Smith's conception of ethics was that it had to do merely with the theory of *appreciation* or *evaluation*. We know, however, that this psychological discussion represented merely preliminaries which in his mind led to the doctrines of practical morals, and that the whole plexus of moral attitudes with reference to which approbation or disapprobation is possible constituted in his mind a plane of human activities distinct from that which for him made up the religious sphere. Then the third division of the problem of understanding human life appeared to Smith to be that which deals with the history and theory of civic justice, the ways and means of attempting to secure an approximation to the principles of morals which ethics treats in the abstract and in the individualistic phases. And, finally, as all moral achievement has to get the use of material bases and media, it was necessary to work out a science of the ways and means by which the necessary material conditions of all spiritual achievement are to be secured. Thus Smith's science of wealth had relatively the same relation to his whole philosophy of life that the technique of marine architecture has to our systems of commercial and admiralty and international law. It was not a science of people in the fulness of their lives. It was merely a science of things and people considered as factors in producing the material equipment of life.

I repeat that we are not at all bound to justify Smith's classification. It is an entirely negligible matter that his analysis of moral phenomena would not now satisfy anyone. The main thing is that he had a definite perception of the mediate, and subordinate, and tributary status of wealth, and that he betrayed relatively slight symptoms of the tendency, which was so strong in the stereotyped classical theory, to assume that the wealth factor is the sole arbiter of social relations. How to build a ship is one thing. How to settle questions of equity between builders, and owners, and officers, and crew, and shippers, and passengers, and consignees, and other navigators, and commercial interests of the nations at large, is a very different thing. The former is analogous with the questions which Smith directly raised in *The Wealth of Nations*. The latter are suggestive analogues of the sort of questions which he

saw the need of raising in his wider moral philosophy, and in spite of himself indirectly raised in his economic discussion.[2]

We have to justify these propositions by a rapid analysis of *The Wealth of Nations* itself.

Chapter I expounds the purely technical theorem:

> The greatest improvement in the productive powers of labor, and the greater part of the skill, dexterity, and judgment with which, it is anywhere directed, or applied, seem to have been the *effects of the division of labour.*

This is a proposition which is as far outside the range of moral relations, as Smith thought of them, as elementary theorems about the increased efficiency of power applied by means of wedge, pulley, screw, or lever.

Smith attributes the increase of work which division of labor makes possible to three factors: *first,* to the increase of dexterity in every particular workman; *second,* to saving of time usually lost in passing from one species of work to another; *third,* to the invention of machines which enable one man to do the work of many.

Under the last head he introduces a consideration which might be generalized beyond the form in which he uses it; viz.:

> All the improvements in machinery, however, have by no means been the inventions of those who had occasion to use the machines. Many improvements have been made by the ingenuity of the makers of the machines, when to make them became the business of a peculiar trade; and some by that of those who are called philosophers or men of speculation, whose trade it is not to do anything, but to observe everything, and who, upon that account, are often capable of combining together the powers of the most distant and dissimilar objects.[3]

Without restricting this factor to its value in the invention of machinery, we may say that the division of labor makes room for activities which have increasingly remote relations to the productive process, and sets free types of action which enrich life, whether or not they have a direct influence upon processes of producing wealth.[4]

The chapter contains a further theorem which squints toward the bearing of economic factors upon social structure; viz.:

> The separation of different trades and employments is a consequence of the efficiency of the division of

labour, and is most extensive in the countries which enjoy the highest degree of industry and improvement.[5]. . .

In its primary purpose the first chapter of *The Wealth of Nations* is no more an essay in moral relations than an agricultural chemist's statement of the reasons why the virgin soil of the Canadian wheat area is more fertile than an abandoned farm in New England. It has been an effective stimulus of later inquiry into moral relations, but it is immediately no more moral, as Smith would use the term, than a comparison of the vegetation of the temperate and torrid zones.

In Chapter II Smith discusses "the principle which gives occasion to the division of labour." The thesis is as follows:

> This division of labour, from which so many advantages are derived, is not originally the effect of any human wisdom, which foresees and intends that general opulence to which it gives occasion. It is the necessary, though very slow and gradual, consequence of a *certain propensity* in human nature which has in view no such extensive utility; *the propensity to truck, barter, and exchange one thing for another.*

Of this proposition we may say, first, it is methodologically an *obiter dictum*. That is, it belongs in a larger range of inquiry, antecedent and fundamental to the technological inquiry to which *The Wealth of Nations* is devoted. It is, moreover, a species of inquiry for which Smith's scheme of moral philosophy apparently does not provide a plane. It is related to the proper subject-matter of economics, as conceived by the author of *The Wealth of Nations,* very much as an inquiry into the ultimate physical reasons for the relative durability of wood and steel would be related to an engineer's account of the comparative economy of these materials, as discovered by experience, for constructing railroad bridges.

In the second place, the exact nature of the question which Smith raises in this chapter is primarily psychological, and secondarily socio-psychological. It is therefore a fair index of the closeness of relationship between the phenomena of industry and the general phenomena of individual and social consciousness. In this connection Smith's work is a premonition of the inevitable awakening of the sociological consciousness with the unavoidable pursuit of inquiries (which may have started among economic phenomena), out into all their relationships as moral and physical phenomena.

In the third place, the particular explanation which Smith proposes is of a piece with the mental philosophizings of his time, but it merely applies a mouth-filling name to an unanalyzed phenomenon. The "propensity to barter" is just as much and just as little a distinct and ultimate force in human affairs as a "propensity to swim," or a "propensity to jump over stone walls," or a "propensity to go to the circus." If we fall into the water, we try to swim, because we have a preference for living. The same fact, appealed to from another direction, stimulates us to make the best of our ability to get over a wall if we are chased by a bull. Certain desires for nervous stimulation find temporary satisfaction in the circus, but a thousand alternative recourses may serve the same purpose. That is, Smith scratched the surface of psychological phenomena, which have since his time furnished problems for more exact psychology and sociology.

In the fourth place, we may observe that this sort of explanation is not yet entirely discredited even among rather prominent scholars. Sombart has thought it worth while to ridicule such pseudo-explanation at some length.[7]

In this same chapter Smith starts another line of inquiry, which is also external to economic technology, but, like the problem of psychical motivation in general, it could not be ignored, even at his preliminary stage of research. It is strictly an essay in anthropology. The facts in the case, quite independent of our apprehension of them, are in their degree responsible for many social differences, while more or less definite theories about the facts are shaping both abstract sociological doctrines and concrete social programs. He says:

> The difference of natural talents in different men, is, in reality, much less than we are aware of, and the very different genius which appears to distinguish men of different professions, when grown up to maturity, is not so much the cause, as the effect of the division of labour. The difference between the most dissimilar characters, between a philosopher and a common street porter, for example, seems to arise not so much from nature, as from habit, custom and education. . . . By nature a philosopher is not in genius and in disposition half so different from a street porter, as a mastiff is from a greyhound, or a greyhound from a spaniel, or this last from a shepherd's dog.[8]

These propositions, taken by themselves, are identical with clauses in the doctrines of nearly all the modern revolutionary philosophers. They are taken for granted by most of the extreme socialists. The truth or error of the propositions is not before us for discussion in this argument. The significant point is that Smith instinctively perceived the close relation between the technological problems of wealth, and the anthropological and psychological and social problems of people.

Chapter III elaborates the thesis that, "as it is the power of exchanging that gives occasion to the division of labour, so the extent of this division must always be limited to the extent of that power, or, in other words, by the extent of the market."

In one sense this proposition is strictly physical. It is no more to be disputed than the proposition that the pressure of water at the bottom of a tube is in proportion to the height of the water in the tube.

On the other hand, Smith does not hint at the broad scope of the question, What makes a market? This is a sociological problem in the most extensive sense. Its answer must come from knowledge of the whole gamut and the most refined combinations of human desires. Li Hung Chang is reported to have said that, if he could persuade every man in China to add a couple of inches to the length of his shirt-tail, he could create a market for all the cotton grown in America. The population of China is not necessarily a market for American cotton. By a decree of the imperial government, if Great Britain could be induced to acquiesce, China might cease to be a market for opium, etc., etc. While, therefore, this chapter contains a very important principle of economic technology, it leaves untouched the much more important sociological question of the origin and variation of markets. . . .

Chapter IV, on "The Origin and Use of Money as a Medium of Exchange," does not probe farther into the sociology and psychology of money than is necessary for immediate explanation of the obvious phenomena of exchange. It therefore has the same relation to ultimate sociology and psychology that a mechanic's explanation of the advantages of lubricating oils would have to physics and chemistry. The chapter contains illustrations in abundance of the psychological nature of the forces that have originated and modified the use of money through varied estimates of convenience. The point of view, however, is exclusively that of the technique of the economic cycle—production, exchange, division of labor, widening of the market, more production, more division of labor, more widening of the market, etc., etc.

At the close of the chapter the author enters upon that thus far unbounded sea of troubles, the theory of value.

We discover at a glance, in the light of the economic discussion of nearly a century, that Smith's treatment of the subject was on a relatively superficial plane. That is, he was discussing the technique, not the psychology, nor the logic, nor the sociology, of money. This appears at once in his forms of expression; e.g.:

> What are the rules [*sic*] which men naturally observe in exchanging them [goods] either for money or for one another, I shall now proceed to examine. Three rules [*sic*] determine what shall be called the relative

or exchangeable value of goods.

> The word *value,* it is to be observed, has two different meanings, and sometimes expresses the utility of some particular object, and sometimes the power of purchasing other goods which the possession of that object conveys. The one may be called "value in use," the other, "value in exchange." . . . In order to investigate the principles which regulate the exchangeable value of commodities, I shall endeavour to show, first, what is the real measure of this exchangeable value; or wherein consists the real price of all commodities; secondly, what are the different parts of which this real price is composed, or made up; and lastly, what are the different circumstances which sometimes raise some or all of these different parts of price above, and sometimes sink them below their natural or ordinary rate; or what are the causes which sometimes hinder the market price, that is, the actual price of commodities from coinciding exactly with what may be called their natural price.[9]

Three chapters follow, on the subjects thus proposed. It is easy to point out, at this late day, that we open up the whole unknown world of the psychology and sociology of value when we begin to observe that some tribes will exchange their goods for wampum, and some for paper promises to pay, and some for gold only. It is easy to find in Adam Smith's discussion the points at which paths lead farther into the by-ways of these subjects than he felt impelled to pry. As a matter of fact, however, we have to follow the whole nineteenth-century history of economic theory, up to the point where we find John Stuart Mill declaring that the theory of value had been settled, and then through another generation, which encounters more difficulties than ever in the theory of value—we have to review this whole evolution, to be aware of the full measure of difference between the technological treatment of value in *The Wealth of Nations,* and the problems that present themselves to modern philosophers when they attempt to formulate the phenomena of money and of value in terms of their ultimate relations.

At the same time, one might easily mistake the first paragraph of the fifth chapter for a royal road, instead of an untrodden path, into the broadest realms of social philosophy. If one did not know the sequel, one might with good reason surmise that an earlier Karl Marx had been discovered. In this paragraph Smith is certainly nearer to the fundamental theorem of Marx than to the major premises of economic theory and practice at the present time, at least in England and the United States. The paragraph reads as follows:

> Every man is rich or poor according to the degree in which he can afford to enjoy the necessaries, conveniences, and amusements of human life. But after the division of labour has once thoroughly

taken place, it is by the very small part of these with which a man's own labour can supply him. The far greater part of them he must derive from the labour of other people, and he must be rich or poor according to the quantity of that labour which he can command, or which he can afford to purchase. The value of any commodity, therefore, to the person who possesses it, and who means not to use or consume it himself, but to exchange it for other commodities, is equal to the quantity of labour which it enables him to purchase or command. Labour, therefore, is the real measure of the exchangeable value of all commodities.[10]

We shall have occasion to observe presently how Smith restrained himself from following this clue in the direction which Marx afterward took. We may notice, in passing, that, although Smith very distinctly reiterated the same theorem when discussing the wages of labor (Chap. VIII), he approached it as an explanation of the problem of value in general and of price in particular. It did not occur to him as a class question at all. He was in the course of explaining the mechanism of civilized exchanges, and his assumption was that the mechanism was working normally. He was not searching for a clue to a situation which he considered abnormal. Practically no grievances were alleged against the essential structure of the economic system. Such charges as were brought against social arrangements at this time were principally political in form, whatever might have been their implicit economic content. The antithesis of labor and capital, as social categories, was at that time virtually unknown. Labor and capital were purely economic categories, and could be treated as abstractions, whether on the debit or credit side of the reckoning, without provoking class prejudice. Precisely the opposite was the case when Marx wrote, and this was at all events an important factor in deciding that in Marx's hands a labor theory of value became directly a class issue instead of a mere technical distinction.

Then we must make note of another effect upon Smith's mind of the presumption that the system which he tried to explain was operating normally. That is, he was phenomenally unconscious, as it appears after a century of closer analysis, that commonplace, everyday exchanges could not be accounted for by his extremely naïve theory of price. It would be easy for us to make an *a-priori* argument to the effect that a man so wise as he could not possibly have overlooked, as he did, some of the plain gaps between the facts and his explanation; but the reason is evidently to be found in his disregard of the artificial and arbitrary social arrangements by which civilization complicates the simple order of human actions. In other words, when he attempted to explain the phenomena of price, his logical process seems to have been, first, a generalization of the simplest conceivable exchanges of the products of

labor into the type of all exchanges. Then, instead of using that generalization merely as a search hypothesis—i.e., to guide a complete induction—he used it as a principle for explaining all exchanges deductively. Of course, this amounts logically to begging the question with respect to every case of exchange which is not used as a means of testing the generalization. That is, such a principle once adopted for such use is a blind leader of the blind. It glosses over the facts instead of exposing them. . . .

When Smith says, for instance, "Labour was the first price, the original purchase money that was paid for all things,"[12] he overpersuades himself, more than he is aware, that the same is true in the same degree in all purchases. For our present purpose it is enough to point out that the result was an intolerable vagueness and approximateness in his theory of exchanges. Thus he says:[13]

> The real price of everything, what everything really costs to the man who wants to acquire it, is the toil and trouble of acquiring it. What everything is really worth to the man who has acquired it, and who wants to dispose of it or exchange it for something else, is the toil and trouble which it can save to himself, and which it can impose upon other people.[14]

It is by no means clear precisely what Smith meant by these propositions, but any version that might be proposed would be ruled out, as an adequate formula of exchanges, by types of cases which could not be so explained. This, however, has been the theme of a voluminous economic literature for nearly a century. Our argument does not call for an examination of the progress of analysis on this point. We may simply note, by way of illustration, that no formulation of the mere mechanism of economic exchanges can possibly express the essential facts of value and price. These are phenomena resulting from more than one variable. They are psychical and social as well as mechanical. There is probably a certain minute portion of the "toil and trouble" element in every case of value, but whether it is the "toil and trouble" which it actually costs the producer to produce it, or the "toil and trouble" which it would cost the purchaser to produce it, or the "toil and trouble" to which the purchaser would be liable if he had to go without it, actual exchanges in civilized society could not be expressed uniformly in terms of either concept. "Toil and trouble" as an equivalent for the term "labor expended in production" can in very few cases be an equally approximate measure of the reason why the seller sells and why the buyer buys. Value or price sometimes has one ratio to the labor-cost of production or of reproduction, and sometimes a quite different ratio. These familiar considerations may be summed up in the platitude: Price or value is a phenomenon of two chief variables; viz., first, the conditions governing the supply, and, second, the conditions governing appreciation as a factor of demand.[15]

In a word, Smith's attempt at an explanation of price and value credited labor-cost with too exclusive significance; or, to express the same thing from the other point of view, it failed to make due allowance for the subjective and social factors in value and price. All this has meanwhile been made evident by the economists themselves, though it is equally evident that the last word has not been said, and that the psychologists and sociologists have a function in tracing the facts to their ultimate elements.

When Smith touches upon the relation of wealth to anything beyond the immediate technicalities of economic processes, his propositions affect the modern reader as relatively less applicable to the real world of today than they were to his own time. . . . They are approximations to truth, but the approach was so much closer when he wrote, that, under the operation of present conditions, some of the paragraphs, when applied to our world, read almost like satire. . . .

In Chapter VI, on "The Component Parts of Commodities," we come upon a turn of the argument which it is by no means easy to understand or to appraise. The first reason for this is that we cannot be sure how clearly Smith drew the distinction between what is and what ought to be in the processes of industry. That is, it is by no means certain that he always confined himself to bare analysis of the occurrences in commerce, and we are not always able to tell when he wanted to be understood as merely formulating the facts, and when he adds to the facts his own appraisals.

For instance, speaking of labor, in an "advanced state of society," he says: "In this state of things, the whole produce of labour does not always belong to the labourer."[21] As a bald statement of fact, this is literally true. Does Smith, or does he not, mean to imply that the extent to which it is true is strictly in accordance with equity? We can answer this question only vaguely. Smith certainly had no thought of any such radical injustice as Marx afterward alleged in this connection. It is not certain that he would assert that there was any injustice at all in the system of distribution operated by the society of his day. This in spite of the fact that in certain concrete cases, like those of the colliers or the salters, he protested against abuses. He had not generalized such items into an indictment against the industrial system at large. Apparently he assumed that the more complicated system of production, consequent upon division of labor, automatically invented a corresponding system of distribution, in which the reward of each participant in production was assigned in strict ratio with the value of his labor in creating the product. Whether he would have asserted precisely this or not, if the question had been distinctly proposed, it is

evident that in his mind there was not yet a problem of distribution which was not settled in advance by the technique of production. . . . Smith goes on to say:

> Neither is the quantity of labour commonly employed in acquiring or producing any commodity the only circumstance which can regulate the quantity which it ought commonly to purchase, command or exchange for. And additional quantity, it is evident, must be due for the profits of the stock which advanced wages and furnished the materials of that labour.

We may not be able to divest our minds of associations formed by study of the economic literature since Adam Smith. We may do our best, however, to judge him for a moment, in the cold light of abstract logic, without reference to disturbing interests. We may claim to be attempting at least to think judicially when we call attention to a significant anomaly in this confident assertion. Is it not remarkable that, so soon after declaring labor to be "the real measure of the exchangeable value of all commodities,"[22] Smith should feel at liberty to take for granted that profits are as evidently due to the capitalist as wages are to the laborer? To be sure, Smith has not in so many words said that labor is the only *source* of wealth. He has merely said that labor is the only real *measure* of wealth. At the same time, his language conveys the impression that in his mind the concepts "source" and "measure" were so associated that they amounted to the same thing. He said, a few pages later: "Wages, profit, and rent are the three principal *sources* of all revenue, as well as of all exchangeable value."[23] Again he remarks: "As in a civilized country there are but few commodities of which the exchangeable value arises *from labour only.* . . . ."[24]

In Smith's mind the claim of capital to profits appeared as evident and immediate as the claim of labor to its wage. Not quite three-quarters of a century later, Marx launched his system of social philosophy centered about absolute denial of the claim of capital to profits.[25] Yet, as we have seen, the two men seem to have held nearly identical views of labor as the ultimate measure of right to wealth. How shall we account for the evolution of the classical political economy and Marxian socialism from so nearly identical conceptions of the relation of labor to wealth?

The truth probably is that Smith's views never actually approached quite so near to the major premise of Marx's system as would appear from the things which Smith left unsaid, or from the partially uncritical form of the things which he actually said. Judged by himself in other connections, as, for example, the propositions last cited, and Chapter IX, "Of the Profits of Stock," Smith never entertained a doubt that the payment of profits to capital is as strictly and fundamentally consistent with the natural order of things as the payment of wages to labor. Whether this state of things represented an undetected contradiction in Smith's mind, or whether it was merely an accident of incomplete formulation of his views, may never be decided. This much is obvious: If Adam Smith had introduced into economic theory a searching critique of the basis of the claims of capital to profits, Marx's economic doctrine would in all probability never have put in an appearance. If it had appeared, it could hardly, under the supposed circumstances, have been fathered by a man of Marx's intellectual power. If justice and only justice had meanwhile been done both to capital and to labor, in the way of working out a valid theory of when and why and in what proportion each deserves a share of the surplus product, Marx might still have become a socialist, but his socialism would certainly have had a different point of detachment from orthodox economic theory.

Profits, as the man on the street uses the word, is a blanket term which may include elements as heterogeneous as wages and graft and loot. To some of these elements one capitalist has as clear a title as the laborer has to his wage. To others of these elements another capitalist has no more title in equity than the bank-breaker has to his stealings. Smith did not feel the necessity of a critique of the title of capital to profits, because his attention was turned in the direction of the productive activities of capitalists, and their consequent title to their reward. Marx was intensely impressed by the political and commercial usurpations which sanctioned arbitrary claims of masters and denied some of the natural claims of workmen. In Marx's time it was becoming necessary to recognize the class cleavage between capitalists and laborers. The contrasts between their situations were so sharp that it was as easy for Marx to assume that the capitalist is not a laborer, and consequently not entitled to a wage in the form of profits, or otherwise, as it was three-quarters of a century earlier for Smith to assume that the capitalist is a laborer, and therefore entitled to a wage in the form of profits.[26] Unconsciously, and doubtless with equal intention to represent things as they are, both Smith and Marx started a fashion of pinning economic faith to a false universal. In the former case it was, "Every capitalist deserves profits." In the latter case it was, "No capitalist deserves profits." For purposes of analysis we may separate the logical from the moral elements in modern social theory and practice. Speaking, then, of the logical phase only, we may say that the phenomenon of Marxian socialism is merely, in Hegelian terms, the inevitable extreme antithesis of Smith's extreme thesis, and that inevitable criticism is now ascertaining the elements of truth in both false universals, and combining them in a synthesis that shall more closely approach a true universal. . . .

The next following five chapters (VII-XI), on the general subject of the factors entering into the price of commodities, might furnish texts for many times that number of chapters on the social variants of "natural" and "market" price. If we should enter upon a subject of this sort, however, it should be with the latest economic formulas as the brief in view of which we should draw up our own plea. It would introduce unnecessary confusion if we should attempt to restate in sociological terms all of Smith's propositions about price. In the first place, they are primarily technological, not sociological. In the second place, they appear in present economic theory with much revision, so that to a considerable extent we should be wasting our strength trying to do over again much that the economists have meanwhile done, if we tried to restate Smith's doctrines in detail. Our cue at this point, therefore, is, first, to note that the argument now becomes relatively technical, with the extra-economic factors relatively negligible; second, that at the outset of this technical inquiry a prime sociological question is waived, and that this sociological question is ever present with us when we face our practical problems of correlating our economic systems with the remainder of our institutions. We must make this last statement more explicit.

At the beginning of Chapter VII Smith introduces the distinction between "natural" price and "market" price. He says:

> There is in every society or neighbourhood an ordinary or average rate both of wages and profit in every different employment of labour and stock. This rate is naturally regulated, as I shall show hereafter, partly by the general circumstances of the society [*sic*], their riches or poverty, their advancing, stationary or declining condition; and partly by the particular nature of each employment.

> There is likewise in every society or neighbourhood an ordinary or average rate of rent, which is regulated too, as I shall show hereafter, partly by the general circumstances [*sic*] of the society or neighbourhood in which the land is situated, and partly by the natural or improved fertility of the land.

> These ordinary or average rates may be called the natural rates of wages, profit, and rent, at the time and place in which they commonly prevail.

> When the price of any commodity is neither more nor less than what is sufficient to pay the rent of the land, the wages of the labourer and the profits of the stock employed in raising, preparing and bringing it to market, according to their natural rates, the commodity is then sold for what may be called its natural price.

The commodity is then sold precisely for what it is worth, or for what it really costs the person who brings it to market. . . . .

The actual price at which any commodity is commonly sold is called its market price. It may either be above, or below, or exactly the same with natural price.[32]

As a rough and ready formal division, the distinction is of course perfectly familiar and obvious and necessary. When we attempt to apply it to a concrete case of price in a modern community, however, we encounter a difficulty, not with the formal principle of division, but with questions of fact which should determine the application of the principle. Perhaps the essence of the matter may be suggested by a mere verbal correction. If we substitute for the phrase "natural price" the term "customary price," we at once raise the question whether there is a difference between the two concepts. If we think the question through, there is little room for doubt that Smith's phrase harbors a fundamental fallacy. The "customary," in price as in other things, may be far from the "natural," if we mean by "natural" that which is most nearly in accord with the permanent or essential nature of things. For instance, suppose a community has for a generation been paying for its illuminating gas a price which includes a profit on watered stock equal to two or three times the market rates of interest on the actual capital invested. If we adopt the contention of the gas company that it is entirely within its rights in watering its stock and in treating the fictitious investment as though it were real, then it would make no difference whether we used the phrase "natural" or "customary" price. In other words, so soon as prices, whether in the element of rent, or profits, or wages, come to be in question on grounds of equity, it makes all the difference in the world with our decision how much of the variable and arbitrary "general circumstances of the society" we assume to be natural and necessary, and so inflexible factors of price.

All the mooted social questions of today over economic claims of various classes are to a greater or less degree contests over the claim that vested or customary rights are natural rights. There is never a question between democracy and privilege, especially if the privilege has actually been exercised, in which it is not contended, openly or tacitly, on the side of the privilege, that the privilege is in accordance with the eternal nature of things. At this moment the extreme "stand-patters" on the subject of the American tariff do their best to make their fellow-citizens believe that the bonus which the law gives them is a price which they have as natural a right to collect of the consumer as the laborer has to collect his hire. The men who have fixed railroad rates in the past want perpetual freedom to make rates without governmental control, and they

claim that such freedom is "natural," while governmental control is unnatural.

That is, all the conventionalities which fix the standard of living in a given community may for a long time be taken for granted, and accordingly the wage of unskilled labor may be less for a month in Russia than the wages for the same class of labor may be for an eight-hour day in some parts of the United States. The Russian employer and the American employee could not be brought to an agreement as to which of these rates of wages, if either, represented the "natural" price of labor. So far as the bookkeeping of a particular industry is concerned, or the conditions of competition in a given market, customary price may be treated as "natural" price. But the moment price becomes a moral question, by being brought into the arena of conflict between groups with antagonistic interests in distribution, then the previous question is always in order; viz.: How much of customary market valuation is not natural but unnatural? To what extent have the conventionalities of society interfered with the natural equilibration of the claims of all the members of society?

Again we must remind ourselves that at Adam Smith's time there was a minimum of occasion for imagining that there could or should ever be any considerable modification in the laws of property in Great Britain. British institutions, on their strictly economic side at least, as distinguished from the politico-economic phases as involved in such a question as restricted or free foreign trade, must have seemed to Smith nearly as firmly settled as the rock-bound coasts of the kingdom. It cost him no stretch of the imagination, no stultification of mind or conscience, to assume that the customary social stratification, from landed gentlemen to navvy, was in rough correspondence with natural law. In the middle of the nineteenth century, on the contrary, especially in Germany, doubts had already disturbed such sunny satisfaction. Today the operation of the same principles which Smith took for granted produces anomalies which no judicially minded person can overlook. We have come to understand that there are really three categories of price, instead of two. We may call these "customary price," "market price," and "normal price." The last phrase means just what the words might have meant to Adam Smith, minus the implication that the third and the first categories necessarily correspond. Everyone who perceives that the last valuation of everything in this world must be in terms of people, not in terms of commodities, is beginning to draw the inference that there is always an open question whether the current scale of prices takes sufficient account of human values to approach as near as possible to normal prices.

I am not at all sure that socialists of the Marxian or any other type are really nearer in sympathy than Adam

Smith was to the practical application of the human measure of value. Socialism seems to be, in fact, in the aggregate, less a contention for application of deeper moral principles, than a contention for admission of a larger number of people to a share in the dividends of the moral principles than now prevail in society. Socialism does not seem to be really a program of more respect for men, but rather of respect for more men. So far as it goes, even this is an impulse in the direction of more authentic democracy. More radically democratic, however, than any socialistic principle, is the perception that the capacity of people to convert material goods and opportunities into higher values is the last measure of price which it is possible to apply. It is always an open social question whether there are artificial and arbitrary restrictions of the equal freedom of all to exercise this capacity. So far as a disposition to entertain this question is an item in "the general circumstances of the society," a force is at work tending either to strengthen prices, because they approximate a scale dictated by due appraisal of human values, or to rearrange prices with more regard for the human term in the calculation.

There is no fig-leaf of economic shame discreetly drawn over Smith's admission that all the products of labor belonged to the laborer till private property in land and the accumulation of stock made a new situation.[33] Although Smith regarded these as artificial, in a sense contrasted with primitive, it does not seem to have occurred to him that they were artificial in a sense opposed to his term "natural" any more than the division of labor itself. There was nothing to excuse about one of these phenomena more than about all. In spite of keen vision for what he would regard as the accidents of a system which was essentially rational or "natural," in spite of such details as that, "We have no acts of parliament against combining to lower the price of work; but many against combining to raise it,"[34] Smith accepted the ground-plan of British economic institutions as unassailable. The inferences drawn by Marx from premises so nearly identical with those of Smith would have seemed to the latter so preposterous that he was under no sort of embarrassment in stating those premises with perfect frankness. No social phenomena had appeared to make Smith doubt that in general the capitalist's claim to profits and the landlord's claim to rent is as clear as the laborer's claim to wages. In other words, slightly varying our previous statement, Smith did not doubt that the wage system was essentially a righteous system, in spite of the fact that it permitted a part of the product to go to the landlord, and another part to the capitalist. . . .

[We] point out the probability that there would have been no Marxism, except as a political movement, if economic theory, from Adam Smith's time, had squarely faced the problem: What are the primary economic elements, and what are the accidental conventional elements, in our system of property rights? We should probably have been spared a large part of the confusion which permits certain types of social agitators to treat all private ownership of land as in principle and in practice absentee landlordism, and all private ownership of capital as in principle and in practice stock-watering and gambling. Modern sociology is a necessary protest as much against the extreme prejudice of the economists as of the socialists.[36]

Notes

[1] *Account of the Life and Writings of Adam Smith,* p. liv.

[2] The *Lectures on Justice,* etc. . . . contain nothing that affects this summary. The treatment is wholly historical and legal, in form and substance, except in Parts II and III, which might be classed as economic rather than legal or historical. At all events, the relation of the lectures to antecedent moral philosophy does not appear to have been unlike that of *The Wealth of Nations* of which . . . the lectures are virtually a first draft.

[3] I, p. 11.

[4] Mallock, *Aristocracy and Evolution* (London, 1898), opposes to what he is pleased to call sociology, on the one hand, and to an equally questionable version of socialism, on the other, a ponderous argument, drawn out through three hundred and eighty pages, the substance of which is merely a variation of this perception of the advantages of the division of labor. The thread of wisdom that runs through the book is entangled in a woeful snarl of irrelevance and inconsequence. His generalizations about sociology fall flat among sociologists, because he apparently bounds sociology by Herbert Spencer, Edward Bellamy, Benjamin Kidd, and Sidney Webb! His account of socialism is equally provincial. The great-man theory which he revises and recommends as a remedy for the errors of both, easily boils down to the fact of the *advantages of specialization*. This is all implicitly, and much of it expressly, in *The Wealth of Nations;* it has been exhibited much more voluminously by Tarde, although under the inadequate labels "imitation" and "invention;" it has been generalized most correctly by my colleague, Professor W. I. Thomas, in his interpretation "pace-making."

Mr. Mallock's volume is an ingeniously elaborated insinuation that the world is shrouding itself in darkness through failure to perceive that, of all specializers, the specializer in money-making is pre-eminently entitled to its forbearance, its admiration, and its fostering favor. The pathos of this appeal so overstimulates the "impartial spectator's" sense of humor that he is embarrassed in doing justice to the elements in the book which deserve serious attention.

[5] P. 7. . . .

[7] *Moderne Kapitalismus,* Vol. I, pp. xxv ff.

[8] Pp. 16 f.

[9] Pp. 28, 29.

[10] Cf. Chap. VI, 4th paragraph, p. 48; also p. 50, 2d paragraph. . . .

[12] P. 30.

[13] *Ibid.*

[14] I refrain from turning any light from the "marginal utility theory" upon Smith. According to the outline of analysis of which this essay is a detail, that development must be noticed in its chronological order.

[15] Cf. Simmel, "A Chapter in the Philosophy of Value," *American Journal of Sociology,* Vol. V, p. 577. For further concrete illustrations of the lack of precision in Smith's labor theory of value, see [Walter] Bagehot, *Economic Studies,* pp. 121 ff. . . .

[21] P. 50.

[22] Chap. V, p. 30.

[23] P. 53.

[24] P. 54.

[25] I am referring, of course, to the *Communist Manifesto,* not to *Capital.*

[26] It is not true, and I do not assert, that Marx utterly overlooked the industrial function of the capitalist. He admitted it, but then he obscured it in such a way that it has been easy for his followers to ignore it, while supposing that they were following his teachings. Using the names of Smith and Marx to label tendencies for which they were partly responsible, I point out the mistaken assumptions of the tendencies, while I am aware that neither Smith nor Marx is justly to be charged with deliberately promulgating the extreme errors to which their theories have lent force. . . .

[32] Pp. 55, 56.

[33] Chap. VIII, p. 65.

[34] P. 67. . . .

[36] The beginnings of the classical subsistence-minimum theory of wages, as contained in Chap. VIII of *The Wealth of Nations,* may be passed over in this discussion, for the reason that the technological aspects are made foremost, and the moral question is not allowed to emerge. . . .

Henry J. Bittermann (essay date 1940)

SOURCE: "Adam Smith's Empiricism and the Law of Nature. I," in *The Journal of Political Economy,* Vol. XLVIII, No. 4, August, 1940, pp. 487-520.

[*In the following excerpt, Bittermann examines Smith's methodology in relation to the doctrine of natural law, arguing that, in formulating his ethical and economic theories, Smith rejected the rationalistic methods of the natural-law school of thought in favor of empirical procedures.*]

I. THE PROBLEM STATED

Adam Smith was both the founder of a science and the prophet of an economic and political creed, and the combination and possible confusion of scientific and normative[2] elements in the **Wealth of Nations** has long provided material for the critics. There were advocates of laisser faire long before Smith, and it may well be contended that economic liberalism was but one aspect of broader philosophic, literary, and political movements of the time directed toward the emancipation of the individual from traditional social controls of thought and action. In formulating his economic theories Smith utilized the arguments and conclusions of a host of writers. His preeminence is due to the fact that he first integrated various theories into a "system"; he showed how an economic order with a minimum of state action could function as a going concern; by comparing the effects of laisser faire and intervention in economic matters, he argued that per capita real income would be greater in the absence of control. With some important qualifications he concluded that the interests of society, by which he understood the interests of the sum of individuals in the group, would be best served by permitting each one to pursue his own interest in his own way.

The transition from analytic conclusion to normative prescription was easily made, often without clear indication. Many of the historians of economic doctrine have held that a harmony of interests was a presupposition of Smith's analysis; that ultimately economic theory and practical program depended on his belief in a natural order of the universe, part of the rational theology of the time. Others have seen a close intellectual kinship with the writers on natural law in jurisprudence and political theory. . . .

The commentators on Smith's naturalism who have noted a close relation to natural law and natural theology have adduced a variety of evidence, some of it direct, as when Smith spoke of "natural" liberty or when he referred to the invisible hand; some of it indirect, as when it is held that the harmony of nature was an assumption derived from Hutcheson's theology. It is evident enough that Smith was indebted to Cicero, Grotius, Pufendorf, and Hutcheson for some of his ideas, illustrations, and expressions, both in the *Theory of Moral Sentiments* and in the *Wealth of Nations*. It is easy, therefore, to attribute to Smith some of the ideas of his predecessors and to supply the gaps in his own exposition from their theories, particularly since he did not always state his assumptions or how he differed from the writers whom he cites. His style itself, especially the florid rhetoric of the *Moral Sentiments,* is a fruitful source of confusion. Thus, he was an individualist with a firm belief in private property. He followed Locke in point of time, was familiar with his works, shared some of his prejudices, and in a few places used phrases that at once suggest Locke. It may then be concluded that Smith followed Locke's reasoning. Smith borrowed ideas from Pufendorf, he discussed economic phenomena in terms of relatively simple regularities, and so it is concluded that he was influenced by the natural-law school of jurisprudence and applied their method to a new area. He admired his teacher, Hutcheson, followed his precedents in his teaching, and accepted some of his theology, so that the critics have found in Smith a development of Hutcheson's views. And no doubt Smith was influenced by all these sources.

But the argument of historical continuity is particularly deceptive when applied to the development of ideas, for it tends to neglect a host of other influences on the thinking of any one man. In Smith's case it neglects the influences of Hume, whom he called "by far the most illustrious philosopher and historian of the present age"[11] and from whom, he said, he differed "a little." While the critics have often noted Hume's influence on specific points, they seem to have neglected Hume's philosophic influence on Smith. Yet Hume's achievements as a philosopher were to upset a rationalist epistemology involving self-evident ideas, to question the assumptions commonly made about causation, and to attack with telling blows the arguments of natural theology. His political theories were directed against natural law and natural rights. It is, of course, quite possible that Smith completely refused to accept his closest friend's conclusions, but he could scarcely have passed over the published arguments without comment, and, in fact, in several places he points out his express disagreement with Hume. The high praise of Hume would probably not have been applied to an author whose conclusions he thought were erroneous. Likewise Hume, though he criticized various points of Smith's ethical and economic theories, did not charge

him with adherence to notions which he himself had refuted.[12] Their silence cannot be regarded wholly as friendly forbearance; rather it indicates considerable agreement on fundamental issues.

It is proposed in this essay to re-examine the question of Smith's naturalism, to analyze his methodology in its bearing on the assumptions of natural law and natural theology, in order to determine to what extent Smith's normative economics rested on these theories. In the course of the discussion the vexed question of the relationship between the *Theory of Moral Sentiments* and the *Wealth of Nations* must be raised, since so many of the critics have used these works to interpret one another. It will be contended that Smith's empiricism gave a quite different orientation to his ideas of science, nature, and theology than that postulated by those who have attributed great importance to natural law and theology.

The long and involved doctrinal development of the natural-law theory cannot be reviewed here, for it has appeared with variations throughout the history of political speculation from Aristotle and the Stoics down to modern times.[13] Only a few aspects which seem most relevant to Adam Smith's position will be noted. Stripped of complications and variations, the theory argued that there was an ethical law of nature, discoverable by reason alone, that was uniform through time and place; that this law was an ideal pattern to which positive laws, public policy, and individual conduct should conform; that this law had a divine origin; and that conformity to it was essential for accomplishing the divine plan.[14] In the form given to the doctrine by Roman Stoicism and Roman law it provided many principles for the scholastics and the legal theorists of the seventeenth and eighteenth centuries. With the Reformation, differing theological theories made it difficult to win acceptance of ideas based on any one interpretation of revelation. With the rise of national states and the internal and external conflicts incident thereto, political and juristic theory needed other sanctions than traditional custom and law, if it was to state principles that would reduce conflict and reform jurisprudence. Hence, with the barest elements of theological reasoning and legal practice as accepted principles, the great theorists of international law reformulated the doctrine of natural law in terms of "pure reason," and in this form, in the opinion of many scholars, it served a valuable purpose.[15] Natural laws were deduced from reason directly or from the social nature of man or from the nature of man and society. Its chief exponents held that the law of nature could not be discovered from empirical evidence, since it was invariable, while positive law exhibited many contradictions.[16] Locke, like Pufendorf, stated his doctrine of natural rights in terms of the conditions prevailing in a state of nature, thought of abstractly rather than historically, in which men lived justly and peacefully, by and large, and from which they preserved their rights to person and property when they formed governments by the social contract. To Locke also the law of nature was reason and the will of God.[17] Francis Hutcheson, however, based his argument on an induction of Divine Providence and regarded as natural laws the rules of conduct which tended most effectually to promote "the greatest happiness and perfection" of mankind. He took "human affections" rather than reason as his point of departure, but when he dealt with many concrete issues his "moral sense" gave certain and direct judgments quite as easily as the right reason of his predecessors. He also accepted Locke's doctrines of the state of nature and natural rights with some qualifications, particularly regarding property rights.[18]

It is fully realized that these brief characterizations of the theories of the men who greatly influenced Smith's thought are not adequate statements, but limitations of space prevent fuller treatment. It will be shown that Smith differed in most important respects from these writers. He rejected reason as an important determinant of conduct; he tried to discover the principles of morals empirically; he recognized the variation of moral rules with time, place, and circumstance; he rejected the notion of a social contract; he saw a coincidence of his empirical results and the implications of Providence but did not draw his most important conclusions from the divine order.

Hume's philosophic influence on Smith, it seems, ought not to be neglected, for Smith accepted many of Hume's conclusions, and, though they may have disagreed on theology, Hume's arguments could not have been wholly without effect. Hume attacked rationalism (in the narrower sense) in ethics and theology. In his strictly empirical epistemology reason consisted merely in the comparison of ideas, the copies of sense impressions; it could note relations among the data of experience; it could determine the probable consequences of action; but it could not oppose the passions or direct the will. Hence, he rejected theories that asserted that moral conduct was "conformity to reason" and found the basis for morals in sentiments, in pleasure and pain. Morality was that which was approved of as conducive to either public or private utility.[19] The uniformity of sentiments is sufficient to infer the existence of moral rules, but not so great as to justify any immutable precepts.[20]

Accordingly, Hume rejected political doctrines which tried to deduce principles from the rational and social nature of man and which asserted the universality and invariability of ethical norms applicable to the state. The Grotius school had made an effective, though erroneous, argument for greater humanity in public affairs. Its error consisted in deriving from reason principles which were to be justified only on the grounds

of utility. The rules of justice were mere artificial conventions which arose historically and were useful in controlling the selfishness of man in a world characterized by material scarcity.[21] Hume also conceded propaganda value to the "philosophic fiction" of the state of nature and the social contract. It had no more historical or philosophic basis than the Leviathan or the theory of patriarchal origin. Rights were merely accepted rules of public utility.[22]

Hume's discussion of natural religion is particularly important in view of the emphasis placed on Smith's natural religion by some of the commentators. Smith undoubtedly knew the *Treatise* and *Enquiries* and probably also had seen the manuscript of the *Dialogues concerning Natural Religion* before he wrote the **Moral Sentiments**.[23] How skeptical of natural theology Hume really was is not certain, and Smith apparently did not consider him a complete skeptic. Hume escaped personal responsibility for his position by the use of the dialogue form, in which the speakers are fictitious Greeks, and the form of an address to the Athenians by Epicurus. When writing *in propria persona,* he asserts some belief in a natural—i.e., nonmiraculous—theology, which conceded the principle of design, though this may have been mere tactical precaution.[24]. . .

II. ADAM SMITH AND THE METHOD OF SCIENCE

Adam Smith's methodology was essentially empirical,[27] deriving its inspiration from Newton and Hume,[28] in contrast to the rationalistic method of the natural-law school of thought. Unfortunately, Smith nowhere in his writings explicitly formulated his own method of investigation in ethics and economics. His major works proceeded at once to subject matter, and his ideas of method can be inferred only from incidental remarks and from the arguments of some minor, posthumously published, essays.[29]

Smith, somewhat like the later positivists, had little respect for the "cobweb science" of metaphysics, which had produced "nothing but subtleties and sophisms."[30] He neglected to state explicitly his own metaphysical assumptions, but he was no mere pragmatist. He believed that ethics and economics could be studied by scientific methods, that their laws were to be discovered by induction from sense data. He denies the possibility of a priori knowledge and refers to the "fallacious experiment" of Socrates and Plato, who tried to obtain knowledge by dialectic.[31] Sensation alone can be the source of knowledge, and complex sensations "are felt as simple and uncompounded sensations."[32] Experience provides the basis for causal connection, which may be established only through repeated observation of similar events. Likewise, "the general maxims of morality are formed, like all other general maxims, from experience and induction."[33] Smith's epistemology had many evident points of resemblance to Hume's, but, since he did not state his position fully, it is difficult to say how close the agreement was.

From a methodological standpoint the best evidence of Smith's position is offered by the posthumous essay on **"The Principles Which Lead and Direct Philosophical Enquiries, Illustrated by the History of Astronomy"**[34] and similarly entitled fragments on ancient physics and ancient logic and metaphysics. These essays were apparently intended to form part of a history of scientific method. They are critical of metaphysics and of a priori methods in science and try to show that the experimental method of Newton was the true path, though Smith showed how Newton's predecessors had made valuable empirical contributions. Thus the process of investigation was from un-co-ordinated generalizations about a limited class of phenomena to more inclusive theories, from the more particular to the more general. The error of the pre-Newtonians lay in their hasty generalization and their tendency to substitute metaphysical notions for the inferences that could have been made from the data. Smith's discussion of the earlier astronomers is almost a critique in terms of the Newtonian "Rules of Reasoning in Philosophy."[35] At each stage of investigation the conclusions are embodied in "systems," which are subject to correction or rejection according to the results of investigation and criticism. Says Smith:

> Systems in many respects resemble machines. A machine is a little system, created to perform, as well as to connect together, in reality, those different movements and effects which the artist has occasion for. A system is an imaginary machine invented to connect together in the fancy those different movements and effects which are already in reality performed. The machines that are first invented to perform any particular movement are always the most complex, and succeeding artists generally discover that, with fewer wheels, with fewer principles of motion, than had originally been employed, the same effects may be more easily produced. The first systems, in the same manner, are always the most complex, and a particular connecting chain, or principle, is generally thought necessary to unite every two seemingly disjointed appearances: but it often happens, that one great connecting principle is afterwards found to be sufficient to bind together all the disconnected phenomena that occur in a whole species of things.[36]

A system in this sense was a theory, based on one or more general propositions, from which all the known phenomena could be deduced or causally explained, though the major premises could be established only by inductive procedures. Smith's ideal was Newton's "System of the World," the synthetic portion of his physics and astronomy, in which the solar system was explained deductively with the gravitational law as the major premise.[37] Smith emphasized the importance of induction without showing precisely what constituted valid induction or without distinguishing carefully between the functions of deductive and inductive reasoning. By "induction" he meant, probably, a procedure analogous to Newton's "experimentalism," which combined both methods, using the terms in the sense of, say, Mill's *Logic*. At least both Smith and Newton used both techniques.[38] The Newtonian method was what Jevons called "inverse deduction." Analysis consisted of a study of a given class of data, observations, or experiments as basis for the formulation of a tentative causal hypothesis, which, in turn, was to be tested by further observation and experiment and accepted or rejected according to agreement or disagreement with fact. A valid generalization might then be used to establish further and more general hypotheses, themselves to be tested in the same way. The final check on this procedure was to take the most general conclusion as a major premise and then to determine whether all the known relevant phenomena could be deduced from it, i.e., synthesis or system-building.[39] The famed Newtonian "hypotheses non fingo" did not imply that hypothesis was not a part of scientific method but only that hypotheses transcending experience were to be rejected.[40] In fact the *Principia* contains more formal mathematics than empirical data. As seen by the Newtonians (and also by Newton probably), the merit of the experimental method was its inference of causes from effects, as opposed to the rationalistic procedure. Results might be tentative; laws would be a succession of approximations; they might be incomplete, but they would rest on the solid ground of data and would not be conjectural inferences from uncertain premises.

The **"History of Astronomy"** illustrated the method of successive approximations, the opposition to metaphysics, and the validity of empirical methods. The same view is maintained in the other methodological fragments, though in a more negative way. Smith's opposition to nonempirical modes of reasoning extended even to a disparagement of formal logic.[41] Since it may safely be assumed that Smith did not hold to a logical dichotomy of *Naturwissenschaft and Geisteswissenschaft*,[42] the ethical and economic works might be expected to imitate the Newtonian method. The *Theory of Moral Sentiments* is an attempt to state valid generalizations about the ethical judgments made by mankind. Its purpose is not primarily normative, in the sense that the author tried to show what ought to be done, though he frequently lapsed into exhortation. Rather it tries to explain the causes of moral decisions, taken as data; it is a sort of sociology and psychology of value judgment.[43]

Smith holds that there is little disagreement among men as to what specific types of conduct are approved or disapproved, except, perhaps, on the part of those directly involved. With these judgments as data, he analyzes the common elements and subsequently combines them into a theory of general approbation and disapprobation. Finally, he discusses earlier theories of ethics in terms of their internal consistency and their consonance with the facts as he understood them. His argument is that the moralists of all schools are in substantial agreement on the data, i.e., the types of conduct regarded as moral; their disagreement is in the explanations given.[44] The earlier theories are regarded as defective for various reasons. Theories "which make virtue consist in propriety"[45] are defective in that "none of these systems either give, or even pretend to give, any precise or distinct measure by which this fitness or propriety of affection can be ascertained or judged of,"[46] that is, they lack precision. Systems based on prudence fail to explain many types of approved conduct, just as systems of benevolence cannot explain universal approval of certain types of self-interested behavior.[47] Mandeville's "licentious system" is sheer sophistry in that it confounds virtue and vice and in any event is wholly unempirical.[48] After thus demonstrating the unsatisfactory character of definitions of virtue, Smith analyzes theories of approbation, which, he concedes, are at least valid empirical generalizations. Simple egoistic theories[49] cannot explain social interests and benevolent acts, for the attempt to explain benevolence in terms of putative self-interest fails because individuals have sentiments of approval, or the contrary, about acts in the past which could not affect them or about events which could not conceivably occur to them.[50] Rationalist theories place undue emphasis on reason, which is merely instrumental and has the limited function of formulating general rules. But "it is altogether absurd and unintelligible to suppose that the first perceptions of right and wrong can be derived from reason," for they are founded upon "immediate sense and feeling."[51] Smith objects to Hutcheson's "moral sense," which had a "peculiar power of perception," because there is no empirical evidence for the existence of such a sense. As an analytic device it is useless, for it cannot explain any sentiment which cannot be explained as well without resort to a "moral sense."

The adequacy or correctness of Smith's theory as an ethical system is not under discussion here. What is significant, however, is that his procedure was an application of the techniques of Newtonian experimentalism to the questions of morals. Experimentation was obviously ruled out by the nature of the subject matter, but the analysis, criticism, and formulation of conclusions was empirical. The adequacy of the observations may be questioned; it is doubtful that the high degree of uniformity of sentiments, which Smith postulated, actually occurs. Smith sometimes departs from the strictly descriptive-analytic method by resort to advice and exhortation.[52]

A detailed discussion of the method of the **Wealth of Nations** is scarcely necessary in this *Journal*. Even a superficial acquaintance with the work should be enough to dispose of the view that it was a series of abstract deductions from a single premise of self-interest. The assumption of egoistic motivation in economic life is obvious enough, but Smith's work is not deductive in the sense that the term could be applied to, say, the major works of Ricardo and Senior. The bulk of Smith's text consists of descriptive, historical, and statistical data, with a few inferences from "conjectural history."[53] There are some deductions from definition and arguments supported only by common knowledge or casual observation, which give parts of the work an abstract tone. But Smith had argued that valid generalizations could be reached only by induction from observation, and he tried to apply this technique. Often his data were not explicitly stated, and, perhaps, they were inadequate to support some of his conclusions. He depended upon casual observation in such matters as wage differentials, costs of production, and the pharmacist's high markup, as indeed was unavoidable considering the available data. In other instances he piled up facts to prove his point, e.g., the long digression on the value of silver, the statistics of wheat prices, and changes in wage rates and profits. In terms of present-day methods his statistical technique was primitive, and he took too few variables into account. The important point, methodologically, is that he used such facts as he had; he believed that his conclusions were valid inferences from his data; he attempted to check his theories by factual observation. He was scientific for his day.

After establishing, to his own satisfaction at least, a large number of theoretical propositions about the statics and dynamics of production and distribution in the first two books, he analyzed the economic policies of Europe and the "systems" of political economy in the third and fourth books. As in his **Moral Sentiments,** he criticizes the earlier systems in terms of their consistency, the validity of their theoretical inferences, and their appropriateness as means of attaining the end postulated, the maximization of per capita real income.[54] This third criterion involved definite normative assumptions, which may be questioned but are unavoidable if economic policy is to be discussed.

Brief note should also be taken of Adam Smith's minor essays. His studies of aesthetics and linguistics[55] were also intended to be empirical investigations, though the essay on languages represents "conjectural history" at its worst, with classic Latin taken as a type of primitive language. Some idea of the probable content of the projected work on jurisprudence may be obtained from the Glasgow lectures of 1763.[56] These lectures compare the principles of public and private law in England and Scotland with Roman law and Continental jurisprudence, and in the latter part they cover the same ground as the fourth and fifth books of the *Wealth of Nations*. The legal sections do not involve many abstract generalizations. As they were reported, they consisted very largely of legal data, with some references to the theories advanced in the *Moral Sentiments* and some criticisms of the doctrine of natural law and natural rights. As reported, Smith's jurisprudence was decidedly empiristic.[57]

The foregoing discussion of Adam Smith's method has been predicated on the assumption that he believed that the experimental method of Newton, which he extolled in a minor essay, could be applied to the moral sciences, with, perhaps, some modifications in technique due to the subject matter and the impossibility of controlled experiment but without change in epistemological position. Conclusions would be valid only in terms of observation and reasoning upon data, sometimes taking the form of mental experiment.[58] The procedure might be quite abstract, but "fact" rather than "reason" or "the nature of things" would be the theoretical point of departure. The *Geisteswissenschaften* presented a special difficulty apart from the problems of inadequate observation and experimentation. They could not easily be confined to the descriptive-analytic since they touched upon the normative at many points. The analysis of economics and ethics might be empirical and positivistic, but the synthesis could not avoid normative implications, especially considering Smith's definition of the scope of political economy.[59] One of the achievements of Adam Smith was to apply the experimental method to the problems of economics and ethics and so to formulate valid "systems." His weakness was, perhaps, the belief that the data observed would yield valid normative ideals.

III. MOTIVATIONS AND MORALS

An examination of Adam Smith's ideas about human motivation seems indispensable to an analysis of his method and its relation to the doctrine of natural law. . . . The relation of the *Theory of Moral Sentiments* to the *Wealth of Nations* also hinges on this question, while the consistency or inconsistency of the two books has an important bearing on his method of investigation. Some of the commentators have construed the works as mutually consistent and complementary. Others have seen definite conflicts in their psychologic, ethical, or metaphysical theories. No logical difficulty is presented in scientific investigations if contrary assumptions or hypotheses are used in tentatively unrelated problems. If, however, generalizations from one set of data are to be combined with inferences from other sets as part of a larger synthesis, contrariety of postulates implies ambiguity in the broader conclusions, while contradiction of postulates makes valid generalization impossible, at least within the framework of non-Hegelian logic.

Since Smith was above all a system builder, these arguments of the critics must be examined, though some may be dismissed briefly. H. T. Buckle, in a passage often cited, holds that both works were essentially deductive, the one starting from the principle of sympathy, the other from self-interest.[60] If this were the case, the charge of inconsistency would not, of itself, be important, though it might cast doubt on the finality of Smith's conclusions. The reasons for not regarding either work as essentially deductive have already been given. Others have held that the ethical theory was written under the influence of Shaftesbury and Hutcheson and that the economic treatise was more influenced by Hobbes and Mandeville. Smith, however, was thoroughly familiar with these writers in 1759, when he criticized them adversely, and he did not withdraw his objections. Whether or not he changed his views is more debatable. The influence of French materialism and physiocracy has been given less emphasis in recent years as a formative influence on Smith's thought, though his theory of distribution shows signs of physiocratic influence.[61] One writer goes as far as to say that the intervening period of seventeen years enabled him to read and appropriate a new body of literature.[62] In any case he may have been inconsistent without being aware of the fact. The rather extensive revision of the text of the sixth edition,[63] published shortly before the author's death in 1790, would indicate that his intellect was not enfeebled and that this edition still represented his views, so that any disagreement with the *Wealth of Nations* cannot be passed over as mere oversight. The Preface of the last edition of the *Moral Sentiments* explains that the *Wealth of Nations* is to be regarded as partial fulfilment of the promise to publish a work on justice. It may be inferred that Smith himself regarded the works as complementary or as parts of a larger whole to be completed by a study of jurisprudence and political theory.[64]. . .

It has been argued that he entertained contrary notions of human motivation in the two works or that his ethical notions contradicted each other. It is a quite correct commonplace that the *Wealth of Nations* assumes that economic behavior is motivated by self-interest, though the author does not deny the existence of benevolent sentiments or their occasional influence on economic acts.[88] Smith merely minimizes the importance of nonselfish or noneconomic motives in economic life. This is exactly the view maintained in the *Moral Sentiments*,[89] where there is also some attempt to explain this egoistic psychology. Where, as rarely, economic matters are mentioned, the assumption is always that self-interest is the motive of action. Tradesmen are expected to try to make money, to practice economy and parsimony,[90] merchants carry on business in terms of utility, i.e., self-interest, and exchange services at an agreed valuation.[91] Moreover, the common sentiment of mankind approves self-seeking, so that the individual, who has an instinctive desire of approval, has a further incentive for acquisitive activity, even to obtain wealth beyond his wants.[92] The acquisitive urge is regarded as quite universal when Smith asks: "From whence, then, arises that emulation which runs through all the different ranks of men, and what are the advantages which we propose by that great purpose of human life which we call bettering our condition?" The *Moral Sentiments* does not differ in its view of human nature from the *Wealth of Nations*. It merely considers many other matters than the "uniform, constant, and uninterrupted effort of every man to better his condition."[93] In both works self-interested conduct is regarded as usual and beneficial to society. Not only does the ordinary business of life depend upon it, but acquisitiveness stimulates industry, invention, and science. The opinion that Smith in the *Moral Sentiments* regarded benevolence as the leading motive, or as the moral motive, rests on an erroneous identification of benevolence and sympathy. In point of fact, however, the psychological device of sympathy is used to explain the approval of egoistic as well as altruistic sentiments.

From the point of view of ethics there also is little or no conflict between Smith's essays, though different arguments are used, as might be expected in studies of such different character. The *Theory of Moral Sentiments* was a purely academic study, an attempt to discover a valid theory of morals by empirical methods. Smith, like other authors of ethical treatises, could not expect his work to have any practical effect beyond the incidental edification of his readers. The *Wealth of Nations* sought valid theoretical conclusions, but it also proposed to apply these conclusions to a radical reform of policy. Paradoxical as it may seem, the theory of ethics was less directly normative than the scientific work on economics. The moral theory was in the main descriptive; the economic theory neatly wove prescriptive elements into its descriptive-predictive fabric.

The ethical propositions of the *Wealth of Nations* are of two sorts: statements of the aims of society or of social policy and evaluations of means of attaining these ends. It seems clear that to Smith the ultimate objective of social policy was the maximization of per capita income.

> Political œconomy, considered as a branch of the science of statesman or legislator, proposes two distinct objects: first, to provide a plentiful revenue or subsistence for the people, or more properly to enable them to provide such a revenue or subsistence for themselves; and secondly, to supply the state or commonwealth with a revenue sufficient for the public services. It proposes to enrich both the people and the sovereign.[94]

The argument of Book V shows that the income of the state depended on the size of the national real income. While Smith in places speaks of the aggregate national income as the end of social policy, the first statement of his objective measures welfare in terms of income per head.[95] Systems of political economy are judged in terms of this criterion, to which Smith sees only one limitation. Economic interests must sometimes be subordinated to military.[96]

Related to his general economic norm is his position with regard to the conflicting interests of economic classes. He prefers the more numerous to the less numerous groups as a matter of general policy; consumers take precedence over producers.

> Consumption is the sole end and purpose of all production; and the interest of the producer ought to be attended to, only so far as it may be necessary for promoting that of the consumer. The maxim is so perfectly self-evident, that it would be absurd to attempt to prove it. But in the mercantile system, the interest of the consumer is almost constantly sacrificed to that of the producer; and it seems to consider production, and not consumption, as the ultimate end and object of all industry and commerce.[97]

The principal reason for condemning monopoly is the injury to consumers,[98] but monopoly also is wasteful[99] and injurious to the interests of capitalists seeking advantageous investments.[100] The mercantile system is a series of monopolies for the benefit of a few merchants and to the detriment of consumers, other merchants, landlords, and laborers.[101] The interests of merchants are in frequent conflict with those of other economic classes.[102] Guild regulations occasion "a very important inequality in the whole of the advantages and disadvantages of the different employments of labour and stock,"[103] i.e., they benefit a small group at the expense of a larger. Combinations of employers, facilitated by law, keep wages low and so are injurious to workers.[104]

It is evident that in these instances Smith did not postulate a harmony of interests but rather emphasized their conflict. He condemned mercantilism and guild restrictions in part because they reduced the national dividend and in part because they were inimical to the welfare of the larger groups in society. There remained his own system as the one most conducive to well-being: national income would be maximized; the free play of competition would enable each individual to obtain the wealth to which his efforts entitled him; government would be impartial in the conflicts of economic interests.

> All systems either of preference or of restraint, therefore, being thus completely taken away, the obvious and simple system of natural liberty

establishes itself of its own accord. Every man, as long as he does not violate the laws of justice, is left perfectly free to pursue his own interest his own way, and to bring both his industry and capital into competition with those of any other man or order of men.[105]

The chief exegetical issue in this passage is the meaning of the "laws of justice." Did Smith here mean the justice implied by the law of property, contract, and tort, or did he imply some ideal ethical justice? The *Wealth of Nations* is not explicit on the point. It defines justice by implication when it mentions the second "duty of the sovereign, that of protecting, as far as possible, every member of the society from the injustice or oppression of every other member of it."[106] Even the *Moral Sentiments* treated justice in only general terms, since Smith had expected to publish a treatise on jurisprudence. What he does say there indicates some possibility of conflict between the ethical and juridical concepts, though he argues that the law is an attempt to formulate the ethical rules. The rules of justice are enforcible by punitive sanctions and so can apply only to conduct arising from the selfish or the unsocial passions. Compulsory benevolence is a contradiction. The common opinion approves of selfish conduct, provided that the individual conforms to the accepted rules of fair play, that is, that he does not interfere with another's opportunity of attaining his selfish ends. The spectators sympathize with all the actors, but where there is a conflict they approve of only moderate action. This is at best an indefinite rule, but in practice certain definite types of conduct are accepted as fair play or are rejected as unwarranted injury, in the light of the experience and habits of society. The laws of justice do not prescribe the ideal conduct, they merely state an ethical minimum. "Mere justice is, upon most occasions, but a negative virtue, and only hinders us from hurting our neighbour."[107] Moreover, there is a cultural lag between the ethical standards set by social approval and the rules of justice administered by courts, and the ethical standard may be used to judge the legal.[108]

> Every system of positive law may be regarded as a more or less imperfect attempt towards a system of natural jurisprudence, or towards an enumeration of the particular rules of justice. . . . Sometimes what is called the constitution of the state, that is, the interest of the government; sometimes the interest of particular orders of men who tyrannize the government, warp the positive laws of the country from what natural justice would prescribe. . . . Systems of positive law, therefore, though they deserve the greatest authority, as the records of the sentiments of mankind in different ages and nations, yet can never be regarded as accurate systems of the rules of natural justice.[109]

It seems probable, then, that the laws of justice which limit individual conduct under the Smithian system are to be understood as legal requirements, even though the law itself could be criticized in terms of social ideals and policy. The *Moral Sentiments* looked upon ethical problems from the standpoint of the individual. As a theory of individual ethics it did not directly formulate social ideals, except incidentally. "All constitutions of government, however, are valued only in proportion as they tend to promote the happiness of those who live under them."[110] Though he agreed with the utilitarians in the practical consequences, Smith based this judgment of social policy upon the sentiments of the spectators rather than upon direct considerations of utility. The correspondence was due to the sentiments happily implanted by Nature.[111]

There is thus no apparent inconsistency in the main ethical presuppositions of the two works of Adam Smith. The earlier one was concerned with individual behavior and only mentions social ethics incidentally. The later work assumes the same standard of individual conduct and, in addition, formulates more distinctly at least one aspect of the happiness of the people living under government, the greatest possible average per capita income. No doubt the economic was only one aspect of happiness to Smith, but it was essentially part of the same criterion applied in the early work. Since the spectators might be presumed to sympathize with all, when there is a conflict of interest, they might be inclined to favor the more numerous group. Smith does not say so distinctly, but this view would not be inconsistent with what he says about social policy and the interests of individuals. In both works he emphasized the greater importance of social than of individual welfare, but in the framework of his individualistic psychology and morals the social well-being could mean only the well-being of larger, as opposed to smaller, groups. In the *Wealth of Nations* the impartial spectator puts in no appearance, unless perhaps Smith cast himself in that role. Nor is the doctrine of sympathy mentioned directly. In this way Smith freed his economics from direct dependence upon his earlier ethical theory, certainly a prudent step from both scientific and practical points of view. But the ethical assumptions are essentially the same. . . .

Notes

. . .[2] Certain concepts are basic to the argument of this essay, and to avoid possible confusion they will be tentatively defined here. By "scientific" propositions are meant those which state, or purport to state, conditions or relations of empirically observed or observable phenomena. The copula of such propositions must be of the form "is" or "is not." As here used the term is equivalent to Pareto's "logico-experimental" or J. N. Keynes's "positive." As used here the term need not imply full acceptance of a positivistic or even completely empiristic position. By "normative" propositions are meant statements of criteria of value judgments, prescriptions, statements of ideals or ends, or the application of such criteria to questions of "fact." The copula is of the form "ought" or "ought not." By "empiricism" is meant the theory that knowledge is, and can be, obtained only from sense experience. Generalizations (principles or laws) are summary statements of observed similarities and regularities of phenomena, whose predictive value rests on probability. "Rationalism" is here defined in the narrower, epistemological sense rather than in the broader sense as used in, say, Lecky's *Rise and Influence of Rationalism in Europe.* Theories are regarded as rationalistic when propositions are derived by deduction from primitive propositions, assumed as given, intuitive, self-evident, or a priori. Such propositions may be epistemological, ethical, political, or even physical. The validity of generalization thus depends upon the correctness of the primitive propositions and the logic of deduction rather than upon agreement or disagreement with observation. In practice philosophers have combined empirical and rationalistic methods—perhaps Hume was the only strict empiricist—but the heuristic value of the distinction is not thereby destroyed. . . .

[11] *Wealth of Nations,* V, i, Part III, art. 3 (Cannan, II, 275). In all references to the *Wealth of Nations* the book and chapter are given in Roman figures; the second part of the citation refers to the volume and page of the edition by Cannan (3d ed.; London, 1922).

[12] J. Y. T. Greig (ed.), *Letters of David Hume* (Oxford, 1932), I, 303-6, 312-13; II, 311-12.

[13] Cf. C. E. Vaughan, *Studies in the History of Political Philosophy* (Manchester, 1925), Vol. I; Otto Gierke, *Natural Law and the Theory of Society, 1500 to 1800,* ed. Ernest Barker (2 vols.; Cambridge, 1934), esp. editor's Introduction; David G. Ritchie, *Natural Rights* (London, 1895), chap. ii; Sir Frederick Pollock, "History of the Law of Nature," *Essays in the Law* (London, 1922), chaps. ii-iii; George H. Sabine, *History of Political Theory* (New York, 1937), chap. xxi.

[14] Cicero in the *Republic* thus states it: "There is in fact a true law—namely right reason—which is in accordance with nature, applies to all men, and is unchangeable and eternal. . . . Its commands and prohibitions always influence good men, but are without effect on the bad. To invalidate this law by human legislation is never morally right, nor is it permissible ever to restrict its operation, and to annul it wholly is impossible. . . . But there will be one law, eternal, and unchangeable, binding at all times upon all peoples; and there will be, as it were, one common master and ruler of men, namely God, who is the author of this law, its

interpreter and its sponsor. . . ." This translation is that of G. H. Sabine and S. B. Smith, *Cicero on the Commonwealth* (Columbus, Ohio, 1929), pp. 215-16 (cf. Cicero, *De re publica,* ed. K. Ziegler [Leipzig, 1915], pp. 95-96). This particular passage was well known in the Middle Ages and to Grotius and Pufendorf.

[15] Cf. Arthur Salz, "Ueber einige Beziehungen des Naturrechtes zur Sozial-philosophie," *Archiv für Sozialwissenschaft und Sozialpolitik,* XXXIX. (1927), 525-56; [J. Jastrow, "Naturrecht und Volkswirtschaft," *Jahrbücher für Nationalökonomie,* CXXVI (1927), 689-730]; Sabine, *op. cit.,* pp. 425-29. Says Professor Salz: "Wenn das Naturrecht ein Irrtum ist, so hat es kaum je einer fruchtbareren gegeben" (p. 538).

[16] For the doctrinal differences cf. Gierke, *op. cit.,* esp. II, 289 ff. Grotius used the criterion of right reason; Pufendorf, "the rational and social nature of man." Cf. Grotius, *De jure belli ac pacis* (1625, 1646), reprinted by the Carnegie Institution (1913), Book I, chap. i, sec. 10, p. 4; sec. 12, p. 6; and, in the same series, see Pufendorf, *De officio hominis et civis* (1673) (New York, 1927), Book I, chap. ii, sec. 16; and *De jure naturae et gentium* (1672) (Oxford, 1934), Book I; Book II, chap. iii.

[17] *Of Civil Government,* chap. i, sec. 6; chap. v, sec. 26 ff.; chap. ix, sec. 135.

[18] *System of Moral Philosophy* (2 vols.; 1755), pp. 1, 29-35, 169-220. For a discussion of the development of Hutcheson's thought see W. R. Scott, *Francis Hutcheson* (Cambridge, 1900).

[19] *Treatise of Human Nature,* Book III, secs. 1-2; *Enquiry concerning Human Understanding,* Sec. VIII, Part I, in L. A. Selby-Bigge (ed.), *Hume's Enquiries* (Oxford, 1936), p. 83; cf. also *Enquiry concerning the Principles of Morals* in *ibid.,* p. 173. There is not complete agreement among the critics as to Hume's ethics or theology. Cf. B. M. Laing, *David Hume* (London, 1932), chap. viii; R. Metz, *David Hume: Leben und Philosophie* (Stuttgart, 1929), chap. ii; John Laird, *Hume's Philosophy of Human Nature* (London, 1932), chaps. vii-viii.

[20] Hume's own uncertainty on this score is evidenced in his "A Dialogue" in T. H. Green and T. H. Grose (eds.), *Essays, Moral, Political and Literary by David Hume* (London, 1882), II, 289-305.

[21] *Treatise,* Book III, Part II, secs. 1-5; *Enquiry concerning Morals,* sec. III.

[22] *Treatise,* Book III, Parts V, VII, IX; *Enquiry. . . . Morals,* secs. III-IV; "Of the Original Contract," Green and Grose, *op. cit.,* I, 443-60; "Of the Origin of Government," *ibid.,* pp. 113-17.

[23] Smith's personal acquaintance with Hume dates from 1750 or possibly earlier. He apparently did not receive a presentation copy of the *Enquiries,* and the tale of their confiscation while he was a student at Oxford, if true, referred to a purchased copy. The *Dialogues* were written about 1751, and the manuscript was circulated among Hume's friends, probably including Smith. They all advised against publication, and Smith was unwilling to have the work appear before his own death. What his "many reasons" were must be a matter of conjecture. From one of his letters it seems that he regarded the *Dialogues* as unfit for general circulation and preferred to have their arguments known only to a few. Cf. John Rae, *Life of Adam Smith* (London, 1895), pp. 15, 45-48, 295-314; W. R. Scott, *Adam Smith as Student and Professor* (Glasgow, 1937), pp. 34-35, 64; Norman Kemp Smith (ed.), *Hume's Dialogues concerning Natural Religion* (Oxford, 1935), pp. 110-21; Greig, *op. cit.,* II, 316-18, 334-36.

[24] There were blasphemy laws in the statues (cf. "Natural History of Religion" in his *Essays,* II, 309-63). . . .

[27] . . . It may be objected that the terms "empiricism" and "rationalism" are inappropriate in discussing eighteenth-century writers, who themselves did not use the terms in this precise sense. This objection does not seem valid if the "rationalistic" elements of theories or arguments can be distinguished from the "empirical." The distinction here made came into use in the sense above defined some time in the early nineteenth century, though Bacon (1626) had used the words in approximately the modern sense (cf. *Oxford Dictionary,* s.v. "rationalist"; V. Cousin, *Cours de l'histoire de la philosophie* [Paris, 1829], I, 445). The British empiricists, e.g., Locke and Hume, contrasted their own method of reasoning with that of the Cartesians and other "rationalists." The immediate followers of Newton were quite explicit in rejecting the a priori method and compared Descartes, Spinoza, and Leibnitz unfavorably with their master, e.g., Roger Cotes in the Preface of his (2d) edition of Newton's *Principia* (1713); Henry Pemberton, *A View of Sir Isaac Newton's Philosophy* (London, 1728), pp. 2-5; Colin Maclaurin, *An Account of Sir Isaac Newton's Philosophical Discoveries* (London, 1748), pp. 14-19, 64 ff., 93-95.

[28] Hume regarded his own work as an application of the Newtonian method to the problems of epistemology and morals. His first work appeared with the title *Treatise on Human Nature: Being an Attempt To Introduce the Experimental Method of Reasoning into Moral Subjects* (1739).

[29] *Essays on Philosophical Subjects* (1795), reprinted in *The Works of Adam Smith, LL.D.* (London, 1811-12), Vol. V.

[30] *Wealth of Nations,* V, i, Part III, art. ii (Cannan, II, 258). In a letter introducing an author to his publisher, Cadell (May 7, 1786), Smith has an interesting comment on this view. He says: "He has a work upon moral Philosophy which, tho' he and I differ a little as David Hume and I used to do, I expect will do him very great honour. It is as free from metaphysics as is possible for any work on that subject to be. Its fault, in my opinion, is that it is too free of them. . . ." (Scott, *Adam Smith,* p. 299).

[31] "History of Ancient Logics and Metaphysics," *Works,* V, 231.

[32] "Of the External Senses," *ibid.,* pp. 333-99. It should be noted that this not profound essay is devoted to the psychology of sensation rather than to epistemology.

[33] *Theory of Moral Sentiments,* VIII, iii (*Works,* I, 567). Except where otherwise noted the references to the *Moral Sentiments* are to the edition in the *Works,* a reprint of the sixth edition, the last from Smith's own hand. For convenience of reference to numerous subsequent editions, the "parts" are indicated by capital Roman numerals and the sections of the parts by lower-case Roman numbers. Some of the parts are divided into chapters without sections.

[34] *Works,* V, 54-190. From internal evidence this essay appears to have been written some time before 1758, though the original draft was revised later, and at Smith's death there were notes for another revision. The author was evidently quite partial to this "fragment of an intended juvenile work." In 1773 he directed Hume to publish it in the event of his death, and in 1790 he preserved it from destruction, along with the other methodological essays, when he ordered his friends to burn sixteen volumes of other manuscript. It is clear that these essays antedate the *Moral Sentiments,* but it is not evident whether they dated from the Oxford period, as might be suggested by Smith's word "juvenile," or from his Edinburgh or early Glasgow lectures. It may be surmised that Smith laid this original plan aside when he began the composition of his two great works. In his letter to Hume in 1773 he describes the essay as containing a history of astronomical systems to the time of Descartes (John Rae, *Life of Adam Smith,* pp. 262-63). Since the form of the essay as published included an elaborate treatment of Newton's system, it seems likely that at least the latter part was written after 1773. Consequently, its views would seem to be those of Smith at his maturity.

[35] Sir Isaac Newton, *Mathematical Principles of Natural Philosophy,* trans. Andrew Motte, ed. N. W. Chittenden (New York, 1846), Book III, pp. 384-85. Omitting Newton's comments, these rules are: "Rule I. We are to admit no more causes of natural things than such as are both true and sufficient to explain their

appearances. Rule II. Therefore to the same natural effects, we must, as far as possible, assign the same causes. Rule III. The qualities of bodies, which admit neither intension nor remission of degrees, and which are found to belong to all bodies within the reach of our experiments, are to be esteemed the universal qualities of all bodies whatsoever. Rule IV. In experimental philosophy we are to look upon propositions collected by general induction from phaenomena as accurately or very nearly true, notwithstanding any hypothesis that may be imagined, till such time as other phaenomena occur, by which they may either be made more accurate, or liable to exceptions."

[36] *Works,* V, 116-17. John Rae seized upon this quotation as the basis for his criticism that Smith's economics was not an empirical science but a philosophic system, useful for didactic or propaganda purposes. . . . Veblen used it for a similar purpose.

[37] Cf. "History of Astronomy," *Works,* V, 175-90. The Newtonian system is "the greatest discovery that ever was made by man, the discovery of an immense chain of most important and sublime truths, all closely connected together, by one capital fact, of the reality of which we have daily experience" (*ibid.,* pp. 189-90).

[38] Newton and some of his followers sometimes speak of deducing principles from phenomena. Their quarrel with the Cartesians was not over deduction as such, but over the "rationalistic" method of deducing effects from assumed a priori causes, which could not be established from empirical data.

[39] Cf. Cotes, *loc. cit.;* Pemberton, *op. cit.,* pp. 5-15; Maclaurin, *op. cit.,* pp. 6-19, 90-93. Newton's methodological remarks were scattered, and his disciples stated his position more systematically. For a modern discussion of Newton's views see Edwin A. Burtt, *The Metaphysical Foundations of Modern Physics* (New York, 1925), pp. 202-23. It seems quite probable that Adam Smith knew these early commentaries on Newton. The catalogue of his library shows that he had Pemberton's edition (1726) of the *Principia,* but it does not indicate that he had the more popular work here cited. Bonar's catalogue lists Maclaurin's *Treatise on Fluxions* but not his study of Newton. Smith in his "History of Astronomy" refers to Maclaurin (*Works,* V, 161). From the context the reference was to his work on Newton or some other work on astronomy, and not to a text on the calculus. From the lists of subscribers prefixed to Pemberton's *View* and Maclaurin's *Account* it appears that Robert Simson, Smith's teacher, colleague, and friend, had both works. The names of several other friends (Lord Kames, Stewart, the merchant) appear as well.

[40] Newton used *fingo* not *utor.*

[41] The Glasgow course in logic as Smith taught it gave only a cursory treatment of formal logic; the major part of the course was rhetoric and belles-lettres (cf. Dugald Stewart's "Account of the Life and Writings of Adam Smith" in Smith's *Works,* V, 412, where he quotes from Professor John Millar, one of Smith's pupils).

[42] "Human society, when we contemplate it in a certain abstract and philosophical light, appears like a great, an immense machine, whose regular and harmonious movements produce a thousand agreeable effects" (*Mor. Sent.,* VIII, iii, p. 560).

[43] Thus he states explicitly: "Let it be considered too, that the present inquiry is not concerning a matter of right, if I may say so, but concerning a matter of fact. We are not at present examining upon what principles a perfect being would approve of the punishment of bad actions; but upon what principles so weak and imperfect a creature as man actually and in fact approves of it" (*ibid.,* II, i, p. 129 [1st ed., p. 167]).

[44] This agreement must be qualified in so far as the approval of conduct varies somewhat with time, place, and cultural development. Infanticide, though approved by the Greeks, would not be approved in modern times (*ibid.,* V, chap. ii).

[45] He names Plato, Aristotle, the Stoics, Clark, Woollaston, and Shaftesbury.

[46] *Mor. Sent.,* VII, ii, chap. i, p. 518.

[47] Epicurus, on the one hand, the Church Fathers, Cudworth, and Hutcheson, on the other, are cited.

[48] In the first five editions La Rochefoucauld was bracketed with Mandeville, but his name was struck out of the sixth. Holbach and Helvetius were not mentioned.

[49] He mentions Hobbes, Pufendorf, and Mandeville. The inclusion of Pufendorf in this category seems unwarranted.

[50] *Mor. Sent.,* VII, iii, p. 563.

[51] *Ibid.,* p. 568.

[52] *The Moral Sentiments* was a redaction of the first part of the Glasgow lectures, which were intended to form the character, as well as train the minds, of undergraduates, many of whom were preparing for the service of the kirk and the bar (cf. Scott, *Francis Hutcheson,* pp. 64-68). This may possibly account for the rhetorical style of the *Moral Sentiments* when compared with the *Wealth of Nations,* written years after Smith had stopped teaching.

[53] The phrase is Dugald Stewart's in his "Account" (*op. cit.,* p. 450); illustrations are the deer and beaver problem and the economy of "the original state of things."

[54] See below, p. 516.[This section not included in the excerpt.]

[55] "Of the Imitative Arts," *Works,* V, 243-318; "Of Certain English and Italian Verses," *ibid.,* pp. 321-30; "Considerations concerning the First Formation of Languages," *ibid.,* pp. 1-48. The "Considerations" appeared first as an appendix to the third edition of the *Moral Sentiments* (1767); the others were posthumous.

[56] Edwin Cannan (ed.), *Lectures on Justice, Police, Revenue and Arms* (Oxford, 1896).

[57] It is possible that the text did not fully report the lecturer's conclusions, and perhaps not accurately. What professor would wish to be preserved to posterity by a student's lecture notes?

[58] Hume regarded the mental experiment as a proper empirical device.

[59] See below, p. 516. [This section not included in the excerpt.]

[60] *History of Civilization in England* (New York, 1890), Vol. II, chap. vi, pp. 340-57.

[61] The discovery of the [*Lectures on Justice, Police, Revenue and Arms*] of 1763 showed that Smith had held the doctrine of laisser faire before his French journey, a view which Dugald Stewart had maintained on other evidence. It was thought that the natural order of the physiocrats greatly influenced Smith's thought. Most of the critics, however, find more of the natural-order doctrine in the *Moral Sentiments* than in the *Wealth of Nations,* but the former work preceded the exposition of the physiocratic order by several years. . . . [The] Smithian conception of natural processes was quite different from the physiocratic.

[62] [Witold von Skar y ski, *Adam Smith als Moralphilosoph und Schoepfer der Nationaloekonomie* (Berlin, 1878)].

[63] The first five editions of the *Moral Sentiments* (1759, 1761, 1767, 1774, and 1781) were not materially changed by the author. The second edition changed the titles and numbering of the parts and sections and added eighteen pages and a footnote (p. 76) in answer to an objection by Hume. Otherwise the text is the same except for the correction of errata and a few verbal changes. The second to fifth editions are identical, page by page, except for changes in spelling and spacing due to typesetting. The third edition added the disser-tation on languages, and the fourth added a subtitle, "The Theory of Moral Sentiments, or an Essay towards an Analysis of the Principles by which Men Naturally Judge concerning the Conduct and Character, First of Their Neighbours, and Afterwards of Themselves." The forms of the title-pages, publishers' names, and colophons also varied.

[64] It seems likely that Smith had written part of this third treatise by 1790. The manuscript may have been among the papers he ordered destroyed just before his death. The *Lectures* give some indication of the probable contents. . . .

[88] "But man has almost constant occasion for the help of his brethren, and it is in vain for him to expect it from their benevolence only. He will be more likely to prevail if he can interest their self-love in his favour, and show them that it is for their own advantage to do for him what he requires of them. . . . It is not from the benevolence of the butcher, the brewer, or the baker, that we expect our dinner, but from regard to their own interest. We address ourselves, not to their humanity, but to their self-love, and never talk to them of our necessities but of their advantages. Nobody but a beggar chuses to depend chiefly upon the benevolence of his fellow citizens. Even a beggar does not depend on it entirely. . . ." (*W. of N.,* I, ii [Cannan, I, 16]).

[89] He advances the argument that the rich man, in hiring labor, has an eye to his own well-being but in fact so provides for the wants of his workers, "all of whom thus derive from his luxury and caprice, that share of the necessaries of life, which they would in vain have expected from his humanity or his justice" (*Mor. Sent.,* IV, chap. i, p. 318).

[90] *Ibid.,* III, chap. vi, pp. 297-98.

[91] *Ibid.,* II, ii, chap. iii, p. 146. "Even a tradesman is thought a poor-spirited fellow among his neighbours, who does not bestir himself to get what they call an extraordinary job or some uncommon advantage," as would be a gentleman "who did not exert himself to gain an estate" or a politician who neglected to campaign or a prince who was not anxious to gain or keep territory (p. 298).

[92] "It is because mankind are disposed to sympathize more entirely with our joy than with our sorrow, that we make parade of our riches and conceal our poverty. . . . nay, it is chiefly from this regard to the sentiments of mankind, that we pursue riches and avoid poverty" (*ibid.,* I, iii, chap. ii, pp. 80-81). (This may be the inspiration of Rae and Veblen.)

[93] *W. of N.,* II, iii (Cannan, I, 325). With slight variations this phrase is repeated elsewhere (Cannan, I, 328; II, 43, 172).

[94] *W. of N.*, IV, Introd. (Cannan, I, 395).

[95] "According therefore, as this produce, or what is purchased with it, bears a greater or smaller proportion to the number of those who are to consume it, the nation will be better or worse supplied with all the necessaries and conveniencies for which it has occasion" (*ibid.*, Introd. [Cannan, I, 1]). The real wealth is equated to the annual produce of land and labor in a number of other places (Cannan, I, 237, 240, 417).

[96] "As defence, however, is of much more importance than opulence, the act of navigation is, perhaps, the wisest of all the commercial regulations of England" (*ibid.*, IV, ii [Cannan, I, 429]).

[97] *Ibid.*, IV, viii (Cannan, II, 159).

[98] "The price of monopoly is upon every occasion the highest which can be got" and "the highest which can be squeezed out of the buyers" (*ibid.*, I, vii [Cannan, I, 63]).

[99] "Monopoly, besides, is a great enemy to good management, which can never be universally established but in consequence of the free and universal competition which forces everybody to have recourse to it for the sake of self-defence" (*ibid.*, I, xi, chap. i [Cannan, I, 148]).

[100] *Ibid.*, V, i, Part III, art. 1 (Cannan, II, 245).

[101] *Ibid.*, IV, vii-viii (Cannan, II, 129, 159).

[102] *Ibid.*, I, ix (Cannan, I, 100); I, xi (Cannan, I, 249-50); IV, vii, Part II (Cannan, II, 112).

[103] *Ibid.*, I, x, Part II (Cannan, I, 131).

[104] *Ibid.*, I, viii (Cannan, I, 68).

[105] *Ibid.*, IV, ix (Cannan, II, 184).

[106] *Ibid.*, V, i, Part II (Cannan, II, 202).

[107] *Moral Sentiments*, II, ii, p. 137.

[108] Presumably this is why Smith condoned smuggling (*W. of N.* [Cannan, II, 381]) and the illegal export of wool in an earlier period (*[Lectures on Justice, Police, Revenue and Arms]*, p. 136).

[109] *Mor. Sent.* VII, iv, pp. 608-9.

[110] *Ibid.*, IV, chap. i, p. 320.

[111] *Ibid.*, VII, ii, pp. 534-35 (cf. p. 325).

A. L. Macfie (lecture date 1955)

SOURCE: "The Scottish Tradition in Economic Thought," in *The Individual in Society: Papers on Adam Smith*, George Allen & Unwin Ltd., 1967, pp. 19-41.

[In the following essay, Macfie places Smith and several other economists, including Francis Hutcheson, David Hume, and James and John Stuart Mill, within the historical context of the Scottish tradition in economic thought. Macfie emphasizes that their approach was sociological rather than analytical and that their methods were strongly influenced by the philosophy of Stoicism and the doctrine of natural law. Macfie's essay was originally delivered as a lecture at the Annual General Meeting of the Scottish Economic Society on March 14, 1955.]

I

This essay must start with a confession. In undertaking, some months ago, to submit an article on some such subject as 'The Scottish Tradition in Economic Thought', I was, it is now clear, in a state of not very creditable ignorance. I had then a rather vague idea that one could in an article say something directly significant on this subject. I had, of course, at various times read the Scots classics in a rather haphazard way; but the effect of reading them all straight through in their proper sequence, in the hope of tracing the individual Scottish thread running through them—the effect of this has been radical. For it has forced the conviction that there is a quite specific doctrine and method in Scots economic thinking, especially clear and influential between roughly 1730 and 1870, and still alive, if not on top. As it shows some of the greatest names—Hume, Smith, the Mills—and also some considerable satellites—Hutcheson, Lauderdale, Rae, McCulloch—it at once appears that a mere article will not do. If there is a Scottish line inspiring these great writings, then only a volume could do it justice. The kind of thesis one would like to examine is the view that between Hutcheson and John Stuart Mill it was that Scottish mode of approach that formed the atmosphere of British economic thought. But this starts many other hares, and the most we can do here is to chase some of them conscientiously.

Our general theme must then be that there is a characteristic Scottish attitude and method which is important in the history of economic thought. It may be called the philosophical approach, though many of us may prefer to call it, equally aptly, the social approach. This is not the dominant approach today in academic teaching—the scientific or analytical method holds that place everywhere—but in Scotland the traditional approach is still alive and influential.

It should then be our business to show that this Scottish method and interpretation grew in a definitely historical setting. It grew out of the Scottish soil and reflected truly the Scottish atmosphere. To establish this one would need to describe at least four influences which nourished it. First, there is the place of Scots social thinking in the stream of European culture and history. The Scots gave it their own typical turn but their thought is in the broad Stoic stream. It was brought to its highest pitch by Hutcheson, Hume and Smith. Rather more speculatively, it was alive and dominant in the Mills. Then this Scottish method has its simple everyday reflection in the teaching and curricula of the Scots universities, especially Glasgow in the period between Carmichael and Smith, and later Edinburgh. This we need to prove the persistence, the natural roots of the method. It has formed the seed-bed of Scots students and teaching—all of them in all our Scottish universities—right back to link up with the Middle Ages. This in turn reflects the character and interests of the Scottish people, and they again have their special contacts and friendships with the Continent, practical contacts shaping the education of the people who provided the leaders in Scotland till after the '45.

It will then be necessary to show how this approach and method were at work in the classical sequence up to and including the Mills. It was indeed working in Marshall, though more as a climate than as the guiding line. Is this not the way in which his faithfulness to the classic line, on which he so insisted, took effect? Certainly Jevons was the more typical English exact scientist. But we must not digress. An equally strong claimant as a fact is the decline of the philosophic method from its dominant position, or from being a pervading atmosphere, after about 1870. Along with this we have to note the relative decline from eminence of Scots economic thinkers. After the Mills no Scot reaches the heights in economic theory, and after Marshall there are no more 'three-deckers', no comprehensive philosophic surveys of economic theory. Whether this is because the Scot can be great only when he may also philosophize is a matter for speculation.

Then finally one 'lone star' influence that demands notice is the fact of Smith's genius. Genius can have strange indirect effects. Its brilliance often extinguishes other valuable, though lesser lights. This is not due to any lack of sources in Smith's work; they are all there. But successors cannot continue on the level of genius. One aspect of the great man, probably that which suits later conditions, is chosen, much of the rest probably rejected. The section of Smith's work which was so chosen and developed till it became supreme was the first two books of the **Wealth of Nations.** The theory of static equilibrium there so carefully sketched has grown into an analytic system and method which has for long dominated English-speaking universities, and our universities today control our

theory as never before in modern times. It is a paradox of history that the analytics of Book I, in which Smith took his own line, should have eclipsed the philosophic and historical methods in which he so revelled and which showed his Scots character. Book I of the **Wealth of Nations** is now a part of world thought, as is the *Origin of Species,* or *Principia Mathematica.* But even so we cannot speak for the future. The positive analytic method is a mere stripling. An immense future stretches ahead; and the past certainly shows that each phase of social development produces its own philosophy and method in all the social disciplines. Do these signs of today which spell out the future show any special call for the sociological method? If so, a Scottish revival is due. An opportunity is opening for Scottish thinkers.

II

We begin then with the thesis that there is a unique Scots method or approach, or interpretation of social issues, as individual as any personal approach, and that it can be described as philosophic or sociological. It rises to maturity in the eighteenth century, especially through the work of Hutcheson, Hume and Adam Smith. They gave it its unique bite and flavour, though the flavour depends on the Scottish soil and cultivation in the propensities and institutions of the people. This is seen in the course of writings taken as their normal education by all the members of this close-knit group— between Edinburgh and Glasgow. The course began with Natural Theology (including some Natural Philosophy), went on to Moral Philosophy, and thence to Justice and Law. It was under the law of contract and private property, with its social aspects, that the broad descriptive and critical comments on political economy arose (the kind of discursive comment *ambulando* which the philosophic method naturally and richly inspires). This accepted sequence is found in all the writers—in Gershom Carmichael, Adam Ferguson and Dugald Stewart as much as in the great trinity. It also dominates the method and point of view of Lauderdale and Rae, though after Smith the more specialized treatment of economics inevitably begins. Each writer may give his work a special slant towards his own special interest: Hutcheson towards morals, Hume towards metaphysical scepticism and also history, Ferguson towards sociology and Smith towards economics. Smith, however, like Hume, adds the crown of genius, and genius is apt to confuse the inevitabilities of logic. It also shapes history in a way which may obscure the roots and setting of the writer. Thus, just because Smith is a world figure, we are apt to ignore his completely Scottish character. We cannot begin to understand him, especially what are often thought of as his weaknesses, if we thus ignore his roots, for the Scottish method was more concerned with giving a broad well balanced comprehensive picture seen from different points of view than with logical rigour. In fact, Smith was, like the others, a philosophic writer, modelled on Hutcheson, whom W. R. Scott truly called the 'preacher-philosopher'.[2] His aim was to present all the relevant facts critically. Modern writers start from a totally different angle. They found on the law of non-contradiction. They aim at isolating one aspect of experience and breaking it down by analysis into its logical components. Thus the older type of writer is often accused of 'inconsistencies', and certainly these are to be found, especially in Hutcheson, whose pupil here Smith certainly was. To the analyst such inconsistencies are anathema. To the modern method they represent failure. But to the philosopher they reflect the facts of our experience. It is part of wisdom to recognize, accept and be able to carry such inconsistencies. While we should of course try to reduce them, we should not insist on avoiding them in our critical descriptions, for then we omit the crux of our fate, and also the practical human problems.

This attitude is still very much alive in the Mills. James is the most sociological of the Benthamites and his valuable historical and psychological expansions are in the true synthetic tradition. The son of course is both the jack and master of all trades. If one reads through the *Logic,* the *Political Economy,* and the main ethical and political writings in one gulp, the sheer wide power, range and status of this mind cannot be missed. But the 'improvement' bacillus is always at work in it, inspiring and driving—the optimistic tough individual practical belief in wide human improvement reflected down from Hutcheson and Smith. The Utilitarian movement is itself, of course, a philosophy. But as a philosophy it is English rather than Scottish, especially in its positivism and its willingness to be dominated by facts. Bentham gave it these main characters; by contrast the Scottish qualities in the Mill writings are unmistakable.

But is the attitude and tradition still alive? Well, it has to be confessed, only in a rather negative way. Scots teachers and writers are today certainly primarily interested in the historical or the social and critical system of Marshall's *Principles.* But that is a world movement. They were themselves brought up in it. The writings of Scots economists are, however, still coloured by the traditional Scottish point of view. One hint, significant if slight, anyone immersing himself in this literature can hardly miss. In the Scots writings up to recent times there is hardly, so far as I can find, one serious example of the use of mathematics to develop analysis. (The Hutcheson example is well known. He removed the mathematical passage in the second edition of the *Inquiry concerning Beauty and Virtue.*) Some may contemplate this fact with relief. The whole Scots sequence cleaves to actual events, to historical and institutional relations growing through them, and to the individual experiences that support and develop the argument. But such individual factors do not lend

themselves to mathematical or purely deductive logical treatment. It is not the case that there is any relative weakness in the Scot in mathematics. The facts certainly prove the opposite in the eighteenth and nineteenth centuries, in Glasgow and Edinburgh.[3] The obvious explanation is that the Scottish philosophical and the mathematical methods do not blend. The assumptions in the first are normative, in the second exact. For this very reason, mathematical processes are especially grateful to the English exact positive scientific approach in economics. It is no doubt a useful contrast of methods within our small island. Ideally, the one should stimulate the other.

It should be noticed here that this approach is reflected in the curricula of the Scots universities, and always has been. It has been bred into Scots thinking over all the generations, and is now steadily acquired as well as inherited. This can be illustrated by the curricula of the eighteenth century. The course was in Humanity and Greek, Philosophy (metaphysical and natural), Logic and Moral Philosophy, and, less securely though it was always there, Mathematics.[4] It is here interesting that in August 1695 'the Faculty at Glasgow appointed "Mr. John Tran . . . to compose the Ethics, Oeconomics and Politics" for the general course in philosophy which the Parliamentary Commission of 1695 was seeking to arrange by agreement between the four Scots universities'. This was only a tidying operation, for the disciplines were already established in all the universities. Lively individual preferences, as might be expected, prevented any common course from ever reaching print, so Mr. Tran's course is not available; but the fact stands out that as early as 1695 'Oeconomics and Politics' were established studies for the graduands.

We should never forget that Adam Smith grew from these roots; that his work is as influenced by them as any writer's could be; and that it could not have grown from any but just such an exactly and richly cultivated soil. This fact has been obscured by the unfortunate inadequacy of Scottish histories of the seventeenth century. Yet, as H. W. Meikle insisted in his Murray Lecture, the foundations for the future cultural growth were in fact largely laid in Scotland in the seventeenth century. Adam Smith was taught in a burgh school in Kirkcaldy, and later in the normal courses of a Scots university he built up the knowledge, methods and aims of his own thinking. He was not building on air or mere personal talent, as popular records are apt to suggest. We should remember such strategic events as these: The Advocates' Library began its modern career in 1682, and, as Dr. Meikle insists, it was one of the vital vehicles of Scottish culture. Again, Stair's *Institutions of the Law of Scotland* appeared in 1681. This is the scientific genesis and inspiration of Scottish jurisprudence, and is itself a unique work by any standard. It was from such stems that Smith's genius was bred. The foundations remain to this day. No Scottish student in Arts can take a pass degree without a philosophy, and the Honours courses are based on the width of the pass degree, as knowledge of at least four subjects is required in it (though modern specialization has made some inroads). This training has no doubt encouraged a people more interested in a philosophic argument (and in persuading other people that he, the teacher, is right) than even in getting what one wants. (Does not the Englishman typically make exactly the opposite choice?) The Scots theological interests and relations should also be mentioned, but cross illustrations will grow as we proceed.

We note next that this local movement of thought was itself also a reflection, though as an original facet; a reflection of what was perhaps the major European stream. It is the great flow from Stoicism. But the Scottish inspiration came rather through the Roman glosses than from the Greek sources. Cicero, Marcus Aurelius, Seneca, Epictetus, these were Hutcheson's mentors (though Leechman mentions the way he encouraged Greek studies). Hume's references are to the same texts, and so it is for all of them. They did not—they were not trying to—dig so deep as the mighty Greeks. They were painting a broad practical sketch of society, expressing all the important balances, not exposing the roots. For these slightly superficial surveys the Roman texts were invaluable models. As an example, take Hutcheson dealing in their typical way, later followed by Hume and Smith, with the advantages of social life. He quotes Cicero (*De Finibus*) on the advantages of a population sufficient to allow of division of labour. The passage has his usual optimistic flavour. It does not appear in his treatment of economy, and it is interesting as showing the social origin of the Scottish treatment of division of labour rather than the more individualistic source described by Locke. But this so fruitful treatment of division of labour is still embedded in an ethical, political, legal argument.[5] It was Smith who was inspired to effect its transference, to form the premiss of a purely economic argument and so give a new science its task and direction.

The Stoic influence in Scottish thought is most apparent in the constant study of Law. Especially on the practical side of this philosophizing, the argument was carried by discussions of property rights and origins, or by questions on contract, particularly in relation to land. This appears in the first teacher of the school, Gershom Carmichael, under whom Hutcheson studied and whose major work was the editing of the text of Puffendorf. So we are back to the broadest river in European culture, the Stoic-inspired Roman jurisprudence, carried practically throughout Europe on the broad currents of Roman and Canon Law. The richest contacts for Scotland came from France and Holland. (The French, like the Scots were more deeply versed and skilled in Latin than in Greek.) In our Glasgow

school this comes through directly in the study of Puffendorf, and especially of Grotius, whom Smith read under Hutcheson. This tradition pervades the *Wealth of Nations,* but in a Scottish dress. It is optimistic, tolerant, always eager for social benefits between as well as within nations, very different from the nervous, individualist, critical, touchy excursions of the revolutionary French writers. This good temper the school owes at least as much to Hutcheson as to Smith. Leechman, who was a pupil of Hutcheson and later became Principal in Glasgow, has described Hutcheson's personal attitude in words which apply equally to Smith, and indeed to Hume and all the Edinburgh writers. In spirit, aim and conduct they were citizens of the world, and they behaved as such. The world was smaller then and more harmonious, but these sympathies and contacts still struggle to live in Scotland today.

These scrappy remarks are all that space allows here. The place of Scottish thought in the main stream of European jurisprudence is a subject that grows in subtlety and scope the more one learns about it. It would need a long chapter in any volume dealing with our subject. Its literature is as massive and difficult as any Europe's thought can show. But there is a more popular level of interpretation, and it may be useful to suggest in a footnote some simple writings that at least serve as introductions or summaries.[6]

The main faith which the Law of Nature and Stoicism inspired in Scotland was a faith in natural liberty in a natural society. Here certainly Smith was Hutcheson's faithful disciple. Of Hutcheson, Leechman tells us: 'As he had occasion every year in the course of his lectures to explain the origin of government, and compare the different forms of it, he took peculiar care, while on that subject, to inculcate the importance of civil and religious liberty to the happiness of mankind: as a warm love of liberty, and manly zeal for promoting it, were ruling principles in his own breast; he always insisted on it at great length, and with the greatest strength of argument and earnestness of persuasion: and he had such success on this important point, that few, if any, of his pupils, whatever contrary prejudices they might bring along with them, ever left him without favourable notions of that side of the question which he espoused and defended'. Smith certainly was so influenced with the others. But our view of natural liberty in the *Wealth of Nations* has received a deceptive twist from history, from the individualism of the industrial developments, and the interpreters, apologists and critics, of the Industrial Revolution. This twist does not do balanced justice to Smith's own feeling about natural liberty: here he followed his teacher, and was in a broad way, at one with his fellow writers. The arguments were thrashed out in relation to the American colonists. On this, though earlier, Hutcheson was at least as liberal and decisive as Smith.[7] And the extent to which Smith's imagination could range is seen in his suggestions for federal government in a unified British family. Here again we have to make an effort of historical imagination to see what our classic fathers wanted and appreciated. We are so apt to read our own wants, especially in terms of some index number of the standard of living, into their more closely-knit social and cultural aspirations. Perhaps this quotation from Hume expresses their hopes as tersely and vividly as we have space for: 'The more these refined arts advance, the more sociable do men become; nor is it possible that, when enriched with science and possessed of a fund of conversation, they should be contented to remain in solitude, or live with their fellow-citizens in that distant manner which is peculiar to ignorant and barbarous nations. They flock into cities; love to receive and communicate knowledge; to show their wit or their breeding; their taste in conversation or living, in clothes or furniture. Curiosity allures the wise; vanity the foolish; and pleasure both. Particular clubs and societies are everywhere formed, both sexes meet in an easy and sociable manner, and the tempers of men, as well as their behaviour, refine apace. So that, besides the improvements which they receive from knowledge and the liberal arts, it is impossible but they must feel an increase of humanity from the very habit of conversing together and contributing to each other's pleasure and entertainment.' Natural liberty is a very different sentiment when inspired by the aim of 'an increase in humanity' from that pervading business specialization. But it was this society as a glorified Athenaeum that these eighteenth century Scotsmen desired, and indeed to a creditable, if limited, extent achieved.

It might here be convenient very briefly to recall some of the more influential factors in these Scottish contacts; especially with France and Holland. The natural enemy was England, and this lingered, so far as influences went, into the early eighteenth century. So the inevitable friends were found in the Low Countries and France. Professor Mackie remarks: 'There was much coming and going between Scotland and France, where until about 1670, the government accorded to the Hugenots the privileges promised by the Edict of Nantes in 1598, and it is obvious that in the world of western scholarship the man from Glasgow could fully hold his own.' That he did so can be gathered, on a popular level, from such a study as *The Scot Abroad* by John Hill Burton. The direct evidence is scattered over the memoirs of scholars, statesmen and fighting men in all the literatures of Europe. The Reformation paved the way for a possible partnership with England but the balance swung decisively only in the eighteenth century. We need merely mention the economic ties with the Low Countries. Only 1707 with its gradual swing towards the west in commercial expansion, displaced these predominant links with the Continent. Of equal influence, especially in the sixteenth and

seventeenth centuries, were the religious contacts. Scottish churchmen in their many see-saw evasions tended towards Holland, Geneva, even France, rather than towards England.

The evidence here is well known. What was important was the personal and social impact of these contacts. It is best realized through the diaries—again a formidable library. But four famous later ones can be recalled—those of 'Jupiter' Carlyle, Ramsay of Ochtertyre and Cockburn, and, most intriguing of all, the recent Boswell volumes. There is also a lesser known one, from which a passage seems worth quotation, because it reflects vividly a swing in Scottish social habit; it comes from *John Fergusson 1727-50 (An Ayrshire Family in the 'Forty-Five)* by James Fergusson. Lord Kilkerran, a Court of Session judge, is concerned about the education of his son, the subject of the biography. He wishes a legal training such as will suit him to care for the Ayrshire estate. 'John's education', we are told[8] 'had advanced to the university stage when, in the autumn of 1743, his father decided that it should be completed in England. It was an unusual decision for those days. For generations past Scottish boys, cspccially students of law, had gone to the continent to seek such instruction as they could not get at home. This was partly because of the long wars with England and the traditions of continental alliances and friendships they left behind. Moreover, English universities were not open to Presbyterians, nor, if they had been, could the Roman Law, on which the Scottish legal system is founded, be studied there so well as in the Netherlands, where Lord Kilkerran himself had gone as a young man, and many of his contemporaries.' The boy was placed at Dr. Dodderidge's (dissenting) Academy at Northampton. In a letter to the reverend doctor the father says, 'The boy is seventeen since July last, and after being taught Latin and Greek at a publick school[9] with the assistance of a tutor, has been one year at the University with Mr. Maclairn, Professor of Mathematicks, whose name will not be unknown to you. What his proficiency has been in the languages I shall not anticipate your judgment, and as they are of great use in life, especially the Latin, for the study of Roman law, to which I intend he shall apply himself, I hope it will not be out of your way to improve him in the knowledge of that language. The Greek I know you are more fond of in England than we are here, and for gentleman educated for the church it is absolutely necessary, but otherwise I consider it only as a part of the belles lettres.'

This no doubt marks a social watershed. Thereafter, in growing volume the contacts are English. In the earlier diaries, however, we feel the strength of the personal influences. They are mainly centred round the Law and the Church. The leaders of Scotland depended on the management of their estates, or aimed to acquire estates. The law they must know was feudal and Roman, and the pre-eminent schools of such law were in Holland and France. Every man of property, intent on the education of his heirs, inevitably sent them on their Continental travels. In this regard, it is one of the smaller compensations of Boswell's swing to good behaviour that he turned (with such agonizing) to Holland and the traditional road for Scottish finish. For one could desire no more complete short account of the type of studies young Scotsmen followed than that in *Boswell in Holland;* and the spice of genius is added, as ever with Boswell. Part of the genius brings us to the heart of the personal life for the many Scots who share in Boswell's gaieties. But they are all very serious also, as one would expect of the breed. We certainly feel their determination to master any knowledge which will help them to manage their Scottish affairs. The same practical spirit and thoughtful comparative study of foreign institutions also flavours Sir James Steuart's volumes.

In their social gatherings the Church and the men-at-arms are the other main contributors. From the diaries we can sense the strength of the eclectic tradition. They are typically curious about people, men at work, about comparative institutions and what we could call 'social statistics'. They are not concerned with logical processes or sequences, or the framing of abstract hypotheses and their analysis to their utmost limits. They wish to build a truly balanced picture of social life as they found it and the forces which controlled it. Here it must be insisted Adam Smith is a true Scot of the eighteenth century. He had the common Latin Continental scholarly basis (how strange to find his library so full of Stoic texts, so almost entirely devoid of technical economic texts). He is not consciously concerned with building a logical model, or even with arguing in the merely logical mode. We should note his inconsistencies, but we should remember that they are the reflections of the method. Each aspect, the analytical, the historical, the contemporary-comparative (or sociological), is dealt with in turn. The inconsistencies arise out of these different aspects, and so out of real conditions. In Book I we have the analytics, and they bore such great issue that Book I has almost obliterated the rest in the world's estimate; but the rest is at least as characteristic of Smith as Book I. It is the *whole* book which represents his meaning.

Next in this family history come that unique father and son, James and John Stuart Mill. That this is fact some may contest; especially outside Scotland they may not be recognized as full-blooded Scots. Their effective lives were spent in the metropolitan circles of British culture, and they spent their lives in advocating a social theory and policy which are generally regarded as English, though they are more truly British. Certainly, we ought to accept the son's own words that *philosophically* he was no Utilitarian. One could spend an article on each of these issues; here we can only summarize. About James Mill there is really no question. To the end of his days he was as Scots as his native Angus (and the breed there is strong). Of his type he is really a very Scots Scotsman, so Scots that the parishioners who heard his early 'tasting' sermons could not thole him. No doubt a church is one of the few places in which a Scotsman submits to being told, but evidently the burning ardour to teach that was James Mill's enduring dynamic in life took intensities which even they were not prepared willingly to stomach.

His story is as typical a Scots success story as one could find. He had the special qualities and virtues of the Scottish approach, and he brought them from Scotland via Edinburgh University. He was interested in all social forces and structures. There are the usual exercises in comparative sociology in both the *Elements* and the *History of British India.* (In the latter there is an interesting reference to the work of John Millar in Glasgow; a direct link between the tradition's source and the modern classical sequence.)[10] And of course he shows the eclectic interests that are so Scottish, especially in his wide psychological insights. The simple clarity of his thought and style reflect his great Scottish predecessors (of the east rather than the west coast). Indeed his very clarity may explain why he has been so constantly underestimated. Obscurity is one way to temporary reputation. Ricardo's *Principles* is, to most non-specialists at least, unintelligible if they try to consider the book as a coherent system.[11] So it is probably Mill's translation of it in his *Elements* that in the earlier period carried the original work into the central consciousness of ordinary British thinking. For Mill's little book is entirely clear, though it is probably as near to what Ricardo meant as anyone is likely to get, which may not be very near. But further, here, and most distinctly, the economic theory is placed in its proper relation to the other social sciences, in the true Scottish manner. 'It is also,' he writes, 'in a peculiar manner, the business of those whose object it is to ascertain the means of raising human happiness to its greatest height, to consider, what is that class of men by whom the greatest happiness is enjoyed. It will not probably be disputed, that they who are raised above solicitude for the means of subsistence and respectability, without being exposed to the vices and follies of great riches, the men of middling fortunes, in short, the men to whom society is generally indebted for its greatest improvements, are the men, who, having their time at their own disposal, freed from the necessity of manual labour, subject to no man's authority, and engaged in the most delightful occupations, obtain, as a class, the greatest sum of human enjoyment. For the happiness, therefore, as well as the ornament of our nature, it is peculiarly desirable that a class of this description should form as large a proportion of each community as possible.' So even James Mill saw visions, and here what a prescient vision! For he foresaw the welfare state, in which we are all to be comfortably middle-class. There is, further, no doubt that on its personal side Mill was the driving power of the whole movement. The tributes of George Grote[12] and of his own son, and his letters with Ricardo leave no doubt about this. Through him the Scottish tradition flows through the veins of the whole Utilitarian movement.

For the son, on the merely factual side, the case is less obviously strong. His mother was English, though she had little, if any, influence on his intellectual life. He lived in England through his formative and most active years. But was it England? Could anyone live under the direct guidance of James Mill without living rather intensely in Scotland? The famous, in some respects infamous, education was his father, and it is just a supreme example or excess of a peculiarly Scottish propensity. It formed Mill through and through. It produced a mind of unique power, speed and range. Reading over his major works—and one has to do this to sense his special power, for it is extensive rather than intensive—one cannot miss the recognition that this is a weapon specially forged, made possible only by the conscious persistence of its maker. Evidence of a type which others may find inconclusive is the simple fact that, in these two, any knowledgeable Scot will recognize his brothers; not in capacity, but rather in their fanaticisms and weak spots. Especially Scottish is their consuming desire to teach everyone they meet. If one were asked to find outstanding examples of this fanaticism, few could stand beside them. Perhaps the Ancient Mariner could. With that goes the typical elimination of the humorous point of view which is so generally accepted in the south as Scottish. The teaching Scot, like the ravening wolf, is too busy to be humorous. If his mind had been disengaged he could no doubt have seen the joke, perhaps as quickly as a Frenchman or a missionary. But he is not interested in the joke. He has to get his message across. It is not argued that this is necessarily a proper attitude. It is merely insisted that it is a Scots attitude, and that the Mills illustrate it pre-eminently. Then again, Mill's 'inconsistencies' are even more famous than Smith's and they arise out of the same method for the same reasons. There are other questions that arise with John Stuart Mill, especially perhaps in regard to his wife's responsibility for the social aspects of his writing, but these we must ignore. They do not alter the broad conclusion as to Mill's responsibility for the sociological emphasis throughout the *Principles,* and especially in the theory of distribution. Yet this is entirely what one would expect of one brought up by his father, who was in turn nourished by the Scots method and interests.

This brings us to about 1870, or indeed later, if we include Marshall. Marshall is the equivocal figure. If the Mills are typically Scots, Marshall is the proper English contrast. The *Principles* of Marshall is in the shape and spirit of the *Principles* of Mill, as Marshall

delighted to insist. One wonders at times if he does not protest too much. Certainly the tone and wide sympathies, especially of Book III and VI, are in the tradition, but the footnotes and Books IV and V introduce the modern monographic abstractly analytic method. The history passes down to the Appendices. Some gremlins have slipped into the cupboards and cellars of the venerable building. As we know, the footnotes and the appendices have grown to separate commands. They have sunk the 'three-deckers', which sail the seas of realistic speculation no more. Perhaps it was Jevons who launched the decisive attack, for he began the long line of modern positive scientific monographs, but the contributions of Marshall towards their ultimate victory are as subtle and deep as was Marshall himself.[13]

However this may be, the fact which stands out for us is clear. The specific Scots tradition ceases to dominate about the middle of the century (sharing rule with Ricardo). There are no great, or even highly placed, Scottish writers in economic theory after Mill, and after Marshall the tradition that Scots thinkers did so much to form, the eclectic, comparative, widely sociological tradition, has faded out. What is still very much alive is the analytic method, the technique of static equilibrium which finds its source, or a main source, in Book I of the **Wealth of Nations**. But this is no longer specifically Scottish—it never was. It is absorbed into the stream of world thought as truly as is the central theory of Darwinian evolution. In its modern, dominantly Marshallian perfection it has captured the Universities. All academic economists have spent their lives teaching it as the core of their subject. And the Universities today control the spirit of social theory far more exclusively than in the eighteenth or even the nineteenth century. Only Smith of our greater Scots economists was an academic, and he was so much more. This (perhaps temporary) eclipse of the Scottish method is then the last fact we must, rather dismally, record.

III

We turn from fact to fiction—here admittedly a distinction of degree. The effect of Smith's genius on the course of the Scottish tradition is a difficult speculation. Yet one cannot ignore it, for it was also Smith's genius which started the modern analytic method on its conquering course. Anyone who studies any pre-Smith Scottish economist (Sir James Steuart, say), then Ricardo, the Mills and Marshall in sequence, will accept this. Here then is the novel individual force that Smith himself contributed. But in his use of history and of broad sociological facts and comparisons to develop his argument and to demonstrate the need for considering all the influences together as seen in actual institutions—in this Smith was not original, he was simply Scottish. His aim was the Scottish, not the modern aim. If here also he shows genius, as he did, it lies in the richness, the apt relevance of his illustrations. It is a mistake here merely to lament the past. The old sociological thinkers of the Scottish school had weaknesses and gaps that to us are glaring. Especially, their view of what can pass as a fact fully deserved Dugald Stewart's inspired description, 'conjectural history' (he did not mean this as a criticism). With their equipment, based as it was on little more than travellers' tales, facts could hardly be more than conjecture. If the older method is ever to revive in economics, we must realize that the task will be much more difficult than it was in the eighteenth century. Then one mind could reasonably absorb all the writings on the social sciences, as a glance through Adam Smith's library will show. Today this is impossible. We are all so specialized that when we stray from our own disciplines the sense that we may be talking weak superficialities is an inadequacy that we must accept and face. May it not be mere arrogance for any of us to expect to survey all the knowledge? Or has the delusion of Faust in reality captured our spirits? A due humility seems to require that we take the risk of these recognized inadequacies. The eighteenth century thinkers were not accustomed to speak with the assured dogmatism of our modern analysts. As we are, with our present one-line specialisms, we run the risk that nowhere will a balanced picture of the whole social adventure, or even sections of it, be drawn. Yet this should always be the crown of our endeavour. Are our trained thinkers then to leave this valuation to journalists and politicians, for it will inevitably be made by someone? It is neither fair nor right that they should be alone in making it. And it seems immensely dangerous to allow them to be alone.

It should not be laid to Smith's account that Benthamite Utilitarianism became the basis of orthodox economic thought. The opposite is the truth, on the ethical side; Smith there went much deeper than Utilitarianism. It is in fact just an accident of history—one of the many which underline the inadequacy of mechanistic interpretations—that the method of static equilibrium originated in his Book I. The central assumptions of Benthamite Utilitarianism are themselves antithetic to the whole spirit of the Scottish social school. The main philosophic contrast is between a mechanistic psychology, which inevitably eliminates any truly moral theory, and the optimistic forward-looking assumptions of the Scottish school; or again it is seen in the fact that the Scots saw the central fact as a *growing* society, a creature quite different from any single individual, whereas to Bentham any society was merely an aggregate of individuals. This broad contrast is of central importance for modern economics simply because Marshall accepted as the basis of his positive economic theory the mechanistic 'ethical' or psychological assumptions of Bentham.[14] The static

equilibrium theory of 'normal' value is therefore itself inevitably mechanistic. It traces the run down, after disturbance, to a position of stable equilibrium. It has great heuristic value. But its practical inadequacy stands out; it is not equipped to deal with changes *away* from equilibrium. Yet these changes seem to dominate our economic fates.

In this context a historical speculation will perhaps be allowed. Suppose Benthamism had not captured the dynastic succession. Is it possible that then the spirit and outlook of Lauderdale and Rae might have gained command? We can at least imagine it. They were both critics of Smith, inevitably though admiringly, but they were both completely in the Scots manner and method. It is, however, the line of their criticism that is significant. They thought Smith's theory should give more weight to the importance of invention, novelty, new arrangements in history. Smith, of course, did much here, but to Lauderadale and Rae invention is picked on as the core of economic growth, and this is suggested as the central issue in theory and practice.[15] One cannot say this of the **Wealth of Nations**. If their interpretation had developed, it would have had to do so through the Scottish type of procedure, by comparative and historical excursions. The analytic equilibrium theory in fact misses change. It cannot cope with the individual causes of change, just because it is analytical. This means that the method deals with laws and characters that are common to different economic situations. But change and innovation cannot be dealt with by such a method, simply because an innovation, an economic novelty or change away from equilibrium, is by definition a fact. It is therefore in the major sense unique, not common. If it is thus unique as history, it must then be dealt with, it can only be dealt with finally, by methods which are proper to the particular, to qualities as well as quantities. Such methods as the historical, the philosophical or the sociological, are in their turn complementary. The Bentham-Marshall analysis has given us keen cutting power where regularities can be traced, and this is invaluable, but the older method has faltered or been absorbed in the sands of specialization. Yet the strong basis for its use, as Lauderdale and Rae saw it, still remains. Enterprise is its most positive pole. It is the individual improving or creative element that finds some place in *every* worker in his degree. This is the drive behind economic growth. There are ample sources for this, as for most lines of theory, in the **Wealth of Nations**. Had it grown, it is possible to imagine the type of theory that Schumpeter has so richly developed in our day, working in broadening circles through the whole range of economic experience over the last two centuries. If this had happened, our economic theory would certainly be a better balanced, a more realistic, more practical equipment than it is today. We might also be nearer control of our main economic evil, the problem of unpredictable growth or decay, inevitably away from economic equilibrium.

IV

If we try to account for the decline in the Scottish influence, we become even more speculative, and because, apart from its influence on the future (on which this article will end), the subject is of no special practical importance, only brief comment is attempted. We should perhaps first remember that the very brilliance of our eighteenth century throws our judgment out of balance. One would not expect the splendour of classical Athens from its modern representatives. The power of the Scottish influence on European thought is indeed surprising as coming from such a small and then rather remote people. That they realized their position is often evident in their remarks. It is taken for granted quite naturally in this letter from David Hume to Gilbert Elliot (1757): 'Is it not strange,' he writes, 'that at a time when we have lost our Princes, our Parliaments, our independent Governments, even the presence of our chief nobility, are unhappy in our Accent or Pronunciation, speak a very corrupt Dialect of the tongue, which we make use of: is it not strange, I say, that in these circumstances, we should really be the people most distinguished for Literature in Europe?' It is the strangeness, not the fact that excites his wonder. The fact was accepted, and Hume was certainly no boaster, and was in a position to judge. To ask why it happened is as hopeless of answer as questions about any broad movement of history.

On the more practical side, the cradle being mainly in Glasgow, there is real occasion for research into the economic setting there over the century, for it showed a vigorous outburst of energy, and opportunities made and taken, such as would stimulate and direct wider social enquiries. The eighteenth century rapidity at least must be rather unique. Later, Glasgow slowed down to the tempo and form of British industrial development in general. But the answers we can offer to 'Why the decline in Scots economists?' are at best negative. The one positive factor we have noted is that an antithetic movement of thought captured the leadership of social thinking, and Scotsmen, like Welshmen, or even Irishmen, have been absorbed into it. We in the Scottish Universities have done our due and proper part in teaching economic theory in the Bentham-Marshall tradition to a rich flow of students. The present article may at times have seemed critical of that tradition, but this is not intended. Any fair estimate must recognize the invaluable services to accuracy of definition, objective consistency and cutting edge that the more positive methods have built and sustained. When we remember the vague guesses of previous speculation we must insist that these disciplines of the experimental and scientific methods are at least an essential stage in the longer journey of knowledge. But are we sufficiently satisfied with their results to regard them as more than a stage, tool-making rather than directly ore-bearing? However that may be, there is little doubt that Scotsmen, while acquiescent, have not been entirely comfortable and luxuriant in modern economic theorizing, and it may well be that men so placed do not tend to excel there. The Scottish mood remains critical. The trend has been to teach the orthodox line, but to do one's special work rather in historical, social or semi-philosophical research. The two obvious Scots rebels should at least be mentioned—Ruskin and Carlyle. That their crusade was largely emotional is not in itself to its discredit. But here we deal with scientific thought, so we need only remark that their protests were typical of the Scottish tradition in that they were broadly social and moralistic. A more closely reasoned academic reaction is to be found in one who taught Marshall's system all his academic life yet came in the end to feel it was not enough. William Smart's *Second Thoughts of an Economist* puts the equilibrium theory of distribution entirely fairly (on the lines of his book on Distribution). He quietly insists that if you are teaching mere economics, you must in logic and common sense distribute according to 'economic worth'. Where he reacts, as he reflects on his work towards its close, is in the conviction that economic theory should itself be based on assumptions which are at once more realistic and more moralistic than those accepted in Marshall's footnote (on page 17). He agrees that the static equilibrium theory of prices follows logically from the assumption that a rising standard of living is a sufficient aim for economic science—but only, he correctly points out, if we think of the standard of living in merely quantitative terms. If exact logic is maintained, Benthamite assumptions can lead only to such conclusions. (Strict logic is not in fact maintained.) Yet, to this experienced business man who later turned to teaching and economic history, it was clear that the quantitative measure was incapable of dealing with the real emotions and forces which inspire business and working men. If pushed to the application we wish to reach, it gives false results. We wish, for workmen also, the economics of free enterprise in a growing society rather than what we have been given, the economics of free competition in a static society. This is the Scottish reaction still at work.

It is difficult to find a kenspeckle link in the tradition between Smart and John Stuart Mill, simply because there are then no kenspeckle Scots economists. In Glasgow the man who bridged these years was Edward Caird. He taught some economic theory in his Moral Philosophy course, but in the only set of notes available (made by a student in his class) the economic theory is slight;[16] it is typically illustrated from classical and Stoic sources, interlaced into their moral theories. He certainly regarded it as part of his duty, though a small part, to teach Political Economy, but when he felt the subject grow beyond his energy he gladly passed it on (in 1887) to William Smart. The following passage,[17] which concludes a public lecture by Caird, shows, however, how conscious he was of the wider social forms in economic life, and how typically Scots was his reaction to them: 'I do not think it will be possible henceforth to separate political economy from the general study of politics, or to discuss the laws of the production and distribution of wealth apart from the consideration of the relation of the distribution of wealth and the modes of distributing it to the other elements of social well-being. The abstraction of science will always be necessary for thorough knowledge of economy, as of everything else; but when we isolate part of *human* existence, it is more important than in relation to any other subject to remember that we *are* abstracting—*i.e.* that we are dealing with fragments of a whole, of which no final account can be given by anatomy. The practical value of the social science of the future will depend not only on the way in which we break up the complete problem of our existence into manageable parts, but as much and even more upon the way in which we are able to gather the elements together again, and to see how they act and react upon each other in the living movement of the social body.'

One might well ask, where has the Scots energy gone, if it has lacked the highest achievement in economics? Some questions merely raise others. After all, the abilities of a people can be spread over all its interests. To academic minds, Theology, Philosophy, the Law, Science, Medicine have always opened wide doors, and there the generations of Scottish scholars have found at once satisfaction and distinction. But more specifically, one may expect a people to follow its aptitudes. If so, Scots interested in sociological or normative processes would not find these very directly in modern analytical economics. Here it may be fair to note the numbers of distinguished Scots in the history of social anthropology. In the eighteenth century they shared almost an oligopoly with the French, but later we have Maine, J. F. McLennan, W. Robertson Smith and Frazer. Closer to home and today, we note W. R. Scott, Sir Alexander Gray and Professor Hamilton in their contributions to economic history. And, in general, anyone who knows the Scots universities from the inside realizes that the most natural approach of Scotsmen is either philosophical or historical, or severely applied in the sense that it confines itself to interpretation based on scientifically established fact. So it is with the students also. No one who has taught Scots students can miss the special response when the philosophic aspect is raised. We cannot explain such tastes. It is just 'the nature of the beast'.

Finally, as to the future, will it be likely to offer new opportunities to Scotsmen to follow their bent? If it does, we may expect a more positive Scottish contribution. Whether Scots today maintain the qualities so impressive in their scholarly past is endlessly debateable because the limits of the argument cannot be fixed. Their interest in the speculative and in the normative type of knowledge is certainly as intense. It appears that the influence of the Church is not dominant as it certainly was in the eighteenth century. It was the Presbyterian structure that then most closely expressed the familial relations of the relatively small society which led the country.[18] This may have diminished, but mainly in form. If one were to add the intellectual impacts of the Church, the Universities, the Law, Medicine, the more scientific side of business, the Scots are certainly as intellectually inclined today as ever they have been. Then again, one might point to some watering of the warm family emotion which formed our earlier loyalties and institutions. Certainly the power of the larger kinship group has passed. But we remain a small tightly knit nation, keenly interested in each other as persons living together. That this still lives is expressed in our poetry, essentially a folk, a family literature. The talented editors of *A Scots Anthology* (stretching from the thirteenth to the twentieth century) remark: 'The main body of Scottish poetry is not in this heroic vein but springs from the normal day to day life of the people, a people who, until the end of the eighteenth century, lived wholly in the country or in small towns where you had only to go down a wynd off the main street to reach the country. It was, too, a remarkably homogeneous people. Rich and poor lived pretty close together and the gap between the great folk and the common folk was not an unbridgeable gap; divisions between the classes did not obscure their common humanity. And so we find that a court poet like Dunbar could leave the lofty, artificial, allegoric strain and be not only familiar, but vulgar; that some of the best of our songs of peasant life and feeling are by writers of the landed and professional classes; that Scott—Sheriff of Selkirk; Laird of Abbotsford, and Baronet—could write of the life and feelings of common folk with an understanding and reverence equalled only by Wordsworth; and that, in our own time, *Fisher Jamie*—that delightful serio-comic elegy on a Tweedside poacher—was composed by a highly cultured Scot who ended his life as Governor-General of Canada and Chancellor of the University of Edinburgh.' If one reads through these five hundred or so pages of living emotion, the continuing sense of personal individual life in a free community is manifest. We may still then feel assured that whether or not we are the size of our fathers, we remain the same kind.

The future, however, will open to us only if we give it what it wants. Are there any signs that there may be a renewed need for the Scottish approach in the social sciences? Here we can only consult our broad impressions. Are we satisfied that the methods of analytic economics are sufficient, or indeed alone suitable, as the theoretical approach to the economic issues now typical in industry? In the nineteenth century the practical effort was specialized as never before. It appeared reasonable to treat by a linear science what was then practised as a rather linear way of life in private business. Even within their own minds, it was customary for business men to keep somewhat separate the standards of business from their more speculative ethical and religious ideals, and a simple code of the economic man could have sufficient appearance of practical relevance, as well as afford a firm intellectual basis. Between them social biology, Freud, the joint-stock company, modern nationalism and wars, the inevitable state direction they foster, have altered the slant of our thought about man in society. The importance of groups as the setting of the individual, perhaps the central awareness of the eighteenth century in Scotland, this awareness is today again dominant; dominant in fact, and therefore to be dealt with by scientists; dominant in the kind of problem which practice proposes to thought, as in all the mixed issues of welfare and defence which make up the traffic of our political life. In this new world, the effort to see the different aspects together in their proper relations again becomes at least as important as the exact definition and analysis of each aspect. The two traditional methods, the analytic and synoptic, are then seen to be complementary, mutually supporting and nourishing each other. We may well have to be patient with sociology. Its difficulties are immense. But if there is a future for sociological economics and politics—and if there is not we shall have to make it—then there is an opportunity for the resurgence of the Scottish tradition and the Scottish genius. May the opportunity make the men!

Notes

. . .² W. R. Scott, *Francis Hutcheson*, p. 70.

³ For the seventeenth century *see* H. W. Meikle, *Some Aspects of the later seventeenth century in Scotland*, p. 25.

⁴ The Chair of Mathematics in Glasgow dates from 1691 but it was not until 1826 that the subject was formally admitted to the curriculum for the degree of M.A. This seems to have kept down the number taking the subject. But the record is creditable, especially in the great period. Cf. Mackie, *The University of Glasgow*, p. 216.

⁵ This passage occurs in vol. I, p. 289, of *A System of Moral Philosophy*, in a discussion of 'the necessity of a social life'. It is quite separate, in place and subject, from his treatment of economic values which occurs in vol. II, Ch. 12, embedded in his consideration of contracts.

⁶ *Legacy of the Middle Ages* (Meynial on Roman Law); *Cambridge Medieval History*, vol. V (Hazeltine, Roman and Canon Law); Vinogradoff, *Roman Law in Medieval Europe;* Bryce, *Studies in History and Juris-*

prudence, Holy Roman Empire; James Macintosh, *Roman Law in Modern Practice;* and J. N. Figgis, *From Gerson to Grotius.*

⁷ Cf. *The William and Mary Quarterly,* vol. XI, No. 2 (April 1954). For Hutcheson the article by Professor Caroline Robbins (a grateful name) is specially interesting. The whole number is very relevant.

⁸ Op. cit., p. 25.

⁹ The High School of Edinburgh. The mathematician is Colin Maclaurin, of the *Treatise on Fluxions.*

¹⁰ Mill quotes Millar as an authority on three occasions: in important footnotes on the English constitution, slavery in primitive times and the position of women in North American tribes. Calling him 'that sagacious contemplator of the progress of society', he later remarks that 'the writings of Mr Millar remain about the only source from which the slightest information on the subject can be drawn', the subject being civilization among the Hindus. I am indebted to Dr R. L. Meek for this reference.

¹¹ Need it be said that no criticism of Ricardo is here intended? His contribution to economics is shining and accepted. But many will agree with Schumpeter's summary: 'Ricardo's *Principles* are the most difficult book on Economics ever written. It is difficult enough even to understand it, more difficult to interpret it, and most difficult to estimate it properly' (*Economic Doctrine and Method,* p. 80).

¹² G. Grote, *Minor Works,* p. 284.

¹³ This paragraph may seem to suggest that Marshall would have sympathized with the predominance of analytics and the specialized monograph. I believe this is the opposite of the truth. Marshall was essentially a perfectionist, seeking to reform the institutions and members of the *society* he knew, and wished us all to know. If so, he was nearer the early classics than the economic theorists of today.

¹⁴ *Principles,* p. 17, n. [One must remember this is volume I. If Marshall had written volume II, he would certainly have dealt with dynamic theory. As to the association psychology, the eighteenth century Scottish school also accepted it but this was *faute de mieux.* This psychology prejudged the emotion *versus* reason argument in favour of the former. It therefore laid thinkers like Smith open to the charge of inconsistency, when they appeared to give reason any determining power.]

¹⁵ For emphasis on the vital importance of what we can summarize as 'know-how', and the suggestion that Smith did not give it sufficient weight, see Lauderdale, *Inquiry into the Nature and Origin of Public Wealth,*

pp. 159-61, 176-7, 184-5, where Smith is criticized for missing the special productivity of capital, its own productivity as distinct from that of labour; cf. also p. 287. For Rae this productivity of capital is the central theme. It inspires the whole of his remarkable *Sociological Theory of Capital*. Mill with his usual wisdom quoted fully from the outstanding passage (Mill's *Principles,* pp. 165-72), but Rae's theme just is that economic progress depends on enterprise, so in turn on the existence of those social conditions which call it forth. Chapters IX, X and XIV are especially relevant.

[16] There may be further sets of his notes in private hands. If so they would be welcomed by the Library of his University, if legible.

[17] Edward Caird, *The Moral Aspect of the Economic Problem* (1888).

[18] Cf. Mackie, *The University of Glasgow,* pp. 186, 212.

Smith on the meaning of the term "value" (1776):

The word VALUE, it is to be observed, has two different meanings, and sometimes expresses the utility of some particular object, and sometimes the power of purchasing other goods which the possession of that object conveys. The one may be called "value in use;" the other, "value in exchange." The things which have the greatest value in use have frequently little or no value in exchange; and on the contrary, those which have the greatest value in exchange have frequently little or no value in use. Nothing is more useful than water: but it will purchase scarce any thing; scarce any thing can be had in exchange for it. A diamond, on the contrary, has scarce any value in use; but a very great quantity of other goods may frequently be had in exchange for it.

In order to investigate the principles which regulate the exchangeable value of commodities, I shall endeavour to shew,

First, what is the real measure of this exchangeable value; or, wherein consists the real price of all commodities.

Secondly, what are the different parts of which this real price is composed or made up.

And, lastly, what are the different circumstances which sometimes raise some or all of these different parts of price above, and sometimes sink them below their natural or ordinary rate; or, what are the causes which sometimes hinder the market price, that is, the actual price of commodities, from coinciding exactly with what may be called their natural price.

Adam Smith, in An Inquiry into the Nature and Causes of the Wealth of Nations, *edited by Edwin Cannan, The Modern Library, 1937.*

T. D. Campbell (essay date 1971)

SOURCE: "Politics and Principles," in *Adam Smith's Science of Morals,* George Allen & Unwin Ltd., 1971, pp. 205-20.

[*In the following essay, Campbell argues that Smith's moral and political philosophies are ultimately based on the principle of utility.*]

The thesis that Smith's theory of morality is essentially a scientific one should not be taken to imply that he does not endorse any moral and political principles of his own. By and large he accepts, as morally justified, the norms which it is his main purpose to explain. His own moral convictions can be seen in the arguments which he uses to justify his confidence in the judgments of the impartial spectator. These convictions are also apparent in the moral assumptions he brings to bear on the political issues of his day and in the recommendations he makes concerning the general conduct of politics. This is not to say that the arguments which he uses to justify his moral and political principles are the same as those which he uses to explain why certain principles are generally accepted. At least they do not correspond to the efficient causes of moral and political principles; although, as we shall see, they do often correspond to the final causes of such principles, or, in other words, to the purposes which are unwittingly served by these efficient causes.

Despite all that Smith has to say against utility as the explanation for the ordinary person's moral and political attitudes, his own normative moral and political philosophy turns out to be, in the end, a form of utilitarianism. It is because men, by following their spontaneous moral sentiments, play their part in a system which is conducive to the happiness of mankind, that Smith recommends that these moral sentiments should continue to serve as guides for conduct. They find their justification in the fact that they are a means towards the production of general happiness. Similarly, when it comes to giving political advice, he relies on the principle of utility to provide the basis on which political decisions ought to be made. For the most part utility dictates that politicians should leave well alone, but this is by no means always the case. Sometimes it is necessary for them to intervene in the natural social processes for the benefit of human happiness. Utility, or the production of happiness, is thus the principle by reference to which he judges that both the natural moral sentiments and the system of natural liberty are desirable. It is also the principle behind his suggestions for refining these sentiments and correcting such defects as may remain even when the condition of natural liberty has been established. We may, therefore, say that, with respect to his own normative philosophy, utility is his supreme moral and political principle.

I. THE THEORY OF GOVERNMENT

Smith's theory of government is the meeting place for his scientific theory of society and his own practical recommendations; it is, therefore, a good point from which to start a consideration of the normative and metaphysical beliefs which lie behind his science of society. The four functions which Smith allocates to government are 'justice, police, revenue and arms'; 'The object of justice is security from injury, and it is the foundation of civil government. The objects of police are the cheapness of commodities, public security and cleanliness'; revenue concerns taxes raised to defray the expenses of government, and the fourth purpose of government is to maintain an army for external defence.[1] The powers of government are legislative, judicial and federal (the power of making war and peace);[2] its main method of operation is, therefore, the law, which Smith defines as the command of the sovereign.[3] He has a deep interest in the development of different types of government in different societies, which he explains partly by economic and partly by military factors.[4] He himself favoured a type of mixed government, corresponding to the constitution of Britain in his own day, which combined a representative legislature, on a limited franchise, with a hereditary monarchy. The descriptions which he gives of the development of government in its various functions are of great sociological interest in themselves, but, from the point of view of the discussion of the relationship between his sociological theory and his normative philosophy, they are only a background for his analysis of political obligation. It is in his analysis of the reasons why men do obey, or ought to obey, their governments that we can discern his own political philosophy.

Government exists where there is law; a law is a commandment whose observance can be enforced; whenever one person or group of persons can successfully get their decisions accepted as law, they constitute a government.[5] Smith sees that this makes the question of the citizens' obligation to obey the commands of the sovereign central to the study of politics, and, in order to answer this question, he finds it necessary to discuss the duties of the sovereign towards the subject. When Smith asks why men 'enter into' civil society, he is still primarily asking a factual question: he wants to know what 'induces men to obey'[6] their government. Because he treats it as a factual question he has no difficulty in rejecting the theory that men obey because of some contract entered into either by themselves or their forbears, for, as he says, (1) men obey where the contract is unknown, (2) they do not give the contract as the reason why they obey, (3) they are not aware of giving their consent, and (4) in those instances where there is a contract, as in the case of resident aliens, this does not result in any trust being placed in the persons who have made the contract to obey.[7] However, it becomes clear that it is not *only* a factual question which he is asking when he includes amongst the objections to the contract theory the moral argument that a person ought not to be bound by a promise made by his ancestors: he goes on to ridicule the notion of tacit consent by saying that most people have no real chance to leave their country and:

> To say that by staying in a country a man agrees to a contract of obedience to government is just the same with carrying a man into a ship and after he is at a distance from land to tell him that by being in the ship he has contracted to obey the master.[8]

In concluding, therefore, that 'the foundation of a duty cannot be a principle with which mankind is entirely unacquainted'[8] Smith appears to be making the psychological point that we cannot have a motive of which we are totally unaware, and the moral point that a man cannot be obliged to obey a contract into which he did not explicitly enter.

His own theory of political obligation is, likewise, a mixture of descriptive and normative theory. Men obey, he argues, because of 'the principles of authority and utility';[9] the first relates to those characteristics of men which make others accept them as superior and worthy of being obeyed, and the second to the subjects' awareness of the private and public utility of the functions of government. It is the principle of authority which has most in common with the doctrine of the **Moral Sentiments** where Smith tends to play down the importance of utility and rely on laws of social psychology to explain men's behaviour.

The four characteristics which give authority are age, long possession of power, wealth, and mental or physical abilities. The first is explained by arguing that the imagination connects the ideas of age with those of wisdom and experience which, to some extent, makes age just as effective as the possession of ability in obtaining authority. In so far as these qualities are admired in themselves, rather than as means to fulfilling the useful functions of government, they come under the principle of authority. But of more importance than either age or wisdom is the long possession of power; this is explained by the association of ideas, and, in particular, by relating it to the expectations and resentments of mankind: we have seen how many rights, especially property rights, arise out of the expectations which an established practice or possession forms in men's minds and the consequent resentment which is aroused by the frustration of these expectations. This is applied to the possession of political power; men are prepared to accept the commands of those who have always given them orders but will reject those of the 'upstart'. Wealth is the fourth, and most important, authority-conferring characteristic; this we have already examined in detail when considering the 'origin and distinction of ranks',[10] and it is necessary, here, only to add that Smith considers the possession of wealth to be the main factor which attracts the respect of other men and to remind ourselves that this is not primarily a matter of the subject's economic dependence on the rich but of the ability of the rich to obtain the admiration and sympathy of the poor on account of the ease with which men sympathize with the imagined pleasures of the wealthy. This source of authority alone is, according to Smith, 'upon ordinary occasions, sufficient to govern the world'.[11]

If the principle of authority is the one which leads men to obey rulers without question, then that of utility induces them to obey because they appreciate the purposes which government serves, particularly its role in maintaining justice and peace in society, for not only does government protect the rich against the poor, but 'by civil institutions the poorest may get redress of injuries from the wealthiest and most powerful'.[12] This is not primarily a sense of private or individual utility, since political obligation may oblige men to act against their own interests:

> It is the sense of public utility, more than of private, which influences men to obedience. It may sometimes be for my interest to disobey, and to wish government overturned, but I am sensible that other men are of a different opinion from me, and would not assist me in the enterprise. I therefore submit to its decision for the good of the whole.[12]

This does not, in fact, contradict Smith's view of the minor place which benevolence holds in the pantheon of motives, since he hints that private utility would hold more sway if the individual was in a position to conduct an individual rebellion.

The principle of utility is on a par with that of authority as an *explanation* for obedience; it acts as a further support for the principle of authority and may, indeed, incorporate the principle of authority in so far as men become aware of the utility of blind obedience to rulers.[13] Smith even suggests some sociological generalizations about the relative weight of the two principles in different types of civil society:

> In all governments both these principles take place in some degree, but in a monarchy the principle of authority prevails, and in a democracy that of utility. In Britain, which is a mixed government, the factions formed some time ago, under the names of Whig and Tory, were influenced by these principles, the former submitted to government on account of its utility and the advantages which they derived from it, while the latter pretended that it was of divine institution, and to offend against it was equally criminal as for a child to rebel against its parent.[14]

But, from the philosophical point of view, the principles are not on the same level, since the principle of utility is used to evaluate the principle of authority. It is clear that Smith does not consider that the principle of authority is self-justifying. He notes, for instance, that it is irrational because it depends on an illusion, created by the imagination, which runs counter to our ordinary moral judgments:

> That kings are the servants of the people, to be obeyed, resisted, deposed, or punished, as the public conveniency may require, is the doctrine of reason and philosophy; but it is not the doctrine of Nature. Nature would teach us to submit to them for their own sake, to tremble and bow down before their exalted station, to regard their smile as a reward sufficient to compensate any services, and to dread their displeasure, though no other evil were to follow from it, as the severest of all mortifications.[15]

On the other hand he points out the usefulness of the principle of authority in promoting the stability and hence the happiness of society.

It would appear, therefore, that Smith elevates the principle of utility into *the* principle of his normative theory of political obligation. Men ought to obey their rulers in so far as their government is effective in producing public happiness by sustaining the internal and external peace of a country; in the end, this is the standard by which all governments must be judged. Such a principle, of course, entails that when a government fails to fulfil these purposes it should cease to command men's obedience (although the principle of authority may still produce *de facto* obedience), and Smith is willing to allow that 'Whatever be the principle of allegiance, a right of resistance must undoubtedly be lawful, because no authority is altogether unlimited.'[16] However, this right of rebellion is severely limited; frequent rebellions lead to instabilities which make it difficult to re-establish *de facto* authority, presumably because it makes it impossible to rely on the principle of long possession. Therefore, on the basis of the principle of utility itself, Smith concludes that, while 'no government is quite perfect', nevertheless 'it is better to submit to some inconveniences than make attempts against it'.[17] But the right to rebel does exist, and Smith argues unequivocally for the justice of the Revolution against James II on the grounds that he ignored the rights of Parliament. Yet even in this case he is primarily concerned to explain *why* the Revolution occurred, namely because James aroused 'the most furious passions, fear, hatred, and resentment',[18] and 'plainly showed his intention to change the religion of the country, which is the most difficult thing in the world',[19] so that men overcame their 'habitual sense of deference'[18] and rose in rebellion.

II. UTILITY AND THE STATESMAN

The principle of utility does not only determine the limits of obligatory obedience to political authority, it is also the principle which Smith uses, in conjunction with his sociological theory, to guide the decisions of statesmen. Rulers ought to act so as to secure the happiness of their citizens. It seems to have been Smith's own conviction that 'All constitutions of government . . . are valued only in proportion as they tend to promote the happiness of those who live under them.'[20] This may be demonstrated by looking in turn at what he has to say about the four purposes of government.

The most important function of government is to enforce the rules of natural justice. In Chapter Nine we saw that Smith does not consider that men in general seek justice for its utility. But it was also noted, in the same chapter, that Smith does not deny that justice has utility. In his final explanation of the sentiments on which the sense of justice is based, Smith emphasizes that justice is essential to the security and thus to the happiness of society:

> Justice . . . is the main pillar that upholds the whole edifice. If it is removed, the great, the immense fabric of human society, that fabric which to raise and support seems in this world, if I may say so, to have been the peculiar and darling care of Nature, must in a moment crumble into atoms. In order to enforce the observation of justice, therefore, Nature has implanted in the human breast that consciousness of ill-desert, those terrors of merited punishment which attend upon its violation, as the great safeguards of the association of mankind, to protect the weak, to curb the violent, and to chastise the guilty.[21]

Thus resentment is useful because it accomplishes 'all the political ends of punishment; the correction of the criminal, and the example to the public'.[22]

Smith's definition of justice is particularly suited to utilitarian interpretations (especially the negative formulation of utilitarianism which advocates the minimization of pain), since it is to do with the prevention of harm or injury, and it is clear that, for all he has to say against utility as the immediate ground of the sentiments of justice, he regards the government's duty to enforce justice as a particular case of its duty to promote the happiness, or at least to ward off the unhappiness, of its subjects:

> The wisdom of every state or commonwealth endeavours as well as it can, to employ the force of the society to restrain those who are subject to its authority, from hurting or disturbing the happiness of one another.[23]

Smith expects that, even in the case of politicians, it will always be immediate resentment against injustice which leads men to support the laws of justice, but in so far as it becomes a matter of debate as to whether or not the state should enforce the rules of natural justice, it is to the principle of utility that Smith considers all men, and especially statesmen, will have recourse. We have seen, in the last chapter, that in certain aspects of justice, such as the infliction of punishment after due judicial processes,[24] and the enforcement of laws of military discipline,[25] Smith notes, probably with approval, that considerations of utility have a place. When it comes to the general philosophical justification of all sentiments of justice, this appeal to the production of happiness and the prevention of pain is used to validate all the rules of natural justice. Apart from the immediate injuries which the administration of justice prevents, it has other, less direct but extremely important, consequences. It is indicated, in the ***Wealth of Nations,*** that justice is useful in promoting prosperity; indeed it is an essential requirement for the development of commercial society:

> Commerce and manufactures can seldom flourish long in any state which does not enjoy a regular administration of justice, in which the people do not feel themselves secure in the possession of their property, in which the faith of contracts is not supported by law, and in which the authority of the state is not supposed to be regularly employed in enforcing the payment of debts from all those who are able to pay.[26]

It is, therefore, the principle of utility that lies behind Smith's recommendation that all governments should enforce the laws of natural justice. And the same principle explains his willingness to allow that, under certain circumstances, it is even right for the government to compel acts of positive benevolence; in some cases, if it is necessary for 'promoting the prosperity of the commonwealth',[27] the magistrate may make laws concerning conduct which was neither right nor wrong before these laws were made. Moreover, Smith frequently insists that it is the statesman's duty to revise the law when it is hindering social development.[28]

It is less clear whether Smith thought that justice, in the sense of fairness, could conflict with utility in the sense of the maximization of happiness and the minimization of pain. The immediate moral sentiments prompt men to feel resentment at injuries being inflicted on *anyone*, which seems to imply that justice protects the happiness of all men equally.[29] Apart from the sentinel example, Smith does not give much consideration to clashes between fairness and utility; he tends to assume that there is no conflict between them: the sovereign owes 'justice and equality of treatment' to 'all the different orders of his subjects',[30] but there is no suggestion that this equality is incompatible with the useful consequences of enforcing the rules of justice. Although his arguments in favour of aristocracy would seem to suggest that he considers that the few should be preferred to the many, it should be remembered that he justified the division of society into ranks because of the contribution this makes to the stability of society[31] and thus to the happiness of all its members. Moreover, we have seen that Smith does not believe that prosperity does bring great happiness, whatever men's imaginations may indicate to the contrary. He seems to think that the essential requirements of a happy life are open to all and clearly approves that this should be so.[32] On the other hand, while he accepts a limited equality of distribution as inevitable and desirable,[33] he is more concerned with equality of opportunity, the removal of restrictions on the individual's chances to make the most of his own abilities and virtues.[34] In this process considerations of merit and demerit lead to justified inequalities. This is part of justice in so far as a person rightly resents being deprived of the fruits of his labours. It is possible therefore, to argue that Smith would put considerations of fairness above the production of greater quantities of happiness as such, but he himself did not feel that he had to choose between these two goals.

The second function of government, namely police, is mainly concerned with the 'cheapness of commodities', and is the central topic of the *Wealth of Nations.* It is, of course, Smith's most famous doctrine that all governments should allow the natural workings of the economy to operate without state intervention. This thesis is partly supported by saying that restrictions on the economic liberty of the subject are unjust, but Smith's main argument is along the lines that government inaction, outside the sphere of justice, is the best means to promote high consumption and therefore the general happiness.[35] For, although Smith realizes that in some ways commercial society reduces men's opportunities for self-development,[36] he is in no doubt that, on the whole, it is greatly beneficial. His advocacy of the system of natural liberty is ultimately based on an assessment of its utility in increasing *per capita* consumption. The fact that this is so can be seen in his willingness to consider exceptions to the policy of non-intervention.[37] On the whole he distrusts governments as inefficient and self-interested, but he sees that in certain matters some government action is necessary for the general welfare; for instance, every government has 'the duty of erecting and maintaining certain public works and certain public institutions, which it can never be for the interest of any individual, or small number of individuals, to erect and maintain'.[38]

Smith is prepared to consider each case for government intervention in economic life on its own merits; in discussing certain regulations concerning banking, for example, he concludes that:

> Such regulations may, no doubt, be considered as in some respect a violation of natural liberty. But those exertions of the natural liberty of a few individuals, which might endanger the security of the whole society, are, and ought to be, restrained by the laws of all governments; of the most free as well as the most despotical.[39]

In fact the system of natural liberty is not so much an absence of all state-supported institutions as the presence of those institutions which are best adapted to make the self-interested actions of individual men work to the advantages of all.[40] Laws which prevent the self-interest of particular groups, such as merchants, from thwarting the checks and balances of open competition are justified.[41] Some state aid for education,[42] and control over religion,[43] are deemed advisable to counter the adverse effects of the division of labour and religious fanaticism. Despite the difficulties inherent in such a task, the statesman has the duty of doing everything in his power to promote the prosperity of the nation. In particular he has to keep laws relating to economics up to date. Restrictions and practices which were useful in their day, such as monopolies and inheritance according to the rules of primogeniture, had, in Smith's time, ceased to fit the changed economic conditions and he therefore recommends their abolition.[44]

The third function of government, the collection of revenue, is subordinate to its other functions in that the revenue is required in order that these other activities can be carried on. But even here utility comes in when he recommends that taxes be gathered in such a way as to raise the maximum revenue while doing as little harm as possible to the economic life of the nation,[45] although he also stresses that taxes should be 'equal', by which he means a proportional equality according to which those who have most at stake in the successful functioning of government, that is, those with most property, should pay most.[46] The final purpose of government is that of seeing to external defence by the provision of an army. This is an end to which Smith was prepared to sacrifice economic freedoms,[47] as he considered it to be a necessary condition of all justice and prosperity that each country should be secure from invasion and defeat in war.

It is not difficult to draw up a list of the many different ways in which Smith's advice to statesmen is governed by his utilitarian presuppositions. In addition to the clear tasks of administering justice and seeing to the security of the nation, there are numerous instances where he is anxious to see governments act in order to correct the defects of the natural order. Yet it should still be remembered that Smith sets strict limitations on the extent to which far-sighted human action can 'turn away the arrow which is aimed at the head of the righteous'.[48] Many of the malfunctionings which he mentions are not such as can be remedied. In the case of government action there is, in addition, the danger that attempts to improve the lot of mankind may lead to disaster because politicians do not realize the intricacy of the mechanism with which they are dealing. Smith comes out strongly against what he calls the 'spirit of system' which leads men to change the constitution and laws of society according to some elaborate plan of their own; he realizes the constant temptation for politicians to hold out schemes for the dramatic improvement of society:

> The leaders of the discontented party seldom fail to hold out some plausible plan of reformation which, they pretend, will not only remove the inconveniences and relieve the distresses immediately complained of, but will prevent, in all time coming, any return of the like inconveniences and distresses.[49]

Moreover,

> The great body of the party are commonly intoxicated with the imaginary beauty of this ideal system, of which they have no experience.[49]

Such plans, Smith believes, always under-rate the natural forces at work in society and over-estimate the power of government to alter the natural course of events.

In contrast to the man of system, he sets out a picture of the wise statesman which is an eloquent and balanced statement of Burkean conservatism, and shows that Smith's alleged complacent optimism is sometimes mixed with more than a tinge of pessimism:

> The man whose public spirit is prompted altogether by humanity and benevolence, will respect the established powers and privileges even of individuals, and still more those of the great orders and societies, into which the state is divided. Though he should consider some of them as in some measure abusive, he will content himself with moderating, what he often cannot annihilate without great violence. When he cannot conquer the rooted prejudices of the people by reason and persuasion, he will not attempt to subdue them by force . . . He will accommodate, as well as he can, his public arrangements to the confirmed habits and prejudices of the people; and will remedy as well as he can, the inconveniences which may flow from the want of those regulations which the people are averse to submit to. When he cannot establish the right, he will not disdain to ameliorate the wrong; but like Solon, when he cannot establish the best system of laws, he will endeavour to establish the best that the people can bear.[50]

This is not to say that statesmen are never to make radical changes in the law or even in the constitution of the state. In normal times the loyal support of the constitution is the best means to make 'our fellow-citizens as safe, respectable and happy as we can', but in disturbed times,

> even a wise man may be disposed to think some alteration necessary in that constitution or form of government, which, in its actual condition, appears plainly unable to maintain the public tranquillity. In such cases, however, it often requires, perhaps, the highest effort of political wisdom to determine when a real patriot ought to support and endeavour to re-establish the authority of the old system, and when he ought to give way to the more daring, but often dangerous spirit of innovation.[51]

The ordinary politician cannot be expected to rise to these heights and act purely with regard to the general interest of society. Men's desire for power and selfish interest, together with normal human short-sightedness, make them unable to act effectively from humanity and benevolence. However, Smith thinks that there is one motive which may indirectly lead men to promote the general welfare. This takes us back to his own peculiar theory of utility, namely that men are fascinated by any machine or system which shows a nice adjustment of means to ends; in the realm of politics it is possible to rouse men to great political and administrative tasks by interesting them in intricate means rather than beneficial ends. This motive accounts for a good deal of the useful acts of politicians.[52]

Even if it is admitted that in the sphere of politics utility is Smith's over-riding moral principle, this does not automatically establish that this is so in non-political matters. But the whole weight of his discussion of final causation would suggest that, in all matters of individual and social morality, utility is the ultimate ground on which he approves of the ordinary moral sentiments. Justice, of course, is part of morality, and this we have already discussed. Prudence is a virtue which clearly promotes the happiness of the individual, and given that each person is best suited to look after his own interests, the practice of prudential behaviour throughout a society would undoubtedly promote the general happiness.[53] Smith makes a point of stressing that benevolence is naturally felt most strongly for those whom we are best able to help and gets weaker and weaker as the persons concerned become more and more remote from our sphere of influence.[54] The restricted nature of the benevolent affections which are approved of by the impartial spectator is ultimately justified by the fact that society is benefited most by each endeavouring to promote the welfare of those whom he is in the position of being able to help. Here, as elsewhere, Smith notes, and approves, the fact that 'Nature' intends the happiness of mankind.[55] Because Smith's statements about final causation reveal his own moral principles, this does not imply that he did not regard these statements as primarily assertions of final causation; he clearly regarded it as explanatory to say that a particular causal process exhibits the purpose of God. But, having demonstrated this, he took a certain satisfaction in being able to sit back and admire the handiwork of God, and this admiration includes approval of the principle on which God is seen to act; it is because God is a utilitarian[56] that we can say that Smith's own moral presuppositions are utilitarian.

III. CONTEMPLATIVE UTILITARIANISM

To argue that Smith is a utilitarian seems paradoxical in view of his recurrent criticism of utilitarianism. But these criticisms are all directed at those who argue that utility can explain the origin of moral judgments or that it ought to be the principle by which men make their day-to-day moral choices. Those who fail to distinguish between Smith's theory of the causes of moral judgments and his practical advice to the ordinary moral agent on the one hand, and his own normative philosophy on the other, inevitably misrepresent his ultimate moral principles.[57]

It is true that he did not think that utility is the basis of everyday moral judgments; for while these judgments take into account the immediate consequences of acts, even this is secondary to the assessment of the appropriateness of an act to its situation. Nor did he think that utility *ought* to be the conscious basis of ordinary moral judgments; men's calculations concerning future consequences are too inaccurate, and they would tend, especially where their own interests are involved, to use considerations of utility as excuses to make exceptions in their own favour.

Sometimes it does appear that Smith commends a form of rule-utilitarianism, in that, although particular acts are to be judged by whether or not they conform to the appropriate moral rules, the rules themselves are to be assessed according to their consequences. For instance, he says that, in assessing the utility of justice, we should consider the consequences of a certain type of behaviour becoming general throughout a society.[58] But he considers that the origin of general rules is to be found in judgments concerning particular acts and that appeal to such judgments is a more effective way of justifying these rules than presentation of calculations about their utility. Such calculations may provide ultimate justification for moral rules but they are uncertain everyday supports for these rules.

Utility is, however, the principle which is necessary for the guidance of those who have to consider the total system of society, whether as scientists, philosophers, or statesmen.[59] It is the principle which provides many final explanations, and which enables us to make ultimate assessments concerning the soundness of ordinary moral judgments and the value of the whole mechanism of society; it is also the principle according to which political reforms ought to be conducted, and on which the citizen ought to base his decisions about political obligation, when this is in doubt.

Utility is, therefore, very much *the* meta-principle for Smith. It is to be found at the basis of his whole moral outlook, but it operates most typically at the level of contemplation, when men adopt a God's-eye-view of society, enter into His universal benevolence and feel admiration and approval for what they observe. At this level of reflection utility provides the key to the interpretation of God's creation. For, as we have seen, Smith considers God to be a utilitarian[60]; probably a rule-utilitarian. God considers the general consequences of types of conduct and arranges it so that men habitually act in such a way as to maximize the general happiness. But, of course, God is a utilitarian whose situation is so unlike that of men that it is difficult to compare His utilitarianism with that of human beings. For instance, God does not, presumably, have to choose between His own happiness and that of other beings, and therefore many of the problems of justice versus utility, or private versus public utility, do not arise.

But we can ask whether it is *only* happiness that God wishes for men. Here the relevant quotations are equally divided between those that speak of the 'happiness and perfection of the species', and those that mention only human happiness.[61] It seems, therefore, that there is some hint of ideal utilitarianism present in what is predominantly a hedonistic utilitarian theory. 'Perfection' may simply mean the multiplication of the species, but it is much more likely to refer to the Stoic idea of man's place in the total system of the universe. It is at this point that Smith's moral ideals merge with his aesthetic or contemplative principles. The 'perfectly virtuous' man acts in accordance with 'the rules of perfect prudence, of strict justice, and of proper benevolence',[62] and it is this 'perfection of human nature' which 'can alone produce among mankind that harmony of sentiments and passions in which consists their whole grace and propriety'.[63] The perfection of the species thus serves to promote the harmony of society as an integral part of the total system which God has created. It is through virtuous behaviour that men become completely adapted to the workings of the social mechanism, a mechanism which they can, to some extent, appreciate and admire. It is clear that Smith did not consider that this concept of perfection conflicted with the ideal of human happiness, since the essential elements of human happiness include the approval of society and of conscience, which can only be obtained by virtuous conduct.

It will be remembered that Smith's analysis of utility includes the aesthetic appreciation of a well-functioning machine in which more attention is paid to means than to ends.[64] This applies to man's appreciation of God's human creation:

> When we consider such actions as making a part of a system of behaviour which tends to promote the happiness either of the individual or of the society, they appear to derive a beauty from this utility, not unlike that which we ascribe to any well-contrived machine.[65]

This brings out the extent to which Smith regarded utility as a principle for directing contemplation rather than an immediate moral guide; it involves an aesthetic appreciation of the design as well as approval of the product. In practical terms it may involve making small improvements in the machine, thus rendering it even more pleasing to behold, and also more beneficial to mankind, but, for most people, its logical implications are that they should concern themselves with their own affairs and adopt an attitude of detachment, even resignation, with respect to the wider world. It certainly does not mean that they should be utilitarians in the manner in which God is a utilitarian, acting in order to achieve the happiness of all men; it is the lot of relatively weak and powerless human beings to look to their own happiness and the welfare of a few close friends and relations; by so doing they promote God's plan for bringing about the general happiness in the manner for which they are best equipped. As politicians, and occasionally as subjects, they may be called upon to transcend this limited outlook and act according to their estimation of the happiness of a whole nation. But to reflect on the happiness of *all* mankind is something that should almost always be reserved for the social scientist, and the philosopher.

Notes

[1] *L.J.*, [*Lectures on Jurisprudence,* edited by Edwin Canaan, Oxford: Clavendon Press, 1896], pp. 3f.

[2] *L.J.*, p. 17.

[3] *T.M.S.* [*The Theory of Moral Sentiments,* 6th ed., London: A. Strahan and T. Cadell, and W. Creech and J. Bell and Co., 1790], III.5 (I.413).

[4] *L.J.*, pp. 14-55.

[5] *L.J.*, p. 15.

[6] *L.J.*, p. 10.

[7] *L.J.*, pp. 11ff.

[8] *L.J.*, p. 12.

[9] *L.J.*, p. 9; cf. *W.N.* [*Wealth of Nations,* 5th ed., edited by A. Cannan, London: Methuen, 1961], V.i.1 (II.232ff.).

[10] Cf. p. 172.

[11] *T.M.S.*, I.iii.2 (I.131).

[12] *L.J.*, p. 10.

[13] *T.M.S.*, I.iii.2 (I.127).

[14] *L.J.*, p. 11. This quotation reveals Smith's preferences both for Whigs against Tories and for utility against authority.

[15] *T.M.S.*, I.iii.2 (I.128).

[16] *L.J.*, p. 68. Here the word 'authority' is clearly used in a *de jure* sense.

[17] *L.J.*, p. 69.

[18] *T.M.S.*, I.iii.2 (I.128).

[19] *L.J.*, p. 71.

[20] *T.M.S.*, IV.1 (I.468).

[21] *T.M.S.*, II.ii.3 (I.215f.).

[22] *T.M.S.*, II.i.1 (I.166).

[23] *T.M.S.*, VI.ii (II.66f.).

[24] Cf. p. 201.

[25] Cf. p. 202.

[26] *W.N.*, V.iii (II.445).

[27] *T.M.S.*, II.ii.1 (I.201).

[28] *W.N.*, III.ii (I.408).

[29] Cf. p. 172.

[30] *W.N.*, IV.viii (II.171).

[31] *T.M.S.*, I.iii.2 (I.127).

[32] *T.M.S.*, III.3 (I.369): 'In the most glittering and exalted situation that our idle fancy can hold out to us, the pleasures from which we propose to derive our real happiness, are almost always the same with those which, in our actual, though humble station, we have at all times at hand, and in our power.'

[33] *W.N.*, I.viii (I.88).

[34] Cf. *W.N.*, I.x.2 (I.136) and IV.ix (II.208).[35] Cf. *W.N.*, IV.ii (I.478).

[36] Cf. *W.N.*, V.i.3 art. 2 (II.303).

[37] Many examples of this are given by Jacob Viner, 'Adam Smith and Laissez-Faire' in *Adam Smith, 1776-1926*, pp. 138-54.

[38] Cf. *W.N.*, IV.ix (II.209).

[39] *W.N.*, II.ii. (I.344f.).

[40] Cf. Nathan Rosenberg, 'Some Institutional Aspects of the *Wealth of Nations*', *Journal of Political Economy*, vol. XLVIII, pp. 557-70.

[41] Cf. *W.N.*, I.xi (I.278).

[42] Cf. *W.N.*, V.i.3. art.2 (II.302).

[43] Cf. *W.N.*, V.i.3. art.3 (II.317).

[44] Cf. *W.N.*, III.ii (I.408).

[45] Cf. *W.N.*, V.ii.2 (II.351).

[46] Cf. *W.N.*, V.ii.2 (II.350).

[47] Cf. *W.N.*, IV.ii (I.484).

[48] *T.M.S.*, III.5 (I.421).

[49] *T.M.S.*, VI.ii.2 (II.107).

[50] *T.M.S.*, VI.ii.2 (II.108ff.).

[51] *T.M.S.*, VI.ii.2. (II.104f.).

[52] Cf. *W.N.*, IV.i (I.469ff.).

[53] Cf. pp. 178ff.

[54] Cf. pp. 182ff.

[55] Cf. *T.M.S.*, VI.ii.Intro. (II.68).

[56] *T.M.S.*, VI.ii.3 (II.118): 'The administration of the great system of the universe . . . the care of the universal happiness of all rational and sensible beings, is the business of God'.

[57] Cf. A. L. Macfie, *The Individual in Society*, pp. 45-8. Macfie, having pointed out that Smith criticizes Hume's theory of utility, concludes that 'Utility for him [Smith] was not basic.'

[58] *T.M.S.*, II.ii.3 (I.223).

[59] It is because the ordinary person is unable to make accurate utilitarian calculations that Smith considers politics to be a specialist occupation and does not favour a universal franchise.

[60] Cf. *T.M.S.*, III.5 (I.413f.): 'The happiness of mankind, as well as of all other rational creatures, seems to have been the original purpose intended by the Author of nature.'

[61] Cf. *T.M.S.*, II.iii.3 (I.267): 'Man was made . . . to promote . . . the happiness of all'; *T.M.S.*, III.5 (I.421): 'The same great end, the order of the world, and the perfection and happiness of human nature'; and *T.M.S.*, II.iii.3 (I.265).

[62] *T.M.S.*, VI.iii (II.120).

[63] *T.M.S.*, I.i.5 (I.47).

[64] Cf. pp. 116ff.

[65] *T.M.S.*, VII.iii (II.356).

Samuel Hollander (essay date 1973)

SOURCE: A conclusion to *The Economics of Adam Smith*, University of Toronto Press, 1973, pp. 305-20.

[*Hollander defends Smith against charges that* The Wealth of Nations *contains numerous inconsistencies and assesses his contribution to formal and applied classical economics. The critic underscores Smith's responsiveness to changing economic conditions brought about by contemporary technological and sociological developments, particularly as displayed in his theory of the competitive allocation of resources.*]

Professor Schumpeter in his celebrated critique has written that Adam Smith's function was merely that of co-ordinator whose 'mental stature was up to mastering the unwieldy material that flowed from many sources and to subjecting it, with a strong hand, to the rule of a small number of coherent principles'; there was not 'a single *analytic* idea, principle, or method that was entirely new in 1776.'[1] There is much to be said for viewing the *Wealth of Nations* as a 'synthesis'; but in our view the downplaying of the achievement implied by Schumpeter's formulation is seriously misleading. For the strength of the work lies precisely in its comprehensiveness—unparalleled at the time— which, as Sir Alexander Gray has observed, reflects a transition in economic literature from partisan pamphlet to scientific treatise.[2] This characteristic of the *Wealth of Nations* is reflected not merely in the extraordinary range of topics treated, but also in Smith's demonstration of a high degree of interdependence between apparently unrelated variables culminating in his development of a more or less consistent 'model' of value and distribution. That steps in this direction had already been taken by Hume, Cantillon, Steuart and Quesnay—reflected for example in a sensitivity regarding method and a growing appreciation of the interdependencies of the system of production and exchange and the organizational function of the profit motive—detracts in no way from Smith's achievement. Apart from this, the adoption of pure novelty in analytical technique as the criterion of 'quality' places too much weight upon a comparison of particular Smithian theories—formulated mathematically—with earlier versions, and neglects the weightings of the variables utilized. Essentially the Schumpeterian view tends to play down Smith's use of historical and contemporary data for analytical purposes, although his genius lay in an ability to find hypotheses to fit his impressions of what the facts were or had been, in which exercise qualitative judgments play a central role.

Indicative of a certain lack of perspective which seems to derive from a preoccupation with novelty is Schumpeter's evaluation of pre-Smithian price theory. All that was lacking, runs the argument, in the analysis of the 'Scholastics' including the later ethical jurists and natural law philosophers—from which Smith's own analysis is said to derive—is the technical apparatus of schedules and the notion of the margin. In our opinion this evaluation is questionable. To *list* some, or even all, of the elements which enter into the determination of competitive price is one thing and, to *combine* them into a consistent theory of allocation is quite another; the moralists including Smith's teachers—while recognizing relevant objective and subjective factors—failed to fuse them into a system of price determination with particular emphasis upon a general tendency towards 'equilibrium.' It is in this light that Smith's contribution may be better appreciated. A preliminary analytical solution was initially developed (in his lectures)—in a general rather than partial equilibrium context—in terms of the mechanism of adaptation of supply to demand achieved by alterations in the distribution of labour (the only factor allowed for) which assures that, in the long run, market prices will reflect production costs or, in Smith's words, which assures 'a natural balance of industry.' This analysis was extended in the *Wealth of Nations* to include capital and land in addition to labour as productive factors entering into the equilibrating process.

The *formal* analysis of 'general equilibrium' in the *Wealth of Nations,* it is true, is given relatively little attention, and is in some respects narrowly constrained. The analysis suggests that factor ratios were technically determined and identical from sector to sector, raising the question of whether Smith was aware of these assumptions and whether he used them consistently.

But the fact is that Smith was not so much concerned with giving a formal statement of general equilibrium as he was to analyse readjustments to changes. It would not be surprising, therefore, it the formal account was no more than a first approximation. Our examination of Smith's general treatment of factor interrelationships *with constant technology*—particularly in the context of the effects of changes in factor prices—confirms that in the manufacturing sector certain key ratios were in fact held to be *data*. Particularly important are the labour-machinery ratio; the materials-labour ratio; and the materials-output ratio. However, when full allowance is made for 'new-type' technology—for the most part adoptable only at large scale—then the possibility of alteration in the machinery-labour ratio is admitted; for an increase in the size of the 'firm' is frequently said to be accompanied by a rising machinery-labour ratio, the capital goods 'embodying' the technology in question. (Even the rigid materials requirement might be overcome by way of new technology permitting reductions in the maintenance of fixed capital.) These new ratios, it is true, are still technically determined and there is no generalized recognition of factor substitutability; in particular, while labour-saving processes involving a higher fixed capital-labour ratio are adopted—according to Smith—at the same time as wage rates are tending upwards, no causal relationship is defined and their adoption is related to increased scale of operation. Nonetheless, the strict condition of constant proportions is in practice relaxed. In the case of agriculture also, the impression is that variation in the intensity of operating given land areas was allowed for although by no means emphasized. Finally, the implicit assumption of identical technical proportions between sectors, which is characteristic of the formal analysis of general equilibrium, is also not consistently maintained.

Smith was thus not bound by the strict assumptions implicit in the formal analysis. His treatment 'of the natural and market price of commodities' was perhaps not a *deliberate* first approximation; he nowhere draws attention to the contrast between the formal analysis and practical applications. But there can be little doubt that the formal statements of this chapter had a well-defined objective—namely the explanation of the broad principles of resource allocation—and in dealing with particular issues Smith drew upon relationships which do not appear available to him if we limit our attention to his 'model-building.' In brief, Smith did not fully specify his formal model of the price mechanism but certain characteristics of it were developed during the treatment of actual problems. Similarly, the role of demand in allocation can only be fully appreciated if attention is paid to particular applications of a theory of choice.

The main purpose of the *Wealth of Nations* was evidently not to provide an analytic framework for its own sake. The object of the work was ultimately to define the necessary conditions for rapid economic development in contemporary circumstances and Smith's treatment of the price mechanism must accordingly, in the final resort, be considered with this end in view. It is, in brief, not merely the elaboration of the mechanisms of resource allocation which requires attention, but also the particular uses to which the analysis was put, and it is in the course of Smith's treatment of the historical sequence of investment priorities according to the principle of profit-rate equalization, that a fundamental equilibrating mechanism is utilized, namely resource allocation governed by the differential pattern of factor endowments between economies. Despite the overwhelming significance of the mechanism, the reader of the *Wealth of Nations* will find no hint thereof in the First Book. It is rather in the 'applied' chapters, dealing with contemporary restraints on importation and with the colonial trade, that full and skillful use is made of the mechanism, casting a new light upon Smith's contribution to both theoretical and applied economics.[3] Smith's fundamental concern in the *Wealth of Nations* was with economic development defined in terms of (real) national income per head. His objective was to demonstrate that reliance upon the free operation of the competitive mechanisms of resource allocation would assure the maximization at any time of the national income generated by the community's given resources, including the force of 'productive labourers,' that is, of labourers in the capitalist sector; it is indeed precisely the assumption of full employment which assured the key role accorded to the micro-economic problems of resource allocation in the *Wealth of Nations*. But what is of particular relevance is Smith's demonstration that during the course of development the community's factor endowments are likely to alter, thereby generating a differential pattern of optimal allocation, in an international setting, from period to period. Demonstration of the non-chaotic nature of the competitive price mechanism was certainly not new with Smith, but the extension thereof to encompass the effects of differential factor proportions upon the pattern of activity superseded even Hume's contribution, which (like that of Gervaise) hinged upon *qualitative* factor differentials between nations. (Benjamin Franklin and Josiah Tucker may have been closer to Smith in this particular respect.) And the application of the principle to the problem of investment priorities *over time* with specific reference to contemporary policy issues represents a formidable achievement; there is much truth in Gray's observation that there is in the *Wealth of Nations* 'no distinction between economic science and economic art.'[4]

The outcome of our argument thus far is that Smith's analysis cannot be adequately appreciated apart from its precise applications. The conclusion is reinforced by consideration of Smith's approach to government intervention as a means of achieving rapid economic expansion. The maximization in each period of national income (or given population of national income per head) guaranteed the greatest achievable surplus—income over subsistence—available for taxation purposes, for capital accumulation, and for current consumption. (In Smith's view the purchaser of services merely transferred to the worker his own 'right' to consume commodities.) It is, of course, capital accumulation which represents in the *Wealth of Nations* the key element in the growth mechanism. Increased investment was essential both as a means of raising productivity—the capital-deepening process—and as a necessary condition for the expansion of the capitalist sector—the capital-widening process. Since the latter process allowed the achievement of scale economies, we conclude that the emphasis, in this case too, was largely upon expanding aggregate income as a means of raising *per capita* income.

Expansion of the 'productive' sector—capital widening—required not only an increased capital stock but also an addition to the available work force in that sector. However, Smith's vision of the contemporary British economy was not one of unemployment or of such rapid population growth that it was possible to take for granted in the Ricardian manner, even as a first approximation, the availability of 'infinite' supplies of labour at the subsistence level. The requisite supply would therefore have to be derived either from the service sector, or from natural population growth in response to average wages in excess of subsistence. In this regard it is essential to recall Smith's assumption of a degree of immobility on the part of service labour (preventing the equalization of wage rates between sectors); and also his assumption that the population mechanism—which received particular attention—applied only to workers in the productive sector. These assumptions imply strongly that Smith accorded greater significance to population expansion as the source of the labour supply required to assure an expansion of the productive sector than to any transfer from the service sector although the latter was certainly not ruled out. The relative significance of the service sector would accordingly fall with economic growth even if its absolute size remained unchanged.

What, however, was categorically ruled out by Smith as a means of raising productive employment was any redirection, by governmental intervention, of a *given* capital stock towards relatively labour-intensive branches of the productive sector. Such intervention, it was expected, must be abortive and in fact must reduce national income *even when an increase in the productive labour force was assured*. For the objective was not simply the expansion of employment of productive labour. Expansion by way of distorting the competitive allocation of resources, Smith insisted, must *re-*

duce the national income and it is the growth of national income, or more specifically, national income per head, that was the relevant objective of policy.

In this respect Smith's position is in sharp contrast with that of his mercantilist predecessors, whose vision was, in the large, one of unemployment or under-employment both voluntary and involuntary. Their concern with the absorption of surplus labour is clear from their repeated proposals for make-work projects and the disciplining of the work force. The national importance of the colonies, of various raw materials, of different forms of trading, of trade with different countries, of different domestic spending patterns, were all evaluated in terms of their effects upon domestic employment. (Hume too, it may be remarked, tended to assume unemployment in his monetary analysis and on grounds of employment was not a free trader.) Now Smith of course also distinguished between sectors on the basis of their employment-generating capacities, but in our view it would be a fundamental misjudgment to regard this discussion as a mercantilist 'residue.' His object was to counter actual forms of governmental interference which had prematurely diverted resources away from the agricultural sector. He pointed in fact to the underutilization of land in Britain and on the continent as evidence of this; conversely, he called for greater investment in the carrying trade—the least 'labour-intensive' category—in the event that the profit rate indicated its desirability. In brief, in contemporary circumstances, the productive labour force might indeed be increased consistently with an increase of national income, but this would result in consequence of the *removal* of impediments to competitive resource allocation. The argument frequently made in the secondary literature that the Smithian logic calls for the redirection of capital to labour-intensive sectors, because the principle of profit-rate equalization generates too little investment in agriculture and too much in manufacturing and trade, in terms of employment, does not apply and the charge of serious inconsistency in the **Wealth of Nations** in this respect is unjustified.

Smith has also frequently been charged with serious inconsistency on the grounds that he condemned mercantilist protection while maintaining an equivocating interest in defence and power. It is indeed sometimes suggested that 'nationalism' was the overriding criterion, so that inconsistency is a misnomer; whatever policy was deemed suitable for the 'national interest' was recommended. Our study suggests that neither interpretation is adequate. It may be accurate to ascribe to Smith an overriding concern with national power; but this in his view would best be achieved by those competitive processes which assured the maximization of the surplus—rather than by intervention in support of particular sectors—whereby the *potential* for national defence at each period is maximized. Of

equal significance is the fact that in the few cases where intervention in support of particular industries or branches of commerce was recommended the economic cost involved was defined quite explicitly. In both respects, therefore, Smith's reference is ultimately to the market mechanism.

Moreover, with regard to the extent and nature of legitimate intervention at the ports, Smith after all was recommending the replacement of a set of heavy protective devices by a less severe set designed largely for the raising of revenue; evidently it seemed desirable to keep in mind as far as possible, during any reform, the likely consequences for growth of duties or taxes—in any event necessitated for revenue purposes—and to utilize this intelligence in the choice of commodities upon which they would be levied. Similarly, Smith's occasional references to the maintenance of British superiority in foreign markets need not be considered a 'mercantilist residue.' It was obviously necessary to avoid imposing revenue-raising devices which would place British industry at a *disadvantage* in world markets. Smith's proposals represent a significant relaxation in light of the heavy protective duties then current; and it must always be recalled that the recommended reform, it was expected, would be undertaken unilaterally.

It is in this context that Smith's prudential and practical approach to reform may best be appreciated. We have noted his insistence that protective duties and prohibitions must be relaxed slowly in order to avoid sudden and heavy unemployment; his concession that a degree of control over corn exports would be justified in order to assure 'the public tranquility' and perhaps as a retaliatory device; and his justification of retaliatory duties as a means of forcing the removal of those imposed abroad on domestic products. While he ridiculed the interventionist schemes of the 'man of system' he conceded the need to call upon the services of 'that insidious and crafty animal, vulgarly called a statesman or politician, whose councils are directed by the momentary fluctuations of affairs.'[5] But there is a world of difference between this prudential outlook and typical mercantilist recommendations.

One crucial category of intervention, however, found some favour in Smith's estimation (apart, of course, from 'defence, justice and public works'), namely fiscal devices designed to alter the pattern of expenditure in favour of investment and at the cost of luxury consumption. The argument for some intervention by fiscal means was much strengthened by Smith's ambivalent attitude, held in common with Hume and others, towards 'excessive' consumption (by all classes). At the same time, despite an evident concern with development, Smith's continual references to the 'natural rights' of men not to be disturbed represents a significant, though not absolute, constraint upon the extent to which intervention directed towards patterns of expenditure between investment and consumption might be justified.

It may at this point be worth remarking that our interpretation is not intended to imply a denial of a frequent appeal to what constitutes, at least from the economic point of view, *'a priori'* arguments.[6] We have encountered numerous instances, such as the contention that 'as to cultivate the ground was the original destination of man, so in every state of his existence he seems to retain a predilection for this primitive employment,' or that the ultimate basis for exchange lies in the propensity of mankind 'to truck, barter, and exchange one thing for another.'[7] The point, however, is that on the whole such appeals can be discarded while the analytical structure remains intact.

A fundamental conclusion of this study is that it is as misleading to regard the British economy of Smith's day as basically 'agricultural' as it is to ascribe to it the features of a highly industrialized, capital-intensive economy. The agricultural sector itself was actually one of the most capital-intensive sectors, and structural change within the manufacturing sector was transforming the nature of the economy. It is clear from Smith's account both of the industry structure and of technological change that he was aware of the beginnings of a transition; and it is the trend which matters. We have attempted to show in fact that Smith recognized and dealt with many of the important technological developments prior to 1776 (with the significant exception of those occurring in the cotton industry) basing his analysis in part upon the economic pressures exerted by changing relative prices. On balance, in light of the attention paid to the determinants of industrial organization, to fixed capital and its maintenance, to the sources of knowledge, and to the differential factor-saving effects of various innovations, we reject the charge that the failed to 'anticipate' the industrial revolution.

Bearing in mind both the role accorded by Smith to the price mechanism in economic development and the analysis of the process of technological progress we may evaluate the relevance of the alleged 'Corn Model' as an accurate representation of Smithian growth theory. In our view the model does not seem appropriate; in fact it would be more suitable for the analysis of the seventeenth-century than the mid-eighteenth-century economy. For it neglects the production function in manufacturing; the significance of raw materials—which in many respects played an even more important role than food in capital as a constraint upon employment—receives no attention; and there is no place for fixed capital and accordingly for almost the entire Smithian process of 'embodied' technical change.[8]

Now we do not intend to deny that Smith frequently accorded particular significance—both quantitative and qualitative—to basic 'necessaries.' We have in mind the unique treatment of price determination in the case of corn; the close relationship defined between corn prices, money wages and commodity prices; the dependence of population growth upon corn supplies; and the wages-fund theory. But Smith was keenly aware of rising working-class living standards in contemporary Britain and of the complications which this entailed. When he utilised corn as *numéraire,* for example, it was because it served better than any alternative but not because it was satisfactory in its own right. The degree of sophistication which characterised working-class budgets rendered quite inadequate any simple set of causal relations. Thus the fact that the real counterpart of money wages could not in practise be reduced to basic necessaries threatened the entire population mechanism and suggested to Smith a possible case for the utilization of excise taxes to induce a change in the pattern of consumption. The reaction of population to high average wages was further complicated by the differential patterns of behaviour on the part of labour in the capitalist and the non-capitalist sectors. It would not, therefore, be legitimate to ascribe to Smith use of models incorporating relatively invariant functional relationships and constant conditions since this abstracts from the very problem which concerned him, namely the 'balance' of forces relevant in particular circumstances.[9] To neglect these complications is to neglect some of the essentials of Smith's economics. Finally, it must be repeated that the special role accorded corn at various stages of the argument positively did not preclude an overwhelming concern with the allocation of resources.

Smith's awareness of contemporary technological and sociological developments, we have concluded, was more profound than is sometimes implied. A few words are in order regarding the state of governmental intervention, for it is frequently suggested that Smith failed to appreciate the contemporary process of rapid decay of internal governmental regulation. Our investigation confirms an exaggeration, on Smith's part, of the severity of regulation, but at the same time indicates some recognition of a diminution in control. Smith's overstatement of the degree of internal regulation may certainly have been simply an error of judgment; the evidence was subject to conflicting interpretation by contemporary authorities. But it may also have been deliberate to some degree. Smith, of course, much feared monopolistic and monopsonistic tendencies, which were, in his view, likely in the last resort to be incurable. From this point of view even occasional cases of legal support were reprehensible in the extreme.[10] Allowance must also be made for his *a priori* principle in favour of free trade based once again upon the 'natural right' of individuals not to be interefered with. While we do not intend to deny a certain 'empirical' or 'utilitarian' outlook—apparently sufficiently power-ful to have led Smith to remain silent on a number of burning social issues of the day—there can be little doubt that the principle of natural liberty played an important role in the present case, implying indeed the belief that an appeal in such terms would not fall upon deaf ears. We have, for example, noted his severe condemnation of British interference with economic activity in the colonies despite a belief that the regu-lations happened to be ineffectual. And the case against the settlement laws contained a similar appeal: the attempt at regulation of the labour market is 'evidently as impertinent as it is oppressive.'[11]

We have observed that when allowance is made for Smith's overriding concern with contemporary issues it is possible to detect a greater degree of consistency in the **Wealth of Nations** than may be apparent at first sight. Thus the serious charge that the Smithian analysis of profit-rate equalization conflicts with that of differential employment-generating capacities of alternative investments is unjustified, for it neglects to take into account distortions in the pattern of ac-tivity the correction of which was Smith's objective. Similarly, there is little justification for a charge of inconsistency regarding the broad issue of priorities in national policy. But there remains an element of truth in the observation that 'consistency was not his shining virtue.'[12] A striking instance is the implica-tion of the existence of unused resources in the 'vent-for-surplus' theory of trade, which contrasts with the assumption of full employment of capital and labour implied in the theory based upon 'absolute advan-tage.' It is true that Smith was engaged in a critique of policies and proposals formally designed to raise employment; we must keep in mind that he was writ-ing a 'tract for the time,' and could better make his case if he could prove his opponents wrong using *their* criteria of policy. Yet it is difficult to resolve entirely the disaccord in this fashion, and we con-clude that the alternative approaches to trade based on differing sets of implicit assumptions are not sat-isfactorily reconciled. (At the same time, the impor-tance of the vent-for-surplus doctrine should not be exaggerated, for it frequently is utilized simply to explain the function of wholesale traders and, in this context, it may be used together with any theory which accounts for regional specialization.)

It is essential to consider the relation between Smith's theory of vent-for-surplus and the so-called 'Smith-Turgot theorem on savings' with an eye to their com-patibility. Smith's eulogy of the advantages of capital accumulation, his correspondingly negative attitude towards luxury consumption, and his insistence that the process of savings involves no leakage from the income stream constitute fundamental divergencies from traditional mercantilist positions, although tentative steps in this direction had already been taken, for ex-ample, by Hutcheson. For despite their 'doctrine of thrift' mercantilist writers, on the whole, gave quali-fied assent to the requirement for luxury consumption as a means of assuring a high level of activity. While the Physiocrats also tended to show a formal concern with hoarding and emphasized the necessity for con-sumption in the interest of productive activity, their position can only be appreciated within the specific context of the French doctrine. It was Turgot, howev-er, who stated with particular clarity that the process of accumulation did not involve any attempt to add to money hoards.

The 'vent-for-surplus' theory has been described as a 'surviving relic of the Mercantile Theory' by J.S. Mill, for international trade—according to orthodox classi-cal doctrine—permits the more efficient use of capi-tal and labour and does not absorb into productive activity resources otherwise idle. But it must be not-ed that Smith's theorem on savings merely implies that no attempt is made to add to money balances from sales proceeds thus, in principle, precluding 'monetary' causes of unemployment and excess ca-pacity; it does not rule out other possible causes. In fact the rationalization for excess capacity in a closed economy suggested by Smith's discussion relates to a severe degree of specificness attributed to domestic resources and high inelasticity attributed to domestic demand for those *particular* products which can tech-nically be produced. There is, therefore, no necessary conflict between the vent-for-surplus doctrine and the theorem on savings.

Smith's forecast of a downward secular trend in the average profit rate with capital accumulation also re-quires attention in the present context. We have seen that the argument already referred to by Hume and Massie was formally based upon the notion of "in-creasing competition.' But this argument was supple-mented by a suggestion that an increasing paucity of investment opportunities lies at the root of the problem (although the only instance given of what he might have had in mind appears in a loose formulation of diminishing returns at the extensive margin in agricul-ture). An explanation along these lines does not, in principle, conflict with the Smith-Turgot theorem. It is true that the profit-rate decline, in Smith's view, might be checked by the acquisition of 'new markets,' but the argument relates to the diversion of *fully utilized* capital towards more profitable branches of activity thus raising the average rate, rather than to the absorp-tion into use of hitherto *idle* capacity. While in our view the position does not necessarily conflict with the orthodox 'law of markets,' classical writers frequently insisted that it did[13] and Ricardo in particular was unable to accept a view of the economic system which envis-aged variations in the secular rate of profit unrelated to inverse variations in the real cost of producing wage goods.[14]

Yet there remains one related phenomenon which appears to be in conflict with the Smith-Turgot theorem. The predicted decline in the rate of profit (and accordingly the natural rate of interest) with increasing accumulation is said ultimately to lead to the stationary state where there occurs no further net investment (and accordingly no new stimulus to an expansion of population). But Smith at the same time much emphasized the tendency, in the normal course of development, for increasing investment to be made in the carrying trade which, it will be recalled, 'is altogether withdrawn from supporting the productive labour of that particular country, to support that of some foreign countries.' Moreover, note is also taken on occasion of direct foreign investment undertaken by various European nations with relatively low rates of interest. If we understand Smith correctly, it would appear to be the case that, at least in an open economy, saving may be undertaken which is not reflected in net domestic investment. Our point is not simply that subsequent effects playing back on the domestic economy are not investigated by Smith, but rather that the existence of a potentially serious conflict with the fundamental proposition regarding the nature of saving is nowhere given formal recognition.

Smith's physiocratic contemporaries approached the problem of economic growth in terms similar to those of the *Wealth of Nations,* insofar as the emphasis is upon accumulation of capital envisaged as 'advances' permitting time-consuming activity, and maximization of the community's disposable surplus—by attention to 'efficiency' in allocation—as the source of new capital. Moreover, in both Smithian and physiocratic economics (and earlier, in the work of Cantillon), in sharp contrast with traditional mercantilist doctrine, population size fell away as an immediate objective of policy. The general unconcern with the magnitude of population as such is reflected, in part, by the fact that neither Smith nor the Physiocrats showed any concern for the potential 'loss' of population to the colonies such as was feared by some contemporaries; much more attention was paid, by Smith, to the outward flow of capital. This position was indeed maintained at a time not far removed from the Stuart rebellion when it might have been expected that concern for a large body of yeomen would have preoccupied him.

Smith's possible 'debt' to the Physiocrats has been the subject of considerable debate, although perhaps what is really important is how much Smith accepted of the French analysts, rather than his debt to them. Professor Cannan has suggested, largely on the basis of close examination of the contrasts between the [*Lectures on Justice, Police, Revenue and Arms*] and the *Wealth of Nations,* that while Smith's distinction between productive and unproductive labour, the thesis that productive labour is maintained from capital advances, the distributive scheme, and the concept of annual produce, seem to have been influenced by his contact with and knowledge of the French economists, his analyses of the division of labour, of price, and of the wage structure were developed independently. Of particular significance, the general case for economic liberalism had long been adopted.[15] But even Cannan's limited attributions are probably exaggerated. There is in the *Lectures* perhaps more attention paid to the role of capital in permitting time-consuming processes than Cannan is prepared to concede, and the issue is touched upon, as we have seen, by Hutcheson, Oswald and Tucker. Several of Smith's immediate predecessors, including Cantillon and Steuart, were placing increasing emphasis upon productive capital as distinct from purely commercial capital opening the road towards a view of profits as a class income received not only by merchants but by capitalist-employers generally. While the basic physiocratic theory implies that only capital invested in agriculture is capable of generating a net return it was Smith's position (and that of Turgot) that a net revenue is yielded in *all* spheres of activity (although the source of the return in the mercantile sector, it will be recalled, is explained by Smith in terms of the traditional principle of 'alienation'). There is, moreover, some evidence that Smith may have drawn upon the work of James Oswald in his division of cost-price into the component parts of rent, wages and profits which constitutes the basis for the distribution of the entire national income between aggregate rent, wages and profits, and the natural-price doctrine was discussed by William Temple in 1758.

But whatever the extent and nature of Smith's 'debts' the fact is that the Physiocrats were severely constrained by their characteristic doctrines regarding agriculture as the sole wealth-creating activity. Equally significant, inadequate attention was paid to the mechanism whereby resources would be allocated in a freely-operating system and it is difficult to escape the impression that their support for free trade both internally and externally as a necessary precondition of rapid development was not based securely upon a well-constructed analytical foundation. There is also justification for the view that their policy proposals were designed as a device to counter the contemporary pattern of intervention but would have been much qualified in other circumstances. This is above all true of their recommendation for free trade in corn, which was, it would appear, maintained conditionally in light of France's circumstance as a net corn exporter. The Physiocrats, in brief, made appeal to a 'superior' principle, namely the effect of policy upon the price and quantity of agricultural produce. By contrast, Smith's 'agricultural bias' did not lead to much distortion in his applied economics and his policy proposals in support of free trade were more firmly based upon the allocative processes of the competitive price system. Yet we have shown also that Smith did not do full justice to his case in favour of non-intervention when envisaged from the point of view of a developing country poorly endowed with natural resources or one which, although adequately endowed, has entered belatedly into competition with other, relatively advanced, 'landed' nations.

It is further argued by Cannan that Smith—particularly by his use of a theory of capital and productive labour, and by his appendage of a scheme of distribution to an existing theory of price—'settled the form of economic treatises of a century at least.'[16] But if this view is considered closely it will be seen to be only partially adequate. Ricardo was not much concerned with the issue of productive and unproductive labour; he diverged markedly in the analyses of price, the 'measure of value,' distribution, and the profit-rate trend; it is not even clear whether some of his discussions—such as that of machinery—were in any way related to micro-economic decision-making units, whether in other words they fall within the 'paradigm' of competitive allocation theory. Even where the Smithian approach accords with that of his successors, it was frequently misunderstood. This is revealed in the charge by McCulloch that the analysis of investment priorities conflicted with the principles of profit-rate equalization; and also in the related, mistaken, belief of Ricardo that Smith championed a large gross revenue. And Smith's recognition of the role of differential factor endowments as a rationale for international trade, and of changes therein over time as an explanation of temporal variations in optimal resource allocation went unnoticed. The impression left upon Smith's successors by the *precise* details of his allocative mechanism, or the *precise* relationship envisaged between the theory of competitive resource allocation and economic development was thus scarcely an extensive one.

Yet there remains an important element of truth in Cannan's proposition. The *general* case in favour of laissez-faire and the *general* workings of the competitive process in assuring a tendency towards the establishment of equilibrium wage-rate and profit-rate structures, and the analysis of the relationship between market and cost prices, represent without question a vital link with the future. Moreover, Smith's early nineteenth-century successors had conveniently available to them what appeared already to be a body of 'received doctrine' upon which they could draw, and of equal importance to which they could direct their critical attention; for without doubt, Smith presented an extensive body of economics in

a manner which they found supremely worthwhile. In particular, Ricardo's analytical structure relating to distribution was formulated in direct response to that of Smith. It is, in our view, impossible to appreciate the Ricardian innovations without keeping to the fore Smith's formulation of the problem to be solved—the effect of wage-rate changes upon profits—and Smith's own solution.

In matters of aggregative economic theory a number of precise relationships may also be discerned. The conception of capital as 'advances'; the view of the savings process as proceeding in a 'hitchless' fashion; the minimization of the monetary determination of the interest rate; the specification of the relationship between the rates of growth of capital and population as the key determinant of working-class living standards are matters which come to occupy the centre of the stage. Equally important regarding the fundamental matters of method and of ultimate objective, Hume, Smith, and the nineteenth-century classical writers—as Lord Robbins has emphasized—had in common a critical concern not merely with social reform but with reform based upon a systematic body of scientific knowledge.[17] The precise theoretical structures utilized certainly differ from case to case and may have been more or less soundly constructed, but the mode of operation and the general objective—the improved welfare of the working-class in particular—was shared by all.

Our discussion leads on to the relationship between Smithian and Marxian analysis. The characteristic element of Smith's work which is most attractive to scholars in the Marxian tradition is his extension of physiocratic doctrine to allow for the generation of surplus-value in *all* sectors: 'The special feature of the [Smithian] pattern which marked it off from those put forward by earlier economists was the inclusion of *profit on capital* as a general category of class income which accrued to all who used "stock" in the employment of wage-labour, and which was qualitatively distinct both from the rent of land and from the wages of labour.'[18] More specifically, if we consider Smith's occasional attribution to *labour* of the ability to generate surplus value—at least in industry and trade—together with the classification of Book II, chapter v which distinguished sectors according to their respective 'constant' and 'variable'—as distinct from 'fixed' and 'circulating'—elements in a given capital stock we are even faced, in principle, with the Marxian problem of profit-rate equalization. For if profits are in some sense a deduction from labour's contribution and if labour-capital ratios differ between sectors, Marx's issue makes an appearance. Smith, of course, never recognized the problem but it lurks in the shadows.

But even when—as is usually the case in the *Wealth of Nations*—a value-creating ability is accorded to land

and capital, the moral justification of property income is questioned. Smith's recommendations, it must at the same time be emphasized, imply a 'reformist' rather than a 'revolutionary' propensity; there is no call for confiscatory measures or any interference with private property rights, despite explicit statements to the effect that 'the affluence of the few supposes the indigence of the many,'[19] or that 'civil government, so far as it is instituted for the security of property, is in reality instituted for the defence of the rich against the poor, or of those who have some property against those who have none at all.'[20] Without doubt Smith (and Hume too) took a hard-headed approach to any schemes for equality in the distribution of wealth; and in the case at hand one may discern (even within the narrow scope of purely economic issues and apart from certain desirable social characteristics attributed by Smith to capitalism in general, and—to a degree—to inequality in particular) a very practical reason for the failure to draw the 'logical' conclusions from such striking observations. Smith was conscious that Britain could not be viewed as an isolated island; any excessive taxation of income would simply assure the transfer of capital elsewhere. This was certainly the basis for his warning against the taxation of pure interest. On the whole, a case might be made according to which Smith championed the *allocative* function of the price mechanism while at the same time he was dissatisfied with the distributional implications thereof. The dilemma was resolved above all by the absence of any practicable alternative to the process of capital accumulation as then undertaken by the recipients of interest and rent, which process in fact provided the best assurance in the circumstances that the labouring classes too would partake of the benefits of economic development. Thus Smith's allowances for monopsony pressure, which in principle imply a rejection of population restraint as the primary solution for depressed living standards, were of little practical relevance during a period of secular expansion such as Smith envisaged. It is equally essential to take into account Smith's outline of the measures which might legitimately be undertaken by the state to alleviate some of the worst defects of the contemporary system.

Notes

[1] [Schumpeter, J.A. *Economic Doctrine and Method.* 1912; London, 1954—*History of Economic Analysis.* New York, 1954.]

[2] *Adam Smith, 1723-1790* (London, 1948), 19.

[3] The contrast between formal statements and practical applications can be further illustrated. The main sectoral differences which are formally recognized in the Second Book are those between agriculture, manufactures, and trade. Differences within manufactur-

ing in the fixed-circulating capital ratio, and differences within either manufactures, or agriculture in the turnover rate of capital are ruled out. Yet in several practical applications such differences do play a part.

A similar interpretation may be suggested for Smith's treatment of the wages-fund theory. The formal analysis suggests that changes in the wage rate cannot exert an influence on the total wage bill, a constraint that is only true if factor proportions are identical everywhere and technologically determined. If these assumptions are taken seriously, then crucial obstacles exist in the way of full employment. But these problems were not necessarily obvious to Smith, and, in fact, it seems from our study to be the case that Smith was unaware of the implicit assumptions of his formal analysis.

See too G.J. Stigler, 'The Classical Economics: An Alternative View,' *Five Lectures on Economic Problems* (London, 1949), 25-36 which distinguishes (in a case study relating to Nassau Senior's analysis in the hand-loom weaver report) between the 'working technique' and the 'formal theory' of classical economists. *Adam Smith,* 20.

[4] *Adam Smith,* 20.

[5] Adam Smith, *Wealth of Nations,* [Modern Library Edition, edited by E. Cannan, New York, 1937], 435.

[6] Moreover, the institutional framework essential for the efficient operation of the price mechanism must be kept in mind throughout. Indispensable accounts are given by N. Rosenberg, 'Some Institutional Aspects of the *Wealth of Nations,*' *Journal of Political Economy,* LXVIII (Dec. 1960); and Warren J. Samuels, *The Classical Theory of Economic Policy* (Cleveland, 1966).

[7] For some peculiar Smithian *obiter dicta* see Arthur H. Cole, 'Puzzles of the *Wealth of Nations,*' *Canadian Journal of Economics and Political Science,* XXIV (Feb. 1958), 1-8.

[8] The growth rate of the economy—defined algebraically . . . as $k(p/w) - 1$—will *in practice* depend upon the relationship between the distribution of the initial stock of wages goods between productive and service labour; the average productivity of labour; and the average wage rate. Unless the order of magnitude of these variables can be given, scarcely anything has been achieved by the mathematical formulation. But it is precisely at this point that the real problems of interpretation arise. For example, while the response of population to wage increases above 'subsistence' was certainly taken into account, much emphasis is placed upon upward pressures on the wage rate, due to scarcity of labour supplies, during a period of expansion. And increased productivity cannot be relied upon to counterbalance exactly increases in wages. We cannot

presume that Smith was concerned with a regularly progressive economy and must accordingly examine the precise determinants of productivity and average wages.

[9] For this same view, see J.J. Spengler, 'Adam Smith's Theory of Economic Growth—Part II,' *Southern Economic Journal*, XXVI (July 1951), 5.

[10] Cf. *Wealth of Nations*, 128-9; 141-2 in particular.

[11] *Ibid.*, 122.

[12] A.L. Macfie, *The Individual in Society: Papers on Adam Smith* (London, 1967), 68. Professor Macfie extends the observation generally to eighteenth-century writers, especially members of the Scottish sociological school (*ibid.*, 126).

[13] Cf. Donald Winch, *Classical Political Economy and Colonies* (London, 1965), 30-1, 42-4, 81-5.

[14] *Principles of Political Economy*, 344-6.

[15] E. Cannan, 'Editor's Introduction,' *Lectures on Justice, Police, Revenue and Arms* (New York, 1964), xxviii-xxxi; 'Editor's Introduction,' *Wealth of Nations*, xxxviii-xliii, and Cannan, *A Review of Economic Theory* (London, 1929), 291f.

At the outset of the *Wealth of Nations*, in the 'Plan of Work,' Smith stated that the growth of national product depended more upon the *efficiency* with which productive labour is used than the relative proportion of the labour force in the productive and service sectors (*ibid.*, lvii-lviii). Cannan has implied ([*Lectures on Justice, Police, Revenue and Arms*], xxix; *Wealth of Nations*, xli) that his weighting suggests that the great emphasis upon productive labour of Book II—accorded to physiocratic influence—had not yet been achieved when the plan was formulated. Yet it must be borne in mind that capital accumulation was essential for the embodiment of new technology as well as for the support of additional productive labour.

[16] 'Introduction,' *Wealth of Nations*, xxxix.

[17] *Theory of Economic Policy*, 169f.

[18] R.L. Meek, 'Adam Smith and the Classical Theory of Profit,' in Meek, *Economics and Ideology and Other Essays* (London, 1967), 18. The contrast with the [*Lectures on Justice, Police, Revenue and Arms*] is emphasized in 'The Physiocratic Concept of Profit,' *ibid.*, 306.

[19] *Wealth of Nations*, 670.

[20] *Ibid.*, 674. Cf. *Lectures*, 15.

R. H. Campbell and A. S. Skinner (essay date 1982)

SOURCE: "The Wealth of Nations," in *Adam Smith*, St. Martin's Press, 1982, pp. 168-85.

[*In the following essay on* The Wealth of Nations, *Campbell and Skinner provide a comprehensive analysis of Smith's economic system, explaining and discussing the interrelationship among his theories of production, labor, wages, price and distribution, profits, savings and investment, interest rates, and capital accumulation. The authors also comment on Smith's policy recommendations concerning government regulation of the economy.*]

The first edition of the **Wealth of Nations** was published on 9 March 1776 by Strahan and Cadell. It appeared in two volumes, at a cost of one pound and sixteen shillings. The second edition appeared in 1778 and the third six years later. The fourth edition is dated 1786, and the fifth and final version to be published in Smith's lifetime appeared in 1789, the year of the French Revolution.

The work has become one of the most influential to be published in the English language and has now been translated into Chinese, Czech, Dutch, Finnish, Italian, Portuguese, Russian, Serbo-Croat, Spanish, Swedish and Turkish. The first edition was sold out in six months, and was translated into Danish (1779-80), French (1778-9, 1788) and German (1776-8) before Smith died.

When the book appeared, many of its major themes would have been familiar to Smith's old students, his friends, and other contemporaries. The long analysis of the public debt in Book V, for example, drew attention to the dangerous influence of the moneyed interest, to the disincentive effects of the high levels of taxation needed to service it, and to the power which a developed government sector could exert in a constitutional sense. Smith also made effective use of the sociological analysis which he had developed in the context of the **Lectures on Jurisprudence,** most notably in the treatment of such necessary public services as defence and justice—areas of analysis where he returned to the problem not only of the costs of providing such services, but also to the links which exist between forms of economic organisation and the relationships between different social groups. In the same vein, Smith introduced his most complete analysis of the breakdown of feudalism and of the causes of the emergence of the modern system of commerce—the fourth stage of his lectures on history which embraced his account of the institutions of the exchange economy.[1] More striking still, perhaps, was Smith's concern with the problems faced by the modern citizen and the extent to which it was possible for him to fulfil the functions and obligations of his classical counterpart.[2] Here the most interesting feature is Smith's appreciation of the point that the division of labour, in his eyes the most important source of increased productivity, was also associated with important social costs. It was in fact his contention, that the individual who is confined to a small specialised function for a large part of the working day, was likely to become 'as stupid and ignorant as it is possible for a human creature to become', thus generating a sort of 'mental mutilation, deformity and wretchedness'. Smith believed that this development would erode martial spirit and adversely affect that capacity for moral judgement which had been considered in the *Theory of Moral Sentiments:*

> His dexterity at his own particular trade seems, in this manner, to be acquired at the expense of his intellectual, social, and martial virtues. But in every improved and civilised society this is the state into which the labouring poor, that is, the great body of the people, must necessarily fall, unless government takes some pains to prevent it.[3]

Such themes were not uncommon in writings published before 1776, especially in the circle of Smith's acquaintance, and yet the book made a great impact among the members of it. David Hume wrote joyously:

> Euge! Belle! Dear Mr Smith: I am much pleas'd with your Performance, and the Perusal of it has taken me from a State of great Anxiety. It was a Work of so much Expectation, by yourself, by your Friends, and by the Public, that I troubled for its Appearance; but am now much relieved.[4]

Hugh Blair commented:

> I Confess you have exceeded my expectations. One writer after another on these Subjects did nothing but puzzle me. I despaired of ever arriving at clear Ideas. You have given me full and Compleat Satisfaction and my Faith is fixed. I do think the Age is highly indebted to you, and I wish they may be duly Sensible of the Obligation. You have done great Service to the World by overturning all that interested Sophistry of Merchants, with which they had Confounded the whole Subject of Commerce. Your work ought to be, and I am perswaded will in some degree become, the Commercial Code of Nations. I did not read one Chapter of it without Acquiring much Light and instruction. I am Convinced that since Montesquieu's *Esprit des Loix,* Europe has not received any Publication which tends so much to Enlarge and Rectify the ideas of mankind.
>
> Your arrangement is excellent. One chapter paves the way for another; and your System gradually erects itself. Nothing was ever better suited than your Style is to the Subject; clear and distinct to the

last degree, full without being too much so, and as tercly as the Subject could admit. Dry as some of the Subjects are, It carried me along. I read the whole with avidity; and have pleasure in thinking that I shall with some short time give it a Second and more deliberate perusal.[5]

Joseph Black, though writing primarily to inform Smith of Hume's declining health began:

> I have no doubt that the Views you have given of many parts of your Subject will be found by experience to be as just as they are new and interesting and although it be admired immediately by discerning and impartial Judges [,] It will require some time before others who are not so quick sighted and whose minds are warped by Prejudice or Interest can understand and relish such a comprehensive System composed with such just and liberal sentiments.[6]

William Robertson had high expectations of the work:

> but it has gone far beyond what I expected. You have formed into a regular and consistent system one of the most intricate and important parts of political science, and if the English be capable of extending their ideas beyond the narrow and illiberal arrangements introduced by the mercantile supporters of Revolution principles . . . I should think your Book will occasion a total change in several important articles both in policy and finance.[7]

Adam Ferguson had:

> been for sometime so busy reading you, and recommending and quoting you, to my students, that I have not had leisure to trouble you with letters. I suppose, however, that of all the opinions on which you have any curiosity, mine is among the least doubtful. You may believe, that on further acquaintance with your work my esteem is not a little increased. You are surely to reign alone on these subjects, to form the opinions and I hope to govern at least the coming generations.[8]

These assessments are interesting precisely because they show how quickly some of Smith's friends grasped his purpose, which was to produce, in the first instance, an analytical system or what a notable critic, Governor Pownall, was to describe as 'an institute of the Principia *of those laws of motion,* by which the operations of the community are directed and regulated, and by which they should be examined'.[9] In making a similar point, Hume felt moved to remark that the book was unlikely to achieve popular appeal, since:

> the Reading of it necessarily requires so much Attention, and the Public is disposed to give so

little, that I shall still doubt for some time of its being at first very popular: But it has Depth and Solidity and Acuteness, and it is so much illustrated by curious Facts, that it must at last take the public Attention.[10]

A week later Hume wrote to William Strahan, who had also published Edward Gibbon's *Decline and Fall*: 'Dr Smith's . . . is another excellent Work that has come from your Press this Winter; but I have ventured to tell him, that it requires too much thought to be as popular as Mr Gibbon's.'[11] Adam Ferguson sized up the situation well: 'You are not to expect the run of a novel, nor even of a true history; but you may venture to assure your booksellers of a steady and continual sale, as long as people wish for information on these subjects.'[12]

In the event the fears of Smith's friends were disproved, precisely because the book appealed differently to separate groups. Smith's friends admired the comprehensive and systematic explanation of economic life which it embodied, but were worried about those features which made it look, in the words of Hugh Blair, 'too much like a publication for the present moment'. But at the same time, it was this practical aspect which appealed to a wider readership. The *Wealth of Nations* was not only an intellectual achievement of the greatest magnitude, embracing as it does the explanation of complex social relations on the basis of a few principles, but also a work which provided practical prescriptions for the problems of the day.

The systematic or analytical aspect of Smith's contribution emerges in a number of different ways. To begin with, there are the links with other aspects of his thought, all of which remind the reader of the interrelations which exist between the different parts of the lectures given from the chair of moral philosophy. In the context of his largely economic analysis, Smith required to make some judgement as to the activities of men, and in fact relied mainly on the self-regarding propensities already detailed in the *Theory of Moral Sentiments*. He did not suggest that these propensities provided of themselves an adequate statement of man's psychology, but simply contended that within the economic sphere man is motivated by a desire for gain. As he put it in a famous passage, 'it is not from the benevolence of the butcher, the brewer, or the baker, that we expect our dinner, but from their regard to their own interest'.[13] Smith also recognised in examining economic phenomena, that he was concerned with only one aspect of the activities of man in society, and that the analysis must depend upon some prior judgement as to the nature of the social bond. The formal analysis of the latter problem is also contained in the *Theory of Moral Sentiments* in the sense that the individual must be restrained from hurting his fellows in respect of their persons and property: the basic minimum condition of justice. The analytical side of Smith's contribution is also related to his historical treatment of jurisprudence, or at least to that aspect of it which helped to explain the origins of the exchange economy and, therefore, some of its leading features.

Smith was concerned with a situation where there were three main forms of economic activity: agriculture, manufacture and trade, all of which were carried on through the use of three factors of production—land, labour and capital. Smith ascribed a great deal of importance to the distinction between factors of production, and to the particular forms of return which they generated for each of the socio-economic groups with which they were associated.

Smith defined wages as a form of return which accrued to those who must earn subsistence through the sale of their labour power, arguing that this particular type of monetary reward is payable by those (undertakers) who require the factor. Rent on the other hand, accrues to the owners (proprietors) of land and is paid by those who need it (the farmers) because the resource is both productive and scarce. Rent thus emerges as a surplus in the sense that it accrues to the owner of land independently of any effort made by him so that the proprietors appear to be the only group 'whose revenue costs them neither labour nor care, but comes to them, as it were, of its own accord'. On the other hand, profit is that type of return which accrues to undertakers (or capitalists to use the modern term) as the reward for the trouble taken, and the risks incurred, in combining the factors of production. As Smith put it:

> As soon as stock has accumulated in the hands of particular persons, some of them will naturally employ it in setting to work industrious people, whom they will supply with materials and subsistence, in order to make a profit by the sale of their work, or by what their labour adds to the value of the materials.[14]

By stock Smith meant either fixed capital (such as that embodied in plant, 'useful machines') or circulating capital (devoted to the purchase of raw materials or labour).

Looked at in this way, all groups in society are in a sense interdependent. The proprietors depend on the undertakers engaged in agriculture for their income; wage-labour depends on the undertakers operating in all three sectors for employment; while the undertakers engaged in different types of activity depend upon each other and the two remaining groups in respect of the services which they provide, and the expenditures which they incur. The parallel with the physiocratic perspective is obvious, and so too is Smith's vision of the pattern of interdependencies which emerge. The point is made with particular clarity in Book II where Smith employs a kind of 'period' analysis in a way which may demonstrate his debt to physiocracy in general and to the work of Turgot in particular.

Suppose, following Smith, that we examine the performance of the economy during a particular year, from the standpoint of the beginning of the period in question. Under these circumstances it is reasonable to assume that there will be certain stocks of goods in existence, reflecting the level of output attained in the previous period, together with the quantities of (consumption and investment) goods purchased during it; stocks which may be divided into three main parts.

First, there is that part of total stock which is reserved for immediate consumption, and which is held by all consumers (capitalists, labour and proprietors). The characteristic feature of this part of the total stock is that it affords no revenue to its possessors since it consists in 'the stock of food, clothes, house-hold furniture, etc., which have been purchased by their proper consumers, but which are not yet entirely consumed.'[15]

Secondly, there is that part of the total stock which may be described as 'fixed capital' and which will again be distributed between the various groups in society. This part of the stock, Smith suggested, is composed of the 'useful machines' purchased in preceding periods and held by the capitalists engaged in manufacture; the quantity of useful buildings and of 'improved land' in the possession of the capitalist farmers and the proprietors, together with the 'aquired and useful abilities' of all the inhabitants.[16]

Thirdly, there is that part of the total stock which may be described as 'circulating capital' and which again has several components, these being:

(a) The quantity of money necessary to carry on the process of circulation. In this connection Smith observed that:

The sole use of money is to circulate consumeable goods. By means of it, provisions, materials, and finished work, are bought and sold, and distributed to their proper consumers. The quantity of money therefore, which can be annually employed in any country must be determined by the value of the consumable goods which can be annually circulated within it.[17]

(b) The stock of provisions and other agricultural products which are available for sale during the current period, but which are still in the hands of either the farmers or merchants.

(c) The stock of raw materials and work in process, which is held by merchants, undertakers, or those capitalists engaged in the agricultural sector (including mining, etc.).

(d) The stock of manufactured goods (consumption and investment) created during the previous period, but which remain in the hands of undertakers and merchants at the beginning of the present year.[18]

Perhaps the logic of the process can be best represented by artificially splitting up the activities involved. Suppose at the beginning of the time period in question, that the major capitalist groups possess the total net receipts earned from the sale of products in the previous period, and that the undertakers engaged in agriculture open by transmitting the total rent due to the proprietors of land, for the use of that factor. The income thus provided will enable the proprietors to make the necessary purchases of consumption (and investment) goods in the current period, thus contributing to reduce the stocks of such goods with which the undertakers and merchants began the period. Secondly, assume that the undertakers engaged in both sectors, together with the merchant groups transmit to wage-labour the content of the wages fund, thus providing this socio-economic class with an income which can be used in the current period. Thirdly, the undertakers in agriculture and manufactures make purchases of consumption and investment goods from each other through the medium of retail and wholesale merchants thus generating a series of expenditures linking the two sectors. Finally the process of circulation may be seen to be completed by the purchases made by individual undertakers within their own sectors. Once again these purchases will include consumption and investment goods, thus contributing still further to reduce the stocks of commodities which were available for sale when the period under examination began.

Given these points, the working of the system can be seen to involve a series of flows whereby income is exchanged for commodities in such a way as to generate a series of withdrawals from the 'circulating' capital of society. As Smith pointed out, the consumption goods thus withdrawn from the existing stock may be entirely used up within the current period, or used to increase the stock 'reserved for immediate consumption' or to replace the more durable goods (e.g. clothes) which had reached the end of their life in the course of the same period. Similarly, the undertakers as a result of their purchases, will add to their stocks of raw materials and/or their fixed capital, or replace the machines which had finally worn out in the current period. Looked at in this way, the 'circular flow' may be seen to involve a certain level of purchases which takes goods from the market but which is at the same time matched by a continuous process of replacement by virtue of the productive activity which is currently carried on.

While this vision of the economic process is important in its own right, Smith also used it to demonstrate the importance of a wide range of economic problems as well as the interconnections which exist between them. The first and most obvious problem in the context of the exchange economy is that of *price* and its determinants. In handling this problem, Smith assumed the existence of what he called 'ordinary' or 'average' rates of wages, profit, and rent; rates of return which may be said to prevail within any given society or neighbourhood during any given time period (such as a year). These rates of return determine the natural or supply price of any commodity, defined by Smith as that amount which is 'neither more nor less than what is sufficient to pay the rent of the land, the wages of the labourer, and the profits of the stock' according to their prevailing and natural rates.[19] By contrast, market price is now defined as that price which may prevail at any given point in time, being regulated by 'the proportion between the quantity which is actually brought to market, and the demand of those who are willing to pay the natural price of the commodity'.[20] The two prices are interrelated in that in a competitive situation any divergence between them will cause the rates of return accruing to factors to rise above or fall below their 'natural' rates, thus generating an inflow or outflow of resources to or from the employment affected—with consequent effects on the supply of the commodity. In short the natural price of commodities emerges as the equilibrium or 'central' price, 'to which the prices of all commodities are continually gravitating'.[21]

Following on from this argument, Smith's next task was to elucidate the forces which determine the level of the ordinary or average rates of return to factors, applying to this problem the same 'demand and supply' type of analysis just considered.

The process of wage determination was seen by Smith to involve a kind of bargain or contract:

> What are the common wages of labour depends every where upon the contract usually made between . . . two parties whose interests are by no means the same. The workmen desire to get as much, the masters to give as little as possible. The former are disposed to combine in order to raise, the latter in order to lower the wages of labour.[22]

While Smith recognised that the balance of advantage would often lie with the masters due to their legal privilege to combine, he also pointed out that demand and supply relationships would frequently cause individual employers 'to voluntarily break through the natural combination of masters not to raise wages'. Indeed the only rate which Smith felt able to define clearly was the subsistence wage:

> A man must always live by his work, and his wages must at least be sufficient to maintain him. They must even upon most occasions be somewhat more; otherwise it would be impossible for him to bring up a family, and the race of workmen could not last beyond the first generation.[23]

Profits, on the other hand, Smith argued, must be affected by the selling price of the commodity and the cost of production (including wages). Profits are likely to be particularly sensitive to changes in demand, together with the 'good or bad fortune' of both rivals and customers; facts which make it difficult to identify an 'ordinary' or 'average' rate of return. However, Smith suggested that the rate of interest would provide a reasonably accurate guide to the prevailing rates, basically on the ground that the rate paid for borrowed funds would be reflected in the profits expected: 'It may be laid down as a maxim, that wherever a great deal can be made by the use of money, a great deal will commonly be given for the use of it; and that wherever little can be made by it, less will commonly be given for it.'[24] At least as a broad generalisation Smith felt able to state that the rate of profit prevailing would be determined by the wage rate and the quantity of stock (capital), taken in conjunction with the outlets for profitable investment.

The final form of return, rent, is in many ways the least satisfactory aspect of Smith's argument, although he did offer a number of interesting insights, later to be taken up by David Ricardo. Rent for Smith was a 'monopoly' price at least in the sense that it is generally the highest which can be got 'in the actual circumstances of the land'.[25] He clearly perceived that rent payments would vary with the fertility of the soil and location—thus making it difficult to speak of a particular rate of rent in the same sense in which we refer to a particular rate of interest. But the analysis does seem to suggest that in any given time period rent payments will be related to the quantity of land in use, which must, in turn, be affected by the level of population. Further, Smith's argument indicates that during any given time period rent payments will be related, not only to the productivity of the soil, but also to the prevailing rates of wages and profit.

The treatment of price and distribution leads directly to another analytical step in Smith's system. It will be recalled that costs of production are incurred by those who create commodities, thus providing individuals with the income needed to purchase them. It follows that if the price of each commodity (in a position of equilibrium) comprehends payments made for rent, wages and profit, according to their natural rates, then 'it must be so for all commodities which compose the whole annual produce of the land and labour of every country, taken complexly'. Smith concluded: 'The whole price or exchangeable value of that annual produce, must resolve itself into the same three parts, and be parcelled out among the different inhabitants.'[26] In this way Smith drew attention to the distribution of total income between wages, profit and rent but also to the relationship between aggregate output and aggregate income. Or, as he put it, 'the gross revenue of all the inhabitants of a great country, comprehends the whole annual produce of their land and labour'.[27] This income, once generated would obviously be used in part to purchase consumption goods—including those services which do not directly contribute to physical output and which cannot therefore be said to contribute to generate that level of income associated with it. Smith suggested that the services of 'players, buffoons, opera singers, and musicians' fall within this class, and added that:

> The sovereign . . . with all the officers both of justice and war who serve under him—the whole army and navy, are unproductive labourers. They are the servants of the publick and are maintained by a part of the annual produce of the industry of other people.[28]

On the other hand, some part of aggregate income will be saved, notably by the entrepreneurial groups, with a view to purchasing items of both fixed and variable capital. The working of the circular flow can thus be visualised in rather different terms from those used at the outset; that is, in terms of an economic system where consumption and investment goods are annually produced, sold, and replaced, in a seemingly endless cycle, and where any changes in the direction of demand for commodities will, by virtue of the operation of the price mechanism, generate changes in the use of available resources.

This particular, and essentially modern, way of looking at the economic process leads on to yet another change of focus represented by Smith's preoccupation with economic growth. Remaining with the period analysis of the previous examples, Smith noted that:

> The annual produce of the land and labour of any nation can be increased in its value by no other means, but by increasing either the number of its productive labourers, or the productive powers of those labourers who had before been employed.[29]

Smith recognised that both sources of increased output would require an additional capital, devoted either to increasing the wages fund or to the purchase of fixed capital equipment which would 'facilitate and abridge labour'. In both cases an increase in the funds devoted to savings is required; a perception which is linked to three characteristic features of his argument. First, Smith suggested that net savings will always be possible during each (annual) period, and that such savings will be prompted by 'the desire of bettering our condition,

a desire which though generally calm and dispassionate, comes with us from the womb, and never leaves us till we go into the grave'.[30] Secondly, he argued that savings once made will always be used effectively, thus stating a basic assumption which was to become one of the features of classical economics: 'What is annually saved is as regularly consumed as what is annually spent, and nearly in the same time too; but it is consumed by a different set of people.'[31] Finally Smith suggested that savings when so used must create successively higher levels of output, since:

> Parsimony, by increasing the fund which is destined for the maintenance of productive hands, tends to increase the number of those hands whose labour adds to the value of the subject upon which it is bestowed. It tends therefore to increase the exchangeable value of the annual produce of the land and labour of the country. It puts into motion an additional quantity of industry, which gives an additional value to the annual produce.[32]

The higher levels of output and income thus attained, make it possible to reach still greater levels of savings and investment in subsequent periods, thus generating further increases in output and income. Once started, the process of capital accumulation may be seen as a self-generating process, indicating that Smith's model of the flow should be seen, not as a circle of given size, but rather as a spiral of constantly expanding dimensions. A further point demands notice, in this connection, namely Smith's perception that the rate of growth will depend on the proportion of income devoted to savings, and on the extent to which the different outlets for productive activity (agriculture, manufacture, trade) put in motion greater or lesser quantities of 'industry' for a given injection of capital. It was Smith's contention that investment in agriculture would be productive of greater levels of surplus than manufacture, and that manufacture would make a more significant contribution to growth than trade.

Although Smith's treatment of distribution was developed in Book I, thus anticipating to some extent the treatment of capital accumulation, it is the latter discussion which helps to explain many of the earlier judgements. If for example subsistence wages were paid during a given annual period and net savings took place, then the consequence would be an increase in demand for labour and the payment of wage rates in excess of the minimum level. Where sustained over a period of time, high market wages would tend to cause an increase in the level of population, thus enhancing the demand for food and the utilisation of land. It was thus Smith's view that wages would always *tend* towards the subsistence level as population increased over time. He also considered that profit levels would tend to decline in the long run, partly in consequence of the gradual increase in stock, and partly because of increasing difficulty in finding 'a profitable method of employing any new capital'.[33] Smith was quite clear in respect of rent however, arguing that rent payments would increase over time, partly in consequence of increased use of the available stock of land, and partly because 'those improvements in the productive powers of labour, which tend directly to reduce the real price of manufactures, tend indirectly to raise the real rent of land'.[34]

It is one thing to talk of tendencies and another of trends—and here Smith pointed out that economies could be stationary (such as China), declining (he cites amongst others the case of Bengal) or advancing. In the last case the examples cited were America and Great Britain. If the latter had a slower growth rate than America, Smith was able to point out that real wages had risen in the eighteenth century while profit rates had been sufficient to sustain the rapid rate of growth required. Obviously such judgements are the reflections of the economic circumstances prevailing, although Smith was quick to point out that one very important reason for them was institutional:

> though the profusion of government must, undoubtedly, have retarded the natural progress of England towards opulence and improvement, it has not been able to stop it. The annual produce of its land and labour is, undoubtedly, much greater at present than it was either at the restoration or at the revolution. The capital, therefore, annually employed in cultivating this land, and in maintaining this labour, must likewise be much greater. In the midst of all the exactions of government, this capital has been silently and gradually accumulated by the private frugality and good conduct of individuals, by their universal, continual, and uninterrupted effort to better their own condition. It is this effort, protected by law and allowed by liberty to exert itself in the manner that is most advantageous, which has maintained the progress of England towards opulence and improvement in almost all former times, and which, it is to be hoped, will do so in all future times.[35]

The account given above is possibly sufficient to show that Smith's system was a considerable intellectual achievement, and to reveal that the system takes two forms. First, there is an account of the economy as a system, and, secondly, the provision of an analytical system which shows the links between those different problems which a review of the economy reveals. But, as the last quotation also implies, the system in both senses draws attention to a number of policy recommendations; recommendations which were more readily grasped than the intellectual work which underpins them, and which help to explain the contemporary popularity of the book.

One of the most striking features of the economic system, in Smith's eyes, was that individuals in pursuing their own interest unwittingly contribute to ends which they did not originally intend to promote—whether reference is made to the working of the allocative mechanism or the process of economic growth. In a policy sense Smith thus recommended that governments should take steps to eliminate legislative arrangements which impeded individual activity, such as the laws of succession and entail, on the ground that they were no longer relevant. In a similar vein, he called for the repeal of those regulations which established the privileges of corporations and regulated the system of apprenticeship: 'The statute of apprenticeship obstructs the free circulation of labour from one employment to another, even in the same place. The exclusive privileges of corporations obstruct it from one place to another, even in the same employment.'[36] Smith also commented on the problems presented by the Poor Laws and the Laws of Settlement and summarised his appeal to government in these terms:

> break down the exclusive privileges of corporations, and repeal the statute of apprenticeship, both which are real encroachments upon natural liberty, and add to these the repeal of the law of settlements, so that a poor workman, when thrown out of employment either in one trade or in one place, may seek for it in another trade or in another place, without the fear . . . of a prosecution.[37]

Smith also objected to positions of privilege, such as monopoly powers, on the ground that they were impolitic and unjust; unjust in that a monopoly position was one of privilege and advantage, and therefore: 'contrary to that justice and equality of treatment which the sovereign owes to all the different orders of his subjects',[38] impolitic in that the prices at which goods so controlled are sold are 'upon every occasion the highest that can be got' so that: 'The monopolists, by keeping the market constantly understocked, by never fully supplying the effectual demand, sell their commodities much above the natural price, and raise their emoluments, whether they consist in wages or profit, greatly above their natural rate.'[39] He added that monopoly is 'a great enemy to good management' and that it had the additional defect of restricting the flow of capital to the trades affected because of the legal barriers to entry which were involved.[40]

Finally, Smith's objection to monopoly in general may also be distinguished from his criticism of one expression of it; namely, the mercantile *system* which he described as the 'modern system' of policy, best understood 'in our own country and in our own times'.[41] Here Smith considered regulations which defined the trade relations between one country and another and which often reflected the state of animosity between them. In this context Smith examined a policy which sought to produce a net inflow of gold by means of such 'engines' as bounties on exportation, drawbacks, and controls over imports. But his main emphasis fell on one of the chief features of the system from a British point of view, the old colonial relationship with North America which was currently breaking up. Smith objected to any policy of control and restraint, because it artificially restricted the extent of the market and, therefore, the possibilities for further extension of the division of labour and economic growth. In particular Smith insisted that this pattern of infringement of liberty was liable to:

> that general objection which may be made to all the different expedients of the mercantile system; the objection of forcing . . . part of the industry of the country into a channel less advantageous than that in which it would run of its own accord.[42]

The belief that regulation will always distort the use of resources by breaking the 'natural balance of industry' dates back to Smith's days as a lecturer in Glasgow and represents his main criticism both of monopoly in general and its manifestation in mercantile policy as a whole. The general position is usefully summarised in the statement that:

> No regulation of commerce can increase the quantity of industry in any society beyond what its capital can maintain. It can only divert a part of it into a direction into which it might not otherwise have gone: and it is by no means certain that this artificial direction is likely to be more advantageous to the society than that into which it would have gone of its own accord.[43]

While many of Smith's specific objections to current policy did not distinguish between legislation and its actual implementation, none the less his recommendations amount to an impressive programme of reform designed to implement the 'obvious and simple' system of natural liberty. Yet it is the direction of change, as distinct from its complete success which was seen by him to be the most important. He was after all eminently realistic, and indeed criticised Quesnay for seeming to have implied that the economy 'would thrive and prosper only under a certain precise regimen of perfect liberty and perfect justice'. As Smith saw, 'If a nation could not prosper without the enjoyment of perfect liberty and perfect justice, there is not in the world a nation which could ever have prospered.'[44]

But even with existing restraints Smith's tone was optimistic, clearly believing that the drive to better our condition was capable of overcoming 'a hundred impertinent obstructions with which the folly of human laws too often encumbers its operations; though the

effect of these obstructions is always more or less to encroach upon its freedom, or diminish its security'.[45] At the same time Smith recognised that the type of economy in question was not without its problems, and drew attention to the need to regulate activities which might affect the general interest in a variety of ways. Hence for example he recommended regulation of the rate of interest, in such a way as to ensure that 'sober people are universally preferred, as borrowers, to prodigals and projectors', together with control over the small note issue.[46] Again in the name of the public interest he supported taxes on the retail sale of liquor to discourage the multiplication of alehouses, and differential taxes on beer and spirits in order to discourage the consumption of the latter. To take another example, Smith advocated higher taxes on those who demanded rent in kind, as a means of discouraging a practice which was injurious to the tenant.[47] Cases of this kind can be multiplied but are of greater importance because they illustrate two principles. First, Smith was prepared to interfere with activities which reflected imperfect knowledge on the part of the individual, while, secondly, he was prepared to control activities, such as the small note issue, where imperfect knowledge was not necessarily the problem. As he remarked by way of answer to those who objected to a proposal of the latter kind, 'The obligation of building party walls, in order to prevent the communication of fire, is a violation of natural liberty, exactly of the same kind with the regulations of the banking trade which are here proposed.'[48] Indeed Smith went further in stating a principle of potentially wide application: 'those exertions of the natural liberty of . . . individuals, which might endanger the security of the whole society, are, and ought to be, restrained by the laws of all governments; of the most free, as well as of the most despotical'.[49] He also added that the state should ensure the provision of public services, ranging from education to canals, harbours, bridges and roads—services which are: 'of such a nature, that the profit could never repay the expence to any individual, or small number of individuals, and which it therefore cannot be expected that any individual or small number of individuals should erect or maintain'.[50] Once more this criteria could be used to justify a very wide range of activities in that it supports intervention in cases of market failure.

Yet two points deserve notice by way of qualification. First it is evident that while Smith might defend the provision of a wide range of services, he always insisted that they should be organised in a way which recognised the facts of human nature, believing as he did in the value of incentive and in the proposition that 'Public services are never better performed than where their reward comes only in consequence of their being performed, and is proportioned to the diligence employed in performing them.'[51]

Secondly, it is appropriate to recall that the optimistic tone found in Smith's assessment of economic growth was qualified by his recognition of the 'oppressive inequality' of the modern state; of the influence exerted on governments by the 'clamourous importunity' of partial and especially mercantile interests,[52] and by that recognition of the social costs of the division of labour which dates back to his days as a lecturer in Glasgow. The mocking tone with which he sometimes treated the pursuit of wealth in the **Theory of Moral Sentiments** ('*place,* that great object which divides the wives of aldermen')[53] is matched only by his sympathy for the isolation of the individual who, finding himself in a large city or manufactory, finds himself also to be 'sunk in obscurity and darkness'.[54]

Notes

[All of the references to Smith's works listed below are cited from *The Glasgow Edition of the Works and Correspondence of Adam Smith,* 7 vols., edited by A.S. Skinner and others (Oxford: Clarendon Press, 1976-)].

[1] See especially, Book III.

[2] For comment, D. Winch *Adam Smith's Politics* (Cambridge, 1978).

[3] *WN, [Wealth of Nations]* V.i.f.50.

[4] *Corr., [Correspondence]* letter 150, David Hume to Adam Smith, 1 April 1776.

[5] *Corr.,* letter 151, Hugh Blair to Adam Smith, 3 April 1776.

[6] *Corr.,* letter 152, Joseph Black to Adam Smith, April 1776.

[7] *Corr.,* letter 153, William Robertson to Adam Smith, 8 April 1776.

[8] *Corr.,* letter 154, Adam Ferguson to Adam Smith, 18 April 1776.

[9] *Corr.,* 354, *A letter from Governor Pownall to Adam Smith.*

[10] *Corr.,* letter 150.

[11] *The Letters of David Hume,* ed. J.Y.T. Greig (Oxford, 1932), ii, 314.

[12] *Corr.,* letter 154.

[13] *WN,* I.ii.2.

[14] Ibid., I.vi.5.

[15] Ibid., II.i.12.

[16] Ibid., II.i.13-17.

[17] Ibid., II.iii.23.

[18] Ibid., II.i.19-22.

[19] Ibid., I.vii.4.

[20] Ibid., I.vii.8.

[21] Ibid., I.vii.15.

[22] Ibid., I.viii.11.

[23] Ibid., I.viii. 15. It should be emphasised that Smith believed wages would be above subsistence in progressive states (*WN,* I.viii.22f). He also anticipated the modern view that high rates of return encourage productivity (*WN,* I.viii.43, 44).

[24] Ibid., I.ix.4.

[25] Ibid., I.xi.a.1.

[26] Ibid., II.ii.2.

[27] Ibid., II.ii.5.

[28] Ibid., II.iii.2.

[29] Ibid., II.iii.32.

[30] Ibid., II.iii.28.

[31] Ibid., II.iii.18.

[32] Ibid., II.iii.17.

[33] See for example, ibid., I.ix.2, and I.ix.10.

[34] Ibid., I.xi.p.4.

[35] Ibid., II.iii.36.

[36] Ibid., I.x.c.42.

[37] Ibid., IV.ii.42.

[38] Ibid., IV.viii.30.

[39] Ibid., I.vii.26.

[40] Ibid., I.xi.b.5., I.vii.26.

[41] Ibid., IV.2.

[42] Ibid., IV.v.a.24.

[43] Ibid., IV.ii.3.

[44] Ibid., IV.ix.28.

[45] Ibid., IV.v.b.43.

[46] Ibid., II.iv.15. Jeremy Bentham objected to the policy of regulation on the ground that it was inconsistent with Smith's general position. See his *Defence of Usury* (1787). The 'letters' are printed in *Corr.*, 386-404.

[47] See in particular, Jacob Viner, 'Adam Smith and Laisser-Faire', in *Adam Smith 1776-1926, Lectures to Commemorate the Sesquicentennial of the Publication of the Wealth of Nations* (Chicago, 1928).

[48] *WN*, II.ii.94.

[49] Ibid.

[50] Ibid., V.i.c.i.

[51] Ibid., V.i.b.20.

[52] See, for example, *WN*, I.xi.p.10, and IV.ii.43.

[53] *TMS*, [*Theory of Moral Sentiments*] I.iii.2.8.

[54] *WN*, V.i.g.12.

D. D. Raphael (essay date 1985)

SOURCE: "Ethics," in *Adam Smith*, Oxford University Press, Oxford, 1985, pp. 29-45.

[*In the following excerpt, Raphael judges the strengths and weaknesses of Smith's theory of moral judgment.*]

The first chapter of the **Moral Sentiments** is entitled 'Of Sympathy'; the first chapter of the **Wealth of Nations** is entitled 'Of the Division of Labour'. In each case the title is a signal of what Smith thinks most fundamental. The main subject of the **Moral Sentiments** is the nature of moral judgement and Smith founds it on sympathy. The main subject of the **Wealth of Nations** is economic growth and Smith founds that on the division of labour.

SYMPATHY

It is a mistake to suppose, as a number of nineteenth-century commentators did, that Adam Smith's first book treats sympathy as the motive of moral action. The role of sympathy in his book is to explain the origin and the nature of moral judgement, of approval and disapproval. For this purpose he uses the word 'sympathy' in a somewhat unusual way to mean not just sharing the feelings of another, but being aware that one shares the feelings of another. As often happens when a philosopher takes a term of common usage and employs it in a special sense, he sometimes forgets his own prescription and slips back into the normal meaning, but in general Smith is clear enough about what he is doing.

He uses his notion of sympathy to explain two different kinds of moral judgement or approval. The first is a judgement about the 'propriety' of an action; in plain language, the judgement that an action is right or wrong. The second is a judgement about an action's merit or demerit, the judgement that it deserves praise or blame, reward or punishment. According to Smith, the feeling of approval which is expressed in a judgement of right or wrong is the result of sympathy with the agent's motive. We can illustrate what he means with a simple example. If I see Alma Goodheart help a lame old lady across the road, I 'sympathize' with her kindness and as a result I approve of it as the appropriate response. I would have responded in the same way if I had been in her shoes and so I must think her response reasonable and proper. I say that her action was the right thing to do. A further judgement that the action is praiseworthy expresses a second form of approval, which arises from sympathy with the old lady's feeling of gratitude. On the other hand, if I see Ira Grumpy kicking a cat that has got in his way, I feel antipathy to Ira's annoyance and sympathy with the cat's resentment. The antipathy produces disapproval of the action as wrong, and the sympathy with resentment produces an additional and different disapproving judgement of the action as blameworthy.

When Smith says that an average spectator (he actually says 'every spectator' but that is rhetoric) would sympathize with the kindness of someone like my Alma Goodheart, he means that if the spectator imagines himself in Alma's shoes, he finds that he too would want to help the old lady; he observes a correspondence between the feeling, the prompting to action, which he would have and that which Alma evidently has. Likewise the spectator's 'sympathy' with the old lady's gratitude is a perception that, if he were in the old lady's situation and were helped, he would have the same feeling of gratitude that the old lady has. Antipathy towards an Ira Grumpy is an awareness, when you imagine yourself in his place, that you would not feel the same annoyance with the cat as he does. It will be seen that Smith's concept of sympathy is linked with the exercise of imagination. The sympathy that causes approval or disapproval is not necessarily awareness of an actual feeling which reproduces here and now the motives of those who act or the reactions of those whom the action affects. It is the thought of a feeling which you would have if you were in their shoes, an awareness that comes from imagining yourself in the situations of those who are actually involved.

The two judgements of approval that arise from sympathy are clearly rational, in Smith's view. A spectator who finds that the feelings of those involved correspond to what his own would be, must regard those feelings as appropriate to the situation.

> The man who resents the injuries that have been done to me, and observes that I resent them precisely as he does, necessarily approves of my resentment. The man whose sympathy keeps time to my grief, cannot but admit the reasonableness of my sorrow. He who admires the same poem, or the same picture, and admires them exactly as I do, must surely allow the justness of my admiration.

Sympathy creates a social bond. This is plainly true of sympathy in its most common meaning of compassion; when one feels compassion for the sorrow or the need of another, one is moved to give comfort or help. Sympathy of this kind, serving as a motive of action, promotes a sense of responsibility to share the burdens of others. Sympathy in Adam Smith's sense is a socializing agent in a different way. Everyone, or nearly everyone, is pleased with the approval of others and uncomfortable with disapproval. I learn from experience that spectators approve when my feelings and reactions correspond to the feelings and reactions which they would have in my situation. If my natural reactions differ from the common norm, I shall meet with disapproval. So I have an inducement to conform, in order to win approval. If, for example, my natural reaction to sorrow or to injury is more vigorous than that of the average spectator, I am taught by his lack of approval to try to tone it down in future.

Such differences in sentiment between the observer and the person observed may arise from differences in the natural constitution of particular individuals. They are, however, also inherent in the process of imaginative sympathy. For all that the imagination allows us, in a sense, to identify ourselves with other people, imagining is not the same as actually experiencing, and the reproduction of feeling cannot match up to the original.

> The person principally concerned is sensible of this, and at the same time passionately desires a more complete sympathy. . . . But he can only hope to obtain this by lowering his passion to that pitch, in which the spectators are capable of going along with him. . . . What they feel, will, indeed, always be, in some respects, different from what he feels . . . These two sentiments, however, may, it is evident, have such a correspondence with one another, as is sufficient for the harmony of society. Though they will never be unisons, they may be concords, and this is all that is wanted or required.

The spectator for his part is also aware that his feelings must fall short of those experienced by 'the person principally concerned'. The spectator too is influenced by the socializing tendencies of sympathy; he too would like to see a more complete concordance of feelings. So he strives to heighten his reaction by a closer identification, trying to take into his imaginative leap all the little details that make an experience more poignant.

These two efforts, on the one side to damp down the violence of experienced feeling, on the other to enliven the weakness of imagined reproduction, produce two different kinds of virtue, the virtue of self-command and the virtue of 'indulgent humanity' or sensibility. Smith's own ethical doctrine (as contrasted with his contribution to ethical theory) emphasized the value of self-command. It was at the forefront, of Stoic ethics, which had impressed him deeply in his early years, especially from his reading of Epictetus. Epictetus was a Greek slave in the time of the Roman Empire, who became emancipated but whose earlier period of slavery had taught him to face the harsh burdens of life with fortitude, with what we would now call the 'stoic' virtue of resignation. One can see from the ***Moral Sentiments*** that Adam Smith was fascinated by Stoic ethics, although he came to see that certain features of the Stoic doctrine were unacceptable. Even so, his own code of ethics is more Stoic than Christian. He thought of himself as putting the two together. 'As to love our neighbour as we love ourselves is the great law of Christianity, so it is the great precept of nature to love ourselves only as we love our neighbour, or what comes to the same thing, as our neighbour is capable of loving us'.

THE IMPARTIAL SPECTATOR

So far I have been dealing with Smith's theory of the moral judgements which we make as spectators of the behaviour and character of other people. What of judgements about ourselves? Smith's answer to this question constitutes the most original and the subtlest part of his ethical theory. According to Smith, I approve or disapprove of my own actions by imagining myself in the shoes of a spectator. Let us go back to my earlier example of judging another person's action to be wrong. Suppose that I, like Ira Grumpy, were annoyed by a cat and were tempted to kick it, but said to myself 'No, that would be wrong.' Smith thinks that my moral disapproval is the result of the disapproval of spectators. I know that most people disapprove of such actions. Obviously they would disapprove of me just as much as they disapprove of Ira Grumpy. If I were somebody else and looked at myself kicking the cat, I should feel the same antipathy as I feel towards Ira. The judgements of conscience, moral judgements about one's own actions, are in the first instance a reflection of the judgements of society. Smith himself uses the image of a mirror.

> Were it possible that a human creature could grow up to manhood in some solitary place, without any communication with his own species, he could no more think of his own character, of the propriety or demerit of his own sentiments and conduct, of the beauty or deformity of his own mind, than of the beauty or deformity of his own face. All these are objects which he cannot easily see . . . and with regard to which he is provided with no mirror which can present them to his view. Bring him into society, and he is immediately provided with the mirror which he wanted before.

> We suppose ourselves the spectators of our own behaviour, and endeavour to imagine what effect it would, in this light, produce upon us. This is the only looking-glass by which we can, in some measure, with the eyes of other people, scrutinize the propriety of our own conduct.

If Smith had stopped there, his theory would be too simple. Spectators can make mistakes; they may be unaware of some of the facts or may misunderstand motives. A man's conscience sometimes tells him that he must go against popular sentiment. This, Smith thinks, is because he is in a better position than spectators to know the relevant facts. Of course, he too may misinterpret facts from partiality to his own interest, and this is why he should try to look at them in the guise of an impartial spectator. In order to avoid self-deceit we must try to see 'ourselves in the light in which others see us, or in which they would see us if they knew all'. It remains true, however, that we may think the judgement of actual spectators to be misguided through ignorance of some of the relevant facts. Even so, says Smith, we reach our moral judgement by imagining ourselves as an ideal impartial spectator, a spectator who knows all the relevant facts but is not personally involved. If we find that this imagined impartial spectator, 'the man within the breast', would sympathize with what we plan to do, or with what we have done, that causes us to approve. If the impartial spectator does not sympathize, we disapprove.

The late Professor A. L. Macfie observed [in *The Individual in Society,* 1967] that Robert Burns, who knew and valued *The Theory of Moral Sentiments,* probably had in mind Smith's phrase, 'if we saw ourselves as others see us', when he wrote

> O wad some Pow'r the giftie gie us
> To see oursels as others see us.

The touch of religious language in that couplet is also to be found in Smith's account of the impartial spectator. Smith most commonly writes of 'nature' as the source of our moral and other capacities but at times he is prepared to use theological language.

> The all-wise Author of Nature has, in this manner, taught man to respect the sentiments and judgments of his brethren . . . He has made man, if I may say so, the immediate judge of mankind; and has, in this respect, as in many others, created him after his own image, and appointed him his vicegerent upon earth, to superintend the behaviour of his brethren.

The association with biblical ideas and phrases does not mean that Smith has abandoned explanation in terms of human nature, what we nowadays call empirical psychology. There is a fair amount of evidence, including some in the *Moral Sentiments* itself, that he had reservations about accepting Christianity, though he did not carry religious scepticism as far as Hume did. Smith was probably a deist. Like a number of other thinkers of the Enlightenment, he considered that observable nature afforded sufficient reason for believing in the existence of God. Smith's account of natural processes can be read as a would-be scientific enterprise, with no need for an underpinning from theology. In his ethics, as in his economics, scientific explanation was what he was after. However, both for Smith himself and for most of his readers an account of natural process was more persuasive, as well as more vivid, if nature were personified or treated as the work of a personal God. The metaphor of legal language, when he speaks of man as the judge of mankind, serves the same purpose. Sympathy and antipathy, with consequent approval and disapproval, take place as a matter of course. Spectators do not set themselves up to imitate earthly judges in courts of law, still less to imitate a heavenly judge. But the effect of their behaviour is analogous to that of intentional judges. Its significance is brought out by the comparison with judges and by the traditional language about God.

In the same spirit Smith is ready to say that the general rules of morality are 'justly' regarded as laws of God. They come to us from experience. Having found that our sympathy and consequent approbation tend to be directed upon the same sort of object on different occasions, we generalize our experience into rules or principles: for example, that it is right to help people in need, wrong to harm those who have intended no harm to us, right to reward the beneficent and to punish the evil-doer. It is equally natural for men to ascribe to their gods those feelings which matter most for the conduct of human life; since moral rules resemble laws, they are treated as divine laws attended by divine sanctions. The natural tendency is refined and confirmed by 'philosophical researches', which lead to monotheistic belief and which also observe 'badges of authority' in moral judgement; these badges or marks of authority are signs that moral judgement was intended by God to direct our lives. The last part of this argument echoes an earlier moralist of the eighteenth century, Bishop Butler, who influenced the mature thought of Smith's teacher, Hutcheson.

SMITH'S MORAL PSYCHOLOGY

Smith's theory is primarily an explanation of the origin of moral judgement, something that nowadays would be assigned to psychology rather than philosophy. The eighteenth century did not distinguish between the two disciplines, and for Adam Smith, as for Hume, psychological explanation was the most fruitful method of dealing with philosophical problems. In consequence Smith's theory about the psychology of moral judgement tended to determine his views on the philosophical problem of the standard of right action. The problem is to find a principle or set of principles for deciding what is the right thing to do. One answer that has immediate attractions is the view of utilitarianism: the proper standard is maximum promotion of the general happiness. Utilitarianism received its name from Jeremy Bentham but its substance was prominent enough earlier in the eighteenth century, and Adam Smith was well aware of its appeal. He was prepared to allow that moral actions do in fact tend, as a whole, to promote the general happiness, and that this is the end intended by God, but he opposed the view that utility is the one and only standard of right action. In practice, he argued, the thought of utility has a subordinate role in the formation of moral judgement. Our approval arises first from sympathy with the motive of the agent and secondly from sympathy with the gratitude of the beneficiary. Thirdly it receives added support from noting that the action conforms to the general rules of morality (which in fact, as he has explained, have their origin in the two kinds of sympathy). Then fourthly it may gain further confirmation from the pleasure which attends the thought of utility. According to Smith, the last consideration is also the least in its contribution to the final judgement of approval.

Smith's objection to utilitarianism is that we do not in practice decide what is right by reference to utility. Now if the problem of the standard of ethics were one of positive psychology, finding out how we do in fact reach our decisions, the objection would be conclusive. But the problem is a normative one; it is concerned with the question 'How *should* we decide?' Smith would still say, however, that the answer is to be gleaned from actual practice. Even if social utility is the ultimate end, nature achieves that end through the workings of sympathy. Defending his view that the concept of ill desert depends on sympathy with resent-

ment, Smith writes:

> . . . the present inquiry is not concerning a matter of right, if I may say so, but concerning a matter of fact. We are not at present examining upon what principles a perfect being would approve of the punishment of bad actions; but upon what principles so weak and imperfect a creature as man actually and in fact approves of it. . . . Though man . . . be naturally endowed with a desire of the welfare and preservation of society, yet the Author of nature has not entrusted it to his reason to find out that a certain application of punishments is the proper means of attaining this end; but has endowed him with an immediate and instinctive approbation of that very application which is most proper to attain it. The economy of nature is in this respect exactly of a piece with what it is upon many other occasions.

The trouble with Smith's method of distinguishing between right and fact is that it ignores the practical problems which often face imperfect men in reaching moral decisions. In a dilemma, with the need to choose between competing goods (or evils), 'immediate and instinctive approbation' fails us. It is then that we want to ask the normative question 'How *should* we decide?'

If you were to ask Smith what is the standard of moral judgement, the criterion whereby you can decide what you ought to do, Smith would say it is the approval of the impartial spectator. That, however, will only tell you whether or not the impartial spectator has the same attitude to a proposed action as you have yourself. If your attitude is hesitation between conflicting goods, each of them affording some valid ground for choice, it does not help to know that the impartial spectator sympathizes. The function of the impartial spectator is to enable you to be impartial; if your initial inclination if affected by partiality, by a concern for your own personal interest, the impartial spectator will help you to take a more objective view. If, however, you have rid yourself of partiality but are still unclear about the respective merits of competing alternatives, the impartial spectator cannot help.

Nevertheless, as a psychological account of the origin of conscience the theory of the impartial spectator is impressive, especially in linking the moral judgements of the individual with those of society. The first stage of Smith's theory, his account of the approval of actual spectators, has a weakness. He says that the approval of a spectator is the result of awareness that he would share the agent's feelings if he were in the same situation. This does not distinguish between moral and other kinds of approval. When introducing his theory that approval depends on sympathy (in the sense of observation of correspondence), Smith himself gives a variety of examples to show that a judgement of propriety need not be a moral judgement.

> The man whose sympathy keeps time to my grief,
> cannot but admit the reasonableness of my sorrow.
> He who admires the same poem, or the same picture,
> and admires them exactly as I do, must surely allow
> the justness of my admiration. He who laughs at the
> same joke, and laughs along with me, cannot well
> deny the propriety of my laughter. . . . If the same
> arguments which convince you convince me
> likewise, I necessarily approve of your conviction.

Sympathy, the recognition of a correspondence, either
of feelings or of opinions, produces approval. But what
determines whether the approval, the judgement of
propriety, is moral as contrasted with aesthetic or intellectual? Smith would say that moral approbation
expresses sympathy with motives, but this seems too
wide. Suppose I go to a concert from a desire to hear
the music on the programme. A spectator who shares
my tastes will approve of my action and its motive.
Yet it would be distinctly odd to call his approbation
moral.

However, this weakness in Smith's explanation of the
judgement of propriety does not affect the value of his
most important contribution to ethical theory, his concept of the impartial spectator. The approval of the
imagined impartial spectator does indeed depend on
Smith's earlier account of approval by actual spectators, so that it could apply to nonmoral as well as
moral approval; but this does not matter. Anyone who
was bothered that his aesthetic tastes or his ambitions
were unduly subjective could consult the judgement of
an imagined impartial spectator. In practice such wor-
ries are concentrated upon moral issues, when we speak
of an exercise of conscience. Even though Smith's
concept of the impartial spectator could cover more
than conscience, it can still be valuable as a psychological explanation of the latter.

Smith's explanation of the origin of conscience is in
principle similar to that of Freud. Straightforward moral
judgements about our own actions, according to Smith,
are built up in the mind as a reflection of the attitudes
of society, mediated especially in childhood through
the influence of parents, teachers, and schoolfellows.
The built-up set of attitudes in the mind acts as a second self passing judgement on the plans or actions of
the natural self.

> When I endeavour to examine my own conduct,
> when I endeavour to pass sentence upon it, and
> either to approve or condemn it, it is evident that,
> in all such cases, I divide myself, as it were, into
> two persons . . . The first is the spectator, whose
> sentiments with regard to my own conduct I
> endeavour to enter into, by placing myself in his
> situation, and by considering how it would appear
> to me, when seen from that particular point of view.
> The second is the agent, the person whom I properly
> call myself, and of whose conduct, under the
> character of a spectator, I was endeavouring to form

some opinion.

Freud writes of a super-ego, a second self built up in
the mind as a reflection, largely, of the attitude of
parents, acquiring the function of a censor to pass
judgement on the desires and actions of the natural
self.

There are significant differences between the two theories. First, Freud places particular emphasis on the
influence of parental attitudes, while Smith thinks more
broadly of social norms and mentions teachers and
schoolfellows as well as parents in inculcating these
norms into the child. Secondly, Freud's super-ego seems
to do much more in the way of disapproval than of
positive approval. It includes an uplifting 'ego ideal'
as well as a repressive 'conscience', but Freud emphasizes the latter element. The primary role of the super-
ego is that of a censor, inhibiting the exuberance of
sexual and associated impulses. Smith thinks of the
impartial spectator as being there both to approve and
to disapprove. There is no perceptible leaning to one
side or the other. Thirdly, Smith adds the vital qualification that 'the man within the breast' can be a superior judge to 'the man without' in being better informed about facts and motives.

Psychoanalysts presumably find Freud's theory useful
in their medical practice. One can well understand that
certain types of neurosis are connected with an excessive sense of inhibition and that this is often the effect
of an excessively censorious parent in childhood. If,
however, Freud's theory is generalized and taken to be
an explanation of the conscience of most normal people, then it seems less satisfactory than the explanation
given by Adam Smith. Parents are no doubt the major
influence in the moral education of children during
their earliest years, but teachers and fellow-pupils, and
then friends and fellow-workers, all have a part to play
later on. A repressive family background can produce
a rigid, censorious conscience, more inclined to 'don't'
than 'do'; but an affectionate background at home and
at school results in a more liberal conscience, encouraging both the development of self and a concern for
others.

What of the third difference between Smith and Freud,
Smith's readiness to make conscience a 'superior tribunal' to the judgement of actual spectators? Having
had our eyes opened by Freud and others to the dark
recesses of the unconscious, we may be inclined to
treat Smith's view as a typical piece of eigheenth-cen-
tury optimism, blind to the prevalence of self-deceit.
That, however, is too simple-minded. Smith knew
nothing of explicit theories of the unconscious but he
was well aware of the strength of self-deceit.

> This self-deceit, this fatal weakness of mankind, is
> the source of half the disorders of human life. If we

saw ourselves in the light in which others see us, or in which they would see us if they knew all, a reformation would generally be unavoidable. We could not otherwise endure the sight.

Hence the need for the impartial spectator, to see ourselves as others see us—or rather, as 'they would see us if they knew all'. We do sometimes think that our own conscience is a better judge than popular opinion, and because of this it is a generally approved maxim that in such circumstances a person ought to follow the dictate of his own conscience. Smith tries to accommodate in his theory the facts of real life.

I have confined this account of Smith's ethics to his theory of moral judgement because that is the main topic of his first book and by far his most important contribution to moral philosophy. *The Theory of Moral Sentiments* has a good deal to say also about cardinal virtues. The earlier version of the book gave some prominence to the distinction between justice and beneficence, treating justice as primarily a negative virtue of avoiding harm to others, and beneficence as the positive virtue of doing them good. It balanced the Christian virtue of love, as the motive of beneficence, with the Stoic virtue of self-command, and it regarded prudence or rational self-interest as a proper object of approval, though not of warm admiration. The enlarged version of the book, put together some years after the publication of the *Wealth of Nations,* gives more prominence to prudence and also adds a little to the emphasis on self-command. This aspect of the *Moral Sentiments* invites comparison with the psychology underlying the *Wealth of Nations*. . . . The *Moral Sentiments* itself, however, has suffered from the preoccupation of scholars with these comparisons. It has been misunderstood, and its primary aim, as a work of moral philosophy, has been neglected.

Kenneth Lux (essay date 1990)

SOURCE: "The Mistake," in *Adam Smith's Mistake: How a Moral Philosopher Invented Economics & Ended Morality,* Shambhala, 1990, pp. 80-93.

[*In the following excerpt, Lux faults Smith's thesis (in* The Wealth of Nations) *that human self-interest is solely responsible for the economic well-being of the public, arguing that this theory fails to take into account the possibility of dishonesty and cheating on the part of economic actors.*]

The central statement of Adam Smith's *Wealth of Nations*—for history, and certainly for economics—is that which affirms the value of self-interest: "It is not from the benevolence of the butcher, the brewer, or the baker, that we expect our dinner, but from their regard to their own self interest." The lines that follow this "butcher-baker" statement are often quoted as well: "We address ourselves, not to their humanity but to their self-love, and never talk to them of our own necessities but of their advantages. Nobody but a beggar chooses to depend chiefly upon the benevolence of his fellow citizens."[1]

In this famous passage Smith seems to be telling us that, within the range of human motives, those in the category of *self-interest,* and not those classed as *benevolence,* are chiefly responsible for our being adequately supplied with provisions for living and the other goods and services that an economy should provide. Economists often debate what, exactly, self-interest means: is it selfishness or something different, perhaps more enlightened? In a while we will give further attention to this debate. But let us first recall that when Smith's predecessors, such as Richard Cumberland and Francis Hutcheson, divided the middle range of human motivation into two categories they were quite clearly talking about "moral sentiments" on the one hand and selfishness on the other. Smith himself takes this division as the starting point of his refutation of selfishness in the opening lines of his *Theory of Moral Sentiments:* "How selfish so ever man may be supposed, there are evidently some principles in his nature, which interest him in the fortune of others, and render their happiness necessary to him, though he derives nothing from it, except the pleasure of seeing it."[2]

With the quickening eclipse of the influence of religion in the eighteenth century, social writers and moral philosophers were constantly occupied with the question of how society could continue to be held together without the traditional guidance of religious teachings. Many even wondered whether society *was* being held together. Smith himself, in the passage quoted from his *Wealth of Nations,* could hardly make it clearer that by *self-interest* he means a concern with the self to the exclusion of a concern with the other: "We address ourselves not to their humanity but to their self-love. . . ."

Indeed, what makes this passage so striking, and what has given it its claim on the modern imagination, is its shock value. Certainly this was true in Smith's day, when the traditional religious conception of morality was still closely adhered to. That which had traditionally been seen as a bad thing—selfishness or self-interest—was advanced by Smith as a good thing, a social benefit. It is not the traditional social benefit of benevolence, says Smith, that nourishes us and sustains us (and note the same linguistic root in *benevolence* and *benefit*), but its essential opposite—selfishness. What a startling revelation was offered to the world in Adam Smith's impressive and distinguished tome!

We now come very close to the point of being able to discern Adam Smith's mistake. It is brought into view when we ask a question of the self-interest passage that is usually not asked: According to Smith's own logic, what would an economy look like if in fact benevolence were the determining motive?

Adam Smith is telling us that the economy in his day, and by extension in our own, is guided by self-interest and not benevolence. How do we know this to be correct? Is Smith a master psychologist capable of probing the minds of people and observing their motives? Perhaps this is the case; Smith has been praised for his keen psychological insight. But Smith's passage seems to carry a definitiveness that precludes any further discussion as to the motives of economic actors in the marketplace. The power of its conviction does not seem to reside so much in its psychology as in its logic. We can see how this is accomplished in the passage when we answer the question that we have posed to it.

An economy based on benevolence would be quite different from our own, as Smith tells us. What, then, would it look like? How would generosity, kindness, and so on translate into the economic sphere? Smith, in his passage, gives us the answer most directly and categorically. In his terms, for benevolence to be operative in the economic sphere, goods would have to be given away, for free. If people have to pay for what they receive then this means self-interest and not benevolence is operating on the part of the butcher, the baker. It is only the beggar (one who is without means of payment) who depends on benevolence. The "appeal" to the self-interest of the butcher and baker that Smith refers to is precisely the exchange of money for their goods. To appeal to their benevolence would be to ask them to give away their goods without exchange—as a free offering.

So we find that Smith is telling us in this passage that in any economy based on exchange—which certainly includes any market economy, and perhaps *any* modern economy—it is only self-interest operating and not benevolence. Thus we can see that, knowingly or not, Smith is being categorical; his logic lies beyond psychological probing, questioning of motives, or any other empirical argument. That is why his passage carries such conviction and power—and why it has been one of the transforming forces in shaping the modern mind and the modern world.

We now are ready to see Smith's mistake. It becomes clear when we go to the second part of his thesis, which says that self-interest, rather than benevolence, promotes the social good and that, in fact, self-interest is *more* effective in promoting the social good than benevolence. Herein lies the big surprise revealed by political economy: the economic actor "intends only his own gain, and he is in this, as in many other cases, led by an invisible hand to promote an end which was

no part of his intention. Nor is it always the worse for the society that it was no part of it. By pursuing his own interest he frequently promotes that of the society more effectually than when he really intends to promote it."[3] But here is a problem, a deep problem indeed, and one that goes to the heart of the matter. For we can ask, what about honesty?

If the butcher or baker can cheat us (say by using short weights on his scale), and he can get away with it, isn't it in his self-interest to do so? The answer must be yes. There is nothing in self-interest that rules out cheating, especially if one is good at it. It is not self-interest that prevents someone from cheating. Self-interest only dictates that they not get caught. As we have seen, history is full of accounts of people deceiving, defrauding, coercing, and essentially stealing from others in their economic dealings. And we only know about those who were caught. Even among them, some have been seen as heroes; they did quite well, with their penalties hardly matching the gains of their crimes. In fact, we will see that economists came to conclude that from the standpoint of self-interest it would be *irrational* for someone *not* to cheat if they could be reasonably sure of getting away with it. "Honesty is the best policy" is not an economic doctrine.

Smith himself, throughout his second book, gives many acute descriptions of these tendencies on the part of entrepreneurial economic actors, and he doesn't mince any words about it. For example, in discussing merchants and dealers, he says it is they "who have generally an interest to deceive and even to oppress the public, and who accordingly have upon many occasions, both deceived and oppressed it."[4]

Smith's forthright talk of businessmen cheating and oppressing the public seems to stand in direct contradiction to his advocacy of self-interest as the sole principle necessary for the achievement of the public good. The saving grace was supposed to be the "invisible hand" of competition. It was competition that would keep these instincts and "expensive vanities" of the merchants, dealers, and landlords in line. Smith would hardly have been surprised at the motives of Rockefeller, but he certainly would have been chagrined at his success. Smith had essentially overlooked the possibility that self-interest would work to undermine and eliminate competition and thus to tie up the invisible hand. It is this outcome of unrestrained self-interest that is the fundamental flaw in any absolute policy of laissez-faire. This was not even adequately recognized by the early advocates of antitrust. When Senator Sherman spoke on behalf of the first antitrust legislation, he said, "The law of selfishness, uncontrolled by competition, compels it to disregard the interest of the consumer." Implicit in Sherman's statement, but seemingly not recognized by him, is the deduction that the law of selfishness also compels it to eliminate competition. For competition to continue to exist as a restraint on the rapacity of self-interest, it would have to be supported by a force or principle other than economic self-interest.

As we have seen, when taken by itself, self-interest naturally leads to cheating and dishonesty. The example of the merchant who cheats the consumer illustrates the problem of self-interest in the interpersonal or social context. But "cheating" also occurs in relation to the physical and natural context—the environment. For the principle of self-interest dictates that the individual seek self-benefit by imposing costs on the natural environment. From the Industrial Revolution and continuing down into the present, self-interest has produced pollution, depletion, and the progressive destruction of the natural world. The evidence begins with the foul streets, sewers, and air of Adam Smith's London and extends to the acid rain, ozone depletion, and "greenhouse effect" of today.

Now, approximately two hundred years after *The Wealth of Nations,* society is just beginning to recognize the destructive consequences of economic self-interest; however, it does not as easily recognize that this state of affairs is implicitly supported by economic theory in its pure Smithian form. For example, in *The Economic Way of Thinking,* Paul Heyne tells us that we don't really *need* such a thing as clean water, because there really are no needs; there are only *wants,* and these are backed up by purchasing power, or *demand.* Demand can always find substitutes, says the economist, for there are "substitutes everywhere." "Who needs water?" Heyne asks. He explains: "People are creatures of habit, in what they think as well as what they do. Perhaps this also explains why so many have trouble recognizing the significance of substitutes and hence such difficulty in appreciating the law of demand. Water provides an excellent example." Heyne goes on to say that "we have confused the issue for ourselves by identifying pollution with environmental damage."[5] So pollution is not environmental damage after all?

What then is pollution? Simply a disagreement over property rights, the economist tells us. Again Heyne: "Pollution exists when people's expectations about what they can and may do come into conflict. Pollution is eliminated when disagreements about property rights are resolved—when those who formerly protested the actions of others consent to those actions."[6] In other words, pollution is not an objective reality. It is only a question of protest on the part of some about what others are doing. In the economist's world of self-interest, all is indeed self, including the environment; there is nothing objective. If the price system can be adjusted so that those who are unhappy about what they believe to be pollution can be paid enough to

keep them quiet, then the so-called pollution will disappear. Following this logic, we can presume that at some point the polluter would find it too expensive to pollute and would therefore cut down on environmentally destructive acts. This assumes, of course, that there really is an environment separate from the self, a fact that economic theory fundamentally seems to deny, as we have just seen.

Heyne concludes: "There may be no more important lesson for us to learn about pollution than that pollution so thoroughly permeates our society that we cannot realistically hope to eliminate it. Pollution exists when teenagers play their transistor radios and thereby infringe on the right of other bus passengers to enjoy peace and quiet; pollution still exists, though in a changed form, when the other bus passengers infringe on the teenagers' right to hear music by enforcing their own desire for peace and quiet."[7] So from the standpoint of economic theory, peace and quiet is pollution for the teenager. And so it goes. Logically, then, pollution must be a constant. Thus we should not be surprised to find that in forums held to discuss the problems facing the natural environment, economists are generally the most resistant to proposed solutions. For example, in a 1988 discussion of the consequences of the warming of the earth as a result of the greenhouse effect, environmental and resource scientists sounded the alarm. Irving R. Mintzer of the World Resources Institute warned, "We are talking about changing the entire fabric of nature." The economist quoted in this discussion, however—a professor at Carnegie-Mellon—is the voice of doing less rather than more: "There is no way to justify spending tens of billions of dollars a year to prevent the greenhouse effect."[8] The economist had studied the law of demand and knew the "real values" involved. More accurately, he or she knew that there are no real values, just as there is nothing objective; there is only personal demand.

Smith's doctrine of self-interest is quite a remarkable one. The celebrated critical economist Joan Robinson is succinct and incisive in this regard: "This is an ideology to end ideologies, for it has abolished the moral problem. It is only necessary for each individual to act egotistically for the good of all to be attained."[9] And there we have the essence of Adam Smith's mistake.

Our review of several periods of history has shown that the good of all is not attained by pure self-interest or egoism. There must be another principle operating in people, a principle that moderates self-interest in favor of the general good. We indicated above that a sense of honesty could be one such moderating tendency. Honesty follows a standard that is outside of self-interest, and this is precisely the definition of morality. Other such principles are fairness, integrity, reasonableness, and a sense of justice.

As a matter of fact, it is according to Smith himself that justice is necessary for the good to be attained. He says this at a point in his book that is far removed from the butcher-baker statement, which occurs on page 14 of the Cannan edition of Smith's work. On page 651, Smith reviews his "obvious and simple system of natural liberty," which is the central idea of his entire text. In fact, his call for liberty, or freedom from the restraints of a mercantile and aristocratic ruling system, and for the just treatment of the working person still rings down through the centuries. It is this call that aligns Smith with the liberty that the American nation was pursuing, coincidentally, in the same year as the publication of his book. Smith says, "Every man, as long as he does not violate the laws of justice, is left perfectly free to pursue his own interests in his own way, and to bring both his industry and capital into competition with those of any other man, or order of men." *As long as he does not violate the laws of justice.* This qualification is critical, yet it is missing from his earlier statement, which has become the hallmark statement for economics and for the place of self-interest in the modern world.

While a respect for justice is not necessarily equivalent to benevolence, it is certainly *closer* to benevolence than to self-interest, and that is why Smith counterbalances self-interest with justice in the grand concluding statement quoted above. Although, in his earlier work, *The Theory of Moral Sentiments,* Smith draws a fine distinction between justice and "beneficence," he clearly classifies both as "the virtues."[10]

We turn now to a final elucidation of the butcher-baker statement. Adam Smith made a mistake. He said, "It is not from the benevolence of the butcher, the brewer, or the baker that we expect our dinner, but from their regard to their own interest." We should now be able to see that Adam Smith left out just one little word—a word which has made a world of difference. And if this mistake is not corrected, then the absence of that word could threaten to unmake a world. That word is *only.* What Adam Smith ought to have said was, "It is not *only* from the benevolence. . . .";￼ then everything would have been all right.

I said before that we would eventually view the butcher-baker statement in an even larger context, and now is the time to do this, because in so doing we will find intriguing confirmation for our account of Adam Smith's mistake. For it turns out that four sentences before this statement we find the missing *only.* Smith, in attempting to explain the origin of the division of labor, contrasts the behavior of animals with that of humans. Animals, he says, are largely independent and have little need for the assistance of other animals. But man, on the other hand,

has almost constant occasion for the help of his

brethren, and it is in vain for him to expect it from their benevolence *only.* He will be more likely to prevail if he can interest their self-love in his favor, and shew them that it is for their own advantage to do for him what he requires of them. Whoever offers to another a bargain of any kind, proposes to do this. Give me that which I want, and you shall have this which you want, is the meaning of every such offer; and it is in this manner that we obtain from one another the far greater part of those good offices which we stand in need of. It is not from the benevolence of the butcher, the brewer, or the baker, that we expect our dinner, but from their regard to their own interest. (italics added)

Of course, we don't mean to imply that Smith *intended* to insert the word *only* before *benevolence,* and that he mistakenly left it out. He intended it to be just the way it is; but in his intention he made a mistake. And what is so fascinating about this analysis of his text is that we can see how close he was to putting it differently. He almost might have said that self-interest wasn't everything, that some measure of benevolence was also needed for society to be benefited. But in the end, and just at the margin of his thought, he made the fateful decision to write on behalf of self-interest to the exclusion of benevolence. What contributed to this, as we have pointed out, is that Smith saw benevolence as operating only in the donation of free gifts or charity, and he did not realize that it also needed to play a part in exchange as well—in the form of honesty, integrity, or fairness. The significance of the omission of *only* in the butcher-baker sentence is clear when we remember that this statement became the basis of the counsel of self-interest in respectable and academic thought.

As we have just seen, Smith's sanctioning of self-interest without any qualifying or restraining force completely eliminated the moral problem in human action. Morality is always a matter of choosing, and situations of moral relevance always involve conflict of interest. One has to choose between the interests of "rightness" (which can be taken to mean honesty, justice, fairness, the concerns of the other, the public, society) and the interests of the self in disregard of rightness. The nature of the latter choice was rather clearly expressed in the now immortal words of John Pierpont Morgan: "I owe the public nothing." Smith's statement equating the pursuit of the interests of the self with the public good completely eliminated the need for choice: Just do what's good for you alone, and the good for all will be attained. There is no more moral problem because there is no conflict of interest. There is only one interest, and that is self-interest.

It is quite striking, and still another confirmation of our analysis of Smith's mistake, to find in the famous "invisible hand" passage almost the same conceptual and moral slippage. In this passage, which appears on page 423, Smith says that the individual

> intends only his own gain, and he is in this, as in many other cases, led by an invisible hand to promote an end which was no part of his intention. Nor is it always the worse for the society that it was no part of it. By pursuing his own interest he frequently promotes that of the society more effectually than when he really intends to promote it. I have never known much good done by those who affected to trade for the public good. It is an affectation indeed, not very common among merchants, and very few words need be employed in dissuading them from it.

Smith states that in the pursuit of self-interest the individual is "led by an invisible hand" to promote the social good, although that is no part of his intention. Furthermore, by pursuing self-interest he will be more likely to promote the social good than if he intentionally sets out to do so. It should be noted how truly remarkable this statement is. Smith would seem to be telling us that if we want to find people who will best promote the public good, we should choose those who are essentially pursuing their own interest. Before the reader has been given the opportunity to realize just how strange this statement is, Smith goes on to say, "I have never known much good done by those who affected to trade for the public good. It is an affectation, indeed, not very common among merchants, and very few words need be employed in dissuading them from it."

We immediately appreciate Smith's dry wit when he says that "very few words" are needed to dissuade the merchant from trading for the public good. It thus appears that Smith is referring to the hypocrisy, perhaps thinly veiled, of those who pretend to trade for the public good. So, the whole passage might then be taken as an ironic invective against such hypocrisy, and we can understand Smith as saying that one who honestly pursues his own self-interest does a lot better for society, or at least does it no harm, than one who deceptively claims to be pursuing the public good. Well and good, and we accept this caution against the ill effects of hypocritical claims in the public interest. But in the previous phrase Smith refers to those who "*really* intend" to promote the public good. Well, if these people really intend to do so, they cannot be the same hypocritical persons that Smith then seems to refer to. Therefore, Smith's adjective *really* is misused and misleading. To be consistent Smith would have had to have said something like, "those who *apparently* intend to promote the public good." To say it as he did leaves the whole passage as a contradiction, and as a remarkable condemnation of truly benevolent intentions.

In both the butcher-baker statement and the invisible hand passage we see that Smith came within a hair's breadth of not slipping into a philosophy of moral failure; the mere use of the right modifying word in each passage would have prevented immorality from finding its intellectual and theoretical justification in the name of economics. The tragedy of all this is that Smith was not a bad man at all. Indeed, Smith was a good man, and all of his intentions were highly honorable, as we will see further on. But in promoting his good ends through the means of justifying self-interest he made a fateful mistake—a mistake which allowed people of much more dubious intentions than Smith, beginning with Thomas Malthus, to find justification for their own self-interests in Smith's name and work.

We have said that in his economics Smith was dealing with the "middle range" of human motivation. This is necessarily the case because economics as a field concerns this middle range. The full range of human motivation involves the *passions* as well as the *interests,* to use Albert Hirschman's delineation of these forces in economic history.[11] We can see human motivation as very simply consisting of a bipolar dimension, with love on one end and hate on the other. These two poles represent the passions. . . .

In the middle range of motivation are the interests, and these can be classified as benevolence and self-interest (or selfishness), to use the Smithian terms.

The conflict of interests that we have been discussing is the conflict between the upward and the downward directions on this continuum (or, more accurately, vector). To put it very starkly, but accurately, the choice between these directions corresponds to the choice between good and bad, or virtue and vice.

While it is easy to make a distinction between the two ends of the vector—between white and black—it is always more difficult to make such moral distinctions in the middle, or gray, area, of the continuum. But a distinction in the middle range is still the same *kind* of distinction; it is a distinction between good and bad.

In his doctrine of self-interest, Smith made what can be called a *transvaluation*. That is, he reversed the poles of the continuum of motivation, at least in the middle range. In effect he said that bad was good and good was bad. We will see shortly how Smith was influenced by a predecessor, Bernard de Mandeville, to make this transvaluation. Mandeville's famous utterance that "private vice is public benefit" was to leave its fateful mark on Smith.

We have seen, then, that transvaluations become the root of moral confusion when the polarity is mislabeled. The economic doctrine of self-interest has introduced just this confusion into modern life, and in an intellectually acceptable form. Modern society has been struggling with this problem ever since the inception of the science of economics in the late 1700s.

Transvaluation is not just a product of economics, of course, and people of ill will in all spheres inevitably use transvaluative language to justify their vices and evil intentions. Perhaps the most well-known literary portrayal of this is in George Orwell's satire *Nineteen Eighty-four,* where mechanistic man, living in a totalitarian regime, talks in the language of doublespeak or even "newspeak." Here war is called peace, and lies are called truths.

The misuse of language, or mislabeling, is an important aspect of transvaluation. For Confucius, the path back to morality lay, at least in part, in what he called "the rectification of names." Immorality flourished, according to the Confucian perspective, when things and actions were not called by their correct names.[12] The most serious instance of such mislabeling is when what is bad is called good, and vice versa.

We also need to be clear, however, that immorality is not just or primarily a problem of mislabeling. It is not only a language problem. Immorality flows from the unchecked ill will of the lower self, or lower pole of motivation. It is unchecked because the counterbalancing force, the higher pole, is overpowered or held in abeyance. Language enters the picture because unchecked ill will inevitably distorts language; transvalued language is then used to render the lower pole, or lower self, dominant over a higher self that has been linguistically disclaimed. It is the central thesis of this book that in its self-interest doctrine economics has served precisely this purpose.

It is the task of the present work, then, to affect a rectification of names in the area of economics, and in social action and policy in general. We want to show that self-interest in essence means selfishness, and selfishness cannot produce the social good because in fact it is the very force that destroys the social good, despite the claim of economics to the contrary. As a matter of fact, this claim provides one of the deep mystifications that bedevil what we call the modern world.

Notes

[1] Smith, *The Wealth of Nations,* ed. Edwin Cannan (New York: Modern Library, 1937), book 1, chap. 2, p. 14.

[2] Smith, *The Theory of Moral Sentiments* (Indianapolis: Liberty Classics, 1976), pt. 1, sec. 1, chap. 1, p. 47.

[3] Smith, *The Wealth of Nations,* book 3, chap. 2, p. 423.

[4] Ibid., book 1, chap. 11, p. 250.

[5] Paul Heyne, *The Economic Way of Thinking,* 4th ed. (Chicago: Science Research Associates, 1983), pp. 22, 245.

[6] Ibid., p. 245.

[7] Ibid., p. 251.

[8] "The Heat Is On: Calculating the Consequences of a Warmer Planet," *New York Times,* 26 June 1988, sec. 4.

[9] Joan Robinson, *Economic Philosophy* (New York: Anchor Books, 1964), p. 54.

[10] Smith, *The Theory of Moral Sentiments,* pt. 2, sec. 2.

[11] Albert O. Hirschman, *The Passions and the Interests* (Princeton: Princeton University Press, 1977).

[12] Cheng-ming in Fung Yu-Lan, *A History of Ancient China,* vol. 1, (Princeton: Princeton University Press, 1952).

Jerry Z. Muller (essay date 1993)

SOURCE: "'A Small Party': Moral and Political Leadership in Commercial Society," in *Adam Smith in His Time and Ours: Designing the Decent Society*, The Free Press, 1993, pp. 164-74.

[*In the following excerpt, Muller analyzes Smith's views on the moral and political roles of the intellectual as social scientist in commercial society.*]

Commercial society, in which every man becomes to some degree a merchant, encourages the spread of characteristics associated with the prudent pursuit of self-interest—the "inferior virtues" of moderation, self-control, frugality, and decent behavior toward others. But that does not mean that the rarer and more demanding virtues, such as valor, strong benevolence, and fortitude, are obsolete. While Smith taught that the road to national wealth lay in commerce rather than in conquest, he believed that the nation still needed the ability to defend itself and therefore required the fortitude and bravery of the military hero. While well-designed institutions minimize the need for ongoing government intervention in social and economic life, commercial society still requires the informed prudence and wisdom of statesmen and legislators devoted to the public weal.[1] In *The Theory of Moral Sentiments,* Smith reminded his readers of the superiority of these virtues and the greater approbation and self-approbation that ought to attend them. And *The Wealth of Nations* was written not for men who sought to increase their own wealth but for those who might be motivated to advance the public good by increasing the wealth of the nation and strengthening its character-building institutions.[2]

Much of the institutional analysis contained in *The Wealth of Nations, The Theory of Moral Sentiments,* and the lectures on jurisprudence is devoted to describing and prescribing how institutions should be structured to develop the inferior virtues. Yet time and again Smith insists that the survival and prosperity of society depend on the cultivation of the superior virtues among at least some of its members. Though he devotes little explicit attention to the institutional means by which this can be achieved, that lapse is more apparent than real. Implicit in Smith's works is the assumption that superior virtue, insofar as it is susceptible to cultivation, can be developed through exposing those who have developed the inferior virtues through institutional means to the stimulus of moral philosophy. To those who are morally and intellectually capable of learning its lessons, moral philosophy teaches that superior virtue may earn them the more intense approbation of their fellow men and assure them the self-approbation that comes with knowing that one has acted not only acceptably but excellently.

The great strength of commercial society, as Smith perceives it, is its ability to control the passions by promoting the inferior virtues associated with striving for rank and fortune and with the prudent pursuit of self-interest. The virtues of "those who are contented to walk in the humble paths of private and peaceable life" are "temperance, decency, modesty, and moderation . . . industry and frugality."[3] The characteristic type of commercial society is the prudent man, who

> is not always very forward to listen to the voice even of noble and great ambition. . . . [He] would be much better pleased that the public business were well managed by some other person, than that he himself should have the trouble, and incur the responsibility, of managing it. In the bottom of his heart he would prefer the undisturbed enjoyment of secure tranquillity, not only to all the vain splendour of successful ambition but to the real and solid glory of performing the greatest and most magnanimous actions.[4]

The prudent man's pursuit of his own health, fortune, rank, and reputation produces a character worthy of our "cold esteem," but these virtues are neither very ennobling nor very endearing.[5] Smith's prudent man closely resembles the "bourgeois" who was to be the target of so much cultural criticism in the years ahead.[6] Yet Smith did not characterize the prudent man as lacking in virtue; to do so would be to disdain the qualities of prudence, deferred gratification, and self-control that make men gentle in their relations with one another and that prompt them to create the univer-

sal opulence which makes possible a decent life for the many. It was this disdain, characteristic of the civic republican tradition, that Smith sought to dispel.

Commercial society is based on the assumption that the benevolence of most people is limited, and that it declines in strength as distance increases from family to friends to neighborhood to country. Although commercial society provides for the "inferior prudence" required for the pursuit of self-interest, it also demands that at least some of its members acquire that "superior prudence" which combines prudence "with many greater and more splendid virtues, with valour, with extensive and strong benevolence, and with a sacred regard to the rules of justice, and all these supported by a proper degree of self-command."[7] Smith values the actions of the man of inferior prudence "contented to walk in the humble paths of private and peaceable life," but he values more highly "the more splendid actions of the hero, the statesman, or the legislator."[8]

Smith stressed the significance of institutions which habituate individuals to develop decent behavior. In Smith's civilizing project, state institutions of coercive social control were rendered less necessary by the self-restraints which were the products of non-political institutions such as the family, the market, and the chapel. Yet he believed that those institutions of moral education needed to be augmented by an intellectual elite which offered a rational explanation and rhetorical encouragement of the inferior virtues of prudent self-control, as well as the superior virtues of benevolence, self-sacrifice, and public-spiritedness. "The wise and the virtuous," Smith believed, were inevitably a "small party."[9] Yet the members of that small party played a number of crucial roles in promoting the moral and economic wealth of the nation.

The term "intellectual"—with its modern connotation of an independent man of letters who tries to mold public opinion and the opinion of legislators—did not come into wide use until the closing years of the nineteenth century. But the type long preceded the term. Smith wrote relatively little about intellectuals and their proper political role. But his conception of that role, including his own, is implicit in the rhetoric of his books and in the observations scattered through them. To reconstruct that conception, we must assemble the fragments into a coherent whole.

THE INTELLECTUAL AS MORALIST

One such fragment appears in *The Theory of Moral Sentiments,* in Smith's description of "the wise and virtuous man." In judging our own behavior, Smith writes, we may orient ourselves to either of two standards of proper behavior. The lower standard is the one that is attained by most of those around us. The higher standard is that of moral perfection, insofar as each of us is capable of understanding that ideal. The ability to comprehend the nature of moral perfection varies with our capacity to reflect on our observations of the character and conduct of those around us, and hence to perfect our sense of what is morally just and proper. The wise and virtuous man aspires to this higher standard and directs his attention to understanding its implications.[10] Because he is aware of his own imperfection, he does not treat those who are more imperfect with scorn or contempt. Instead, he attempts "by his advice and by his example" to "promote their further advancement."[11]

Smith believed that this impulse is deeply ingrained in human nature. "The desire of being believed, the desire of persuading, of leading and directing other people, seems to be one of the strongest of all our natural desires. . . ." This desire to influence the judgments of others marks a stage in the rise to perfection. "As from admiring other people we come to wish to be admired ourselves; so from being led and directed by other people we learn to wish to become ourselves leaders and directors," Smith writes. And just as the desire to be regarded as admirable by others motivates us to act admirably, the desire to be believed by others motivates us to act in a manner worthy of belief.[12] The "great ambition" to guide the conduct of others, therefore, is both morally legitimate and a goad to moral self-improvement.

Smith's purpose in *The Theory of Moral Sentiments* is to encourage the desire to become the proper object of self-approval among those who are potentially virtuous.[13] Just as the style and rhetoric of *The Wealth of Nations* are designed to motivate legislators to advance the public interest, so the style and rhetoric of *The Theory of Moral Sentiments* are designed to make its readers more virtuous. The market was to structure the incentives for material gain so that man's search for the attention of others would lead him toward decent forms of behavior. Social settings such as the family, neighborhood and chapel provided a structure of incentives in which the passion for approbation would lead toward some degree of benevolent behavior. But what structure of incentives could develop the passion of self-approbation, the desire to act in a way we know we ought to approve of even if those around us do not?

Smith gives an implicit answer to this question in *The Theory of Moral Sentiments,* where he criticizes the "casuistry" of moralizing works that try to determine the precise degree of vice and virtue but fail "to animate us to what is generous and noble . . . to soften us to what is gentle and humane."[14] The proper role of "books of morality" is to excite emotions in the heart, to present moral cases in a way that will make us *want* to act as we *ought* to.[15] Smith's strat-

egy is to reveal the implicit logic of social judgment in what he calls "common life" by describing the social disapproval and self-disapproval provoked by bad deeds, and the approbation and self-approbation aroused by good ones. The lesson of *The Theory of Moral Sentiments* is that self-command pays: it gratifies either the desire for approbation, or—more valuably—the desire for self-approbation. The intention is to strengthen the reader's sense that self-satisfaction results from acting virtuously.

One role of the intellectual, then, is that of the moral philosopher who guides the conscience of his readers or listeners.[16] He must direct them toward the proper pursuit of prudence, toward obedience to the rules of justice, and toward benevolence.[17] This role demands the use of reason in order to discover general rules of prudence, justice, and benevolence based upon induction from experience.[18] But the task of the moral philosopher is not merely to distinguish between virtuous and vicious actions: he must do so in such a way as to encourage the members of his audience to improve their own behavior.

Despite Smith's awareness of the limits of rational persuasion as a motive for moral action, he believed that the conceptions of morality offered by philosophers influence the judgments and actions of those who are moved by conscience to try to act virtuously. One responsibility of the moral philosopher is to criticize philosophies that fail to make relevant moral distinctions, because bad philosophy can undermine virtuous behavior. This conviction explains Smith's vigorous criticism of Mandeville. Because Mandeville emphasized the psychological motives behind moral action, his work has "an air of truth and probability which is very apt to impose upon the unskillful." Mandeville's system, Smith complains, is "wholly pernicious" in that it seems to eliminate entirely the distinction between virtue and vice.[19] "The question concerning the nature of virtue necessarily has some influence upon our notions of right and wrong in many particular cases," Smith noted. By reducing all virtuous actions to egoistic vices, Mandeville undermined the desire to act virtuously.[20]

The deleterious effect of Mandeville's philosophy, Smith believed, could be traced to his inability to make relevant distinctions. His fallacy was "to represent every passion as wholly vicious, which is so in any degree and in any direction." For example, he labeled as vices "the love of pleasure and the love of sex." Yet, Smith insisted, it is perfectly moral to indulge those passions so long as they are controlled by temperance and marital fidelity.[21] Similarly, by classifying the desire for approbation as "vanity," Mandeville failed to distinguish the morally laudable desire for *earned* approbation from the desire for *unearned* approbation, which is the proper definition of vanity.[22] Though Smith shared Mandeville's emphasis on the passionate sources of behavior, Smith regarded his own moral philosophy as a corrective to Mandeville's intellectual errors and to their morally pernicious effects.

One role of the intellectual, as Smith conceived it, is as moral analyst and guide to individual behavior. The other role is as policy analyst, who makes use of social scientific knowledge to guide the actions of legislators toward the public interest.

THE INTELLECTUAL AND THE POLITICIAN

Like much else in commercial society, the role of the intellectual as policy analyst is a result of the division of labor. For the variety of occupations in a commercial society

> present an almost infinite variety of objects to the contemplation of those few, who, being attached to no particular occupation themselves, have leisure and inclination to examine the occupations of other people. The contemplation of so great a variety of objects necessarily exercises their minds in endless comparisons and combinations, and renders their understandings, in an extraordinary degree, both acute and comprehensive. Unless those few, however, happen to be placed in some very particular situations, their great abilities, though honourable to themselves, may contribute very little to the good government or happiness of their society."[23]

Smith suggested no mechanism by which those few could be placed in the "particular situations" in which their abilities could be made to serve the happiness of their society—perhaps because he and other Scottish intellectuals were already in situations of influence thanks to the patronage of the rulers of Scotland and England. To proclaim that fact would be at best superfluous, at worst impolitic. But occupying a position of potential influence merely created the *possibility* of bringing one's intellectual abilities to bear on government. To realize that possibility demanded a style of writing which appealed to potential readers in positions of power—the Townshends and the Buccleuchs, the Shelburnes and the Pitts.

It is Smith's concern for the effect of his writing on his intended audience that accounts for the radically different portraits of the merchant in *The Theory of Moral Sentiments* and *The Wealth of Nations*. In *The Theory of Moral Sentiments* the portrait is positive, whereas in *The Wealth of Nations* the merchant is capable of threatening public welfare by exercising undue political influence. This was a warning to politicians, most of whom were men of landed wealth, to resist the attempts of merchants to get laws passed that would serve their own interests.

The Wealth of Nations tries to influence the politician by appealing to his concern for the public good and by the aesthetic attraction exerted by the systematic exposition of the "system of natural liberty."

Ultimately it is only the legislator who can prevent special interests from dominating the decisions of government. To do so requires politicians motivated to put the welfare of the country above their personal and particular interests. Under modern conditions politicians have need for men whose intellectual aptitudes and whose position in the division of labor allow them to think systematically about "the science of the legislator." But even with such advisers, the politician needs to be guided by prudence, an awareness of the gap between what is desirable and what is possible.

Smith wrote relatively little about what he regarded as the best structure of government. To portray him either as a supporter or an opponent of modern representative democracy is simply anachronistic: in a country where most people were benighted to the point of illiteracy, the possibility of their participation in government was hardly conceivable. In his lectures of 1762, Smith's few comments on "democracy"—a term he used in the traditional sense of direct popular participation in government—noted that it had not been much of a success the few times that it had been tried and in each case had been abandoned.[24] In his genealogy of commercial society, as we have seen, Smith depicted the consolidation of royal power over the feudal landlords as a gain for civilization. He clearly approved of the division of power as it had developed in England from the Glorious Revolution through the age of Walpole. Legislative power lay in the elected House of Commons, but the monarch could influence the Commons through the preferments at his disposal.[25] In the vocabulary of his day, Smith was a Whig, a supporter of a strong central government dominated by a modernizing and commercialized aristocracy. But he was a sceptical, scientific Whig, uncommitted to any faction.[26]

Smith maintained that the institutions of commercial society guided men's passions into some degree of benevolence, but benevolence was limited, and its intensity diminished with social distance. The other side of the coin of limited benevolence is group self-interest, a reality with which the prudent statesman must reckon. Each state, Smith wrote, is made up of numerous "orders and societies, each of which has its own particular powers, privileges, and immunities." Though all these orders and communities depend upon the state for their prosperity and protection, individuals are naturally concerned to protect the interests of their particular order or community over those of others. "This partiality, though it may sometimes be unjust, may not, upon that account, be useless," Smith remarked. For the effort" to preserve whatever is the established balance among the different orders and societies into which the state is divided . . . contributes in reality to the stability and permanency of the whole system."[27]

The importance of stability pervades Smith's remarks on government. Only a stable government can guarantee the security of person and property which is so essential to the flourishing of commercial society. Under modern conditions, he believed, that stability rests on the opinion the governed have of the governors. The importance of public opinion in a legitimate regime was one of the arguments Smith advanced for the promotion of mass education. It was also central to his view of political prudence: because government in commercial society rested ultimately upon public opinion, he was wary of government attempts to institute radical change, no matter how well intentioned or well advised. He cautioned enlightened monarchs against attempts to hasten reform by usurping the power and privileges of the nobility, of cities and provinces, or of the other established orders of society.[28]

Smith believed that statesmen needed to be guided by ideals as they set policy, and he tried to make his social science attractive to them. But he warned of the dangers of trying to implement those policy ideals all at once. To do so was to commit the error of "the man of system," who "is often so enamoured with the supposed beauty of his own ideal plan of government, that he cannot suffer the smallest deviation from any part of it." Such attempts are bound to fail, Smith warned, because of the resistance arising from existing socio-economic interests and deeply rooted beliefs. The man of system, in other words, is insufficiently attuned to the peculiarities of his countrymen to make proper use of mechanisms for the institutional direction of the passions:

> He seems to imagine that he can arrange the different members of a great society with as much ease as the hand arranges the different pieces upon a chess-board. He does not consider that the pieces upon the chess-board have no other principle of motion besides that which the hand impresses upon them; but that, in the great chess-board of human society, every single piece has a principle of motion of its own, altogether different from that which the legislature might choose to impress upon it. If those two principles coincide and act in the same direction, the game of human society will go on easily and harmoniously, and is very likely to be happy and successful. If they are opposite or different, the game will go on miserably. . . . [29]

Systematic social thought necessarily simplifies the motives of human behavior. Men are not like chess-pieces, because of the complexity of human motiva-

tions. Hence, unlike the rules of a game, the rules of society are never fully spelled out, and political actions often have unanticipated consequences. *It is the role of social science to anticipate these consequences more fully, but the limits of prediction commend caution in reform.*

And so, even as Smith tried to encourage the politician to act like a good citizen who wishes to "promote, by every means in his power, the welfare of the whole society of his fellow-citizens," he cautioned the benevolent "man of public spirit" to

> respect the established powers and privileges even of individuals, and still more those of the great orders and societies, into which the state is divided. . . . He will content himself with moderating, what he often cannot annihilate without great violence. When he cannot conquer the rooted prejudices of the people by reason and persuasion, he will not attempt to subdue them by force. . . . He will accommodate, as well as he can, his public arrangements to the confirmed habits and prejudices of the people. . . . When he cannot establish the right, he will not disdain to ameliorate the wrong; but like Solon, when he cannot establish the best system of laws, he will endeavour to establish the best that the people can bear.[30]

Smith's policy recommendations reflect his awareness of the need to accommodate existing interests in order to preserve governmental legitimacy and stability. Though he argued strongly that most tariffs served private interests, he recommended that the protectionist tariffs then in effect in industries involving large investments of capital and employing many workers be lifted gradually and with adequate warning, thus providing "equitable regard" to the interests of investors and preventing sudden mass unemployment.[31] In both *The Theory of Moral Sentiments* and *The Wealth of Nations* he cautioned against the excessive use of government force to implement even well-motivated policy reforms; and in *The Wealth of Nations,* he expressed approval of the manner in which the English Parliament was being "managed" through the accommodation of existing interests, in contrast to the forceful attempts of the French monarch to overcome the resistance of the *parlements.*[32]

For Smith, then, one role of the intellectual was to influence men of power, to encourage their public spirit, and to provide them with concepts and information through which they could anticipate the probable consequences of government action. Yet, Smith insisted, even well-motivated and well-informed politicians had to be guided by prudence, the knowledge of the possible, and by sensitivity to the situation of the moment. The "science of a legislator," in which the social scientist specialized, deals with "general principles which are always the same"; but the implementation of policy depends on "the skill of that insidious and crafty animal, vulgarly called a statesman or politician, whose councils are directed by the momentary fluctuations of affairs."[33] In other words, the skills, knowledge, motivations, and considerations of the politician are different from—and no less important than—those of the intellectual.

Notes

[1] *TMS, [The Theory of Moral Sentiments],* VI.i.15, p. 216.

[2] On the overlap between classical and modern virtues in Smith and in the Scottish Enlightenment, see the compressed and penetrating comments of J. G. A. Pocock, "The political limits to premodern economics," in John Dunn (ed.), *The Economic Limits to Modern Politics* (Cambridge, 1990), pp. 121-41, pp. 134-40.

[3] *TMS,* VI.iii.13, p. 242.

[4] *TMS,* VI.1.13, p. 216.

[5] *TMS,* VI.1.14, p. 216.

[6] For a brilliant evocation of the origins and recurrent laments of this criticism, see Allan Bloom, "Commerce and 'Culture,'" in his *Giants and Dwarfs: Essays 1960-1990* (New York, 1990), pp. 277-94.

[7] *TMS,* VI.1.15, p. 216.

[8] *TMS,* VI.iii.13, p. 242.

[9] *TMS,* I.iii.2, p. 62.

[10] *TMS,* VI.iii.25, p. 247.

[11] *TMS,* VI.iii.25, p. 248.

[12] *TMS,* VII, iv, 24-25, p. 336.

[13] In this purpose, Smith was continuing the tradition of his teacher, Francis Hutcheson. See Duncan Forbes, *Hume's Philosophical Politics* (Cambridge, 1978), p. 56; Richard F. Teichgraeber III, *"Free Trade" and Moral Philosophy: Rethinking the Sources of Adam Smith's Wealth of Nations* (Durham, 1986), pp. 123-33; and Richard Sher, *Church and University in the Scottish Enlightenment* (Princeton, 1985), pp. 166-68.

[14] *TMS,* VII.iv.33, p. 339.

[15] *TMS,* VII.iv.33, p. 340.

[16] *TMS,* VII.ii.1.47, p. 293.

[17] *TMS,* VI.iii.concl.1, p. 262.

[18] *TMS,* VII.ii.2.6, pp. 319-20.

[19] *TMS,* VII.ii.4.6, p. 308.

[20] *TMS,* VII.iii.intro.3, p. 315.

[21] *TMS,* VII.ii.4.11, p. 312.

[22] *TMS,* VII.ii.4.8, p. 309.

[23] *WN [The Wealth of Nations],* V.iv.f.51, p. 783.

[24] *LJ [Lectures on Jurisprudence]* (A), pp. 242, 289.

[25] *LJ* (A), pp. 268-69; *LJ* (B), pp. 420-22; *WN,* V.i.g.19, pp. 798-99.

[26] On Smith's Whiggism, see Duncan Forbes, "Sceptical Whiggism, Commerce, and History," in Andrew S. Skinner and Thomas Wilson (eds.), *Essays on Adam Smith* (Oxford, 1975); and J. G. A. Pocock, "The varieties of Whiggism from Exclusion to Reform: A history of ideology and discourse," in his *Virtue, Commerce, and History* (Cambridge, 1985), pp. 215-310.

[27] *TMS,* VI.ii.2.9, pp. 230-31.

[28] *TMS,* VI.ii.2.18, p. 234.

[29] *TMS,* VI.ii.2.17, p. 234.

[30] *TMS,* VI.ii.2.16, p. 233.

[31] *WN,* IV.ii.40-44, p. 469-71.

[32] *WN,* V.i.g.19, pp. 798-99.

[33] *WN,* IV.ii.39, p. 468.

FURTHER READING

Biography

Ross, Ian Simpson. *The Life of Adam Smith.* Oxford, England: Clarendon Press, 1995, 495 p.
　　A biography that includes discussion of Smith's writings and their critical reception. Ross, one of the editors of *The Glasgow Edition of the Works and Correspondence of Adam Smith*, provides a bibliography of primary and secondary sources.

Criticism

Blaug, Mark. *Economic Theory in Retrospect.* 4th ed. Cambridge: Cambridge University Press, 1985, 737 p.

A history of economic theory from mercantilist times to the twentieth century, with a chapter on Smith's *Wealth of Nations*.

Bonar, James. *Moral Sense*. Library of Philosophy, edited by J. H. Muirhead. London: George Allen & Unwin, 1930, 304 p.

A study of the theory of moral philosophy prevailing in Scotland during the eighteenth century, which Bonar defines as "a special theory of the origin of Ethics — the theory that right decisions, if not indeed right principles, were due to a Moral Sense conceived as a special faculty." Bonar focuses on the writings and thought of the founders of this philosophy, Anthony Ashley Cooper Shaftesbury and Francis Hutcheson, their leading followers, and their principal critics, among them Smith.

Brown, Maurice. *Adam Smith's Economics: Its Place in the Development of Economic Thought*. London: Croom Helm, 1988, 189 p.

An examination of Smith's economic theory that takes into account his epistemology, methodology, and understanding of social institutions, politics, and history.

Hont, Istvan, and Michael Ignatieff, eds. *Wealth and Virtue: The Shaping of Political Economy in the Scottish Enlightenment*. Cambridge: Cambridge University Press, 1983, 371 p.

Thirteen essays on the origins of Scottish jurisprudence, moral philosophy, and political economy. Three of the essays are specifically devoted to Smith, and he is also a subject of discussion in the others, many of which assess the role of the civic humanist and natural jurisprudence traditions in the development of the Scottish political economy.

Jones, Peter, and Andrew S. Skinner, eds. *Adam Smith Reviewed*. Edinburgh: Edinburgh University Press, 1992, 252 p.

A collection of ten essays by noted scholars of Smith covering a variety of aspects of his thought and career, from his aesthetic philosophy and lectures on belles lettres and rhetoric to his economic and ethical theories and his writings on jurisprudence.

Lerner, Max. An introduction to *An Inquiry into the Nature and Causes of the Wealth of Nations*, by Adam Smith, edited by Edwin Cannan, The Modern Library, 1937, pp. v-x.

Explains the reasons for the book's enormous impact on Western economic history.

Lindgren, J. Ralph. *The Social Philosophy of Adam Smith*. The Hague, Netherlands: Martinus Nijhoff, 1973, 164 p.

Attempts to interpret Smith's social philosophy from Smith's own perspective, taking into account his interests, methods, and objectives.

Mizuta, Hiroshi, and Chuhei Sugiyama, eds. *Adam Smith: International Perspectives*. New York: St. Martin's Press, 1993, 328 p.

A collection of seventeen essays describing the reception and application of Smith's ideas in a variety of countries, including Germany, France, Italy, the United States, Russia, India, China, and Japan.

Morrow, Glenn R. *The Ethical and Economic Theories of Adam Smith: A Study in the Social Philosophy of the Eighteenth Century*. New York: Longmans, Green, and Co., 1923, 91 p.

Examines Smith's moral and economic theories within the context of eighteenth-century rationalistic thought, with emphasis on the relationship between the doctrine of natural law and Smith's ethical doctrine of sympathy.

Samuels, Warren J. "Adam Smith and the Economy as a System of Power." *Review of Social Economy* XXXI, No. 2 (October 1973): 123-37.

Suggests an alternative analysis to the traditional neoclassical interpretation of the *Wealth of Nations*, arguing that the book is "a model not just of economic actors allocating their limited resources so as to maximize their welfare but a model also of a struggle for command of resources and market position and thus of welfare maximizing through power and mutual coercion."

Skinner, Andrew S. *A System of Social Science: Papers Relating to Adam Smith*. Oxford, England: Clarendon Press, 1979, 278 p.

A collection of essays that, according to the author, makes "a single commentary on Smith's system of social science." Among the subjects discussed by Skinner are Smith's moral, political, and economic theories and his thoughts concerning mercantilist policy, the proper function of government, and the relationship between science and the imagination.

————, and Thomas Wilson, eds. *Essays on Adam Smith*. Oxford, England: Clarendon Press, 1975, 647 p.

Twenty-six essays on Smith and his works written in observance of the bicentenary of the *Wealth of Nations* and published in conjunction with *The Glasgow Edition of the Works and Correspondence of Adam Smith*. The volume is divided into two parts, the first of which mainly concerns Smith's philosophical and political philosophies and the second of which deals primarily with his economic thought.

Wood, John Cunningham, ed. *Adam Smith: Critical Assessments*. 4 vols. London: Croom Helm, 1984.

Reprints 150 important critical assessments of Smith's writings dating from Smith's own day to the present. The collection consists entirely of articles published in English-language journals and is arranged thematically, with separate volumes devoted to: 1) The Life of Adam Smith and Perspectives on His Thought; 2) Smith's *Wealth of Nations*; 3)Smithian Economic Analysis; and 4) Specialized Topics.

How to Use This Index

The main references

Calvino, Italo
1923-1985.....CLC 5, 8, 11, 22, 33, 39,
73; SSC 3

list all author entries in the following Gale Literary Criticism series:

BLC = *Black Literature Criticism*
CLC = *Contemporary Literary Criticism*
CLR = *Children's Literature Review*
CMLC = *Classical and Medieval Literature Criticism*
DA = *DISCovering Authors*
DC = *Drama Criticism*
HLC = *Hispanic Literature Criticism*
LC = *Literature Criticism from 1400 to 1800*
NCLC = *Nineteenth-Century Literature Criticism*
PC = *Poetry Criticism*
SSC = *Short Story Criticism*
TCLC = *Twentieth-Century Literary Criticism*
WLC = *World Literature Criticism, 1500 to the Present*

The cross-references

See also CANR 23; CA 85-88;
obituary CA 116

list all author entries in the following Gale biographical and literary sources:

AAYA = *Authors & Artists for Young Adults*
AITN = *Authors in the News*
BEST = *Bestsellers*
BW = *Black Writers*
CA = *Contemporary Authors*
CAAS = *Contemporary Authors Autobiography Series*
CABS = *Contemporary Authors Bibliographical Series*
CANR = *Contemporary Authors New Revision Series*
CAP = *Contemporary Authors Permanent Series*
CDALB = *Concise Dictionary of American Literary Biography*
CDBLB = *Concise Dictionary of British Literary Biography*
DLB = *Dictionary of Literary Biography*
DLBD = *Dictionary of Literary Biography Documentary Series*
DLBY = *Dictionary of Literary Biography Yearbook*
HW = *Hispanic Writers*
JRDA = *Junior DISCovering Authors*
MAICYA = *Major Authors and Illustrators for Children and Young Adults*
MTCW = *Major 20th-Century Writers*
NNAL = *Native North American Literature*
SAAS = *Something about the Author Autobiography Series*
SATA = *Something about the Author*
YABC = *Yesterday's Authors of Books for Children*

Literature
Criticism from
1400 to 1800

Cumulative Indexes

Literary Criticism Series
Cumulative Author Index

Abasiyanik, Sait Faik   1906-1954
See Sait Faik
See also CA 123

Abbey, Edward   1927-1989 . . . . . . CLC 36, 59
See also CA 45-48; 128; CANR 2, 41

Abbott, Lee K(ittredge)   1947- . . . . . . CLC 48
See also CA 124; CANR 51; DLB 130

Abe, Kobo
1924-1993 . . . . CLC 8, 22, 53, 81;
DAM NOV
See also CA 65-68; 140; CANR 24; MTCW

Abelard, Peter   c. 1079-c. 1142 . . . CMLC 11
See also DLB 115

Abell, Kjeld   1901-1961 . . . . CLC 15
See also CA 111

Abish, Walter   1931- . . . . CLC 22
See also CA 101; CANR 37; DLB 130

Abrahams, Peter (Henry)   1919- . . . . . CLC 4
See also BW 1; CA 57-60; CANR 26;
DLB 117; MTCW

Abrams, M(eyer) H(oward)   1912- . . . CLC 24
See also CA 57-60; CANR 13, 33; DLB 67

Abse, Dannie
1923- . . . CLC 7, 29; DAB; DAM POET
See also CA 53-56; CAAS 1; CANR 4, 46;
DLB 27

Achebe, (Albert) Chinua(lumogu)
1930- . . . . . CLC 1, 3, 5, 7, 11, 26, 51, 75;
BLC; DA; DAB; DAC; DAM MST,
MULT, NOV; WLC
See also AAYA 15; BW 2; CA 1-4R;
CANR 6, 26, 47; CLR 20; DLB 117;
MAICYA; MTCW; SATA 40;
SATA-Brief 38

Acker, Kathy   1948- . . . . CLC 45
See also CA 117; 122; CANR 55

Ackroyd, Peter   1949- . . . . CLC 34, 52
See also CA 123; 127; CANR 51; DLB 155;
INT 127

Acorn, Milton   1923- . . . . CLC 15; DAC
See also CA 103; DLB 53; INT 103

Adamov, Arthur
1908-1970 . . . . CLC 4, 25; DAM DRAM
See also CA 17-18; 25-28R; CAP 2; MTCW

Adams, Alice (Boyd)
1926- . . . . CLC 6, 13, 46; SSC 24
See also CA 81-84; CANR 26, 53;
DLBY 86; INT CANR-26; MTCW

Adams, Andy   1859-1935 . . . . TCLC 56
See also YABC 1

Adams, Douglas (Noel)
1952- . . . . CLC 27, 60; DAM POP
See also AAYA 4; BEST 89:3; CA 106;
CANR 34; DLBY 83; JRDA

Adams, Francis   1862-1893 . . . . NCLC 33

Adams, Henry (Brooks)
1838-1918 . . . . . . TCLC 4, 52; DA; DAB;
DAC; DAM MST
See also CA 104; 133; DLB 12, 47

Adams, Richard (George)
1920- . . . . CLC 4, 5, 18; DAM NOV
See also AAYA 16; AITN 1, 2; CA 49-52;
CANR 3, 35; CLR 20; JRDA; MAICYA;
MTCW; SATA 7, 69

Adamson, Joy(-Friederike Victoria)
1910-1980 . . . . CLC 17
See also CA 69-72; 93-96; CANR 22;
MTCW; SATA 11; SATA-Obit 22

Adcock, Fleur   1934- . . . . CLC 41
See also CA 25-28R; CAAS 23; CANR 11,
34; DLB 40

Addams, Charles (Samuel)
1912-1988 . . . . CLC 30
See also CA 61-64; 126; CANR 12

Addison, Joseph   1672-1719 . . . . LC 18
See also CDBLB 1660-1789; DLB 101

Adler, Alfred (F.)   1870-1937 . . . . . . TCLC 61
See also CA 119

Adler, C(arole) S(chwerdtfeger)
1932- . . . . CLC 35
See also AAYA 4; CA 89-92; CANR 19,
40; JRDA; MAICYA; SAAS 15;
SATA 26, 63

Adler, Renata   1938- . . . . CLC 8, 31
See also CA 49-52; CANR 5, 22, 52;
MTCW

Ady, Endre   1877-1919 . . . . TCLC 11
See also CA 107

Aeschylus
525B.C.-456B.C. . . . . CMLC 11; DA;
DAB; DAC; DAM DRAM, MST

Afton, Effie
See Harper, Frances Ellen Watkins

Agapida, Fray Antonio
See Irving, Washington

Agee, James (Rufus)
1909-1955 . . . . TCLC 1, 19; DAM NOV
See also AITN 1; CA 108; 148;
CDALB 1941-1968; DLB 2, 26, 152

Aghill, Gordon
See Silverberg, Robert

Agnon, S(hmuel) Y(osef Halevi)
1888-1970 . . . . CLC 4, 8, 14
See also CA 17-18; 25-28R; CAP 2; MTCW

Agrippa von Nettesheim, Henry Cornelius
1486-1535 . . . . LC 27

Aherne, Owen
See Cassill, R(onald) V(erlin)

Ai   1947- . . . . CLC 4, 14, 69
See also CA 85-88; CAAS 13; DLB 120

Aickman, Robert (Fordyce)
1914-1981 . . . . CLC 57
See also CA 5-8R; CANR 3

Aiken, Conrad (Potter)
1889-1973 . . . . CLC 1, 3, 5, 10, 52;
DAM NOV, POET; SSC 9
See also CA 5-8R; 45-48; CANR 4;
CDALB 1929-1941; DLB 9, 45, 102;
MTCW; SATA 3, 30

Aiken, Joan (Delano)   1924- . . . . CLC 35
See also AAYA 1; CA 9-12R; CANR 4, 23,
34; CLR 1, 19; DLB 161; JRDA;
MAICYA; MTCW; SAAS 1; SATA 2,
30, 73

Ainsworth, William Harrison
1805-1882 . . . . NCLC 13
See also DLB 21; SATA 24

Aitmatov, Chingiz (Torekulovich)
1928- . . . . CLC 71
See also CA 103; CANR 38; MTCW;
SATA 56

Akers, Floyd
See Baum, L(yman) Frank

Akhmadulina, Bella Akhatovna
1937- . . . . CLC 53; DAM POET
See also CA 65-68

Akhmatova, Anna
1888-1966 . . . . CLC 11, 25, 64;
DAM POET; PC 2
See also CA 19-20; 25-28R; CANR 35;
CAP 1; MTCW

Aksakov, Sergei Timofeyvich
1791-1859 . . . . NCLC 2

Aksenov, Vassily
See Aksyonov, Vassily (Pavlovich)

Aksyonov, Vassily (Pavlovich)
1932- . . . . CLC 22, 37
See also CA 53-56; CANR 12, 48

Akutagawa, Ryunosuke
1892-1927 . . . . TCLC 16
See also CA 117; 154

Alain   1868-1951 . . . . TCLC 41

Alain-Fournier . . . . TCLC 6
See also Fournier, Henri Alban
See also DLB 65

Alarcon, Pedro Antonio de
1833-1891 . . . . NCLC 1

Alas (y Urena), Leopoldo (Enrique Garcia)
1852-1901 . . . . TCLC 29
See also CA 113; 131; HW

Albee, Edward (Franklin III)
1928- . . . . . . CLC 1, 2, 3, 5, 9, 11, 13, 25,
53, 86; DA; DAB; DAC; DAM DRAM,
MST; WLC
See also AITN 1; CA 5-8R; CABS 3;
CANR 8, 54; CDALB 1941-1968; DLB 7;
INT CANR-8; MTCW

Alberti, Rafael   1902- . . . . CLC 7
See also CA 85-88; DLB 108

Albert the Great   1200(?)-1280 . . . . CMLC 16
See also DLB 115

Alcala-Galiano, Juan Valera y
See Valera y Alcala-Galiano, Juan

Alcott, Amos Bronson 1799-1888 .. NCLC 1
See also DLB 1

Alcott, Louisa May
1832-1888 ..... NCLC 6, 58; DA; DAB;
DAC; DAM MST, NOV; WLC
See also CDALB 1865-1917; CLR 1, 38;
DLB 1, 42, 79; DLBD 14; JRDA;
MAICYA; YABC 1

Aldanov, M. A.
See Aldanov, Mark (Alexandrovich)

Aldanov, Mark (Alexandrovich)
1886(?)-1957 .... TCLC 23
See also CA 118

Aldington, Richard 1892-1962...... CLC 49
See also CA 85-88; CANR 45; DLB 20, 36,
100, 149

Aldiss, Brian W(ilson)
1925- .... CLC 5, 14, 40; DAM NOV
See also CA 5-8R; CAAS 2; CANR 5, 28;
DLB 14; MTCW; SATA 34

Alegria, Claribel
1924- .... CLC 75; DAM MULT
See also CA 131; CAAS 15; DLB 145; HW

Alegria, Fernando 1918-........... CLC 57
See also CA 9-12R; CANR 5, 32; HW

Aleichem, Sholom .... TCLC 1, 35
See also Rabinovitch, Sholem

Aleixandre, Vicente
1898-1984 .... CLC 9, 36; DAM POET;
PC 15
See also CA 85-88; 114; CANR 26;
DLB 108; HW; MTCW

Alepoudelis, Odysseus
See Elytis, Odysseus

Aleshkovsky, Joseph 1929-
See Aleshkovsky, Yuz
See also CA 121; 128

Aleshkovsky, Yuz .... CLC 44
See also Aleshkovsky, Joseph

Alexander, Lloyd (Chudley) 1924- .. CLC 35
See also AAYA 1; CA 1-4R; CANR 1, 24,
38, 55; CLR 1, 5; DLB 52; JRDA;
MAICYA; MTCW; SAAS 19; SATA 3,
49, 81

Alexie, Sherman (Joseph, Jr.)
1966- .... CLC 96; DAM MULT
See also CA 138; NNAL

Alfau, Felipe 1902-............... CLC 66
See also CA 137

Alger, Horatio, Jr. 1832-1899..... NCLC 8
See also DLB 42; SATA 16

Algren, Nelson 1909-1981 .... CLC 4, 10, 33
See also CA 13-16R; 103; CANR 20;
CDALB 1941-1968; DLB 9; DLBY 81,
82; MTCW

Ali, Ahmed 1910- .... CLC 69
See also CA 25-28R; CANR 15, 34

Alighieri, Dante 1265-1321 .... CMLC 3, 18

Allan, John B.
See Westlake, Donald E(dwin)

Allen, Edward 1948-.............. CLC 59

Allen, Paula Gunn
1939- .... CLC 84; DAM MULT
See also CA 112; 143; NNAL

Allen, Roland
See Ayckbourn, Alan

Allen, Sarah A.
See Hopkins, Pauline Elizabeth

Allen, Woody
1935- .... CLC 16, 52; DAM POP
See also AAYA 10; CA 33-36R; CANR 27,
38; DLB 44; MTCW

Allende, Isabel
1942- .... CLC 39, 57, 97; DAM MULT,
NOV; HLC
See also AAYA 18; CA 125; 130;
CANR 51; DLB 145; HW; INT 130;
MTCW

Alleyn, Ellen
See Rossetti, Christina (Georgina)

Allingham, Margery (Louise)
1904-1966 .... CLC 19
See also CA 5-8R; 25-28R; CANR 4;
DLB 77; MTCW

Allingham, William 1824-1889 ... NCLC 25
See also DLB 35

Allison, Dorothy E. 1949- .... CLC 78
See also CA 140

Allston, Washington 1779-1843.... NCLC 2
See also DLB 1

Almedingen, E. M. .... CLC 12
See also Almedingen, Martha Edith von
See also SATA 3

Almedingen, Martha Edith von 1898-1971
See Almedingen, E. M.
See also CA 1-4R; CANR 1

Almqvist, Carl Jonas Love
1793-1866 .... NCLC 42

Alonso, Damaso 1898-1990 .... CLC 14
See also CA 110; 131; 130; DLB 108; HW

Alov
See Gogol, Nikolai (Vasilyevich)

Alta 1942-...................... CLC 19
See also CA 57-60

Alter, Robert B(ernard) 1935-...... CLC 34
See also CA 49-52; CANR 1, 47

Alther, Lisa 1944-.............. CLC 7, 41
See also CA 65-68; CANR 12, 30, 51;
MTCW

Altman, Robert 1925-............. CLC 16
See also CA 73-76; CANR 43

Alvarez, A(lfred) 1929-.......... CLC 5, 13
See also CA 1-4R; CANR 3, 33; DLB 14,
40

Alvarez, Alejandro Rodriguez 1903-1965
See Casona, Alejandro
See also CA 131; 93-96; HW

Alvarez, Julia 1950-.............. CLC 93
See also CA 147

Alvaro, Corrado 1896-1956 .... TCLC 60

Amado, Jorge
1912- .... CLC 13, 40; DAM MULT,
NOV; HLC
See also CA 77-80; CANR 35; DLB 113;
MTCW

Ambler, Eric 1909-........... CLC 4, 6, 9
See also CA 9-12R; CANR 7, 38; DLB 77;
MTCW

Amichai, Yehuda 1924- ...... CLC 9, 22, 57
See also CA 85-88; CANR 46; MTCW

Amiel, Henri Frederic 1821-1881 .. NCLC 4

Amis, Kingsley (William)
1922-1995 ..... CLC 1, 2, 3, 5, 8, 13, 40,
44; DA; DAB; DAC; DAM MST, NOV
See also AITN 2; CA 9-12R; 150; CANR 8,
28, 54; CDBLB 1945-1960; DLB 15, 27,
100, 139; INT CANR-8; MTCW

Amis, Martin (Louis)
1949- .... CLC 4, 9, 38, 62
See also BEST 90:3; CA 65-68; CANR 8,
27, 54; DLB 14; INT CANR-27

Ammons, A(rchie) R(andolph)
1926- .... CLC 2, 3, 5, 8, 9, 25, 57;
DAM POET; PC 16
See also AITN 1; CA 9-12R; CANR 6, 36,
51; DLB 5, 165; MTCW

Amo, Tauraatua i
See Adams, Henry (Brooks)

Anand, Mulk Raj
1905- .... CLC 23, 93; DAM NOV
See also CA 65-68; CANR 32; MTCW

Anatol
See Schnitzler, Arthur

Anaya, Rudolfo A(lfonso)
1937- .... CLC 23; DAM MULT, NOV;
HLC
See also CA 45-48; CAAS 4; CANR 1, 32,
51; DLB 82; HW 1; MTCW

Andersen, Hans Christian
1805-1875 .... NCLC 7; DA; DAB;
DAC; DAM MST, POP; SSC 6; WLC
See also CLR 6; MAICYA; YABC 1

Anderson, C. Farley
See Mencken, H(enry) L(ouis); Nathan,
George Jean

Anderson, Jessica (Margaret) Queale
.... CLC 37
See also CA 9-12R; CANR 4

Anderson, Jon (Victor)
1940- .... CLC 9; DAM POET
See also CA 25-28R; CANR 20

Anderson, Lindsay (Gordon)
1923-1994 .... CLC 20
See also CA 125; 128; 146

Anderson, Maxwell
1888-1959 ...... TCLC 2; DAM DRAM
See also CA 105; 152; DLB 7

Anderson, Poul (William) 1926- .... CLC 15
See also AAYA 5; CA 1-4R; CAAS 2;
CANR 2, 15, 34; DLB 8; INT CANR-15;
MTCW; SATA 90; SATA-Brief 39

Anderson, Robert (Woodruff)
1917- .... CLC 23; DAM DRAM
See also AITN 1; CA 21-24R; CANR 32;
DLB 7

Anderson, Sherwood
1876-1941 .... TCLC 1, 10, 24; DA;
DAB; DAC; DAM MST, NOV; SSC 1;
WLC
See also CA 104; 121; CDALB 1917-1929;
DLB 4, 9, 86; DLBD 1; MTCW

Andier, Pierre
See Desnos, Robert

Andouard
See Giraudoux, (Hippolyte) Jean

Andrade, Carlos Drummond de . . . . . . **CLC 18**
See also Drummond de Andrade, Carlos

Andrade, Mario de 1893-1945 . . . . . **TCLC 43**

Andreae, Johann V(alentin)
1586-1654 . . . . **LC 32**
See also DLB 164

Andreas-Salome, Lou 1861-1937 . . . **TCLC 56**
See also DLB 66

Andrewes, Lancelot 1555-1626 . . . . **LC 5**
See also DLB 151, 172

Andrews, Cicily Fairfield
See West, Rebecca

Andrews, Elton V.
See Pohl, Frederik

Andreyev, Leonid (Nikolaevich)
1871-1919 . . . . **TCLC 3**
See also CA 104

Andric, Ivo 1892-1975 . . . . **CLC 8**
See also CA 81-84; 57-60; CANR 43;
DLB 147; MTCW

Angelique, Pierre
See Bataille, Georges

Angell, Roger 1920- . . . . **CLC 26**
See also CA 57-60; CANR 13, 44; DLB 171

Angelou, Maya
1928- . . . . **CLC 12, 35, 64, 77; BLC; DA;
DAB; DAC; DAM MST, MULT, POET,
POP**
See also AAYA 7; BW 2; CA 65-68;
CANR 19, 42; DLB 38; MTCW;
SATA 49

Annensky, Innokenty Fyodorovich
1856-1909 . . . . **TCLC 14**
See also CA 110

Anon, Charles Robert
See Pessoa, Fernando (Antonio Nogueira)

Anouilh, Jean (Marie Lucien Pierre)
1910-1987 . . . . . . **CLC 1, 3, 8, 13, 40, 50;
DAM DRAM**
See also CA 17-20R; 123; CANR 32;
MTCW

Anthony, Florence
See Ai

Anthony, John
See Ciardi, John (Anthony)

Anthony, Peter
See Shaffer, Anthony (Joshua); Shaffer,
Peter (Levin)

Anthony, Piers 1934- . . **CLC 35; DAM POP**
See also AAYA 11; CA 21-24R; CANR 28;
DLB 8; MTCW; SAAS 22; SATA 84

Antoine, Marc
See Proust, (Valentin-Louis-George-Eugene-)
Marcel

Antoninus, Brother
See Everson, William (Oliver)

Antonioni, Michelangelo 1912- . . . . . **CLC 20**
See also CA 73-76; CANR 45

Antschel, Paul 1920-1970
See Celan, Paul
See also CA 85-88; CANR 33; MTCW

Anwar, Chairil 1922-1949 . . . . **TCLC 22**
See also CA 121

Apollinaire, Guillaume
1880-1918 . . . . **TCLC 3, 8, 51;
DAM POET; PC 7**
See also Kostrowitzki, Wilhelm Apollinaris
de
See also CA 152

Appelfeld, Aharon 1932- . . . . **CLC 23, 47**
See also CA 112; 133

Apple, Max (Isaac) 1941- . . . . **CLC 9, 33**
See also CA 81-84; CANR 19, 54; DLB 130

Appleman, Philip (Dean) 1926- . . . . . **CLC 51**
See also CA 13-16R; CAAS 18; CANR 6,
29

Appleton, Lawrence
See Lovecraft, H(oward) P(hillips)

Apteryx
See Eliot, T(homas) S(tearns)

Apuleius, (Lucius Madaurensis)
125(?)-175(?) . . . . **CMLC 1**

Aquin, Hubert 1929-1977 . . . . **CLC 15**
See also CA 105; DLB 53

Aragon, Louis
1897-1982 . . . . . **CLC 3, 22; DAM NOV,
POET**
See also CA 69-72; 108; CANR 28;
DLB 72; MTCW

Arany, Janos 1817-1882 . . . . **NCLC 34**

Arbuthnot, John 1667-1735 . . . . **LC 1**
See also DLB 101

Archer, Herbert Winslow
See Mencken, H(enry) L(ouis)

Archer, Jeffrey (Howard)
1940- . . . . **CLC 28; DAM POP**
See also AAYA 16; BEST 89:3; CA 77-80;
CANR 22, 52; INT CANR-22

Archer, Jules 1915- . . . . **CLC 12**
See also CA 9-12R; CANR 6; SAAS 5;
SATA 4, 85

Archer, Lee
See Ellison, Harlan (Jay)

Arden, John
1930- . . . . . **CLC 6, 13, 15; DAM DRAM**
See also CA 13-16R; CAAS 4; CANR 31;
DLB 13; MTCW

Arenas, Reinaldo
1943-1990 . . . . . . **CLC 41; DAM MULT;
HLC**
See also CA 124; 128; 133; DLB 145; HW

Arendt, Hannah 1906-1975 . . . . . **CLC 66, 98**
See also CA 17-20R; 61-64; CANR 26;
MTCW

Aretino, Pietro 1492-1556 . . . . **LC 12**

Arghezi, Tudor . . . . **CLC 80**
See also Theodorescu, Ion N.

Arguedas, Jose Maria
1911-1969 . . . . **CLC 10, 18**
See also CA 89-92; DLB 113; HW

Argueta, Manlio 1936- . . . . **CLC 31**
See also CA 131; DLB 145; HW

Ariosto, Ludovico 1474-1533 . . . . **LC 6**

Aristides
See Epstein, Joseph

Aristophanes
450B.C.-385B.C. . . . . **CMLC 4; DA;
DAB; DAC; DAM DRAM, MST; DC 2**

Arlt, Roberto (Godofredo Christophersen)
1900-1942 . . . . . **TCLC 29; DAM MULT;
HLC**
See also CA 123; 131; HW

Armah, Ayi Kwei
1939- . . . . **CLC 5, 33; BLC;
DAM MULT, POET**
See also BW 1; CA 61-64; CANR 21;
DLB 117; MTCW

Armatrading, Joan 1950- . . . . **CLC 17**
See also CA 114

Arnette, Robert
See Silverberg, Robert

**Arnim, Achim von (Ludwig Joachim von
Arnim)** 1781-1831 . . . . **NCLC 5**
See also DLB 90

Arnim, Bettina von 1785-1859 . . . . **NCLC 38**
See also DLB 90

Arnold, Matthew
1822-1888 . . . . . **NCLC 6, 29; DA; DAB;
DAC; DAM MST, POET; PC 5; WLC**
See also CDBLB 1832-1890; DLB 32, 57

Arnold, Thomas 1795-1842 . . . . . . **NCLC 18**
See also DLB 55

Arnow, Harriette (Louisa) Simpson
1908-1986 . . . . **CLC 2, 7, 18**
See also CA 9-12R; 118; CANR 14; DLB 6;
MTCW; SATA 42; SATA-Obit 47

Arp, Hans
See Arp, Jean

Arp, Jean 1887-1966 . . . . **CLC 5**
See also CA 81-84; 25-28R; CANR 42

Arrabal
See Arrabal, Fernando

Arrabal, Fernando 1932- . . . **CLC 2, 9, 18, 58**
See also CA 9-12R; CANR 15

Arrick, Fran . . . . **CLC 30**
See also Gaberman, Judie Angell

Artaud, Antonin (Marie Joseph)
1896-1948 . . . **TCLC 3, 36; DAM DRAM**
See also CA 104; 149

Arthur, Ruth M(abel) 1905-1979 . . . . **CLC 12**
See also CA 9-12R; 85-88; CANR 4;
SATA 7, 26

Artsybashev, Mikhail (Petrovich)
1878-1927 . . . . **TCLC 31**

Arundel, Honor (Morfydd)
1919-1973 . . . . **CLC 17**
See also CA 21-22; 41-44R; CAP 2;
CLR 35; SATA 4; SATA-Obit 24

Arzner, Dorothy 1897-1979 . . . . **CLC 98**

Asch, Sholem 1880-1957 . . . . **TCLC 3**
See also CA 105

Ash, Shalom
See Asch, Sholem

Baker, Russell (Wayne) 1925- . . . . . . **CLC 31**
See also BEST 89:4; CA 57-60; CANR 11,
41; MTCW

Bakhtin, M.
See Bakhtin, Mikhail Mikhailovich

Bakhtin, M. M.
See Bakhtin, Mikhail Mikhailovich

Bakhtin, Mikhail
See Bakhtin, Mikhail Mikhailovich

Bakhtin, Mikhail Mikhailovich
1895-1975 . . . . **CLC 83**
See also CA 128; 113

Bakshi, Ralph 1938(?)- . . . . **CLC 26**
See also CA 112; 138

Bakunin, Mikhail (Alexandrovich)
1814-1876 . . . . **NCLC 25, 58**

Baldwin, James (Arthur)
1924-1987 . . . . . . **CLC 1, 2, 3, 4, 5, 8, 13,**
15, 17, 42, 50, 67, 90; BLC; DA; DAB;
DAC; DAM MST, MULT, NOV, POP;
DC 1; SSC 10; WLC
See also AAYA 4; BW 1; CA 1-4R; 124;
CABS 1; CANR 3, 24;
CDALB 1941-1968; DLB 2, 7, 33;
DLBY 87; MTCW; SATA 9;
SATA-Obit 54

Ballard, J(ames) G(raham)
1930- . . . . **CLC 3, 6, 14, 36; DAM NOV,**
POP; SSC 1
See also AAYA 3; CA 5-8R; CANR 15, 39;
DLB 14; MTCW

Balmont, Konstantin (Dmitriyevich)
1867-1943 . . . . **TCLC 11**
See also CA 109

Balzac, Honore de
1799-1850 . . . . **NCLC 5, 35, 53; DA;**
DAB; DAC; DAM MST, NOV; SSC 5;
WLC
See also DLB 119

Bambara, Toni Cade
1939-1995 . . . . . . **CLC 19, 88; BLC; DA;**
DAC; DAM MST, MULT
See also AAYA 5; BW 2; CA 29-32R; 150;
CANR 24, 49; DLB 38; MTCW

Bamdad, A.
See Shamlu, Ahmad

Banat, D. R.
See Bradbury, Ray (Douglas)

Bancroft, Laura
See Baum, L(yman) Frank

Banim, John 1798-1842 . . . . **NCLC 13**
See also DLB 116, 158, 159

Banim, Michael 1796-1874 . . . . . . **NCLC 13**
See also DLB 158, 159

Banks, Iain
See Banks, Iain M(enzies)

Banks, Iain M(enzies) 1954- . . . . **CLC 34**
See also CA 123; 128; INT 128

Banks, Lynne Reid . . . . **CLC 23**
See also Reid Banks, Lynne
See also AAYA 6

Banks, Russell 1940- . . . . **CLC 37, 72**
See also CA 65-68; CAAS 15; CANR 19,
52; DLB 130

Banville, John 1945- . . . . **CLC 46**
See also CA 117; 128; DLB 14; INT 128

Banville, Theodore (Faullain) de
1832-1891 . . . . **NCLC 9**

Baraka, Amiri
1934- . . . . **CLC 1, 2, 3, 5, 10, 14, 33;**
BLC; DA; DAC; DAM MST, MULT,
POET, POP; DC 6; PC 4
See also Jones, LeRoi
See also BW 2; CA 21-24R; CABS 3;
CANR 27, 38; CDALB 1941-1968;
DLB 5, 7, 16, 38; DLBD 8; MTCW

Barbauld, Anna Laetitia
1743-1825 . . . . **NCLC 50**
See also DLB 107, 109, 142, 158

Barbellion, W. N. P. . . . . **TCLC 24**
See also Cummings, Bruce F(rederick)

Barbera, Jack (Vincent) 1945- . . . . . . **CLC 44**
See also CA 110; CANR 45

Barbey d'Aurevilly, Jules Amedee
1808-1889 . . . . **NCLC 1; SSC 17**
See also DLB 119

Barbusse, Henri 1873-1935 . . . . **TCLC 5**
See also CA 105; 154; DLB 65

Barclay, Bill
See Moorcock, Michael (John)

Barclay, William Ewert
See Moorcock, Michael (John)

Barea, Arturo 1897-1957 . . . . **TCLC 14**
See also CA 111

Barfoot, Joan 1946- . . . . **CLC 18**
See also CA 105

Baring, Maurice 1874-1945 . . . . **TCLC 8**
See also CA 105; DLB 34

Barker, Clive 1952- . . . **CLC 52; DAM POP**
See also AAYA 10; BEST 90:3; CA 121;
129; INT 129; MTCW

Barker, George Granville
1913-1991 . . . . . **CLC 8, 48; DAM POET**
See also CA 9-12R; 135; CANR 7, 38;
DLB 20; MTCW

Barker, Harley Granville
See Granville-Barker, Harley
See also DLB 10

Barker, Howard 1946- . . . . **CLC 37**
See also CA 102; DLB 13

Barker, Pat(ricia) 1943- . . . . **CLC 32, 94**
See also CA 117; 122; CANR 50; INT 122

Barlow, Joel 1754-1812 . . . . **NCLC 23**
See also DLB 37

Barnard, Mary (Ethel) 1909- . . . . **CLC 48**
See also CA 21-22; CAP 2

Barnes, Djuna
1892-1982 . . . **CLC 3, 4, 8, 11, 29; SSC 3**
See also CA 9-12R; 107; CANR 16, 55;
DLB 4, 9, 45; MTCW

Barnes, Julian (Patrick)
1946- . . . . **CLC 42; DAB**
See also CA 102; CANR 19, 54; DLBY 93

Barnes, Peter 1931- . . . . **CLC 5, 56**
See also CA 65-68; CAAS 12; CANR 33,
34; DLB 13; MTCW

Baroja (y Nessi), Pio
1872-1956 . . . . **TCLC 8; HLC**
See also CA 104

Baron, David
See Pinter, Harold

Baron Corvo
See Rolfe, Frederick (William Serafino
Austin Lewis Mary)

Barondess, Sue K(aufman)
1926-1977 . . . . **CLC 8**
See also Kaufman, Sue
See also CA 1-4R; 69-72; CANR 1

Baron de Teive
See Pessoa, Fernando (Antonio Nogueira)

Barres, Maurice 1862-1923 . . . . **TCLC 47**
See also DLB 123

Barreto, Afonso Henrique de Lima
See Lima Barreto, Afonso Henrique de

Barrett, (Roger) Syd 1946- . . . . **CLC 35**

Barrett, William (Christopher)
1913-1992 . . . . **CLC 27**
See also CA 13-16R; 139; CANR 11;
INT CANR-11

Barrie, J(ames) M(atthew)
1860-1937 . . . . **TCLC 2; DAB;**
DAM DRAM
See also CA 104; 136; CDBLB 1890-1914;
CLR 16; DLB 10, 141, 156; MAICYA;
YABC 1

Barrington, Michael
See Moorcock, Michael (John)

Barrol, Grady
See Bograd, Larry

Barry, Mike
See Malzberg, Barry N(athaniel)

Barry, Philip 1896-1949 . . . . **TCLC 11**
See also CA 109; DLB 7

Bart, Andre Schwarz
See Schwarz-Bart, Andre

Barth, John (Simmons)
1930- . . . . . . **CLC 1, 2, 3, 5, 7, 9, 10, 14,**
27, 51, 89; DAM NOV; SSC 10
See also AITN 1, 2; CA 1-4R; CABS 1;
CANR 5, 23, 49; DLB 2; MTCW

Barthelme, Donald
1931-1989 . . . . . . **CLC 1, 2, 3, 5, 6, 8, 13,**
23, 46, 59; DAM NOV; SSC 2
See also CA 21-24R; 129; CANR 20;
DLB 2; DLBY 80, 89; MTCW; SATA 7;
SATA-Obit 62

Barthelme, Frederick 1943- . . . . **CLC 36**
See also CA 114; 122; DLBY 85; INT 122

Barthes, Roland (Gerard)
1915-1980 . . . . **CLC 24, 83**
See also CA 130; 97-100; MTCW

Barzun, Jacques (Martin) 1907- . . . . **CLC 51**
See also CA 61-64; CANR 22

Bashevis, Isaac
See Singer, Isaac Bashevis

Bashkirtseff, Marie 1859-1884 . . . **NCLC 27**

Basho
See Matsuo Basho

Bass, Kingsley B., Jr.
See Bullins, Ed

Bass, Rick 1958- . . . . **CLC 79**
See also CA 126; CANR 53

Belser, Reimond Karel Maria de 1929-
See Ruyslinck, Ward
See also CA 152

Bely, Andrey . . . . **TCLC 7; PC 11**
See also Bugayev, Boris Nikolayevich

Benary, Margot
See Benary-Isbert, Margot

Benary-Isbert, Margot 1889-1979 . . . **CLC 12**
See also CA 5-8R; 89-92; CANR 4;
CLR 12; MAICYA; SATA 2;
SATA-Obit 21

Benavente (y Martinez), Jacinto
1866-1954 . . . . . **TCLC 3; DAM DRAM,
MULT**
See also CA 106; 131; HW; MTCW

Benchley, Peter (Bradford)
1940- . . . . . **CLC 4, 8; DAM NOV, POP**
See also AAYA 14; AITN 2; CA 17-20R;
CANR 12, 35; MTCW; SATA 3, 89

Benchley, Robert (Charles)
1889-1945 . . . . **TCLC 1, 55**
See also CA 105; 153; DLB 11

Benda, Julien 1867-1956 . . . . **TCLC 60**
See also CA 120; 154

Benedict, Ruth 1887-1948 . . . . **TCLC 60**

Benedikt, Michael 1935- . . . . **CLC 4, 14**
See also CA 13-16R; CANR 7; DLB 5

Benet, Juan 1927- . . . . **CLC 28**
See also CA 143

Benet, Stephen Vincent
1898-1943 . . . . . . **TCLC 7; DAM POET;
SSC 10**
See also CA 104; 152; DLB 4, 48, 102;
YABC 1

Benet, William Rose
1886-1950 . . . . . . **TCLC 28; DAM POET**
See also CA 118; 152; DLB 45

Benford, Gregory (Albert) 1941- . . . . **CLC 52**
See also CA 69-72; CANR 12, 24, 49;
DLBY 82

Bengtsson, Frans (Gunnar)
1894-1954 . . . . **TCLC 48**

Benjamin, David
See Slavitt, David R(ytman)

Benjamin, Lois
See Gould, Lois

Benjamin, Walter 1892-1940 . . . . . . **TCLC 39**

Benn, Gottfried 1886-1956 . . . . **TCLC 3**
See also CA 106; 153; DLB 56

Bennett, Alan
1934- . . . **CLC 45, 77; DAB; DAM MST**
See also CA 103; CANR 35, 55; MTCW

Bennett, (Enoch) Arnold
1867-1931 . . . . **TCLC 5, 20**
See also CA 106; CDBLB 1890-1914;
DLB 10, 34, 98, 135

Bennett, Elizabeth
See Mitchell, Margaret (Munnerlyn)

Bennett, George Harold 1930-
See Bennett, Hal
See also BW 1; CA 97-100

Bennett, Hal . . . . **CLC 5**
See also Bennett, George Harold
See also DLB 33

Bennett, Jay 1912- . . . . **CLC 35**
See also AAYA 10; CA 69-72; CANR 11,
42; JRDA; SAAS 4; SATA 41, 87;
SATA-Brief 27

Bennett, Louise (Simone)
1919- . . . . . **CLC 28; BLC; DAM MULT**
See also BW 2; CA 151; DLB 117

Benson, E(dward) F(rederic)
1867-1940 . . . . **TCLC 27**
See also CA 114; DLB 135, 153

Benson, Jackson J. 1930- . . . . **CLC 34**
See also CA 25-28R; DLB 111

Benson, Sally 1900-1972 . . . . **CLC 17**
See also CA 19-20; 37-40R; CAP 1;
SATA 1, 35; SATA-Obit 27

Benson, Stella 1892-1933 . . . . **TCLC 17**
See also CA 117; 154; DLB 36, 162

Bentham, Jeremy 1748-1832 . . . . . **NCLC 38**
See also DLB 107, 158

Bentley, E(dmund) C(lerihew)
1875-1956 . . . . **TCLC 12**
See also CA 108; DLB 70

Bentley, Eric (Russell) 1916- . . . . . . **CLC 24**
See also CA 5-8R; CANR 6; INT CANR-6

Beranger, Pierre Jean de
1780-1857 . . . . **NCLC 34**

Berdyaev, Nicolas
See Berdyaev, Nikolai (Aleksandrovich)

Berdyaev, Nikolai (Aleksandrovich)
1874-1948 . . . . **TCLC 67**
See also CA 120

Berendt, John (Lawrence) 1939- . . . . **CLC 86**
See also CA 146

Berger, Colonel
See Malraux, (Georges-)Andre

Berger, John (Peter) 1926- . . . . . . **CLC 2, 19**
See also CA 81-84; CANR 51; DLB 14

Berger, Melvin H. 1927- . . . . **CLC 12**
See also CA 5-8R; CANR 4; CLR 32;
SAAS 2; SATA 5, 88

Berger, Thomas (Louis)
1924- . . . . **CLC 3, 5, 8, 11, 18, 38;
DAM NOV**
See also CA 1-4R; CANR 5, 28, 51; DLB 2;
DLBY 80; INT CANR-28; MTCW

Bergman, (Ernst) Ingmar
1918- . . . . **CLC 16, 72**
See also CA 81-84; CANR 33

Bergson, Henri 1859-1941 . . . . **TCLC 32**

Bergstein, Eleanor 1938- . . . . **CLC 4**
See also CA 53-56; CANR 5

Berkoff, Steven 1937- . . . . **CLC 56**
See also CA 104

Bermant, Chaim (Icyk) 1929- . . . . . . **CLC 40**
See also CA 57-60; CANR 6, 31

Bern, Victoria
See Fisher, M(ary) F(rances) K(ennedy)

Bernanos, (Paul Louis) Georges
1888-1948 . . . . **TCLC 3**
See also CA 104; 130; DLB 72

Bernard, April 1956- . . . . **CLC 59**
See also CA 131

Berne, Victoria
See Fisher, M(ary) F(rances) K(ennedy)

Bernhard, Thomas
1931-1989 . . . . **CLC 3, 32, 61**
See also CA 85-88; 127; CANR 32;
DLB 85, 124; MTCW

Berriault, Gina 1926- . . . . **CLC 54**
See also CA 116; 129; DLB 130

Berrigan, Daniel 1921- . . . . **CLC 4**
See also CA 33-36R; CAAS 1; CANR 11,
43; DLB 5

Berrigan, Edmund Joseph Michael, Jr.
1934-1983
See Berrigan, Ted
See also CA 61-64; 110; CANR 14

Berrigan, Ted . . . . **CLC 37**
See also Berrigan, Edmund Joseph Michael,
Jr.
See also DLB 5, 169

Berry, Charles Edward Anderson 1931-
See Berry, Chuck
See also CA 115

Berry, Chuck . . . . **CLC 17**
See also Berry, Charles Edward Anderson

Berry, Jonas
See Ashbery, John (Lawrence)

Berry, Wendell (Erdman)
1934- . . . . **CLC 4, 6, 8, 27, 46;
DAM POET**
See also AITN 1; CA 73-76; CANR 50;
DLB 5, 6

Berryman, John
1914-1972 . . . . . . **CLC 1, 2, 3, 4, 6, 8, 10,
13, 25, 62; DAM POET**
See also CA 13-16; 33-36R; CABS 2;
CANR 35; CAP 1; CDALB 1941-1968;
DLB 48; MTCW

Bertolucci, Bernardo 1940- . . . . **CLC 16**
See also CA 106

Bertrand, Aloysius 1807-1841 . . . . **NCLC 31**

Bertran de Born c. 1140-1215 . . . . . **CMLC 5**

Besant, Annie (Wood) 1847-1933 . . . **TCLC 9**
See also CA 105

Bessie, Alvah 1904-1985 . . . . **CLC 23**
See also CA 5-8R; 116; CANR 2; DLB 26

Bethlen, T. D.
See Silverberg, Robert

Beti, Mongo . . . . **CLC 27; BLC; DAM MULT**
See also Biyidi, Alexandre

Betjeman, John
1906-1984 . . . . **CLC 2, 6, 10, 34, 43;
DAB; DAM MST, POET**
See also CA 9-12R; 112; CANR 33;
CDBLB 1945-1960; DLB 20; DLBY 84;
MTCW

Bettelheim, Bruno 1903-1990 . . . . . . **CLC 79**
See also CA 81-84; 131; CANR 23; MTCW

Betti, Ugo 1892-1953 . . . . **TCLC 5**
See also CA 104

Betts, Doris (Waugh) 1932- . . . . **CLC 3, 6, 28**
See also CA 13-16R; CANR 9; DLBY 82;
INT CANR-9

Bevan, Alistair
See Roberts, Keith (John Kingston)

Bialik, Chaim Nachman
1873-1934 . . . . **TCLC 25**

Bickerstaff, Isaac
See Swift, Jonathan

Bidart, Frank   1939- . . . .   CLC 33
See also CA 140

Bienek, Horst   1930- . . . .   CLC 7, 11
See also CA 73-76; DLB 75

Bierce, Ambrose (Gwinett)
1842-1914(?) . . . . TCLC 1, 7, 44; DA;
DAC; DAM MST; SSC 9; WLC
See also CA 104; 139; CDALB 1865-1917;
DLB 11, 12, 23, 71, 74

Biggers, Earl Derr   1884-1933 . . . . . TCLC 65
See also CA 108; 153

Billings, Josh
See Shaw, Henry Wheeler

Billington, (Lady) Rachel (Mary)
1942- . . . .   CLC 43
See also AITN 2; CA 33-36R; CANR 44

Binyon, T(imothy) J(ohn)   1936- . . . .   CLC 34
See also CA 111; CANR 28

Bioy Casares, Adolfo
1914- . . . . CLC 4, 8, 13, 88;
DAM MULT; HLC; SSC 17
See also CA 29-32R; CANR 19, 43;
DLB 113; HW; MTCW

Bird, Cordwainer
See Ellison, Harlan (Jay)

Bird, Robert Montgomery
1806-1854 . . . . NCLC 1

Birney, (Alfred) Earle
1904- . . . . CLC 1, 4, 6, 11; DAC;
DAM MST, POET
See also CA 1-4R; CANR 5, 20; DLB 88;
MTCW

Bishop, Elizabeth
1911-1979 . . . . . . CLC 1, 4, 9, 13, 15, 32;
DA; DAC; DAM MST, POET; PC 3
See also CA 5-8R; 89-92; CABS 2;
CANR 26; CDALB 1968-1988; DLB 5,
169; MTCW; SATA-Obit 24

Bishop, John   1935- . . . .   CLC 10
See also CA 105

Bissett, Bill   1939- . . . .   CLC 18; PC 14
See also CA 69-72; CAAS 19; CANR 15;
DLB 53; MTCW

Bitov, Andrei (Georgievich)   1937- . . .   CLC 57
See also CA 142

Biyidi, Alexandre   1932-
See Beti, Mongo
See also BW 1; CA 114; 124; MTCW

Bjarme, Brynjolf
See Ibsen, Henrik (Johan)

Bjornson, Bjornstjerne (Martinius)
1832-1910 . . . . TCLC 7, 37
See also CA 104

Black, Robert
See Holdstock, Robert P.

Blackburn, Paul   1926-1971 . . . . . .   CLC 9, 43
See also CA 81-84; 33-36R; CANR 34;
DLB 16; DLBY 81

Black Elk
1863-1950 . . . . . TCLC 33; DAM MULT
See also CA 144; NNAL

Black Hobart
See Sanders, (James) Ed(ward)

Blacklin, Malcolm
See Chambers, Aidan

Blackmore, R(ichard) D(oddridge)
1825-1900 . . . . TCLC 27
See also CA 120; DLB 18

Blackmur, R(ichard) P(almer)
1904-1965 . . . . CLC 2, 24
See also CA 11-12; 25-28R; CAP 1; DLB 63

Black Tarantula
See Acker, Kathy

Blackwood, Algernon (Henry)
1869-1951 . . . . TCLC 5
See also CA 105; 150; DLB 153, 156

Blackwood, Caroline   1931-1996 . . .   CLC 6, 9
See also CA 85-88; 151; CANR 32;
DLB 14; MTCW

Blade, Alexander
See Hamilton, Edmond; Silverberg, Robert

Blaga, Lucian   1895-1961 . . . .   CLC 75

Blair, Eric (Arthur)   1903-1950
See Orwell, George
See also CA 104; 132; DA; DAB; DAC;
DAM MST, NOV; MTCW; SATA 29

Blais, Marie-Claire
1939- . . . . CLC 2, 4, 6, 13, 22; DAC;
DAM MST
See also CA 21-24R; CAAS 4; CANR 38;
DLB 53; MTCW

Blaise, Clark   1940- . . . .   CLC 29
See also AITN 2; CA 53-56; CAAS 3;
CANR 5; DLB 53

Blake, Nicholas
See Day Lewis, C(ecil)
See also DLB 77

Blake, William
1757-1827 . . . . NCLC 13, 37, 57; DA;
DAB; DAC; DAM MST, POET; PC 12;
WLC
See also CDBLB 1789-1832; DLB 93, 163;
MAICYA; SATA 30

Blake, William J(ames)   1894-1969 . . .   PC 12
See also CA 5-8R; 25-28R

Blasco Ibanez, Vicente
1867-1928 . . . . TCLC 12; DAM NOV
See also CA 110; 131; HW; MTCW

Blatty, William Peter
1928- . . . . CLC 2; DAM POP
See also CA 5-8R; CANR 9

Bleeck, Oliver
See Thomas, Ross (Elmore)

Blessing, Lee   1949- . . . .   CLC 54

Blish, James (Benjamin)
1921-1975 . . . . CLC 14
See also CA 1-4R; 57-60; CANR 3; DLB 8;
MTCW; SATA 66

Bliss, Reginald
See Wells, H(erbert) G(eorge)

Blixen, Karen (Christentze Dinesen)
1885-1962
See Dinesen, Isak
See also CA 25-28; CANR 22, 50; CAP 2;
MTCW; SATA 44

Bloch, Robert (Albert)   1917-1994 . . .   CLC 33
See also CA 5-8R; 146; CAAS 20; CANR 5;
DLB 44; INT CANR-5; SATA 12;
SATA-Obit 82

Blok, Alexander (Alexandrovich)
1880-1921 . . . . TCLC 5
See also CA 104

Blom, Jan
See Breytenbach, Breyten

Bloom, Harold   1930- . . . .   CLC 24
See also CA 13-16R; CANR 39; DLB 67

Bloomfield, Aurelius
See Bourne, Randolph S(illiman)

Blount, Roy (Alton), Jr.   1941- . . . . .   CLC 38
See also CA 53-56; CANR 10, 28;
INT CANR-28; MTCW

Bloy, Leon   1846-1917 . . . .   TCLC 22
See also CA 121; DLB 123

Blume, Judy (Sussman)
1938- . . . CLC 12, 30; DAM NOV, POP
See also AAYA 3; CA 29-32R; CANR 13,
37; CLR 2, 15; DLB 52; JRDA;
MAICYA; MTCW; SATA 2, 31, 79

Blunden, Edmund (Charles)
1896-1974 . . . . CLC 2, 56
See also CA 17-18; 45-48; CANR 54;
CAP 2; DLB 20, 100, 155; MTCW

Bly, Robert (Elwood)
1926- . . . . CLC 1, 2, 5, 10, 15, 38;
DAM POET
See also CA 5-8R; CANR 41; DLB 5;
MTCW

Boas, Franz   1858-1942 . . . .   TCLC 56
See also CA 115

Bobette
See Simenon, Georges (Jacques Christian)

Boccaccio, Giovanni
1313-1375 . . . . CMLC 13; SSC 10

Bochco, Steven   1943- . . . .   CLC 35
See also AAYA 11; CA 124; 138

Bodenheim, Maxwell   1892-1954 . . .   TCLC 44
See also CA 110; DLB 9, 45

Bodker, Cecil   1927- . . . .   CLC 21
See also CA 73-76; CANR 13, 44; CLR 23;
MAICYA; SATA 14

Boell, Heinrich (Theodor)
1917-1985 . . . . CLC 2, 3, 6, 9, 11, 15, 27,
32, 72; DA; DAB; DAC; DAM MST,
NOV; SSC 23; WLC
See also CA 21-24R; 116; CANR 24;
DLB 69; DLBY 85; MTCW

Boerne, Alfred
See Doeblin, Alfred

Boethius   480(?)-524(?) . . . .   CMLC 15
See also DLB 115

Bogan, Louise
1897-1970 . . . . CLC 4, 39, 46, 93;
DAM POET; PC 12
See also CA 73-76; 25-28R; CANR 33;
DLB 45, 169; MTCW

Bogarde, Dirk . . . .   CLC 19
See also Van Den Bogarde, Derek Jules
Gaspard Ulric Niven
See also DLB 14

Brandes, Georg (Morris Cohen)
1842-1927 .... TCLC 10
See also CA 105

Brandys, Kazimierz 1916- .... CLC 62

Branley, Franklyn M(ansfield)
1915- .... CLC 21
See also CA 33-36R; CANR 14, 39;
CLR 13; MAICYA; SAAS 16; SATA 4,
68

Brathwaite, Edward Kamau
1930- .... CLC 11; DAM POET
See also BW 2; CA 25-28R; CANR 11, 26,
47; DLB 125

Brautigan, Richard (Gary)
1935-1984 .... CLC 1, 3, 5, 9, 12, 34, 42;
DAM NOV
See also CA 53-56; 113; CANR 34; DLB 2,
5; DLBY 80, 84; MTCW; SATA 56

Brave Bird, Mary 1953-
See Crow Dog, Mary (Ellen)
See also NNAL

Braverman, Kate 1950- .... CLC 67
See also CA 89-92

Brecht, Bertolt
1898-1956 ...... TCLC 1, 6, 13, 35; DA;
DAB; DAC; DAM DRAM, MST; DC 3;
WLC
See also CA 104; 133; DLB 56, 124; MTCW

Brecht, Eugen Berthold Friedrich
See Brecht, Bertolt

Bremer, Fredrika 1801-1865 ..... NCLC 11

Brennan, Christopher John
1870-1932 .... TCLC 17
See also CA 117

Brennan, Maeve 1917- .... CLC 5
See also CA 81-84

Brentano, Clemens (Maria)
1778-1842 .... NCLC 1
See also DLB 90

Brent of Bin Bin
See Franklin, (Stella Maraia Sarah) Miles

Brenton, Howard 1942- .... CLC 31
See also CA 69-72; CANR 33; DLB 13;
MTCW

Breslin, James 1930-
See Breslin, Jimmy
See also CA 73-76; CANR 31; DAM NOV;
MTCW

Breslin, Jimmy .... CLC 4, 43
See also Breslin, James
See also AITN 1

Bresson, Robert 1901- .... CLC 16
See also CA 110; CANR 49

Breton, Andre
1896-1966 ..... CLC 2, 9, 15, 54; PC 15
See also CA 19-20; 25-28R; CANR 40;
CAP 2; DLB 65; MTCW

Breytenbach, Breyten
1939(?)- ...... CLC 23, 37; DAM POET
See also CA 113; 129

Bridgers, Sue Ellen 1942- .... CLC 26
See also AAYA 8; CA 65-68; CANR 11,
36; CLR 18; DLB 52; JRDA; MAICYA;
SAAS 1; SATA 22, 90

Bridges, Robert (Seymour)
1844-1930 ...... TCLC 1; DAM POET
See also CA 104; 152; CDBLB 1890-1914;
DLB 19, 98

Bridie, James .... TCLC 3
See also Mavor, Osborne Henry
See also DLB 10

Brin, David 1950- .... CLC 34
See also CA 102; CANR 24;
INT CANR-24; SATA 65

Brink, Andre (Philippus)
1935- .... CLC 18, 36
See also CA 104; CANR 39; INT 103;
MTCW

Brinsmead, H(esba) F(ay) 1922- .... CLC 21
See also CA 21-24R; CANR 10; MAICYA;
SAAS 5; SATA 18, 78

Brittain, Vera (Mary)
1893(?)-1970 .... CLC 23
See also CA 13-16; 25-28R; CAP 1; MTCW

Broch, Hermann 1886-1951 ...... TCLC 20
See also CA 117; DLB 85, 124

Brock, Rose
See Hansen, Joseph

Brodkey, Harold (Roy) 1930-1996 .. CLC 56
See also CA 111; 151; DLB 130

Brodsky, Iosif Alexandrovich 1940-1996
See Brodsky, Joseph
See also AITN 1; CA 41-44R; 151;
CANR 37; DAM POET; MTCW

Brodsky, Joseph .. CLC 4, 6, 13, 36, 50; PC 9
See also Brodsky, Iosif Alexandrovich

Brodsky, Michael Mark 1948- ..... CLC 19
See also CA 102; CANR 18, 41

Bromell, Henry 1947- .... CLC 5
See also CA 53-56; CANR 9

Bromfield, Louis (Brucker)
1896-1956 .... TCLC 11
See also CA 107; DLB 4, 9, 86

Broner, E(sther) M(asserman)
1930- .... CLC 19
See also CA 17-20R; CANR 8, 25; DLB 28

Bronk, William 1918- .... CLC 10
See also CA 89-92; CANR 23; DLB 165

Bronstein, Lev Davidovich
See Trotsky, Leon

Bronte, Anne 1820-1849......... NCLC 4
See also DLB 21

Bronte, Charlotte
1816-1855 ..... NCLC 3, 8, 33, 58; DA;
DAB; DAC; DAM MST, NOV; WLC
See also AAYA 17; CDBLB 1832-1890;
DLB 21, 159

Bronte, Emily (Jane)
1818-1848 .... NCLC 16, 35; DA; DAB;
DAC; DAM MST, NOV, POET; PC 8;
WLC
See also AAYA 17; CDBLB 1832-1890;
DLB 21, 32

Brooke, Frances 1724-1789 .... LC 6
See also DLB 39, 99

Brooke, Henry 1703(?)-1783 .... LC 1
See also DLB 39

Brooke, Rupert (Chawner)
1887-1915 ...... TCLC 2, 7; DA; DAB;
DAC; DAM MST, POET; WLC
See also CA 104; 132; CDBLB 1914-1945;
DLB 19; MTCW

Brooke-Haven, P.
See Wodehouse, P(elham) G(renville)

Brooke-Rose, Christine 1926- ...... CLC 40
See also CA 13-16R; DLB 14

Brookner, Anita
1928- .... CLC 32, 34, 51; DAB;
DAM POP
See also CA 114; 120; CANR 37; DLBY 87;
MTCW

Brooks, Cleanth 1906-1994 ..... CLC 24, 86
See also CA 17-20R; 145; CANR 33, 35;
DLB 63; DLBY 94; INT CANR-35;
MTCW

Brooks, George
See Baum, L(yman) Frank

Brooks, Gwendolyn
1917- ...... CLC 1, 2, 4, 5, 15, 49; BLC;
DA; DAC; DAM MST, MULT, POET;
PC 7; WLC
See also AITN 1; BW 2; CA 1-4R;
CANR 1, 27, 52; CDALB 1941-1968;
CLR 27; DLB 5, 76, 165; MTCW;
SATA 6

Brooks, Mel..................... CLC 12
See also Kaminsky, Melvin
See also AAYA 13; DLB 26

Brooks, Peter 1938- .... CLC 34
See also CA 45-48; CANR 1

Brooks, Van Wyck 1886-1963...... CLC 29
See also CA 1-4R; CANR 6; DLB 45, 63,
103

Brophy, Brigid (Antonia)
1929-1995 .... CLC 6, 11, 29
See also CA 5-8R; 149; CAAS 4; CANR 25,
53; DLB 14; MTCW

Brosman, Catharine Savage 1934-.... CLC 9
See also CA 61-64; CANR 21, 46

Brother Antoninus
See Everson, William (Oliver)

Broughton, T(homas) Alan 1936- ... CLC 19
See also CA 45-48; CANR 2, 23, 48

Broumas, Olga 1949- .... CLC 10, 73
See also CA 85-88; CANR 20

Brown, Charles Brockden
1771-1810 .... NCLC 22
See also CDALB 1640-1865; DLB 37, 59,
73

Brown, Christy 1932-1981......... CLC 63
See also CA 105; 104; DLB 14

Brown, Claude
1937- ..... CLC 30; BLC; DAM MULT
See also AAYA 7; BW 1; CA 73-76

Brown, Dee (Alexander)
1908- .... CLC 18, 47; DAM POP
See also CA 13-16R; CAAS 6; CANR 11,
45; DLBY 80; MTCW; SATA 5

Brown, George
See Wertmueller, Lina

Brown, George Douglas
1869-1902 .... TCLC 28

Brown, George Mackay
1921-1996 . . . . CLC 5, 48
See also CA 21-24R; 151; CAAS 6;
CANR 12, 37; DLB 14, 27, 139; MTCW;
SATA 35

Brown, (William) Larry 1951- . . . . . CLC 73
See also CA 130; 134; INT 133

Brown, Moses
See Barrett, William (Christopher)

Brown, Rita Mae
1944- . . . . . CLC 18, 43, 79; DAM NOV,
POP
See also CA 45-48; CANR 2, 11, 35;
INT CANR-11; MTCW

Brown, Roderick (Langmere) Haig-
See Haig-Brown, Roderick (Langmere)

Brown, Rosellen 1939- . . . . CLC 32
See also CA 77-80; CAAS 10; CANR 14, 44

Brown, Sterling Allen
1901-1989 . . . . CLC 1, 23, 59; BLC;
DAM MULT, POET
See also BW 1; CA 85-88; 127; CANR 26;
DLB 48, 51, 63; MTCW

Brown, Will
See Ainsworth, William Harrison

Brown, William Wells
1813-1884 . . . . NCLC 2; BLC;
DAM MULT; DC 1
See also DLB 3, 50

Browne, (Clyde) Jackson 1948(?)- . . . CLC 21
See also CA 120

Browning, Elizabeth Barrett
1806-1861 . . . . . NCLC 1, 16; DA; DAB;
DAC; DAM MST, POET; PC 6; WLC
See also CDBLB 1832-1890; DLB 32

Browning, Robert
1812-1889 . . . . NCLC 19; DA; DAB;
DAC; DAM MST, POET; PC 2
See also CDBLB 1832-1890; DLB 32, 163;
YABC 1

Browning, Tod 1882-1962 . . . . CLC 16
See also CA 141; 117

Brownson, Orestes (Augustus)
1803-1876 . . . . NCLC 50

Bruccoli, Matthew J(oseph) 1931- . . CLC 34
See also CA 9-12R; CANR 7; DLB 103

Bruce, Lenny . . . . CLC 21
See also Schneider, Leonard Alfred

Bruin, John
See Brutus, Dennis

Brulard, Henri
See Stendhal

Brulls, Christian
See Simenon, Georges (Jacques Christian)

Brunner, John (Kilian Houston)
1934-1995 . . . . . . CLC 8, 10; DAM POP
See also CA 1-4R; 149; CAAS 8; CANR 2,
37; MTCW

Bruno, Giordano 1548-1600 . . . . LC 27

Brutus, Dennis
1924- . . . . . CLC 43; BLC; DAM MULT,
POET
See also BW 2; CA 49-52; CAAS 14;
CANR 2, 27, 42; DLB 117

Bryan, C(ourtlandt) D(ixon) B(arnes)
1936- . . . . CLC 29
See also CA 73-76; CANR 13;
INT CANR-13

Bryan, Michael
See Moore, Brian

Bryant, William Cullen
1794-1878 . . . . . NCLC 6, 46; DA; DAB;
DAC; DAM MST, POET
See also CDALB 1640-1865; DLB 3, 43, 59

Bryusov, Valery Yakovlevich
1873-1924 . . . . TCLC 10
See also CA 107

Buchan, John
1875-1940 . . . . TCLC 41; DAB;
DAM POP
See also CA 108; 145; DLB 34, 70, 156;
YABC 2

Buchanan, George 1506-1582 . . . . LC 4

Buchheim, Lothar-Guenther 1918- . . . CLC 6
See also CA 85-88

Buchner, (Karl) Georg
1813-1837 . . . . NCLC 26

Buchwald, Art(hur) 1925- . . . . CLC 33
See also AITN 1; CA 5-8R; CANR 21;
MTCW; SATA 10

Buck, Pearl S(ydenstricker)
1892-1973 . . . . CLC 7, 11, 18; DA; DAB;
DAC; DAM MST, NOV
See also AITN 1; CA 1-4R; 41-44R;
CANR 1, 34; DLB 9, 102; MTCW;
SATA 1, 25

Buckler, Ernest
1908-1984 . . CLC 13; DAC; DAM MST
See also CA 11-12; 114; CAP 1; DLB 68;
SATA 47

Buckley, Vincent (Thomas)
1925-1988 . . . . CLC 57
See also CA 101

Buckley, William F(rank), Jr.
1925- . . . . CLC 7, 18, 37; DAM POP
See also AITN 1; CA 1-4R; CANR 1, 24,
53; DLB 137; DLBY 80; INT CANR-24;
MTCW

Buechner, (Carl) Frederick
1926- . . . . . . CLC 2, 4, 6, 9; DAM NOV
See also CA 13-16R; CANR 11, 39;
DLBY 80; INT CANR-11; MTCW

Buell, John (Edward) 1927- . . . . CLC 10
See also CA 1-4R; DLB 53

Buero Vallejo, Antonio 1916- . . . CLC 15, 46
See also CA 106; CANR 24, 49; HW;
MTCW

Bufalino, Gesualdo 1920(?)- . . . . CLC 74

Bugayev, Boris Nikolayevich 1880-1934
See Bely, Andrey
See also CA 104

Bukowski, Charles
1920-1994 . . . . CLC 2, 5, 9, 41, 82;
DAM NOV, POET
See also CA 17-20R; 144; CANR 40;
DLB 5, 130, 169; MTCW

Bulgakov, Mikhail (Afanas'evich)
1891-1940 . . . . TCLC 2, 16;
DAM DRAM, NOV; SSC 18
See also CA 105; 152

Bulgya, Alexander Alexandrovich
1901-1956 . . . . TCLC 53
See also Fadeyev, Alexander
See also CA 117

Bullins, Ed
1935- . . . . CLC 1, 5, 7; BLC;
DAM DRAM, MULT; DC 6
See also BW 2; CA 49-52; CAAS 16;
CANR 24, 46; DLB 7, 38; MTCW

Bulwer-Lytton, Edward (George Earle Lytton)
1803-1873 . . . . NCLC 1, 45
See also DLB 21

Bunin, Ivan Alexeyevich
1870-1953 . . . . TCLC 6; SSC 5
See also CA 104

Bunting, Basil
1900-1985 . . . . CLC 10, 39, 47;
DAM POET
See also CA 53-56; 115; CANR 7; DLB 20

Bunuel, Luis
1900-1983 . . . . CLC 16, 80;
DAM MULT; HLC
See also CA 101; 110; CANR 32; HW

Bunyan, John
1628-1688 . . . . . . LC 4; DA; DAB; DAC;
DAM MST; WLC
See also CDBLB 1660-1789; DLB 39

Burckhardt, Jacob (Christoph)
1818-1897 . . . . NCLC 49

Burford, Eleanor
See Hibbert, Eleanor Alice Burford

Burgess, Anthony
CLC 1, 2, 4, 5, 8, 10, 13, 15, 22, 40, 62,
81, 94; DAB
See also Wilson, John (Anthony) Burgess
See also AITN 1; CDBLB 1960 to Present;
DLB 14

Burke, Edmund
1729(?)-1797 . . . . . . LC 7, 36; DA; DAB;
DAC; DAM MST; WLC
See also DLB 104

Burke, Kenneth (Duva)
1897-1993 . . . . CLC 2, 24
See also CA 5-8R; 143; CANR 39; DLB 45,
63; MTCW

Burke, Leda
See Garnett, David

Burke, Ralph
See Silverberg, Robert

Burke, Thomas 1886-1945 . . . . TCLC 63
See also CA 113

Burney, Fanny 1752-1840 . . . . NCLC 12, 54
See also DLB 39

Burns, Robert 1759-1796 . . . . PC 6
See also CDBLB 1789-1832; DA; DAB;
DAC; DAM MST, POET; DLB 109;
WLC

Burns, Tex
See L'Amour, Louis (Dearborn)

Burnshaw, Stanley 1906- . . . . . CLC 3, 13, 44
See also CA 9-12R; DLB 48

Burr, Anne 1937- . . . . CLC 6
See also CA 25-28R

Capote, Truman
1924-1984 ...... **CLC 1, 3, 8, 13, 19, 34, 38, 58; DA; DAB; DAC; DAM MST, NOV, POP; SSC 2; WLC**
See also CA 5-8R; 113; CANR 18; CDALB 1941-1968; DLB 2; DLBY 80, 84; MTCW; SATA 91

Capra, Frank 1897-1991.......... **CLC 16**
See also CA 61-64; 135

Caputo, Philip 1941-.............. **CLC 32**
See also CA 73-76; CANR 40

Card, Orson Scott
1951- ...... **CLC 44, 47, 50; DAM POP**
See also AAYA 11; CA 102; CANR 27, 47; INT CANR-27; MTCW; SATA 83

Cardenal, Ernesto
1925- .... **CLC 31; DAM MULT, POET; HLC**
See also CA 49-52; CANR 2, 32; HW; MTCW

Cardozo, Benjamin N(athan)
1870-1938 .... **TCLC 65**
See also CA 117

Carducci, Giosue 1835-1907....... **TCLC 32**

Carew, Thomas 1595(?)-1640....... **LC 13**
See also DLB 126

Carey, Ernestine Gilbreth 1908-.... **CLC 17**
See also CA 5-8R; SATA 2

Carey, Peter 1943-......... **CLC 40, 55, 96**
See also CA 123; 127; CANR 53; INT 127; MTCW

Carleton, William 1794-1869...... **NCLC 3**
See also DLB 159

Carlisle, Henry (Coffin) 1926-...... **CLC 33**
See also CA 13-16R; CANR 15

Carlsen, Chris
See Holdstock, Robert P.

Carlson, Ron(ald F.) 1947-......... **CLC 54**
See also CA 105; CANR 27

Carlyle, Thomas
1795-1881 .... **NCLC 22; DA; DAB; DAC; DAM MST**
See also CDBLB 1789-1832; DLB 55; 144

Carman, (William) Bliss
1861-1929 .... **TCLC 7; DAC**
See also CA 104; 152; DLB 92

Carnegie, Dale 1888-1955 .... **TCLC 53**

Carossa, Hans 1878-1956........ **TCLC 48**
See also DLB 66

Carpenter, Don(ald Richard)
1931-1995 .... **CLC 41**
See also CA 45-48; 149; CANR 1

Carpentier (y Valmont), Alejo
1904-1980 .... **CLC 8, 11, 38; DAM MULT; HLC**
See also CA 65-68; 97-100; CANR 11; DLB 113; HW

Carr, Caleb 1955(?)-.............. **CLC 86**
See also CA 147

Carr, Emily 1871-1945........... **TCLC 32**
See also DLB 68

Carr, John Dickson 1906-1977 ...... **CLC 3**
See also CA 49-52; 69-72; CANR 3, 33; MTCW

Carr, Philippa
See Hibbert, Eleanor Alice Burford

Carr, Virginia Spencer 1929-....... **CLC 34**
See also CA 61-64; DLB 111

Carrere, Emmanuel 1957- .... **CLC 89**

Carrier, Roch
1937- ... **CLC 13, 78; DAC; DAM MST**
See also CA 130; DLB 53

Carroll, James P. 1943(?)-......... **CLC 38**
See also CA 81-84

Carroll, Jim 1951- .... **CLC 35**
See also AAYA 17; CA 45-48; CANR 42

Carroll, Lewis .... **NCLC 2, 53; WLC**
See also Dodgson, Charles Lutwidge
See also CDBLB 1832-1890; CLR 2, 18; DLB 18, 163; JRDA

Carroll, Paul Vincent 1900-1968.... **CLC 10**
See also CA 9-12R; 25-28R; DLB 10

Carruth, Hayden
1921- ...... **CLC 4, 7, 10, 18, 84; PC 10**
See also CA 9-12R; CANR 4, 38; DLB 5, 165; INT CANR-4; MTCW; SATA 47

Carson, Rachel Louise
1907-1964 .... **CLC 71; DAM POP**
See also CA 77-80; CANR 35; MTCW; SATA 23

Carter, Angela (Olive)
1940-1992 ...... **CLC 5, 41, 76; SSC 13**
See also CA 53-56; 136; CANR 12, 36; DLB 14; MTCW; SATA 66; SATA-Obit 70

Carter, Nick
See Smith, Martin Cruz

Carver, Raymond
1938-1988 .... **CLC 22, 36, 53, 55; DAM NOV; SSC 8**
See also CA 33-36R; 126; CANR 17, 34; DLB 130; DLBY 84, 88; MTCW

Cary, Elizabeth, Lady Falkland
1585-1639 .... **LC 30**

Cary, (Arthur) Joyce (Lunel)
1888-1957 .... **TCLC 1, 29**
See also CA 104; CDBLB 1914-1945; DLB 15, 100

Casanova de Seingalt, Giovanni Jacopo
1725-1798 .... **LC 13**

Casares, Adolfo Bioy
See Bioy Casares, Adolfo

Casely-Hayford, J(oseph) E(phraim)
1866-1930 .... **TCLC 24; BLC; DAM MULT**
See also BW 2; CA 123; 152

Casey, John (Dudley) 1939-........ **CLC 59**
See also BEST 90:2; CA 69-72; CANR 23

Casey, Michael 1947-.............. **CLC 2**
See also CA 65-68; DLB 5

Casey, Patrick
See Thurman, Wallace (Henry)

Casey, Warren (Peter) 1935-1988... **CLC 12**
See also CA 101; 127; INT 101

Casona, Alejandro................. CLC 49
See also Alvarez, Alejandro Rodriguez

Cassavetes, John 1929-1989....... **CLC 20**
See also CA 85-88; 127

Cassill, R(onald) V(erlin) 1919-... **CLC 4, 23**
See also CA 9-12R; CAAS 1; CANR 7, 45; DLB 6

Cassirer, Ernst 1874-1945 .... **TCLC 61**

Cassity, (Allen) Turner 1929- .... **CLC 6, 42**
See also CA 17-20R; CAAS 8; CANR 11; DLB 105

Castaneda, Carlos 1931(?)-......... **CLC 12**
See also CA 25-28R; CANR 32; HW; MTCW

Castedo, Elena 1937- .... **CLC 65**
See also CA 132

Castedo-Ellerman, Elena
See Castedo, Elena

Castellanos, Rosario
1925-1974 ...... **CLC 66; DAM MULT; HLC**
See also CA 131; 53-56; DLB 113; HW

Castelvetro, Lodovico 1505-1571..... **LC 12**

Castiglione, Baldassare 1478-1529 ... **LC 12**

Castle, Robert
See Hamilton, Edmond

Castro, Guillen de 1569-1631........ **LC 19**

Castro, Rosalia de
1837-1885 ...... **NCLC 3; DAM MULT**

Cather, Willa
See Cather, Willa Sibert

Cather, Willa Sibert
1873-1947 .... **TCLC 1, 11, 31; DA; DAB; DAC; DAM MST, NOV; SSC 2; WLC**
See also CA 104; 128; CDALB 1865-1917; DLB 9, 54, 78; DLBD 1; MTCW; SATA 30

Catton, (Charles) Bruce
1899-1978 .... **CLC 35**
See also AITN 1; CA 5-8R; 81-84; CANR 7; DLB 17; SATA 2; SATA-Obit 24

Catullus c. 84B.C.-c. 54B.C. ..... **CMLC 18**

Cauldwell, Frank
See King, Francis (Henry)

Caunitz, William J. 1933-1996 ..... **CLC 34**
See also BEST 89:3; CA 125; 130; 152; INT 130

Causley, Charles (Stanley) 1917-..... **CLC 7**
See also CA 9-12R; CANR 5, 35; CLR 30; DLB 27; MTCW; SATA 3, 66

Caute, David 1936-.... **CLC 29; DAM NOV**
See also CA 1-4R; CAAS 4; CANR 1, 33; DLB 14

Cavafy, C(onstantine) P(eter)
1863-1933 .... **TCLC 2, 7; DAM POET**
See also Kavafis, Konstantinos Petrou
See also CA 148

Cavallo, Evelyn
See Spark, Muriel (Sarah)

Cavanna, Betty .... **CLC 12**
See also Harrison, Elizabeth Cavanna
See also JRDA; MAICYA; SAAS 4; SATA 1, 30

Cavendish, Margaret Lucas
1623-1673 .... **LC 30**
See also DLB 131

Childress, Alice
1920-1994 .... **CLC 12, 15, 86, 96; BLC;
DAM DRAM, MULT, NOV; DC 4**
See also AAYA 8; BW 2; CA 45-48; 146;
CANR 3, 27, 50; CLR 14; DLB 7, 38;
JRDA; MAICYA; MTCW; SATA 7, 48,
81

Chislett, (Margaret) Anne 1943- .... **CLC 34**
See also CA 151

Chitty, Thomas Willes 1926- .... **CLC 11**
See also Hinde, Thomas
See also CA 5-8R

Chivers, Thomas Holley
1809-1858 .... **NCLC 49**
See also DLB 3

Chomette, Rene Lucien 1898-1981
See Clair, Rene
See also CA 103

Chopin, Kate
.... **TCLC 5, 14; DA; DAB; SSC 8**
See also Chopin, Katherine
See also CDALB 1865-1917; DLB 12, 78

Chopin, Katherine 1851-1904
See Chopin, Kate
See also CA 104; 122; DAC; DAM MST,
NOV

Chretien de Troyes
c. 12th cent. - .... **CMLC 10**

Christie
See Ichikawa, Kon

Christie, Agatha (Mary Clarissa)
1890-1976 ...... **CLC 1, 6, 8, 12, 39, 48;
DAB; DAC; DAM NOV**
See also AAYA 9; AITN 1, 2; CA 17-20R;
61-64; CANR 10, 37; CDBLB 1914-1945;
DLB 13, 77; MTCW; SATA 36

Christie, (Ann) Philippa
See Pearce, Philippa
See also CA 5-8R; CANR 4

Christine de Pizan 1365(?)-1431(?) .... **LC 9**

Chubb, Elmer
See Masters, Edgar Lee

Chulkov, Mikhail Dmitrievich
1743-1792 .... **LC 2**
See also DLB 150

Churchill, Caryl 1938- ... **CLC 31, 55; DC 5**
See also CA 102; CANR 22, 46; DLB 13;
MTCW

Churchill, Charles 1731-1764 .... **LC 3**
See also DLB 109

Chute, Carolyn 1947- .... **CLC 39**
See also CA 123

Ciardi, John (Anthony)
1916-1986 .... **CLC 10, 40, 44;
DAM POET**
See also CA 5-8R; 118; CAAS 2; CANR 5,
33; CLR 19; DLB 5; DLBY 86;
INT CANR-5; MAICYA; MTCW;
SATA 1, 65; SATA-Obit 46

Cicero, Marcus Tullius
106B.C.-43B.C. .... **CMLC 3**

Cimino, Michael 1943- .... **CLC 16**
See also CA 105

Cioran, E(mil) M. 1911-1995 .... **CLC 64**
See also CA 25-28R; 149

Cisneros, Sandra
1954- ..... **CLC 69; DAM MULT; HLC**
See also AAYA 9; CA 131; DLB 122, 152;
HW

Cixous, Helene 1937- .... **CLC 92**
See also CA 126; CANR 55; DLB 83;
MTCW

Clair, Rene .... **CLC 20**
See also Chomette, Rene Lucien

Clampitt, Amy 1920-1994 .... **CLC 32**
See also CA 110; 146; CANR 29; DLB 105

Clancy, Thomas L., Jr. 1947-
See Clancy, Tom
See also CA 125; 131; INT 131; MTCW

Clancy, Tom ..... **CLC 45; DAM NOV, POP**
See also Clancy, Thomas L., Jr.
See also AAYA 9; BEST 89:1, 90:1

Clare, John
1793-1864 .... **NCLC 9; DAB;
DAM POET**
See also DLB 55, 96

Clarin
See Alas (y Urena), Leopoldo (Enrique
Garcia)

Clark, Al C.
See Goines, Donald

Clark, (Robert) Brian 1932- .... **CLC 29**
See also CA 41-44R

Clark, Curt
See Westlake, Donald E(dwin)

Clark, Eleanor 1913-1996 .... **CLC 5, 19**
See also CA 9-12R; 151; CANR 41; DLB 6

Clark, J. P.
See Clark, John Pepper
See also DLB 117

Clark, John Pepper
1935- .... **CLC 38; BLC; DAM DRAM,
MULT; DC 5**
See also Clark, J. P.
See also BW 1; CA 65-68; CANR 16

Clark, M. R.
See Clark, Mavis Thorpe

Clark, Mavis Thorpe 1909- .... **CLC 12**
See also CA 57-60; CANR 8, 37; CLR 30;
MAICYA; SAAS 5; SATA 8, 74

Clark, Walter Van Tilburg
1909-1971 .... **CLC 28**
See also CA 9-12R; 33-36R; DLB 9;
SATA 8

Clarke, Arthur C(harles)
1917- .... **CLC 1, 4, 13, 18, 35;
DAM POP; SSC 3**
See also AAYA 4; CA 1-4R; CANR 2, 28,
55; JRDA; MAICYA; MTCW; SATA 13,
70

Clarke, Austin
1896-1974 ...... **CLC 6, 9; DAM POET**
See also CA 29-32; 49-52; CAP 2; DLB 10,
20

Clarke, Austin C(hesterfield)
1934- .... **CLC 8, 53; BLC; DAC;
DAM MULT**
See also BW 1; CA 25-28R; CAAS 16;
CANR 14, 32; DLB 53, 125

Clarke, Gillian 1937- .... **CLC 61**
See also CA 106; DLB 40

Clarke, Marcus (Andrew Hislop)
1846-1881 .... **NCLC 19**

Clarke, Shirley 1925- .... **CLC 16**

Clash, The
See Headon, (Nicky) Topper; Jones, Mick;
Simonon, Paul; Strummer, Joe

Claudel, Paul (Louis Charles Marie)
1868-1955 .... **TCLC 2, 10**
See also CA 104

Clavell, James (duMaresq)
1925-1994 .... **CLC 6, 25, 87;
DAM NOV, POP**
See also CA 25-28R; 146; CANR 26, 48;
MTCW

Cleaver, (Leroy) Eldridge
1935- ..... **CLC 30; BLC; DAM MULT**
See also BW 1; CA 21-24R; CANR 16

Cleese, John (Marwood) 1939- ..... **CLC 21**
See also Monty Python
See also CA 112; 116; CANR 35; MTCW

Cleishbotham, Jebediah
See Scott, Walter

Cleland, John 1710-1789 .... **LC 2**
See also DLB 39

Clemens, Samuel Langhorne 1835-1910
See Twain, Mark
See also CA 104; 135; CDALB 1865-1917;
DA; DAB; DAC; DAM MST, NOV;
DLB 11, 12, 23, 64, 74; JRDA;
MAICYA; YABC 2

Cleophil
See Congreve, William

Clerihew, E.
See Bentley, E(dmund) C(lerihew)

Clerk, N. W.
See Lewis, C(live) S(taples)

Cliff, Jimmy .... **CLC 21**
See also Chambers, James

Clifton, (Thelma) Lucille
1936- .... **CLC 19, 66; BLC;
DAM MULT, POET**
See also BW 2; CA 49-52; CANR 2, 24, 42;
CLR 5; DLB 5, 41; MAICYA; MTCW;
SATA 20, 69

Clinton, Dirk
See Silverberg, Robert

Clough, Arthur Hugh 1819-1861 .. **NCLC 27**
See also DLB 32

Clutha, Janet Paterson Frame 1924-
See Frame, Janet
See also CA 1-4R; CANR 2, 36; MTCW

Clyne, Terence
See Blatty, William Peter

Cobalt, Martin
See Mayne, William (James Carter)

Cobbett, William 1763-1835 ..... **NCLC 49**
See also DLB 43, 107, 158

Coburn, D(onald) L(ee) 1938- ...... **CLC 10**
See also CA 89-92

Cocteau, Jean (Maurice Eugene Clement)
1889-1963 .... **CLC 1, 8, 15, 16, 43; DA;
DAB; DAC; DAM DRAM, MST, NOV;
WLC**
See also CA 25-28; CANR 40; CAP 2;
DLB 65; MTCW

Codrescu, Andrei
1946- .... **CLC 46; DAM POET**
See also CA 33-36R; CAAS 19; CANR 13,
34, 53

Coe, Max
See Bourne, Randolph S(illiman)

Coe, Tucker
See Westlake, Donald E(dwin)

Coetzee, J(ohn) M(ichael)
1940- ...... **CLC 23, 33, 66; DAM NOV**
See also CA 77-80; CANR 41, 54; MTCW

Coffey, Brian
See Koontz, Dean R(ay)

Cohan, George M. 1878-1942 ..... **TCLC 60**

Cohen, Arthur A(llen)
1928-1986 .... **CLC 7, 31**
See also CA 1-4R; 120; CANR 1, 17, 42;
DLB 28

Cohen, Leonard (Norman)
1934- .... **CLC 3, 38; DAC; DAM MST**
See also CA 21-24R; CANR 14; DLB 53;
MTCW

Cohen, Matt 1942- .... **CLC 19; DAC**
See also CA 61-64; CAAS 18; CANR 40;
DLB 53

Cohen-Solal, Annie 19(?)- .... **CLC 50**

Colegate, Isabel 1931- .... **CLC 36**
See also CA 17-20R; CANR 8, 22; DLB 14;
INT CANR-22; MTCW

Coleman, Emmett
See Reed, Ishmael

Coleridge, Samuel Taylor
1772-1834 ..... **NCLC 9, 54; DA; DAB;**
DAC; DAM MST, POET; PC 11; WLC
See also CDBLB 1789-1832; DLB 93, 107

Coleridge, Sara 1802-1852 ...... **NCLC 31**

Coles, Don 1928- .... **CLC 46**
See also CA 115; CANR 38

Colette, (Sidonie-Gabrielle)
1873-1954 .... **TCLC 1, 5, 16;**
DAM NOV; SSC 10
See also CA 104; 131; DLB 65; MTCW

Collett, (Jacobine) Camilla (Wergeland)
1813-1895 .... **NCLC 22**

Collier, Christopher 1930- .... **CLC 30**
See also AAYA 13; CA 33-36R; CANR 13,
33; JRDA; MAICYA; SATA 16, 70

Collier, James L(incoln)
1928- .... **CLC 30; DAM POP**
See also AAYA 13; CA 9-12R; CANR 4,
33; CLR 3; JRDA; MAICYA; SAAS 21;
SATA 8, 70

Collier, Jeremy 1650-1726 .... **LC 6**

Collier, John 1901-1980 .... **SSC 19**
See also CA 65-68; 97-100; CANR 10;
DLB 77

Collingwood, R(obin) G(eorge)
1889(?)-1943 .... **TCLC 67**
See also CA 117

Collins, Hunt
See Hunter, Evan

Collins, Linda 1931- .... **CLC 44**
See also CA 125

Collins, (William) Wilkie
1824-1889 .... **NCLC 1, 18**
See also CDBLB 1832-1890; DLB 18, 70,
159

Collins, William
1721-1759 .... **LC 4; DAM POET**
See also DLB 109

Collodi, Carlo 1826-1890 .... **NCLC 54**
See also Lorenzini, Carlo
See also CLR 5

Colman, George
See Glassco, John

Colt, Winchester Remington
See Hubbard, L(afayette) Ron(ald)

Colter, Cyrus 1910- .... **CLC 58**
See also BW 1; CA 65-68; CANR 10;
DLB 33

Colton, James
See Hansen, Joseph

Colum, Padraic 1881-1972 .... **CLC 28**
See also CA 73-76; 33-36R; CANR 35;
CLR 36; MAICYA; MTCW; SATA 15

Colvin, James
See Moorcock, Michael (John)

Colwin, Laurie (E.)
1944-1992 .... **CLC 5, 13, 23, 84**
See also CA 89-92; 139; CANR 20, 46;
DLBY 80; MTCW

Comfort, Alex(ander)
1920- .... **CLC 7; DAM POP**
See also CA 1-4R; CANR 1, 45

Comfort, Montgomery
See Campbell, (John) Ramsey

Compton-Burnett, I(vy)
1884(?)-1969 ...... **CLC 1, 3, 10, 15, 34;**
DAM NOV
See also CA 1-4R; 25-28R; CANR 4;
DLB 36; MTCW

Comstock, Anthony 1844-1915 .... **TCLC 13**
See also CA 110

Comte, Auguste 1798-1857 .... **NCLC 54**

Conan Doyle, Arthur
See Doyle, Arthur Conan

Conde, Maryse
1937- .... **CLC 52, 92; DAM MULT**
See also Boucolon, Maryse
See also BW 2

Condillac, Etienne Bonnot de
1714-1780 .... **LC 26**

Condon, Richard (Thomas)
1915-1996 .... **CLC 4, 6, 8, 10, 45;**
DAM NOV
See also BEST 90:3; CA 1-4R; 151;
CAAS 1; CANR 2, 23; INT CANR-23;
MTCW

Confucius
551B.C.-479B.C. .... **CMLC 19; DA;**
DAB; DAC; DAM MST

Congreve, William
1670-1729 .... **LC 5, 21; DA; DAB;**
DAC; DAM DRAM, MST, POET;
DC 2; WLC
See also CDBLB 1660-1789; DLB 39, 84

Connell, Evan S(helby), Jr.
1924- .... **CLC 4, 6, 45; DAM NOV**
See also AAYA 7; CA 1-4R; CAAS 2;
CANR 2, 39; DLB 2; DLBY 81; MTCW

Connelly, Marc(us Cook)
1890-1980 .... **CLC 7**
See also CA 85-88; 102; CANR 30; DLB 7;
DLBY 80; SATA-Obit 25

Connor, Ralph .... **TCLC 31**
See also Gordon, Charles William
See also DLB 92

Conrad, Joseph
1857-1924 .... **TCLC 1, 6, 13, 25, 43, 57;**
DA; DAB; DAC; DAM MST, NOV;
SSC 9; WLC
See also CA 104; 131; CDBLB 1890-1914;
DLB 10, 34, 98, 156; MTCW; SATA 27

Conrad, Robert Arnold
See Hart, Moss

Conroy, Donald Pat(rick)
1945- ... **CLC 30, 74; DAM NOV, POP**
See also AAYA 8; AITN 1; CA 85-88;
CANR 24, 53; DLB 6; MTCW

Constant (de Rebecque), (Henri) Benjamin
1767-1830 .... **NCLC 6**
See also DLB 119

Conybeare, Charles Augustus
See Eliot, T(homas) S(tearns)

Cook, Michael 1933- .... **CLC 58**
See also CA 93-96; DLB 53

Cook, Robin 1940- .... **CLC 14; DAM POP**
See also BEST 90:2; CA 108; 111;
CANR 41; INT 111

Cook, Roy
See Silverberg, Robert

Cooke, Elizabeth 1948- .... **CLC 55**
See also CA 129

Cooke, John Esten 1830-1886 ..... **NCLC 5**
See also DLB 3

Cooke, John Estes
See Baum, L(yman) Frank

Cooke, M. E.
See Creasey, John

Cooke, Margaret
See Creasey, John

Cook-Lynn, Elizabeth
1930- .... **CLC 93; DAM MULT**
See also CA 133; NNAL

Cooney, Ray .... **CLC 62**

Cooper, Douglas 1960- .... **CLC 86**

Cooper, Henry St. John
See Creasey, John

Cooper, J. California
.... **CLC 56; DAM MULT**
See also AAYA 12; BW 1; CA 125;
CANR 55

Cooper, James Fenimore
1789-1851 .... **NCLC 1, 27, 54**
See also CDALB 1640-1865; DLB 3;
SATA 19

Coover, Robert (Lowell)
1932- .... **CLC 3, 7, 15, 32, 46, 87;**
DAM NOV; SSC 15
See also CA 45-48; CANR 3, 37; DLB 2;
DLBY 81; MTCW

Author Index

Davies, (William) Robertson
1913-1995 ..... **CLC 2, 7, 13, 25, 42, 75, 91; DA; DAB; DAC; DAM MST, NOV, POP; WLC**
See also BEST 89:2; CA 33-36R; 150; CANR 17, 42; DLB 68; INT CANR-17; MTCW

Davies, W(illiam) H(enry)
1871-1940 .... **TCLC 5**
See also CA 104; DLB 19, 174

Davies, Walter C.
See Kornbluth, C(yril) M.

Davis, Angela (Yvonne)
1944- .... **CLC 77; DAM MULT**
See also BW 2; CA 57-60; CANR 10

Davis, B. Lynch
See Bioy Casares, Adolfo; Borges, Jorge Luis

Davis, Gordon
See Hunt, E(verette) Howard, (Jr.)

Davis, Harold Lenoir 1896-1960.... **CLC 49**
See also CA 89-92; DLB 9

Davis, Rebecca (Blaine) Harding
1831-1910 .... **TCLC 6**
See also CA 104; DLB 74

Davis, Richard Harding
1864-1916 .... **TCLC 24**
See also CA 114; DLB 12, 23, 78, 79; DLBD 13

Davison, Frank Dalby 1893-1970 ... **CLC 15**
See also CA 116

Davison, Lawrence H.
See Lawrence, D(avid) H(erbert Richards)

Davison, Peter (Hubert) 1928- ..... **CLC 28**
See also CA 9-12R; CAAS 4; CANR 3, 43; DLB 5

Davys, Mary 1674-1732............. **LC 1**
See also DLB 39

Dawson, Fielding 1930- .... **CLC 6**
See also CA 85-88; DLB 130

Dawson, Peter
See Faust, Frederick (Schiller)

Day, Clarence (Shepard, Jr.)
1874-1935 .... **TCLC 25**
See also CA 108; DLB 11

Day, Thomas 1748-1789............. **LC 1**
See also DLB 39; YABC 1

Day Lewis, C(ecil)
1904-1972 .... **CLC 1, 6, 10; DAM POET; PC 11**
See also Blake, Nicholas
See also CA 13-16; 33-36R; CANR 34; CAP 1; DLB 15, 20; MTCW

Dazai, Osamu .... **TCLC 11**
See also Tsushima, Shuji

de Andrade, Carlos Drummond
See Drummond de Andrade, Carlos

Deane, Norman
See Creasey, John

de Beauvoir, Simone (Lucie Ernestine Marie Bertrand)
See Beauvoir, Simone (Lucie Ernestine Marie Bertrand) de

de Brissac, Malcolm
See Dickinson, Peter (Malcolm)

de Chardin, Pierre Teilhard
See Teilhard de Chardin, (Marie Joseph) Pierre

Dee, John 1527-1608 .... **LC 20**

Deer, Sandra 1940-............... **CLC 45**

De Ferrari, Gabriella 1941-........ **CLC 65**
See also CA 146

Defoe, Daniel
1660(?)-1731 .... **LC 1; DA; DAB; DAC; DAM MST, NOV; WLC**
See also CDBLB 1660-1789; DLB 39, 95, 101; JRDA; MAICYA; SATA 22

de Gourmont, Remy(-Marie-Charles)
See Gourmont, Remy (-Marie-Charles) de

de Hartog, Jan 1914-............. **CLC 19**
See also CA 1-4R; CANR 1

de Hostos, E. M.
See Hostos (y Bonilla), Eugenio Maria de

de Hostos, Eugenio M.
See Hostos (y Bonilla), Eugenio Maria de

Deighton, Len .... **CLC 4, 7, 22, 46**
See also Deighton, Leonard Cyril
See also AAYA 6; BEST 89:2; CDBLB 1960 to Present; DLB 87

Deighton, Leonard Cyril 1929-
See Deighton, Len
See also CA 9-12R; CANR 19, 33; DAM NOV, POP; MTCW

Dekker, Thomas
1572(?)-1632 ..... **LC 22; DAM DRAM**
See also CDBLB Before 1660; DLB 62, 172

Delafield, E. M. 1890-1943 .... **TCLC 61**
See also Dashwood, Edmee Elizabeth Monica de la Pasture
See also DLB 34

de la Mare, Walter (John)
1873-1956 .... **TCLC 4, 53; DAB; DAC; DAM MST, POET; SSC 14; WLC**
See also CDBLB 1914-1945; CLR 23; DLB 162; SATA 16

Delaney, Franey
See O'Hara, John (Henry)

Delaney, Shelagh
1939- .... **CLC 29; DAM DRAM**
See also CA 17-20R; CANR 30; CDBLB 1960 to Present; DLB 13; MTCW

Delany, Mary (Granville Pendarves)
1700-1788 .... **LC 12**

Delany, Samuel R(ay, Jr.)
1942- .... **CLC 8, 14, 38; BLC; DAM MULT**
See also BW 2; CA 81-84; CANR 27, 43; DLB 8, 33; MTCW

De La Ramee, (Marie) Louise 1839-1908
See Ouida
See also SATA 20

de la Roche, Mazo 1879-1961...... **CLC 14**
See also CA 85-88; CANR 30; DLB 68; SATA 64

Delbanco, Nicholas (Franklin)
1942- .... **CLC 6, 13**
See also CA 17-20R; CAAS 2; CANR 29, 55; DLB 6

del Castillo, Michel 1933-......... **CLC 38**
See also CA 109

Deledda, Grazia (Cosima)
1875(?)-1936 .... **TCLC 23**
See also CA 123

Delibes, Miguel .... **CLC 8, 18**
See also Delibes Setien, Miguel

Delibes Setien, Miguel 1920-
See Delibes, Miguel
See also CA 45-48; CANR 1, 32; HW; MTCW

DeLillo, Don
1936- ..... **CLC 8, 10, 13, 27, 39, 54, 76; DAM NOV, POP**
See also BEST 89:1; CA 81-84; CANR 21; DLB 6, 173; MTCW

de Lisser, H. G.
See De Lisser, H(erbert) G(eorge)
See also DLB 117

De Lisser, H(erbert) G(eorge)
1878-1944 .... **TCLC 12**
See also de Lisser, H. G.
See also BW 2; CA 109; 152

Deloria, Vine (Victor), Jr.
1933- .... **CLC 21; DAM MULT**
See also CA 53-56; CANR 5, 20, 48; MTCW; NNAL; SATA 21

Del Vecchio, John M(ichael)
1947- .... **CLC 29**
See also CA 110; DLBD 9

de Man, Paul (Adolph Michel)
1919-1983 .... **CLC 55**
See also CA 128; 111; DLB 67; MTCW

De Marinis, Rick 1934-........... **CLC 54**
See also CA 57-60; CAAS 24; CANR 9, 25, 50

Dembry, R. Emmet
See Murfree, Mary Noailles

Demby, William
1922- ..... **CLC 53; BLC; DAM MULT**
See also BW 1; CA 81-84; DLB 33

Demijohn, Thom
See Disch, Thomas M(ichael)

de Montherlant, Henry (Milon)
See Montherlant, Henry (Milon) de

Demosthenes 384B.C.-322B.C. .... **CMLC 13**

de Natale, Francine
See Malzberg, Barry N(athaniel)

Denby, Edwin (Orr) 1903-1983..... **CLC 48**
See also CA 138; 110

Denis, Julio
See Cortazar, Julio

Denmark, Harrison
See Zelazny, Roger (Joseph)

Dennis, John 1658-1734............ **LC 11**
See also DLB 101

Dennis, Nigel (Forbes) 1912-1989.... **CLC 8**
See also CA 25-28R; 129; DLB 13, 15; MTCW

De Palma, Brian (Russell) 1940-.... **CLC 20**
See also CA 109

De Quincey, Thomas 1785-1859 ... **NCLC 4**
See also CDBLB 1789-1832; DLB 110; 144

Deren, Eleanora 1908(?)-1961
See Deren, Maya
See also CA 111

Deren, Maya .... CLC 16
See also Deren, Eleanora

Derleth, August (William)
1909-1971 .... CLC 31
See also CA 1-4R; 29-32R; CANR 4;
DLB 9; SATA 5

Der Nister 1884-1950........... TCLC 56

de Routisie, Albert
See Aragon, Louis

Derrida, Jacques 1930-........ CLC 24, 87
See also CA 124; 127

Derry Down Derry
See Lear, Edward

Dersonnes, Jacques
See Simenon, Georges (Jacques Christian)

Desai, Anita
1937- .... CLC 19, 37, 97; DAB;
DAM NOV
See also CA 81-84; CANR 33, 53; MTCW;
SATA 63

de Saint-Luc, Jean
See Glassco, John

de Saint Roman, Arnaud
See Aragon, Louis

Descartes, Rene 1596-1650 ...... LC 20, 35

De Sica, Vittorio 1901(?)-1974 ..... CLC 20
See also CA 117

Desnos, Robert 1900-1945........ TCLC 22
See also CA 121; 151

Destouches, Louis-Ferdinand
1894-1961 .... CLC 9, 15
See also Celine, Louis-Ferdinand
See also CA 85-88; CANR 28; MTCW

Deutsch, Babette 1895-1982 .... CLC 18
See also CA 1-4R; 108; CANR 4; DLB 45;
SATA 1; SATA-Obit 33

Devenant, William 1606-1649 .... LC 13

Devkota, Laxmiprasad
1909-1959 .... TCLC 23
See also CA 123

De Voto, Bernard (Augustine)
1897-1955 .... TCLC 29
See also CA 113; DLB 9

De Vries, Peter
1910-1993 .... CLC 1, 2, 3, 7, 10, 28, 46;
DAM NOV
See also CA 17-20R; 142; CANR 41;
DLB 6; DLBY 82; MTCW

Dexter, John
See Bradley, Marion Zimmer

Dexter, Martin
See Faust, Frederick (Schiller)

Dexter, Pete
1943- .... CLC 34, 55; DAM POP
See also BEST 89:2; CA 127; 131; INT 131;
MTCW

Diamano, Silmang
See Senghor, Leopold Sedar

Diamond, Neil 1941- .... CLC 30
See also CA 108

Diaz del Castillo, Bernal 1496-1584 .. LC 31

di Bassetto, Corno
See Shaw, George Bernard

Dick, Philip K(indred)
1928-1982 .... CLC 10, 30, 72;
DAM NOV, POP
See also CA 49-52; 106; CANR 2, 16;
DLB 8; MTCW

Dickens, Charles (John Huffam)
1812-1870 ...... NCLC 3, 8, 18, 26, 37,
50; DA; DAB; DAC; DAM MST, NOV;
SSC 17; WLC
See also CDBLB 1832-1890; DLB 21, 55,
70, 159, 166; JRDA; MAICYA; SATA 15

Dickey, James (Lafayette)
1923- .... CLC 1, 2, 4, 7, 10, 15, 47;
DAM NOV, POET, POP
See also AITN 1, 2; CA 9-12R; CABS 2;
CANR 10, 48; CDALB 1968-1988;
DLB 5; DLBD 7; DLBY 82, 93;
INT CANR-10; MTCW

Dickey, William 1928-1994 ..... CLC 3, 28
See also CA 9-12R; 145; CANR 24; DLB 5

Dickinson, Charles 1951-......... CLC 49
See also CA 128

Dickinson, Emily (Elizabeth)
1830-1886 .... NCLC 21; DA; DAB;
DAC; DAM MST, POET; PC 1; WLC
See also CDALB 1865-1917; DLB 1;
SATA 29

Dickinson, Peter (Malcolm)
1927- .... CLC 12, 35
See also AAYA 9; CA 41-44R; CANR 31;
CLR 29; DLB 87, 161; JRDA; MAICYA;
SATA 5, 62

Dickson, Carr
See Carr, John Dickson

Dickson, Carter
See Carr, John Dickson

Diderot, Denis 1713-1784 .... LC 26

Didion, Joan
1934- .. CLC 1, 3, 8, 14, 32; DAM NOV
See also AITN 1; CA 5-8R; CANR 14, 52;
CDALB 1968-1988; DLB 2, 173;
DLBY 81, 86; MTCW

Dietrich, Robert
See Hunt, E(verette) Howard, (Jr.)

Dillard, Annie
1945- .... CLC 9, 60; DAM NOV
See also AAYA 6; CA 49-52; CANR 3, 43;
DLBY 80; MTCW; SATA 10

Dillard, R(ichard) H(enry) W(ilde)
1937- .... CLC 5
See also CA 21-24R; CAAS 7; CANR 10;
DLB 5

Dillon, Eilis 1920-1994........... CLC 17
See also CA 9-12R; 147; CAAS 3; CANR 4,
38; CLR 26; MAICYA; SATA 2, 74;
SATA-Obit 83

Dimont, Penelope
See Mortimer, Penelope (Ruth)

Dinesen, Isak....... CLC 10, 29, 95; SSC 7
See also Blixen, Karen (Christentze
Dinesen)

Ding Ling...................... CLC 68
See also Chiang Pin-chin

Disch, Thomas M(ichael) 1940-... CLC 7, 36
See also AAYA 17; CA 21-24R; CAAS 4;
CANR 17, 36, 54; CLR 18; DLB 8;
MAICYA; MTCW; SAAS 15; SATA 54

Disch, Tom
See Disch, Thomas M(ichael)

d'Isly, Georges
See Simenon, Georges (Jacques Christian)

Disraeli, Benjamin 1804-1881 .. NCLC 2, 39
See also DLB 21, 55

Ditcum, Steve
See Crumb, R(obert)

Dixon, Paige
See Corcoran, Barbara

Dixon, Stephen 1936-..... CLC 52; SSC 16
See also CA 89-92; CANR 17, 40, 54;
DLB 130

Dobell, Sydney Thompson
1824-1874 .... NCLC 43
See also DLB 32

Doblin, Alfred .... TCLC 13
See also Doeblin, Alfred

Dobrolyubov, Nikolai Alexandrovich
1836-1861 .... NCLC 5

Dobyns, Stephen 1941-........... CLC 37
See also CA 45-48; CANR 2, 18

Doctorow, E(dgar) L(aurence)
1931- ..... CLC 6, 11, 15, 18, 37, 44, 65;
DAM NOV, POP
See also AITN 2; BEST 89:3; CA 45-48;
CANR 2, 33, 51; CDALB 1968-1988;
DLB 2, 28, 173; DLBY 80; MTCW

Dodgson, Charles Lutwidge 1832-1898
See Carroll, Lewis
See also CLR 2; DA; DAB; DAC;
DAM MST, NOV, POET; MAICYA;
YABC 2

Dodson, Owen (Vincent)
1914-1983 .... CLC 79; BLC;
DAM MULT
See also BW 1; CA 65-68; 110; CANR 24;
DLB 76

Doeblin, Alfred 1878-1957....... TCLC 13
See also Doblin, Alfred
See also CA 110; 141; DLB 66

Doerr, Harriet 1910- .... CLC 34
See also CA 117; 122; CANR 47; INT 122

Domecq, H(onorio) Bustos
See Bioy Casares, Adolfo; Borges, Jorge
Luis

Domini, Rey
See Lorde, Audre (Geraldine)

Dominique
See Proust, (Valentin-Louis-George-Eugene-)
Marcel

Don, A
See Stephen, Leslie

Donaldson, Stephen R.
1947- .... CLC 46; DAM POP
See also CA 89-92; CANR 13, 55;
INT CANR-13

Donleavy, J(ames) P(atrick)
1926- .... CLC 1, 4, 6, 10, 45
See also AITN 2; CA 9-12R; CANR 24, 49;
DLB 6, 173; INT CANR-24; MTCW

Donne, John
1572-1631 ...... **LC 10, 24; DA; DAB; DAC; DAM MST, POET; PC 1**
See also CDBLB Before 1660; DLB 121, 151

Donnell, David 1939(?)- .... **CLC 34**

Donoghue, P. S.
See Hunt, E(verette) Howard, (Jr.)

Donoso (Yanez), Jose
1924- .... **CLC 4, 8, 11, 32; DAM MULT; HLC**
See also CA 81-84; CANR 32; DLB 113; HW; MTCW

Donovan, John 1928-1992 .... **CLC 35**
See also CA 97-100; 137; CLR 3; MAICYA; SATA 72; SATA-Brief 29

Don Roberto
See Cunninghame Graham, R(obert) B(ontine)

Doolittle, Hilda
1886-1961 ..... **CLC 3, 8, 14, 31, 34, 73; DA; DAC; DAM MST, POET; PC 5; WLC**
See also H. D.
See also CA 97-100; CANR 35; DLB 4, 45; MTCW

Dorfman, Ariel
1942- .... **CLC 48, 77; DAM MULT; HLC**
See also CA 124; 130; HW; INT 130

Dorn, Edward (Merton) 1929-... **CLC 10, 18**
See also CA 93-96; CANR 42; DLB 5; INT 93-96

Dorsan, Luc
See Simenon, Georges (Jacques Christian)

Dorsange, Jean
See Simenon, Georges (Jacques Christian)

Dos Passos, John (Roderigo)
1896-1970 ...... **CLC 1, 4, 8, 11, 15, 25, 34, 82; DA; DAB; DAC; DAM MST, NOV; WLC**
See also CA 1-4R; 29-32R; CANR 3; CDALB 1929-1941; DLB 4, 9; DLBD 1; MTCW

Dossage, Jean
See Simenon, Georges (Jacques Christian)

Dostoevsky, Fedor Mikhailovich
1821-1881 ...... **NCLC 2, 7, 21, 33, 43; DA; DAB; DAC; DAM MST, NOV; SSC 2; WLC**

Doughty, Charles M(ontagu)
1843-1926 .... **TCLC 27**
See also CA 115; DLB 19, 57, 174

Douglas, Ellen .... **CLC 73**
See also Haxton, Josephine Ayres; Williamson, Ellen Douglas

Douglas, Gavin 1475(?)-1522 .... **LC 20**

Douglas, Keith 1920-1944 .... **TCLC 40**
See also DLB 27

Douglas, Leonard
See Bradbury, Ray (Douglas)

Douglas, Michael
See Crichton, (John) Michael

Douglass, Frederick
1817(?)-1895 .... **NCLC 7, 55; BLC; DA; DAC; DAM MST, MULT; WLC**
See also CDALB 1640-1865; DLB 1, 43, 50, 79; SATA 29

Dourado, (Waldomiro Freitas) Autran
1926- .... **CLC 23, 60**
See also CA 25-28R; CANR 34

Dourado, Waldomiro Autran
See Dourado, (Waldomiro Freitas) Autran

Dove, Rita (Frances)
1952- .... **CLC 50, 81; DAM MULT, POET; PC 6**
See also BW 2; CA 109; CAAS 19; CANR 27, 42; DLB 120

Dowell, Coleman 1925-1985 .... **CLC 60**
See also CA 25-28R; 117; CANR 10; DLB 130

Dowson, Ernest (Christopher)
1867-1900 .... **TCLC 4**
See also CA 105; 150; DLB 19, 135

Doyle, A. Conan
See Doyle, Arthur Conan

Doyle, Arthur Conan
1859-1930 .... **TCLC 7; DA; DAB; DAC; DAM MST, NOV; SSC 12; WLC**
See also AAYA 14; CA 104; 122; CDBLB 1890-1914; DLB 18, 70, 156; MTCW; SATA 24

Doyle, Conan
See Doyle, Arthur Conan

Doyle, John
See Graves, Robert (von Ranke)

Doyle, Roddy 1958(?)- .... **CLC 81**
See also AAYA 14; CA 143

Doyle, Sir A. Conan
See Doyle, Arthur Conan

Doyle, Sir Arthur Conan
See Doyle, Arthur Conan

Dr. A
See Asimov, Isaac; Silverstein, Alvin

Drabble, Margaret
1939- .... **CLC 2, 3, 5, 8, 10, 22, 53; DAB; DAC; DAM MST, NOV, POP**
See also CA 13-16R; CANR 18, 35; CDBLB 1960 to Present; DLB 14, 155; MTCW; SATA 48

Drapier, M. B.
See Swift, Jonathan

Drayham, James
See Mencken, H(enry) L(ouis)

Drayton, Michael 1563-1631 .... **LC 8**

Dreadstone, Carl
See Campbell, (John) Ramsey

Dreiser, Theodore (Herman Albert)
1871-1945 .... **TCLC 10, 18, 35; DA; DAC; DAM MST, NOV; WLC**
See also CA 106; 132; CDALB 1865-1917; DLB 9, 12, 102, 137; DLBD 1; MTCW

Drexler, Rosalyn 1926- .... **CLC 2, 6**
See also CA 81-84

Dreyer, Carl Theodor 1889-1968 .... **CLC 16**
See also CA 116

Drieu la Rochelle, Pierre(-Eugene)
1893-1945 .... **TCLC 21**
See also CA 117; DLB 72

Drinkwater, John 1882-1937 ..... **TCLC 57**
See also CA 109; 149; DLB 10, 19, 149

Drop Shot
See Cable, George Washington

Droste-Hulshoff, Annette Freiin von
1797-1848 .... **NCLC 3**
See also DLB 133

Drummond, Walter
See Silverberg, Robert

Drummond, William Henry
1854-1907 .... **TCLC 25**
See also DLB 92

Drummond de Andrade, Carlos
1902-1987 .... **CLC 18**
See also Andrade, Carlos Drummond de
See also CA 132; 123

Drury, Allen (Stuart) 1918- .... **CLC 37**
See also CA 57-60; CANR 18, 52; INT CANR-18

Dryden, John
1631-1700 .... **LC 3, 21; DA; DAB; DAC; DAM DRAM, MST, POET; DC 3; WLC**
See also CDBLB 1660-1789; DLB 80, 101, 131

Duberman, Martin 1930- .... **CLC 8**
See also CA 1-4R; CANR 2

Dubie, Norman (Evans) 1945- ...... **CLC 36**
See also CA 69-72; CANR 12; DLB 120

Du Bois, W(illiam) E(dward) B(urghardt)
1868-1963 .... **CLC 1, 2, 13, 64, 96; BLC; DA; DAC; DAM MST, MULT, NOV; WLC**
See also BW 1; CA 85-88; CANR 34; CDALB 1865-1917; DLB 47, 50, 91; MTCW; SATA 42

Dubus, Andre
1936- .... **CLC 13, 36, 97; SSC 15**
See also CA 21-24R; CANR 17; DLB 130; INT CANR-17

Duca Minimo
See D'Annunzio, Gabriele

Ducharme, Rejean 1941- .... **CLC 74**
See also DLB 60

Duclos, Charles Pinot 1704-1772 ..... **LC 1**

Dudek, Louis 1918- .... **CLC 11, 19**
See also CA 45-48; CAAS 14; CANR 1; DLB 88

Duerrenmatt, Friedrich
1921-1990 ...... **CLC 1, 4, 8, 11, 15, 43; DAM DRAM**
See also CA 17-20R; CANR 33; DLB 69, 124; MTCW

Duffy, Bruce (?)- .... **CLC 50**

Duffy, Maureen 1933- .... **CLC 37**
See also CA 25-28R; CANR 33; DLB 14; MTCW

Dugan, Alan 1923- .... **CLC 2, 6**
See also CA 81-84; DLB 5

du Gard, Roger Martin
See Martin du Gard, Roger

Eichendorff, Joseph Freiherr von
1788-1857 . . . . **NCLC 8**
See also DLB 90

Eigner, Larry . . . . **CLC 9**
See also Eigner, Laurence (Joel)
See also CAAS 23; DLB 5

Eigner, Laurence (Joel) 1927-1996
See Eigner, Larry
See also CA 9-12R; 151; CANR 6

Einstein, Albert 1879-1955 . . . . **TCLC 65**
See also CA 121; 133; MTCW

Eiseley, Loren Corey 1907-1977 . . . . . **CLC 7**
See also AAYA 5; CA 1-4R; 73-76;
CANR 6

Eisenstadt, Jill 1963- . . . . **CLC 50**
See also CA 140

Eisenstein, Sergei (Mikhailovich)
1898-1948 . . . . **TCLC 57**
See also CA 114; 149

Eisner, Simon
See Kornbluth, C(yril) M.

Ekeloef, (Bengt) Gunnar
1907-1968 . . . . **CLC 27; DAM POET**
See also CA 123; 25-28R

Ekelof, (Bengt) Gunnar
See Ekeloef, (Bengt) Gunnar

Ekwensi, C. O. D.
See Ekwensi, Cyprian (Odiatu Duaka)

Ekwensi, Cyprian (Odiatu Duaka)
1921- . . . . . . **CLC 4; BLC; DAM MULT**
See also BW 2; CA 29-32R; CANR 18, 42;
DLB 117; MTCW; SATA 66

Elaine . . . . **TCLC 18**
See also Leverson, Ada

El Crummo
See Crumb, R(obert)

Elia
See Lamb, Charles

Eliade, Mircea 1907-1986 . . . . **CLC 19**
See also CA 65-68; 119; CANR 30; MTCW

Eliot, A. D.
See Jewett, (Theodora) Sarah Orne

Eliot, Alice
See Jewett, (Theodora) Sarah Orne

Eliot, Dan
See Silverberg, Robert

Eliot, George
1819-1880 . . . . . **NCLC 4, 13, 23, 41, 49;**
DA; DAB; DAC; DAM MST, NOV;
WLC
See also CDBLB 1832-1890; DLB 21, 35, 55

Eliot, John 1604-1690 . . . . **LC 5**
See also DLB 24

Eliot, T(homas) S(tearns)
1888-1965 . . . . . **CLC 1, 2, 3, 6, 9, 10, 13,**
15, 24, 34, 41, 55, 57; DA; DAB; DAC;
DAM DRAM, MST, POET; PC 5;
WLC 2
See also CA 5-8R; 25-28R; CANR 41;
CDALB 1929-1941; DLB 7, 10, 45, 63;
DLBY 88; MTCW

Elizabeth 1866-1941 . . . . **TCLC 41**

Elkin, Stanley L(awrence)
1930-1995 . . . . . . **CLC 4, 6, 9, 14, 27, 51,**
91; DAM NOV, POP; SSC 12
See also CA 9-12R; 148; CANR 8, 46;
DLB 2, 28; DLBY 80; INT CANR-8;
MTCW

Elledge, Scott . . . . **CLC 34**

Elliot, Don
See Silverberg, Robert

Elliott, Don
See Silverberg, Robert

Elliott, George P(aul) 1918-1980 . . . . . **CLC 2**
See also CA 1-4R; 97-100; CANR 2

Elliott, Janice 1931- . . . . **CLC 47**
See also CA 13-16R; CANR 8, 29; DLB 14

Elliott, Sumner Locke 1917-1991 . . . **CLC 38**
See also CA 5-8R; 134; CANR 2, 21

Elliott, William
See Bradbury, Ray (Douglas)

Ellis, A. E. . . . . **CLC 7**

Ellis, Alice Thomas . . . . **CLC 40**
See also Haycraft, Anna

Ellis, Bret Easton
1964- . . . . **CLC 39, 71; DAM POP**
See also AAYA 2; CA 118; 123; CANR 51;
INT 123

Ellis, (Henry) Havelock
1859-1939 . . . . **TCLC 14**
See also CA 109

Ellis, Landon
See Ellison, Harlan (Jay)

Ellis, Trey 1962- . . . . **CLC 55**
See also CA 146

Ellison, Harlan (Jay)
1934- . . . . . . **CLC 1, 13, 42; DAM POP;**
SSC 14
See also CA 5-8R; CANR 5, 46; DLB 8;
INT CANR-5; MTCW

Ellison, Ralph (Waldo)
1914-1994 . . . . **CLC 1, 3, 11, 54, 86;**
BLC; DA; DAB; DAC; DAM MST,
MULT, NOV; WLC
See also AAYA 19; BW 1; CA 9-12R; 145;
CANR 24, 53; CDALB 1941-1968;
DLB 2, 76; DLBY 94; MTCW

Ellmann, Lucy (Elizabeth) 1956- . . . . **CLC 61**
See also CA 128

Ellmann, Richard (David)
1918-1987 . . . . **CLC 50**
See also BEST 89:2; CA 1-4R; 122;
CANR 2, 28; DLB 103; DLBY 87;
MTCW

Elman, Richard 1934- . . . . **CLC 19**
See also CA 17-20R; CAAS 3; CANR 47

Elron
See Hubbard, L(afayette) Ron(ald)

Eluard, Paul . . . . **TCLC 7, 41**
See also Grindel, Eugene

Elyot, Sir Thomas 1490(?)-1546 . . . . . **LC 11**

Elytis, Odysseus
1911-1996 . . . . **CLC 15, 49; DAM POET**
See also CA 102; 151; MTCW

Emecheta, (Florence Onye) Buchi
1944- . . **CLC 14, 48; BLC; DAM MULT**
See also BW 2; CA 81-84; CANR 27;
DLB 117; MTCW; SATA 66

Emerson, Ralph Waldo
1803-1882 . . . . . **NCLC 1, 38; DA; DAB;**
DAC; DAM MST, POET; WLC
See also CDALB 1640-1865; DLB 1, 59, 73

Eminescu, Mihail 1850-1889 . . . . . **NCLC 33**

Empson, William
1906-1984 . . . . **CLC 3, 8, 19, 33, 34**
See also CA 17-20R; 112; CANR 31;
DLB 20; MTCW

Enchi Fumiko (Ueda) 1905-1986 . . . . **CLC 31**
See also CA 129; 121

Ende, Michael (Andreas Helmuth)
1929-1995 . . . . **CLC 31**
See also CA 118; 124; 149; CANR 36;
CLR 14; DLB 75; MAICYA; SATA 61;
SATA-Brief 42; SATA-Obit 86

Endo, Shusaku
1923-1996 . . . . **CLC 7, 14, 19, 54;**
DAM NOV
See also CA 29-32R; 153; CANR 21, 54;
MTCW

Engel, Marian 1933-1985 . . . . **CLC 36**
See also CA 25-28R; CANR 12; DLB 53;
INT CANR-12

Engelhardt, Frederick
See Hubbard, L(afayette) Ron(ald)

Enright, D(ennis) J(oseph)
1920- . . . . **CLC 4, 8, 31**
See also CA 1-4R; CANR 1, 42; DLB 27;
SATA 25

Enzensberger, Hans Magnus
1929- . . . . **CLC 43**
See also CA 116; 119

Ephron, Nora 1941- . . . . **CLC 17, 31**
See also AITN 2; CA 65-68; CANR 12, 39

Epsilon
See Betjeman, John

Epstein, Daniel Mark 1948- . . . . **CLC 7**
See also CA 49-52; CANR 2, 53

Epstein, Jacob 1956- . . . . **CLC 19**
See also CA 114

Epstein, Joseph 1937- . . . . **CLC 39**
See also CA 112; 119; CANR 50

Epstein, Leslie 1938- . . . . **CLC 27**
See also CA 73-76; CAAS 12; CANR 23

Equiano, Olaudah
1745(?)-1797 . . . . **LC 16; BLC;**
DAM MULT
See also DLB 37, 50

Erasmus, Desiderius 1469(?)-1536 . . . . **LC 16**

Erdman, Paul E(mil) 1932- . . . . **CLC 25**
See also AITN 1; CA 61-64; CANR 13, 43

Erdrich, Louise
1954- . . . . **CLC 39, 54; DAM MULT,**
NOV, POP
See also AAYA 10; BEST 89:1; CA 114;
CANR 41; DLB 152; MTCW; NNAL

Erenburg, Ilya (Grigoryevich)
See Ehrenburg, Ilya (Grigoryevich)

Feinstein, Elaine 1930-............ **CLC 36**
  See also CA 69-72; CAAS 1; CANR 31;
  DLB 14, 40; MTCW

Feldman, Irving (Mordecai) 1928-.... **CLC 7**
  See also CA 1-4R; CANR 1; DLB 169

Fellini, Federico 1920-1993 ..... **CLC 16, 85**
  See also CA 65-68; 143; CANR 33

Felsen, Henry Gregor 1916- .... **CLC 17**
  See also CA 1-4R; CANR 1; SAAS 2;
  SATA 1

Fenton, James Martin 1949-....... **CLC 32**
  See also CA 102; DLB 40

Ferber, Edna 1887-1968........ **CLC 18, 93**
  See also AITN 1; CA 5-8R; 25-28R; DLB 9,
  28, 86; MTCW; SATA 7

Ferguson, Helen
  See Kavan, Anna

Ferguson, Samuel 1810-1886..... **NCLC 33**
  See also DLB 32

Fergusson, Robert 1750-1774 .... **LC 29**
  See also DLB 109

Ferling, Lawrence
  See Ferlinghetti, Lawrence (Monsanto)

Ferlinghetti, Lawrence (Monsanto)
  1919(?)-............. **CLC 2, 6, 10, 27;**
                      DAM POET; PC 1
  See also CA 5-8R; CANR 3, 41;
  CDALB 1941-1968; DLB 5, 16; MTCW

Fernandez, Vicente Garcia Huidobro
  See Huidobro Fernandez, Vicente Garcia

Ferrer, Gabriel (Francisco Victor) Miro
  See Miro (Ferrer), Gabriel (Francisco
  Victor)

Ferrier, Susan (Edmonstone)
  1782-1854 .... **NCLC 8**
  See also DLB 116

Ferrigno, Robert 1948(?)-......... **CLC 65**
  See also CA 140

Ferron, Jacques 1921-1985 ... **CLC 94; DAC**
  See also CA 117; 129; DLB 60

Feuchtwanger, Lion 1884-1958 ..... **TCLC 3**
  See also CA 104; DLB 66

Feuillet, Octave 1821-1890 ...... **NCLC 45**

Feydeau, Georges (Leon Jules Marie)
  1862-1921 ..... **TCLC 22; DAM DRAM**
  See also CA 113; 152

Ficino, Marsilio 1433-1499 .... **LC 12**

Fiedeler, Hans
  See Doeblin, Alfred

Fiedler, Leslie A(aron)
  1917- .... **CLC 4, 13, 24**
  See also CA 9-12R; CANR 7; DLB 28, 67;
  MTCW

Field, Andrew 1938-............. **CLC 44**
  See also CA 97-100; CANR 25

Field, Eugene 1850-1895 .... **NCLC 3**
  See also DLB 23, 42, 140; DLBD 13;
  MAICYA; SATA 16

Field, Gans T.
  See Wellman, Manly Wade

Field, Michael .... **TCLC 43**

Field, Peter
  See Hobson, Laura Z(ametkin)

Fielding, Henry
  1707-1754 ..... **LC 1; DA; DAB; DAC;**
                DAM DRAM, MST, NOV; WLC
  See also CDBLB 1660-1789; DLB 39, 84,
  101

Fielding, Sarah 1710-1768 .... **LC 1**
  See also DLB 39

Fierstein, Harvey (Forbes)
  1954- ..... **CLC 33; DAM DRAM, POP**
  See also CA 123; 129

Figes, Eva 1932-................. **CLC 31**
  See also CA 53-56; CANR 4, 44; DLB 14

Finch, Robert (Duer Claydon)
  1900- .... **CLC 18**
  See also CA 57-60; CANR 9, 24, 49;
  DLB 88

Findley, Timothy
  1930- ...... **CLC 27; DAC; DAM MST**
  See also CA 25-28R; CANR 12, 42;
  DLB 53

Fink, William
  See Mencken, H(enry) L(ouis)

Firbank, Louis 1942-
  See Reed, Lou
  See also CA 117

Firbank, (Arthur Annesley) Ronald
  1886-1926 .... **TCLC 1**
  See also CA 104; DLB 36

Fisher, M(ary) F(rances) K(ennedy)
  1908-1992 .... **CLC 76, 87**
  See also CA 77-80; 138; CANR 44

Fisher, Roy 1930-................ **CLC 25**
  See also CA 81-84; CAAS 10; CANR 16;
  DLB 40

Fisher, Rudolph
  1897-1934 .... **TCLC 11; BLC;**
                      DAM MULT
  See also BW 1; CA 107; 124; DLB 51, 102

Fisher, Vardis (Alvero) 1895-1968.... **CLC 7**
  See also CA 5-8R; 25-28R; DLB 9

Fiske, Tarleton
  See Bloch, Robert (Albert)

Fitch, Clarke
  See Sinclair, Upton (Beall)

Fitch, John IV
  See Cormier, Robert (Edmund)

Fitzgerald, Captain Hugh
  See Baum, L(yman) Frank

FitzGerald, Edward 1809-1883 .... **NCLC 9**
  See also DLB 32

Fitzgerald, F(rancis) Scott (Key)
  1896-1940 .... **TCLC 1, 6, 14, 28, 55;**
            DA; DAB; DAC; DAM MST, NOV;
                          SSC 6; WLC
  See also AITN 1; CA 110; 123;
  CDALB 1917-1929; DLB 4, 9, 86;
  DLBD 1; DLBY 81; MTCW

Fitzgerald, Penelope 1916-... **CLC 19, 51, 61**
  See also CA 85-88; CAAS 10; DLB 14

Fitzgerald, Robert (Stuart)
  1910-1985 .... **CLC 39**
  See also CA 1-4R; 114; CANR 1; DLBY 80

FitzGerald, Robert D(avid)
  1902-1987 .... **CLC 19**
  See also CA 17-20R

Fitzgerald, Zelda (Sayre)
  1900-1948 .... **TCLC 52**
  See also CA 117; 126; DLBY 84

Flanagan, Thomas (James Bonner)
  1923- .... **CLC 25, 52**
  See also CA 108; CANR 55; DLBY 80;
  INT 108; MTCW

Flaubert, Gustave
  1821-1880 .... **NCLC 2, 10, 19; DA;**
        DAB; DAC; DAM MST, NOV; SSC 11;
                                    WLC
  See also DLB 119

Flecker, Herman Elroy
  See Flecker, (Herman) James Elroy

Flecker, (Herman) James Elroy
  1884-1915 .... **TCLC 43**
  See also CA 109; 150; DLB 10, 19

Fleming, Ian (Lancaster)
  1908-1964 ...... **CLC 3, 30; DAM POP**
  See also CA 5-8R; CDBLB 1945-1960;
  DLB 87; MTCW; SATA 9

Fleming, Thomas (James) 1927- .... **CLC 37**
  See also CA 5-8R; CANR 10;
  INT CANR-10; SATA 8

Fletcher, John 1579-1625...... **LC 33; DC 6**
  See also CDBLB Before 1660; DLB 58

Fletcher, John Gould 1886-1950... **TCLC 35**
  See also CA 107; DLB 4, 45

Fleur, Paul
  See Pohl, Frederik

Flooglebuckle, Al
  See Spiegelman, Art

Flying Officer X
  See Bates, H(erbert) E(rnest)

Fo, Dario 1926-..... **CLC 32; DAM DRAM**
  See also CA 116; 128; MTCW

Fogarty, Jonathan Titulescu Esq.
  See Farrell, James T(homas)

Folke, Will
  See Bloch, Robert (Albert)

Follett, Ken(neth Martin)
  1949- ...... **CLC 18; DAM NOV, POP**
  See also AAYA 6; BEST 89:4; CA 81-84;
  CANR 13, 33, 54; DLB 87; DLBY 81;
  INT CANR-33; MTCW

Fontane, Theodor 1819-1898 ..... **NCLC 26**
  See also DLB 129

Foote, Horton
  1916- .... **CLC 51, 91; DAM DRAM**
  See also CA 73-76; CANR 34, 51; DLB 26;
  INT CANR-34

Foote, Shelby
  1916- ...... **CLC 75; DAM NOV, POP**
  See also CA 5-8R; CANR 3, 45; DLB 2, 17

Forbes, Esther 1891-1967.......... **CLC 12**
  See also AAYA 17; CA 13-14; 25-28R;
  CAP 1; CLR 27; DLB 22; JRDA;
  MAICYA; SATA 2

Forche, Carolyn (Louise)
  1950- .... **CLC 25, 83, 86; DAM POET;**
                                    PC 10
  See also CA 109; 117; CANR 50; DLB 5;
  INT 117

Ford, Elbur
  See Hibbert, Eleanor Alice Burford

Frost, Robert (Lee)
1874-1963 .... CLC **1, 3, 4, 9, 10, 13, 15, 26, 34, 44; DA; DAB; DAC; DAM MST, POET; PC 1; WLC**
See also CA 89-92; CANR 33; CDALB 1917-1929; DLB 54; DLBD 7; MTCW; SATA 14

Froude, James Anthony
1818-1894 .... NCLC **43**
See also DLB 18, 57, 144

Froy, Herald
See Waterhouse, Keith (Spencer)

Fry, Christopher
1907- ..... CLC **2, 10, 14; DAM DRAM**
See also CA 17-20R; CAAS 23; CANR 9, 30; DLB 13; MTCW; SATA 66

Frye, (Herman) Northrop
1912-1991 .... CLC **24, 70**
See also CA 5-8R; 133; CANR 8, 37; DLB 67, 68; MTCW

Fuchs, Daniel 1909-1993 .... CLC **8, 22**
See also CA 81-84; 142; CAAS 5; CANR 40; DLB 9, 26, 28; DLBY 93

Fuchs, Daniel 1934- .... CLC **34**
See also CA 37-40R; CANR 14, 48

Fuentes, Carlos
1928- ...... CLC **3, 8, 10, 13, 22, 41, 60; DA; DAB; DAC; DAM MST, MULT, NOV; HLC; SSC 24; WLC**
See also AAYA 4; AITN 2; CA 69-72; CANR 10, 32; DLB 113; HW; MTCW

Fuentes, Gregorio Lopez y
See Lopez y Fuentes, Gregorio

Fugard, (Harold) Athol
1932- .... CLC **5, 9, 14, 25, 40, 80; DAM DRAM; DC 3**
See also AAYA 17; CA 85-88; CANR 32, 54; MTCW

Fugard, Sheila 1932- .... CLC **48**
See also CA 125

Fuller, Charles (H., Jr.)
1939- .... CLC **25; BLC; DAM DRAM, MULT; DC 1**
See also BW 2; CA 108; 112; DLB 38; INT 112; MTCW

Fuller, John (Leopold) 1937- .... CLC **62**
See also CA 21-24R; CANR 9, 44; DLB 40

Fuller, Margaret .... NCLC **5, 50**
See also Ossoli, Sarah Margaret (Fuller marchesa d')

Fuller, Roy (Broadbent)
1912-1991 .... CLC **4, 28**
See also CA 5-8R; 135; CAAS 10; CANR 53; DLB 15, 20; SATA 87

Fulton, Alice 1952- .... CLC **52**
See also CA 116

Furphy, Joseph 1843-1912 .... TCLC **25**

Fussell, Paul 1924- .... CLC **74**
See also BEST 90:1; CA 17-20R; CANR 8, 21, 35; INT CANR-21; MTCW

Futabatei, Shimei 1864-1909 ...... TCLC **44**

Futrelle, Jacques 1875-1912 ...... TCLC **19**
See also CA 113

Gaboriau, Emile 1835-1873 ...... NCLC **14**

Gadda, Carlo Emilio 1893-1973 .... CLC **11**
See also CA 89-92

Gaddis, William
1922- ..... CLC **1, 3, 6, 8, 10, 19, 43, 86**
See also CA 17-20R; CANR 21, 48; DLB 2; MTCW

Gage, Walter
See Inge, William (Motter)

Gaines, Ernest J(ames)
1933- .... CLC **3, 11, 18, 86; BLC; DAM MULT**
See also AAYA 18; AITN 1; BW 2; CA 9-12R; CANR 6, 24, 42; CDALB 1968-1988; DLB 2, 33, 152; DLBY 80; MTCW; SATA 86

Gaitskill, Mary 1954- .... CLC **69**
See also CA 128

Galdos, Benito Perez
See Perez Galdos, Benito

Gale, Zona
1874-1938 ...... TCLC **7; DAM DRAM**
See also CA 105; 153; DLB 9, 78

Galeano, Eduardo (Hughes) 1940-... CLC **72**
See also CA 29-32R; CANR 13, 32; HW

Galiano, Juan Valera y Alcala
See Valera y Alcala-Galiano, Juan

Gallagher, Tess
1943- .. CLC **18, 63; DAM POET; PC 9**
See also CA 106; DLB 120

Gallant, Mavis
1922- .... CLC **7, 18, 38; DAC; DAM MST; SSC 5**
See also CA 69-72; CANR 29; DLB 53; MTCW

Gallant, Roy A(rthur) 1924- .... CLC **17**
See also CA 5-8R; CANR 4, 29, 54; CLR 30; MAICYA; SATA 4, 68

Gallico, Paul (William) 1897-1976 ... CLC **2**
See also AITN 1; CA 5-8R; 69-72; CANR 23; DLB 9, 171; MAICYA; SATA 13

Gallo, Max Louis 1932- .... CLC **95**
See also CA 85-88

Gallois, Lucien
See Desnos, Robert

Gallup, Ralph
See Whitemore, Hugh (John)

Galsworthy, John
1867-1933 ...... TCLC **1, 45; DA; DAB; DAC; DAM DRAM, MST, NOV; SSC 22; WLC 2**
See also CA 104; 141; CDBLB 1890-1914; DLB 10, 34, 98, 162

Galt, John 1779-1839 .... NCLC **1**
See also DLB 99, 116, 159

Galvin, James 1951- .... CLC **38**
See also CA 108; CANR 26

Gamboa, Federico 1864-1939 ...... TCLC **36**

Gandhi, M. K.
See Gandhi, Mohandas Karamchand

Gandhi, Mahatma
See Gandhi, Mohandas Karamchand

Gandhi, Mohandas Karamchand
1869-1948 ..... TCLC **59; DAM MULT**
See also CA 121; 132; MTCW

Gann, Ernest Kellogg 1910-1991.... CLC **23**
See also AITN 1; CA 1-4R; 136; CANR 1

Garcia, Cristina 1958- .... CLC **76**
See also CA 141

Garcia Lorca, Federico
1898-1936 ... TCLC **1, 7, 49; DA; DAB; DAC; DAM DRAM, MST, MULT, POET; DC 2; HLC; PC 3; WLC**
See also CA 104; 131; DLB 108; HW; MTCW

Garcia Marquez, Gabriel (Jose)
1928- .... CLC **2, 3, 8, 10, 15, 27, 47, 55, 68; DA; DAB; DAC; DAM MST, MULT, NOV, POP; HLC; SSC 8; WLC**
See also AAYA 3; BEST 89:1, 90:4; CA 33-36R; CANR 10, 28, 50; DLB 113; HW; MTCW

Gard, Janice
See Latham, Jean Lee

Gard, Roger Martin du
See Martin du Gard, Roger

Gardam, Jane 1928- .... CLC **43**
See also CA 49-52; CANR 2, 18, 33, 54; CLR 12; DLB 14, 161; MAICYA; MTCW; SAAS 9; SATA 39, 76; SATA-Brief 28

Gardner, Herb(ert) 1934- .... CLC **44**
See also CA 149

Gardner, John (Champlin), Jr.
1933-1982 ..... CLC **2, 3, 5, 7, 8, 10, 18, 28, 34; DAM NOV, POP; SSC 7**
See also AITN 1; CA 65-68; 107; CANR 33; DLB 2; DLBY 82; MTCW; SATA 40; SATA-Obit 31

Gardner, John (Edmund)
1926- .... CLC **30; DAM POP**
See also CA 103; CANR 15; MTCW

Gardner, Miriam
See Bradley, Marion Zimmer

Gardner, Noel
See Kuttner, Henry

Gardons, S. S.
See Snodgrass, W(illiam) D(e Witt)

Garfield, Leon 1921-1996.......... CLC **12**
See also AAYA 8; CA 17-20R; 152; CANR 38, 41; CLR 21; DLB 161; JRDA; MAICYA; SATA 1, 32, 76; SATA-Obit 90

Garland, (Hannibal) Hamlin
1860-1940 .... TCLC **3; SSC 18**
See also CA 104; DLB 12, 71, 78

Garneau, (Hector de) Saint-Denys
1912-1943 .... TCLC **13**
See also CA 111; DLB 88

Garner, Alan
1934- .... CLC **17; DAB; DAM POP**
See also AAYA 18; CA 73-76; CANR 15; CLR 20; DLB 161; MAICYA; MTCW; SATA 18, 69

Garner, Hugh 1913-1979 .... CLC **13**
See also CA 69-72; CANR 31; DLB 68

Garnett, David 1892-1981 .... CLC **3**
See also CA 5-8R; 103; CANR 17; DLB 34

Garos, Stephanie
See Katz, Steve

Garrett, George (Palmer)
1929- .... CLC **3, 11, 51**
See also CA 1-4R; CAAS 5; CANR 1, 42;
DLB 2, 5, 130, 152; DLBY 83

Garrick, David
1717-1779 ...... LC **15**; DAM DRAM
See also DLB 84

Garrigue, Jean 1914-1972 .... CLC **2, 8**
See also CA 5-8R; 37-40R; CANR 20

Garrison, Frederick
See Sinclair, Upton (Beall)

Garth, Will
See Hamilton, Edmond; Kuttner, Henry

Garvey, Marcus (Moziah, Jr.)
1887-1940 .... TCLC **41**; BLC;
DAM MULT
See also BW 1; CA 120; 124

Gary, Romain .... CLC **25**
See also Kacew, Romain
See also DLB 83

Gascar, Pierre .... CLC **11**
See also Fournier, Pierre

Gascoyne, David (Emery) 1916- .... CLC **45**
See also CA 65-68; CANR 10, 28, 54;
DLB 20; MTCW

Gaskell, Elizabeth Cleghorn
1810-1865 .. NCLC **5**; DAB; DAM MST
See also CDBLB 1832-1890; DLB 21, 144,
159

Gass, William H(oward)
1924- ... CLC **1, 2, 8, 11, 15, 39**; SSC **12**
See also CA 17-20R; CANR 30; DLB 2;
MTCW

Gasset, Jose Ortega y
See Ortega y Gasset, Jose

Gates, Henry Louis, Jr.
1950- .... CLC **65**; DAM MULT
See also BW 2; CA 109; CANR 25, 53;
DLB 67

Gautier, Theophile
1811-1872 ...... NCLC **1**; DAM POET;
SSC **20**
See also DLB 119

Gawsworth, John
See Bates, H(erbert) E(rnest)

Gay, Oliver
See Gogarty, Oliver St. John

Gaye, Marvin (Penze) 1939-1984 ... CLC **26**
See also CA 112

Gebler, Carlo (Ernest) 1954- .... CLC **39**
See also CA 119; 133

Gee, Maggie (Mary) 1948- .... CLC **57**
See also CA 130

Gee, Maurice (Gough) 1931- .... CLC **29**
See also CA 97-100; SATA 46

Gelbart, Larry (Simon) 1923- ... CLC **21, 61**
See also CA 73-76; CANR 45

Gelber, Jack 1932- .... CLC **1, 6, 14, 79**
See also CA 1-4R; CANR 2; DLB 7

Gellhorn, Martha (Ellis) 1908- .. CLC **14, 60**
See also CA 77-80; CANR 44; DLBY 82

Genet, Jean
1910-1986 ...... CLC **1, 2, 5, 10, 14, 44,
46**; DAM DRAM
See also CA 13-16R; CANR 18; DLB 72;
DLBY 86; MTCW

Gent, Peter 1942- .... CLC **29**
See also AITN 1; CA 89-92; DLBY 82

Gentlewoman in New England, A
See Bradstreet, Anne

Gentlewoman in Those Parts, A
See Bradstreet, Anne

George, Jean Craighead 1919- ...... CLC **35**
See also AAYA 8; CA 5-8R; CANR 25;
CLR 1; DLB 52; JRDA; MAICYA;
SATA 2, 68

George, Stefan (Anton)
1868-1933 .... TCLC **2, 14**
See also CA 104

Georges, Georges Martin
See Simenon, Georges (Jacques Christian)

Gerhardi, William Alexander
See Gerhardie, William Alexander

Gerhardie, William Alexander
1895-1977 .... CLC **5**
See also CA 25-28R; 73-76; CANR 18;
DLB 36

Gerstler, Amy 1956- .... CLC **70**
See also CA 146

Gertler, T. .... CLC **34**
See also CA 116; 121; INT 121

gfgg .... CLC **XvXzc**

Ghalib .... NCLC **39**
See also Ghalib, Hsadullah Khan

Ghalib, Hsadullah Khan 1797-1869
See Ghalib
See also DAM POET

Ghelderode, Michel de
1898-1962 .... CLC **6, 11**; DAM DRAM
See also CA 85-88; CANR 40

Ghiselin, Brewster 1903- .... CLC **23**
See also CA 13-16R; CAAS 10; CANR 13

Ghose, Zulfikar 1935- .... CLC **42**
See also CA 65-68

Ghosh, Amitav 1956- .... CLC **44**
See also CA 147

Giacosa, Giuseppe 1847-1906 ...... TCLC **7**
See also CA 104

Gibb, Lee
See Waterhouse, Keith (Spencer)

Gibbon, Lewis Grassic .... TCLC **4**
See also Mitchell, James Leslie

Gibbons, Kaye
1960- .... CLC **50, 88**; DAM POP
See also CA 151

Gibran, Kahlil
1883-1931 .... TCLC **1, 9**; DAM POET,
POP; PC **9**
See also CA 104; 150

Gibran, Khalil
See Gibran, Kahlil

Gibson, William
1914- .... CLC **23**; DA; DAB; DAC;
DAM DRAM, MST
See also CA 9-12R; CANR 9, 42; DLB 7;
SATA 66

Gibson, William (Ford)
1948- .... CLC **39, 63**; DAM POP
See also AAYA 12; CA 126; 133; CANR 52

Gide, Andre (Paul Guillaume)
1869-1951 .... TCLC **5, 12, 36**; DA;
DAB; DAC; DAM MST, NOV; SSC **13**;
WLC
See also CA 104; 124; DLB 65; MTCW

Gifford, Barry (Colby) 1946- .... CLC **34**
See also CA 65-68; CANR 9, 30, 40

Gilbert, W(illiam) S(chwenck)
1836-1911 ..... TCLC **3**; DAM DRAM,
POET
See also CA 104; SATA 36

Gilbreth, Frank B., Jr. 1911- .... CLC **17**
See also CA 9-12R; SATA 2

Gilchrist, Ellen
1935- .... CLC **34, 48**; DAM POP;
SSC **14**
See also CA 113; 116; CANR 41; DLB 130;
MTCW

Giles, Molly 1942- .... CLC **39**
See also CA 126

Gill, Patrick
See Creasey, John

Gilliam, Terry (Vance) 1940- .... CLC **21**
See also Monty Python
See also AAYA 19; CA 108; 113;
CANR 35; INT 113

Gillian, Jerry
See Gilliam, Terry (Vance)

Gilliatt, Penelope (Ann Douglass)
1932-1993 .... CLC **2, 10, 13, 53**
See also AITN 2; CA 13-16R; 141;
CANR 49; DLB 14

Gilman, Charlotte (Anna) Perkins (Stetson)
1860-1935 .... TCLC **9, 37**; SSC **13**
See also CA 106; 150

Gilmour, David 1949- .... CLC **35**
See also CA 138, 147

Gilpin, William 1724-1804 .... NCLC **30**

Gilray, J. D.
See Mencken, H(enry) L(ouis)

Gilroy, Frank D(aniel) 1925- .... CLC **2**
See also CA 81-84; CANR 32; DLB 7

Ginsberg, Allen
1926- ...... CLC **1, 2, 3, 4, 6, 13, 36, 69**;
DA; DAB; DAC; DAM MST, POET;
PC **4**; WLC **3**
See also AITN 1; CA 1-4R; CANR 2, 41;
CDALB 1941-1968; DLB 5, 16, 169;
MTCW

Ginzburg, Natalia
1916-1991 .... CLC **5, 11, 54, 70**
See also CA 85-88; 135; CANR 33; MTCW

Giono, Jean 1895-1970 .... CLC **4, 11**
See also CA 45-48; 29-32R; CANR 2, 35;
DLB 72; MTCW

Giovanni, Nikki
    1943- . . . . . . **CLC 2, 4, 19, 64; BLC; DA;**
        DAB; DAC; DAM MST, MULT, POET
    See also AITN 1; BW 2; CA 29-32R;
        CAAS 6; CANR 18, 41; CLR 6; DLB 5,
        41; INT CANR-18; MAICYA; MTCW;
        SATA 24

Giovene, Andrea 1904- . . . . **CLC 7**
    See also CA 85-88

Gippius, Zinaida (Nikolayevna) 1869-1945
    See Hippius, Zinaida
    See also CA 106

Giraudoux, (Hippolyte) Jean
    1882-1944 . . . . **TCLC 2, 7; DAM DRAM**
    See also CA 104; DLB 65

Gironella, Jose Maria 1917- . . . . **CLC 11**
    See also CA 101

Gissing, George (Robert)
    1857-1903 . . . . **TCLC 3, 24, 47**
    See also CA 105; DLB 18, 135

Giurlani, Aldo
    See Palazzeschi, Aldo

Gladkov, Fyodor (Vasilyevich)
    1883-1958 . . . . **TCLC 27**

Glanville, Brian (Lester) 1931- . . . . . . **CLC 6**
    See also CA 5-8R; CAAS 9; CANR 3;
        DLB 15, 139; SATA 42

Glasgow, Ellen (Anderson Gholson)
    1873(?)-1945 . . . . **TCLC 2, 7**
    See also CA 104; DLB 9, 12

Glaspell, Susan 1882(?)-1948 . . . . . **TCLC 55**
    See also CA 110; 154; DLB 7, 9, 78;
        YABC 2

Glassco, John 1909-1981 . . . . **CLC 9**
    See also CA 13-16R; 102; CANR 15;
        DLB 68

Glasscock, Amnesia
    See Steinbeck, John (Ernst)

Glasser, Ronald J. 1940(?)- . . . . **CLC 37**

Glassman, Joyce
    See Johnson, Joyce

Glendinning, Victoria 1937- . . . . **CLC 50**
    See also CA 120; 127; DLB 155

Glissant, Edouard
    1928- . . . . **CLC 10, 68; DAM MULT**
    See also CA 153

Gloag, Julian 1930- . . . . **CLC 40**
    See also AITN 1; CA 65-68; CANR 10

Glowacki, Aleksander
    See Prus, Boleslaw

Gluck, Louise (Elisabeth)
    1943- . . . . **CLC 7, 22, 44, 81;**
        DAM POET; PC 16
    See also CA 33-36R; CANR 40; DLB 5

Gobineau, Joseph Arthur (Comte) de
    1816-1882 . . . . **NCLC 17**
    See also DLB 123

Godard, Jean-Luc 1930- . . . . **CLC 20**
    See also CA 93-96

Godden, (Margaret) Rumer 1907- . . . **CLC 53**
    See also AAYA 6; CA 5-8R; CANR 4, 27,
        36, 55; CLR 20; DLB 161; MAICYA;
        SAAS 12; SATA 3, 36

Godoy Alcayaga, Lucila 1889-1957
    See Mistral, Gabriela
    See also BW 2; CA 104; 131; DAM MULT;
        HW; MTCW

Godwin, Gail (Kathleen)
    1937- . . . . **CLC 5, 8, 22, 31, 69;**
        DAM POP
    See also CA 29-32R; CANR 15, 43; DLB 6;
        INT CANR-15; MTCW

Godwin, William 1756-1836 . . . . . . **NCLC 14**
    See also CDBLB 1789-1832; DLB 39, 104,
        142, 158, 163

Goethe, Johann Wolfgang von
    1749-1832 . . . . **NCLC 4, 22, 34; DA;**
        DAB; DAC; DAM DRAM, MST,
        POET; PC 5; WLC 3
    See also DLB 94

Gogarty, Oliver St. John
    1878-1957 . . . . **TCLC 15**
    See also CA 109; 150; DLB 15, 19

Gogol, Nikolai (Vasilyevich)
    1809-1852 . . . . **NCLC 5, 15, 31; DA;**
        DAB; DAC; DAM DRAM, MST; DC 1;
        SSC 4; WLC

Goines, Donald
    1937(?)-1974 . . . . **CLC 80; BLC;**
        DAM MULT, POP
    See also AITN 1; BW 1; CA 124; 114;
        DLB 33

Gold, Herbert 1924- . . . . **CLC 4, 7, 14, 42**
    See also CA 9-12R; CANR 17, 45; DLB 2;
        DLBY 81

Goldbarth, Albert 1948- . . . . **CLC 5, 38**
    See also CA 53-56; CANR 6, 40; DLB 120

Goldberg, Anatol 1910-1982 . . . . **CLC 34**
    See also CA 131; 117

Goldemberg, Isaac 1945- . . . . **CLC 52**
    See also CA 69-72; CAAS 12; CANR 11,
        32; HW

Golding, William (Gerald)
    1911-1993 . . . . **CLC 1, 2, 3, 8, 10, 17, 27,**
        58, 81; DA; DAB; DAC; DAM MST,
        NOV; WLC
    See also AAYA 5; CA 5-8R; 141;
        CANR 13, 33, 54; CDBLB 1945-1960;
        DLB 15, 100; MTCW

Goldman, Emma 1869-1940 . . . . . . **TCLC 13**
    See also CA 110; 150

Goldman, Francisco 1955- . . . . **CLC 76**

Goldman, William (W.) 1931- . . . . **CLC 1, 48**
    See also CA 9-12R; CANR 29; DLB 44

Goldmann, Lucien 1913-1970 . . . . . . **CLC 24**
    See also CA 25-28; CAP 2

Goldoni, Carlo
    1707-1793 . . . . **LC 4; DAM DRAM**

Goldsberry, Steven 1949- . . . . **CLC 34**
    See also CA 131

Goldsmith, Oliver
    1728-1774 . . . . . . **LC 2; DA; DAB; DAC;**
        DAM DRAM, MST, NOV, POET;
        WLC
    See also CDBLB 1660-1789; DLB 39, 89,
        104, 109, 142; SATA 26

Goldsmith, Peter
    See Priestley, J(ohn) B(oynton)

Gombrowicz, Witold
    1904-1969 . . . . **CLC 4, 7, 11, 49;**
        DAM DRAM
    See also CA 19-20; 25-28R; CAP 2

Gomez de la Serna, Ramon
    1888-1963 . . . . **CLC 9**
    See also CA 153; 116; HW

Goncharov, Ivan Alexandrovich
    1812-1891 . . . . **NCLC 1**

Goncourt, Edmond (Louis Antoine Huot) de
    1822-1896 . . . . **NCLC 7**
    See also DLB 123

Goncourt, Jules (Alfred Huot) de
    1830-1870 . . . . **NCLC 7**
    See also DLB 123

Gontier, Fernande 19(?)- . . . . **CLC 50**

Goodman, Paul 1911-1972 . . . . **CLC 1, 2, 4, 7**
    See also CA 19-20; 37-40R; CANR 34;
        CAP 2; DLB 130; MTCW

Gordimer, Nadine
    1923- . . . . **CLC 3, 5, 7, 10, 18, 33, 51, 70;**
        DA; DAB; DAC; DAM MST, NOV;
        SSC 17
    See also CA 5-8R; CANR 3, 28;
        INT CANR-28; MTCW

Gordon, Adam Lindsay
    1833-1870 . . . . **NCLC 21**

Gordon, Caroline
    1895-1981 . . . **CLC 6, 13, 29, 83; SSC 15**
    See also CA 11-12; 103; CANR 36; CAP 1;
        DLB 4, 9, 102; DLBY 81; MTCW

Gordon, Charles William 1860-1937
    See Connor, Ralph
    See also CA 109

Gordon, Mary (Catherine)
    1949- . . . . **CLC 13, 22**
    See also CA 102; CANR 44; DLB 6;
        DLBY 81; INT 102; MTCW

Gordon, Sol 1923- . . . . **CLC 26**
    See also CA 53-56; CANR 4; SATA 11

Gordone, Charles
    1925-1995 . . . . . **CLC 1, 4; DAM DRAM**
    See also BW 1; CA 93-96; 150; CANR 55;
        DLB 7; INT 93-96; MTCW

Gorenko, Anna Andreevna
    See Akhmatova, Anna

Gorky, Maxim . . . . **TCLC 8; DAB; WLC**
    See also Peshkov, Alexei Maximovich

Goryan, Sirak
    See Saroyan, William

Gosse, Edmund (William)
    1849-1928 . . . . **TCLC 28**
    See also CA 117; DLB 57, 144

Gotlieb, Phyllis Fay (Bloom)
    1926- . . . . **CLC 18**
    See also CA 13-16R; CANR 7; DLB 88

Gottesman, S. D.
    See Kornbluth, C(yril) M.; Pohl, Frederik

Gottfried von Strassburg
    fl. c. 1210- . . . . **CMLC 10**
    See also DLB 138

Gould, Lois . . . . **CLC 4, 10**
    See also CA 77-80; CANR 29; MTCW

Gourmont, Remy (-Marie-Charles) de
 1858-1915 .... **TCLC 17**
 See also CA 109; 150

Govier, Katherine 1948-.......... **CLC 51**
 See also CA 101; CANR 18, 40

Goyen, (Charles) William
 1915-1983 .... **CLC 5, 8, 14, 40**
 See also AITN 2; CA 5-8R; 110; CANR 6;
 DLB 2; DLBY 83; INT CANR-6

Goytisolo, Juan
 1931- ..... **CLC 5, 10, 23; DAM MULT;**
                                          HLC
 See also CA 85-88; CANR 32; HW; MTCW

Gozzano, Guido 1883-1916 .... **PC 10**
 See also CA 154; DLB 114

Gozzi, (Conte) Carlo 1720-1806 .. **NCLC 23**

Grabbe, Christian Dietrich
 1801-1836 .... **NCLC 2**
 See also DLB 133

Grace, Patricia 1937-............. **CLC 56**

Gracian y Morales, Baltasar
 1601-1658 .... **LC 15**

Gracq, Julien................. **CLC 11, 48**
 See also Poirier, Louis
 See also DLB 83

Grade, Chaim 1910-1982 .... **CLC 10**
 See also CA 93-96; 107

Graduate of Oxford, A
 See Ruskin, John

Graham, John
 See Phillips, David Graham

Graham, Jorie 1951-............. **CLC 48**
 See also CA 111; DLB 120

Graham, R(obert) B(ontine) Cunninghame
 See Cunninghame Graham, R(obert)
 B(ontine)
 See also DLB 98, 135, 174

Graham, Robert
 See Haldeman, Joe (William)

Graham, Tom
 See Lewis, (Harry) Sinclair

Graham, W(illiam) S(ydney)
 1918-1986 .... **CLC 29**
 See also CA 73-76; 118; DLB 20

Graham, Winston (Mawdsley)
 1910- .... **CLC 23**
 See also CA 49-52; CANR 2, 22, 45;
 DLB 77

Grahame, Kenneth
 1859-1932 .... **TCLC 64; DAB**
 See also CA 108; 136; CLR 5; DLB 34, 141;
 MAICYA; YABC 1

Grant, Skeeter
 See Spiegelman, Art

Granville-Barker, Harley
 1877-1946 ...... **TCLC 2; DAM DRAM**
 See also Barker, Harley Granville
 See also CA 104

Grass, Guenter (Wilhelm)
 1927- ..... **CLC 1, 2, 4, 6, 11, 15, 22, 32,**
            49, 88; DA; DAB; DAC; DAM MST,
                                    NOV; WLC
 See also CA 13-16R; CANR 20; DLB 75,
 124; MTCW

Gratton, Thomas
 See Hulme, T(homas) E(rnest)

Grau, Shirley Ann
 1929- .... **CLC 4, 9; SSC 15**
 See also CA 89-92; CANR 22; DLB 2;
 INT CANR-22; MTCW

Gravel, Fern
 See Hall, James Norman

Graver, Elizabeth 1964-........... **CLC 70**
 See also CA 135

Graves, Richard Perceval 1945- .... **CLC 44**
 See also CA 65-68; CANR 9, 26, 51

Graves, Robert (von Ranke)
 1895-1985 ...... **CLC 1, 2, 6, 11, 39, 44,**
       45; DAB; DAC; DAM MST, POET;
                                        PC 6
 See also CA 5-8R; 117; CANR 5, 36;
 CDBLB 1914-1945; DLB 20, 100;
 DLBY 85; MTCW; SATA 45

Graves, Valerie
 See Bradley, Marion Zimmer

Gray, Alasdair (James) 1934- ...... **CLC 41**
 See also CA 126; CANR 47; INT 126;
 MTCW

Gray, Amlin 1946-............... **CLC 29**
 See also CA 138

Gray, Francine du Plessix
 1930- .... **CLC 22; DAM NOV**
 See also BEST 90:3; CA 61-64; CAAS 2;
 CANR 11, 33; INT CANR-11; MTCW

Gray, John (Henry) 1866-1934 .... **TCLC 19**
 See also CA 119

Gray, Simon (James Holliday)
 1936- .... **CLC 9, 14, 36**
 See also AITN 1; CA 21-24R; CAAS 3;
 CANR 32; DLB 13; MTCW

Gray, Spalding 1941-.. **CLC 49; DAM POP**
 See also CA 128

Gray, Thomas
 1716-1771 ...... **LC 4; DA; DAB; DAC;**
                    DAM MST; PC 2; WLC
 See also CDBLB 1660-1789; DLB 109

Grayson, David
 See Baker, Ray Stannard

Grayson, Richard (A.) 1951-....... **CLC 38**
 See also CA 85-88; CANR 14, 31

Greeley, Andrew M(oran)
 1928- .... **CLC 28; DAM POP**
 See also CA 5-8R; CAAS 7; CANR 7, 43;
 MTCW

Green, Anna Katharine
 1846-1935 .... **TCLC 63**
 See also CA 112

Green, Brian
 See Card, Orson Scott

Green, Hannah
 See Greenberg, Joanne (Goldenberg)

Green, Hannah .... **CLC 3**
 See also CA 73-76

Green, Henry 1905-1973 ..... **CLC 2, 13, 97**
 See also Yorke, Henry Vincent
 See also DLB 15

Green, Julian (Hartridge) 1900-
 See Green, Julien; CA 21-24R; CANR 33; DLB 4, 72;
 MTCW

Green, Julien............... **CLC 3, 11, 77**
 See also Green, Julian (Hartridge)

Green, Paul (Eliot)
 1894-1981 ...... **CLC 25; DAM DRAM**
 See also AITN 1; CA 5-8R; 103; CANR 3;
 DLB 7, 9; DLBY 81

Greenberg, Ivan 1908-1973
 See Rahv, Philip
 See also CA 85-88

Greenberg, Joanne (Goldenberg)
 1932-..................... **CLC 7, 30**
 See also AAYA 12; CA 5-8R; CANR 14,
 32; SATA 25

Greenberg, Richard 1959(?)-....... **CLC 57**
 See also CA 138

Greene, Bette 1934-.............. **CLC 30**
 See also AAYA 7; CA 53-56; CANR 4;
 CLR 2; JRDA; MAICYA; SAAS 16;
 SATA 8

Greene, Gael .... **CLC 8**
 See also CA 13-16R; CANR 10

Greene, Graham
 1904-1991 .... **CLC 1, 3, 6, 9, 14, 18, 27,**
       37, 70, 72; DA; DAB; DAC; DAM MST,
                                NOV; WLC
 See also AITN 2; CA 13-16R; 133;
 CANR 35; CDBLB 1945-1960; DLB 13,
 15, 77, 100, 162; DLBY 91; MTCW;
 SATA 20

Greer, Richard
 See Silverberg, Robert

Gregor, Arthur 1923-.............. **CLC 9**
 See also CA 25-28R; CAAS 10; CANR 11;
 SATA 36

Gregor, Lee
 See Pohl, Frederik

Gregory, Isabella Augusta (Persse)
 1852-1932 .... **TCLC 1**
 See also CA 104; DLB 10

Gregory, J. Dennis
 See Williams, John A(lfred)

Grendon, Stephen
 See Derleth, August (William)

Grenville, Kate 1950-............. **CLC 61**
 See also CA 118; CANR 53

Grenville, Pelham
 See Wodehouse, P(elham) G(renville)

Greve, Felix Paul (Berthold Friedrich)
 1879-1948
 See Grove, Frederick Philip
 See also CA 104; 141; DAC; DAM MST

Grey, Zane
 1872-1939 .... **TCLC 6; DAM POP**
 See also CA 104; 132; DLB 9; MTCW

Grieg, (Johan) Nordahl (Brun)
 1902-1943 .... **TCLC 10**
 See also CA 107

Grieve, C(hristopher) M(urray)
 1892-1978 .... **CLC 11, 19; DAM POET**
 See also MacDiarmid, Hugh; Pteleon
 See also CA 5-8R; 85-88; CANR 33;
 MTCW

Griffin, Gerald 1803-1840 .... NCLC 7
See also DLB 159

Griffin, John Howard 1920-1980.... CLC 68
See also AITN 1; CA 1-4R; 101; CANR 2

Griffin, Peter 1942- .... CLC 39
See also CA 136

Griffiths, Trevor 1935-......... CLC 13, 52
See also CA 97-100; CANR 45; DLB 13

Grigson, Geoffrey (Edward Harvey)
1905-1985 .... CLC 7, 39
See also CA 25-28R; 118; CANR 20, 33;
DLB 27; MTCW

Grillparzer, Franz 1791-1872...... NCLC 1
See also DLB 133

Grimble, Reverend Charles James
See Eliot, T(homas) S(tearns)

Grimke, Charlotte L(ottie) Forten
1837(?)-1914
See Forten, Charlotte L.
See also BW 1; CA 117; 124; DAM MULT,
POET

Grimm, Jacob Ludwig Karl
1785-1863 .... NCLC 3
See also DLB 90; MAICYA; SATA 22

Grimm, Wilhelm Karl 1786-1859 .. NCLC 3
See also DLB 90; MAICYA; SATA 22

Grimmelshausen, Johann Jakob Christoffel
von 1621-1676 .... LC 6
See also DLB 168

Grindel, Eugene 1895-1952
See Eluard, Paul
See also CA 104

Grisham, John 1955- .. CLC 84; DAM POP
See also AAYA 14; CA 138; CANR 47

Grossman, David 1954- .... CLC 67
See also CA 138

Grossman, Vasily (Semenovich)
1905-1964 .... CLC 41
See also CA 124; 130; MTCW

Grove, Frederick Philip .... TCLC 4
See also Greve, Felix Paul (Berthold
Friedrich)
See also DLB 92

Grubb
See Crumb, R(obert)

Grumbach, Doris (Isaac)
1918- .... CLC 13, 22, 64
See also CA 5-8R; CAAS 2; CANR 9, 42;
INT CANR-9

Grundtvig, Nicolai Frederik Severin
1783-1872 .... NCLC 1

Grunge
See Crumb, R(obert)

Grunwald, Lisa 1959-............. CLC 44
See also CA 120

Guare, John
1938- .... CLC 8, 14, 29, 67;
DAM DRAM
See also CA 73-76; CANR 21; DLB 7;
MTCW

Gudjonsson, Halldor Kiljan 1902-
See Laxness, Halldor
See also CA 103

Guenter, Erich
See Eich, Guenter

Guest, Barbara 1920-............. CLC 34
See also CA 25-28R; CANR 11, 44; DLB 5

Guest, Judith (Ann)
1936- .... CLC 8, 30; DAM NOV, POP
See also AAYA 7; CA 77-80; CANR 15;
INT CANR-15; MTCW

Guevara, Che .... CLC 87; HLC
See also Guevara (Serna), Ernesto

Guevara (Serna), Ernesto 1928-1967
See Guevara, Che
See also CA 127; 111; DAM MULT; HW

Guild, Nicholas M. 1944-......... CLC 33
See also CA 93-96

Guillemin, Jacques
See Sartre, Jean-Paul

Guillen, Jorge
1893-1984 ...... CLC 11; DAM MULT,
POET
See also CA 89-92; 112; DLB 108; HW

Guillen, Nicolas (Cristobal)
1902-1989 .... CLC 48, 79; BLC;
DAM MST, MULT, POET; HLC
See also BW 2; CA 116; 125; 129; HW

Guillevic, (Eugene) 1907-.......... CLC 33
See also CA 93-96

Guillois
See Desnos, Robert

Guillois, Valentin
See Desnos, Robert

Guiney, Louise Imogen
1861-1920 .... TCLC 41
See also DLB 54

Guiraldes, Ricardo (Guillermo)
1886-1927 .... TCLC 39
See also CA 131; HW; MTCW

Gumilev, Nikolai Stephanovich
1886-1921 .... TCLC 60

Gunesekera, Romesh.............. CLC 91

Gunn, Bill .... CLC 5
See also Gunn, William Harrison
See also DLB 38

Gunn, Thom(son William)
1929- .... CLC 3, 6, 18, 32, 81;
DAM POET
See also CA 17-20R; CANR 9, 33;
CDBLB 1960 to Present; DLB 27;
INT CANR-33; MTCW

Gunn, William Harrison 1934(?)-1989
See Gunn, Bill
See also AITN 1; BW 1; CA 13-16R; 128;
CANR 12, 25

Gunnars, Kristjana 1948-......... CLC 69
See also CA 113; DLB 60

Gurganus, Allan
1947- .... CLC 70; DAM POP
See also BEST 90:1; CA 135

Gurney, A(lbert) R(amsdell), Jr.
1930- .... CLC 32, 50, 54; DAM DRAM
See also CA 77-80; CANR 32

Gurney, Ivor (Bertie) 1890-1937 ... TCLC 33

Gurney, Peter
See Gurney, A(lbert) R(amsdell), Jr.

Guro, Elena 1877-1913.......... TCLC 56

Gustafson, Ralph (Barker) 1909-.... CLC 36
See also CA 21-24R; CANR 8, 45; DLB 88

Gut, Gom
See Simenon, Georges (Jacques Christian)

Guterson, David 1956-............ CLC 91
See also CA 132

Guthrie, A(lfred) B(ertram), Jr.
1901-1991 .... CLC 23
See also CA 57-60; 134; CANR 24; DLB 6;
SATA 62; SATA-Obit 67

Guthrie, Isobel
See Grieve, C(hristopher) M(urray)

Guthrie, Woodrow Wilson 1912-1967
See Guthrie, Woody
See also CA 113; 93-96

Guthrie, Woody................... CLC 35
See also Guthrie, Woodrow Wilson

Guy, Rosa (Cuthbert) 1928-........ CLC 26
See also AAYA 4; BW 2; CA 17-20R;
CANR 14, 34; CLR 13; DLB 33; JRDA;
MAICYA; SATA 14, 62

Gwendolyn
See Bennett, (Enoch) Arnold

H. D. .... CLC 3, 8, 14, 31, 34, 73; PC 5
See also Doolittle, Hilda

H. de V.
See Buchan, John

Haavikko, Paavo Juhani
1931- .... CLC 18, 34
See also CA 106

Habbema, Koos
See Heijermans, Herman

Hacker, Marilyn
1942- .... CLC 5, 9, 23, 72, 91;
DAM POET
See also CA 77-80; DLB 120

Haggard, H(enry) Rider
1856-1925 .... TCLC 11
See also CA 108; 148; DLB 70, 156, 174;
SATA 16

Hagiosy, L.
See Larbaud, Valery (Nicolas)

Hagiwara Sakutaro 1886-1942 .... TCLC 60

Haig, Fenil
See Ford, Ford Madox

Haig-Brown, Roderick (Langmere)
1908-1976 .... CLC 21
See also CA 5-8R; 69-72; CANR 4, 38;
CLR 31; DLB 88; MAICYA; SATA 12

Hailey, Arthur
1920- .... CLC 5; DAM NOV, POP
See also AITN 2; BEST 90:3; CA 1-4R;
CANR 2, 36; DLB 88; DLBY 82; MTCW

Hailey, Elizabeth Forsythe 1938-... CLC 40
See also CA 93-96; CAAS 1; CANR 15, 48;
INT CANR-15

Haines, John (Meade) 1924-....... CLC 58
See also CA 17-20R; CANR 13, 34; DLB 5

Hakluyt, Richard 1552-1616........ LC 31

Haldeman, Joe (William) 1943-..... CLC 61
See also CA 53-56; CAAS 25; CANR 6;
DLB 8; INT CANR-6

Haley, Alex(ander Murray Palmer)
 1921-1992 .... CLC 8, 12, 76; BLC; DA;
  DAB; DAC; DAM MST, MULT, POP
 See also BW 2; CA 77-80; 136; DLB 38;
  MTCW

Haliburton, Thomas Chandler
 1796-1865 .... NCLC 15
 See also DLB 11, 99

Hall, Donald (Andrew, Jr.)
 1928- .. CLC 1, 13, 37, 59; DAM POET
 See also CA 5-8R; CAAS 7; CANR 2, 44;
  DLB 5; SATA 23

Hall, Frederic Sauser
 See Sauser-Hall, Frederic

Hall, James
 See Kuttner, Henry

Hall, James Norman 1887-1951 ... TCLC 23
 See also CA 123; SATA 21

Hall, (Marguerite) Radclyffe
 1886-1943 .... TCLC 12
 See also CA 110; 150

Hall, Rodney 1935- .... CLC 51
 See also CA 109

Halleck, Fitz-Greene 1790-1867 .. NCLC 47
 See also DLB 3

Halliday, Michael
 See Creasey, John

Halpern, Daniel 1945- .... CLC 14
 See also CA 33-36R

Hamburger, Michael (Peter Leopold)
 1924- .... CLC 5, 14
 See also CA 5-8R; CAAS 4; CANR 2, 47;
  DLB 27

Hamill, Pete 1935- .... CLC 10
 See also CA 25-28R; CANR 18

Hamilton, Alexander
 1755(?)-1804 .... NCLC 49
 See also DLB 37

Hamilton, Clive
 See Lewis, C(live) S(taples)

Hamilton, Edmond 1904-1977....... CLC 1
 See also CA 1-4R; CANR 3; DLB 8

Hamilton, Eugene (Jacob) Lee
 See Lee-Hamilton, Eugene (Jacob)

Hamilton, Franklin
 See Silverberg, Robert

Hamilton, Gail
 See Corcoran, Barbara

Hamilton, Mollie
 See Kaye, M(ary) M(argaret)

Hamilton, (Anthony Walter) Patrick
 1904-1962 .... CLC 51
 See also CA 113; DLB 10

Hamilton, Virginia
 1936- .... CLC 26; DAM MULT
 See also AAYA 2; BW 2; CA 25-28R;
  CANR 20, 37; CLR 1, 11, 40; DLB 33,
  52; INT CANR-20; JRDA; MAICYA;
  MTCW; SATA 4, 56, 79

Hammett, (Samuel) Dashiell
 1894-1961 .... CLC 3, 5, 10, 19, 47;
                                     SSC 17
 See also AITN 1; CA 81-84; CANR 42;
  CDALB 1929-1941; DLBD 6; MTCW

Hammon, Jupiter
 1711(?)-1800(?) .... NCLC 5; BLC;
  DAM MULT, POET; PC 16
 See also DLB 31, 50

Hammond, Keith
 See Kuttner, Henry

Hamner, Earl (Henry), Jr. 1923- ... CLC 12
 See also AITN 2; CA 73-76; DLB 6

Hampton, Christopher (James)
 1946- .... CLC 4
 See also CA 25-28R; DLB 13; MTCW

Hamsun, Knut .... TCLC 2, 14, 49
 See also Pedersen, Knut

Handke, Peter
 1942- .... CLC 5, 8, 10, 15, 38;
  DAM DRAM, NOV
 See also CA 77-80; CANR 33; DLB 85,
  124; MTCW

Hanley, James 1901-1985 ... CLC 3, 5, 8, 13
 See also CA 73-76; 117; CANR 36; MTCW

Hannah, Barry 1942-....... CLC 23, 38, 90
 See also CA 108; 110; CANR 43; DLB 6;
  INT 110; MTCW

Hannon, Ezra
 See Hunter, Evan

Hansberry, Lorraine (Vivian)
 1930-1965 ...... CLC 17, 62; BLC; DA;
  DAB; DAC; DAM DRAM, MST,
                         MULT; DC 2
 See also BW 1; CA 109; 25-28R; CABS 3;
  CDALB 1941-1968; DLB 7, 38; MTCW

Hansen, Joseph 1923-............. CLC 38
 See also CA 29-32R; CAAS 17; CANR 16,
  44; INT CANR-16

Hansen, Martin A. 1909-1955..... TCLC 32

Hanson, Kenneth O(stlin) 1922- .... CLC 13
 See also CA 53-56; CANR 7

Hardwick, Elizabeth
 1916- .... CLC 13; DAM NOV
 See also CA 5-8R; CANR 3, 32; DLB 6;
  MTCW

Hardy, Thomas
 1840-1928 ...... TCLC 4, 10, 18, 32, 48,
  53; DA; DAB; DAC; DAM MST, NOV,
  POET; PC 8; SSC 2; WLC
 See also CA 104; 123; CDBLB 1890-1914;
  DLB 18, 19, 135; MTCW

Hare, David 1947- .... CLC 29, 58
 See also CA 97-100; CANR 39; DLB 13;
  MTCW

Harford, Henry
 See Hudson, W(illiam) H(enry)

Hargrave, Leonie
 See Disch, Thomas M(ichael)

Harjo, Joy 1951- ... CLC 83; DAM MULT
 See also CA 114; CANR 35; DLB 120;
  NNAL

Harlan, Louis R(udolph) 1922- ..... CLC 34
 See also CA 21-24R; CANR 25, 55

Harling, Robert 1951(?)- .... CLC 53
 See also CA 147

Harmon, William (Ruth) 1938- ..... CLC 38
 See also CA 33-36R; CANR 14, 32, 35;
  SATA 65

Harper, F. E. W.
 See Harper, Frances Ellen Watkins

Harper, Frances E. W.
 See Harper, Frances Ellen Watkins

Harper, Frances E. Watkins
 See Harper, Frances Ellen Watkins

Harper, Frances Ellen
 See Harper, Frances Ellen Watkins

Harper, Frances Ellen Watkins
 1825-1911 .... TCLC 14; BLC;
  DAM MULT, POET
 See also BW 1; CA 111; 125; DLB 50

Harper, Michael S(teven) 1938- .. CLC 7, 22
 See also BW 1; CA 33-36R; CANR 24;
  DLB 41

Harper, Mrs. F. E. W.
 See Harper, Frances Ellen Watkins

Harris, Christie (Lucy) Irwin
 1907- .... CLC 12
 See also CA 5-8R; CANR 6; DLB 88;
  JRDA; MAICYA; SAAS 10; SATA 6, 74

Harris, Frank 1856-1931 .... TCLC 24
 See also CA 109; 150; DLB 156

Harris, George Washington
 1814-1869 .... NCLC 23
 See also DLB 3, 11

Harris, Joel Chandler
 1848-1908 .... TCLC 2; SSC 19
 See also CA 104; 137; DLB 11, 23, 42, 78,
  91; MAICYA; YABC 1

Harris, John (Wyndham Parkes Lucas)
  Beynon 1903-1969
 See Wyndham, John
 See also CA 102; 89-92

Harris, MacDonald .... CLC 9
 See also Heiney, Donald (William)

Harris, Mark 1922- .... CLC 19
 See also CA 5-8R; CAAS 3; CANR 2, 55;
  DLB 2; DLBY 80

Harris, (Theodore) Wilson 1921-.... CLC 25
 See also BW 2; CA 65-68; CAAS 16;
  CANR 11, 27; DLB 117; MTCW

Harrison, Elizabeth Cavanna 1909-
 See Cavanna, Betty
 See also CA 9-12R; CANR 6, 27

Harrison, Harry (Max) 1925-...... CLC 42
 See also CA 1-4R; CANR 5, 21; DLB 8;
  SATA 4

Harrison, James (Thomas)
 1937- .... CLC 6, 14, 33, 66; SSC 19
 See also CA 13-16R; CANR 8, 51;
  DLBY 82; INT CANR-8

Harrison, Jim
 See Harrison, James (Thomas)

Harrison, Kathryn 1961- .... CLC 70
 See also CA 144

Harrison, Tony 1937-............. CLC 43
 See also CA 65-68; CANR 44; DLB 40;
  MTCW

Harriss, Will(ard Irvin) 1922- ...... CLC 34
 See also CA 111

Harson, Sley
 See Ellison, Harlan (Jay)

Hart, Ellis
 See Ellison, Harlan (Jay)

Horovitz, Israel (Arthur)
1939- .... **CLC 56; DAM DRAM**
See also CA 33-36R; CANR 46; DLB 7

Horvath, Odon von
See Horvath, Oedoen von
See also DLB 85, 124

Horvath, Oedoen von 1901-1938... **TCLC 45**
See also Horvath, Odon von
See also CA 118

Horwitz, Julius 1920-1986......... **CLC 14**
See also CA 9-12R; 119; CANR 12

Hospital, Janette Turner 1942-..... **CLC 42**
See also CA 108; CANR 48

Hostos, E. M. de
See Hostos (y Bonilla), Eugenio Maria de

Hostos, Eugenio M. de
See Hostos (y Bonilla), Eugenio Maria de

Hostos, Eugenio Maria
See Hostos (y Bonilla), Eugenio Maria de

Hostos (y Bonilla), Eugenio Maria de
1839-1903 .... **TCLC 24**
See also CA 123; 131; HW

Houdini
See Lovecraft, H(oward) P(hillips)

Hougan, Carolyn 1943- .... **CLC 34**
See also CA 139

Household, Geoffrey (Edward West)
1900-1988 .... **CLC 11**
See also CA 77-80; 126; DLB 87; SATA 14;
SATA-Obit 59

Housman, A(lfred) E(dward)
1859-1936 ..... **TCLC 1, 10; DA; DAB;**
DAC; DAM MST, POET; PC 2
See also CA 104; 125; DLB 19; MTCW

Housman, Laurence 1865-1959..... **TCLC 7**
See also CA 106; DLB 10; SATA 25

Howard, Elizabeth Jane 1923- ... **CLC 7, 29**
See also CA 5-8R; CANR 8

Howard, Maureen 1930- ..... **CLC 5, 14, 46**
See also CA 53-56; CANR 31; DLBY 83;
INT CANR-31; MTCW

Howard, Richard 1929- ...... **CLC 7, 10, 47**
See also AITN 1; CA 85-88; CANR 25;
DLB 5; INT CANR-25

Howard, Robert Ervin 1906-1936... **TCLC 8**
See also CA 105

Howard, Warren F.
See Pohl, Frederik

Howe, Fanny 1940- .... **CLC 47**
See also CA 117; SATA-Brief 52

Howe, Irving 1920-1993.......... **CLC 85**
See also CA 9-12R; 141; CANR 21, 50;
DLB 67; MTCW

Howe, Julia Ward 1819-1910 ..... **TCLC 21**
See also CA 117; DLB 1

Howe, Susan 1937-............... **CLC 72**
See also DLB 120

Howe, Tina 1937-............... **CLC 48**
See also CA 109

Howell, James 1594(?)-1666 .... **LC 13**
See also DLB 151

Howells, W. D.
See Howells, William Dean

Howells, William D.
See Howells, William Dean

Howells, William Dean
1837-1920 .... **TCLC 7, 17, 41**
See also CA 104; 134; CDALB 1865-1917;
DLB 12, 64, 74, 79

Howes, Barbara 1914-1996 .... **CLC 15**
See also CA 9-12R; 151; CAAS 3;
CANR 53; SATA 5

Hrabal, Bohumil 1914-......... **CLC 13, 67**
See also CA 106; CAAS 12

Hsun, Lu
See Lu Hsun

Hubbard, L(afayette) Ron(ald)
1911-1986 .... **CLC 43; DAM POP**
See also CA 77-80; 118; CANR 52

Huch, Ricarda (Octavia)
1864-1947 .... **TCLC 13**
See also CA 111; DLB 66

Huddle, David 1942- .... **CLC 49**
See also CA 57-60; CAAS 20; DLB 130

Hudson, Jeffrey
See Crichton, (John) Michael

Hudson, W(illiam) H(enry)
1841-1922 .... **TCLC 29**
See also CA 115; DLB 98, 153, 174;
SATA 35

Hueffer, Ford Madox
See Ford, Ford Madox

Hughart, Barry 1934-............. **CLC 39**
See also CA 137

Hughes, Colin
See Creasey, John

Hughes, David (John) 1930- .... **CLC 48**
See also CA 116; 129; DLB 14

Hughes, Edward James
See Hughes, Ted
See also DAM MST, POET

Hughes, (James) Langston
1902-1967 ..... **CLC 1, 5, 10, 15, 35, 44;**
BLC; DA; DAB; DAC; DAM DRAM,
MST, MULT, POET; DC 3; PC 1;
SSC 6; WLC
See also AAYA 12; BW 1; CA 1-4R;
25-28R; CANR 1, 34; CDALB 1929-1941;
CLR 17; DLB 4, 7, 48, 51, 86; JRDA;
MAICYA; MTCW; SATA 4, 33

Hughes, Richard (Arthur Warren)
1900-1976 ...... **CLC 1, 11; DAM NOV**
See also CA 5-8R; 65-68; CANR 4;
DLB 15, 161; MTCW; SATA 8;
SATA-Obit 25

Hughes, Ted
1930- .... **CLC 2, 4, 9, 14, 37; DAB;**
DAC; PC 7
See also Hughes, Edward James
See also CA 1-4R; CANR 1, 33; CLR 3;
DLB 40, 161; MAICYA; MTCW;
SATA 49; SATA-Brief 27

Hugo, Richard F(ranklin)
1923-1982 .... **CLC 6, 18, 32;**
DAM POET
See also CA 49-52; 108; CANR 3; DLB 5

Hugo, Victor (Marie)
1802-1885 .... **NCLC 3, 10, 21; DA;**
DAB; DAC; DAM DRAM, MST, NOV,
POET; WLC
See also DLB 119; SATA 47

Huidobro, Vicente
See Huidobro Fernandez, Vicente Garcia

Huidobro Fernandez, Vicente Garcia
1893-1948 .... **TCLC 31**
See also CA 131; HW

Hulme, Keri 1947- .... **CLC 39**
See also CA 125; INT 125

Hulme, T(homas) E(rnest)
1883-1917 .... **TCLC 21**
See also CA 117; DLB 19

Hume, David 1711-1776............. **LC 7**
See also DLB 104

Humphrey, William 1924-......... **CLC 45**
See also CA 77-80; DLB 6

Humphreys, Emyr Owen 1919-..... **CLC 47**
See also CA 5-8R; CANR 3, 24; DLB 15

Humphreys, Josephine 1945-.... **CLC 34, 57**
See also CA 121; 127; INT 127

Huneker, James Gibbons
1857-1921 .... **TCLC 65**
See also DLB 71

Hungerford, Pixie
See Brinsmead, H(esba) F(ay)

Hunt, E(verette) Howard, (Jr.)
1918-....................... **CLC 3**
See also AITN 1; CA 45-48; CANR 2, 47

Hunt, Kyle
See Creasey, John

Hunt, (James Henry) Leigh
1784-1859 ...... **NCLC 1; DAM POET**

Hunt, Marsha 1946-.............. **CLC 70**
See also BW 2; CA 143

Hunt, Violet 1866-1942 .... **TCLC 53**
See also DLB 162

Hunter, E. Waldo
See Sturgeon, Theodore (Hamilton)

Hunter, Evan
1926- .... **CLC 11, 31; DAM POP**
See also CA 5-8R; CANR 5, 38; DLBY 82;
INT CANR-5; MTCW; SATA 25

Hunter, Kristin (Eggleston) 1931-... **CLC 35**
See also AITN 1; BW 1; CA 13-16R;
CANR 13; CLR 3; DLB 33;
INT CANR-13; MAICYA; SAAS 10;
SATA 12

Hunter, Mollie 1922-............. **CLC 21**
See also McIlwraith, Maureen Mollie
Hunter
See also AAYA 13; CANR 37; CLR 25;
DLB 161; JRDA; MAICYA; SAAS 7;
SATA 54

Hunter, Robert (?)-1734............. **LC 7**

Hurston, Zora Neale
1903-1960 .... **CLC 7, 30, 61; BLC; DA;**
DAC; DAM MST, MULT, NOV; SSC 4
See also AAYA 15; BW 1; CA 85-88;
DLB 51, 86; MTCW

Huston, John (Marcellus)
1906-1987 .... **CLC 20**
See also CA 73-76; 123; CANR 34; DLB 26

Hustvedt, Siri 1955-.............. **CLC 76**
See also CA 137

Hutten, Ulrich von 1488-1523....... **LC 16**

Huxley, Aldous (Leonard)
1894-1963 ..... **CLC 1, 3, 4, 5, 8, 11, 18,**
35, 79; DA; DAB; DAC; DAM MST,
NOV; WLC
See also AAYA 11; CA 85-88; CANR 44;
CDBLB 1914-1945; DLB 36, 100, 162;
MTCW; SATA 63

Huysmans, Charles Marie Georges
1848-1907
See Huysmans, Joris-Karl
See also CA 104

Huysmans, Joris-Karl.............. **TCLC 7**
See also Huysmans, Charles Marie Georges
See also DLB 123

Hwang, David Henry
1957-.... **CLC 55; DAM DRAM; DC 4**
See also CA 127; 132; INT 132

Hyde, Anthony 1946-............. **CLC 42**
See also CA 136

Hyde, Margaret O(ldroyd) 1917-... **CLC 21**
See also CA 1-4R; CANR 1, 36; CLR 23;
JRDA; MAICYA; SAAS 8; SATA 1, 42,
76

Hynes, James 1956(?)-............ **CLC 65**

Ian, Janis 1951- .... **CLC 21**
See also CA 105

Ibanez, Vicente Blasco
See Blasco Ibanez, Vicente

Ibarguengoitia, Jorge 1928-1983.... **CLC 37**
See also CA 124; 113; HW

Ibsen, Henrik (Johan)
1828-1906 ...... **TCLC 2, 8, 16, 37, 52;**
DA; DAB; DAC; DAM DRAM, MST;
DC 2; WLC
See also CA 104; 141

Ibuse Masuji 1898-1993........... **CLC 22**
See also CA 127; 141

Ichikawa, Kon 1915-.............. **CLC 20**
See also CA 121

Idle, Eric 1943-.................. **CLC 21**
See also Monty Python
See also CA 116; CANR 35

Ignatow, David 1914-...... **CLC 4, 7, 14, 40**
See also CA 9-12R; CAAS 3; CANR 31;
DLB 5

Ihimaera, Witi 1944- .... **CLC 46**
See also CA 77-80

Ilf, Ilya....................... **TCLC 21**
See also Fainzilberg, Ilya Arnoldovich

Illyes, Gyula 1902-1983........... **PC 16**
See also CA 114; 109

Immermann, Karl (Lebrecht)
1796-1840 .... **NCLC 4, 49**
See also DLB 133

Inclan, Ramon (Maria) del Valle
See Valle-Inclan, Ramon (Maria) del

Infante, G(uillermo) Cabrera
See Cabrera Infante, G(uillermo)

Ingalls, Rachel (Holmes) 1940-..... **CLC 42**
See also CA 123; 127

Ingamells, Rex 1913-1955 .... **TCLC 35**

Inge, William (Motter)
1913-1973 .. **CLC 1, 8, 19; DAM DRAM**
See also CA 9-12R; CDALB 1941-1968;
DLB 7; MTCW

Ingelow, Jean 1820-1897 .... **NCLC 39**
See also DLB 35, 163; SATA 33

Ingram, Willis J.
See Harris, Mark

Innaurato, Albert (F.) 1948(?)-.. **CLC 21, 60**
See also CA 115; 122; INT 122

Innes, Michael
See Stewart, J(ohn) I(nnes) M(ackintosh)

Ionesco, Eugene
1909-1994 .... **CLC 1, 4, 6, 9, 11, 15, 41,**
86; DA; DAB; DAC; DAM DRAM,
MST; WLC
See also CA 9-12R; 144; CANR 55;
MTCW; SATA 7; SATA-Obit 79

Iqbal, Muhammad 1873-1938 ..... **TCLC 28**

Ireland, Patrick
See O'Doherty, Brian

Iron, Ralph
See Schreiner, Olive (Emilie Albertina)

Irving, John (Winslow)
1942- ..... **CLC 13, 23, 38; DAM NOV,**
POP
See also AAYA 8; BEST 89:3; CA 25-28R;
CANR 28; DLB 6; DLBY 82; MTCW

Irving, Washington
1783-1859 ..... **NCLC 2, 19; DA; DAB;**
DAM MST; SSC 2; WLC
See also CDALB 1640-1865; DLB 3, 11, 30,
59, 73, 74; YABC 2

Irwin, P. K.
See Page, P(atricia) K(athleen)

Isaacs, Susan 1943- ... **CLC 32; DAM POP**
See also BEST 89:1; CA 89-92; CANR 20,
41; INT CANR-20; MTCW

Isherwood, Christopher (William Bradshaw)
1904-1986 .... **CLC 1, 9, 11, 14, 44;**
DAM DRAM, NOV
See also CA 13-16R; 117; CANR 35;
DLB 15; DLBY 86; MTCW

Ishiguro, Kazuo
1954- ...... **CLC 27, 56, 59; DAM NOV**
See also BEST 90:2; CA 120; CANR 49;
MTCW

Ishikawa, Hakuhin
See Ishikawa, Takuboku

Ishikawa, Takuboku
1886(?)-1912 .... **TCLC 15;**
DAM POET; PC 10
See also CA 113; 153

Iskander, Fazil 1929-............. **CLC 47**
See also CA 102

Isler, Alan .... **CLC 91**

Ivan IV 1530-1584 .... **LC 17**

Ivanov, Vyacheslav Ivanovich
1866-1949 .... **TCLC 33**
See also CA 122

Ivask, Ivar Vidrik 1927-1992....... **CLC 14**
See also CA 37-40R; 139; CANR 24

Ives, Morgan
See Bradley, Marion Zimmer

J. R. S.
See Gogarty, Oliver St. John

Jabran, Kahlil
See Gibran, Kahlil

Jabran, Khalil
See Gibran, Kahlil

Jackson, Daniel
See Wingrove, David (John)

Jackson, Jesse 1908-1983 .... **CLC 12**
See also BW 1; CA 25-28R; 109; CANR 27;
CLR 28; MAICYA; SATA 2, 29;
SATA-Obit 48

Jackson, Laura (Riding) 1901-1991
See Riding, Laura
See also CA 65-68; 135; CANR 28; DLB 48

Jackson, Sam
See Trumbo, Dalton

Jackson, Sara
See Wingrove, David (John)

Jackson, Shirley
1919-1965 .... **CLC 11, 60, 87; DA;**
DAC; DAM MST; SSC 9; WLC
See also AAYA 9; CA 1-4R; 25-28R;
CANR 4, 52; CDALB 1941-1968; DLB 6;
SATA 2

Jacob, (Cyprien-)Max 1876-1944 ... **TCLC 6**
See also CA 104

Jacobs, Jim 1942-................ **CLC 12**
See also CA 97-100; INT 97-100

Jacobs, W(illiam) W(ymark)
1863-1943 .... **TCLC 22**
See also CA 121; DLB 135

Jacobsen, Jens Peter 1847-1885 .. **NCLC 34**

Jacobsen, Josephine 1908-......... **CLC 48**
See also CA 33-36R; CAAS 18; CANR 23,
48

Jacobson, Dan 1929- .... **CLC 4, 14**
See also CA 1-4R; CANR 2, 25; DLB 14;
MTCW

Jacqueline
See Carpentier (y Valmont), Alejo

Jagger, Mick 1944-............... **CLC 17**

Jakes, John (William)
1932- ...... **CLC 29; DAM NOV, POP**
See also BEST 89:4; CA 57-60; CANR 10,
43; DLBY 83; INT CANR-10; MTCW;
SATA 62

Jalal al-Din Rumi 1297-1373..... **CMLC 20**

James, Andrew
See Kirkup, James

James, C(yril) L(ionel) R(obert)
1901-1989 .... **CLC 33**
See also BW 2; CA 117; 125; 128; DLB 125;
MTCW

James, Daniel (Lewis) 1911-1988
See Santiago, Danny
See also CA 125

James, Dynely
See Mayne, William (James Carter)

James, Henry Sr. 1811-1882..... **NCLC 53**

Jones, Gayl
1949- .... CLC 6, 9; BLC; DAM MULT
See also BW 2; CA 77-80; CANR 27;
DLB 33; MTCW

Jones, James 1921-1977.... CLC 1, 3, 10, 39
See also AITN 1, 2; CA 1-4R; 69-72;
CANR 6; DLB 2, 143; MTCW

Jones, John J.
See Lovecraft, H(oward) P(hillips)

Jones, LeRoi .... CLC 1, 2, 3, 5, 10, 14
See also Baraka, Amiri

Jones, Louis B. .... CLC 65
See also CA 141

Jones, Madison (Percy, Jr.) 1925- ... CLC 4
See also CA 13-16R; CAAS 11; CANR 7,
54; DLB 152

Jones, Mervyn 1922- .... CLC 10, 52
See also CA 45-48; CAAS 5; CANR 1;
MTCW

Jones, Mick 1956(?)- .... CLC 30

Jones, Nettie (Pearl) 1941- .... CLC 34
See also BW 2; CA 137; CAAS 20

Jones, Preston 1936-1979 .... CLC 10
See also CA 73-76; 89-92; DLB 7

Jones, Robert F(rancis) 1934- .... CLC 7
See also CA 49-52; CANR 2

Jones, Rod 1953- .... CLC 50
See also CA 128

Jones, Terence Graham Parry
1942- .... CLC 21
See also Jones, Terry; Monty Python
See also CA 112; 116; CANR 35; INT 116

Jones, Terry
See Jones, Terence Graham Parry
See also SATA 67; SATA-Brief 51

Jones, Thom 1945(?)- .... CLC 81

Jong, Erica
1942- .... CLC 4, 6, 8, 18, 83;
DAM NOV, POP
See also AITN 1; BEST 90:2; CA 73-76;
CANR 26, 52; DLB 2, 5, 28, 152;
INT CANR-26; MTCW

Jonson, Ben(jamin)
1572(?)-1637 ...... LC 6, 33; DA; DAB;
DAC; DAM DRAM, MST, POET;
DC 4; WLC
See also CDBLB Before 1660; DLB 62, 121

Jordan, June
1936- ..... CLC 5, 11, 23; DAM MULT,
POET
See also AAYA 2; BW 2; CA 33-36R;
CANR 25; CLR 10; DLB 38; MAICYA;
MTCW; SATA 4

Jordan, Pat(rick M.) 1941- .... CLC 37
See also CA 33-36R

Jorgensen, Ivar
See Ellison, Harlan (Jay)

Jorgenson, Ivar
See Silverberg, Robert

Josephus, Flavius c. 37-100 ...... CMLC 13

Josipovici, Gabriel 1940- .... CLC 6, 43
See also CA 37-40R; CAAS 8; CANR 47;
DLB 14

Joubert, Joseph 1754-1824 .... NCLC 9

Jouve, Pierre Jean 1887-1976 ...... CLC 47
See also CA 65-68

Joyce, James (Augustine Aloysius)
1882-1941 .... TCLC 3, 8, 16, 35, 52;
DA; DAB; DAC; DAM MST, NOV,
POET; SSC 3; WLC
See also CA 104; 126; CDBLB 1914-1945;
DLB 10, 19, 36, 162; MTCW

Jozsef, Attila 1905-1937 .... TCLC 22
See also CA 116

Juana Ines de la Cruz 1651(?)-1695 ... LC 5

Judd, Cyril
See Kornbluth, C(yril) M.; Pohl, Frederik

Julian of Norwich 1342(?)-1416(?) .... LC 6
See also DLB 146

Juniper, Alex
See Hospital, Janette Turner

Junius
See Luxemburg, Rosa

Just, Ward (Swift) 1935- .... CLC 4, 27
See also CA 25-28R; CANR 32;
INT CANR-32

Justice, Donald (Rodney)
1925- .... CLC 6, 19; DAM POET
See also CA 5-8R; CANR 26, 54;
DLBY 83; INT CANR-26

Juvenal c. 55-c. 127 .... CMLC 8

Juvenis
See Bourne, Randolph S(illiman)

Kacew, Romain 1914-1980
See Gary, Romain
See also CA 108; 102

Kadare, Ismail 1936- .... CLC 52

Kadohata, Cynthia .... CLC 59
See also CA 140

Kafka, Franz
1883-1924 .... TCLC 2, 6, 13, 29, 47, 53;
DA; DAB; DAC; DAM MST, NOV;
SSC 5; WLC
See also CA 105; 126; DLB 81; MTCW

Kahanovitsch, Pinkhes
See Der Nister

Kahn, Roger 1927- .... CLC 30
See also CA 25-28R; CANR 44; DLB 171;
SATA 37

Kain, Saul
See Sassoon, Siegfried (Lorraine)

Kaiser, Georg 1878-1945 .... TCLC 9
See also CA 106; DLB 124

Kaletski, Alexander 1946- .... CLC 39
See also CA 118; 143

Kalidasa fl. c. 400- .... CMLC 9

Kallman, Chester (Simon)
1921-1975 .... CLC 2
See also CA 45-48; 53-56; CANR 3

Kaminsky, Melvin 1926-
See Brooks, Mel
See also CA 65-68; CANR 16

Kaminsky, Stuart M(elvin) 1934- ... CLC 59
See also CA 73-76; CANR 29, 53

Kane, Francis
See Robbins, Harold

Kane, Paul
See Simon, Paul (Frederick)

Kane, Wilson
See Bloch, Robert (Albert)

Kanin, Garson 1912- .... CLC 22
See also AITN 1; CA 5-8R; CANR 7;
DLB 7

Kaniuk, Yoram 1930- .... CLC 19
See also CA 134

Kant, Immanuel 1724-1804 ...... NCLC 27
See also DLB 94

Kantor, MacKinlay 1904-1977 ...... CLC 7
See also CA 61-64; 73-76; DLB 9, 102

Kaplan, David Michael 1946- ...... CLC 50

Kaplan, James 1951- .... CLC 59
See also CA 135

Karageorge, Michael
See Anderson, Poul (William)

Karamzin, Nikolai Mikhailovich
1766-1826 .... NCLC 3
See also DLB 150

Karapanou, Margarita 1946- .... CLC 13
See also CA 101

Karinthy, Frigyes 1887-1938 ...... TCLC 47

Karl, Frederick R(obert) 1927- ..... CLC 34
See also CA 5-8R; CANR 3, 44

Kastel, Warren
See Silverberg, Robert

Kataev, Evgeny Petrovich 1903-1942
See Petrov, Evgeny
See also CA 120

Kataphusin
See Ruskin, John

Katz, Steve 1935- .... CLC 47
See also CA 25-28R; CAAS 14; CANR 12;
DLBY 83

Kauffman, Janet 1945- .... CLC 42
See also CA 117; CANR 43; DLBY 86

Kaufman, Bob (Garnell)
1925-1986 .... CLC 49
See also BW 1; CA 41-44R; 118; CANR 22;
DLB 16, 41

Kaufman, George S.
1889-1961 ...... CLC 38; DAM DRAM
See also CA 108; 93-96; DLB 7; INT 108

Kaufman, Sue .... CLC 3, 8
See also Barondess, Sue K(aufman)

Kavafis, Konstantinos Petrou 1863-1933
See Cavafy, C(onstantine) P(eter)
See also CA 104

Kavan, Anna 1901-1968 ...... CLC 5, 13, 82
See also CA 5-8R; CANR 6; MTCW

Kavanagh, Dan
See Barnes, Julian (Patrick)

Kavanagh, Patrick (Joseph)
1904-1967 .... CLC 22
See also CA 123; 25-28R; DLB 15, 20;
MTCW

Kawabata, Yasunari
1899-1972 .... CLC 2, 5, 9, 18;
DAM MULT; SSC 17
See also CA 93-96; 33-36R

Kaye, M(ary) M(argaret) 1909- ..... CLC 28
See also CA 89-92; CANR 24; MTCW;
SATA 62

Kaye, Mollie
See Kaye, M(ary) M(argaret)

Kaye-Smith, Sheila 1887-1956..... **TCLC 20**
See also CA 118; DLB 36

Kaymor, Patrice Maguilene
See Senghor, Leopold Sedar

Kazan, Elia 1909-........... **CLC 6, 16, 63**
See also CA 21-24R; CANR 32

Kazantzakis, Nikos
1883(?)-1957 .... **TCLC 2, 5, 33**
See also CA 105; 132; MTCW

Kazin, Alfred 1915- .... **CLC 34, 38**
See also CA 1-4R; CAAS 7; CANR 1, 45;
DLB 67

Keane, Mary Nesta (Skrine) 1904-1996
See Keane, Molly
See also CA 108; 114; 151

Keane, Molly.................... **CLC 31**
See also Keane, Mary Nesta (Skrine)
See also INT 114

Keates, Jonathan 19(?)-........... **CLC 34**

Keaton, Buster 1895-1966 .... **CLC 20**

Keats, John
1795-1821 .... **NCLC 8; DA; DAB;**
DAC; DAM MST, POET; PC 1; WLC
See also CDBLB 1789-1832; DLB 96, 110

Keene, Donald 1922- .... **CLC 34**
See also CA 1-4R; CANR 5

Keillor, Garrison.................. **CLC 40**
See also Keillor, Gary (Edward)
See also AAYA 2; BEST 89:3; DLBY 87;
SATA 58

Keillor, Gary (Edward) 1942-
See Keillor, Garrison
See also CA 111; 117; CANR 36;
DAM POP; MTCW

Keith, Michael
See Hubbard, L(afayette) Ron(ald)

Keller, Gottfried 1819-1890....... **NCLC 2**
See also DLB 129

Kellerman, Jonathan
1949- .... **CLC 44; DAM POP**
See also BEST 90:1; CA 106; CANR 29, 51;
INT CANR-29

Kelley, William Melvin 1937-...... **CLC 22**
See also BW 1; CA 77-80; CANR 27;
DLB 33

Kellogg, Marjorie 1922-............ **CLC 2**
See also CA 81-84

Kellow, Kathleen
See Hibbert, Eleanor Alice Burford

Kelly, M(ilton) T(erry) 1947-....... **CLC 55**
See also CA 97-100; CAAS 22; CANR 19,
43

Kelman, James 1946-.......... **CLC 58, 86**
See also CA 148

Kemal, Yashar 1923- .... **CLC 14, 29**
See also CA 89-92; CANR 44

Kemble, Fanny 1809-1893 .... **NCLC 18**
See also DLB 32

Kemelman, Harry 1908-............ **CLC 2**
See also AITN 1; CA 9-12R; CANR 6;
DLB 28

Kempe, Margery 1373(?)-1440(?) ..... **LC 6**
See also DLB 146

Kempis, Thomas a 1380-1471 .... **LC 11**

Kendall, Henry 1839-1882...... **NCLC 12**

Keneally, Thomas (Michael)
1935- ...... **CLC 5, 8, 10, 14, 19, 27, 43;**
DAM NOV
See also CA 85-88; CANR 10, 50; MTCW

Kennedy, Adrienne (Lita)
1931- ..... **CLC 66; BLC; DAM MULT;**
DC 5
See also BW 2; CA 103; CAAS 20; CABS 3;
CANR 26, 53; DLB 38

Kennedy, John Pendleton
1795-1870 .... **NCLC 2**
See also DLB 3

Kennedy, Joseph Charles 1929-
See Kennedy, X. J.
See also CA 1-4R; CANR 4, 30, 40;
SATA 14, 86

Kennedy, William
1928- ... **CLC 6, 28, 34, 53; DAM NOV**
See also AAYA 1; CA 85-88; CANR 14,
31; DLB 143; DLBY 85; INT CANR-31;
MTCW; SATA 57

Kennedy, X. J..................... **CLC 8, 42**
See also Kennedy, Joseph Charles
See also CAAS 9; CLR 27; DLB 5;
SAAS 22

Kenny, Maurice (Francis)
1929- .... **CLC 87; DAM MULT**
See also CA 144; CAAS 22; NNAL

Kent, Kelvin
See Kuttner, Henry

Kenton, Maxwell
See Southern, Terry

Kenyon, Robert O.
See Kuttner, Henry

Kerouac, Jack ..... **CLC 1, 2, 3, 5, 14, 29, 61**
See also Kerouac, Jean-Louis Lebris de
See also CDALB 1941-1968; DLB 2, 16;
DLBD 3; DLBY 95

Kerouac, Jean-Louis Lebris de 1922-1969
See Kerouac, Jack
See also AITN 1; CA 5-8R; 25-28R;
CANR 26, 54; DA; DAB; DAC;
DAM MST, NOV, POET, POP; MTCW;
WLC

Kerr, Jean 1923-.................. **CLC 22**
See also CA 5-8R; CANR 7; INT CANR-7

Kerr, M. E..................... **CLC 12, 35**
See also Meaker, Marijane (Agnes)
See also AAYA 2; CLR 29; SAAS 1

Kerr, Robert .... **CLC 55**

Kerrigan, (Thomas) Anthony
1918- .... **CLC 4, 6**
See also CA 49-52; CAAS 11; CANR 4

Kerry, Lois
See Duncan, Lois

Kesey, Ken (Elton)
1935- ...... **CLC 1, 3, 6, 11, 46, 64; DA;**
DAB; DAC; DAM MST, NOV, POP;
WLC
See also CA 1-4R; CANR 22, 38;
CDALB 1968-1988; DLB 2, 16; MTCW;
SATA 66

Kesselring, Joseph (Otto)
1902-1967 ..... **CLC 45; DAM DRAM,**
MST
See also CA 150

Kessler, Jascha (Frederick) 1929-.... **CLC 4**
See also CA 17-20R; CANR 8, 48

Kettelkamp, Larry (Dale) 1933- .... **CLC 12**
See also CA 29-32R; CANR 16; SAAS 3;
SATA 2

Key, Ellen 1849-1926............ **TCLC 65**

Keyber, Conny
See Fielding, Henry

Keyes, Daniel
1927- .... **CLC 80; DA; DAC;**
DAM MST, NOV
See also CA 17-20R; CANR 10, 26, 54;
SATA 37

Keynes, John Maynard
1883-1946 .... **TCLC 64**
See also CA 114; DLBD 10

Khanshendel, Chiron
See Rose, Wendy

Khayyam, Omar
1048-1131 .... **CMLC 11; DAM POET;**
PC 8

Kherdian, David 1931-........... **CLC 6, 9**
See also CA 21-24R; CAAS 2; CANR 39;
CLR 24; JRDA; MAICYA; SATA 16, 74

Khlebnikov, Velimir .... **TCLC 20**
See also Khlebnikov, Viktor Vladimirovich

Khlebnikov, Viktor Vladimirovich 1885-1922
See Khlebnikov, Velimir
See also CA 117

Khodasevich, Vladislav (Felitsianovich)
1886-1939 .... **TCLC 15**
See also CA 115

Kielland, Alexander Lange
1849-1906 .... **TCLC 5**
See also CA 104

Kiely, Benedict 1919-.......... **CLC 23, 43**
See also CA 1-4R; CANR 2; DLB 15

Kienzle, William X(avier)
1928- .... **CLC 25; DAM POP**
See also CA 93-96; CAAS 1; CANR 9, 31;
INT CANR-31; MTCW

Kierkegaard, Soren 1813-1855.... **NCLC 34**

Killens, John Oliver 1916-1987..... **CLC 10**
See also BW 2; CA 77-80; 123; CAAS 2;
CANR 26; DLB 33

Killigrew, Anne 1660-1685.......... **LC 4**
See also DLB 131

Kim
See Simenon, Georges (Jacques Christian)

Kincaid, Jamaica
1949- .... **CLC 43, 68; BLC;**
DAM MULT, NOV
See also AAYA 13; BW 2; CA 125;
CANR 47; DLB 157

King, Francis (Henry)
1923- .... **CLC 8, 53; DAM NOV**
See also CA 1-4R; CANR 1, 33; DLB 15,
139; MTCW

King, Martin Luther, Jr.
1929-1968 .... **CLC 83; BLC; DA; DAB; DAC; DAM MST, MULT**
See also BW 2; CA 25-28; CANR 27, 44; CAP 2; MTCW; SATA 14

King, Stephen (Edwin)
1947- .... **CLC 12, 26, 37, 61; DAM NOV, POP; SSC 17**
See also AAYA 1, 17; BEST 90:1; CA 61-64; CANR 1, 30, 52; DLB 143; DLBY 80; JRDA; MTCW; SATA 9, 55

King, Steve
See King, Stephen (Edwin)

King, Thomas
1943- ..... **CLC 89; DAC; DAM MULT**
See also CA 144; NNAL

Kingman, Lee .... **CLC 17**
See also Natti, (Mary) Lee
See also SAAS 3; SATA 1, 67

Kingsley, Charles 1819-1875 ..... **NCLC 35**
See also DLB 21, 32, 163; YABC 2

Kingsley, Sidney 1906-1995 .... **CLC 44**
See also CA 85-88; 147; DLB 7

Kingsolver, Barbara
1955- .... **CLC 55, 81; DAM POP**
See also AAYA 15; CA 129; 134; INT 134

Kingston, Maxine (Ting Ting) Hong
1940- .... **CLC 12, 19, 58; DAM MULT, NOV**
See also AAYA 8; CA 69-72; CANR 13, 38; DLB 173; DLBY 80; INT CANR-13; MTCW; SATA 53

Kinnell, Galway
1927- .... **CLC 1, 2, 3, 5, 13, 29**
See also CA 9-12R; CANR 10, 34; DLB 5; DLBY 87; INT CANR-34; MTCW

Kinsella, Thomas 1928- .... **CLC 4, 19**
See also CA 17-20R; CANR 15; DLB 27; MTCW

Kinsella, W(illiam) P(atrick)
1935- .... **CLC 27, 43; DAC; DAM NOV, POP**
See also AAYA 7; CA 97-100; CAAS 7; CANR 21, 35; INT CANR-21; MTCW

Kipling, (Joseph) Rudyard
1865-1936 ...... **TCLC 8, 17; DA; DAB; DAC; DAM MST, POET; PC 3; SSC 5; WLC**
See also CA 105; 120; CANR 33; CDBLB 1890-1914; CLR 39; DLB 19, 34, 141, 156; MAICYA; MTCW; YABC 2

Kirkup, James 1918- .... **CLC 1**
See also CA 1-4R; CAAS 4; CANR 2; DLB 27; SATA 12

Kirkwood, James 1930(?)-1989 ...... **CLC 9**
See also AITN 2; CA 1-4R; 128; CANR 6, 40

Kirshner, Sidney
See Kingsley, Sidney

Kis, Danilo 1935-1989 .... **CLC 57**
See also CA 109; 118; 129; MTCW

Kivi, Aleksis 1834-1872 .... **NCLC 30**

Kizer, Carolyn (Ashley)
1925- ..... **CLC 15, 39, 80; DAM POET**
See also CA 65-68; CAAS 5; CANR 24; DLB 5, 169

Klabund 1890-1928 .... **TCLC 44**
See also DLB 66

Klappert, Peter 1942- .... **CLC 57**
See also CA 33-36R; DLB 5

Klein, A(braham) M(oses)
1909-1972 .... **CLC 19; DAB; DAC; DAM MST**
See also CA 101; 37-40R; DLB 68

Klein, Norma 1938-1989 .... **CLC 30**
See also AAYA 2; CA 41-44R; 128; CANR 15, 37; CLR 2, 19; INT CANR-15; JRDA; MAICYA; SAAS 1; SATA 7, 57

Klein, T(heodore) E(ibon) D(onald)
1947- .... **CLC 34**
See also CA 119; CANR 44

Kleist, Heinrich von
1777-1811 .... **NCLC 2, 37; DAM DRAM; SSC 22**
See also DLB 90

Klima, Ivan 1931- ..... **CLC 56; DAM NOV**
See also CA 25-28R; CANR 17, 50

Klimentov, Andrei Platonovich 1899-1951
See Platonov, Andrei
See also CA 108

Klinger, Friedrich Maximilian von
1752-1831 .... **NCLC 1**
See also DLB 94

Klopstock, Friedrich Gottlieb
1724-1803 .... **NCLC 11**
See also DLB 97

Knebel, Fletcher 1911-1993 .... **CLC 14**
See also AITN 1; CA 1-4R; 140; CAAS 3; CANR 1, 36; SATA 36; SATA-Obit 75

Knickerbocker, Diedrich
See Irving, Washington

Knight, Etheridge
1931-1991 .... **CLC 40; BLC; DAM POET; PC 14**
See also BW 1; CA 21-24R; 133; CANR 23; DLB 41

Knight, Sarah Kemble 1666-1727 ..... **LC 7**
See also DLB 24

Knister, Raymond 1899-1932 ...... **TCLC 56**
See also DLB 68

Knowles, John
1926- ...... **CLC 1, 4, 10, 26; DA; DAC; DAM MST, NOV**
See also AAYA 10; CA 17-20R; CANR 40; CDALB 1968-1988; DLB 6; MTCW; SATA 8, 89

Knox, Calvin M.
See Silverberg, Robert

Knye, Cassandra
See Disch, Thomas M(ichael)

Koch, C(hristopher) J(ohn) 1932- ... **CLC 42**
See also CA 127

Koch, Christopher
See Koch, C(hristopher) J(ohn)

Koch, Kenneth
1925- .... **CLC 5, 8, 44; DAM POET**
See also CA 1-4R; CANR 6, 36; DLB 5; INT CANR-36; SATA 65

Kochanowski, Jan 1530-1584 .... **LC 10**

Kock, Charles Paul de
1794-1871 .... **NCLC 16**

Koda Shigeyuki 1867-1947
See Rohan, Koda
See also CA 121

Koestler, Arthur
1905-1983 .... **CLC 1, 3, 6, 8, 15, 33**
See also CA 1-4R; 109; CANR 1, 33; CDBLB 1945-1960; DLBY 83; MTCW

Kogawa, Joy Nozomi
1935- ...... **CLC 78; DAC; DAM MST, MULT**
See also CA 101; CANR 19

Kohout, Pavel 1928- .... **CLC 13**
See also CA 45-48; CANR 3

Koizumi, Yakumo
See Hearn, (Patricio) Lafcadio (Tessima Carlos)

Kolmar, Gertrud 1894-1943 .... **TCLC 40**

Komunyakaa, Yusef 1947- ...... **CLC 86, 94**
See also CA 147; DLB 120

Konrad, George
See Konrad, Gyoergy

Konrad, Gyoergy 1933- ...... **CLC 4, 10, 73**
See also CA 85-88

Konwicki, Tadeusz 1926- ..... **CLC 8, 28, 54**
See also CA 101; CAAS 9; CANR 39; MTCW

Koontz, Dean R(ay)
1945- ...... **CLC 78; DAM NOV, POP**
See also AAYA 9; BEST 89:3, 90:2; CA 108; CANR 19, 36, 52; MTCW

Kopit, Arthur (Lee)
1937- ..... **CLC 1, 18, 33; DAM DRAM**
See also AITN 1; CA 81-84; CABS 3; DLB 7; MTCW

Kops, Bernard 1926- .... **CLC 4**
See also CA 5-8R; DLB 13

Kornbluth, C(yril) M. 1923-1958 .... **TCLC 8**
See also CA 105; DLB 8

Korolenko, V. G.
See Korolenko, Vladimir Galaktionovich

Korolenko, Vladimir
See Korolenko, Vladimir Galaktionovich

Korolenko, Vladimir G.
See Korolenko, Vladimir Galaktionovich

Korolenko, Vladimir Galaktionovich
1853-1921 .... **TCLC 22**
See also CA 121

Korzybski, Alfred (Habdank Skarbek)
1879-1950 .... **TCLC 61**
See also CA 123

Kosinski, Jerzy (Nikodem)
1933-1991 .... **CLC 1, 2, 3, 6, 10, 15, 53, 70; DAM NOV**
See also CA 17-20R; 134; CANR 9, 46; DLB 2; DLBY 82; MTCW

Kostelanetz, Richard (Cory) 1940- .. **CLC 28**
See also CA 13-16R; CAAS 8; CANR 38

Kostrowitzki, Wilhelm Apollinaris de
1880-1918
See Apollinaire, Guillaume
See also CA 104

Kotlowitz, Robert 1924- .... **CLC 4**
See also CA 33-36R; CANR 36

Kotzebue, August (Friedrich Ferdinand) von
    1761-1819 .... NCLC 25
    See also DLB 94

Kotzwinkle, William   1938- ... CLC 5, 14, 35
    See also CA 45-48; CANR 3, 44; CLR 6;
    DLB 173; MAICYA; SATA 24, 70

Kozol, Jonathan   1936-............ CLC 17
    See also CA 61-64; CANR 16, 45

Kozoll, Michael   1940(?)-.......... CLC 35

Kramer, Kathryn   19(?)-........... CLC 34

Kramer, Larry   1935- .. CLC 42; DAM POP
    See also CA 124; 126

Krasicki, Ignacy   1735-1801 .... NCLC 8

Krasinski, Zygmunt   1812-1859 .... NCLC 4

Kraus, Karl   1874-1936............ TCLC 5
    See also CA 104; DLB 118

Kreve (Mickevicius), Vincas
    1882-1954 .... TCLC 27

Kristeva, Julia   1941- .... CLC 77
    See also CA 154

Kristofferson, Kris   1936-.......... CLC 26
    See also CA 104

Krizanc, John   1956-.............. CLC 57

Krleza, Miroslav   1893-1981........ CLC 8
    See also CA 97-100; 105; CANR 50;
    DLB 147

Kroetsch, Robert
    1927- .... CLC 5, 23, 57; DAC;
                                  DAM POET
    See also CA 17-20R; CANR 8, 38; DLB 53;
    MTCW

Kroetz, Franz
    See Kroetz, Franz Xaver

Kroetz, Franz Xaver   1946- .... CLC 41
    See also CA 130

Kroker, Arthur   1945-.............. CLC 77

Kropotkin, Peter (Aleksieevich)
    1842-1921 .... TCLC 36
    See also CA 119

Krotkov, Yuri   1917-.............. CLC 19
    See also CA 102

Krumb
    See Crumb, R(obert)

Krumgold, Joseph (Quincy)
    1908-1980 .... CLC 12
    See also CA 9-12R; 101; CANR 7;
    MAICYA; SATA 1, 48; SATA-Obit 23

Krumwitz
    See Crumb, R(obert)

Krutch, Joseph Wood   1893-1970.... CLC 24
    See also CA 1-4R; 25-28R; CANR 4;
    DLB 63

Krutzch, Gus
    See Eliot, T(homas) S(tearns)

Krylov, Ivan Andreevich
    1768(?)-1844 .... NCLC 1
    See also DLB 150

Kubin, Alfred (Leopold Isidor)
    1877-1959 .... TCLC 23
    See also CA 112; 149; DLB 81

Kubrick, Stanley   1928-............ CLC 16
    See also CA 81-84; CANR 33; DLB 26

Kumin, Maxine (Winokur)
    1925- ..... CLC 5, 13, 28; DAM POET;
                                  PC 15
    See also AITN 2; CA 1-4R; CAAS 8;
    CANR 1, 21; DLB 5; MTCW; SATA 12

Kundera, Milan
    1929- .... CLC 4, 9, 19, 32, 68;
                        DAM NOV; SSC 24
    See also AAYA 2; CA 85-88; CANR 19,
    52; MTCW

Kunene, Mazisi (Raymond)   1930-... CLC 85
    See also BW 1; CA 125; DLB 117

Kunitz, Stanley (Jasspon)
    1905- .... CLC 6, 11, 14
    See also CA 41-44R; CANR 26; DLB 48;
    INT CANR-26; MTCW

Kunze, Reiner   1933-.............. CLC 10
    See also CA 93-96; DLB 75

Kuprin, Aleksandr Ivanovich
    1870-1938 .... TCLC 5
    See also CA 104

Kureishi, Hanif   1954(?)-........... CLC 64
    See also CA 139

Kurosawa, Akira
    1910- .... CLC 16; DAM MULT
    See also AAYA 11; CA 101; CANR 46

Kushner, Tony
    1957(?)- .... CLC 81; DAM DRAM
    See also CA 144

Kuttner, Henry   1915-1958........ TCLC 10
    See also CA 107; DLB 8

Kuzma, Greg   1944-................ CLC 7
    See also CA 33-36R

Kuzmin, Mikhail   1872(?)-1936 .... TCLC 40

Kyd, Thomas
    1558-1594 .... LC 22; DAM DRAM;
                                  DC 3
    See also DLB 62

Kyprianos, Iossif
    See Samarakis, Antonis

La Bruyere, Jean de   1645-1696...... LC 17

Lacan, Jacques (Marie Emile)
    1901-1981 .... CLC 75
    See also CA 121; 104

Laclos, Pierre Ambroise Francois Choderlos
    de   1741-1803 .... NCLC 4

Lacolere, Francois
    See Aragon, Louis

La Colere, Francois
    See Aragon, Louis

La Deshabilleuse
    See Simenon, Georges (Jacques Christian)

Lady Gregory
    See Gregory, Isabella Augusta (Persse)

Lady of Quality, A
    See Bagnold, Enid

La Fayette, Marie (Madelaine Pioche de la
    Vergne Comtes   1634-1693....... LC 2

Lafayette, Rene
    See Hubbard, L(afayette) Ron(ald)

Laforgue, Jules
    1860-1887 .... NCLC 5, 53; PC 14;
                                  SSC 20

Lagerkvist, Paer (Fabian)
    1891-1974 .... CLC 7, 10, 13, 54;
                        DAM DRAM, NOV
    See also Lagerkvist, Par
    See also CA 85-88; 49-52; MTCW

Lagerkvist, Par .... SSC 12
    See also Lagerkvist, Paer (Fabian)

Lagerloef, Selma (Ottiliana Lovisa)
    1858-1940 .... TCLC 4, 36
    See also Lagerlof, Selma (Ottiliana Lovisa)
    See also CA 108; SATA 15

Lagerlof, Selma (Ottiliana Lovisa)
    See Lagerloef, Selma (Ottiliana Lovisa)
    See also CLR 7; SATA 15

La Guma, (Justin) Alex(ander)
    1925-1985 .... CLC 19; DAM NOV
    See also BW 1; CA 49-52; 118; CANR 25;
    DLB 117; MTCW

Laidlaw, A. K.
    See Grieve, C(hristopher) M(urray)

Lainez, Manuel Mujica
    See Mujica Lainez, Manuel
    See also HW

Laing, R(onald) D(avid)
    1927-1989 .... CLC 95
    See also CA 107; 129; CANR 34; MTCW

Lamartine, Alphonse (Marie Louis Prat) de
    1790-1869 ..... NCLC 11; DAM POET;
                                  PC 16

Lamb, Charles
    1775-1834 .... NCLC 10; DA; DAB;
                        DAC; DAM MST; WLC
    See also CDBLB 1789-1832; DLB 93, 107,
    163; SATA 17

Lamb, Lady Caroline   1785-1828 .. NCLC 38
    See also DLB 116

Lamming, George (William)
    1927- .... CLC 2, 4, 66; BLC;
                        DAM MULT
    See also BW 2; CA 85-88; CANR 26;
    DLB 125; MTCW

L'Amour, Louis (Dearborn)
    1908-1988 .... CLC 25, 55; DAM NOV,
                                  POP
    See also AAYA 16; AITN 2; BEST 89:2;
    CA 1-4R; 125; CANR 3, 25, 40;
    DLBY 80; MTCW

Lampedusa, Giuseppe (Tomasi) di ... TCLC 13
    See also Tomasi di Lampedusa, Giuseppe

Lampman, Archibald   1861-1899 .. NCLC 25
    See also DLB 92

Lancaster, Bruce   1896-1963........ CLC 36
    See also CA 9-10; CAP 1; SATA 9

Landau, Mark Alexandrovich
    See Aldanov, Mark (Alexandrovich)

Landau-Aldanov, Mark Alexandrovich
    See Aldanov, Mark (Alexandrovich)

Landis, Jerry
    See Simon, Paul (Frederick)

Landis, John   1950-.............. CLC 26
    See also CA 112; 122

Landolfi, Tommaso   1908-1979... CLC 11, 49
    See also CA 127; 117

Levine, Norman   1924- . . . . CLC 54
    See also CA 73-76; CAAS 23; CANR 14;
    DLB 88

Levine, Philip
    1928- . . . . CLC 2, 4, 5, 9, 14, 33;
                                            DAM POET
    See also CA 9-12R; CANR 9, 37, 52;
    DLB 5

Levinson, Deirdre   1931- . . . . CLC 49
    See also CA 73-76

Levi-Strauss, Claude   1908- . . . . CLC 38
    See also CA 1-4R; CANR 6, 32; MTCW

Levitin, Sonia (Wolff)   1934- . . . . CLC 17
    See also AAYA 13; CA 29-32R; CANR 14,
    32; JRDA; MAICYA; SAAS 2; SATA 4,
    68

Levon, O. U.
    See Kesey, Ken (Elton)

Lewes, George Henry
    1817-1878 . . . . NCLC 25
    See also DLB 55, 144

Lewis, Alun   1915-1944 . . . . TCLC 3
    See also CA 104; DLB 20, 162

Lewis, C. Day
    See Day Lewis, C(ecil)

Lewis, C(live) S(taples)
    1898-1963 . . . . . CLC 1, 3, 6, 14, 27; DA;
        DAB; DAC; DAM MST, NOV, POP;
                                                WLC
    See also AAYA 3; CA 81-84; CANR 33;
    CDBLB 1945-1960; CLR 3, 27; DLB 15,
    100, 160; JRDA; MAICYA; MTCW;
    SATA 13

Lewis, Janet   1899- . . . . CLC 41
    See also Winters, Janet Lewis
    See also CA 9-12R; CANR 29; CAP 1;
    DLBY 87

Lewis, Matthew Gregory
    1775-1818 . . . . NCLC 11
    See also DLB 39, 158

Lewis, (Harry) Sinclair
    1885-1951 . . . . . TCLC 4, 13, 23, 39; DA;
        DAB; DAC; DAM MST, NOV; WLC
    See also CA 104; 133; CDALB 1917-1929;
    DLB 9, 102; DLBD 1; MTCW

Lewis, (Percy) Wyndham
    1884(?)-1957 . . . . TCLC 2, 9
    See also CA 104; DLB 15

Lewisohn, Ludwig   1883-1955 . . . . . . TCLC 19
    See also CA 107; DLB 4, 9, 28, 102

Leyner, Mark   1956- . . . . CLC 92
    See also CA 110; CANR 28, 53

Lezama Lima, Jose
    1910-1976 . . . . CLC 4, 10; DAM MULT
    See also CA 77-80; DLB 113; HW

L'Heureux, John (Clarke)   1934- . . . . CLC 52
    See also CA 13-16R; CANR 23, 45

Liddell, C. H.
    See Kuttner, Henry

Lie, Jonas (Lauritz Idemil)
    1833-1908(?) . . . . TCLC 5
    See also CA 115

Lieber, Joel   1937-1971 . . . . CLC 6
    See also CA 73-76; 29-32R

Lieber, Stanley Martin
    See Lee, Stan

Lieberman, Laurence (James)
    1935- . . . . CLC 4, 36
    See also CA 17-20R; CANR 8, 36

Lieksman, Anders
    See Haavikko, Paavo Juhani

Li Fei-kan   1904-
    See Pa Chin
    See also CA 105

Lifton, Robert Jay   1926- . . . . CLC 67
    See also CA 17-20R; CANR 27;
    INT CANR-27; SATA 66

Lightfoot, Gordon   1938- . . . . CLC 26
    See also CA 109

Lightman, Alan P.   1948- . . . . CLC 81
    See also CA 141

Ligotti, Thomas (Robert)
    1953- . . . . CLC 44; SSC 16
    See also CA 123; CANR 49

Li Ho   791-817 . . . . PC 13

Liliencron, (Friedrich Adolf Axel) Detlev von
    1844-1909 . . . . TCLC 18
    See also CA 117

Lilly, William   1602-1681 . . . . LC 27

Lima, Jose Lezama
    See Lezama Lima, Jose

Lima Barreto, Afonso Henrique de
    1881-1922 . . . . TCLC 23
    See also CA 117

Limonov, Edward   1944- . . . . CLC 67
    See also CA 137

Lin, Frank
    See Atherton, Gertrude (Franklin Horn)

Lincoln, Abraham   1809-1865 . . . . . NCLC 18

Lind, Jakov . . . . CLC 1, 2, 4, 27, 82
    See also Landwirth, Heinz
    See also CAAS 4

Lindbergh, Anne (Spencer) Morrow
    1906- . . . . CLC 82; DAM NOV
    See also CA 17-20R; CANR 16; MTCW;
    SATA 33

Lindsay, David   1878-1945 . . . . TCLC 15
    See also CA 113

Lindsay, (Nicholas) Vachel
    1879-1931 . . . . TCLC 17; DA; DAC;
                            DAM MST, POET; WLC
    See also CA 114; 135; CDALB 1865-1917;
    DLB 54; SATA 40

Linke-Poot
    See Doeblin, Alfred

Linney, Romulus   1930- . . . . CLC 51
    See also CA 1-4R; CANR 40, 44

Linton, Eliza Lynn   1822-1898 . . . . NCLC 41
    See also DLB 18

Li Po   701-763 . . . . CMLC 2

Lipsius, Justus   1547-1606 . . . . LC 16

Lipsyte, Robert (Michael)
    1938- . . . . CLC 21; DA; DAC;
                                        DAM MST, NOV
    See also AAYA 7; CA 17-20R; CANR 8;
    CLR 23; JRDA; MAICYA; SATA 5, 68

Lish, Gordon (Jay)   1934- . . CLC 45; SSC 18
    See also CA 113; 117; DLB 130; INT 117

Lispector, Clarice   1925-1977 . . . . CLC 43
    See also CA 139; 116; DLB 113

Littell, Robert   1935(?)- . . . . CLC 42
    See also CA 109; 112

Little, Malcolm   1925-1965
    See Malcolm X
    See also BW 1; CA 125; 111; DA; DAB;
    DAC; DAM MST, MULT; MTCW

Littlewit, Humphrey Gent.
    See Lovecraft, H(oward) P(hillips)

Litwos
    See Sienkiewicz, Henryk (Adam Alexander
    Pius)

Liu E   1857-1909 . . . . TCLC 15
    See also CA 115

Lively, Penelope (Margaret)
    1933- . . . . CLC 32, 50; DAM NOV
    See also CA 41-44R; CANR 29; CLR 7;
    DLB 14, 161; JRDA; MAICYA; MTCW;
    SATA 7, 60

Livesay, Dorothy (Kathleen)
    1909- . . . . CLC 4, 15, 79; DAC;
                                    DAM MST, POET
    See also AITN 2; CA 25-28R; CAAS 8;
    CANR 36; DLB 68; MTCW

Livy   c. 59B.C.-c. 17 . . . . CMLC 11

Lizardi, Jose Joaquin Fernandez de
    1776-1827 . . . . NCLC 30

Llewellyn, Richard
    See Llewellyn Lloyd, Richard Dafydd
    Vivian
    See also DLB 15

Llewellyn Lloyd, Richard Dafydd Vivian
    1906-1983 . . . . CLC 7, 80
    See also Llewellyn, Richard
    See also CA 53-56; 111; CANR 7;
    SATA 11; SATA-Obit 37

Llosa, (Jorge) Mario (Pedro) Vargas
    See Vargas Llosa, (Jorge) Mario (Pedro)

Lloyd Webber, Andrew   1948-
    See Webber, Andrew Lloyd
    See also AAYA 1; CA 116; 149;
    DAM DRAM; SATA 56

Llull, Ramon   c. 1235-c. 1316 . . . . . CMLC 12

Locke, Alain (Le Roy)
    1886-1954 . . . . TCLC 43
    See also BW 1; CA 106; 124; DLB 51

Locke, John   1632-1704 . . . . LC 7, 35
    See also DLB 101

Locke-Elliott, Sumner
    See Elliott, Sumner Locke

Lockhart, John Gibson
    1794-1854 . . . . NCLC 6
    See also DLB 110, 116, 144

Lodge, David (John)
    1935- . . . . CLC 36; DAM POP
    See also BEST 90:1; CA 17-20R; CANR 19,
    53; DLB 14; INT CANR-19; MTCW

Loennbohm, Armas Eino Leopold   1878-1926
    See Leino, Eino
    See also CA 123

Loewinsohn, Ron(ald William)
    1937- . . . . CLC 52
    See also CA 25-28R

Maloff, Saul 1922- . . . . CLC 5
See also CA 33-36R

Malone, Louis
See MacNeice, (Frederick) Louis

Malone, Michael (Christopher)
1942- . . . . CLC 43
See also CA 77-80; CANR 14, 32

Malory, (Sir) Thomas
1410(?)-1471(?) . . . . . . LC 11; DA; DAB;
DAC; DAM MST
See also CDBLB Before 1660; DLB 146;
SATA 59; SATA-Brief 33

Malouf, (George Joseph) David
1934- . . . . CLC 28, 86
See also CA 124; CANR 50

Malraux, (Georges-)Andre
1901-1976 . . . . . . CLC 1, 4, 9, 13, 15, 57;
DAM NOV
See also CA 21-22; 69-72; CANR 34;
CAP 2; DLB 72; MTCW

Malzberg, Barry N(athaniel) 1939- . . . CLC 7
See also CA 61-64; CAAS 4; CANR 16;
DLB 8

Mamet, David (Alan)
1947- . . . . CLC 9, 15, 34, 46, 91;
DAM DRAM; DC 4
See also AAYA 3; CA 81-84; CABS 3;
CANR 15, 41; DLB 7; MTCW

Mamoulian, Rouben (Zachary)
1897-1987 . . . . CLC 16
See also CA 25-28R; 124

Mandelstam, Osip (Emilievich)
1891(?)-1938(?) . . . . . . TCLC 2, 6; PC 14
See also CA 104; 150

Mander, (Mary) Jane 1877-1949. . . TCLC 31

Mandeville, John fl. 1350- . . . . CMLC 19
See also DLB 146

Mandiargues, Andre Pieyre de. . . . . . CLC 41
See also Pieyre de Mandiargues, Andre
See also DLB 83

Mandrake, Ethel Belle
See Thurman, Wallace (Henry)

Mangan, James Clarence
1803-1849 . . . . NCLC 27

Maniere, J.-E.
See Giraudoux, (Hippolyte) Jean

Manley, (Mary) Delariviere
1672(?)-1724 . . . . LC 1
See also DLB 39, 80

Mann, Abel
See Creasey, John

Mann, (Luiz) Heinrich 1871-1950. . . TCLC 9
See also CA 106; DLB 66

Mann, (Paul) Thomas
1875-1955 . . . . TCLC 2, 8, 14, 21, 35, 44,
60; DA; DAB; DAC; DAM MST, NOV;
SSC 5; WLC
See also CA 104; 128; DLB 66; MTCW

Mannheim, Karl 1893-1947 . . . . TCLC 65

Manning, David
See Faust, Frederick (Schiller)

Manning, Frederic 1887(?)-1935 . . . TCLC 25
See also CA 124

Manning, Olivia 1915-1980 . . . . . CLC 5, 19
See also CA 5-8R; 101; CANR 29; MTCW

Mano, D. Keith 1942- . . . . CLC 2, 10
See also CA 25-28R; CAAS 6; CANR 26;
DLB 6

Mansfield, Katherine
. . TCLC 2, 8, 39; DAB; SSC 9, 23; WLC
See also Beauchamp, Kathleen Mansfield
See also DLB 162

Manso, Peter 1940- . . . . CLC 39
See also CA 29-32R; CANR 44

Mantecon, Juan Jimenez
See Jimenez (Mantecon), Juan Ramon

Manton, Peter
See Creasey, John

Man Without a Spleen, A
See Chekhov, Anton (Pavlovich)

Manzoni, Alessandro 1785-1873 . . NCLC 29

Mapu, Abraham (ben Jekutiel)
1808-1867 . . . . NCLC 18

Mara, Sally
See Queneau, Raymond

Marat, Jean Paul 1743-1793 . . . . LC 10

Marcel, Gabriel Honore
1889-1973 . . . . CLC 15
See also CA 102; 45-48; MTCW

Marchbanks, Samuel
See Davies, (William) Robertson

Marchi, Giacomo
See Bassani, Giorgio

Margulies, Donald. . . . . CLC 76

Marie de France c. 12th cent. -. . . . CMLC 8

Marie de l'Incarnation 1599-1672. . . . LC 10

Mariner, Scott
See Pohl, Frederik

Marinetti, Filippo Tommaso
1876-1944 . . . . TCLC 10
See also CA 107; DLB 114

Marivaux, Pierre Carlet de Chamblain de
1688-1763 . . . . LC 4

Markandaya, Kamala . . . . CLC 8, 38
See also Taylor, Kamala (Purnaiya)

Markfield, Wallace 1926-. . . . . CLC 8
See also CA 69-72; CAAS 3; DLB 2, 28

Markham, Edwin 1852-1940 . . . . . . TCLC 47
See also DLB 54

Markham, Robert
See Amis, Kingsley (William)

Marks, J
See Highwater, Jamake (Mamake)

Marks-Highwater, J
See Highwater, Jamake (Mamake)

Markson, David M(errill) 1927- . . . . CLC 67
See also CA 49-52; CANR 1

Marley, Bob. . . . . CLC 17
See also Marley, Robert Nesta

Marley, Robert Nesta 1945-1981
See Marley, Bob
See also CA 107; 103

Marlowe, Christopher
1564-1593 . . . . . LC 22; DA; DAB; DAC;
DAM DRAM, MST; DC 1; WLC
See also CDBLB Before 1660; DLB 62

Marlowe, Stephen 1928-
See Queen, Ellery
See also CA 13-16R; CANR 6, 55

Marmontel, Jean-Francois
1723-1799 . . . . LC 2

Marquand, John P(hillips)
1893-1960 . . . . CLC 2, 10
See also CA 85-88; DLB 9, 102

Marques, Rene
1919-1979 . . . . . . CLC 96; DAM MULT;
HLC
See also CA 97-100; 85-88; DLB 113; HW

Marquez, Gabriel (Jose) Garcia
See Garcia Marquez, Gabriel (Jose)

Marquis, Don(ald Robert Perry)
1878-1937 . . . . TCLC 7
See also CA 104; DLB 11, 25

Marric, J. J.
See Creasey, John

Marrow, Bernard
See Moore, Brian

Marryat, Frederick 1792-1848 . . . . NCLC 3
See also DLB 21, 163

Marsden, James
See Creasey, John

Marsh, (Edith) Ngaio
1899-1982 . . . . . . CLC 7, 53; DAM POP
See also CA 9-12R; CANR 6; DLB 77;
MTCW

Marshall, Garry 1934-. . . . . CLC 17
See also AAYA 3; CA 111; SATA 60

Marshall, Paule
1929- . . . . CLC 27, 72; BLC;
DAM MULT; SSC 3
See also BW 2; CA 77-80; CANR 25;
DLB 157; MTCW

Marsten, Richard
See Hunter, Evan

Marston, John
1576-1634 . . . . LC 33; DAM DRAM
See also DLB 58, 172

Martha, Henry
See Harris, Mark

Martial c. 40-c. 104 . . . . PC 10

Martin, Ken
See Hubbard, L(afayette) Ron(ald)

Martin, Richard
See Creasey, John

Martin, Steve 1945- . . . . CLC 30
See also CA 97-100; CANR 30; MTCW

Martin, Valerie 1948-. . . . . CLC 89
See also BEST 90:2; CA 85-88; CANR 49

Martin, Violet Florence
1862-1915 . . . . TCLC 51

Martin, Webber
See Silverberg, Robert

Martindale, Patrick Victor
See White, Patrick (Victor Martindale)

Martin du Gard, Roger
1881-1958 . . . . TCLC 24
See also CA 118; DLB 65

Martineau, Harriet 1802-1876. . . . NCLC 26
See also DLB 21, 55, 159, 163, 166;
YABC 2

McCauley, Stephen (D.) 1955- ..... CLC 50
See also CA 141

McClure, Michael (Thomas)
1932- .... CLC 6, 10
See also CA 21-24R; CANR 17, 46;
DLB 16

McCorkle, Jill (Collins) 1958-...... CLC 51
See also CA 121; DLBY 87

McCourt, James 1941-............. CLC 5
See also CA 57-60

McCoy, Horace (Stanley)
1897-1955 .... TCLC 28
See also CA 108; DLB 9

McCrae, John 1872-1918........ TCLC 12
See also CA 109; DLB 92

McCreigh, James
See Pohl, Frederik

McCullers, (Lula) Carson (Smith)
1917-1967 .... CLC 1, 4, 10, 12, 48; DA;
DAB; DAC; DAM MST, NOV; SSC 24;
WLC
See also CA 5-8R; 25-28R; CABS 1, 3;
CANR 18; CDALB 1941-1968; DLB 2, 7,
173; MTCW; SATA 27

McCulloch, John Tyler
See Burroughs, Edgar Rice

McCullough, Colleen
1938(?)- .... CLC 27; DAM NOV, POP
See also CA 81-84; CANR 17, 46; MTCW

McDermott, Alice 1953- .... CLC 90
See also CA 109; CANR 40

McElroy, Joseph 1930- .... CLC 5, 47
See also CA 17-20R

McEwan, Ian (Russell)
1948- .... CLC 13, 66; DAM NOV
See also BEST 90:4; CA 61-64; CANR 14,
41; DLB 14; MTCW

McFadden, David 1940-.......... CLC 48
See also CA 104; DLB 60; INT 104

McFarland, Dennis 1950- .... CLC 65

McGahern, John
1934- .... CLC 5, 9, 48; SSC 17
See also CA 17-20R; CANR 29; DLB 14;
MTCW

McGinley, Patrick (Anthony)
1937- .... CLC 41
See also CA 120; 127; INT 127

McGinley, Phyllis 1905-1978 ...... CLC 14
See also CA 9-12R; 77-80; CANR 19;
DLB 11, 48; SATA 2, 44; SATA-Obit 24

McGinniss, Joe 1942-............. CLC 32
See also AITN 2; BEST 89:2; CA 25-28R;
CANR 26; INT CANR-26

McGivern, Maureen Daly
See Daly, Maureen

McGrath, Patrick 1950-.......... CLC 55
See also CA 136

McGrath, Thomas (Matthew)
1916-1990 .... CLC 28, 59; DAM POET
See also CA 9-12R; 132; CANR 6, 33;
MTCW; SATA 41; SATA-Obit 66

McGuane, Thomas (Francis III)
1939- .... CLC 3, 7, 18, 45
See also AITN 2; CA 49-52; CANR 5, 24,
49; DLB 2; DLBY 80; INT CANR-24;
MTCW

McGuckian, Medbh
1950- .... CLC 48; DAM POET
See also CA 143; DLB 40

McHale, Tom 1942(?)-1982....... CLC 3, 5
See also AITN 1; CA 77-80; 106

McIlvanney, William 1936-....... CLC 42
See also CA 25-28R; DLB 14

McIlwraith, Maureen Mollie Hunter
See Hunter, Mollie
See also SATA 2

McInerney, Jay
1955- .... CLC 34; DAM POP
See also AAYA 18; CA 116; 123;
CANR 45; INT 123

McIntyre, Vonda N(eel) 1948- ..... CLC 18
See also CA 81-84; CANR 17, 34; MTCW

McKay, Claude
.... TCLC 7, 41; BLC; DAB; PC 2
See also McKay, Festus Claudius
See also DLB 4, 45, 51, 117

McKay, Festus Claudius 1889-1948
See McKay, Claude
See also BW 1; CA 104; 124; DA; DAC;
DAM MST, MULT, NOV, POET;
MTCW; WLC

McKuen, Rod 1933-............. CLC 1, 3
See also AITN 1; CA 41-44R; CANR 40

McLoughlin, R. B.
See Mencken, H(enry) L(ouis)

McLuhan, (Herbert) Marshall
1911-1980 .... CLC 37, 83
See also CA 9-12R; 102; CANR 12, 34;
DLB 88; INT CANR-12; MTCW

McMillan, Terry (L.)
1951- .... CLC 50, 61; DAM MULT,
NOV, POP
See also BW 2; CA 140

McMurtry, Larry (Jeff)
1936- .... CLC 2, 3, 7, 11, 27, 44;
DAM NOV, POP
See also AAYA 15; AITN 2; BEST 89:2;
CA 5-8R; CANR 19, 43;
CDALB 1968-1988; DLB 2, 143;
DLBY 80, 87; MTCW

McNally, T. M. 1961- .... CLC 82

McNally, Terrence
1939- ... CLC 4, 7, 41, 91; DAM DRAM
See also CA 45-48; CANR 2; DLB 7

McNamer, Deirdre 1950-......... CLC 70

McNeile, Herman Cyril 1888-1937
See Sapper
See also DLB 77

McNickle, (William) D'Arcy
1904-1977 ...... CLC 89; DAM MULT
See also CA 9-12R; 85-88; CANR 5, 45;
NNAL; SATA-Obit 22

McPhee, John (Angus) 1931- ...... CLC 36
See also BEST 90:1; CA 65-68; CANR 20,
46; MTCW

McPherson, James Alan
1943- .... CLC 19, 77
See also BW 1; CA 25-28R; CAAS 17;
CANR 24; DLB 38; MTCW

McPherson, William (Alexander)
1933- .... CLC 34
See also CA 69-72; CANR 28;
INT CANR-28

Mead, Margaret 1901-1978........ CLC 37
See also AITN 1; CA 1-4R; 81-84;
CANR 4; MTCW; SATA-Obit 20

Meaker, Marijane (Agnes) 1927-
See Kerr, M. E.
See also CA 107; CANR 37; INT 107;
JRDA; MAICYA; MTCW; SATA 20, 61

Medoff, Mark (Howard)
1940- .... CLC 6, 23; DAM DRAM
See also AITN 1; CA 53-56; CANR 5;
DLB 7; INT CANR-5

Medvedev, P. N.
See Bakhtin, Mikhail Mikhailovich

Meged, Aharon
See Megged, Aharon

Meged, Aron
See Megged, Aharon

Megged, Aharon 1920-............ CLC 9
See also CA 49-52; CAAS 13; CANR 1

Mehta, Ved (Parkash) 1934-....... CLC 37
See also CA 1-4R; CANR 2, 23; MTCW

Melanter
See Blackmore, R(ichard) D(oddridge)

Melikow, Loris
See Hofmannsthal, Hugo von

Melmoth, Sebastian
See Wilde, Oscar (Fingal O'Flahertie Wills)

Meltzer, Milton 1915-............ CLC 26
See also AAYA 8; CA 13-16R; CANR 38;
CLR 13; DLB 61; JRDA; MAICYA;
SAAS 1; SATA 1, 50, 80

Melville, Herman
1819-1891 ..... NCLC 3, 12, 29, 45, 49;
DA; DAB; DAC; DAM MST, NOV;
SSC 1, 17; WLC
See also CDALB 1640-1865; DLB 3, 74;
SATA 59

Menander
c. 342B.C.-c. 292B.C......... CMLC 9;
DAM DRAM; DC 3

Mencken, H(enry) L(ouis)
1880-1956 .... TCLC 13
See also CA 105; 125; CDALB 1917-1929;
DLB 11, 29, 63, 137; MTCW

Mercer, David
1928-1980 .... CLC 5; DAM DRAM
See also CA 9-12R; 102; CANR 23;
DLB 13; MTCW

Merchant, Paul
See Ellison, Harlan (Jay)

Meredith, George
1828-1909 .. TCLC 17, 43; DAM POET
See also CA 117; 153; CDBLB 1832-1890;
DLB 18, 35, 57, 159

Meredith, William (Morris)
1919- .. CLC 4, 13, 22, 55; DAM POET
See also CA 9-12R; CAAS 14; CANR 6, 40;
DLB 5

Merezhkovsky, Dmitry Sergeyevich
1865-1941 . . . . **TCLC 29**

Merimee, Prosper
1803-1870 . . . . **NCLC 6; SSC 7**
See also DLB 119

Merkin, Daphne 1954- . . . . **CLC 44**
See also CA 123

Merlin, Arthur
See Blish, James (Benjamin)

Merrill, James (Ingram)
1926-1995 . . . . **CLC 2, 3, 6, 8, 13, 18, 34,**
91; DAM POET
See also CA 13-16R; 147; CANR 10, 49;
DLB 5, 165; DLBY 85; INT CANR-10;
MTCW

Merriman, Alex
See Silverberg, Robert

Merritt, E. B.
See Waddington, Miriam

Merton, Thomas
1915-1968 . . **CLC 1, 3, 11, 34, 83; PC 10**
See also CA 5-8R; 25-28R; CANR 22, 53;
DLB 48; DLBY 81; MTCW

Merwin, W(illiam) S(tanley)
1927- . . . . . . **CLC 1, 2, 3, 5, 8, 13, 18, 45,**
88; DAM POET
See also CA 13-16R; CANR 15, 51; DLB 5,
169; INT CANR-15; MTCW

Metcalf, John 1938- . . . . **CLC 37**
See also CA 113; DLB 60

Metcalf, Suzanne
See Baum, L(yman) Frank

Mew, Charlotte (Mary)
1870-1928 . . . . **TCLC 8**
See also CA 105; DLB 19, 135

Mewshaw, Michael 1943- . . . . **CLC 9**
See also CA 53-56; CANR 7, 47; DLBY 80

Meyer, June
See Jordan, June

Meyer, Lynn
See Slavitt, David R(ytman)

Meyer-Meyrink, Gustav 1868-1932
See Meyrink, Gustav
See also CA 117

Meyers, Jeffrey 1939- . . . . **CLC 39**
See also CA 73-76; CANR 54; DLB 111

Meynell, Alice (Christina Gertrude Thompson)
1847-1922 . . . . **TCLC 6**
See also CA 104; DLB 19, 98

Meyrink, Gustav . . . . **TCLC 21**
See also Meyer-Meyrink, Gustav
See also DLB 81

Michaels, Leonard
1933- . . . . **CLC 6, 25; SSC 16**
See also CA 61-64; CANR 21; DLB 130;
MTCW

Michaux, Henri 1899-1984 . . . . . . **CLC 8, 19**
See also CA 85-88; 114

Michelangelo 1475-1564 . . . . **LC 12**

Michelet, Jules 1798-1874 . . . . . . **NCLC 31**

Michener, James A(lbert)
1907(?)- . . . . **CLC 1, 5, 11, 29, 60;**
DAM NOV, POP
See also AITN 1; BEST 90:1; CA 5-8R;
CANR 21, 45; DLB 6; MTCW

Mickiewicz, Adam 1798-1855 . . . . . **NCLC 3**

Middleton, Christopher 1926- . . . . . . **CLC 13**
See also CA 13-16R; CANR 29, 54;
DLB 40

Middleton, Richard (Barham)
1882-1911 . . . . **TCLC 56**
See also DLB 156

Middleton, Stanley 1919- . . . . **CLC 7, 38**
See also CA 25-28R; CAAS 23; CANR 21,
46; DLB 14

Middleton, Thomas
1580-1627 . . . . **LC 33; DAM DRAM,**
MST; DC 5
See also DLB 58

Migueis, Jose Rodrigues 1901- . . . . . **CLC 10**

Mikszath, Kalman 1847-1910 . . . . . **TCLC 31**

Miles, Josephine (Louise)
1911-1985 . . . . **CLC 1, 2, 14, 34, 39;**
DAM POET
See also CA 1-4R; 116; CANR 2, 55;
DLB 48

Militant
See Sandburg, Carl (August)

Mill, John Stuart 1806-1873 . . **NCLC 11, 58**
See also CDBLB 1832-1890; DLB 55

Millar, Kenneth
1915-1983 . . . . **CLC 14; DAM POP**
See also Macdonald, Ross
See also CA 9-12R; 110; CANR 16; DLB 2;
DLBD 6; DLBY 83; MTCW

Millay, E. Vincent
See Millay, Edna St. Vincent

Millay, Edna St. Vincent
1892-1950 . . . . . . **TCLC 4, 49; DA; DAB;**
DAC; DAM MST, POET; PC 6
See also CA 104; 130; CDALB 1917-1929;
DLB 45; MTCW

Miller, Arthur
1915- . . . . **CLC 1, 2, 6, 10, 15, 26, 47, 78;**
DA; DAB; DAC; DAM DRAM, MST;
DC 1; WLC
See also AAYA 15; AITN 1; CA 1-4R;
CABS 3; CANR 2, 30, 54;
CDALB 1941-1968; DLB 7; MTCW

Miller, Henry (Valentine)
1891-1980 . . . . **CLC 1, 2, 4, 9, 14, 43, 84;**
DA; DAB; DAC; DAM MST, NOV;
WLC
See also CA 9-12R; 97-100; CANR 33;
CDALB 1929-1941; DLB 4, 9; DLBY 80;
MTCW

Miller, Jason 1939(?)- . . . . **CLC 2**
See also AITN 1; CA 73-76; DLB 7

Miller, Sue 1943- . . . . . **CLC 44; DAM POP**
See also BEST 90:3; CA 139; DLB 143

Miller, Walter M(ichael, Jr.)
1923- . . . . **CLC 4, 30**
See also CA 85-88; DLB 8

Millett, Kate 1934- . . . . **CLC 67**
See also AITN 1; CA 73-76; CANR 32, 53;
MTCW

Millhauser, Steven 1943- . . . . **CLC 21, 54**
See also CA 110; 111; DLB 2; INT 111

Millin, Sarah Gertrude 1889-1968 . . **CLC 49**
See also CA 102; 93-96

Milne, A(lan) A(lexander)
1882-1956 . . . . . . **TCLC 6; DAB; DAC;**
DAM MST
See also CA 104; 133; CLR 1, 26; DLB 10,
77, 100, 160; MAICYA; MTCW;
YABC 1

Milner, Ron(ald)
1938- . . . . . **CLC 56; BLC; DAM MULT**
See also AITN 1; BW 1; CA 73-76;
CANR 24; DLB 38; MTCW

Milosz, Czeslaw
1911- . . . . **CLC 5, 11, 22, 31, 56, 82;**
DAM MST, POET; PC 8
See also CA 81-84; CANR 23, 51; MTCW

Milton, John
1608-1674 . . . . . . **LC 9; DA; DAB; DAC;**
DAM MST, POET; WLC
See also CDBLB 1660-1789; DLB 131, 151

Min, Anchee 1957- . . . . **CLC 86**
See also CA 146

Minehaha, Cornelius
See Wedekind, (Benjamin) Frank(lin)

Miner, Valerie 1947- . . . . **CLC 40**
See also CA 97-100

Minimo, Duca
See D'Annunzio, Gabriele

Minot, Susan 1956- . . . . **CLC 44**
See also CA 134

Minus, Ed 1938- . . . . **CLC 39**

Miranda, Javier
See Bioy Casares, Adolfo

Mirbeau, Octave 1848-1917 . . . . **TCLC 55**
See also DLB 123

Miro (Ferrer), Gabriel (Francisco Victor)
1879-1930 . . . . **TCLC 5**
See also CA 104

Mishima, Yukio
. . . . **CLC 2, 4, 6, 9, 27; DC 1; SSC 4**
See also Hiraoka, Kimitake

Mistral, Frederic 1830-1914 . . . . . . **TCLC 51**
See also CA 122

Mistral, Gabriela . . . . **TCLC 2; HLC**
See also Godoy Alcayaga, Lucila

Mistry, Rohinton 1952- . . . . . . **CLC 71; DAC**
See also CA 141

Mitchell, Clyde
See Ellison, Harlan (Jay); Silverberg, Robert

Mitchell, James Leslie 1901-1935
See Gibbon, Lewis Grassic
See also CA 104; DLB 15

Mitchell, Joni 1943- . . . . **CLC 12**
See also CA 112

Mitchell, Joseph (Quincy)
1908-1996 . . . . **CLC 98**
See also CA 77-80; 152

Mitchell, Margaret (Munnerlyn)
1900-1949 . . . . . . **TCLC 11; DAM NOV,**
POP
See also CA 109; 125; CANR 55; DLB 9;
MTCW

Mitchell, Peggy
See Mitchell, Margaret (Munnerlyn)

Mitchell, S(ilas) Weir 1829-1914 . . **TCLC 36**

Mitchell, W(illiam) O(rmond)
1914- ...... **CLC 25; DAC; DAM MST**
See also CA 77-80; CANR 15, 43; DLB 88

Mitford, Mary Russell 1787-1855.. **NCLC 4**
See also DLB 110, 116

Mitford, Nancy 1904-1973........ **CLC 44**
See also CA 9-12R

Miyamoto, Yuriko 1899-1951 ..... **TCLC 37**

Mo, Timothy (Peter) 1950(?)- ...... **CLC 46**
See also CA 117; MTCW

Modarressi, Taghi (M.) 1931- ...... **CLC 44**
See also CA 121; 134; INT 134

Modiano, Patrick (Jean) 1945- ..... **CLC 18**
See also CA 85-88; CANR 17, 40; DLB 83

Moerck, Paal
See Roelvaag, O(le) E(dvart)

Mofolo, Thomas (Mokopu)
1875(?)-1948 .... **TCLC 22; BLC;**
DAM MULT
See also CA 121; 153

Mohr, Nicholasa
1935- ..... **CLC 12; DAM MULT; HLC**
See also AAYA 8; CA 49-52; CANR 1, 32;
CLR 22; DLB 145; HW; JRDA; SAAS 8;
SATA 8

Mojtabai, A(nn) G(race)
1938- .... **CLC 5, 9, 15, 29**
See also CA 85-88

Moliere
1622-1673 ..... **LC 28; DA; DAB; DAC;**
DAM DRAM, MST; WLC

Molin, Charles
See Mayne, William (James Carter)

Molnar, Ferenc
1878-1952 ..... **TCLC 20; DAM DRAM**
See also CA 109; 153

Momaday, N(avarre) Scott
1934- ..... **CLC 2, 19, 85, 95; DA; DAB;**
DAC; DAM MST, MULT, NOV, POP
See also AAYA 11; CA 25-28R; CANR 14,
34; DLB 143; INT CANR-14; MTCW;
NNAL; SATA 48; SATA-Brief 30

Monette, Paul 1945-1995.......... **CLC 82**
See also CA 139; 147

Monroe, Harriet 1860-1936....... **TCLC 12**
See also CA 109; DLB 54, 91

Monroe, Lyle
See Heinlein, Robert A(nson)

Montagu, Elizabeth 1917- .... **NCLC 7**
See also CA 9-12R

Montagu, Mary (Pierrepont) Wortley
1689-1762 .... **LC 9; PC 16**
See also DLB 95, 101

Montagu, W. H.
See Coleridge, Samuel Taylor

Montague, John (Patrick)
1929- .... **CLC 13, 46**
See also CA 9-12R; CANR 9; DLB 40;
MTCW

Montaigne, Michel (Eyquem) de
1533-1592 ...... **LC 8; DA; DAB; DAC;**
DAM MST; WLC

Montale, Eugenio
1896-1981 .... **CLC 7, 9, 18; PC 13**
See also CA 17-20R; 104; CANR 30;
DLB 114; MTCW

Montesquieu, Charles-Louis de Secondat
1689-1755 .... **LC 7**

Montgomery, (Robert) Bruce 1921-1978
See Crispin, Edmund
See also CA 104

Montgomery, L(ucy) M(aud)
1874-1942 .... **TCLC 51; DAC;**
DAM MST
See also AAYA 12; CA 108; 137; CLR 8;
DLB 92; DLBD 14; JRDA; MAICYA;
YABC 1

Montgomery, Marion H., Jr. 1925-.. **CLC 7**
See also AITN 1; CA 1-4R; CANR 3, 48;
DLB 6

Montgomery, Max
See Davenport, Guy (Mattison, Jr.)

Montherlant, Henry (Milon) de
1896-1972 .... **CLC 8, 19; DAM DRAM**
See also CA 85-88; 37-40R; DLB 72;
MTCW

Monty Python
See Chapman, Graham; Cleese, John
(Marwood); Gilliam, Terry (Vance); Idle,
Eric; Jones, Terence Graham Parry; Palin,
Michael (Edward)
See also AAYA 7

Moodie, Susanna (Strickland)
1803-1885 .... **NCLC 14**
See also DLB 99

Mooney, Edward 1951-
See Mooney, Ted
See also CA 130

Mooney, Ted .... **CLC 25**
See also Mooney, Edward

Moorcock, Michael (John)
1939- .... **CLC 5, 27, 58**
See also CA 45-48; CAAS 5; CANR 2, 17,
38; DLB 14; MTCW

Moore, Brian
1921- ...... **CLC 1, 3, 5, 7, 8, 19, 32, 90;**
DAB; DAC; DAM MST
See also CA 1-4R; CANR 1, 25, 42; MTCW

Moore, Edward
See Muir, Edwin

Moore, George Augustus
1852-1933 .... **TCLC 7; SSC 19**
See also CA 104; DLB 10, 18, 57, 135

Moore, Lorrie .... **CLC 39, 45, 68**
See also Moore, Marie Lorena

Moore, Marianne (Craig)
1887-1972 .... **CLC 1, 2, 4, 8, 10, 13, 19,**
47; DA; DAB; DAC; DAM MST, POET;
PC 4
See also CA 1-4R; 33-36R; CANR 3;
CDALB 1929-1941; DLB 45; DLBD 7;
MTCW; SATA 20

Moore, Marie Lorena 1957-
See Moore, Lorrie
See also CA 116; CANR 39

Moore, Thomas 1779-1852....... **NCLC 6**
See also DLB 96, 144

Morand, Paul 1888-1976 .. **CLC 41; SSC 22**
See also CA 69-72; DLB 65

Morante, Elsa 1918-1985........ **CLC 8, 47**
See also CA 85-88; 117; CANR 35; MTCW

Moravia, Alberto....... CLC 2, 7, 11, 27, 46
See also Pincherle, Alberto

More, Hannah 1745-1833 .... **NCLC 27**
See also DLB 107, 109, 116, 158

More, Henry 1614-1687............. **LC 9**
See also DLB 126

More, Sir Thomas 1478-1535 .... **LC 10, 32**

Moreas, Jean.................... TCLC 18
See also Papadiamantopoulos, Johannes

Morgan, Berry 1919-.............. **CLC 6**
See also CA 49-52; DLB 6

Morgan, Claire
See Highsmith, (Mary) Patricia

Morgan, Edwin (George) 1920-..... **CLC 31**
See also CA 5-8R; CANR 3, 43; DLB 27

Morgan, (George) Frederick
1922-...................... **CLC 23**
See also CA 17-20R; CANR 21

Morgan, Harriet
See Mencken, H(enry) L(ouis)

Morgan, Jane
See Cooper, James Fenimore

Morgan, Janet 1945- .... **CLC 39**
See also CA 65-68

Morgan, Lady 1776(?)-1859...... **NCLC 29**
See also DLB 116, 158

Morgan, Robin 1941-.............. **CLC 2**
See also CA 69-72; CANR 29; MTCW;
SATA 80

Morgan, Scott
See Kuttner, Henry

Morgan, Seth 1949(?)-1990........ **CLC 65**
See also CA 132

Morgenstern, Christian
1871-1914 .... **TCLC 8**
See also CA 105

Morgenstern, S.
See Goldman, William (W.)

Moricz, Zsigmond 1879-1942 ..... **TCLC 33**

Morike, Eduard (Friedrich)
1804-1875 .... **NCLC 10**
See also DLB 133

Mori Ogai .... TCLC 14
See also Mori Rintaro

Mori Rintaro 1862-1922
See Mori Ogai
See also CA 110

Moritz, Karl Philipp 1756-1793 ...... **LC 2**
See also DLB 94

Morland, Peter Henry
See Faust, Frederick (Schiller)

Morren, Theophil
See Hofmannsthal, Hugo von

Morris, Bill 1952-................ **CLC 76**

Morris, Julian
See West, Morris L(anglo)

Morris, Steveland Judkins 1950(?)-
See Wonder, Stevie
See also CA 111

Morris, William 1834-1896 .... **NCLC 4**
See also CDBLB 1832-1890; DLB 18, 35,
57, 156

Morris, Wright 1910-... **CLC 1, 3, 7, 18, 37**
See also CA 9-12R; CANR 21; DLB 2;
DLBY 81; MTCW

Morrison, Chloe Anthony Wofford
See Morrison, Toni

Morrison, James Douglas 1943-1971
See Morrison, Jim
See also CA 73-76; CANR 40

Morrison, Jim .... **CLC 17**
See also Morrison, James Douglas

Morrison, Toni
1931- .... **CLC 4, 10, 22, 55, 81, 87;
BLC; DA; DAB; DAC; DAM MST,
MULT, NOV, POP**
See also AAYA 1; BW 2; CA 29-32R;
CANR 27, 42; CDALB 1968-1988;
DLB 6, 33, 143; DLBY 81; MTCW;
SATA 57

Morrison, Van 1945- .... **CLC 21**
See also CA 116

Mortimer, John (Clifford)
1923- ...... **CLC 28, 43; DAM DRAM,
POP**
See also CA 13-16R; CANR 21;
CDBLB 1960 to Present; DLB 13;
INT CANR-21; MTCW

Mortimer, Penelope (Ruth) 1918-.... **CLC 5**
See also CA 57-60; CANR 45

Morton, Anthony
See Creasey, John

Mosher, Howard Frank 1943-...... **CLC 62**
See also CA 139

Mosley, Nicholas 1923- .... **CLC 43, 70**
See also CA 69-72; CANR 41; DLB 14

Mosley, Walter
1952- ..... **CLC 97; DAM MULT, POP**
See also AAYA 17; BW 2; CA 142

Moss, Howard
1922-1987 .... **CLC 7, 14, 45, 50;
DAM POET**
See also CA 1-4R; 123; CANR 1, 44;
DLB 5

Mossgiel, Rab
See Burns, Robert

Motion, Andrew (Peter) 1952-...... **CLC 47**
See also CA 146; DLB 40

Motley, Willard (Francis)
1909-1965 .... **CLC 18**
See also BW 1; CA 117; 106; DLB 76, 143

Motoori, Norinaga 1730-1801 .... **NCLC 45**

Mott, Michael (Charles Alston)
1930- .... **CLC 15, 34**
See also CA 5-8R; CAAS 7; CANR 7, 29

Mountain Wolf Woman
1884-1960 .... **CLC 92**
See also CA 144; NNAL

Moure, Erin 1955- .... **CLC 88**
See also CA 113; DLB 60

Mowat, Farley (McGill)
1921- .... **CLC 26; DAC; DAM MST**
See also AAYA 1; CA 1-4R; CANR 4, 24,
42; CLR 20; DLB 68; INT CANAR-24;
JRDA; MAICYA; MTCW; SATA 3, 55

Moyers, Bill 1934-............. **CLC 74**
See also AITN 2; CA 61-64; CANR 31, 52

Mphahlele, Es'kia
See Mphahlele, Ezekiel
See also DLB 125

Mphahlele, Ezekiel
1919- ..... **CLC 25; BLC; DAM MULT**
See also Mphahlele, Es'kia
See also BW 2; CA 81-84; CANR 26

Mqhayi, S(amuel) E(dward) K(rune Loliwe)
1875-1945 .... **TCLC 25; BLC;
DAM MULT**
See also CA 153

Mrozek, Slawomir 1930-........ **CLC 3, 13**
See also CA 13-16R; CAAS 10; CANR 29;
MTCW

Mrs. Belloc-Lowndes
See Lowndes, Marie Adelaide (Belloc)

Mtwa, Percy (?)-................. **CLC 47**

Mueller, Lisel 1924-........... **CLC 13, 51**
See also CA 93-96; DLB 105

Muir, Edwin 1887-1959 .... **TCLC 2**
See also CA 104; DLB 20, 100

Muir, John 1838-1914 .... **TCLC 28**

Mujica Lainez, Manuel
1910-1984 .... **CLC 31**
See also Lainez, Manuel Mujica
See also CA 81-84; 112; CANR 32; HW

Mukherjee, Bharati
1940- .... **CLC 53; DAM NOV**
See also BEST 89:2; CA 107; CANR 45;
DLB 60; MTCW

Muldoon, Paul
1951- .... **CLC 32, 72; DAM POET**
See also CA 113; 129; CANR 52; DLB 40;
INT 129

Mulisch, Harry 1927-............. **CLC 42**
See also CA 9-12R; CANR 6, 26

Mull, Martin 1943-............... **CLC 17**
See also CA 105

Mulock, Dinah Maria
See Craik, Dinah Maria (Mulock)

Munford, Robert 1737(?)-1783 .... **LC 5**
See also DLB 31

Mungo, Raymond 1946-.......... **CLC 72**
See also CA 49-52; CANR 2

Munro, Alice
1931- ...... **CLC 6, 10, 19, 50, 95; DAC;
DAM MST, NOV; SSC 3**
See also AITN 2; CA 33-36R; CANR 33,
53; DLB 53; MTCW; SATA 29

Munro, H(ector) H(ugh) 1870-1916
See Saki
See also CA 104; 130; CDBLB 1890-1914;
DA; DAB; DAC; DAM MST, NOV;
DLB 34, 162; MTCW; WLC

Murasaki, Lady................. **CMLC 1**

Murdoch, (Jean) Iris
1919- ...... **CLC 1, 2, 3, 4, 6, 8, 11, 15,
22, 31, 51; DAB; DAC; DAM MST,
NOV**
See also CA 13-16R; CANR 8, 43;
CDBLB 1960 to Present; DLB 14;
INT CANR-8; MTCW

Murfree, Mary Noailles
1850-1922 .... **SSC 22**
See also CA 122; DLB 12, 74

Murnau, Friedrich Wilhelm
See Plumpe, Friedrich Wilhelm

Murphy, Richard 1927-........... **CLC 41**
See also CA 29-32R; DLB 40

Murphy, Sylvia 1937-............. **CLC 34**
See also CA 121

Murphy, Thomas (Bernard) 1935-... **CLC 51**
See also CA 101

Murray, Albert L. 1916-.......... **CLC 73**
See also BW 2; CA 49-52; CANR 26, 52;
DLB 38

Murray, Les(lie) A(llan)
1938- .... **CLC 40; DAM POET**
See also CA 21-24R; CANR 11, 27

Murry, J. Middleton
See Murry, John Middleton

Murry, John Middleton
1889-1957 .... **TCLC 16**
See also CA 118; DLB 149

Musgrave, Susan 1951- .... **CLC 13, 54**
See also CA 69-72; CANR 45

Musil, Robert (Edler von)
1880-1942 .... **TCLC 12; SSC 18**
See also CA 109; CANR 55; DLB 81, 124

Muske, Carol 1945- .... **CLC 90**
See also Muske-Dukes, Carol (Anne)

Muske-Dukes, Carol (Anne) 1945-
See Muske, Carol
See also CA 65-68; CANR 32

Musset, (Louis Charles) Alfred de
1810-1857 .... **NCLC 7**

My Brother's Brother
See Chekhov, Anton (Pavlovich)

Myers, L. H. 1881-1944.......... **TCLC 59**
See also DLB 15

Myers, Walter Dean
1937- ..... **CLC 35; BLC; DAM MULT,
NOV**
See also AAYA 4; BW 2; CA 33-36R;
CANR 20, 42; CLR 4, 16, 35; DLB 33;
INT CANR-20; JRDA; MAICYA;
SAAS 2; SATA 41, 71; SATA-Brief 27

Myers, Walter M.
See Myers, Walter Dean

Myles, Symon
See Follett, Ken(neth Martin)

Nabokov, Vladimir (Vladimirovich)
1899-1977 ..... **CLC 1, 2, 3, 6, 8, 11, 15,
23, 44, 46, 64; DA; DAB; DAC;
DAM MST, NOV; SSC 11; WLC**
See also CA 5-8R; 69-72; CANR 20;
CDALB 1941-1968; DLB 2; DLBD 3;
DLBY 80, 91; MTCW

Nagai Kafu.................... **TCLC 51**
See also Nagai Sokichi

Nagai Sokichi 1879-1959
See Nagai Kafu
See also CA 117

Nagy, Laszlo 1925-1978........... **CLC 7**
See also CA 129; 112

Naipaul, Shiva(dhar Srinivasa)
1945-1985 ..... **CLC 32, 39; DAM NOV**
See also CA 110; 112; 116; CANR 33;
DLB 157; DLBY 85; MTCW

Naipaul, V(idiadhar) S(urajprasad)
1932- .... **CLC 4, 7, 9, 13, 18, 37; DAB;**
DAC; DAM MST, NOV
See also CA 1-4R; CANR 1, 33, 51;
CDBLB 1960 to Present; DLB 125;
DLBY 85; MTCW

Nakos, Lilika 1899(?)-............ **CLC 29**

Narayan, R(asipuram) K(rishnaswami)
1906- .... **CLC 7, 28, 47; DAM NOV**
See also CA 81-84; CANR 33; MTCW;
SATA 62

Nash, (Fredric) Ogden
1902-1971 .... **CLC 23; DAM POET**
See also CA 13-14; 29-32R; CANR 34;
CAP 1; DLB 11; MAICYA; MTCW;
SATA 2, 46

Nathan, Daniel
See Dannay, Frederic

Nathan, George Jean 1882-1958 ... **TCLC 18**
See also Hatteras, Owen
See also CA 114; DLB 137

Natsume, Kinnosuke 1867-1916
See Natsume, Soseki
See also CA 104

Natsume, Soseki .... **TCLC 2, 10**
See also Natsume, Kinnosuke

Natti, (Mary) Lee 1919-
See Kingman, Lee
See also CA 5-8R; CANR 2

Naylor, Gloria
1950- ..... **CLC 28, 52; BLC; DA; DAC;**
DAM MST, MULT, NOV, POP
See also AAYA 6; BW 2; CA 107;
CANR 27, 51; DLB 173; MTCW

Neihardt, John Gneisenau
1881-1973 .... **CLC 32**
See also CA 13-14; CAP 1; DLB 9, 54

Nekrasov, Nikolai Alekseevich
1821-1878 .... **NCLC 11**

Nelligan, Emile 1879-1941....... **TCLC 14**
See also CA 114; DLB 92

Nelson, Willie 1933-.............. **CLC 17**
See also CA 107

Nemerov, Howard (Stanley)
1920-1991 .... **CLC 2, 6, 9, 36;**
DAM POET
See also CA 1-4R; 134; CABS 2; CANR 1,
27, 53; DLB 5, 6; DLBY 83;
INT CANR-27; MTCW

Neruda, Pablo
1904-1973 ..... **CLC 1, 2, 5, 7, 9, 28, 62;**
DA; DAB; DAC; DAM MST, MULT,
POET; HLC; PC 4; WLC
See also CA 19-20; 45-48; CAP 2; HW;
MTCW

Nerval, Gerard de
1808-1855 ..... **NCLC 1; PC 13; SSC 18**

Nervo, (Jose) Amado (Ruiz de)
1870-1919 .... **TCLC 11**
See also CA 109; 131; HW

Nessi, Pio Baroja y
See Baroja (y Nessi), Pio

Nestroy, Johann 1801-1862..... **NCLC 42**
See also DLB 133

Neufeld, John (Arthur) 1938- ...... **CLC 17**
See also AAYA 11; CA 25-28R; CANR 11,
37; MAICYA; SAAS 3; SATA 6, 81

Neville, Emily Cheney 1919-....... **CLC 12**
See also CA 5-8R; CANR 3, 37; JRDA;
MAICYA; SAAS 2; SATA 1

Newbound, Bernard Slade 1930-
See Slade, Bernard
See also CA 81-84; CANR 49;
DAM DRAM

Newby, P(ercy) H(oward)
1918- .... **CLC 2, 13; DAM NOV**
See also CA 5-8R; CANR 32; DLB 15;
MTCW

Newlove, Donald 1928- .... **CLC 6**
See also CA 29-32R; CANR 25

Newlove, John (Herbert) 1938-..... **CLC 14**
See also CA 21-24R; CANR 9, 25

Newman, Charles 1938-.......... **CLC 2, 8**
See also CA 21-24R

Newman, Edwin (Harold) 1919- .... **CLC 14**
See also AITN 1; CA 69-72; CANR 5

Newman, John Henry
1801-1890 .... **NCLC 38**
See also DLB 18, 32, 55

Newton, Suzanne 1936-.......... **CLC 35**
See also CA 41-44R; CANR 14; JRDA;
SATA 5, 77

Nexo, Martin Andersen
1869-1954 .... **TCLC 43**

Nezval, Vitezslav 1900-1958 ..... **TCLC 44**
See also CA 123

Ng, Fae Myenne 1957(?)-.......... **CLC 81**
See also CA 146

Ngema, Mbongeni 1955- .... **CLC 57**
See also BW 2; CA 143

Ngugi, James T(hiong'o)........ **CLC 3, 7, 13**
See also Ngugi wa Thiong'o

Ngugi wa Thiong'o
1938- ..... **CLC 36; BLC; DAM MULT,**
NOV
See also Ngugi, James T(hiong'o)
See also BW 2; CA 81-84; CANR 27;
DLB 125; MTCW

Nichol, B(arrie) P(hillip)
1944-1988 .... **CLC 18**
See also CA 53-56; DLB 53; SATA 66

Nichols, John (Treadwell) 1940-.... **CLC 38**
See also CA 9-12R; CAAS 2; CANR 6;
DLBY 82

Nichols, Leigh
See Koontz, Dean R(ay)

Nichols, Peter (Richard)
1927-................. **CLC 5, 36, 65**
See also CA 104; CANR 33; DLB 13;
MTCW

Nicolas, F. R. E.
See Freeling, Nicolas

Niedecker, Lorine
1903-1970 .... **CLC 10, 42; DAM POET**
See also CA 25-28; CAP 2; DLB 48

Nietzsche, Friedrich (Wilhelm)
1844-1900 .... **TCLC 10, 18, 55**
See also CA 107; 121; DLB 129

Nievo, Ippolito 1831-1861 .... **NCLC 22**

Nightingale, Anne Redmon 1943-
See Redmon, Anne
See also CA 103

Nik. T. O.
See Annensky, Innokenty Fyodorovich

Nin, Anais
1903-1977 ...... **CLC 1, 4, 8, 11, 14, 60;**
DAM NOV, POP; SSC 10
See also AITN 2; CA 13-16R; 69-72;
CANR 22, 53; DLB 2, 4, 152; MTCW

Nishiwaki, Junzaburo 1894-1982 .... **PC 15**
See also CA 107

Nissenson, Hugh 1933-........... **CLC 4, 9**
See also CA 17-20R; CANR 27; DLB 28

Niven, Larry .... **CLC 8**
See also Niven, Laurence Van Cott
See also DLB 8

Niven, Laurence Van Cott 1938-
See Niven, Larry
See also CA 21-24R; CAAS 12; CANR 14,
44; DAM POP; MTCW

Nixon, Agnes Eckhardt 1927-...... **CLC 21**
See also CA 110

Nizan, Paul 1905-1940........... **TCLC 40**
See also DLB 72

Nkosi, Lewis
1936- ..... **CLC 45; BLC; DAM MULT**
See also BW 1; CA 65-68; CANR 27;
DLB 157

Nodier, (Jean) Charles (Emmanuel)
1780-1844 .... **NCLC 19**
See also DLB 119

Nolan, Christopher 1965-.......... **CLC 58**
See also CA 111

Noon, Jeff 1957-................. **CLC 91**
See also CA 148

Norden, Charles
See Durrell, Lawrence (George)

Nordhoff, Charles (Bernard)
1887-1947 .... **TCLC 23**
See also CA 108; DLB 9; SATA 23

Norfolk, Lawrence 1963-.......... **CLC 76**
See also CA 144

Norman, Marsha
1947- .... **CLC 28; DAM DRAM**
See also CA 105; CABS 3; CANR 41;
DLBY 84

Norris, Benjamin Franklin, Jr.
1870-1902 .... **TCLC 24**
See also Norris, Frank
See also CA 110

Norris, Frank
See Norris, Benjamin Franklin, Jr.
See also CDALB 1865-1917; DLB 12, 71

Norris, Leslie 1921-.............. **CLC 14**
See also CA 11-12; CANR 14; CAP 1;
DLB 27

North, Andrew
See Norton, Andre

North, Anthony
See Koontz, Dean R(ay)

North, Captain George
See Stevenson, Robert Louis (Balfour)

North, Milou
See Erdrich, Louise

Northrup, B. A.
See Hubbard, L(afayette) Ron(ald)

North Staffs
See Hulme, T(homas) E(rnest)

Norton, Alice Mary
See Norton, Andre
See also MAICYA; SATA 1, 43

Norton, Andre 1912- . . . . **CLC 12**
See also Norton, Alice Mary
See also AAYA 14; CA 1-4R; CANR 2, 31;
DLB 8, 52; JRDA; MTCW; SATA 91

Norton, Caroline 1808-1877. . . . . . **NCLC 47**
See also DLB 21, 159

Norway, Nevil Shute 1899-1960
See Shute, Nevil
See also CA 102; 93-96

Norwid, Cyprian Kamil
1821-1883 . . . . **NCLC 17**

Nosille, Nabrah
See Ellison, Harlan (Jay)

Nossack, Hans Erich 1901-1978 . . . . . **CLC 6**
See also CA 93-96; 85-88; DLB 69

Nostradamus 1503-1566. . . . . **LC 27**

Nosu, Chuji
See Ozu, Yasujiro

Notenburg, Eleanora (Genrikhovna) von
See Guro, Elena

Nova, Craig 1945-. . . . . **CLC 7, 31**
See also CA 45-48; CANR 2, 53

Novak, Joseph
See Kosinski, Jerzy (Nikodem)

Novalis 1772-1801 . . . . **NCLC 13**
See also DLB 90

Nowlan, Alden (Albert)
1933-1983 . . **CLC 15; DAC; DAM MST**
See also CA 9-12R; CANR 5; DLB 53

Noyes, Alfred 1880-1958 . . . . **TCLC 7**
See also CA 104; DLB 20

Nunn, Kem 19(?)-. . . . . **CLC 34**

Nye, Robert
1939- . . . . **CLC 13, 42; DAM NOV**
See also CA 33-36R; CANR 29; DLB 14;
MTCW; SATA 6

Nyro, Laura 1947- . . . . **CLC 17**

Oates, Joyce Carol
1938- . . . . . . **CLC 1, 2, 3, 6, 9, 11, 15, 19,
33, 52; DA; DAB; DAC; DAM MST,
NOV, POP; SSC 6; WLC**
See also AAYA 15; AITN 1; BEST 89:2;
CA 5-8R; CANR 25, 45;
CDALB 1968-1988; DLB 2, 5, 130;
DLBY 81; INT CANR-25; MTCW

O'Brien, Darcy 1939-. . . . . **CLC 11**
See also CA 21-24R; CANR 8

O'Brien, E. G.
See Clarke, Arthur C(harles)

O'Brien, Edna
1936- . . . . **CLC 3, 5, 8, 13, 36, 65;
DAM NOV; SSC 10**
See also CA 1-4R; CANR 6, 41;
CDBLB 1960 to Present; DLB 14;
MTCW

O'Brien, Fitz-James 1828-1862. . . **NCLC 21**
See also DLB 74

O'Brien, Flann. . . . . . . **CLC 1, 4, 5, 7, 10, 47**
See also O Nuallain, Brian

O'Brien, Richard 1942- . . . . **CLC 17**
See also CA 124

O'Brien, Tim
1946- . . . . **CLC 7, 19, 40; DAM POP**
See also AAYA 16; CA 85-88; CANR 40;
DLB 152; DLBD 9; DLBY 80

Obstfelder, Sigbjoern 1866-1900. . . **TCLC 23**
See also CA 123

O'Casey, Sean
1880-1964 . . . . . **CLC 1, 5, 9, 11, 15, 88;
DAB; DAC; DAM DRAM, MST**
See also CA 89-92; CDBLB 1914-1945;
DLB 10; MTCW

O'Cathasaigh, Sean
See O'Casey, Sean

Ochs, Phil 1940-1976. . . . . **CLC 17**
See also CA 65-68

O'Connor, Edwin (Greene)
1918-1968 . . . . **CLC 14**
See also CA 93-96; 25-28R

O'Connor, (Mary) Flannery
1925-1964 . . . . **CLC 1, 2, 3, 6, 10, 13, 15,
21, 66; DA; DAB; DAC; DAM MST,
NOV; SSC 1, 23; WLC**
See also AAYA 7; CA 1-4R; CANR 3, 41;
CDALB 1941-1968; DLB 2, 152;
DLBD 12; DLBY 80; MTCW

O'Connor, Frank. . . . . **CLC 23; SSC 5**
See also O'Donovan, Michael John
See also DLB 162

O'Dell, Scott 1898-1989. . . . . **CLC 30**
See also AAYA 3; CA 61-64; 129;
CANR 12, 30; CLR 1, 16; DLB 52;
JRDA; MAICYA; SATA 12, 60

Odets, Clifford
1906-1963 . . . . **CLC 2, 28, 98;
DAM DRAM; DC 6**
See also CA 85-88; DLB 7, 26; MTCW

O'Doherty, Brian 1934-. . . . . **CLC 76**
See also CA 105

O'Donnell, K. M.
See Malzberg, Barry N(athaniel)

O'Donnell, Lawrence
See Kuttner, Henry

O'Donovan, Michael John
1903-1966 . . . . **CLC 14**
See also O'Connor, Frank
See also CA 93-96

Oe, Kenzaburo
1935- . . . . . **CLC 10, 36, 86; DAM NOV;
SSC 20**
See also CA 97-100; CANR 36, 50;
DLBY 94; MTCW

O'Faolain, Julia 1932-. . . . . . . **CLC 6, 19, 47**
See also CA 81-84; CAAS 2; CANR 12;
DLB 14; MTCW

O'Faolain, Sean
1900-1991 . . . . **CLC 1, 7, 14, 32, 70;
SSC 13**
See also CA 61-64; 134; CANR 12;
DLB 15, 162; MTCW

O'Flaherty, Liam
1896-1984 . . . . **CLC 5, 34; SSC 6**
See also CA 101; 113; CANR 35; DLB 36,
162; DLBY 84; MTCW

Ogilvy, Gavin
See Barrie, J(ames) M(atthew)

O'Grady, Standish James
1846-1928 . . . . **TCLC 5**
See also CA 104

O'Grady, Timothy 1951-. . . . . **CLC 59**
See also CA 138

O'Hara, Frank
1926-1966 . . . . **CLC 2, 5, 13, 78;
DAM POET**
See also CA 9-12R; 25-28R; CANR 33;
DLB 5, 16; MTCW

O'Hara, John (Henry)
1905-1970 . . . . **CLC 1, 2, 3, 6, 11, 42;
DAM NOV; SSC 15**
See also CA 5-8R; 25-28R; CANR 31;
CDALB 1929-1941; DLB 9, 86; DLBD 2;
MTCW

O Hehir, Diana 1922- . . . . **CLC 41**
See also CA 93-96

Okigbo, Christopher (Ifenayichukwu)
1932-1967 . . . . **CLC 25, 84; BLC;
DAM MULT, POET; PC 7**
See also BW 1; CA 77-80; DLB 125;
MTCW

Okri, Ben 1959- . . . . **CLC 87**
See also BW 2; CA 130; 138; DLB 157;
INT 138

Olds, Sharon
1942- . . . . . **CLC 32, 39, 85; DAM POET**
See also CA 101; CANR 18, 41; DLB 120

Oldstyle, Jonathan
See Irving, Washington

Olesha, Yuri (Karlovich)
1899-1960 . . . . **CLC 8**
See also CA 85-88

Oliphant, Laurence
1829(?)-1888 . . . . **NCLC 47**
See also DLB 18, 166

Oliphant, Margaret (Oliphant Wilson)
1828-1897 . . . . **NCLC 11**
See also DLB 18, 159

Oliver, Mary 1935-. . . . . **CLC 19, 34, 98**
See also CA 21-24R; CANR 9, 43; DLB 5

Olivier, Laurence (Kerr)
1907-1989 . . . . **CLC 20**
See also CA 111; 150; 129

Olsen, Tillie
1913- . . . . . **CLC 4, 13; DA; DAB; DAC;
DAM MST; SSC 11**
See also CA 1-4R; CANR 1, 43; DLB 28;
DLBY 80; MTCW

Olson, Charles (John)
1910-1970 . . . . . **CLC 1, 2, 5, 6, 9, 11, 29;
DAM POET**
See also CA 13-16; 25-28R; CABS 2;
CANR 35; CAP 1; DLB 5, 16; MTCW

Olson, Toby 1937- . . . . CLC 28
See also CA 65-68; CANR 9, 31

Olyesha, Yuri
See Olesha, Yuri (Karlovich)

Ondaatje, (Philip) Michael
1943- . . . . CLC 14, 29, 51, 76; DAB;
DAC; DAM MST
See also CA 77-80; CANR 42; DLB 60

Oneal, Elizabeth 1934-
See Oneal, Zibby
See also CA 106; CANR 28; MAICYA;
SATA 30, 82

Oneal, Zibby . . . . CLC 30
See also Oneal, Elizabeth
See also AAYA 5; CLR 13; JRDA

O'Neill, Eugene (Gladstone)
1888-1953 . . . . . . TCLC 1, 6, 27, 49; DA;
DAB; DAC; DAM DRAM, MST; WLC
See also AITN 1; CA 110; 132;
CDALB 1929-1941; DLB 7; MTCW

Onetti, Juan Carlos
1909-1994 . . . . CLC 7, 10; DAM MULT,
NOV; SSC 23
See also CA 85-88; 145; CANR 32;
DLB 113; HW; MTCW

O Nuallain, Brian 1911-1966
See O'Brien, Flann
See also CA 21-22; 25-28R; CAP 2

Oppen, George 1908-1984 . . . . CLC 7, 13, 34
See also CA 13-16R; 113; CANR 8; DLB 5,
165

Oppenheim, E(dward) Phillips
1866-1946 . . . . TCLC 45
See also CA 111; DLB 70

Origen c. 185-c. 254 . . . . CMLC 19

Orlovitz, Gil 1918-1973 . . . . CLC 22
See also CA 77-80; 45-48; DLB 2, 5

Orris
See Ingelow, Jean

Ortega y Gasset, Jose
1883-1955 . . . . . TCLC 9; DAM MULT;
HLC
See also CA 106; 130; HW; MTCW

Ortese, Anna Maria 1914- . . . . CLC 89

Ortiz, Simon J(oseph)
1941- . . . . CLC 45; DAM MULT, POET
See also CA 134; DLB 120; NNAL

Orton, Joe . . . . CLC 4, 13, 43; DC 3
See also Orton, John Kingsley
See also CDBLB 1960 to Present; DLB 13

Orton, John Kingsley 1933-1967
See Orton, Joe
See also CA 85-88; CANR 35;
DAM DRAM; MTCW

Orwell, George
. . . . . TCLC 2, 6, 15, 31, 51; DAB; WLC
See also Blair, Eric (Arthur)
See also CDBLB 1945-1960; DLB 15, 98

Osborne, David
See Silverberg, Robert

Osborne, George
See Silverberg, Robert

Osborne, John (James)
1929-1994 . . . . . CLC 1, 2, 5, 11, 45; DA;
DAB; DAC; DAM DRAM, MST; WLC
See also CA 13-16R; 147; CANR 21;
CDBLB 1945-1960; DLB 13; MTCW

Osborne, Lawrence 1958- . . . . CLC 50

Oshima, Nagisa 1932- . . . . CLC 20
See also CA 116; 121

Oskison, John Milton
1874-1947 . . . . . TCLC 35; DAM MULT
See also CA 144; NNAL

Ossoli, Sarah Margaret (Fuller marchesa d')
1810-1850
See Fuller, Margaret
See also SATA 25

Ostrovsky, Alexander
1823-1886 . . . . NCLC 30, 57

Otero, Blas de 1916-1979 . . . . CLC 11
See also CA 89-92; DLB 134

Otto, Whitney 1955- . . . . CLC 70
See also CA 140

Ouida . . . . TCLC 43
See also De La Ramee, (Marie) Louise
See also DLB 18, 156

Ousmane, Sembene 1923- . . . . CLC 66; BLC
See also BW 1; CA 117; 125; MTCW

Ovid
43B.C.-18(?) . . . CMLC 7; DAM POET;
PC 2

Owen, Hugh
See Faust, Frederick (Schiller)

Owen, Wilfred (Edward Salter)
1893-1918 . . . . . . TCLC 5, 27; DA; DAB;
DAC; DAM MST, POET; WLC
See also CA 104; 141; CDBLB 1914-1945;
DLB 20

Owens, Rochelle 1936- . . . . CLC 8
See also CA 17-20R; CAAS 2; CANR 39

Oz, Amos
1939- . . . . CLC 5, 8, 11, 27, 33, 54;
DAM NOV
See also CA 53-56; CANR 27, 47; MTCW

Ozick, Cynthia
1928- . . . . CLC 3, 7, 28, 62; DAM NOV,
POP; SSC 15
See also BEST 90:1; CA 17-20R; CANR 23;
DLB 28, 152; DLBY 82; INT CANR-23;
MTCW

Ozu, Yasujiro 1903-1963 . . . . CLC 16
See also CA 112

Pacheco, C.
See Pessoa, Fernando (Antonio Nogueira)

Pa Chin . . . . CLC 18
See also Li Fei-kan

Pack, Robert 1929- . . . . CLC 13
See also CA 1-4R; CANR 3, 44; DLB 5

Padgett, Lewis
See Kuttner, Henry

Padilla (Lorenzo), Heberto 1932- . . . CLC 38
See also AITN 1; CA 123; 131; HW

Page, Jimmy 1944- . . . . CLC 12

Page, Louise 1955- . . . . CLC 40
See also CA 140

Page, P(atricia) K(athleen)
1916- . . . . CLC 7, 18; DAC; DAM MST;
PC 12
See also CA 53-56; CANR 4, 22; DLB 68;
MTCW

Page, Thomas Nelson 1853-1922 . . . . SSC 23
See also CA 118; DLB 12, 78; DLBD 13

Paget, Violet 1856-1935
See Lee, Vernon
See also CA 104

Paget-Lowe, Henry
See Lovecraft, H(oward) P(hillips)

Paglia, Camille (Anna) 1947- . . . . CLC 68
See also CA 140

Paige, Richard
See Koontz, Dean R(ay)

Pakenham, Antonia
See Fraser, (Lady) Antonia (Pakenham)

Palamas, Kostes 1859-1943 . . . . TCLC 5
See also CA 105

Palazzeschi, Aldo 1885-1974 . . . . CLC 11
See also CA 89-92; 53-56; DLB 114

Paley, Grace
1922- . . . . CLC 4, 6, 37; DAM POP;
SSC 8
See also CA 25-28R; CANR 13, 46;
DLB 28; INT CANR-13; MTCW

Palin, Michael (Edward) 1943- . . . . . CLC 21
See also Monty Python
See also CA 107; CANR 35; SATA 67

Palliser, Charles 1947- . . . . CLC 65
See also CA 136

Palma, Ricardo 1833-1919 . . . . TCLC 29

Pancake, Breece Dexter 1952-1979
See Pancake, Breece D'J
See also CA 123; 109

Pancake, Breece D'J . . . . CLC 29
See also Pancake, Breece Dexter
See also DLB 130

Panko, Rudy
See Gogol, Nikolai (Vasilyevich)

Papadiamantis, Alexandros
1851-1911 . . . . TCLC 29

Papadiamantopoulos, Johannes 1856-1910
See Moreas, Jean
See also CA 117

Papini, Giovanni 1881-1956 . . . . TCLC 22
See also CA 121

Paracelsus 1493-1541 . . . . LC 14

Parasol, Peter
See Stevens, Wallace

Parfenie, Maria
See Codrescu, Andrei

Parini, Jay (Lee) 1948- . . . . CLC 54
See also CA 97-100; CAAS 16; CANR 32

Park, Jordan
See Kornbluth, C(yril) M.; Pohl, Frederik

Parker, Bert
See Ellison, Harlan (Jay)

Parker, Dorothy (Rothschild)
1893-1967 . . . . CLC 15, 68;
DAM POET; SSC 2
See also CA 19-20; 25-28R; CAP 2;
DLB 11, 45, 86; MTCW

Parker, Robert B(rown)
1932- ...... CLC 27; DAM NOV, POP
See also BEST 89:4; CA 49-52; CANR 1,
26, 52; INT CANR-26; MTCW

Parkin, Frank 1940- .... CLC 43
See also CA 147

Parkman, Francis, Jr.
1823-1893 .... NCLC 12
See also DLB 1, 30

Parks, Gordon (Alexander Buchanan)
1912- ... CLC 1, 16; BLC; DAM MULT
See also AITN 2; BW 2; CA 41-44R;
CANR 26; DLB 33; SATA 8

Parnell, Thomas 1679-1718 .... LC 3
See also DLB 94

Parra, Nicanor
1914- ...... CLC 2; DAM MULT; HLC
See also CA 85-88; CANR 32; HW; MTCW

Parrish, Mary Frances
See Fisher, M(ary) F(rances) K(ennedy)

Parson
See Coleridge, Samuel Taylor

Parson Lot
See Kingsley, Charles

Partridge, Anthony
See Oppenheim, E(dward) Phillips

Pascal, Blaise 1623-1662 .... LC 35

Pascoli, Giovanni 1855-1912 ...... TCLC 45

Pasolini, Pier Paolo
1922-1975 .... CLC 20, 37
See also CA 93-96; 61-64; DLB 128;
MTCW

Pasquini
See Silone, Ignazio

Pastan, Linda (Olenik)
1932- .... CLC 27; DAM POET
See also CA 61-64; CANR 18, 40; DLB 5

Pasternak, Boris (Leonidovich)
1890-1960 ...... CLC 7, 10, 18, 63; DA;
DAB; DAC; DAM MST, NOV, POET;
PC 6; WLC
See also CA 127; 116; MTCW

Patchen, Kenneth
1911-1972 ... CLC 1, 2, 18; DAM POET
See also CA 1-4R; 33-36R; CANR 3, 35;
DLB 16, 48; MTCW

Pater, Walter (Horatio)
1839-1894 .... NCLC 7
See also CDBLB 1832-1890; DLB 57, 156

Paterson, A(ndrew) B(arton)
1864-1941 .... TCLC 32

Paterson, Katherine (Womeldorf)
1932- .... CLC 12, 30
See also AAYA 1; CA 21-24R; CANR 28;
CLR 7; DLB 52; JRDA; MAICYA;
MTCW; SATA 13, 53

Patmore, Coventry Kersey Dighton
1823-1896 .... NCLC 9
See also DLB 35, 98

Paton, Alan (Stewart)
1903-1988 ...... CLC 4, 10, 25, 55; DA;
DAB; DAC; DAM MST, NOV; WLC
See also CA 13-16; 125; CANR 22; CAP 1;
MTCW; SATA 11; SATA-Obit 56

Paton Walsh, Gillian 1937-
See Walsh, Jill Paton
See also CANR 38; JRDA; MAICYA;
SAAS 3; SATA 4, 72

Paulding, James Kirke 1778-1860 .. NCLC 2
See also DLB 3, 59, 74

Paulin, Thomas Neilson 1949-
See Paulin, Tom
See also CA 123; 128

Paulin, Tom .... CLC 37
See also Paulin, Thomas Neilson
See also DLB 40

Paustovsky, Konstantin (Georgievich)
1892-1968 .... CLC 40
See also CA 93-96; 25-28R

Pavese, Cesare
1908-1950 ..... TCLC 3; PC 13; SSC 19
See also CA 104; DLB 128

Pavic, Milorad 1929- .... CLC 60
See also CA 136

Payne, Alan
See Jakes, John (William)

Paz, Gil
See Lugones, Leopoldo

Paz, Octavio
1914- .... CLC 3, 4, 6, 10, 19, 51, 65;
DA; DAB; DAC; DAM MST, MULT,
POET; HLC; PC 1; WLC
See also CA 73-76; CANR 32; DLBY 90;
HW; MTCW

p'Bitek, Okot
1931-1982 .... CLC 96; BLC;
DAM MULT
See also BW 2; CA 124; 107; DLB 125;
MTCW

Peacock, Molly 1947- .... CLC 60
See also CA 103; CAAS 21; CANR 52;
DLB 120

Peacock, Thomas Love
1785-1866 .... NCLC 22
See also DLB 96, 116

Peake, Mervyn 1911-1968 .... CLC 7, 54
See also CA 5-8R; 25-28R; CANR 3;
DLB 15, 160; MTCW; SATA 23

Pearce, Philippa .... CLC 21
See also Christie, (Ann) Philippa
See also CLR 9; DLB 161; MAICYA;
SATA 1, 67

Pearl, Eric
See Elman, Richard

Pearson, T(homas) R(eid) 1956- .... CLC 39
See also CA 120; 130; INT 130

Peck, Dale 1967- .... CLC 81
See also CA 146

Peck, John 1941- .... CLC 3
See also CA 49-52; CANR 3

Peck, Richard (Wayne) 1934- ...... CLC 21
See also AAYA 1; CA 85-88; CANR 19,
38; CLR 15; INT CANR-19; JRDA;
MAICYA; SAAS 2; SATA 18, 55

Peck, Robert Newton
1928- .. CLC 17; DA; DAC; DAM MST
See also AAYA 3; CA 81-84; CANR 31;
JRDA; MAICYA; SAAS 1; SATA 21, 62

Peckinpah, (David) Sam(uel)
1925-1984 .... CLC 20
See also CA 109; 114

Pedersen, Knut 1859-1952
See Hamsun, Knut
See also CA 104; 119; MTCW

Peeslake, Gaffer
See Durrell, Lawrence (George)

Peguy, Charles Pierre
1873-1914 .... TCLC 10
See also CA 107

Pena, Ramon del Valle y
See Valle-Inclan, Ramon (Maria) del

Pendennis, Arthur Esquir
See Thackeray, William Makepeace

Penn, William 1644-1718 .... LC 25
See also DLB 24

Pepys, Samuel
1633-1703 ..... LC 11; DA; DAB; DAC;
DAM MST; WLC
See also CDBLB 1660-1789; DLB 101

Percy, Walker
1916-1990 .... CLC 2, 3, 6, 8, 14, 18, 47,
65; DAM NOV, POP
See also CA 1-4R; 131; CANR 1, 23;
DLB 2; DLBY 80, 90; MTCW

Perec, Georges 1936-1982 .... CLC 56
See also CA 141; DLB 83

Pereda (y Sanchez de Porrua), Jose Maria de
1833-1906 .... TCLC 16
See also CA 117

Pereda y Porrua, Jose Maria de
See Pereda (y Sanchez de Porrua), Jose
Maria de

Peregoy, George Weems
See Mencken, H(enry) L(ouis)

Perelman, S(idney) J(oseph)
1904-1979 ...... CLC 3, 5, 9, 15, 23, 44,
49; DAM DRAM
See also AITN 1, 2; CA 73-76; 89-92;
CANR 18; DLB 11, 44; MTCW

Peret, Benjamin 1899-1959 .... TCLC 20
See also CA 117

Peretz, Isaac Loeb 1851(?)-1915... TCLC 16
See also CA 109

Peretz, Yitzkhok Leibush
See Peretz, Isaac Loeb

Perez Galdos, Benito 1843-1920... TCLC 27
See also CA 125; 153; HW

Perrault, Charles 1628-1703 .... LC 2
See also MAICYA; SATA 25

Perry, Brighton
See Sherwood, Robert E(mmet)

Perse, St.-John .... CLC 4, 11, 46
See also Leger, (Marie-Rene Auguste) Alexis
Saint-Leger

Perutz, Leo 1882-1957 .... TCLC 60
See also DLB 81

Peseenz, Tulio F.
See Lopez y Fuentes, Gregorio

Pesetsky, Bette 1932- .... CLC 28
See also CA 133; DLB 130

Peshkov, Alexei Maximovich 1868-1936
See Gorky, Maxim
See also CA 105; 141; DA; DAC;
DAM DRAM, MST, NOV

Pessoa, Fernando (Antonio Nogueira)
1888-1935 . . . . **TCLC 27; HLC**
See also CA 125

Peterkin, Julia Mood 1880-1961. . . . **CLC 31**
See also CA 102; DLB 9

Peters, Joan K. 1945- . . . . **CLC 39**

Peters, Robert L(ouis) 1924- . . . . **CLC 7**
See also CA 13-16R; CAAS 8; DLB 105

Petofi, Sandor 1823-1849 . . . . **NCLC 21**

Petrakis, Harry Mark 1923- . . . . **CLC 3**
See also CA 9-12R; CANR 4, 30

Petrarch
1304-1374 . . . . **CMLC 20; DAM POET;**
PC 8

Petrov, Evgeny . . . . **TCLC 21**
See also Kataev, Evgeny Petrovich

Petry, Ann (Lane) 1908- . . . . . . **CLC 1, 7, 18**
See also BW 1; CA 5-8R; CAAS 6;
CANR 4, 46; CLR 12; DLB 76; JRDA;
MAICYA; MTCW; SATA 5

Petursson, Halligrimur 1614-1674 . . . . **LC 8**

Philips, Katherine 1632-1664 . . . . **LC 30**
See also DLB 131

Philipson, Morris H. 1926- . . . . **CLC 53**
See also CA 1-4R; CANR 4

Phillips, Caryl
1958- . . . . **CLC 96; DAM MULT**
See also BW 2; CA 141; DLB 157

Phillips, David Graham
1867-1911 . . . . **TCLC 44**
See also CA 108; DLB 9, 12

Phillips, Jack
See Sandburg, Carl (August)

Phillips, Jayne Anne
1952- . . . . **CLC 15, 33; SSC 16**
See also CA 101; CANR 24, 50; DLBY 80;
INT CANR-24; MTCW

Phillips, Richard
See Dick, Philip K(indred)

Phillips, Robert (Schaeffer) 1938- . . . **CLC 28**
See also CA 17-20R; CAAS 13; CANR 8;
DLB 105

Phillips, Ward
See Lovecraft, H(oward) P(hillips)

Piccolo, Lucio 1901-1969 . . . . **CLC 13**
See also CA 97-100; DLB 114

Pickthall, Marjorie L(owry) C(hristie)
1883-1922 . . . . **TCLC 21**
See also CA 107; DLB 92

Pico della Mirandola, Giovanni
1463-1494 . . . . **LC 15**

Piercy, Marge
1936- . . . . **CLC 3, 6, 14, 18, 27, 62**
See also CA 21-24R; CAAS 1; CANR 13,
43; DLB 120; MTCW

Piers, Robert
See Anthony, Piers

Pieyre de Mandiargues, Andre 1909-1991
See Mandiargues, Andre Pieyre de
See also CA 103; 136; CANR 22

Pilnyak, Boris . . . . **TCLC 23**
See also Vogau, Boris Andreyevich

Pincherle, Alberto
1907-1990 . . . . . **CLC 11, 18; DAM NOV**
See also Moravia, Alberto
See also CA 25-28R; 132; CANR 33;
MTCW

Pinckney, Darryl 1953- . . . . **CLC 76**
See also BW 2; CA 143

Pindar 518B.C.-446B.C. . . . . **CMLC 12**

Pineda, Cecile 1942- . . . . **CLC 39**
See also CA 118

Pinero, Arthur Wing
1855-1934 . . . . . **TCLC 32; DAM DRAM**
See also CA 110; 153; DLB 10

Pinero, Miguel (Antonio Gomez)
1946-1988 . . . . **CLC 4, 55**
See also CA 61-64; 125; CANR 29; HW

Pinget, Robert 1919- . . . . **CLC 7, 13, 37**
See also CA 85-88; DLB 83

Pink Floyd
See Barrett, (Roger) Syd; Gilmour, David;
Mason, Nick; Waters, Roger; Wright,
Rick

Pinkney, Edward 1802-1828 . . . . . **NCLC 31**

Pinkwater, Daniel Manus 1941- . . . . **CLC 35**
See also Pinkwater, Manus
See also AAYA 1; CA 29-32R; CANR 12,
38; CLR 4; JRDA; MAICYA; SAAS 3;
SATA 46, 76

Pinkwater, Manus
See Pinkwater, Daniel Manus
See also SATA 8

Pinsky, Robert
1940- . . **CLC 9, 19, 38, 94; DAM POET**
See also CA 29-32R; CAAS 4; DLBY 82

Pinta, Harold
See Pinter, Harold

Pinter, Harold
1930- . . . . . **CLC 1, 3, 6, 9, 11, 15, 27, 58,**
73; DA; DAB; DAC; DAM DRAM,
MST; WLC
See also CA 5-8R; CANR 33; CDBLB 1960
to Present; DLB 13; MTCW

Piozzi, Hester Lynch (Thrale)
1741-1821 . . . . **NCLC 57**
See also DLB 104, 142

Pirandello, Luigi
1867-1936 . . . . . . **TCLC 4, 29; DA; DAB;**
DAC; DAM DRAM, MST; DC 5;
SSC 22; WLC
See also CA 104; 153

Pirsig, Robert M(aynard)
1928- . . . . **CLC 4, 6, 73; DAM POP**
See also CA 53-56; CANR 42; MTCW;
SATA 39

Pisarev, Dmitry Ivanovich
1840-1868 . . . . **NCLC 25**

Pix, Mary (Griffith) 1666-1709 . . . . . . **LC 8**
See also DLB 80

Pixerecourt, Guilbert de
1773-1844 . . . . **NCLC 39**

Plaidy, Jean
See Hibbert, Eleanor Alice Burford

Planche, James Robinson
1796-1880 . . . . **NCLC 42**

Plant, Robert 1948- . . . . **CLC 12**

Plante, David (Robert)
1940- . . . . **CLC 7, 23, 38; DAM NOV**
See also CA 37-40R; CANR 12, 36;
DLBY 83; INT CANR-12; MTCW

Plath, Sylvia
1932-1963 . . . . . **CLC 1, 2, 3, 5, 9, 11, 14,**
17, 50, 51, 62; DA; DAB; DAC;
DAM MST, POET; PC 1; WLC
See also AAYA 13; CA 19-20; CANR 34;
CAP 2; CDALB 1941-1968; DLB 5, 6,
152; MTCW

Plato
428(?)B.C.-348(?)B.C. . . . . . **CMLC 8; DA;**
DAB; DAC; DAM MST

Platonov, Andrei . . . . **TCLC 14**
See also Klimentov, Andrei Platonovich

Platt, Kin 1911- . . . . **CLC 26**
See also AAYA 11; CA 17-20R; CANR 11;
JRDA; SAAS 17; SATA 21, 86

Plautus c. 251B.C.-184B.C. . . . . **DC 6**

Plick et Plock
See Simenon, Georges (Jacques Christian)

Plimpton, George (Ames) 1927- . . . . . **CLC 36**
See also AITN 1; CA 21-24R; CANR 32;
MTCW; SATA 10

Plomer, William Charles Franklin
1903-1973 . . . . **CLC 4, 8**
See also CA 21-22; CANR 34; CAP 2;
DLB 20, 162; MTCW; SATA 24

Plowman, Piers
See Kavanagh, Patrick (Joseph)

Plum, J.
See Wodehouse, P(elham) G(renville)

Plumly, Stanley (Ross) 1939- . . . . **CLC 33**
See also CA 108; 110; DLB 5; INT 110

Plumpe, Friedrich Wilhelm
1888-1931 . . . . **TCLC 53**
See also CA 112

Poe, Edgar Allan
1809-1849 . . . . **NCLC 1, 16, 55; DA;**
DAB; DAC; DAM MST, POET; PC 1;
SSC 1, 22; WLC
See also AAYA 14; CDALB 1640-1865;
DLB 3, 59, 73, 74; SATA 23

Poet of Titchfield Street, The
See Pound, Ezra (Weston Loomis)

Pohl, Frederik 1919- . . . . **CLC 18**
See also CA 61-64; CAAS 1; CANR 11, 37;
DLB 8; INT CANR-11; MTCW;
SATA 24

Poirier, Louis 1910-
See Gracq, Julien
See also CA 122; 126

Poitier, Sidney 1927- . . . . **CLC 26**
See also BW 1; CA 117

Polanski, Roman 1933- . . . . **CLC 16**
See also CA 77-80

Poliakoff, Stephen 1952- . . . . **CLC 38**
See also CA 106; DLB 13

Police, The
See Copeland, Stewart (Armstrong);
Summers, Andrew James; Sumner,
Gordon Matthew

Polidori, John William
1795-1821 .... **NCLC 51**
See also DLB 116

Pollitt, Katha 1949- .... **CLC 28**
See also CA 120; 122; MTCW

Pollock, (Mary) Sharon
1936- .... **CLC 50; DAC; DAM DRAM,
MST**
See also CA 141; DLB 60

Polo, Marco 1254-1324 .... **CMLC 15**

Polonsky, Abraham (Lincoln)
1910- .... **CLC 92**
See also CA 104; DLB 26; INT 104

Polybius c. 200B.C.-c. 118B.C. .... **CMLC 17**

Pomerance, Bernard
1940- .... **CLC 13; DAM DRAM**
See also CA 101; CANR 49

Ponge, Francis (Jean Gaston Alfred)
1899-1988 ..... **CLC 6, 18; DAM POET**
See also CA 85-88; 126; CANR 40

Pontoppidan, Henrik 1857-1943 ... **TCLC 29**

Poole, Josephine .... **CLC 17**
See also Helyar, Jane Penelope Josephine
See also SAAS 2; SATA 5

Popa, Vasko 1922-1991 .... **CLC 19**
See also CA 112; 148

Pope, Alexander
1688-1744 ...... **LC 3; DA; DAB; DAC;
DAM MST, POET; WLC**
See also CDBLB 1660-1789; DLB 95, 101

Porter, Connie (Rose) 1959(?)- ..... **CLC 70**
See also BW 2; CA 142; SATA 81

Porter, Gene(va Grace) Stratton
1863(?)-1924 .... **TCLC 21**
See also CA 112

Porter, Katherine Anne
1890-1980 ...... **CLC 1, 3, 7, 10, 13, 15,
27; DA; DAB; DAC; DAM MST, NOV;
SSC 4**
See also AITN 2; CA 1-4R; 101; CANR 1;
DLB 4, 9, 102; DLBD 12; DLBY 80;
MTCW; SATA 39; SATA-Obit 23

Porter, Peter (Neville Frederick)
1929- .... **CLC 5, 13, 33**
See also CA 85-88; DLB 40

Porter, William Sydney 1862-1910
See Henry, O.
See also CA 104; 131; CDALB 1865-1917;
DA; DAB; DAC; DAM MST; DLB 12,
78, 79; MTCW; YABC 2

Portillo (y Pacheco), Jose Lopez
See Lopez Portillo (y Pacheco), Jose

Post, Melville Davisson
1869-1930 .... **TCLC 39**
See also CA 110

Potok, Chaim
1929- .... **CLC 2, 7, 14, 26; DAM NOV**
See also AAYA 15; AITN 1, 2; CA 17-20R;
CANR 19, 35; DLB 28, 152;
INT CANR-19; MTCW; SATA 33

Potter, Beatrice
See Webb, (Martha) Beatrice (Potter)
See also MAICYA

Potter, Dennis (Christopher George)
1935-1994 .... **CLC 58, 86**
See also CA 107; 145; CANR 33; MTCW

Pound, Ezra (Weston Loomis)
1885-1972 ...... **CLC 1, 2, 3, 4, 5, 7, 10,
13, 18, 34, 48, 50; DA; DAB; DAC;
DAM MST, POET; PC 4; WLC**
See also CA 5-8R; 37-40R; CANR 40;
CDALB 1917-1929; DLB 4, 45, 63;
MTCW

Povod, Reinaldo 1959-1994 .... **CLC 44**
See also CA 136; 146

Powell, Adam Clayton, Jr.
1908-1972 .... **CLC 89; BLC;
DAM MULT**
See also BW 1; CA 102; 33-36R

Powell, Anthony (Dymoke)
1905- .... **CLC 1, 3, 7, 9, 10, 31**
See also CA 1-4R; CANR 1, 32;
CDBLB 1945-1960; DLB 15; MTCW

Powell, Dawn 1897-1965 .... **CLC 66**
See also CA 5-8R

Powell, Padgett 1952-............. **CLC 34**
See also CA 126

Power, Susan .... **CLC 91**

Powers, J(ames) F(arl)
1917- .... **CLC 1, 4, 8, 57; SSC 4**
See also CA 1-4R; CANR 2; DLB 130;
MTCW

Powers, John J(ames) 1945-
See Powers, John R.
See also CA 69-72

Powers, John R. .... **CLC 66**
See also Powers, John J(ames)

Powers, Richard (S.) 1957- .... **CLC 93**
See also CA 148

Pownall, David 1938-............. **CLC 10**
See also CA 89-92; CAAS 18; CANR 49;
DLB 14

Powys, John Cowper
1872-1963 .... **CLC 7, 9, 15, 46**
See also CA 85-88; DLB 15; MTCW

Powys, T(heodore) F(rancis)
1875-1953 .... **TCLC 9**
See also CA 106; DLB 36, 162

Prager, Emily 1952-............... **CLC 56**

Pratt, E(dwin) J(ohn)
1883(?)-1964 .... **CLC 19; DAC;
DAM POET**
See also CA 141; 93-96; DLB 92

Premchand..................... **TCLC 21**
See also Srivastava, Dhanpat Rai

Preussler, Otfried 1923-........... **CLC 17**
See also CA 77-80; SATA 24

Prevert, Jacques (Henri Marie)
1900-1977 .... **CLC 15**
See also CA 77-80; 69-72; CANR 29;
MTCW; SATA-Obit 30

Prevost, Abbe (Antoine Francois)
1697-1763 .... **LC 1**

Price, (Edward) Reynolds
1933- .... **CLC 3, 6, 13, 43, 50, 63;
DAM NOV; SSC 22**
See also CA 1-4R; CANR 1, 37; DLB 2;
INT CANR-37

Price, Richard 1949- .... **CLC 6, 12**
See also CA 49-52; CANR 3; DLBY 81

Prichard, Katharine Susannah
1883-1969 .... **CLC 46**
See also CA 11-12; CANR 33; CAP 1;
MTCW; SATA 66

Priestley, J(ohn) B(oynton)
1894-1984 .... **CLC 2, 5, 9, 34;
DAM DRAM, NOV**
See also CA 9-12R; 113; CANR 33;
CDBLB 1914-1945; DLB 10, 34, 77, 100,
139; DLBY 84; MTCW

Prince 1958(?)- .... **CLC 35**

Prince, F(rank) T(empleton) 1912- .. **CLC 22**
See also CA 101; CANR 43; DLB 20

Prince Kropotkin
See Kropotkin, Peter (Aleksieevich)

Prior, Matthew 1664-1721.......... **LC 4**
See also DLB 95

Pritchard, William H(arrison)
1932- .... **CLC 34**
See also CA 65-68; CANR 23; DLB 111

Pritchett, V(ictor) S(awdon)
1900- .... **CLC 5, 13, 15, 41;
DAM NOV; SSC 14**
See also CA 61-64; CANR 31; DLB 15,
139; MTCW

Private 19022
See Manning, Frederic

Probst, Mark 1925- .... **CLC 59**
See also CA 130

Prokosch, Frederic 1908-1989.... **CLC 4, 48**
See also CA 73-76; 128; DLB 48

Prophet, The
See Dreiser, Theodore (Herman Albert)

Prose, Francine 1947-............. **CLC 45**
See also CA 109; 112; CANR 46

Proudhon
See Cunha, Euclides (Rodrigues Pimenta) da

Proulx, E. Annie 1935- .... **CLC 81**

**Proust, (Valentin-Louis-George-Eugene-)
Marcel**
1871-1922 .... **TCLC 7, 13, 33; DA;
DAB; DAC; DAM MST, NOV; WLC**
See also CA 104; 120; DLB 65; MTCW

Prowler, Harley
See Masters, Edgar Lee

Prus, Boleslaw 1845-1912 .... **TCLC 48**

Pryor, Richard (Franklin Lenox Thomas)
1940- .... **CLC 26**
See also CA 122

Przybyszewski, Stanislaw
1868-1927 .... **TCLC 36**
See also DLB 66

Pteleon
See Grieve, C(hristopher) M(urray)
See also DAM POET

Puckett, Lute
See Masters, Edgar Lee

Puig, Manuel
1932-1990 . . . . CLC 3, 5, 10, 28, 65;
DAM MULT; HLC
See also CA 45-48; CANR 2, 32; DLB 113;
HW; MTCW

Purdy, Al(fred Wellington)
1918- . . . . CLC 3, 6, 14, 50; DAC;
DAM MST, POET
See also CA 81-84; CAAS 17; CANR 42;
DLB 88

Purdy, James (Amos)
1923- . . . . CLC 2, 4, 10, 28, 52
See also CA 33-36R; CAAS 1; CANR 19,
51; DLB 2; INT CANR-19; MTCW

Pure, Simon
See Swinnerton, Frank Arthur

Pushkin, Alexander (Sergeyevich)
1799-1837 . . . . . NCLC 3, 27; DA; DAB;
DAC; DAM DRAM, MST, POET;
PC 10; WLC
See also SATA 61

P'u Sung-ling 1640-1715 . . . . LC 3

Putnam, Arthur Lee
See Alger, Horatio, Jr.

Puzo, Mario
1920- . . . . . CLC 1, 2, 6, 36; DAM NOV,
POP
See also CA 65-68; CANR 4, 42; DLB 6;
MTCW

Pygge, Edward
See Barnes, Julian (Patrick)

Pym, Barbara (Mary Crampton)
1913-1980 . . . . CLC 13, 19, 37
See also CA 13-14; 97-100; CANR 13, 34;
CAP 1; DLB 14; DLBY 87; MTCW

Pynchon, Thomas (Ruggles, Jr.)
1937- . . . . . CLC 2, 3, 6, 9, 11, 18, 33, 62,
72; DA; DAB; DAC; DAM MST, NOV,
POP; SSC 14; WLC
See also BEST 90:2; CA 17-20R; CANR 22,
46; DLB 2, 173; MTCW

Qian Zhongshu
See Ch'ien Chung-shu

Qroll
See Dagerman, Stig (Halvard)

Quarrington, Paul (Lewis) 1953- . . . . CLC 65
See also CA 129

Quasimodo, Salvatore 1901-1968 . . . CLC 10
See also CA 13-16; 25-28R; CAP 1;
DLB 114; MTCW

Quay, Stephen 1947- . . . . CLC 95

Quay, The Brothers
See Quay, Stephen; Quay, Timothy

Quay, Timothy 1947- . . . . CLC 95

Queen, Ellery. . . . . CLC 3, 11
See also Dannay, Frederic; Davidson,
Avram; Lee, Manfred B(ennington);
Marlowe, Stephen; Sturgeon, Theodore
(Hamilton); Vance, John Holbrook

Queen, Ellery, Jr.
See Dannay, Frederic; Lee, Manfred
B(ennington)

Queneau, Raymond
1903-1976 . . . . CLC 2, 5, 10, 42
See also CA 77-80; 69-72; CANR 32;
DLB 72; MTCW

Quevedo, Francisco de 1580-1645. . . . LC 23

Quiller-Couch, Arthur Thomas
1863-1944 . . . . TCLC 53
See also CA 118; DLB 135, 153

Quin, Ann (Marie) 1936-1973 . . . . . . CLC 6
See also CA 9-12R; 45-48; DLB 14

Quinn, Martin
See Smith, Martin Cruz

Quinn, Peter 1947- . . . . CLC 91

Quinn, Simon
See Smith, Martin Cruz

Quiroga, Horacio (Sylvestre)
1878-1937 . . . . . TCLC 20; DAM MULT;
HLC
See also CA 117; 131; HW; MTCW

Quoirez, Francoise 1935-. . . . . CLC 9
See also Sagan, Francoise
See also CA 49-52; CANR 6, 39; MTCW

Raabe, Wilhelm 1831-1910 . . . . TCLC 45
See also DLB 129

Rabe, David (William)
1940- . . . . . . CLC 4, 8, 33; DAM DRAM
See also CA 85-88; CABS 3; DLB 7

Rabelais, Francois
1483-1553 . . . . . . LC 5; DA; DAB; DAC;
DAM MST; WLC

Rabinovitch, Sholem 1859-1916
See Aleichem, Sholom
See also CA 104

Rachilde 1860-1953 . . . . TCLC 67
See also DLB 123

Racine, Jean
1639-1699 . . . . LC 28; DAB; DAM MST

Radcliffe, Ann (Ward)
1764-1823 . . . . NCLC 6, 55
See also DLB 39

Radiguet, Raymond 1903-1923 . . . . TCLC 29
See also DLB 65

Radnoti, Miklos 1909-1944 . . . . TCLC 16
See also CA 118

Rado, James 1939- . . . . CLC 17
See also CA 105

Radvanyi, Netty 1900-1983
See Seghers, Anna
See also CA 85-88; 110

Rae, Ben
See Griffiths, Trevor

Raeburn, John (Hay) 1941-. . . . . CLC 34
See also CA 57-60

Ragni, Gerome 1942-1991 . . . . CLC 17
See also CA 105; 134

Rahv, Philip 1908-1973 . . . . CLC 24
See also Greenberg, Ivan
See also DLB 137

Raine, Craig 1944- . . . . CLC 32
See also CA 108; CANR 29, 51; DLB 40

Raine, Kathleen (Jessie) 1908- . . . CLC 7, 45
See also CA 85-88; CANR 46; DLB 20;
MTCW

Rainis, Janis 1865-1929 . . . . TCLC 29

Rakosi, Carl . . . . CLC 47
See also Rawley, Callman
See also CAAS 5

Raleigh, Richard
See Lovecraft, H(oward) P(hillips)

Raleigh, Sir Walter 1554(?)-1618 . . . . LC 31
See also CDBLB Before 1660; DLB 172

Rallentando, H. P.
See Sayers, Dorothy L(eigh)

Ramal, Walter
See de la Mare, Walter (John)

Ramon, Juan
See Jimenez (Mantecon), Juan Ramon

Ramos, Graciliano 1892-1953 . . . . . TCLC 32

Rampersad, Arnold 1941-. . . . . CLC 44
See also BW 2; CA 127; 133; DLB 111;
INT 133

Rampling, Anne
See Rice, Anne

Ramsay, Allan 1684(?)-1758 . . . . LC 29
See also DLB 95

Ramuz, Charles-Ferdinand
1878-1947 . . . . TCLC 33

Rand, Ayn
1905-1982 . . . . . . CLC 3, 30, 44, 79; DA;
DAC; DAM MST, NOV, POP; WLC
See also AAYA 10; CA 13-16R; 105;
CANR 27; MTCW

Randall, Dudley (Felker)
1914- . . . . . . CLC 1; BLC; DAM MULT
See also BW 1; CA 25-28R; CANR 23;
DLB 41

Randall, Robert
See Silverberg, Robert

Ranger, Ken
See Creasey, John

Ransom, John Crowe
1888-1974 . . . . CLC 2, 4, 5, 11, 24;
DAM POET
See also CA 5-8R; 49-52; CANR 6, 34;
DLB 45, 63; MTCW

Rao, Raja 1909- . . . CLC 25, 56; DAM NOV
See also CA 73-76; CANR 51; MTCW

Raphael, Frederic (Michael)
1931- . . . . CLC 2, 14
See also CA 1-4R; CANR 1; DLB 14

Ratcliffe, James P.
See Mencken, H(enry) L(ouis)

Rathbone, Julian 1935- . . . . CLC 41
See also CA 101; CANR 34

Rattigan, Terence (Mervyn)
1911-1977 . . . . CLC 7; DAM DRAM
See also CA 85-88; 73-76;
CDBLB 1945-1960; DLB 13; MTCW

Ratushinskaya, Irina 1954- . . . . CLC 54
See also CA 129

Raven, Simon (Arthur Noel)
1927- . . . . CLC 14
See also CA 81-84

Rawley, Callman 1903-
See Rakosi, Carl
See also CA 21-24R; CANR 12, 32

Rawlings, Marjorie Kinnan
1896-1953 . . . . TCLC 4
See also CA 104; 137; DLB 9, 22, 102;
JRDA; MAICYA; YABC 1

Rosa, Joao Guimaraes 1908-1967 . . . **CLC 23**
See also CA 89-92; DLB 113

Rose, Wendy
1948- . . . . **CLC 85; DAM MULT; PC 13**
See also CA 53-56; CANR 5, 51; NNAL;
SATA 12

Rosen, Richard (Dean) 1949- . . . . **CLC 39**
See also CA 77-80; INT CANR-30

Rosenberg, Isaac 1890-1918 . . . . . . **TCLC 12**
See also CA 107; DLB 20

Rosenblatt, Joe . . . . **CLC 15**
See also Rosenblatt, Joseph

Rosenblatt, Joseph 1933-
See Rosenblatt, Joe
See also CA 89-92; INT 89-92

Rosenfeld, Samuel 1896-1963
See Tzara, Tristan
See also CA 89-92

Rosenstock, Sami
See Tzara, Tristan

Rosenstock, Samuel
See Tzara, Tristan

Rosenthal, M(acha) L(ouis)
1917-1996 . . . . **CLC 28**
See also CA 1-4R; 152; CAAS 6; CANR 4,
51; DLB 5; SATA 59

Ross, Barnaby
See Dannay, Frederic

Ross, Bernard L.
See Follett, Ken(neth Martin)

Ross, J. H.
See Lawrence, T(homas) E(dward)

Ross, Martin
See Martin, Violet Florence
See also DLB 135

Ross, (James) Sinclair
1908- . . . . . . **CLC 13; DAC; DAM MST;**
SSC 24
See also CA 73-76; DLB 88

Rossetti, Christina (Georgina)
1830-1894 . . . . . **NCLC 2, 50; DA; DAB;**
DAC; DAM MST, POET; PC 7; WLC
See also DLB 35, 163; MAICYA; SATA 20

Rossetti, Dante Gabriel
1828-1882 . . . . **NCLC 4; DA; DAB;**
DAC; DAM MST, POET; WLC
See also CDBLB 1832-1890; DLB 35

Rossner, Judith (Perelman)
1935- . . . . **CLC 6, 9, 29**
See also AITN 2; BEST 90:3; CA 17-20R;
CANR 18, 51; DLB 6; INT CANR-18;
MTCW

Rostand, Edmond (Eugene Alexis)
1868-1918 . . . . . . **TCLC 6, 37; DA; DAB;**
DAC; DAM DRAM, MST
See also CA 104; 126; MTCW

Roth, Henry 1906-1995 . . . . **CLC 2, 6, 11**
See also CA 11-12; 149; CANR 38; CAP 1;
DLB 28; MTCW

Roth, Joseph 1894-1939 . . . . **TCLC 33**
See also DLB 85

Roth, Philip (Milton)
1933- . . . . . . **CLC 1, 2, 3, 4, 6, 9, 15, 22,**
31, 47, 66, 86; DA; DAB; DAC;
DAM MST, NOV, POP; WLC
See also BEST 90:3; CA 1-4R; CANR 1, 22,
36, 55; CDALB 1968-1988; DLB 2, 28,
173; DLBY 82; MTCW

Rothenberg, Jerome 1931- . . . . **CLC 6, 57**
See also CA 45-48; CANR 1; DLB 5

Roumain, Jacques (Jean Baptiste)
1907-1944 . . . . **TCLC 19; BLC;**
DAM MULT
See also BW 1; CA 117; 125

Rourke, Constance (Mayfield)
1885-1941 . . . . **TCLC 12**
See also CA 107; YABC 1

Rousseau, Jean-Baptiste 1671-1741 . . . **LC 9**

Rousseau, Jean-Jacques
1712-1778 . . . . **LC 14, 36; DA; DAB;**
DAC; DAM MST; WLC

Roussel, Raymond 1877-1933 . . . . . **TCLC 20**
See also CA 117

Rovit, Earl (Herbert) 1927- . . . . **CLC 7**
See also CA 5-8R; CANR 12

Rowe, Nicholas 1674-1718 . . . . **LC 8**
See also DLB 84

Rowley, Ames Dorrance
See Lovecraft, H(oward) P(hillips)

Rowson, Susanna Haswell
1762(?)-1824 . . . . **NCLC 5**
See also DLB 37

Roy, Gabrielle
1909-1983 . . . . **CLC 10, 14; DAB; DAC;**
DAM MST
See also CA 53-56; 110; CANR 5; DLB 68;
MTCW

Rozewicz, Tadeusz
1921- . . . . **CLC 9, 23; DAM POET**
See also CA 108; CANR 36; MTCW

Ruark, Gibbons 1941- . . . . **CLC 3**
See also CA 33-36R; CAAS 23; CANR 14,
31; DLB 120

Rubens, Bernice (Ruth) 1923- . . . **CLC 19, 31**
See also CA 25-28R; CANR 33; DLB 14;
MTCW

Rubin, Harold
See Robbins, Harold

Rudkin, (James) David 1936- . . . . . . **CLC 14**
See also CA 89-92; DLB 13

Rudnik, Raphael 1933- . . . . **CLC 7**
See also CA 29-32R

Ruffian, M.
See Hasek, Jaroslav (Matej Frantisek)

Ruiz, Jose Martinez . . . . **CLC 11**
See also Martinez Ruiz, Jose

Rukeyser, Muriel
1913-1980 . . . . **CLC 6, 10, 15, 27;**
DAM POET; PC 12
See also CA 5-8R; 93-96; CANR 26;
DLB 48; MTCW; SATA-Obit 22

Rule, Jane (Vance) 1931- . . . . **CLC 27**
See also CA 25-28R; CAAS 18; CANR 12;
DLB 60

Rulfo, Juan
1918-1986 . . . . **CLC 8, 80; DAM MULT;**
HLC
See also CA 85-88; 118; CANR 26;
DLB 113; HW; MTCW

Runeberg, Johan 1804-1877 . . . . . . **NCLC 41**

Runyon, (Alfred) Damon
1884(?)-1946 . . . . **TCLC 10**
See also CA 107; DLB 11, 86, 171

Rush, Norman 1933- . . . . **CLC 44**
See also CA 121; 126; INT 126

Rushdie, (Ahmed) Salman
1947- . . . . . **CLC 23, 31, 55; DAB; DAC;**
DAM MST, NOV, POP
See also BEST 89:3; CA 108; 111;
CANR 33; INT 111; MTCW

Rushforth, Peter (Scott) 1945- . . . . . **CLC 19**
See also CA 101

Ruskin, John 1819-1900 . . . . **TCLC 63**
See also CA 114; 129; CDBLB 1832-1890;
DLB 55, 163; SATA 24

Russ, Joanna 1937- . . . . **CLC 15**
See also CA 25-28R; CANR 11, 31; DLB 8;
MTCW

Russell, George William 1867-1935
See Baker, Jean H.
See also CA 104; 153; CDBLB 1890-1914;
DAM POET

Russell, (Henry) Ken(neth Alfred)
1927- . . . . **CLC 16**
See also CA 105

Russell, Willy 1947- . . . . **CLC 60**

Rutherford, Mark . . . . **TCLC 25**
See also White, William Hale
See also DLB 18

Ruyslinck, Ward 1929- . . . . **CLC 14**
See also Belser, Reimond Karel Maria de

Ryan, Cornelius (John) 1920-1974 . . . **CLC 7**
See also CA 69-72; 53-56; CANR 38

Ryan, Michael 1946- . . . . **CLC 65**
See also CA 49-52; DLBY 82

Rybakov, Anatoli (Naumovich)
1911- . . . . **CLC 23, 53**
See also CA 126; 135; SATA 79

Ryder, Jonathan
See Ludlum, Robert

Ryga, George
1932-1987 . . **CLC 14; DAC; DAM MST**
See also CA 101; 124; CANR 43; DLB 60

S. S.
See Sassoon, Siegfried (Lorraine)

Saba, Umberto 1883-1957 . . . . **TCLC 33**
See also CA 144; DLB 114

Sabatini, Rafael 1875-1950 . . . . **TCLC 47**

Sabato, Ernesto (R.)
1911- . . . . **CLC 10, 23; DAM MULT;**
HLC
See also CA 97-100; CANR 32; DLB 145;
HW; MTCW

Sacastru, Martin
See Bioy Casares, Adolfo

Sacher-Masoch, Leopold von
1836(?)-1895 . . . . **NCLC 31**

Author Index

Seferis, George .... CLC 5, 11
  See also Seferiades, Giorgos Stylianou

Segal, Erich (Wolf)
  1937- .... CLC 3, 10; DAM POP
  See also BEST 89:1; CA 25-28R; CANR 20,
  36; DLBY 86; INT CANR-20; MTCW

Seger, Bob 1945-................. CLC 35

Seghers, Anna .... CLC 7
  See also Radvanyi, Netty
  See also DLB 69

Seidel, Frederick (Lewis) 1936-..... CLC 18
  See also CA 13-16R; CANR 8; DLBY 84

Seifert, Jaroslav
  1901-1986 .... CLC 34, 44, 93
  See also CA 127; MTCW

Sei Shonagon c. 966-1017(?) ...... CMLC 6

Selby, Hubert, Jr.
  1928- .... CLC 1, 2, 4, 8; SSC 20
  See also CA 13-16R; CANR 33; DLB 2

Selzer, Richard 1928-............. CLC 74
  See also CA 65-68; CANR 14

Sembene, Ousmane
  See Ousmane, Sembene

Senancour, Etienne Pivert de
  1770-1846 .... NCLC 16
  See also DLB 119

Sender, Ramon (Jose)
  1902-1982 .. CLC 8; DAM MULT; HLC
  See also CA 5-8R; 105; CANR 8; HW;
  MTCW

Seneca, Lucius Annaeus
  4B.C.-65...... CMLC 6; DAM DRAM;
                                  DC 5

Senghor, Leopold Sedar
  1906- ..... CLC 54; BLC; DAM MULT,
                                  POET
  See also BW 2; CA 116; 125; CANR 47;
  MTCW

Serling, (Edward) Rod(man)
  1924-1975 .... CLC 30
  See also AAYA 14; AITN 1; CA 65-68;
  57-60; DLB 26

Serna, Ramon Gomez de la
  See Gomez de la Serna, Ramon

Serpieres
  See Guillevic, (Eugene)

Service, Robert
  See Service, Robert W(illiam)
  See also DAB; DLB 92

Service, Robert W(illiam)
  1874(?)-1958 ...... TCLC 15; DA; DAC;
                      DAM MST, POET; WLC
  See also Service, Robert
  See also CA 115; 140; SATA 20

Seth, Vikram
  1952- .... CLC 43, 90; DAM MULT
  See also CA 121; 127; CANR 50; DLB 120;
  INT 127

Seton, Cynthia Propper
  1926-1982 .... CLC 27
  See also CA 5-8R; 108; CANR 7

Seton, Ernest (Evan) Thompson
  1860-1946 .... TCLC 31
  See also CA 109; DLB 92; DLBD 13;
  JRDA; SATA 18

Seton-Thompson, Ernest
  See Seton, Ernest (Evan) Thompson

Settle, Mary Lee 1918- .... CLC 19, 61
  See also CA 89-92; CAAS 1; CANR 44;
  DLB 6; INT 89-92

Seuphor, Michel
  See Arp, Jean

Sevigne, Marie (de Rabutin-Chantal) Marquise
  de 1626-1696 .... LC 11

Sexton, Anne (Harvey)
  1928-1974 .... CLC 2, 4, 6, 8, 10, 15, 53;
       DA; DAB; DAC; DAM MST, POET;
                                  PC 2; WLC
  See also CA 1-4R; 53-56; CABS 2;
  CANR 3, 36; CDALB 1941-1968; DLB 5,
  169; MTCW; SATA 10

Shaara, Michael (Joseph, Jr.)
  1929-1988 .... CLC 15; DAM POP
  See also AITN 1; CA 102; 125; CANR 52;
  DLBY 83

Shackleton, C. C.
  See Aldiss, Brian W(ilson)

Shacochis, Bob .... CLC 39
  See also Shacochis, Robert G.

Shacochis, Robert G. 1951-
  See Shacochis, Bob
  See also CA 119; 124; INT 124

Shaffer, Anthony (Joshua)
  1926- .... CLC 19; DAM DRAM
  See also CA 110; 116; DLB 13

Shaffer, Peter (Levin)
  1926- ...... CLC 5, 14, 18, 37, 60; DAB;
                      DAM DRAM, MST
  See also CA 25-28R; CANR 25, 47;
  CDBLB 1960 to Present; DLB 13;
  MTCW

Shakey, Bernard
  See Young, Neil

Shalamov, Varlam (Tikhonovich)
  1907(?)-1982 .... CLC 18
  See also CA 129; 105

Shamlu, Ahmad 1925- .... CLC 10

Shammas, Anton 1951-............ CLC 55

Shange, Ntozake
  1948- .... CLC 8, 25, 38, 74; BLC;
                      DAM DRAM, MULT; DC 3
  See also AAYA 9; BW 2; CA 85-88;
  CABS 3; CANR 27, 48; DLB 38; MTCW

Shanley, John Patrick 1950-....... CLC 75
  See also CA 128; 133

Shapcott, Thomas W(illiam) 1935- .. CLC 38
  See also CA 69-72; CANR 49

Shapiro, Jane..................... CLC 76

Shapiro, Karl (Jay) 1913- .. CLC 4, 8, 15, 53
  See also CA 1-4R; CAAS 6; CANR 1, 36;
  DLB 48; MTCW

Sharp, William 1855-1905 .... TCLC 39
  See also DLB 156

Sharpe, Thomas Ridley 1928-
  See Sharpe, Tom
  See also CA 114; 122; INT 122

Sharpe, Tom..................... CLC 36
  See also Sharpe, Thomas Ridley
  See also DLB 14

Shaw, Bernard.................. TCLC 45
  See also Shaw, George Bernard
  See also BW 1

Shaw, G. Bernard
  See Shaw, George Bernard

Shaw, George Bernard
  1856-1950 ... TCLC 3, 9, 21; DA; DAB;
              DAC; DAM DRAM, MST; WLC
  See also Shaw, Bernard
  See also CA 104; 128; CDBLB 1914-1945;
  DLB 10, 57; MTCW

Shaw, Henry Wheeler
  1818-1885 .... NCLC 15
  See also DLB 11

Shaw, Irwin
  1913-1984 .... CLC 7, 23, 34;
                      DAM DRAM, POP
  See also AITN 1; CA 13-16R; 112;
  CANR 21; CDALB 1941-1968; DLB 6,
  102; DLBY 84; MTCW

Shaw, Robert 1927-1978 .... CLC 5
  See also AITN 1; CA 1-4R; 81-84;
  CANR 4; DLB 13, 14

Shaw, T. E.
  See Lawrence, T(homas) E(dward)

Shawn, Wallace 1943- .... CLC 41
  See also CA 112

Shea, Lisa 1953-................. CLC 86
  See also CA 147

Sheed, Wilfrid (John Joseph)
  1930-................ CLC 2, 4, 10, 53
  See also CA 65-68; CANR 30; DLB 6;
  MTCW

Sheldon, Alice Hastings Bradley
  1915(?)-1987
  See Tiptree, James, Jr.
  See also CA 108; 122; CANR 34; INT 108;
  MTCW

Sheldon, John
  See Bloch, Robert (Albert)

Shelley, Mary Wollstonecraft (Godwin)
  1797-1851 .... NCLC 14; DA; DAB;
              DAC; DAM MST, NOV; WLC
  See also CDBLB 1789-1832; DLB 110, 116,
  159; SATA 29

Shelley, Percy Bysshe
  1792-1822 .... NCLC 18; DA; DAB;
          DAC; DAM MST, POET; PC 14; WLC
  See also CDBLB 1789-1832; DLB 96, 110,
  158

Shepard, Jim 1956-............... CLC 36
  See also CA 137; SATA 90

Shepard, Lucius 1947- .... CLC 34
  See also CA 128; 141

Shepard, Sam
  1943- .... CLC 4, 6, 17, 34, 41, 44;
                      DAM DRAM; DC 5
  See also AAYA 1; CA 69-72; CABS 3;
  CANR 22; DLB 7; MTCW

Shepherd, Michael
  See Ludlum, Robert

Sherburne, Zoa (Morin) 1912-...... CLC 30
  See also AAYA 13; CA 1-4R; CANR 3, 37;
  MAICYA; SAAS 18; SATA 3

Sheridan, Frances 1724-1766........ LC 7
  See also DLB 39, 84

Somerville & Ross
See Martin, Violet Florence; Somerville, Edith

Sommer, Scott 1951- . . . . CLC 25
See also CA 106

Sondheim, Stephen (Joshua)
1930- . . . . CLC **30, 39; DAM DRAM**
See also AAYA 11; CA 103; CANR 47

Sontag, Susan
1933- . . . . CLC **1, 2, 10, 13, 31;**
DAM POP
See also CA 17-20R; CANR 25, 51; DLB 2, 67; MTCW

Sophocles
496(?)B.C.-406(?)B.C. . . . . CMLC **2; DA;**
DAB; DAC; DAM DRAM, MST; DC 1

Sordello 1189-1269 . . . . CMLC **15**

Sorel, Julia
See Drexler, Rosalyn

Sorrentino, Gilbert
1929- . . . . CLC **3, 7, 14, 22, 40**
See also CA 77-80; CANR 14, 33; DLB 5, 173; DLBY 80; INT CANR-14

Soto, Gary
1952- . . . . CLC **32, 80; DAM MULT;**
HLC
See also AAYA 10; CA 119; 125; CANR 50; CLR 38; DLB 82; HW; INT 125; JRDA; SATA 80

Soupault, Philippe 1897-1990 . . . . . . CLC **68**
See also CA 116; 147; 131

Souster, (Holmes) Raymond
1921- . . . CLC **5, 14; DAC; DAM POET**
See also CA 13-16R; CAAS 14; CANR 13, 29, 53; DLB 88; SATA 63

Southern, Terry 1924(?)-1995 . . . . CLC **7**
See also CA 1-4R; 150; CANR 1, 55; DLB 2

Southey, Robert 1774-1843 . . . . NCLC **8**
See also DLB 93, 107, 142; SATA 54

Southworth, Emma Dorothy Eliza Nevitte
1819-1899 . . . . NCLC **26**

Souza, Ernest
See Scott, Evelyn

Soyinka, Wole
1934- . . . . CLC **3, 5, 14, 36, 44; BLC;**
DA; DAB; DAC; DAM DRAM, MST,
MULT; DC 2; WLC
See also BW 2; CA 13-16R; CANR 27, 39; DLB 125; MTCW

Spackman, W(illiam) M(ode)
1905-1990 . . . . CLC **46**
See also CA 81-84; 132

Spacks, Barry (Bernard) 1931- . . . . . CLC **14**
See also CA 154; CANR 33; DLB 105

Spanidou, Irini 1946- . . . . CLC **44**

Spark, Muriel (Sarah)
1918- . . . . . CLC **2, 3, 5, 8, 13, 18, 40, 94;**
DAB; DAC; DAM MST, NOV; SSC 10
See also CA 5-8R; CANR 12, 36; CDBLB 1945-1960; DLB 15, 139; INT CANR-12; MTCW

Spaulding, Douglas
See Bradbury, Ray (Douglas)

Spaulding, Leonard
See Bradbury, Ray (Douglas)

Spence, J. A. D.
See Eliot, T(homas) S(tearns)

Spencer, Elizabeth 1921- . . . . CLC **22**
See also CA 13-16R; CANR 32; DLB 6; MTCW; SATA 14

Spencer, Leonard G.
See Silverberg, Robert

Spencer, Scott 1945- . . . . CLC **30**
See also CA 113; CANR 51; DLBY 86

Spender, Stephen (Harold)
1909-1995 . . . . . . CLC **1, 2, 5, 10, 41, 91;**
DAM POET
See also CA 9-12R; 149; CANR 31, 54; CDBLB 1945-1960; DLB 20; MTCW

Spengler, Oswald (Arnold Gottfried)
1880-1936 . . . . TCLC **25**
See also CA 118

Spenser, Edmund
1552(?)-1599 . . . . LC **5; DA; DAB; DAC;**
DAM MST, POET; PC 8; WLC
See also CDBLB Before 1660; DLB 167

Spicer, Jack
1925-1965 . . . . CLC **8, 18, 72;**
DAM POET
See also CA 85-88; DLB 5, 16

Spiegelman, Art 1948- . . . . CLC **76**
See also AAYA 10; CA 125; CANR 41, 55

Spielberg, Peter 1929- . . . . CLC **6**
See also CA 5-8R; CANR 4, 48; DLBY 81

Spielberg, Steven 1947- . . . . CLC **20**
See also AAYA 8; CA 77-80; CANR 32; SATA 32

Spillane, Frank Morrison 1918-
See Spillane, Mickey
See also CA 25-28R; CANR 28; MTCW; SATA 66

Spillane, Mickey . . . . CLC **3, 13**
See also Spillane, Frank Morrison

Spinoza, Benedictus de 1632-1677 . . . . LC **9**

Spinrad, Norman (Richard) 1940- . . . CLC **46**
See also CA 37-40R; CAAS 19; CANR 20; DLB 8; INT CANR-20

Spitteler, Carl (Friedrich Georg)
1845-1924 . . . . TCLC **12**
See also CA 109; DLB 129

Spivack, Kathleen (Romola Drucker)
1938- . . . . CLC **6**
See also CA 49-52

Spoto, Donald 1941- . . . . CLC **39**
See also CA 65-68; CANR 11

Springsteen, Bruce (F.) 1949- . . . . . . CLC **17**
See also CA 111

Spurling, Hilary 1940- . . . . CLC **34**
See also CA 104; CANR 25, 52

Spyker, John Howland
See Elman, Richard

Squires, (James) Radcliffe
1917-1993 . . . . CLC **51**
See also CA 1-4R; 140; CANR 6, 21

Srivastava, Dhanpat Rai 1880(?)-1936
See Premchand
See also CA 118

Stacy, Donald
See Pohl, Frederik

Stael, Germaine de
See Stael-Holstein, Anne Louise Germaine Necker Baronn
See also DLB 119

Stael-Holstein, Anne Louise Germaine Necker
Baronn 1766-1817 . . . . NCLC **3**
See also Stael, Germaine de

Stafford, Jean 1915-1979 . . . CLC **4, 7, 19, 68**
See also CA 1-4R; 85-88; CANR 3; DLB 2, 173; MTCW; SATA-Obit 22

Stafford, William (Edgar)
1914-1993 . . . CLC **4, 7, 29; DAM POET**
See also CA 5-8R; 142; CAAS 3; CANR 5, 22; DLB 5; INT CANR-22

Staines, Trevor
See Brunner, John (Kilian Houston)

Stairs, Gordon
See Austin, Mary (Hunter)

Stannard, Martin 1947- . . . . CLC **44**
See also CA 142; DLB 155

Stanton, Maura 1946- . . . . CLC **9**
See also CA 89-92; CANR 15; DLB 120

Stanton, Schuyler
See Baum, L(yman) Frank

Stapledon, (William) Olaf
1886-1950 . . . . TCLC **22**
See also CA 111; DLB 15

Starbuck, George (Edwin)
1931-1996 . . . . CLC **53; DAM POET**
See also CA 21-24R; 153; CANR 23

Stark, Richard
See Westlake, Donald E(dwin)

Staunton, Schuyler
See Baum, L(yman) Frank

Stead, Christina (Ellen)
1902-1983 . . . . CLC **2, 5, 8, 32, 80**
See also CA 13-16R; 109; CANR 33, 40; MTCW

Stead, William Thomas
1849-1912 . . . . TCLC **48**

Steele, Richard 1672-1729 . . . . LC **18**
See also CDBLB 1660-1789; DLB 84, 101

Steele, Timothy (Reid) 1948- . . . . CLC **45**
See also CA 93-96; CANR 16, 50; DLB 120

Steffens, (Joseph) Lincoln
1866-1936 . . . . TCLC **20**
See also CA 117

Stegner, Wallace (Earle)
1909-1993 . . . CLC **9, 49, 81; DAM NOV**
See also AITN 1; BEST 90:3; CA 1-4R; 141; CAAS 9; CANR 1, 21, 46; DLB 9; DLBY 93; MTCW

Stein, Gertrude
1874-1946 . . . . . . CLC **1, 6, 28, 48; DA;**
DAB; DAC; DAM MST, NOV, POET;
WLC
See also CA 104; 132; CDALB 1917-1929; DLB 4, 54, 86; MTCW

Steinbeck, John (Ernst)
1902-1968 ...... CLC 1, 5, 9, 13, 21, 34,
45, 75; DA; DAB; DAC; DAM DRAM,
MST, NOV; SSC 11; WLC
See also AAYA 12; CA 1-4R; 25-28R;
CANR 1, 35; CDALB 1929-1941; DLB 7,
9; DLBD 2; MTCW; SATA 9

Steinem, Gloria 1934-............. CLC 63
See also CA 53-56; CANR 28, 51; MTCW

Steiner, George
1929-............ CLC 24; DAM NOV
See also CA 73-76; CANR 31; DLB 67;
MTCW; SATA 62

Steiner, K. Leslie
See Delany, Samuel R(ay, Jr.)

Steiner, Rudolf 1861-1925........ TCLC 13
See also CA 107

Stendhal
1783-1842 .... NCLC 23, 46; DA; DAB;
DAC; DAM MST, NOV; WLC
See also DLB 119

Stephen, Leslie 1832-1904........ TCLC 23
See also CA 123; DLB 57, 144

Stephen, Sir Leslie
See Stephen, Leslie

Stephen, Virginia
See Woolf, (Adeline) Virginia

Stephens, James 1882(?)-1950...... TCLC 4
See also CA 104; DLB 19, 153, 162

Stephens, Reed
See Donaldson, Stephen R.

Steptoe, Lydia
See Barnes, Djuna

Sterchi, Beat 1949-............... CLC 65

Sterling, Brett
See Bradbury, Ray (Douglas); Hamilton,
Edmond

Sterling, Bruce 1954-............. CLC 72
See also CA 119; CANR 44

Sterling, George 1869-1926....... TCLC 20
See also CA 117; DLB 54

Stern, Gerald 1925- .... CLC 40
See also CA 81-84; CANR 28; DLB 105

Stern, Richard (Gustave) 1928-... CLC 4, 39
See also CA 1-4R; CANR 1, 25, 52;
DLBY 87; INT CANR-25

Sternberg, Josef von 1894-1969..... CLC 20
See also CA 81-84

Sterne, Laurence
1713-1768 ...... LC 2; DA; DAB; DAC;
DAM MST, NOV; WLC
See also CDBLB 1660-1789; DLB 39

Sternheim, (William Adolf) Carl
1878-1942 .... TCLC 8
See also CA 105; DLB 56, 118

Stevens, Mark 1951- .... CLC 34
See also CA 122

Stevens, Wallace
1879-1955 .... TCLC 3, 12, 45; DA;
DAB; DAC; DAM MST, POET; PC 6;
WLC
See also CA 104; 124; CDALB 1929-1941;
DLB 54; MTCW

Stevenson, Anne (Katharine)
1933- .... CLC 7, 33
See also CA 17-20R; CAAS 9; CANR 9, 33;
DLB 40; MTCW

Stevenson, Robert Louis (Balfour)
1850-1894 ..... NCLC 5, 14; DA; DAB;
DAC; DAM MST, NOV; SSC 11; WLC
See also CDBLB 1890-1914; CLR 10, 11;
DLB 18, 57, 141, 156, 174; DLBD 13;
JRDA; MAICYA; YABC 2

Stewart, J(ohn) I(nnes) M(ackintosh)
1906-1994 .... CLC 7, 14, 32
See also CA 85-88; 147; CAAS 3;
CANR 47; MTCW

Stewart, Mary (Florence Elinor)
1916- .... CLC 7, 35; DAB
See also CA 1-4R; CANR 1; SATA 12

Stewart, Mary Rainbow
See Stewart, Mary (Florence Elinor)

Stifle, June
See Campbell, Maria

Stifter, Adalbert 1805-1868...... NCLC 41
See also DLB 133

Still, James 1906-................ CLC 49
See also CA 65-68; CAAS 17; CANR 10,
26; DLB 9; SATA 29

Sting
See Sumner, Gordon Matthew

Stirling, Arthur
See Sinclair, Upton (Beall)

Stitt, Milan 1941-................ CLC 29
See also CA 69-72

Stockton, Francis Richard 1834-1902
See Stockton, Frank R.
See also CA 108; 137; MAICYA; SATA 44

Stockton, Frank R................ TCLC 47
See also Stockton, Francis Richard
See also DLB 42, 74; DLBD 13;
SATA-Brief 32

Stoddard, Charles
See Kuttner, Henry

Stoker, Abraham 1847-1912
See Stoker, Bram
See also CA 105; DA; DAC; DAM MST,
NOV; SATA 29

Stoker, Bram
1847-1912 .... TCLC 8; DAB; WLC
See also Stoker, Abraham
See also CA 150; CDBLB 1890-1914;
DLB 36, 70

Stolz, Mary (Slattery) 1920-....... CLC 12
See also AAYA 8; AITN 1; CA 5-8R;
CANR 13, 41; JRDA; MAICYA;
SAAS 3; SATA 10, 71

Stone, Irving
1903-1989 .... CLC 7; DAM POP
See also AITN 1; CA 1-4R; 129; CAAS 3;
CANR 1, 23; INT CANR-23; MTCW;
SATA 3; SATA-Obit 64

Stone, Oliver (William) 1946-...... CLC 73
See also AAYA 15; CA 110; CANR 55

Stone, Robert (Anthony)
1937- .... CLC 5, 23, 42
See also CA 85-88; CANR 23; DLB 152;
INT CANR-23; MTCW

Stone, Zachary
See Follett, Ken(neth Martin)

Stoppard, Tom
1937- ..... CLC 1, 3, 4, 5, 8, 15, 29, 34,
63, 91; DA; DAB; DAC; DAM DRAM,
MST; DC 6; WLC
See also CA 81-84; CANR 39;
CDBLB 1960 to Present; DLB 13;
DLBY 85; MTCW

Storey, David (Malcolm)
1933- ..... CLC 2, 4, 5, 8; DAM DRAM
See also CA 81-84; CANR 36; DLB 13, 14;
MTCW

Storm, Hyemeyohsts
1935- .... CLC 3; DAM MULT
See also CA 81-84; CANR 45; NNAL

Storm, (Hans) Theodor (Woldsen)
1817-1888 .... NCLC 1

Storni, Alfonsina
1892-1938 ..... TCLC 5; DAM MULT;
HLC
See also CA 104; 131; HW

Stout, Rex (Todhunter) 1886-1975 ... CLC 3
See also AITN 2; CA 61-64

Stow, (Julian) Randolph 1935-.. CLC 23, 48
See also CA 13-16R; CANR 33; MTCW

Stowe, Harriet (Elizabeth) Beecher
1811-1896 ..... NCLC 3, 50; DA; DAB;
DAC; DAM MST, NOV; WLC
See also CDALB 1865-1917; DLB 1, 12, 42,
74; JRDA; MAICYA; YABC 1

Strachey, (Giles) Lytton
1880-1932 .... TCLC 12
See also CA 110; DLB 149; DLBD 10

Strand, Mark
1934- .. CLC 6, 18, 41, 71; DAM POET
See also CA 21-24R; CANR 40; DLB 5;
SATA 41

Straub, Peter (Francis)
1943- .... CLC 28; DAM POP
See also BEST 89:1; CA 85-88; CANR 28;
DLBY 84; MTCW

Strauss, Botho 1944- .... CLC 22
See also DLB 124

Streatfeild, (Mary) Noel
1895(?)-1986 .... CLC 21
See also CA 81-84; 120; CANR 31;
CLR 17; DLB 160; MAICYA; SATA 20;
SATA-Obit 48

Stribling, T(homas) S(igismund)
1881-1965 .... CLC 23
See also CA 107; DLB 9

Strindberg, (Johan) August
1849-1912 ...... TCLC 1, 8, 21, 47; DA;
DAB; DAC; DAM DRAM, MST; WLC
See also CA 104; 135

Stringer, Arthur 1874-1950....... TCLC 37
See also DLB 92

Stringer, David
See Roberts, Keith (John Kingston)

Strugatskii, Arkadii (Natanovich)
1925-1991 .... CLC 27
See also CA 106; 135

Strugatskii, Boris (Natanovich)
1933- .... CLC 27
See also CA 106

Tate, Ellalice
See Hibbert, Eleanor Alice Burford

Tate, James (Vincent) 1943- ... **CLC 2, 6, 25**
See also CA 21-24R; CANR 29; DLB 5, 169

Tavel, Ronald 1940- .... **CLC 6**
See also CA 21-24R; CANR 33

Taylor, C(ecil) P(hilip) 1929-1981... **CLC 27**
See also CA 25-28R; 105; CANR 47

Taylor, Edward
1642(?)-1729 .... **LC 11; DA; DAB; DAC; DAM MST, POET**
See also DLB 24

Taylor, Eleanor Ross 1920- .... **CLC 5**
See also CA 81-84

Taylor, Elizabeth 1912-1975 ... **CLC 2, 4, 29**
See also CA 13-16R; CANR 9; DLB 139; MTCW; SATA 13

Taylor, Henry (Splawn) 1942- ...... **CLC 44**
See also CA 33-36R; CAAS 7; CANR 31; DLB 5

Taylor, Kamala (Purnaiya) 1924-
See Markandaya, Kamala
See also CA 77-80

Taylor, Mildred D. .... **CLC 21**
See also AAYA 10; BW 1; CA 85-88; CANR 25; CLR 9; DLB 52; JRDA; MAICYA; SAAS 5; SATA 15, 70

Taylor, Peter (Hillsman)
1917-1994 ..... **CLC 1, 4, 18, 37, 44, 50, 71; SSC 10**
See also CA 13-16R; 147; CANR 9, 50; DLBY 81, 94; INT CANR-9; MTCW

Taylor, Robert Lewis 1912- .... **CLC 14**
See also CA 1-4R; CANR 3; SATA 10

Tchekhov, Anton
See Chekhov, Anton (Pavlovich)

Teasdale, Sara 1884-1933 .... **TCLC 4**
See also CA 104; DLB 45; SATA 32

Tegner, Esaias 1782-1846 .... **NCLC 2**

Teilhard de Chardin, (Marie Joseph) Pierre
1881-1955 .... **TCLC 9**
See also CA 105

Temple, Ann
See Mortimer, Penelope (Ruth)

Tennant, Emma (Christina)
1937- .... **CLC 13, 52**
See also CA 65-68; CAAS 9; CANR 10, 38; DLB 14

Tenneshaw, S. M.
See Silverberg, Robert

Tennyson, Alfred
1809-1892 .... **NCLC 30; DA; DAB; DAC; DAM MST, POET; PC 6; WLC**
See also CDBLB 1832-1890; DLB 32

Teran, Lisa St. Aubin de .... **CLC 36**
See also St. Aubin de Teran, Lisa

Terence 195(?)B.C.-159B.C. ...... **CMLC 14**

Teresa de Jesus, St. 1515-1582 ...... **LC 18**

Terkel, Louis 1912-
See Terkel, Studs
See also CA 57-60; CANR 18, 45; MTCW

Terkel, Studs .... **CLC 38**
See also Terkel, Louis
See also AITN 1

Terry, C. V.
See Slaughter, Frank G(ill)

Terry, Megan 1932- .... **CLC 19**
See also CA 77-80; CABS 3; CANR 43; DLB 7

Tertz, Abram
See Sinyavsky, Andrei (Donatevich)

Tesich, Steve 1943(?)-1996 ...... **CLC 40, 69**
See also CA 105; 152; DLBY 83

Teternikov, Fyodor Kuzmich 1863-1927
See Sologub, Fyodor
See also CA 104

Tevis, Walter 1928-1984 .... **CLC 42**
See also CA 113

Tey, Josephine .... **TCLC 14**
See also Mackintosh, Elizabeth
See also DLB 77

Thackeray, William Makepeace
1811-1863 .... **NCLC 5, 14, 22, 43; DA; DAB; DAC; DAM MST, NOV; WLC**
See also CDBLB 1832-1890; DLB 21, 55, 159, 163; SATA 23

Thakura, Ravindranatha
See Tagore, Rabindranath

Tharoor, Shashi 1956- .... **CLC 70**
See also CA 141

Thelwell, Michael Miles 1939- ..... **CLC 22**
See also BW 2; CA 101

Theobald, Lewis, Jr.
See Lovecraft, H(oward) P(hillips)

Theodorescu, Ion N. 1880-1967
See Arghezi, Tudor
See also CA 116

Theriault, Yves
1915-1983 .. **CLC 79; DAC; DAM MST**
See also CA 102; DLB 88

Theroux, Alexander (Louis)
1939- .... **CLC 2, 25**
See also CA 85-88; CANR 20

Theroux, Paul (Edward)
1941- .... **CLC 5, 8, 11, 15, 28, 46; DAM POP**
See also BEST 89:4; CA 33-36R; CANR 20, 45; DLB 2; MTCW; SATA 44

Thesen, Sharon 1946- .... **CLC 56**

Thevenin, Denis
See Duhamel, Georges

Thibault, Jacques Anatole Francois
1844-1924
See France, Anatole
See also CA 106; 127; DAM NOV; MTCW

Thiele, Colin (Milton) 1920- .... **CLC 17**
See also CA 29-32R; CANR 12, 28, 53; CLR 27; MAICYA; SAAS 2; SATA 14, 72

Thomas, Audrey (Callahan)
1935- .... **CLC 7, 13, 37; SSC 20**
See also AITN 2; CA 21-24R; CAAS 19; CANR 36; DLB 60; MTCW

Thomas, D(onald) M(ichael)
1935- .... **CLC 13, 22, 31**
See also CA 61-64; CAAS 11; CANR 17, 45; CDBLB 1960 to Present; DLB 40; INT CANR-17; MTCW

Thomas, Dylan (Marlais)
1914-1953 ... **TCLC 1, 8, 45; DA; DAB; DAC; DAM DRAM, MST, POET; PC 2; SSC 3; WLC**
See also CA 104; 120; CDBLB 1945-1960; DLB 13, 20, 139; MTCW; SATA 60

Thomas, (Philip) Edward
1878-1917 ...... **TCLC 10; DAM POET**
See also CA 106; 153; DLB 19

Thomas, Joyce Carol 1938- .... **CLC 35**
See also AAYA 12; BW 2; CA 113; 116; CANR 48; CLR 19; DLB 33; INT 116; JRDA; MAICYA; MTCW; SAAS 7; SATA 40, 78

Thomas, Lewis 1913-1993 .... **CLC 35**
See also CA 85-88; 143; CANR 38; MTCW

Thomas, Paul
See Mann, (Paul) Thomas

Thomas, Piri 1928- .... **CLC 17**
See also CA 73-76; HW

Thomas, R(onald) S(tuart)
1913- .... **CLC 6, 13, 48; DAB; DAM POET**
See also CA 89-92; CAAS 4; CANR 30; CDBLB 1960 to Present; DLB 27; MTCW

Thomas, Ross (Elmore) 1926-1995 .. **CLC 39**
See also CA 33-36R; 150; CANR 22

Thompson, Francis Clegg
See Mencken, H(enry) L(ouis)

Thompson, Francis Joseph
1859-1907 .... **TCLC 4**
See also CA 104; CDBLB 1890-1914; DLB 19

Thompson, Hunter S(tockton)
1939- .... **CLC 9, 17, 40; DAM POP**
See also BEST 89:1; CA 17-20R; CANR 23, 46; MTCW

Thompson, James Myers
See Thompson, Jim (Myers)

Thompson, Jim (Myers)
1906-1977(?) .... **CLC 69**
See also CA 140

Thompson, Judith .... **CLC 39**

Thomson, James
1700-1748 ..... **LC 16, 29; DAM POET**
See also DLB 95

Thomson, James
1834-1882 ..... **NCLC 18; DAM POET**
See also DLB 35

Thoreau, Henry David
1817-1862 ..... **NCLC 7, 21; DA; DAB; DAC; DAM MST; WLC**
See also CDALB 1640-1865; DLB 1

Thornton, Hall
See Silverberg, Robert

Thucydides c. 455B.C.-399B.C. .... **CMLC 17**

Thurber, James (Grover)
1894-1961 .... **CLC 5, 11, 25; DA; DAB;
DAC; DAM DRAM, MST, NOV; SSC 1**
See also CA 73-76; CANR 17, 39;
CDALB 1929-1941; DLB 4, 11, 22, 102;
MAICYA; MTCW; SATA 13

Thurman, Wallace (Henry)
1902-1934 .... **TCLC 6; BLC;
DAM MULT**
See also BW 1; CA 104; 124; DLB 51

Ticheburn, Cheviot
See Ainsworth, William Harrison

Tieck, (Johann) Ludwig
1773-1853 .... **NCLC 5, 46**
See also DLB 90

Tiger, Derry
See Ellison, Harlan (Jay)

Tilghman, Christopher 1948(?)-..... **CLC 65**

Tillinghast, Richard (Williford)
1940- .... **CLC 29**
See also CA 29-32R; CAAS 23; CANR 26,
51

Timrod, Henry 1828-1867 .... **NCLC 25**
See also DLB 3

Tindall, Gillian 1938-.............. **CLC 7**
See also CA 21-24R; CANR 11

Tiptree, James, Jr. .... **CLC 48, 50**
See also Sheldon, Alice Hastings Bradley
See also DLB 8

Titmarsh, Michael Angelo
See Thackeray, William Makepeace

**Tocqueville, Alexis (Charles Henri Maurice
Clerel Comte)** 1805-1859..... **NCLC 7**

Tolkien, J(ohn) R(onald) R(euel)
1892-1973 .... **CLC 1, 2, 3, 8, 12, 38;
DA; DAB; DAC; DAM MST, NOV,
POP; WLC**
See also AAYA 10; AITN 1; CA 17-18;
45-48; CANR 36; CAP 2;
CDBLB 1914-1945; DLB 15, 160; JRDA;
MAICYA; MTCW; SATA 2, 32;
SATA-Obit 24

Toller, Ernst 1893-1939 .... **TCLC 10**
See also CA 107; DLB 124

Tolson, M. B.
See Tolson, Melvin B(eaunorus)

Tolson, Melvin B(eaunorus)
1898(?)-1966 .... **CLC 36; BLC;
DAM MULT, POET**
See also BW 1; CA 124; 89-92; DLB 48, 76

Tolstoi, Aleksei Nikolaevich
See Tolstoy, Alexey Nikolaevich

Tolstoy, Alexey Nikolaevich
1882-1945 .... **TCLC 18**
See also CA 107

Tolstoy, Count Leo
See Tolstoy, Leo (Nikolaevich)

Tolstoy, Leo (Nikolaevich)
1828-1910 ...... **TCLC 4, 11, 17, 28, 44;
DA; DAB; DAC; DAM MST, NOV;
SSC 9; WLC**
See also CA 104; 123; SATA 26

Tomasi di Lampedusa, Giuseppe 1896-1957
See Lampedusa, Giuseppe (Tomasi) di
See also CA 111

Tomlin, Lily .... **CLC 17**
See also Tomlin, Mary Jean

Tomlin, Mary Jean 1939(?)-
See Tomlin, Lily
See also CA 117

Tomlinson, (Alfred) Charles
1927- .... **CLC 2, 4, 6, 13, 45;
DAM POET**
See also CA 5-8R; CANR 33; DLB 40

Tonson, Jacob
See Bennett, (Enoch) Arnold

Toole, John Kennedy
1937-1969 .... **CLC 19, 64**
See also CA 104; DLBY 81

Toomer, Jean
1894-1967 ...... **CLC 1, 4, 13, 22; BLC;
DAM MULT; PC 7; SSC 1**
See also BW 1; CA 85-88;
CDALB 1917-1929; DLB 45, 51; MTCW

Torley, Luke
See Blish, James (Benjamin)

Tornimparte, Alessandra
See Ginzburg, Natalia

Torre, Raoul della
See Mencken, H(enry) L(ouis)

Torrey, E(dwin) Fuller 1937-....... **CLC 34**
See also CA 119

Torsvan, Ben Traven
See Traven, B.

Torsvan, Benno Traven
See Traven, B.

Torsvan, Berick Traven
See Traven, B.

Torsvan, Berwick Traven
See Traven, B.

Torsvan, Bruno Traven
See Traven, B.

Torsvan, Traven
See Traven, B.

Tournier, Michel (Edouard)
1924- .... **CLC 6, 23, 36, 95**
See also CA 49-52; CANR 3, 36; DLB 83;
MTCW; SATA 23

Tournimparte, Alessandra
See Ginzburg, Natalia

Towers, Ivar
See Kornbluth, C(yril) M.

Towne, Robert (Burton) 1936(?)-.... **CLC 87**
See also CA 108; DLB 44

Townsend, Sue 1946- .. **CLC 61; DAB; DAC**
See also CA 119; 127; INT 127; MTCW;
SATA 55; SATA-Brief 48

Townshend, Peter (Dennis Blandford)
1945- .... **CLC 17, 42**
See also CA 107

Tozzi, Federigo 1883-1920........ **TCLC 31**

Traill, Catharine Parr
1802-1899 .... **NCLC 31**
See also DLB 99

Trakl, Georg 1887-1914........... **TCLC 5**
See also CA 104

Transtroemer, Tomas (Goesta)
1931- .... **CLC 52, 65; DAM POET**
See also CA 117; 129; CAAS 17

Transtromer, Tomas Gosta
See Transtroemer, Tomas (Goesta)

Traven, B. (?)-1969............. **CLC 8, 11**
See also CA 19-20; 25-28R; CAP 2; DLB 9,
56; MTCW

Treitel, Jonathan 1959- .... **CLC 70**

Tremain, Rose 1943-.............. **CLC 42**
See also CA 97-100; CANR 44; DLB 14

Tremblay, Michel
1942- ...... **CLC 29; DAC; DAM MST**
See also CA 116; 128; DLB 60; MTCW

Trevanian .... **CLC 29**
See also Whitaker, Rod(ney)

Trevor, Glen
See Hilton, James

Trevor, William
1928- ..... **CLC 7, 9, 14, 25, 71; SSC 21**
See also Cox, William Trevor
See also DLB 14, 139

Trifonov, Yuri (Valentinovich)
1925-1981 .... **CLC 45**
See also CA 126; 103; MTCW

Trilling, Lionel 1905-1975 .... **CLC 9, 11, 24**
See also CA 9-12R; 61-64; CANR 10;
DLB 28, 63; INT CANR-10; MTCW

Trimball, W. H.
See Mencken, H(enry) L(ouis)

Tristan
See Gomez de la Serna, Ramon

Tristram
See Housman, A(lfred) E(dward)

Trogdon, William (Lewis) 1939-
See Heat-Moon, William Least
See also CA 115; 119; CANR 47; INT 119

Trollope, Anthony
1815-1882 ..... **NCLC 6, 33; DA; DAB;
DAC; DAM MST, NOV; WLC**
See also CDBLB 1832-1890; DLB 21, 57,
159; SATA 22

Trollope, Frances 1779-1863 ..... **NCLC 30**
See also DLB 21, 166

Trotsky, Leon 1879-1940........ **TCLC 22**
See also CA 118

Trotter (Cockburn), Catharine
1679-1749 .... **LC 8**
See also DLB 84

Trout, Kilgore
See Farmer, Philip Jose

Trow, George W. S. 1943-........ **CLC 52**
See also CA 126

Troyat, Henri 1911-.............. **CLC 23**
See also CA 45-48; CANR 2, 33; MTCW

Trudeau, G(arretson) B(eekman) 1948-
See Trudeau, Garry B.
See also CA 81-84; CANR 31; SATA 35

Trudeau, Garry B.................. **CLC 12**
See also Trudeau, G(arretson) B(eekman)
See also AAYA 10; AITN 2

Truffaut, Francois 1932-1984....... **CLC 20**
See also CA 81-84; 113; CANR 34

Trumbo, Dalton 1905-1976 .... **CLC 19**
See also CA 21-24R; 69-72; CANR 10;
DLB 26

Van Druten, John (William)
1901-1957 .... TCLC **2**
See also CA 104; DLB 10

Van Duyn, Mona (Jane)
1921- .... CLC **3, 7, 63; DAM POET**
See also CA 9-12R; CANR 7, 38; DLB 5

Van Dyne, Edith
See Baum, L(yman) Frank

van Itallie, Jean-Claude 1936-....... CLC **3**
See also CA 45-48; CAAS 2; CANR 1, 48;
DLB 7

van Ostaijen, Paul 1896-1928 ..... TCLC **33**

Van Peebles, Melvin
1932- .... CLC **2, 20; DAM MULT**
See also BW 2; CA 85-88; CANR 27

Vansittart, Peter 1920-........... CLC **42**
See also CA 1-4R; CANR 3, 49

Van Vechten, Carl 1880-1964 ...... CLC **33**
See also CA 89-92; DLB 4, 9, 51

Van Vogt, A(lfred) E(lton) 1912-..... CLC **1**
See also CA 21-24R; CANR 28; DLB 8;
SATA 14

Varda, Agnes 1928- .... CLC **16**
See also CA 116; 122

Vargas Llosa, (Jorge) Mario (Pedro)
1936-.... CLC **3, 6, 9, 10, 15, 31, 42, 85;**
DA; DAB; DAC; DAM MST, MULT,
NOV; HLC
See also CA 73-76; CANR 18, 32, 42;
DLB 145; HW; MTCW

Vasiliu, Gheorghe 1881-1957
See Bacovia, George
See also CA 123

Vassa, Gustavus
See Equiano, Olaudah

Vassilikos, Vassilis 1933-......... CLC **4, 8**
See also CA 81-84

Vaughan, Henry 1621-1695 .... LC **27**
See also DLB 131

Vaughn, Stephanie.................. CLC **62**

Vazov, Ivan (Minchov)
1850-1921 .... TCLC **25**
See also CA 121; DLB 147

Veblen, Thorstein (Bunde)
1857-1929 .... TCLC **31**
See also CA 115

Vega, Lope de 1562-1635 .... LC **23**

Venison, Alfred
See Pound, Ezra (Weston Loomis)

Verdi, Marie de
See Mencken, H(enry) L(ouis)

Verdu, Matilde
See Cela, Camilo Jose

Verga, Giovanni (Carmelo)
1840-1922 .... TCLC **3; SSC 21**
See also CA 104; 123

Vergil
70B.C.-19B.C...... CMLC **9; DA; DAB;**
DAC; DAM MST, POET; PC 12

Verhaeren, Emile (Adolphe Gustave)
1855-1916 .... TCLC **12**
See also CA 109

Verlaine, Paul (Marie)
1844-1896 .... NCLC **2, 51;**
DAM POET; PC 2

Verne, Jules (Gabriel)
1828-1905 .... TCLC **6, 52**
See also AAYA 16; CA 110; 131; DLB 123;
JRDA; MAICYA; SATA 21

Very, Jones 1813-1880........... NCLC **9**
See also DLB 1

Vesaas, Tarjei 1897-1970......... CLC **48**
See also CA 29-32R

Vialis, Gaston
See Simenon, Georges (Jacques Christian)

Vian, Boris 1920-1959 .... TCLC **9**
See also CA 106; DLB 72

Viaud, (Louis Marie) Julien 1850-1923
See Loti, Pierre
See also CA 107

Vicar, Henry
See Felsen, Henry Gregor

Vicker, Angus
See Felsen, Henry Gregor

Vidal, Gore
1925- ..... CLC **2, 4, 6, 8, 10, 22, 33, 72;**
DAM NOV, POP
See also AITN 1; BEST 90:2; CA 5-8R;
CANR 13, 45; DLB 6, 152;
INT CANR-13; MTCW

Viereck, Peter (Robert Edwin)
1916- .... CLC **4**
See also CA 1-4R; CANR 1, 47; DLB 5

Vigny, Alfred (Victor) de
1797-1863 ...... NCLC **7; DAM POET**
See also DLB 119

Vilakazi, Benedict Wallet
1906-1947 .... TCLC **37**

Villiers de l'Isle Adam, Jean Marie Mathias
Philippe Auguste Comte
1838-1889 .... NCLC **3; SSC 14**
See also DLB 123

Villon, Francois 1431-1463(?) .... PC **13**

Vinci, Leonardo da 1452-1519....... LC **12**

Vine, Barbara .... CLC **50**
See also Rendell, Ruth (Barbara)
See also BEST 90:4

Vinge, Joan D(ennison)
1948- .... CLC **30; SSC 24**
See also CA 93-96; SATA 36

Violis, G.
See Simenon, Georges (Jacques Christian)

Visconti, Luchino 1906-1976....... CLC **16**
See also CA 81-84; 65-68; CANR 39

Vittorini, Elio 1908-1966...... CLC **6, 9, 14**
See also CA 133; 25-28R

Vizinczey, Stephen 1933-......... CLC **40**
See also CA 128; INT 128

Vliet, R(ussell) G(ordon)
1929-1984 .... CLC **22**
See also CA 37-40R; 112; CANR 18

Vogau, Boris Andreyevich 1894-1937(?)
See Pilnyak, Boris
See also CA 123

Vogel, Paula A(nne) 1951-........ CLC **76**
See also CA 108

Voight, Ellen Bryant 1943-........ CLC **54**
See also CA 69-72; CANR 11, 29, 55;
DLB 120

Voigt, Cynthia 1942- .... CLC **30**
See also AAYA 3; CA 106; CANR 18, 37,
40; CLR 13; INT CANR-18; JRDA;
MAICYA; SATA 48, 79; SATA-Brief 33

Voinovich, Vladimir (Nikolaevich)
1932-.................... CLC **10, 49**
See also CA 81-84; CAAS 12; CANR 33;
MTCW

Vollmann, William T.
1959- ...... CLC **89; DAM NOV, POP**
See also CA 134

Voloshinov, V. N.
See Bakhtin, Mikhail Mikhailovich

Voltaire
1694-1778 ..... LC **14; DA; DAB; DAC;**
DAM DRAM, MST; SSC 12; WLC

von Bingen, Hildegard
1098(?)-1179 .... CMLC **20**

von Daeniken, Erich 1935- .... CLC **30**
See also AITN 1; CA 37-40R; CANR 17,
44

von Daniken, Erich
See von Daeniken, Erich

von Heidenstam, (Carl Gustaf) Verner
See Heidenstam, (Carl Gustaf) Verner von

von Heyse, Paul (Johann Ludwig)
See Heyse, Paul (Johann Ludwig von)

von Hofmannsthal, Hugo
See Hofmannsthal, Hugo von

von Horvath, Odon
See Horvath, Oedoen von

von Horvath, Oedoen
See Horvath, Oedoen von

von Liliencron, (Friedrich Adolf Axel) Detlev
See Liliencron, (Friedrich Adolf Axel)
Detlev von

Vonnegut, Kurt, Jr.
1922-..... CLC **1, 2, 3, 4, 5, 8, 12, 22,**
40, 60; DA; DAB; DAC; DAM MST,
NOV, POP; SSC 8; WLC
See also AAYA 6; AITN 1; BEST 90:4;
CA 1-4R; CANR 1, 25, 49;
CDALB 1968-1988; DLB 2, 8, 152;
DLBD 3; DLBY 80; MTCW

Von Rachen, Kurt
See Hubbard, L(afayette) Ron(ald)

von Rezzori (d'Arezzo), Gregor
See Rezzori (d'Arezzo), Gregor von

von Sternberg, Josef
See Sternberg, Josef von

Vorster, Gordon 1924-............ CLC **34**
See also CA 133

Vosce, Trudie
See Ozick, Cynthia

Voznesensky, Andrei (Andreievich)
1933-...... CLC **1, 15, 57; DAM POET**
See also CA 89-92; CANR 37; MTCW

Waddington, Miriam 1917-........ CLC **28**
See also CA 21-24R; CANR 12, 30;
DLB 68

Wagman, Fredrica 1937-........... CLC **7**
See also CA 97-100; INT 97-100

Watkins, Gloria 1955(?)-
See hooks, bell
See also BW 2; CA 143

Watkins, Paul 1964-............. **CLC 55**
See also CA 132

Watkins, Vernon Phillips
1906-1967 .... **CLC 43**
See also CA 9-10; 25-28R; CAP 1; DLB 20

Watson, Irving S.
See Mencken, H(enry) L(ouis)

Watson, John H.
See Farmer, Philip Jose

Watson, Richard F.
See Silverberg, Robert

Waugh, Auberon (Alexander) 1939-.. **CLC 7**
See also CA 45-48; CANR 6, 22; DLB 14

Waugh, Evelyn (Arthur St. John)
1903-1966 ...... **CLC 1, 3, 8, 13, 19, 27,
44; DA; DAB; DAC; DAM MST, NOV,
POP; WLC**
See also CA 85-88; 25-28R; CANR 22;
CDBLB 1914-1945; DLB 15, 162; MTCW

Waugh, Harriet 1944- .... **CLC 6**
See also CA 85-88; CANR 22

Ways, C. R.
See Blount, Roy (Alton), Jr.

Waystaff, Simon
See Swift, Jonathan

Webb, (Martha) Beatrice (Potter)
1858-1943 .... **TCLC 22**
See also Potter, Beatrice
See also CA 117

Webb, Charles (Richard) 1939-...... **CLC 7**
See also CA 25-28R

Webb, James H(enry), Jr. 1946-.... **CLC 22**
See also CA 81-84

Webb, Mary (Gladys Meredith)
1881-1927 .... **TCLC 24**
See also CA 123; DLB 34

Webb, Mrs. Sidney
See Webb, (Martha) Beatrice (Potter)

Webb, Phyllis 1927-............... **CLC 18**
See also CA 104; CANR 23; DLB 53

Webb, Sidney (James)
1859-1947 .... **TCLC 22**
See also CA 117

Webber, Andrew Lloyd............. **CLC 21**
See also Lloyd Webber, Andrew

Weber, Lenora Mattingly
1895-1971 .... **CLC 12**
See also CA 19-20; 29-32R; CAP 1;
SATA 2; SATA-Obit 26

Webster, John
1579(?)-1634(?) ...... **LC 33; DA; DAB;
DAC; DAM DRAM, MST; DC 2; WLC**
See also CDBLB Before 1660; DLB 58

Webster, Noah 1758-1843 .... **NCLC 30**

Wedekind, (Benjamin) Frank(lin)
1864-1918 ...... **TCLC 7; DAM DRAM**
See also CA 104; 153; DLB 118

Weidman, Jerome 1913-............ **CLC 7**
See also AITN 2; CA 1-4R; CANR 1;
DLB 28

Weil, Simone (Adolphine)
1909-1943 .... **TCLC 23**
See also CA 117

Weinstein, Nathan
See West, Nathanael

Weinstein, Nathan von Wallenstein
See West, Nathanael

Weir, Peter (Lindsay) 1944- .... **CLC 20**
See also CA 113; 123

Weiss, Peter (Ulrich)
1916-1982 .... **CLC 3, 15, 51;
DAM DRAM**
See also CA 45-48; 106; CANR 3; DLB 69,
124

Weiss, Theodore (Russell)
1916- .... **CLC 3, 8, 14**
See also CA 9-12R; CAAS 2; CANR 46;
DLB 5

Welch, (Maurice) Denton
1915-1948 .... **TCLC 22**
See also CA 121; 148

Welch, James
1940- ..... **CLC 6, 14, 52; DAM MULT,
POP**
See also CA 85-88; CANR 42; NNAL

Weldon, Fay
1933- .... **CLC 6, 9, 11, 19, 36, 59;
DAM POP**
See also CA 21-24R; CANR 16, 46;
CDBLB 1960 to Present; DLB 14;
INT CANR-16; MTCW

Wellek, Rene 1903-1995.......... **CLC 28**
See also CA 5-8R; 150; CAAS 7; CANR 8;
DLB 63; INT CANR-8

Weller, Michael 1942-......... **CLC 10, 53**
See also CA 85-88

Weller, Paul 1958-............... **CLC 26**

Wellershoff, Dieter 1925-.......... **CLC 46**
See also CA 89-92; CANR 16, 37

Welles, (George) Orson
1915-1985 .... **CLC 20, 80**
See also CA 93-96; 117

Wellman, Mac 1945- .... **CLC 65**

Wellman, Manly Wade 1903-1986 .. **CLC 49**
See also CA 1-4R; 118; CANR 6, 16, 44;
SATA 6; SATA-Obit 47

Wells, Carolyn 1869(?)-1942 ...... **TCLC 35**
See also CA 113; DLB 11

Wells, H(erbert) G(eorge)
1866-1946 .... **TCLC 6, 12, 19; DA;
DAB; DAC; DAM MST, NOV; SSC 6;
WLC**
See also AAYA 18; CA 110; 121;
CDBLB 1914-1945; DLB 34, 70, 156;
MTCW; SATA 20

Wells, Rosemary 1943-............ **CLC 12**
See also AAYA 13; CA 85-88; CANR 48;
CLR 16; MAICYA; SAAS 1; SATA 18,
69

Welty, Eudora
1909- ...... **CLC 1, 2, 5, 14, 22, 33; DA;
DAB; DAC; DAM MST, NOV; SSC 1;
WLC**
See also CA 9-12R; CABS 1; CANR 32;
CDALB 1941-1968; DLB 2, 102, 143;
DLBD 12; DLBY 87; MTCW

Wen I-to 1899-1946 .... **TCLC 28**

Wentworth, Robert
See Hamilton, Edmond

Werfel, Franz (V.) 1890-1945 ...... **TCLC 8**
See also CA 104; DLB 81, 124

Wergeland, Henrik Arnold
1808-1845 .... **NCLC 5**

Wersba, Barbara 1932-............ **CLC 30**
See also AAYA 2; CA 29-32R; CANR 16,
38; CLR 3; DLB 52; JRDA; MAICYA;
SAAS 2; SATA 1, 58

Wertmueller, Lina 1928- .... **CLC 16**
See also CA 97-100; CANR 39

Wescott, Glenway 1901-1987....... **CLC 13**
See also CA 13-16R; 121; CANR 23;
DLB 4, 9, 102

Wesker, Arnold
1932- .... **CLC 3, 5, 42; DAB;
DAM DRAM**
See also CA 1-4R; CAAS 7; CANR 1, 33;
CDBLB 1960 to Present; DLB 13;
MTCW

Wesley, Richard (Errol) 1945-....... **CLC 7**
See also BW 1; CA 57-60; CANR 27;
DLB 38

Wessel, Johan Herman 1742-1785 .... **LC 7**

West, Anthony (Panther)
1914-1987 .... **CLC 50**
See also CA 45-48; 124; CANR 3, 19;
DLB 15

West, C. P.
See Wodehouse, P(elham) G(renville)

West, (Mary) Jessamyn
1902-1984 .... **CLC 7, 17**
See also CA 9-12R; 112; CANR 27; DLB 6;
DLBY 84; MTCW; SATA-Obit 37

West, Morris L(anglo) 1916-..... **CLC 6, 33**
See also CA 5-8R; CANR 24, 49; MTCW

West, Nathanael
1903-1940 ..... **TCLC 1, 14, 44; SSC 16**
See also CA 104; 125; CDALB 1929-1941;
DLB 4, 9, 28; MTCW

West, Owen
See Koontz, Dean R(ay)

West, Paul 1930- .... **CLC 7, 14, 96**
See also CA 13-16R; CAAS 7; CANR 22,
53; DLB 14; INT CANR-22

West, Rebecca 1892-1983 .. **CLC 7, 9, 31, 50**
See also CA 5-8R; 109; CANR 19; DLB 36;
DLBY 83; MTCW

Westall, Robert (Atkinson)
1929-1993 .... **CLC 17**
See also AAYA 12; CA 69-72; 141;
CANR 18; CLR 13; JRDA; MAICYA;
SAAS 2; SATA 23, 69; SATA-Obit 75

Westlake, Donald E(dwin)
1933- .... **CLC 7, 33; DAM POP**
See also CA 17-20R; CAAS 13; CANR 16,
44; INT CANR-16

Westmacott, Mary
See Christie, Agatha (Mary Clarissa)

Weston, Allen
See Norton, Andre

Wetcheek, J. L.
See Feuchtwanger, Lion

Wetering, Janwillem van de
See van de Wetering, Janwillem

Wetherell, Elizabeth
See Warner, Susan (Bogert)

Whale, James 1889-1957 . . . . TCLC 63

Whalen, Philip 1923- . . . . CLC 6, 29
See also CA 9-12R; CANR 5, 39; DLB 16

Wharton, Edith (Newbold Jones)
1862-1937 . . . . . . TCLC 3, 9, 27, 53; DA;
DAB; DAC; DAM MST, NOV; SSC 6;
WLC
See also CA 104; 132; CDALB 1865-1917;
DLB 4, 9, 12, 78; DLBD 13; MTCW

Wharton, James
See Mencken, H(enry) L(ouis)

Wharton, William (a pseudonym)
. . . . CLC 18, 37
See also CA 93-96; DLBY 80; INT 93-96

Wheatley (Peters), Phillis
1754(?)-1784 . . . . LC 3; BLC; DA; DAC;
DAM MST, MULT, POET; PC 3; WLC
See also CDALB 1640-1865; DLB 31, 50

Wheelock, John Hall 1886-1978 . . . . CLC 14
See also CA 13-16R; 77-80; CANR 14;
DLB 45

White, E(lwyn) B(rooks)
1899-1985 . . CLC 10, 34, 39; DAM POP
See also AITN 2; CA 13-16R; 116;
CANR 16, 37; CLR 1, 21; DLB 11, 22;
MAICYA; MTCW; SATA 2, 29;
SATA-Obit 44

White, Edmund (Valentine III)
1940- . . . . CLC 27; DAM POP
See also AAYA 7; CA 45-48; CANR 3, 19,
36; MTCW

White, Patrick (Victor Martindale)
1912-1990 . . CLC 3, 4, 5, 7, 9, 18, 65, 69
See also CA 81-84; 132; CANR 43; MTCW

White, Phyllis Dorothy James 1920-
See James, P. D.
See also CA 21-24R; CANR 17, 43;
DAM POP; MTCW

White, T(erence) H(anbury)
1906-1964 . . . . CLC 30
See also CA 73-76; CANR 37; DLB 160;
JRDA; MAICYA; SATA 12

White, Terence de Vere
1912-1994 . . . . CLC 49
See also CA 49-52; 145; CANR 3

White, Walter F(rancis)
1893-1955 . . . . TCLC 15
See also White, Walter
See also BW 1; CA 115; 124; DLB 51

White, William Hale 1831-1913
See Rutherford, Mark
See also CA 121

Whitehead, E(dward) A(nthony)
1933- . . . . CLC 5
See also CA 65-68

Whitemore, Hugh (John) 1936- . . . . . CLC 37
See also CA 132; INT 132

Whitman, Sarah Helen (Power)
1803-1878 . . . . NCLC 19
See also DLB 1

Whitman, Walt(er)
1819-1892 . . . . . NCLC 4, 31; DA; DAB;
DAC; DAM MST, POET; PC 3; WLC
See also CDALB 1640-1865; DLB 3, 64;
SATA 20

Whitney, Phyllis A(yame)
1903- . . . . CLC 42; DAM POP
See also AITN 2; BEST 90:3; CA 1-4R;
CANR 3, 25, 38; JRDA; MAICYA;
SATA 1, 30

Whittemore, (Edward) Reed (Jr.)
1919- . . . . CLC 4
See also CA 9-12R; CAAS 8; CANR 4;
DLB 5

Whittier, John Greenleaf
1807-1892 . . . . NCLC 8
See also DLB 1

Whittlebot, Hernia
See Coward, Noel (Peirce)

Wicker, Thomas Grey 1926-
See Wicker, Tom
See also CA 65-68; CANR 21, 46

Wicker, Tom . . . . CLC 7
See also Wicker, Thomas Grey

Wideman, John Edgar
1941- . . . . CLC 5, 34, 36, 67; BLC;
DAM MULT
See also BW 2; CA 85-88; CANR 14, 42;
DLB 33, 143

Wiebe, Rudy (Henry)
1934- . . . . CLC 6, 11, 14; DAC;
DAM MST
See also CA 37-40R; CANR 42; DLB 60

Wieland, Christoph Martin
1733-1813 . . . . NCLC 17
See also DLB 97

Wiene, Robert 1881-1938 . . . . TCLC 56

Wieners, John 1934- . . . . CLC 7
See also CA 13-16R; DLB 16

Wiesel, Elie(zer)
1928- . . . . . . CLC 3, 5, 11, 37; DA; DAB;
DAC; DAM MST, NOV
See also AAYA 7; AITN 1; CA 5-8R;
CAAS 4; CANR 8, 40; DLB 83;
DLBY 87; INT CANR-8; MTCW;
SATA 56

Wiggins, Marianne 1947- . . . . CLC 57
See also BEST 89:3; CA 130

Wight, James Alfred 1916-
See Herriot, James
See also CA 77-80; SATA 55;
SATA-Brief 44

Wilbur, Richard (Purdy)
1921- . . . CLC 3, 6, 9, 14, 53; DA; DAB;
DAC; DAM MST, POET
See also CA 1-4R; CABS 2; CANR 2, 29;
DLB 5, 169; INT CANR-29; MTCW;
SATA 9

Wild, Peter 1940- . . . . CLC 14
See also CA 37-40R; DLB 5

Wilde, Oscar (Fingal O'Flahertie Wills)
1854(?)-1900 . . . . TCLC 1, 8, 23, 41; DA;
DAB; DAC; DAM DRAM, MST, NOV;
SSC 11; WLC
See also CA 104; 119; CDBLB 1890-1914;
DLB 10, 19, 34, 57, 141, 156; SATA 24

Wilder, Billy . . . . CLC 20
See also Wilder, Samuel
See also DLB 26

Wilder, Samuel 1906-
See Wilder, Billy
See also CA 89-92

Wilder, Thornton (Niven)
1897-1975 . . . . . . CLC 1, 5, 6, 10, 15, 35,
82; DA; DAB; DAC; DAM DRAM,
MST, NOV; DC 1; WLC
See also AITN 2; CA 13-16R; 61-64;
CANR 40; DLB 4, 7, 9; MTCW

Wilding, Michael 1942- . . . . CLC 73
See also CA 104; CANR 24, 49

Wiley, Richard 1944- . . . . CLC 44
See also CA 121; 129

Wilhelm, Kate . . . . CLC 7
See also Wilhelm, Katie Gertrude
See also CAAS 5; DLB 8; INT CANR-17

Wilhelm, Katie Gertrude 1928-
See Wilhelm, Kate
See also CA 37-40R; CANR 17, 36; MTCW

Wilkins, Mary
See Freeman, Mary Eleanor Wilkins

Willard, Nancy 1936- . . . . CLC 7, 37
See also CA 89-92; CANR 10, 39; CLR 5;
DLB 5, 52; MAICYA; MTCW;
SATA 37, 71; SATA-Brief 30

Williams, C(harles) K(enneth)
1936- . . . . CLC 33, 56; DAM POET
See also CA 37-40R; DLB 5

Williams, Charles
See Collier, James L(incoln)

Williams, Charles (Walter Stansby)
1886-1945 . . . . TCLC 1, 11
See also CA 104; DLB 100, 153

Williams, (George) Emlyn
1905-1987 . . . . . . CLC 15; DAM DRAM
See also CA 104; 123; CANR 36; DLB 10,
77; MTCW

Williams, Hugo 1942- . . . . CLC 42
See also CA 17-20R; CANR 45; DLB 40

Williams, J. Walker
See Wodehouse, P(elham) G(renville)

Williams, John A(lfred)
1925- . . . CLC 5, 13; BLC; DAM MULT
See also BW 2; CA 53-56; CAAS 3;
CANR 6, 26, 51; DLB 2, 33;
INT CANR-6

Williams, Jonathan (Chamberlain)
1929- . . . . CLC 13
See also CA 9-12R; CAAS 12; CANR 8;
DLB 5

Williams, Joy 1944- . . . . CLC 31
See also CA 41-44R; CANR 22, 48

Williams, Norman 1952- . . . . CLC 39
See also CA 118

Williams, Sherley Anne
1944- . . . . . CLC 89; BLC; DAM MULT,
POET
See also BW 2; CA 73-76; CANR 25;
DLB 41; INT CANR-25; SATA 78

Williams, Shirley
See Williams, Sherley Anne

Williams, Tennessee
1911-1983 ..... **CLC 1, 2, 5, 7, 8, 11, 15,
19, 30, 39, 45, 71; DA; DAB; DAC;
DAM DRAM, MST; DC 4; WLC**
See also AITN 1, 2; CA 5-8R; 108;
CABS 3; CANR 31; CDALB 1941-1968;
DLB 7; DLBD 4; DLBY 83; MTCW

Williams, Thomas (Alonzo)
1926-1990 .... **CLC 14**
See also CA 1-4R; 132; CANR 2

Williams, William C.
See Williams, William Carlos

Williams, William Carlos
1883-1963 .... **CLC 1, 2, 5, 9, 13, 22, 42,
67; DA; DAB; DAC; DAM MST, POET;
PC 7**
See also CA 89-92; CANR 34;
CDALB 1917-1929; DLB 4, 16, 54, 86;
MTCW

Williamson, David (Keith) 1942-.... **CLC 56**
See also CA 103; CANR 41

Williamson, Ellen Douglas 1905-1984
See Douglas, Ellen
See also CA 17-20R; 114; CANR 39

Williamson, Jack.................. **CLC 29**
See also Williamson, John Stewart
See also CAAS 8; DLB 8

Williamson, John Stewart 1908-
See Williamson, Jack
See also CA 17-20R; CANR 23

Willie, Frederick
See Lovecraft, H(oward) P(hillips)

Willingham, Calder (Baynard, Jr.)
1922-1995 .... **CLC 5, 51**
See also CA 5-8R; 147; CANR 3; DLB 2,
44; MTCW

Willis, Charles
See Clarke, Arthur C(harles)

Willy
See Colette, (Sidonie-Gabrielle)

Willy, Colette
See Colette, (Sidonie-Gabrielle)

Wilson, A(ndrew) N(orman) 1950- .. **CLC 33**
See also CA 112; 122; DLB 14, 155

Wilson, Angus (Frank Johnstone)
1913-1991 .. **CLC 2, 3, 5, 25, 34; SSC 21**
See also CA 5-8R; 134; CANR 21; DLB 15,
139, 155; MTCW

Wilson, August
1945- .... **CLC 39, 50, 63; BLC; DA;
DAB; DAC; DAM DRAM, MST,
MULT; DC 2**
See also AAYA 16; BW 2; CA 115; 122;
CANR 42, 54; MTCW

Wilson, Brian 1942-.............. **CLC 12**

Wilson, Colin 1931- .... **CLC 3, 14**
See also CA 1-4R; CAAS 5; CANR 1, 22,
33; DLB 14; MTCW

Wilson, Dirk
See Pohl, Frederik

Wilson, Edmund
1895-1972 .... **CLC 1, 2, 3, 8, 24**
See also CA 1-4R; 37-40R; CANR 1, 46;
DLB 63; MTCW

Wilson, Ethel Davis (Bryant)
1888(?)-1980 .... **CLC 13; DAC;
DAM POET**
See also CA 102; DLB 68; MTCW

Wilson, John 1785-1854.......... **NCLC 5**

Wilson, John (Anthony) Burgess 1917-1993
See Burgess, Anthony
See also CA 1-4R; 143; CANR 2, 46; DAC;
DAM NOV; MTCW

Wilson, Lanford
1937- ..... **CLC 7, 14, 36; DAM DRAM**
See also CA 17-20R; CABS 3; CANR 45;
DLB 7

Wilson, Robert M. 1944-......... **CLC 7, 9**
See also CA 49-52; CANR 2, 41; MTCW

Wilson, Robert McLiam 1964- ..... **CLC 59**
See also CA 132

Wilson, Sloan 1920-.............. **CLC 32**
See also CA 1-4R; CANR 1, 44

Wilson, Snoo 1948-.............. **CLC 33**
See also CA 69-72

Wilson, William S(mith) 1932- ..... **CLC 49**
See also CA 81-84

Winchilsea, Anne (Kingsmill) Finch Counte
1661-1720 .... **LC 3**

Windham, Basil
See Wodehouse, P(elham) G(renville)

Wingrove, David (John) 1954-...... **CLC 68**
See also CA 133

Winters, Janet Lewis .... **CLC 41**
See also Lewis, Janet
See also DLBY 87

Winters, (Arthur) Yvor
1900-1968 .... **CLC 4, 8, 32**
See also CA 11-12; 25-28R; CAP 1;
DLB 48; MTCW

Winterson, Jeanette
1959- .... **CLC 64; DAM POP**
See also CA 136

Winthrop, John 1588-1649.......... **LC 31**
See also DLB 24, 30

Wiseman, Frederick 1930-......... **CLC 20**

Wister, Owen 1860-1938 .... **TCLC 21**
See also CA 108; DLB 9, 78; SATA 62

Witkacy
See Witkiewicz, Stanislaw Ignacy

Witkiewicz, Stanislaw Ignacy
1885-1939 .... **TCLC 8**
See also CA 105

Wittgenstein, Ludwig (Josef Johann)
1889-1951 .... **TCLC 59**
See also CA 113

Wittig, Monique 1935(?)-.......... **CLC 22**
See also CA 116; 135; DLB 83

Wittlin, Jozef 1896-1976 .... **CLC 25**
See also CA 49-52; 65-68; CANR 3

Wodehouse, P(elham) G(renville)
1881-1975 ... **CLC 1, 2, 5, 10, 22; DAB;
DAC; DAM NOV; SSC 2**
See also AITN 2; CA 45-48; 57-60;
CANR 3, 33; CDBLB 1914-1945;
DLB 34, 162; MTCW; SATA 22

Woiwode, L.
See Woiwode, Larry (Alfred)

Woiwode, Larry (Alfred) 1941-... **CLC 6, 10**
See also CA 73-76; CANR 16; DLB 6;
INT CANR-16

Wojciechowska, Maia (Teresa)
1927- .... **CLC 26**
See also AAYA 8; CA 9-12R; CANR 4, 41;
CLR 1; JRDA; MAICYA; SAAS 1;
SATA 1, 28, 83

Wolf, Christa 1929- .... **CLC 14, 29, 58**
See also CA 85-88; CANR 45; DLB 75;
MTCW

Wolfe, Gene (Rodman)
1931- .... **CLC 25; DAM POP**
See also CA 57-60; CAAS 9; CANR 6, 32;
DLB 8

Wolfe, George C. 1954-........... **CLC 49**
See also CA 149

Wolfe, Thomas (Clayton)
1900-1938 ..... **TCLC 4, 13, 29, 61; DA;
DAB; DAC; DAM MST, NOV; WLC**
See also CA 104; 132; CDALB 1929-1941;
DLB 9, 102; DLBD 2; DLBY 85; MTCW

Wolfe, Thomas Kennerly, Jr. 1931-
See Wolfe, Tom
See also CA 13-16R; CANR 9, 33;
DAM POP; INT CANR-9; MTCW

Wolfe, Tom .... **CLC 1, 2, 9, 15, 35, 51**
See also Wolfe, Thomas Kennerly, Jr.
See also AAYA 8; AITN 2; BEST 89:1;
DLB 152

Wolff, Geoffrey (Ansell) 1937- ..... **CLC 41**
See also CA 29-32R; CANR 29, 43

Wolff, Sonia
See Levitin, Sonia (Wolff)

Wolff, Tobias (Jonathan Ansell)
1945-...................... **CLC 39, 64**
See also AAYA 16; BEST 90:2; CA 114;
117; CAAS 22; CANR 54; DLB 130;
INT 117

Wolfram von Eschenbach
c. 1170-c. 1220 .... **CMLC 5**
See also DLB 138

Wolitzer, Hilma 1930-............. **CLC 17**
See also CA 65-68; CANR 18, 40;
INT CANR-18; SATA 31

Wollstonecraft, Mary 1759-1797...... **LC 5**
See also CDBLB 1789-1832; DLB 39, 104,
158

Wonder, Stevie .... **CLC 12**
See also Morris, Steveland Judkins

Wong, Jade Snow 1922-........... **CLC 17**
See also CA 109

Woodcott, Keith
See Brunner, John (Kilian Houston)

Woodruff, Robert W.
See Mencken, H(enry) L(ouis)

Woolf, (Adeline) Virginia
1882-1941 .... **TCLC 1, 5, 20, 43, 56;
DA; DAB; DAC; DAM MST, NOV;
SSC 7; WLC**
See also CA 104; 130; CDBLB 1914-1945;
DLB 36, 100, 162; DLBD 10; MTCW

Woollcott, Alexander (Humphreys)
1887-1943 .... **TCLC 5**
See also CA 105; DLB 29

Woolrich, Cornell 1903-1968 . . . . . . **CLC 77**
See also Hopley-Woolrich, Cornell George

Wordsworth, Dorothy
1771-1855 . . . . **NCLC 25**
See also DLB 107

Wordsworth, William
1770-1850 . . . . **NCLC 12, 38; DA; DAB;**
DAC; DAM MST, POET; PC 4; WLC
See also CDBLB 1789-1832; DLB 93, 107

Wouk, Herman
1915- . . **CLC 1, 9, 38; DAM NOV, POP**
See also CA 5-8R; CANR 6, 33; DLBY 82;
INT CANR-6; MTCW

Wright, Charles (Penzel, Jr.)
1935- . . . . **CLC 6, 13, 28**
See also CA 29-32R; CAAS 7; CANR 23,
36; DLB 165; DLBY 82; MTCW

Wright, Charles Stevenson
1932- . . . . **CLC 49; BLC 3;**
DAM MULT, POET
See also BW 1; CA 9-12R; CANR 26;
DLB 33

Wright, Jack R.
See Harris, Mark

Wright, James (Arlington)
1927-1980 . . . . **CLC 3, 5, 10, 28;**
DAM POET
See also AITN 2; CA 49-52; 97-100;
CANR 4, 34; DLB 5, 169; MTCW

Wright, Judith (Arandell)
1915- . . . . **CLC 11, 53; PC 14**
See also CA 13-16R; CANR 31; MTCW;
SATA 14

Wright, L(aurali) R. 1939- . . . . **CLC 44**
See also CA 138

Wright, Richard (Nathaniel)
1908-1960 . . . . **CLC 1, 3, 4, 9, 14, 21, 48,**
74; BLC; DA; DAB; DAC; DAM MST,
MULT, NOV; SSC 2; WLC
See also AAYA 5; BW 1; CA 108;
CDALB 1929-1941; DLB 76, 102;
DLBD 2; MTCW

Wright, Richard B(ruce) 1937- . . . . . . **CLC 6**
See also CA 85-88; DLB 53

Wright, Rick 1945- . . . . **CLC 35**

Wright, Rowland
See Wells, Carolyn

Wright, Stephen Caldwell 1946- . . . . **CLC 33**
See also BW 2

Wright, Willard Huntington 1888-1939
See Van Dine, S. S.
See also CA 115

Wright, William 1930- . . . . **CLC 44**
See also CA 53-56; CANR 7, 23

Wroth, LadyMary 1587-1653(?) . . . . . **LC 30**
See also DLB 121

Wu Ch'eng-en 1500(?)-1582(?) . . . . **LC 7**

Wu Ching-tzu 1701-1754 . . . . **LC 2**

Wurlitzer, Rudolph 1938(?)- . . **CLC 2, 4, 15**
See also CA 85-88; DLB 173

Wycherley, William
1641-1715 . . . . . **LC 8, 21; DAM DRAM**
See also CDBLB 1660-1789; DLB 80

Wylie, Elinor (Morton Hoyt)
1885-1928 . . . . **TCLC 8**
See also CA 105; DLB 9, 45

Wylie, Philip (Gordon) 1902-1971 . . . **CLC 43**
See also CA 21-22; 33-36R; CAP 2; DLB 9

Wyndham, John . . . . **CLC 19**
See also Harris, John (Wyndham Parkes
Lucas) Beynon

Wyss, Johann David Von
1743-1818 . . . . **NCLC 10**
See also JRDA; MAICYA; SATA 29;
SATA-Brief 27

Xenophon
c. 430B.C.-c. 354B.C. . . . . **CMLC 17**

Yakumo Koizumi
See Hearn, (Patricio) Lafcadio (Tessima
Carlos)

Yanez, Jose Donoso
See Donoso (Yanez), Jose

Yanovsky, Basile S.
See Yanovsky, V(assily) S(emenovich)

Yanovsky, V(assily) S(emenovich)
1906-1989 . . . . **CLC 2, 18**
See also CA 97-100; 129

Yates, Richard 1926-1992 . . . . . **CLC 7, 8, 23**
See also CA 5-8R; 139; CANR 10, 43;
DLB 2; DLBY 81, 92; INT CANR-10

Yeats, W. B.
See Yeats, William Butler

Yeats, William Butler
1865-1939 . . . . . **TCLC 1, 11, 18, 31; DA;**
DAB; DAC; DAM DRAM, MST,
POET; WLC
See also CA 104; 127; CANR 45;
CDBLB 1890-1914; DLB 10, 19, 98, 156;
MTCW

Yehoshua, A(braham) B.
1936- . . . . **CLC 13, 31**
See also CA 33-36R; CANR 43

Yep, Laurence Michael 1948- . . . . . . **CLC 35**
See also AAYA 5; CA 49-52; CANR 1, 46;
CLR 3, 17; DLB 52; JRDA; MAICYA;
SATA 7, 69

Yerby, Frank G(arvin)
1916-1991 . . . . **CLC 1, 7, 22; BLC;**
DAM MULT
See also BW 1; CA 9-12R; 136; CANR 16,
52; DLB 76; INT CANR-16; MTCW

Yesenin, Sergei Alexandrovich
See Esenin, Sergei (Alexandrovich)

Yevtushenko, Yevgeny (Alexandrovich)
1933- . . . . **CLC 1, 3, 13, 26, 51;**
DAM POET
See also CA 81-84; CANR 33, 54; MTCW

Yezierska, Anzia 1885(?)-1970 . . . . . **CLC 46**
See also CA 126; 89-92; DLB 28; MTCW

Yglesias, Helen 1915- . . . . **CLC 7, 22**
See also CA 37-40R; CAAS 20; CANR 15;
INT CANR-15; MTCW

Yokomitsu Riichi 1898-1947 . . . . . . **TCLC 47**

Yonge, Charlotte (Mary)
1823-1901 . . . . **TCLC 48**
See also CA 109; DLB 18, 163; SATA 17

York, Jeremy
See Creasey, John

York, Simon
See Heinlein, Robert A(nson)

Yorke, Henry Vincent 1905-1974 . . . **CLC 13**
See also Green, Henry
See also CA 85-88; 49-52

Yosano Akiko 1878-1942 . . **TCLC 59; PC 11**

Yoshimoto, Banana . . . . **CLC 84**
See also Yoshimoto, Mahoko

Yoshimoto, Mahoko 1964-
See Yoshimoto, Banana
See also CA 144

Young, Al(bert James)
1939- . . . . . **CLC 19; BLC; DAM MULT**
See also BW 2; CA 29-32R; CANR 26;
DLB 33

Young, Andrew (John) 1885-1971 . . . . **CLC 5**
See also CA 5-8R; CANR 7, 29

Young, Collier
See Bloch, Robert (Albert)

Young, Edward 1683-1765 . . . . **LC 3**
See also DLB 95

Young, Marguerite (Vivian)
1909-1995 . . . . **CLC 82**
See also CA 13-16; 150; CAP 1

Young, Neil 1945- . . . . **CLC 17**
See also CA 110

Young Bear, Ray A.
1950- . . . . **CLC 94; DAM MULT**
See also CA 146; NNAL

Yourcenar, Marguerite
1903-1987 . . . . **CLC 19, 38, 50, 87;**
DAM NOV
See also CA 69-72; CANR 23; DLB 72;
DLBY 88; MTCW

Yurick, Sol 1925- . . . . **CLC 6**
See also CA 13-16R; CANR 25

Zabolotskii, Nikolai Alekseevich
1903-1958 . . . . **TCLC 52**
See also CA 116

Zamiatin, Yevgenii
See Zamyatin, Evgeny Ivanovich

Zamora, Bernice (B. Ortiz)
1938- . . . . . **CLC 89; DAM MULT; HLC**
See also CA 151; DLB 82; HW

Zamyatin, Evgeny Ivanovich
1884-1937 . . . . **TCLC 8, 37**
See also CA 105

Zangwill, Israel 1864-1926 . . . . **TCLC 16**
See also CA 109; DLB 10, 135

Zappa, Francis Vincent, Jr. 1940-1993
See Zappa, Frank
See also CA 108; 143

Zappa, Frank . . . . **CLC 17**
See also Zappa, Francis Vincent, Jr.

Zaturenska, Marya 1902-1982 . . . . **CLC 6, 11**
See also CA 13-16R; 105; CANR 22

Zelazny, Roger (Joseph)
1937-1995 . . . . **CLC 21**
See also AAYA 7; CA 21-24R; 148;
CANR 26; DLB 8; MTCW; SATA 57;
SATA-Brief 39

Zhdanov, Andrei A(lexandrovich)
1896-1948 . . . . **TCLC 18**
See also CA 117

Literary Criticism Series
Cumulative Topic Index

This index lists all topic entries in Gale's *Classical and Medieval Literature Criticism, Contemporary Literary Criticism, Literature Criticism from 1400 to 1800, Nineteenth-Century Literature Criticism,* and *Twentieth-Century Literary Criticism.*

Topic Index

Topic Index

LC Cumulative Nationality Index

LC Cumulative Title Index

Title Index

Title Index

Title Index

Title Index

Title Index

Title Index

Title Index

Title Index

Title Index

Title Index

Title Index

Title Index

Title Index

ISBN 0-7876-1130-1